R 300.3

A DICTIONARY OF THE SOCIAL SCIENCES

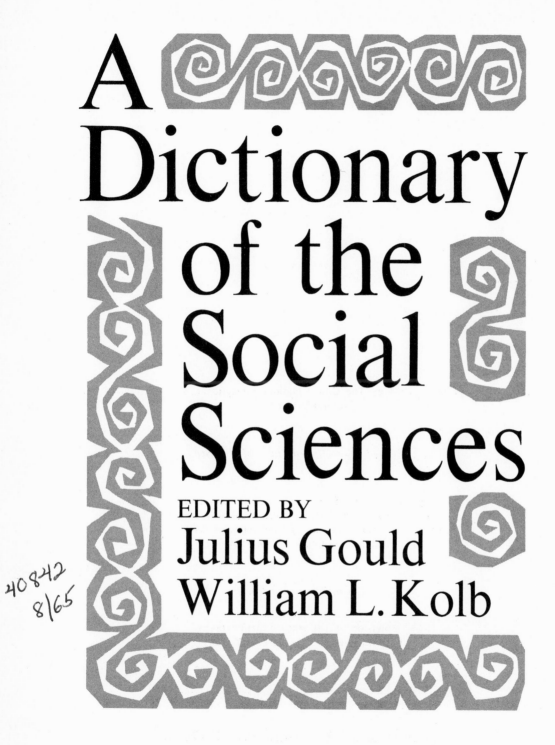

A Dictionary of the Social Sciences

EDITED BY
Julius Gould
William L. Kolb

Compiled under the auspices of The United Nations
Educational, Scientific, and Cultural Organization

THE FREE PRESS

A DICTIONARY OF THE SOCIAL SCIENCES

Compiled under the auspices of UNESCO

EDITORS

JULIUS GOULD
Professor of Sociology, University of Nottingham

WILLIAM L. KOLB
Dean of the College, Beloit College

ADVISORY COMMITTEE TO THE BRITISH EDITOR

Political Science   **W. HARRISON**
Professor of Politics, University of Warwick

J. C. REES
Reader in the Department of Political Theory and Government,
University College of Swansea

W. A. ROBSON
Professor Emeritus of Public Administration,
University of London

K. B. SMELLIE
Professor of Political Science, University of London

Social Anthropology   **I. SCHAPERA**
Professor of Social Anthropology, University of London

A. P. STIRLING
Lecturer in Anthropology, University of London

Social Psychology   **W. J. H. SPROTT**
formerly Professor of Psychology, University of Nottingham

Sociology   **M. GINSBERG**
Professor of Sociology, University of London

ADVISORY COMMITTEE TO THE AMERICAN EDITOR

Assistant Editor   **ROBERT C. STONE**
Director, Institute for Social Science Research,
San Francisco State College

Anthropology   **DAVID BIDNEY**
Professor of Anthropology and Philosophy,
University of Indiana

Economics   **DAVID McCORD WRIGHT**
Professor of Economics, University of Georgia

Political Science   **DAVID B. TRUMAN**
Dean of the College, Columbia College, Columbia University

Social Psychology   **EDMUND H. VOLKART**
Dean of the Graduate School, Oregon State University

Sociology   **HERBERT BLUMER**
Professor of Sociology, University of California
at Berkeley

CONTRIBUTORS

BRITISH COMMONWEALTH

V. L. Allen
S. Andreski
Michael Argyle

F. G. Bailey
Z. Barbu
L. F. Baric
J. Beattie
Ronald M. Berndt
N. Birnbaum
H. S. Booker
A. Briggs
P. A. Bromhead
J. M. Brown
Tom Burns

A. H. Christie
J. Cohen
G. D. H. Cole
D. C. Coleman

C. de Monchaux
A. L. Diamond
M. Douglas

N. Elias
J. S. Erös

S. E. Finer
R. W. Firth
Ronald Fletcher
Jean Floud
L. P. Foldes
Maurice Freedman
W. Friedmann

E. A. Gellner
G. L. Goodwin

J. Gould
E. Grebenik
J. A. G. Griffith

J. Hajnal
Lady Laura M. Hall
J. E. Hall Williams
P. Halmos
Wilfrid Harrison
H. L. A. Hart
A. Hazlewood
H. Himmelweit
W. H. N. Hotopf
R. N. Carew Hunt

E. O. James
D. H. N. Johnson

F. Kräupl Taylor

E. R. Leach
Sir Aubrey Lewis
K. Little
D. Lockwood

R. B. McCallum
R. T. McKenzie
D. G. MacRae
H. Maddick
C. Madge
L. P. Mair
G. Marshall
J. Middleton
J. D. B. Miller
J. Mogey
G. C. Moodie
H. S. Morris
G. R. G. Mure

F. S. Northedge

A. N. Oppenheim
G. N. Ostergaard

R. H. Pear
T. H. Pear
E. H. Phelps Brown
W. Pickles
J. P. Plamenatz
D. R. Price-Williams

J. C. Rees
T. H. R. Rigby
K. C. Rosser

R. V. Sampson
P. J. O. Self
G. H. N. Seton-Watson
R. L. Sharwood
K. B. Smellie
J. H. Smith
W. Stark
A. P. Stirling
P. Streeten

V. W. Turner

S. V. Utechin

D. V. Verney
P. E. Vernon

Barbara E. Ward
J. H. Warrender
D. C. Watt
C. Wilson
C. Winsten

vi

CONTRIBUTORS

UNITED STATES OF AMERICA

Franz Adler
Charles Aikin
Clark Lee Allen
C. Arnold Anderson
William Anderson
Robert C. Angell
Lowell D. Ashby

Elizabeth E. Bacon
Read Bain
E. C. Banfield
H. G. Barnett
Harry W. Basehart
Howard Becker
Hubert Bice
David Bidney
Robert Bierstedt
V. W. Bladen
Herbert Blumer
Hugh A. Bone
Hubert Bonner
George H. Borts
Raymond V. Bowers
Mary Jean Bowman
Royall Brandis
Harvey C. Bunke
Ernest W. Burgess

Holbert N. Carroll
J. S. G. Carson
Joseph B. Casagrande
Alfred F. Chalk
Ely Chinoy
Carl F. Christ
Richard V. Clemence
Robert E. Clute
Lewis A. Coser
Cornelius P. Cotter
Fred Cottrell
Paul G. Craig
Joan Criswell

H. Otto Dahlke
Alfred de Grazia

Richard Dewey
Kathleen E. Dunlop

James S. Earley
David Easton
William Ebenstein
Luke Ebersole
Munro S. Edmonson
Henry W. Ehrmann
Allan W. Eister
Frederick Elkin
Alona E. Evans
Cortez A. M. Ewing

Robert E. L. Faris
David G. Farrelly
Robert Ferber
James W. Fesler
Joseph H. Fichter
Walter Firey
John L. Fischer
Nelson N. Foote
C. J. Friedrich
H. J. Friedsam

Bert Gerow
Harlan W. Gilmore
Ray L. Gold
Melvin L. Greenhut

Carl H. Hamburg
Robert J. Harris
Eugene L. Hartley
Frederick H. Hartmann
Frank E. Hartung
Robert J. Havighurst
Amos H. Hawley
C. Addison Hickman
Ernest R. Hilgard
Joseph S. Himes
Werner Z. Hirsch
E. Adamson Hoebel
Burkart Holzner
John J. Honigmann
Rex D. Hopper
John M. Howell

Marie Jahoda
Edward C. Jandy
Ralph Jones

Harold F. Kaufman
Felix M. Keesing
Alan C. Kerckhoff
Arden R. King
Clyde Kluckhohn
William L. Kolb
Irving B. Kravis
Thomas Ktsanes
Manford Kuhn

Weston La Barre
Werner S. Landecker
Kurt Lang
Russell L. Langworthy
Earl Latham
William S. Laughlin
Richard H. Leftwich
Avery Leiserson
Daniel Lerner
W. A. Lessa
H. H. Liebhafsky
Leslie Lipson
Charles P. Loomis

Harold McCarty
Stephen L. McDonald
Robert McGinnis
Gerard J. Mangone
Margaret Mead
Frank Miller
William L. Miller
Harry E. Moore
Heyward Moore

Raoul Naroll
Fred Warner Neal
Theodore M. Newcomb
Meyer F. Nimkoff
Edward Norbeck

Henry Oliver

FOREWORD

by the Secretariat of Unesco

The present volume is the first to appear in a series of unilingual dictionaries in the social sciences to be published with the help of Unesco. It is designed to describe and define approximately one thousand basic concepts used in the social sciences.

This work has been prepared in pursuance of Unesco's programme which, from 1952 onwards, has made provision for the clarification of social science terminology and the preparation of social science dictionaries in the main languages of the world. Preliminary studies were carried out by the Unesco Secretariat, which convened in 1954 an international meeting of experts—social scientists as well as linguists—in order to explore the problems raised by the implementation of such a project. In accordance with the recommendations made on this occasion, a pilot project was undertaken by national working parties using the English, French, or Spanish languages, and operating in Belgium, France, Great Britain, Saarland, Spain, Switzerland, and the USA. The terms were drawn from the vocabulary used in writings on technological change, and numbered approximately two hundred. The draft definitions prepared were reviewed in 1956 at a second meeting of experts held at Unesco House. It was then recommended that two inter-disciplinary dictionaries, one in English and one in French, dealing with general social science terminology should be prepared, to be followed at a later date by others in Spanish and Arabic. These dictionaries were intended to define the key concepts most widely employed in the various social science disciplines. The experts further recommended that the everyday usages of the terms defined should be given as well as the most widely accepted scientific usages, which should be illustrated by short quotations from the literature. The aim was to find synthetic scientific definitions that would constitute a common denominator to the different usages. The purpose of the volume is twofold: to afford the reader, whether student or practitioner, a general introduction to the main problems and developments occurring in the domain of the social sciences, and to provide for specialists in other disciplines a source of understanding of the main concepts used in fields outside their own.

For the English-language edition, the compilation of the Dictionary was entrusted to two groups, one in the United Kingdom and the other in the United States of America. These comprised some 270 social scientists, whose names are recorded on pages vi–viii, and whose scholarship, skill, interest, and patience instilled life in the project and alone made it feasible. The activities of the British group were co-ordinated by Professor Julius Gould, now of the University of Nottingham (and formerly of the London School of Economics and Political Science). The American group was headed by Dean William L. Kolb, formerly of Tulane University and Carleton College, Northfield, Minnesota, and now Dean of the College, Beloit College, Wisconsin. It is thanks to their unsparing effort and pioneering enterprise that the work has been brought to fulfilment. It is to be hoped that it will meet a long-standing need among social scientists and the learned public and that it will be the forerunner of similar volumes in other languages.

EDITORS' INTRODUCTION

In the foreword to this volume, the Secretariat of Unesco has described the history of the social science dictionary project as initiated by the Department of Social Sciences at Unesco. The purpose of this introduction is to indicate—albeit briefly—some of the considerations that have governed the work of the Editors.

After the broad directive for the work had been agreed upon, its interpretation was left to us, under the guidance of two national Advisory Committees.[1] It was obviously important that great care should be taken in the early planning stage—when both the scope and the coverage of the Dictionary would be determined and the style for the entries developed. It was recognized from the start that the selection of approximately one thousand 'general' concepts and terms used in the social sciences would be a difficult and, in part, arbitrary undertaking. Tentative selections were made from a study of the literature in the fields of political science, social anthropology, economics, social psychology, and sociology—the aim being to select terms that were general and/or in some way basic to the disciplines concerned. For the most part we aimed to omit terms that were unduly technical or appeared to be used only in the analysis of minor or local phenomena. Judgements of value clearly entered into this process of selection and into the subsequent discussion by experts in both Britain and the USA concerning the coverage attained by the initial selection. In an English-language volume of this kind the emphasis was bound to fall upon usages in contemporary literature and research in the USA, in Great Britain, and in Commonwealth countries. But no effort was made to set up artificial boundaries within the language—increasingly international—of the social sciences.

An attempt, in the main successful, was made throughout to exclude those terms about whose meaning there was little to dispute and concerning which little need be, or could be, added to a standard dictionary definition such as might be found, for example, in the *Oxford English Dictionary*. In deciding upon the number of terms to be drawn from each discipline, we were guided by our wish to secure a roughly equal balance as between disciplines. In the outcome, however, concepts drawn from political science and sociology were in the majority. On the other hand, it was noted that many of the concepts included are, so to speak, 'general' in a special sense—in that they are used in two or more social science disciplines. Thus a purely arithmetical count of the number of terms assignable to each discipline is bound, in obvious ways, to be misleading.

The instructions given to the contributors emphasized the importance of clarity in style and content so that the Editors might fulfil their primary obligations. These

---

[1] The American Editor was also assisted by a local Advisory Committee at Tulane University: he wishes to record his thanks to the members of this Committee - Professors David Deener, Munro Edmonson, Carl Hamburg, and Howard Schaller.

obligations were understood to centre on the preparation of a dictionary of selected concepts or terms which would aim at fuller and more comprehensive treatment than had proved possible in other works styled as dictionaries and published in recent years. Such works had attempted the impossible task of expounding a great complexity of usage in two or three lines. Nevertheless, it was not our aim, nor was it possible, to produce an encyclopaedia. The readers whom we specially had in mind were (*a*) students in any one of the disciplines seeking information concerning the usage of terms and concepts in related disciplines, and (*b*) students and research workers in areas of the world which have been, and are currently, seeking to develop a vocabulary of social science in their own different languages.

No doubt if we had to plan this work afresh we would proceed, in places, on rather different lines: the balance and the choices, in the light of our experience, would not be made in exactly the same way. In other words we would make rather different mistakes. . . .

The many contributors to this volume agreed to work within the points of guidance that we evolved—largely in the light of the pilot project in which we had both participated. There were some minor variations in procedure as between the British and American preparations; but no serious differences emerged. We hope that we have achieved a style that standardized, without confining, the work of the contributors. We are most grateful to them for allowing us to draw so heavily on their learning and patience.

We would like here to say something further on the question of arrangement. All except a few entries in this volume are divided into sections—prefixed by the letters of the alphabet in bold type. Section A. is designed to set out concisely the core meaning or meanings of the term as used in one or more of the social sciences. Most entries also contain a Section B.—which provides, variously, a historical background to these meanings and/or a more detailed discussion. In the longer entries other Sections (C., D., E., etc.) are included. These Sections develop the historical or analytical discussion in further detail. It is here that controversies and divergences of meaning have been explored and an attempt made to place them in perspective. We would emphasize that there has been no intention to play down such divergences, inevitable as they are in the social sciences, or to legislate dogmatically in favour of one or more of the meanings discussed. These divergences often stem from complex theoretical debates—and such differences cannot be summarily dispelled. The aim has been to clarify, in brief compass, the extent and sources of divergence, and to describe the many convergences that can be noted. The contributors, moreover, themselves proceeded from a wide range of assumptions, and no attempt has been made to impose on these pages an artificial, formal consistency.

The Sections C., D., etc. have also been used for a distinct but related purpose. Many of the longer entries are concerned with terms that have a special significance in different social sciences. In these cases, therefore, the additional sections take up these emphases in separate detail.

In a very small number of cases a British *and* an American contributor have each offered a view on the usage of a term; but, in general, this procedure did not seem either appropriate or—we are happy to say—necessary.

An important point arose over the differences, in obvious instances, between

British and American spelling. It was decided to follow British usage (as set out in the *Oxford English Dictionary*) throughout the text, except in direct quotation from American publications.

The views expressed in each entry of this volume are those of the individual contributors. They are not those of the Editors, or of Unesco, or of the two national Advisory Committees. The Editors and members of both Committees made suggestions as to content and revisions. The British Committee was composed of scholars nominated by the Association of Social Anthropologists of the Commonwealth, the British Sociological Association, and the Political Studies Association of the United Kingdom. The American Committee was selected by the American Editor.

The names of the contributors are given on pages vi–viii above in two separate lists. Under the heading 'British Commonwealth' are included the names of those whose entries were initially requested by the British Editor; under the heading 'United States of America' are the names of those whose entries were requested by the American Editor.

We are jointly responsible for the preparation of the volume—for both the British and American contributions. Our names are listed alphabetically but, in an enterprise in which we have been equal partners, there is no question of seniority.

A special word of recognition is due to Dr K. Szczerba-Likiernik, now Secretary-General of the International Social Science Council, and Dr S. Friedman, Head of the Division for the International Development of Social Sciences of Unesco. We owe a great debt to them for their unwavering support.

We would like also to record, with pleasure and gratitude, the help we received from the members of the British and American Advisory Committees—both individually and collectively. These Committees did not, of course, sponsor this volume, nor do they carry any responsibility for it. The advice provided by Committee members, on points of both policy and detail, was, however, of genuine value to us.

Although the major costs of the enterprise were borne by Unesco, the Social Science Research Council in New York generously provided contributions towards meetings of the American Advisory Committee, certain aspects of the editorial work, and the typing of the manuscript. Tulane University and Carleton College also were helpful in furnishing support. The British Editor wishes to express his gratitude to the Rockefeller Foundation (and in particular to Dr Gerald Freund) which permitted him to spend one month of a Fellowship visit to the USA in constant consultation with his American colleague.

Special thanks are owed to Helen Webster Kolb, wife of the American Editor, for editorial, secretarial, and supervisory work throughout the project. Thanks are also due to Mr M. C. Albrow and Mr E. Krausz who helped in the checking of citations; to Mrs M. E. Jones, Mrs M. Richardson, Mrs Daniel Wogan, Mrs W. L. Beson, and Mrs R. D. Scott for typing assistance, involving work on many drafts of the material; and to Miss Joan Aiken for assistance in proof-reading.

Our wives and families have borne with our preoccupations as Editors: to them a final word of thanks (and apology) is more than appropriate.

JULIUS GOULD
WILLIAM L. KOLB

ACKNOWLEDGEMENTS

Thanks are due to the individuals and publishers concerned for permission to reproduce excerpts from the following works. For convenience, British and American sources have been listed separately, but works published by different publishers in the two countries appear in both sections.

GREAT BRITAIN

George Allen & Unwin, Limited
Condliffe, J. P., *The Commerce of Nations* (New York: W. W. Norton; London: Allen & Unwin). Schumpeter, J. A., *History of Economic Analysis*, edited by E. B. Schumpeter (New York: Oxford University Press; London: Allen & Unwin).

Cambridge University Press
Furnivall, J. S., *Netherlands India* (London: Cambridge University Press).

Controller of Her Majesty's Stationery Office
General Register Office, *Classification of Occupations, 1950* (London: H.M.S.O.).

Macmillan & Company, Limited
Dicey, A. V., *Introduction to the Study of the Law of the Constitution* (London: Macmillan; New York: St Martin's Press). Emmet, D. M., *Function, Purpose and Powers* (London: Macmillan; New York: St Martin's Press).

Methuen & Company, Limited
McDougall, W., *Outline of Psychology* (London: Methuen).

Routledge & Kegan Paul, Limited
Durkheim, E., *Suicide* (London: Routledge & Kegan Paul; New York: The Free Press). Mill, J. S., *Auguste Comte and Positivism* (London: Routledge & Kegan Paul). Ogden, C. K. & Richards, I. A., *The Meaning of Meaning* (London: Routledge & Kegan Paul; New York: Harcourt, Brace & World).

Royal Anthropological Institute
Haldane, J. B. S., 'The Argument from Animals to Men', Huxley Memorial Lecture, 1956, *Journal of the Royal Anthropological Institute*, July–December 1956, p. 5.

Trustees of the Estate of the late Lord Keynes and Macmillan & Company, Limited
Keynes, J. M., *The General Theory of Employment, Interest and Money* (London: Macmillan; New York: Harcourt, Brace & World).

C. A. Watts & Company, Limited
Firth, R., *Elements of Social Organization* (London: Watts).

UNITED STATES OF AMERICA

Addison-Wesley Publishing Co., Inc.
Hebb, D. O. & Thompson, W. R., 'The Social Significance of Animal Studies', in Lindzey, G. (ed.), *Handbook of Social Psychology*, vol. I (Cambridge, Mass.: Addison-Wesley).

American Anthropological Association
Wallace, A. F. C., 'Revitalization Movements', *American Anthropologist*, vol. 59, 1956, pp. 267-8.

American Law Institute Publisher
Restatement of the Law of Property, vol. I (St. Paul: American Law Institute).

American Psychological Association
Joint Committee of the American Psychological Association, American Educational Research Association, and National Council of Measurement in Education, *Psychological Bulletin*, Supplement, vol. 51, 1954, p. 29. Behan, R. A., 'Expectancies and Hullian Theory', *Psychological Review*, vol. 60, p. 252.

The Editor of *American Scientist*, and Dr G. E. Hutchinson
Hutchinson, G. E., 'Marginalia', *American Scientist*, vol. 38, 1950, p. 283.

Appleton-Century-Crofts, Inc.
Marx, K. & Engels, F., *The Communist Manifesto*, edited by S. H. Beer (New York: Appleton-Century-Crofts).

The Trustees of Columbia University in the City of New York
Macmahon, A. W., 'The Problems of Federalism: A Survey', in Macmahon, A. W. (ed.), *Federalism Mature and Emergent* (New York: Doubleday).

Columbia University Press
Kardiner, A. & Linton, R., *The Psychological Frontiers of Society* (New York: Columbia University Press).

Harcourt, Brace & World, Inc.
Keynes, J. M., *The General Theory of Employment, Interest and Money* (London: Macmillan; New York: Harcourt, Brace & World). Kroeber, A. L., *Anthropology* (New York:

Harcourt, Brace & World). Malinowski, B., 'The Problem of Meaning in Primitive Language', in Ogden, C. K. & Richards, I. A., *The Meaning of Meaning* (New York: Harcourt, Brace & World; London: Routledge & Kegan Paul).

Harvard University Press

Cicero, *De Legibus*, Loeb Classical Library edition translated by Keys (Cambridge, Mass.: Harvard University Press). Emerson, R., *From Empire to Nation* (Cambridge, Mass.: Harvard University Press). Langer, S. K., *Philosophy in a New Key* (Cambridge, Mass.: Harvard University Press). Parsons, T. & Shils, E. A., *Toward a General Theory of Action* (Cambridge, Mass.: Harvard University Press).

D. C. Heath & Company

Eubank, E. D., *Concepts of Sociology* (Boston: D. C. Heath). Schermerhorn, R. A., *These Our People* (Boston: D. C. Heath).

Holt, Rinehart & Winston, Inc.

Allport, G. W., *Personality: A Psychological Interpretation* (New York: Henry Holt). Freeman, E., *Principles of General Psychology* (New York: Henry Holt). Odum, H. W. & Moore, H. E., *American Regionalism* (New York: Henry Holt). Peak, H., 'Problems of Objective Observation', in Festinger, L. & Katz, D. (eds.), *Research Methods in the Behavioral Sciences* (New York: Dryden Press).

Houghton Mifflin Company

Berry, B., *Race and Ethnic Relations* (Boston: Houghton Mifflin).

Richard D. Irwin, Inc.

Halm, G. N., *Monetary Theory*, 2nd edition (Homewood, Ill.: Irwin).

Alfred A. Knopf, Inc.

Rose, A., *Sociology: The Study of Human Relations* (New York: Alfred A. Knopf). Truman, B., *The Governmental Process* (New York: Alfred A. Knopf). de Tocqueville, A., *Democracy in America*, translated by H. Reeve (New York: Alfred A. Knopf).

Liveright Publishing Corporation

Kohler, W., *Gestalt Psychology* (New York: Liveright).

McGraw-Hill Book Co., Inc.

Kemmerer, E. W., *Gold and the Gold Standard* (New York and London: McGraw-Hill).

National Bureau of Economic Research

Brown, W. A., Fr., *The International Gold Standard Reinterpreted*, vol. II (New York: National Bureau of Economic Research).

W. W. Norton and Company, Inc.

Condliffe, J. P., *The Commerce of Nations* (New York: W. W. Norton; London: Allen & Unwin).

Oxford University Press, Inc.

Murray, H. A., *Explorations in Personality* (New York: Oxford University Press). Schumpeter, J. A., *History of Economic Analysis*, edited by E. B. Schumpeter (New York: Oxford University Press; London: Allen & Unwin).

Prentice-Hall, Inc.

Findlay Mackenzie (ed.), *Planned Society: Yesterday, Today, Tomorrow.* © 1937, by permission of Prentice-Hall, Inc., Englewood Cliffs, New Jersey.

Public Affairs Press

Pribram, K., *Conflicting Patterns of Thought* (Washington: Public Affairs Press).

Random House, Inc.

Smith, A., *The Wealth of Nations* (New York: The Modern Library).

St. Martin's Press, Inc.

Emmet, D. M., *Function, Purpose and Powers* (New York: St. Martin's Press; London: Macmillan). Dicey, A. V., *Introduction to the Study of the Law of the Constitution* (New York: St. Martin's Press; London: Macmillan).

University of Chicago Press

Knight, F. H., *Social Economic Organization* (Chicago: University of Chicago Bookstore), Copyright 1942 by The University of Chicago. Kroeber, A. L., *The Nature of Culture* (Chicago: University of Chicago Press), Copyright 1952 by The University of Chicago. Mead, G. H., *Mind, Self and Society* (Chicago: University of Chicago Press), Copyright 1934 by The University of Chicago. Park, R. E. and Burgess, E. W., *Introduction to the Science of Sociology* (Chicago: University of Chicago Press), Copyright 1921 by The University of Chicago. Redfield, R., 'The Folk Society', *American Journal of Sociology*, vol. LII, 1946–7, pp. 293, 298, Copyright 1947 by The University of Chicago. Simmel, G., 'Fashion', *American Journal of Sociology*, May, 1957, pp. 541–58, Copyright 1957 by The University of Chicago.

A DICTIONARY OF THE SOCIAL SCIENCES

A

Abnormal (Also **Normal**)

A. *Abnormal* has the following senses: (a) that which deviates from the average; (b) that which is opposite to, or qualitatively different from, a general (absolute) norm or value; (c) unfit, inefficient, unbalanced, i.e. not functioning according to some given design or end; (d) socially maladjusted. *Normal* denotes: (a) average; (b) that which fits into, or is identical with, an absolute norm or value; (c) fit, efficient, balanced, i.e. functioning according to some given design or end; (d) adjusted to a specific socio-ethical code.

B. 1. In a statistical sense *normal* denotes some kind of average, or that which lies within the limits of the first standard deviation in a frequency distribution. *Abnormal* denotes in this case that which deviates from the normal. Two main difficulties are involved in this use of the terms:

(a) The concept of abnormality is ambiguous, i.e. it refers at the same time to what is above, or superior to, the normal, and to what is below, or inferior to, the normal.

(b) This use involves a high degree of relativity in the meaning of the terms; what is normal in one group can be abnormal in another.

2. The terms can be used in a normative sense. According to a common-sense opinion as well as to some trends in present-day psychiatry, 'normality-abnormality' connotes sanity-insanity. In this case the terms are dichotomous; people are either 'sane' or 'insane'. The abnormal (diseased) mind is functionally, i.e. qualitatively, different from the normal mind. Normality and abnormality in this usage cannot be represented on a continuum.

In a way different from this usage, Freud and most of his followers work with the hypothesis of 'continuity'. The 'normal' individual struggles with the same 'complexes' as the 'abnormal', the difference lying mainly in the manner in which he handles them. Though on this point opinion among Freudians varies widely, one can say that the condition of normality, or abnormality, is essentially determined by the ego—helped by the superego—whose function is to control, organize, and adjust to reality the impulses, feelings, and phantasies generated in the unconscious structure of the mind. The onset of war neuroses can be taken as an illustrative example. The weakening of the ego, as well as the re-orientation and regression of the superego, resulting from a drastic change in the conditions of life, may cause a transition from *real anxiety*—which in the given circumstances is a normal condition—to *neurotic anxiety*. While *real anxiety* is objectively confined and rationally understandable (being related to the danger involved in the external situation), *neurotic anxiety* is a diffuse, generalized, free-floating emotional state which can be understood only by reference to unconscious sources of anxiety created by early experiences in the life of the individual. In this case, normality connotes a preponderance of conscious, rational determinants of behaviour, while abnormality connotes a preponderance of conscious, irrational determinants; normality facilitates adjustment to reality, physical and social, while abnormality leads to maladjustment, i.e. to delusional behaviour. It has to be said, however, that this difference is essentially one of degree.

3. *Normal* can sometimes denote fitness and efficiency. For instance, an organism is normal when functioning according to its design and nature. This implies, firstly, capacity for survival, and, secondly, cohesive growth, viz. harmonious development of the basic needs of the organism. Abnormality denotes, in this case, one-sided or unbalanced development. In connection with this one can mention the tendency in psychology and in psychopathology in particular to identify normality with a balanced and well-integrated personality structure. Strong repression is often considered as a sign of abnormality, for it leads to the inhibition of some basic drives. The uses indicated under this point suffer from the vagueness involved in the concepts of 'design' and 'nature'.

4. The terms denote also social adjustment and conformity. A person is 'normal' to the extent to which he is adjusted to, or in harmony with, the ethico-cultural code of his society. 'From the psychiatric point of view, a

Absentee Ownership

psychically normal person is one who is in harmony with himself, and with his environment. He conforms with the cultural requirements, or injunctions of his community' (L. E. Hinsie & J. Shatsky, *Psychiatric Dictionary*, New York: Oxford University Press, 1940, p. 372). In this sense normality tends to be equated with conventionality, and abnormality with 'anti-social conduct'. This use encounters two main difficulties:

(a) It introduces a high degree of cultural relativity in the concept of normality-abnormality; one has to establish and to admit specific standards for each culture.

(b) It raises the question of maladjusted societies, i.e. of societies displaying traits which can be called abnormal. For example, there are cultures which encourage the drinking of polluted water, or cultures which encourage superstition. There are also cultures which encourage self-destructive processes by stimulating in their members strong in-group feelings and aggression towards out-groups. This points to the need to work out standards for establishing when a culture or a society is normal, and when abnormal. For the present there is little consensus on this point among social scientists.

Z. Barbu

See also: ADJUSTMENT
        CONFORMITY
        DEVIANT BEHAVIOUR
        NEUROSIS
        PSYCHOSIS

Absentee Ownership

A. *Absentee ownership*—sometimes *absenteeism*—denotes the situation in which ownership of property and control of its use, particularly in the productive process, are to some degree separated, but in which the owner receives income from the use of the property through claims on profit or through rent. The degree of control relinquished may be relatively slight, or it may be almost total.

B. Originally, *absentee ownership* referred to the activities of landlords and members of the nobility who lived away from their estates and left their management to other people, while deriving income from the land in the form of rent and shares, or in the form of profits produced by having the land worked directly under the manager of the estate. In the history of western civilization in modern times the two best examples of absentee ownership are to be found in the practices of the court nobility of the days of Louis XIV in pre-revolutionary France, and of English landlords in the 19th century who were accused of exploiting Ireland and the Irish tenant. The leading economists of the day, J. R. McCulloch, M. Longfield, and N. W. Senior, took an active part in discussing the 'Irish Question' and the effects of absenteeism.

C. In the United States from the 1870s until the coming of the New Deal in the 1930s the problem of the absentee ownership of agricultural land and of farm tenantry received considerable attention. The problem today is considered by many no longer to be serious, although a certain amount of such land ownership exists, notably among professionals. Much of this land worked by other than the actual owners is not held for the purpose of earning a profitable return, but is held as a place for rest, recreation, or retirement.

D. The first quarter of the 20th century saw the term *absentee ownership* carried over into the field of business primarily in application to the joint stock company. D. H. Robertson states that the joint stock company '... system operates to produce an almost complete control of the business and the ownership of the capital embarked in it' (*The Controls of Industry*, Cambridge: Cambridge University Press, 1955, p. 65). In such an analysis the emphasis is placed on absence from the day-to-day process of directing production, rather than on residential location. In this view, because of the diversification of ownership of the joint stock company through the use of stocks, ownership cannot be anything but absentee, and control of the company must be in the hands of salaried employees called the managerial class, who, in the United States, may or may not own stocks in the company. This approach is at least debatable, however, if it is taken to apply to the formulation of overall company policy or to managerial control of the economic structure. T. Veblen believed that some of the most powerful men in the economic sphere in modern times were the absentee owners whom he called 'captains of industry' (*Absentee Ownership and Business Enterprise in Recent Times*, New York: B. W. Huebsch, 1923). These men, he claimed, did not themselves participate directly in the productive processes, but by means of their control over money and investments were able to keep a controlling influence over industrial prices and output. More orthodox writers have stressed the advantages of absentee stock ownership and transfer in making possible a much larger and more flexible supply of capital for development than would otherwise be the case.

Kathleen E. Dunlop

See also: PROPERTY

Absolute Advantage (See Comparative Cost Advantage)

Absolute Monarchy (See Monarchy)

Absolutism

A. *Absolutism* denotes the type of political structure characterized by: (a) the absence of customary or legal limitations on the authority of the government; (b) the extremely wide scope of actually exercised authority. In large polities the second criterion implies the existence of a centralized administrative apparatus. The question of other features of political structure is not prejudged by the proposed definition. Absolutism, autocracy (q.v.), and despotism (q.v.) are concepts whose denotations intersect but do not coincide. On the other hand, whereas totalitarianism implies absolutism, the reverse is not true.

B. 1. The term as used by historians generally does not refer to *any* government enjoying unlimited authority but to the monarchies of the northern and western parts of the European continent in the 17th and 18th centuries, and the features which they had in common.

2. From the point of view of general sociology this usage is not very helpful, because there are good grounds for believing that a number of these features were but contingently connected with the unlimited nature of authority. Moreover, seen against a broader comparative background, the authority of the so-called absolute monarchs of 18th-century Europe appears to have been much more limited—above all by the privileges of the nobility and the clergy—than that of many other rulers: such as, for instance, Mongol khans, Turkish sultans, kings of Fiji, and a number of modern dictators. It remains true, however, that the monarchs in question claimed absolute authority and that their de facto authority was much nearer to this ideal than that of their feudal precursors or constitutional successors.

3. In elaborating a definition of *absolutism* as a sociological category, it must be borne in mind that *absolutes* never materialize, i.e. there can be no such thing as literally absolute authority—no network of social relations which would ensure obedience to all imaginable commands (even if we exclude those commands whose execution is physically impossible); yet while the scope of authority cannot be measured, it is sufficient for the purpose of the definition that cases which differ markedly can be ranked according to the width of this scope.

S. Andreski

See also: AUTOCRACY
DESPOTISM
DICTATORSHIP
TOTALITARIANISM
TYRANNY

Acceleration Principle

A. In contemporary usage this term refers to the magnified effect on the demand for producers' goods that *may* be induced by changes in the demand for consumers' goods. The term *relation*, formerly used as a synonym, has virtually disappeared from the current literature. Numerical models in which the acceleration principle is assumed to operate require that some value be assigned to the effect in question. The number of times by which an increase in income is multiplied in increased demand for investment goods is the *acceleration coefficient* or *accelerator*.

B. The term *acceleration principle* is usually associated with the work of the American economist J. M. Clark, who attempted an exact formulation of the relationship between the demands for products and for means of production in his 1917 article ('Business Acceleration and the Law of Demand', *Journal of Political Economy*, vol. XXV, 1917, pp. 217-35). Although Clark did not himself employ the term, it was implicit in his treatment as the following paragraph shows: 'The demand for enlarging the means of production (including stocks of finished goods on the way to the consumer) varies, not with the volume of the demand for the finished product, but rather with the acceleration of that demand, allowance being made for the fact that the equipment cannot be adjusted as rapidly as demand changes, and so may be unusually scarce or redundant to start with in any given period. The demand for equipment may decrease as a result of this law even though the demand for the finished product is still growing' (*Preface to Social Economics: Essays on Economic Theory and Social Problems*, New York: Farrar & Rinehart,

Acceptance

1936, p. 348). R. F. Harrod used the term *relation* to designate the same concept, and the two expressions were used synonymously for some time thereafter (R. F. Harrod, *The Trade Cycle*, Oxford: Oxford University Press, 1936, ch. 2). P. A. Samuelson writes, for example, '... Professor Hansen has developed a new model sequence which ingeniously combines the multiplier analysis with that of the *acceleration* principle or *relation*' (P. A. Samuelson, 'Interactions Between the Multiplier Analysis and the Principle of Acceleration', *Review of Economic Statistics*, vol. XXI, 1939, p. 76)

C. Although the principle is frequently stated as a relation between income and investment, it specifically refers to the relation between increases or decreases in the demand for consumers' goods and the increase or decrease in the demand for producers' goods. According to G. Haberler, 'It is the proposition that, for technological reasons, slight changes in the demand for consumers' goods produce much more violent variations in the demand for producers' goods' (*Prosperity and Depression*, Lake Success: United Nations, 1946, p. 86).

1. For example, provided we assume the usual model, if a consumers' goods industry replaces its equipment at 10 per cent a year and an increase in income is reflected in a 10 per cent increase in demand which requires a 10 per cent increase in equipment, this represents a 100 per cent increase in demand for producers' goods—equipment—from the point of view of the producers' goods industry.

2. If the rate of increase in the demand for the consumers' goods remains constant and is reflected in corresponding orders for new equipment, then the demand for producers' goods will remain absolutely constant from year to year. If the rate of increase of demand slackens, this will be reflected in an absolute decrease in demand for producers' goods.

D. It has been necessary in numerical models to assign a value to the effect produced by the *acceleration principle*. 'The multiple by which investment is increased for each dollar of increase in income is called the *acceleration coefficient* or simply the *accelerator*' (A. H. Hansen, *Business Cycles and National Income*, New York: Norton, 1951, p. 173).

E. In business-cycle analysis where the acceleration principle is usually used, frequently in conjunction with the concept of the multiplier (q.v.), the acceleration principle does not always hold, and it sometimes holds without regard to an increase in national income. The following are examples of the kinds of conditions which must be considered.

1. First, it is obvious that an increase in income is translated into an increase in consumption demand only in proportion to the marginal propensity to consume (q.v.).

2. Second, if the trade or business cycle is at its bottom, there is likely to be an excess of consumers' goods plant, so that an increase in demand is not followed by an increase in net investment, but simply by increased use of plant and increased inventories.

3. In a down swing of the business cycle an increase in demand may not be followed by an increase in demand for producers' goods because of the difficulty of borrowing money.

4. Under appropriate circumstances—unfavourable price-cost expectations, for example—the pessimism of the management of consumers' goods industry may keep them from translating an increase in consumer demand into a demand for producers' goods.

5. On the other hand a substantial shift in the nature of consumers' demand may produce an accelerator effect due to the fact that the decrease in demand in one industry does not produce a net disinvestment equivalent to the increased investment occurring in the industry on which the new demand is concentrated (R. F. Bretherton, F. A. Burchardt, & R. S. G. Rutherford, *Public Investment and the Trade Cycle in Great Britain*, Oxford: Oxford University Press, 1941, pp. 6-12).

6. D. McC. Wright and others have shown that a bunching of innovations on one level of capital goods production can also produce an acceleration in the higher stages of production (D. McC. Wright, *The Economics of Disturbance*, New York: The Macmillan Co., 1947, chs. V & VI).

Richard V. Clemence

See also: DEMAND
PROPENSITY TO CONSUME
SUPPLY

Acceptance (Also Rejection)

A. *Acceptance-rejection* may be used to denote a continuum of openness and closedness on the part of a person or group toward experience, objects, people, or groups. Neither of the terms is meaningful alone, and where a

4

degree of acceptance is noted a degree of rejection is implied, and vice versa, except in rare polar cases.

B. Although the matter is not always or even usually stated in the manner above, and though the terms *acceptance* and *rejection* are themselves not always used, and practically never defined, the various states of affairs that can be described as falling along the acceptance-rejection continuum are among the most important in personality theory and in the theory of interpersonal relations.

1. Thus the open and closed minds which M. Rokeach and others have studied recently fall along an acceptance-rejection continuum with respect to ideas. That this is so is indicated, for example, by the phrase *acceptance-rejection* used by Rokeach and R. N. Vidulich with respect to the subjects' response to the experimental situation (M. Rokeach & R. N. Vidulich, 'The Formation of New Belief Systems: The Roles of Memory and the Capacity to Entertain', in M. Rokeach, *The Open and Closed Mind*, New York: Basic Books, 1960, p. 199). When concerned with the acceptance or non-acceptance of an idea or an experience in this manner, the continuum refers to somewhat the same phenomena dealt with by the concept of repression (q.v.). Actually repression is a sub-form of rejection.

2. When used with respect to interpersonal relations, the continuum may be used to denote a wide scale of relationships. Thus one relationship over toward the pole of rejection may take the form of a relationship of open antagonism on the part of one or both parties, while another may involve a more subtle rejection of an emotional relationship with the continued acceptance of an overt, formal social relationship. In the area of interpersonal relations the continuum has been regarded as most important with regard to relations between spouses and between parents and children, in that much of what happens with regard to personality strength, etc. is due to patterns of acceptance and rejection (see, for example, E. H. Erikson, *Childhood and Society*, New York: W. W. Norton, 1950, pp. 169, 181, 247).

3. Attitudes and orientations of a person toward himself also fall along this continuum, and the degree and nature of self-acceptance or self-rejection is regarded by many social psychologists as one of the central problematic features of personality both with regard to its causes and its results in other areas of life (see, for example,

A. H. Maslow, *Motivation and Personality*, New York: Harper & Brothers, 1954, pp. 206-8).

William L. Kolb

See also: ALIENATION
AMBIVALENCE
EMPATHY
IDENTIFICATION
LOVE
PROJECTION
REPRESSION

Accommodation

A. *Accommodation* refers to a social process (q.v.) or product which follows, reduces, or avoids conflict (q.v.)—implying that the resolution of the conflict is necessary for maintenance of the social order, but without implying a complete resolution of conflict mutually satisfactory to the contenders. The term can refer to individual behaviour, thus having psychological implications, or to group behaviour, thus having implications for social structure.

B. According to E. W. Burgess ('Accommodation', in E. R. A. Seligman (ed.), *Encyclopedia of the Social Sciences*, New York: The Macmillan Co., 1930, vol. I, pp. 403-4), the term was first used in the social sciences by J. M. Baldwin (*Mental Development in the Child and the Race*, New York: The Macmillan Co., 1895, pp. 452-7). It was considered to be the social equivalent of biological adaptation, both being forms of adjustment to the environment. F. H. Giddings used the term frequently, considering it as one of several modes of conflict. G. Tarde defined accommodation as the resolution of conflict between two opposing ways of acting and the emergence of a new pattern of behaviour.

R. E. Park & E. W. Burgess (*Introduction to the Science of Sociology*, Chicago: University of Chicago Press, 1921, ch. X), following G. Simmel, considered it a basic social process in a sequence that formed something of a natural cycle whenever groups came into contact with each other: competition (q.v.), conflict, accommodation, and assimilation (q.v.). They regarded it as the basis of social organization (q.v.), just as competition was the basis of the economic order, conflict of the political order, and assimilation of the moral order (q.v.). 'Social organization is the sum total of accommodations to past and present situations. All the social heritages, traditions, sentiments, culture, technique, are accommodations. ...

5

Acculturation

Accommodation [is] the process of making social adjustments to conflict situations by maintaining social distance between groups and persons which might otherwise come into conflict (E. W. Burgess, 'Accommodation', p. 403).

C. Most contemporary users of the term in America and in Europe (e.g. L. von Wiese) have followed Park and Burgess, generally without considering it to be so central in the development of social organization.

1. J. L. Gillin & J. P. Gillin (*Cultural Sociology*, New York: The Macmillan Co., 1948, p. 505), for example, say: 'Accommodation is the term used by sociologists to describe a process in the field of social relationships analogous to the term *adaptation* used by the biologists to describe the process by which living things become adjusted to the environment. By this term the sociologist means the process by which competing and conflicting individuals and groups adjust their relationships to each other in order to overcome the difficulties which arise in competition, contravention, or conflict. ... Accommodation applies to those social changes such as habits, attitudes, patterns of behavior, techniques, institutions, traditions, etc. which are handed down from one generation to another by example and precept.'

2. R. M. MacIver offers another, *variant* definition, emphasizing a psychological aspect: '... [by the term accommodation] we mean the process in which the person or the group comes to fit into a given situation and to feel "at home" within it ...

'The difference between "adjustment" and "accommodation", as we use these terms, is simply that the latter stresses the psychological aspect rather than the valuational one. Accommodation is attained in the sense of harmony between man and his environment. This emphasis is perhaps implied in the use of the term by "the ecological school" ' (R. M. MacIver, *Society, Its Structure and Changes*, New York: Ray Long & Richard R. Smith, 1931, p. 350.)

D. G. Myrdal has attacked the sociologists' use of the term *accommodation* as having a hidden value assumption that it is good because it eliminates conflict. Not only would he have this value assumption be made explicit, and the conditions under which social order arises out of resolution of conflict through accommodation be specified, but he holds that this assumption is not precise enough to serve a scientific purpose: 'In the Negro problem prac-

tically every situation, except where a race riot is on, can be, and is often actually in the literature, described as an "accommodation", and *status quo* in every aspect can thus be, and is, implicitly justified because it preserves cooperation and the social order' (G. Myrdal, with R. Sterner & A. Rose, *An American Dilemma*, New York: Harper & Brothers, 1944, pp. 1050, 1055). Myrdal would thus avoid use of the term except where it is much more narrowly and rigorously defined than has been the case.

Arnold M. Rose

See also: CONFLICT
PROCESS

Accountability (See Responsibility)

Acculturation

A. *Acculturation* may be defined as that process of culture change (q.v.) in which more or less continuous contact between two or more culturally distinct groups results in one group taking over elements of the culture of the other group or groups. The term is also used to designate the resultant state. While there is general agreement among anthropologists that the definition of the term should not be made too rigid, as the phenomena concerned are highly variable and overlap with those covered by other terms in the field of culture change, it is clear that acculturation does refer to one broad type of process through which culture change is accomplished and to the resultant state of the group concerned.

1. It is concerned with results of the contact and interaction of at least two distinct cultural groups.

2. It assumes a baseline of time from which the process commences.

3. It makes one group's culture the point of reference, and focuses upon the events and processes by which that group responds to more or less continuous contact by variously accepting, reformulating, or rejecting elements of the other culture or cultures.

B. This term gained currency within anthropology, particularly in the United States, during the late 19th century.

1. As early as 1880 J. W. Powell, director of the Bureau of American Ethnology, wrote of the 'force of acculturation' which was changing indigenous traditions under the 'overwhelming presence of millions of civilized people' (*Introduction to the Study of Indian Languages*, Washington, D.C.: Government Printing Office,

6

1880, p. 46). W. J. McGee wrote in 1898 of 'piratical acculturation', by which he meant cultural interchange which is 'inimical and adventitious' rather than 'friendly and purposive' ('Piratical Acculturation', *American Anthropologist*, vol. 11, 1898, pp. 243–9).

2. Scattered use of the term in anthropological and other social science writings of the earlier 20th century shows it often employed interchangeably with diffusion (q.v.), assimilation (q.v.), borrowing, and other terms. British studies of the time usually spoke of 'culture contact'.

3. In 1936 a sub-committee of the U.S. Social Science Research Council, consisting of R. Redfield, R. Linton, and M. J. Herskovits, concerned with the definition of the term, issued a report stating: 'Acculturation comprehends those phenomena which result when groups of individuals having different cultures come into continuous first-hand contact, with subsequent changes in the original culture patterns of either or both groups' ('Memorandum for the Study of Acculturation', *American Anthropologist*, vol. 38, 1936, pp. 149–52). This 1936 definition became the point of departure for all subsequent discussions of the term.

C. Various reservations and clarifications have been made in the rapidly expanding literature on acculturation (F. M. Keesing, *Culture Change: An Analysis and Bibliography of Anthropological Sources to 1952*, Stanford: Stanford University Press, 1953). These strictures have been primarily concerned with the relation of individuals to acculturation; the relation of preliterate cultures to complex civilizations; and the relation of culture change to change in the total social structure.

1. M. J. Herskovits was subsequently critical of the phrases 'groups of individuals' and 'continuous first-hand contact' in the 1936 definition, arguing that one missionary making sporadic visits could bring about extensive acculturation (*Man and His Works*, New York: Alfred A. Knopf, 1948, pp. 523–6).

2. G. P. Murdock in a dictionary definition of the term stressed 'the assumption of culture through contact, especially with a people of higher civilization' (H. P. Fairchild (ed.), *Dictionary of Sociology*, Ames, Iowa: Littlefield, Adams, 1955, p. 3). Even if this emphasis on civilization is warranted with respect to contemporary developments, its relevance for the whole period of culture history is dubious.

3. G. D. Spindler, in a later critique, emphasizes the complexity of acculturation study and expands the definition to 'the total adaptive process that occurs in cultural patterning and value systems, group alignments, systems of control, social organization, and economy, and in the psychological structures and functions of individuals, as adaptations are made to the changing conditions of existence created by the impact of populations and their cultures upon each other' (*Sociocultural and Psychological Processes in Menomini Acculturation*, Berkeley: University of California Press, 1955, pp. 3–4).

D. Use of the term in the other social sciences has tended to follow that in anthropology, although it has been used very occasionally to designate (a) the transmission of culture from generation to generation; (b) the adaptation of an out-group member to the behaviour patterns of an in-group; and (c) the impact of a central authority or an urban community upon isolated rural groups.

E. Different types of acculturative situations have been distinguished, based on such variables as the relative sizes of the groups in contact, their momentum (e.g. aggressive, passive), their prestige or hierarchical positions (superordinate, equal, subordinate), their attitudes to one another (e.g. friendly, antagonistic), and the extent of congruence or compatibility between their customs. Degrees or levels of acculturation have also been examined in given populations ranging from initial contacts possibly to the total assimilation of one group by the other. The selective processes of culture transfer and the phenomena of cultural and personal reformulation have also received much attention (see the report of a Social Science Research Council seminar, 'Acculturation: an Exploratory Formulation', *American Anthropologist*, vol. 56, 1954, pp. 973–1002).

Felix M. Keesing

See also: ASSIMILATION
           DIFFUSION

Achieved Status (See **Pattern Variables**)

Act (See **Bill; Social Act**)

Acting Crowd (See **Crowd**)

Action (See **Social Act; Behaviour**)

Action Anthropology (See **Applied Anthropology**)

Adaptation

Adaptation

A. *Adaptation* may be defined as the process, and the resultant condition, in which changes in an organism, system of social organization, group, or culture aid the survival, functioning, maintenance, or achievement of purpose on the part of an organism, personality, group, culture, or any part thereof.

1. As can be seen the present usage of the term has become so broad as to be diffuse and almost meaningless.

2. Yet any return to strict usage must be so heavily biological as to reduce the usefulness of the term for the social sciences.

3. One possibility of restricted social science definition, however, would refer the *outcome* of adaptation to biological survival only, but would refer the *process* to personality, group, and culture as well as organism.

B. The term was originally, and is still, used to apply to all biological forms. In this usage adaptation signified '... those processes whereby a living organism is fitted to its physical and organic environments' (F. H. Hankins, 'Adaptation', in E. R. A. Seligman (ed.), *Encyclopedia of the Social Sciences*, New York: The Macmillan Co., 1930, vol. I, p. 435). The outcome of the process in this context is the biological survival of the individual organism, the species, or the population aggregate. Personality, society, and culture can be considered as adapting, adaptive, or adapted within this context provided the outcome still refers to biological survival.

1. The sources of threats to survival are always partly internal and partly external to the organism. If the organisms were not constituted in a certain way, then certain external conditions, like cold, food scarcity, viruses, and radiation would be potentially fatal.

2. At the level of biological inheritance, mutation and natural selection accomplish adaptive changes for the species or race. From having once regarded racial characteristics as being without adaptive significance, anthropologists have now adopted quite the contrary point of view. Genetically controlled racial differences '... serve, in the long run, to suit races to different environments, or to different phases of a single environment' (C. S. Coon, S. M. Garn, & T. B. Birdsell, *Races: A Study of the Problems of Race Formation in Man*, Springfield: Charles C. Thomas, 1950, p. 4).

3. Adaptation for survival becomes increasingly dependent on learning as one moves from the non-primates to the primates, and within that order to man. The importance of learning reflects the increasing loss of unlearned responses.

4. At the human level learning both increases the range of possible responses which are adaptive, and creates new problems of survival for which new adaptive responses are required.

(a) Lethal threats not only originate in the geographic environment, and in the distribution of the members of the group by age, sex, and number; but they also arise in problems of social organization, social cohesion, and social integration, as well as in culture itself—one's own or the enemy's.

(b) Threats from these and other sources may be modified not by biological mutation, but by more or less successfully changing existing cultural and social structures and their functions. A given population increasing in density may, for example, threaten survival. Inventions for birth control, political mechanisms for controlling interpersonal relations, or migration may counteract the threat.

C. Despite the fact that adaptation may refer to changes in personality, society, or culture necessary for survival, the tendency has been to broaden the usage so that the term applies to changes which aid in the functioning or maintenance of a system, or to the achievement of purpose. Once the precise reference to survival is lost, usage becomes vague, because to date there exists no set of categories by which all the phenomena which in some sense might be aided by adaptive change can be ordered. Nevertheless such usage is the dominant one in social science today, and must therefore be recorded as such. Examples of this usage follow.

1. The toboggan and snowshoe may be said to be adapted to a northern forest environment characterized by deep but loose snow, whereas the sled of the Eskimo is adapted to the hard-packed snow of the Arctic tundra.

2. Modern schools are said to be adapted to provide general training for the young in a highly specialized and mechanized society marked by free choice of occupation.

3. A nation may be said to be forced to adapt its foreign policites to the exigencies of both the international and domestic political situations, thereby contributing both to the stability of the social system and to the maintenance of peace.

John J. Honigmann

See also: EVOLUTION
ORGANISM
SURVIVAL

Adjudication

A. Convenience supports the broad use of the term to cover all authoritative processes of dispute settlement which are peaceful and aim at justice between the parties, even if other objectives such as the maintenance of peace, the determination of facts, the realization of policies, and the maintenance of law are important. *Adjudication* may therefore be defined as the process of deciding matters in dispute by the decision of a court, tribunal, commission, or other body binding on the parties.

B. *Adjudication* is a term of law and political science. It is sometimes used, especially in law, in a narrow sense to refer to the *judicial* settlement of disputes whether between individuals or between nations. In a broader sense *adjudication* is used to refer to the process of settling disputes peacefully by anybody with authority to make a decision or award binding on the parties. J. B. Moore supports this usage in his compilation, which includes awards of mixed commissions and arbitral tribunals as well as decisions of permanent international courts (*International Adjudications*, New York: Oxford University Press, 1929, 6 vols., vol. 1, pp. xii, xxxvii). He distinguishes, however, between international adjudication on the one hand and the procedures of mediation (q.v.), conciliation, and investigation which result only in recommendations to the parties, on the other. These latter procedures are merely aids to negotiation which may not result in agreement, and therefore lack the *authoritative* character of adjudication.

Broadly defined, *adjudication* includes dispute settlement by a political body such as the United Nations Security Council or a national legislature in whose decision-making *political interests* are important; by international commissions or administrative agencies in whose decision-making *technical knowledge* and *skill* predominate; and by arbitral tribunals selected by the parties for a particular dispute in which *specialized knowledge*, a *spirit of compromise*, or *intuitions of natural justice* may have more influence than legal knowledge. All such bodies, however, are supposed to administer justice and to be guided by considerations of equity when dealing with disputes; and in so far as they are competent to give a decision or award binding on the parties, their activities are commonly called *adjudication* by political scientists.

Quincy Wright

See also: JUSTICE

Adjustment (Also Maladjustment)

A. In its most general sense, *adjustment* denotes the process whereby an organism, organ, or individual entity enters into a relationship of 'harmony' or 'equilibrium' with its environment; and the condition of having attained such a relationship. The antithesis *maladjustment* denotes the absence of such a process and/or the inability to attain such a condition.

B. 1. In its psychological and sociological senses the word occurs more often in America than in Great Britain. No specific meanings of this kind are in the *Shorter Oxford Dictionary* (ed. C. T. Onions, Oxford: Clarendon Press, 1947) nor is the term listed in J. Drever's *Dictionary of Psychology* (Harmondsworth: Penguin Books, 1952). It is, however, discussed at some length by P. Halmos in his book *Towards a Measure of Man* (London: Routledge & Kegan Paul, 1957) who indicates that 'as a process leading up to a goal' adjustment implies 'no finality' in the condition that characterizes the 'goal'. Such a condition 'is at best an intermediary state. For the life process cannot reach a static position; both the individual and its environment are in a constant process of change' (ibid., p. 40).

2. Some of the problems involved in the use of the term may be illustrated by a recent formulation by two American scholars (L. D. Crow & A. Crow, *Understanding Our Behavior*, New York: A. A. Knopf, 1956). They point out that *adjustment* 'refers to the extent to which an object fits the purpose to which it is intended' (ibid., p. 3) and go on to suggest that 'an individual's adjustment is adequate, wholesome or healthful to the extent that he has established a harmonious relationship between himself and the conditions, situations and persons who comprise his physical and social environment' (ibid., p. 4). The ideas of 'purpose', 'harmony', and 'health' which mark all such formulations are themselves often ambiguous and unclear—and their exact connotation is not necessarily uniform in all the spheres (e.g. occupational, vocational, familial, educational, etc.) in which questions of adjustment arise. There are also difficulties which derive from the differing standards of 'health' and 'normality' which mark differing societies and groups within those societies.

3. Usage is made imprecise, further, in so far as (a) the term is often defined in contrast to accommodation (q.v.) and adaptation (q.v.); (b) no clear distinction is drawn between individual adjustment and social adjustment—the

Administration

latter overlaps with the former, both terms denoting the relationships of the individual to the multiple groups which form his 'social environment'; (c) the term is implicitly normative—embodying built-in judgements of value. Especial value is often uncritically attributed to a particular localized set of conditions; and adjustment slides over into conformity (q.v.) to those conditions. Thus, in vocational assessment, tests of 'personality' have frequently been introduced in order to examine an employee's adjustment to the work-situation or the corporate framework. Accepting the physical and psychological requirements of a job and the values implied in it, and being inwardly as well as outwardly loyal to one's employers, are looked upon by many as proof of successful adjustment. This view has not lacked its critics. Similarly it has been objected that an important aim, not only of the vocational counsellor, but also of the priest, teacher, and psychiatrist, is to persuade a person regarded by him as 'maladjusted' to accept and embrace standards against which he may have revolted—whether actively or passively. Such an approach to individual idiosyncrasy seems to ignore the fact that no culture yet described in detail utilizes or emphasizes more than a small sector of its available values, motives, and incentives. To demand an uncritical level or form of adjustment may thus be to neglect and close a number of viable lines of conduct other than those which are, for the time being, conventionally esteemed in the society under review.

T. H. Pear

See also: CONFORMITY

Administered Price (See **Price**)

Administration

A. 1. *Administration* is used to refer to certain special cases of action in which something is served by one person to another; e.g. the administration of a sacrament, or of medicine, or the law (or justice) (see H. Slessor's *The Administration of the Law*, London: Hutchinson's University Library, 1948, and the reference on p. 8 of this work to 'administration of justice').

2. It is also used to denote management (a use found in English from the 16th century).

(a) One special variant persists in the legal usage indicating the management and disposal by an executor or administrator of a deceased person's estate (involving 'letters of administration').

(b) In social and political contexts the term is used most commonly to refer in a general way to activities of management (in the broad as opposed to the narrower sense of management, i.e. to something wider than management conceived as industrial, commercial, or personnel supervision); it is also used more narrowly to indicate special planning and supervisory functions at higher levels (e.g. the functions of the Administrative Class of the British Civil Service).

3. A third usage (in Britain and the United States) refers to the *Government of the day*, or to that part of it which constitutes the Ministry (q.v.) or Presidency (q.v.) (normally prefixed by the possessive form of the Prime Minister's or President's name; e.g. W. E. Hearn (*The Government of England*, London: Longmans, Green, 2nd edn., 1887, p. 219) '... Lord North's administration can scarcely be called a Ministry as we now understand the term'. The first section of Hearn's ch. VIII on the Cabinet is headed 'Description of Modern Administrations'. This use is rare today.

4. In the U.S.A. a further extension makes the term refer to the total of governmental administrative officers; e.g. 'Individuals ... are so at the mercy of administrative officers ... that some form of protection must be offered. ... The Administration is often thrown into relations with individual citizens which must necessarily be hostile' (F. J. Goodnow, *The Principles of the Administrative Law of the United States*, New York: G. P. Putnam's Sons, 1905, bk. VI, 'Control over the Administration', p. 368).

B. Current usage centres on the first two senses of A 2. (b) above, i.e. reference is mainly to the activities involved in co-operative activity within an organization, conceived as serving certain ends which are not necessarily those of the co-operating participants and which is also conceived as being organized for this purpose in a hierarchical manner and as enjoying authority, but possibly also as being under authority.

1. So defined, the areas to which the term could refer are very wide, including at one extreme the affairs of a household, and at the other the affairs of the State. In general, however, the term is not used in connection with smaller and more informal organizations such as families, but tends to be confined to larger and formal organizations. These would include, as well as public and business concerns, such examples as hospitals, churches, and universities.

10

Administration

2. The definition taken literally also does not rule out, as spheres in which administration is involved in internal affairs, both legislatures and courts; but again *administration* is not normally used in connection with the internal affairs of such bodies; nor does it seem to be used very frequently in connection with the internal affairs of political parties or pressure groups. All of these bodies, of course, may be described as being concerned with administration. But by this is normally meant that they participate in, or in some way have contact with, some form of administration taking place outside themselves.

This conventional restrictive use is artificial; to exclude by definition 'judicial administration, for instance, including the docketing and hearing of cases, assigning of judges, laying out of judicial districts' is 'in the strict sense arbitrary' (H. Stein, *Public Administration and Policy Development*, New York: Harcourt, Brace, 1952, p. x).

(a) One reason for this 'arbitrary' limitation is probably that the kinds of formal bodies mentioned in the two previous paragraphs are thought of as having as their primary business *something other than administration*, e.g. legislatures are thought of as existing in order to legislate; the primary business of a court is thought of as being to determine the application of law in specific cases. Allied to this is perhaps the further conception that the relation between administration and its clientele is different from that between these other bodies and their clienteles. Actions within administration proceed all the way from the formulation of broad plans to the face-to-face giving of instructions, rendering of services, etc., to particular persons, whereas legislatures, judiciaries, political parties, and pressure groups are often thought of as relating in a more general, and sometimes more impersonal, way to individuals. (However, at least in the case of political parties the practice of canvassing indicates that this idea is inaccurate.)

(b) A further reason, however, for excluding these other bodies has been that administration has been thought of as being concerned neither with policy (q.v.) (which is a primary concern of legislatures, political parties, and pressure groups), nor with the making or developing of legal rules. Administration has been thought of as being concerned rather with the implementing of policy received from outside and above itself, and as having to act within limits set by rules prescribed and interpreted outside itself. The command theory of law has also supported this view (see W. F. Hearn, *The Government of England*, ch. IV: 'The Legal Expression of the Royal Will in Administration', the exposition in which is in terms of 'the Royal Commands'; see also H. A. Simon on the conceptions of the 1937 report of the President's Committee on Administrative Management in 'Recent Advances in Organization Theory' in S. K. Bailey et al., *Research Frontiers in Politics and Government*, Washington: The Brookings Institution, 1955, p. 24: 'Administration (was) the neutral instrument of policy, according to this doctrine').

This way of looking at administration has increasingly been challenged as attention has come to be drawn to ways in which administration inevitably generates its own internal policies and rules, and also very often inevitably contributes at least part of the content of the policies 'under' which it proceeds, and of the rules which 'regulate' its external rules.

(c) A further consideration allied to the foregoing has again relatively recently been emphasized, namely, that while administration involves formal hierarchical organization, the understanding of the administrative process and the decisions it involves requires examination of the informal structure of administrative bodies as social organizations within which more is at work than the rational transmission of rationally devised policy. Moreover, such administrative bodies can clearly play at least the part of pressure groups, and in some cases may acquire full directing authority (see *Bureaucracy*).

However, other administrative bodies are equally clearly under the direction of persons or bodies outside themselves; whence it would appear to follow that there is justification for the older conception of administration as the implementing of policy being retained as indicating adequately the *primary* characteristic of administration (just as a particular form of policy formation might be the primary characteristic of a legislature, or board of directors, or a political party).

C. Differences have arisen on whether *administration* refers to 'a science' or 'an art', and whether it is possible fruitfully to look for 'principles of administration'. The last conception is treated sceptically by H. A. Simon in *Administrative Behavior* (New York: The Macmillan Co., 1947, pp. 20–44). Writers on management have influenced the conception of administration as science (cf. W. J. M. Mackenzie, 'The Study of Public Administration in the United States', *Public Administration*,

Administrative Law

vol. XXIX, 1951, p. 132) '... in the first phase of American study (theorists) claimed to be founding a "science" of administration. ... the doctrines of "Scientific Management" ... were taken over ...' The British practice has been rather to look on administration as an art. Some recent writings, however, have moved towards allowing something to both science and art (see H. A. Simon, D. W. Smithburgh & V. A. Thompson, *Public Administration*, New York: Alfred A. Knopf, 1950, p. 19 ff; H. Stein, *Public Administration and Policy Development*, pp. xvii–xix; D. Waldo, *The Administrative State: A Study of the Political Theory of American Public Administration*, New York: The Ronald Press, 1948; *The Study of Public Administration*, New York: Random House, 1955, pp. 2–3. This broader interpretation has also been accompanied by a tendency to modify the sharpness of the initial reaction to older formal views of administration. Thus H. A. Simon, 'Recent Advances in Organization Theory', pp. 30 and 36): 'We have come to be suspicious ... of ostensible rational behavior ... nevertheless most behavior in organizations is *intendedly rational behavior*' and 'rationality must be brought about by the design of the organization itself'.

Wilfrid Harrison

See also: PUBLIC ADMINISTRATION

Administrative Law

A. *Administrative law* and *constitutional law* together cover an area which includes all manifestations of state power derived from statute, the common law and the prerogative and the ways in which that power is controlled both by official institutions such as Parliament, the Courts, and local councils and, in certain cases, by unofficial groups or forces. But to distinguish administrative law and constitutional law or to define the former without reference to the latter is only possible in part. At one extreme, we can say that cabinet conventions, parliamentary representation, and the structure of the Courts are matters of constitutional, not administrative, law and that the substantive provision of statutes relating to central and local government functions are matters of administrative law. But in between come a host of matters which can be regarded as either or both: such as delegated legislation, administrative tribunals, local inquiries, ministerial responsibility, the structure of nationalized industries and other public corporations. It is simplest to use another word

and to say that public law consists of two parts viz. (a) constitutional and administrative law (b) criminal law; and to give up any attempt to subdivide the first.

B. Austin defined constitutional law as that branch of public law which 'merely determines the person who shall bear the sovereignty'. With this he compared administrative law as that which 'determines the ends and modes to and in which the sovereign powers shall be exercised: shall be exercised directly by the monarch or sovereign number, or shall be exercised directly by the subordinate political superiors to whom portions of those powers are delegated or committed in trust' (*The Province of Jurisprudence Determined*, London: John Murray, 1861 edn., p. cxi). Maitland observes that Austin's definition of constitutional law is very narrow and contrasts it with that of Holland, of whom he says: 'I think that we catch his idea if we say that, while constitutional law deals with structure, administrative law deals with function. ... His ultimate opinion seems to be that constitutional law deals with structure and with the broader rules which regulate function, while the details of function are left to administrative law.' This, says Maitland, 'is fairly comfortable to our ordinary usage, but ... the line between the constitutional and the administrative departments is one which it is very hard to draw' (*The Constitutional History of England*, Cambridge: Cambridge University Press, 1926, pp. 531, 533, 535, 536).

I. Jennings has written: 'Administrative law is the law relating to the Administration. It determines the organization, powers and duties of administrative authorities' (*The Law and the Constitution*, London: University of London Press, 3rd edn., 1943, p. 194). This is wide enough to embrace most aspects of constitutional law. K. C. Davis, from an American viewpoint, defines administrative law as 'the law concerning the powers and procedures of administrative agencies. An administrative agency is an organ of government, other than a court and other than a legislature, which affects the rights of private parties through either adjudication or rule making. Administrative law consists of constitutional law, statutory law, common law, and agency-made law; the great bulk of it is created by courts in the process of constitutional and statutory interpretation' (*Administrative Law*, St Paul, Minn.: West Publishing Co., 1951, pp. 1, 2). An English administrative lawyer would not have added that last clause; he would consider that the great bulk of it is contained in statutes, statutory instruments, and the decisions of public authorities and administrative tribunals. He would, that is, include substantive public health, housing, town and country planning, and police law with all other statutory provisions relating to central and local governmental activities as part of administrative law, as well as the controlling processes of the Courts and Parliament.

J. A. G. Griffith

See also: CONSTITUTIONAL LAW
LAW

Affect

A. *Affect*, in the broadest sense as used in psychology, refers to the feeling quality of experience, i.e. 'affection' as distinct from cognition (q.v.) and conation (q.v.).

More specifically and most commonly, the term is used as equivalent to emotion (q.v.) and, even more narrowly, to refer to the subjective aspect of emotional states, in contrast to their observable signs.

In all usages, the term covers both positive and negative states, including, for instance, anger and anxiety (q.v.) as well as affection in the sense of love (q.v.).

B. 1. *Affect* has been used in psychology as an inclusive term to cover *a wide range* of experiences 'which involve a feeling tone to any degree and of whatever character' (C. A. Ruckmick, *The Psychology of Feeling and Emotion*, New York: McGraw-Hill, 1936, p. 57). In this broad sense, *affects* stand in contrast to *thoughts* and *actions* in the threefold division of mental life into affective, cognitive, and conative functions.

2. (a) *Affect* is also used rather more narrowly, as interchangeable with emotion. Thus: '... the affective quality of each instinctive process and the sum of the visceral and bodily changes in which it expresses itself are peculiar and distinct; hence language provides special names for such modes of affective experience, names such as anger, fear, curiosity; and the generic name for them is emotion' (W. McDougall, *Introduction to Social Psychology*, Boston: John W. Luce, 3rd edn., 1912, p. 46).

(b) A similar usage is to be found in psychoanalysis, where affect and action are contrasted: 'Affectivity manifests itself essentially in motor (secretory and vasomotor) discharge resulting in an internal alteration of the subject's own body without reference to the external world; motility, in actions designed to effect changes in the external world' (S. Freud, 'The Unconscious', 1915, in *The Standard Edition of the Complete Psychological Works of Sigmund Freud*, ed. by J. Strachey, London: Hogarth Press and the Institute of Psycho-analysis, 24 vols., 1953, vol. XIV, p. 179). In psychoanalytic theory, affects are regarded as having the functions both of *lowering drive tension* through internal physical discharge (largely through autonomic nervous system functions) and of giving *internal subjective signals for adaptive action to be carried out in relation to external stimuli*. In this theory, special stress has been laid upon the importance of adequate expression of affects for the personality as a whole. If affects are inhibited or 'strangulated', through unconscious fear of their results, the general level of emotional excitation may become intolerable, and relief may be sought in the unrealistic, substitute forms of outlet that are typical of neurosis. The long-term inhibition of affects has also been shown to be related significantly to functional and even structural disorders in the bodily organs which effect emotional discharge, producing psychosomatic illness.

3. A further narrowing of the term *affect* was suggested by J. T. MacCurdy (*The Psychology of Emotion, Morbid and Normal*, New York: Harcourt, Brace, 1928, p. 44), who distinguished between affect as a subjective, conscious experience, and emotion as the objective manifestation (including both expressive and physiological changes).

C. de Monchaux

See also: COGNITION
CONATION
EMOTION
WILL

Affinity

A. *Affinity* may be defined as a social relationship between individuals and groups established on the basis of marriage, or of descent (q.v.) and marriage. In the anthropological literature of social organization (q.v.) the meanings assigned are relatively uniform.

1. Affinal kinsmen are '... those whose relationship, real or by adoption, can be demonstrated genealogically by marriage, or by marriage and descent' (R. Piddington, *An Introduction to Social Anthropology*, Edinburgh: Oliver & Boyd, 1950, p. 111).

Age and Area Hypothesis

2. The contrast with the biological connections of consanguinity (q.v.) is stressed in G. P. Murdock's statement that 'Whenever the connection between two relatives ... includes one or more marital links, the two have no necessary biological relationship and are classed as affinal relatives' (G. P. Murdock, *Social Structure*, New York: The Macmillan Co., 1949, p. 95).

B. Reports of field research and theoretical analyses in recent years yield fresh insight into the significance of networks of affinal linkages among individuals and groups in relation to problems of social structure.

1. This is particularly evident in the emphasis of Lévi-Strauss on the consequences for human society '... of substituting the mechanism of a sociologically determined affinity for that of a biologically determined consanguinity' (C. Lévi-Strauss, 'Language and the Analysis of Social Laws', *American Anthropologist*, vol. 53, 1951, p. 158).

2. Similarly, L. Bohannan's distinction between '... rights in a woman as a wife—rights *in uxorem*—and rights in a woman as to the children she may bear, rights *in genetricem*' contributes to a deeper understanding of the mechanisms through which affinity may bind together persons and groups 'Dahomean Marriage: A Revaluation', *Africa*, vol. XIX, 1949, pp. 285–6).

Harry W. Basehart

See also: Consanguinity
        Family
        Kinship and Kinship System
        Kinship Terminology

Age and Area Hypothesis

A. The *age and area hypothesis* may be defined as the theoretically and empirically grounded inference that the age of culture traits can be determined by observing the distribution of such traits over a large area and that the determination can be checked by archaeological study of the culture centre. Thus it serves as the basis for a method of reconstructing the culture history of a region by combining ethnological and archaeological data. 'It is a method of inferring probable reconstructions of what happened in particular situations that resemble other situations in which the principle has actually been known to be operative' (A. L. Kroeber, *Anthropology*, New York: Harcourt, Brace, 1948, p. 561).

1. The hypothesis rests on the assumption that important traits tend to diffuse from a single centre like ripples spreading on a pond when a stone is thrown.

(a) At any given point of time, ripples of culture may be found encircling the culture centre from which they originated.

(b) The farther out the ripples are from the centre, the earlier they left the centre, so that cultures on the periphery or margin of the area still display traits characteristic of the centre in the earliest period. Those successively closer to the centre display traits characteristic of the centre at successively later periods.

2. A corresponding assumption underlying the hypothesis is that the culture centre shows traits not found on the periphery, due to the modification of the centre over time.

B. While anthropologists generally agree as to the meaning of the hypothesis, they tend to disagree on the extent to which it can be successfully used to reconstruct culture history (M. J. Herskovits, *Cultural Anthropology*, New York: Knopf, 1955, pp. 468–70).

Raoul Naroll

See also: Diffusion
        Kulturkreise

Age-Class, Age-Grade, Age-Set

A. These three terms are used with reference to *social groups based on age*. They have not always been clearly distinguished or precisely defined.

1. H. Schurtz, who first called attention to the importance of this principle of grouping, used *age-classes* as a comprehensive term to refer to all groups based on age (*Altersklassen und Männerbünde*, Berlin: Reimer, 1902), and this use was followed by R. H. Lowie (*Primitive Society*, New York: Boni & Liveright, 1920.

2. The term *age-grade* became current in reference to the system characteristic of the Hamitic and Hila-Hamitic peoples of East Africa. In this system men who have passed through the rites of initiation into adult status during a fixed period are organized into permanent groups, and advance as groups through further recognized stages, each of which has its appropriate social tasks (J. H. Driberg, 'Age Grades', *Encyclopaedia Britannica*, 14th edn., 1929).

3. Within an age-grade system so defined, the term *age-set* is commonly used to denote the groups of persons initiated during the same period. This period, however, is usually one of several years, and the persons who actually went through the ritual together form a sub-division of the group who advance through life together. Some writers (e.g. G. W. B. Huntingford, *The Nandi of Kenya*, London: Routledge & Kegan Paul, 1953) refer to these divisions as *sub-sets*. Others (e.g. H. E. Lambert, *Kikuyu Social and Political Institutions*, London: Oxford University Press, 1956) call the sub-division a set and the aggregate of sets (in his sense) a *regiment*.

4. Mention should also be made of the age-organization characteristics of the Yoruba people of Nigeria. In this system individuals pass through a series of grades; entry to a higher grade is secured, when the appropriate age is reached, by the giving of a feast to those who are already members. The members of each grade can be called upon for public services deemed appropriate to their age. In practice contemporaries move up together, but there is no organization into sets nor any alternative ceremony for passing from one grade to the next.

B. The formation of age-sets grouping together persons who have been initiated at one time is characteristic of many societies which do *not* have the age-grade system as defined above. A committee of social anthropologists in the United Kingdom has defined *age-set* as 'a formally organized group of age-fellows', and where this use is followed an *age-grade* is one of the stages through which age-sets pass in an age-grade system—'stages each of which has distinctive status, ceremonial, military or other activities' (Royal Anthropological Institute, *Notes and Queries on Anthropology*, London: Routledge & Kegan Paul, 6th edn., 1951, pp. 67–8). If this use is followed, the appropriate term for the group of persons initiated during the same ceremonies is *sub-set*.

C. A very broad sense of the terms *age-grading* and *age-grade* is found in some writers—signifying, respectively, *any* social differentiation based on *age* and *any* status ascribed on the basis of *age*. Thus 'Virtually every phase of collective life—every institution—involves a system of age-grades' (A. H. Hawley, *Human Ecology*, New York: Ronald Press, 1950, p. 187). But these terms are more appropriately confined to the type of organization in which formally constituted groups of people pass together through socially recognized stages.

L. P. Mair

Aggregate

A. The term *aggregate* is used in social science both as a noun to refer to a type of social unit and as a verb to designate a type of social process. Its use as a noun is frequently qualified by such adjectives as social, status, and statistical. The core reference of aggregate as a social unit is to a temporary fortuitous gathering of individuals within a delimitable geographic area. It should be distinguished from the term category (q.v.) or social category, which denotes sections of a population distinguished externally by one or more common characteristics.

B. 1. The term is sometimes used to refer to any kind of more or less permanent social unit or collectivity. This usage is illustrated by T. Parsons (*The Structure of Social Action*, Glencoe, Ill.: The Free Press, 1949, pp. 279, 744, *et passim*) in the analysis of Pareto's 'persistence of aggregates' and 'residues', in conclusion on 'systems of action and their units', etc.

2. Usually, however, *aggregate* is differentiated from group (q.v.) as a type of social collectivity. Its meaning may be considered at three levels.

(a) At the first level *aggregate* is defined as lacking any significant binding or cohesive social force. The unifying social component that is missing in the aggregate is variously called 'significantly permanent binding consensus', 'organization or interaction', 'social relationships' among individuals, 'consciousness of kind', or 'self-consciousness'. T. M. Newcomb writes: 'We shall limit our definition of "group" by excluding mere *aggregates*—i.e. gatherings of people who have no social relationship to one another except the temporary one of a common physical location' (*Social Psychology*, New York: Dryden Press, 1950, pp. 491–2).

(b) At the second level of analysis the definitions seek to identify factors that assemble individuals into aggregates. At this level the concept has two different referents.

(i) In one context it refers to a gathering of individuals occupying a common geographical location. G. A. Lundberg, C. C. Schrag, and O. N. Larsen using aggregate and aggregation as synonyms state: '*An aggregation designates any human plurel in which the members are in geographical proximity*. That is, gatherings of people who have no relationship to one another except the temporary one of a common physical location are called aggregates' (*Sociology*, New York: Harper & Brothers, 1958, pp. 382–3).

(ii) In another context the term *aggregate*

Aggression

refers to numbers of individuals who are classified or thought of together because of some distinguishing social characteristics, even though they may not be located in the same geographical area. Similarity of observable characteristics like education and income or of overt behaviour such as admiring a hero constitute such distinguishing criteria.

(c) At the third level of analysis *aggregate* is defined as a temporary, fortuitous, and unstable human plurel. The assemblage of individuals, whether concentrated or dispersed, is not regarded as being consciously purposeful, permanent in existence, or having clearly defined boundaries. As a consequence, the included individuals are not 'members' in the strict sense of that word.

Joseph S. Himes

See also: CATEGORY

Aggression (Political Science)

A. *Aggression* has long been a concept of international politics, but only since the establishment of the League of Nations has there been an extensive effort to define it as a term of international law (Q. Wright, 'The Prevention of Aggression', *American Journal of International Law*, vol. 50, 1956, p. 519). There seems to be considerable agreement with the position of W. N. Hogan when he says that '... an acceptable definition of aggression and a reliable procedure for determining when an act of aggression has occurred are essential to a practicable system of collective security' (*International Conflict and Collective Security*, Lexington: University of Kentucky Press, 1955, p. 50). The Security Council of the United Nations—and now, pursuant to the Uniting for Peace Resolution, the General Assembly—is authorized to call specific actions *aggression*, but the divided state of the world impedes a body of practice sufficient to develop a definition, and efforts at definition—apart from actual cases—have not been fruitful. There appears to be no immediate prospect of consensus among diplomats, students of international law, or students of political and social behaviour.

B. Attempts at formal definition in the area of international relations have generally followed one of two approaches: (a) definition by enumeration of specific acts; (b) definition by abstract statement.

1. The standard example of definition by enumeration is the so-called Soviet definition used in conventions between the Soviet Union and other countries in 1933 and 1934. (See *League of Nations Treaty Series*, vol. CXLVII, 1934, no. 3391, pp. 67–77; for a more recent, but similar, Soviet definition see U.N. Document A/C.6/L.208, U.N. General Assembly: Sixth Session; Sixth Committee; Report of the International Law Commission covering the work of its third session: Questions of Defining Aggression). Ignoring the possibility of provocation the definition declares that the aggressor shall be considered to be that state which is the first to commit any of the following actions: '(1) Declaration of war upon another State; (2) Invasion by its armed forces, with or without a declaration of war, of the territory of another State; (3) Attack by its land, naval or air forces, with or without a declaration of war, on the territory, vessels or aircraft of another State; (4) Naval blockade of the coasts or ports of another State; (5) Provision of support to armed bands formed in its territory which have invaded the territory of another State, or refusal, notwithstanding the request of the invaded State, to take in its own territory all the measures in its power to deprive those bands of all aid or protection'.

2. A typical example of attempt at abstract definition is that by Q. Wright: 'An act of aggression is the use or threat to use armed force across an internationally recognized frontier, for which a government, *de facto* or *de jure*, is responsible because of act or negligence, unless justified by a necessity for individual or collective self-defence, by the authority of the United Nations to restore international peace and security, or by consent of the state within whose territory armed force is being used' ('The Prevention of Aggression', p. 526). The Harvard Research defines *aggression* as '...resort to armed force by a State when such resort has been duly determined, by a means which that State is bound to accept, to constitute a violation of an obligation' ('Draft Convention on Rights and Duties of States in Case of Aggression', *American Journal of International Law*, vol. 33, Supplement, 1939, p. 827).

Wright notes the attempt to define an aggressor by the 'provisional orders method'. By this method, the international agency orders a cease-fire after hostilities begin and the party which refuses to end the conflict ... would brand itself as aggressor' ('The Prevention of Aggression', p. 520). Other questions that have been raised include (a) whether aggression should include 'indirect aggression' by economic pressure or ideological infiltration; (b) whether aggression includes in some circumstances civil strife; (c) whether aggression includes threats or potential threats of aggression; (d) whether the aggressor must always be a state (ibid., p. 522).

C. An effort at a sociological or political definition of *aggression* as a term designating a wide range of individual or group acts might furnish the context within which a definition of *aggression* as among states might be worked out. But although the term is sometimes used in such a way no serious effort has been made to grapple with problems of definition. Thus it is simply used synonomously with *encroachment* as a term in ordinary usage. Social analysis does, of course, complicate the problem of definition by stressing the fact that as the term is used both popularly and legally in a power situation what is one nation's definition of an act of aggression is another's act of self-defence. Psychological analysis of aggression is no more helpful, in that it is restricted to the analysis of individual attitudes and the correlated acts and has not been successfully extended to group analysis. (See *aggression* (Social Psychology)). Indeed among students of international politics the psychological dimension has only confused the issue more. J. Stone, for example, lists as one of the difficulties of definition the 'psychological attitude' which is involved in aggression and notes that a state '... has no psyche capable of objective examination' (*Legal Controls of International Conflict*, London: Stevens, 1954, p. 330). And the International Law Commission of the United Nations has dealt with 'aggressive intention' and has indicated that it is '... not susceptible to definition' ('Report of the International Law Commission covering its Third Session, May 16–July 27, 1951', *American Journal of International Law*, vol. 45, 1951, Supplement, p. 119).

John M. Howell

See also: WAR

Aggression (Social Psychology)
A. *Aggression* in its most general usage, stemming from its basic meaning (the act of stepping towards or approaching), has reference to the initiation of physical assault or offensive action.

B. 1. Current and recent use of the term (and the related terms, e.g. aggressiveness) cover the qualities denoted in earlier psychological writings by such terms as pugnacity or self-assertion.

The significance of the term as denoting a fundamental trait or disposition has been much debated. It is perhaps advisable to distinguish the reality of observable *acts of aggression* from the assumed, and unverifiable, trait of 'aggressiveness' attributed to persons or groups. There need be no positive correlation between the propensity to perform such acts and the frequency of e.g. gestures, expressions, etc. which may, in ignorance of cultural diversities, be erroneously attributed to hypothetical traits of aggressiveness.

2. Additional shades of meaning have been primarily the result of psychoanalytic theory— the factor held common in most usages seems to have been the absence of social feeling whether, to use J. Drever's formulation (*Dictionary of Psychology*, Harmondsworth: Penguin Books, 1952), aggressiveness be regarded as 'a manifestation ... of the will to power (Adler) over other people or a projection of the death impulse (Freud)'.

It should be noted that Freud's view shifted from his earlier work in which aggressiveness was conceived as a response to frustration of impulse to his later view that it is an original and independent instinctive disposition (M. Ginsberg, *On the Diversity of Morals*, London: Heinemann, 1956, p. 303). This latter position developed into Freud's theory of Eros and Thanatos (life and death instincts) and the wider social theory which he attempted to develop in *Civilization and Its Discontents* (London: Hogarth Press, 1949).

On this Freudian position see T. H. Pear's observation '... (Freud) developed the notion of two classes of instinct: Eros, or the sexual instinct, and a death instinct, the task of which is to lead organic matter back into the inorganic state. This was criticized by W. McDougall in *Psychoanalysis and Social Psychology*, and some of Freud's followers felt themselves compelled to diverge from him at this point' (T. H. Pear, *The Nature of Conflict*, Paris: Unesco, 1957, p. 131).

T. H. Pear

See also: AGGRESSION (Political Science)
FRUSTRATION

Agitation (Also **Agitator**)
A. In modern usage *agitation* has a double meaning: (a) public excitement, a disturbance arising from disorderly behaviour of the masses; (b) the attempt to bring about some sort of excited, although not necessarily disorderly,

Agnation

attitude among the masses of people especially for political purposes. Thus an *agitator* is a man who attempts to influence the thought and behaviour of a great number of men and women in the direction of such excitement.

B. 1. The term *agitator* obtained a certain prominence during the English civil war of the 17th century (1647) when each regiment of the Cromwellian army elected representatives who were called 'agitators'.

2. During the French Revolution the word was used to denote men who irresponsibly tried to create civil disturbances. The term *agitation* was used generally in this sense (i.e. creation of civic disorder) by the spokesmen of Conservative governments afraid of national, democratic, or socialist movements after the French Revolution, especially in continental Europe.

3. On the other hand, especially in England, the term was also used to describe peaceful and orderly campaigns to mobilize public opinion for some legislative reform, to be carried out by parliament.

4. The term *agitation* has been retained in a different sense by the various revolutionary movements of the Right and Left of our time. By the leaders and followers of these movements, *agitation* is regarded as a legitimate means to arouse public opinion against an oppressive or otherwise objectionable government and social system. The agitator of the revolutionary or extreme opposition parties addresses popular assemblies, strikers, students, etc., in order to bring about a radical change in government.

5. A special Communist usage should be noted. All Communist parties have special organizations for 'agitation and propaganda', but of course, these departments do not organize subversive movements in countries in which a Communist government is in power, but serve the general indoctrination policy of the governing party.

C. Although agitation is obviously an integral part of any propaganda campaign, it has usually denoted an activity influencing people through *speech*, whereas propaganda denotes activities designed to influence the masses through the written word. Broadcasting and television, of course, bring the spoken word of an *agitator* to a nationwide audience which before was only attainable through the written word, so that the two terms (agitation and propaganda) tend to coalesce in our time.

J. S. Erös

See also: PROPAGANDA

Agnatic (See Agnation)

Agnation
A. In contemporary anthropology *agnation* (and the adjective *agnatic*) implies common descent through males only. The criteria of common residence and authority (derived from Roman law) have been dropped, and the term is occasionally used without reference to any organization of groups at all. The term *patrilineal* is used as a synonym for agnatic.

B. In Roman law *agnati* were kin who traced their relationship by descent through males only from a common ancestor, who were under the authority of a single *paterfamilias*, and who resided together. *Agnati* could be adopted. They included women, but not kin linked through a woman (see H. S. Maine, *Ancient Law*, London: John Murray, 1905, p. 148).

J. Middleton

See also: MATRILINEAL
UNILINEAL

Agrarian
The term *agrarian* seems to be used in two ways by modern social scientists.

1. It may be used as an adjective referring to all socio-economic structures, policies, programmes, problems, public measures, and laws which have to do with distribution and tenure of farm or agricultural land and with the social, economic, and political status of those who either live on agricultural land or are dependent on agriculture for a livelihood. It may be used as a noun to refer to one who lives in such a relation to agriculture. It is as an adjective with this meaning that D. Mitrany (*Marx Against the Peasant*, London: Weidenfeld & Nicolson, 1951, p. 135) uses the term when he describes the ways which have been advocated for 'dealing with the agrarian problem in eastern Europe'.

It will be noted that in this first sense the word expresses or reflects no preferences for a way of life and no political interests or objectives. It is simply descriptive of the social and economic organization of agricultural life and of policies, laws, and programmes having to do with that life.

2. In the second usage of the term, *agrarian* signifies a value preference, the advocacy of certain interests, and the conception that life is conditioned by the fact of living in a rural environment. Again the term may be used as a noun or an adjective. As an adjective it may be used to describe a social movement (q.v.) or a philosophy which advocates the values of a rural, agricultural economy as a way of life and the interests of those who live such a way of life. When S. M. Lipset (*Agrarian Socialism: The Cooperative Commonwealth Federation in Saskatchewan*, Berkeley: University of California Press, 1950) uses *agrarian* to modify *socialism*, he implies not only that such socialism had its origin among farmers, but also that it was developed to benefit the interests of those dependent upon agriculture and that it valued the way of life of those engaged in agriculture. Similarly as a noun the term denotes those individuals who espouse the interests of the farmer and/or his way of life. In this meaning of the term an *agrarian* may but need not be himself engaged in agriculture. From this usage of *agrarian* comes *agrarianism* to denote the movements built on these interests and values or the philosophy of such movements.

Mulford Q. Sibley

See also: AGRICULTURE
SOCIAL MOVEMENT

Agrarianism (See **Agrarian**)

Agriculture (Also Horticulture)

A. In its most general sense *agriculture* is the cultivation of the soil to produce edible food crops—primarily roots and cereals.

B. 1. In 19th-century ethnological theory, human societies were supposed to have developed through three economic stages: hunting, herding, and agriculture. The third, because it included animal husbandry and cultivation by ploughing, was presumed to have followed the domestication of animals. However, in view of the fact that many communities cultivate without having owned any livestock, the terms agriculture and horticulture, as denoting two types of tillage, were later distinguished.

Horticulture was used to refer to the *more primitive stage of hand tillage* or hoe-culture, which was correlated with other traits (notably responsibility of women for cultivation, and relatively small size of field).

Agriculture was reserved for a later stage of evolution, in which the soil was cultivated over a relatively wide area, generally with the use of animal traction or ploughs.

2. This evolutionary scheme is now discarded, it being recognized that all peoples do not pass inevitably through the same series of developmental stages, but the distinction between *agriculture* and *horticulture* (i.e. the cultivation of the soil with hand tools) is often maintained, both in anthropology and in archaeology.

M. Douglas

See also: SUBSISTENCE ECONOMY

Alienation

A. *Alienation* as most generally used in social science, denotes an estrangement or separation between parts or the whole of the personality and significant aspects of the world of experience.

1. Within this general denotation the term may refer to (a) an objective state of estrangement or separation; (b) the state of feeling of the estranged personality; (c) a motivational state tending toward estrangement.

2. The separation denoted by the term may be between (a) the self and the objective world; (b) the self and aspects of the self that have become separated and placed over against the self, e.g. alienated labour; (c) the self and the self.

B. Although there are several sources for the idea of alienation in various philosophic treatments of the place of man in the world, its primary source in the social sciences was the social theory of Marx supported perhaps by the sociology of Freud (K. Marx, *Economic and Philosophic Manuscripts of 1844*, London: Lawrence & Wishart, 1959, pp. 67–84; S. Freud, *Civilization and Its Discontents*, trans. by J. Riviere, London: Hogarth Press, 1953). In Marxian theory some men are alienated from their labour objectively by the relations of economic production and the systems of class domination. This separation from their work and the products of their work results also in their being alienated from nature and from themselves. In Freudian theory *alienation* (the term must be imputed although the idea is clear enough) occurs primarily as the result of the needs of civilization, although H. Marcuse suggests that Freud was aware that the demands of social structure hostile to the core of the self could be made worse by the existence of class domination (H. Marcuse, *Eros and Civilization*, Boston: The Beacon Press, 1955, p. 45 ff).

This usage views *alienation* as the state of or the result of conformity with institutional expectations in segmented roles, where the performance of specialized functions, determined by the division of labour and the system of dominance of certain groups, deprives the total personality of opportunities to exercise

Allegiance

substantively rational judgment and thereby to apply its creative powers in influencing the conditions of its own existence. Conformity without involvement takes the form of submission to necessity as represented by objective and alien demands, rather than subjective personal needs, while the role-performance ('alienated labour') perpetuates the conditions of this estranged existence. According to E. Fromm (*The Sane Society*, New York: Rinehart, 1955, p. 120), man leads an alienated life when 'he does not experience himself as the centre of his world, as the creator of his own acts—but his acts and their consequences have become his masters, whom he obeys, or whom he may even worship'.

C. From this conception of alienation as an objective state of separation, there comes the usage of *alienation* as the malaise that results from such a state, sometimes accompanied by a shift of emphasis from structures of domination to the value content of the culture as the primary causal factor. In this usage the estrangement of the self from the self is stressed. There is a loss of emotions which are part of normal experience. The withdrawal of emotional interest from an external world, because it is threatening, leads to an exaggerated concern with oneself. This may express itself either in extreme sensitivity and altered feelings, or in depersonalization and isolation of affect where the overcharged feelings are repressed or dissociated from the conscious personality. A passage from K. Horney discusses alienation as lack of comprehension of the self: 'We cannot suppress or eliminate essential parts of ourselves without becoming estranged from ourselves. ... The person simply becomes oblivious to what he really feels, likes, rejects, believes—in short, to what he really is. Without knowing it he may live the life of his image. ... The person loses interest in life because it is not he who lives it; he cannot make decisions because he does not know what he really wants; if difficulties mount he may be pervaded by a sense of unreality—an accentuated expression of his permanent condition of being unreal to himself' (*Our Inner Conflicts*, London: Routledge & Kegan Paul, 1946, p. 111).

D. While the motivational tendency toward the rejection of internalized or external expectations of others may be derived from the conflict between the objective order of the world and the inner core of the self, stress in much sociological theory today tends to fall not on this conflict which may exist but on the failure to overcome it. A passage from T. Parsons and E. A. Shils (*Toward a General Theory of Action*, Cambridge, Mass.: Harvard University Press, 1951, p. 156 ff.) illustrates this usage: 'Insofar as internalization occurs without exceptionally great unmastered conflict, ego will develop need-dispositions to conform with expectations; while faulty internalization (internalization attended by ineffective defense mechanisms or incomplete resolution of conflicts) may produce alienative need-dispositions, which are derivative need-dispositions to refuse to fulfil expectations'. Partial internalization is thus a prerequisite for alienation to occur, otherwise the attitude would be considered one of indifference. Many alienative tendencies do, however, remain covert, since they exist only as the negative component of an ambivalent conformity-alienation disposition.

Kurt Lang

See also: CONFORMITY AND NON-CONFORMITY

Allegiance

A. The most general use of the term has long been to describe the ties and emotions (romantic and legal) which bind an individual to a group or its symbols.

B. 1. For historians the term involves the medieval concepts of liege-homage as they developed in feudal times and the early modern period. Hence the legal concept of *allegiance* is peculiar to English law and has no exact counterpart in German, French, or Italian jurisprudence. This is because the development of feudal institutions in Europe did not favour the confirmation of the idea of 'liege homage' as it did in England. The concept came to be variously interpreted. Thus, in the days of Edward III and Richard II allegiance was linked with treason (q.v.) by statutes which made treasonous the intent or purpose of killing or deposing the King without any overt act. This concept was extended by James I in the Church-State contest. A breach of allegiance now became also a form of heresy.

In the 17th and 18th centuries allegiance became due to the body politic. The individual owed allegiance from the moment of his birth on British soil; as a corollary, only natural-born subjects had a right to own land. The British Naturalisation Act of 1870 deprived the concept of much of its significance.

20

2. In the United States the doctrine of absolute and perpetual allegiance has been regarded as inadmissible. The American revolution settled for Americans the question of perpetual allegiance. Mr Justice Story (1779–1845) could say 'allegiance is nothing more than the tie or duty of obedience of a subject to the sovereign under whose protection he is' (Inglis v. Sailor's Snug Harbor, 3, Peters 99–155 (1830)). In the United States allegiance is now demonstrated by an oath to support the Constitution and laws of the United States—not to support the government of the United States.

3. (a) Contemporary legal usage is illustrated by reference to the declaration of Justice Story quoted above, i.e. allegiance involves the legal duty which is owed by an inhabitant towards the sovereign and the territory in which he resides. Allegiance and protection are the two correlative factors denoting the reciprocal duties of subjects and rulers, i.e. if one requires the protection of a sovereign, one must swear to uphold and obey the sovereign's orders, and if the sovereign wishes for support, he will naturalize and protect one from injury by his enemies at home or abroad.

(b) More generally *allegiance* refers to attachment to social institutions and symbols. Here failure to maintain such attachments is attended by social rather than legal penalties.

R. H. Pear

See also: LOYALTY
          TREASON

Alliance

The social science usage of the term follows ordinary usage, although social scientists may make highly sophisticated analyses of the causes and consequences of the phenomena denoted by it.

1. In its most general meaning *alliance* denotes the joining together of two or more persons or groups in a co-operative venture which faces active opposition (actual, potential, or figurative). In this general sense one may speak, for example, of an alliance between two political leaders against another leader, or between science and money against disease.

2. In the area of international politics, however, the meaning of the term is more restricted. The element of co-operation is present as is the facing of actual or potential opposition. But the co-operation always contains the pledge or the actual provision of mutual military assistance under certain agreed-upon circumstances.

Frederick H. Hartmann and Heyward Moore

Allocation of Resources

Allocation of Resources

A. The *allocation of resources* is the apportioning of available productive agents, human and non-human, among firms and industries engaged in the production of goods and services. Scarcity of means which have alternative uses is an almost ubiquitous condition of human behaviour (L. Robbins, *An Essay on the Nature and Significance of Economic Science*, London: Macmillan, 1932, p. 15). If the goal of economic activity be taken to be a level of want satisfaction as high as the economy can provide, the best possible productive techniques must be used, resources must be fully employed, and resources must be properly allocated or distributed among their alternative uses in the satisfaction of wants of consumers.

B. The problem of resource allocation grows out of the fact that an economy's capacity to produce is inherently limited whereas human wants are virtually unlimited. One of the central problems of economics is the determination of how large each of the specialized users of resources should be. In a completely planned economy, the extreme form of which would be a slave state with a small class of rulers, resources might be allocated in a highly arbitrary manner designed to serve the best interests of the governing class. In a completely free economy resources would be allocated in accordance with the wishes of consumers as expressed in the market place. A shortage of a commodity would be reflected by a higher price; this would tend to reduce consumption and increase production. In this way the economy's resources would be utilized to produce such goods and in such amounts as were dictated by consumer preference. Price (q.v.) plays the central role in the allocation of resources in a free-enterprise economy.

The economist is concerned with the efficiency conditions for the optimum utilization of society's resources. Factors of production (what a firm buys) must be used in the most efficient combinations. This requires that in equilibrium the marginal rate of substitution between any two factors must be the same for any good using both, and the marginal rate of substitution between any two goods used by the consumer must be equal to the technological rate of transformation between them. In an economy characterized by pure competition in all markets price everywhere in equilibrium will equal marginal cost, a situation which summarizes the previous two conditions. Provided that the

21

Ambilateral

amounts of factors in the economy are fixed, and that there is no divergence between private and social marginal cost, universal marginal cost pricing is a necessary condition for an 'optimum' equilibrium position, this being defined as a position from which no individual can be made better off without at least one other being made worse off.

It may be fairly stated that the economist's traditional suspicion of monopoly rests on the fact that in equilibrium the presence of monopolistic forces in either input or output markets distorts the allocation of resources and results in a failure of the economy to achieve optimal efficiency. So much for equilibrium analysis. Some writers, however, shift the argument to growth and emphasize that large corporations often have the ability and opportunity to exploit economies of scale and engage in extensive research; and that, although bigness (not the same thing as monopoly) and various deviations from pure competition may entail relatively inefficient allocation of resources at any moment of time, they may encourage a more rapid long-run development rate than would prevail under purely competitive market conditions. From this point of view the efficient allocation goal becomes less significant if economic development proceeds at a rapid rate (J. A. Schumpeter, *Capitalism, Socialism, and Democracy*, New York: Harper & Brothers, 3rd edn., 1950, pp. 104–5).

In the contemporary world free-market prices have not been depended upon exclusively for the allocation of resources, but to a considerable degree resource allocation has become a function of public authority. The optimum allocation of resources has, in fact, lost its place as a prime function of the economic system; other objectives such as the full employment of resources, better distribution of income, economic growth, and, particularly for the underdeveloped countries, rapid industrialization, have taken priority over resource allocation as the chief functions of public policy (S. E. Harris, *International and Interregional Economics*, New York: McGraw-Hill, 1957, p. 226).

Clark Lee Allen

See also: MARGINAL ANALYSIS
MARKET ECONOMY
MONOPOLY
PRICE

Alternative Cost (See **Cost**)

Amalgamation (See **Assimilation**)

Ambilateral

Ambilateral is sometimes used in kinship studies to refer to non-unilineal systems in which an individual may choose to align himself with either of his parental groups. R. Firth argues that 'The admission to membership through descent from either males or females—or both conjoined—shows that the *hapu* is not a unilateral group of the strict type. It may be called, in fact, an *ambilateral* group, since both parents are eligible for the purposes of kinship affiliation' (R. Firth, *Economics of the New Zealand Maori*, Wellington, N.Z.: R. E. Owen, 1959, p. 112).

Maurice Freedman

See also: DESCENT

Ambivalence

A. In its more general sense in psychological and psychoanalytic writings, *ambivalence* means the co-existence in one person, of opposing emotional attitudes, e.g. of love and hate, towards another person or object.

B. 1. The term was coined by E. Bleuler (*Vortrag von Prof. Bleuler über Ambivalenz*, Report in *Zentralblatt für Psychoanalyse*, 1910), to describe the co-existence in one person, of opposing emotional attitudes, e.g. of love and hate, towards the same object. Ambivalence was considered by Bleuler to be a fundamental characteristic of the emotional life of those suffering from schizophrenia (Bleuler's term for *dementia praecox*). He showed that *emotional ambivalence* often extended into other areas of the personality, producing *ambivalence of the will* (e.g. a patient wishes at the same time to eat and not to eat: he brings the spoon to his mouth dozens of times but never completes the act) or *intellectual ambivalence* (e.g. a patient says in the same breath: 'I am Dr H., I am not Dr H.') (E. Bleuler, *Dementia Praecox, or the Group of Schizophrenias*, trans. by J. Zinkin, New York: International Universities Press, 1950, pp. 53–4).

2. Freud adopted the term, using it primarily in the sense of an oscillation between love and hate, although on rare occasions he used it also to describe the co-existence in one person of the active and passive forms of an instinctual impulse, e.g. of sadism and masochism, or of scopophilia and exhibitionism (see J. Strachey's editorial footnote 2 to Freud's *Instincts and their Vicissitudes*, standard edn., London: Hogarth Press, 1957, vol. XIV, p. 131). Freud also extended the range of application of the term to include *neurotic* versions, as well as the extreme *psychotic* forms reported by Bleuler. Further, he regarded ambivalence as a fundamental *characteristic of infantile emotional life*, a necessary consequence of the dependence of the child upon the mother (or mother substitute). Primitive, unorganized drives of a sexual and aggressive nature are exercised at first upon the one object, which is the most powerful source both of satisfaction and of frustration.

C. de Monchaux

See also: AFFECT
EMOTION
LOVE

Amendment

A. The term *amendment*, whenever used, has the core denotation of alteration or change. Historically the change or alteration denoted was for the sake of correction or improvement. In the realities and controversies of politics, however, the nature of correction or improvement becomes uncertain, so that alteration or change remains the only indisputable meaning as the term is applied. Historically also, the term has denoted *formal* change or alteration in court proceedings, parliamentary motions or written constitutions; but the term in recent years has also come to refer to the informal, sometimes unintended, changes in law or constitutions.

B. In its usage to denote formal procedure or the result of such procedure, *amendment* is found in court proceedings, parliamentary procedure, and the dealings with the language of written constitutions.

1. In Anglo-American law since the time of Blackstone, at least, an amendment in a court proceeding is the correction of error committed in any process, pleading or procedure. The correction may be made by the litigants, either as a matter of course or of mutual consent, or on the motion of the court.

2. In parliamentary procedure the term refers to alterations proposed or made in the language of any bill, measure, resolution, or motion, before its submission, during its consideration, or after its enactment. This usage applies not only to the legislative bodies of states, but also to any bodies organized along parliamentary lines.

3. Probably the most fundamental type of formal amendment is that which is constituted by the alteration of the formal language of written constitutions. The importance of the amending procedure in a time of serious social change has been stated by C. J. Friedrich: '... a well-drawn constitution will provide for its own amendment in such a way as to forestall, as far as is humanly possible, revolutionary upheavals. That being the case, the provisions for amendment form a vital part of most modern constitutions' (*Constitutional Government and Democracy*, Boston: Ginn, 1941, p. 135).

The *formal* amending process has meaning only in those constitutions designated as 'rigid'. E. McC. Sait has said, 'The flexible constitution places constitutional law and ordinary law on the same level, in the sense that both are enacted in the same way and proceed from the same source. The rigid constitution possesses a special and higher status, standing above the ordinary law and being more difficult to change' (*Political Institutions*, New York: D. Appleton-Century, 1938, p. 331). In the modern world, the principal example of the flexible constitution is that of the United Kingdom, which is alterable by act of a majority of the Parliament.

In states with rigid constitutions, the amending process generally requires action that goes beyond the normal requirements for passage of a bill. In some cases more than a simple majority vote of the major legislative body is required. In addition co-operative action of local governmental units is sometimes required.

C. It has become increasingly apparent that change in constitutions, written or unwritten, formal or informal, comes about frequently through means other than that of formal amendment. Perhaps the first extension of the term *amendment* beyond the meaning restricted to a formal process of change with respect to an inflexible constitution was the use of it to denote the alteration and the process of alteration of flexible constitutions. But the term is also coming to be used of those changes in constitutional law, even under a written, supposedly inflexible constitution, that come about through administrative decisions, court actions, etc. In this sense all constitutions are undergoing a continuous process of amendment, and formal amendment becomes a limiting case.

Earl Latham

See also: CONSTITUTION

American Government

A. *American government*, in addition to its obvious meaning, denotes a specialized subfield of American political science centred on the study of and teaching about local, state, and national government and politics of the United States.

American Government

B. 1. Perhaps only the comparative government field in American political science is independent of the subject-matter of American government. Yet American government is regarded as a special field because it is the general subject of the introductory course in political science for the great majority of college students. In this role, it has acquired a life of its own, and many professors are specialists in American government: national, state, and local, without necessarily being specialized either in another field or in a sub-field of this rather inchoate area.

The latest extensive study of the prevalence of introductory courses in American government was made in 1951 by the American Political Science Association. Of 252 institutions that reported, 172 (70 per cent) offered American government as the beginning course. An additional 10 per cent appeared to offer a course largely in American government. Thirty-eight departments called their beginning course 'principles of' or 'introduction to' political science, these being combinations of philosophy, theory, principles, comparative government, and international affairs.

2. Of what does *American government* as a course of study consist? Partly the scope of the field is defined by texts on American government for college freshmen and sophomores. Texts in this field correspond to the texts in introductory economics, sociology, and psychology with respect to placement in the curriculum, but they take an entirely different approach, being primarily descriptive treatises on American institutions and law, rather than attempts to state principles of human behaviour. The authors of texts are usually unclear as to whether they want to teach ethics or be objective. As a result their values usually sidle in silently, but they are usually present, and are frequently justified as a necessary means of value indoctrination. Thus, for instance, F. O. Wilcox ('The Introductory Course in Government', *American Political Science Review*, vol. XLI, 1947, p. 487) declares: 'The dominating objective should be to encourage an appreciation of the nature and value of popular government—what difference it makes whether we have it or not—what the alternatives are—what institutions would seem to be essential for its preservation'. Even on the assumption that every college student must be indoctrinated with the values of the existing society, its institutions, its 'goals', its 'progress', the status of the field of American government might be clarified if it

were also recognized that every student should have a chance to learn objective political science in an atmosphere freed of political justifications and moral tensions. While universities should be responsible for civic instruction, just as churches are responsible for religious instruction, the burden should not be placed upon political science departments but upon the university as a whole. Thus thoroughly objective courses in American government should be offered, although under these new conditions, it is quite unlikely that the course would retain its name or shape for very long.

3. Research and writing in the field seem to favour certain topics. The Presidency is one. Electoral college reform is another. Reapportionment is another. The treaty power is a fourth. Congressional investigations and security measures constitute yet another. Negro rights, political participation, and executive reorganization are also favourites. States' rights have declined as a subject of interest but federalism still receives much attention.

State and local governments are inadequately studied. Most of the best scholars specialize in the national government, notwithstanding that the possibilities of a political science are better in the state and local field, where many cases present themselves for analysis and comparison, and moreover, that state and local governments are in themselves important enough to warrant the interest of a fair proportion of the best minds.

The complaint may also be made that the field is still too juridical. The courts are followed too closely as giving a true version of what occurs in politics and what is important to government. Also, many believe that the field lingers too readily on controversies that are 'cheap'; that is, they are easy to come by, anyone can have an opinion on them, and they are current. Prominent among these are civil rights issues, taken without reference to the total context of social action; public power, taken as a black-and-white opposition to private power; and the 'problem of the non-voter', where undiluted indignation may be vented on the apathy of the public.

Lastly, integration with the materials of economics and sociology lags, although the evidences of the integration of social and economic factors in real politics and government abound, and though other fields of political science are pressing towards greater integration. As a result of this lag, the important para-constitutional and quasi-public groups in the

24

United States are just beginning to be studied as essentials to knowing American government. Churches, unions, corporations, trade associations, foundations, universities, and other groups are greatly influential in the political and governing processes; their structures, functions, networks of contacts, leadership, and increasing participation in government are largely ignored in the texts and in much of the research. It takes a decade for advanced ideas and work to be integrated into the textbooks and lower division courses. Since the last few years have seen remarkable progress at the formal level, the next few years may witness a number of positive responses to the criticisms detailed above.

Alfred de Grazia

See also: FOREIGN AND COMPARATIVE
GOVERNMENT

Anarchism

A. *Anarchism* is the political doctrine, theory, or philosophy which maintains that political authority, in whatever guise, is unnecessary and undesirable. While the central emphasis of the theory is thus hostility to the State, it is frequently associated with attitudes which would repudiate not only political authority but organized social and religious authority as well. Anarchism stresses the possibilities of voluntary co-operation and mutual aid in the life of man and attacks co-operation brought by force or the threat of external coercion.

While anarchism is united in its basic repudiation of the State, it is divided with respect to its doctrine of property. Individualist anarchism believes that property in material things should be vested in each person; while communist anarchism, generally speaking, holds that property should be administered primarily by voluntary groups.

B. While the exact formulations differ from one another in some degree, the meaning ascribed to *anarchism* by students of political science (and the social sciences generally) is fairly uniform. 'Aetiologically', E. V. Zenker maintains (*Anarchism: A Criticism and History of the Anarchist Theory*, Eng. trans., London: Methuen, 1898, p. 264), 'anarchism may be defined ... as disbelief in the suitability of constituted society'. B. R. Tucker (*Individual Liberty*, New York: Vanguard Press, 1926, p. 7) terms it 'the doctrine that all the affairs of men should be managed by individuals or voluntary associations, and that the State should be abolished'.

B. Russell (*Roads to Freedom*, London: Allen & Unwin, 2nd edn., 1919, p. 50) defines it as 'the theory which is opposed to every kind of forcible government'. F. W. Coker (*Recent Political Thought*, New York: D. Appleton-Century, 1934, p. 192) thinks of it as 'the doctrine that political authority, in any of its forms, is unnecessary and undesirable' and he goes on to suggest that anarchism 'has usually been associated with opposition to the institution of private property and also with hostility to organized religious authority'. According to H. W. Laidler (*Social-Economic Movements*, New York: Thomas F. Crowell, 1944, p. 283), in general individualist anarchism would not disturb the principle of private property ownership, while communist anarchism 'would substitute for private ownership a system of community or producers' ownership and operation of land and capital without the interference of the political state'.

Mulford Q. Sibley

See also: FREEDOM
RADICALISM

Ancestor Worship

A. *Ancestor worship* may be defined as a set of attitudes, beliefs, and practices associated with the treatment as deified of a wide range of deceased persons in a community—particularly the dead within a kinship grouping, however this may be circumscribed. While certain aspects of the definition should be modified to suit the particular form and function of ancestor worship as it appears in various societies, it does appear universally to require a belief that the ancestral dead may interfere in human life and must, therefore, be placated, or conversely that human activity itself may promote the well-being of the ancestral dead in an after-life.

1. A careful distinction should be made between reverence accorded to ancestors and the worship of ancestors as though they were deities, the latter constituting an actual cult of the dead. Except in speaking of such a cult, the use of the expression *ancestor worship* is not justified.

2. Similarly the term excludes cults of the dead which are not ancestrally directed. Although the worship of dead kings may be included, if such worship is grounded in kinship concepts, reverence for heroes and totemism are specifically excluded.

B. While students of comparative religion have employed the term, its use has been pre-emi-

Animism

nently determined by anthropologists. A representative anthropological use is that of P. Radin, where he speaks of ancestor worship as the '... equation of one's ancestors, both remote and immediate, or of persons standing in the place of ancestor or titular household head, with spirits and gods, and the transference to them of all specifically religious acts and attitudes which are usually associated with the worship of the spirits and gods' ('Ancestor Worship', in E. R. A. Seligman (ed.), *Encyclopedia of the Social Sciences*, New York: The Macmillan Co., vol. II, 1931, p. 54).

C. Until fairly recently, most anthropologists have concerned themselves with the distribution of the forms of ancestor worship, but the attention which is currently given in the anthropological sciences to structure and function has created some impatience with a purely geographical treatment.

1. Special attention to the appearance of the cult of ancestors was given by J. G. Frazer and by his contemporaries who were interested in demonstrating an evolution of religious forms (*The Golden Bough*, New York: The Macmillan Co., abridged edn., 1936).

2. Later writers, such as R. H. Lowie and W. D. Wallis, were content to note the appearance of the phenomenon of ancestor worship in different parts of the world (R. H. Lowie, *Primitive Religion*, New York: Boni & Liveright, 1924; W. D. Wallis, *Religion in Primitive Society*, New York: Crofts, 1939).

3. Contemporary writers agree that such a phenomenon as ancestor worship demands a definition with respect to each individual society and to a careful consideration of that society's cultural attitudes and promises (W. Howells, *The Heathens*, New York: Doubleday, 1946; W. J. Goode, *Religion Among the Primitives*, Glencoe, Ill.: The Free Press, 1951).

(a) Thus F. L. K. Hsu has shown that the ancestral cult among the Chinese has the function of stabilizing the family system and providing a rationale for it (*Under the Ancestors' Shadow*, New York: Columbia University Press, 1948).

(b) Conversely, in Dahomey, ancestor worship is only one of a complex series of beliefs surrounding an elaborate pantheon tied into the political structure (cf. M. J. Herskovits, *Dahomey*, New York: Augustin, 1938).

Robert F. Spencer

Androcracy (See **Patriarchy**)

Animism (Also **Animatism**)

A. *Animism* may be defined as the belief in the existence of a separable soul-entity, potentially distinct and apart from any concrete embodiment in a living individual or material organism. *Animatism* denotes the belief in the inhabitation of natural objects by impersonal supernatural forces.

B. 1. In his famous 'minimal definition', the distinguished British anthropologist, E. B. Tylor, defined religion as 'a belief in spiritual beings' (*Primitive Culture*, New York: Holt, 1st American, from 2nd English edn., 1874, 2 vols., vol. I, pp. 424–5). The ethnographic ubiquity of animism, Tylor believed, must depend upon experiences which are universal among all men. These, according to Tylor, would include the phenomena of *life* and *death*, *sleep*, and abnormal psychic states such as *ecstasy* (literally, '[the soul's] standing outside [the body]').

2. Somewhat allied historically with Tylor's animism is Spencer's theory that religion arose and evolved as forms of ghost-worship (*The Principles of Sociology*, New York: Appleton-Century-Crofts, 1876–96, 3 vols., vol. I, pp. 322–3, ch. 20). Spencer's theory can perhaps best be schematized by imaging the ethnographic world as a series of concentric circles, the outermost of which consists in the most ancient, widespread and generalized belief in ghosts or spirits; then, successively within this are other circles, embodying more and more specialized forms of polytheism, ancestor worship and the like until the latest and highest form, monotheism, has evolved. However, Spencer's numerous critics have argued that many nature gods might well have arisen from a direct contemplation of nature and an imputing to natural phenomena of animating spirits that need not have passed through a human body at any time as a ghost.

3. Modern psychologists have added to our understanding of animistic thinking as described by Tylor. W. James (*The Varieties of Religious Experience*, New York: Longmans, Green, 1952) has shown that the 'mystical experience' or *ecstasy* is a psychological state of partial ego-abeyance, as in dreams, which might lead to a belief in the 'ecstatic' soul. J. Piaget (*The Child's Conception of the World*, New York: Harcourt, Brace, 1929) has collected materials on the animistic thinking of children which indicate that this is a naturally recurring stage of ego-differentiation in the child's view of the world. W. Dennis ('Animistic Thinking among College and University Students', *Scientific Monthly*, vol. 76, 1953, pp. 247–9) has further shown that much of the thinking of contemporary young adults is animistic also.

4. In the same Tylorian tradition W. La Barre (*The Human Animal*, Chicago: University of Chicago Press, 1954, pp. 276, 295–6) has suggested that a primitive misunderstanding of the nature of *breath* and metabolic *warmth* would account for the belief in a quasi-material soul as air or fire, which is evidently behind the Indo-European concepts of the soul (anima, spiritus, pneuma, atman, logos, etc.); that is, since breath and warmth depart from the dead body, these must therefore constitute the life-principle or soul. The animist thus explains 'life' as something *additive*, rather than as a *process* in a living organism (as modern biology views the matter); the *anima* is thus a kind of insubstantial unknown substance X, the algebraic difference between the living and the dead body.

5. All the above writers, like Tylor himself, have sought rationalist and positivist explanations for animistic thinking. They accord to primitive men rational and logical minds, but minds that reason from a different premise the hypothesis of the *anima* or soul. That is, they believe that primitive men had real empirical data, naturalistically occurring, which they tried to explain by means of an animistic hypothesis; and that, meanwhile, the various modern sciences of biology, psychology, anthropology, and linguistics have alternative and different explanations for these same naturalistic phenomena. It is relevant to emphasize here that there are, of course, many other alternative explanations of the origin and nature of religion (e.g. Durkheim's important thesis that religious rites are a celebration of the mystic 'ingroupness' of the ingroup); but at the same time these interesting and valuable hypotheses are not relevant to a discussion of *animism*.

C. 1. Tylor's concept of animism has been criticized on two grounds, its intellectualism and its evolutionism. In general, critics of Tylor would consider that he neglected the emotional aspects of religion, and some would even argue the priority of feeling over thinking in religious phenomena. That is, animism might be less a rational explanation of events than a way of rationalizing basic feelings about death and immortality or the like. For example, Tylor's successor at Oxford, R. R. Marett (*The Threshold of Religion*, London: Methuen, 1914, pp. 102–21) believed that Tylor gave too little place to the emotions of awe and wonder in the

origins of religion (in which most modern students would agree with Marett). Marett also argued an evolutionary stage prior to Tylor's universal original animism (in which most modern students would agree with neither, by rejecting cultural evolutionism as such). After the researches of Bishop Codrington and others on Melanesian religion, Marett produced an alternative theory, that of *animatism*, which he believed had preceded *animism* as an evolutionary stage of thinking. But 'This, too, involves an intellectualistic emphasis', as F. M. Keesing has pointed out (*Cultural Anthropology*, New York: Rinehart, 1958, p. 326). The issue has perhaps been best formulated by M. J. Herskovits (*Cultural Anthropology*, New York: Knopf, 1955, p. 211): 'For Marett, the concepts of *mana* and its counterpart, *tabu*, represented the most generalized, and hence the basic, force of religious belief. This he held to be especially true when mana was compared to animism which was intellectualistic and lacked "the emotions of awe, wonder, and the like". To the sense "of the attribution of life and animation which many peoples have toward inanimate objects", Marett gave the name *animatism*. Thus he distinguished this belief from the narrower category of the *animae*, the spirits that actuate men and beasts and objects of nature and which, for Tylor, constituted animism'. Marett's *animatism* is a belief in the 'animation' of natural objects by the impersonal force of *mana* (compare the Siouan *wakan*, Algonkian *manitou*, Iroquoian *orenda*, and many other similar concepts in other parts of the world).

2. The cultural evolutionist controversy involved in the special theories of Tylor and Marett, as to whether *animatism* preceded *animism* or the reverse, is now a dead issue. Modern anthropologists are simply not interested in postulating pseudo-history or universal sequences on intellectualist logical grounds. The classic Tylor-Marett difference of interpretation has also softened with time. Thus R. Benedict can write of 'animatism, or the belief in mana; and animism, or the belief in spirits' ('Religion', in F. Boas (ed.), *General Anthropology*, New York: D. C. Heath, 1938, pp. 627–65), a matter that hinges entirely on the spiritual nature of *mana*. 'Benedict suggests that the distinction here comes from application by man to spiritual theory of his experiences respectively with *persons* [animism] and with *things* [animatism]' (F. M. Keesing, *Cultural Anthropology*, p. 337). Similarly, in Keesing's own definitions (ibid, p. 426), of 'Animatism:

Animism

belief in impersonal spiritual power or force, e.g. mana' and 'Animism: belief in personalized, indwelling spirits throughout nature', the distinction hinges only on the issue of personal/impersonal. Again, in A. Hoebel (*Man in the Primitive World*, New York: McGraw-Hill, 2nd edn., 1949, p. 643) the definitions 'Animatism, the attribution of life to inanimate objects' and 'Animism, the belief in the existence of spiritual beings' might almost be exchanged with one another; while in H. H. Turney-High (*General Anthropology*, New York: Crowell, 1949, p. 569) 'Animatism: The belief that all objects are living, sentient beings' and 'Animism: The belief in spiritual beings' the distinction would seem to disappear entirely.

D. In recent years the Tylor-Marett controversy has been not so much settled in its own terms as abandoned for alternative ways of viewing the phenomena. That is, culture-evolutionary explanations have been largely replaced by psychological understandings, and what contemporary anthropoligists see is not *stages* but *kinds* of attitudes toward nature. If we may omit Frazer's own evolutionist biases and theories of priority, the distinction between animism and animatism can be seen to consist in the contrast of soul/mana and personal/impersonal forces imputed to nature, that is in Frazer's old contrast of magic/religion (*The Golden Bough*, 1 vol. edn., New York: The Macmillan Co., 1930, pp. 11–12). All evolutionist controversies forgotten, magic depends on a belief in the automatic operation of impersonal forces which man can embody and control, viz. *mana*; while religion depends on the contingent wills of independent personalized spirits whom man must placate or persuade or submit to. That the two may be intimately mixed in any ethnographically-encountered 'religion' is not to impugn the usefulness of Frazer's typological distinction. Furthermore, we may all assent to a neo-Marettian position, viz., that magic and religion represent discernibly different emotional *attitudes* toward reality. It is not so much a question of mana and magic as being *concepts* appropriate toward things, and spirits and gods as being *concepts* appropriate toward persons, with one or the other being prior historically or phylogenetically. It is, rather, that magic and religion are both anthropomorphic projections on to nature, representing different ontogenetic stages or *emotional styles* of viewing reality. (An additional, and emotionally different, style or world-view is, of course, that of science).

Modern dynamic psychology thus sees man's projective patterning of the unknown (the not-self, the object) as being derived from his own consciousness of himself (the experienced, the subject). What a man sees in the Rorschach-unknown is not so much a function of that unknown as it is of himself and his own projective paradigms. Similarly, modern dynamic psychiatry would state that the *nature* of what he sees and the *manner* of his seeing it both depend upon the stage of differentiation or discrimination of ego-boundaries that the individual perceiver has attained to emotionally in his ontogenetic experience of persons and of things. The classic analytic position is that animistic (or animatistic) thinking derives from an archaic and infantile stage in individual development when there is still an imperfect discrimination of the ego and the world. Not knowing the world in mature 'object-relationship', experientially and emotionally, as something discrete and different from the subjective consciousness and will, the narcissistic and immature (undifferentiated) ego imputes its own crude perception of the self to an as yet only vaguely discerned not-self.

Whether this perception is properly to be described as 'animatistic' or 'animistic' would therefore depend on the degree of differentiation in the perceiving individual. If the world and his will are undiscriminated; if material reality is seen as animate, responsive to volition, and imbued with power (mana); if the mana is ambiguously inside-outside or may be incorporated by the individual; and if the mana is 'impersonal', since this world-view precedes the full discrimination of other persons as objects—then we have the world-view of the magician, whose unique will sways a world of impersonal forces. This stage or style is that of animatism, of impersonal mana, and of magic. In this an undisenchanted 'infantile omnipotence' operates with the arrogance and epistemological naïveté of the magician, who commands a world in which the expression of his wish is equivalent to its accomplishment (an 'omnipotence of thought' also characteristic of magic thinking in the schizophrenic, who has essentially remained in or regressed to this stage of thinking).

In contrast, in a later familial or 'oedipal' stage of emotional development, when other persons are better discriminated as discrete and will-possessing objects, like but apart from the subjective self, then the world may be seen projectively in terms of many personalized polytheistic sibling spirits or in terms of personalized

28

parental gods, primarily of the father as creator, law-giver, omnipotent ruler of reality, and the like. The chastened narcissism of the individual in the oedipal stage of religion thus imputes omnipotence to an outside anthropomorphic Person and Father, and amends his emotional and ritual behaviour accordingly. Hence the oedipal stance of religion is psychologically more mature than the preoedipal stance of magic. (Again, a transoedipal stance is also possible, that of science, in which omnipotence is attributed neither to the self nor to the not-self, but in which paradigmatic son and father are endowed with equal but finite potency).

However, the psychological as well as the evolutionary theories of the animistic origin and nature of religious behaviour must be subject to the same stringent caution: child, psychotic, primitive, and primeval man are by no means identical and each must be methodologically discriminated from the others. Neither the psychologically infantile nor the ethnographically primitive should be confounded with the historically archaic. Biology is not ethnography, nor is psychology history.

Weston La Barre

See also: ANCESTOR WORSHIP
MAGIC
MANA
POLYTHEISM
RELIGION
SOCIOLOGY OF RELIGION

Anomy (Anomie)

A. The term has three different, though related, meanings. These are (a) personal disorganization of the sort that results in a disoriented or lawless individual, with little reference to the rigidity of the social structure or the character of its norms; (b) social situations in which the norms themselves are in conflict and the individual runs into trouble in his efforts to conform to contradictory requirements; and (c) a social situation that, in the limiting case, contains no norms and one that is, in consequence, the contrary of 'society' as 'anarchy' is the contrary of 'government'. There would seem to be a grammatical warrant for the adoption of the third of these usages in preference to the other two, but custom will doubtless dictate, in due course, the final outcome.

B. The word appeared in English as early as 1591 and was frequently used in 17th century theology to mean disregard of law, especially divine law. The word appears in addition in Dr Johnson's dictionary of 1755. The word appears both in its English and French spelling, more usually, perhaps, in the latter. The French spelling predominates because of its introduction into the vocabulary of sociology by Durkheim, in his classic study of suicide (1897). Durkheim distinguished between three kinds of suicide and the following passage is a relevant summary of his position: 'Anomy, therefore, is a regular and specific factor in suicide in our modern societies; one of the springs from which the annual contingent feeds. So we have here a new type to distinguish from the others. It differs from them in its dependence, not on the way in which individuals are attached to society, but on how it regulates them. Egoistic suicide results from man's no longer finding a basis for existence in life; altruistic suicide, because this basis for existence appears to man situated beyond life itself. The third sort of suicide, the existence of which has just been shown, results from man's activity's lacking regulation and his consequent sufferings. By virtue of its origin we shall assign this last variety the name of *anomic suicide*' (E. Durkheim, *Suicide*, trans. by J. A. Spaulding & G. Simpson, ed. by G. Simpson, London: Routledge & Kegan Paul, 1952, p. 258). Although Simpson, in this translation, uses the English form, several American writers have retained the French *anomie*.

C. R. M. MacIver recommends that the English form be adopted. He defines *anomy* as 'the fulfilment of the process of desocialization, the retreat of the individual into his own ego, the sceptical rejection of all social bonds'. He goes on to say that anomy is not simply lawlessness; it 'signifies the state of mind of one who has been pulled up from his moral roots, who has no longer any standards but only disconnected urges, who has no longer any sense of continuity, of folk, of obligation'. MacIver finds three types of anomic persons—those who have 'lost the compass' of their lives, those who thereupon pursue external values like power, and those who are hopelessly disoriented. Those last, in the most profound sense of all, are 'displaced persons', the victims of social alienation. MacIver concludes that anomy is an enemy of democracy, and thus gives it a political connotation (*The Ramparts We Guard*, New York: The Macmillan Co., 1950, p. 77).

In his 'Social Structure and Anomie', R. K. Merton equates anomy with instability and refers also in this connection to 'demoralization' and 'de-institutionalization' (reprinted in

Antagonistic Co-operation

R. K. Merton, *Social Theory and Social Structure*, rev. edn., Glencoe: The Free Press, 1957, p. 136). T. Parsons sees anomy as 'the polar antithesis of full institutionalization', as 'the absence of structured complementarity of the interaction process or, what is the same thing, the complete breakdown of normative order' (*The Social System*, Glencoe: The Free Press, 1951, p. 39). He regards it as a limiting concept, however, and one that is 'never descriptive of a concrete social system'.

Robert Bierstedt

See also: SOCIAL DISORGANIZATION

Antagonistic Co-operation

A. The term was introduced by W. G. Sumner in his *Folkways* (Boston: Ginn, 1906). Sumner's definition runs as follows: 'Antagonistic co-operation ... is a high action of the reason to overlook lesser antagonisms in order to work together for great interests' (ibid., p. 18).

It would seem that Sumner's definition was drawn from his study of classical economics which asserted, since the days of Adam Smith, that the division of labour is the expression of man's constant need for the co-operation and assistance of his fellows in the pursuit of his self-interest. Smith wrote: 'Man has almost constant occasion for the help of his brethren, and it is in vain for him to expect it from their benevolence only. ... It is not from the benevolence of the butcher, the brewer or the baker that we expect our dinner, but from their regard to their own interest' (A. Smith, *The Wealth of Nations*, The Modern Library Edition, New York: Random House, 1937, p. 14).

B. An attempt has been made to restrict the reference of the term to economic phenomena. Thus E. T. Hiller (*Social Relations and Structures*, New York: Harper, 1947, pp. 154-5) restricts the use of the term to the economic field when he writes: 'Although co-operation is necessary for production, disagreements arise over the division of the returns between the participants. This mixture of sociative and dissociative, agreeing and disagreeing relation is called competitive co-operation or antagonistic co-operation'. But it is only in sociology that the term has found acceptance.

Lewis A. Coser

See also: CO-OPERATION

Anthropomorphism

In its most general sense, *anthropomorphism* denotes the ascription of human or man-like characteristics to a variety of non-human forms. Most frequent usage is concerned with the ascriptions made in beliefs about supernatural beings. Such beliefs may be religious—e.g. spirits; or non-religious—e.g. gnomes. The ascribed characteristics may be anatomical, physiological, psychological, affective or emotional, behavioural, or symbolic. The forms may be faunal, floral, celestial, inanimate material, or non-material. Use of the term in social science follows general use, viz. *anthropomorphism* is a component of beliefs concerning supernatural beings. It tends to differ from theological and literary usages in that its main emphasis does not centre on *theistic* beliefs, but also includes animistic beliefs relating to spirits.

Verne F. Ray

See also: ANIMISM

Anti-Colonialism

The term *anti-colonialism* has arisen to describe the movement against colonialism (q.v.), and particularly against the powers said to practise colonialism. It is thus used to describe the movement against the political, economic, or cultural domination by the European powers or by the United States, over nations, peoples, or communities which are non-European. 'The "anti-colonialism" of the Asian countries is easier to explain as it stems largely from strong racial feeling and from resentment of the long-standing European domination of the world, of which the oversea colonies are the surviving symbols' (A. C. Burns, *In Defence of Colonies*, London: Allen & Unwin, 1957, p. 19).

H. Maddick

See also: COLONIALISM
COLONY

Anxiety

A. *Anxiety* may be defined as a reaction of apprehension ranging from uneasiness to complete panic preceded by a real or a symbolic condition of threat which the subject perceives diffusely and to which he reacts with an intensity that tends to be disproportionate.

B. The interpretation of anxiety varies according to theoretical perspective and methods of research employed.

1. One view, advocated mainly by experimental psychologists, regards anxiety as a reaction found in both man and animals. It is constituted by an association of a non-noxious stimulus with a noxious stimulus, either in a simple Pavlovian form of a conditioning of the non-noxious stimulus so that it provokes the reaction or in more complex forms (W. N. Schoenfeld, 'An Experimental Approach to Anxiety, Escape and Avoidance Behaviour', in P. H. Hoch & J. Zubin (eds.), *Anxiety*, New York: Grune & Stratton, 1950, pp. 70–99). Animals may experience a simple anxiety response as the result of the association of a non-noxious stimulus with such elementary shocking stimuli as electric shock or air blast. Humans experience a more complicated and symbolic anxiety reaction. The reactions are continuous but differ quantitatively.

2. Another view common to social and clinical psychologists sees anxiety as a distinctive reaction of human beings which requires symbols, temporal orientation, and a scheme of imagery. According to this viewpoint, animals experience fear or the alertness and suspicion which leads to vigilance, but not anxiety. Even infants have a startle reaction which is distinct from anxiety. Socialized humans experience anxiety in part because they react to emotionally charged symbols and images that they can anticipate or recall as well as experience in the present.

C. Anxiety may be categorized into neurotic and normal types.

1. Neurotic anxiety is constituted by a reaction of helplessness disproportionate to the diffuse threat which provokes it. The afflicted person becomes apprehensive, diffident, and uncertain about how to cope with the threat, and hence perceives it as a persistent menacing problem. Since he cannot muster an effective response to handle the danger, he resorts to defences to avert the panic inherent in anxiety. For some psychiatrists and analysts neurotic anxiety is a core disorder because other neurotic symptoms and even some psychotic symptoms may be interpreted as defences against it. In K. Horney's *The Neurotic Personality of our Time* (New York: W. W. Norton, 1937, p. 23) anxiety is 'the motor which sets the neurotic process going and keeps it in motion'. This stress on anxiety differs from the view which considers anxiety as a special neurotic syndrome parallel but not necessarily basic to other neuroses. In either interpretation anxiety is thought to be primarily a product of unconscious psychic processes and threats, since the ostensible threat does not seem sufficient to produce the intensity of the response.

2. The definition of anxiety as being a response disproportionate to the consciously perceived situation affects the conception of so-called *normal anxiety*, so that it cannot be identified with fear which is specific and directed in proportionate measure toward the situation. In this sense there is always an aspect of 'abnormality' about anxiety.

(a) *Normal anxiety* may denote anxiety which is shared by a group. Thus A. I. Hallowell ('The Social Function of Anxiety in a Primitive Society', *American Sociological Review*, vol. 6, 1941, p. 881) maintains that the Saulteaux Indians 'invest certain disease situations with a traumatic quality which is a function of the beliefs held rather than of the actual danger threatened by the illness itself'.

(b) The term, *normal anxiety*, may also be used to refer to a reaction resulting from a genuine outside danger where the response, though disproportionate is only so to a minimal degree. In this case as in (a) above some investigators have questioned whether the term 'normal' is appropriate since the response may be seriously incapacitating.

(c) The third use of *normal anxiety* to denote a reaction of mild apprehension and uncertainty in relation to the achievement of a vital but somewhat vague goal is perhaps most appropriate. This reaction is illustrated by the American middle-class child's striving for success in a highly competitive milieu. A. Davis maintains that anxiety in this sense is essential for success: 'The development of adaptive, socialized anxiety in middle-status life is all the more essential because the social and prestige awards of this status must necessarily be postponed during the prolonged training of the child and adolescent' (A. Davis, 'Socialization and Adolescent Personality', in T. M. Newcomb & E. L. Hartley (eds.), *Readings in Social Psychology*, New York: Henry Holt, 1947, p. 143).

D. Comparison of the incidence, focus, and intensity of anxiety between social groups may be made. Thus the Alorese seem more anxiety-ridden than Americans. Americans become intensely anxious about failure in their careers, the Saulteaux about diseases which do not respond to treatment, and the Siriono about the possible loss of food. A group dimension of anxiety is also present in the anxiety found in unstructured groups and in the dissolution of organized groups, as in the case of collective panic where each person becomes so concerned about his own safety that he cannot respond in

Applied Anthropology

an orderly manner in accord with group demands.

S. Kirson Weinberg

See also: ABNORMAL
NEUROSIS

Applied Anthropology

A. *Applied anthropology* may be defined as the professional application of any one of the disciplines included in anthropology to human affairs. Application may be direct or indirect, on behalf of a client, a government, the anthropologist himself, or the anthropologist in conjunction with the groups studied.

B. The idea of applying anthropology goes back many years, but according to H. I. Hogbin the first actual use of the term, *applied anthropology*, was by Radcliffe-Brown in the title of an article published in 1930 (H. I. Hogbin, 'Anthropology as Public Service and Malinowski's Contribution to It', in R. Firth (ed.), *Man and Culture*, London: Routledge & Kegan Paul, 1957, p. 245n.; the article referred to was A. R. Radcliffe-Brown, 'Applied Anthropology', *Report of the Twentieth Meeting of the Australian and New Zealand Association for the Advancement of Science*, 1930, pp. 267–80). Malinowski used the term, *practical anthropology*, in much the same way (H. I. Hogbin, 'Anthropology as Public Service and Malinowski's Contribution to It', p. 252).

C. The use of such terms did not at first suggest the possibility of a profession of applied anthropology with an appropriate ethic of professional responsibility, but this conception gradually developed.

1. There were a few government anthropologists appointed in various parts of the British Empire and Commonwealth and British Trust Territories during the period between World Wars I and II, and anthropologists began to be employed in problems relating to American Indians during the same period. The problems of dealing with ethnic minorities, colonial peoples, and underdeveloped areas has increased the use of anthropologists by government during and since World War II.

2. In 1941, The Society for Applied Anthropology was formed in the United States. It was based '... upon the premise that a science of human relations can only be developed if theories are tested in practice', and it called for testing the results of analysis and hypothesis by application to concrete problems ('Editorial Statement', *Applied Anthropology*, vol. 1, 1941, pp. 1–2). In 1949, the Society drew up a code of professional ethics which stated in part '... that the applied anthropologist must take responsibility for the effects of his recommendations, never maintaining that he is merely a technician unconcerned with the ends toward which his applied scientific skills are directed'; and that '... the specific area of responsibility of the applied anthropologist is to promote a state of dynamic equilibrium within systems of human relationships' (M. Mead, E. D. Chapple & G. G. Brown, 'Report of the Committee on Ethics', *Human Organization*, vol. 8, 1949, p. 20).

3. Although the term has been used more extensively for the work of social or cultural anthropologists in government, industry, race relations, and the technical assistance field, it may be more generally applied when a specialist in any field of anthropology, culture, linguistics, physical anthropology, or archaeology draws professionally on his discipline to solve some practical problem.

D. As was to be expected, several terms have been used synonomously with applied anthropology. Malinowski's use of *practical anthropology* has already been mentioned. Where stress has been placed on deliberate social change, the term has sometimes been used interchangeably with *experimental anthropology*. S. Tax and his students have given the name *action anthropology* to non-directive intervention in cultural change among American Indian groups.

E. There is some difference at present between (a) those who would regard applied anthropology as a profession for which anthropologists, in addition to a theoretical education in some branch of anthropology, must be specially trained and within which professional standards should prevail; and (b) those who identify applied anthropology with a form of anthropological research which either continuously or at some point becomes a part of, and affects, the process of change which it studies. It must be stressed that either view involves a search for values, rooted in the discipline of anthropology, which can guide the applied anthropologist in any use of his knowledge at any level of intervention in human affairs.

Margaret Mead

See also: SOCIAL ANTHROPOLOGY

Appointive Office (See **Public Office**)

Apportionment

A. The most important usage of the term *apportionment* as it is understood in the United States, particularly in constitutional law, is to denote the process by which representation in legislative bodies may be distributed according to the population of various legally defined areas. The term is also used to denote (a) the distribution of either a tax burden or the income from a tax according to population and area; (b) the distribution of civil service appointments among the states according to population and area; (c) the distribution of delegates to party conventions on the basis of population and contribution to party vote; (d) the allotment of funds to various agencies of government; and (e) the distribution of right and responsibility proportionate to time or degree of participation with respect to a transaction.

B. The ordinary usage of the term *apportionment* simply denotes the distribution of something. Thus it is possible to say that in the United States the apportionment of Senators in the Federal Congress is fixed by the Constitution at two for each state. In modern democratic societies, however, the term has become peculiarly associated with the distribution of representation on the basis of population and geographic area, particularly in the United States. The use of the term to denote such distribution in the United States has probably come about because of the language of the U.S. Federal Constitution which provides that 'Representatives and direct taxes shall be apportioned among the several States which may be included within this Union, according to their numbers ...' (Article 1, Section 2). To that end, the same section of the Constitution provides that a census 'shall be made every ten years, together with an apportionment of seats in the lower house in a manner directed by the Congress'. Thus the language of the Constitution has tied the term to the principle of distribution according to population and geographic area. This has been reinforced by the fact that many state constitutions base distribution of representation on geographic area and population, and use the term *apportionment* in this context.

The principle which the term *apportionment* denotes in the United States is also found in Britain, although the term itself is not necessarily associated with the principle. Thus D. L. Keir (*The Constitutional History of Modern Britain Since 1485*, London: A. & C. Black, 6th edn., 1960, p. 460) writes: 'The representation of "interests" has been abandoned in favour of proportioning representation to population. New and largely artificial units have been constructed for this purpose, comprising aggregations of population reckoned on a purely numerical basis, existing only for parliamentary elections, and often possessing no other principle of life'.

C. The principle of *apportionment* (according to population and geographic area) in the United States extends beyond legislative representation. Under the Pendleton Act of 1883, apportionment is applied in connection with the Civil Service. Also the general practice of both major political parties has been to determine the number of delegates to the party convention on a basis ultimately related to the various states' populations *and* their contribution to the party vote. Taxation and revenue may be distributed on the basis of area and population.

D. Despite the close association of the term with distribution according to population and geographic area in the United States, it has retained in some contexts the simple meaning of distribution. Thus *apportionment* is frequently used with respect to allotment of funds to various agencies of government, the purpose being to control and prevent deficits: 'These apportionments, which require careful advance planning of the year's work are then submitted to the mayor, manager, governor, or finance director ...' (L. D. White, *Introduction to the Study of Public Administration*, New York: The Macmillan Co., rev. edn., 1939, p. 237). So also in law *apportionment* may denote the allotment of shares to be paid on a collective debt by each owing it, or it may have reference to the amount of rent to be paid when tenancy is terminated at an irregular interval.

Oscar Svarlien

Appropriation

A. *Appropriation* is a legislative action or process authorizing expenditures of public funds to be made for stated purposes.

'Appropriations are authorizations to make expenditures from the general fund of the Treasury or from the various special funds' (*The Budget of the United States Government for the Fiscal Year Ending June 30, 1961*, Washington: Government Printing Office, 1960, p. 3). '... by the Appropriation Act, Parliament

Appropriation

"appropriates" the supply which it grants to particular purposes, these purposes being shown under the various Votes of the Annual Estimates' (J. Woods, 'Treasury Control', *Political Quarterly*, vol. XXV, 1954, pp. 370–1).

B. Although the term may relate to the taking of property (cf. the opposite *expropriation*), attention here is confined to its bearing on the four phases of government expenditure: (a) estimating of expenditure; (b) appropriation; (c) execution of the expenditures authorized by the appropriations; and (d) audit. In British and American national practice the preparation of expenditure estimates (i.e. drafting of the budget) and the execution of the authorized spending programme are executive responsibilities, while appropriation and audit are legislative responsibilities.

Two factors largely determine the meaning of *appropriation:* the technical problems of accounting in an untidy political and administrative world; and the relations between the legislative and executive branches, to which historic battles over the power of the purse have made varying contributions in different countries.

1. *Appropriation* as the authorization of expenditure of public funds must be distinguished from three related things.

(a) The granting of authority to do something which costs money is not the same as the granting of the authority to spend the money. In the United States this leads to the distinction between an *appropriation act* and an *enabling act*. The latter establishes substantive policy, and authorizes an executive agency to do particular things. But an enabling act does not carry money for its execution; this must be separately provided by one or a series of appropriation acts. In turn, an appropriation act in the United States does not normally include substantive enabling provisions, but simply finances already authorized activities.

(b) An appropriation is distinct from the *budget of estimated expenditures* submitted by the Executive. The budget is informational and recommendatory in purpose and therefore more detailed than the language of appropriation acts.

(c) Appropriations may overlap, but not be identical, with authority to commit or obligate public funds. The authorization to commit public funds enables an agency to sign contracts for construction, equipment and supplies, and services that commit the government to pay the contract sums when the contract is fulfilled. In the United States, congressional appropriations include such authority, but Congress may vote the authority without at the same time appropriating the funds to meet the obligation.

2. British and American appropriation acts differ in their relation to a given fiscal year. Parliament appropriates funds for payments actually to be made during the fiscal year; Congress appropriates funds part of which will be spent during the current year (e.g. on salaries and wages), part of which will be set aside to discharge obligations incurred during the fiscal year but to be paid in later years, and part of which will be carried over into succeeding years to provide continuity in certain programmes even though these have not been translated into firm contractual obligations. Neither Parliament nor Congress appropriates annually the full sums to be spent by the whole Government. Permanent appropriations account for perhaps a fourth of British expenditure and a tenth of American expenditure; interest on the public debt is among the items thus covered. In the United States an additional third of the annual expenditure is financed by appropriations carried over from prior years (though not 'permanent').

Failure of annual appropriation acts to be passed prior to the fiscal year to which they pertain leads legislatures to vote authorization of month-to-month continuation of the already established spending rate so that agencies do not have to suspend operations. Unanticipated needs, agencies' improvidence, and political advantages in making the initial major appropriation acts appear modest lead to the need for supplemental and deficiency appropriation acts during the course of the fiscal year.

3. The nature of legislative-executive relations helps to define the meaning of *appropriation*. (a) The United States Congress and the state legislatures have a relatively free hand in determining what appropriations shall be. But the British Parliament may only decrease or delete items; it may not increase them and it may not introduce new items. As the House of Lords is powerless with respect to money bills and the British Cabinet commands majority support in the House of Commons and may make any appropriation vote a question of confidence, the executive has the whip hand. In the United States the legislative majority may be unsympathetic to the chief executive, and the two legislative chambers are in fact equal, although by tradition appropriation bills are initiated in the House of Representatives.

(b) The degree of detail in appropriation acts is greater in the United States. Whereas the British appropriations fall into about 150 'votes', the current appropriation items in the United States are about 625. Degree of detail in appropriation acts affects the scope for executive flexibility.

(c) While the question does not arise in Great Britain, the ability or inability of the American chief executive to veto items in an appropriation bill has important bearing on his strength in the appropriation process. The President must veto a whole bill to make effective his objection to any part of it; most state governors can veto individual items in an appropriation bill while permitting the remainder of the bill to become law.

James W. Fesler

See also: BUDGET

Appropriation Act (See **Appropriation**)

Arbitration (See **Mediation**)

Archaeology

A. *Archaeology* may be defined as the study of the old as this pertains to man's society and culture. As a discipline, it addresses itself both to the particulars of the past in specific times and places and to generalizations about past events. Although rooted in a humanistic tradition, archaeology is a science in so far as it uses methods of empirical verification in determining and relating its data and also organizes its findings for the investigation of social and cultural processes.

B. In the United States archaeology is considered a sub-field of anthropology, and although not so considered in England it is obviously closely related to that branch of human knowledge.

1. It is related to physical anthropology in that the remains of man are found and studied in archaeological contexts.

2. It is related to ethnology in that living peoples preserve cultural continuity with the past.

3. It is related to linguistics in that written language is often a part of archaeological findings.

4. It is related to social and cultural anthropology in that theories of cultural change and of man's cultural and social behaviour may be advanced and tested upon the bases of archaeological evidence.

C. Archaeology tends to merge with history and the line separating the two disciplines is neither clear nor exact. In a general way, human events recorded in contemporaneous written records are the domain of history, while those recorded only in material residue—artifacts, burials, ruined buildings, etc.—in the earth belong to archaeology. Yet there are exceptions to this as in Egyptian or Mayan hieroglyphic texts where such writings provide but a limited amount of information concerning a past society and are usually regarded as falling within the purview of the archaeologist.

D. Areas of investigation constitute specialities in archaeology. Distinct fields of interest are designated by such terms as biblical archaeology, prehistoric archaeology, and classical archaeology whose modifying adjectives indicate clearly the temporal era on which each field is concentrated. In Europe a distinction is sometimes made between archaeology and prehistory. It is customary for archaeology to have reference to the study of Classical or Mediterranean civilizations, while the earlier Neolithic, Mesolithic, and Palaeolithic cultures are treated under prehistory. In the Americas, on the other hand, the entire range of Pre-Columbian time back to the earliest Lithic stages is embraced in archaeology.

E. Archaeology has developed a body of special methods and techniques which distinguish it from other sub-fields of anthropology and from history. These methods and techniques derive from the long time-perspective of archaeology and from the necessity of archaeological concern with material objects.

1. The archaeologist must carefully exhume and preserve artifacts and structures from the past.

2. He must determine the ages of such structures and artifacts, relatively or exactly, by their associations and their position in geological strata. In these efforts he uses the aid of other relevant sciences.

3. Assemblages of artifacts are related to soil strata and, with the help of geologists, palaeontologists, and palaeobotanists, to ancient natural environments.

4. Through all this the archaeologist must remain aware of the fact that material objects are not culture but the products of culture. They are, in effect, the fossilized imprints of past social and cultural behaviour. To reconstruct such behaviour, it becomes the archaeological

Area Co-Tradition

task to infer and attribute function to these objects by analogy with living situations.

Gordon R. Willey

See also: PREHISTORY

Area Co-Tradition

A. Discussion and application of the *area co-tradition* concept in archaeology have yet to provide an agreed-upon formal definition.

1. One usage of the term regards area co-tradition as the culture area (q.v.) with time depth.

2. Another usage restricts *area co-tradition* to a culture area with a single co-tradition, the latter being considered a series of traditions—a series of sequences of 'culture phases' or 'whole cultures'—having a common origin.

3. A third possible usage would accept the limitation of co-tradition to 'whole cultures' but would allow *area co-tradition* to be applied to culture areas having more than one co-tradition.

B. The concept was introduced into archaeological literature by W. C. Bennett, although Bennett acknowledged that the term was coined by R. Linton. Bennett never actually defined the term, but rather gave a specific example, the Peruvian area co-tradition ('The Peruvian Co-Tradition', in *A Reappraisal of Peruvian Archeology*, Memoirs of the Society for American Archeology, no. 4, 1948). The term was apparently used by Bennett to cover the overall history of an area in which the component cultures had been interrelated over a long period of time. In his 'New World Culture History: South America' (in A. L. Kroeber (ed.), *Anthropology Today—An Encyclopedic Inventory*, Chicago: University of Chicago Press, 1953, p. 214), Bennett comments, 'The area co-tradition approach assumes cultural continuity within the region and mutual influence of the component cultures both in space and in time'.

C. G. R. Willey has indicated that the concept is an aid to archaeological-historical interpretation because it provides time depth, and on that basis has used the term to mean the culture area with time depth. 'It affords the archeologist a working device in place of the culture area, for the latter lacked the time dimension and was unsuited to problems of prehistory. The area co-tradition is, in effect, the culture area with time depth' ('Archeological Theories and Interpretation: New World', in *Anthropology Today*, p. 374). Willey has suggested that in the eastern United States there are three co-traditions and that perhaps two exist in the Eskimo area.

D. I. Rouse has felt that some misinterpretations of the concepts held by Bennett have crept into the literature and has attempted to formulate a general definition after criticizing the use of area co-tradition by others.

1. Rouse insists that Bennett meant something more by area co-tradition than the culture area with time depth, since, he argues, the culture area concept itself necessarily contains the implication of relationships through time (I. Rouse, 'Culture Area and Co-Tradition', *Southwestern Journal of Anthropology*, vol. 13, 1957, pp. 123–33, esp. pp. 124–5). The 'something more' can be determined only by separating for the moment the parts of the concept, 'area' and 'co-tradition'.

2. In discussing co-tradition, Rouse indicates that Willey and Phillips have used the term tradition—and by implication, co-tradition—to apply to elements and complexes of elements as well as to cultural wholes, whereas Bennett used co-tradition to refer only to whole cultures. Rouse then proceeds to define tradition as consisting of '... a single linear series of phases [whole cultures] which has developed through a relatively long span of time but not necessarily within a single area'. He further defines co-tradition as '... a series of traditions which have a common origin' ('Culture Area and Co-Tradition', p. 128).

3. Rouse then argues that writers such as P. S. Martin and J. B. Rinaldo have misapplied the 'area' part of the area co-tradition concept by using it to designate Southwestern cultural history as an area co-tradition, the reason being that there are at least two co-traditions in that area, and Bennett meant the term to apply only where there was one co-tradition present (I. Rouse, 'Culture Area and Co-Tradition', p. 129; the reference here is to P. S. Martin and J. B. Rinaldo, 'The Southwestern Co-tradition', *Southwestern Journal of Anthropology*, vol. 7, 1951, pp. 215–29).

4. On the basis of this analysis Rouse emerges with a general definition to the effect that area co-tradition refers to an area with a single series of sequences of 'culture phases' or 'whole cultures' having a common origin. If an area has more than one co-tradition it is not an area co-tradition.

E. While the restriction of the term to 'whole cultures' or 'culture phases' would seem justified by Bennett's use of the term, the effort to exclude areas with more than one co-tradition seems dubious, particularly in light of Bennett's

36

own reference to the Martin-Rinaldo usage without quarrelling with it. (W. C. Bennett, 'Area Archeology', *American Anthropologist*, vol. 55, 1953, pp. 5–16, esp. p. 10).

W. A. Lessa

See also: CULTURE AREA

Aristocracy

A. *Aristocracy* denotes the theory and practice of government by an elite—generally hereditary —designated as best at ruling. This is its basic meaning and it implies a moral justification for rule by such an elite.

B. There is, of course, much difficulty in finding universally acceptable criteria whereby 'the best' in any given society may be defined or selected— and in practice such criteria have seldom been applied.

1. In Greek political philosophy *aristocracy* denotes government of those who most nearly attain to the ideal of human perfection. Aristotle classifies the possible good constitutions as kingship, aristocracy, and constitutional government. This echoes down the ages e.g. 'Every supreme government is a *monarchy* (properly so called) or an *aristocracy* (in the generic meaning of the expression). In other words, it is a government of one or a government of a number' (J. Austin, *The Province of Jurisprudence Determined* (1832). London: Weidenfeld & Nicolson, 1954, p. 217).

2. Aristotle himself had distinguished between *oligarchy* and *aristocracy* in the following terms: 'Election by wealth is oligarchic and election by merit aristocratic' (*Politics*, 273a, Loeb edn.), and 'Virtue is the defining factor of aristocracy as wealth is of oligarchy and freedom of democracy' (ibid., 1294a). But from the earliest times the word aristocracy was practically synonymous with oligarchy. Thus Carthage and Venice were cited as great aristocracies of wealth.

3. At a later stage of European history (i.e. before the French Revolution) *aristocracy* was opposed to *monarchy*. 'Aristocracy is when a company of men, met in counsel, ascribe to themselves whatsoever power is due to any rightful monarch ... Such men were the Roman Senate' (R. Coke, *Elements of Power and Subjection*, London: Badell & Collins, 1660, p. 55).

C. Usage with reference to a form of government passes over into that of the class to which such a ruling body belongs, a patrician order, the collective body of those who form a privileged class with regard to the government of the country: it is extended to those who by birth or fortune occupy a position distinctly above the rest of the community. The political power and prestige of such an 'upper class' have long been in dissolution.

K. B. Smellie

See also: OLIGARCHY

Artifact

A. The term *artifact* is used within the field of cultural anthropology, particularly archaeology, to denote an individual form of material culture or a deliberate product of human workmanship, in contrast to objects produced accidentally by natural forces.

1. In practice, it is not always a simple task to distinguish intentional man-made forms from natural forms. For example, in the recognition of the earliest Palaeolithic tools, much controversy has arisen as to whether some chipped stone forms—eoliths—which are simple and poorly standardized, might not be the end-products of natural forces, such as stream action and thermal change.

2. Although historically most artifacts seem to be the products of single individuals and therefore relatively small, there seems to be no objective basis for excluding larger and group-produced forms, such as castles, airplanes, etc.

3. By figurative extension the term is sometimes used to include the outcomes in sociological research of the use of particular methods or research designs.

B. Controversy concerning the term has occurred more with respect to the theoretical contexts in which it has been included, than with respect to its denotative content.

1. One of the issues has concerned the possibility of studying artifacts as elements of culture on a historical or cross-cultural basis independent of their functions within total cultural configurations.

2. It has been a central concept in the discussion of geological time, carbon dating, and conceptions of evolution in archaeology. This has been particularly true with respect to the matter of sequence of stages, and the relativity in time of such sequences.

Bert Gerow

See also: ARCHAEOLOGY
CULTURAL EVOLUTION
MATERIAL CULTURE

Assembly

Ascribed Status (See **Pattern Variables**)

Assembly

A. In its most general sense the term denotes a gathering together of people in a place, frequently in order to engage in some form of political expression, deliberation, or demonstration. It is also sometimes used as the proper name for a legislative or deliberative body, as in the case of the French *Assemblée Nationale* or the General Assembly of the United Nations.

B. In its historical usage *assembly* in politics refers both to the *simple* forms of law- and decision-making units in which, because total numbers are small, *all* qualified participants can gather together to comprise such a unit; and also to gatherings of sub-groups of larger political systems bent upon protest or petition to the governing body.

The first really *national* assembly was that of France in 1789, when upon the convocation of the States-General by Louis XVI, the nobles and clergy refused to deliberate in the same chamber with the third estate, the latter constituted themselves an *Assemblée Nationale*, serving first the function of political protest and expression, and later that of the making of law and political decisions. Perhaps because of the historical association of *assembly* with the Revolution, most French works of reference lavish great attention on every assembly which in the history of the world might be supposed to have had the public interest or liberty in mind; while the British and Americans—despite the guarantee of freedom of peaceable assembly regulated in reasonable degree in the interest of public convenience and good order—tend to limit their attention to *unlawful* assemblies. Furthermore, in its English connotation one has the feeling that *assembly* is a noun of multitude signifying little if anything. But in France *Assemblée* has the connotation of its appearance—an army terrible with banners.

K. B. Smellie

See also: LEGISLATIVE BODY
PETITION

Assimilation

A. The term literally means the process of becoming 'alike' or 'more alike'; as used in sociology, it denotes (a) the process whereby a group, generally a minority or immigrant group, is through contact absorbed into the culture of another group or groups; (b) the result of such absorption.

Thus *assimilation* denotes the process in which one set of cultural traits is relinquished and a new set acquired, through communication and participation. The change is gradual and may take place in any degree. The concept is distinct from the biological process of racial merging through interbreeding, or amalgamation. Full assimilation means the incorporation of new members into a society so that they are not distinguishable from former members. It is frequently pointed out that immigrants may not only adopt another culture but may contribute to it by introducing certain of their own traits to the dominant culture; this indicates that the passage of elements is not an exclusively one-way process.

B. The term became current in sociology with reference to the process whereby migrants discarded the culture traits of their land of origin and acquired the culture of their new country. The process has been of special interest in the United States in view of the large amount of immigration to that country; the popular term 'Americanization' has had a similar meaning. According to R. E. Park and E. W. Burgess, 'Assimilation is a process of interpenetration and fusion in which persons and groups acquire the memories, sentiments, and attitudes of other persons or groups, and, by sharing their experience and history, are incorporated with them in a common cultural life' (*Introduction to the Science of Sociology*, Chicago: University of Chicago Press, 1921, p. 735). These authors further indicate (ibid., p. 759) that there is no implication of resulting uniformity; the corporate character of societies is based on organization of complementary differences, and assimilation means the successful incorporation of a variety of persons into the new society.

C. While there is little important variation in the sociological usage of this concept, some scholars, especially in anthropology, have used *acculturation* in a closely related sense. 'The process by which a minority group finds a place for itself in the wider society may be said to be one both of assimilation and acculturation. By the use of the former term we may undertake an analysis of the way in which the minority becomes incorporated into the system of social relations which constitute the greater society. Employing the second term we may study how the cultural characteristics of the minority change in response to those of the surrounding majority' (M. Freedman (ed.), *A Minority in*

Britain, London: Vallentine, Mitchell, 1955, p. 240).

Robert E. L. Faris

See also: ACCOMMODATION
ACCULTURATION
COMPETITION
CONFLICT
PROCESS

Association

A. In its most general usage the term denotes the process by which people become allied to one another and the groups which form as a result of such an alliance.

B. It is sometimes used in 'formal sociology' to describe the basic unit of social behaviour, i.e. a grouping, large or small, for carrying out an activity. It can consist of any number of individuals from two (a dyad) to an entire population, provided that they are in contact and have at least the elements of organization.

It seems probable that G. Simmel first crystallized the idea of a 'pure' or 'formal' sociology concerned with the 'forms of association' (*die Formen der Vergesellschaftung*). As A. Small's translations of Simmel's writings were published in the *American Journal of Sociology* from 1896 onwards, the idea may be assumed to have influenced the earlier American sociologists as well as more recent writers. H. Becker in his *Systematic Sociology* (New York: John Wiley, 1932), a free adaptation of L. Von Wiese's 'Allgemeine Soziologie', contrasts association and dissociation as the two basic forms of social behaviour.

C. A more frequent usage follows R. M. MacIver and C. H. Page, who define association as 'a group organized for the pursuit of an *interest or group of interests* in common' (R. M. MacIver & C. H. Page, *Society*, London: The Macmillan Co., 1955, p. 12).

This usage, defining associations as interest-conscious unities with definite organization, distinguishes association from institution (q.v.). Thus, for example, a trade union is an association and collective bargaining an institution. Many other writers however use the terms more or less interchangeably.

It also distinguishes associations from two other major types of group: (a) inclusive territorial unities; (b) interest-conscious unities without definite organization, e.g. social class, ethnic group.

D. The work by F. Tönnies, *Gemeinschaft und Gesellschaft*, is translated by C. P. Loomis as *Community and Association* (London: Routledge & Kegan Paul, 1955) but *association* is not reserved exclusively for the *Gesellschaft* (q.v.) type of social organization depending on contractual rather than traditional obligations. Thus Loomis translates Tönnies as writing that 'the essence of both Gemeinschaft and Gesellschaft is found interwoven in all kinds of associations' (ibid., p. 18).

C. Madge

See also: COMMUNITY
GESELLSCHAFT
GROUP
INSTITUTION

Atomism

A. *Atomism* is the name of a theory or kind of theory. (The derivative adjective 'atomistic' can apply to views or things consonant with some form of atomism). In its most general sense the term refers to any doctrine which maintains that the *subject-matter of a given discipline is divisible into a set of units which are not divisible further and which are thus its ultimate constituents.* Alternatively, the term can also be applied to a doctrine which allows further divisibility of units, but insists that all larger units are merely aggregates of smaller ones. (For instance, a social theory is atomistic if it insists that all social institutions and events are to be seen as composed of the actions of individual men and nothing else, even if the doctrine allows that individual men may be seen as divisible by some other science.) In general, atomistic doctrines tend to be inspired by the view that unless the process of division and subdivision comes to a rest when it reaches some kind of ultimate unit, there can be nothing real to investigate, for systems or aggregates do not 'really exist' over and above the 'parts'. In practice, it is not so much the theoretical defects of this argument, as the practical difficulties of locating and identifying plausible 'atoms' and showing that real structures and their behaviour can be exhaustively explained in terms of them, which have led to doubts about atomism.

B. *Atomism* becomes the name of a specific doctrine rather than of a type of doctrine when the context in which it is to be applied is either tacitly understood or specified, usually by an adjective (e.g. physical, logical, social).

1. Thus, in sociology or political science, *atomism* may designate a theory to the effect

Attitude

that social processes and groups are by-products of the doings of social atoms. Individual people or their individual acts may be identified as these atoms.

2. In the psychology of perception or in epistemology, *atomism* will designate a theory to the effect that there are ultimate units of perception or sensation, and that percepts and perceptible objects generally are to be understood in terms of them.

3. In logic and in ontology, *atomism* is to be understood as the doctrine that there are ultimate units of discourse, or of existence, from which all meaningful assertion, or all being is built up.

E. A. Gellner

See also: REDUCTIONISM

Attitude

A. 1. The essential components of the concept of *attitude* are two:

(a) The notion of attitude has been found useful, if not indispensable, because it provides a conceptual bridge between persisting psychological states of the individual and persisting objects of orientation (including whole classes of objects) in that individual's world. To understand the conditions under which attitudes are formed, endure, and change is thus equivalent to understanding the conditions of a very great deal of behaviour.

(b) This important conceptual tool must be so defined as to come to grips with the facts of intra-individual psychological organization (including the individual's taxonomy of objects, whether concrete or abstract), and also with the facts of persistence and change. Since we understand things best when we understand the conditions under which they do and do not change, an adequate definition must face the Heraclitean problems of persistence in spite of change. It must, moreover, remain accessible to the empirical facts of observed behaviour, from which alone attitudes can be inferred.

2. Some such definition as the following therefore seems required: An *attitude* is the individual's organization of psychological processes, as inferred from his behaviour, with respect to some aspect of the world which he distinguishes from other aspects. It represents the residue of his previous experience with which he approaches any subsequent situation including that aspect and, together with the contemporary influences in such a situation, determines his behaviour in it. Attitudes are enduring in the sense that such residues are carried over to new situations, but they change in so far as new residues are acquired through experience in new situations.

B. Psychologists and sociologists, to whom the notion has more conceptual significance than to other social scientists, differ contextually rather than conceptually in their usage of the term. Historically, both disciplines have, in one way or another, regarded attitudes as tendencies to act with regard to some specifiable entity.

1. Many sociologists, following W. I. Thomas and F. Znaniecki, have viewed attitudes primarily in the context of social value which they define as 'any datum having an empirical content accessible to the members of some social group and a meaning with regard to which it is or may be an object of activity' (*The Polish Peasant in Europe and America*, New York: Knopf, 1927, vol. I, p. 21). Attitudes and values are, in fact, defined interdependently: 'A value is the objective counterpart of the attitude' (ibid., p. 22); and 'The attitude is thus the individual counterpart of the social value' (ibid., p. 22). 'It is the individual tendency to react, either positively or negatively, to a given social value' (ibid., p. 24).

2. Psychologists have characteristically been concerned with relationships between attitudes and other psychological characteristics of individuals, and their social-psychological treatises, at least since the beginning of the 1930s (cf. G. & L. B. Murphy, *Experimental Social Psychology*, New York: Harper & Brothers, 1931), have devoted much space to such topics. Among their many definitions, two have probably been most influential: 'An attitude is a mental and neural state of readiness, organized through experience, exerting a directive or dynamic influence upon the individual's response to all objects and situations with which it is related' (G. W. Allport, 'Attitudes', in C. Murchison (ed.), *Handbook of Social Psychology*, Worcester, Mass.: Clark University Press, 1935, p. 810); and 'An attitude can be defined as an enduring organization of motivational, emotional, perceptual, and cognitive processes with respect to some aspect of the individual's world' (D. Krech & R. S. Crutchfield, *Theory and Problems of Social Psychology*, New York: McGraw-Hill, 1948, p. 152).

3. Attitudes have occasionally been defined, both by sociologists (cf. W. M. Fuson, 'Attitudes: A Note on the Concept and Its Research Context', *American Sociological Review*, vol. 7, 1942, pp. 856–7) and by psychologists (cf. D. T.

Campbell, 'The Indirect Assessment of Social Attitudes', *Psychological Bulletin*, vol. 47, 1950, pp. 15–38) simply in terms of the probability of the occurrence of a specified behaviour in a specified situation. Such definitions, while relatively devoid of conceptual content, serve to remind us that the ultimate referent of attitudes is behaviour.

4. Often, though not invariably, motives, like attitudes, are distinguished from one another by labels which refer to objects of orientation. Perhaps the principal distinctions between motives and attitudes are the following: (a) motives are conceptualized as existing only during those periods in which organisms are actually being activated in some manner, while attitudes are thought of as persisting, even during periods of behavioural quiescence; and (b) a wide range of specific and transitory motives may be aroused in the same individual who may be said to have a single, general attitude toward a whole class of specific objects—e.g. an entomologist with a favourable attitude toward lepidoptera is, at a given moment, motivated to catch a particular butterfly. Thus attitudes are generally both more persistent and more inclusive than motives, and a 'motive' which is described as both persistent and general is indistinguishable from an attitude.

Theodore M. Newcomb

See also: MOTIVATION
SYSTEMS OF ORIENTATION
VALUE

Attribute (See **Variable**)

Audience

A. In social science usage an *audience* is an aggregate (q.v.) of people, spatially contiguous or dispersed, whose attention is focused on a common object (usually another person or persons) and whose response is either covert and passive or, if overt and active, is limited to symbolic manifestations of approval or disapproval.

B. While an audience which is 'concrete', in the sense that its members are spatially contiguous, may have a non-human object or an unaware human object as the focus of its attention, the more typical case is one in which the object is human and is aware. From the viewpoint of the aware human object of attention, the audience enters as a conception of a plurality of observers toward whom his behaviour is oriented at least

in part. Such orientation may range from an unintended modification of behaviour to deliberate efforts at communication.

1. The concrete audience may extend to include the presence of any other person or persons whose attention may influence the behaviour of the person who is the object of attention. This influence may be felt even in the complete absence of verbal communication. In summarizing experimental studies of group problem solving, H. H. Kelly refers to four possible modes of influence on group performance stemming from the presence of others: '(a) passive audiences, (b) other persons doing the same task, (c) other persons competing with the subjects, and (d) an audience which reacts to the subjects' ('Experimental Studies of Group Problem Solving and Process', in G. Lindzey (ed.), *Handbook of Social Psychology*, Cambridge, Mass.: Addison-Wesley, 1954, p. 748).

2. The assumption that the presence of spectators has some influence can also be applied to natural groupings such as crowds (q.v.). R. H. Turner and L. M. Killian emphasize the importance to leaders of support from persons who are part of a crowd but whose passivity constitute them an 'audience': 'The majority of crowd members often play a relatively passive role and are somewhat in the relationship of an audience to the active nucleus' (*Collective Behavior*, New York: Prentice-Hall, 1957, pp. 117 ff).

3. The distinction between leadership and active followership, on the one hand, and those who are mere spectators, on the other, has led some students of crowd behaviour to consider the audience as a *passive crowd*, whose participants observe in order to be entertained or to assent or dissent, but do not initiate or carry out any collective action. What characterizes this formal sociological view of the audience is the polarization of interaction between a speaker or performer, on one side, and the spectators or passive followers, on the other. 'In the audience ... the influence of the leader is by far the most important, and the effect of the other members of the crowd upon each other is relatively slight' (H. Clark, 'The Crowd', in J. M. Bentley (ed.), *Studies in Social and General Psychology from the University of Illinois*, Princeton, N.J.: Psychological Review Co., 1916, p. 30).

C. The *mass audiences* created by technological advances in the speed of communication over a wide area extend far beyond the limits of any *concrete audience*. This kind of audience is made up of those who make convergent

Authoritarianism

selections from the diverse contents of mass communication. The audience for any content can be determined if we know, for example, who reads what magazines, who sees what kinds of movies, etc. But 'the field of audience research includes not only those studies aiming at accurate description of the audience to various media, channels, or items of communication. In addition it deals with the factors responsible for the types of communication exposure which do exist as well as with the motivations for seeing, reading, and listening' (B. Berelson & M. Janowitz, *Reader in Public Opinion and Communication*, Glencoe, Ill.: The Free Press, 1950, p. 335).

D. The conception of an *audience* enters also as a social determinant into the thought processes that precede the framing of a message by influencing its logic, its symbolism, and the appeals used. Working within the framework of the theory of G. H. Mead, C. W. Mills writes that 'the generalized other is the internalized audience with which the thinker converses: a focalized and abstracted organization of attitudes of those implicated in the social fields of behavior and experience' ('Language, Logic and Culture', *American Sociological Review*, vol. 5, 1939, p. 672).

Kurt Lang

See also: COMMUNICATION
CROWD
MASS CULTURE
MASS MEDIA
MASS SOCIETY
SOCIAL INTERACTION

Authoritarianism

A. *Authoritarianism* can be used in at least three distinct ways:

1. In a psychological sense, when we speak, for instance, of authoritarian *character*—it denotes a disposition uniting zealous obedience to an hierarchic superior, obsequiousness and sycophancy towards the stronger in general, with overbearing and scornful demeanour towards those who are in one's power.

2. In describing the manner of conducting administration, it denotes reliance on apodictic orders and threats of punishment, and aversion to employing either consultation or persuasion.

3. Finally it denotes an *ideology* which advocates the propagation, or applauds the prevalence, of authoritarian *administrative procedures*, and extols the paragon of authoritarian *character*.

B. 1. The relationship between authoritarian propensities, procedures, and ideologies is that of mutual facilitation. Persons with authoritarian propensities naturally tend to resort to authoritarian administrative procedures, and espouse authoritarian ideologies, while the prevalence of authoritarian procedures forms authoritarian characters, and increases the number of people who have vested interest in authoritarian ideologies—in addition to making these ideologies seem more 'natural'. In view of this the use of the word *authoritarianism* without further qualification might be justified in the description of a condition of a social entity when reference is made *to a joint occurrence of authoritarian propensities, procedures, and ideologies*.

2. It should be noted that:

(a) this usage does not allow for variations in the proportions of these *ingredients*. From the point of view of social dynamics these variations might be of the utmost importance.

(b) it is not easy to assess the degree of authoritarianism. For example: (i) various aspects of social life may not be equally pervaded by it, even if on the whole there is a trend towards consistency; (ii) there may be great differences in this respect between various parts of social structure. Thus, for instance, in medieval Europe the manor was a very authoritarian entity, whereas the feudal hierarchy was in fact thoroughly unauthoritarian.

S. Andreski

See also: AUTOCRACY
DESPOTISM
DICTATORSHIP
FEUDALISM
TOTALITARIANISM

Authority

A. When the confusions between *authority* and power (q.v.) and *authority* and legitimacy (q.v.) are cleared away it will be found that a common meaning underlies the varying usages of the term. When it is especially difficult or impossible to demonstrate rationally the adequacy of a course of action to the requirements of a situation, assent may be secured by relating technical requirements to values, beliefs, or truths that transcend the particular judgements involved. *Authority* denotes this mode of securing assent.

B. Authority is frequently used in a pejorative sense. Thus C. S. Peirce observes 'When the method of authority prevailed, the truth meant little more than the Catholic faith' ('How to Make Our Ideas Clear', *Collected Papers of Charles Sanders Peirce*, ed. by C. Hartshorne & P. Weiss, Cambridge, Mass.: Harvard University Press, vol. 5, 1934, p. 267). Peirce, like so many others, did not realize that Catholic authority offers only one particular content, and that he himself relied and had to rely on authority too. G. C. Lewis, in an important study (*An Essay on the Influence of Authority in Matters of Opinion*, London: John W. Parker, 1849, p. 7) suggested that the 'principle' of authority consisted in 'adopting the belief of others, on a matter of opinion, without reference to the particular grounds on which that belief may rest'. It is characteristic for most writings on authority to this day that they are preoccupied with what causes authority to be 'accepted', or 'guaranteed', or 'believed in', without prior inquiry into what it *is*. This failing is illustrated in M. Weber, *The Theory of Social and Economic Organization* (trans. by A. M. Henderson & T. Parsons, Glencoe, Ill.: The Free Press, 1947, pp. 56 ff, 324 ff). That it is a quality seems clear enough, when persons possessing this quality are referred to as 'authorities'. But what this quality is, seems not to be clearly understood. If we consider the several factors which Weber (ibid.) thought 'guaranteed' authority, namely (a) tradition, (b) rationality and legality, and (c) charisma, we may conclude that since these are the several possible bases of any political order, authority is an ineluctable feature of such a political order. But what is the particular or specific character of this feature? This question remains unanswered; for power, e.g., is likewise such a feature, and authority and power ought clearly to be distinguished.

T. D. Weldon (*The Vocabulary of Politics*, Harmondsworth: Penguin Books, 1953, p. 50 et seq.) makes the crucial observations that when people possess authority they seem to possess the capacity to produce reasons, if challenged, or at any rate are believed to have this capacity. At the same time 'People do what he (who possesses authority) tells them without asking questions'. But then in trying to distinguish authority from power, he does not pursue this valuable lead, but turns again to the problem of 'whence authority is derived'. As a consequence he does not arrive at the identification of a sharply defined referent for the term. But he rejects one such referent which is often found, authority as power.

Authority is frequently said to be 'force

rightly or justly applied'. It is rightful power (J. Hall, 'Authority and the Law', in C. J. Friedrich (ed.), *Authority*, Cambridge, Mass.: Harvard University Press, 1958, p. 58). If thus defined, authority becomes indistinguishable from legitimacy; for rightful power is legitimate power, and rightful force is legitimate force. The difficulty with such a concept is that it makes authority a kind of power, when actually it has been customary to use the term authority in dialectic juxtaposition to power to describe a situation in which a claim to obedience may be largely neglected. It is then said that a person has authority, but no power. By analogy, the authority of a great physician is not measurable in terms of the number of persons who follow his advice.

The crux of this dilemma was made the basis of another approach to authority by H. Lasswell and A. Kaplan, who proposed to define authority as 'formal power' (*Power and Society*, New Haven: Yale University Press, 1950, p. 133). It seems to them 'power of low weight'. But while authority undoubtedly is a source of power, the amount of power it generates is not a crucial consideration; this can be very great, or rather small, but the quality which creates it, namely authority, is something separate and distinct from power.

Writers in sociology and anthropology, as well as law, have defined authority in various ways. B. Malinowski, for example, would define it 'as the legally vested power to establish norms, to take decisions and to enforce them through the use of sanctions by coercion' (*Freedom and Civilization*, New York: Roy Publishers, 1944, p. 187 ff). Here, too and throughout the literature of law, we find the confusion of power and authority.

A resolution of these difficulties might have been found, had not, in the vast and discordant writings on authority, freedom and reason, the dialectic relation of authority and reason been often neglected. Writers like Lewis and Weldon offer a clue. Authority is a kind of 'hidden reasoning'. It might in this perspective be called 'the faculty of gaining another man's assent' (B. de Jouvenel, *Sovereignty*, Cambridge: The University Press, 1957, p. 29). It is the capacity for the kind of reasoning that relates technical requirements to transcendent values and beliefs. With regard to the contingent aspects of decisions, actions, and opinions, the role of authority is that of bridging the gap between rational demonstration and the requirements of the concrete situation. It does not matter whether

Autistic Thinking

rational demonstration is prevented by lack of time, lack of knowledge or insight on the part of those accepting authority, or by a variety of other limitations of man's finite nature. Typically, therefore, authority is a quality of communications which possess this potentiality of being elaborated by valuational as well as technical reasoning. That the originator of such communications is called an 'authority' may, from a scientific standpoint, be considered a figure of speech. Whether seen as a quality of communications, or as that of communicants, authority is a basic constituent of all political and social existence, generating power and influence through the consent it engenders, and thus making power legitimate. Freedom (q.v.), therefore, cannot be understood, except within the context of authority, whether it be the freedom from arbitrary interference or the freedom of effective participation in the political community. Only a community of beings with infinite capacity for rational demonstration and infinite time to await the conclusions of such demonstrative reasoning would be able to dispense with the dependence upon communications which are framed in terms of a potential reasoned elaboration, that is to say, would dispense with authority.

C. J. Friedrich

See also: FREEDOM
LEGITIMACY
POWER

Autistic Thinking

A. *Autistic thinking* denotes cognitive processes relatively little constrained by considerations of reality. Frequent but not necessary concomitants are (a) the limitation or absence of communication and (b) the need-satisfying quality of the content of such cognitive processes, frequently serving in place of satisfactions not obtained in ways related to reality.

B. 1. Freud, though he did not use the term, emphasized the wishful-thinking aspects of thought-processes; as early as 1900 (S. Freud, *The Interpretation of Dreams*, in A. A. Brill (trans. and ed.), *The Basic Writings of Sigmund Freud*, New York: Random House, 1938) he described the influence of the id (q.v.) on thought, and in 1911 he drew the now familiar distinction between the pleasure principle (q.v.) and the reality principle (q.v.) ('Formulations Regarding the Two Principles in Mental Functioning', in *Collected Papers*, London: Hogarth Press, 1924, vol. II, pp. 113–21).

The concept, although not the term, entered the psychiatric literature in 1916 in E. Bleuler's use of *dereistic thinking* (*Textbook of Psychiatry*, trans. by A. A. Brill, New York: The Macmillan Co., 1924, pp. 45–6). Bleuler's special concern was with phantasies in adult psychotics, but he also saw the importance of the almost universal prevalence of phantasy-like processes among normal humans. He drew the distinction between realistic thought, most clearly illustrated in rational problem solving, and the autistic thought processes which characterize daydreams.

2. Psychologists have freely borrowed the term, though their interest in thought processes long antedates it. One of the earliest systematic attempts to explore the content of daydreams was made by the Belgian psychologist, J. Varendonck (*The Psychology of Daydreams*, London: Allen & Unwin, 1921), who analysed excerpts from his own diary, kept while in the trenches during World War I. Summarized by R. White ('Interpretation of Imaginative Productions', in J. McV. Hunt (ed.), *Personality and the Behavior Disorders*, New York: Ronald Press, 1944, vol. 1, p. 217), Varendonck enumerated the following characteristics of autistic thought: '(1) a turning away from reality so that inner life assumes the dominant position, (2) spontaneous drift without the toil and fatigue which attends working for communication by means of speech, and (3) guidance of associations by some tendency or striving, often of a pleasant kind'.

C. An interesting contrast in the treatment of autistic thinking with respect to symbolism and communication is found in the works of J. Piaget and H. S. Sullivan.

1. Piaget (*The Language and Thought of the Child*, trans. by M. Warden, New York: Harcourt, Brace, 1932, p. 43) places emphasis on the private, uncommunicable, organic aspects of autistic thought. 'Intelligence, just because it undergoes a gradual process of socialization, is enabled through the bond established by language between thought and words to make an increasing use of concepts; whereas autism, just because it remains individual, is still tied to imagery, to organic activity, and even to organic movements' (ibid., p. 45).

2. Sullivan (*The Interpersonal Theory of Psychiatry*, ed. by H. S. Perry & M. L. Gavel, New York: W. W. Norton, 1953, pp. 181–3, 221–5), while recognizing that autistic thought is private, still believes that private symbols are used in such thought, and that through such symbols the person is engaged in private communication with himself.

D. Since the work of Freud and Bleuler efforts have been made to link autistic thinking with the creation of such cultural products as myth (q.v.) and religion (q.v.). Such efforts imply, of course, a sense of autism which embodies (rather than excludes) interpersonal communication and the analysis of the processes of communication through which autistic thought becomes myth.

Theodore M. Newcomb

See also: COGNITION
COMMUNICATION
MIND
SOCIAL INTERACTION

Autocracy

A. *Autocracy* denotes a structure of power characterized by: (a) clear ascendancy of one person at the top of its administrative hierarchy; (b) lack of any laws or customs in virtue of which the ruler might be called upon to account for his actions; (c) absence of any customary or legal limitations on the exercise of authority by the ruler. The last of these criteria does not imply that autocracy and totalitarianism (q.v.) are identical, as the absence of institutional limitations of the ruler's authority does not necessarily lead to the establishment of systematic governmental control over the totality of social life of the subjects. While an autocracy may be based primarily on the loyalty of the subjects, or on the fear of punishment, in practice both ingredients are always present, with great variations in their relative importance.

The proposed definition leaves equally open the question of whether the supreme authority is bestowed in accordance with pre-established norms or whether it is conquered (be it merely through a *threat* of violence); in the former case we have a legitimate autocracy (hereditary or co-optative); in the latter a dictatorship.

B. 1. Some writers use autocracy in a very wide sense. For example, M. Duverger (*Les Régimes politiques*, Paris: Presses Universitaires, 1948, p. 12) writes: 'Autocratic regimes have this in common that they do not permit the choice of the rulers to be influenced by actions of the ruled ...' On this interpretation autocracy signifies *non-elective government*.

2. More commonly, by autocracy is meant a type of government where one man (called the autocrat) wields overwhelming power. It might be advisable to adhere basically to this meaning, while making it more precise.

S. Andreski

See also: DICTATORSHIP
TOTALITARIANISM

Automation

A. *Automation* denotes the production of goods by machines without manual control. This requires that the control be continuous or nearly continuous from the start to the finish of a production process, and thus differs from previous use of machinery which normally required manual handling of the product or manual control of the machine. The control involved in automation can be accomplished by the use of electronic control devices which guide the movement of the product from one machine to the next and which are capable of correcting problems arising during production. Automation designates a 'closed' operation as the machinery deals with the difficulties arising during the operation and selects the best solution to the immediate problem without human intervention.

B. The term *automation* actually refers to two related phenomena.

1. In a very general sense automation means a continuation of the process of mechanization in the production of goods which has been in progress for hundreds of years. In this sense automation is nothing new. In its broadest application this definition is correct, but automation more specifically refers to recent drastic changes in the *method* of machine production.

2. *Automation* in its more specific usage designates a process that goes further than mechanization. 'Mechanization basically substitutes mechanical effort for human effort, but man must still operate and control the machine. In true automation, manual control of machines is eliminated' (F. F. Mauser & D. J. Schwartz, *Introduction to American Business*, New York: American Book Company, 1956, p. 230). This is made possible by the introduction of electronic control devices in industrial operations which '... have made possible a wide variety of self-correcting and self-programming machines, capable of automatically performing a sequence of logical operations. They can correct the errors which occur during their own operations and can choose, according to built-in criteria, from

Autonomy

among several predetermined plans of action. These are the technical bases on which automatic factories can be built' (J. Diebold, *Automation*, digested by H. F. Klingman, New York: Controllership Foundation, 1954, p. 1).

Thus automation is characterized by machine 'supervision' of the work in progress. A machine might be constructed so that '... information on the progress of the job is automatically fed into a computer so that there is a check on results at short intervals. The computer then interprets the information and sends back instructions in a numerical code on perforated ... tape or film as to the next step that is necessary and the machine automatically responds. Here we have the highest development of the feedback principle, where information from the problem itself automatically influences the end result' (*Automation and Job Trends*, Chicago: Council for Technological Advancement, 1955, p. 5).

While a limited amount of automatic machinery of this sort has existed for a number of years in a few production processes, the prospect of the widespread use of such machinery has brought the term automation into popular usage in recent years.

Norman J. Wood

See also: TECHNOLOGY

Autonomy

A. In its most general psychological sense *autonomy* refers to the maintenance of the integrity of the self (q.v.). There is the tendency in every individual to resist the pressures of enculturation (q.v.) and to persist in certain forms of behaviour that in the past have helped him to cope with his problems. In successful and wholesome socialization (q.v.), the struggle between the child's wishes and persistent motives results in the individual's developing self-control and an increasing sense of self-esteem, which in turn generates an abiding *sense* of autonomy in the person.

B. The problem of autonomy in social psychology is handled in four distinct but related ways depending on which feature of behaviour is being emphasized, viz., ego psychology, motivation, learning, or personality dissociation. The common denominator of the four ways of looking at autonomy is the continuance of response, the 'fixation' of behaviour at a level that originally brought satisfaction to the individual, in the absence of a specific stimulus or stimulus situation that would normally arouse the response.

1. In ego psychology, which is propounded mostly by psychoanalytically oriented psychologists, autonomy refers to the tendency of the healthy organism to retain its identity. H. Hartmann ('On Rational and Irrational Action', in G. Roheim (ed.), *Psycho-analysis and the Social Sciences*, London: Imago Publishing Company, 1947, vol. I, p. 359 f.) divides this striving for self-identity into two forms: (a) *primary autonomy*, consisting of 'inborn ego dispositions', and (b) *secondary autonomy*, consisting of those ego-characteristics which are acquired in the service of defence of the self. W. Stern (*Psychology of Early Childhood*, London: Allen & Unwin, 1930, p. 492), describes the autonomy of the self on the basis of the child's awareness of the extent to which he 'realizes himself as a living entity, a one complete centre of power', in contrast to his earlier helplessness and his submission to his parents' will. E. Erikson ('Growth and Crises of the "Healthy Personality" ', in C. Kluckhohn, H. A. Murray & D. M. Schneider (eds.), *Personality in Nature, Society, and Culture*, London: Jonathan Cape, 1953, p. 204), vividly describes the ego's determination to maintain its independence in the face of irrational authority by the phrase, 'don't fence me in'.

2. The motivational approach to autonomy is widely used in contemporary psychology. Many motives, especially physiological drives like hunger and thirst, persist because they are cyclical organic tensions and because their satisfaction aids in the preservation of the organism. Acquired motives, on the other hand, tend to function independently of any further reinforcement of the physiological conditions which brought them into being. They take on a *functional* autonomy. R. Woodworth (*Dynamic Psychology*, New York: Columbia University Press, 1918, p. 67), who first formulated this principle, describes the process by saying that 'the mechanism furnishes its own drive'. G. W. Allport (*Personality: A Psychological Interpretation*, New York: Henry Holt, 1937, p. 194), who gave the principle its name, and who made it an important basis of his theory of personality, regards adult motives as 'self-sustaining, *contemporary* systems, growing out of antecedent systems, but functionally independent of them'. Personality in this view is a self-sustaining, self-maintaining behaviour organization, historically related to its prior motives but functionally an autonomous, self-governing structure.

3. Closely related to motivational autonomy and differing from ego psychology is the approach that considers autonomy as a product of learning. Like all learned behaviour, autonomy improves with practice. That it differs from ego psychology is shown by the claim of learning theorists that autonomous behaviour usually occurs without arousing self-reactions to it, so that, as N. Cameron has pointed out (*The Psychology of Behavior Disorder*, Boston: Houghton Mifflin, 1947, p. 370), during and after its occurrence 'the autonomous act may remain inaccessible ... or "unconscious" '.

4. The concept of autonomy is used extensively in describing certain types of behaviour disorder, especially hysteria and multiple personality. Cameron (ibid., p. 350) defines hysterical autonomy as '*the appearance of an isolated behavior fragment ... which is out of keeping with the shared environmental context or with the person's prior behavior ... in the absence of ... tissue pathology adequate to account for it*'. The fragmented, autonomous behaviour is a reaction to anxiety. As in the functional autonomy of motives and in behaviour that persists in the absence of constant reinforcement so in dissociative behaviour disorders there is a functional but not an historical break in the continuity of behaviour. As early as 1920 S. Freud (*Beyond the Pleasure Principle*, London: The International Psycho-analytical Press, 1922, p. 18 f.) formulated substantially the same idea as a 'repetition compulsion', or the continuance, in the absence of any known motive, of behaviour which originally acted in the service of a drive. Today this concept in an extended form is widely used to describe the persistence of defences which were once useful in coping with anxiety but which no longer have an adjustive function.

Hubert Bonner

See also: ENCULTURATION
SOCIALIZATION

Average Propensity to Consume (See Propensity to Consume)

Average Propensity to Save (See Propensity to Consume)

Average Revenue (See Revenue)

Avoidance Relationship (See Joking Relationship)

Avunculate

A. *Avunculate* denotes the institutionalization of authority by the mother's brother over the sister's son and the latter being made the heir and companion of the former.

B. Many early writers, Bachofen, Morgan, and others, maintained that the avunculate was necessarily linked with matrilineal descent, and that where it was found with patrilineal or other descent it was to be regarded as a survival of a previous matrilineal system. It was also linked with matriarchy. This view has long been shown to have been both unnecessary and mistaken (see, among others, R. H. Lowie, *Primitive Society*, London: George Routledge, 1921, pp. 171–3; A. R. Radcliffe-Brown, 'The Mother's Brother in South Africa', in *Structure and Function in Primitive Society*, London: Cohen & West, 1952, pp. 15–31.)

J. Middleton

Avunculocal (See Residence)

B

Balance of Payments

A. The *balance of payments* is a concept referring to (a) the relationship between the payments-claims of one nation against the rest of the world and the payments-obligations of that nation to the rest of the world, and (b) a factual accounting of this relationship.

B. The claims of a nation for payment and the counterclaims of all other nations for payment are at the core of the concept. The claims, or *credits*, denote payments coming into the nation. The counter claims, or *debits*, refer to payments going to other nations. This concept, encompassing, as it does, not only trade in goods but also services and capital movements, is much broader and for most purposes much more useful than the once-prevalent concept of balance of trade, which dealt only with merchandise movements.

1. Technically the balance of payments of a nation are always in balance in the sense that credits equal debits. This may be accomplished, however, by entering as credits moneys borrowed on a long- or short-term basis that are used to pay for items entered as debits.

2. The basic categories of the balance of payments are (a) the current account, (b) the long-term capital account, and (c) the short-term capital account. While the total balance of payments must balance in the accounting sense mentioned above, in any particular period one of the sub-categories may be in imbalance. Thus if long- or short-term capital borrowing is employed to pay for imports, the current account will be out of balance, and the balance of payments restored through items in the capital account.

3. More important is the question of the *equilibrium* of the balance of payments. If for example the payment for debits is accomplished by means of borrowing capital which falls into the long-term capital account, and the imports are themselves producers' goods designed for the long-run growth of the economy, the balance of payments may be considered to be in equilibrium even though the current account is out of balance and the total balance of payments balances because of borrowing. On the other hand, if the borrowing to meet debit payments is not part of a long-term pattern of stability, a condition likely to be reflected in the short-term capital account, the situation is inherently unstable and adjustments will ultimately have to be made. 'If a nation's balance of payments balances only precariously, the condition is referred to as one of *disequilibrium in its balance of payments*' (S. Enke & V. Salera, *International Economics*, New York: Prentice-Hall, 1947, p. 152). The continued use of foreign reserves or the exporting of gold may indicate the same precarious condition (ibid., p. 151).

C. In a specific sense, the *balance of payments* refers to a special kind of simplified national accounting statement. 'A complete national statement of debits and credits over a given period, a statement of items for which payment was made and of items for which payment was received by a specific country, is termed the *balance of international payments* of that country' (P. T. Ellsworth, *The International Economy*, New York: The Macmillan Co., 1950, p. 260). It is usually calculated for a calendar year, although longer or shorter periods may be used for some special purpose.

1. This balance of payments statement has been developed more or less independently over the years by most of the larger countries, with some consultation. Hence, practices have frequently differed in detail and sometimes also on major questions of categorization and presentation. In recent years, the international economic agencies, notably the International Monetary Fund, have been making efforts to bring about greater stabilization in form.

2. The balance of payments statement provides a clear reflection of the composition of the international transactions of a nation; it shows whether a nation is borrowing or lending and whether its currency is getting 'stronger' or 'weaker'. Trade policy can often be illuminated by examination of the balance of payments. A comparison and contrast of successive balance of payments statements often clearly reveals significant trends in the structure of an economy as well as in the international economic relations of a nation.

Yet, the balance of payments statement usually does not of itself give all the information that might be required for analysis of the international economic relations of a country (L. Tarshis, *Introduction to International Trade and Finance*, New York: John Wiley, 1955, pp. 265–6). The major analytic problem is to sort out those entries which preserve balance in the accounting sense, and are induced by changes elsewhere in the account, from those entries which are autonomously generated by the trading and financing activities of a country. There are, in addition, certain technical problems. In the balance of payments statement as prepared by some countries, there is not enough detail. As a statement of a nation's economic transactions with all other nations, in the aggregate, it does not tell specifically where trade and capital are moving. It does not reveal the assets and liabilities that relate one country to another; it does not establish the debtor or creditor status of a nation. It only reveals changes from one year to the next.

C. Addison Hickman

See also: INTERNATIONAL ECONOMICS

Balance of Power

A. The term *balance of power* is frequently used solely for propaganda purposes, in justifying or condemning policies not ipso facto related to any *balance* in the strict sense. Thus in the most general, loose usage it has also at times been equated with 'power politics' (generally in a derogatory sense) or with any kind of 'distribution of power', whether or not related to a condition of equilibrium.

In stricter parlance the term denotes either (a) a political system marked by a particular configuration of power relationships; or (b) a foreign policy which is held to be the one most likely to further the interests of a particular state.

B. The term may describe a fundamental principle of international politics, namely, the tendency for any state (or group of states) which threatens so to increase its relative power as to dominate the rest, to become subject almost automatically to countervailing pressure from the remaining states with the result that a rough equilibrium of power is preserved.

The term itself came into use only with the rise of national states at the time of the Renaissance, but Hume in his essay *Of the Balance of Power* rightly points out that although Thucydides did not use the precise *term* he was well acquainted with the *idea*. From the 16th until well into the 20th century the balance of power was generally regarded as part of the 'common law of Europe'. Thus Vattel saw as an integral part of the European political system 'that famous scheme of the political balance, or the equilibrium of power, by which is understood such a disposition of things, as that no one potentate be able absolutely to predominate, and prescribe laws to the others' (*Le Droit des gens*, 1758, Eng. trans. by J. Chitty, 1834, p. 311). The peace settlements of Westphalia (1648), Utrecht (1713), and Vienna (1815) were also shaped by the maxim *ad conservandum in Europa equilibrium*.

A distinction needs to be drawn here between the *multiple* balance, which writers like Vattel had in mind, and a *simple* or *two-sided* balance. A multiple balance is made up of a constellation of several independent states of not very unequal strength, such as existed, for instance, for the greater part of the 19th century.

1. The *multiple* balance, with its 'perpetual quadrille' of changing alignments, is said to have made for greater tranquillity in the body politic of Europe by acting as a check on aggrandisement, by limiting the incidence and scope of wars, and by protecting the smaller states. 'Europe has known almost as much peace as war; and it has owed these periods of peace to the Balance of Power. No one state has ever been strong enough to eat up all the rest, and the mutual jealousy of the Great Powers has preserved even the small states, which could not have preserved themselves' (A. J. P. Taylor, *The Struggle for Mastery in Europe*, Oxford: The University Press, 1954, p. xix).

2. On the other hand, critics of the balance of power during and after World War I (President Wilson—'The great game now for ever discredited of the Balance of Power') have claimed that the *multiple* balance almost invariably turns sooner or later into a *simple* or *two-sided* balance —the balance of a pair of scales—of two aggregates of power (e.g. the Triple Alliance and the Triple Entente) more or less equally balanced against each other. This kind of balance they regard as synonymous with competing military alliances and armaments races, one which because of its rigidity, competitiveness, and instability leads inevitably to war. After both World Wars, many hoped that it would be replaced by a 'community of power' operating through a system of collective security, first under the League of Nations and then under the United Nations.

49

Ballot

C. The attainment or preservation of a balance of power may also be *prescribed* as the policy best calculated to further the interests of a particular state or group of states. In other words, in this sense it provides a *maxim* to be followed by statesmen for the purpose of national advantage rather than an axiomatic truth of international politics.

It should be noted, however, that although the attainment of a stable balance may be a policy's avowed aim, the real aim may well be a *margin* or *preponderance* of power rather than an exact equilibrium. In other words, states have habitually considered that real security lies not in being *just* as strong as a potential enemy, but in being a *little stronger*. As A. F. Pollard contends: 'One has a shrewd suspicion that those who believe in a balance of power, do so because they think it is like a balance at the bank, something better than mere equality, an advantage which they possess' ('The Balance of Power', *Journal of the British Institute of International Affairs*, vol. II, 1923, p. 59).

G. L. Goodwin

See also: ALLIANCE

Ballot

A. The term *ballot* is used in politics and political science synonymously with voting (q.v.) to denote the process by which the selections of voters are registered; usually designating also the printed piece of paper (ballot paper or ballot) containing the names of candidates for office and/or a statement of the proposal which the voter is expected to approve or reject. In democratic systems the ballot has normally been so arranged and administered that the voter has free and secret choices among genuine alternatives. 'Balloting' may also take place in non-democratic systems where political pressures make the 'secrecy' of the ballot impossible.

B. 1. The secret ballot, sometimes called the 'Australian ballot' came into general use in Anglo-Saxon countries in the latter half of the 19th century after it was first used in Australia in 1856. The British Parliament adopted it in 1872 despite the opposition of J. S. Mill on the ground that voting was a public function, and that every man's vote was a public matter. The introduction of the Australian ballot into the United States took place in Kentucky in 1888. By 1950, it was in use in each of the forty-eight states.

2. The systems of balloting naturally differ from country to country. The following comments relate to the United States procedure. According to A. Ranney and W. Kendall, all the American states use the Australian ballot but the form of the ballot may be one of four kinds (*Democracy and the American Party System*, New York: Harcourt, Brace, 1956, p. 324). The *party-column* type lists all candidates by party vertically and by office horizontally. The *office-group* ballot arrays together all of the candidates for a single office. The *party-circle* type provides a circle at the top of the ballot so that the voter may vote for all the candidates of a particular party without marking each of the names. The *party-emblem* type provides an identifying emblem against the name of the party or the party's candidates to help in identifying the proper choices. Finally, most ballots provide space for writing in or pasting in (with stickers brought to the polling-booth) the names of others who do not appear in the printed lists. When a voter chooses not to vote for all of a party's nominees but divides his choices among candidates from other parties, it is said that he 'splits the ticket'.

As V. O. Key has said, 'Whether the ballot is in form a party-column or an office-block ballot, it is usually a long ballot containing a large number of names and perhaps constitutional amendments and other propositions on which the voters are asked to express an opinion' (*Politics, Parties and Pressure Groups*, New York: Thomas Y. Crowell, 4th edn., 1958, p. 695). Because a voter in the United States will be a resident of many constituencies and electoral districts, although he maintains but a single residence, the ballot on which he records his choices may be so long as to be unwieldy. Reform of the ballot, to shorten it to those offices and candidates about whom the voter may have time to inform himself, dates at least from the establishment in 1909 of the National Short Ballot Organization. Although some reform has been achieved in some states, the gains have not been notable and the average American ballot imposes a formidable complexity of choices.

Earl Latham

See also: ELECTION
          VOTING

Bargaining

A. *Bargaining* denotes (a) the process of argument, persuasion, threat, proposal- and counter-proposal by which the potential parties to a transaction discuss its terms and possibly reach agreement on them; (b) reaching or endeavouring to reach an agreement whereby the concessions or favours given by one party are compensated by those given by the other. If actions are guided in this way when, it is held, they should be governed by principle, then the sense is pejorative.

B. 1. Bargaining can provide a distinct factor in the determination of the terms of a transaction wherever there is a range of terms at any one of which both parties are willing to deal: for example, rather than not sell his horse to B, A is willing to take as little as £50; rather than not get A's horse, B is willing to give as much as £60; both are willing to deal at any price in the range £50-60, and the actual point may be decided by bargaining. The range within which the terms are not determined by the conditions of supply and demand is reduced in proportion as either party has access to others with whom he might alternatively deal, and knows what terms they offer him—the limiting case is a wide market in which at any one time there is a going price at which all can deal. But bargaining can go on in a market containing many buyers and sellers if, as in a bazaar, these do not disclose from the outset the terms on which each is willing to deal.

2. Agreements are often made, not to carry out a particular transaction, but *to observe certain terms* in any transactions which the parties, or others whom they represent, may choose to initiate subsequently: e.g. agreements are made between trade unions and employers not for the hiring of specified amounts of labour at specified rates, but for the observance of certain terms as a minimum in such hirings as may occur from week to week thereafter. The process by which such terms are arrived at is also described as bargaining, but its scope cannot be represented by the simple range of indeterminacy of the horse-trade, because each party has to consider not the possible present terms alone, but their effects on subsequent transactions. Bargaining in this sense can be regarded in part simply as a tussle for shares in a given product, in part as expressing differences of opinion about a decision of policy.

C. There is no agreement on an analytical framework for the arbitraments of bargaining. When the term *bargaining power* is used to cover all factors which bear on the terms of settlement, it comprehends all manner of personal and political as well as economic circumstances. When, with strike and lock-out in mind, it is used to mean power to impose greater loss on the other party than oneself by withholding consent to offered terms, its content can hardly be distinguished from the forces of supply and demand that bear on the settlement; the loss imposed on firms by a strike, for example, depends on the current demand for their product.

D. The term *collective bargaining* was first used by Beatrice Potter (Mrs. Sidney Webb) in *The Cooperative Movement in Great Britain* (London: Swan Sonnenschein, 1891, p. 217), to describe the arrangement by which a number of workmen agree that in making their individual contracts of employment they shall observe common terms as a minimum, and through representatives negotiate those terms with the employer or association of employers.

E. H. Phelps Brown

See also: COMPROMISE

Bargaining Power (See **Bargaining**)

Basic Personality Structure
A. The term is an explanatory construct inferred from observations that people of a given culture tend to be somewhat alike in personality. Inasmuch as essentially all writers on basic personality structure utilize the definition and approach of A. Kardiner and R. Linton (*The Psychological Frontiers of Society*, New York: Columbia University Press, 1945), it seems that Linton's definition is appropriate: *basic personality structure* denotes '... that personality configuration which is shared by the bulk of the society's members as a result of the early experiences which they have in common. It does not correspond to the total personality of the individual but rather to the projective systems or, in different phraseology, the value-attitude systems which are basic to the individual's personality configuration. Thus the same basic personality types may be reflected in many different forms of behavior and may enter into many different total personality configurations' (ibid., p. viii).

B. 1. Kardiner (*The Individual and His Society*, New York: Columbia University Press, 1939, p. 12) first used the term to denote 'that group of psychic and behavioral characteristics derived from contact with the same institutions, such as language, specific connotations, etc.' Again, Kardiner gives the term as meaning 'the

Basic Personality Structure

effective adaptive tools of the individual which are common to every individual in the society' (A. Kardiner & R. Linton, *The Psychological Frontiers of Society*, p. 237).

In the same work Linton speaks of basic personality as being a configuration of elements involving the following propositions (ibid., p. vi-viii): (a) that the individual's early experiences exert a lasting effect upon his personality, especially upon the development of his projective system; (b) that similar experiences will tend to produce similar personality configurations in the individuals who are subjected to them; (c) that the techniques which the members of any society employ in the care and rearing of children are culturally patterned and will tend to be similar, although never identical, for various families within the society. To the extent that these propositions are supported by evidence it follows that the members of any given society will have a common societal basic personality structure.

2. A. Inkeles and D. J. Levinson apply the term to 'those dispositions, conceptions, modes of relating to others, and the like, that make the individual maximally receptive to cultural ways and ideologies, and that enable him to achieve adequate gratification and security within the existing order' ('National Character: The Study of Modal Personality and Sociocultural Systems', in G. Lindzey (ed.), *Handbook of Social Psychology*, Cambridge, Mass.: Addison-Wesley, 1954, p. 980).

C. Other terms closely allied to basic personality structure are *modal personality*, *national character*, *social character*, and *standardized personality*.

1. M. Mead ('National Character', in A. L. Kroeber (ed.), *Anthropology Today*, Chicago: University of Chicago Press, 1953, p. 642) says that *national character* studies 'attempt to delineate how the innate properties of human beings, the idiosyncratic elements in each human being, and the general and individual patterns of human maturation are integrated within a shared social tradition in such a way that certain regularities appear in the behaviour of all members of the culture which can be described as a *culturally regular* character'.

National character is mostly commonly distinguished from basic personality structure in that it has been applied to modern nations, whereas the latter has been applied to the study of 'small, relatively well integrated groups, either "primitive" tribes or rural communities'

(R. Linton, 'What We Know and Don't Know', in F. L. K. Hsu (ed.), *Aspects of Culture and Personality*, New York: Abelard-Schuman, 1954, pp. 206-7).

2. The conception of *modal personality* is fully presented by Linton when he uses the statistical concept of mode to refer to a personality pattern which appears with the greatest frequency among the variety of personality patternings in a given society. He says that modal personality and basic personality 'differ mainly in stressing different aspects of the same phenomenon ...'. 'The "Modal Personality" for any society can be established directly and objectively by studying the frequencies of various personality configurations among a society's members. ... The term "Basic Personality" or "Basic Personality Type" reflects a dynamic approach to this phenomenon of Modal Personality' ('Problems of Status Personality', in S. S. Sargent & M. W. Smith (eds.), *Culture and Personality*, New York: The Viking Press, 1949, p. 163).

3. Other related terms are used to denote the personality or character structure of a concrete individual. Thus E. Fromm says, 'The sociopsychological approach which has been suggested in my own writing centers around the concept of the "social character". By social character I refer to the nucleus of the character structure which is shared by most members of the same culture in contradistinction to the *individual character* in which people belonging to the same culture differ from each other' ('Psychoanalytic Characterology and Its Application to the Understanding of Culture, *Culture and Personality*, p. 4).

Kardiner uses the term 'character' for the 'personal variant of the basic personality structure' (*The Individual and His Society*, p. 12). E. Beaglehole uses the term 'personality' in this sense: 'Personality refers to the variation on this common organization [basic personality structure] that persons possess as persons' ('Character Structure', *Psychiatry*, vol. 7, 1944, p. 151).

D. The concept of basic personality should not be confused with an occasional clinical usage of the term 'basic personality structure' or 'basic character structure'. As Inkeles and Levinson ('National Character: The Study of Modal Personality and Sociocultural Systems', p. 980), say, 'The term "basic" in this connection [cultural anthropology] refers to the sociocultural matrix rather than to that which is "deepest" in the person. The basic personality must be common or modal in the society, and is psychologically central in the sense that it is a generic feature on which diverse behavioral manifestations may be based'.

E. The concept has not gone uncriticized in contemporary social science. Causal links between personality and culture are in any case very complex and difficult to disentangle both from each other and from other relevant causal links. The more complex (i.e. more differentiated the society), the more difficult becomes the task of specifying such links. Some attempts to specify these links have, of necessity, been speculative rather than empirically grounded. A recent comment upon the 'basic personality' approach to the study of national character notes the 'potential importance' of the approach but adds three important qualifications. Firstly, the heterogeneity of modern societies may result in there being 'not one but a number of core types'. Secondly, where such a core type does exist, it would still be impossible to attribute actual behaviour (e.g. political choices) directly or solely to the core type. Thirdly, propositions about the general character of a culture are inadequate guides or predictors for more specific analyses. 'If the representative personality of a culture is aggressive, for example, this does not tell us what the object of the aggression will be' (L. Broom & P. Selznick, *Sociology*, Evanston, Ill.: Row, Peterson, 1958, p. 114).

Robert J. Havighurst

See also: CHARACTER STRUCTURE
PERSONALITY SYSTEM

Behaviour

A. *Behaviour* in its most general sense denotes the change, movement, or response of any entity or system in relation to its environment or situation. According to R. E. Park ('Behavior and Conduct', in R. E. Park and E. W. Burgess, *Introduction to the Science of Sociology*, Chicago: University of Chicago Press, 1924, p. 188), 'The fact is that every science is everywhere seeking to describe and explain the movements, changes, and reactions, that is to say the behavior, of some portion of the world about us'. In the social sciences, of course, the concern is with *human behaviour*, including the internal and external aspects of what men do and do not do. Although any movement or response of the human being may be considered behaviour, and is so considered by some, others

prefer to restrict the word *behaviour* to movement or response which has implications for the environment or situation. Thus E. C. Tolman says, 'That is, a behavior, or an action, differs from a mere movement or response in that a behavior or action can be fully identified and described in terms only of the organism-environment rearrangement which it produces. A mere movement or a response can, on the other hand, be identified in purely intra-organism terms, e.g. as consisting of such-and-such muscle contractions or glandular secretions' ('A Psychological Model', in T. Parsons & E. A. Shils (eds.), *Toward a General Theory of Action*, Cambridge, Mass.: Harvard University Press, 1951, p. 279).

B. Variations in usage of the term derive from differences in epistemological assumptions, conceptual schemes, and notions of what is important and unimportant in science. Controversy has centred on whether or not 'non-observable' intervening variables should be employed in the prediction of behaviour and on the nature of such variables if they are to be used.

1. Beginning with J. B. Watson (*Psychology from the Standpoint of a Behaviorist*, Philadelphia: J. B. Lippincott, 1919), there has been a tradition in psychology that the phenomena of human behaviour must be directly observable and measurable in some fashion, thus ruling out of the field subjective states and introspective accounts. Although this 'hard-boiled' doctrine seems to have softened, it still survives in the social sciences. B. F. Skinner (*Science and Human Behavior*, New York: The Macmillan Co., 1953, p. 35), for example, argues that intervening variables should be omitted, not on the grounds 'that they do not exist, but that they are not relevant in a functional analysis'.

2. At the opposite extreme from the 'behaviourist' position is that which considers behaviour within the 'action frame of reference'. This mode of thought stems from Weber's theory of 'action'. 'In "action" is included all human behavior when and in so far as the acting individual attaches a subjective meaning to it. Action in this sense may be either overt or purely inward or subjective; it may consist of positive intervention or passively acquiescing in the situation' (*The Theory of Social and Economic Organization*, trans. by A. M. Henderson & T. Parsons, New York: Oxford University Press, 1947, p. 88). T. Parsons and E. A. Shils further state that 'any behavior of a living

Behaviourism

organism might be called action; but to be so called, it must be analysed in terms of the anticipated states of affairs toward which it is directed, the situation in which it occurs, the normative regulation (e.g. the intelligence) of the behavior, and the expenditure of energy or "motivation" involved' ('Values, Motives and Systems of Action', in T. Parsons & E. A. Shils (eds.), *Toward a General Theory of Action*, p. 53).

3. The decision to include intervening variables in the analysis of behaviour does not necessarily, however, commit one to the 'action frame of reference'. As Tolman ('A Psychological Model', pp. 281–3) points out, some who have employed intervening variables have attributed neurophysiological properties to them and others have gone to the opposite extreme of phenomenology and accepted subjective categories as they are given in the experience of the person behaving. Still others, and this tends to be true of those using the 'action frame of reference', have drawn on the subjective experience of the person whose behaviour is being observed, but have nevertheless employed categories and concepts which reformulate this experience in ways relevant to the scientific observer rather than restricting it to the interpretation placed upon it by the person whose experience it was.

Edmund H. Volkart

See also: Behaviourism
          Intervening Variable

Behaviourism

A. *Behaviourism* denotes a movement in American psychology which is characterized by (a) interest in the study of learning and cognition, in man and other animals; (b) a concern with the operational definition of concepts, that is, definitions which specify the observations necessary for identifying the thing defined; (c) minimizing the importance of concepts which refer to 'mental' or 'subjective' processes; (d) a preference for research through laboratory experimentation; and (e) the use of the word behaviour (q.v.) to refer to speech and to inner processes such as thinking as well as to overt acts.

B. 1. The first major spokesman in this school of psychology was J. B. Watson. In *Behaviorism* (New York: The People's Institute Publishing Co., 1925, p. 3) he states, 'Possibly the easiest way to bring out the contrast between the old psychology [the "introspective psychology" of James, Wundt, Kulpe, Titchener, Angell, Judd, and McDougall] and the new is to say that all schools of psychology except that of behaviorism claim that *"consciousness" is the subject matter of psychology*. Behaviorism, on the contrary, holds that the subject matter of human psychology is the *behavior or activities of the human being*. Behaviorism claims that "consciousness" is neither a definable nor a usable concept; that it is merely another word for the "soul" of more ancient times.' Watson goes on (ibid., p. 6), 'Let us limit ourselves to things that can be observed, and formulate laws concerning only those things. Now what can we observe? Well, we can observe *behavior*—what *the organism does or says*. And let me make this fundamental point at once: that *saying* is doing—that is, *behaving*. Speaking overtly or to ourselves (thinking) is just as objective a type of behavior as baseball. The rule, or measuring rod, which the behaviorist puts in front of him always is: Can I describe this bit of behavior I see in terms of "stimulus and response?"' '

2. Watson was the forerunner of a major trend in American psychology, with his interest in the process of learning, his preference for experimental investigation of presently-occurring events, his epistemological position favouring the 'operational definition' of concepts (that is, definitions which specify the observations necessary for identifying the thing defined), and his broad use of the word *behaviour* to mean acts, words, and thoughts.

Behaviourism as a school no longer exists, chiefly because these aforementioned qualities of it characterize practically all of American psychology today, as W. W. Lambert states in 'Stimulus-Response Contiguity and Reinforcement Theory in Social Psychology' (G. Lindzey (ed.), *The Handbook of Social Psychology*), Cambridge, Mass.: Addison-Wesley, 1954, pp. 57–90). Since the 1930s, the study of learning (including cognition) in the behaviouristic style has received more attention than any other topic in American psychology. Pavlov's work on conditioning was an important early stimulating factor in this trend, and so was the work of E. Thorndike on the effect of reward and punishment on learning. Prominent American learning theorists include C. Hull, O. H. Mowrer, E. R. Guthrie, E. C. Tolman, D. O. Hebb, and K. Lewin. Learning theory of one school or another has been utilized in social psychology in studies of imitative behaviour, psychotherapy, child development, identification, attitude change, and achievement (ibid., pp. 81–85; see also M. Scheerer, 'Cognitive Theory', *Handbook of Social Psychology*, pp. 91–142).

C. Behaviourism has had important consequences for sociology as well as for psychology. On the one hand the extreme emphasis of some behaviourists on the exclusion of such concepts as motives, attitudes, and values, aroused considerable opposition among sociologists. Thus R. M. MacIver was impelled to say, 'Incompetent to deal with the subjectivity of experience the behaviorists would discard it altogether. Seeking to get rid of subjective terms they get rid of the social fact, since it is fact only as created by and known to experience' (*Society: Its Structure and Changes*, New York: Ray Long & Richard R. Smith, 1931, pp. 529–30). At the same time, however, the behaviourist focus on overt behaviour encouraged sociologists to develop theories in which concepts such as attitude, motive, and value were related to and derived from overt behaviour in interaction, e.g. the work of G. H. Mead. Perhaps the most important long-run effect of behaviourism on sociology and social psychology has been that greater attention is now given to the testing of hypotheses and to the operational definition of concepts.

Dorrian Apple Sweetser

See also: Behaviour
　　　　　Intervening Variable
　　　　　Social Interaction

Betrothal

The term denotes the formal engagement to marry. The achieving of marital status is a complex process, with many aspects, which develop through recognized stages. In many societies it is difficult to determine where marriage (q.v.) starts and betrothal ends. In some cases there may be a formal act of betrothal, which, if either party breaks the contract to marry, entitles the other to indemnity. Among the Todas, where infant betrothal was customary, the rate of indemnity differed for men and for women.

Sometimes betrothal gives the future spouses limited rights in each other even before the marriage is consummated, e.g. a suitor may claim damages for the seduction of his betrothed. Among the Bemba of Northern Rhodesia he gains this right when he makes his contribution to her initiation ceremonies (A. I. Richards, *Bemba Marriage and Present Eco-*

nomic Conditions, Livingstone: Rhodes-Livingstone Papers, no. 4, 1940, pp. 51–8).

M. Douglas

See also: Marriage

Bias

A. The term *bias* has currently a very wide reference often being equated with prejudice (q.v.), the state of being loaded, incomplete, and unrepresentative (see B. 2, 3, 4, and 5 below). The following, however, is an attempt based on usage in statistics (see B. 1 below) at a general but narrower definition: *bias* refers to an inaccurate estimate of phenomena which is based on a sample of observations and in which the inaccuracy results at least in part from systematic distortion in the collection and/or analysis of the observations.

In this sense, a biased definition of a situation may lead to a prejudiced attitude toward the situation, but the attitude itself is not biased because it is an *evaluation* of an estimate rather than an *estimate*. A question may yield a biased estimate if it is loaded or inadequate just as a sample may yield a biased estimate if it is drawn so as to be systematically unrepresentative of its parent population. The questions and samples, however, are not themselves biased according to the above definition.

B. 1. In the language of statistics *bias* refers to a condition of an estimate of a distribution parameter or of a test of some hypothesis. An estimator, say X, of a frequency or distribution function parameter, say θ, is said to be biased if the sum of all possible values of X, each value weighted by the probability of its occurrence, is unequal to θ. This weighted sum is an arithmetic mean, called the mathematical expectation of X, and is usually written $E(X)$. Thus, an estimator, X, of a parameter, θ, is biased whenever $E(X) \neq \theta$ — the difference between the two values being the 'bias'.

A statistical test is used in the process of deciding whether an hypothesis about some parameter is correct or whether an alternate to the hypothesis is correct. Two important characteristics of any statistical test are its size and power function. The former is the probability that the test will reject the hypothesis when it is correct. The latter is the probability that it will be rejected when some alternate is correct. A statistical test is said to be biased whenever the ordinate of the power function for some alternate is less than the size of the test.

2. When it is used in connection with the

term attitude, bias is synonymous with prejudice. Thus, a biased attitude toward a situation is one which is distorted by the predilections of the individual with respect to that situation. M. W. Riley, J. W. Riley Jr. and J. Toby use the word in this sense when they warn that an important task for social scientists is '... to make method less "subjective"—to dissociate it from the bias of the investigator' (*Sociological Studies in Scale Analysis*, New Brunswick: Rutgers University Press, 1954, p. 20).

3. In the phrase 'biased question' the bias denoted is usually constituted by one of two conditions. A biased question sometimes means one which yields enough information to classify the respondent when it is fully answered, but which may result in a false classification of the respondent's true state because of the phrasing of the question.

In this sense, L. Guttman sets the following as a criterion of useful questions: 'Is the question unbiased in its division of people into "favorable" and "unfavorable"?' ('The Problem of Attitude and Opinion Measurement', in S. A. Stouffer, et al., *Measurement and Prediction: Studies in Social Psychology in World War Two*, Princeton, N.J.: Princeton University Press, 1950, vol. 4, p. 48). In the second sense, a biased question may be one which yields accurate but inadequate information. In this light, Stouffer evaluates the question 'What kind of work do you think you will do right after the war?' as follows: 'This brought responses in terms of job plans, but was biased against the reporting of plans for further schooling' ('Two Case Studies in Prediction: Introductory Comments', in S. A. Stouffer, et al., ibid., pp. 480–1).

4. A biased sample usually refers to one which is drawn in such a manner as to render it non-representative of its parent population with respect to one or more distributions. In this sense, W. J. Goode and P. K. Hatt state that 'Departures from randomness will cause biases in the resulting sample' (*Methods in Social Research*, New York: McGraw-Hill, 1952, p. 218). On the same page these authors use bias as a synonym of attitudinal prejudice.

5. *Response bias* is a term used in survey research to denote the extent to which the research procedures used admit of responses (to questions) which on average yield results other than the 'true' results. Thus C. A. Moser observes that 'the effect of response bias is similar to that of sampling bias. In both cases the expected value of the estimate—let us say the average amount of pub-going—differs from the true value for the population. In the one case that is because people systematically misreport their behaviour, in the other because the sampling procedure is biased, for instance if interviewing is done in the evenings and the "regulars" are missed' (*Survey Methods in Social Investigation*, London: Heinemann, 1958, p. 248).

Robert McGinnis

See also: PREJUDICE

Bicameral (Also **Unicameral**)

A. *Bicameral* and *unicameral* are used as adjectives, primarily in connection with legislative organization; and as signifying a two-chambered (bicameral) or one-chambered (unicameral) legislative structure. The reference is, however, not primarily to the room or rooms in which the house or houses sit, but to the separate bodies of members and their status and powers in the legislative organization and with respect to each other. A member of one chamber will not be also a member of the other.

B. The usage is most common in democratic countries, where legislatures have significant powers, and it was actually developed mainly in English-speaking countries.

1. A house or chamber signifies, then, an organized body of members, that meets by itself for legislative purposes. It may be a national, state (in a federal system), or local legislative body. In bicameral systems one house usually has considerably more members than the other. This larger body is ordinarily called the lower house, the other the upper house or chamber, but the words 'upper' and 'lower' tell nothing about the relative powers of the two bodies.

The members of the lower house are generally elected directly by the voters; those of the upper house may be so elected, as is the case with the Senate of the United States and the senates of the forty-nine state legislatures that are bicameral. Nebraska has a unicameral system.

In many countries, however, the members of the upper house receive a right to their seats by other methods, e.g. by inheritance (as is the case with many members of the British House of Lords); by executive appointment (as in the parliament of the Dominion of Canada); by indirect election (as was once the case with the United States Senate, whose members until 1913 were elected by the state legislatures); and by constitutional designation of certain public officers to serve ex officio as upper house members. Various combinations of these and other methods are also to be found.

While the bicameral system of organizing national legislative bodies has become the most widely adopted system in democratic countries, this is most clearly true of their central legislative bodies. In the member states of federal systems, there are a number of departures from the bicameral system, and in local legislative bodies a bicameral arrangement is the rare exception.

2. The existence of a bicameral system does not imply that the two houses are equal in constitutional powers. Quite the contrary is true. There is probably no example of a bicameral legislative body in which the two houses have completely equal constitutional powers. One or the other may have distinctive powers over financial measures, treaties, or appointments, or may exercise special judicial or other powers. What is most common is that the consent of both chambers is usually required before an ordinary law may be enacted or altered, but even on this point some of the more recent constitutions provide means whereby in certain circumstances one house may legally enact a measure despite the opposition of the other. This is especially noticeable in systems of parliamentary government, where the executive is directly responsible to the legislature. To be equally responsible to two different chambers at once is difficult and in some cases practically impossible. The larger or 'lower' house, which is the one normally looked upon as most directly responsible to the people, tends to become the dominant one in parliamentary systems of government. In such systems it is often seriously questioned whether the upper or second chamber serves any useful function whatever.

3. Various reasons have been advanced in favour of having two chambers. These have special significance in federal systems of government, where the political structure takes on the characteristics of both a union of autonomous states and a single nation with unitary interests. The notion that one house should represent the member states as such or in their particular interests, and the other represent the national electorate, i.e. 'the people', as a whole, is widely diffused through the literature on federal systems of government.

William Anderson

See also: LEGISLATIVE BODY

Bifurcate Collateral Terminology (See **Kinship Terminology**)

Bifurcate Merging Terminology (See **Kinship Terminology**)

Bilateral

In kinship studies this term is used in several ways. (a) All kinship is said to be *bilateral* in the sense that, whatever the principle of descent, an individual has kinship ties to and through both parents. (b) Only some systems are said to be bilateral; these are the non-unilineal systems, in which kinship ties traced through both parents have, or may have, equal social weight. (c) In the context of cross-cousin marriage, bilateral is used as a synonym for symmetrical; i.e. bilateral cross-cousin marriage is the marriage of either kind of cross-cousin.

Maurice Freedman

See also: COGNATIC
          CROSS-COUSINS
          DESCENT

Bilateral Monopoly (See **Monopoly**)

Bilateral Trade (See **Multilateralism**)

Bilateralism (See **Multilateralism**)

Bilinear (See **Lineal**)

Bill

A. In the legislative process, the term *bill* denotes a draft of a proposed statute which is presented to a legislative body for enactment.

B. A strict definition might hold that a bill becomes an *act* once it has been passed by the legislature. Thus, in Great Britain, 'A Bill is a draft of a legislative proposal which, when it has been passed by both Houses, and received the Royal Assent, will become an Act of Parliament or Statute' (G. Campion, *An Introduction to the Procedure of the House of Commons*, London: Macmillan, 1950, p. 109–10). Of American practice H. Walker observed, 'When a proposal is ready for introduction in a legislative body, it is called a bill: when approved by the legislative body it becomes an act: when approved by the executive, and all other prescribed formalities have been observed, it becomes a law' (*The Legislative Process*, New York: Ronald Press, 1948, p. 225). However, American writers seldom observe this distinction, and thus usually speak of the President or a governor as signing or vetoing a bill.

1. It is common practice to distinguish between a public bill and a private bill. The latter

Birth Rate

is a bill whose applicability is confined to the specified individual, locality, organization, or other special interest on behalf of which it is introduced. A public bill is one which, if enacted, would affect the entire public. Different procedures govern the passage of each type of bill.

2. In reference to parliamentary-type governments, especially those with strong cabinets, it is likewise common practice to distinguish between a government bill, which is a public bill sponsored by the cabinet, and a private member's bill, which is a public bill sponsored by a member of the parliament who is not a member of the cabinet or ministry.

3. Two additional uses of the term *bill* as it relates to government may be mentioned: (a) A bill may be a special act which is passed by a legislature 'in the exercise of a quasi judicial power' (Black's Law Dictionary). An example is a bill of attainder. (b) A formal and historic declaration of human rights and liberties contained in a statute or written constitution is often designated as a 'bill of rights'.

Howard Scarrow

See also: LAW
STATUTE

Bilocal (See Residence)

Birth Rate

1. *Birth rate* denotes in a general sense the frequency of births in a population (see *fertility*).

2. It also denotes a particular commonly used index more precisely known as the *crude birth rate*; for a single calendar year, it is the number of births in a population in that year divided by the total population at mid-year or the mean population during the year (usually the resulting quotient is multiplied by 1,000, to give the birth rate 'per 1,000').

3. Contrasted with crude birth rates there are (a) *specific birth rates* (e.g. *age-specific birth rate, duration-specific birth rate,* etc.) relating to subsections of the population. (Such indices are commonly called *fertility rates*, rather than *birth rates*); (b) *adjusted* or *standardized birth rates* similar to the more frequently used standardized death rates (q.v.).

J. Hajnal

See also: DEATH RATE
FERTILITY

Blood Brother

This term denotes a relation of alliance or consociation by which individuals not related by kinship acquire ties of pseudo-kinship, the rights and duties that compose the relationship being modelled on those of brotherhood. The institution is 'a common device by which people are enabled to visit or traverse the territory of potentially hostile neighbours' (A Committee of the Royal Anthropological Institute, *Notes and Queries on Anthropology*, London: Routledge & Kegan Paul, 6th edn., 1951, p. 135). There may be rituals performed to create and to reaffirm the relationship.

J. Middleton

See also: KINSHIP TERMINOLOGY

Blood Feud (See Feud)

Board (See Commission; Committee)

Bolshevism

A. 1. The term *Bolshevism* (from Russian *bol'she*, more) was adopted by V. I. Lenin in 1909, having been occasionally used by other writers in previous years. The expression *Bolshevik* had been in general use as a noun to describe a member of that faction of the Russian Social Democratic Labour Party which had achieved the majority towards the end of the 2nd Congress of the Party in 1903, and as an adjective to denote the specific characteristics of the faction and its members.

(a) As seen by the Bolsheviks themselves, these characteristics were chiefly the adherence to orthodox Marxism as against revisionism; acceptance of a centralized hierarchical form of party organization with a core of professional revolutionaries as its guiding and directing element as opposed to the concept of a broad and loosely organized party; and revolutionary, as opposed to reformist, tactics.

(b) To their opponents in the party, the *Mensheviks*, however, Bolshevism had the connotations of dogmatism and doctrinarism; power-seeking by the faction and its leader; lack of concern for workers' genuine interests and disregard for their views; proneness to intrigue and adventurism.

(c) Since 1917, when the Bolsheviks seized power in Russia, their activities affected increasingly diverse spheres of life and the numbers of their adherents and sympathizers and of their opponents throughout the world increased; as a result, the original attributes of Bolshevism became surrounded by a host of derivative and analogous meanings, until almost any politically or socially relevant quality that was meant to appear positive could be called Bolshevik by sympathizers and *vice versa*.

2. The word *Bolsheviks* was a part of the official designation of the Russian Communist Party from 1912 to 1952.

B. V. I. Lenin (*Works*, Moscow: State Publishing House—Party Publishing House, 3rd Russian edn., 1928–36, vol. XIV, p. 33), gave two definitions of Bolshevism: (a) 'revolutionary Marxism ... in Russia'; and (b) 'the application of revolutionary Marxism to the special conditions of the epoch' (ibid., vol. XV, p. 283). He distinguished two aspects in it, and spoke of Bolshevism 'as a trend of political thought and as a political party' (ibid., vol. XXV, p. 174). I. V. Stalin considered Bolshevism to be identical with Leninism, saying that these were two names for the same object. The *Large Soviet Encyclopaedia* (Moscow: State Scientific Publishing House, 2nd edn., 1950, vol. 5) defines Bolshevism as 'the theory and tactics of Leninism embodied in the party of a new type, the party of Bolsheviks created by V. I. Lenin and I. V. Stalin', and describes it as 'the only consistent revolutionary Marxist trend in the international labour movement ...'.

C. Outside Russia in the 1920s and 1930s Bolshevism tended to be classified as one of the left-wing, radical, "progressive" movements; whereas in the 1940s and 1950s it has usually been treated as a variety of modern totalitarianism. Thus W. Gurian (*Bolshevism, An Introduction to Soviet Communism*, Notre Dame, Indiana: University of Notre Dame Press, 1952, p. 170), describes Bolshevism as 'that modern Communism which achieved power in Russia through the October revolution of 1917, and since has developed into a movement of world importance'. The author distinguishes three aspects of Bolshevism: (a) a secular pseudo-religion which 'replaces a transcendental God by a political and social order, the classless society' (ibid., p. 6); (b) 'the Russian reality of Bolshevism ... its rule and behaviour, ... typical policies and basic methods' of the Soviet regime (ibid., p. 3); (c) 'a world power that owes its successes not only to such material factors as the strength of the empire under its control, but also to the exploitation of social and psychological crises in western society of the 20th century' (ibid., p. 3).

S. V. Utechin

See also: COMMUNISM

Borrowing (See **Diffusion**)

Boss (See **Political Boss**)

Bourgeois (Also **Bourgeoisie**)

The most general use of these terms has reference to the mercantile or 'middle' strata in various societies, but their significance varies, depending both upon context and upon the extent to which the terms are used in polemic rather than in description.

1. Thus, until the coming of Marxism, the terms were used to describe either 'the mercantile or shopkeeping middle class of any country' (*Oxford English Dictionary*, 1933) or such town-dwellers in France, and later (by extension) elsewhere, as enjoyed political rights.

2. The Marxist theory of the class war gave them a new meaning. In the Marxian view, 'modern bourgeois society' had 'sprouted from the ruins of feudal society' (K. Marx & F. Engels, *Manifesto of the Communist Party*, 1st edn., 1848, London: Martin Lawrence, 1934, p. 10). The bourgeoisie had 'developed', increased its capital, and pushed into the background every class handed down from the Middle Ages' (ibid., p. 11), until it had 'conquered for itself, in the modern representative State, exclusive political sway' (ibid., p. 12). The executive of the modern State thus became 'a committee for managing the common affairs of the whole bourgeoisie' (ibid., p. 12). But the bourgeoisie, in accordance with the dialectical process, had 'not only ... forged the weapons that bring death to itself' (ibid., p. 15), it had also 'called into existence the men who are to wield those weapons—the modern working class—the proletarians' (ibid., p. 15). For Marx the bourgeoisie was thus one of the two elements in a new dialectic struggle, one of the two combatants in a new class war. It was the whole class of those who owned the land, the factories, and the instruments of labour, together with their dependents and hangers-on.

3. The word *bourgeois* and *bourgeoisie* thus passed into the vocabulary of continental Socialists, who were mainly Marxist from the early 1890s onwards, and to some extent inevitably penetrated also the vocabulary of their opponents, and, through translations, the English language too. They therefore came to be used with two or three meanings which to non-Marxists are by no means synonymous with 'middle-class' and often cause confusion; namely 'capitalist', 'non-socialist', 'non-Marxist'. Thus, in Marxist usage, 'bourgeois society'

Bride-Price

mostly means 'capitalist society', 'bourgeois parties' means 'non-Socialist parties' and 'bourgeois socialism', 'non-Marxist socialism'. Sometimes, however, two or all three of these senses are present in the one word, and sometimes also the original meaning of 'middle-class', along with one or two or all three of the other senses. This may well happen not only in Marxist works or in translations from continental writings, but also in the works of English-speaking authors who have borrowed the word, with or without a full appreciation of its semantic content. Caution is therefore required in any appreciation of its meaning.

W. Pickles

See also: MIDDLE CLASS
SOCIAL CLASS
STRATIFICATION

Bride-Price (Also **Bride-Wealth** and **Marriage Payments**)

A. These terms denote a gift made by the bridegroom and his kinsmen to the father and kinsmen of the bride, which carries legal and social implications varying from society to society.

B. 1. Payment of this kind is often a factor in establishing a legal marriage, and its acceptance signifies the transfer of those rights to which a husband is entitled in marriage. *Bride-price* is the oldest form, and was current when the institution was much disapproved by Europeans first meeting it in Africa. In 1848 Sir Harry Smith urged the Africans to abandon 'the sin of buying wives'. As familiarity with the institution in different societies proved that it did not necessarily contain any commercial element, the term was found by some to be unsatisfactory. In a long correspondence in *Man* between 1929 and 1931 various other terms were suggested, 'dower', 'espousal fee', 'earnest', 'settlement', 'marriage indemnity', but none of these has gained acceptance except *bride-wealth* and *marriage payments*.

2. The institution varies considerably in its form and functions. In Islamic societies the emphasis is not on the legality of the marriage so much as on a gift to the bride. It is found most highly elaborated in societies with agnatic descent, where the payment provides the means of attaching children to lineages, as its payment is the test of the validity of a marriage and its refund the mechanism of establishing divorce. For instance, it is the cornerstone of innumerable institutions among the Nuer of the Sudan where nearly all kinship categories are defined,

and incest laws justified, in terms of rights to receive and to contribute to marriage cattle. The custom is widespread in Africa, in Islamic cultures, Burma, China, Indonesia, Melanesia, but it is not universal. For instance, it is not part of the tradition of European cultures derived from Roman Law; it is not typical of Australia nor of many peoples of the North American continent.

3. *Bride-price* paid by the family of the groom is often reciprocated by a payment to them of a gift from the family of the bride, which may variously be called dowry, countergift, or return payment. Since the rule of polygamy tends to create a shortage of unmarried girls, their parents can require a high brideprice, and the institution, among its other functions, becomes a means of delaying the age of marriage for men, of enhancing their dependence on their kinsmen for acquiring the wherewithal to marry, and so also a means of distributing scarce females. Conversely, where monogamy, and a greater proportion of females to males in the population, are found together, one tends to find more emphasis on dowry than on bride-price, and women with no dowry are less likely to get married. In European peasant communities, such as in Poland or Ireland, it was usual for the bride's dowry in cash to be matched to the value of the farm the groom would inherit, and the cash to be used to settle the groom's brothers in other occupations.

M. Douglas

See also: MARRIAGE
POLYGAMY

Bride-Wealth (See **Bride-Price**)

Budget

A. In principle *budget* can refer to the plan of allocating any scarce resource over a period of time. Usually, however, it is restricted to the allocation of financial resources. In this sense, *budget* usually refers to a blueprint or plan of expected revenues and expenditures, with variations of form in relation to its use for business, person, family, or government.

B. The term *budget* has relevance for all four broad areas of finance: government, business, family, and personal. In each area, however, the term is used somewhat differently.

1. When the word *budget* is used in connection with personal or family finance, it generally connotes a financial plan whereby individuals or families attempt to balance their income and expenditures. Moreover, family or personal budgets generally '... presuppose the establishment of certain goals, such as the desire to reduce some expenses, get out of debt, or save a specified amount each year' (J. F. Bradley & R. H. Wherry, *Personal & Family Finance*, New York: Rinehart, 1957, p. 15).

2. In business, a budget or budgeting has a somewhat different connotation. Budgeting may be regarded as '... a method for combining the co-ordinated intelligence of an entire organization into a plan of action based upon past performances and governed by a rational judgment of factors that will influence the course of the business future' (A. Matz, et al., *Cost Accounting*, Dallas: Southwestern Pub., 1957, p. 473). The budget, then, is used for business management as a tool for formulating intelligent decisions as well as for control and forecasting. While this meaning is mostly used to refer to the financial plans of business, it does contain the possibility of an extra-financial use.

3. In government finance *budget* has two primary meanings. In its narrowest sense, it is an accounting document which serves as a control mechanism over a sub-agency which is authorized by a larger agency to carry on certain authorized spending activities. The budget, when used in this sense, is a spending authorization request made by the spending agent to the controlling agent. If and when the budget is approved it serves as the guide for the expending and, possibly, collecting of funds by the agency in question.

Most of the literature on the subject of government budgets treats the broader aspect of government budgeting. In this conception the budget is a financial plan for the government based on past, present, and future revenue and expenditure. As such, the 'budget document' consists of both control and plan. K. E. Poole uses this concept when he states that a budget is a '... comprehensive advance plan of governmental revenues and expenditures. It is intended to achieve a desired relation between planned expenditures and the taxes and other revenues required to finance them' (*Public Finance and Economic Welfare*, New York: Rinehart, 1956, p. 58).

4. In British public finance the term denotes, as U. K. Hicks indicates, 'an annual plan of financial policy' introduced, in ordinary circumstances, annually by the Chancellor of the Exchequer and consisting of 'the details of the taxes it is proposed to levy during the year'

(*Public Finance*, London: Pitman, 1948, pp. 39, 48). Such proposals are incorporated into the Finance Bill for the year.

Bernard F. Sliger

See also: FISCAL POLICY
        PUBLIC FINANCE

Bureaucracy

A. The literal meaning of this term is 'rule by the office' or 'rule by officials'. In the popular usage it often carries a pejorative sense. In the social sciences usage tends to follow the classic definition given by Weber (H. H. Gerth & C. W. Mills, *From Max Weber: Essays in Sociology*, London: Routledge & Kegan Paul, 1948, pp. 196–8). In Weber's usage (in sharp contrast to popular usage) the term has no invidious connotations.

The term carries three related meanings, analytically separable but empirically closely connected.

1. *Bureaucracy*, conceived of as an ideal type, refers to principles of organization that find varying degrees of expression in a wide variety of organizations. The characteristics of the ideal type are rationality in decision making, impersonality in social relations, routinization of tasks, and centralization of authority.

2. Weber's set of structural characteristics of bureaucracy previously listed constitute a definition for taxonomic purposes. These are: (a) fixed and official areas of jurisdiction for members; (b) a graded system of centralized authority; (c) a system of central files; (d) a set of special skills called office management; (e) official activities which demand the full time of personnel, and as a corollary the divorce of the official life of the employee from his personal life, particularly with reference to finances; (f) systematic and general rules which define procedure and which are followed.

3. One of the recurring tendencies in bureaucratic organization is the development of red tape, rigid rules, and procedural emphasis. This tendency is also labelled *bureaucracy*.

B. Most sociologists cite Weber as authority for discussions of bureaucracy. R. K. Merton (*Social Theory and Social Structure*, Glencoe, Ill.: The Free Press, 1957, p. 196), however, also argues that the popular conception of bureaucracy and Weber's definition are functionally related. Merton offers the proposition that bureaucratic organization, as defined by Weber, has as its consequences red tape, formalism, and rigid rules.

Business Cycles and Business Fluctuations

T. Parsons in his writings follows Weber's definition of bureaucracy quite closely emphasizing the central notion of rationality. In his volume on *The Sociology of Work* (Minneapolis: University of Minnesota Press, 1954, p. 149). T. Caplow comments on key elements in bureaucratic organization. These are rationality and impersonality. To this two other key characteristics might be added: centralization of authority, and routinization of tasks. In pointing to the key elements of the quintessence of bureaucracy writers have been quick to point out that Weber's definition is an 'ideal type' never more than approximated in reality.

Robert C. Stone

See also: ADMINISTRATION
DECISION-MAKING
RATIONALITY

Business Cycles and Business Fluctuations

A. *Business cycles* and *business fluctuations* refer to movements in the overall level of economic activity which are not attributable to a long-term trend of the economic system toward growth or decline. *Cycle* implies significant regularity of the movements but neither periodicity with respect to calendar time nor equal amplitude of successive movements. *Fluctuation* does not imply periodicity, equal amplitude, or regularity of movements.

B. Since the operation of an economic system is a dynamic process, one aspect of economic activity is change. Three broad types of change which occur in a private-enterprise capitalistic economy may be delineated, only one of which has applied to it the concepts of business cycles or business fluctuations.

1. A part of an economic system may undergo change without significant net effect on the overall level of economic activity. For example, the price of wheat may rise, the price of cotton decline, or employment in coalmining fall while employment in the oil industry rises. Such changes are never considered as falling into the category of business fluctuations or cycles, except, perhaps, in studies of the particular industries concerned.

2. An economy may move in the direction of long-run growth or decline as measured by an index as that of per capita real income over a period of many years—perhaps as much as a century. *Fluctuation* and *cycle* are not employed to designate such trends.

3. There may be shifts in the level of activity of an economic system as measured by movement in such indices as number of unemployed, wholesale prices, and the national income. It is in this area of change that the expressions *business cycles* and *business fluctuations* are used.

C. The distinction between business fluctuations and business cycles is not always clear-cut. While A. F. Burns says in one place 'Business cycles are not merely fluctuations in aggregate economic activity' he adds two pages later that 'the science of economic fluctuations is only beginning to pass into an inductive stage. Even today the descriptions of business cycles by economists ...' ('Mitchell on What Happens During the Business Cycle', in A. F. Burns, *The Frontiers of Economic Knowledge*, New York and Princeton: National Bureau of Economic Research by Princeton University Press, 1954, pp. 187, 189). Such usage suggests that at times the terms are used interchangeably while in other contexts a distinction is made. A. H. Hansen suggests that those whose approach to the problem is empirical are more likely to favour the term *business fluctuation* because of the many irregularities in the data while the abstract theorists will tend to use *business cycles* since theoretical models exhibiting regularity of change are much the simpler in construction (*Fiscal Policy and Business Cycles*, New York: W. W. Norton, 1941, pp. 13–14). Unfortunately for this distinction, the National Bureau of Economic Research, the leader in empirical research in this field, favours the use of the term *business cycles*.

D. While by no means standard practice, when a distinction between *business cycles* and *business fluctuations* is made, the writer uses *fluctuation* when he does not want to imply *regularity* or *periodicity* to the movements of aggregate economic activity, while he reserves *business cycle* to imply *regularity* and to a decreasing extent *periodicity*.

1. W. C. Mitchell says, 'Business cycles are a species of fluctuations in the economic activities of organized communities. The adjective business restricts the concept to fluctuations in activities which are systematically conducted on a commercial basis. The noun "cycles" bars out fluctuations which do not occur with a measure of regularity' (*Business Cycles, The Problem and Its Setting*, New York: National Bureau of Economic Research, 1927, p. 468). He denies, however, that the term includes the concept of periodicity.

2. J. A. Schumpeter also excludes periodicity over calendar time in the proper use of the term, although there *is*, according to Schumpeter, '... a process which systematically produces alternating phases of prosperity and depression ...' (*Business Cycles*, 2 vols., New York: McGraw-Hill, 1939, vol. 1, p. 143).

3. What has happened is that empirical studies have shown that what are called business cycles do not demonstrate periodicity with respect to calendar time, although they may show regularities of other sorts. Originally, there was an expectation that periodicity was characteristic of the business cycle. In the popular mind, and very likely, in the minds of many economists, the term *business cycle* still contains overtones of periodicity. This probably explains the growing use of the alternate term *business fluctuations*.

E. British usage, as for example, in the titles of R. F. Harrod's book, *The Trade Cycle* (Oxford: Oxford University Press, 1936) and of J. R. Hicks' book, *A Contribution to the Theory of the Trade Cycle* (Oxford: Oxford University Press, 1950), is to use the term *trade cycle* rather than *business cycle*. There appears to be no substantive difference in the two terms.

Royall Brandis

Business Enterprise

A. *Business enterprise* may refer to (a) a production treated by the unit theory of capitalist production, (b) a factor of production, (c) the system of capitalist production and distribution, or (d) the spirit or attitude of the system or the individual entrepreneur (q.v.). Furthermore, while the first three usages are ostensibly those of a value-free economics, valuational elements may be added to their definition which depend largely on the account given of and the attitude taken toward business enterprise as spirit, attitude, or informing principle.

B. 1. In the economic theory of production, a business enterprise is described as a production unit through which inputs of the factors of production are combined to make and sell goods for a profit. For example, K. E. Boulding states that the firm or business enterprise '... may be defined as an institution which buys things, transforms them in some way, and then sells them with the purpose of making a profit' (*Economic Analysis*, New York: Harper Bros., 3rd edn., 1955, p. 491). This definition neutrally stresses the combination of the factors of production for profit and organization of the productive process.

2. In the economic theory of distribution, *business enterprise* is sometimes used to designate a factor of production representing the contribution of entrepreneurs to the productive process. When used in this way the term is closely akin to and sometimes synonomous with such terms as *enterprise, entrepreneurship,* and *management*, as these are used to describe factors of production.

3. The term could be applied to a system of production made up of the inter-relationships of business enterprise units, or one in which business enterprise is a major factor of production, although it rarely is. More frequent are the terms *enterprise system* or *free enterprise system*, the latter generally carrying positive connotations.

4. While the term *business enterprise* need not carry evaluative overtones when it is applied to a unit of production, a factor of production, or an economic system, there is no doubt that historically it frequently has, and on occasion still does. *Enterprise* alone has the general meaning of daring, courage, imagination, and initiative or of an undertaking which involves such qualities. When these are seen as applying either to the productive process or to the search for profit, these latter are positively valued and the person, unit, or system which embodies them is also. On the other hand there have been critics who have identified business enterprise with the pecuniary motive and have judged this motive to be in conflict with a concern for the production of goods and their equitable distribution. Despite his claims to the contrary, Veblen saw business enterprise in this critical light (*The Theory of Business Enterprise*, New York: C. Scribner's Sons, 1923). He applied this conception to the individual entrepreneur and the single enterprise unit. Moreover, since he saw the attitudes and activities of such men and units as the directing force of modern society, the negative connotation applied also to the total system.

William H. Wesson

See also: ENTREPRENEUR
　　　　　MARKET ECONOMY

C

Cabinet

A. The term *cabinet* originally denoted the private room wherein the confidential advisers or ministers of the head of state met together, and today denotes (a) what is transacted there; (b) the body of persons who meet in such a cabinet; and more specifically (c) that limited number of the ministers who are in a more confidential position and have, in effect, together with the chief minister and/or the head of the state, supreme direction of national affairs.

B. The original implication of the term, in the European countries of its origin, is that of *secret and confidential*.

   1. Thus in Britain the term first appears at the beginning of the 17th century as an adjective, qualifying the word 'counsel' (i.e. 'advice') (e.g. Bacon's Essaies of Counsell in *The Essaies*, London: John Beale, 1612, p. 63). At the accession of Charles I (1625) reference is made to a 'Cabinet council'. The distinction grew up between the formal council of the monarch's advisers, i.e. the Privy Council, whose importance waned from the 17th century, and the inner ring of advisers or Cabinet Council, whose importance increased. (The exact relationship between the two bodies is still in dispute.)

   2. In France, the sense is similar, e.g. Montesquieu, *Esprit des Lois* (vol. XII, p. viii)—where he writes 'ce furent bien le cabinet et les favoris qui établirent ce crime'.

   3. In Germany, the development is similar: under the absolute princes of the 16th and 17th centuries there developed the *Geheime Rat*, the council of the monarch's highest officials and advisers; but during the 18th century, in certain of the states, the princes tended to withdraw themselves from their *Geheime Rat* into a narrow circle of personal advisers called collectively the *Geheime Kabinett*.

   4. The U.S.A. borrowed the term from English practice. The Constitution makes no mention of it, and at first Washington tried to use the Senate as a kind of Privy Council, a development checked by the Senate's clear dislike of such a role. In 1793, Washington called together the Attorney General and his Secretaries of State, War, and Navy; this Conference was, circa 1810, recognized as the official council or 'cabinet' of the President. The first recorded use of the term in this context is *Annals of the 6th Congress* (1799–1801, Washington: Gales & Seaton, 1851, p. 1077): 'The President of the U.S. was to take his Cabinet from among the people of the U.S.' The U.S. Cabinet was and is a select body of Presidential advisers.

C. The following specifies certain current differences in national usage.

   1. In Great Britain it denotes the smaller body of ministers (as contrasted with the full number who are known collectively as 'The Government' (q.v.)) who form the advisory council of the Crown and by whom the general policy of the executive and also the more important legislative measures introduced by the government into Parliament are decided. It is recognized by statute law only indirectly, notably in the Ministers of the Crown Act, 1937, which provided for an increased salary for those ministers who were also members of the Cabinet. (*Cabinet rank* appears to mean merely that the holder of the appointment so designated shall receive the same salary as ministers who are members of the Cabinet). The choice of persons who are to be members rests with the Prime Minister; recently it has been confined to some eighteen persons.

   Sir Ivor Jennings (*Cabinet Government*, Cambridge: Cambridge University Press, 1st edn., 1936, p. 174) describes it as 'the directing body of the national policy. Consisting of the principal leaders of the party in power, it is able to forward that policy by reason of its control of the House of Commons. Consisting, too, of the heads of the more important Government departments, it is able to forward its policy by laying down the principles to be followed by the central administrative machine. Their service under the crown is the legal explanation of the political fact that ministers hold important Government offices. Membership of the Privy Council is a historical survival'.

   2. In the United States it denotes the heads of certain executive departments serving in an advisory capacity to the President in whom alone, under the Constitution (II.i) the 'executive power' is vested. The present membership comprises: the Secretary of State, of the Treasury, of Defence, of the Interior, of Agriculture, of Commerce, of Labour, and of Health, Education and Welfare; together with the Attorney-General and the Postmaster-General.

The phrase *Kitchen-cabinet* is sometimes used to denote a President's private and unofficial clique of advisers: first used during the first term of President Andrew Jackson (1829–33).

3. In France, (a) the original flavour of 'cabinet' as something confidential and informal is preserved in the French distinction between the formal body, the *Conseil des Ministres* presided over by the President of the Republic and which alone is mentioned in the Constitution; and *le Cabinet*, presided over by the Prime Minister, a more informal and more 'political' body; (b) the phrase *le cabinet de ministre* denotes the small group of some half a dozen personal or political friends whom each minister brings into office with him as his personal staff.

S. E. Finer

See also: CABINET GOVERNMENT

Cabinet Government

A. *Cabinet government* denotes a regime in which the Cabinet works within the framework of a representative system of government and which is marked by the following characteristics:

1. The executive power with all its prerogatives is *formally* given to a head of state (q.v.) in whose name and by whose order executive actions are performed.

2. All such actions, however, or at least the most important of them must first have been decided by certain ministers meeting as a corporate body called the Cabinet (q.v.).

3. While the nominal head of state has the formal authority to appoint and dismiss his ministers, his power to do so is limited by three conditions: (a) these ministers must be supported by the majority party in the legislature or, if no one party has a clear majority, by a group of parties taking part in a coalition. (b) the Cabinet must act as a collective body. (c) as a collective body it is responsible for its policy to the legislature.

B. Such a regime is generally contrasted with *presidential government* as found in the U.S.A.; it is a feature of the political system of Great Britain and of Commonwealth countries. It has also been in evidence elsewhere, e.g. in France

from the Restoration of 1814 and in Germany under the Weimar Republic set up in 1919.

S. E. Finer

See also: CABINET
HEAD OF STATE
LEGISLATIVE BODY
PARLIAMENTARY GOVERNMENT
PRESIDENCY

Cannibalism

A. The anthropological use of the term (and the alternative term *anthropophagy*) denotes the institutionalized and regularized practice of eating human flesh—approved and linked with other cultural features. Authentically substantiated cases of cannibalism are less common in anthropological literature than one might expect. They are mostly confined to the non-literate world: a notable exception are the Aztecs who are rarely referred to as cannibals, but among whom sacrificial victims were cut up after death and distributed for eating. Conventionally, headhunting-ritual and cannibalism (human sacrifice) are often taken as linked (*Notes and Queries on Anthropology*, London: Routledge & Kegan Paul, 6th edn., 1951, p. 177), but in fact they are rarely reported in combination.

1. Among many peoples (especially in the non-literate world) the term is used in a pejorative sense in reference to neighbouring groups or to enemies.

2. Isolated instances (e.g. among the Eskimos and Shoshones, in the course of acute food shortage during bad seasons, or as occasionally reported among shipwrecked Europeans, or in certain wartime situations) do not warrant the application of the term *cannibals* to all the members of the group concerned.

3. Some writers consider that teknophagy (eating children) should be distinguished from cannibalism as such, since (and the type situation is aboriginal Australia) small children are eaten only occasionally in the event of extreme hunger, or to increase the strength of an older child, or, in the case of a child who has died from natural or other causes, to encourage its spirit to be reborn in a new body from the same mother.

4. H. Basedow (*The Australian Aboriginal*, Adelaide: F. W. Preece, 1925, pp. 21, 189) holds that if human flesh is consumed only to avert death from starvation, or as a feature of mortuary ritual (as in certain areas of aboriginal Australia, where parts of a dead body might be

Capital

eaten), we are not justified in speaking of cannibalism. There is not general agreement on this point, however. The term *ritual-cannibalism* is sometimes used to isolate this as a special category.

5. Various attempts have been made to 'explain' cannibalism. Thus for the eastern highlands of New Guinea; as for other regions, institutionalized, regularized cannibalism has been explained as an attempt to compensate for an inadequate diet, containing much starchy food and little protein ('Short Extract of B. de Sahagun, *A History of Ancient Mexico*', in C. S. Coon (ed.), *A Reader in General Anthropology*, London: Jonathan Cape, 1950, p. 446).

B. Psychoanalytic usage is based on the type situation of the Oedipal family, with the killing and eating of the 'primal father' (see particularly the work of S. Freud and G. Roheim). The phrase *symbolic cannibalism* is used to denote the practice (e.g. in aboriginal Australia) of eating one's own totem or that of another known person.

Ronald M. Berndt

See also: SACRIFICE

Capital

A. Definitions of *capital* that have taken forms which deserve emphasis are as follows:

1. The accountant distinguishes between the net assets of the proprietor and the total assets used in the business. The former is called the *proprietor's capital*, *net worth*, or just *capital*. The latter represents the *total capital*. These uses stress the monetary view of capital. Because good-will can be included and because for some special purposes one may even include the skill of workers employed by the business as part of the total capital, the distinction should be clear between capital in the accounting sense and in the sense of an apparatus or thing used in production.

2. An economic definition in widespread use is that which relates capital to producers' goods. In this context capital consists of those goods produced by man and used in further production. For some purposes trained skills might be included. Consumer durable goods and natural resources are excluded and so too is labour from this concept of capital.

3. Still a third definition may be proposed. This definition includes land and durable goods along with all kinds of producers' goods. It divides capital into two broad categories: (a) *consumers' capital* consisting of consumer durable goods; and (b) *producers' capital* including inventories and goods in process as well as physical equipment and land.

4. There are several sub-forms of the term capital which are used primarily in economics and accounting:

(a) *Circulating capital* has been defined in accounting and in national income accounting as that capital which changes its form within a given period of time, customarily designated as a year. In a slightly different context other writers relate circulating capital to the output of a firm. It is that capital which reappears in the form of the final product. Thus coal, lubricating oil, the raw materials that go into a productive process and their like are circulating capital under either of these concepts.

(b) *Fixed capital* is durable. It is not used up within the year period and hence maintains its own form for a considerable period of time. Machines, furnaces, and factory buildings are examples of fixed capital.

(c) *Free capital* is that capital which may be used in many different ways. It is not limited to a single type of productive process or a few closely related sets of productive processes, but rather is usable in the production of quite different things. Some circulating capital, such as coal and lubricating oil, is also free capital. It may be used in the manufacture of clothes, bags, food products, and other things. On the other hand, other raw materials may not be free capital, as their use may be restricted to a given industry and product.

(d) *Specialized capital* is that capital which can be used in only one kind of productive process or a few closely related lines of production. Many of the processes used in the fabrication of automobiles are specialized to that industry.

(e) *Equity capital* refers to the interest in a business of the owner. It is distinguishable from the *borrowed capital* of a business. What equity capital means to the economist is therefore what capital means to the accountant.

(f) *Working capital* means the net current assets of a business. It is primarily a concept in accounting. Working capital may be computed by taking the difference between the firm's current assets and its current liabilities.

B. The term *capital* is used in accounting to refer to the interest of the proprietor in the assets of the business. Alternatively, the terms *proprietorship* or *net worth* are used to convey the same idea (H. S. Noble & C. R. Niswonger,

Accounting Principles, Cincinnati: South-Western Publishing Co., 6th edn., 1953, p. 5). Occasionally businessmen employ this accounting usage, though according to H. G. Guthmann & H. E. Dougall (*Corporate Financial Policy*, New York: Prentice-Hall, 1948, pp. 71–3), capital more frequently indicates to them the total assets that are employed to operate a business. This businessman's idea of capital as the total assets used in a business has an historic origin that dates from before the industrial revolution. It implies a financial fund, a valuation, or investment. Capital signifies in this usage a sum or quantity which can be expressed readily in monetary terms and which serves as a source of income.

C. Economists have wavered between the monetary usage of *capital* and a usage which stresses producers' goods and, sometimes, trained skills. According to F. A. Fetter ('Capital', in E. R. A. Seligman (ed.), *Encyclopedia of the Social Sciences*, New York: The Macmillan Co., vol. III, 1930, pp. 187–90), the classicists, Smith, Mill, and others, vacillated in this respect. In some places they stressed the technological side of capital; at others, the valuational side. The use of one term to express distinctively different ideas could only result in difficulties. One of these is the tendency to capitalize income at the going rate of interest—a tendency related to the conceiving of capital as a fund—rather than relating income to (a) the replacement cost of items which created the income or to (b) the securing of items which would yield the same income (F. H. Knight, 'Interest', in E. R. A. Seligman (ed.), *Encyclopedia of the Social Sciences*, vol. VIII, 1932, pp. 131–43). These difficulties can to some extent be dissipated if one notes that the physical and technological embodiment of capital is manifest within a short-run perspective; while in the long run the monetary counterpart may be viewed. This kind of distinction is emphasized in J. Robinson's *Economics of Imperfect Competition* (London: Macmillan, 1946, p. 19). In the same general key, J. S. Bain (*Pricing, Distribution and Employment*, New York: Holt, rev. edn., 1953, pp. 573 ff.) distinguishes between the capital goods and its investable fund counterpart holding the physical good to be the primary meaning of *capital* and the money counterpart to be a complementary meaning.

Another difficulty, at least supported by viewing capital primarily as a fund, is that of conceiving labour as the agent which uses and re-

produces capital, thus denying productive contributions to factors other than labour, including capital. In fact, as F. Knight ('The Ricardian Theory of Production and Distribution', *Canadian Journal of Economics*, vol. 1, 1935, pp. 171–96, esp. fn. 41) has pointed out the 'relation is symmetrically mutual'. In mid-20th-century economics, the imputation process is conceived to be applicable to all factors of production, with capital being regarded primarily as physical goods and skills.

D. Unfortunately even regarding *capital* as composed of productive elements does not lead to totally consistent definition. Marshall (*Principles of Economics*, London: Macmillan, 8th edn., 1920, p. 71) defines *capital* as consisting of *all* things other than land which yield income and which are generally regarded as doing so in common discourse. Basic texts in economics use the term in a comparably broad manner. Thus C. L. Allen, J. M. Buchanan & M. R. Colberg (*Prices, Income, and Public Policy*, New York: McGraw-Hill, 1954, p. 93) let *capital* stand for all types of productive factors other than labour. The context in which the term is used then controls its precise meaning. Marshall excludes land; Allen, Buchanan, and Colberg exclude labour and consumer goods. G. J. Stigler (*The Theory of Price*, New York: Macmillan, 1947, pp. 321 ff.) holds that capital consists of consumers' goods as well as productive resources, excepting labour, the services of which continue for a significant period of time. Finally we might recall that marginal productivity theory emphasizes the similarity of all factors of production, so that a generalized concept of capital could include labour as well as land along with capital goods. This concept of capital is due in part to I. Fisher (*The Theory of Interest*, New York: The Macmillan Co., 1930). Its chief importance lies in the fact that it points to the possibility of simplifying the theory of distribution by abolishing the classical distinction between theories of wages, rent, interest, and profit; all that is needed is a single theory of the hire and selling prices of factors of production. However, Fisher did admit the necessity of a rough working distinction between labour and other valuable things—capital in the narrow sense—in a society without slavery. Manifestly the value of any definition can be estimated only by reference to the theoretical system of which it is a part.

E. Most accountants use 'historical cost' con-

Capital Goods

cepts and make little allowance for changes in the value of money. Economists, however, allow for changes in reproduction cost and for inflation and deflation. Thus a concern may have much 'capital' in the eyes of an accountant, while having little or no 'capital' in the view of an economist; or in other cases the opposite may be true. It is impractical to equate the usual measure of the accountant with that of the economist.

Melvin L. Greenhut

See also: CAPITAL GOODS
CAPITAL-LABOUR RATIO
MARGINAL EFFICIENCY OF CAPITAL

Capital Consumption Allowance
(See **Depreciation**)

Capital Goods
A. Both from an analytical and from a statistical point of view it seems sound to define the term as the existing stock of produced goods, either single-use or multiple-use, but not immediately perishable, capable of rendering services to the consumers and the producers of the relevant economic entity under consideration. This definition constitutes an adaptation of the definition of capital (q.v.) used by S. Kuznets in his statistical study, *Commodity Flow and Capital Formation* (New York: National Bureau of Economic Research, 1938, vol. I, p. 3).

1. By 'single-use' is meant goods which disappear in yielding the gratification or service for which they were created. You can't drink your bottle of beer twice. But since bottled beer is durable a stock may be accumulated. But goods which are both immediately perishable *and* single-use can scarcely be called capital goods.

2. Where such practice is useful or relevant to a given classification or analysis, descriptive limiting adjectives should be used to establish the subdivisions *consumers' capital goods* and *producers' capital goods*.

3. Within the two subdivisions of *capital goods*, further sub-types may be usefully identified. Thus the two major subdivisions can be further categorized into (a) *durables*, (b) *semi-durables*, and (c) *non-durables*. Still further subdivisions may be accomplished to distinguish among such sub-types (i) at destination and (ii) in circulation; and on the basis of whether they are (iii) finished or (iv) unfinished. The degree of fineness in the classification must depend on the nature of the problem under consideration and in the solution of which the definition is to serve as a tool (cf. S. Kuznets, *Commodity Flow and Capital Formation*, pp. 5–7, and L. Metzler, 'Factors Governing the Length of Inventory Cycles', *Review of Economic Statistics*, vol. 29, pp. 1–15).

B. As J. A. Schumpeter notes, until 1870 many writers used the term *capital* (q.v.) both in a physical, or technological, sense and in a monetary sense (*History of Economic Analysis*, New York: Oxford University Press, 1954, pp. 898–9). This fact apparently accounts for the relatively recent development of the *capital goods* concept. The term was invented by J. B. Clark for the purpose of distinguishing between his abstract conception of 'Pure Capital' as a 'fund of value' and the 'combination of objects such as tools' in which the capital fund 'temporarily resides' ('Capital and Its Earnings', *Publications of the American Economic Association*, vol. 3, 1889, p. 92). In *The Distribution of Wealth*, Clark amplified the distinction by an analogy: 'Pure Capital' is a stationary waterfall, while capital goods are the particular things which enter and leave the waterfall 'as an endless succession of drops of falling water ... eminently material and concrete' (*The Distribution of Wealth*, New York: The Macmillan Co., 1899, p. 121). Clark included land within the term; most later writers have not done so.

A. Marshall noted Clark's use of the term, but did not adopt it, and suggested the use of the alternative definitions of *instrumental capital* to include generally all goods aiding labour in production, and of *consumption capital* to include goods affording 'direct sustenance to workers' (*Principles of Economics*, London: Macmillan, 8th edn., 1920, pp. 73–5). I. Fisher adopted the term *capital goods* as a general term to include 'both capital instruments and capital property', the latter being a 'quantum of property rights existing at any instant'. Both were to be counted in units and to be distinguished from *capital value* counted in dollars (*The Nature of Capital and Income*, New York: The Macmillan Co., 1927, p. 67). Since that time the term has come into increasing use.

C. L. M. Fraser summarizes his detailed analysis of the logic and usefulness of various capital goods concepts by saying: '... capital as a goods concept may stand for the whole of a community's equipment at a given moment of time; or for production goods as opposed to consumption goods; or for long-lived goods as opposed to short-lived goods; or for exchange use goods as opposed to personal use goods' (*Economic Thought and Language*, London: A. & C. Black, 1937, p. 305). The confusions resulting from these multiple usages can be reduced by defining *capital goods* as producers' goods capable of rendering services, and then subdividing these goods into classes by the use of appropriate categories. Thus the fact that some modern writers do not include inventories of finished goods within the meaning of the term *capital goods* and others do can be reconciled by speaking of *finished* capital goods and *unfinished* capital goods. Similarly the dichotomy between those who would restrict capital goods to producers' goods and those who would not, and between those who stress fixed position as opposed to circulation, can be overcome by the use of appropriate adjectives. Thus the Conference on Research in Income and Wealth speaks of *producers' capital goods* and includes the following items in its statistical estimates of such goods: (a) *fixed capital goods*, including non-farm business structures, farm structures, producer durables; and (b) *circulating capital goods*, including livestock, crops, and private non-farm inventories (*Studies in Income and Wealth*, New York: National Bureau of Economic Research, vol. 12, 1950, pp. 18–19). There is little reason why this cannot be done with respect to other uses of the term.

H. H. Liebhafsky

See also: CAPITAL

Capital-Labour Ratio

A. *Capital-labour ratio* may be defined as the ratio of the quantity of capital to the quantity of labour available as inputs to or in a given economic entity at a given time or during a given period of time. Use of the concept would seem to require that the methods of measuring the particular elements entering into the ratio, the relevant time period, and the nature of the entity using the inputs, i.e. individual, firm, or nation, be specified.

B. The term *capital-labour ratio* is used principally in economics in the theory of income distribution. P. H. Douglas provides a detailed account of early uses of the concept in the works of Longfield, Von Thunen, J. B. Clark, and others (*The Theory of Wages*, New York: The Macmillan Co., 1934, pp. 17–96). Then, as now, the concept was understood to refer to the amount of capital relative to the amount of labour available as inputs to or within an economic entity at a given time or during a given period of time.

C. Modern writers who use the concept in explaining the principle of diminishing returns (q.v.) and the marginal productivity theory of distribution generally assume that the proportions are completely variable in which capital can be combined with labour in producing a given output. 'Variations of form' of physical capital are generally achieved in these discussions by introducing time and a value or monetary concept of capital into the analysis. For example, G. J. Stigler notes that the 'entrepreneur can sometimes sell the inappropriate form of [capital] equipment and replace it … and he can always wear [it] out … and replace it' (*The Theory of Prices*, New York: The Macmillan Co., rev. edn., 1952, p. 117).

However, some writers in the field of macroeconomic theory have adopted a strict physical concept of capital and rejected the notion of the infinite divisibility of capital (see, for example, A. Murad, 'Net Investment and Industrial Progress', in K. K. Kurihara (ed.), *Post Keynesian Economics*, New Brunswick: Rutgers University Press, 1954, p. 234). Other writers have assumed infinite divisibility in their discussion of the effects, under static assumptions, of changes in factor supplies, technological progress, and inventions upon the relative returns received by capital and labour (J. R. Hicks, *The Theory of Wages*, London: Macmillan, 1932; and J. Robinson, *Essays in the Theory of Employment*, London: Macmillan, 1937, pp. 75–100). Much of the debate springs from failure to distinguish new invention from change in methods actually used. There is always a stock of known but unused methods which a change in the planned ratio may make profitable.

D. In their attempt to solve the problem of the influence of capital and labour on production in the United States during the years 1899–1922, P. H. Douglas and C. W. Cobb give precise definitions of all the magnitudes entering into their ratio. They measure capital (C) as equal to money additions to capital in given years deflated by an index number of the cost of capital goods, labour (L) as equal to the average number employed in manufacturing in given years, and product (P) as an index of physical production, in which physical quantities of a variety of products are reduced to index numbers and weighted by relative values added by

Capitalism

manufacturing in given years (P. H. Douglas, *The Theory of Wages*, pp. 129–40; for a bibliography of criticism of this work as well as for a reply by Douglas, see P. H. Douglas & G. T. Gunn, 'Further Measurements of Marginal Productivity', *Quarterly Journal of Economics*, vol. LIV, 1940, pp. 399-428).

C. G. Clark (*The Conditions of Economic Progress*, London: Macmillan, 1940, pp. 37–45) notes the difficulty involved in attempts to measure capital and argues that real capital can only be measured by dividing a market value—original cost or reproduction cost—by an index number. J. Robinson, on the other hand, defines the term *capital* as used in the ratio by saying 'capital must be conceived in physical terms, that is, as a stock of capital goods, and it is most conveniently measured in terms of cost units' ('The Classification of Inventions', in American Economic Association, *Readings in the Theory of Income Distribution*, Philadelphia: Blakiston, 1946, p. 176, fn. 3). There is in fact no wholly satisfactory means of measuring the capital stock over time. Physical units omit the influence of change in method and output composition. Value units bring in the index number problem. Cost units are not independent of method changes and changes in the stock.

G. Grossman has utilized the related concept of *incremental capital-intensity* defined as 'the volume of (gross) fixed capital investment divided by the increment in the number of workers and employees' ('Trends in Soviet Capital Formation', in National Bureau of Economic Research, *Capital Formation and Economic Growth*, Princeton: Princeton University Press, 1955, p. 176). N. M. Kaplan has commented on Grossman's concept: 'Average capital-intensity as a measure of the stock of capital available per worker is certainly relevant to problems of economic growth. ... Emphasis on average capital-intensity is ... warranted by the absence of aggregate measures of technological advance and by the reflection in increased average capital-intensity of significant aspects of technological advance. ...' ('Comment', in National Bureau of Economic Research, *Capital Formation and Economic Growth*, p. 207). However, Kaplan then demonstrates mathematically that incremental and average capital-intensity are '... not so related that inferences about one can be drawn from observations of the other' (ibid.). In his analysis of the 'structural part of the theory of dynamic processes' of capital growth, A. Lowe defines

capital-intensity as 'the value of the capital stock' divided by the 'value of payrolls of the workers operating it over a stated period' ('Structural Analysis of Real Capital Formation', in National Bureau of Economic Research, *Capital Formation and Economic Growth*, pp. 595–6). He then utilizes the concept in a dynamic analysis of 'labor-displacing and labor-attracting technical changes'.

H. H. Liebhafsky

See also: CAPITAL
　　　　　CAPITAL GOODS

Capitalism

A. The term *capitalism* denotes an economic system in which the greater proportion of economic life, particularly ownership of and investment in production goods, is carried on under private (i.e. non-governmental) auspices through the process of economic competition (q.v.) and the avowed incentive of profit.

B. 1. The word comes from the Latin, *caput*, head, and from capital, which seems to have been used in Latin as an adjective, in the phrase *pars capitalis debiti* (the capital part, or principal, of a debt), in reference to a sum of money owed. From this it was extended to other things besides money, still mainly as an adjective, as in the phrase 'capital stock', signifying either the value of assets embodied in trade or production or those assets themselves. At least by the early 17th century *capital* was sometimes used as a noun. The lexicographer, Cotgrave, defined it in 1680 as 'wealth, worth; a stocke, a man's principall, or chiefe, substance'. It is also used as a noun in 1635 in Dufferne's *Merchant Mirrour*; but it continued to be more commonly used as an adjective until the 19th century. From *capital* came *capitalist*, an owner of capital, used by Arthur Young as early as 1792, and from *capitalist*, *capitalism*, a system dominated by such persons—used by W. M. Thackeray in 1854, but not in frequent use until the 1880s. Marx called his magum opus of 1867 *Das Kapital*, but spoke more often of the bourgeoisie than of the capitalists and of bourgeois production than of capitalism.

2. The word *capitalism* was largely popularized by socialists as a name for the economic system they were attacking. By it they meant a system under which the means of production are mainly owned by private persons, who use them to extract profit by paying the labourers less than what the socialists considered the full value of their product—though not less than the value of their labour-power as determined under conditions of private ownership of the means of production. Anti-socialists have often rejected the name *capitalism* for this system, which they have preferred to regard as one in which the product is divided among the factors of production according to their marginal productivity. This involves treating private ownership of means of production as a legitimate and productive source of income, which socialists deny, asserting rather that labour is the sole source of value and should receive the full product or that the entire product should be collectively owned and redistributed in accordance with the requirements of general utility and/or social justice.

C. The word is not as a rule precisely defined, and is in fact used in several overlapping senses; but the idea of private ownership of the means of production and their employment in quest of profit is common to them all, whereas that of the exploitation of the labouring by the capitalist class is peculiar to socialists.

1. Capital and capitalists are often contrasted, as man-made factors of production and their ownership, with land as a natural factor; but in settled countries the natural properties of the land have usually been greatly affected, for good or ill, by the application of capital and labour to them; and in highly industrialized countries in particular the distinction between land and capital has lost most of its economic importance, at any rate where a class of great landowners, clearly distinct from other capitalists, has ceased to exist.

2. Capitalism, as the word is ordinarily used, frequently involves the existence of owners of large amounts of capital: one would hardly describe as capitalistic a society where industry was mainly in the hands of small-scale producers, whom Marx calls petty bourgeois as distinct from the bourgeoisie proper, who operate on a larger scale.

3. Capitalism is often regarded as passing through three successive stages, beginning with commercial capitalism, under which large-scale operators come to dominate the processes of exchange, running on (with the Industrial Revolution) into the stage of industrial capitalism, dominated by the owners of large factories, mines, and other industrial enterprises, and then to the stage of finance, or financial, capitalism, in which control passes more and more into the hands of bankers and financiers dominating industrial enterprises to which they advance

money, or to great investors divorced from the day-to-day management of industrial enterprises, but controlling them and extracting profit from them by their financial power. These stages are not, of course, mutually exclusive: the earlier do not cease to exist when the later are superimposed upon them. Reference is sometimes made to a fourth form, state capitalism, defined by Lenin as a system under which the State takes over and exploits means of production in the interest of the class which controls the state; but the phrase, 'state capitalism', is also used to describe any system of state collectivisation, without reference to its use for the benefit of a particular class.

Still a fifth form is frequently described in the literature concerned with those economies in which there is an increased element of state intervention either in terms of welfare programmes or of responsibility for employment and lessening the impact of the business cycle. This form is denoted by such phrases as *welfare capitalism* or *protected capitalism*.

D. According to non-socialist economists who accept the name *capitalism* as denoting an economic system resting on private ownership and investment, such a system, if left to operate freely with a minimum of state interference, maximizes production and results in a rational distribution of scarce resources and efforts among alternative uses. Socialists, in addition to rejecting the legitimacy of a part of the product accruing to private owners, usually deny that rational distribution will occur in the absence of a production plan, including a planned distribution of incomes. They point out that the rich man's shilling and the poor man's have the same purchasing power in the market, and that, as the utility of money decreases with the amount possessed, highly unequal distribution creates far less aggregate value than more even distribution, and is therefore irrational as well as unjust. It also results in preference being given to luxuries over relative necessaries, and thus distorts the productive structure, which should be designed to produce the maximum response to real wants and needs, rather than to adjust production to the existing structure of purchasing power. The defenders of capitalism usually retort that maximum production requires the offer of large incentives to entrepreneurs, who take the risks of combining the factors of production, and that less unequal distribution would have the effect of reducing total output. Socialists retort partly by denying this,

Capitalization

and partly by refusing to accept maximum production as the *sole* criterion of the merits of an economic system, fairness and an approach to equality in distribution being in their view also important.

G. D. H. Cole

Capitalization (Also **Capitalization of Income**)

A. *Capitalization* or *capitalization of income* may be defined as the determination of the present value of a resource by the determination of the present discounted value of prospective net receipts from the use of the resource. In mathematical terms this may be represented as follows:

$$V = \frac{R_0}{(1+r)^0} + \frac{R_1}{(1+r)^1} + \frac{R_2}{(1+r)^2} \ldots\ldots + \frac{R_n}{(1+r)^n}$$

where the R_s constitute the dated prospective net receipts, r represents some discount rate—such as the market rate of interest—expressed as a decimal fraction, and V is the present value of the resource. In the special case where returns are constant and perpetual it can be shown that the expression above reduces to $V = \frac{R}{r}$. This definition holds only under conditions of certainty. Uncertainty, however, can greatly complicate the determination of present discounted values.

B. There exist in recent literature many echoes of past controversy concerning the proper definition of *income* (q.v.). However, the term *capitalization of income* or *capitalization* conceived as a process which establishes the present value of any resource appears to occasion little or no divergence of opinion or usage. '... the value of the good itself is the discounted value (however determined) of its future services' (I. Fisher, *The Theory of Interest*, New York: The Macmillan Co., 1930, p. 16). 'What is discounted in the valuation of property is future yield (*Ertrag*), which may or may not be consumed. What are discounted are yields, not "consumptions"' (H. C. Simons, *Personal Income Taxation*, Chicago: University of Chicago Press, 1938, p. 90). 'Under absolute certainty, every asset will be capitalized *by the price bids of buyers and sellers* in the market place at the *present discounted value* of all its future net receipts ... the cash dollar rentals ... *minus* all cash outlays ...' (P. A. Samuelson, *Economics*, New York: McGraw-Hill, 3rd edn., 1955, p. 575).

1. The present value of a resource may, for example, consist in value placed upon structures, machines, animals, land, or securities. Considered in this broad way all 'resources' have the prospect of giving rise to net receipts in some time pattern. If we think of the already committed or 'sunk' cost of a resource, these net receipts in prospect give rise to an implicit net rate of return. Alternatively, if we think of the resource as an investment opportunity to be valued, these same prospective net receipts together with an acceptable net rate of return—such as the market rate of interest—will give rise to the capitalized present value.

2. It follows that if the owner of a resource can discern alternative streams of net receipts flowing therefrom he should select that one whose discounted present value—capitalized value—is greatest. This provides a rule governing the rate at which resources should be 'used up'. In the case of the owner of a bond the fixed terms of the security itself usually offer no such alternatives, though the opportunity to sell at present capitalized value and use the proceeds to buy alternative income streams of equal value is always present.

3. As the negative of net receipt is net payment, the capitalized value of a series of obligatory prospective net payments constitutes a negative resource or liability. Thus in the literature of public finance there is frequent reference to *tax capitalization*. In the most general case the value of a resource or liability may constitute the present discounted value of a mixture of prospective net receipts and net payments.

4. It has been noted that uncertainty can greatly complicate the determination of present discounted values. The several dimensions of uncertainty may involve the size of future net receipts or net payments, future market rates of interest, and the future general price levels among others. In practical affairs the valuation is often a very difficult one and the errors made in the process give rise to windfall losses for some and offsetting windfall gains for others. In general the more distant the horizon within which the individual sees all factors clearly, the less the uncertainty.

Lowell D. Ashby

See also: RISK AND UNCERTAINTY

Career

A. The term *career* occurs frequently in sociological and psychological literature and, following popular usage, is virtually a synonym for occupation (q.v.) or profession (q.v.) carrying, usually, the implication of a high degree of job stability, a life's work. A more detailed definition, following usage in the literature would define *career* and its related term *career pattern* as follows: A career or career pattern is a series of adjustments made to the institutions, formal organizations, and informal social relationships involved in the occupation, or sequence of occupations, which make up the work history of a person or group of persons.

B. O. Hall in his work on medical careers ('The Stages of a Medical Career', *American Journal of Sociology*, vol. LIII, 1947–8, p. 327) observes: 'Medicine, like other professions, is practised in a network of institutions, formal organizations, and informal social relationships. The medical career may be conceived as a set of more or less successful adjustments to these institutions and to the formal and informal organization'. He adds that 'a career, so conceived ... [is] by no means unique to the medical profession. Presumably one could investigate similar phenomena in the academic field, in law, in the ministry, in engineering, and so forth'. Using Hall's definition as a point of departure, H. S. Becker ('The Career of the Chicago Public School-teacher', *American Journal of Sociology*, vol. LVII, 1951–2, p. 470) differentiates between 'mobility through a hierarchy of ranked positions ... as the *vertical* aspect of the career', and 'what might, in contrast, be called the *horizontal* aspect ... movement among the positions available at one level of such a hierarchy'.

C. With the increasing realization that the work history of most persons is not limited to a single occupation or profession, the concept of *career pattern* has come into wide use (see, for example, P. E. Davidson & H. D. Anderson, *Occupational Mobility in an American Community*, Stanford University, California: Stanford University Press, 1937; D. C. Miller & W. H. Form, *Industrial Sociology*, New York: Harper & Brothers, 1951, p. 861; D. E. Super, *The Psychology of Careers*, New York: Harper & Brothers, 1957) to denote, according to Miller and Form, a 'sequence of jobs that follow some orderly development', or, according to Super, 'the sequence of occupations in the life of an individual or of a group of individuals. This sequence may be analysed in order to ascertain

the major work periods which constitute a career'.

H. J. Friedsam

See also: OCCUPATION
PROFESSIONS

Cargo Cult

This term was popularly used in the Australian Mandated Territory of New Guinea from about 1935 to describe a number of millenary movements which arose in many parts of the area, and were characterized by the belief that the millennium would be ushered in with the appearance of a miraculous cargo of trade goods. Later it came to be loosely used of many anti-European movements of different kinds throughout the South-West Pacific area.

The term correctly describes a millenary movement in which it is believed that the millennium will be inaugurated by the return of the spirits of the dead bringing with them large quantities of the goods normally possessed by Europeans, for distribution to the adherents of the movement.

L. P. Mair

See also: NATIVISM
REVITALIZATION MOVEMENT

Cartel

A. *Cartel* refers to any arrangements between business firms possessing some characteristics of independence of each other, which arrangements are designed to reduce competition among these firms in a market, without destroying their freedom of action in areas not covered by the cartel agreement. The market to which the arrangements refer may be defined by geographical area, type of product sold, class of customer, or other consideration important to the members of the cartel.

B. The first use of the word *cartel* to refer to the structure of an industry is said by R. Piotrowski (*Cartels and Trusts*, London: Allen & Unwin, 1933, p. 11) to have been by a member of the German Reichstag in 1879. There has always been a distinction between *cartel* and *trust*. *Cartel* refers to an agreement among independent business firms to exercise monopoly power in a market *without* destroying the organizational independence of the participating firms or even their freedom of action in other markets not covered by the agreement. Thus R. Liefman (*Cartels, Concerns, and Trusts*, trans. by D. H.

Case Study Method

Macgregor, London: Methuen, 1932, p. 7) defines cartels as '… voluntary agreements between—or … associations of—independent enterprises of similar type to secure a monopoly of the market'.

C. In general, cartels, as defined above, have been illegal in the United States since 1890. Consequently, American economists have tended to treat the term as implying a European form of monopoly organization of an industry. More recently they have tended to use the word *cartel* to refer to international monopoly agreements by independent producers domiciled in more than one nation. Thus, G. W. Stocking and M. W. Atkins say (*Cartels in Action*, New York: The Twentieth Century Fund, 1946, p. 3), 'In this country [the United States] it [cartel] now commonly refers to international marketing arrangements'. F. Machlup ('The Nature of the International Cartel Problem', in C. D. Edwards (ed.), *A Cartel Policy for the United Nations*, New York: Columbia University Press, 1945, p. 5), on the other hand, uses the term *international cartels* to refer to 'Business arrangements which have the purpose or effect of reducing or regulating competition in international trade …' while retaining the older meaning of cartel to refer to either domestic or international business arrangements of this type.

Royall Brandis

See also: Economic Competition
          Monopoly

Case Method (See Case Study Method)

Case Study Method

A. The *case study method* consists of a mode of analysis rather than a set of research procedures. It is 'an approach which views any social unit as a whole' (W. J. Goode & P. K. Hatt, *Methods in Social Research*, New York: McGraw-Hill, 1952, p. 331). The unit being studied may be an individual, a family, an institution, an association, even a society.

H. W. Odum and K. Jocher have suggested that 'the earliest applications of the case method … were the historians' descriptive accounts of peoples and nations, followed later by detailed studies of smaller groups, factions, and individuals', (*An Introduction to Social Research*, New York: Henry Holt, 1929, p. 229). The first systematic use of case studies in social research is to be found in the work of LePlay, where it was linked with typological and statistical analysis. But it was not until the publication of W. Healy's *The Individual Delinquent* (Boston: Little, Brown, 1915) and especially W. I. Thomas's & F. Znaniecki's *The Polish Peasant in Europe and America* (Chicago: The University of Chicago Press, 1918) that the case study method achieved widespread recognition as a distinctive and independent approach to the study of social phenomena.

The term *case method* (case work) has also been used in social work to refer to the techniques of analysis and treatment of individuals and families who come to social agencies for aid in dealing with their personal problems. Its resemblance to the case study method in research lies in the insistence that treatment be based upon a full record of the individual (or family) history and circumstances.

The case method is also a pedagogical technique used in law, business and public administration, and other fields. Its particular value varies from field to field. In law, where the case method of teaching began, cases constitute significant legal 'acts' from whose analysis the student derives both the principles of law and training in its practice. In such fields as business and public administration, cases are descriptions of problem situations from which the student gains some understanding of the complex facts with which he must eventually deal.

B. The value of the case study method, it has been suggested, lies in its effort to discover all the variables relevant to a given case. It tries to convey an understanding of a class or type of phenomena by the full description and detailed analysis of one or a series of cases belonging to that class. Most enquiries labelled as case studies have been focused upon 'individual behavior in its total social setting' (C. R. Shaw, 'Case Study Method', *Publications of the American Sociological Society*, Chicago: University of Chicago Press, 1927, vol. XXI, p. 149), and the case method has therefore been deemed to be of particular value in exploring the individual's values, attitudes, and definitions of situations. The type of data and research procedures usually linked with the case study method reflect this interest in the relationship between individual behaviour and social context: personal documents, letters, diaries, records of social agencies, and, more recently, intensive interviews.

Case studies, it has been argued, provide an insight into social reality unattainable through statistical analysis; conversely, they have been attacked as unscientific because they do not lead to tested generalizations. The seeming conflict between case studies and statistical research no longer excites attention; there is now general agreement that each has a legitimate place in the research process. The detailed examination of cases can provide the categories to be used and hypotheses to be tested by statistical analysis; the significance of relationships discovered through statistical analysis can be explored by the close study of individual cases. Case studies which are not systematically compared with one another or used in some form of at least implicit statistical form may give a first-hand 'feel' for the realities of social life, but they cannot yield scientific generalizations.

Ely Chinoy

See also: CULTURE CASE STUDY

Caste

A. The term *caste* refers to: (a) the form of social organization found in India based on religious beliefs in the supremacy of the Brahman, rigid ranking according to birth, and restrictions on occupation and marriage; (b) one of the Indian hereditary groups within this social system; (c) any hereditary and exclusive class elsewhere (usually pejoratively with connotations of discrimination or unfair privilege).

Few terms in the whole field of the social sciences have presented as many difficulties in definition or aroused such sharp differences of opinion as the term *caste*. The literature on caste is immense—J. H. Hutton (*Caste in India*, London: Oxford University Press, 1951, Foreword) refers to a list of over five thousand published works on this subject—and the number of attempts at definition is equally formidable. Since its first use by the Portuguese in Goa in the 16th century, the term has been used freely and without dispute in descriptions of Indian society. In general, though any definition that has been advanced has met with disagreement and criticism, there has been little controversy as regards use within India. As numerous authorities have pointed out, it is easy to distinguish one caste from another even if it is impossible to define an individual caste. The sharpest controversies have arisen over the use of this term outside India. It is therefore necessary to consider these two fields separately.

B. The first usage to be considered is that applied to India.

1. One common source of confusion can be disposed of immediately: the term *caste* is not used for the traditional and largely imaginary classification of Hindu society into four orders or *varna*—Brahman or priests, Kshatriya or warriors, Vaisya, farmers and traders, and Sudra, the servile classes. That the contemporary situation is both largely unrelated to and infinitely more complex than this four-fold Brahmanical model has been constantly emphasized by all authorities. 'There are thought to be some 3000 castes in India ... Some are derived from tribal or racial elements, some are occupational, ... some are territorial, some religious, and so forth' (ibid., p. 2). Further, most of these castes (*jat*) are internally divided, some with several levels of segmentation, into smaller endogamous units called sub-castes. A village or local region may contain as a maximum between twenty and thirty different endogamous castes or sub-castes varying in status from the Brahmans at the top of the scale to the untouchable castes at the bottom.

2. The difficulties of definition have arisen from two sources: firstly, the extreme diversity, taking India as a whole, of these social units, and secondly, disagreements among authorities as to the essential characteristics either of the individual caste or of the system as a whole. Aware of the difficulties, many authors have avoided attempts at definition and have concentrated upon listing the features of the system as a whole. G. S. Ghurye, for example (in his *Caste and Race in India*, London: Routledge & Kegan Paul, 1932, ch. I), discerns six fundamental characteristics of the Indian caste system: (a) the segmental division of society into distinct groups with membership determined by birth; (b) hierarchy according to a definite scheme of social precedence with the Brahman as the head of the hierarchy; (c) restrictions on inter-dining and social intercourse arising out of notions of ritual pollution; (d) varying civil and religious disabilities and privileges of the different segments; (e) restrictions on occupation; (f) endogamy.

While few authorities would disagree fundamentally with Ghurye's list, or with earlier lists of this type, there has been much variance of opinion as to the relative importance of the characteristics discerned.

(i) Ghurye himself, arguing the primacy of notions of racial and ritual purity, sees endogamy as the principal feature of the system, quoting E. Westermarck (*History of Human Marriage*, London: Macmillan, 5th edn., 1925, vol. II, p. 59): 'endogamy is the essence of the

75

Caste

caste system'. This view has been heavily supported by many eminent Indian authorities, notably Hutton, Hocart, S. C. Roy, N. K. Dutt, and more recently by M. N. Srinivas (*Religion and Society among the Coorgs of South India*, London: Oxford University Press, 1952, p. 26) and by H. N. C. Stevenson: 'These beliefs [concerning purity and pollution] ... form the major cause of caste fission' ('Status Evaluation in the Hindu Caste System', *Journal of the Royal Anthropological Institute*, vol. 84, 1954, p. 46).

(ii) A contrary emphasis is expressed by H. A. Rose (*A Glossary of the Tribes and Castes of the Punjab*, Lahore: Government Printing Press, 1911, vol. I, p. iii): 'The more one studies castes in the works of Nesfield, Ibbetson, Risley, and other writers, the more one sees, I think, that caste like law may be defined as a function of economics'. Here the emphasis is on occupational differentiation as the primary basis of caste formation, and on the relation between caste status and political and economic power. These writers note that change in the political and economic status of a caste is accompanied by a change in its ritual status, and that the latter change is invariably preceded by the former. '... social standing, which is all that caste means, depends very largely on political importance, whether present or belonging to the recent past. ... The rise in the social scale which accompanies increased political importance will presently be followed by a rise in caste'. Sir Denzil Ibbetson, *Panjab Castes*, Lahore: Government Printing Press, 1916, p. 6). Ibbetson goes on to describe how, given increased political and economic importance, a caste may raise its 'social standing' through observance of what he calls 'the artificial standards' (i.e. the rules of ritual avoidance) of Brahmanical Hinduism. Caste, says Ibbetson, 'has no necessary connection with the Hindu religion'.

(iii) A third emphasis discernible particularly in general works of sociology, is on the hierarchical aspect of the system. Caste is here treated as an extreme form of social stratification, characterized by fixed birth status, social discrimination, and a complete absence of vertical mobility for individuals. Notions of ritual purity and religious sanctions are seen not as fundamental but rather as rationalizations by the dominant castes to justify and maintain their superiority. Here caste is viewed as the extreme case of absolutely rigid social class. For example, 'It seems best ... not to limit the word "caste" to the Hindu groups, but to recognize a continuum of graded classes, with castes merely representing the extreme of fixity' (R. H. Lowie, *Social Organization*, London: Routledge & Kegan Paul, 1950, p. 274).

C. Varying emphases such as those above have largely governed attitudes towards the use of the term outside India.

1. Those who hold that notions of ritual purity are the essential feature of the Indian phenomena have noted 'analogous institutions' elsewhere (as in divisions of populations into endogamous estates in Ancient Rome or Greece, in Medieval Europe, and so forth) but, pointing out the absence of religious sanctions and beliefs about pollution, have denied the use of the term *caste* for these institutions (cf. J. H. Hutton, *Caste in India*, ch. IX, for a typical discussion).

2. Those who emphasize hierarchical grading and political and economic factors, tend to see this restriction of the term to India as an unprofitably extreme position. Of recent years there has been a noticeable tendency towards a widespread use of the term with the connotation of rigid hierarchy combined with endogamous segregation. See, for example, M. Tumin's account of a Guatemalan village divided into two ranked segments—Ladinos and Indians (*Caste in a Peasant Society*, Princeton: Princeton University Press, 1952) or Lowie's (ibid., p. 274 ff.) use of the term for American Negroes, Jews in Hitler's Germany, and for endogamous and ranked divisions among certain East African tribes.

3. The most heated debates on the use of *caste* have arisen over the application of this term in studies of race relations, particularly as regards Negro-White relations in the United States. Though in this context the term seems to have been in use with reference to Negroes for at least a hundred years, it has recently been systematically employed, particularly by W. L. Warner and his associates at the University of Chicago (cf. G. Myrdal, *An American Dilemma*, New York: Harper, 1944, vol. II, p. 1377, for references), in sociological studies of the relations between Negroes and Whites. Here the term appears to be used for two reasons; firstly, because the authors believe that the essential features of caste structure generally as they discern them (primarily, segmental division, rigid endogamy, hierarchy, absence of individual mobility, and social discrimination) occur together in this context, and secondly, to avoid the use of the term *race*. Myrdal (ibid., vol. I, ch. 31) discusses at length the usefulness of the term *caste* in such studies. He defends the use of the term, pointing out that the 'former term "race" is, as we have shown [in an earlier chapter], inappropriate in a scientific enquiry, since it has biological and genetic connotations which are incorrect in this context and which are particularly dangerous as they run parallel to widely spread false racial beliefs' (ibid., vol. I, p. 667). He stresses that these racial beliefs of the Whites with 'a kernel of magical logic, signified by the notion of "blood" ' are rationalizations to uphold the interests of the superior White caste. Those who support this use point to the rigid 'caste line' separating the Negroes from the Whites, and to the existence of class stratification on either side of this line which, though inter-caste relations may change, 'remains rigid and unblurred'. 'The dividing line between two castes is by definition clear-cut, consciously felt by every member of each caste, and easily observable' (ibid., vol. I, p. 675).

It should however be pointed out that many social scientists oppose this use of the term *caste* on the grounds that it embodies assumptions which are false, static, mystical, and/or irrelevant to the problems.

4. Finally it should be noted that some authors seek to avoid the difficulties here by explicit statements as regards the use of the term. For example, 'The term "caste" is used here as a mere verbal convenience to describe the two groups studied, whose status in relation to each other is fixed almost immutably by biological ancestry. We do not equate the caste system of India with the institutionalized relations between American Negroes and Whites' (F. R. Westie & M. L. Westie, 'The Social Distance Pyramid: Relationships between Caste and Class', *American Journal of Sociology*, vol. LXIII, 1957–8, p. 192, fn. no. 5). This quotation well demonstrates both the wide divergences in the use of the term, and the current confused and unsatisfactory position from the point of view of general sociological theory.

K. C. Rosser

See also: SOCIAL CLASS
STRATIFICATION

Category

A. A *category* denotes either the *name* given to any class of things, actions, or relationships which recur with sufficient (relative) uniformity and frequency as to render the class a useful subject of a predication; or the *class* itself. When rigorously defined and placed in a system of classes, it becomes a scientific category.

B. *Category* is a term in logic and is used in the social sciences in much the same way as in all other forms of rigorous communication. Most natural scientists use *category* simply as a classificatory term which implies nothing pertaining to epistemology or ontology. The categories of physical and biological science are more rigorous and definitive than those of the social sciences, because they are based on more, and more valid, empirical research, and because the physical and biological taxonomies are more strictly systematized. The social sciences still engage in more description than generalization, and social scientists still tend to make their own individual definitions and classifications.

All technical terms and concepts in the social sciences are categories in the sense that they denote or name, a class of observable things, actions, or relations. Nothing can be observed as a datum for science that cannot be named or categorized; hence all observations require symbols and concepts, which to some extent determine what is observed. Many social science categories, usually more qualitative than quantitative, have received wide acceptance. Of these some have proved susceptible to quantification and to more strict delimitation in time and space. In this social science is repeating the history of the physical and biological sciences. While social science categories based on statistical research are perhaps most useful for strictly scientific purposes, qualitative categories, rigorously defined, are also useful.

Read Bain

See also: FRAME OF REFERENCE
POSTULATE

Catharsis

A. *Catharsis* may be defined as the release, liberation, or reduction of emotional tension through bringing into consciousness by abreaction—talking out or acting out, or by some other means—repressed, traumatic, symptom-producing, affect-loaded experiences. This definition commits one neither to the position that therapeutic catharsis occurs at all, or that it is produced by any one or several therapeutic techniques, nor to a particular theory as to the rationale of its occurrence.

B. 1. The term (the Greek word meaning cleansing or purification) was used by Aristotle in his survey of tragic drama. Such drama produced the experience of fear and pity, effected a purification or cleansing of the emotions which he called 'catharsis'. Freud and Breuer during

Cathexis

their early studies of hysteria proposed that, through hypnosis, abreaction (or a re-experiencing of a repressed or unconscious, symptom-producing emotion) occurred and with it came a cathartic effect, that is, a return to consciousness of the emotion, with a release of tension, or a reduction of its intensity and symptom-forming capacity. They referred to this procedure as 'cathartic therapy'. When Freud substituted free association for hypnosis as a means for inducing abreaction, he continued to refer to 'cathartic therapy'.

2. The term was adopted by S. Freud & J. Breuer (*Studies on Hysteria*, trans. by J. Strachey, *The Standard Edition of the Complete Psychological Works of S. Freud*, London: Hogarth Press, 1955, vol. 2, published originally as *Studien über Hysterie*, Leipzig & Vienna: Deuticke, 1895) for use somewhat in the Aristotelian sense to denote changes occurring as a result of a psychotherapeutic procedure.

3. In contemporary literature the basic meaning of the term is essentially unchanged, though catharsis may occasionally be restricted to particular therapeutic techniques. J. B. Rotter (*Social Learning and Clinical Psychology*, New York: Prentice-Hall, 1954, p. 372 ff.) has distinguished between several usages of the term which restrict catharsis to ventilation, or verbalization, of previous traumatic experience or physical exercise and callisthenics, or release of hostility against a symbolic object. The common denominator of all adaptations of the concept to particular therapeutic techniques or rationales is reduction of tension or release of unpleasant affect through re-experiencing an originally tension-producing or traumatic episode.

4. A careful survey reveals differences of opinion, sometimes based on attempted experimental tests, as to whether or not there is a true cathartic effect with any technique; or, assuming that there is catharsis, there are debates as to the proper technique for producing it or as to the rationale of the technique chosen. But throughout this literature the basic meaning of the term is unchanged.

Dorothy W. Seago

See also: AFFECT

Cathexis

A. *Cathexis* may be defined as the involvement or investment of energy or affect in a particular stimulus situation—object, person, action, event. The term may be used to denote degree of affect or interest or attention, or to indicate the goal towards which a particular action is oriented. It has no consistent or necessary association with a particular theoretical position as to the nature, source, or distribution of energy.

B. The term *cathexis* (*Besetzung*) was first used by Freud in 1893 to mean 'charge of psychic energy'. He used it as a noun (ego cathexis), as a verb (to cathect an object), and as an adjective (cathectic fidelity). It was used frequently, casually, without careful definition, as a general utility word with some reference to energy manifestations: as a charge of energy, physiological or psychic; as impulse; as the relative potency of instincts or drives; or as a predisposition to react towards a particular situation or a preference for a particular object, person, or action. It was used to refer to the source of energy (libidinal cathexis); to indicate direction of the flow or investment of energy (narcissistic or ego cathexis vs. anaclitic or object cathexis), or to indicate degree of affect or interest in or attention to an object, person, or action (low cathexis, no cathexis, maximum cathexis).

C. In recent sociological and psychological studies the term *cathexis* has been given a somewhat more specific meaning. For example, Parsons (T. Parsons & E. A. Shils, *Toward a General Theory of Action*, Cambridge, Mass.: Harvard University Press, 1951, p. 10) defines it as 'a state of the organism—a state of euphoria or dysphoria—*in relationship to some object. ...* It is *object-oriented affect. ...* It involves attaching affective significance to an object'. In this sense it is used in studies on 'body cathexis', 'parent cathexis', 'self-image cathexis', and so on. In no case, apparently, does the term imply a particular theoretical framework nor does its use commit the writer to a particular theoretical position.

Dorothy W. Seago

See also: AFFECT

Caucus

A. A *caucus* is a meeting of members of a party or faction for the purpose of selecting party leaders, nominating candidates for public office, or for drafting policy. It is usually a meeting of a small group within the larger party group, and, with the exception of local nominating caucuses, the small group is usually composed of a few select leaders meeting for the purpose of considering organization and policy matters in terms of party regularity. For this and other reasons the term is often used in a pejorative sense.

Caucus is also sometimes used as a verb to denote the concerting of plans by any group of leaders or aspirants for leadership.

B. The term was coined in American politics, and first appeared in Boston during the latter part of the colonial period. In early American usage it had an unfavourable connotation. John Adams's diary in 1763 speaks of a 'Caucus Club' meeting at intervals 'in the garret of Tom Dawes. ... There they smoke tobacco till you cannot see from one end of the garret to the other. There they drink flip I suppose and they choose a moderator who puts questions to the vote regularly; and select men, assessors, collectors, wardens, firewards, and representatives are regularly chosen before they are chosen in the town ...' (J. Adams, *The Works of J. Adams*, Boston: C. Little & J. Brown, 1850, vol. II, p. 144). Decisions presumably were made by a cabal in a 'smoke-filled room' away from democratic controls.

C. The term came to be used in the United States to denote various sorts of political meetings, sometimes without the implication of concealment and deviousness.

1. Among the most important kinds of caucus was that for purposes of nominating candidates (nominating caucus). Nominating caucuses were of two types.

(a) One was a precinct caucus of all enrolled party members called for the purpose of nominating candidates; in some towns the caucus was and is provided for by law. In effect this type of caucus resembles a direct primary (q.v.). Some caucuses choose delegates to conventions which in turn nominate candidates for certain offices.

(b) The other type of nominating caucus was composed of party members in legislatures. For a time after 1793, nominations for governor were made by the party members in the state legislatures; this became known as the 'legislative caucus'. Some legislative districts had no party membership in the state legislature, so local party leaders went to the state capitol to sit in with the legislative caucus, an arrangement referred to as a 'mixed caucus'. On the national level from 1800 to 1824, a 'congressional caucus' performed a similar function in designating the party candidates for president and vice-president. All these caucuses have long since been superseded by nominating conventions and direct primaries.

2. The nominating caucus may be distinguished from a caucus composed of a party's members in a legislature for the purpose of deciding party positions such as floor leader and whip, committee assignments, patronage and related matters, and the party's position on public issues. These caucuses are usually referred to as the Senate Republican caucus, the House Democratic caucus, etc. In the U.S. Congress, the Republicans have substituted the word *conference* for caucus. In times past, the caucus attempted to bind members to a party line vote. Party leaders have found it difficult to bind members to a caucus decision in recent years and, indeed, have voiced the view that members cannot be bound by a caucus in policy matters.

D. In England the term has been more rarely used. It was used around 1867 to refer to a system of party organization by committees (the Birmingham caucus) which helped the Liberals win three seats at Birmingham in the General Election of 1868; and it has been used in its general sense. The term, though used in other countries too, has remained largely American.

Hugh A. Bone

See also: CONVENTION
NOMINATION
PARTY

Causation (See Social Causation)

Censorship

A. *Censorship* denotes the restriction by authority (political, religious, or other) of any public expression regarded as dangerous to that authority and to the political or moral order that it sustains. It may also denote a self-imposed restriction in conformity with a widespread public attitude or group pressure.

B. 1. The practice of censorship dates back to the earliest political and theocratic societies. It was familiar to Ancient Greece and Rome, and to the Middle Ages, but it became more strict after the invention of printing. Thus in the 16th century, the first Index of prohibited books was made by the Catholic Church. The Protestants also instituted censorship in the era of the Reformation.

2. Censorship in our time has been classified into two main categories: the preventative and the punitive, depending on whether it is exercised before or after the issuance of the material in question. In the United States, much has been written concerning 'previous restraint' (preventative censorship) as antagonistic to the Constitutional guarantees of free speech and press. The first case, however, in which the Supreme Court had to pass on the question was *Near v. Minnesota* (283 U.S. 697, 1931). In this case the Court invalidated the so-called Minnesota Gag Law as 'an improper deprivation of liberty of the press, by a five to four decision' (Z. Chafee, Jr., *Free Speech in the United States*, Cambridge, Mass.: Harvard University Press, 1948, p. 377). According to Blackstone (*Commentaries on the Laws of England*, London: Murray, 1862, vol. IV, p. 152): 'To subject the Press to the restrictive power of a licenser, as was formerly done, both before and since the revolution, is to subject all freedom of sentiment to the prejudices of one man, and make him the arbitrary and infallible judge of all controverted points in learning, religion, and government.'

3. Other important distinctions may be made between official and unofficial censorship, and between censorship which is imposed directly by authority and that which results from informal agreements or decisions 'not to publish'. The practice of censorship at these levels may be encountered, e.g. in the dilemmas of publishers concerning matters affecting national security (in peace or war) or matters which may be discerned on various criteria to be 'obscene'. Clearly, national practices differ very widely—depending upon the constitutional guarantees of free press and other forms of publication, the self-imposed limitations on publication of 'secret' or 'classified' material, and the shifting interpretations of what may be considered an obscene publication, etc., etc.

C. Censorship is today taken to be an institution found mainly in authoritarian and totalitarian societies (see, for example, R. Kindersley, *The First Russian Revisionists*, Oxford: Clarendon Press, 1962, pp. 73 et seq., for a description of censorship in Tsarist Russia. For the contemporary situation in a wide variety of politically authoritarian contexts see International Press Institute, *The Press in Authoritarian Countries*, Zurich: International Press Institute, 1959). But both in its self-imposed form and in its official form, it is far from unknown in countries where the governing process is democratic in nature.

1. Even though the 1st Amendment to the Constitution of the United States says that 'Congress shall make no law ... abridging the freedom of speech, or of the press ...' both state and federal courts have held that it could not have been the intention of the constitutional guarantees to sanction defamatory utterances and publications or to give private individuals a free hand in the dissemination of obscene or fraudulent matter by speech or print (see C. C. Maxey, *The American Problem of Government*, New York: Crofts, 1939). Censorship has been tolerated with respect to the mails, the importation of foreign books, the stage, the motion picture, and radio and television. But Mr. Justice Holmes, in a dissenting opinion in *Abrams v. the United States* (250 U.S. 616, 1919) contended that 'the ultimate good desired is better reached by free trade in ideas ...'

The present situation in the United States is described as follows by F. Castberg (*Freedom of Speech in the West*, Oslo: Oslo University Press, 1960, p. 146): 'An official system of control with compulsory licensing is now deemed by the Supreme Court to be censorship contrary to the Constitution'.

2. In France one also finds patterns of press control. Castberg (ibid., p. 47) cites the advance censorship imposed by the Pflimlin ministry in May 1958 and comments that 'The limits of press freedom are now expressed through the medium of advance censorship: but in principle they are primarily established by the criminal provisions of the legislation, as applied to printed matter'. The legislation meant is the provision of Article 30 of the 1959 Penal Code which empowers the prefects of departments and the Paris Prefect of Police 'to undertake all acts necessary with a view to preventing crimes and violations of the internal or external security of the State'.

Oscar Svarlien

See also: CIVIL LIBERTIES

Census

A. The term denotes the collection (through governmental initiative) of information as to the numbers of a country's population, i.e. a total count of the number of its inhabitants on a given day of the year (as in Great Britain) or over a period of weeks (as in the U.S.A.). The count is generally taken at stated intervals (in the U.S.A. and in Great Britain at decennial intervals). It further denotes the collection, at the same time and/or on the same schedule as the population-count, of other data concerning the population counted. The range of this data varies according to differing national practice and changing conceptions of the information required for social policy. The word is also used to describe non-governmental inquiries where simple classificatory information is sought.

B. 1. An official census customarily collects information as to the numbers at each sex and age, together with facts about whether these persons are single, married, widowed or divorced. It may also include data on the fertility experience of the persons counted; their educational experience; their occupations; the housing which they occupy; their nationality or their spoken language. This is not, of course, an exhaustive list—and practice differs according to the requirements of public administration and social policy.

2. In Great Britain the schedule is filled in by the individual householders. In the U.S. Census of 1960 householders were asked themselves to complete an Advanced Census Report and hand this to the enumerator. On his visit the enumerator ascertained certain other data by observation.

3. From its historical usage with regard to population counting the term has often been implicitly reserved for *total or complete* analysis of a given population—as contrasted with a partial analysis (or survey) conducted through sampling procedures. For this latter type of enquiry greater skill may be required on the part of the interviewers (compared to census enumerators): the interviews may be longer and more intensive; and the results may be presented in a more elaborate fashion than is often the case with census reports. Nevertheless no hard and fast line may be drawn between the two types of enquiry. Furthermore, the census enumeration may now itself include recourse to sampling. For example in the United States Census 'most of the information obtained in the 1960 Censuses was obtained on a sample basis. Every fourth housing unit visited was selected for the sample' (U.S. Bureau of the Census, *U.S. Censuses of Population and Housing*, 1960: *Principal Data-Collecting Forms and Procedures*, Washington, D.C.: U.S. Government Printing Office, 1961, p. 3). Enumerators delivered a second questionnaire with respect to the sample population and housing at every fourth household. 'Some of the data elicited in this way were intended to be tabulated for a 5 per cent sample and others for only a 20 per cent sample of the housing units' (ibid., p. 4).

In the British Census of 1961 part of the Census schedule was administered to a 10 per cent sample only. In 1946 the term *Family Census* was used to describe the *sample* study

of fertility conducted by the British Royal Commission on Population.

C. The term has been applied not only to censuses of population and housing but also to official surveys of agriculture (as in the U.S.) and of industrial production and distribution (e.g. as provided for in Great Britain by the Census of Production Act 1906 and the Statistics of Trade Act 1947).

J. Mogey

See also: DEMOGRAPHY
 POPULATION

Centralization (Also **Decentralization**)

A. *Centralization* denotes a high concentration of power (measured by criteria of weight, scope, and domain) by a few within an organized social group. Sub-categories of centralization would be of a geographical, functional, or other kind. *Decentralization* is a low concentration of power. For special purposes, the term might be restricted by specifying the 'degree of concentration' and by defining the respective 'organized social group', denoting either geographical scope or power distribution among hierarchically superior or inferior loci.

Centralization is frequently used pejoratively, while *decentralization* usually carries a positive connotation. Other abstract terms are now used in the same area of meaning (e.g. control, integration, autonomy, hierarchy, discipline, co-ordination, etc.) which make it perfectly possible to treat at length of *centralization* and *decentralization* without even mentioning the terms.

B. *Centralization* came to be used frequently in the early 19th century, particularly in France, to denote a process of increasing governmental powers, especially over local political areas. The term was given wide currency by de Tocqueville who wrote: 'Centralization is a word in general and daily use, without any precise meaning being attached to it. Nevertheless, there exist two distinct kinds of centralization, which it is necessary to discriminate with accuracy. Certain interests are common to all parts of a nation, such as the enactment of its general laws. ... Other interests are peculiar to certain parts of the nation, such, for instance, as the business of the several townships. ... When the power that directs the former or general interests is concentrated in one place or the same persons, it constitutes a centralized government. To concentrate in like manner in one place the direction

Ceremony

of the latter or local interests, constitutes what may be termed a centralized administration. ... It is not the *administrative* but the *political* effects of decentralization that I most admire in America' (A. de Tocqueville, *Democracy in America* (1st edn., 1835) trans. by H. Reeve, New York: Knopf, 1945, pp. 86, 94).

C. Various forms of *centralization* (and *decentralization*) may be distinguished:

1. H. Kelsen (*General Theory of Law and State*, Cambridge, Mass.: Harvard University Press, 1945, p. 304) declares, 'The conception of a centralized legal order implies that all its norms are valid throughout the whole territory over which it extends'.

2. A. Lepawsky (*Administration*, New York: Knopf, 1949, p. 377) speaks of the 'possibility of combining economic and social decentralization with a high degree of political centralization'.

3. In a negative evaluation of trends of centralization, D. E. Lilienthal (*T.V.A.—Democracy on the March*, Harmondsworth: Penguin Books, 1944, p. 131) spoke of 'over centralization [as] the tendency all over the world, in business as well as government'. Similarly J. R. Pennock (*Liberal Democracy*, New York: Rinehart, 1950, p. 178) points to a 'steady and rapid movement towards centralization of government' both in England and the U.S.

4. H. Lasswell and A. Kaplan (*Power and Society*, New Haven: Yale University Press, 1950, p. 225) treat *centralization* and *decentralization* in terms of 'the territorial and/or functional distribution of power'. For them 'a *unitary* state is one in which the rule is centralized; a *federal* state, decentralized territorially; *syndicalist*, decentralized functionally. ... The scope, weight, and domain of power are all three involved in centralization-decentralization'.

Alfred de Grazia

See also: POWER

Centralized Tribe (See **Tribe**)

Ceremony

A. *Ceremony* may be defined as the expression of shared feelings and attitudes through more or less formally ordered actions of an essentially symbolic nature performed on appropriate occasions. The term may, but need not, contain orientations toward objects, empirical or non-empirical, capable of inspiring attitudes of loyalty, respect, or reverence. In either event it implies careful attention to the form of behaviour

and the selection of forms which are appropriate for expressing sentiments attached to a particular social situation. Sentiment is inseparable from the act.

1. According to Radcliffe-Brown this definition is very old: Confucian philosophers of the 2nd and 3rd centuries B.C. spoke of 'ceremony' as the orderly expression of feelings appropriate to a social situation (*Taboo*, Cambridge: Cambridge University Press, 1939, p. 33).

2. A recent example of the use of this definition is the description by W. L. Warner of the ceremonies of Memorial Day in the United States as orderly actions expressing man's feelings of 'triumph over death' as well as 'the sentiments of equality and unity of all the living among themselves, of all the living with all the dead, and of all the living and the dead, as a group, with the gods' (*Democracy in Jonesville*, New York: Harper & Brothers, 1949, pp. 290–2).

B. In addition to the feelings expressed *ceremony* may be constituted by one or more of the following elements, through which the feelings appropriate to the situation are given symbolic expression.

1. In ceremonial context, human bodies and things are manipulated: people bow or genuflect, tip the hat, present arms, slaughter cattle, pour libations, extinguish a fire, wave a lamp, or even perform sexual intercourse. It is essential to know the meaning which such acts possess in the ceremonial situation in order to grasp the sentiments which they express.

2. People interact in ceremonies, and frequently ceremony involves a stepping up of interaction. Such intensification may be achieved with alcohol, through dancing, or in other deliberate ways.

3. Avoidance is a widespread element in *ceremony*, i.e. people avoid performing certain acts, contact with certain objects, or interaction with certain other people. Avoidance enhances the significance of the occasion and thereby sets it apart as special or sacred.

4. *Ceremony* often involves the use of objects such as flags, crosses, wine, kava, turkey, and representations of various sorts. These objects possess symbolic meaning.

5. Non-empirical objects or supernatural entities constitute targets of many ceremonies. Whether these are regarded as 'master symbols' or as objects in the eyes of the actor whose reality status is left open, they tend to canalize emotion in the ceremonial context. However, many ceremonies may be purely secular in nature.

C. Ceremonies can be said to perform certain general functions for the social group.

1. They help to express, perpetuate, and transmit those elements of the value and sentiment system.

2. They help to preserve such values and sentiments from doubt and opposition.

3. They help to intensify the solidarity of persons who participate in the ceremony.

D. Particular functions may be performed by certain classes of ceremonies.

1. Rites of passage help the individual to effect a status change.

2. Rites of deference acknowledge super-ordination and subordination, as well as friendship, and so help to maintain a given social structure.

3. Rites of intensification occur periodically at times of crisis that 'involve relatively great changes of interaction rates'. They function to increase the solidarity of the group and to reduce the tension present so that they serve to counter-act the crisis (E. D. Chapple & C. S. Coon, *Principles of Anthropology*, New York: Henry Holt, 1942, p. 398). In such ceremonies the activities engaged in may be designed instrumentally by the actors to effect some end: for example, to produce more fish, promote rain or cure a sick person.

E. *Ceremony* is frequently used synonymously with ritual (q.v.), but there are uses of the terms which at least in nuance are not identical.

1. Ritual generally seems to refer primarily to the normative or psychologically compulsive necessity for minute adherence to formulated rules of expressive or magical behaviour, while ceremony stresses at least equally the linkage of value and sentiment with the expressive act. Thus R. L. Beals and H. Hoijer define ritual as 'a prescribed way of performing religious acts...' while they define ceremony as involving '... a number of interconnected and related rituals, performed at a given time' (*An Introduction to Anthropology*, New York: The Macmillan Co., 1953, pp. 496–7).

2. Because of this slight difference in emphasis it appears possible for ritual to be used as designating types of action in which the term ceremony or its adjectival form, ceremonious, would hardly be used. Thus R. K. Merton describes the response to an inadequate relationship between institutionalized means and culturally valued goals which involves the fact that '... though one draws in one's horizons, one continues to abide almost compulsively by institutional norms' as ritualistic ('Social Structure and Anomie', *Social Theory and Social Structure*, Glencoe, Ill.: The Free Press, 1957, p. 150). Similarly F. Alexander in discussing obsessive ideas and actions describes compulsive, repetitive performance as 'ritualistic' (*Our Age of Unreason*, New York: Lippincott, 1951, pp. 132–3). It is difficult to imagine using the terms ceremony, ceremonious, or ceremonial to describe either of these modes of behaviour.

John J. Honigmann

See also: RITUAL

Character (See **Character Structure**)

Character Structure

A. *Character structure* is an explanatory construct inferred from habitual or significant actions of an individual, which denotes an interrelated set of attitudes, values, learned motives, drives, ego defences, and learned forms of impulse expression. This structure develops through time as an outcome of the experience of the individual. The character structure is generally conceived of as a relatively enduring and organized pattern of behaviour; hence it is predictable and research can be done on it. Because of its social consequences and because induced change in character is possible, character structure may be evaluated with reference to standards, moral or otherwise.

The more important aspects of the concept *character structure* are (a) that it describes a relatively permanent configuration; (b) that it accounts for the habitual or characteristic aspects of an individual's behaviour; (c) that the latter include the characteristic modes of defence; (d) that characteristic modes of behaviour are integrated with one another and not isolated.

B. 1. The term *character structure* is used in three related fields of social science: psychoanalysis (where it appears to have originated), clinical and 'dynamic' psychology, and cultural anthropology. In psychoanalytic writings it is often used interchangeably and synonymously with *character* (however, *character* is sometimes used with different emphases in 'non-dynamic' psychology, sociology, and education, and in theories of biological constitution, as well as in common speech). E. Fromm ('Psychoanalytic Characterology and its Application to the Understanding of Culture' in S. S. Sargent & M. W. Smith (eds.), *Culture and Personality*,

Charisma

New York: Wenner-Gren Foundation, 1949, p. 1) describes its origin in psychoanalysis: 'Psychoanalytic characterology dates back to Freud's paper on "Character and Anal Eroticism", published in 1908. This paper marks the shift of attention from the neurotic *symptom* to the neurotic *character*. Freud and his fellow workers became increasingly aware of the fact that any symptom was embedded in a person's character, hence that in order to understand and cure a symptom one has to understand the total character structure. They proceeded from the analysis of the symptom to the analysis of the character'.

2. *Character structure* is, first of all, an *organization* of behaviour tendencies, with a considerable degree of permanence. It is described by O. Fenichel (*The Psychoanalytic Theory of Neurosis*, New York: W. W. Norton, 1945, p. 467) as 'the ego's habitual modes of adjustment to the external world, the id, and the superego, and the characteristic types of combining these modes with one another'. In clinical psychology the term *ego structure* is more commonly used. *Ego structure*, however, tends to emphasize the hierarchy of values and the cognitive functions of the individual, while *character structure* places more emphasis on defences, reaction formations, and sublimations, i.e. on the more devious and less direct means by which the individual deals with the conflicts between impulses and external forces.

3. The term is sometimes given a slightly different usage in anthropology, to stress the fact that people of similar cultural experience have similar character structures. E. Beaglehole ('Character Structure', *Psychiatry*, vol. 7, 1944, p. 148) says that 'character structure may be thought of as an organization of the needs and emotions within each person that fits him to respond adaptively to the major social values of the group'. E. H. Erikson ('Childhood and Tradition in Two American Indian Tribes' in C. Kluckhohn & H. A. Murray (eds.), *Personality in Nature, Society, and Culture*, New York: Knopf, 1949, p. 194) speaks of 'the collective or official character structure of the Yurok'.

4. The term *character* is sometimes used by non-psychoanalytic writers in a sense very similar to *character structure*, but not generally containing all of the implications of the latter. For example, G. H. Mead (*Mind, Self and Society*, Chicago: University of Chicago Press, 1934, pp. 162–3) emphasizes the organized and structural nature, the developmental process, and the culturally common aspect, as well as the moral and ethical relevance of character: 'The structure ... on which the self is built is this response which is common to all. ... Such responses are abstract attitudes, but they constitute just what we term a man's character. ... (The "generalized other") guides conduct controlled by principles, and a person who has such an organized group of responses is a man who we say has character, in the moral sense'.

Robert J. Havighurst

See also: BASIC PERSONALITY STRUCTURE
PERSONALITY SYSTEM
SELF

Charisma

A. In theological usage *charisma* means an endowment of divine grace. In its sociological usage the term (and the related adjective *charismatic*) has come by a process of transference to refer to the qualities of those who claim or are believed to possess powers of leadership derived from some unusual sanction—divine, magical, diabolic—or merely exceptional individuality.

B. The term came into social science usage through the writings of Weber, who borrowed it from R. Sohm. For Weber a charismatic figure is an individual who (a) restores emotion, awe, and magic to the conduct of affairs and (b) would appear to himself and/or others to be endowed with an authority analagous to that of the original, i.e. theological, meaning of the word (*From Max Weber*, trans. and ed. by H. H. Gerth & C. W. Mills, London: Kegan Paul, Trench, Trubner, 1947, pp. 245–52). Search for such a figure, Weber thought, would be a central part of a search for a new social order in societies affected by extreme rationalization and the high development of science.

It is now frequently argued that *all* leadership involves not merely authority, somehow or other legitimated, but also some ascription of charismatic quality. This is probably to extend the word too widely for the concept to be genuinely useful. It is true to say, however, that most, if not all, cases of legal or traditional dominance and authority have developed out of charismatic leadership through a process of routinization made necessary by the exigencies of everyday life.

D. G. MacRae

See also: AUTHORITY
LEADERSHIP

Chauvinism

A. The term *chauvinism* was first used in France to denote an extreme type of nationalism. Nicolas Chauvin was a brave French soldier serving in the armies of the Revolution and of Napoleon I. His fanatical and naïve patriotic utterances were noted by his comrades with surprise. His figure was popularized by Scribe, whose play *Le Soldat laboureur* presented Chauvin on the French stage. French journalists and politicians then used the term *chauvinism* to denounce the extreme nationalism of the Bonapartists and their successors.

B. 1. Use of the term in political literature denotes patterns of ideas associated with extreme forms of nationalism and national pride. Thus, according to B. C. Shafer, a 'Chauvinist' (or a Jingo) is a zealotic and fanatical nationalist obsessed by 'fervent, blind patriotism' who assumes 'uninformed, narrow views' on the peoples of the world. He is also 'anti-everything not of his nation', that is, anti-foreigner, distrusting and disliking men of other races´ (*Nationalism, Myth and Reality*, London: Gollancz, 1955, p. 207).

L. von Wiese regards 'Chauvinism and similar types of extreme nationalism' as a form of 'radicalization; salvation from real or imagined disadvantages is sought through assaults upon other peoples or states'. According to von Wiese, radicalization is 'fanatical belief in some one-sided principle which dominates behavior in total disregard of qualifying facts and tendencies' (L. von Wiese, adapted and amplified by H. Becker, *Systematic Sociology*, New York: John Wiley, 1932, pp. 389, 391).

2. Chauvinism was used pejoratively by French liberal, democratic, and socialist politicians at the turn of the century, in order to denounce ideas and attitudes of an *extremist minority*. In the 20th century the term is still used pejoratively, but the attitudes criticized are no longer minority attitudes. These attitudes have taken various forms: e.g. Fascism in Italy, National Socialism or Hitlerism in Germany; Zdhanovism or Stalinism in the Soviet Union, Pan-Arabism or Nasserism in the Middle East. But whenever they become widespread, whether in Right-wing or Left-wing movements, in 'imperialist' or 'ex-colonialist' areas of the world they have reflected and accentuated the movement away from individualism and internationalism and towards a deeper, often extreme

and anti-democratic, emphasis of nationalist programmes and ideas.

J. S. Erös

See also: NATIONALISM

Checks and Balances

A. In modern usage the phrase *checks and balances* denotes a particular expedient for maintaining in practice the principle of the separation of powers (q.v.) among the organs of government provided for in a constitution. It is a system which so contrives 'the interior structure of the government as that its several constituent parts may, by their mutual relations, be the means of keeping each other in their proper places' (A. Hamilton, J. Jay, J. Madison, *The Federalist*, No. 51, 1788.

'While recognizing the principle of separation of powers among the legislative, executive, and judicial powers, this system seeks to protect each of them against the others, and the people against all, by requiring the approval of one department of certain acts of another' (E. C. Smith & A. J. Zurcher, *New Dictionary of American Politics*, New York: Barnes & Noble, 1949, p. 59).

B. 1. Although it is mainly used with regard to expedients designed to limit the exercise of power within political institutions, it also has a wider reference, e.g. to problems arising within the formal structure of many types of social groups.

2. The idea which the term implies has long been current in political literature—but in its most specific meaning it has come, within American experience, to denote a means of implementing the separation of powers. Those who framed the Constitution of 1787 divided the functions of government according to a threefold classification—legislative, executive, and judicial. They then authorized each branch to participate in the affairs of the other two for the purpose of preventing power from being abused. For example, the Legislature was given responsibility for enacting statutes, yet the Executive was empowered to approve or to veto bills passed by the Legislature, and the courts, exercising the power of judicial review, could interpret the statutes or declare them void. Thus in essence the phrase *checks and balances* comes to indicate a means whereby different organs of government are kept within their constitutional limits by giving powers to rival branches. The checks provided in any particular system

Chief

may be either numerous or few; in practice some checks have proved to be ineffective, and political arrangements have sometimes been made to offset the intended functioning of the principle.

David G. Farrelly

See also: SEPARATION OF POWERS

Chief

A. The term *chief* is used in various societies to describe *persons who are recognized as in some way pre-eminent*. The nature of this pre-eminence, and the social consequences of recognition, vary so widely in different cases that it is impossible to make any generalizations about it beyond the fact that a chief is always of higher rank than one who is not a chief.

B. There are a number of usages which are clearly distinct, though it cannot safely be assumed that the cases covered by one usage are alike in every respect. These arise from the use of the word *chief* to represent words in different native languages which, literally translated, have by no means the same meaning.

1. The term may refer to an individual recognized as holding a unique position of supremacy, whether merely in rank or also in authority, *in a political community*. In political communities of state type, sub-divisions of the political unit may have their own chiefs; in this case the superior chief is generally called a *paramount chief*.

2. It may be used to denote an individual who has qualified by *some socially approved achievement to be regarded as eminent*. In this sense the word translates the Crow Indian *batse'tse*, a word probably derived from roots meaning 'man' and 'good' or 'valiant'. This designation can be earned by a number of specified warlike exploits (cf. R. H. Lowie, *The Crow Indians*, New York: Farrar & Rinehart, 1935, p. 5).

3. It may be used for an individual holding any *one of a limited number of hereditary titles which are ranked in order*. In this sense the word translates the Samoan *ali'i*. The holder of the highest ranked title in such a system or in one of its sub-divisions may be described as paramount.

4. The phrase *talking chief* is sometimes used (e.g. in M. Mead, *Coming of Age in Samoa*, New York: William Morrow, 1928, p. 75). as a translation of the Samoan word *tulafale*, describing the counsellors who were associated with the title-holders, regulated the succession to titles and settled disputes as to precedence. Most ethnographers, however, prefer to translate this term by *orator*.

5. In recent writing on the Nilotes of the Sudan the word has been used of persons who hold a *special, but not unique, ritual position and are not accorded any formal marks of superior status in recognition of this*. The *leopard skin chief* of the Nuer is a person who has a special ritual relationship with the earth giving him the power to bless or curse, to cleanse a killer from the pollution which he has incurred by shedding blood, and to perform the appropriate ceremony of reconciliation between persons who are ready to terminate a blood-feud. E. E. Evans-Pritchard considers that the word *chief* is 'sufficiently vague to be retained' as a designation for such a person 'in the absence of a more suitable English word' (*The Nuer*, Oxford: Oxford University Press, 1940, p. 5).

6. In Africa *persons who have been endowed with executive authority by* European governments are normally designated as *chiefs* regardless of the position which they may hold in the social structure of the people over whom they are given this authority.

L. P. Mair

Church

A. Usage in sociology has been strongly influenced by the work of E. Troeltsch, who, in his book *The Social Teaching of the Christian Churches* (trans. O. Wyon, New York: The Macmillan Co., 1931, esp. vol. I, p. 331 ff.) held that *church* must be considered along with *sect* (q.v.). Troeltsch regarded the church as an essentially conservative religious organization, which adapts itself to the secular order, both dominating and being dominated by it. The individual is born into the church and may partake of the benefits it offers in virtue of its possession of an 'objective treasury of grace'. The church appears as the 'great educator of the nations' seeking somehow to 'cover the whole life of humanity'. The asceticism found in the church consists of heroic renunciations and mortifications practised by a specialized personnel and designed to compensate for the worldliness and mere pedestrian morality of others.

B. Troeltsch's distinction may be found essentially reproduced, while at the same time efforts are made to develop it further in some fashion, in H. R. Niebuhr's *The Social Sources of*

Denominationalism (New York: Henry Holt, 1929, esp. pp. 17–21 and 128–32), in L. Pope's *Millhands and Preachers* (New Haven: Yale University Press, 1942, ch. 7), in J. M. Yinger's *Religion, Society and the Individual* (New York: The Macmillan Co., 1957, pp. 142–55). Yinger's interest is a strongly typological one affording a six-fold distinction. (There are indeed indications in Troeltsch's own work that he was dissatisfied with his dichotomous split.) While not relinquishing the typological interest, Niebuhr and Pope have shown a special concern with problems connected with the transformation of sect into church or church-like form, as in the case of the changing sect which caters to class-mobile people taking over urban ways and values.

C. In addition to these typological and 'dynamic' interests, there is a not unrelated interest in close analytical scrutiny of the bases of the original distinction between church and sect (exemplified in a recent paper by B. Johnson, 'A Critical Appraisal of the Church-Sect Typology', *American Sociological Review*, vol. 22, 1957, pp. 88–92). The discontent that this kind of scrutiny engenders is shown in Johnson's comment that the church-sect dichotomy, originally proposed as an opposition of ideal types (so that it would be expected that concrete organizations labelled church or sect would not show all characteristics imputed to the 'pure forms'), has, in virtue of 'the low state of development of ideal-type methodology', come to be a matter of two opposed concepts each of which 'refers to a loosely integrated listing of empirical characteristics' (ibid., p. 88).

Louis Schneider

See also: CULT
RELIGION
SECT

Circulation of Elites

A. The phrase *circulation of elites* denotes the recruitment and/or ejection of members of a leading or ruling group in a society as a whole, in one or more of its separate institutions, or in some particular social category which may have only the most rudimentary social structure—for example, a group of artists or scholars.

B. In modern sociology the problem of elite circulation has been the focus of three different types of concern.

1. Darwinian ideas when applied to society have resulted in a considerable concern with the eugenic recruitment of a biologically superior elite in those societies where there is considerable differential fertility between social classes and/or ethnic groups.

2. In recent social investigation motivated by international competition in the areas of economic growth and the development of science, there has been considerable concern that societies make maximum use of their human resources. This is to be accomplished by conducting a search for talent among those social classes and ethnic groups which have lacked access to the elite-producing educational facilities in the past and by making higher education accessible to those who are found to have talent (cf. M. Young, *The Rise of the Meritocracy*, London: Thames & Hudson, 1958).

3. The most thoroughgoing development of a theory of elite circulation is that which stemmed from the anti-parliamentarian reaction of V. Pareto in Italy and G. Sorel in France. This theory, taking its sources largely in the eighteenth chapter of Machiavelli's *The Prince*, found its fullest expression in Pareto's *The Mind and Society* (translated from *Trattato di Sociologia generale* by A. Bongiorno & A. Livingston, ed. by A. Livingston, New York: Harcourt, Brace, 1935, 4 vols., vols. 3 & 4, paragraphs 2026–54, 2178–202).

This theory of circulation of elites—or rather of alternation of elites in which changing conditions of circulation play an important part—can be briefly summarized as follows: All societies are oligarchic in character. The governing elite is characterized by changing proportions of the residues of 'persistence of aggregates' (characterized by willingness to use force, faith, anti-intellectualism, belief in righteousness of cause, etc.) and 'instinct for combinations' (characterized by intellectualism and cunning, scepticism, reluctance to use force, enjoyment of the results of leadership rather than belief in righteousness of cause). Immediately following a revolution the residues of 'persistence of aggregates' among the elite are likely to be stronger than the residues of 'instinct for combination'. This is because lion-like strength of conviction and the willingness to use force are necessary conditions for the seizure of power, although there must be some of the fox-like qualities of intellect and cunning in order to develop the strategy and tactics of seizing power.

The conditions of retaining power and the softening effects of enjoying its privileges, however, gradually change the proportion of resi-

Citizenship

dues so that 'foxes' come to outnumber 'lions' among the elite. This is in part the result of the changing character structure of people who are already members of the elite, and partly the result of the recruitment of 'foxes' from the non-elite. This circulation of 'foxes' into the elite, deprives the masses of intelligent leadership but gradually increases the proportion of the residues of 'persistence of aggregates' among them. Finally, the stage is reached where the elite has become totally unwilling to use force and has lost faith in its destiny, and the 'lions' of the masses are ready to use force, are convinced of the righteousness of their cause, and possess enough residues of 'instinct for combinations' or fox-like qualities, or, alternatively, are able to recruit 'foxes' either from disaffected members of the elite or members of the masses who have not been recruited into the elite so that tactical and strategic planning is possible. The result is revolution and a new beginning of the cycle.

D. G. MacRae

See also: ELITE
RESIDUES

Citizenship

A. *Citizenship* may be defined (a) as a status of relationship existing between a natural person and a political society, known as the state (q.v.), by which the former owes allegiance and the latter protection. This status or relationship between the individual and the state is determined by municipal law, and recognized by the law of nations (this is the predominant usage in legal contexts); (b) as the status of the citizen in a society based upon the rule of law and the principles of equality.

B. 1. Citizenship in international law also denotes nationality. 'Citizenship, as distinct from nationality, is a creature solely of domestic law. It refers to rights which a State sees fit to confer upon certain individuals who are also its nationals' (C. C. Hyde, *International Law Chiefly as Interpreted and Applied by the United States*, Boston: Little, Brown, 2nd rev. edn., 1947, 3 vols., vol. 2, p. 1066). The law of nationality has gained in importance in recent years, and the term *national* has acquired a generic connotation that includes both *citizens* and *subjects*. 'Yet a state may have nationals who do not enjoy the status of citizens. The British Nationality Act of 1948, Section 13, distinguishes between British subjects who are citizens of the United Kingdom and colonies and those who are subjects without such citizenship' (O. Svarlien, *An Introduction to the Law of Nations*, New York: McGraw-Hill, 1955, p. 422). Likewise, in the United States, the Immigration and Nationality Act of 1952 makes a distinction between nationals and citizens (82nd Cong., 2nd Sess., Public Law 414 (H. R. 5678); 66 Stat. L. 163). *Nationality* is a term generally regarded as having a broader meaning than the word *citizenship*. The term *citizen*, in its general acceptation, is applicable only to a natural person who is endowed with full political and civil rights in the body politic of the state. A corporation, for example, has nationality but no citizenship. According to a British authority, the term *citizen*, in its widest sense, simply stands in opposition to the term alien, and would thus include all members of the state. But in a state where the government is elected through a widely extended suffrage, 'it is not uncommon to mean by the "citizens" only those who have a right to vote in such elections —leaving out of sight the usually larger part of the community that has not this right' (H. Sidgwick, *The Elements of Politics*, London: Macmillan, 4th edn., 1919, p. 387). In English usage, furthermore, the term *citizen* adheres more closely to its original meaning as shown by its derivation (*civis*, a free inhabitant of a city), while the term *subject* is generally used with reference to a person amenable to the laws of the nation.

In the United States, citizenship is defined by the 14th Amendment to the Constitution as follows: 'All persons born or naturalized in the United States and subject to the jurisdiction thereof are citizens of the United States and of the State wherein they reside'. Thus in the United States there exists dual citizenship in that a citizen of the nation as a whole is also at the same time a citizen of the state of the Union in which he resides. The resultant rights consequent upon citizenship of the Union as well as of the state of residence are not the same, however. The definition of citizenship contained in the 14th Amendment 'makes national citizenship primary and more fundamental than state citizenship' (J. M. Mathews, *The American Constitutional System*, New York: McGraw-Hill, 2nd edn., 1940, p. 348).

2. Citizenship is not to be confused with domicile nor citizen with inhabitant. One may be a citizen of a state without being an inhabitant of the same, or an inhabitant without being a citizen. One may also be a citizen of the United States of America without being a citizen of any state in the Union. The status of citizenship, furthermore, is determined by the municipal laws of independent states, generally in conformity with the principle of *jus soli* (place of birth) or *jus sanguinis* (nationality of parents). Inasmuch as individual states are free to determine for themselves the conditions of citizenship, it is quite possible that two or more states may claim the same person as their citizen, creating a situation of dual or multiple citizenship. This condition is recognized in international law no less than that of statelessness. In the latter case the individual is without citizenship or nationality.

C. In political science and in sociology the term *citizenship* is used in a somewhat wider sense. The sociologist L. T. Hobhouse (*Morals in Evolution* (1st edn., 1916), London: Chapman & Hall, 7th edn., 1950, p. 60) observes that 'the subjects of a government have become citizens of a state and the citizen has rights which are no less important than his duties. These rights hold good against the government just as they hold against other individuals, for it is a prime characteristic of the State based on citizenship that it establishes the reign of law, and subjects its own officers to this impersonal sovereign'. Following in the tradition of Hobhouse, T. H. Marshall (*Citizenship and Social Class*, Cambridge: Cambridge University Press, 1950) discussed the evolution of citizenship in the light of the changing conception of rights and duties in 19th-century England. For him the movement was one from legal rights to political rights and thence in the exercise of political rights to social rights. More recently D. W. Brogan has argued that the idea of citizenship has 'two aspects. The first ... is the assumption that every citizen has the right to be consulted in the conduct of the political society and the duty of having something to contribute to the general consultation. The second aspect is the converse of the first. The citizen who has a right to be consulted is bound by the results of the consultation' (*Citizenship Today*, Chapel Hill: University of North Carolina Press, 1960, pp. 4–5).

Oscar Svarlien

See also: NATIONALITY
STATE

City (See Urbanization)

City State
A. *City State* is a term denoting political systems (primarily but not solely in the ancient world) in which political activity and leadership is concentrated in a single town or city—such concentration being deemed to express an 'ideal' of social organization.

B. 1. The term has been used in England since the late 19th century to denote a self-governing city along with its dependent territory, i.e. in the sense of the *polis* in Greek antiquity. In the days of the *polis*, the city was the state, a republic formed by the people who lived within the same walls. This form was conserved or reproduced in the medieval Italian cities, and in Geneva in more recent times. It is worthy of remark that until the late 19th century, the word *city* alone was used in this context. The French have always used the word *cité* to refer to political communities of this type.

2. At some point in the latter half of the 19th century English writers began to use the term *City State*, even *City-State*. Thus 'It is then a City-State that we have to deal with in Greek and Roman history; a State in which the whole life and energy of the people, political, intellectual, religious, is focused at one point, and that point a city' (W. Warde Fowler, *The City-State of the Greeks and Romans*, London: Macmillan, 1893, p. 9). This, of course, is most confusing because the *polis* was not a city nor was it a state in any connotation of 'city' later than the middle ages or of 'state' in any connotation later than the 16th century. H. Sidgwick discusses the City-State in contrast with the country state, pointing out that until the late 4th century B.C. 'a Greek ... could hardly conceive of a high degree of political organization being attained by a community whose political life did not centre in a single town' (*The Development of European Polity*, London: Macmillan, 1903, p. 67). The Greek idea of 'the city community, i.e. a community inhabiting a district with a city for centre' came to be fixed as 'the highest and ultimate form of human association' (ibid., p. 70).

C. The explanation of the English usage is in part illustrated by the philosophical and normative quality of the term as indicated by Sidgwick. Some idea of the factors responsible for the usage may be gained from the following considerations: (a) The *polis* was based on a city and the modern state on a country; (b) of great relevance was the revival of the study of both Plato and Aristotle, and (c) the idealist philosophers demonstrated that a modern state was

Civil Law

not a collection but a unity of a special kind. 'This public person ... formerly took the name of *City*, and now takes that of *Republic* or *body politic*' (J. J. Rousseau, *Social Contract* (1762), bk. 1, ch. V, in *The Social Contract and Discourses*, London: J. M. Dent, 1913, p. 13). Bosanquet in *The Philosophical Theory of the State* (London: Macmillan, 1899) proposed to do for the nation state what Plato and Aristotle had done for the *polis* or City State. The word *polis* came to Aristotle, W. K. Newman writes in his *Politics of Aristotle* (Oxford: Clarendon, 1887, vol. 1, p. 40), 'fresh from popular use and full of associations of a definite kind'. They were that it implied a certain quality of life possible only where certain conditions were satisfied—a centre which was a city or citadel, a whole of which the individual was a part and a unity in which production, trade, science, and religion were as much phenomena of the state as government. The art of *politike* (politics) was that of regulating all human activities and of providing for their harmonious co-operation for a common end. Just as Plato thought that the city was the individual writ large, so the 19th-century commentators thought that the nation state was or might be the *polis* writ large. Thus the English and Americans, under the influence of the idealists, talk about a City State while the French under the influence of Rousseau and Napoleon stick to *cité*.

K. B. Smellie

See also: NATION
          STATE

Civil Jurisdiction (See Jurisdiction)

Civil Law

The epithet *civil* is applied to law in several distinct senses.

1. It is sometimes used to indicate Roman law—a usage which is medieval in origin, stemming from the contrast between Justinian's *corpus juris civilis* and the body of church or *canon* law.

2. More usually *civil law* denotes the whole body of law which is concerned with *civil* as distinct from criminal proceedings. Thus A. K. R. Kiralfy writes that 'Civil proceedings are taken in order to assist individuals to recover property or enforce obligations in their favour. Criminal proceedings are taken to suppress crime and punish criminals, and are under the control of the State' (*The English Legal System*, London: Sweet & Maxwell, 1960, p. 9). Kiralfy adds a warning on the dangers of making this distinction too sharp.

3. *Civil law* is also used in contrast to *common law*—in the sense of that term that refers to the Common Law of England and, with modifications, other 'common law' countries. It should be noted that the term *common law* is often used in a sense other than that implied by this particular contrast; i.e. it may be used in contrast with (a) *equity* in its legal sense; 'those principles of law which were administered before 1875 by the Courts of Equity (mainly the Court of Chancery)' (O. Hood Phillips, *A First Book of English Law*, London: Sweet & Maxwell, 1960, p. 6) and (b) law drawn from the decisions of Judges.

4. R. M. Jackson points out that in law 'the term "civil" is sometimes used to mean the whole law of some particular state in contrast to international law' (*The Machinery of Justice in England*, Cambridge: Cambridge University Press, 1960, p. 9).

J. Gould

See also: LAW

Civil Liberties

A. *Civil liberties* denotes those personal and social freedoms derived from one's civil relationships which are guaranteed by law against restraint except for the common good or the public interest. Civil liberties become civil rights (q.v.) when they are claimed and enforced through judicial or administrative action.

B. 1. 'Civil liberty is a concept, basic to modern democratic political thought, which in its most general usage connotes freedom of the individual with respect to personal action, the possession and use of property, religious belief and worship, and the expression of opinion. This freedom is conceived to imply a right to protection against both governmental and private interference, but it is essentially a right of the individual as against the authoritarian state' (R. E. Cushman, 'Civil Liberties', in E. R. A. Seligman (ed.), *Encyclopedia of the Social Sciences*, New York: The Macmillan Co., 1930, vol. III, p. 509). Some definitions, however, restrict the term *civil liberty* to the exemption from interference with one's person, property, or opinion by arbitrary governmental action alone (*Webster's Collegiate Dictionary*, Springfield, Mass.: G. & C. Merriam Co., 5th edn., 1939, p. 186).

2. Since liberty under law is never absolute,

there has been much controversy over its limits. Therefore, some users of the term emphasize the notion that there are limits to freedom. Civil liberty in this sense is the liberty of a member of society, being man's natural liberty, so far restrained by human laws (and no further) as is necessary and expedient for the general advantage of the public or the common interest. Or again, 'liberal-legal cultures recognize that liberty must be limited by custom, morals, taste, and self-restraint, or by laws protecting others' welfare and freedom' (T. D. Eliot, 'Civil Liberties', *Encyclopaedia Britannica*, Chicago: Encyclopaedia Britannica, 1954, vol. 5, p. 743A).

Sometimes civil liberties are merely referred to by way of enumeration, such as 'freedom claimed by or accorded to persons to speak, write, publish, assemble and organize without interference or penalty' (H. P. Fairchild (ed.), *Dictionary of Sociology*, New York: Philosophical Library, 1957). When this definition-by-enumeration is employed, it is widely recognized that any list of civil liberties varies with time and place; hence, no static listing is possible for all societies under every condition.

3. Further to complicate the problem of usage, some writers distinguish between civil liberties and civil rights; others equate the terms or fail to differentiate between them; a third group subordinates civil liberties under a more general term *civil rights*; and others make civil liberties the overall term to include civil rights. To illustrate: I. de S. Pool and G. Schueller refer to civil liberties as freedoms which may be exercised without necessarily involving positive action on the part of someone else, whereas civil rights impose positive duties. In essence the distinction here is that liberties do not require action by another person, but rights do ('The Constitution of the State', in O. K. Flechtheim (ed.), *Fundamentals of Political Science*, New York: Ronald Press, 1952, p. 255). C. O. Johnson may be cited as one who refers to civil liberties or civil rights, apparently making no distinction (*American National Government*, New York: Crowell, 1951). A third group makes civil rights the more inclusive term under which are included civil liberties, political liberty, individual security, etc. (President's Committee on Civil Rights, *To Secure These Rights*, Washington: U.S. Government Printing Office, 1947). In the fourth category is E. McK. Erickson's definition (*Dictionary of American History*, New York: Scribner's Sons, 1951, 6 vols., vol. I, p. 381): 'Civil liberties is a term generally used in the U.S. to indicate not only civil rights, privileges, prerogatives, franchises and freedoms in general but also the concept of immunity or protection of individuals or groups from undue interference by the government.'

David G. Farrelly

See also: CITIZENSHIP
CIVIL RIGHTS

Civil Rights

A. The term *civil rights* denotes the claims to certain basic social freedoms in the enjoyment of which a citizen has the 'right' to be confirmed by courts or administrative agencies. Their guaranteed enjoyment is the basic content of the status of citizen.

B. 1. The word *rights* is generic, embracing any powers and privileges vested in a person by positive law or custom and lawfully claimed by him. *Civil rights* are both substantive and procedural, and they pertain to either life, liberty, or property. They are guaranteed by constitutions and statutes against arbitrary and oppressive conduct on the part of the state. Statutory law may often be used to protect certain civil rights from violation by individuals or groups. Further, courts may refuse to apply the usual judicial remedies (e.g. injunction) for the enforcement of private agreements that violate civil rights (*Shelley* v. *Kraemer*, U.S. Supreme Court Reports, 334 U.S. 1, 92 L.Ed. 1161 68 S.Ct. 836).

2. The recognition and enjoyment of specific civil rights depends upon the nation or territory in which a person lives, his status in the community, the form of government, and the prevailing political situation. Thus, civil rights are relative, not absolute; any listing of them is necessarily conditioned by time and place. However, the Universal Declaration of Human Rights (General Assembly of the United Nations, December 10, 1948) includes an enumeration of basic civil rights which should be available to all persons in the world. In 1947 the President's Committee on Civil Rights attempted to reformulate the essential rights of Americans as: (a) safety and security of person (often referred to as individual or personal rights); (b) citizenship and its privileges (elsewhere called political rights); (c) freedom of conscience and expression (often referred to as civil liberties); (d) equality of opportunity (*To Secure These Rights*, *Report of the President's Committee on Civil Rights*, Washington: U.S. Government Printing Office, 1947).

Civil Service

3. Some writers attempt to draw a distinction between civil liberties (q.v.) and civil rights. For example, they classify freedom of speech as a liberty and trial by jury as a right. Others fail to differentiate, thus listing among civil liberties the right to freedom of speech and the right of criminal justice (R. K. Carr, D. H. Morrison et al., *American Democracy in Theory and Practice*, New York: Rinehart, 1951). The distinction and confusion between the terms might be avoided if it were recognized and accepted that civil liberties become civil rights when one claims that a freedom has been denied and a court or administrative agency upholds the claimant. In other words, liberties do not require action from others, but rights do.

C. 1. In the United States there has existed a restricted definition of the term civil rights. By this usage civil rights are those rights secured by the 13th and 14th Amendments to the U.S. Constitution and by certain acts of Congress which abolished the civil incidence of involuntary servitude. This usage gained currency with reference to the status of the Negro, in the years before and just after the Civil War (J. Dickinson, 'Civil Rights', in E. R. A. Seligman (ed.), *Encyclopedia of the Social Sciences*, New York: Macmillan, 1930, vol. III, pp. 513–5). Thus in 1866 an Act was passed 'to protect all persons in the United States in their Civil Rights and to furnish the Means of Their Vindication'. There followed further legislation, including the Act of 1875; cases arising out of this Act came before the Supreme Court (Supreme Court of the U.S., 1883, 109 US 3.27 L.Ed. 835 3 Sup Ct 18) and became known as the Civil Rights Cases. Thus, according to M. R. Konvitz, the term contemplates the rights enumerated in the federal Civil Rights Act of 1875 and the various acts against discrimination found on the statute books of eighteen states (*The Constitution and Civil Rights*, New York: Columbia University Press, 1947).

2. From this background a modern usage has developed in the United States which is both technical and limited; it stems from concern with the problems of discrimination because of race, colour, or creed. Civil rights here refers to the rights of persons to employment, and to equal accommodations in hotels, restaurants, common carriers, and other places open to the public (ibid.). Similarly, E. S. Newman considers civil rights as relating to non-descrimination in employment, housing, education, health, and welfare (*The Law of Civil Rights and Civil Liberties, Legal Almanac Series No.* 13, New York: Oceana Publishers, 1958).

David G. Farrelly

See also: CITIZENSHIP
CIVIL LIBERTIES

Civil Service

A. The term *civil service* denotes generally the body of central government officials of a permanent and non-political status, who are members neither of the judiciary nor of the armed forces.

B. 1. The term was originally applied to that part of the East India Company's administration carried on by the covenanted servants who did not belong to its armed forces.

2. In England, the term first appeared with the meaning set out in Acts *c.* 1853. Sir Robert Peel was writing, *c.* 1841–2 of 'employment in the Civil Service of the country', and of 'the civil servants of the Crown', meaning thereby to distinguish these from 'political' and 'ministerial' servants (cf. E. Hughes, 'Civil Service Reform 1853–1855' *Public Administration*, vol. XXXII, 1954, pp. 17–19). It was the Trevelyan-Northcote *Report on the Organization of the Permanent Civil Service* (pub. 1854) that gave the term its popularity, and thereafter it was used as the official expression.

3. In the U.S.A., the term first appears *c.* 1863 as an adoption from Britain. It was recognized officially in 1871 in the Statute of that year granting the President permission 'to regulate the admission of persons into the civil service of the U.S.'. The reason for the borrowing of this British term is that the reform movement which ended in the establishment of the U.S. Civil Service Commission in 1883 was begun by T. A. Jenckes (Representative 1863–71) and C. Schurz, who turned to Britain for their inspiration and who corresponded with British reformers, e.g. Trevelyan.

C. 1. (a) In Gt. Britain the standard definition is that given in the Report of the Royal Commission of the Civil Service, 1929–31 (known as the Tomlin Commission): 'Those servants of the Crown, other than holders of political or judicial offices, who are employed in a civil capacity and whose remuneration is paid, wholly and directly, out of monies voted by Parliament' (Cmd. 3909, London: H.M.S.O., 1931, para. 9).

(b) The officials of local authorities do not style themselves 'the Local Civil Service' but 'the Local Government Service' and individually as 'Local Government Officers'. Manual workers are not deemed to be part of this 'Local Government Service' and are individually styled 'Local Government Servants'.

2. (a) In the U.S.A. *civil service* means those groups of positions in the Federal Government set aside to be filled by appointees chosen, not on the basis of political favour, but of merit as demonstrated in examinations prescribed by the Civil Service Commissioners. Hence the terms *civil service*, *competitive service*, and *the classified service* are broadly synonymous.

(b) The term is also by extension applied to similar groups of positions in states and cities of the United States.

S. E. Finer

See also: ADMINISTRATION
MINISTER
OFFICE

Civilization

A. In the numerous uses of *civilization* in ordinary speech and writing, the humanities, and the social sciences, no single meaning or theme can be selected as definitive. Even within the social sciences there is no one dominant use. By restricting a survey of uses to the social sciences, however, some order can be introduced into the variety of meanings and two themes can be found to pervade the various definitions.

1. The major theme is that civilization is conceived of as a form of culture (q.v.). Within this theme there are three major forms of use.

(a) Civilization and culture are synonyms.

(b) Civilization is culture when the latter is characterized by a *greater degree of complexity and a sizeable number of traits*.

(c) Civilization is culture when the latter is characterized by *qualitatively* more advanced elements and traits as measured by some *criteria of progress*.

2. A second (minor) theme contrasts culture and civilization. Culture shifts its meaning to become those human ideas and creations concerned with myth, religion, art, and literature; while civilization is the realm of human creativity concerned with technology and science.

B. Early writers in modern cultural anthropology tended to equate culture and civilization. Although E. B. Tylor was not consistent in his use he writes, 'Culture or Civilization, taken in its wide ethnographic sense, is that complex whole which includes knowledge, belief, art, morals, law, custom, and any other capabilities and habits acquired by man as a member

of society' (*Primitive Culture*, London: John Murray, 1871, vol. I, p. 1).

C. Although, logically, a use which defined civilization as simply a type of culture marked by greater differentiation, complexity, and sheer quantity of cultural items would seem to be the next step, such is not the case chronologically. Simultaneously with the use of culture and civilization as synonyms, there arose the definition of civilization as a form of culture qualitatively different from other forms. This use has persisted to the present day.

1. This usage is rooted in the fact that in the 19th century civilization was meant to convey the idea of civilizing, of making the peoples of non-Western societies more like those of the Western nations. Tylor, for example, wrote that 'Human life may be roughly classed into three great stages, Savage, Barbaric, Civilized ...' and indicated that '... civilized life may be taken as beginning with the art of writing ...' (*Anthropology*, New York: Macmillan, 1895, pp. 23–4). His illustrations of the three stages are '... a savage of the Brazilian forests, a barbarous New Zealander or Dahoman, and a civilized European ...' (ibid., p. 25).

2. Anthropologists using evaluative criteria for describing a culture as civilized have been reluctant to use *moral* standards as such criteria; rather they have used criteria in which measurement is possible according to a *norm of internal efficiency*. Thus writing, technology, and science have been those most commonly used. Together with these, other characteristics frequently associated with them in empirical observation of cultures have also been used: the presence of cities, of population heterogeneity linked with a complex division of labour, and of concentrations of economic and political power. Thus V. G. Childe describes the differentiating characteristics of a civilization as '... the aggregation of large populations in cities; the differentiation within these of primary producers (fishers, farmers, etc.), full-time specialist artisans, merchants, officials, priests, and rulers; an effective concentration of economic and political power; the use of conventional symbols for recording and transmitting information (writing), and equally conventional standards of weights and measures, of time and space, leading to some mathematical and calendrical science' (*Social Evolution*, London: Watts, 1951, p. 161).

3. A few anthropologists have been willing to differentiate civilizations not only on the basis of easily measurable criteria, but also on the

Clan

basis of differentiation in the moral order. Here, again, however, the characteristics of the moral order used are those most easily linked with the criteria based on the norm of efficiency and do not penetrate to the core of the moral systems of various cultures. Thus R. Redfield writes that '... the moral order, though it is shaken by civilization, is also, in civilization, taken by reason into charge'. Further, 'The moral order in early civilization is taken in charge by specialists as a philosophical problem ...' (*The Primitive World and Its Transformations*, Ithaca, New York: Cornell University Press, 1953, pp. 119–20). For A. L. Kroeber an increase in technological complexity tends to be linked with a decrease in magic and 'superstition', a decrease in the obsession with physiological or anatomical considerations in social situations, and a lack of concern with death and decay; and therefore these characteristics can be used as criteria of the progress of civilization (*Anthropology*, New York: Harcourt, Brace, 1949, pp. 298–304).

D. Some anthropologists, recoiling from the complexities involved in attempting comparative evaluations of cultures as civilized and uncivilized, have attempted to adopt a purely quantitative and 'presence of complexity' definition of civilization. While it is difficult to see how such a definition can remain separate from one using criteria of progress such as writing and the division of labour, the intent to refrain from evaluation is apparent. R. L. Beals and H. Hoijer, for example, write 'All civilizations, including the great ones of today and ancient times, are but special instances of culture, distinctive in the quantity of their content and the complexity of their patterning, but not qualitatively different from the cultures of so-called uncivilized peoples' (*An Introduction to Anthropology*, New York: The Macmillan Co., 1953, p. 227).

E. While anthropologists and most sociologists have followed the usages just described, a few sociologists and anthropologists have attempted to separate the meanings of culture and civilization from one another. They do this by restricting culture to 'expressions of life' such as religion, art, literature, and ultimate moral ends. In this manner civilization comes to consist of '... the whole mechanism and organization which man has devised in his endeavour to control the conditions of his life. It would include not only our systems of social organization but also our techniques and our material

instruments' (R. M. MacIver, *Society, Its Structure and Changes*, New York: Long & Smith, 1931, p. 226). Here again is seen the distinction between that which is cumulative and easily measurable and that which is seen as non-cumulative and essentially qualitative. Only this time instead of using the former as criteria for determining the civilized status of a culture, they are used to differentiate one part of the realm of human creativity from another part; and hence, by this definition, culture and civilization exist side by side in every human society.

Although this usage of civilization may continue in the German social sciences, as in the work of Alfred Weber, from whom MacIver adopted it, it is probably disappearing from American and English usage. The distinction so designated is coming to be called by other terms. Thus MacIver in his more recent work speaks of myth and technique, and Kroeber writes of 'reality culture' and 'value culture' (R. M. MacIver, *The Web of Government*, New York: The Macmillan Co., 1947, pp. 3–12; A. L. Kroeber, 'Reality Culture and Value Culture', *The Nature of Culture*, Chicago: University of Chicago Press, 1952, pp. 152–68).

Arden R. King

See also: CULTURE
            MYTH
            TECHNOLOGY

Clan

A. *Clan* denotes a unilineal descent group. It may be either patrilineal or matrilineal, but not necessarily be corporate, exogamous, totemic, or localized.

B. 1. *Clan* was used originally in anthropology to refer to Teutonic and Scottish society. According to B. S. Philpotts, clans are 'large groups of kindred organized on an agnatic basis' and a clan is 'a fixed agnatic kindred' (*Kindred and Clan*, Cambridge: Cambridge University Press, 1913, pp. 2, 245).

2. The usual criterion for defining a clan is unilineal descent; some writers have also included exogamy and totemism. Among some American anthropologists a clan is a matrilineal *sib* (q.v.), the word *gens* being used for a patrilineal *sib*; a *sib* is defined as 'a unilateral kinship group ... [it] traces kinship through *either* parent to the total neglect of the other' (R. H. Lowie, *Primitive Society*, London: Routledge, 1929, p. 105). The *sib* is called *clan* in English usage.

3. It may be segmented into sub-clans and/or

lineages. Within it exact genealogical relationships need not be traced, although it is always believed to have a single founding ancestor or ancestress.

4. In recent years a large number of clan systems has been described, referring both to clans in which descent is traced through males only for which W. E. Lawrence ('Alternating Generations in Australia', in G. P. Murdock (ed.), *Studies in the Science of Society*, New Haven: Yale University Press, 1937, p. 319), suggests the composite term *patri-clan*, and those in which it is traced through females only (*matri-clan*). Different authors have used the term to refer to various types of descent group A. R. Radcliffe-Brown ('Introduction' to A. R. Radcliffe-Brown & D. Forde (eds.), *African Systems of Kinship and Marriage*, London: Oxford University Press, 1950, p. 40) has summed up the position: 'The term "clan" has often been used without any clear definition. There are ... many different kinds of clan systems, but the term should be used only for a group having unilineal descent in which all the members regard one another as in some specific sense kinsfolk'. Clans may be localized or dispersed, and they may or may not form corporate groups.

Because of its original connection with Celtic clans, some efforts have been made to find substitutes; e.g. Lang and Frazer suggested 'totemkin'. But in fact the term's lack of very precise definition has been a factor in its general popularity and usefulness.

J. Middleton

See also: DESCENT
GENS
LINEAGE
SIB
UNILINEAL

Class (See Social Class)

Class-Consciousness

1. *Class-consciousness* is used by writers in the Marxian tradition to denote the process whereby the members of a class (generally the 'proletarian' class) become 'aware' of themselves, i.e. of their collective identity and destiny; and the outcome of such a process. It is thus intimately connected with the idea of revolutionary class conflict and denotes the presumed will of the workers to recognize their common 'enemy'—the capitalists—, their common 'misery', and their common goal—triumph of the proletariat.

According to K. R. Popper, it shows how 'the objective class situation (class interest as well as class struggle) gains consciousness in the minds of its members, or, to express the same thought in a language less dependent on Hegel, by which members of a class become conscious of their class situation (*The Open Society and Its Enemies*, London: Routledge & Kegan Paul, 3rd rev. edn., 1957, vol. II, p. 115).

2. Outside the Marxist context the term may be used in an operational sense to denote a given 'high' degree of sharing of attitudes of isolation, solidarity, and collective purpose within a national sub-group, most of whose members also share a common skill, relation to the means of production, and style of life. In simpler (and less specific) language, one may say that class-consciousness is a group's feeling that its social achievements are specially dependent upon its fortunes as a group. More specifically, again, one may say that class-consciousness exists when a 'considerable' grouping in a society, possessing similar economic traits, achieves similar, high scores on tests of their perception of common traits, common needs, and common collective aims. In this sense it can be expressed in a constructed index. As such, it may then be usefully related and lend new meaning to historical events, personality characteristics, indices of social mobility, the imminence of rapid social change (including political violence), and a host of other phenomena and indices.

Thus O. Glantz, designating 'class conscious' persons in Philadelphia on a basis of a combination of 'allegiance' and 'orientation', attempted through questionnaire research to relate 'class-consciousness' with 'political cohesiveness' ('Class Consciousness and Political Solidarity', *American Sociological Review*, vol. 23, 1958, p. 375 et seq.)

Alfred de Grazia

See also: CLASS STRUGGLE
SOCIAL CLASS

Class Struggle

A. The term denotes the manifestation of mutual hostility, displayed through varying degrees of intellectual and/or physical violence between and within groups in society, and based upon the location of the persons and groups involved in the system of stratification (q.v.). The social classes which serve as the root of the struggle need not be differentiated simply by their economic interests, but may be based upon separate or combined factors of cultural, eco-

Class Struggle

nomic, historical, political, social, and religious factors.

B. In its modern usage the phrase is employed by two principal groups: (a) by Marxists and Syndicalists; (b) by non-Marxist and non-Syndicalist social scientists.

1. Marxist usage of *class struggle* denotes the 'inevitable' conflicts arising between and amongst the exploiting and exploited classes throughout the succeeding epochs of history (feudalism, capitalism, etc.). These inevitable conflicts comprise the motive power of the materialist dialectic which, to the Marxists, is the complete explanation for the entire panorama of history. 'The history of all hitherto existing society is the history of class struggles . . . Freeman and slave, patrician and plebeian, lord and serf, guildmaster and journeyman, in a word, oppressor and oppressed, stood in constant opposition to one another . . . In the earlier epochs of history, we find almost everywhere a complicated arrangement of society into various orders, a manifold gradation of social rank. In ancient Rome we have patricians, knights, plebeians, slaves; in the Middle Ages, feudal lords, vassals, guildmasters, journeymen, apprentices, serfs; in almost all of these classes, again, subordinate gradations. . . . Our epoch, the epoch of the bourgeoisie, possesses, however, this distinctive feature: It has simplified the class antagonisms. Society as a whole is more and more splitting up into two great hostile camps, . . . bourgeoisie and proletariat' (K. Marx & F. Engels, *The Communist Manifesto* (1848), ed. by S. H. Beer, New York: Appleton-Century-Crofts, 1955, pp. 9–10)

It is salient to note the reduction of antagonistic groups to two in the capitalistic epoch. From that point onward, orthodox Marxists next predict the destruction of capitalist domination of society through violent revolution. The chaos ensuing will be followed by the epoch of socialism during which all vestiges of capitalism are to be liquidated by a dictatorship of the victorious proletariat. With the completed liquidation of capitalism, and thus of the antagonistic element of proletarian society, the class struggle will cease and the historical dialectic at this level will terminate. 'In place of the old bourgeois society, with its classes and class antagonism, we shall have an association, in which the free development of each is the condition for the free development of all' (ibid., p. 32). All Marxist commentators, from Marx and Engels themselves to Krushchev, have made moderating or qualifying statements concerning the greater or lesser intensity and the means of carrying out the class struggle, but in the pronouncements of all it stands as the inevitable 'motor' of the historical dialectic process.

The Syndicalist usage of *class struggle*—also based upon economic determinism—envisages an inevitable violent conflict between the proletariat and the bourgeoisie manifested in its highest stage of development as a 'myth' of the General Strike. Unlike the rationalism of the Marxian interpretation, the Syndicalists provide no systematic programme, but see the class struggle and its myth as meritorious in themselves. It is almost purely an irrationalistic interpretation: 'The strike brings the working-men face to face with the employers in a clash of interests. A strike clears up, as if by a flash of lightning, the deep antagonism which exists between those who employ and those who work for employers. It further deepens the chasm between them, consolidating the employers on the one hand, and the working-men on the other. ... It is a revolutionary fact of great value' (L. Lorwin, *Syndicalism in France*, New York: Columbia University Press, 1914, pp. 126–7, quoted in J. H. Hallowell, *Main Currents in Modern Political Thought*, New York: Holt, 1950, p. 459).

2. The non-Marxist, non-Syndicalist usage denotes, much more ambiguously, conflict or conflicts between and amongst various groups rooted in social strata and classes, based not only on economic factors, but also upon other contributing causes such as the disparate distribution of power or privilege. Exemplifying this position is R. M. MacIver's view that '. . . while the economic issue is so often the rallying point in the struggle of groups or classes only by a gross simplification can we treat it as an adequate explanation of that struggle. It is the groups that struggle, not just their economic interests, and each group is internally integrated, as well as divided from others, by a complex of conditions that have worked historically to bring the group into being *as a group* . . .' (*The Web of Government*, New York: The Macmillan Co., 1947, p. 135).

A. B. Winter

See also: Class-Consciousness
Myth
Social Class
Stratification
Syndicalism

Classificatory Kinship System (See Kinship Terminology)

Clique

A. A *clique* is a sub-group within a larger structure whose members prefer to associate with each other on the basis of sheer liking or common interests; this preference emerges spontaneously among the individuals concerned, and their relationships with each other are marked by frequency of interaction, ease of communication, and a sense of 'we-feeling'. In other words, a clique is a primary group (C. H. Cooley, *Social Organization*, New York: Charles Scribner's Sons, 1909, pp. 23–31) and it may be analysed either from the point of view of interpersonal relations or as a structural element in community life and the class system.

B. The term *clique* is most frequently encountered in the fields of sociology, social psychology, and sociometry. Through all of these the meaning remains relatively consistent, although slightly different emphases are found depending on conceptual frameworks and fields of observation. While in ordinary usage the term is often used to denote pejoratively certain kinds of groups and their behaviour, social science usage tries to avoid this normative application.

1. In sociometric studies members of some formally defined group (classroom, factory division, military unit) may be asked to indicate which other members they like or dislike, accept or reject. The indicated patterns of attraction and repulsion among the members thus reveal the actual preferential sub-groups within the larger group. From this standpoint, a clique is 'any subgroup *all* of whose positive choices and *none* of whose rejections are made among themselves' (T. M. Newcomb, *Social Psychology*, New York: The Dryden Press, 1950, p. 641).

2. In a like vein, but with more emphasis on actual interaction (as opposed to sociometric choice), G. C. Homans writes: 'When we speak of a number of men as forming a clique, we only mean that they form a subgroup within a larger unit; that is, their interactions with one another are more frequent than they are with outsiders or members of other subgroups' (*The Human Group*, London: Routledge & Kegan Paul, 1951, p. 133).

3. Whereas the above definitions emphasize frequency of in-group choices or in-group interaction, M. Sherif emphasizes that cliques are '*informally* or *spontaneously* structured small groups' ('A Preliminary Experimental Study of Intergroup Relations', in J. H. Rohrer & M. Sherif (eds.), *Social Psychology at the Cross-roads*, New York: Harper & Brothers, 1951, p. 392).

4. The concept is also used in the analysis of broader social structures, particularly in sociological studies of stratification at the community level. Thus, in the Yankee City series, clique is defined as an 'intimate nonkin group, membership in which may vary in numbers from two to thirty or more people … . The clique is an informal association because it has no explicit rules of entrance, of membership, or of exit. … It has no elected officers nor any formally recognized hierarchy of leaders … but all its members know each other intimately and participate in frequent face-to-face relations' (W. L. Warner & P. S. Lunt, *The Social Life of a Modern Community*, New Haven: Yale University Press, 1941, pp. 110–1). Further, the overlap in clique membership tends to integrate 'almost the entire population of a community in a single vast system of clique relations' (ibid., p. 111).

A similar viewpoint is adopted by A. B. Hollingshead, who also points out that clique members are most frequently from the same social class, and adds that cliques 'are the smallest organized units within a class …' (*Elmtown's Youth*, New York: John Wiley, 1949, p. 80 fn., pp. 205–6). Being concerned with adolescents, Hollingshead also distinguishes between the 'clique' and the 'gang'. They are similar social forms, the difference being in 'the importance placed upon predacious activity that almost invariably leads to conflict in the gang. The clique is a socially accepted group which normally does not develop conflict relations to the point where an undeclared war exists between itself and society, or, for that matter, other cliques' (ibid., p. 206, fn).

Edmund H. Volkart

See also: Gang
            Group

Closed Primary (See **Primary**)

Cluster Sampling (See **Sampling**)

Coalition

A. *Coalition* denotes a combination of political groups or forces, temporary in nature and for specific objectives. Although the term is usually applied in connection with political parties aligning for parliamentary or electoral purposes, and sometimes to groupings cutting across party lines, it may also refer to a temporary alliance of nation states for joint action.

Coercion

B. 1. Most commonly the term is used in connection with political parties, particularly in multi-party systems. It may, however, refer to an alliance of forces within a party or of groups cutting across party lines.

2. (a) Party coalitions are usually formed for the parliamentary purpose of forming and maintaining a government. Coalition governments often have as their objective the assertion of unity in crisis or are brought into being on similar broad political grounds. In such situations the largest party may form a coalition with one or more smaller parties in order to obtain a majority. In other circumstances several smaller parties may form a coalition for the purpose of keeping a larger party out of power. Usually such coalitions involve ministerial posts for members of all parties in the coalition in relation to their strength.

(b) Coalitions may also be formed for the purpose of defeating a government. In post-World War II France, the frequent agreement of the Communists and the extreme right in opposing the coalition government was sometimes referred to as a 'negative coalition'.

(c) Coalition may also refer to combinations of political parties for electoral purposes. Under the French electoral system of the Fourth Republic, for example, parties could form coalitions for the purpose of pooling votes in multi-member constituencies. French practice distinguished between a coalition and an alliance, which involves a virtual party merger to offer a single list of candidates.

(d) In the two-party system of the United States, coalition has a slightly different meaning. Ordinarily it refers to groupings which cut across party lines on specific issues in Congress. An example is the coalition of Southern Democrats and Northern Republicans to oppose certain measures advocated by the Roosevelt and Truman administrations.

C. *Coalition* may also refer to combinations of nation states grouped together for joint action.

In international politics, a coalition of states is considered more informal as well as more temporary and limited than an alliance, although the two are sometimes used interchangeably. Thus the wartime unity of the United States, the Soviet Union, and Great Britain is sometimes referred to as a coalition, sometimes as an alliance.

Fred Warner Neal

See also: ALLIANCE

Coercion

A. *Coercion* signifies, in general, the imposition of external regulation and control upon persons, by the threat or use of force and power (q.v.). Distinctions are commonly drawn between violent and non-violent, physical and non-physical, legitimate and illegitimate forms of coercion.

B. Coercion is an important concept in social science, because the legitimate use of force (internally through police power, and externally through military power) is frequently regarded as the ultimate instrumentality or sanction of the state (q.v.). The theory and practice of democracy (q.v.) contrast coercion with consent and impose severe limits upon the area of internal conflicts open to solution by coercion. International politics are also marked by efforts to control and limit the use of coercion by sovereign states.

C. Social scientists have been concerned with non-legal coercion as a means of control used by persons and groups. Here the question of legitimate and illegitimate coercion becomes much more complex, and the borderline between coercion and forms of manipulative influence becomes blurred. The questions arising in this area of investigation involve the state, as well as other social institutions, and ethical and psychological as well as technical and political issues.

Daniel Lerner

See also: INFLUENCE
POWER
SOCIAL CONTROL

Cognatic

Cognatic is used in kinship studies to describe the relationship between two or more people who share ancestry traced indifferently through males and females. The term is also used for kinship systems (otherwise called *non-unilineal* or *bilateral*) in which there is no unilineal principle. 'Persons are cognatic kin or cognates when they are descended from a common ancestor or ancestress counting descent through males and females' (A. R. Radcliffe-Brown, 'Introduction' to A. R. Radcliffe-Brown & D. Forde (eds.), *African Systems of Kinship and Marriage*, London: Oxford University Press, 1950, p. 4). 'One principle [of descent] that may be adopted is the simple cognatic principle. To define the kin of a given person his descent is traced back a certain number of generations, to his four grandparents, his eight great-grand-parents, or still farther, and all descendants of his recognized ancestors, through both males and females, are his cognates' (ibid., p. 13).

Maurice Freedman

See also: BILATERAL

Cognition

A. *Cognition* is a generic term used to indicate all the various aspects of knowing, including perception, judgement, reasoning and remembering, thinking and imagining. Traditionally it has been used to represent a mode of experience which is different from *conation* (q.v.), *affect* (q.v.).

B. The term has come down to us from the writings of Plato and Aristotle. Plato had distinguished three aspects of the soul: intellectual, emotional, and moral, or cognitive, affective, and conative. Aristotle modified this to differentiate the dianoetic (cognitive or intellectual) and the orectic (emotional and moral) capacities of the mind. The triad: cognition, feeling or affect, and conation, was revived in the 18th century as a scheme of classifying mental functions by Tetens (1736–1807) and Kant (1724-1804). While thus pointing towards the predominantly intellectual aspect of the organism, the term has only a pertinent meaning when employed in a classification of mental functions, based, in turn, upon the framework of subjective states of consciousness or unconsciousness.

C. With the development of behaviourism in psychology, the status of the phenomena designated by cognition became controversial. Emphasis upon the conceptualization of directly observable phenomena and the tendency to conceive them within the framework of stimulus-response has eliminated the concept of cognition from a great deal of psychological theory and research. On the other hand, even among social behaviourists the possibility of treating cognitive phenomena as intervening variables tightly linked with overt action and the idea that behaviour has dimensions of organization that cannot be contained within the stimulus-response framework have led to the continued development of cognitive theory (cf. M. Scheerer, 'Cognitive Theory', in G. Lindzey (ed.), *Handbook of Social Psychology*, Cambridge: Addison-Wesley, 1954, vol. I, pp. 91–142). At the level of social psychology and sociology interest in cognition has centred on the sharing of cognitive culture and also the

conditions and consequences of cognitive disagreement among members of a group (cf. T. Parsons, *The Social System*, Glencoe, Ill.: The Free Press, 1951, pp. 326–83; and L. Festinger, *A Theory of Cognitive Dissonance*, Evanston, Ill.: Row, Peterson, 1957).

D. A recent development in the study of cognition has been the simulation of cognitive processes, including decision processes, through the use of computers. Although the term *cognition* is rarely if ever used in these studies, cognitive processes such as communication, control of behaviour through feed-back of information, 'thinking', and calculation of risk and probabilities are the focus of attention. In this work there has been the further effort to move from simulation of these processes in the machine to cautious generalization from the machine to the human being and the human group (see for example, W. Sluckin, *Minds and Machines*, Baltimore: Penguin Books, rev. edn., 1960).

D. R. Price-Williams

See also: AFFECT
COMMUNICATION
CONATION
CYBERNETICS
GAME THEORY
REASON

Cohesion

A. The use of this term among sociologists refers to a close alignment among the components of a collectivity—a use which parallels that of the more widely used term *integration*. *Cohesion* does not ordinarily have a specifically sociological definition framed in terms of group properties. On the other hand, the socio-psychological use of the term *cohesiveness* is well established, and it would seem impractical to differentiate between *cohesion* and *cohesiveness*. Thus, it appears wise to give preference to the socio-psychological definition presented in the 'group dynamics' literature. This definition refers to the attraction which a group has for its members, taking into account all motivating forces, no matter whether originating inside or outside the individual, by which his feelings toward the group are affected. This formulation not only avoids duplication of a more strictly sociological conception of integration; it also suggests the empirical task of determining the extent to which cohesion varies with integration, a problem of significance to social psychologists and sociologists alike.

Collective Behaviour

B. Sociologists have made sporadic use of this concept to indicate the unitary quality of a collectivity. E. Durkheim uses the term in this fashion (*On the Division of Labor in Society*, trans. by G. Simpson, New York: The Macmillan Co., 1933, pp. 49–69). Being more specifically concerned with the unifying functions of social homogeneity, on the one hand, and of social differentiation, on the other, he seems to designate their joint product sometimes by the term *cohesion* and sometimes by presumably synonymous terms such as *integration* or *equilibrium* (q.v.). In fact, so broad is his notion of cohesion that it allows a formulation of socio-psychological import, namely in terms of 'the variable intensity of the forces which hold the individual more or less strictly attached to his group' (ibid., p. 148). The view of cohesion as a product of such forces, while only of incidental significance for Durkheim, many years later became characteristic of the socio-psychological approach to cohesion.

C. In the current socio-psychological literature, a frequently used version of the concept is *cohesiveness*. In this form, the concept plays a major role in the area of social psychology called *group dynamics* (q.v.), which is concerned with the functioning of groups in a total field of psychological forces. L. Festinger, S. Schachter and K. Back define 'cohesiveness' as 'the total field of forces which act on members to remain in the group' (*Social Pressures in Informal Groups*, New York: Harper & Brothers, 1950, p. 164). Apparently in the same sense, D. Cartwright and A. Zander use the often-quoted phrase 'attraction to the group' (*Group Dynamics*, Evanston, Ill.: Row, Peterson, 1953, p. 76). In the last analysis, the concept is concerned with the motivation of the individual to maintain his membership in a specified group.

Werner S. Landecker

See also: SOCIAL EQUILIBRIUM
SOCIAL INTEGRATION

Collective Bargaining (See **Bargaining**)

Collective Behaviour

A. *Collective behaviour* is that form of group behaviour which emerges and develops in undefined and emotional situations; it is marked by a process of interaction in which impulses and moods are aroused, spread, organized, and mobilized on specific objects of action. It should be distinguished from that form of group behaviour which, while collective, is organized in terms of established cultural norms and lines of social structure.

B. 1. In his article on 'Collective Behavior' (in E. R. A. Seligman (ed.), *Encyclopedia of the Social Sciences*, New York: The Macmillan Co., 1930, vol. III, p. 631), R. E. Park, the originator of the term, speaks of collective behaviour as the behaviour which results from any assemblage of human beings in which 'every individual ... is moved to think and act under the influence of a mood or a state of mind, in which each shares and to which each contributes'.

2. The term *collective behaviour* is in use chiefly among American sociologists, although it is being adopted increasingly by social psychologists and political scientists. It designates an *area* of group behaviour which seems to stand apart with a distinctive character. The nature of this area is suggested by the following kinds of groups and of group behaviour: collective excitement, social unrest, crowd behaviour, riots, manias, crazes, fads, mass alarms, mass hysteria, public revolts, protest movements, rebellions, primitive religious behaviour, reform movements, and revolutionary movements. It is believed that collective behaviour, as represented by such illustrative instances, has a common nature that distinguishes it from other forms of human group behaviour. This common nature consists of a combination of the following characteristics:

(a) The behaviour involves the participation of sizeable numbers of people who are caught in a process of lively interstimulation. They are led to develop common moods, impulses, and feelings which tie them together into a collectivity.

(b) The behaviour strikes against prevailing orderly forms of group behaviour. Since it is a challenge to, and a departure from, the existing norms and forms of group behaviour, collective behaviour cannot be explained in terms of such norms and forms. Thus the chief theoretical tools of sociology—the concepts of culture and social structure—are inadequate to account for collective behaviour.

(c) The behaviour is built up or forged in the relatively fluid or undefined situation in which it occurs. Starting usually as a spontaneous and unguided expression of impulse and feeling, collective behaviour may develop and take form along many diverse lines, depending on how the initial impulses and feelings are mobilized in the process of interaction taking place among the participants. The study of this process of interaction—which is not covered by pre-existing culture and social organization—becomes the chief interest of study.

Herbert Blumer

See also: CROWD
FAD
FASHION
MASS SOCIETY
SOCIAL INTERACTION

Collectivism

A. *Collectivism* denotes the beliefs, objectives, or methods of those who advocate comprehensive central political control over social (and especially economic) arrangements—or the extension of such controls.

B. 1. The term, as used extensively in Europe since the Basel Congress of the First Socialist International in 1869, and in Great Britain more particularly since the 1880s, has for many authorities a close affiliation to the term socialism (q.v.). It appears to have originally been employed to distinguish a third school of Socialist activity at the period of the Basel Congress—the other two schools being those of Proudhon and Marx. The intention was to offer a non-authoritarian form of socialism or communism. 'Collectivism, as Bakunin and his followers used the word, had reference to the local face-to-face group of co-operating producers and consumers: it had nothing in common with the later usage in which the word came to mean "State Socialism"—ownership by the great "collective" which was represented by the democratized State ...' (G. D. H. Cole, *History of Socialist Thought*, London: Macmillan, 1954, vol. II, p. 339). Cole also notes the distinction made by Kropotkin 'between two stages in the coming revolutionary society—collectivism and Communism. Collectivism, he says, is a transitional stage, during which the conception of ownership will survive and will take the form of ownership by the Communes (ibid., p. 354).

2. The term has been widened to cover (a) forms of socialist doctrine and control (particularly, but not only authoritarian forms) and (b) (mostly in a pejorative sense) doctrines, 'socialist' or not, which imply increased state intervention, especially in the economic sphere, i.e. state planning for the economy. In (b) the distinction between 'socialism' and 'collectivism' has been attempted by various writers either (i) on the ground that 'socialism' is but one instance of a species of doctrines and practice which may be called 'collectivism' or 'planning' (F. A. von Hayek, *Road to Serfdom*,

London: Routledge, 1944, p. 23); also 'Political collectivism is the belief that the aims of society are best achieved by conscious central direction' (F. A. von Hayek, *The Counter Revolution of Science*, Glencoe, Ill.: The Free Press, 1952, p. 92); or (ii) on the ground that collectivism as contrasted with individualism (q.v.) is a looser, more indefinite term than socialism—and that such a looser term is, for certain purposes, required, e.g. A. V. Dicey (*Law and Public Opinion in England*, London: Macmillan, 2nd edn., 1926, p. 64) says, 'A person may be a collectivist, that is to say entertain ideas which are not in harmony with the ideas of individualism ...'.

J. Gould

See also: COMMUNISM
SOCIALISM

Colonialism

1. (a) The term *colonialism* was used until recent times to indicate the Colonial practice or idiom, e.g. the phrase 'the place was going ahead' was described in 1887 as a 'colonialism'. Similarly, in the 1940s, H. J. Laski wrote '... Americans had an inferiority complex about Europe. ... There was a colonialism about their attitude' (*The American Democracy*, London: Allen & Unwin, 1949, p. 63).

(b) It was also used to denote the *system of government as generally applied to colonial possessions*. Thus A. V. Dicey in *England's Case against Home Rule* (London: John Murray, 1886), having distinguished between the federal and the colonial aspects, goes on to refer to federalism and colonialism. Thus he says 'English colonialism works well enough' (ibid., p. 273). This was distinguished at the time from *imperialism* (q.v.). The *Standard*, 20 May, 1889, describes the dominant political forces in South Africa as 'Colonialism, Republicanism and Imperialism'.

2. The term now refers to a state of inferiority or of servitude experienced by a community, a country, or a nation which is dominated politically and/or economically and/or culturally by another and more developed community or nation; applied especially when the dominant nation is European or North American, and the less-developed, a non-European people.

Three relevant points may be made in comment on this definition:

(a) The date of origin of this usage is roughly in the early 1950s. President Truman, writing of the 'Point Four Programme', used 'colonialism' in his memoirs (H. S. Truman, *Years of Trial*

Colony

and Hope, London: Hodder & Stoughton, 1956, p. 246, and *Year of Decisions*, London: Hodder & Stoughton, 1955, p. 196). Yet in 1949 his announcement of this programme referred not to colonialism but to imperialism—'the old imperialism—exploitation for foreign profit' (*Years of Trial and Hope*, p. 242).

By 1952, Lord Hailey had written ('A Turning Point in Colonial Rule', *International Affairs*, vol. 28, 1952, p. 181) 'That [colonialism] seems to be a term now used by the weaker national units in order to describe any action taken against their wishes by a stronger national unit'.

(b) (i) The political use of the term is directed especially at the practices of European powers with colonial territories. 'The older word, "Imperialism" ... the domination of one community by another ... applied ... to the expansive policies of Russia and China. Colonialism ... could be narrowed so as to apply to the "Colonial" powers (notably Britain and France)' (V. T. Harlow, ' "Colonialism" and the Transfer of Power', *United Empire*, September-October, 1956, pp. 189–92).

(ii) The greatest publicity for the new use was given at the Bandoeng Conference in April 1955. President Sukarno of Indonesia on 18 April referred to colonialism which, he said, 'has also its modern dress, in the form of economic control, intellectual control and actual physical control, by a small but alien community within a nation' (*Keesing's Contemporary Archives*, London: Keesing's Publications, 7-14 May 1955, col. 14181). The Russian Juridical Dictionary cites this conference as the first use of *colonialism* in this sense.

3. The term has been qualified and extended in such a way as to apply to the practice of powers other than the traditionally criticized European 'colonial powers', i.e. to the U.S.S.R., and more recently it has been applied to the interaction of Asiatic powers. Thus *The Times* (London, 13 January 1958, p. 7) quoted the Prime Minister of Pakistan as referring to 'the brown colonialism of India' (with regard to Kashmir).

H. Maddick

See also: ANTI-COLONIALISM
COLONY

Colony

1. In its broadest usage *colony* denotes a settlement of a body of citizens of one state in another country with administrative and/or constitutional connection between the parent state and the new settlement. This connection has traditionally been one which *subordinates* the colony to the parent state. Usually supreme legislative powers have been retained by the mother state—what Blackstone in his *Commentaries on the Laws of England* (1765-9) terms, 'the general superintending power of the legislature of the mother-country'.

While Blackstone made a distinction between the legal system of colonies acquired by peaceful means and those acquired by force, a more common distinction was between colonies in which permanent settlers were expected to multiply and expand, e.g. settlers in North America, and, say, the Spaniards and Portugese in South America, where a native population was subjected to the rule of foreigners who were expatriated only temporarily. The aspect of subjugation led Canada to substitute *Dominion* (q.v.) in 1865—a term adopted by other self-governing British colonies in 1907.

2. By World War II the meaning had shifted. *Colony* now meant a territory, subordinate in various ways—political, cultural, or economic—to a more developed country. Supreme legislative power and much of the administration rested with the controlling country, which was usually of a different ethnic group from the colony. Thus *colony* today denotes an underdeveloped country controlled to a varying degree by another state, usually European or North American.

H. Maddick

See also: ANTI-COLONIALISM
COLONIALISM
DOMINION

Colour Bar

A. In its most general and literal sense *colour bar* denotes a policy regulating the relations of social groups (especially social distance (q.v.) and the distribution of privileges) in terms of differences observed, or supposed, in skin pigmentation and/or 'race'.

B. There are *two* more specific usages:

1. One usage implies prejudice on the part of the group which imposes the policy.

(a) Here it has special reference to the policy of racial separation practised in a number of countries in which non-European groups are under the political control of Europeans or people of European descent. Such a policy may be formal and statutory (i.e. embodied in the legal and constitutional framework of the state) and/or informal and conventional. In such contexts the colour bar (i) ostensibly aims to keep persons of different race and culture, or allegedly different race and culture, from mixing too closely with each other; (ii) in actual effect it discriminates in favour of the politically dominant group aiming at ensuring the political supremacy of that group and its monopoly of most of the economic opportunities.

(b) Non-whites may erect a colour bar (or a counter colour bar) vis-à-vis 'whites'. Such a bar, where it occurs, is informal and conventional. Thus certain African and North American Indian tribes look down upon light-skinned persons, and educated Africans and American Negroes of the upper class sometimes practise a form of ostracism in relations with 'whites'.

2. The other usage which does not involve such prejudice but is rather aimed at protecting indigenous rights against possible encroachment by outsiders. For example, the British government did not allow land in its West African colonies to be bought by Europeans, and the Danes have kept out those who are not Eskimo from Greenland.

K. Little

See also: ACCOMMODATION
DISCRIMINATION
SEGREGATION

Commensalism

A. In human ecology, *commensalism* generally denotes a relation involving both *competition* (q.v.) and *co-operation* (q.v.) among those who participate in an integrated division of labour. When differentiated from *symbiosis* (q.v.) and used as a technical ecological concept, *commensalism* designates relations among men who occupy *similar* specialized positions within an integrated division of labour (q.v.).

B. The etymology of the term, from the Latin *com* (with or together) + *mensa* (table) + *ism*, meaning the relation of eating at a common table, provides by extension the biological and sociological meanings. In biology it refers to relations among organisms (either like or unlike) which ordinarily eat together. It implies some degree of reciprocal advantage. Social scientists rarely use commensalism as a means of describing group relations among plants or animals. A few of them specifically use the concepts for analysing group relations among men. Three of the latter are cited here:

1. T. L. Smith uses *commensalism* synonymously with *symbiosis*. More particularly, he uses both terms to designate a relation of mutual

aid such as is characteristic of pioneer settlements and other small neighbourhood groups (*The Sociology of Rural Life*, New York: Harper & Brothers, 1953, p. 523). Most authors who see no reason for distinguishing *commensalism* and *symbiosis* employ the latter concept and omit the former.

2. E. E. Bergel mentions 'commensality' as useful in analysing social class structure in that only persons of the same prestige level habitually dine together as friends, whereas members of higher strata exclude those of lower positions from this relation which implies intimacy and equality (*Urban Sociology*, New York: McGraw-Hill, 1955, p. 181).

3. *Commensalism* is differentiated from *symbiosis* and used critically as a distinct ecological concept by A. H. Hawley (*Human Ecology*, New York: The Ronald Press, 1950, p. 39). It designates relations among men who occupy *similar* specialized positions as producers or consumers within a division-of-labour structure. In contrast, *symbiosis* refers to relations among men who hold *different* kinds of functional positions within this structure. Commensal relations are predominantly competitive, although they also involve an underlying co-operation. According to Hawley, commensalism underlies 'categoric' groups (composed of similar members) as contrasted with 'corporate' groups (composed of dissimilar members and based on symbiosis), and these two kinds of groups together form the basic social structure of a complex human community (q.v.).

James A. Quinn

See also: COMMUNITY
COMPETITION
CO-OPERATION
DIVISION OF LABOUR
ECOLOGY
SYMBIOSIS

Commercial Law

The term *commercial law* has been used since the 18th century to describe in general terms those branches of law having reference to trade and commerce. *Mercantile law* and *business law* may be regarded as synonyms. The *law merchant* (the unusual position of the adjective derives from the Latin *lex mercatoria*) is generally used in an historical sense to describe the custom of merchants once applied in local courts such as customary Courts of Fairs and Boroughs and statutory Courts of the Staple. The law merchant was absorbed into the common law of England during the 18th century.

Commercial Law

There is no general agreement as to the precise extent of *commercial law* but most authorities would agree on the inclusion of some or all of the following branches of law:

1. (a) *Contract:* the law of contract has of course a wider concern than commercial dealings alone, but much of the more specialized branches of commercial law is based on the general principles of the law of contract. Since not all promises or agreements are recognized by, or enforceable in, the courts of law, the aim of this subject is to ascertain what promises are legally enforceable or have other legal effect, what meaning such promises have, and what legal results follow from carrying them out, or failing to carry them out, in different circumstances.

(b) *Agency:* an important sub-division of the law of contract is formed by those rules which enable one person to enter into a contract in the name of, or on behalf of, another, and which prescribe the legal effect of this situation.

2. *Goods:* of the branches of law concerned with business dealings with goods, the most important are:

(a) *The sale of goods:* 'the supreme object of commerce is the sale of goods' (H. W. Disney, *The Elements of Commercial Law*, London: MacDonald & Evans, 1908, p. 3). The basic principle of the law is that the legal effect of a contract for buying and selling goods, whether written or oral, is a matter for agreement by the parties themselves. In the absence of such an agreement the law governs the passing of the ownership of (or the 'property' in) the goods from seller to buyer; the performance of the contract by each (including detailed rules as to delivery and payment); the terms of the contract (including the obligation of the seller to supply goods of the proper nature and quality); and the remedies of each party if the other defaults. In England and Scotland many of the rules, originally laid down by the courts in decided cases, are now to be found in the Sale of Goods Act, 1893. Many of the United States had adopted the similar Uniform Sales Act. Since 1954 nineteen of the United States have adopted the new and comprehensive Uniform Commercial Code.

(b) *Bailment:* this branch of the law deals with the situation where one person ('the bailee') is in possession of goods belonging to another ('the bailor'). Common examples are hire, and storage or warehousing. In England 'hire purchase' is a bailment where the bailee may become the owner of the goods; it is dis-tinguished from a sale of goods on credit terms ('credit sale' or 'instalment sale') by the fact that the bailee is not necessarily in breach of contract if he fails to acquire the property in the goods.

(c) *The carriage of goods:* this is a special type of bailment, of great importance, especially in regard to carriage by sea (or 'the contract of affreightment' as it is sometimes called). Closely associated with this branch of the law are 'marine insurance' and the general rules regulating merchant shipping.

3. *Finance:* commercial transactions depend today on an elaborate financial organization, and branches of law include:

(a) *Banking law:* the legal rules governing the relationship between the bank and its customer, and between one bank and another, although based largely on general principles of the common law, now form a highly specialized subject, closely allied to negotiable instruments.

(b) *Negotiable instruments:* these rules govern the transfer by one person to another of documents representing abstract legal rights, or the right to the payment of money, the most common of which are cheques and other bills of exchange, the law as to which was codified in England and Scotland by the Bills of Exchange Act, 1882, and in the United States by the Uniform Negotiable Instruments Law.

(c) *The contract of guarantee or suretyship:* this is a contract whereby one person undertakes liability in the event of another's failure to carry out a specified obligation.

(d) *Insurance:* this, too, is a special type of contract, involving a promise by one person or a body of persons ('the insurer') to pay money to another ('the insured') on the occurrence of a specified event which may cause loss to the insured. Except in the case of insurance against death or personal injury, the general principle is that the insurer is not bound to pay more than the value of the loss suffered by the insured.

4. *Business organization:* there are two main ways in which persons may associate together for the purpose of carrying on a business:

(a) *Partnerships:* as against other persons, the rights and obligations of the partnership (or 'firm') are those of all the individual partners; as between the partners themselves, the rights and obligations are, in the absence of contrary agreement, prescribed by the law. In England and Scotland most of the rules are to be found in the Partnership Act, 1890.

(b) *Corporations:* in England an association of persons may acquire a separate legal personality, distinct from that of its members, only by a grant from the State. This grant may be by Royal Charter or by a special Act of Parliament, but the common method adopted by commercial associations is by registration under the Companies Act, 1948 (or an earlier Act). This branch of the law is commonly called 'company law' in England and Scotland, and corresponds with the American *corporation law*.

5. *Insolvency:* sometimes regarded as a branch of commercial law are those rules relating to a person's inability to pay his debts as they fall due, a condition known as *insolvency*. In some cases court proceedings of a special type may be taken whereby the administration of the insolvent's property for the benefit of his creditors is undertaken under the control of the court, and the insolvent is subject to certain legal disabilities: this is known as *bankruptcy*.

A. L. Diamond

See also: CONTRACT
LAW

Commission

A. *Commission* may refer either to a certificate of office or to a body of men to whom some public function has been entrusted.

B. 1. In the first sense, i.e. a certificate of office, a commission is 'letters-patent granted by the government, under the public seal, to a person appointed to an office, giving him authority to perform the duties of his office. The commission is not the office, but only evidence of it, and, as soon as it is signed and sealed, vests the office in the appointee' (*Bouvier's Law Dictionary*, Baldwin's Student edn., Cleveland: Banks-Baldwin Law Publishing Company, 1946).

2. The second usage of *commission* to denote a group of men jointly performing a public function has not been formulated with precision. Legislatures and chief executives that create and name agencies have not developed a nice discrimination among *commission*, *board*, and *committee*. In the U.S.A. the President's *Committee* on Administrative Management had much the same task as the later *Commission* on Organization of the Executive Branch of the Government; the National Labor Relations *Board* has the same legal status as the Federal Trade *Commission*.

(a) In the United States the principal usages of *commission* are three: (i) *commission government*, a form of local government organization;

(ii) the *independent regulatory commission;* and (iii) the temporary *commission of inquiry* to study and report.

(i) Under the commission form of local government the voters elect usually five commissioners who collectively serve as the municipal legislative body and individually serve as heads of particular administrative departments.

(ii) The independent regulatory commission is defined by R. E. Cushman (*The Independent Regulatory Commissions*, New York: Oxford University Press, 1941, p. 4) as 'any commission, board, or authority which lies outside the regular executive departments and which has for its major job the exercise of some form of restrictive or disciplinary control over private conduct or private property'. M. H. Bernstein has identified seven agencies that qualify for the category, and groups them as follows (*Regulating Business by Independent Commission*, Princeton: Princeton University Press, 1955): two which regulate transportation carriers (the Interstate Commerce Commission and Civil Aeronautics Board), two which regulate other utilities (the Federal Power Commission and Federal Communications Commission), and three which regulate practices in special fields (the Federal Trade Commission, National Labor Relations Board, and Securities and Exchange Commission).

The independent regulatory commission is an anomaly in a government constitutionally committed to the separation of powers (q.v.). It combines legislative, judicial, and executive functions. It is statutorily protected against direct control by the President. Typically this is achieved by requiring that no more than a bare majority of the members of the commission be members of the same political party, by providing terms of office longer than the President's, by staggering the terms so a majority of the positions on a commission do not become vacant in one President's term, and especially by protecting commissioners against presidential removal save for inefficiency, neglect of duty, or malfeasance in office. In American state governments the members of some regulatory commissions are popularly or legislatively elected.

(iii) Temporary commissions of inquiry are established by Congress, the President, or both, typically are composed of men and women of considerable distinction in the country, assemble small staffs or rely upon existing agencies for staff work, in some cases hold hearings and

Committee

request written submittals of views of interested persons and organizations, and conclude their work with the publication of a report on the subject assigned them. Illustrative are the President's Commission on Immigration and Naturalization (which reported in 1953), the first and second Commissions on Organization of the Executive Branch of the Government (1949 and 1955), and the Commission on Intergovernmental Relations (1955). While the first was a presidential creation, the others named were established by act of Congress and some of their members were appointed by the President of the United States, some by the President of the Senate, and some by the Speaker of the House of Representatives; further, members of Congress were among those appointed.

(b) In British practice the *Royal Commission* is the most important example of the term's use. However, its prestige rather than its subject-matter assignment or quality of contribution is what distinguishes it from advisory bodies appointed by a Minister heading a department or by any other high official of the Government. The Lord High Chancellor's Committee on Minister's Powers (1932) and Committee on Administrative Tribunals and Enquiries (1957) are hardly less significant than, say, the Royal Commission on the University of Durham (1935). According to H. Finer, 'A Royal Commission is, in legal form, a command by the Crown, on the initiative and responsibility of ministers or a minister, requiring that certain persons named shall examine into a subject of inquiry, which is then stated in what are called the Terms of Reference' (*Governments of Greater European Powers*, New York: Henry Holt, 1956, p. 124). Though basically similar to the American commissions of inquiry already described (which are often consciously imitative of the British model), the British Royal Commission fills a more obvious need. This is because committees of Parliament lack the specialization and time for the exhaustive inquiries often undertaken in the United States by standing and special committees of the Congress.

Both in the U.S.A. and in Britain an occasional commission of inquiry has its origin in diversionary and dilatory political tactics. Its creation may be a partial concession to heavy pressure for action, while at the same time it postpones decision. A commission may also 'depoliticalize' a critical issue, partly because the commission's procedure and tone of report appear fair and judicious, and partly because its membership is usually either bipartisan or 'neutral'.

C. The term is also used in the titles of specialized agencies of the U.N. both *functional* (e.g. the Commission on Human Rights, the Commission on Narcotic Drugs) and *regional* (e.g. the Economic Commission for Europe, the Economic Commission for Asia and the Far East, set up by the Economic and Social Council of the U.N.).

James W. Fesler

See also: COMMITTEE

Committee

A. The term *committee* denotes a body of persons charged with some specific function or functions. There appear to be three qualifying characteristics, namely that:

1. This body should, in some sense, be derivative from, or dependent upon, another, and usually larger body. The etymology of the word itself suggests that it is a body to which something has been *committed*.

2. It is usually smaller than the body from which it derives its status.

3. Usually the procedure in a committee is more informal than procedure in the body from which it derives.

B. There are, however, cases where a committee is constituted by the parent body resolving itself 'into a committee'. For example, it is not uncommon for local councils in Britain to resolve themselves into a committee in order to ensure secrecy of their proceedings.

The most striking example of a committee whose personnel is identical with that of its parent body, is the Committee of the Whole House in the Parliament of Great Britain, and, of course, in parliaments modelled upon it. The Committee of the Whole House is defined in T. E. May (*Parliamentary Practice*, G. Campion & T. G. B. Cocks (eds.), London: Butterworth, 15th edn., 1950, p. 579) thus: 'It is, in fact, the House itself in a less formal guise, presided over by a chairman, instead of by the Speaker, and conducting its business according to more flexible rules of procedure. For instance, a Member may speak more than once to the same question, and a motion does not require a seconder'.

This particular sitting of the House has two of the three characteristics mentioned above, viz.: (a) it uses a freer procedure than the

House as such, and, (b) it has to report to the House as such after its deliberations have been concluded. What then of the third characteristic, viz. size? When the practice was begun, it was not anticipated that all members of the House would, *in fact*, be present to discuss and to deliberate; and the reason for having a committee of the *whole* House instead of some smaller and representative committee was that by making the nominal position of a committee as large as possible one guarantees that there is a large attendance. This practice of making committees much larger than mere despatch and efficiency would dictate is frequently followed today for precisely the same reason: namely, that if the committee is a small one, the members actually attending would be few and might even fall short of a quorum. In short, the Committee of the Whole is, in fact, smaller than the 'House'. For these reasons the Committee of the Whole House illustrates the three-fold characteristics above more than it invalidates them.

C. The word *committee* is often qualified by an adjective, and these adjectives fall into three main types:

1. Adjectives of the first type are descriptive of the parent body from which they derive. Among these is the *legislative committee*, for instance, the specialized functional committees of the Senate and the House of Representatives in the U.S.A., which have the duty of scrutinizing Bills and reporting thereon to the appropriate chamber and of instigating inquiries in the particular field with which they are concerned; and also the committees of the British House of Commons, viz.: the Committees of the Whole House (and its two special forms, the Committee of Supply, and the Committee of Ways and Means), the Standing Committees which consider Bills that have received their second reading, and the Select Committees to inquire and report, e.g. the Select Committee of Estimates (which is a sessional committee), or the Select Committee of the House of Commons Disqualification Bills, 1956, which is an ad hoc Select Committee, i.e. established for a specific task and then disbanded.

A second type is the departmental committee, e.g. Departmental Committee of Allotments (1922).

A third type is the local authority committee, e.g. in Britain, local authorities operate through a system of Committees, some of which are *permissive*, i.e. it is within the discretion of the local authority to set them up or not, and others

of which are *statutory*, i.e. they must be established by statute.

2. Adjectives of the second type are descriptive of the work the committees perform. K. C. Wheare (*Government by Committee*, Oxford: Oxford University Press, 1955, p. 2) classifies committees into six types, viz.: 'committees to advise, committees to inquire, committees to negotiate, committees to legislate, committees to administer and committees to scrutinize and control'. Broadly speaking, this classification is consistent with the previous classification. For instance, a local authority's committees might well contain samples of all these six types. The only difficulty in joining the two classifications lies in Wheare's fourth type, viz.: committees to legislate. It might have been just as well to substitute the term *committees to deliberate* rather than the term *to legislate* (strictly speaking, the Standing Committees of the House of Commons, do not, in fact, legislate). If, then, the expression 'committees to deliberate' be substituted for 'committees to legislate' above, the foregoing six-fold classification of committees according to the functions they fulfil can be used in conjunction with the three-fold classification in (1) above.

3. Adjectives of the third type are descriptive of the operational role of the committees. This classification relates to the part played by committees which administer. First of all, one may make a two-fold distinction into territorial committees and into functional committees. The quality of the first is that their work, whatever this may be, is circumscribed territorially. Examples of this would be a Divisional Health Executive of a British local authority, this executive being formally a sub-committee of the local council, which sub-committee has specific duties relating to health which it carries out within a circumscribed territory. The second class of committee, the *functional* committee may be divided into two classes, viz.: *horizontal* and *vertical*. The *horizontal* committee is one which is entrusted with some particular part of several different services, e.g. finance, establishments, whilst the vertical committee is a committee which supervises a single service or group of services, e.g. the Education Service, the Fire Service. It will be seen that a committee can be both functional and territorial as in the example of the functional health executive quoted above, which administers *one* service for *one* particular area.

D. Many bodies are committees according to

Commodity

the definition given above, but go by different names. For example, some go by the name of council, e.g. the Council of Foreign Relations (U.S.A.), or the Whitley Councils in Great Britain. Some go by the name of bureau, and some by the name of panel. Two recent synonyms for committees are *working party* (Great Britain) and *task force* (U.S.A.). The former derives from British military usage, meaning a party of people sent out under supervision to go and perform some duty; the latter derives from American military terminology designating some force which is assigned a particular operational role. It is difficult to see what purpose is served by these demotic neologisms, other than to give a false air of informality and egalitarianism to bodies that in every respect could perfectly well be designated (and indeed are) *committees*.

One particularly confusing synonym for committee is the expression *commission* (q.v.). There are legal differences between the British *Royal* Commission and other kinds of committee, but apart from this the words *commission* and *committee* are frequently used without any clear distinction between them. For instance in the UNO there exist a Committee of Information from Non-Self-Governing Territories, and a Commission on the Status of Women; and the former receives annual reports based on information supplied by the latter.

E. A *sub-committee* is a body standing in much the same relationship to a committee as a committee stands in relationship to the parent body.

S. E. Finer

See also: COMMISSION

Commodity

A. No single, clear-cut definition of commodity is in use because of differences on the inclusion of free goods and on the inclusion of services. Present-day economists tend to use the phrase *goods and services* rather than the word *commodity*. *Commodity* is, however, sometimes used in a meaning very close to that given it by W. S. Jevons: 'By a commodity, we shall understand any object, substance, action or service which can afford pleasure or ward off pain' (*The Theory of Political Economy*, London: The Macmillan Co., 4th edn., 1924, pp. 37–8). In all cases the element of usefulness with respect to human needs is present in the meanings.

B. Several similar but not identical uses of the term *commodity* can be distinguished.

1. Many writers have used the word in such a manner as to indicate clearly that a commodity was *any* useful article including free goods. Hence in this meaning air is a commodity.

2. The British classical economists, on the other hand, often use the word as a synonym for *economic good*, i.e. one that is scarce enough to require a price. Thus A. Smith wrote, 'Every commodity besides is more frequently exchanged for and thereby compared with other commodities' (*The Wealth of Nations*, London: Methuen, 5th edn., 1930, bk. 1, ch. 5, p. 33). Thus Smith thought of commodities as economic goods, having an exchange value.

3. Because labour services were considered the wellspring of value by the classical economists, services were not classed as commodities by Smith and other classical economists. As the attitude toward the source of value shifted, so also did the question arise as to whether services having an exchange value, as opposed to material objects having an exchange value, should be considered as commodities. Here Jevons's statement, that 'by a commodity, we shall understand any object, substance, action or service which can afford pleasure or ward off pain', becomes relevant. In this statement he includes services which the earlier economists ordinarily did not. He also includes free goods and services, which, at least by implication, the earlier economists did not include.

4. In the American business community, *commodity* is often used in a way that indicates that the word applies especially to raw materials, e.g. commodity exchanges; but it is difficult to find any documentary sanction for this usage.

R. W. Pfouts

See also: ECONOMIC GOODS

Common Good

1. In its most general straightforward use *common good* has a distributive sense. The statement that (or inquiry whether) a certain institution, policy, etc., is 'for the *common good*', implies that 'it' is at least ultimately, for the good, i.e. the *well-being* of *every* member of the community or group under discussion.

2. (a) By a simple transition, *the common good* sometimes refers to *the institutions, policies, etc.*, which are or would be *for* the common good in (1) above. Similarly *a common good* may sometimes refer to *an* institution, etc., which is or would be *for* the common good in sense (1).

(b) In discussions, however, of general

principles of governmental action, 'government for the *common good*' seems to be readily accepted as a synonym for *impartial* government—evidently because, though it be logically possible that not everyone will benefit from the policies of an impartial government, such a government nevertheless *considers* the good of everyone equally. The distinction between this use of *common good*, and the general use in (1) above, seems to be recognized, a little obscurely, in J. Laird's remark (*A Study in Moral Theory*, London: Allen & Unwin, 1926, p. 241) that 'the phrase ... is radically ambiguous, since it may mean either the good which is common to each (or at least to a majority which takes heed of the minority interests as well as of its own), or the good of the community organized as a whole'.

(c) A special and perhaps artificial use of *common good* seems to date back to T. H. Green (*Prolegomena to Ethics* (1883), Oxford: Clarendon Press, 2nd edn., 1884; *Principles of Political Obligation*, London: Longmans, Green, 1913). Green held that *virtue* is man's highest good, so that conduciveness to virtue is the test of right action, including governmental action. But he linked this with the customary formula that government should be 'for the common good' (i) by assuming that this formula means that government should promote '*a* common good', and (ii) by suggesting that virtue is such a common good, is 'the only truly common good' (this latter assertion Green justified on the somewhat heterogeneous grounds that virtue is (a) a non-competitive good, (b) the same good in and for everyone, (c) promotable, or realizable, only in society). Writers directly or indirectly referring back to Green, even when critical of him, seem to have been influenced (i) into writing as if '*a* common good' (and not '*the* common good') were the *standard* phrase, and (ii) into taking 'common good' not in the sense of 'something that is *for* everyone's good', but rather in the sense of 'an ultimate good that is essentially "common" in character'. This development has caused difficulty, as may be seen in E. F. Carritt (*The Theory of Morals*, London: Oxford University Press, 1928, ch. 7), J. Laird (*The Device of Government*, Cambridge: Cambridge University Press, 1944, pp. 138–40), and especially J. D. Mabbott (*The State and the Citizen*, London: Hutchinson's University Library, 1948, pp. 86–94), who discuss in some perplexity the question whether any kind of ultimate good can properly or usefully be described as a 'common' good. It may be questioned whether this 'difficult' concept is, as these writers appear to assume, involved in the ordinary uses of *common good*.

(d) J. Laird (ibid., p. 241) suggests that 'common good' besides having 'a distributive sense' (sense (1) above) has also 'a collective sense', because an organization, e.g. a state, may be in a condition, e.g. military powerfulness, which neither is nor can be a condition of any of its members individually but which these members regard as a good condition of the *organization*.

Perhaps it may be doubted, however, whether the good condition of an organization, thus understood, is ever *naturally* described as a common good, or as being for the common good, except where it is also for the good of the members individually.

(e) Terms sometimes synonomous with *common good* are *public welfare*, *public good*, and *public interest*.

J. M. Brown

See also: WELFARE

Common Law (See Civil Law)

Common Property (Communal Property)

Common or communal property in its comparatively rare, pure form denotes that which is held collectively by a group as against others, and in which there are no individual or sectional rights (e.g. tribal territory among the lower hunting peoples is held in this way). But with the advance of economic techniques it is increasingly usual to find recognition of individual or family rights within the tribal territory, or even the limitation of strictly common ownership to certain woodlands or pastures (cf. L. T. Hobhouse, G. C. Wheeler & M. Ginsberg, *The Material Culture and Social Institutions of the Simpler Peoples*, London: University of London, 1930, pp. 243–53). In so far, however, as 'title ... has a community character' and the relation of individual and family to the land is 'usufructuary rather than absolute' (C. K. Meek, *Land, Law and Custom in the Colonies*, London: Oxford University Press, 1946, p. 26) it seems reasonable to speak of 'common' or 'communal' ownership.

Jean Floud

See also: PROPERTY

Commonwealth

A. The most common usage of *commonwealth* today is in the phrase 'the Commonwealth of

Commonwealth

Nations', or 'the Commonwealth', used to describe the association between Britain, Canada, Australia, New Zealand, India, Pakistan, Ceylon, Ghana, Nigeria, and Malaya.

1. In this context the term dates from the 1880s and 1890s, and the search for a way of describing the self-government colonies within the British Empire. The first use of 'commonwealth of nations' seems to have been by Lord Rosebery in 1884; it was given wider circulation in the decade before World War I by Lionel Curtis, as a name for the form of Imperial Federation which he advocated.

2. The full term 'British Commonwealth of Nations', used by General Smuts in 1917 to describe Britain and the Dominions (by which name the self-governing colonies had been known since 1907), was given official sanction in the Anglo-Irish Treaty of 1921 (see N. Mansergh, *The Name and Nature of the British Commonwealth*, Cambridge: Cambridge University Press, 1954, pp. 1–5). It achieved official explanation in 1926, when the Imperial Conference laid down (through the pen of Lord Balfour) that Britain and the Dominions were 'autonomous Communities within the British Empire, equal in status, in no way subordinate one to another in any aspect of their domestic or external affairs, though united by a common allegiance to the Crown, and freely associated as members of the British Commonwealth of Nations' (Cmd. 2768, London: H.M.S.O., 1926, p. 14). On this interpretation, the Dominions and Britain formed the British Commonwealth of Nations, which, along with Britain's colonial territories and India, comprised the British Empire. The essence of the position was that the Dominions were accorded equal status with Britain, with full sovereign rights; but there were doubts about what connections between them were implied by 'common allegiance' and 'free association'. *The Statute of Westminster* (1931) gave legal force to the situation.

3. Since 1926 the British Commonwealth of Nations has evolved into the Commonwealth of Nations by a process in which it has become clear that now (a) common allegiance on the part of the states which recognize the Queen as their Head of State does not involve either a common foreign policy or a common attitude to peace and war; (b) free association includes the right of members to dissociate or secede; (c) republics, and countries with other Heads of State than the Queen, can be members of the Commonwealth, as long as they recognize the Queen as Head of the Commonwealth, as the symbol of the free association of member-nations; (d) membership involves no obligations except the recognition of a symbol, and the practice of consultation with other members when it seems appropriate. The Commonwealth of Nations is thus an association of sovereign states, comprising Britain and a number of other countries which were formerly her dependencies. Each is separately sovereign; although they recognize the Queen as Head of the Commonwealth, this symbolic function carries with it no common sovereignty.

B. 1. The term began as a synonym for the public welfare, and as an approximate translation of the Latin *res publica*. In the 16th century it was current in two meanings which frequently blended into one: it meant (a) the common good (q.v.); (b) a free community organized on the principle of the common good (see W. K. Hancock, 'A Veray and True Comyn Wele', *Politics in Pitcairn*, London: Macmillan, 1947, p. 95). In the second of these senses the word was used as an alternative for state (q.v.), but always with distinct overtones of public benefit.

2. When the reign of the Stuarts came temporarily to an end in 1649, Parliament declared that it was setting up 'a Commonwealth and Free State' to take the place of the monarchy; and it was as 'the Commonwealth of England' that the country functioned without a king. This gave the word *Commonwealth* an association with *republicanism* (q.v.) which persisted for at least two centuries more. The association was not absolute: Locke used it to mean 'any independent community'; Johnson said a republican was 'one who thinks a commonwealth without monarchy the best government'; and Hallam called the Kings of England 'the chiefs of the English commonwealth'. Nevertheless, Sir George Cornewall Lewis's *Remarks on the Use and Abuse of some Political Terms*, which was first published in 1832 and from which these three examples are taken, equated commonwealth with republic to mean 'a general name for all governments in which the sovereign power resides in several persons, whether they be few or many' (ibid., edn. of 1898, p. 68).

3. By the end of the 19th century, *commonwealth* could once again be accommodated to monarchy: the Commonwealth of Australia was established in 1901 as an integral part of the British Empire. At the same time, the Socialist movement retained something of the original sense of the term, in its demands for a 'co-operative Commonwealth' and a 'Socialist

Commonwealth'. Recent usages of the term to describe a particular state can be found in the Commonwealth of the Philippines (between 1934 and 1946) and the Commonwealth of Puerto Rico (since 1952). In both cases no monarchical element is present: the usage, under strong American influence, looks back to the 17th century and echoes the fact that Commonwealth is the official designation of four American states—Massachusetts, Pennsylvania, Virginia, and Kentucky.

C. The overtones of active public benefit which the word had in its application to a single state became fainter when it was applied to an association of sovereign states which proved to have frequently divergent interests. The notions of unity and common good can be used only with caution about the Commonwealth of Nations. Nevertheless, the sense of mutual goodwill inherent in the word has some relevance to the intimacy and confidence which mark the relations of most members of the Commonwealth.

J. D. B. Miller

See also: DOMINION
STATE

Communal Property (See Common Property)

Communalism

There are three distinct usages of *communalism*: the first and second may be regarded as obsolete; the third is the most recent and scientific.

1. In European discussions, the word was used to describe a system whereby communes, or similar small political entities, had considerable legislative powers delegated to them by the central government. It was used to describe both an existing state of affairs, and a form of government to be aimed at.

2. Following the Paris Commune of 1871, an adherent of the Commune was described as a Communalist.

3. In English in the 20th century, the word has been used to describe 'the phenomenon of collision or tension between several communities coexisting on a single territory' (W. K. Hancock, *Survey of British Commonwealth Affairs*, London: Oxford University Press, 1937, vol. I, p. 430). In this context, communities are regarded as based upon race, language or religion. Ambiguities arise in *defining* the communities. In practical politics, a community is one which, by reason of race, language, reli-

gion, or historical memory, *considers* itself to be one, and acts accordingly.

The phrase gained currency through the practice of providing separate representation for Hindus, Muslims, and other communities in British India, especially under the Morley-Minto reforms of 1909. It has been used also to describe conditions in such places as Ceylon, Palestine, East Africa, and even Northern Ireland and Canada (see, e.g. Sir I. Jennings, *The Approach to Self-Government*, Cambridge: Cambridge University Press, 1956, ch. II).

J. D. B. Miller

See also: COMMONWEALTH

Communication

A. While definitions of *communication* vary according to the theoretical frame of reference employed and the stress placed on certain aspects of the total process, they all include five fundamental factors: (a) an initiator, (b) a recipient, (c) a mode or vehicle, (d) a message, and (e) an effect. Thus in its most general form *communication* denotes a process in which an initiator emits or sends a message via some vehicle to some recipient and produces an effect. Most definitions also include the idea of interaction in which the initiator is simultaneously or successively a recipient and the recipient simultaneously or successively an initiator.

1. In most definitions the initiator is an organism, as is the recipient. In recent work in communication engineering the initiator or the recipient may also be a physical system other than an organism. In some definitions 'true' communication is restricted to human beings, although the grounds for such restriction vary.

2. In those definitions applicable to all organisms the mode of communication may be any behaviour of the organism capable of stimulating response in another organism. In non-organic systems of communication, physical vehicles of different sorts may be employed.

3. There is considerable controversy over the nature of the message or meaning (q.v.) in communication and of the range of phenomena which may be embraced in the message, but there is the common element that the message somehow involves the vehicle's being able to direct the recipient's, and sometimes the initiator's, attention and behaviour to some range of phenomena beyond the vehicle. It is in this sense that signs (q.v.) and symbols (q.v.) are always involved in communication.

4. Communication always implies some sort of differential effect in the behaviour of the recipient, and, in some definitions, in the

Communication

behaviour of the initiator. Unless some differential effect in the behaviour of the recipient occurs, communication has not taken place.

B. Three broad approaches to the definition and study of communication can be discerned in the social sciences.

1. Sociologists and psychologists, together with biologists, have approached the study of communication through the comparative analysis of the behaviour of different species of animals including man. These studies, based on a broad conception of each of the components of communication, have not been so much concerned with the content of communication as with the levels of complexity of the behaviour involved in communication and the possibility of continuity among the various levels as one approaches the communication of men. Thus D. O. Hebb & W. R. Thompson ('The Social Significance of Animal Studies', in G. Lindzey (ed.), *Handbook of Social Psychology*, Cambridge, Mass.: Addison-Wesley, 1954, vol. I, pp. 537–40) classify communication by three levels of complexity:

(a) *Reflexive communication* is communication in which there is no objective evidence of purpose or intention on the part of the initiator although the recipient responds in a fashion that goes beyond the stimulus or vehicle. The stimulus or vehicle emitted by the initiator seems tightly linked as a response to some stimulus unrelated to the potential response of the recipient. Thus the alarm response of a primate may result in the flight of the group, but continues long after such flight has taken place. Therefore it seems reflexibly bound to the danger stimulus, but not related in a purposive sense to flight, for it does not cease with flight (see *phatic communication*).

(b) *Purposive but non-syntactic communication* is that communication in which 'the sender remains sensitive to the receiver's responses during sending, and by modification of his sending shows that his behaviour is, in fact, guided by the intention (expectancy) of achieving a particular behavioural effect in the receiver' (ibid., p. 538). The 'broken wing' behaviour of the grouse is purposive in this sense.

(c) *Syntactic communication*, present only in humans, is constituted by the capacity to combine and readily recombine representational acts (vehicles). Thus, according to Hebb and Thompson, language (q.v.) 'combines *two or more* representative gestures or noises purpose-

fully, for a single effect; and ... it uses the *same* gestures in different combinations for different effects, changing readily with the circumstances' (ibid., p. 539).

2. Some social psychologists and sociologists have confined their interest in communication largely to the study of language and the analysis of the vehicles and messages (signs, symbols, and their meanings) in communication, although they have also been interested in the functional effects of communication. A typical definition of communication is given by G. A. Lundberg, C. C. Schrag, & O. N. Larsen (*Sociology*, New York: Harper & Brothers, 1954, p. 360): 'Communication may be defined as the transmission of meanings through the use of symbols. When men interact by means of symbols they are engaged in communication. The sender and receiver of symbols have communicated, however, only if they identify themselves with each other's situation'. The vital elements in this definition revolve around the notion of shared meanings. Despite the fact that an effort has been made to give a behavioural base to the concept of shared meanings through the idea that what this means is that the vehicle has the capacity to call out the same learned response in both the initiator and the recipient, this approach to the study of communication through the analysis of meanings has, to date, been fundamentally antithetical to a rigorous behaviouristic study of language.

3. In recent years a new approach to communication in the social sciences has been borrowed from the work of communications engineers. This approach rather than concentrating on meanings and the functions of communication, or its levels of complexity, stresses the total process. In this approach 'Communication is said to occur when a source of messages transmits signals over a channel to a receiver at the destination. The transmitted signals usually have representative function and are combined according to rules agreed upon in advance by the source and the destination' (G. A. Miller, 'Psycholinguistics', in G. Lindzey (ed.), *Handbook of Social Psychology*, vol. II, p. 701). This framework for studying communication has been labelled 'information theory', and its proponents point out that not only human and animal, but also physical systems as well, may be analysed within this framework. Thus it could 'include the procedures by means of which one mechanism (say automatic equipment to track an airplane and to compute its probable future positions) affects another mechanism (say a guided missile chasing this airplane)' (C. E. Shannon & W. Weaver, *The Mathematical Theory of Communication*, Urbana: University of Illinois Press, 1949, p. 95).

Eugene L. Hartley

See also: MEANING
        SIGN
        SOCIAL INTERACTION
        SYMBOL
        SYMBOLISM

Communism

A. 1. Broadly *Communism* denotes the theory or practice of those social reformers who have advocated e.g. 'community living' free from hierarchical controls as well as the 'common' enjoyment of property, amenities etc.—either for the whole of a society or for its ruling elite. Some but not all of these reformers have been supporters of anarchism or syndicalism.

2. The term also is currently, and often loosely, used to describe the activities and beliefs of certain states or political bodies in many countries even where some such states or bodies do not describe themselves as 'communist'.

3. The term, in discussions within the U.S.S.R., denotes the *future* social conditions which state and party policy purports to create: to such conditions the present arrangements (socialism) are deemed a preliminary stage.

B. 1. The situations to which the first usage refers are many and various—ranging from the 'elite communism' proposed by Plato (on the model of ancient Sparta) or the life led by some of the 16th-century Anabaptists in Munster to the Hutterite communities of the New World, the phalansteries proposed by Fourier, and so on. Such are the social arrangements surveyed for the U.S.A., by A. E. Bestor (*Backwoods Utopias*, Philadelphia: University of Pennsylvania Press, 1950) and for Britain by W. H. G. Armytage (*Heavens Below*, London: Routledge & Kegan Paul, 1961). Such settlements were geared to egalitarian conditions of life—in the consumption of food, distribution of income with regard to need, etc.

2. Communism and Communist are used to describe the activities or policies of the governments of the U.S.S.R. and the Chinese People's Republic: the governments of the Warsaw Pact countries; other governments associated with them; and also political organizations which are outside the countries ruled by such governments but which support their aims and policies. Not all such governments or organizations call themselves communist. Thus, the terms 'popular democracies', 'workers' parties' are used instead; and in countries where communist parties have been banned they may operate under other names.

3. The terms, of course, have a long history—antedating their use in Marxian contexts.

(a) The word 'communist' (from the Latin *communis*) was not coined by any of the early socialist schools, but was first employed by the obscure secret societies which grew up in France under the July Monarchy (1830–48). By the end of the 1830s these societies were concerning themselves with social rather than with political reforms, and it was in connection with the latter that the expression 'Communauté' was used in 1839.

(b) The word 'Communiste' appeared in 1840, and was introduced into England in that year in the letters which the Owenite, John Goodwyn Barmby, was sending from France for publication in the *New Moral World*, when he used it with reference to the followers of Etienne Cabet, who had been much influenced by Owenism (*The New Moral World*, Leeds, 1840, vol. 1, no. 5, p. 75). 'Communisme' made its first appearance in 1841, and was thereafter used to designate the more proletarian and militant section of the Socialist movement.

(c) Thus it was that Marx and Engels gave the name 'Communist' to their famous manifesto of 1848, drawn up to provide a programme for the Communist League, which had grown out of one of the secret societies above mentioned. They pointed out that 'Communists do not form a separate party as opposed to other working-class parties', that 'they do not set up any sectarian principles of their own', and that they are simply 'the most advanced and resolute section of the working-class parties of every country, that section which pushes forward all others'. As Engels explained in the preface to the English edition of the Manifesto (1888) they 'could not have called it a *Socialist* Manifesto' because, at the time when it was written, the Socialists were either the adherents of one of the 'various Utopian systems' which were 'gradually dying out', or were 'social quacks' who were attempting to redress grievances 'without any danger to capital and profit'. Thus he declared that Socialism was a 'middle-class movement' whereas Communism was a 'working-class movement'. The one was regarded as 'respectable', and the other was not.

As late as the Gotha Congress of 1875, Marx objected to the use of the term 'socialist' in the

Community

name 'German Socialist Workers' Party' given to the union of his followers with those of Lassalle.

4. The Russian Marxists called their party 'Socialist', and it was not until the Seventh Congress of March 1918 that the Bolsheviks changed the name of their own from 'Social Democratic' to 'Communist', thus giving effect to a proposal made by Lenin a year earlier in his 'April Theses'. None the less, Lenin continued to describe the October Revolution and the economy it had set up as 'Socialist', since Marx had laid down that society must pass through this stage in its transition from capitalism into the 'higher stage' of Communism when it would at last become possible to apply the principle of 'From each according to his abilities to each according to his needs' instead of, as was necessary under Socialism, 'to each according to his work'. It should also be noted that in the period from 1918 to 1921 certain experiments in nationalization and distribution in Russia were styled *War Communism*—but they proved to be a transitory phase, followed by the New Economic Policy.

In a lengthy article in the *Large Soviet Encyclopaedia*, Moscow, passed for publication on 9 September 1953, *Communism* was described as 'the highest formation of society which replaces the capitalist formation', and which is reached through the 'lower formation' of Socialism—Socialism of the Soviet type being, of course, understood. In neither do there any longer exist hostile classes, seeing that 'exploitation'—the cause of the hostility—has disappeared with capitalism. The transition into Communism will be effected by strengthening the Socialist order and without a revolution. Under Communism, the means of production will be common property, everyone will work with selfless devotion and the state, represented at that time by Stalin as the instrument which is guiding society to its final goal, will have 'withered' away. The inevitability of this *dénouement* is then shown to be attested by the Marxist-Leninist 'scientific' demonstration of the laws which govern the development of society.

The present position is set out in the Programme of the Communist Party of the Soviet Union as adopted by the Twenty-Second Party Congress on 31 October 1961: '*What is Communism? Communism is a classless social system with one form of public ownership of the means of production and full social equality of all members of society; under it, the all-round develop-*

ment of people will be accompanied by the growth of the productive forces through continuous progress in science and technology; all sources of public wealth will gush forth abundantly and the great principle "From each according to his ability, to each according to his needs" will be implemented. Communism is a highly organized society of free, socially conscious working people in which public self government will be established, a society in which labour for the good of society will become the prime vital requirement of everyone, a necessity recognized by all, and the ability of each person will be employed to the greatest benefit of the people' (Supplement to *New Times*, no. 48, 29 November 1961, p. 27). The same document later observes 'The main economic task of the party and the Soviet people is to create *the material and technical basis of communism* within two decades' (ibid., p. 29).

These and other passages in the Programme raise many questions relative to the role both of the State and the Communist Party under these future conditions (see ibid., p. 43 et seq. for the official Soviet view on the role of the State; also L. Schapiro (ed.), *The U.S.S.R. and the Future*, New York: Praeger, 1962).

R. N. Carew Hunt
J. Gould

See also:　ANARCHISM
SOCIALISM
SYNDICALISM

Community

A. After reviewing 94 definitions of *community*, G. A. Hillery reaches the conclusion that 'beyond the concept that people are involved in community, there is no complete agreement as to the nature of community' ('Definitions of Community: Areas of Agreement', *Rural Sociology*, vol. 20, 1955, p. 119). Although the term has been variously employed as a synonym for *society, social organization*, or *social system*, many writers agree that it has a specific territorial locus, often limited in character. And this appears to be the way it is most commonly used by researchers. If we accept this perspective, a modification of T. Parsons's definition in *The Social System* (Glencoe, Ill.: The Free Press, 1951, p. 91) has much to recommend it: a community is a collectivity of actors sharing a limited territorial area as the base for carrying out the greatest share of their daily activities. This definition implies that persons interact within a *local* institutional complex which provides a wide range of basic services, yet it also takes into consideration the fact that the community is not necessarily a self-sufficient unit.

B. Some writers employ the term *community* without formally defining it, but appear to equate it with *society, group, social system*, and *social organization*—e.g. W. J. Goode ('Community Within a Community: The Professions', *American Sociological Review*, 1957, vol. XXII, pp. 194–200). R. A. Nisbet (*The Quest for Community*, New York: Oxford University Press, 1953) seems to use community synonymously with society or social system, but he also makes the additional qualification that integration or a 'sense of belonging' characterizes a community.

C. Most writers assume that a community has a specified territorial base. Within this context there are still variations in usage:

1. Some sociologists view the community in biological rather than in socio-cultural terms. Thus E. C. Hughes describes community, in contrast to society, 'in terms of *competition, symbiosis*, and the *division of labor* by which it gains sustenance from its environment' ('Institutions and the Community', in R. E. Park (ed.), *An Outline of the Principles of Sociology*, New York: Barnes & Noble, 1939, p. 310).

2. Other sociologists view community in both biological and socio-cultural terms.

3. Still others define community only in socio-cultural terms. Among those who stress this orientation, a variety of social characteristics are emphasized in defining community. Some writers emphasize (a) subjective criteria such as identification, others (b) objective criteria. Still others employ combinations of these. According to B. E. Mercer, for example, 'A human community is a functionally related aggregate of people who live in a particular geographic locality at a particular time, share a common culture, are arranged in a social structure, and exhibit an awareness of their uniqueness and separate identity as a group' (*The American Community*, New York: Random House, 1956, p. 27).

D. A third issue involves specifying the boundaries of a community. G. P. Murdock et al. state, 'The term "community" connotes the maximal group of persons who normally reside together in face-to-face association' (*Outline of Cultural Materials*, New Haven: Yale University Press, 3rd rev. edn., 1950, p. 93). However, R. M. MacIver and C. Page, although acknowledging

the need for a territorial base, apply the concept community to such varying units as 'a pioneer settlement, a village, a city, a tribe, or a nation' (*Society: An Introductory Analysis*, New York: Rinehart, 1949, p. 8). Other writers utilize the term specifically to refer to a local unit which can be larger than that designated by Murdock but not so large as to include a nation or a region.

Gideon Sjoberg

See also: ECOLOGY
GROUP
SOCIETY

Company Law (See **Commercial Law**)

Comparative Cost Advantage
A. The principle of *comparative cost advantage* sets forth the conditions under which trade between two areas is of mutual economic advantage. In its present form, it can be stated succinctly in the following form: exchange beneficial to the areas concerned can take place when the cost ratios of producing any two commodities are initially different in the different areas in question. 'A country should expand or curtail the production of different commodities until her ratios of marginal cost are the same as those abroad and export the surplus or import the deficiency so generated' (R. F. Harrod, *International Economics*, New York: Pitman Publishing Corporation, 1947, p. 19).

B. The germ of the 'doctrine' or 'law' of comparative advantage dates back to Adam Smith when he said, '... if a foreign country can supply us with a commodity cheaper than we ourselves can make it, better buy it of them with some part of the product of our own industry, employed in a way in which we have some advantage' (*Wealth of Nations* (1st edn., 1776), London: Methuen, 5th edn., 1930, p. 422). This statement from Smith is a rather concise formulation of *absolute* advantage. To D. Ricardo, however, must go the credit for introducing the doctrine of *comparative* advantage into economics. Ricardo stated that trade would take place between nations when differences in cost of production were relative rather than absolute, for, to quote his example, '... exchange might even take place notwithstanding that the commodity imported by Portugal could be produced there with less labour than in England' (*Political Economy and Taxation*, London: John Murray, 1817, p. 159). Ricardo's formulation of the principle is that if trade is

115

Comparative Method

left free, each country in the long run exports those commodities in whose production it enjoys a comparative advantage in *labour costs*, and imports those commodities which could be produced at home only at a comparative disadvantage in labour costs.

Though the principle as formulated by Ricardo and other writers in the classical tradition was successful in repudiating mercantilism and in getting men of affairs to realize the advantages of free trade, it was unduly shackled by the limitations of the doctrine of the labour theory of value. As H. G. Brainard has said '... the [Ricardian] principle of comparative advantage, as an explanation of the reason for international trade, cannot be accepted ... because of the inadequacy of the labor theory of value as a tool of analysis. The classical doctrine of international trade is now primarily of interest only from an historical point of view, rather than a theory which gives acceptable answers to the questions of why trade takes place'. (*International Economics and Public Policy*, New York: Henry Holt, 1954, p. 127).

C. Modern economic theory answers the question of why trade takes place because of comparative cost advantage without reference to the labour theory of value (R. F. Harrod, *International Economics*, ch. 2; P. A. Samuelson, *Economics*, New York: McGraw-Hill, 2nd edn., 1951, pp. 694–701). The analysis is similar to the classical one in stressing the idea that trade occurs when goods can be purchased more cheaply away from home than at home; that such purchases are possible because of cost differences among nations and regions; and that the greatest gains occur from trading when specialization among nations is developed to a high degree. Here, however, similarity ends. The modern theory of comparative advantage includes analysis of the cost differences with respect to all factors of production and does not require that the cost-unit in one nation be identical with that in another. All that is required is that there be a unit of account within each nation for the measurement of production costs.

The following example may clarify the method of comparative cost advantage analysis: Suppose that the cost of producing 1 unit of steel in country A is equal to the cost of producing 1 unit of cloth, as measured by cost unit a; and that in a second country, B, the cost of producing 1 unit of steel is twice that of producing 1 unit of cloth, as measured by cost

unit b. Each cost measurement unit need make measurement possible by a common standard *only* within each country, and there need be no relationship between the measure used in country A with that of country B. Given such measurement it can be stated that, prior to trade between the two nations, 1 unit of steel in A traded for 1 unit of cloth, and in B, 1 unit of steel traded for 2 units of cloth. Both countries can gain by specializing and trading with each other. In country A, 1 unit of steel and 1 unit of cloth can be produced equally efficiently; while in country B, 1 unit of steel can be produced only one-half as efficiently as a unit of cloth. Country B, by giving up a unit of steel, can produce two units of cloth, and country A, by transferring resources from cloth to steel, produces as many units of steel as it gives up units of cloth. The advantages for country B are obvious, and A may profit both from increased specialization and from bargaining with B for part of the gain B achieves by giving up steel and producing cloth.

Bernard F. Sliger
Hubert Bice

See also: COST

Comparative Method

A. *Comparative method* is a general term denoting the procedures which, by clarifying the resemblances and differences displayed by phenomena (or classes of phenomena) deemed, on various criteria, to be 'comparable', aim at eliciting and classifying (a) causal factors in the emergence and development of such phenomena (or classes); (b) patterns of interrelation both within and between such phenomena (or classes).

B. The use of comparative methods in the study of social and historical data was not, of course, unknown at earlier times—the work of Vico and Montesquieu, among the 'precursors' of modern sociology, would suffice to show how central their use has been to the growth of the social sciences. But it was in the latter half of the 19th century that the use of the methods of comparison, in their application to social phenomena, came to be explicitly and articulately invoked. Methods of this kind had been employed with success in the late 18th century developments of the natural sciences by which Comte had been so much impressed. Comte himself insisted upon the use of such methods in what he designated as 'sociology'—such methods involving 'a rational comparison of different and independent coexisting states of human society scattered over the earth' (K. E. Bock, *The Acceptance of Histories*, Berkeley & Los Angeles: University of California Press, 1956, p. 6). The use of the method in later 19th-century sociology and anthropology was further encouraged by the significant uses to which it was put by Darwin and by students of the history of language. Darwin himself was well aware of the difficulty of using such methods to yield *historical* accounts of growth as distinct from morphologies based upon *contemporaneous* data. Such limitations were not always observed in the 19th-century application of such methods to social phenomena—with familiar pseudo-historical and evolutionary results. Though Comte himself was clearly aware of some of these pitfalls, his own use of the terms 'comparative or historical method' formed part of a philosophy of history in which implicit assumptions about man and society tended to outweigh analysis of, or concern with, empirical data (see K. E. Bock, ibid.); and in the work of anthropologists influenced by evolutionary ideas the comparative method was often loosely employed to yield elaborate and untenable conclusions. But, as M. Ginsberg points out, the use of the method neither proves nor implies the existence of genetic affinities or chronological sequences (*Studies in Sociology*, London: Methuen, 1932, p. 65 et. seq.). Nor were such affinities or sequences assumed in the work of all those who were influenced so fruitfully by Darwin (e.g. E. B. Tylor, 'On a Method of Investigating the Development of Institutions; Applied to Laws of Marriage and Descent', *Journal of the Royal Anthropological Institute*, vol. 18, 1889, pp. 245–6). Indeed, by 1906 the philosopher H. W. B. Joseph argued that 'what is called the *historical* or *comparative* method has in the last few generations revolutionised many branches of enquiry. It is but an application of the general principle of varying the circumstances in order better to discover the causes of a phenomenon' (*An Introduction to Logic*, Oxford: Clarendon Press, 1906, p. 522). And in the work of Durkheim and Hobhouse the use of the comparative method was explicitly regarded as at the core of theoretical and empirical sociology.

Something of a reaction set in with the growth of new techniques and approaches in modern social anthropology in the period after World War I. It was a response to the exaggerations and misapplications which marred much earlier use of the method. In some quarters it was deemed incompatible with the approach of 'functionalism' in that the functionalist approach insisted upon contextual analysis, whereas the comparative method had involved the comparison of social institutions torn from their contexts. Much of this debate between the two approaches now seems out of date and academic. In so far as extreme forms of functionalism insist, theoretically, on the uniqueness of social systems, the comparative method, in some of its earlier applications, is certainly minimized. But as R. Fletcher has argued, ('Functionalism as a Social Theory', *Sociological Review*, vol. 4, new series, 1956, p. 43) the functional approach in practice does 'seek to establish generalisations about the interrelationships of institutions in all societies *of certain types* ... to classify societies, to group them together in so far as they approximate to a certain type, and thereafter to compare like with like in the attempt to establish the existence of, or the absence of, certain uniformities'. Powerful support for the use of the comparative method in social anthropology came from S. F. Nadel, who stresses the need to examine social facts 'in the artificial isolation entailed in any comparison and increasing with its range' and insists that 'The anthropologist (or any scientist) whose motto is "never depart from contexts" ignores that we possess intellectual means for isolating elements from their settings without disastrous loss of meaning' (*Foundations of Social Anthropology*, Glencoe, Ill.: The Free Press, 1958, p. 228).

Few would claim, however, that contemporary work in comparative study has fully overcome some of the traditional difficulties, e.g. the problems of defining discrete units of study, of allowing for the different degrees of complexity and variability within such units, of establishing adequate criteria of comparability, and of ensuring that units selected for study have been selected on non-arbitrary grounds. In an evaluation of comparative anthropological work, I. Schapera has argued strongly for a more restricted application of the comparative method to 'an intensive study of a given region embracing all the peoples living there about whom information is available. By carefully comparing the forms taken among these people by the particular social phenomena with which we are concerned we try to establish, by a process of generalization, one or more basic types into which the various forms can be classified' ('Some Comments on Com-

Competition

parative Method in Social Anthropology', *American Anthropologist*, vol. 55, 1953, p. 359). Commenting upon Schapera's approach, M. Singer dissented from such a restrictive use of the method. Arguing that method is dictated by problem, he believed that Schapera had over-simplified the task of securing satisfactory 'basic types'. 'Where the aim is to give a com-prehensive survey of the kinship systems of all parts of the world, or of a large area, a method like that of intensive regional comparison is probably more appropriate—for other prob-lems and purposes other and perhaps novel methods and concepts will be required' ('Sum-mary of Comments and Discussion', *American Anthropologist*, vol. 55, 1953, p. 364).

J. Gould

See also: CULTURAL EVOLUTION
FUNCTION
HISTORICISM
IDEAL-TYPE ANALYSIS

Competition

A. In recent usage *competition* is that form of interaction which involves a struggle for goals which are scarce or are believed to be scarce; the interaction is normatively regulated, may be direct or indirect, personal, or impersonal, and tends to exclude the use of force and violence.

B. Since the time of C. H. Cooley, sociologists have drawn attention to the fact that the pur-suit of scarce ends which others are also pursu-ing may be carried on without awareness of the others, or if with awareness without conflict (q.v.). In his essay 'Personal Competition', Cooley wrote that 'competition is not neces-sarily a hostile contention, nor even something of which the competing individual is always conscious. ... It is eligibility to perform some social function that makes a man a competitor, and he may or may not be aware of it, or, if aware of it, he may or may not be consciously opposed to others' ('Personal Competition', in his *Sociological Theory and Social Research*, New York: Henry Holt, 1930, p. 165).

C. Strongly influenced by the biological and economic views of the late 19th and early 20th centuries, R. E. Park and E. W. Burgess (*Introduction to the Science of Sociology*, Chi-cago: University of Chicago Press, 2nd edn., 1924) made competition, *conceived as uncon-scious and impersonal*, the cornerstone of the field of human ecology (q.v.). They described

competition as 'the elementary, universal, and fundamental form' of interaction, and added that it is 'strictly speaking ... interaction with-out social contact' (ibid., p. 506). The function of competition was described as the creation of 'an impersonal social order in which each individual, being free to pursue his own profit, and, in a sense, compelled to do so, makes every other individual a means to that end' (ibid., p. 507). This was qualified, however, by the statement that 'in human society competition is always complicated with other processes [of interaction]' and that 'Competition among men ... has been very largely converted into rivalry and conflict', which were regarded as conscious and personal (ibid., pp. 506, 512).

D. Recent usage tends to broaden the meaning of *competition* to make it refer to the conscious or unconscious, personal or impersonal, pur-suit of scarce ends within a framework of rules. It tends to emphasize Cooley's point that where competition is impersonal, it is so because the individual is oriented toward the goal rather than toward his competitors. K. Young defines competition as 'a less violent form of opposition in which two or more persons or groups struggle for some end or goal but in the course of which attention is focused chiefly on reward rather than on the competitor' (*Sociology: A Study of Society and Culture*, New York: American Book Company, 1949, p. 64). Personal rivalry may still be considered competition, however, if it occurs under the governance of rules which exclude fraud and violence, and limit attention to the rival's relationship to the scarce goal. K. Davis makes this the key to his distinction between competition and conflict '... competition simply aims to outdo the com-petitor in achieving some mutually desired goal. ... It implies that there are rules of the game to which the competitors must conform and that behind these rules, justifying and maintaining them, is a common set of values superior to the competitive interest. It also implies an absence of coercion. ... The rules of competition limit the means that may be used. ... When competition breaks through the rules it transforms itself into conflict' (*Human Society*, New York: The Macmillan Co., 1949, p. 162).

E. Current psychological usage accepts the idea of scarce goals as characteristic of the competi-tive situation and does not concern itself explicitly with the questions of impersonality and normative regulation. For example,

L. Doob writes that, 'From a psychological viewpoint, competition involves a goal which, being scarce, cannot be shared by or appears unsharable to the individuals concerned' (*Social Psychology*, New York: Henry Holt, 1952, p. 210).

H. J. Friedsam

See also: CONFLICT
ECOLOGY
ECONOMIC COMPETITION
PROCESS

Complementary Filiation (See Descent)

Compromise

A. The term *compromise* has not developed any specialized meaning within any of the disciplines in the social sciences. It would therefore appear that the ordinary Webster dictionary definition is acceptable, that is, 'A settlement by arbitration or by consent reached by mutual concessions; a reciprocal abatement of extreme demands or rights, resulting in an agreement ...' However, the use of the word arbitration in this definition might be objectionable to some students of international law and relations, for reasons explained in B.3 below.

B. 1. In sociology the term denotes a sub-process of accommodation (q.v.) or a form of co-ordinate accommodation, in resolving or adjusting group conflicts. 'In order to avoid fruitless struggle the contestants may agree to a compromise. In compromise, each party to the dispute makes some concessions ...' (W. F. Ogburn & M. F. Nimkoff, *Sociology*, Boston: Houghton Mifflin, 1946, p. 376). The term appears to have received less attention in sociology in recent years (compare ibid., with the third edition of the same work in 1958).

2. Compromise as a form of accommodation in the political process has received considerable attention in the discipline of political science (see, for example, C. E. Merriam, *Prologue to Politics*, Chicago: University of Chicago Press, 1939, p. 55). Here the meaning is that covered by such political arrangements as The Great Compromise at the Philadelphia Convention during the formation of the United States Constitution or the Missouri Compromise of 1820 and the Compromise of 1850 in regard to the issue of slavery.

3. Public International Law and diplomacy differentiate between methods for the pacific settlement of disputes based on compromise (i.e. through a balancing of political factors) as opposed to those based on a legal decision. Negotiation (q.v.), good offices, mediation (q.v.), and conciliation (q.v.) are specific designations for types of pacific settlement which belong to the former group, whereas adjudication (q.v.) belongs to the latter. Some writers would include arbitration in the latter group. (P. E. Corbett, *Post-War Worlds*, New York: Farrar & Rinehart, 1942, pp. 152–3; L. Oppenheim, *International Law*, London: Longmans, Green, 7th edn., 1952, vol. II, p. 3 ff.). However, past practice has on occasion revealed that although arbitral decisions may be rendered on the basis of law they may also be based on compromises rather heavily influenced by political factors having little to do with adjudication.

Robert E. Clute

See also: ADJUDICATION
CONCILIATION
MEDIATION
NEGOTIATION

Conation

A. *Conation* has been used traditionally to emphasize the striving aspect of experience, manifesting itself in desires and impulses. It has been variously employed to represent the inception of purposive activity, the mental state accompanying a desire to act and the conscious tendency to act (H. C. Warren, *Dictionary of Psychology*, Boston: Houghton Mifflin, 1934).

B. 1. As with cognition (q.v.) the word has a meaning of theoretical importance when employed in the triadic classification of mental functions, originated by Plato and Aristotle, and later formulated by Tetens and Kant. The analogy presented by Plato (*Phaedrus*) of a charioteer who holds the reins, and two pairs of horses which draw the chariot, illustrates the difference between the guiding element of cognition, and the dynamic elements of affect and conation.

2. Again as with cognition, the co-ordinate term *conation* has been used variously, along with the third term *affect*, in different schemes of psychological schools. Perhaps the last time in which the term was used in an important theoretical manner was in 1918, when J. Ward published his book *Psychological Principles* (Cambridge: Cambridge University Press). Ward discarded the classical 'state of mind or consciousness' with the three sub-divisions of cognition, emotion, and conation, and substituted a division based upon the direction of attention.

Concept

Thus (a) where attention is determined non-voluntarily, where feeling follows the act of attention, Ward postulated a sensory or receptive attitude; and (b) where feeling precedes the act of attention, a voluntary determination of attention, Ward postulated a motor or active attitude. Conation is then fitted into this scheme by regarding it as coming under the latter type of direction of attention.

3. Ward's scheme, though now largely only of historical importance, has been outlined here to show the gradual displacement of the term *conation*. Attention has lost its theoretical importance, but the sensory and motor aspects of experience have endured under the modern framework of stimulus-response psychology. *Conation* therefore is still used in a loose generic sense to emphasize the 'inner' determinants of action, with the subordinate features of motives and dispositions or attitudes (q.v.) But analysis is focused upon motivation and the tendency to act while in no way using conation as a classification of some importance in contradistinction to other modes of experience.

D. R. Price-Williams

See also: AFFECT
COGNITION
MOTIVATION

Concept

A. In general usage the term mainly denotes 'idea' or 'notion'. It is envisaged as an abstract or psychological thing presupposing conscious minds which at least potentially 'have' the concept, i.e. understand it, operate with it, apply it, etc. In philosophy and the social sciences (and other sciences too) concepts enter as (a) the most general *tools* of inquiry as such and as (b) the content or object of some specific inquiries, notably in comparative studies. What follows refers principally to (a) rather than (b).

The nature of concepts, and their relation to the things 'of which they are the concepts', and to the minds which use or contemplate them, are among the most hotly disputed subjects in philosophy. The present definition is not intended to prejudge or settle any of these issues, even if limitations of space make it appear to do so.

B. Defined as an aspect of thought, a *concept* is a kind of unit in terms of which one thinks; a unit smaller than a judgement, proposition, or theory, but one which necessarily enters into these. In an assertion, something is predicated

of a concept, and the predicate itself can generally be re-described as a concept. At the same time, however, the concept is by no means an ultimate or indivisible unit, for concepts can be augmented or diminished by addition or subtraction of some feature. (For instance, one may say that someone's concept of social class does, or fails to, include the notion of differences in material rewards.) Moreover, while concepts occur *within* assertions or theories and are thus *distinct* from *them*, a *proposition or theory or thesis* as a whole can in turn be referred to as a further *concept*. For instance R. Firth writes that 'some of Dr. Leach's concepts are of a special order ... I refer to his thesis that seeking for power is the basis of social choice' (Foreword to E. R. Leach, *Political Systems of Highland Burma*, London: G. Bell, 1954, p. vii).

C. Concepts correspond to or '*are the meaning of*' all meaningful words, with certain qualifications: (a) only one concept corresponds to two or more words with the same meaning; (b) there is a tendency to speak of concepts only with regard to words which do, or at least can, refer either to something that can exist or be imagined or to an operation that can be performed, and not in connection with words whose role is grammatical rather than designative (for instance, one may speak of the concept of sovereignty, of infinity, of addition, but not of the concept of 'and'—though one must add that the drawing of the lines between these kinds of meaning is a difficult, unsettled, and controversial part of philosophy; (c) there is a tendency to speak of concepts in connection with general rather than singular terms (one is unlikely to speak of a 'concept of John' or of a 'concept of London'; in those cases the term 'conception' is more likely to be used. There are, however, exceptions, e.g. 'the concepts of God').

The fact that concepts may be seen as the meanings of terms should not lead one to suppose that concepts are in some narrow sense linguistic entities: although concepts may be defined in terms of the rules governing the use of the words said to designate them, those rules determine (a) what things in the world are classed together (as 'falling under the same concept'), (b) what features are grouped together (as 'being various characteristics of the same thing'), (c) what operations of measurement, classification, discrimination, etc., are performed by the man 'using the concept', and so on.

120

D. Discussions of concepts in the social sciences tend to be a matter of the choice of terms and, more importantly, of their definitions. One may talk both of discovering and of inventing concepts; also of changing and developing concepts. In as far as given theories require certain concepts, and in as far as concepts can be said to incorporate theories, there is no sharp line between choice of theories and choice of concepts. Nevertheless, while theories are thought of primarily as true or false, concepts are more naturally described as applicable or inapplicable, valid or invalid, useful or useless.

E. A. Gellner

See also: CATEGORY

Conciliation

A. *Conciliation* denotes the action of bringing into harmony or effecting a settlement between conflicting groups or individuals. The process generally involves a board, commission, agency, or some other group which studies the facts, makes proposals to the disputants, and attempts to arrive at a settlement of the conflict. Proposals are in the form of a recommendation and are not a binding award or judgement. The disputants are therefore free to accept or reject the findings and proposals of the conciliators.

B. 1. The term *conciliation* is utilized in sociology to designate a sub-process of accommodation (q.v.) or a form of co-ordinate accommodation to bring about the adjustment of conflicting individuals or groups. R. E. Park and E. W. Burgess distinguish conciliation from compromise in that the latter merely averts or adjourns conflict, whereas the former involves 'repudiation or expression of regret with reference to the struggle' and is thus 'a removal of the roots of the conflict' (*Introduction to the Science of Sociology*, Chicago: University of Chicago Press, 1924, p. 708).

2. From the standpoint of international law and relations, conciliation is, 'the process of settling a dispute by referring it to a commission of persons whose task it is to elucidate the facts and (usually after hearing the parties and endeavouring to bring them to an agreement) to make a report containing proposals for a settlement, but which does not have the binding character of an award or judgment' (L. Oppenheim, *International Law*, London: Longmans, Green, 7th edn., 1952, vol. II, p. 12). Conciliation differs from good offices and mediation in that the latter are an attempt to persuade the disputants to decide for themselves, whereas in the former the conciliators are expected to propose or recommend a settlement (J. L. Brierly, *The Law of Nations*, Oxford: The Clarendon Press, 5th edn., 1955, pp. 293–4). It differs from arbitration or adjudication in that the award is not legally binding on the disputants. P. E. Corbett writes: 'The object contemplated here is rather amiable compromise than judgment, the recommendations of the conciliators may override legal rights and their findings are in any case not binding on the parties ...' (*Post-War Worlds*, New York: Farrar & Rinehart, 1942, p. 153).

3. Conciliation is used in the solution of labour disputes, but in this area one does not find the sharp distinction between mediation and conciliation which exists in international law and relations. K. Braun evidences this trend in his definition of the term. He writes: 'Mediation (or conciliation) is an attempt to settle disputes with the help of an outsider who assists the disputants in their negotiations'. He continues: 'Following common practice, we shall use the terms "mediation" and "conciliation" interchangeably' (*Labor Disputes and Their Settlement*, Baltimore: The Johns Hopkins Press, 1955, pp. 53–4). It differs from negotiation in which no outside party participates and from arbitration in that its finding is a suggestion or recommendation and is not a legally binding award. Conciliation is sometimes termed compulsory or voluntary, not to designate the recommendation for settlement (which may never be compulsory), but to designate cases in which a public agency may have the power to attempt conciliation on its own volition without first receiving the consent of the disputants, as opposed to cases where the disputants have voluntarily requested conciliation. Modern governments usually provide conciliating machinery for labour disputes. Examples in the United States Government would be the Federal Mediation and Conciliation Service and the National Mediation Board.

Robert E. Clute

See also: ACCOMMODATION
COMPROMISE

Concubinage

1. *Concubinage* generally denotes the cohabiting of a man and a woman who are not legally married; the practice of having or the state of being a concubine; that form of socially recognized sexual mating to which the term marriage is denied in any given society, but in which the woman has a socially recognized position in the household of the man.

Conditioning

2. The main usage in social anthropology follows (1) above.

(a) In some cases the term applies to sexual unions which are distinguished from marriage as 'matings of inferior status in the social scheme of values' (R. H. Lowie, 'Marriage', in E. R. A. Seligman (ed.), *Encyclopedia of the Social Sciences*, London: Macmillan, 1933, vol. X, p. 146) i.e. marriage is more approved, and concubinage is less approved.

(b) In other cases the distinction lies, not in any greater honour or approval attached to marriage, *but only in the different legal consequences of the union*. Among the Nuer of the Sudan, if a widow chooses not to accept to live in leviratic marriage (q.v.) with a brother of her late husband, she may be allowed to cohabit with a lover of her choosing. As the marriage bonds between her and her dead husband remain undissolved, she cannot make a new marriage, and any children she may subsequently bear are still counted as the children of the dead man, her legal husband. Neither the man nor the woman has any legally enforceable rights over the other, but the status of living in concubinage is not disapproved (E. E. Evans-Pritchard, *Kinship and Marriage among the Nuer*, London: Oxford University Press, 1951, p. 116-7).

3. There is an alternative usage (probably a development from the now obsolete sense of 'concubine' as a *man* living in concubinage) i.e. the union of a man with one or more women outside the bond of marriage—as contrasted with *cicisbeism* (from Italian, *Cicisbeo*, the recognized gallant of a married woman) for the corresponding union of a married woman with one or more men. E. Smith notes among the Ila, '... in addition to the forms of marriage ... a kind of cicisbeism named *lubembo*, which is really a species of polyandry. It differs from an ordinary system of paramours in that there is a public ceremony, so that everybody knows of it, even the woman's husband' (*The Ila-Speaking Peoples of N. Rhodesia*, London: Macmillan, 1920, vol. II, pp. 67-9).

M. Douglas

See also: MARRIAGE

Conditioned Reflex (See Conditioning)

Conditioned Response (See Conditioning)

Conditioning

A. *Conditioning* denotes the process by which stimuli originally not linked with a reflex or response come to be so linked.

B. The term has a technical scientific meaning only in psychology, in which discipline two main classes of conditioning experiments are commonly distinguished: *classical conditioning*, which follows the paradigm of Pavlov's conditioned salivation experiments, and *instrumental* or *operant conditioning*, for which the reference experiment is rat lever-pressing as investigated by B. F. Skinner (I. P. Pavlov, *Conditioned Reflexes*, London: Oxford University Press, 1927; E. R. Hilgard & D. G. Marquis, *Conditioning and Learning*, New York: D. Appleton-Century, 1940, p. 27; B. F. Skinner, *The Behavior of Organisms*, New York: D. Appleton-Century, 1938; J. Konorski & S. Miller, 'On Two Types of Conditioned Reflex', *Journal of General Psychology*, vol. 16, 1937, pp. 264-72).

1. Classical conditioning conforms to the pattern of Pavlov's conditioned salivation experiment in dogs (though, of course, applicable to other organisms and other responses). The main feature is that the originally neutral conditioned stimulus, through repeated pairing with the unconditioned stimulus, acquires the response originally given to the unconditioned stimulus (or some fraction or replica of this response).

2. In instrumental or operant conditioning, the reinforcing stimulus (equivalent to Pavlov's unconditioned stimulus) occurs if, and only if, the instrumental or operant (conditioned) response occurs; thus the response that is strengthened is that which *produces* or *leads to* the reinforcing stimulus rather than that elicited by the reinforcing stimulus.

C. In psychology *conditioning* is sometimes used without reference to specific experimental arrangements to denote the stimulus-substitution conception of associative learning (E. R. Guthrie, *The Psychology of Learning*, New York: Harper & Brothers, 1935). In this usage, Pavlov's experiment is a special case of a more general principle of learning. If learning and conditioning are assumed to be synonymous, anything acquired through training or experience must, ipso facto, have been 'conditioned'. In sociology and social psychology this somewhat loose usage has been adopted by some as a basis for refuting the argument that social behaviour is instinctive. Thus, for example, W. I. Thomas said that 'Since Pavlov's first experiments on the conditioned reflex, the conditioned reaction has had growing recognition, and to some of us, the characteristic behavior traits of individuals, races, and nationalities appear so largely a result of a series of conditionings that the questions of biological heredity, germ plasm, and constitutional differences recede greatly in importance ...' (*Social Behavior and Personality*, ed. by E. H. Volkart, New York: Social Science Research Council, 1951, p. 188).

Preferred usage appears to be, however, to have *conditioning* refer to the experimental arrangements under which specific forms of learning take place, without begging the question whether or not all learning (social or otherwise) takes place according to the processes brought to light within these arrangements. According to this more limited view something has been acquired by conditioning only if it has been learnt within arrangements closely corresponding to those of either classical or instrumental conditioning. Of those who argue that social learning does for the most part occur under such conditions, only B. F. Skinner has developed the several steps of the theoretical argument upon which such a claim might be based (*Science and Human Behavior*, New York: The Macmillan Co., 1953). Many social psychologists, for various reasons, are convinced that conditioning is not an adequate explanation for complex forms of social thought and action, and even those who believe that the concept may ultimately serve such a purpose, agree that the demonstration of such explanation has not yet occurred.

Ernest R. Hilgard

See also: LEARNING
        REINFORCEMENT

Conflict

A. *Conflict* may be defined as 'a struggle over values and claims to scarce status, power and resources in which the aims of the opponents are to neutralize, injure or eliminate their rivals' (L. A. Coser, *The Functions of Social Conflict*, Glencoe, Ill.: The Free Press, 1956, p. 8).

B. An analysis of the literature reveals that the term *conflict* is defined with a number of different emphases. According to one school of thought, which might be said to stem from the work of G. Simmel (*Conflict and The Web of Group Affiliations*, trans. by K. H. Wolff & R. Bendix, Glencoe, Ill.: The Free Press, 1955, p. 13) and to have been developed in America by R. E. Park and his co-workers, conflict is seen as one of the central forms of interaction. Simmel writes, 'If every interaction among men

is a sociation, conflict ... must certainly be considered as sociation. ... Conflict is ... designed to resolve divergent dualisms; it is a way of achieving some kind of unity, even if it be through the annihilation of one of the conflicting parties'. R. E. Park & E. W. Burgess (*Introduction to the Science of Sociology*, Chicago: University of Chicago Press, 1921, p. 574) likewise treat conflict, as well as competition, as 'forms of interaction'. In contrast to this view a number of scholars have seen in conflict a dissociative process (q.v.). Thus G. A. Lundberg (*The Foundations of Sociology*, New York: The Macmillan Co., 1939, p. 275) finds that conflict is characterized by 'a suspension of communication between the opposing parties'. L. Wilson & W. L. Kolb (*Sociological Analysis*, New York: Harcourt, Brace, 1949, p. 714) likewise define conflict as 'a disjunctive process'.

C. Those who see in conflict a form of social interaction have been led to attempt to distinguish it from competition (q.v.). Park and Burgess say that conflict, as distinct from competition, is always conscious and involves direct communication: 'Both are forms of interaction, but competition is a struggle between individuals, or groups of individuals, who are not necessarily in contact and communication, while conflict is a contest in which contact is an indispensable condition. Competition ... is unconscious. Conflict is always conscious. ... Both competition and conflict are forms of struggle. Competition, however, is continuous and impersonal, conflict is intermittent and personal' (R. E. Park & E. W. Burgess, *Introduction to the Science of Sociology*, p. 574).

D. A number of scholars have attempted to distinguish between conflict and competition mainly in terms of the means used by goal-oriented antagonists. Thus R. M. MacIver, while defining conflict as 'all activity in which men contend against one another for any objective', proceeds to distinguish between what he terms 'direct conflict' and 'indirect conflict' (which is roughly equivalent to competition) (*Society*, New York: Farrar & Rinehart, 1937, p. 51). Direct conflict 'occurs where individuals or groups thwart or impede or restrain or injure or destroy one another in the effort to attain some goal' (ibid., p. 51). Indirect conflict occurs 'where individuals or groups do not actually impede the efforts of one another but nevertheless seek to attain their ends in ways which obstruct the attainment of the same end

Conformity

by others' (ibid., p. 51). Similarly R. M. Williams, Jr., defines conflict as 'a struggle over values (distributive or non-distributive) in which the immediate aims of the opponents are to neutralize, injure or eliminate their rivals. Conflict results from conscious pursuit of exclusive values' (*The Reduction of Intergroup Tensions*, New York: Social Science Research Council, 1947, p. 43). Competition, to Williams, is focused upon reaching a goal rather than removing competitors.

Lewis A. Coser

See also: COMPETITION
PROCESS

Conformity (Also Non-Conformity)

A. There is no disagreement as to the meaning of these terms but considerable confusion as to the appropriate area in which they should be used. In brief, there are three connected yet distinctly different areas:

1. The first is that of the individual's basic personality structure—here we may speak of *conformity tendencies*, yet this should be resisted for other terms, such as *submission, compliance, love, identification, introspection*, and *imitation*, are more proper and more specific in this sector. We may also speak of conformity and its opposite when we assess an individual's acts behaviouristically. But the behaviourist cannot afford to speak of *conformity tendencies*; he never sees tendencies, he only infers them.

2. Then we may speak of the *conformity behaviour* of the individual; here again the terms listed in (1) would suffice and the use of the term *conformity* without reference to the social context in which it occurs would be superfluous.

3. In observing social aggregates we may truly refer to their homogeneity as *conformity*. The proper context of application is sociology and the social or even biological sciences but not psychology. The latter is well supplied with more pertinent terms to convey the appropriate meanings.

B. 1. In England the Acts of Conformity prescribed adherence to the established Church and forbade all other religious allegiance (1551–1662). Later from this religious designation, arose the term *non-conformist*.

2. For the contemporary sociological application of the term, 'to conform' is to comply with any usage or practice. Its simplest definition is implied in the words, 'We attempt to find out what is being done and do it' (J. J. B. Morgan, *Psychology*, New York: Rinehart, 1947, p. 146). A more elaborate definition of conformity may throw more light on its nature. 'When a group of individuals react *repeatedly* in a characteristic way to a stimulus situation, we infer that the members of the group have an established social attitude in relation to it. This characteristic reaction of groups of people is sometimes called "conforming behavior"' (M. Sherif & H. Cantril, *The Psychology of Ego-Involvements*, New York: Wiley, 1947, p. 29). One may say that *non-conformity* or deviance does not require a specific definition; this is by no means certain. At any rate T. Parsons's definition of deviance is useful for it draws attention to the psychological and sociological contexts in which conformity and non-conformity may occur: 'Deviance and the mechanisms of social control may be defined in two ways, according to whether the individual actor or the interactive system is taken as the point of reference. In the first context deviance is a motivated tendency for an actor to behave in contravention of one or more institutionalized normative patterns. ... In the second context, that of the interactive system, deviance is the tendency on the part of one or more of the component actors to behave in such a way as to disturb the equilibrium of the interactive process. Deviance, therefore, is defined by its tendency to result either in change in the state of the interactive system, or in re-equilibration by counteracting forces the latter being the mechanisms of social control' (*The Social System*, Glencoe, Ill.: The Free Press, 1952, p. 250).

C. The classification of both conformity and non-conformity phenomena may lead to a more stringent definition of these terms than those cited.

1. Conformity may relate to the majority or it may relate to elites, oppressed groups, professional groups, and other minorities.

2. Conformities may be comprehensive or may apply only to specific role-expectations.

3. They may be temporary or permanent.

4. They must be analysed as to their depth of consolidation: do they amount to mere outward compliance or do they also include inward acceptance?

5. A classification is clearly necessary on the following grounds: is it a deviance from (a) the law, (b) morals, (c) conventions, (d) or is it neither of these but only a kind of rare behaviour?

6. Following T. Parsons (*The Social System*, p. 257) and R. K. Merton ('Social Structure and Anomie', *American Sociological Review*, vol. 3, 1938, pp. 672–82), both conformity and non-conformity may be expressed in dominative and submissive ways, i.e. dominative conformity is 'compulsive performance orientation' (Parsons), submissive conformity is 'compulsive acquiescence in status and expectations' (Parsons), while dominative non-conformity is rebelliousness, or 'innovation' (Merton), and submissive non-conformity is withdrawal or 'retreatism' (Merton).

7. There is Merton's own classification (ibid.) of the conformity-non-conformity dimension: does the dimension relate to culture goals or institutionalized means? to both or to neither?

8. Yet another classification might be developed from a recent examination of D. Riesman's thesis (as set out in *The Lonely Crowd*, New York: Yale University Press, 1950) of an increase in American 'other-directedness' (conformity) at the expense of 'inner-directedness': 'It would be a sad thing if our conceptual tools did not allow us to differentiate a thoughtful and warm receptiveness toward others from a wholesale, undiscriminating fashionableness, and a non-messianic, informed, independent kind of thinking from a know-it-all, aggressive self-righteousness' (A. J. Brodbeck, P. Nogee, & A. Di Mascio, 'Two Kinds of Conformity: A Study of the Riesman Typology applied to Standards of Parental Discipline', *Journal of Psychology*, vol. 41, 1956, p. 38).

9. Another basis of classification hinges on the dominant motive for conformity; this could be briefly indicated by the terms 'love-conformity' and 'fear-conformity' or 'conformity for acceptance' and 'conformity for fear of rejection'; indeed, these two may be logically equated, yet clearly the psychological emphases are distinct.

10. A distinction may be drawn between those kinds of non-conformities which are institutionalized and those which are not. Example of the former would be the licence and non-conformities of the culture hero, the genius, the intellectual, or artist whose deviation from the norm is tolerated, even respected and secretly envied, but not held up to the ordinary folk as an example to be followed.

11. Classification may be grounded in a political context: in the contrast between 'conformity imposed' and 'conformity chosen'; the social and psychological significance of this classification is well summed up by C. Kluckhohn and H. A. Murray, 'Greater behavioral conformity often leads to an accumulation of resentment and thus to an increase in emotional incompatibility. It is as if the individual's hatred of society rose with each renunciation that was involved in the process of adjustment' (*Personality in Nature, Society, and Culture*, New York: Knopf, 1949, p. 26).

12. Finally, conformity and non-conformity have often been discovered to furnish all the meanings that there were in terms such as 'normality' and 'abnormality' or 'adjustment' and 'maladjustment'. The invidiousness of this practice of using positive sociological terms normatively can be shown up by drawing attention to the cases which are 'pathological' by virtue of being 'conforming', and to cases which are deemed 'excellent' by virtue of their being inventively novel and therefore 'non-conforming'. Accordingly, one might classify both conformity and non-conformity into 'pathological' and 'creative' subtypes. (Cf. P. Halmos, *Towards a Measure of Man*, Routledge & Kegan Paul, London, 1957).

P. Halmos

See also: ADJUSTMENT
DEVIANT BEHAVIOUR

Conjugal Family (See Family)

Consanguine Family (See Family)

Consanguinity

A. *Consanguinity* may be defined as a social relationship established on the basis of descent from a common ancestor, actual or assumed. Consanguinity may be lineal, where one person is the direct ancestor of another; or collateral, where there is an ultimate common ancestor, but persons are not linked by a direct line of descent.

1. The definition of L. H. Morgan remains basic; he referred to 'consanguinity, or blood' relationships in his discussion of Roman kinship, specifying that this involved 'the relation of persons descended from the same ancestor' (*Systems of Consanguinity and Affinity of the Human Family*, Smithsonian Contributions to Knowledge, vol. XVII, Washington: Smithsonian Institution, 1871, p. 17).

2. Definitions similar to those of Morgan are frequent in anthropological literature. For example, G. P. Murdock's influential study, *Social Structure* (New York: The Macmillan Co., 1949, p. 95) conforms to this usage by

Conscience

designating consanguineal relatives as those '... between whom every connecting link is one of blood or common ancestry ...'.

3. It was also Morgan who further distinguished between lineal consanguinity '... which subsists among persons of whom one is descended from the other', and collateral consanguinity '... which exists among persons who are descended from a common ancestor, but not from each other' (ibid., p. 17).

B. The idea of 'blood ties' which is obviously suggested by the Latin root of consanguinity can lead to difficulty. First, relationships of descent may include adoptive or fictional 'blood-ties'. Second, it may appear that blood-ties do not necessarily involve a common ancestor.

1. M. Titiev, for example, resolves the first problem simply by saying that ' "Blood" ties, whether they be real or fictitious, are described as consanguineous ...' (*The Science of Man: An Introduction to Anthropology*, New York: Henry Holt, 1954, p. 378). A. R. Radcliffe-Brown, however, objects to the use of *consanguinity* and would substitute *kinship*, arguing that the former refers to a biological blood relationship, whereas in anthropology '... we have to deal with a specifically social relationship' ('Introduction', to A. R. Radcliffe-Brown & D. Forde (eds.), *African Systems of Kinship and Marriage*, London: Oxford University Press, 1950, p. 4). He refers to the distinction between *genitor*, biological father, and *pater*, sociological father, and instances of adoption as support for his position. There would be more difficulties, however, in using *kinship* to designate descent from a common ancestor even though fictitious 'social' descent is involved, since kinship refers to affinal relations as well, than there would be in continuing to use consanguinity in these instances.

2. K. Davis and W. L. Warner suggest that the conception of blood-ties includes both relationship by common ancestor and relationship of husband and wife through common offspring when they write that '... kinship may be defined as social relations based on connection through birth. This holds for relationships by affinity as well as for those by consanguinity—for although husband and wife may have no recognized common ancestry, they are nonetheless related by blood through their common offspring' ('Structural Analysis of Kinship', *American Anthropologist*, vol. 39, 1937, pp. 292–313). If this is true and if *consanguinity* is defined

as relationship through blood-ties, then the term would have to be broadened to include affinal relations as well as relations through a common ancestor. This would render meaningless the use of the terms *affinity* and *consanguinity* as Davis and Warner have used them in the quotation above.

Harry W. Basehart

See also: KINSHIP

Conscience

A. 1. A broad, general definition such as that in *Webster's New International Dictionary*, London: G. Bell, 2nd edn., 1947, p. 567), may fairly represent the average popular view: i.e. 'Consciousness of the moral goodness or blame worthiness of one's own conduct, intentions or character, together with a feeling of obligation to do or be that which is recognized as good; often with special reference to feelings of guilt or remorse for ill-doing'.

2. As used in psychology and ethics the term may be said to have an historical rather than a current interest. This is especially so in psychological writings where the word is still encountered, but such terms as *guilt*, *introjection*, *superego* have the position of technical terms.

The term denotes the sense which an individual has concerning (a) his own behaviour; (b) the qualities of *right* and *wrong* which such behaviour manifests; and (c) what follows from, or is implied by, such behaviour.

B. The term, explicitly or implicitly, has a sharp reference to the role of the *individual* in the formation and/or acceptance of social norms and moral standards. This may be illustrated by two recent examples of its usage:

1. 'The introjected social norms are experienced by the individual as his own conscience; they are not only a mirror of external coercion and authority, but also a projection of his own individuality. Conscience is at least partly the expression of the individual in his relationships with others in various circumstances. It is not only a result of the individual adaptation, but also his own self-realization' (Z. Barbu, *Democracy and Dictatorship*, London: Routledge & Kegan Paul, 1956, p. 64).

2. '... clearly discernible in the history of morality is the internalisation and individualisation of the conscience. There gradually emerges the notion that goodness is something which the mind can apprehend as self-sustained and independent of external sanctions'

(M. Ginsberg, *Reason and Unreason in Society*, London: Longmans, Green, 1947, p. 309).

T. H. Pear

See also: GENERALIZED OTHER
SUPEREGO

Consciousness

A. *Consciousness* denotes a reflective mental attitude enabling an individual to become aware of himself and of his environment in various degrees of clarity and complexity. This includes: (a) awareness of his own mental and bodily functions; (b) awareness of objects in the external world; (c) the perception of himself as an individuality; (d) the perception of himself as a member of a group.

B. 1. In its widest sense *consciousness* denotes reflective mental activity leading to self-knowledge, i.e. 'the insight which the mind has into its own states and processes' (A. Lalande, *Vocabulaire Technique et Critique de la Philosophie*, Paris: Felix Alcan, 1928, p. 127). In philosophy the term has various usages indicating specific modes and degrees of self-awareness. The Stoics, for instance, defined *suneidesis* as an inner sense by which the soul perceives its own tensions. For St Thomas Aquinas *conscientia* connoted knowledge of something. Leibniz was the first who distinguished between *conscious* and *unconscious* mental acts; the unconscious *petites perceptions* become by accumulation a conscious *apperception*.

2. Physiologists have been concerned with the bodily organ of consciousness. According to one theory there are in the brain specific nerve cells which produce consciousness whenever they are stimulated. Another theory holds that consciousness emanates from each cell of the body. A third theory holds that consciousness is closely connected with some aspect of the simple nerve impulse.

3. Present-day psychology tends to eliminate *consciousness* as a technical term. The main reasons for this are two: (a) a reaction from the 19th century 'Psychology of consciousness', and (b) the minor role (of 'epiphenomenon') assigned to consciousness by physiological and depth psychology.

4. Since the discovery of the unconscious aspect of mental activities the general tendency has been to describe consciousness by comparison with the unconscious (q.v.). The main points of difference between these two aspects of the mind can be formulated as follows: (a) The unconscious mental life is continuous, while consciousness is discontinuous; (b) unconscious experiences are vague, inarticulate, and without a clear representation of their object, while consciousness is, on the other hand, ratiocinative; (c) according to Freud the unconscious and consciousness are contradictory mental structures. Mental life in the unconscious is irrational and not shaped by specific forms of adjustment, while in consciousness it is rational and adjusted to a specific type of environment. In consciousness mental energy is associated with, and therefore transformed by verbal symbols (see: F. Alexander, *Fundamentals of Psychoanalysis*, London: Allen & Unwin, 1949, p. 17; E. Jones, *Freud, Life and Works*, London: Hogarth Press, 1955, vol. II, p. 364).

5. Consciousness in 'social' contexts has several meanings.

(a) It may denote the individual's awareness of himself as a member of a group. This point is systematically elaborated by G. H. Mead, who maintains that consciousness originates in a social act. The process of communication enables the individual not only to become aware of the non-self, the other, but also to look back at himself from this perspective, in Mead's terms, to take the role of the other. This internalized other is an essential condition in the rise of consciousness, for it implies a reflective process, i.e. the self becoming an object to itself. 'One attains self-consciousness only as he (the individual) takes, or finds himself stimulated to take the attitude of the other. Then he is in the position of reacting in himself to that attitude of the other' (G. H. Mead, *Mind, Self and Society*, Chicago: University of Chicago Press, 1934, p. 194). Apart from its specific significance for psychology, Mead's thesis has the merit of stressing the fact that consciousness is a relational reality; it implies both self-awareness and awareness of the non-self, persons or things.

(b) *Class-consciousness* is a term frequently used by Marxian ideologues denoting the identity between the individual as a conscious being and the interests of his social class. In Soviet ideology the term denotes the individual's awareness of himself as a member of the Party.

Z. Barbu

See also: CLASS-CONSCIOUSNESS
SELF
UNCONSCIOUS

Consensus

Consensus

A. *Consensus* may be defined as that general agreement in thought and feeling which tends to produce order where there was disorder. Such general agreement may be accompanied by differences of view on detail.

B. Consensus is regularly used to mean more than *rational* agreement—it implies sharing of *sentiment* as well as idea. This is no doubt because the unity of thought is believed to spring in part from a unity of feeling. There are marked differences in usage, however, which seem to be related to interest in differing time spans.

1. Within the long sweep of social evolution, all societal culture traits are seen as evidence of consensus. Thus R. E. Park and E. W. Burgess say that folkways, mores, technique, and ideals 'may all be reduced to the one term "consensus" ' (*Introduction to the Science of Sociology*, Chicago: University of Chicago Press, 1924, p. 163). And again, 'Considered concretely, it [society] is a complex of organized habits, sentiments, and social attitudes—in short, consensus' (ibid., p. 163). This usage obviously stems from Comte, who thought of consensus as the bond which holds societies together. It does not include an element which is always present when short time spans are in view: the implication of former disagreement. Since the consensus has become customary there is no clear suggestion that where now there is agreement there was disagreement. Since there are other terms such as *cultural unity* or *culture* (q.v.) itself to denote what Park and Burgess were getting at, it seems feasible to narrow the meaning of *consensus*.

2. This might be done by utilizing the standpoint of H. M. Kallen's article—'Consensus' in the *Encyclopedia of the Social Sciences* (E. R. A. Seligman (ed.), New York: The Macmillan Co., 1931, vol. IV, p. 225). He thinks of consensus as the co-operative resolution of conflict, an agreement won among those of somewhat equal power, thus stressing the element of short-time span and the idea of former disagreement. He differentiates it from conformity—voluntary acceptance of a way of behaviour which confronts one in the environment—and coercion, which results in involuntary acquiescence. Consensus is then the culmination of a process in which public sentiment and public opinion are brought to bear on a problem. It preserves features of many of the discrete and conflicting ideas that have been put forward in the earlier stage.

While the Park and Burgess usage is too broad, the Kallen usage is too narrow in the sense of implying the existence of earlier conflict in every case. It seems wise to include cases where there has been *any* preceding difference, even when it was only random confusion.

Robert C. Angell

See also: CULTURAL INTEGRATION
CULTURE
MORAL ORDER
SOCIAL INTEGRATION

Conservation

A. In the fields of economics, political science, and law *conservation* means the husbanding of persons, creatures, and of specific categories of such things, simple and complex, as trees, fishes, rivers, forests, lakes, beaches, and soils; or the preservation of such items from unnecessary, excessive, wasteful, and destructive uses or influences. At the same time, *conservation* implies use, which of itself is not necessarily prohibited so long as such use is wise, temperate, prudent, and appropriate—and is especially for the benefit of mankind and generally on the long- rather than the short-term basis.

B. The term has both positive and negative connotations: as applied positively, conservation may be accomplished or promoted through the utilization of men, materials, and equipment in simple or complex processes, procedures, and practices with or upon an object or objects and directed toward specified goals. A simple example of such positive application would be the 'stubble-mulching' practice of the United States Soil Conservation Service. Conservation in the negative sense may be accomplished through the arresting, ceasing, or enjoining of imprudent or wasteful processes, procedures, and practices, e.g. the objectives of the ancient statute providing for penalties 'for taking of salmons at certain times of the year' (anno. 13 Ed., Stat. I, cap. 47 (1285), *The Statutes at Large: from Magna Charta to the 25th Year of the Reign of King George the Third inclusive*, A New Edition in 10 vols. Revised, Corrected and Continued by C. Runnington, London: Eyre, Strahan & Woodfall, 1786, vol. I, p. 110).

C. The legislative meaning of *conservation* in the United States, as applied to selected natural resources in the Soil Conservation and Domestic Allotment Act of 1936 included '... (1) preservation and improvement of soil fertility; (2) promotion of the economic use ... of land; (3) diminution of exploitation and wasteful and unscientific use of national soil resources; (4) the protection of rivers and harbors against the results of soil erosion in aid of maintaining the navigability of waters and water courses and in aid of flood control ...' (49 *Stat.* 1148, *The Statutes at Large of the U.S.A.*, Washington: U.S. Government Printing Office, vol. XLIX, part I, 1936). The modern Congressional use of the word appears to vary little or not at all from its Elizabethan employment as, for example, in the statute entitled 'An act for the preservation of spawn and fry of fish' where it was required: 'That the lord admiral of England ... and all and every other person ... which by grant or other lawful ways and means ... have or ought to have any conservation or preservation of any rivers and streams ... have full power ... to enquire of all offences ... done contrary to ... this act' (1 Eliz. 17, 1558, *The Statutes at Large: from Magna Charta ...* vol. II, pp. 520–21).

A. B. Winter

Conservatism

A. The term *conservatism* is derived from the same root as the adjective, *conservative*, which connotes a disposition to preserve things as they are. It is used to designate a set of beliefs about society and government, among them being an attitude of respect towards the existing social and political arrangements, especially when these have been gradually formed over a long period.

The name *Conservative* began to be widely used in England in the 1830s in place of the historic *Tory*, though the latter has never fallen out of currency, and in the British system of politics the Conservative Party has always been one of the major parties. The Conservative tradition, as it has been developed by such men as Burke, Coleridge, Peel, and Disraeli, has a claim to be regarded as a coherent account of man's place in society and under government—though it has never been reduced to a schematic doctrine.

The most commonly emphasized elements of this account, as it has been elaborated in England, are summarized below, with the caution that any summary does violence to a 'philosophy' which has never received systematic exposition (see S. P. Huntington, 'Conservatism as an Ideology', *American Political Science Review*, vol. LI, 1957, pp. 454–73).

B. 1. 'Conservatism arose to resist Jacobinism, and that is to this day its most essential and fundamental characteristic' (Lord Hugh Cecil, *Conservatism*, London: Williams & Norgate, 1912, p. 249). The conservative sees in Jacobinism a willingness to destroy institutions on a large scale in pursuance of purely doctrinal aims, 'to form political institutions on abstract principles of theoretic science, instead of permitting them to spring from the course of events, and to be naturally created by the necessities of nations' (Disraeli). And of the abstract principles the most dangerous is that man is capable of perfection, for nothing is more destructive of genuine improvement than to be moved by the shining vision of Utopia. The idea of original sin is near the truth, for man must take the bad along with the good. Politics is modest in what it can achieve and quite inferior among the joys of existence. 'The oldest and most harmful of all forms of materialism is the attempt to set up the Kingdom of God by force' (K. Pickthorn, *Principles or Prejudices*, London: Signpost Press, 1943, p. 10).

2. Closely connected with the limited view of what the state can achieve is the conception of society as a complex whole comprising interdependent parts, akin to an organism rather than a machine; an intricate web of human relationships whose delicate balance can all too easily be disrupted by grandiose and hurried schemes of reform. Moreover, it is an organism whose growth is to be measured in terms of ages, tested over time and proved in the fact of survival. So with the organic view of society goes 'this respect for precedent, this clinging to prescription, this reverence for antiquity' (Disraeli). The conservative is therefore reluctant to dispense with the accumulated experience of generations and seeks to reform in accordance with the spirit of what is already there. 'I would not exclude alteration ... but even when I changed, it should be to preserve. ... In what I did, I should follow the example of our ancestors. I would make the reparation as nearly as possible in the style of the building' (E. Burke, *Reflections on the French Revolution, and other Essays*, Everyman edn., London: J. M. Dent, 1910, p. 243).

3. Conservatism stresses *diffusion of power*. The conservative approves of the richness in voluntary associations manifested by British society. The large number and diverse character and aim of these groups are a means to many-sided development for individuals but they also constitute a barrier to the concentration of

Conspicuous Consumption

power, act as a buffer between the state and the individual. 'To be attached to the sub-division' said Burke, 'to love the little platoon we belong to in society, is the first principle ... of public affections' (ibid., p. 44). And in our own day, Quintin Hogg has said, 'One of the marks of a healthy society is the rich profusion of social forms which it throws up ... for political liberty is nothing else but the diffusion of power' (Q. Hogg, *The Case for Conservatism*, Harmondsworth: Penguin Books, 1947, pp. 29 & 62). The recently declared aim of a 'property-owning democracy' is an example of this attitude, as is Quintin Hogg's vigorous defence of large personal fortunes which he considers 'an indispensable counterpoise to the vast complex of economic power controlled by the modern state' (ibid., p. 63).

4. Respect for duly constituted authority is one of the most ancient Tory principles. Conservatives reject the liberal doctrine of conditional obedience, though there have been times (e.g. over Ireland on the eve of World War I) when the strain on their allegiance has approached breaking-point. Hence, as Lord Hugh Cecil remarked, 'the most that can be said is that on the whole Conservatives would lean rather more to the side of authority than the Radicals' (*Conservatism*, p. 80). Conservatives have not shrunk from the use of state intervention to relieve distress and to extend benefits and it is only in recent decades that, in the face of growing state activity, they have sought to redress the balance by leaning towards the old Liberal arguments for *laissez-faire*.

Because a number of its leading tenets—respect for authority, caution in reform, inequality of reward and possessions—lend such clear support to the existing order, Conservatism is regarded by some writers merely as an ideology cut to the needs of the propertied classes. And the nature of the social support for the Conservative Party is taken to lend strength to the claim. But conservatism represents a view of society and politics whose validity can be examined on its own merits, quite apart from its 'historical function'.

J. C. Rees

See also: LIBERALISM

Conspicuous Consumption

A. *Conspicuous consumption* may be defined as the lavish and wasteful use of goods and services for the purpose of symbolizing or establishing one's position as a member of a particular social class (q.v.), especially of the upper classes and, more specifically still, of a leisure class.

B. The term first appeared in T. Veblen's *The Theory of the Leisure Class* (1899). Its meaning involves many of Veblen's cognate terms: conspicuous leisure, conspicuous waste, pecuniary canons of taste, predatory culture, pecuniary reputation, etc. These terms are employed both to point out a fact about societies and also to make a value judgement about that fact. They constitute one set of terms in Veblen's conceptual dichotomy, the other set involving such terms as instinct of workmanship, industrial economic institutions, engineers, machine technology, useful work, etc. Though Veblen disclaimed any moral intent, he does hold that the former set of terms designate archaic and barbarous survivals in an evolving new age constituted by the phenomena designated by the second set of terms. The coming into existence of the industrial-technological culture is impeded or subverted by the predatory, aristocratic antecedents as these are reformulated in the pecuniary valuations of a business culture.

Conspicuous consumption involves invidious class distinctions, a pattern of conduct set by the top group, the leisure class, and emulated in its own fashion by each lower social class. Leisure refers to the non-productive consumption of time '(1) from a sense of the unworthiness of productive work, and (2) as an evidence of pecuniary ability to afford a life of idleness' (T. Veblen, *The Theory of the Leisure Class*, London: Allen & Unwin, 1924, p. 43). 'It appears that the utility of both [conspicuous leisure and consumption] alike for the purposes of reputability lies in the element of waste that is common to both. In the one case it is a waste of time and effort, in the other it is a waste of goods. Both are methods of demonstrating the possession of wealth, and the two are conventionally accepted as equivalents' (ibid., p. 85). Veblen attempts to trace conspicuous consumption as a general cultural fact, ranging from family life, living and taste standards, dress, religious observances, government, industry, and higher learning.

C. The term has had a limited but significant diffusion in the social sciences. Many social scientists are familiar with it and other of Veblen's terms. It appears occasionally in the literature of social psychology, where it is used in relation to the discussion of status (q.v.). It is used very rarely in economic writings to indicate

130

very briefly a deviant type of consumer purchasing. It has had a wider acceptance in sociology, but until very recently its use has been largely restricted to the earlier American writers, such as Cooley, Ross, and Lumley. In the last several years, social critics have again recalled Veblen's use of the term not so much to stress the conspicuousness of consumption, as to stress his early insight into the non-rational, symbolic relation of consumption to social status and social stratification (see D. Riesman, *The Lonely Crowd*, New Haven: Yale University Press, 1950, p. 122; C. A. R. Crosland, *The Future of Socialism*, London: Cape, 1956, p. 176).

H. Otto Dahlke

See also: SOCIAL CLASS
STRATIFICATION

Constituency

A. The term *constituency* is used to denote an electoral district, the qualified voters of which elect one or more representatives to a parliament or some other representative assembly. The voters who together elect a representative were described as his *constituents* long before the term *constituency* came into use; *constituency* is still used, even now, to designate the voters rather than the district.

B. There are variations (a) in the size of constituencies and (b) in the number of representatives which each returns. In some countries each constituency returns only one member to the assembly; other countries prefer larger constituencies, in which it is easier for the different shades of political opinion to obtain parliamentary representation proportionate to the electoral support which they enjoy.

When a country has an electoral system based on single-member constituencies, there should be as nearly as possible the same number of voters in each constituency. It is, however, impossible to achieve exact equality save at the expense of total disregard of natural and administrative boundaries. Thus in Britain the normal range is between 45,000 and 75,000 voters, though very thinly populated parts of Scotland have, in some cases, well under 40,000. Furthermore, populations of districts rise or fall, so in order to preserve an adequate degree of equality in population the boundaries between constituencies must be rearranged from time to time. In Britain this is now done every ten years. It is possible to make this rearrangement in such a way as to give an unfair advantage to one party (gerrymandering). In order to prevent such gerrymandering, responsibility for arranging the constituency boundaries is often given to impartial bodies such as, in Great Britain, the Boundary Commissions.

P. A. Bromhead

See also: APPORTIONMENT
ELECTION
PROPORTIONAL REPRESENTATION
REPRESENTATION
VOTING

Constitution

A. Aside from literal usage, and infrequent usages such as that denoting an act of establishing, *constitution* designates something about government. In a formal sense it may refer to (a) a fundamental legal document, or (b) the fundamental institutions of a state—the laws, customs, and great conventions, or (c) the total system of laws and customs. In the sense of constitutionalism (q.v.), a *constitution* is a set of devices to subject the freedom of the holders of political power to limitations and restraints.

In a literal sense, everything has a constitution—in the sense of the sum of its parts. Although often used in this non-technical sense, usage has given it narrower meaning. Scholarly analysis and definition have been confined almost exclusively to the constitution of the state, yet most concepts derived therefrom apply equally well to constitutions of other organizations.

B. As a formal term, constitution has evolved from broad to relatively narrow meanings.

1. The Greek *politeia*, usually translated as constitution, designated the numerous characteristics—economic, social, and governmental—of a state, in the same sense as we speak of the constitution of matter. Later, down to the 16th century, constitution meant a secular or ecclesiastical edict or regulation and was used interchangeably with such words as *lex* or *edictum*, as distinguished from *consuetudo* or custom.

2. In subsequent usage the term came to mean government, and usually a particular aspect of it—its framework or fundamentals. For example, according to H. Finer, 'The system of fundamental political institutions is the constitution ... [it] is the autobiography of a power relationship' (*The Theory and Practice of Modern Government*, London: Methuen, 1949, p. 116). To Bryce the term was more inclusive. It was '... the aggregate of the laws and customs

Constitutional Law

through and under which the public life of a state goes on'; or 'the complex totality of laws embodying the principles and rules whereby the community is organized, governed, and held together' (J. Bryce, *Studies in History and Jurisprudence*, Oxford: at the Clarendon Press, 1901, vol. I, pp. 159, 256). Laws of 'superior importance', 'fundamental laws', 'only matters affecting the sovereign power of government', are typical characterizations of constitution. *Fundamental* is obviously an indefinite term on which opinions differ.

3. Along with the practice, beginning in the 16th century, of attempting to codify the essentials of government in legal documents, there was a tendency on the part of many people, legislators and scholars, to adopt a 'documentation' usage of *constitution*. The codification became the constitution. Although most political science definitions are broader, in usage they frequently designate a document. Probably no such codifications include all that is fundamental nor omit all that is superficial.

C. Although 'fundamentals' are a part of most definitions of constitution, implicitly or explicitly the majority also inject a note of constitutionalism, such as laws and customs 'to which the community hath agreed', 'the rights of the governed', and so forth. E. M. Sait objects: 'Not one of these qualifications can be accepted. In the light of present good usage it is impossible to contend that a state, however autocratic the government may be, can exist without a constitution, or that the frame of government is not a constitution ...' unless it contains limitations on government (*Political Institutions*, New York: D. Appleton-Century, 1938, p. 314).

Those who define *constitution* in the light of constitutionalism grudgingly concede that *constitution* may refer simply to framework, but argue that a 'true' constitution always restrains. 'But whatever its form, a true constitution will have the following facts about it very clearly marked: first, how the various agencies are organized; secondly, what power is entrusted to those agencies; and thirdly, in what manner such power is to be exercised. ... The objects of a constitution ... are to limit the arbitrary action of the government, to guarantee the rights of the governed, and to define the operation of the sovereign power' (C. F. Strong, *Modern Political Constitutions*, London: Sidgwick & Jackson, 1949, p. 10). C. J. Friedrich speaks of constitutions in a functional sense arguing that 'to render a government constitu-

tional required establishing and maintaining effective restraints' (*Constitutional Government and Democracy*, Boston: Ginn, 1946, p. 121).

Charles P. Schleicher

See also: CONSTITUTIONALISM

Constitutional Government
(See **Constitutionalism**)

Constitutional Law

A. *Constitutional law* denotes the legal rules which define and delimit the structure and powers of the organs of government in a state.

B. Aristotle defined a constitution as 'an organisation of offices in a state, by which the method of their distribution is fixed, the sovereign authority is determined, and the nature of the end to be pursued by the association and all its members is prescribed' (in *The Politics of Aristotle*, trans. by E. Barker, Oxford: at the Clarendon Press, 1946, p. 156).

The first two features of Aristotle's definition may perhaps be compared with that of A. V. Dicey writing at the end of the 19th century: 'Constitutional law, as the term is used in England, appears to include all rules which directly or indirectly affect the distribution or the exercise of the sovereign power in the state' (*Introduction to the Study of the Law of the Constitution*, London: Macmillan, 9th edn., 1939, p. 23). The formulation owes something to Austin and may be thought too narrow since (unless the word 'exercise' be interpreted in a very broad sense) there are many provisions relating to the organization of government and the formal machinery of state which do not on the face of it have any clear connection with the exercise of sovereign power but are normally considered to be of constitutional importance. A recent and wider definition refers to the collection of rules which 'govern the government' (K. C. Wheare, *Modern Constitutions*, London: Oxford University Press, 1951, p. 1).

1. Where, as is almost universally the case, apart from the United Kingdom, a collection of the rules relating to the organization of government is contained in a written document, *constitutional law* or *the constitution* refers primarily to these codified rules, though it might extend to legal interpretation of them in the courts. Written constitutions may contain provisions which are directory or which indicate or describe the duties of government but are not rules of law enforceable by legal means.

2. In the United Kingdom a great many conventional rules and principles are generally thought of as forming part of the constitution. In 1832 G. C. Lewis (*Use and Abuse of Political Terms*, Oxford: James Thornton, 1877, p. 19) remarked that the words constitutional and unconstitutional 'convey little more than a general sentiment of approbation or dislike'. 'Maxims of the constitution' were 'supposed rules' to which in the speaker's judgement 'the constitution ought to conform, though in fact they have never been observed'. This use (or abuse) of the term is still common in Great Britain, but it presupposes the existence of 'maxims' in a stricter sense, namely the conventions of the constitution which are inferences about the correct behaviour *inter se* of the organs of government drawn from rules which *have* been obeyed. Dicey included these rules within the term 'constitutional law' (*Introduction to the Study of the Law of the Constitution*, p. 25) but distinguished them from rules contained in or inferred from statutes or decisions of courts which might be enforced by legal processes. Sir Ivor Jennings similarly specifies four categories of rules which would figure in a written constitution if one were drawn up in the United Kingdom: (a) legislation; (b) case law; (c) the law and custom of Parliament; (d) conventions.

C. Historically, systems of constitutional law have been classified as falling into a number of categories, the distinguishing criteria being based upon predominant features of organization (e.g. according to the description of the titular head of state, as in *monarchical* or *republican*; according to the relation between executive and legislature, as in *cabinet government* or *presidential government*; or according to the manner of distribution of legislative power, as in *federal* or *unitary* government). A different type of distinction has turned upon the status of the constitutional instrument itself in relation to the powers created by it. Thus Lord Bryce (*Studies in History and Jurisprudence*, Oxford: Oxford University Press, 1901, vol. 1, pp. 151–4) distinguished between 'rigid' and 'flexible' systems. In systems of the second kind, 'there is ... only one legislative authority competent to pass laws in all cases and for all purposes'. H. Kelsen (*General Theory of Law and State*, trans. by A. Wedberg, Cambridge, Mass.: Harvard University Press, 1945, pp. 124–9) classifies constitutions into *formal* and *material* on a similar basis. A *material* consti-

tution exists where there is no special formality for particular classes of legislation or for amendment of constitutional law (see *Sovereignty*). A distinction is sometimes made (where the question is not settled by a written document) between constitutional law and administrative law, the former relating only to the main legislative, executive, and judicial organs of government and the latter to administrative structure and powers only. In many cases a legal rule could be described as either administrative or constitutional and the term *Public Law* offers a convenient general phrase.

G. Marshall

See also: LAW

Constitutional Monarchy (See **Monarchy**)

Constitutionalism

A. *Constitutionalism* (or *constitutional government*) denotes a system of effective regularized restraints upon the authoritative decision-makers in a political society. In short, it is the rule of law or limited government in contrast to arbitrary rule. All governments fall somewhere between the extremes of 'no restraint' and 'complete restraint'; constitutional government is a matter of degree and of definition. The British, for example, have become used to equating 'limited government' with restraints on the substance of governmental and legislative power, whereas the rule of law may mean simply procedural restraint in the sense of equality before the law, *nulla poena sine lege*, etc.; and some would regard the latter procedural safeguards as a sufficient indicator of constitutionalism.

Standards in the form of conventions, morals, and law are essential, but to modern constitutionalists insufficient. Hence standards, plus institutionalized safeguards, are the essentials for the realization of constitutionalism.

B. The primary basis of constitutionalism is a standard or norm against which governmental action is measured; constitutional government is conformance with the norms. From the Greek to the modern age these norms have been visualized as some kind of natural or divine order, custom, or positive law.

1. Modern constitutionalism begins with attempts to provide legal techniques and political machinery for controlling rulers who employed their power despotically in disregard of 'constitutional' obligations. Many writers see the beginning of modern constitutionalism in the Conciliar Movement directed against the Church, and gradually carried over into the

Constructs

state, where it was applied against absolutism by religious dissenters from a state-controlled church, and by trading groups which found themselves hampered by mercantilist policies. Calvin endorsed constitutionalism by acknowledging that people might resist rulers who governed contrary to God's will. Coke waged his battle against the Stuarts in the name of constitutionalism. The Glorious Revolution of 1688 is usually regarded as marking the triumph of constitutionalism in England. The American Revolution was fought under the banner of revolt against 'Acts of pretended Legislation'.

2. The methods of holding wielders of political power responsible are the distinctive marks of modern constitutionalism.

(a) In the case of the United Kingdom, under its uncodified constitution and parliamentary legal omnipotence, most writers see the main restraint as 'powerful tradition'.

(b) C. J. Friedrich (*Constitutional Government and Democracy*, Boston: Ginn, 1946, pp. 121-2) thinks that perhaps the most important is '... the alteration of government between two or three parties ...'.

(c) The codification of fundamentals in a basic legal document (constitution) restrains by clarifying powers and limitations; moreover, the resulting document tends to become a political force of its own. Such devices are apparently increasingly regarded as a necessary part of the 'impedimenta of statehood'.

(d) Judicial review, of executive actions in Great Britain and of legislation as well in the United States, is generally regarded as among the more effective restraints. Since constitutional law is supposedly more basic than ordinary law, constitutionalism frequently expresses itself by imposing greater obstacles in the way of changing the former.

(e) Friedrich argues that the division of powers is the basis of civilized government, and that that is 'what is meant by constitutionalism' (ibid., p. 4). Again '... the maintenance of all restraints depends in the end upon a balance of groups and classes in the community to whose government they apply' (ibid., p. 124). It follows, therefore, that various forms of functional and geographic separation of power, serve to check power, and thus limit it on the domestic scene as the balance of power (q.v.) is supposed to do internationally.

Charles P. Schleicher

See also: CONSTITUTION
RULE OF LAW

134

Constructed Type (See **Ideal-type Analysis**)

Constructs

Constructs are hypothetical categories (q.v.) which possess heuristic or interpretive value even though they do not purport to describe accurately any observable reality. They may be (a) models of behaviour based on explicit norms or principles; (b) hypothetical entities or processes whose existence can be inferred only from their causes, consequences, or manifestations; (c) *ideal* or *constructed* types that combine selected variables in order to focus attention upon common elements in diverse concrete situations or to provide an heuristic device for examining relationships among the selected variables. Economists are the best example of those using models based on explicit norms or principles, although some sociologists, particularly M. Weber, use 'rational action' as a 'pure type' without empirical reference. Sociologists usually, however, create constructs by abstracting related characteristics from observed phenomena. Psychologists, on the other hand, at times postulate entities, processes, or events, the presence of which can be inferred only from their presumed causes, their manifestations, or their consequences. Familiar examples are the Freudian id (q.v.), ego (q.v.), and superego (q.v.). Some behaviourist psychologists have also expressed the view that 'hypothetical constructs' that 'refer to processes or entities that are not directly observed' and do not 'merely abstract the empirical relationships' can be useful theoretical tools (K. MacCorquodale & P. E. Meehl, 'On a Distinction Between Hypothetical Constructs and Intervening Variables', *Psychological Review*, vol. 55, 1948, pp. 104, 106).

When employed self-consciously and critically, constructs constitute a legitimate and frequently invaluable device for analysing and explaining human behaviour. When used without a clear identification and awareness of their nature as hypothetical categories, they may be reified and confused with 'reality', i.e. observable phenomena.

Ely Chinoy

See also: CATEGORY
IDEAL-TYPE ANALYSIS
MODEL

Consumers' Capital (See **Capital**)

Consumers' Surplus (See **Surplus**)

Agreements intending to create but not actually creating binding obligations for reasons of fact, law, or both are mentioned in the definition. In strict logic these agreements may be outside the precise meaning of contract. The general rule is that any agreement is a contract so long as it satisfies jurisdictional requirements as to capacity of the parties, legality of the objectives set out, and formality as to preparation. Limitations upon contract, therefore, are discovered largely through the study of real and apparent exceptions to this rule. Thus reference is often made to, for example, *void contracts* (which have no real standing and hence no legal effect), *voidable contracts* (valid unless and until abrogated at the option of the disadvantaged party), *unenforceable contracts* (where performance is permissible although the law will give no remedy for the breach), and even *illegal contracts* (where enforcement is never a possibility and the instrument may be the foundation for legal proceedings against the parties).

B. The detailed law of contract is both occasioned by and developed in the commercial era of social development. Early law was concerned largely with the land-tenure system and problems of keeping the peace. Moreover, personal relationships during early stages of legal development revolved around the conception of status far more than around contract as the latter term is now understood. Significantly, some of the most essential features of the modern law of contract (at least in Anglo-American law which is based very little upon the law of Rome) were not arrived at until about the middle of the 19th century.

It has been well said that progressive societies proceed from a system of status to one of contract. However, it should be noticed that even today an individual often enters by agreement into relationships which seem to involve surviving overtones of status. Thus, while marriage may be effected by an agreement which is essentially contractual in nature, much of the law relating to marriage comes into operation without relation to any express terms in the agreement. Moreover, many marriage obligations cannot be obviated by agreement between the parties. A second observation is that in modern industrial relations it is commonplace for an individual to entrust his bargaining power to some association. He may enter and leave such a relationship by agreement, but contractual negotiations thereunder are more

between association and association than between individual and individual.

However much of the law of contract may be retaining, or even extending, its scope in modern society, there remains the observation that many relations between employer and employee which once were left to individual agreement within the principle of contract have now been brought within the sphere of governmental control through industrial legislation.

Ralph Jones

See also: COMMERCIAL LAW
STATUS

Control Group (See **Experiment**)

Conurbation

A. *Conurbation* denotes a large geographical area, extending across several local government boundaries, forming in socio-economic terms a single continuous urban region.

B. The term was first used by P. Geddes in the early years of the present century in his discussions of city regions. Further studies of urban aggregates in Great Britain (largely upon the basis of census material) were made in the inter-war years by C. B. Fawcett (*Sociological Review*, vol. XIV, 1922, p. 111, and 'Distribution of the Urban Population in Great Britain', *Geographical Journal*, vol. 79, 1932, pp. 100 ff.). In the 1922 paper Professor Fawcett lists 73 urban areas as conurbations, with populations ranging from about $7\frac{1}{2}$ million (Greater London) to 51,300. The definition from which he operated was stated in his 1932 article as follows: 'I use it [conurbation] in the strict sense of a continuously urban area ... an area occupied by a continuous series of dwellings, factories and other buildings, harbour and docks, urban parks and playing fields, etc., which are not separated from each other by rural land; though in many cases in this country such an urban area includes enclaves of rural land which is still in agricultural occupation' 'Distribution of the Urban Population in Great Britain', p. 100).

Criticism of this definition has proceeded on two lines:

1. It does not place sufficient emphasis upon socio-economic factors: does not ask with sufficient emphasis the following question: how far does a particular centre act as a focal point in trade, industry and commerce?

2. A clear indication is required of where the

Convention

outer boundaries of the continuous urban area are to be drawn.

C. These considerations were taken into account in the preparation of the British 1951 Census in the reports of which the term *conurbation* is officially used for the first time to describe 'Continuously urbanised areas surrounding large population centres, which are, to a greater or lesser extent, focal points of economic and social activity' (*Census 1951 Great Britain One Per Cent Sample Tables*, Part II, Appendix D, p. xvii, London: Her Majesty's Stationery Office, 1952). Examination of these reports show that these areas are 'all large units with populations approaching or in excess of a million persons in each case' (*Census 1951, Preliminary Report*, p. xxii). They are clearly not exhaustive lists of those urban areas in Great Britain to which the term may quite accurately be applied.

D. For a full discussion of particular criteria in determining boundaries see the paper 'Conurbations in England and Wales' contributed to the World Population Conference, 1954, by L. M. Feery, of the General Register Office, London (*Proceedings of the World Population Conference, 1954*, U.N., vol. IV, p. 624). 'The term conurbation is used in Great Britain to describe an urban area, comprising two or more local administrative districts, which can be regarded as a single entity for the purpose of many demographic, economic and social studies. Its unit is based mainly on continuity of streets and buildings with other features of urban development, though it may contain some sparsely populated areas particularly on the outer fringe. Population density is a factor which, allied to local knowledge, helps to determine where the boundaries of a conurbation should lie, some allowance being made for further expansion in order to avoid the need to revise boundaries at frequent intervals to the detriment of statistical comparability' (L. M. Feery, 'Conurbations in England and Wales', p. 624).

J. Gould

See also: METROPOLITAN AREA

Convention

A. 1. *Convention* may be defined as a practice, usage, or rule of conduct or behaviour on what may or may not be done by members of a given group or community.

2. *Convention* when used to designate an international contractual instrument may be defined as a written or oral agreement between one or more states, or organizations of states, intended to create legal rights and duties which are binding on the signatories.

3. The term *convention* may also be used to refer to a meeting of delegates or representatives for some special purpose as in the case of professional associations, interest groups or political parties.

B. The term convention as applied to a rule or standard of conduct although generally utilized in the social sciences does not appear to have acquired any esoteric meaning in regard to any one of the individual disciplines. An examination of the literature reveals that sociology tends to use terms with a more precise meaning such as *folkways* (q.v.) or *norms* (q.v.). Political science tends to use the term *custom and usage*.

C. International contractual instruments between states or between states and international organizations may be called by a variety of names such as *convention*, *declaration*, *pact*, *protocol*, or *treaty*. Although such instruments are popularly known as treaties, the vast majority of such agreements concluded between 1864 and 1945 were called conventions (D. P. Myers, 'The Names and Scope of Treaties', *American Journal of International Law*, vol. 51, 1957, p. 576 ff.). In the past names have more or less been chosen at random with little thought as to their signficance. For instance in 1824 the United States concluded a Convention of Peace, Amity, Navigation and Commerce with Columbia which did not differ from similar agreements with other countries which had received the title *treaty* and the preamble of the instrument referred to it as a 'treaty or general convention' (*U.S. Statutes at Large*, Foreign Treaties, vol. VIII, Boston: Little, Brown, 1853, p. 306). In the past writers and codifiers have generally contended that any technical distinction between these names is difficult to maintain; that they are equally binding and that they have the same legal force (L. Oppenheim, *International Law*, London: Longmans, Green, 8th edn., 1955, vol. 1, and H. W. Briggs, *The Law of Nations*, London: Stevens, 2nd edn., 1953, p. 836 ff.). However, of late there has been a tendency to differentiate more sharply in terminology. Myers ('The Names and Scope of Treaties', p. 583) admits that there is often no difference between a treaty and a convention, but finds a trend in modern practice for the term to take on a more particular meaning. He writes in part: 'Convention has become the standard name of instruments produced by multilateral bodies, which in particular instances study specific phases of a general subject. ... A convention does not deal with questions of high policy between the parties, and the subjects with which it does deal do not require comprehensive treatment of a field of relations' (ibid., pp. 578, 583). This latter view gives cognizance to the increasing use of multilateral conventions by nations and international organizations to cover a wide variety of subjects vital to the conduct of relations between states, such as postal regulations, control of communications, treatment of prisoners of war, and control of opium traffic, which though often not of great political import are so necessary for the well-being of the international community. In the not too far distant future the term convention may be used entirely for such instruments, but in general practice it still has a much wider meaning.

D. The term *convention* is also used in political science to designate a system of delegate conventions devised by political parties on local, state, and national levels as a vehicle for making party nominations and adopting party platforms. The Constitution of the United States does not make provision for political parties or their organization and procedures. The parties initially utilized a caucus (q.v.) composed of the national senators and representatives of the party to select party candidates, but this system did not give proper voice to the minorities and gave undue influence to legislators. By the 1830s the caucus was abandoned in favour of a national convention. At the turn of the century the system was being greatly discredited by abuses of party bosses and machines which packed the conventions with their followers through dubious means and kept these bodies from being truly representative. By the first decade of the 19th century conventions in many states gave way to a system of direct primary elections for the selection of party candidates through normal election facilities at state expense. However, the national convention has persisted. It meets every four years to nominate candidates for the Presidency and Vice-Presidency and to adopt a national party platform. Both parties have adopted formulae by which each state is assured national representation, but is given a larger share of delegates in proportion to the success of the party in that state during the previous elections. The national convention provides an instrument through which opposing sections and interest groups can effect a compromise as is noted by V. O. Key, Jr. (*Politics, Parties and Pressure Groups*, New York: Thomas Y. Crowell Co., 4th edn., 1958, p. 473) when he writes '... the total performance of the national convention, as an instrumentality for weaving together the diverse and geographically scattered elements of each party into a national whole, constitutes an impressive political achievement'.

Robert E. Clute

See also: CAUCUS
TREATY

Convergence (See **Cultural Convergence**)

Co-operation(Economics)(Also **Co-operative; Co-operative Society**)

A. *Co-operation*, in general, indicates any form of working together as contrasted with competition or opposition. In economics and social history it is used (as is the related adjective *co-operative*) to describe any form of social or economic organization in which the stress is laid on working together in harmony as against competition.

B. In this more specific semi-technical usage it refers to the aims and activities of the Co-operative Movement (most sections of which are now organized in the International Co-operative Alliance founded in 1895). During the 19th century, the movement developed variously in different European countries—the consumers' co-operatives (see under C (1)) developing earliest in Great Britain, the producers' co-operatives (see C (2) below) striking deeper roots in continental countries, especially France, Germany, and Italy.

C. Co-operation takes many forms of which the following are the most important.

1. A consumers' co-operative society is a form of economic organization in which consumers are joined together (a) (primarily) for the purchase of goods in retail stores under the collective ownership of the members, and/or (b) for wholesale trade and production.

Most such co-operative societies profess to follow the original principles (the Rochdale principles laid down by the Rochdale Pioneer Society in 1844), viz.: (i) open membership; (ii) one member, one vote, irrespective of the number of shares held; (iii) a limited but variable greater interest on shares; (iv) distribution of surplus to purchasers of goods.

139

Co-operation

Three further requirements, included in a statement of the Rochdale principles drawn up in 1951 by a special Committee of the I.C.A. found less universal acceptance: (v) political and religious neutrality; (vi) cash trading; (vii) promotion of education.

2. A producers' co-operative society is a form of economic organization in which producers join together for common production or the provision of common services.

Clearly the 'co-operative principles' (e.g. open membership; non-profit rule) outlined above cannot always apply in full in this sphere. Instead of open membership, membership is (a) *restricted* by the scale of operation, (b) *limited* to employees and certain former employees. Again a surplus, *over and above interest on capital* may be distributed either in the form of additions to employees' wages or in the form of dividends to those who consume the product.

3. An agricultural co-operative society is a form of economic organization among a group of farmers or peasants, either for the purchase of one or more of a range of farm requisites, or for the collective sale of farm produce, or for the purpose of making advances of capital or credit to the member, either out of their own resources or out of money borrowed for the purpose on their joint guarantee, or advanced by a government.

D. Co-operative is a description sometimes accorded to the collective farms of the Soviet Union (kolkhozi); but, whereas most agricultural co-operatives are based on individual peasant farming, the kolkhozi are associations for collective cultivation of the land, which they possess under the State, selling collectively their collective produce. Both producers' co-operatives (artels) and consumers' co-operatives (in the villages, but not in the towns) also exist in the Soviet Union, but are subject to state control, which is regarded as contrary to co-operative principles by most of the national bodies affiliated to the I.C.A.

G. D. H. Cole

See also: CO-OPERATION (Sociology)

Co-operation (Sociology)

A. *Co-operation* denotes common action towards shared goals which may be corporate or distributive. It may occur through a *division of labour* comprised of like or unlike tasks. It generally occurs in response to shared social norms, and may be valued in itself as well as instrumentally.

B. Even though the term is explicitly considered in sociology as a basic social process or relation, there is considerable confusion concerning its meaning. One finds such logical peculiarities as the following: rivals co-operate in rivalry; the exploited co-operate with their exploiter to be exploited; those in conflict co-operate to maintain the conflict. In such cases it seems that language has lost its meaning, and this tendency is also evidenced in such logical hybrids as *competitive co-operation, antagonistic co-operation* (q.v.), *co-operative conflict, coerced co-operation*, and finally the lumping together of *co-operation-competition* as one concept. Such an amalgam of logical contraries may represent an effort to depict nuances in human relations, but the result is that each term is self-contradictory. New concepts should be developed to cover these subtleties. If the minimum notion of co-operation is some kind of working together, then it is quite clear that rivals by definition do not co-operate, and the same holds true for relations of exploitation or conflict.

C. Co-operation is the sine qua non of society, and in certain respects also of organic nature, as Kropotkin and many recent interpretations have attempted to demonstrate. This continuity between the organic and the cultural is pointed out by many writers and finds its most explicit expression in human ecology (q.v.). Ecologists, however, tend to stress the competitive elements in the human ecological order and consequently minimize the co-operative aspects. The symbiotic relations obtaining among different species have been reformulated at the human level as relations where 'the utilitarian element predominates and where persons use one another as mere tools' (E. T. Hiller, *Principles of Sociology*, New York: Harper & Brothers, 1933, p. 148). Competitive and/or antagonistic co-operation is another idea arising out of this heritage. It should be pointed out, however, that if the antagonisms are suppressed or latent, as it is frequently put, then they are of no relevance to the co-operative relation; and if there is quarrelling over the distribution of the results, then some term other than co-operation should be used to designate that relation. Use of the term co-operation generally implies that the relation is voluntary.

D. Both individuals and groups co-operate, though the literature stresses group co-operation. Group co-operation refers to both the internal

140

activities of a group and relations among groups. In either case 'group co-operation is agreed-upon joint action', or 'any uniting of either similar or dissimilar efforts for the promotion of life or common aims' (L. Broom & P. Selznick, *Sociology*, Evanston, Ill.: Row, Peterson, 1955, p. 34; E. T. Hiller, *Principles of Sociology*, p. 200). The uniting of like efforts or functions has been divided into companionable labour—done with others for pleasure and congeniality; and supplementary labour—done for reasons of efficiency, although frequently accompanied by congeniality. The uniting of like efforts has generally taken place in a folk society and/or primary group context; and of unlike efforts in more complex civilizations. The terms *primary* and *secondary co-operation* have been applied to these distinctions. In general, there is co-operation within the group with the discouraging of opposition and conflict. The relation to other groups is frequently viewed as one of struggle. However, in a highly differentiated society the temporary hostilities among groups should not blind one to the basic co-operation that takes place, for such a society is a highly interdependent one.

H. Otto Dahlke

See also: COMPETITION
             CONFLICT

Corporate Property (See **Property**)

Corporation (See **Property**)

Corporatism (Also **Corporativism**)

A. *Corporatism* (also *corporativism*) denotes the theory, developed in fascist Italy, justifying the organization of the economic system into 'corporations' subordinate to the state and claiming that such a reorganized economic system renders superfluous political representative institutions.

B. 1. Attacking both socialism and capitalism, Italian fascism sought to reorganize the economic life and structure of Italy through a mechanism of control called *corporatism*. The economy was divided into associations of workers, employers, and the professions, and such associations were called syndicates. Only one syndicate was allowed in each branch of industry or business, and though membership in the syndicates was not a legal requirement, the payment of dues was. The officials of the syndicates were either fascist politicians or persons

of reliable loyalty to the fascist regime. In effect, these associations of workers and employers were nothing but instruments of state policy, with little will or life of their own.

To make this dependency of the vocational associations (or syndicates) of capital and labour even more certain and obvious, the fascist government, in 1934, established *corporations*, the purpose of which was to unite the associations of workers and employers in a given industry in one administrative agency. According to law, the syndicates were autonomous, but, *de facto*, were run by the state. The corporation, supreme instrument of fascist economic organization and control, made no pretence of autonomy, as it was nothing but an administrative agency of the state, in no way different from the police, the judiciary, and other tools of fascist government using totalitarian methods. To emphasize the role of the corporations as governmental agencies, a new 'Ministry of Corporations' was set up, directly dependent, as were all other ministries, on the dictator, Benito Mussolini.

2. The philosophy of corporatism rested on two assumptions. First, man should not be politically articulate as a *citizen*, but only as a worker, entrepreneur, farmer, doctor, or lawyer; general political problems are assumed to be too complicated for the mass of the people, who are only expected to understand issues that bear directly on their professional or vocational work. Second, members of a small ruling class are supposed to understand broad issues that effect the whole society, and they alone are therefore qualified to govern the community. This conception is Platonic in origin, and in modern times anti-democratic thinkers like Burke and Hegel have supported it against the claims of democratic theory. In his speech of November 14, 1933, Mussolini stated that the essential bases of corporatism were a single party, a totalitarian government, and an atmosphere of strong ideal tension. The fascist party provided the first two elements, and the strong ideal tension was supplied by the ceaseless propaganda of expansionist imperialism.

Wherever Italian fascism was copied, corporatism was eagerly adopted, as in Portugal in 1933, in Austria in 1934, in Spain in 1939, and in the Western Hemisphere in Brazil in 1937, and finally in Argentina during the dictatorship of Peron (1943–55). As soon as the totalitarian system is replaced by a liberal regime, as happened in Austria (1945), Brazil (1944), and Argentina (1955), corporatism gives way at

Corruption

once for the free associations of workers and employers, independent of the state in law and in fact.

C. The fascist corporations were, as D. Mack Smith points out, 'more an aspiration than a reality' (*Italy*, Ann Arbor: University of Michigan Press, 1959, p. 395). For many years after 1926—when they were provided for by law—they were non-existent. 'On May 9, 1934 the Central Corporative Committee, Mussolini presiding, finally decided to bring into existence, in June, 1934, twenty-two corporations representing various occupations' (W. Ebenstein, *Fascist Italy*, New York: American Book Co., 1939, p. 140). In 1939 the Chamber of Fasces and Corporations was set up—to replace the last vestiges of the parliamentary system. The corporations were, in fact, 'little more than an attempt to keep a tight hold on the workers in strictly centralised unions' D. Mack Smith, *Italy*, p. 395). But Mussolini and his circle attempted to stress the corporate motif in their ideology as a significant and crucial innovation. They claimed that it signalled the end of economic liberalism and that corporatism was 'disciplined and hence controlled economics'.

D. The fascist corporation is not to be confused with the ancient Roman corporation which owed its existence and operation to the free will of individual citizens who banded together for multifarious purposes, as long as such purposes were not against the law or public order and morality. Nor is the fascist corporation to be confused with the American or British business corporation—a company of limited liability, owned and operated by private citizens, and generally engaged in business. Above all, the American business corporation, like the ancient Roman corporation, is not a creature of the state, but comes into existence when individual citizens spontaneously band together for whatever purpose, as long as it is legal.

William Ebenstein

See also: FASCISM

Corruption

A. *Corruption* in public life is the use of public power for private profit, preferment, or prestige, or for the benefit of a group or class, in a way that constitutes a breach of law or of standards of high moral conduct.

B. Corruption involves a violation of a public duty or a departure from high moral standards in exchange for (or in anticipation of) personal pecuniary gain, power, or prestige. Such conduct may be illegal or may constitute departure from ethical standards without violation of law. Legislation that defines and outlaws improper conduct in connection with elections (see the British Corrupt and Illegal Practices Act of 1883, a law that has been widely copied elsewhere in the world), the bribery of public officers, the falsification of public records, the embezzlement of public funds, and the fraudulent sale of public lands and other natural resources constitutes the principal body of law dealing with corruption. Partiality in the grant of licences, the 'sale' of honours, favouritism in the making of contracts, the making of tax refunds that outrage public standards of good conduct, favouritism in the enforcement of statutes against such immoral conduct as prostitution, the deposit of public funds in friendly banks, the disclosure to friends or to former or prospective business or professional associates of information on the basis of which these individuals may reap pecuniary benefits, and providing protection for certain class interests, while not always made illegal, often are viewed as examples of corruption in public life.

Corruption is characteristic of no one period in political history, nor of any one country. While the form it takes varies in history and from nation to nation, it is endemic in both authoritarian and party systems of government. Marked increases in the incidence of corruption often are associated with change in the structure of political and social power (J. J. Senturia, 'Political Corruption', in E. R. A. Seligman, (ed.), *Encyclopedia of the Social Sciences*, New York: The Macmillan Co., 1931, vol. IV, pp. 448–52; C. J. Friedrich, *Constitutional Government and Democracy*, Boston: Little, Brown, 1941, p. 300; see also R. K. Carr et al., *American Democracy in Theory and Practice* New York: Rinehart, 1951; H. Finer, *Theory and Practice of Modern Government*, New York: Henry Holt, 1949).

Charles Aikin

See also: NEPOTISM
PATRONAGE

Cosmology (Also **Cosmogony**)

A. *Cosmology* is that aspect of religious or philosophical belief which concerns the fundamental character of the universe. *Cosmogony* is that part of cosmology concerned specifically with the creation of the universe. While the cosmology and cosmogony of a society may find expression in the science of that society and may in part be shaped by that science, fundamentally they are parts of the religious and philosophical belief system and tend to be embedded, even in civilized societies, in myth (q.v.) and ritual (q.v.).

B. Cosmology and cosmogony as such do not invariably attract the attention of present-day social scientists. As might be suspected, those interested are generally those whose study of cosmology and cosmogony is part of their study of religion (q.v.) and mythology. In such studies the meaning is more often assumed than defined; and attention is centred upon how cosmology and cosmogony (as well as other elements of myth) are related to other aspects of religion such as ritual and value (q.v.).

Mischa Titiev

See also: MYTH
RITUAL

Cost

A. *Cost*, in economics, is that which is sacrificed in order to obtain anything. It implies the destruction or surrender of value or the performance of activity which is irksome at the margin, if not in and of itself (J. Viner, 'Cost', in E. R. A. Seligman (ed.), *Encyclopedia of the Social Sciences*, New York: The Macmillan Co., 1931, vol. 4, pp. 466–7). It may be measured in money or in economic goods, pain, or disutility. If measured in money it is termed *money cost*; if in goods, pain, or disutility, *real cost*.

B. Rational economic behaviour of the enterprise is usually taken to imply an effort to maximize the positive difference between total revenue and total cost, and profits are maximized at the output where marginal costs and marginal revenue are equal. Since the firm is expected to choose the lowest-cost method of producing a given product, costs of production enter significantly into the allocation of scarce resources and the location of industrial activity. While the costs of production are real, they are usually measured in money terms, because stress is placed on those factors which are bought and sold in the market and hence already have a money price. There are, however, cost problems which can only be handled by using the sub-concepts of *outlay* and *implicit costs; opportunity* or *alternative costs; variable,*

fixed, total and *unit costs;* and, finally, *marginal cost.*

1. The profit and loss statement of an enterprise generally lists the costs that are paid for the factors of production that come from outside the enterprise. These costs are known as *outlay*. This frequently means that in small, individually owned enterprises, the cost of management is hidden since it is furnished from within the enterprise and remains an *implicit cost*. Before true profit can be calculated this cost must be determined (E. Whittaker, *Economic Analysis*, New York: John Wiley, 1956, pp. 212–14).

2. The determination of implicit cost, as well as other managerial decisions, must be based on the concept of alternative or opportunity costs, which measures cost in terms of the alternatives or opportunities that are foregone. Thus the owner of the self-managed enterprise may calculate the implicit costs of his management in terms of the income he has foregone by staying out of the market in that area where he could command the highest income. The use of calculated opportunity or alternative costs need not be restricted to the relation of outlay and implicit costs, however. If, after a factor of production has already been contracted for, the use of that factor for alternative purposes may be determined by which use offers the best return, even though neither use will totally offset the outlay originally made.

3. The economist divides the costs of the enterprise into two major categories: those that vary in the aggregate as output varies and those that remain constant with changes in output. Current usage among economists is to describe the former as *variable costs*, the latter as *fixed costs*. Total cost is then the summation of all variable and fixed costs. Usually the cost accountant and frequently the economist is primarily concerned with *unit* rather than *total* costs; average total *unit cost* is the summation of average variable cost and average fixed cost. Variation in price levels produces great distortion in the real value of fixed cost, as historically recorded. A firm making money profits may be making real losses.

4. Fundamental to much in economics is the concept of *marginal cost* which may be approximately defined as the addition to total cost involved in producing one more unit of output.

C. *Social costs* as contrasted with the costs that are relevant only to the enterprise are much

Cost of Living

more complex, and must frequently be calculated only as real costs because they cannot be measured in money. There may be a great divergence between social and private costs: the smoke nuisance of a factory constitutes a social cost of production, but it does not enter into the profit-and-loss statement of the firm (A. C. Pigou, *The Economics of Welfare*, London: Macmillan, 2nd edn., 1924, p. 162). Nevertheless, efforts must be made to calculate such costs, and some of the cost concepts, particularly those of opportunity or alternative costs, are relevant.

1. It may be said, for example, that the real cost to a community of producing a commodity is the alternatives which are foregone. Thus in a war economy additional munitions can be produced after full employment of resources has been attained only at the cost of giving up the production of some consumer goods. During a widespread business depression, on the other hand, idle workers can be employed on public work projects at virtually no real costs.

2. At the level of international trade, opportunity or alternative costs for the society must be related to the *comparative cost* of producing similar goods in one or more nations, and the relations of these costs will determine the *comparative cost advantage* (q.v.).

Clark Lee Allen

Cost of Living

A. The *cost of living* may be defined as the *monetary* cost of maintaining a given standard or level of living by any particular group or groups within a population. While the concept *real cost of living* may be said to have some meaning in that it designates the actual sacrifices of effort or pain necessary for the maintenance of a level or standard of living, the difficulties of determining the crucial sacrifices are so great, that the term cannot at this time be given substantive definition.

B. The *cost of living* concept is usually used to express the monetary cost of maintaining a specified level or standard of living. The standard or level of living against which the cost of living is measured can be any given standard or level. Often the concept relates to the maintenance of what is considered to be an adequate standard of living. In this context the cost of living is '... the sum spent for those things which are considered to be necessary for proper existence ...' (National Industrial Conference Board, *Cost of Living in the United States, 1914–1926*, New York: National Industrial Conference Board, 1930, p. 11). Difficulties arise, however, when an effort is made to measure the cost of living as related to an actual level of living or an ideal standard of living held by a total population or a sub-group thereof. While a *cost of living index* may be constructed, which may be used to measure changes in the cost of living over time, by assembling and weighting the items of a given level or standard of living and then expressing the monetary cost at any particular time as a percentage of the cost of the same level or standard during some base year, controversy over such an index is almost inevitable. Even the measurement of the cost of living through the use of an index for a particular group is difficult, especially with regard to the weighting of the various items of the index, since the desires and purchases of the consumers do not remain constant, but vary from month to month. Comparison of the cost of living of the same group over long periods of time, or of the costs of living of various groups historically, simultaneously within a society, or across national boundaries, is difficult, if not impossible, because the standards and levels of living are simply not the same. The most that can usually be done is to formulate a statement as to what the comparative money costs *would be*, if the various groups actually wanted or did consume the same amount and kinds of goods and services.

C. It is obvious that the monetary cost of a given level of living measures only one of the variables that determine what might be called the *real cost of living*. If the money prices for a given level or standard of living are the same for an individual at two points in time at which his monetary income varies, even while he remains in the same occupation, it is obvious that the *real* cost of living, in at least one possible meaning of the term, is not the same at the two points in time. So also if two persons with similar occupations in different economic systems pay the same money prices for their consumer goods, but one man must work twice as long for the same amount of money, it is hardly realistic to say that their real costs of living are the same, even though their monetary costs are. The difficulty in speaking of *real cost of living* arises from two sources, however. (a) How can it be conceptually separated from other concepts which get at the same variables? What is the difference between *real cost of living* and *real income*? Or rather how can they be related to one another, since their measurements overlap? (b) What are the real costs of living and how do various real costs relate to one another? The work which one does is a real cost of maintaining a level of living, but so also are the alternative consumer goods that are given up, provided they are desired. Perhaps the best that can be done is to restrict the term *cost of living* to the monetary cost factor, recognizing its limitations, and then to use it in as unambiguous a manner as possible to measure *one* of the variables that determine the actual economic status of groups and individuals.

Norman J. Wood

See also: COST
         INDEX

Couvade

A. *Couvade* denotes a variety of customs involving the simulation by a husband of the experiences of childbirth.

B. 1. The customs include, e.g. fasting and taking to bed. The ethnographic evidence for such customs, and their significance, are discussed in E. B. Tylor, *Researches into the Early History of Mankind* (London: John Murray, 3rd rev. edn., 1878, p. 291, et seq.). Tylor also uses the term to cover certain other activities on the part of the father, e.g. among the Land Dayaks of South Borneo the father is obliged to refrain from certain activities *before* his wife's childbirth. He also uses the term to cover various kinds of taboos which are imposed in some societies on a father while his child is in early infancy. But since it has been found to be very general in primitive societies for taboos of some kind to be observed by both parents before or after the birth of a child, the term *couvade* has been restricted to cases where the experiences of the wife are actually simulated.

2. The phrase 'faire la couvade' was said to be in use in Béarn, in the south of France, as recently as the early 19th century. Another authority describes a custom which was current among the Basques as late as the middle of the last century whereby, when a child was born, its father went to bed, taking the baby with him, and was complimented by his neighbours while his wife went about her normal tasks (F. Michel, *Le Pays basque*, Paris: Firmin-Didot, 1857, p. 201, quoted in E. B. Tylor, *Researches into the Early History of Mankind*, p. 302).

L. P. Mair

Covert or Implicit Culture

Covert or Implicit Culture

A. *Covert* or *implicit culture* is that sector of culture (q.v.)—unstated premises and crypto-categories—which is not ordinarily verbalized by culture carriers and which must be reconstructed by the analyst whether the analyst comes from within or without the culture.

B. Anthropologists have long sensed that there was more to cultures than could be generalized directly from the evidence of the eye and the ear. They realized that the distinctive quality of each culture arose largely from underlying but very pervasive principles which even the most articulate informant could not verbalize.

1. E. Sapir was very sensitive to such highest common factors or least common denominators in cultures, and he came close to stating the idea of *covert* or *implicit* culture ('Culture, Genuine and Spurious', *American Journal of Sociology*, vol. XXIX, 1923–4, pp. 401–29; 'The Unconscious Patterning of Behavior in Society', in E. S. Dummer (ed.), *The Unconscious*, New York: Knopf, 1927).

2. A. R. Radcliffe-Brown also recognized the need to go beyond what participants in the culture could tell the investigator: 'We can ... find, beneath the diversities, a limited number of general principles applied and combined in various ways' ('The Study of Kinship Systems', *Journal of the Royal Anthropological Institute*, vol. LXXI, 1941, p. 17).

C. C. Kluckhohn introduced the term *covert culture* in 1941 '[A feature of the covert culture] is reducible to a "principle" which is, so to speak, "behind" the structural regularities of the overt culture, which "accounts for" two or more specific patterns' ('Patterning as Exemplified in Navaho Culture', in L. Spier et al. (eds.), *Language, Culture and Personality*, Menasha, Wisconsin: Sapir Memorial Publication Fund, 1941, p. 114). In 1943 he defined *covert culture* as 'that sector of the culture of which the members of the society are unaware or minimally aware' and discussed one aspect: 'the implicit or suppressed premises which tend to be characteristic of members of a certain group' (C. Kluckhohn, 'Covert Culture and Administrative Problems', *American Anthropologist*, vol. 45, 1943, pp. 217–18).

1. Kluckhohn's concept of covert culture was derived largely from Sapir, but the term was taken from unpublished lectures of R. Linton who later published his own definition: '[culture] ... includes phenomena of at least three

Credit

different orders: material, that is products of industry; kinetic, that is, overt behavior (since this necessarily involves movement); and psychological, that is, the knowledge, attitudes, and values shared by the members of a society … the phenomena of the first two orders may be classed together as constituting the *overt* aspect of a culture. Those of the third order, that is, psychological phenomena, constitute the *covert* aspect of a culture' (*The Cultural Background of Personality*, New York: D. Appleton-Century, 1945, p. 38).

2. The term *covert* has been frequently used by American social scientists in Linton's or in Kluckhohn's sense or a mixture, but rarely by British social scientists.

D. Kluckhohn and W. Kelly in 1945 avoided the word *covert* and substituted *implicit* because many students and social scientists reacted to *covert* as signifying what participants in the culture regarded as to be hidden on grounds of being either sacred or unpleasant ('The Concept of Culture', in R. Linton (ed.), *The Science of Man in the World Crisis*, New York: Columbia University Press, 1945, pp. 100–1 et passim). A. L. Kroeber's attempt to meet the tendency to regard *covert* as implying secretiveness is important: ' "covertness" here does not imply intent of concealment, as it does so often in interpersonal motivations, rather only lack of awareness. It is probably a case of cultural forms being relatively more and less in focus of awareness along a sliding scale partly of occasion and partly of generic situations. Thus rules of conduct, which serve as protections to personality, are likely to be formulated with awareness and explicitness, though also subject to attempted warpings by self-interest. At the other end of the scale, rules of grammar in speech, which normally serve to connect personalities when they feel relaxed and in least need of protection, are unformulated, except as a result of the highly sophisticated curiosity of linguists, and can properly be described as having grown up both anonymously and unconsciously' (*The Nature of Culture*, Chicago: University of Chicago Press, 1952, p. 130).

Clyde Kluckhohn

See also: CULTURE

Credit

A. *Credit* may refer to (a) the condition of being credit-worthy, that is, of being able to secure credit on favourable terms; (b) credit transactions, in which money, goods, or a promise to make a pecuniary payment for a debtor is given by the creditor in exchange for the debtor's promise to repay, normally at a future time; or (c) the institution of credit, by which through credit transactions command of economic resources is shifted from some hands and uses to others. The fundamental economic features of credit are that (a) it involves transactions completed over an extended period of time, and (b) credit and debt are inextricably related. Credit transactions normally, but not necessarily, involve the charging and payment of interest (q.v.).

B. The foundation of credit extension is the expectation that the debt contract will be honoured. This gives rise to the denotation of the word *credit* signifying the credit-worthiness of a person or institution, based on his integrity and capability. It is often said that the 'four Cs' of credit are Character, Capacity, Capital, and Collateral, the last being property specifically pledged to repayment of a debt. Capacity here refers to the debtor's income-earning potential, and it is upon income rather than property that the servicing of debt normally depends.

C. The question of what is exchanged in a *credit transaction* reveals many significant differences in viewpoint. Older economists conceived of credit as the exchange of present *goods* for future goods, or of present value (q.v.) for future value. A more modern view emphasizes the transfer of 'purchasing power', or general command over economic resources (G. N. Halm, *Monetary Theory*, Philadelphia: The Blakiston Co., 2nd edn., 1946).

The evolution of monetary and credit institutions and of modern monetary theory, however, have led towards recognizing credit transactions as uniquely pecuniary. Thus R. G. Hawtrey, after pointing out that 'Credit, in fact, is best understood as simply another name for debt', states, 'A debt is a pecuniary obligation; it is expressed as a number in terms of a unit which is called a "money of account"' ('Credit', in E. R. A. Seligman (ed.), *Encyclopedia of the Social Sciences*, New York: The Macmillan Co., 1931, vol. 4, p. 545). Analysis shows, furthermore, that what is used as money as a 'means of payment' in highly developed modern economies is itself mainly the promises or debts of banking institutions, expressed in units of the money of account. Today commercial banking is, in one of its most important aspects, a system of 'clearing'—

offsetting—credits and debts, and we have in effect a credit money, appropriate to our credit economy, as it differs from an economy of barter or of simple monetary exchange.

Credit is classified in numerous ways: (a) by the time span of the obligation, as short-term, intermediate, long-term, or payable on demand; (b) with regard to its purpose, as to finance production, consumption, or governmental operations; (c) by type of credit, as private, trade, and bank credit; (d) by its form, as book accounts, acceptances, promissory notes, bonds, etc.; and (e) with respect to security for the debt, as unsecured notes or bonds or those secured by various pledges of income or property.

D. A well-developed credit system, such as exists in modern credit economies, depends on the use of *credit instruments*, legal documents evidencing the existence and terms of credit or debt contracts. These fall in either one of two classes: (a) orders to pay, e.g. cheques and drafts, and (b) promises to pay, e.g. promissory notes or bonds. The evolution of the modern credit institution was contingent upon the development of these instruments and their *negotiability*, a legal characteristic which permits them to be taken with confidence by third parties.

In many cases credit extension takes the form of the debtor pledging his credit—promise to repay—to the creditor, who in turn pledges his credit to third parties. Commercial and accepting banks notably perform this function. The major economic effects of this are to substitute stronger credit for weaker or less well-known credit, and thus to increase the 'liquidity' as well as the quality of debt.

E. Once credit becomes an institution pervading the economic structure, the question remains as to its functions for the economy. While it is agreed that credit serves to transfer purchasing power and ultimately economic resources from creditor to debtor, some authorities hold that credit *only* transfers existing wealth, and cannot create additional wealth or income. This distinction often takes the form of contrasting credit, as merely an exchange of resources, with saving (q.v.) which purportedly creates capital (q.v.) representing real power to produce. While under conditions of full use of resources, expanded credit may lead only to inflation (q.v.), it would be a mistake to underrate the productive leverage which the institution of credit exerts in the modern economy.

Credit not only puts resources into the hands of those who may use them more effectively than others, but it serves a vital role in helping toward insuring that resources do not remain involuntarily idle. Hence public supervision of credit—and thereby of money (q.v.)—is recognized as one of the vital tasks of economic regulation.

James S. Earley

See also: Capital
Money
Money and Banking

Crime (Also **Criminal Law**)
A. A good account of both the common and legal usages of the term *crime* may be found in the remark of Lord Atkin—'The domain of criminal jurisprudence can only be ascertained by examining what acts at any particular period are declared by the State to be crimes, and the only common nature they will be found to possess is that they are prohibited by the State and that those who commit them are punished' (*Proprietary Articles Trade Association* v. *Att-Gen. of Canada*, The Law Reports [1931] Appeal Cases, pp. 310 ff. at p. 324).

A more recent attempt at a detailed statement of the scope of criminal law may be found in the argument of the *Wolfenden Committee Report on Homosexual Offences and Prostitution* (1957, Cmnd. 247). So far as concerned the scope of their inquiry, the function of the criminal law could be defined as follows: 'to preserve public order and decency, to protect the citizen from what is offensive or injurious, and to provide sufficient safeguards against exploitation and corruption of others, particularly those who are specially vulnerable because they are young, weak in body or mind, inexperienced, or in a state of special physical, official or economic dependence' (ibid., pp. 9–10).

B. In its most general sense *crime* is an act prohibited by law upon pain of punishment, i.e. an offence against the criminal law.

More specifically there are important variations. States differ in regard to what is declared to be criminal (there are wide differences in the sphere of sexual offences); even the same state may have defined the content of the criminal law otherwise at different historical periods (witchcraft as a crime used to be punishable in England and the United States). Similarly some states (the states of the U.S.A., many European countries, and British dominions and colonies)

Criminology

enjoy a comprehensive criminal code whereas the U.K. does not.

It is however possible to detect certain underlying unities in the notion of offences against the criminal law. (a) Such conduct is usually socially harmful and morally blameworthy. (b) Such conduct is also sufficiently serious for it to merit state intervention; it is not simply left to the individuals who may have been wronged to seek redress by way of civil action in the courts.

It should, however, be noted that: (a) By no means all antisocial conduct is criminal; (b) The test of moral wrong is not infallible, for many acts which are highly immoral may be quite outside criminal law. (c) It has been strongly suggested that some acts which are at present regarded as criminal offences should no longer be so treated, e.g. homosexual behaviour between consenting adult males, and attempted suicide. The Wolfenden Report contends that there must be a realm of private morality and immorality which is not the law's concern because crime and sin cannot be equated (ibid., p. 24).

C. Some criminologists have sought to widen the definition of crime so as to include types of socially deviant behaviour which are not punishable as offences in the courts but which are regarded as sociologically significant. For example, E. Sutherland, in his book on *White Collar Crime* (New York: The Dryden Press, 1949) writes about forms of business or commercial activity which are essentially dishonest or socially harmful, but may not *legally* constitute a criminal offence. This approach may be valuable in revealing the shortcomings of the criminal law or the true nature of deviant behaviour. However, it would be wise for criminologists not to stray too far from the consideration of behaviour legally defined as criminal (see J. Hall, *General Principles of Criminal Law*, Indianapolis: Bobbs-Merrill, 1947, pp. 10–11; D. R. Taft, *Criminology*, New York: The Macmillan Co., 1956, pp. 15–16).

J. E. Hall Williams

See also: CRIMINOLOGY

Criminology (Also **Penology**)

A. *Criminology* and *penology* are those subfields of sociology in which the investigator attempts to formulate and test theories as to why criminal law becomes law, why people break such laws, why societies do what they do to those who break such laws, and what the effects of varying modes of law enforcement are. Thus it is apparent that the two disciplines are concerned with the enforcement, by means of formal sanctions, of conformity to social norms, and with the conditions which produce nonconformity; and being so concerned are logically a part of the general field of social control (q.v.).

B. Contemporary criminology and penology give attention mostly to 'civilized' societies with formalized government. In such a context the criminologist has been forced to define crime as the violation of any law interpreted as protecting the public welfare, violation of which results in the charging of the state's law enforcement agencies with the responsibility of apprehension and punishment of the offender. Such a definition is necessary, even though many of these laws have never been the result of consensus (q.v.). Despite the heterogeneity of the laws which may be defined as criminal laws, and of the acts which may be defined as crimes, there is considerable unanimity among criminologists as to the major areas of investigation. These are: (a) statistical data on crimes and criminals; (b) police systems for apprehending violators; (c) court systems for trying the accused; (d) systems for treating or punishing the convicted; (e) systematic analysis of social conditions predictive of criminal behaviour and possibilities of rehabilitation.

C. By virtue of the nature of their subject matter, criminology and penology are applied sciences. The whole law enforcement machinery of society is an effort to prevent law violation. Thus the development of a body of theory concerning the causes of crime and the possibilities of modifying these causes is an integral part of the task of the criminologist. Similarly, the penologist is confronted with the task of evaluating and perhaps inventing systems of punishment and treatment.

Harlan W. Gilmore

See also: CRIME (also CRIMINAL LAW)
SOCIAL CONTROL
SOCIAL DISORGANIZATION

Cross-Cousins

A. In modern English a cousin is a cognate of the same generation as the person in reference. A first cousin is the child of a sibling (i.e. brother or sister) of a parent. A *cross-cousin* is a first cousin who is the child of a father's sister

148

or mother's brother (i.e. where the parental siblings are of opposite sex).

B. Cross-cousins assume importance in anthropological analysis because they lie outside the common prohibition of marriage with parallel cousins and because they are sometimes designated as preferred or even prescribed mates. Cross-cousin marriage may be symmetrical (or bilateral), in which case a man may marry either his father's sister's daughter or his mother's brother's daughter, or asymmetrical (or unilateral), in which case he may marry only one of the two kinds of cross-cousin. In the context of cross-cousin marriage a cross-cousin is not necessarily a first cousin; she may be any woman standing in the appropriate generation and descent class.

Maurice Freedman

See also: BILATERAL
 COGNATIC
 PARALLEL COUSIN
 UNILATERAL

Crowd

A. Considering the diversity and contradictions of the characteristics used by various social scientists to define *crowd*, it is difficult if not impossible to arrive at a universally acceptable definition. An effort at definition can be made, however, by focusing on those characteristics on which there is substantial agreement, by eliminating some of the most controversial characteristics, by speaking of the crowd-like features of some social groupings, and by the development of sub-concepts.

Thus a *crowd* proper might be defined as an aggregate of human beings in physical proximity, brought into direct and temporary contact, with strong rapport and mutual stimulation. Groupings which are not in physical proximity; audiences which have a predictable organization and are likely to be more reflective; and panic aggregates in which the participants do not feel rapport may be excluded. Crowds may develop spontaneously or through manipulation; and may or may not have a distinct central objective or differentiation among the participants in feelings, behaviour, and status positions. A common sub-classification based on the presence or absence of a central objective is that of the *acting crowd* in which attention is directed toward some common objective and the *expressive crowd* in which there is no distinct central focus and the participants engage only in excited movements.

Groupings such as audiences or street corner aggregates may become crowds; and a population at war or in panic may have certain crowd characteristics.

B. Although social scientists usually begin consideration of crowds with certain similar observations, the selection of different characteristics as essential and their extension to other contexts frequently results in variation and confusion in the use of the term. The primary questions about which there is disagreement are the following:

1. Is physical proximity of individuals necessary? Most authors agree with K. Davis, who writes, 'One criterion of the crowd is physical presence. ... Without such physical presence there can be no crowd' (*Human Society*, New York: The Macmillan Co., 1949, p. 347). A few social scientists, however, affirm that proximity is not necessary. Thus, C. A. Dawson and W. E. Gettys say, 'Physical proximity is not requisite to crowd formation. What is necessary is that the individuals composing the crowd must be in contact through communication' (*Introduction to Sociology*, New York: The Ronald Press, 1948, p. 608).

2. How far does the range of the term extend? Does it include the audience and the participants in panics? R. Brown, defining crowds as 'collectivities that are congregated and polarized on a temporary-irregular basis and which usually involve only temporary identification', includes both ('Mass Phenomena', in G. Lindzey (ed.), *Handbook of Social Psychology*, Cambridge, Mass.: Addison-Wesley, 1954, p. 840). Other authors disagree. S. S. Sargent, for example, speaks of the audience as 'a highly structured group. ... Its members are oriented toward the speaker or performance and only incidentally toward each other'; and says regarding panic that, while crowd members interact with each other, in a panic 'everyone flees the source of danger, or supposed danger, in a thoroughly individualistic way' (*Social Psychology*, New York: The Ronald Press, 1950, pp. 374–5, 265).

3. To what degree do the members of a crowd feel and behave similarly? H. Cantril defines a crowd as a 'congregate group of individuals who have temporarily identified themselves with common values and who are experiencing similar emotions' (*Psychology of Social Movements*, New York: John Wiley, 1941, p. 80). R. H. Turner and L. M. Killian suggest that the members of a crowd may be 'at

Crown

various stages of the development of crowd action, feeling, thinking, and acting quite differently, yet contributing to the development of a common line of action' (*Collective Behavior*, Englewood Cliffs, N.J.: Prentice-Hall, 1957, p. 103).

C. In addition to direct contradictions embodied in definitions, authors point up different characteristics:

1. T. D. Eliot includes the statement that 'the ordinary and "rational" controls of personality are relaxed or in abeyance, making a crowd subject to suggestion and to hysterical or mob behaviors' ('Crowd', in H. P. Fairchild (ed.), *Dictionary of Sociology*, New York: Philosophical Library, 1944, p. 79).

2. H. Blumer, again, stresses the importance of the distinction between the *active crowd* which has a focus of attention and the *expressive crowd* which has no focus ('Collective Behavior', in A. M. Lee (ed.), *New Outline of the Principles of Sociology*, New York: Barnes & Noble, 1951, pp. 180–5).

3. R. E. Park stresses among other things the necessity of having rapport, 'Such a collectivity becomes a crowd ... only when a condition of *rapport* has been established' ('The Crowd Defined', in R. E. Park & E. W. Burgess, *Introduction to the Science of Sociology*, Chicago: The University of Chicago Press, 2nd edn., 1924, p. 893).

4. L. Wilson and W. L. Kolb stress the relation of the crowd to its social and cultural environment: 'The attitudes ... are either a part of the culture pattern of the community, or they have been created alike in each individual. ... Thus the crowd ... is a product of the community and its system of social relations' (*Sociological Analysis*, New York: Harcourt, Brace, 1949, p. 307).

5. W. A. Westley argues that crowds need not be spontaneous, and designates as one of his sub-categories of crowd *planned crowds* 'which have been deliberately organized, and which congregate with the assent of the participating members' (*The Formation, Nature and Control of Crowds*, Ottawa: Defence Research Board, Directorate of Atomic Research, 1956, p. 15).

Frederick Elkin

See also: AUDIENCE
MOB

Crown

A. The term *Crown* denotes the Monarch and/or his (her) authority and powers. In certain contexts it denotes, by a variety of legal fictions, the exercise of such authority and powers by persons who, *formally*, act on the Monarch's behalf.

B. 1. In the Middle Ages '... the Crown had an hereditary revenue from various sources which satisfied many of the needs of government. If the King wanted more he asked for and obtained a grant ...'(W. R. Anson, *Law and Custom of the Constitution*, 5th edn., 1922, vol. I, p. 31). This usage is still often applied to non-parliamentary monarchies.

2. In parliamentary monarchies with Cabinet Government (q.v.) the term often refers to (a) the Monarch in his official capacity, e.g. 'the pardon of the Crown' (cf. the use of *Kungliga majestät* in Sweden); (b) the authority of the Ministry other than that vested in individual Ministers by Statute ('Ministers of the Crown'); (c) unity of authority. The Executive is divided into a Head of State (q.v.) and a Government of Ministers with whom real political power lies. There are two advantages in obscuring this division:

(i) It allows for flexibility. The Monarch may lose more of his Prerogatives to the Ministry but they still constitutionally pertain to the Crown. In the Norwegian and Swedish Constitutions the fiction of the Monarch as Head both of State and Government is preserved (e.g. 'The King alone shall govern the Realm', *Regeringsform*, Sweden, Art. 4).

(ii) It enables states to reduce the political influence of the Monarchy while retaining its mystique. Property belongs to 'the Crown', not to 'the State', and oaths of loyalty are taken to the Monarch, not to the Government. The traditional forms are preserved despite the adoption of a system of government where the realities of power lie elsewhere. In such contexts *Crown* acts as a substitute for more loaded expressions such as 'the State' or 'the People'.

D. V. Verney

See also: HEAD OF STATE

Cube Law

The term denotes a 'law' first pronounced by the Rt. Hon. James Parker Smith before the British Royal Commission on Electoral Systems in 1909. He pointed out that under the British electoral system, when two major parties between them poll all or almost all the votes, then the ratio of seats won by the parties may be expected to be at least the cube of the ratio between the votes cast for them, i.e. if the ratio between the votes cast for the two major parties is A : B, the ratio between seats would be at least A^3 : B^3 (see D. E. Butler, 'An Examination of the Result', in H. G. Nicholas, *The British General Election of* 1950, London: Macmillan, 1951, p. 328 ff.).

1. For a statistical explanation of the working of the cube law, see M. G. Kendall & A. Stuart, 'Cubic Proportion in Election Results' (*British Journal of Sociology*, vol. 1, 1950, p. 183).

2. For an examination of the application of the cube law to the British General Election of 1951, see M. G. Kendall & A. Stuart, 'La loi du cube dans les élections britanniques' (*Revue Française de Science Politique*, vol. 2, 1952, p. 270); and D. E. Butler, *The British General Election of 1951* (London: Macmillan, 1952, p. 275). For a similar discussion with respect to the 1955 election, see D. E. Butler, *The British General Election of 1955* (London: Macmillan, 1955, p. 206).

R. T. McKenzie

Cult

A. Three major uses of *cult* may be discerned—two anthropological, one sociological.

1. Some anthropologists define cult as the totality of the religious institutions of a society —particularly pre-literate societies.

2. Most anthropologists define cult as a body of religious beliefs and practices associated with a particular god or set of gods, constituting a specialized part of the religious institutions of a society. By inclusion the officiants and practitioners in such a part of the religious structure of a society are sometimes called a cult.

3. For sociologists a cult is an almost structureless, individual-centred minority religious group, whose characteristics are determined by the isolation and alienation of its members from the structure of the larger society and from its formalized religious institutions.

B. In the works of such British anthropologists as J. G. Frazer, R. R. Marett, and A. Lang, cult was identified with the total religious system of a society, particularly with the 'primitive' religion of a pre-literate society. A good example is found in the phrase from W. D. Wallis, 'The Status of Woman in the Cult', by which he means the activities of women in the total religious domain of any pre-literate culture (*Religion in Primitive Society*, New York: F. S. Crofts, 1939, p. 288).

C. Most anthropologists today use the term with reference to some specialization or emphasis in one part of the religious institutions of a society and so would follow some such use as the following: 'A cult is the sum total of organized beliefs and ritual concerned with a specific spirit or spirits, generally associated with particular objects and places, together with the ritual worship and officiants' (Royal Anthropological Institute of Great Britain and Ireland, *Notes and Queries on Anthropology*, London: Routledge & Kegan Paul, 6th edn. 1951, p. 180).

1. M. Lantis, for example ('The Alaskan Whale Cult and Its Affinities', *American Anthropologist*, vol. 40, 1938, pp. 438–64), in describing Alaskan Eskimo religion, chooses to stress the 'whaling cult', one particular aspect of a total religious system. Parallel uses are to be found in the description of 'ancestral cults', such as those of Africa or China, 'sun cults', 'fertility cults', and the like.

2. This anthropological definition can be extended to historic cultures and civilizations without difficulty; e.g. in Egypt, Babylonia, Greece, etc., various kinds of cults—solar cults, mystery cults—existed, as, for instance, the solar cult created by the pharaoh, Ikhnaton.

D. While sociologists have on occasion followed the two primarily anthropological definitions, they tend increasingly to regard a *cult* as a very loose form of religious organization characteristic of a rapidly secularizing society or one which is atomistic and disorganized. Its members are those people who have been isolated and alienated from the larger social structure to such a degree that they are concerned only for their own religious experience and the relief from stress and meaninglessness which it may bring. Hence the cult is highly individualistic, loosely organized, mystical, and led by a charismatic leader.

1. The most systematic account of this type of religious group has been given by H. Becker: 'Tendencies toward religion of a strictly private, personal character ... come to full fruition in the cult. ... The goal of the adherent ... is that of purely personal ecstatic experience, salvation, comfort, and mental or physical healing'. 'Only a highly atomized and essentially secular social order gives rise to extensive cult belief'. 'The cult is the most ephemeral of all types of religious structure ...' ('The Development and Interaction of the Ecclesia, the Sect, the Denomination, and the Cult as Illustrative of the

Cultural Accumulation

Dilemma of the Church', in L. Von Wiese & H. Becker, *Systematic Sociology*, New York: Wiley, 1932, pp. 624–42, esp. pp. 627–8).

2. J. M. Yinger, following Becker, stresses the criteria for defining a cult: 'The term cult is used in many different ways, usually with the connotations of small size, search for a mystical experience, lack of an organizational structure, and presence of a charismatic leader' (*Religion, Society and the Individual*, New York: The Macmillan Co., 1957, p. 154). He describes it as being at the extreme of personal non-institutionalized religious experience. In a more highly organized and self-conscious form it becomes a sect (q.v.) (*Religion in the Struggle for Power*, Durham, N.C.: Duke University Press, 1946, p. 22).

William L. Kolb

See also: Cargo Cult
         Peyotism
         Religion
         Sect

Cultural Accumulation

A. *Cultural accumulation* denotes a process of cultural growth whereby new cultural elements or traits are added by invention, discovery, and borrowing to those already present, with a resultant increase in the total number of traits or elements.

B. Cultural accumulation and its synonyms are widely employed by anthropologists to characterize the incremental nature of cultural growth and development. Thus L. A. White describes culture as '... a symbolic, continuous, cumulative, and progressive process' (*The Science of Culture*, New York: Farrar, Straus, 1949, p. 140). A. L. Kroeber writes that '... broadly speaking, the process of cultural development is an additive and therefore accumulative one, whereas the process of organic evolution is primarily a substitutive one' (*Anthropology*, New York: Harcourt, Brace, 1948, p. 297).

C. The usage exemplified by White and Kroeber stresses the progressive and developmental nature of culture and thus implies more than a simple increase in the total number of traits and elements. At the same time it must be recognized that culture *can* accumulate in a simple numerical way without creating progress as measured by any useable criteria.

1. Thus while Kroeber (*The Nature of Culture*, Chicago: University of Chicago Press, 1952, p. 152) later offered a more restrictive formulation, i.e. ... the property of accumulativeness is characteristic not of the whole of culture but chiefly of its scientific-technological component', this is true only if cultural accumulation is restricted to incremental development and progress measured by the criterion of instrumental efficiency.

2. Cultural additions can be made in the realm of religion and art, for example, without superseding other items and traits, thus increasing the total number of items and traits in the culture.

3. Whether or not there can and does occur progressive, incremental development in cultural realms other than those of science and technology cannot be determined unless other criteria of progress than those of instrumental efficiency are employed. That an aesthetic or religious belief system can *and* does unfold and occasions developmental cultural accumulation in such realms, seems obvious.

D. Attempts have been made to specify the *processes* of cultural accumulation. Thus H. C. Moore ('Cumulation and Cultural Processes', *American Anthropologist*, vol. 56, 1954, pp. 347–57) distinguishes three types of cultural accumulation.

1. The development of more complex cultural patterns out of simpler antecedent forms, Moore calls 'progressive cumulation'.

2. The introduction of novel elements or cultural alternatives of about the same level of complexity he terms 'agglutinative accumulations'.

3. A third type in which an incremental change leads to the eventual replacement of a trait is called by Moore 'cumulation-becoming-substitution'.

Joseph B. Casagrande

See also: Cultural Substitution

Cultural Alternative

A. *Cultural alternative* is used to denote those different traits and patterns in culture offering choice to the individual in meeting comparable situations, achieving similar ends through varying means, or of achieving varying ends for the satisfaction of similar needs.

B. The term *cultural alternative* together with the companion terms *cultural speciality* (q.v.) and *cultural universal* (q.v.) give recognition to the fact of variability in the degree to which individuals participate in, and control knowledge of, the different aspects of their culture.

While the meaning of these terms is implicit in their ordinary usage, they were first defined as anthropological terms by R. Linton in 1936 (*The Study of Man*, New York: Appleton-Century, 1936, pp. 272–4). He also included a fourth, residual category of extra-cultural behaviour, 'individual peculiarities'.

C. R. Redfield has pointed out that Linton used the term *cultural alternative* for culture traits or patterns of two different types (*The Folk Culture of Yucatan*, Chicago: University of Chicago Press, 1941, pp. 347–8): (a) those traits or patterns shared by some but not all members of a society or even by all members of its sub-groups; (b) those known to all normal adult members of a society or to all members of particular socially recognized sub-groups, but among which the individual may exercise choice.

It is important to note that this ambiguity actually points to overlappings that can be eliminated only by using the terms in an analytic and abstract way rather than as complete concrete descriptions. Thus a given occupation (q.v.) in a particular culture may as a concrete phenomenon be designated by *all three terms*, which point analytically to three different aspects of occupation:

1. As a body of knowledge and skills known only to the members of the occupational group, the occupation can be regarded as a *speciality*.

2. In so far as the occupation is recognized by all the sane adult members of the society as a legitimate mode of activity contributing certain services to the society, it can be considered a *cultural universal*.

3. If the society is a society of achieved rather than ascribed occupational statuses, then the occupation can be regarded as a *cultural alternative*.

Joseph B. Casagrande

See also: CULTURAL SPECIALTY
 CULTURAL UNIVERSAL
 CULTURE

Cultural Anthropology
(See Social Anthropology)

Cultural Configuration
It is impossible to give a single definition of the term *cultural configuration* although it is closely related to the concept *culture pattern* (q.v.).

1. C. Kluckhohn has proposed that *configuration* be applied to patterning in the *covert culture* (q.v.), while culture pattern be reserved for the patterning of *overt culture*: 'A pattern is a generalization *of* behavior or of ideals *for* behavior. A configuration is a generalization *from* behavior. Both patterns and configurations are thus abstractions. ... Configurations ... tend to be purely inferential constructs. Configuration looks to an *inner* coherence in terms of the larger structuralizing principles which prevail in the *covert* culture. Patterns are forms: configurations are, so to speak, inter-relationships between forms' ('Patterning as Exemplified in Navaho Culture', in L. Spier (ed.), *Language, Culture, and Personality*, Menasha, Wis.: Sapir Memorial Publication Fund, 1941, p. 126).

2. A. L. Kroeber, however, uses *configuration* to mean a set of relationships in space, time, and achievement among historical phenomena; and often appears to treat *cultural configuration* and *culture pattern* as synonyms (*Configurations of Culture Growth*, Berkeley: University of California Press, 1944, esp. p. 844). His usage of *configuration* is distinct from, though related to, that of the Gestalt psychologists. Referring to culture, Kroeber's *configuration* is linked more directly with the *style* of the art historians and notions of pattern-style-configuration as employed by Spengler and other general historians. Although P. A. Sorokin uses *configuration*, as well as *pattern*, infrequently and unsystematically, his distinction between the 'internal and external aspects of culture' and his characterization of cultural 'mentalities' as *ideational*, *sensate*, and *idealistic* belong in the same broad tradition which stresses cultural configuration (*Social and Cultural Dynamics*, Boston: Porter Sargent, 1957, pp. 20 ff.).

Clyde Kluckhohn

See also: CULTURE
 CULTURE PATTERN

Cultural Convergence
A. *Cultural convergence* is a process of change by which heterogeneous features in the cultures of geographically separated peoples grow more and more alike with the passage of time until they reach a relatively high degree of similarity, or identity, without any historical factor such as diffusion (q.v.) or acculturation (q.v.) having contributed to the likeness. The nature of the theoretical interest in culture growth determines the degree and kind of similarity which must be present in the end products in order to class them as examples of convergence.

1. *Convergence* is to be understood only in conjunction with the associated concept of *parallelism*. In both cases, the phenomena

Cultural Convergence

are cultural features in geographically separate places which exhibit a sufficient degree of similarity to suggest a common origin, but for which no historical connection and no evidence of diffusion can be found to account for the resemblance.

2. *Convergence* has come to be applied to those instances of resemblance where the evidence indicates that antecedent forms were more and more different as viewed in reverse time sequence. Thus, the contemporary resemblance is spurious so far as what it suggests about history is concerned. Like results have grown from unlike origins.

B. The interpretation of particular phenomena of resemblance as convergence rather than simple parallelism can only rationally be made if there be evidence of unlike origins. The nature of this evidence and the scientific predilections of the investigator generally result in an hypothesis, if not a theory, to account for the process.

1. P. Ehrenreich, who, although he credited Thilenius and von Luschan with the earliest use of the term, first gave it a solid theoretical basis, proposed three explanatory factors: similar environment, similar psychology, and similar cultural conditions, with the first being of relatively small importance ('Zur Frage der Beurteilung und Bewertung ethnographischer Analogien', *Correspondenzblatt der deutschen Gesellschaft für Anthropologie, Ethnologie und Urgeschichte*, 1903, pp. 176–80).

2. F. Graebner, leader of the *Kulturkreis* (q.v.) group, insisted, on the other hand, that likeness in the natural environment was the only important factor in the independent development of similar culture features, if it is granted that such independence exists at all. This latter qualification indicates his fundamental opposition, as a diffusionist, to the ideas of parallelism and convergence (*Methode der Ethnologie*, Heidelberg: C. Winter, 1911).

C. Graebner's opposition to the ideas of parallelism and convergence stimulated rejoinders from the American anthropologists, R. H. Lowie and A. A. Goldenweiser, which are perhaps the most important statements made on *convergence*, and in Goldenweiser's case, on the ancillary principle of *limited possibilities* (R. H. Lowie, 'On the Principle of Convergence in Ethnology', *Journal of American Folklore*, vol. 25, 1912, pp. 24–42; A. A. Goldenweiser, 'The Principle of Limited Possibilities in the Development of Culture', *Journal of American Folklore*, vol. 26, 1913, pp. 259–90).

1. In Lowie's discussion the methodologically distinct concepts of convergence and independent development are confused, and he uses the term *convergent evolution*. In agreement with F. Boas, Lowie denies the principle of complete convergence: '... if we found *exact* parallels of very complicated phenomena, their occurrence in two areas, no matter how widely separated, could not reasonably be explained by convergence' ('On the Principle of Convergence in Ethnology', p. 30). Boas's phrasing is: 'Nobody claims that convergence means an absolute identity of phenomena derived from heterogeneous sources; but we think we have ample proof to show that the most diverse ethnic phenomena, when subject to similar psychical conditions, or when referring to similar activities, will give similar results (not equal results) which we group naturally under the same category when viewed, not from an historical standpoint, but from that of psychology, technology or other similar standpoints. The problem of convergence lies in the correct interpretation of the significance of ethnic phenomena that are apparently identical, but in many respects distinct ...' ('Review of Graebner, *Methode der Ethnologie*', *Science*, vol. 34, 1911, p. 807).

The antagonism of Boas and Lowie to the recognition of great likeness as constituting *identity*, blinded them to the significance of reasonable likenesses, so that neither capitalized upon the interpretational possibilities of the concept of convergence. Indeed, Lowie even doubted that genuine convergence was anything more than an unlikely theoretical possibility.

2. Goldenweiser rejects the term *convergent evolution*, declaring that nothing comparable to the organically unified process of biological evolution is involved in cultural convergence; rather convergence is '... merely a term for certain cultural similarities brought about by processes that are neither historically connected nor parallel' ('The Principle of Limited Possibilities in the Development of Culture', p. 263). He distinguishes *genuine* convergence as that which involves psychologically similar cultural traits, in contrast to *false* convergence in which the similarities are not psychological but merely objective or classificatory. He applies the separate term *dependent convergence* to those similarities which develop from different sources but under the influence of a common cultural medium.

Every instance of parallelism involves, of necessity, a convergence according to Goldenweiser. He reaches this conclusion on the basis of the principle that the probability of a parallel series is roughly inversely proportional to the length of the series. Goldenweiser does not consider the equally likely process of divergence. The latter would seem to require historical data which are not available, but other possible solutions are not ruled out—the question has simply been neglected by all save the linguists.

Goldenweiser refined and expanded the theory of *limited possibilities* and integrated it with his analysis of convergence as the principal explanatory factor: '... every culture is characterized by a limited number of culture traits. ... This limitation in number and character of cultural traits, when compared to the multiplicity of possible historical and psychological sources, constitutes a limitation in the possibilities of development, and necessitates convergence. *The principle of limited possibilities in cultural development is thus constituted an* a priori *argument in favor of convergence*' ('The Principle of Limited Possibilities in the Development of Culture', p. 290).

D. Much recent discussion has centred on the issues raised by Goldenweiser.

1. J. J. Honigmann has stated that: 'Convergence is based on the limited possibilities governing change in a given situation' (*The World of Man*, New York: Harper & Brothers, 1959, p. 206). This generalization is difficult if not impossible to defend. Limited possibilities may be the most frequently operating mechanism but certainly not the only one. As one example from many, the whole field of *psychic unity* would be eliminated. In literature, language, and ceremonial life, as G. P. Murdock has pointed out, limitations are slight and variation may be enormous ('The Common Denominators of Cultures', in R. Linton (ed.), *The Science of Man in the World Crisis*, New York: Columbia University Press, 1945, p. 139).

2. In an important paper treating of convergence, C. Erasmus states that: 'It would seem that the differences between the "psychic unity" and the "limited possibilities" types of explanation is one of degree rather than kind' ('Patolli, Pachisi, and the Limitation of Possibilities', *Southwestern Journal of Anthropology*, vol. 6, 1950, p. 386). However, his statement is categorical rather than supported and undoubtedly is thrown out principally to give impetus to further research.

Verne F. Ray

See also: CULTURAL PARALLELISM

Cultural Determinism

A. *Cultural determinism* is the conception that a cultural system or way of life exerts or is capable of exerting a determining influence upon other aspects of human behaviour, i.e. that the influence is such that these aspects are what they are because of such influence. In some forms it holds that cultural factors determine cultural factors: that a cultural system is its own invariable predictor—the expression 'invariable predictor' being used to retain the stress on invariance while avoiding controversy on the nature of 'cause'. This stress itself can be lightened, but the term would then more properly become *cultural influence* or *cultural conditioning*. Sometimes it is used in a weaker sense simply to denote the view that cultural systems are themselves determined—without specifying that they are determined culturally.

B. There can be little doubt that culture influences culture, but to extend this to mean that culture determines culture without reference to other elements of behaviour and of the situation seems illegitimate.

1. Nineteenth-century speculative evolutionary anthropologists called attention to the regular growth of culture in which, e.g. one form of marriage, mode of subsistence, or religious belief succeeded another in regular fashion (L. H. Morgan, *Ancient Society*, London: Macmillan, 1877). Presumably some form of cultural determinism or conditioning was at work but its nature remained unclarified. While speculative evolutionary theory was abandoned in the 20th century, archaeological data concerning successive phases of culture permitted formulation of a more explicit theory of culture growth, in which a subsequent phase of culture could be shown to be rooted in and dependent upon earlier developments. For example, in many parts of the world the development of agriculture in place of food gathering encouraged population growth, sedentary village life, complex forms of administration, increase of trade, and division of labour by skill. Among exponents of this way of viewing culture are V. G. Childe and J. Steward (V. G. Childe, *What Happened in History*, New York: Penguin Books, 1942, p. 22; J. Steward, 'Cultural Causality and Law', *American Anthropologist*, vol. 51, 1946, pp. 1–27).

2. Not only historically but synchronically, as functionalists have pointed out, a culture at any moment is, at least in part, the product of all its components. Thus if the shift from hoe to

Cultural Drift

plough cultivation is likely to be followed by a shift from matrilocal to patrilocal residence, then it follows that at any moment matrilocal residence is supported by hoe cultivation and patrilocal residence by plough cultivation (G. P. Murdock, *Social Structure*, New York: The Macmillan Co., 1949, p. 206).

3. Yet culture is not to be explained solely in its own terms. One area of socially shared behaviour is not simply determined by the other parts of the cultural system. Every cultural system exists in a larger context, 'the situation', by which it is also influenced. The situation includes the human component, i.e. biological organisms with certain limits and potentialities; the environmental component, including all features except the human organism and artifacts; and, finally, the demographic component, 'the population ... served by a culture' (J. P. Gillin, *The Ways of Men*, New York: D. Appleton-Century, 1948, ch. 10, pp. 198–208).

C. Again there can be little doubt that culture is a pervasive influence in all of human behaviour, but it is doubtful that the relationship is invariant.

1. Culture consists of socially created and shared patterns of human behaviour which are to some degree symbolically formulated. Since any item of motivated human behaviour is seldom totally separated from behaviour that can be defined as culture, it follows that such an item of behaviour is substantially influenced by culture. This idea is expressed in phrases like 'culture determines human behaviour', a position sometimes assumed to combat racism and other organic theories of culture. '...those explanations of custom which derive our economic scheme from human competitiveness, ... and all the rest of the ready explanations that we meet in every magazine ... have for the anthropologist a hollow ring' (R. Benedict, *Patterns of Culture*, London: Routledge, 1935, p. 232).

2. It is possible, however, to interpret too literally the term *cultural determinism* in this context. L. White, for example, argues that slavery, war, race prejudice, and other elements of culture can be explained better by the assumption that it is not people who possess preferences for such custom: '... they do not "have them" at all; rather *it is the cultures which possess the people who have been born into them*' (*The Science of Culture*, New York: Farrar, Straus, 1949, p. 126). Culture may even be described as possessing an extrasomatic character and to be subject to laws of its own.

It cannot be explained by the laws which explain individual behaviour.

3. Such ways of speaking, however, obscure the fact that culture basically is behaviour and exists only in persons, in their physiological, biochemical, and psychological reactions. Only for convenience are cultural phenomena frozen on the cultural level and culture treated as though it were an autonomous realm (A. L. Kroeber, 'White's View of Culture', *American Anthropologist*, vol. 50, 1948, pp. 405–14). It is necessary to guard against the culturalistic fallacy, which claims that culture is all and ignores the role of the individual, and the biologistic fallacy, that would derive culture solely from organismic factors.

John J. Honigmann

See also: DETERMINISM
SOCIAL CAUSATION

Cultural Drift

A. *Cultural drift* denotes a process of internal change in a cultural system (q.v.) constituted by the unconscious selection of small changes in culture, such changes being cumulative and tending in some special direction. It imposes certain limits on the possibilities of further alteration, and consequently provides a basis for assessing the significance of particular cultural variants, and for understanding differential resistance or receptivity to internal or external innovation. Denoting direction, the concept is compatible with unilinear or multilinear theories of change.

B. The term is important but it has not been used widely even by anthropologists, who are responsible for its introduction and elaboration. The term was first used with respect to language and was then extended to other areas of culture.

1. Probably the earliest use was that of E. Sapir who said, 'The drift of a language is constituted by the unconscious selection on the part of its speakers of those individual variations that are cumulative in some special direction' (*Language*, New York: Harcourt, Brace, 1921, pp. 165–6).

2. F. Eggan adapted the concept from Sapir and applied it to the study of a series of changes in northern Philippine culture which appeared to have a particular direction. He remarked, 'Changes, which on the surface seemed to be the result of Spanish or American contacts, turned out on closer inspection to be native cultural changes. Resistance to change, on the one hand, or rapid acceptance, on the other, seemed explicable in many cases in terms of this "drift" '('Some Aspects of Culture Change in the Northern Philippines', *American Anthropologist*, vol. 43, 1941, p. 13).

3. M. J. Herskovits views *drift* as a major process in cultural change, defining the process as '... those changes that represent the accumulation of small variations, whose total effect, over a period of time, is to bring about alterations that, viewed from day to day, are scarcely noticeable' (*Man and His Works*, New York: Knopf, 1948, p. 580). In Herskovits's interpretation, cultural drift explains direction of change, why some variations are important and others not, and why some culture traits are accepted and others rejected.

4. A process of change analogous to 'linguistic drift' is stressed by G. P. Murdock in his theory of the evolution of social organization. Both processes possess the following features: 'limitation in the possibilities of change, a strain toward consistency, shifts from one to another relatively stable equilibrium, compensatory internal readjustments, resistance to any influence from diffusion that is not in accord with the drift' (*Social Structure*, New York: The Macmillan Co., 1949, p. 199).

C. Among sociologists concerned with problems of long-term change, the concept of *immanent change* although broader, seems to be the closest approach to *cultural drift* (cf. P. A. Sorokin, *Society, Culture and Personality: Their Structure and Dynamics*, New York: Harper & Brothers, 1947, pp. 154–5).

Harry W. Basehart

See also: CULTURE
           CULTURE CHANGE

Cultural Evolution

A. *Cultural evolution* denotes a temporal-formal process, continuous and usually accumulative and progressive, by which cultural phenomena, systemically organized, undergo change, one form or stage succeeding another. Cultural evolutionism is the application of the general theory of evolution to cultural phenomena as distinguished from biological or physical phenomena. In the latter half of the 19th century cultural evolution was frequently termed *development* and the same equivalence is common today. The essentials of the theory of cultural evolution were set forth by E. B. Tylor in 1881: '... it appears that wherever there are found elaborate arts, abstruse knowledge, complex institu-

tions, these are the results of gradual development from an earlier, simpler, and ruder stage of life. No stage of civilization comes into existence spontaneously, but grows or is developed out of the stage before it' (*Anthropology*. London: Murray, 1881, p. 20).

B. Theories of cultural evolution may be unilinear, in which one treats the culture of mankind as a unity; or they may be multilinear, in which one treats the culture of mankind as consisting of parts. Both views are valid; the one implies the other. One can trace the course of the evolution of culture of mankind as a whole, or any portion of the cultural totality that can be treated as a unit or a system. One can work out the evolution, or evolutions, of writing, currency, clan organization, or the plough. But one cannot work out the evolution of the human family, as L. H. Morgan tried to do, because the family cannot be treated as a closed system; it is always and everywhere merely a part of a larger social configuration. One can speak of the evolution of the culture of a people, such as the Chinese, or of an area, such as the Andean highlands, only in so far as it can be considered as a closed system; otherwise the occurrence of diffusion would make the establishment of stages impossible. Some theorists hold that multilinear theories of cultural evolution enable one to reconstruct the culture history of specific areas or peoples, but they are confusing the evolution of culture with the culture history of peoples or areas. Cultural evolutionism is concerned only with cultural phenomena as such—with tools, implements, customs, institutions, ideologies—and not with the cultural historical experiences of a people— a tribe or nation: '... this scheme [of the early evolutionists] purports, not to unravel the history of given cultures or peoples, but only to sum up the evolution of culture as such. It is the evolution of *culture* that is being summed, not the history of *a* culture or of *a* people' (R. L. Beals & H. Hoijer, *An Introduction to Anthropology*, New York: The Macmillan Co., 1953, p. 606).

Cultural evolution is not synonymous with progress, but on the whole it has been progressive. Nor is the direction invariably from the simple to the complex; it may be just the reverse.

The validity of theories of cultural evolution has been much debated in anthropological circles. After having been rejected by many anthropologists, they are currently being revived and refined and tested (see L. A. White, *The*

Cultural Integration

Evolution of Culture, New York: McGraw-Hill, 1959; J. H. Steward, *Theory of Culture Change*, Urbana: University of Illinois Press, 1955; V. Gordon Childe, *Social Evolution*, New York: H. Schuman, 1951).

Leslie A. White

See also: CULTURE
   CULTURE CHANGE
   EVOLUTION
   SUPERORGANIC

Cultural Integration

A. *Cultural integration* may be defined as (a) the processes whereby a *culture* becomes whole or entire or (b) the state wherein a culture is whole or entire. The state is recognized or the process realized in (a) a logical, emotional, or aesthetic consistency among cultural meanings; (b) a congruence of cultural norms with behaviour; and (c) the critical or functional interdependence and reinforcement of the different component customs and institutions of the system. There is considerable overlap if not complete identity with the term social integration (q.v.).

B. In every instance of its use the term *cultural integration* recognizably shares the sense of 'wholeness' and of the whole as greater than the sum of its parts. There are, however, at least three somewhat distinct senses of *cultural integration* in anthropology, the field of its primary relevance.

1. It is used to refer to 'the strain of consistency' and the relative consistency present in cultural systems among objects and meanings, customs and beliefs, norms and actions (W. G. Sumner, *Folkways*, Boston: Ginn, 1906, p. 5). 'If the elements of a culture require, for its full exposition, exposition of other elements, this aspect of culture organization exists' (R. Redfield, *The Folk Culture of Yucatan*, Chicago: University of Chicago Press, 1941, pp. 350–1). 'Functionalism' of any variety, essentially an emphasis upon the study of the interrelatedness of different parts of culture or social behaviour, derives from the basic postulate of cultural integration, in contrast to the various historical approaches which '... tend to view single cultures as congeries of disconnected traits, disparate in origin and history ...' (R. L. Beals & H. Hoijer, *An Introduction to Anthropology*, New York: The Macmillan Co., 1953, p. 617).

2. A special sense of *cultural integration*, not contradictory to the first, is that of R. Benedict. For her the integration of a culture is 'patterning' which can be expressed in some, though not all, cultures as a master principle or *culture pattern* (q.v.). 'A culture, like an individual, is a more or less consistent pattern of thought and action. Within each culture there come into being characteristic purposes not necessarily shared by other types of society. In obedience to these purposes each people further and further consolidates its experience, and in proportion to the urgency of these drives the heterogeneous items of behaviour take more and more congruous shape' (*Patterns of Culture*, London: Routledge, 1935, p. 46). In seeming contradiction, however, Benedict also refers to a '... lack of integration ... as characteristic of certain cultures as extreme integration is of others' (ibid., p. 223).

3. For many writers, often the same ones who use the term in one of the foregoing senses, *cultural integration* is the process whereby the cultural system, as it undergoes change through time, maintains an approximation of such order as is implied in the foregoing (R. Linton, *The Study of Man*, New York: D. Appleton-Century, 1936, p. 348). This usage of the term is especially applicable to the incorporation of new customs or beliefs into a culture and is commonly said to be reflected in three ways: (a) the selectivity of innovation; (b) the modification of the form, function, meaning, or use of a borrowed item to bring it into fuller harmony with the culture (ibid., pp. 401–21); (c) the adaptation of the cultural system itself to fit the new usage at any point of stress. *Cultural lag* (q.v.) is, for example, a temporary disharmony due to failure to adapt in this fashion (W. F. Ogburn, *Social Change*, London: Allen & Unwin, 1923, pp. 200–13).

C. Since it is a standard assumption of cultural anthropology and sociology that cultures differ in the completeness of their integration, a measure whereby the degree of integration in different cultures might be compared is felt by some to be an important methodological need of these disciplines.

James B. Watson

See also: CULTURAL PATTERN
   CULTURAL SYSTEM
   FUNCTION
   SOCIAL INTEGRATION
   SOCIAL SYSTEM

Cultural Lag

A. *Cultural lag* is a term employed in the study either of culture change (q.v.) or of social disorganization (q.v.) (cf. e.g. A. Boskoff, 'Social Change', in H. Becker & A. Boskoff (eds.), *Modern Sociological Theory in Continuity and Change*, New York: The Dryden Press, 1957, pp. 299–301; and also D. Martindale, 'Social Disorganization', in ibid., pp. 349–54). It may be defined as the period between that point in time at which one cultural element approximates a cultural goal, valued by the society or by the observer, and that point at which another element or other elements achieve such a degree of approximation; or, as the difference in the rate of change of two or more cultural elements about whose inter-relationships the observer makes no normative predication or claim either explicitly or implicitly. It is treated as a major aspect of social change, and as a causal factor in social disorganization.

B. The term was coined by W. F. Ogburn who used it to designate the time which passes between a change in 'material' culture (e.g. the supply of forests) and the adjustive change in 'adaptive' culture (e.g. policy of using the forests), without excluding the possibility of adaptive culture changing before material culture or non-material culture changing without the material culture changing likewise (*Social Change*, New York: Viking Press, 1922, pp. 200–13).

C. With the gradual disappearance of the use of the term 'material culture' to designate technological objects, and the increasing emphasis on the symbolic aspects of even technological culture, it was necessary to redefine *cultural lag*. Thus T. Parsons considers Ogburn's use of the term to be a variant of Veblen's proposition that 'pragmatic' or 'predatory' actions and institutions lag behind 'workmanlike' or technological ones ('Sociological Elements in Economic Thought', in H. E. Barnes, H. Becker & F. B. Becker, *Contemporary Social Theory*, New York: D. Appleton-Century, 1940, p. 618). The restriction of the term to a time gap between the development of technological and non-technological culture as such is abandoned in H. Hart's conception of cultural lag as the 'time interval between two phases in the development of a culture complex or of two different culture complexes, where the length of the interval requires shortening in order better to promote generally accepted social ends and where such shortening is regarded as potentially possible through social planning' ('The Hypothesis of Cultural Lag: A Present-Day View', in F. R. Allen, et al., *Technology and Social Change*, New York: Appleton-Century-Crofts, 1957, p. 424).

D. J. H. Mueller distinguishes between 'spurious lag' where because the two categories of culture examined are incommensurable, the lag cannot be established but only proclaimed and where it may disappear on redefinition; and 'true lag' where the lagging element is either an effect of another element which precedes it in time or not a time-lag at all but a 'measure of the qualitative disparity between a norm and a given achievement', 'Present Status of the Cultural Lag Hypothesis', *American Sociological Review*, vol. 3, 1938, pp. 320–7).

Kurt H. Wolff

See also: Social Change
        Social Disorganization

Cultural Parallelism

A. *Cultural parallelism* is the presence in two or more places of a feature of culture which, in its geographically separate manifestations, is sufficiently similar in significant aspects to justify its being treated as one for purposes of theoretical interpretation; and for which the available evidence indicates no historically common origin nor diffusion which could account for the presence of the feature in the separate places.

B. When unadorned by a distinct theoretical interpretation or specific historical reference, parallelism merely refers to the presence of a particular feature of culture among two or more peoples geographically distinct one from the other. The geographical distance may be great or small, the cultural feature may be a vast complex or a mere element, the degree of similarity may be virtual identity or may be so slight as to be apparent only to an observer with a lively imagination. Only when theoretical considerations are brought to bear do these differences become critical, and only in connection with such theories does the term have significance.

C. Theoretical usage falls into several broad categories which, while not mutually exclusive, are different in kind.

1. The first broad category of theoretical interpretation of cultural parallels is that espoused by A. Bastian (1826–1905). He held that all mankind shares elementary ideas—*Elementargedanken*—which make for similar responses modified only moderately by environmental conditions and historical factors. This *psychic unity* of mankind naturally resulted in the constant repetition of *inventions* among peoples despite isolation. Thus parallelism for Bastian was merely the evidence which proved psychic unity. His influence was great both in Europe and America. His American follower, D. Brinton, explained even the similarities of adjacent tribes as due to psychic unity. Perhaps the best-known English exponent was Sir James G. Frazer whose *Golden Bough* (London: Macmillan, 3rd edn., 1922–6) is a twelve-volume monument to psychic unity.

2. The second category is that of *cultural evolution* (q.v.) where the assumption is that all societies proceed through the same or closely similar stages of development. This is not the same as *psychic unity*, although the two are not necessarily antagonistic. Nevertheless, as R. H. Lowie properly points out, the *concept* of biological evolution, from which the idea of cultural evolution derives, does not suggest parallelism, although the facts provide numerous *examples*. The *principle* is one of unique events producing discrete results. Lowie recognizes this but does not dispose of the theoretical implications of the facts. He concludes that 'Parallelism was possible only on the principle that the psychic unity of mankind constantly impelled societies to duplicate one another's ideas' (*The History of Ethnological Theory*, New York: Farrar & Rinehart, 1937, p. 29). Lowie characteristically uses the terms parallelism and psychic unity almost interchangeably.

3. A third type of explanation for parallels involves simply recognition of the fact that man is far more inventive than would appear from the reasoning of Bastian and his followers, the cultural evolutionists, and a majority of the diffusionists. E. Nordenskiöld repeatedly made this point (e.g. in his 'The American Indian as Inventor', *Journal of the Royal Anthropological Institute*, vol. 59, 1929, pp. 273–309). That we cannot deny resourcefulness to any people, and that we must recognize the magnitude of the small changes that characterize the daily reworkings of culture as well as the revolutionary changes that follow upon major innovations, are points appropriately emphasized by M. Herskovits (*Man and His Works*, New York: Knopf, 1948, pp. 499–500). This being the case, numerous 'accidental' examples of parallelism are bound to emerge, given the limitations of human cultural life. F. Boas was impressed by man's inventiveness, too, but he did not proceed from the facts to theory. His conclusion was that 'the distribution of isolated customs in regions far apart hardly admits of the argument that they were transmitted from tribe to tribe and lost in intervening territory' ('The Aims of Anthropological Research', *Science*, n.s., vol. 76, 1932, p. 610).

4. Anthropologists have placed considerable emphasis on a more particularistic phrasing, *the principle of limited possibilities*. It is concerned with the technological or structural limitations inherent in an aspect of culture. For example, the nuclear family (q.v.) admits of but a small number of fundamental variants. Hence parallels are inevitable since the family as a generic form is universal. G. P. Murdock subscribes enthusiastically to the idea of man's inventiveness, and to the principle of limited possibilities. He observes that 'parallelism or independent invention is relatively easy and common in the field of social organization, and that any structural form can be developed anywhere if conditions are propitious. The explanation seems to lie in the principle of limited possibilities' (*Social Structure*, New York: The Macmillan Co., 1949, p. 200). He goes further to conclude that 'the search for the source of change must be shifted from the external factors to the social structure itself' (ibid.).

D. The amount of attention given to parallelism and its theoretical counterparts has gradually lessened with the passing of years. This has been due in part to the discrediting of simplistic and non-empirical theories such as the early interpretations of 'psychic unity'. Equally important has been the recognition that most of the phenomena which earlier appeared to call for a simple determination of diffusion vs. independent invention are now recognized as 'a series of special problems, each of which has to be answered on its own merits. ... The quarrel, except for amateurs and extremists, is not about which principle is the only one or the dominant one. ... Rather, the problem is: What happened in such and such particular case ...' (A. L. Kroeber, *Anthropology*, New York: Harcourt, Brace, 1948, pp. 540–1).

Verne F. Ray

See also: CULTURAL CONVERGENCE
CULTURAL EVOLUTION

Cultural Relativity

A. *Cultural relativity* designates the idea that any item of behaviour must be judged *first* in relation to its place in the unique structure of the culture in which it occurs and in terms of the particular value system of that culture. Thus it embodies a *principle of contextualism*. The term has, on occasion, been used to suggest that cultural items (such as ethical norms) may only be judged within their context or are so unique that comparative appraisals are ruled out; but this need not be the case.

B. During the 19th century, anthropologists tended to stress the unity of mankind and the diversity of the inanimate environment. At about the turn of the century, however, this emphasis came to be largely reversed. This was due in considerable part to F. Boas. He stated explicitly and repeatedly that anthropology was interested in historically created diversities, leaving to psychology the exploration of common human nature. He also stressed the position that every aspect of a culture from the sounds of speech to the forms of marriage must be considered in the *total context in which it occurred*. This is essentially the doctrine of cultural relativity. Cultural relativity need not be taken in an extreme sense but it is so taken by a considerable number of anthropologists.

1. For example, one of the best known and extreme statements was made by Boas's pupil, R. Benedict, when she spoke of '... the co-existing and equally valid patterns of life which mankind has created for itself from the raw materials of existence' (*Patterns of Culture*, London: Routledge, 1935, p. 278).

2. Such extreme emphasis on the principle of contextualism has led many to believe the emphasis is intrinsic to the concept. Thus C. Winick defines *cultural relativism* as: 'The principle that experience is interpreted by each person in terms of his own background, frame of reference, and social norms, and that these factors will influence perception and evaluations, so that there is no single scale of values applicable to all societies' (*Dictionary of Anthropology*, New York: Philosophical Library, 1956, p. 454).

C. There has, however, been a recent counter-current in anthropological thought—one stressing *cultural universals* brought about by the similarities in the human situation throughout time and space.

1. F. Boas himself wrote: 'The dynamic forces that mould social life are the same now as those that moulded life thousands of years ago'

(*The Mind of Primitive Man*, New York: The Macmillan Co., 1938, p. 195).

2. But R. Linton is squarely in the mainstream of contemporary anthropological opinion when he writes: 'Behind the seemingly endless diversity of culture patterns there is a fundamental uniformity' ('Universal Ethical Principles: An Anthropological View', in R. N. Anshen (ed.), *Moral Principles of Action*, New York: Harper & Brothers, 1952, p. 646).

3. Similarly C. Kluckhohn has indicated that while 'there are ... few genuine uniformities in culture content unless one states the content in extremely general form ... there are a considerable number of categories and of structural principles found in all cultures' ('Universal Categories of Culture', in A. L. Kroeber (ed.), *Anthropology Today*, Chicago: University of Chicago Press, 1953, pp. 519–20).

D. The reaction against radical relativity, the restress upon universals, likewise appears frequently in recent sociological and psychological writing.

1. W. L. Kolb observes: 'The basic field conditions for the emergence of the human psyche have been relatively the same since man has been man: society, culture, symbolic interaction, and the potentialities of the biological organism interacting in the basic progress of socialization. All social psychologists recognize these universal conditions and processes. Yet, impressed by the facts of social and cultural differences among societies, they have failed to inquire into the qualities of the universal emergent: human nature' ('A Social-Psychological Conception of Human Freedom', *Ethics*, vol. LXIII, 1953, p. 185).

2. T. Parsons and E. A. Shils comment on ethical relativity: '... the proponents of this view have even asserted that every moral standard is necessarily unique. There is much aesthetic sensibility underlying and justifying this contention, but it is neither convincing logically nor fruitful scientifically ('Values, Motives, and Systems of Action', in T. Parsons & E. A. Shils (eds.), *Toward a General Theory of Action*, Cambridge, Mass.: Harvard University Press, 1951, p. 171).

3. The British psychoanalysts H. V. Dicks and R. Money-Kyrle are convinced that there is a universal and natural morality. The latter says: 'The basis of morality is therefore neither a priori and universal as the metaphysicians have claimed, nor empirical and relative as critical philosophers and anthropologists maintain, but

Cultural Specialty

empirical and universal in the sense that it is a quality, like binocular vision or an articulated thumb, which is found to be common to all mankind' (R. E. Money-Kyrle, 'Towards a Common Aim—A Psycho-Analytical Contribution to Ethics', *British Journal of Medical Psychology*, vol. XX, 1944, p. 111; see also H. V. Dicks, 'In Search of Our Proper Ethic', *British Journal of Medical Psychology*, vol. XXIII, 1950, pp. 1–14).

Clyde Kluckhohn

See also: CULTURAL VARIATION

CULTURE

Cultural Specialty

Cultural specialty is a term designating one category of a three-fold classification of culture by R. Linton, based on the recognition of variability in the degree to which individuals participate in, and control knowledge of, the different aspects of their culture (see *cultural alternative*). It may be defined as a culture trait or pattern shared by the members of a socially recognized category of individuals but not shared by the total population. It usually refers to skills and more or less technical forms of knowledge and practice (*The Study of Man*, New York: D. Appleton-Century, 1936, pp. 272–3).

Joseph B. Casagrande

See also: CULTURAL ALTERNATIVE

CULTURAL UNIVERSAL

CULTURE

Cultural Substitution

A. *Cultural substitution* denotes the process in which one element of culture takes the place of another, wholly or partially.

B. Cultural substitution is a process of cultural change. In the analysis of change the focus of interest is usually the way in which new items come about rather than the relation between the new and the old. Thus discussions of change treat invention, diffusion (q.v.), and acculturation (q.v.), more frequently than substitution. A. L. Kroeber (*Anthropology*, New York: Harcourt, Brace, 1948, p. 381) suggests that this emphasis reflects a basic principle of change: 'Replacements, modifications, and substitutions are, broadly speaking, more characteristic of the changes of organic evolution; additive increments are more typical of the changes of human culture'.

Kroeber treats substitution as an elementary concept which does not require definition, and uses 'replacement' and 'displacement' as synonyms. He does not deny that cultural substitution takes place, for it is clear that new elements of culture sometimes take the place of older ones. But he maintains that '... the displacement is often only partial ... the older elements survive, though with diminished or specialized scope' (ibid., p. 378). Candles are cited as an example.

H. G. Barnett (*Innovation: The Basis of Cultural Change*, New York: McGraw-Hill, 1953, p. 16) discusses substitution in the terms of his view that 'every innovation is a combination of ideas. ... The only bonds between its parts in a cultural setting are mental connections ...'. Substitution, for Barnett, is a psychological rather than a cultural process. This view is considered here because the process is concerned with culture conceived as ideas rather than as actions or things. One merit of Barnett's approach is his precise definition of substitution. It is through assimilation or projection that one configuration or set of elements is substituted for another. (a) Given two configurations (CAB and CXY) with a common element, and assuming that CAB serves as the reference point for the innovator, assimilation occurs when CX is substituted for CA to give a new configuration CXB. In other words, '... we may speak of CAB assimilating CX ...' (ibid., p. 208). (b) Projection occurs when CA is substituted for CX to yield another new configuration CAY. 'CA is, after a manner of speaking, projected upon the stimulus field' (ibid., p. 210). Thus substitution is not a unitary process; rather it takes the form of one of these two alternatives.

P. Sorokin (*Social and Cultural Dynamics*, New York: American Book Company, 1937, vol. 4, p. 727) maintains that the idea of substitution is appropriate only when there is 'total change of the total system or of all its essential components ...'. Substitution is not modification or development in which something is added and something else subtracted, but rather total replacement. This restricted view clearly conflicts with Kroeber's more widely accepted usage.

Frank Miller

See also: ACCULTURATION

DIFFUSION

INNOVATION

Cultural System

A. *Cultural system* is used to designate *a culture* when the observer asserts at a minimum that its parts are unified by some kind and degree of interdependence, and that its internal connections define the limits of, and give a character to, the whole. The nature of the relationships of the components of a cultural system depends upon the definition of culture (q.v.) employed. The more culture is abstracted from the social system the more it is conceived as consisting of ideas and its systematic qualities to lie in logical and aesthetic consistency. The less it is abstracted, the more its systematic properties are seen as similar to those of the social system, namely functional interdependence and normative conformity.

B. The use of the term *cultural system* in referring to a culture is relatively recent. The several historical schools of anthropology have tended to view cultures as '... congeries of disconnected traits, disparate in origin and history ...' (R. L. Beals & H. Hoijer, *An Introduction to Anthropology*, New York: The Macmillan Co., 1953, p. 617). *Cultural system*, on the other hand, focuses attention on the interrelatedness of the elements of a culture. Order, linkage, cultural integration (q.v.), and culture pattern (q.v.) are the key words. 'All nature consists of materials. But the manner in which matter is organized into entities is as significant as the substance or the function served within a given system' (A. L. Kroeber & C. Kluckhohn, *Culture: A Critical Review of Concepts and Definitions*, Cambridge, Mass.: Harvard University Peabody Museum of American Archeology and Ethnology, 1952, p. 63).

C. The main properties of a cultural system have been variously conceived. Mostly the formulations stress one or another property, thus constituting complementary emphases rather than contradictory ones.

1. Some conceptions stress the patterning of culture, the *culture pattern*.

2. Overlapping the concept of culture pattern is that of *cultural integration* referring usually to the consistency and interdependency of the elements of a cultural system.

3. Stress is frequently placed on the 'boundary-maintaining' character of the cultural system, its ability to maintain its distinctness as a system over against the environment.

4. Closely related to boundary-maintenance is the concept of system autonomy. 'An autonomous cultural system is one which is self-sustaining—that is, it does not need to be maintained by a complementary, reciprocal, subordinate, or other indispensable connection with a second system' (*The Social Science Seminar on Acculturation*, 'Acculturation: An Exploratory Formulation', *American Anthropologist*, vol. 56, 1954, p. 974).

5. Occasionally the concept of a guide or plan is added to the idea of a system. 'A culture is a historically derived system of explicit and implicit designs for living, which tends to be shared by all or specially designated members of a group' (C. Kluckhohn & W. H. Kelly, 'The Concept of Culture', in R. Linton (ed.), *The Science of Man in the World Crisis*, New York: Columbia University Press, 1945, p. 98).

H. G. Barnett

See also: CULTURAL CONFIGURATION
CULTURAL INTEGRATION
CULTURE
CULTURE PATTERN
FUNCTION
SOCIAL SYSTEM

Cultural Theme

A. *Cultural theme* may be defined as '... a postulate or position, declared or implied, and usually controlling behavior or stimulating activity, which is tacitly approved or openly promoted in a society' (M. E. Opler, 'Themes as Dynamic Forces in Culture', *American Journal of Sociology*, vol. LI, 1945–6, p. 198).

B. The search for significant categories, objective and unbound by the observer's culture, which will both sharpen the description of given cultures and facilitate their comparison, has led in anthropology to the development of a surprising number of concepts, among them *cultural theme*. The cultural comparisons so far envisaged in the use of the concept *theme*, as well as the descriptive purpose to which it has been applied, are essentially qualitative. It aims at characterizing cultural content by means of invariant criteria.

1. Such qualitative, content categories as *theme* are to be distinguished from what G. P. Murdock calls '... the true *universals* of culture ... not identities in habit, in definable behavior' but 'similarities in classification ...' like families, marriage, education, medicine, etc. ('The Common Denominator of Cultures', in R. Linton (ed.), *The Science of Man in the World Crisis*, New York: Columbia University Press, 1945, p. 125). Themes are universal only in the sense that every culture has them or in the sense that R. Linton uses universal as a unit of culture shared by every sane adult

Cultural Universal

member of a particular society. Every society does not have the same themes, of course; nor even themes which cover—though differently—the same universal purposive categories of behaviour, such as education, medicine, etc.

2. Rather than being universals in Murdock's sense, cultural themes represent the effort of the observer '... to develop relatively uniform criteria for describing a culture in terms of its own values on the basis of inductive, objective evidence' (M. E. Opler, 'Rejoinder to Albert K. Cohen', *American Journal of Sociology*, vol. LII, 1946–47, p. 43). Viewed in such a perspective the following general statements can be made about themes: (a) Every culture has multiple themes; (b) while there is necessarily some harmony among the themes of a given culture, there is no assumption of a complete lack of conflict; (c) each theme is likely to have multiple expressions; (d) a theme may find its expressions in one or several parts of the institutional structure; (e) a theme in one culture can presumably be similar to that in another regardless of whether their expressions occur in all the same parts of the institutional structure; (f) themes may be a part of implicit or explicit culture.

James B. Watson

See also: CULTURAL UNIVERSAL
CULTURE
CULTURE PATTERN

Cultural Universal

Cultural universal has two separate and distinct usages which cannot be reconciled.

1. *Cultural universal* is used as a term designating one category of a three-fold classification of culture by R. Linton, based on the recognition of variability in the degree to which individuals participate in, and control knowledge of, the different aspects of their culture (see *cultural alternative*). It may be defined as an element of culture '... common to all sane, adult members of the society' (*The Study of Man*, New York: D. Appleton-Century, 1936, p. 272).

Joseph B. Casagrande

2. *Cultural universal* is one of several terms used to denote aspects of culture believed to exist among all men and attributed in most cases to the necessity of meeting needs common to all men. The other term most commonly used is *universal pattern of culture* (see *culture pattern*).

Clyde Kluckhohn

See also: CULTURAL ALTERNATIVE
CULTURAL SPECIALTY
CULTURE
CULTURE PATTERN

Cultural Variation

A. *Cultural variation* generally refers to the differences in culture (q.v.) among the different communities of mankind, and, on a larger scale, among the different regions of the occupied globe. In a stricter sense it may be used to denote those human differences of belief and behaviour which are learnt through processes of symbolic interaction as distinct from features of human life which are biopsychic in origin or which arise simply and on a non-symbolizing level from the elemental conditions of hominid social life.

B. There are a number of different classes of problems in connection with cultural variation, and anthropologists are not all agreed as to their relative importance.

1. Perhaps of first importance is the problem of the magnitude of cultural variation.

(a) Theoretical positions on this issue run from the extremes of the polygenists and racists, on the one hand, who take different 'racial psychologies' or 'folk souls' each as sui generis; and the doctrinaire culture relativists who—though for other reasons—closely follow them in the pluralistic treatment of cultures; to the opposite monistic pole of the sentimental pan-humanist, for whom the lives of all men are basically the same, the variations being largely incidental.

(b) Differences with respect to the importance of cultural variation have had a bearing upon the sorts of studies attempted. According to C. Kluckhohn, '... in general, from about this time on [1911], the attention of anthropologists throughout the world appears to have been directed overwhelmingly to the distinctiveness of each culture and to the differences in human custom as opposed to the similarities. The latter, where recognized, were explained historically rather than in terms of the common nature of man and certain invariant properties of the human situation' ('Universal Categories of Culture', in A. L. Kroeber (ed.), *Anthropology Today*, Chicago: University of Chicago Press, 1953, p. 511).

2. Second only to the problem of the magnitude of variability is the question of the correlates or causes of comparable differences or similarities of various cultural systems. Here the

range of theories has moved from that of unique historical causes to those which insist on structural-functional studies into the whole range of custom and its corollaries; and from single-factor determinisms, whether racial, geographic, or economic, through sometimes rather vague multi-factor analyses, to stress on the free, though conditioned, response of human creativity.

3. Closely related to the problem of causation is the problem of the growth and developmental processes in the emergence of given cultural varieties or of cultural variation generally. Here the stress has been on the problems of cultural evolution (q.v.), equilibrium and cultural determinism (q.v.).

4. For those concerned with history, there has been the problem of the history and historical interconnections of local and regional cultural varieties, leading ultimately, through archaeology and ethnology, to an inclusive culture history (q.v.).

5. Finally there has been the task of delineating major types of cultures with the eventual aim of an exhaustive typology.

James B. Watson

See also: CULTURAL RELATIVITY
CULTURE

Culture

A. It is difficult to settle upon a single definition of this complex and extremely important term, but the following definitions may each be useful for somewhat different purposes.

1. A. L. Kroeber and C. Kluckhohn present a synthesis that embodies the elements positively accepted by most contemporary social scientists: 'Culture consists of patterns, explicit and implicit, of and for behavior acquired and transmitted by symbols, constituting the distinctive achievements of human groups, including their embodiments in artifacts; the essential core of culture consists of traditional (i.e. historically derived and selected) ideas and especially their attached values; culture systems may, on the one hand, be considered as products of action, on the other as conditioning elements of further action' (*Culture: A Critical Review of Concepts and Definitions, Papers of the Peabody Museum of American Archeology and Ethnology*, vol. 47, no. 1, 1952, p. 181).

2. A biologist, G. E. Hutchinson, gives a brief definition: 'The class of all the behavior exhibited by the group is called the culture of the group' ('Marginalia', *American Scientist*, vol. 38, 1950, p. 283). But some purists would find this definition unacceptable on the ground that the differentiae of culture are comprised of only that behaviour which is distinctive of a group. This purist view premises that we are talking about culture only when a people shows a stylized preference for one path to a goal when—from the observer's perspective—two or more are equally open, physically possible, and functionally effective. It would insist, for example, that to enumerate 'fishing' as an aspect of a maritime culture would be meaningless unless the way or style of fishing were specified in detail. On the other hand, if a people who had access to fish failed to utilize them, such a datum would be significant in defining the culture.

3. A serious lack in the foregoing definitions is the absence of an operational dimension. Hutchinson approaches this in the following: 'Given a group and a newborn spatiotemporal individual, if the individual is placed in the group and later observed, it will exhibit behavior which cannot be distinguished from that constituting the culture of the group in which it has developed. If the individual should actually be moved at birth from a second group having a different culture, then its behavior would be sharply distinguishable from that constituting this second culture. There will usually be difficulty in obtaining cases of quite the sharpness used in stating the generalization, but anyone who wishes to examine its validity can easily do so in contemporary North America. ... The operational method of stating this generalization indicates that the *culture* of the anthropologist has the same degree of abstraction as the *field* of the physicist' (G. E. Hutchinson, 'Marginalia', p. 283).

This line of thinking coincides with the recent stress laid by social scientists upon 'significant discontinuities' as the crucial criterion for isolating cultural units. Upon this basis C. Lévi-Strauss ('Social Structure', in A. L. Kroeber (ed.), *Anthropology Today*, Chicago: University of Chicago Press, 1953, p. 536) may be paraphrased so as to offer the following as a relatively compact and somewhat operational definition which adheres closely to what most social scientists say and to how they actually practice field work and analysis: 'A culture is a set of patterns, of and for behavior, prevalent among a group of human beings at a specified time period and which, from the point of view of the research at hand and of the scale on which it is being carried out, presents, in relation to other such sets, observable and sharp discontinuities'.

Culture

The words 'set' and 'sets' are to be understood as referring in a quasi-technical sense to the 'set theory' branch of topological mathematics.

B. *Culture* signifying *husbandry* appears in English as early as 1420. The technical term in anthropology was introduced into English by E. B. Tylor (*Researches into the Early History and Development of Civilization*, London: John Murray, 1865, pp. 4, 369) in 1865 and systematically defined and made a central concept by the same author six years later: 'Culture ... taken in its wide ethnographic sense, is that complex whole which includes knowledge, belief, art, morals, law, custom, and any other capabilities and habits acquired by man as a member of society' (*Primitive Culture*, London: John Murray, 1871, p. 1).

C. Through the years definitions of culture as a central concept of anthropology and the other social sciences have proliferated. A. L. Kroeber & C. Kluckhohn (*Culture: A Critical Review of Concepts and Definitions*) have analysed 160 definitions in English by anthropologists, sociologists, psychologists, psychiatrists, and others. These appeared, as judged by principal emphasis, to fall into six major groups which were labelled as follows: (1) enumeratively descriptive, (2) historical, (3) normative, (4) psychological, (5) structural, (6) genetic.

1. Tylor's classic definition is echoed in that of F. Boas, representative of the enumeratively descriptive definition: 'Culture embraces all the manifestations of social habits of a community, the reactions of the individual as affected by the habits of the group in which he lives, and the products of human activities as determined by these habits' (F. Boas, 'Anthropology', in E. R. A. Seligman (ed.) *Encyclopedia of the Social Sciences*, New York: The Macmillan Co., 1930, vol. 2, p. 79). The distinctive criteria of this group of definitions are: (a) culture as a comprehensive totality, and (b) enumeration of aspects of culture content.

2. The definitions of the second group, the historical, select one feature of culture, social inheritance or social tradition, rather than define culture substantively: '... the social heredity is called culture. As a general term, *culture* means the total social heredity of mankind, while as a specific term, *a culture* means a particular strain of social heredity' (R. Linton, *The Study of Man*, New York: D. Appleton-Century, 1936, p. 78).

3. The third group emphasizes culture either as a distinctive way of life or as dynamically forceful normative ideas and their consequences. O. Klineberg, for example, defines culture simply as '... that whole "way of life" which is determined by the social environment' (*Race Differences*, New York: Harper & Brothers, 1935, p. 255); while P. Sorokin says: 'The cultural aspect of the superorganic universe consists of meanings, values, norms, their interaction and relationships, their integrated and unintegrated groups ... as they are objectified through overt actions and other vehicles in the empirical socio-cultural universe' (*Society, Culture, and Personality*, New York: Harper & Brothers, 1947, p. 313).

4. The fourth group is 'psychological' in the sense that processes such as adjustment, learning, and habit are singled out. Culture is seen primarily as a set of techniques for satisfying needs, for solving problems, and for adjusting both to the external environment and to other men. C. S. Ford, for example, says: 'Culture consists of traditional ways of solving problems. ... Culture ... is composed of responses which have been accepted because they have met with success; in brief, culture consists of learned problem-solutions' ('Culture and Human Behavior', *Scientific Monthly*, vol. 55, 1942, pp. 555, 557). A few definitions in this group attempt to reduce culture to the concepts of one psychological school: 'By culture we shall understand the sum of all sublimations, all substitutes, or reaction formations, in short, everything in society that inhibits impulses or permits their distorted satisfaction' (G. Roheim, *The Riddle of the Sphinx*, London: Hogarth Press, 1934, p. 216).

5. Only four of the definitions in the fifth, structural, group antedate 1945 and only one was published prior to 1939. These definitions make central the systematic quality of each culture, the organized interrelation of the isolable aspects of culture. Culture becomes abstract, a conceptual model that must be based on and interpret behaviour but which is not behaviour itself. For example, C. Kluckhohn and W. H. Kelly assert that: 'A culture is an historically derived system of explicit and implicit designs for living, which tends to be shared by all or specially designated members of a group' ('The Concept of Culture', in R. Linton (ed.), *The Science of Man in the World Crisis*, New York: Columbia University Press, 1945, p. 98). Not all anthropologists accept the notion of culture as a logical construct—a 'model' based on abstractions from behaviour. However, while on occasion such anthropologists, e.g. R. Linton, D. Bidney, and, in part, L. White, insist that culture comprises actual behaviour, they nevertheless tend to use such expressions as 'patterned ways of behaviour', '*forms* of behaviour', and the like.

6. The sixth, genetic, group focuses on the questions: How has culture come to be? What are the factors that have made culture possible or caused it to come into existence? Other properties are mentioned, but the stress is on the genetic side. L. J. Carr puts much content into nine words: 'The accumulated transmissable results of past behavior in association' ('Situational Psychology', *American Journal of Sociology*, vol. LI, 1945–6, p. 137).

D. Since roughly 1935, many British social anthropologists have tended to use *social structure* (q.v.) rather than culture as a core concept. While there has been this tendency to deprecate the concept of culture and to avoid its use, such British definitions as have appeared fall well within the range of variation of American definition. As illustration, R. Firth's synthetic statement could equally well have been written by an American: 'If ... society is taken to be an organized set of individuals with a given way of life, culture is that way of life. If society is taken to be an aggregate of social relations, then culture is the content of those relations. Society emphasizes the human component, the aggregate of people and the relations between them. Culture emphasizes the component of accumulated resources, immaterial as well as material, which the people inherit, employ, transmute, add to, and transmit. Having substance, if in part only ideational, this component acts as a regulator to action. From the behavioural aspect, culture is all learned behaviour which has been socially acquired. It includes the residual effects of social action. It is necessarily also an incentive to action' (*Elements of Social Organization*, London: Watts, 1951, p. 27).

1. The only striking British innovation is M. Fortes's proposal that culture designate the qualitative aspect of social facts, whereas the term *structure* be applied '... to those features of social events which are actually or ideally susceptible of quantitative description and analysis' ('Time and Social Structure', in M. Fortes (ed.), *Social Structure*, Oxford: Clarendon Press, 1949, p. 57).

2. Firth expresses surprise that Kroeber and Kluckhohn in their treatment of culture devote so little attention to the concept of function, and this remark presumably reflects a view held by many British social anthropologists ('Function', in W. L. Thomas, Jr. (ed.), *Current Anthropology*, Chicago: University of Chicago Press, 1956, p. 246).

E. There are no genuinely consistent tendencies characteristic of the various academic disciplines. Definitions by psychologists, for instance, appear in each of the six major groups of definitions. Indeed, leaving occasional eccentric definitions aside, it may be said that all social scientists using the term *culture* in its anthropological sense differ only in what points they choose to emphasize and how much they feel it necessary to make explicit.

1. Archaeologists have often emphasized artifacts in their definitions, yet statements like the following are becoming more frequent: 'Everything acquired by man after birth, a product of nurture within society, a purely sociological grouping' (A. J. N. Goodwin, *Method in Prehistory*, Cape Town: South African Archaeological Society, 1953, p. 21).

2. A few American sociologists, e.g. R. M. MacIver, have shown some disposition to follow German authors such as A. Weber by identifying culture with subjective religion, philosophy, and art, while using *civilization* to designate the objective technological and informational activities of society. This position takes civilization as accumulative and irreversible with the cultural component seen as highly variable, unique, and non-additive.

F. It is recognized as proper to speak of culture in general—whether in a descriptive or explanatory way—and of particular cultures.

1. The lines of demarcation of any cultural unit chosen for description and analysis are in large part a matter of level of abstraction and convenience for the problem at hand. Occidental culture, Graeco-Roman culture, 19th century European culture, German culture, Swabian culture, the peasant culture of the Black Forest in 1900—these are all equally legitimate abstractions if carefully defined.

2. The term *sub-culture* is often used. M. M. Gordon defines it as follows: '... a subdivision of a national culture, composed of a combination of factorable social situations such as class status, ethnic background, regional and rural or urban residence, and religious affiliation, but *forming in their combination a functioning unity which has an integrated impact on the*

Culture Area

participating individual' ('The Concept of the Sub-Culture and its Application', *Social Forces*, vol. 26, 1947, p. 40).

Clyde Kluckhohn

See also: CIVILIZATION
SOCIETY

Culture Area

A. A *culture area* is a unit of geographic space in which similar culture or cultures are found. Thus it is simply a mode of the 'spatial classification' of culture (A. L. Kroeber, *Cultural and Natural Areas of Native North America*, University of California Publications in American Archeology and Ethnology, Berkeley: University of California Press, 1939, p. 1). The term is equivalent to the term *culture province* as used by Ratzel and more recently by H. Baumann (*Völkerkunde von Afrika*, Essen: Essener, 1939). It should however, be distinguished from *Kulturkreis* (q.v.).

The classical image of a culture area, as exemplified by such areas as the Northwest coast and the Plains of North America, and expounded by Wissler, Kroeber, and Herskovits, is of a clearly defined geographical area with a characteristic ecology, economy, material culture, art style, and set of social values. The characteristic traits of the area are most clearly exemplified in its cultural—not necessarily geographic—centre and thin out toward the edges; along the boundaries between two areas are found marginal tribes with some of the characteristics of each area.

B. One of the earliest uses of the term was that by O. T. Mason, who, evidently influenced by Ratzel's concept of 'culture provinces'—*Kulturprovinzen*, divided the native cultures of the New World into eighteen 'environments or culture areas' ('Influence of Environment on Human Industries or Arts', *Smithsonian Institution, Annual Report*, 1895, Washington: U.S. Government Printing Office, 1896, p. 646). Thus the culture area concept began as a museum classification category, when curators wished to arrange ethnological specimens for display by geographic area of origin rather than by taxonomic type or place in some supposed evolutionary scheme. A culture area was simply some region, defined by a map, whose cultures were considered a significant group in contrast to those of neighbouring regions.

C. The first attempt at a formal theoretical definition of the term was made by C. Wissler

and reflects the empirical origin of the concept: '... we saw that the natives of the New World could be grouped according to single culture traits, giving us food areas, textile areas, ceramic areas, etc. If, however, we take all the traits into simultaneous consideration and shift our point of view to the social, or tribal units, we are able to form fairly definite groups. This will give us culture areas, or classification of culture groups according to their culture traits' (*The American Indian*, New York: Oxford University Press, 2nd edn., 1922, pp. 217–18).

M. J. Herskovits has also contributed to the sharpening of the concept: '... it has been found that when a large region, such as a continent, is surveyed for any particular culture trait or group of traits, the distribution of those traits will be such that they can be plotted on a map in continuous areas' ('Preliminary Consideration of the Culture Areas of Africa', *American Anthropologist*, vol. 26, 1924, p. 50). Much later he wrote: '... when cultures are viewed objectively, they are seen to form clusters, so to speak, sufficiently homogeneous that the regions in which they occur can be delimited on a map. *The area in which similar cultures are found is* called a culture area' (*Man and His Works*, New York: Knopf, 1948, p. 183).

The primary weakness of the *culture area* concept is that no clear agreement can be found on principles of classification which will permit the drawing of comparable area boundaries. It is impossible to resolve, for example, the gross differences between Herskovits's culture areas of Africa and Baumann's 'culture-provinces' of Africa, though both are 'spatial classifications' which claim to map areas 'in which similar cultures are found'.

Raoul Naroll

See also: AGE AND AREA HYPOTHESIS
AREA CO-TRADITION
REGION

Culture Case Study

A. *Culture* is taken in a sense closely related to that of J. L. Myres: '... "culture" is not a state or a condition only, but a process; as in *agriculture* or *horticulture* we mean not the condition of the land but the whole round of the farmer's year, and all that he does in it; "culture", then, is what remains of men's past, working on their present, to shape their future' (*The Political Ideas of the Greeks*, London: Edward Arnold, 1927, p. 2). As used in the combination, the stress is strongly on non-material culture, and especially on the normative aspect thereof.

Case refers to a 'whole' that has social-scientific relevance. It is defined as a whole by the social-scientific problem for which a solution is being sought. Thus it is viewed as 'a whole by interrogation' rather than as a 'whole by intuition'.

Study has to do with the investigation of the case as a relatively unique whole, with the intention of generating from it a tentative answer to the problem initially posed; which answer, stripped of its unique elements, is then to be used in the development of a hypothesis applicable to other cases, considered comparable or identical for the purposes in hand. Through any or all appropriate social-scientific procedures and techniques, this hypothesis is then to be subjected to tests leading to its acceptance or rejection. (For further definition less compressed, see H. Becker, 'Culture Case Study and Greek History: Comparison Viewed Sociologically', *American Sociological Review*, vol. 23, 1958, pp. 489–504).

B. These three words in combination apparently were first used in the lectures of R. E. Park in discussing certain works by E. Durkheim and M. Weber, but occur nowhere in Park's published writings. The combination seems first to have appeared in print in articles by H. Becker, in 1930 and 1931 ('Forms of Population Movement', *Social Forces*, vol. IX, 1930–31, pp. 147–60 and pp. 351–61). Thereafter its use has been largely restricted to Becker's writings and those of students working with him.

Howard Becker

See also: CASE STUDY METHOD

Culture Change
A. Substantively *culture change* may be defined as the modification of culture (q.v.) through time. This definition becomes more precise only when the situations and processes of such modification are fully analysed. Such analysis depends upon the varying definitions of culture (q.v.), society (q.v.), and personality. It is closely related to the term social change (q.v.).

1. The term is often used interchangeably with 'cultural dynamics'.

2. Culture change has been most used by American anthropologists. Social change has been stressed by sociologists and social psycho-logists, and also has been favoured by British social anthropologists.

3. Many American anthropologists and sociologists now speak of *cultural and social change* together, and sometimes use *socio-cultural* change to cover the full range of phenomena concerned.

B. Studies of culture change have been a dominant anthropological interest from the beginnings of the science, but through the years have been given different theoretical emphases.

1. In the middle 19th century when cultural anthropology and sociology were becoming differentiated from history and social philosophy, the initial concern was to explain 'progress' from savagery to civilization. Beginning in the 1860s the dominant task of theory was to uncover grand laws of the evolution of culture and society, as in the works of Morgan and Spencer.

2. From 1896 on Rivers, Boas, and others attacked over-simple evolutionary generalization, and shifted attention to specific culture history (q.v.). So-called historical and diffusionist theories of growth and change held the stage, with their often unduly atomistic and mechanistic reconstructions of the invention and diffusion (q.v.) of trait elements, together with distributional studies of the placement of elements in cultures and culture areas (q.v.).

3. In the 1920s, although the stress on function (q.v.) and functionalism tended to distract attention from culture change, so-called culture-contact and acculturation (q.v.) studies were gaining momentum. From initially studying the impact of Western influences so as to be able to discard intrusive elements and reconstruct traditional cultures, anthropologists came to recognize that an understanding of the events and processes of change could be of vital importance. By the 1930s acculturation studies became the major approach in the time-dimensional analysis of culture. This period was also marked by a strong growth of applied anthropology (q.v.) providing in a broad sense laboratory-like experiments for the further understanding of change.

C. Both basic and applied studies of culture change underwent great expansion during World War II; and subsequently the whole front of the subject has been actively worked. In anthropology alone some three hundred books and papers are currently being published

Culture Complex

yearly in the culture change field (see, for example, F. M. Keesing, *Culture Change: A Survey and Bibliography of Anthropological Sources to 1952*, Stanford: Stanford University Press, 1953). Sociology and social psychology also have their growing literature on related problems, usually dealt with under *social change*.

1. The study of long-term historical process, generally in eclipse since the breakdown of the older evolutionist and diffusionist systems of thought, has been revived, as in the works of L. White, V. G. Childe, and J. Steward. Even the term *social evolution* as applied to generalized processes of cultural growth has been considerably rehabilitated.

2. Acculturation studies have been placed in their proper perspective as one broad type of culture change marked by interaction and culture transfer between two or more cultural systems (q.v.). Other types have also been taken into account, such as changes in a single system, urbanization, change in complex systems such as a large national society, innovation, transfer, reformulation, and forced change through outside intervention. Among other notable problems of contemporary interest in culture change are rates of change, disorganization and reorganization, the role of cults and other dynamic movements, the role of the individual in change, the relation of change to stability, and resistance to change.

Felix M. Keesing

See also: CULTURE
               SOCIAL CHANGE

Culture Complex

A. A *culture complex* may be defined as a functionally integrated grouping of culture traits (q.v.) which persists as a unit in space and time, is cross-culturally diffusible, and is restricted to one aspect of a total culture (q.v.). The term is sometimes loosely and derivatively used, as by some archaeologists, to designate a category of traits associated in space and time whose functional interdependence has not yet been established, or exists only ex hypothesi.

B. The term was first used and developed in the historical analysis of the growth and spread of culture, and was intimately related to the conceptions of the culture trait (q.v.), the cultural configuration (q.v.), the culture pattern (q.v.), and the culture area (q.v.). Although the term was originally used within the theoretical framework of culture history, it has quite obvious

functional implications, and has served as one of the bridge terms for those who believe that the study of culture requires both an historical and a functional approach.

1. The early development of the concept is seen in the writings of C. Wissler and R. B. Dixon (C. Wissler, *Man and Culture*, New York: Thomas Y. Crowell, 1923; R. B. Dixon, *The Building of Cultures*, New York: Charles Scribner's Sons, 1928).

2. Perhaps the best recent statement concerning *culture complex* is that of A. L. Kroeber in defining the essentially synonymous term, *systemic culture pattern* (cf. *culture pattern*): 'A second kind of pattern consists of a system or complex of cultural material that has proved its utility as a system and therefore tends to cohere and persist as a unit; it is modifiable superficially, but modifiable only with difficulty as to its underlying plan. Any one such systemic pattern is limited primarily to one aspect of culture, such as subsistence, religion, or economics; ... it can be diffused cross-culturally from one people to another' (*Anthropology*, New York: Harcourt, Brace, 1948, p. 312).

C. A somewhat less precise conception of *culture complex* is associated with archaeology as it has developed in the United States. Although much of this conception of the term lies in the *incompleteness* of archaeological materials there has been little attempt to achieve more than a list of archaeological culture traits which occur together as an assemblage and to compare these assemblages of culture traits from one site or area to another. There is little emphasis on the integrative or functional attributes of these materials, and in contradistinction to the previously mentioned usage the total cultural remains in a specific site are termed a culture complex. The most notable development of this view is found in the writings of W. C. McKern on the Midwestern Taxonomic Method ('The Midwestern Taxonomic Method as an Aid to Archeological Culture Study', *American Antiquity*, vol. 4, 1939, pp. 301–13).

A similar view is expressed by R. K. Beardsley, et al., when they define a 'community pattern' which 'is the organization of economic, socio-political, and ceremonial inter-relationships within a community, and is largely synonymous with culture complex' ('Functional and Evolutionary Implications of Community Patterning', in R. Wauchope (ed.), *Seminars in Archeology: 1955, Memoirs of the Society for American Archeology*, vol. 11, 1956, p. 134).

This view more successfully approximates that of other usages of the term.

Arden R. King

See also: CULTURE
CULTURE PATTERN

Culture History

A. *Culture history* may be defined as an integrated picture of cultural events as they occur diachronically—i.e. through time—constructed from materials selected from the totality of known cultural data. The methodology of historiography dictates the selection of data and provides the means for interpretation and integration. Historiography in anthropology, as contrasted with document-based history, characteristically involves the derivation of the time element from synchronic data. Numerous techniques are employed in this method, prominent among which is the turning of spatial relationships of cultural interaction or geographical distribution into time relationships or sequences.

B. In the 20th century the term *culture history* has appeared with great frequency in the writings of anthropologists in the sub-fields of ethnology and archaeology. Indeed, the usage is so common that a definition is seldom deemed necessary. Upon analysis, however, it becomes clear that the two sub-disciplines characteristically use these words with significantly different, though not necessarily contradictory meanings.

1. In the archaeologist's routine use of the term, the emphasis is upon the word *culture*. History is taken for granted since archaeology, by its very nature, is predominantly concerned with the recreating of the time sequence, at least as a first step. However, time sequence as represented by stratigraphic succession is of no interest unless cultural materials are involved; hence the emphasis upon culture.

(a) In practice, archaeologists frequently use *culture history* as synonymous with archaeology. For example, the subject of the 75th Anniversary Volume of the Anthropological Society of Washington is New World *archaeology*, as stated by M. T. Newman in the preface, but the title is *New Interpretations of Aboriginal American Culture History* (Washington, 1955, p. vii). In *Anthropology Today* (A. L. Kroeber (ed.), Chicago: University of Chicago Press, 1953) five prominent archaeologists write under the heading 'Problems of the Historical Approach' and three of these employ the term *culture history* in their titles.

(b) The relative importance of ethnology in culture history has sometimes been called into question (without assuming that ethnologists may not, nevertheless, be culture historians). I. Rouse, for example, recognizes that 'Some have argued that archaeology deserves to be regarded as the central discipline for culture-historical research, since it deals with a much longer time perspective than ethnology and has developed sounder techniques for establishing chronology'. However, Rouse goes on to say that 'In the Americas, at least, archaeologists are coming to recognize that their studies of culture history must take into consideration the pertinent ethnological data, and vice versa ... [Archaeology's] descriptive data are so fragmentary that it must yield to ethnology with respect to matters of content, particularly of nonmaterial culture' ('The Strategy of Culture History', in A. L. Kroeber (ed.), *Anthropology Today*, p. 57. See also G. F. Ekholm, 'New World Culture History', in *Yearbook of Anthropology*, New York: Wenner-Gren Foundation for Anthropological Research, 1955, p. 99).

2. In ethnology—in contrast to the archaeological view—the emphasis with respect to *culture history* is upon *history*. Stress upon culture can be taken for granted. Because there are other methods of interpreting culture—e.g. functional and evolutionary—the object is to call attention to the chronological dimension, either for its own sake or for purposes of interpretation or integration. Documentary evidence is not demanded nor even expected, but will be used in those rare instances where available. The methodology of ethnology provides the means for ascertaining history from cultural data as they appear in spatial distribution.

(a) Consistent with the general recognition in ethnology of *culture history* as but one of several methods or approaches in the discipline, there are few ethnologists who employ this method alone and none who equates the terms ethnology and culture history.

(b) Some strong expressions of opinion as to the importance of culture history in anthropology include F. W. Maitland's declaration that 'By and by anthropology will have the choice of being history or nothing' and P. Radin's repetition of the statement as an introductory dictum in his book *The Method and Theory of Ethnology* (New York: McGraw-Hill, 1933, p. vii). K. Birket-Smith observes that 'The present is not understood except as a result of the past, and therefore the vital problem of ethnology, as I understand it, must be a

Culture History

historical one' (in S. Tax et al. (eds.), *An Appraisal of Anthropology Today*, Chicago: University of Chicago Press, 1953, p. 68). E. Sapir opened his classical Time Perspective paper by stating that 'Cultural anthropology is more and more rapidly getting to realize itself as a strictly historical science. Its data cannot be understood, either in themselves or in relation to one another, except as the end points of specific sequences of events reaching back into the remote past ... it is highly important that an historical understanding of the facts be held up as the properly ethnological goal of the student' (*Time Perspective in Aboriginal American Culture, a Study in Method*, Ottawa: Canada Geological Survey, Memoir 90, 1916, pp. 1–2).

(c) The relative importance of ethnology and archaeology in culture history has called forth a few strongly worded opinions from ethnologists. W. Schmidt is convinced that 'The specific task of ethnology in history is something exceedingly valuable, in fact something absolutely necessary, which no other science can accomplish in such vivid fullness. ... Ethnology shares this privilege with pre-history; but it surpasses the latter through the incomparable richness ... it presents to us, while pre-history can but offer the Lifeless and the Maimed data, which become all the more rare the farther back the people go and the older they are' (*The Culture Historical Method of Ethnology*, New York: Fortuny, 1939, pp. 9–10). Schmidt, of course, speaks only for adherents of the *Kulturkreislehre*. Others see the matter differently. C. von Fürer-Haimendorf, for example, states that 'The most significant trend in the anthropological approach to culture history during the years 1952–54 has been the increasing dependence of ethnologists on the findings of prehistoric archaeology' ('Culture History and Cultural Development', in W. L. Thomas, Jr. (ed.), *Current Anthropology*, Chicago: University of Chicago Press, 1956, p. 149).

C. The *culture history* concept is meaningful and significant only in terms of methodology. This methodology is two-dimensional: anthropological and historiographic. Anthropology provides the approaches by which time considerations are revealed and conceptualized in otherwise static cultural data. Historiography provides the means by which such findings are turned into valid and useful historical perspectives of the peoples concerned. The result is *culture history*, a theoretically distinct and uniquely useful aspect of anthropology, serving

alongside social anthropology, cultural psychology, and other methodologically distinct approaches, to give us the answers we seek with respect to man.

1. The methodological contribution of *anthropology* involves 'the translation of a two-dimensional photographic picture of reality into the three-dimensional picture which lies back of it ... the arrangement in an as orderly temporal sequence as possible, within as definitely circumscribed absolute time limits as circumstances will allow of the processes studied by our science' (E. Sapir, *Time Perspective in Aboriginal American Culture*, p. 4). The ethnological approach falls into the general classification of scientific methodology since an ordering of natural phenomena is involved. Kroeber observed that 'Every sound "natural" classification of culture is also inevitably a sound genetic history of culture, as in biology it yields a history of life. We even possess in archaeology a factual partial check on our inferences from cultural pattern to cultural history—a sort of life-line—a counterpart of the substantiation which paleontology gives to classificatory and evolutionary biology' (in 'Concluding Review', S. Tax et al. (eds.), *An Appraisal of Anthropology Today*, p. 367).

2. *Ethnology* and *archaeology* play complementary roles in their utilization and advancement of anthropological methods. Both are concerned with turning space relationships into time relationships. In ethnology the space is lateral, that is, geographic; in archaeology more often vertical, that is, stratigraphic.

3. Valid culture history emerges when the facts and time relationships brought to light by archaeology and ethnology are soundly integrated and evaluated by the methods of *historiography*. C. D. Forde calls this the achievement of 'conceptual integration of individual phenomena ("facts" or "events") in terms of specified time and place' ('Human Geography, History and Sociology', in *The Scottish Geographical Magazine*, vol. 55, 1939, p. 224).

(a) Historiography is lucidly defined by W. W. Taylor, Jr. as 'the discipline characterized by the construction of cultural contexts abstracted from the totality of past actuality. More specifically, it is *projected contemporary thought about past actuality, integrated and synthesized into contexts in terms of cultural man and sequential time*' (*The Study of Archeology*, American Anthropological Association, Mem. 79, 1948, pp. 34–5). So far as *culture history* is concerned, the 'totality of past actuality' is limited to facts revealed by archaeological and ethnological researches, a selective inventory limited by theoretical interest and the fortunes of recovery.

(b) Historiography is concerned with time and period incidentally, not centrally. 'Being "historical" does not mean having a concern merely with time; to have that is being "chronological" ... being "historical" does not mean having a concern merely with the past; to have that is being "antiquarian" ' (*The Study of Archeology*, p. 35). A. L. Kroeber, likewise, cautions against equating history and chronology. He states that he does not want to belittle the time factor but that 'Space relations can and sometimes must take its place' ('History in Science', *American Anthropologist*, vol. 37, 1935, p. 547).

(c) 'Real history' and 'historical reconstruction' have sometimes been fallaciously contrasted in the context of culture history. Taylor's admirable statement succinctly disposes of the matter: 'The words *reconstruction* and *resynthesis* are fundamentally erroneous and have been responsible for much loss of confidence, particularly among the anthropologists. ... The work of all historical disciplines really leads to construction and synthesis, not reconstruction and resynthesis' (*The Study of Archeology*, p. 35).

D. Finally, a 'definition' of culture history is incomplete if it does not take into account the fact that all culture historians of breadth and insight look to a use of their materials beyond the purely historical, if not now and by themselves, then later and by others. 'When we once have enough sound classification and history of cultures, we should be able to take the next step and, with some genuine solidity, to extricate the processes at work, to generalize the story of culture into its causal factors' (A. L. Kroeber, 'Concluding Review', p. 367).

Verne F. Ray

See also: CULTURAL EVOLUTION
FUNCTION

Culture Pattern
A. *Culture pattern* may be defined as a determinate organization of cultural features—an exactness and constancy of relationship irrespective of content and dimensions. (This definition paraphrases and extends a statement by B. L. Whorf, 'Linguistics as an Exact Science', *Technology Review*, vol. 43, 1940, p. 82).

B. *Pattern* has been used by anthropologists as a portmanteau word since at least as early as 1871 (E. B. Tylor, *Primitive Culture*, London: John Murray, 1871, vol. 2, p. 246). This loose usage continued. An example is C. Wissler's reference to 'the following of existing patterns' ('The Functions of Primitive Ritualistic Ceremonies', *Popular Science Monthly*, vol. 87, 1915, p. 202). Increasingly since the 1920s the term has been used—usually without precise definition—by sociologists, psychologists, and other social scientists.

C. The exploration of the nuances of *pattern*, the attempt to differentiate it with precise meanings, has been an American rather than a British venture, and has been carried out almost exclusively by anthropologists.

1. Particularly important in this undertaking was the linguist-anthropologist, E. Sapir. He defined a culture pattern as '... a generalized mode of conduct that is imputed to society rather than to the individual ...' ('The Unconscious Patterning of Behavior in Society', in E. S. Dummer (ed.), *The Unconscious*, New York: Knopf, 1927, pp. 114–42, esp. pp. 118–19. See also E. Sapir, 'Sound Patterns in Language', *Language*, vol. 1, 1925, pp. 37–51). Sapir constantly insisted that cultures could be understood only if as much analysis were given to their constituent forms as to the content embodied in these forms. In particular, he urged that one look at the forms that are, as it were, beneath the surface of the culture [*covert culture* (q.v.)] '... culture ... cannot be adequately defined by a description of those more colorful patterns of behavior in society which lie open to observation' ('Language' in E. R. A. Seligman (ed.), *Encyclopedia of the Social Sciences*, New York: The Macmillan Co., 1933, vol. IX, p. 157).

2. R. Benedict did not give a systematic definition of culture patterns but indicated that they were equivalent to 'characteristic purposes' or to the 'motives, and emotions and values that are institutionalized in that culture' (*Patterns of Culture*, London: Routledge, 1935, pp. 46, 49). Benedict's usage is equivocal. Sometimes she appears to be referring to modalities for behaviour ('ideal' or 'regulatory' patterns) and of behaviour (behavioural patterns); at other points her attention appears to be upon the values central to the implicit culture or to the outstanding emotional principle or principles of particular cultures.

3. C. Kluckhohn tried to define the conceptual core of the phenomenon of patterning in

Culture Trait

general as follows: 'Structure ... is the foremost constituent in the nuclear idea of pattern. The reference is predominantly to form, not content. But a cultural pattern is not merely a structure—it is a structure to which there is some degree of conformance on the part of a number of persons. "Pattern" preserves what is ... historically its dominant meaning: "something to be copied". Pattern, then, in its most general meaning is a structural regularity' ('Patterning as Exemplified in Navaho Culture', in L. Spier (ed.), *Language, Culture and Personality*, Menasha, Wis.: Sapir Memorial Publication Fund, 1941, p. 112).

4. Another specific definition of *culture pattern* is that of A. L. Kroeber: '... basic patterns are nexuses of culture traits which have assumed a definite and coherent structure, which function successfully, and which acquire major historic weight and persistence' ('Structure, Function, and Pattern in Biology and Anthropology', *Scientific Monthly*, vol. LVI, 1943, p. 112). Building upon the content of this article, he has distinguished universal, systematic, societal or whole-culture, and style patterns (A. L. Kroeber, *Anthropology*, New York: Harcourt, Brace, 1948, pp. 311–43). (a) The concept of the universal pattern of culture comes from C. Wissler (*Man and Culture*, New York: Thomas Y. Crowell, 1923, p. 74). It consists of a series of nine categories: speech, material traits, art, knowledge, religion, society, property, government, and war. 'It is a general outline that will more or less fit all cultures' (A. L. Kroeber, *Anthropology*, p. 311). (b) The systematic pattern '... consists of a system or complex of cultural material that has proved its utility as a system and therefore tends to cohere and persist as a unit; it is modifiable superficially, but modifiable only with difficulty as to its underlying plan' (ibid., p. 313). (c) The whole-culture pattern is the concept referring to the systematization and coherence found in a total culture. (d) A style pattern is the result of '... choosing or evolving one line of procedure out of several possible ones, and sticking to it' (ibid., p. 329).

Clyde Kluckhohn

See also: CULTURAL CONFIGURATION
CULTURAL THEME
CULTURE

Culture Trait

A. *Culture trait* may be defined as 'the smallest identifiable unit in a given culture' (M. J. Herskovits, *Man and His Works*, New York: Knopf, 1948, p. 170).

B. *Culture trait*, together with culture complex (q.v.), cultural configuration (q.v.), culture pattern (q.v.), and culture area (q.v.), was one of the concepts employed by C. Wissler and others in the historical analysis of cultural data during the 1920s (C. Wissler, *Man and Culture*, New York: Thomas Y. Crowell, 1923). The *trait* concept has made it possible to draw up listings of the elements of a culture, and has also permitted the functional analysis of larger organizations of culture. The major conceptual problem with regard to the *culture trait* has been that of ascertaining in operational terms what 'the smallest identifiable unit' may be. It has become increasingly apparent that this will vary according to context.

Arden R. King

See also: CULTURAL CONFIGURATION
CULTURE
CULTURE AREA
CULTURE PATTERN

Culturology

A. *Culturology* may be defined as the scientific study and interpretation of cultural phenomena per se.

B. The term *culturology* was first used by the eminent German chemist and philosopher, W. Ostwald; it appeared, as *kulturologie*, in his writings as early as 1909, and was employed in many of his writings thereafter ('Das System der Wissenschaften', in *Die Forderung des Tages*, Leipzig: Akademische Verlagsgesellschaft, 1910, p. 129; see also 'The System of the Sciences', *Rice Institute Pamphlet*, vol. II, no. 3, 1915, pp. 101–90). Ostwald distinguished culturology from sociology. The latter term is too broad, he said, since its focus upon social interaction would include all living species; 'social' and 'cultural' are not synonymous. And the focus upon interaction excludes, or admits only incidentally, tools, utensils, dwellings, philosophies, art, and other elements of culture. The term was not borrowed and used by social scientists at this time, however.

C. L. A. White invented the term independently of Ostwald and introduced it into anthropological literature in 1939, after having used it for years in his lectures ('A Problem of Kinship Terminology', *American Anthropologist*, vol. 41,

1939, p. 571). White has used culturology to designate that which E. B. Tylor defined as 'the science of culture'. In the perspective of culturology, *culture* (q.v.) is an organization of things and events dependent upon symbols—language, custom, tools, beliefs, etc.—considered in an extra-somatic context, and further considered as a process sui generis, quite apart from its human carriers. Culturology, therefore, is the scientific study and interpretation of cultural phenomena per se. 'During the last hundred years', says R. H. Lowie ('Cultural Anthropology: A Science', *American Journal of Sociology*, vol. XLII, 1936–37, p. 301), 'it has become increasingly clear that culture ... represents ... a distinct domain'. Such a domain demands for its investigation a distinct science and culturology fulfils this need.

Objection to culturology and to separating the science of the social—social anthropology and sociology—from this science of culture generally takes the two-fold position that culture is not a reality sui generis, i.e. it cannot be understood as a super-organic, super-psychic phenomenon, and that social and cultural phenomena must be studied as functional wholes (see D. Bidney, *Theoretical Anthropology*, New York: Columbia University Press, 1953, pp. 96–106).

Leslie A. White

See also: Superorganic

Currency (See Money)

Currency Reform (Also Monetary Reform)

A. In economics *currency* or *monetary reform* is generally used to refer not so much to any legislative or administrative change in the monetary and banking system as to governmental action to effect rapid reduction in the claims against the economy which individuals and business firms hold in the form of money and time and savings deposits. Some economists think the term ought also apply to removal of deflationary restraints upon the monetary system (J. M. Keynes, *A Tract on Monetary Reform*, New York: Harcourt, Brace, 1924). For example such reform may involve abandonment and modification of the Gold Standard.

B. *Currency* (now more usually styled *monetary*) *reform* is usually regarded as a step in terminating hyperinflation or toward preventing inflation which impends. Successful reform usually requires reduction in or removal of governmental deficits, a major source of inflation under modern circumstances. Ends generally secondary, but sometimes of primary importance, may be to facilitate termination of price and ration controls, to permit elimination of black markets in democratic countries or free markets in totalitarian countries, to trap tax evaders, to constitute a part of a more comprehensive capital levy, to reallocate current output by reducing claims of holders of previously accumulated cash balances, and in non-democratic countries to reduce the stake of some in a free market system in order to speed up adjustment to totalitarian regimes. The reform itself involves the use of one or more of the following techniques which are designed to reduce claims against society held by individuals and private business firms in the form of monetary balances and time and savings deposits.

1. Holders of money—currency and demand deposits—and savings deposits may be required to exchange them for fewer units, say 10 old for 1 new as in the 1947 monetary reform in Western Germany (F. H. Klopstock, 'Monetary Reform in Western Germany', *The Journal of Political Economy*, vol. 57, 1949, p. 282; H. C. Wallich, *Mainsprings of the German Revival*, New Haven: Yale University Press, 1955, p. 69). This step reduced the aggregates affected by 90 per cent, the equivalent of moving the decimal one point to the left. It must not be assumed that a uniform conversion ratio is always applied. During the monetary reform of 1947 in the U.S.S.R. the ratio 10 : 1 was applied for currency, but for bank deposits the conversion ratios were 1 : 1 up to 3,000 roubles, 3 : 2 for balances in the range 3,000–10,000, and 2 : 1 for balances above 10,000 (M. V. Condoide, *The Soviet Financial System*, Columbus: Ohio State University, The Bureau of Business Research, 1951, p. 69; J. G. Gurley, 'Excess Liquidity and European Monetary Reforms, 1944–1952', *The American Economic Review*, vol. XLIII, 1953, p. 81). The employment of this device in varying degrees is a feature common to most if not all monetary reforms. Professor J. G. Gurley records 24 separate European monetary reforms during the period 1944–52 in which this technique was employed (ibid., pp. 79–80).

2. The holders of money may be required or induced to purchase non-negotiable government bonds, bonds which cannot be converted into money until governmental permission is granted. In 1919 Czechoslovakia and, after liberation from Germany during World War II, several countries, including Czechoslovakia,

Custom

Belgium, Netherlands, and Denmark made use of this means of reducing liquidity (R. G. Hawtrey, *Currency and Credit*, London: Longmans, Green, 4th edn., 1950, pp. 198–9; F. H. Klopstock, 'Monetary Reform in Liberated Europe', *The American Economic Review*, vol. XXXVI, 1946, p. 590).

3. A highly progressive tax may be levied on monetary wealth as in Yugoslavia in 1945 or a part of bank balances may be cancelled as in Western Germany after the 10 : 1 exercise described above and as in Austria after a similar experience (J. G. Gurley, 'Excess Liquidity and European Monetary Reform, 1944–1952', p. 86; F. H. Klopstock, 'Monetary Reform in Liberated Europe', p. 591; H. C. Wallich, *Mainsprings of the German Revival*, p. 69). The difference between this procedure and formal conversion is purely technical.

4. The foregoing actions can be taken without technical blocking of accounts, that is without serving notice that the owners of monetary balances cannot spend them until further notice. Of the 24 cases of European monetary reform during 1944–52, 8 were carried through without formal blocking. In 12 instances monetary balances were blocked preparatory to establishment or announcement of conversion ratios, forced purchases of blocked bonds, or cancellation. In the 4 remaining cases monetary balances remained blocked for longer periods (J. G. Gurley, 'Excess Liquidity and European Monetary Reform, 1944–1952', pp. 80–8).

William L. Miller

See also: DEFLATION
DEVALUATION
GOLD STANDARD
INFLATION
MONEY
MONEY AND BANKING

Custom

A. It is extremely difficult to formulate a precise definition of *custom*. The common core of meaning refers to non-technical social practice or usage that is shared in the group as tradition and learned by the individual as habit. The group within which it is shared may be a society (q.v.) or a sub-group of society.

B. The term acquired prominence as a concept of anthropology in the descriptive interpretation of culture (q.v.). E. B. Tylor included custom in his famous definition of culture, i.e. as one of 'the capabilities and habits acquired by man as a member of society' (*Primitive Culture*, London; John Murray, 1871, vol. I, p. 1). E. Sapir has noted that 'custom is a variable common sense concept which has served as the matrix for the development of the more refined and technical anthropological concept of culture' ('Custom', in E. R. A. Seligman (ed.), *Encyclopedia of the Social Sciences*, New York: The Macmillan Co., 1931, vol. IV, p. 658). A recent anthropological definition is that of J. Gillin: 'a habit which is socially learned, socially performed, and socially transmitted' (*The Ways of Men*, New York and London: D. Appleton-Century, 1948, p. 181).

C. The term entered sociology from descriptive anthropology. Little difference in basic meaning appears, although in sociology there has been some effort to give it a specialized meaning or to assign it various positions in the hierarchy of culture terms.

1. The efforts to distinguish *custom* from folkways (q.v.), mores (q.v.), and other culture concepts by using such adjectives as traditional, spontaneous, non-codified, prescribed, sanctioned, permanent, socially meaningful, and the like, are indecisive and ambiguous, and add little to the definition of the concept.

2. The attempt to assign the term to a particular position of inclusiveness or exclusiveness has also failed. Thus R. M. MacIver and C. H. Page treat custom as a subdivision of the folkways and mores, while K. Davis makes it the inclusive concept of which the folkways and mores are special types (R. M. MacIver & C. H. Page, *Society*, New York: The Macmillan Co., 1955, p. 19; K. Davis, *Human Society*, New York: The Macmillan Co., 1949, p. 73).

Joseph S. Himes

See also: CULTURE
FOLKWAYS
MORES
NORM
VALUE

Cybernetics

A. *Cybernetics* denotes a body of theory and research concerned with men, other organisms, and machines. This theory and research is focused on (a) the self-maintenance and self-control of mechanical and organic systems through the process of feedback, and (b) the communication of information in mechanical and organic systems. In its modern usage in social science the term was coined by N. Wiener (*Cybernetics, or Control and Communication in* *the Animal and the Machine*, New York: John Wiley, 1949).

B. Research and theory in cybernetics fall into two separate yet related categories: control and communication.

1. In the theory of machines it has, for some time, been apparent in the case of servo-mechanisms that one part of the machine may furnish energy and power, another, control of the amount of energy or power. In the simplest servo-mechanisms the control part must be immediately manipulated by the person. For example, in older heating appliances if the temperature dropped, the human being experiencing the drop in temperature might either turn up the draught or manipulate a mechanism furnishing fuel to the appliance. It is possible to see a network here in which feedback goes through the human organism. With the use of the modern thermostat, the person may set it for a certain temperature, so that when the temperature reaches that level the mechanism controlling the furnace will shut it off, and when the temperature drops below that level will turn it on. Thus an equilibrium or homeostatic condition may be maintained, once programmed, without human intervention. It is possible to complicate the system even more to control the thermostat with a mechanism which changes the temperature setting after a period of time. Theoretical thinking about this use of machines has resulted in formulations that have proved fruitful when applied to organisms, including men: (a) It becomes apparent that in any goal-directed behaviour there must be a network in which behaviour is controlled by means of feedback. (b) In complex systems there will be a hierarchy of such controls. (c) Wherever networks and feedback are found it seems probable that behaviour is goal-oriented.

It is apparent from the above that the cybernetic theory of control is a theory of function which places stress not on the consequence of any item of behaviour for the system (although this is implied) but rather on the manner in which the directly functional mechanism is controlled through feedback (cf. G. T. Guilbaud, *What is Cybernetics?*, trans. by V. MacKay, London: Heinemann, 1959, pp. 9–44; and W. Sluckin, *Minds and Machines*, Baltimore: Penguin Books, 1960, pp. 69–99).

2. In the theory of control through feedback, the concept of communication is implied. For what is transmitted back to the control mechanism from the functioning machine or the environment is generally much smaller in dimension than the dimensions of the effect produced (this generally can be measured in terms of energy, although this is not to say that the information transmitted in feedback is energy) and constitutes a signal. The same may also be said for the signals transmitted from the control mechanism to the other parts. Thus the networks conceived by cybernetic theory may be thought of as systems of communication as well as systems of control. The mathematical theory of information concerned with these systems is not centred on the 'semantic' content of the signals transmitted but upon the information capacity of such signals compared with other systems of signals and with the 'noise' or 'equivocation' which may distort the message as it passes through the channel of communication.

The measure of information capacity indicates clearly the lack of concern for semantic content, for it permits the comparison of information capacity of two systems of signals, even though they may not be carrying meaningful information at all. For example, a typewriter keyboard of 85 characters will produce a message—of 25 lines and 60 characters to a line—of 1500 characters. If one wished to use a telegraphic keyboard of two signals to reproduce all possible 1500 character messages from the typewriter keyboard, meaningful or not (the total number of such messages would be 85^{1500}) he would find that it would take approximately 9,614 telegraphic signals to do so. Thus the information-carrying capacity of the two keyboards is indicated by the ratio $\frac{9614}{1500}$ or $\frac{641}{100}$ or by the figure 6.41 (this example is adapted from G. T. Guilbaud, *What is Cybernetics?*, pp. 49–57).

The example is more important than it might seem at first glance, for in the measurement of the information capacity of a signal, reference is always made to a base of two possible equiprobable signals. The appearance of one signal of such a two-signal system carries one binary unit (bit) of information. The appearance of one signal of a system of eight possible equiprobable signals carries three bits of information. This can be illustrated as follows: If one has a system of eight possible, equiprobable signals, e.g. ABCDEFGH, the appearance of A informs the recipient of the signal that it is A and not BCDEFGH. To supply the same information through the two-signal system would require three signals. The first such signal would carry one bit of information, that the group of eight

Cybernetics

possible alphabetical signals was to be reduced to ABCD not EFGH; the second signal could convey that ABCD was to be reduced to AB not CD; and the third signal could convey A not B. Thus it takes three binary steps to reduce ABCDEFGH to A; if there is some means of directly showing A, the same information is conveyed in one step, so that a system of eight equiprobable signals is three times as efficient in information-carrying capacity than is a two-signal system. In the case of the typewriter keyboard example, each typewriter character conveys 6·41 bits of information, or, saying it another way, it would take 6·41 binary steps to reduce 85 characters to one character, whereas the typewriter keyboard can do it in one step.

In the above examples it has been assumed that the probability of a signal, i.e. its frequency of appearance in all possible messages, is equal to that of the other signals in the system of signals. Where the probabilities of the signals in a set of signals are not equal, the average information carried by a particular signal can still be calculated by finding the logarithm to the base two (still relating the measure to the binary base) of $1/p(s)$ where $p(s)$ is the probability of the signal (this is the same formula as in the case where the signals are equiprobable, but in that case the probability of the signal is simply $1/N$ where N is the number of possible signals, and where the signals are not equiprobable the probability must be calculated in other ways). Thus in the case of the 8 equiprobable signals used earlier, the amount of information per signal is given by $\log_2 1/\frac{1}{8}$ or $\log_2 8$ or 3. If in the case of signal A of the 8 signal system ABCDEFGH it is found that A occurs 1/4 of the time rather than 1/8 of the time, then the amount of information per signal A is $\log_2 1/\frac{1}{4}$ or $\log_2 4$ or 2, and A would convey two bits of information. By being able to measure the amount of information per signal when the signals are not equiprobable, it is possible to measure information as conveyed by those systems where the probabilities are not equiprobable because the rules of combining semantically meaningful signals result in the greater frequency of some signals and the lesser frequency of others as in the case of the English alphabet. In this way the theory of information is indirectly related to semantic information.

It is more difficult to establish a direct relation between cybernetic information theory and semantic information to measure actual amounts of semantic information conveyed. It can be done in some simple situations. For example, if one knows that a train is leaving on the minute within the next 8 minutes, and asks when it is leaving, there are 8 possible answers: 1, 2, 3, 4, 5, 6, 7, or 8 minutes. If the respondent says 'one minute' it can be said that three bits of semantic information have been conveyed, for if the person answering could only answer 'yes' or 'no' it would have taken the information seeker three questions to get the same information (this illustration has been adapted from G. T. Guilbaud, *What is Cybernetics?*, pp. 60–1).

For a series of messages, once a measure of information is established it is possible to derive the amount of information transmitted by subtracting the amount of information added in transmission (noise) from the output of information or by subtracting the amount of information lost in transmission (equivocation) from the input of information (W. Sluckin, *Minds and Machines*, pp. 86–7).

As indicated earlier it is possible to treat any system of control through feedback as a system of communication, and hence it is possible to treat individual organisms and groups as systems of communication utilizing some system of signals (this includes not only what we ordinarily regard as communication (q.v.) but also the relationship between an organism and *any* stimuli). Because of this possibility of analogy, it has been possible to use the theory of information in some areas of psychological and sociological research (see, for example, B. McMillan, et al., *Current Trends in Information Theory*, Pittsburgh: University of Pittsburgh Press, 1953).

C. 1. It is possible to conceive of *game theory* also as part of cybernetics, since the mechanisms of control, feedback, and communication in men and machines are obviously involved in any of the thinking and decision processes based on probabilistic estimates in situations of uncertainty.

2. In 'Cybernetics and Social Science' (*British Journal of Sociology*, vol. II, 1951, p. 144 et seq.), D. G. MacRae concludes an account of the work of N. Wiener and his predecessors with some comments upon the relationship of cybernetics to sociological work. For the most part he is sceptical of any claims which might be made that the fruitful analogies, central to cybernetics, will of themselves revolutionize social science or replace more traditional approaches: 'The social universe ... does not provide a suitable population for the mathematical expression of those relations with which cybernetics is most concerned. On the other hand, I have not the slightest doubt that attempting to think oneself into this new attitude with its new language, makes clearer the nature of a significant number of dynamic social processes' (ibid., p. 148). 'The difficulties of cybernetics are the difficulties of all kinds of behaviouristic psychology, for in part, this is what cybernetics essentially is' (ibid., p. 149). MacRae sees scope for social inquiry, however, in the study of the consequences, e.g. for class structure, of applying the techniques of cybernetics to the working of social organizations.

William L. Kolb

See also: COMMUNICATION
GAME THEORY

D

Death Rate

A. The meanings of *death rate* may be classified in analogy with *birth rate* (q.v.):

1. It is used to denote the frequency of death in a population in a general sense (cf. *mortality* (q.v.).

2. It denotes a particular commonly used index more precisely known as the *crude death rate*; for a single calendar year, it is the number of deaths in a population in that year divided by the total number in that population at mid-year or by the mean population during the year (usually the resulting quotient is multiplied by 1000, to give the death rate 'per 1000'). For periods other than one year adjustment is made to bring the crude death rate to a yearly basis.

3. Contrasted with *crude death rates* there are (a) *specific death rates* (e.g. *age specific death rates:* the number of deaths of persons of a given age per 1000 persons of that age) relating to sub-sections of the total population and (b) refined general indices termed *standardized, adjusted* or *corrected death rates, true death rates, life table death rates*, etc. These relate to the total population but are calculated in various ways by combining specific death rates.

B. Comparisons of crude death rates frequently reflect not so much differences between the age specific death rates of the populations being compared, as differences between their age compositions (e.g. districts where there are many elderly people have a high crude death rate even if health conditions are good). That is why the refined indices just mentioned (para-graph A3b) are helpful. Among these refine-ments, standardization is the most frequently employed. There are two forms of standardiza-tion, known as 'direct' and 'indirect', of which the former is more commonly found and is generally meant when the term 'standardiza-tion' is used without qualification. A directly standardized death rate 'tells us what the rate would be if the population being studied had the same age and sex composition as some other population which is used as the *standard*' (W. S. Thompson, *Population Problems*, New York: McGraw-Hill, 1953, p. 229). When death rates for two populations are standardized for age

and sex on the same standard society, differ-ences found are not then due to differences in age and sex composition. Standardized compari-sons using other specific factors can also be made, but this is not often done.

J. Hajnal

See also: BIRTH RATE

Decentralization (See Centralization)

Decision-Making

A. The standard convention is to reserve the term *decision-maker* for one who has formal responsibilities for formulating the policies of an organization, usually an institution of government. *Decision-making*, however, denotes the dynamic process of interaction among all participants who determine a particular policy choice, officials as well as non-officials. The scope of the decision-making process is empiric-ally defined according to the range of partici-pants who can be shown to have had influence in shaping the particular decision. Decision-making studies are studies that focus on all factors relevant to a policy choice and not just on the formal-legal relationships of decision-makers. In particular, they tend to include an analysis of the informal relationships among decision-makers, the role of actors outside the organization, and all the non-rational as well as rational considerations that influenced the behaviour of all who were involved in making the decision.

B. 1. Classical political theory, beginning with Aristotle's discussions of the relationship of forms of government to wisdom in public policy, has recognized the making of decisions to be a prime function of government. Historians, like-wise, have given considerable attention to the study of this function. But, in the social sciences, the concept of decision-making has, in recent years been developed within the context of a 'behavioural' approach to politics. The basic assumption in the approach which makes use of this concept is that, in the last analysis the actions of any institution or organization depend upon the acts, and hence the decisions, of some specific individual or individuals within the structure. This highly pragmatic view has provided the basis for a dynamic approach in which decisions are seen as the product of an interaction process involving the informal as well as formal relationships of the leaders with one another and with the led. The decision-making approach to political studies, in recognizing the importance of non-legal and informal considerations, has also provided a framework for incorporating systematically psychological factors in studying the behaviour of institutions and organizations.

2. In the development of this approach the work of H. Lasswell had a central place. By defining power as participation in the making of decisions, he developed the view that the political process is essentially a decision-making process, and all factors relevant to the making of decisions, including the personalities and life experiences of the participants, can be subjected to systematic empirical examination. In the field of social psychology K. Lewin demonstrated the value of studying the ways in which decisions are arrived at as a key to understanding the dynamics of small group behaviour. F. S. Dunn, in pioneering the decision-making approach in the fields of International Relations and International Law, introduced a realistic, but not cynical, basis for going beyond the narrow and traditional confines of formal, legal analysis of inter-state phenomena.

3. In general it may be said that the decision-making approach has provided an empirical basis for relating knowledge derived from individual and group psychology and from sociology to the study of organizations and institutions. Usually this type of analysis emphasizes not only the elements of rational choice but also the limits placed on rationality by psychological and socio-political considerations and the imperfect information available to decision-makers. The approach has already stimulated a growing body of literature consisting largely of case studies of decision-making under various conditions.

Lucian W. Pye

See also: Leadership
Politics
Public Administration

Defence Mechanism

A. *Defence mechanism* (or ego-, self-defence-mechanism) is an unconscious technique used by an individual or a group of individuals in order to cope with impulses, feelings, or ideas which are not acceptable at their conscious level. Though the rationale of most defence mechanisms is the avoidance of anxiety (q.v.), whether their functioning leads to normal adjustment (q.v.) or not, can only be determined within a wider context.

B. The history of the term *ego-* or *self-defence mechanism* is closely connected with the development of psychoanalysis.

1. The first attempt to define 'defence' as a psychic mechanism was made by S. Freud in 1894. Such a mechanism is, according to him, set up by situations in which 'the ego is confronted by an experience, an idea, a feeling arousing an effect so painful that the person resolves to forget it. ...' or 'to push the thing out, not to think of it, to suppress it' (*The Defence Psycho-neuroses*, Collected Papers, trans. by Joan Riviere, London: International Psycho-analytical Press, 1924, vol. I, pp. 60–1). It is to be noted that at this early period, Freud does not distinguish clearly between a defence mechanism, on the one hand, and intentional forgetting, or 'suppression', on the other.

2. The term has, however, gradually come to denote the unconscious techniques used by the ego to cope with unwelcome instinctual tendencies. The need for such techniques can properly be understood only in terms of psychoanalytical thinking according to which the ego is the unifying and balancing structure of the mind. Thus, it defends itself against any instinctual drive, feeling, or idea which threatens its integrity. Generally speaking any anxiety-arousing mental state calls for measures of defence by the ego. Sometimes the ego-defence mechanisms are called anxiety-dispelling mechanisms.

3. Opinions vary with regard to the number and the names of the ego-defence mechanisms. These are the most frequently used: *repression* (q.v.), (exclusion from consciousness of an anxiety-arousing impulse); *reaction-formation* (change into its opposite of a tendency unacceptable to the conscious-self); *projection* (q.v.) (unconscious attempt to rid oneself of an obnoxious tendency by assigning it to another person); *rationalization* (q.v.) (unconscious attempt to give a rational justification to an absurd impulse or idea); *displacement* (q.v.) (unconscious re-orientation of an impulse or feeling from a normally adequate object or situation towards an inadequate one); *sublimation* (q.v.) (transformation of a socially unacceptable into a socially acceptable impulse); *regression* (q.v.) (reversion of an adult person to early stages of his mental development).

Definition of the Situation

A. Freud includes among the ego-mechanisms, or 'ego-institutions': *introjection*; *isolation*; *undoing*; *turnings against the self*; and *reversal* (*The Ego and the Mechanisms of Defence*, London: Hogarth Press, 1948, p. 47).

C. Freud and his followers have emphasized the intra-psychic and pathological functions of 'ego-defence'. The so-called culturally-oriented psychoanalysts have broadened the meaning and the application of such a term by defining it in the functioning of social relations and structures. Thus K. Horney speaks about timidity as 'a defence against exposing oneself to rebuff' (*The Neurotic Personality of our Time*, London: Kegan Paul, 1937, p. 137). E. Fromm refers to the authoritarian social structure as a 'mechanism of escape' from an unbearable feeling of isolation and insecurity (*The Fear of Freedom*, London: Kegan Paul, 1949, p. 25). J. Monnerot, a French sociologist, sees in '*le déplacement du sacré*'—the displacement of religious feelings from a transcendental to a secular authority—a psychic mechanism contributing to the rise of modern Communism (*La Sociologie du Communisme*, Paris: Gallimard, 1949, pp. 428–60).

Z. Barbu

See also: DISPLACEMENT
 INTROJECTION
 ISOLATION
 MECHANISM
 PROJECTION
 RATIONALIZATION
 REPRESSION

Definition of the Situation

A. The phrase *definition of the situation* denotes (a) the individual agent's or actor's perception and interpretation of any situation in which he may find himself (the actor's definition of the situation) or (b) culturally formulated, embodied, and shared perceptions and interpretations of situations considered identical or similar (cultural or social definition of the situation). There is a two-fold connection between these two kinds of *definitions of the situation*. The *cultural definition* enters and becomes part of the *actor's definition* through social interaction (q.v.), primarily socialization (q.v.); the actor's definition may produce change in the cultural definition.

B. *Definition of the situation* was first used by W. I. Thomas and F. Znaniecki. According to Znaniecki, 'We do not know who first coined this term. It was occasionally used in *The Polish Peasant* and much more extensively in the comparative study of typical patterns of *Primitive Behavior* by Thomas' (F. Znaniecki, *Cultural Sciences*, Urbana: University of Illinois Press, 1952, p. 243). It quickly became, in American sociology and social psychology, the dominant phrase for denoting two facets of the theory of social acts (q.v.). (a) It pointed to the requirement of determining the meaning of a situation to the actor, thus involving social science in the use of categories of meaning, motive, and attitude. (b) It stressed the fact that a dimension of such meaning was cultural in character: i.e. shared, symbolically formulated, and transmitted through the process of socialization; internalized in the personality of the actor and yet also confronting him as the shared attitudes and beliefs of his fellows.

C. Less used synonyms for one or the other meanings of the phrase have been R. M. MacIver's 'dynamic assessment', and Znaniecki's 'humanistic coefficient' (R. M. MacIver, *Social Causation*, Boston: Ginn, 1942; F. Znaniecki, *The Method of Sociology*, New York: Farrar & Rinehart, 1934). In recent years T. Parsons's 'orientation' and M. Weber's 'meaning' have assumed increasing importance as synonyms (T. Parsons, *The Social System*, Glencoe, Ill.: The Free Press, 1951; M. Weber, *The Theory of Social and Economic Organization*, trans. by A. R. Henderson & T. Parsons, London: William Hodge, 1947).

Kurt H. Wolff

See also: SYSTEM OF ORIENTATION

Deflation

A. *Deflation* denotes a situation in which the money demand for output declines relatively to output, the situation being manifested in the form of falling prices per unit of output and, if prices fall relatively to costs, decreasing employment and output. This definition is neutral with respect to possible causes or initial sources of deflation and no confusion need arise in applying the term in a more specific way (e.g. deflation of the money supply) or with modifying adjectives and prefixes.

1. Most of the problems and inequities of what is called deflation stem from decreases in the general level of prices, as measured by some representative wholesale or retail price index, at a rate in excess of that warranted by advancing productivity and correspondingly declining costs. The inequities spring from the fact that in deflation, as in inflation, the prices of different goods and services do not change proportionately. Such price behaviour is implied or explicitly denoted in popular discussion and understanding of the term, as well as in the prevailing usage among economists.

2. However, it is desirable to retain symmetry with the definition of inflation, for the sake of both etymological consistency and formal precision. It is further desirable to conform to the well-established usage of applying the term to one or more of the variables which determine general price levels. The definition above is in keeping with these considerations.

B. Use of the term deflation is confined largely to the scientific and popular literature of economics. When the term is employed in other social sciences, e.g. history or political science, the usage is derived from economics. While no single definition is agreed upon among economists, deflation is usually associated with an actual or potential decline in the general level of prices, which is to say, an increase in the purchasing power of the monetary unit, *and* a reduction of employment and output. Because of the latter aspect of it, the concept of deflation —as it is most commonly used and understood —is not fully symmetrical with that of inflation, extended discussions of it usually running in terms of 'slump', 'recession' or 'unemployment' (cf. J. M. Keynes, *The General Theory of Employment, Interest and Money*, London: Macmillan, 1936, p. 291). By the same token, deflation is not always associated with the sort of decline in the general price level which merely reflects increase in the productivity of economic agents and processes and therefore leads to no reduction of employment and output.

The asymmetry of some definitions of inflation and deflation is illustrated in those of A. G. Hart. According to Hart, inflation is an 'upward movement of price levels', while deflation is a 'downward movement of production and employment, and of such prices as are flexible' (*Money, Debt and Economic Activity*, New York: Prentice-Hall, 2nd edn., 1953, p. 256). It is implicit in these definitions that prices are the more sensitive variable under inflationary pressures, particularly at or near 'full-employment' levels of output, while employment and output are the more sensitive variables under deflationary pressures.

C. Many writers, however, define deflation as the strict opposite of inflation. To them it is not the concepts but the consequences of inflation and deflation that are asymmetrical. E. W. Kemmerer takes such a view, at the same time ascribing deflation to decreases in the quantity of money. Thus, 'Deflation is the reverse of inflation. It occurs whenever the supply of money and deposit currency decreases, relatively to the demand for them, in such a way as to cause a decline in the general price level' (*Kemmerer on Money*, Philadelphia: John C. Winston, 1934, p. 46). A definition stemming from the income-expenditure approach to the value of money, and which is the exact reverse of that given for inflation, is subscribed to by J. H. Rogers and L. V. Chandler. According to these writers, deflation is 'a decrease in the general level of prices growing out of a decrease in expenditures while goods available for purchase are not correspondingly decreased in amount' ('Inflation and Deflation' in E. R. A. Seligman (ed.), *Encyclopedia of the Social Sciences*, New York: The Macmillan Co., 1937, vol. VIII, p. 29).

D. The definition of A. C. Pigou is a notable exception to the usual association of deflation with falling output and price levels. Pigou defines inflation, adding, 'In opposite conditions deflation is taking place'. His definition accordingly would run, 'Deflation is taking place when money income is shrinking relatively to the output of work—not the output of goods and services (real income)—by productive agents, for which it is the payment ...' (*The Veil of Money*, London: Macmillan, 1956, p. 14). Following Pigou, deflation is compatible with rising, constant, or falling prices, depending upon the relative decrease of money income per unit of work and of output per unit of work.

E. Although the concept of deflation is usually swallowed up in that of 'slump' or 'recession', there is one significant episode in recent history (Britain's return to the gold standard in 1925 at the prewar gold price) which, although entailing widespread unemployment and other symptoms of depression in Britain, was generally discussed in terms of deflation. With particular reference to just such an imminent occurrence, J. M. Keynes once defined deflation as 'the policy of reducing the ratio between the volume of a country's currency, and its requirements of purchasing power in the form of money, so as to increase the exchange value of the currency in terms of gold or of commodities (*A Tract on Monetary Reform*, London: Macmillan, 1924,

Delegation of Power

p. 154). The connotation here is a deliberately engineered increase in the value of the monetary unit, as distinguished from that resulting from a (wholly unwanted) 'slump'.

In an analysis of changes in the value of money with particular reference to their effect upon inducements to alter the rate of output, Keynes made the distinction between income deflation and profit deflation. Income deflation is defined as a fall in money earnings of productive factors relative to real output (*A Treatise on Money*, New York: Harcourt, Brace, 1930, vol. I, pp. 138, 155). Profit deflation is a fall in entrepreneurial incomes below the 'normal' level, i.e. below the level which would provide just sufficient inducement to maintain the rate of output unchanged (ibid., pp. 125, 155). The former, per se, has no effect upon output, while the latter, by definition, does. Clearly income deflation may take place in connection with increasing productivity of economic agents and processes without necessarily entailing profit deflation and declining output.

F. Beyond this, the term deflation is rarely used in connection with a modifying adjective or prefix. There are no close equivalents on the side of deflation of such terms as hyperinflation and repressed inflation. The more usual expressions, which carry their own special connotations, are 'major depression' and 'price support' or 'price stabilization'. There would not appear to be even a rough counterpart of 'creeping' inflation.

Stephen L. McDonald

See also: Cost of Living
Inflation

Delegation of Power
A. *Delegation of power* is the act by which an individual or collective body possessing political or legal powers transfers the right to exercise any or all of them to some subordinate individual or collectivity.

B. The power of a delegate may sometimes be contrasted with that of a representative, as when Edmund Burke in 1774 argued that a member of Parliament ought not to accept instructions from those who had elected him as their representative. 'Authoritative instructions, mandates issued, which the member is bound to... argue for, though contrary to the clearest conviction of his judgement and conscience—these are things utterly unknown to the laws of this land' ('Speech to the Electors of Bristol', *Works*, The World's Classics, London: Oxford University Press, 1930, vol. II, p. 165). The term *delegation* used of a *group of appointees* (e.g. to an international body or conference) may reflect the distinction, but the term *representative* is frequently used without the implication of freedom from mandatory instructions.

C. A distinction is commonly drawn between delegation by a sovereign authority and delegation by a subordinate authority.

1. According to the maxim '*delegatus non potest delegare*' a non-sovereign authority may delegate powers only to the extent that it is specifically authorized to do so by the body from which it derives its powers. A sovereign authority may delegate powers either partially or entirely to the extent of abdication. Thus the legislature in Great Britain is able to delegate functions of a general and legislative nature to administrative authorities.

2. Where a constitution confers powers on a legislature and/or contains a doctrine of separation of powers the body on whom legislative authority is conferred frequently cannot in principle delegate or transfer powers which are so wide as to be considered legislative. This doctrine was established by judicial decision in the United States (e.g. *Schechter Poultry Corp.* v. *United States*, 295 U.S. 495 (1935)), and was stated in explicit terms in the constitution of the Fourth French Republic (Art. 13): the National Assembly alone has the right to legislate and it cannot delegate this right. Legislatures in the British Commonwealth, created by British statute, may delegate powers to subordinate agencies since the Privy Council has decided that they are not delegates of the United Kingdom Parliament but are to be treated as possessing attributes of sovereignty for this purpose though subject to the authority of their constitutions (see, for example, *R.* v. *Burah* (3 App. Cas. 889), *Powell* v. *Apollo Candle Co. Ltd.* (1885) (10 App., Cas. 282)).

G. Marshall

See also: Separation of Powers

Demagogy
A. *Demagogy* is consistently applied as a term of opprobrium to denote an unacceptable form of political leadership. Unfortunately, the standards by which to judge forms of leadership are seldom presented explicitly, and those which are suggested implicitly are neither identical nor

free from ambiguity and subjectivity. Among the factors that have been considered as the determining criteria of demagogy are the motivation, intent, and sincerity of the leader, the methods by which he appeals to his public, and the consequences of his appeals and leadership to his followers.

B. Usage of the term suggests that several related but distinct criteria are being applied.

1. It usually refers to the authority of one who proposes to his political public programmes of action which he knows to be fallacious or impracticable in order to gain personal or political advantage.

2. Since adherence to these criteria complicates analysis, involving, for example, estimates of motivation, attention is frequently directed to the manner in which the political figure seeks to attract support from his public, e.g. the frequency of irrational appeals, attention-getting devices, attempts to sway emotions, and so forth. The adequacy of this approach seems doubtful. Gross simplification of complex issues, involving degrees of irrationality and emotionality, is a constant factor in all mass appeals. Therefore, unless the factors of 'irrational appeal' and 'emotion-swaying' techniques are meaningfully defined, the ambiguity and subjectivity surrounding the use of *demagogy* are merely transferred to other words. Restriction of the meaning of demagogy to 'insincere' advocates also provides no firm measurement, e.g. what of the zealous bigot?

3. If the making of 'irrational appeals' to the public by leaders is inherent in democratic politics and if the motivation of the leader is not the determining criterion then perhaps the most appropriate distinction between demagogy and other forms of leadership lies in the area of *consequences*. Thus, by this standard, a demagogue would be one who leads his followers to an emotional attachment to his person, the effects of which are to block their awareness either of the real sources of their discontents or of the real alternatives of action capable of satisfying their grievances. Whether this usage of the term permits a more rigorous and objective delineation of demagogy than the other standards is problematical.

Allan P. Sindler

See also: POLITICAL BOSS

Demand

A. *Demand* may be defined as a schedule of maximum quantities of a commodity which buyers will purchase at different prices taking tastes, money income, and prices of other commodities as 'given'. Thus the term designates not the amount that will be taken at a given price under given conditions, but *the conditions which determine the varying amounts* that will be taken as price varies. '... a change in demand occurs only when there is a change in sales without a change in price ...' (F. H. Knight, 'Demand', in E. R. A. Seligman (ed.), *The Encyclopedia of the Social Sciences*, New York: The Macmillan Co., 1931, vol. V, p. 69). The change in the quantity of commodity purchased as a result of a change in its price, given demand, can be looked upon as consisting of two parts, one of which is due to the change in the real income which results from the change in the price of the commodity and the other to the opportunity of substitution between the commodity whose price has changed and other commodities. The generalized relation between demand and the amounts taken at varying prices is the *demand function*.

B. Use of the term *demand* to indicate the functional relationship between the quantity purchased and the price of a particular commodity at a certain time under certain conditions stems primarily from the appearance of A. Marshall's *Principles of Economics* in 1890 (London: Macmillan), although A. A. Cournot had stated the concept in somewhat similar terms as early as 1838 (*Researches into the Mathematical Principles of the Theory of Wealth*, trans. by N. J. Bacon, New York: Macmillan, 1897). Marshall did not, however, present a complete definition of the demand curve or schedule, since he did not include a statement of all the variables to be held constant for all points on the curve and of the variables that are to be allowed to vary. As a result a good deal of attention has been given by other economists to the formulation of more rigorous definitions which could serve as a basis for theoretical and empirical applications of demand theory. Refinements in the area of partial equilibrium analysis have centred mainly around the question of what other things were to remain the same while the price and quantity of the particular item under consideration were being varied. The typical interpretation has been to include (a) tastes and preferences of the group of consumers concerned; (b) their money incomes; and (c) the price of every other commodity among the 'other things' to be held constant (see, for example, F. Y. Edgeworth,

Demand

'Demand Curves', in *Palgrave's Dictionary of Political Economy*, London: Macmillan, 1926; and G. J. Stigler, *The Theory of Price*, New York: The Macmillan Co., 1946).

C. Demand theory, as developed by Cournot and Marshall, employed the concept of cardinal utility and its maximization on the part of consumers as the psychological underpinning. The notion of indifference curves (q.v.), introduced first by Edgeworth and developed more fully by Pareto, provided a foundation for building the demand function without resting upon the concept of measurable utility (F. Y. Edgeworth, *Mathematical Psychics*, London: C. Kegan Paul, 1881; V. Pareto, *Manuel d'économie politique*, trans. by A. Bonnet, Paris: Giard & Brière, 1909). While Pareto's generalized definition of demand was conceptually superior to Marshall's partial equilibrium definition it was less suitable as a tool for empirical research. This limitation was largely overcome when E. Slutsky, and later J. R. Hicks and R. G. D. Allen, showed that the change in the quantity of a commodity which is purchased as a result of a fall in its price can be looked upon as '... consisting of two parts, one of which is due to the increase in real income which a fall in the price of (Y) entails, the other to the opportunity of substituting (Y) for other goods which results from the fall in the relative price of (Y)' (E. Slutsky, 'Sulla teoria del bilancio del consumatore', *Giornale degli Economisti*, vol. LI, 1915, pp. 1–26; J. R. Hicks & R. G. D. Allen, 'A Reconsideration of the Theory of Value', *Economica*, New Series, vol. I, 1934, pp. 52–76, 196–219). These two effects of the change in price on the quantity purchased have subsequently been termed the *income* and *substitution effects* (J. R. Hicks, *Value and Capital*, Oxford: The Clarendon Press, 1939, and *A Revision of Demand Theory*, Oxford: The Clarendon Press, 1956). M. Friedman has attempted to show that an interpretation of the demand curve which excluded the income effect would both provide a more useful analytical tool and be closer to Marshall's intent than a demand curve defined to include both effects ('The Marshallian Demand Curve', *Journal of Political Economy*, vol. LVII, 1949, pp. 463–95).

D. The appearance of J. Von Neuman and O. Morgenstern's *Theory of Games and Economic Behavior* (Princeton: Princeton University Press, 1944) stimulated interest in the idea of making use of choices involving measur-able risk to derive a utility function with respect to income that is measurable except for scale and origin. M. Friedman and L. J. Savage, and J. Marschak have gone on to show that maximization of a numerical utility function does provide a plausible rationalization of consumer behaviour in choosing among alternatives in which risk is involved, '... the ordinal properties of utility functions can be used to rationalize riskless choice, the numerical properties to rationalize choices involving risk' (M. Friedman & L. J. Savage, 'The Utility Analysis of Choices Involving Risk', *Journal of Political Economy*, vol. LVI, 1948, pp. 279–304; J. Marschak, 'Rational Behavior, Uncertain Prospects, and Measurable Utility', *Econometrica*, vol. XVIII, 1950, pp. 111–41).

E. The analysis of *empirical demand relationships* has followed, though with considerable lag, the theoretical developments discussed above. Following the early work by H. L. Moore, and its critical analysis by H. Working, R. Frisch, and H. Schultz, empirical demand analysis by the use of least squares regression techniques was increasingly conducted within the framework and assumptions of the Marshallian partial equilibrium approach (H. L. Moore, *Economic Cycles: Their Law and Cause*, New York: The Macmillan Co., 1914 and *Forecasting the Yield and Price of Cotton*, New York: The Macmillan Co., 1917; summarized in H. Schultz, *The Theory and Measurement of Demand*, Chicago: University of Chicago Press, 1938). The publication of T. Haavelmos's article on 'The Statistical Implications of a System of Simultaneous Equations' (*Econometrica*, vol. XI, 1943, pp. 1–12) stimulated efforts to conduct empirical demand analysis within a general equilibrium framework in which '... economic data are generated by systems of relations that are, in general, stochastic, dynamic, and simultaneous'. Work by K. A. Fox and others at the United States Department of Agriculture and by H. Wold and L. Jureen has raised some doubt as to whether the simultaneous equation procedure '... will improve or even change the results of the single equation approach within the limits of sampling error' (K. A. Fox, *The Analysis of Demand for Farm Products*, United States Department of Agriculture Technical Bulletin 1081, Washington: United States Department of Agriculture, 1953; H. Wold & L. Jureen, *Demand Analysis*, New York: John Wiley, 1953). J. S. Dusenberry, in his formal treatment of interdependent utilities, conceived the notion of individual demand being related, among other things, to the amount of the product being purchased by others (*Income, Saving, and the Theory of Consumer Behavior*, Cambridge, Mass.: Harvard University Press, 1952).

Vernon W. Ruttan

See also: SUPPLY

Demand Function (See Demand)

Demilitarization (See Neutralization)

Democracy

A. In its most general sense, *democracy* denotes a way of life in a society in which each individual is believed to be entitled to an equality of concern as regards the chances of his participating freely in the values of that society. In a more limited sense, *democracy* denotes the opportunity of the members of the society to participate freely in the decisions, in whatever realm of life, which affect their lives individually and collectively. In its most restricted sense, the term denotes the opportunity of the citizens of a state to participate freely in the narrowly political decisions which affect their individual and collective lives.

B. The meanings of the term *democracy* have moved historically from the most restricted to the most general, although some of the more general conceptions have existed in the past without being associated with the term. As far as democracy as a theory of government in the narrowly political sense is concerned, there are two main concepts which in practice can become almost antithetical. One concept stresses the obedience owed to the people's will, the other the free participation of the individual person in the formation of that will. The one concept begins with the obligation of obeying the enacted will of the majority—either through the expression of 'pure' or 'direct' democracy, such as the New England Town Meeting where all citizens directly made decisions, and representative democracy in which people elect representatives to make decisions for them (cf. J. Madison, *The Federalist Papers*, no. 10 (1787)). This obligation is recognized by those who stress free participation, as long as the civil liberties (q.v.) of the minority are recognized so that its members can attempt to become the majority. Majoritarian democracy, however, can move in the direction of denying such liberties in the name of the will of the people as an absolute force that not only may but must impose itself on all members of the society. It may do this on the basis of an absolutizing of the majority; it may also do it on the basis of one reading of Rousseau's *volonté générale*, on the basis of expressing the will of a social class, as in the dictatorship of the proletariat, or on the basis of a mystical expression of a nation or a folk, as in the case of National Socialism in Germany. In these latter cases the will of the group need not express itself through majority vote, but may be formulated by a vanguard of the proletariat or be embodied in a leader.

Against this, the conception of Western democracy has stressed equality of citizens before the law, a government responsible to majority vote, and the obligations to obey law expressing the will of the majority, provided that there is 'universal' suffrage by free secret ballot, regular elections with more than one political party, and freedom of speech, press, and religion as well as other civil liberties. On the other hand, the Marxist view, which embodies the conception of absolute majoritarian democracy in the form of the dictatorship of the proletariat under the leadership of the vanguard of the proletariat, is that these civil libertarian elements are simply parts of the 'superstructure' of the state, and that as long as there is private ownership of the means of production they are manipulated in such a way as to serve only the interests of the owning class. Marxist theory sees the state as always and inevitably the instrument of the dominant economic class. Thus, it is held, until private ownership is abolished, the real will of the majority is blocked and the civil liberties of individuals are only formal and without substance. Thus J. Hazard points out that government in the U.S.S.R. is carried on in the name of democracy and with democratic symbols (*The Soviet System of Government*, Chicago: University of Chicago Press, 1957, ch. 1), but the Soviet government is avowedly not a political democracy in the Western sense.

C. Democracy as denoting popular participation in decision-making in spheres other than the state, can have almost unlimited relevance, and indeed one finds such participation discussed today in such areas as the family, where heretofore it was not so discussed. Historically, it has had the greatest relevance of this sort in the area of religious polity and economic life, and the latter constitutes, perhaps, the focus of contemporary discussion. In the West, democracy with respect to economic decision-making

Demography

has been associated with 19th-century liberalism and its philosophy of individual property rights both as itself a matter of liberty and as a necessary condition of political democracy. Socialist thought, on the other hand, has concerned itself with the possibility of decision-making in industry on the part of the worker and has encouraged government intervention or ownership as a means of securing such participation. L. Wasserman in his *Modern Political Philosophies* (Philadelphia: Blakiston, 1944) has emphasized that 'Democracy must not be thought of as a completed pattern of society, of government or of an economic system ... Democratic theory specifies no particular form of economy' (ibid., pp. 12, 24); and further says that 'A capitalist economy would remain consistent with democracy as long as it contributed a maximum of material welfare and did not violate the superior requirements of personal and social progress' (ibid., p. 25). On the other hand, the Soviet experiment has indicated to many that state control of the economic system may threaten political democracy. Thus N. Thomas, in his *Democratic Socialism: A New Approach* (New York: Norton, 1951), warns that the state under the most democratic theory and practice is likely to become undemocratic if it seeks to control directly all total economic activity. Some have come to view a mixed economy with the intervention of the state in welfare and the equalizing of economic power as the most workable solution to the problem (J. K. Galbraith, *American Capitalism: The Concept of Countervailing Power*, Boston: Houghton Mifflin, 1952).

D. In its widest and most recent usage, the emphasis on democracy has come to be more and more on a levelling of society in some sense. There is general agreement that political democracy means more than mere forms of government, especially because there is evidence of increasing lip-service paid to democratic forms without practice of the substance of political democracy. There is a widespread notion that in order for democratic forms to work out in practice there must be a modicum of general education, and, if not economic well-being, then at least the absence of widespread poverty (cf. S. M. Lipset, *Political Man*, Garden City, N.Y.: Doubleday, 1960). Increasingly, therefore, there is the feeling that for a society to be democratic in its broadest sense there must be not only political freedom and political equality, but also economic freedom and economic equality. In its

minimum form it consists of the demand for equality of economic opportunity, but beyond this there is an increasing conception of setting minimum standards of living below which no person should be allowed to fall. Furthermore, equality of economic opportunity itself is seen as requiring concern for the total life pattern and the motivation of all men. With this there is also growing emphasis on social equality of all men, an equality of respect that transcends status, wealth, and power, and an equality of concern which seeks for each man the fullest realization of the potentialities of his personality as judged by some criteria of humanness.

Fred Warner Neal

See also: AUTHORITARIANISM
CAPITALISM
COMMUNISM
CONSERVATISM
DICTATORSHIP
LIBERALISM
SOCIALISM

Demography

A. *Demography* is concerned with the numbers of populations (q.v.), changes in numbers, and the way in which such changes come about, e.g. by an excess of births over deaths, or by migration. It also deals with the division of populations into certain sub-groups, by sex, age, and marital status, and changes in these structures. The methods used are primarily quantitative and statistical, and special techniques have been evolved to deal with demographic data. However, demography is sometimes taken to include the study of long-term population movements and theoretical speculations about the causes of such movements.

The term *demography* is also occasionally applied to the study of animal populations.

B. This term was first introduced by A. Guillard in 1855. He defined it as 'the natural and social history of the human species, or, in a narrower sense, the mathematical study of populations, their general movements, and their physical, civil, intellectual and moral conditions' (*Eléments de statistique humaine ou démographic comparée*, Paris: Guillaumin, 1855.).

More recently it has been defined as 'the study of human populations by statistical methods, and deals with such questions as the numbers of people living, dying or being born in a country or region and the measurement of fertility, mortality and marriage rates. For some purposes, qualitative as well as quantitative

188

factors are included within the scope of the subject' (**P. R. Cox**, *Demography*, Cambridge: Cambridge University Press, 1950, p. 1). The U.N. multilingual demographic dictionary defines demography as 'the scientific study of human populations, primarily with respect to their size, their structure and their development' *U.N. Population Studies*, No. 29, New York, 1958, p. 3).

E. Grebenik

See also: POPULATION

Dependency (Political Science)

A. Since at least the 17th century, the term in its political context has denoted a country or province subject to the control of another of which it does not form an integral part.

B. The classic statement is G. C. Lewis's *An Essay on the Government of Dependencies*, published in 1841. Lewis thought that the relations between a dominant and a dependent community formed one of the three divisions of the science of politics, the others being the nature and form of a sovereign government, and the relations between the sovereign governments of independent communities. He considered the relationship of dependency to be one 'between two political communities, of which one is dominant and the other dependent; both being governed by a common supreme government, the one directly and the other indirectly; and the latter being governed directly by a subordinate government' (*An Essay on the Government of Dependencies*, ed. C. P. Lucas, Oxford: At the Clarendon Press, 1891, pp. 3–4). While the former is a sovereign state, the latter is not, and is regarded as part of the dominant sovereign state in questions of domestic jurisdiction at such occasions as the meetings of the United Nations.

C. In common usage a dependency is more often called a *colony* (q.v.). But such an equation is ambiguous. With respect to the British Commonwealth, the 'Crown Colonies' are not the full complement of the territories over which Britain has jurisdiction—some such countries are known as *trust territories* and *protectorates*. *Dependency* is the wider, more inclusive term both for British possessions and those of other 'colonial powers'.

J. D. B. Miller

See also: COLONIALISM
COLONY

Dependency (Social Psychology)

A. *Dependency* in its widest meaning denotes an *affiliative need* found in all individuals. It is the need to relate oneself to, rely upon, and find gratification in, another person.

B. To the extent that no one is completely self-sustaining, a point on which all the writers on the subject agree, it must be supposed that everyone feels some degree of dependency. In this sense dependency is a universal and normal coping mechanism. It ceases to be a normal nurturance-need when it becomes the individual's dominant technique of striving for a desired goal. In this case it may range all the way from passivity and irresponsibility to neurotic and psychotic helplessness. In whatever form or degree it manifests itself it is always basically an ego-attitude in response to a feeling of inadequacy and is necessary for human survival. While it looks like a handicap when we compare the human infant's dependence on his mother with that of other animals, it is responsible for man's greater adaptibility. The latter's prolonged period of dependency helps to account for the great variety of personalities found in the human species. Used in this sense the term *dependency* has the widest applicability. At one end of the dependency-independency continuum it describes the need and pursuit of safety and at the other end the desire and striving for productive association with others. In either case it is a need that must be gratified, and when gratification is thwarted, it issues in hostility, aggression, or mental disorder.

C. 1. Dependency arises out of the infant's feeling of helplessness and recurs normally in adults in situations of extreme threat and distress. Infantile helplessness and dependency are not, however, identical. Helplessness results from a biologically determined need of depending upon others for physical survival. Dependency arises in the interpersonal relations of a child with his parents, and is therefore a function of socialization.

2. In adulthood, dependency is the wish for the continuance of the magic control of childhood, and when it becomes a habitual way of meeting crises it is a neurotic manifestation of what Freud (*The Problem of Anxiety*, New York: Norton, 1936) called the 'omnipotence of thought'.

3. The condition of dependency has been most widely discussed in reference to pathological behaviour. In these discussions it is

Depreciation

defined in one way or another as a neurotic defence mechanism. While it is, as indicated before, a coping mechanism in all people in unusually stressful situations, it is considered abnormal or neurotic when, as A. Kardiner points out (*The Individual and His Society*, New York: Columbia University Press, 1939, pp. 32–5), it persists throughout life as the dominant technique of adjustment. The abnormal forms which are most frequently encountered are character disorder and certain psychosomatic ailments. In character disorder the dependency manifests itself most frequently in such personality traits as self-effacement, dread of loneliness, ingratiation, and indecision (A. Maslow & B. Mittelmann, *Principles of Abnormal Psychology*, New York: Harper & Brothers, 1951, pp. 392–4). Psychosomatic manifestations are such disorders as colon spasm, bronchial asthma, and peptic ulcers (J. Ruesch, 'Social Technique, Social Status, and Social Change in Illness', in C. Kluckhohn, H. A. Murray, & D. M. Schneider, *Personality in Nature, Society, and Culture*, New York: Knopf, 1953, pp. 123–36).

D. The nature of dependency cannot be fully understood apart from the knowledge of its source. Regarding the latter there is virtually no disagreement. Dependency is traced back by most investigators to the early weeks and months of a child's life. While it starts out as a biological helplessness it is conceived by practically all behavioural scientists as an attitude of soliciting support or protection. In the psychological, as distinguished from the biological, source its nature is determined, as Kardiner (*The Individual and His Society*, pp. 319–20) points out, by a feeling of limited resources, ability, or self-reliance. This feeling of inadequacy or inability to cope with stressful life-situations usually originates in the attitudes of parents and their mode of taking care of the child's needs. This mode may have been 'maternal overprotection', as D. M. Levy (*Maternal Overprotection*, New York: Columbia University Press, 1943) calls it; rejection or denial of 'mothering' which generates a feeling of complete desertion in the child, according to M. A. Ribble (*The Rights of Infants*, New York: Columbia University Press, 1943, p. 95–6); or with the severity of such basic disciplines as feeding, weaning, and toilet training (R. Sears, J. Whiting, H. Nowlis, & P. Sears, 'Some Child-rearing Antecedents of Aggression and Dependency', *Genetic Psychology Monographs*, vol. 47,

1953, pp. 135–234). Many psychoanalytic investigators relate dependency to the absence or inadequacy of breastfeeding. This condition F. Goldman-Eisler ('Breastfeeding and Character Formation', in Kluckhohn et al., *Personality in Nature, Society, and Culture*, pp. 146–84), has described as productive of the *orally ungratified* type of character who is marked by helplessness, insecurity, and the tendency to seek love and protection from others.

Hubert Bonner

See also: Autonomy
Need

Dependent Variable (See **Variable**)

Depletion (See **Depreciation**)

Depopulation (See **Population**)

Depreciation

A. In its most specific sense *depreciation* refers to the diminished value and shortened life of capital goods that results from wear and tear. More broadly *depreciation* may refer to the diminished value and shortened life of any capital good or asset providing a flow of services over a significant period of time. Included in this broadened definition would be not only the results of wear and tear, but of *depletion*—the using up of resources that are not replaceable by the efforts of human beings—and *obsolescence*—the inadequacy of the asset relative to newer models. In this latter usage the term becomes synonomous with the *capital consumption allowance*.

B. Accounting texts define *depreciation* as the shortening of the life-expectancy of capital. The idea that depreciation relates to the wear and tear of the apparatus of production is well established. H. S. Noble and C. R. Niswonger have noted that all fixed assets, other than land, decline in total usefulness because of wear, the elements, and the passage of time. This decline in total usefulness is called *depreciation* (*Accounting Principles*, Dallas: South-Western Pub., 6th edn., 1953, p. 241). A. W. Johnson writes: 'As time goes on, the fixed assets of a business lose their dollar value because of a decline in the amount of service still to be received from them. A piece of machinery may last for years but, eventually, its usefulness will come to an end. ... The investment will have been converted into an expense' (*Intermediate Accounting*, New York: Rinehart, 1947, p. 251). In this use of *depreciation* the concept is readily distinguished from *obsolescence* and *depletion*. *Obsolescence* appears when the economic life of an asset is shortened to less than the ordinary physical life because it has become inadequate relative to newer models. *Depletion* applies to resources that are used up and are not replaceable by the efforts of human beings.

C. A broader usage of *depreciation* is suggested by C. A. Smith and J. G. Ashburne when they distinguish between the depreciation that results from physical causes and that which results from functional causes (*Financial and Administrative Accounting*, New York: McGraw-Hill, 1955, pp. 152, 193). Functional factors are considered as a matter of adequacy or obsolescence. Similarly J. R. Hicks and A. G. Hart refer to depreciation as the difference between the total production of capital and the net addition to capital within a period of time ('Measuring Economic Growth', in A. Naftalin et al. (eds.), *An Introduction to Social Science*, Chicago: Lippincott, 1953, bk. 2, p. 79). If loss by fire, storm, and similar items, along with physical and functional elements are included in this difference, *depreciation* becomes synonomous with what economists call the *capital consumption allowance*. This sum subtracted from gross investment leaves net investment. Comparably, it marks in national income accounting the difference between the gross national product and the net national product. In another extension of usage the individual may regard his consumer goods of capital types, e.g. refrigerators and automobiles, as subject to depreciation. In this broad context, depreciation measures the decline in the life of an asset which yields repeat services to its possessor and whose decline results from wear and tear, the elements, and the developments that take place over time.

D. Economists and accountants tend to differ in the ways in which they determine depreciation. For economists there are two sorts of fundamental depreciation charges (J. Dean, *Managerial Economics*, Englewood Cliffs, N.J.: Prentice-Hall, 1951, pp. 17–18). The first of these is the opportunity cost of equipment over a given year, when the alternative opportunity to the use of the equipment in question is to sell it at the beginning of the year. The charge made is that of the difference of the disposal value of the equipment at the beginning of the year and at the end of the year. The second kind of depreciation is that of the exhaustion of a year's

part of limited life (ibid.) where this is figured on the basis of estimated replacement cost at the end of the life of the equipment.

In economics the concept of depreciation is closely related to that of investment. Gross investment is the new creation of capital during a period, depreciation is the decline in value during the period of the capital assets existing at the beginning of the period, and net investment is the difference between the two. Depreciation may be a negative quantity, since changes in prices and interest rates may increase the value of an asset even though the end of its physical life is approaching. All the definitions of depreciation in common use lead to paradoxical results in certain cases, because of various difficulties connected with the concept of maintaining capital intact over time. It is necessary to consider carefully the properties of a definition before using it for the analysis of a particular problem. Some theorists think that because of these difficulties it is desirable to avoid using the concept of depreciation (and with it the concepts of net investment and net income) in pure economic theory.

Accountants ignore opportunity cost as a depreciation charge altogether, and tend to measure depreciation in terms of the distribution of original cost rather than replacement cost. One method of estimating depreciation is to spread it evenly over time. Known as the straight line method, it considers the tangible unit to be used up in equal amounts each year of its life. Because this assumption often violates reality, while at the same time failing to provide the most advantageous profit and loss results for a given enterprise, alternative techniques are used. The hourly rate method, for example, is of this kind. Under it, the depreciation is estimated on the basis of the number of hours that the fixed asset is used over a given accounting period. In turn, the hour use in a given period is compared with the total number of life hours estimated for the fixed asset.

Another area of dispute is that economists believe that allowance should be made for changes in the price level and/or in the reproduction cost of the asset, whereas most accountants still cling to the actual historical cost—which results from the economist's point of view in a great distortion of the alleged profit figures.

Melvin L. Greenhut

See also: CAPITAL
INVESTMENT

Derivation

Depression (See **Business Cycles**)

Dereistic Thinking (See **Autistic Thinking**)

Derivation

A. The word *derivation* has a specific and technical sense in V. Pareto's general theory of social action, viz. the forms of variable logical or sophistic reasoning in which non-logical conduct is clothed (*The Mind and Society*, trans. from *Trattato di Sociologia generale*, by A. Bongiorno & A. Livingston, A. Livingston (ed.), 4 vols., London: Cape, 1935, para. 798). The term is used frequently by Pareto in association with the term *residue* (q.v.) 'The residues are manifestations of sentiments. The derivations comprise logical reasonings, unsound reasonings, and manifestations of sentiments used for purposes of derivation: they are manifestations of the human being's hunger for thinking' (para. 1401). Some, but not all, derivations can be regarded as rationalization (q.v.); all of them can be regarded as the result of man's desire to understand and explain his non-logical actions.

B. There are four major classes of derivations according to Pareto (*The Mind and Society*): (a) assertions (paras. 1430–3); (b) authority (paras. 1434–63); (c) accords with sentiments or principles (paras. 1464–1542); (d) verbal proofs, or paralogisms (paras. 1543–1686).

It would indeed be possible to regard all of these as, in their usual forms, verbal proofs through which concrete non-logical actions are interpreted and justified.

D. G. MacRae

See also: RESIDUES

Descent

A. 1. In one sense of the term sociological and anthropological usage follows a common meaning: an individual is of X *descent* (where X is a local, regional, national, racial, ethnic, or religious description) when one or more of his ancestors was/were of the X group. A statement in this form does not necessarily imply that the individual is himself a member of X group, and it may not connote any flow of rights and duties or any characteristics, political, cultural, or social, from the ancestor(s) in question. In this sense the term has a useful vagueness. Examples: 'He is of British descent' (when perhaps he is a Frenchman in all respects, but had a grandfather who came from England); 'he is of Chinese descent' (when he is 'racially' Chinese but politically and culturally an American).

2. In anthropological discourse the term stands at the centre of kinship studies. It is used in two related but different senses:

(a) In one sense anthropological usage is similar to that of conventional Western genealogy: descent means a kinship tie between two individuals such that either one individual is the ancestor of the other or both share a common ancestor (A is descended from B; A and C are of common descent). The individuals from whom descent is traced need not be progenitors in a biological sense (and here anthropological usage diverges from that of Western genealogy); the links between individuals tied by descent are links of socially defined parenthood, whether or not children were in fact engendered by their social parents. (This distinction is often made by contrasting *genitor* with *pater* and *genetrix* with *mater*; we are concerned now with *patres* and *matres*.) Descent denotes an assertion of rights and duties; by means of it individuals lay claim to status, privileges, and resources or ascribe these things to other people. In a society in which kinship is relatively unimportant in the ascription of rights and duties a statement of the form 'A is descended from B' may mean nothing more than that a certain ill-defined prestige attaches to A because of his connexion with B. In a society where kinship is a framework on which much social life depends, a similar statement is likely to be an assertion that A can command from B, or from other people in virtue of their relation to B, certain definable rights, and that he has corresponding duties. Descent is often bracketed with inheritance and succession (q.v.) to cover the totality of rights which pass from one kinsman to another; in such cases the term descent is being used to indicate the transmission of status shorn of its office-holding and economic aspects.

Descent is traced through both parents, but the manner and extent to which it is traced are aspects of the kinship system as a whole. In some societies (said variously to have bilateral, cognatic, or non-unilineal systems of kinship) an individual conceives of himself as standing at the centre of a circle with relatives fanning out symmetrically through both father and mother. His status vis-à-vis a relative on his father's side (say, father's father) is formally of the same kind as his status vis-à-vis the genealogically similar relative on his mother's side (mother's father). In a unilineal kinship system these two relatives would be of entirely different status.

(b) This leads us to the second sense in which descent is used within the context of kinship: membership in a certain kind of defined group. Unilineal kinship systems divide society into non-overlapping groups (clans, lineages, etc.). *Descent* is used for the status, rights, and duties which accrue from membership in such a group. When we say that a society has patrilineal descent we imply that every individual in it has a certain kind of rights and duties vis-à-vis his fellow patrilineal (agnatic) kinsmen who are members of his group which he does not have in regard to kinsmen who are outside this group.

It will be seen that the term *descent systems* may cover both systems in which non-overlapping (discrete) groups emerge (patrilineal, matrilineal, and double unilineal) and systems in which the tracing of descent, when it leads to the formation of groups, produces a situation in which an individual is a member of more than one of like order. A non-unilineal kinship system may have no descent groups at all. (A kindred, a grouping of kinsmen defined with reference to a given individual, is not a descent group; the people included within it are not all descended from a common ancestor.) It may have a form of bilateral descent group such that an individual is a member of one group consisting of people descended from a particular ancestor and at the same time a member of other and similar groups defined in relation to ancestors traced differently. There is, however, a tertium quid between these two major types of descent system. In some non-unilineal systems an individual, while potentially a member of more than one descent group, must throw in his lot with only one of them. The resulting discrete group (i.e. one which does not overlap in membership with the other groups) is sometimes called a *ramage*.

3. Descent is sometimes used in the context of those naming systems in which the ties between the generations are symbolized. The English and Chinese surname systems, for example, in which the father's surname is borne by his children are sometimes both given as examples of patrilineal descent; whereas in reality the English system of kinship is non-unilineal (although some argue that it has a 'patrilineal bias') while the Chinese is in fact one of unilineal descent in the narrowest sense. The transmission of patronymics (as among Muslims, where a man is known as B son of A and his son as C son of B) is similarly sometimes seen as a form of descent.

B. The special meaning which the word descent takes on in the context of unilineal descent group leads some anthropologists to question the usefulness of continuing to use it in a wide sense. One argument runs that unilineal descent is a politico-legal attachment to a permanent corporation and that other forms of attachment are better described as filiation (q.v.). On this view, membership in a 'bilateral descent group' is based not on descent but on a tie of filiation, that is, the tie between a child and a parent. The analytical distinction here is between a continuous thread (descent) and a series of links between members of adjacent generations (filiation). Within the context of unilineal descent systems themselves the contrast between descent and filiation is shewn, inter alia, by the difference of the nature of the tie with one's own unilineal group from that of the tie with the unilineal group of the parent through whom descent is not traced (*complementary filiation*).

C. The various historical elements in the development of usage in the anthropological literature can be conveniently illustrated in the following brief quotations. L. H. Morgan: 'The gens, though a very ancient social organization founded upon kin, does not include all the descendants of a common ancestor. ... In the ancient gens descent was limited to the female line ... the children of [a woman's] sons, and the children of her male descendants, through males, would belong to other gentes...' (*Ancient Society*, New York: Henry Holt, 1877, pp. 67–8). W. H. R. Rivers: 'Whenever I use this term it will apply to membership of a group, and to this only. We speak of descent as patrilineal when a child belongs to the social group of his father, and as matrilineal when he belongs to the social group of his mother ... the use of the term is only of value when the group is unilateral' (*Social Organization*, London: Kegan Paul, Trench, Trubner, 1924, but written some years earlier, p. 86). R. H. Lowie: 'Further, *some* correlation assuredly exists between the rule of inheritance and the rule of descent, as follows from the part the transmission of property played in establishing a unilateral group of kin' (*Primitive Society*, London: Routledge, 1921, pp. 158–9). A. R. Radcliffe-Brown: 'Two persons who are kin are related in one or other of two ways: either one is descended from the other, or they are both descended from a common ancestor. It is to be remembered that "descent" here

Despotism

refers to the social relationship of parents and children, not to the physical relation. Kinship is thus based on descent, and what first determines the character of a kinship system is the way in which descent is recognized and reckoned' ('Introduction', to A. R. Radcliffe-Brown & D. Forde (eds.), *African Systems of Kinship and Marriage*, London: Oxford University Press, 1950, p. 13). G. P. Murdock: 'A rule of descent affiliates an individual at birth with a particular group of relatives with whom he is especially intimate and from whom he can expect certain kinds of services that he cannot demand of non-relatives, or even of other kinsmen' (*Social Structure*, New York: The Macmillan Co., 1949, p. 15).

Maurice Freedman

See also: Consanguinity
Filiation
Kinship and Kinship System

Descriptive Kinship System (See Kinship Terminology)

Despotism

A. *Despotism* may be defined as a type of authority exhibiting the following features: (a) absence of customary or legal limitations on the scope of authority; (b) an arbitrary (unpredictable) manner of exercising it. It frequently has a pejorative sense but it is still possible to speak of benevolent or enlightened despotism.

B. Whereas (a) above makes (b) very probable, it does not necessitate it, because, for the sake of order and efficiency, a ruler might restrain his whims, promulgate rules prescribing his and his agents' behaviour, and adhere to them. Prussia under Frederick II provided an almost perfect example of this possibility. Some economically successful slave owners followed a similar policy. Despotism, as thus defined, is most commonly accompanied by autocracy (q.v.) because a directorate, no matter how narrow, must reach decisions according to some rules, if it is to endure. Nevertheless, observance of the rules by the wielders of authority in their dealings with the members of the privileged stratum is compatible with despotic treatment of the lower strata, e.g. the case of ancient Sparta.

C. Recently K. A. Wittfogel reintroduced the term *oriental despotism* into sociological discussions (*Oriental Despotism*, New Haven:

Yale University Press, 1957). By oriental despotism Wittfogel means not merely a type of government but a type of social structure in its entirety (which he sometimes calls 'hydraulic society') characterized by: (a) autocracy; (b) centralized bureaucratic administration; (c) lack of stable nobility; (d) subordinate position of the merchants; (e) unimportance of slavery; (f) irrigation agriculture dependent on large-scale waterworks. The last feature is, according to Wittfogel, crucial, and necessitates the others. This concept is open to several objections. In the first place, the 'oriental' is slightly misleading because not all politics which existed in Asia displayed these characteristics; and, on the other hand, Wittfogel himself finds examples of his type outside Asia (the Incas, the Aztecs, Muscovy). Secondly, it is wrong to assert that all these features are necessarily linked. Features (a), (b), (c), (d), and (e) can appear not only in different incomplete combinations, but also jointly without the sixth (e.g. Late Roman empire, Byzantium, Ottoman sultanate, Muscovy, early Tokugawa Japan). Furthermore, irrigation on a considerable scale was known in Mesopotamia before the growth of centralized states. So, all that can be confidently asserted is that: (i) only centralized administration can build and maintain very large irrigational systems; (ii) the dependence of the population on such a system strengthens the central government—i.e. fosters centralization. The third objection is that Asiatic societies—even those whose agriculture always remained dependent on large-scale irrigation—underwent many changes, so that it is impossible to cast them into one static type. In fact it would be nearer the truth to assert that pre-machine supra-tribal agrarian societies oscillated between feudal or semi-feudal dispersion of authority, and autocratic-bureaucratic centralization. More fitly, then, we could speak of *agrarian bureaucracy* as a social type.

S. Andreski

See also: Authoritarianism
Dictatorship
Tyranny

Determinism

A. The term *determinism* denotes a doctrine which claims that all objects or events, or all objects or events of some kind (for instance, falling within the range of some scientific discipline) are determined, that is to say *must* be as they are and as they will be, in virtue of some laws or forces which necessitate their being so.

B. Determinism is in fact the name of a whole class of theories which have the above feature in common. The term becomes the name of a specific doctrine when the *kind* of determinism is indicated, implicitly or explicitly. The specification may indicate either *the class of things* that are determined, or *the type of thing* that does the determining, or both. For instance, *economic determinism* tends to mean the doctrine that economic factors determine others, *historical determinism* tends to mean the theory that events in history are determined, *sociological determinism* is likely to mean the assertion that social facts are determined, *and* that they are determined by social factors.

C. An important characterization of determinism, cutting across the sub-division in terms of field or subject, arises from describing it as *causal determinism*, which means the doctrine that events are determined causally. This idea can be opposed, for instance, to statistical or to theological determinism, i.e. to theories which claim that events are determined *non-causally* by statistical probabilities, or by the deity. It is arguable whether these types of determination should be seen as fundamentally non-causal, or whether ultimately they are but a special case of causation. It may be argued that statistical probabilities are to be interpreted as consequences of causes too complex or minute to be isolated in individual cases and that even transcendental determinants are to count as causes.

E. A. Gellner

See also: Cultural Determinism
Social Causation

Detribalization

Etymologically this word should signify the process of losing a characteristic which could be described as *tribal* or the condition of having lost this. Confusion is caused by the ambiguity of the word *tribal*, which may be taken to refer either to a social grouping or to a mode of life.

1. The term may be used, and is so used among British anthropologists, to refer to individuals who have become detached from a group to which they originally belonged, and which is at a cultural and social level appropriately described as tribal. Thus a commission appointed to fix the boundaries of land to be allotted to the tribes of Kenya also considered what provision should be made for the *detribalized*. 'Reserves for detribalized natives'

already existed, but the commission remarked that there was 'no accepted test of detribalization' (*Kenya Land Commission Report*, London: H.M.S.O., 1934, p. 333). Later, however, the commission described the descendants of persons who had been brought into the country as slaves as 'truly detribalised' (ibid., p. 340). This usage is also implied by I. Schapera when, arguing that all the Africans who go from Bechuanaland to work in South Africa do not become 'detribalised', he remarks that they keep in touch with fellow-tribesmen at work, and with relatives at home, in ways which indicate that 'they have not finally abandoned the territory' (*Migrant Labour and Tribal Life*, London: Oxford University Press, 1947, p. 169).

In this sense the word is almost synonymous with *urbanization*, since in the vast majority of cases the process is a feature of migration from rural to urban areas; there may, however, also be farm labourers who are in this sense detribalized.

Most sociologists find this word too imprecise to be of much value, and use it only when examining the validity of the assumptions popularly associated with it.

2. American anthropologists use detribalization as in (1) above, but they also extend its meaning to include an individual or group which has lost its tribal way of life. Thus a native may be detribalized even when living among his own tribe if his cultural ways no longer conform to those of his group. And the culture of a group itself may be detribalized under missionary influence without any one leaving the group.

L. P. Mair

See also: Acculturation
Marginal Man
Tribe

Devaluation

A. In defining *devaluation* economists have followed legislative and administrative usage instead of looking purely to economic results. *Devaluation* denotes an act of government explicitly aimed toward the reduction of the international value of its monetary unit in terms of those of other countries. Accordingly partial devaluation by means of discriminatory exchange rates is not usually classed as devaluation. If the stated goal is devaluation, the intent and not the ex-post results is taken at its face value. Occasionally *devaluation* means reduction of metallic content of coins, as when the monarch of former times debased or 'raised'

Deviant Behaviour

coins (J. A. Schumpeter, *History of Economic Analysis*, New York: Oxford University Press, 1954, pp. 99–100, 209–99).

B. As generally used in economics, *devaluation* indicates action by a government to lower the international value of its monetary unit in terms of those of other countries (R. G. Hawtrey, *Currency and Credit*, London: Longmans, Green, 4th edn., 1950, pp. 207–8, 223, 239–40, 431; L. Tarshis, *Introduction to International Trade and Finance*, New York: J. Wiley, 1955, pp. 337–8). Thus if the government of the United Kingdom reduces the pound from \$5 =£1 to \$4=£1, the dollar price of pound balance is, temporarily at least, reduced by 20 per cent and the pound price of dollars has been increased by 25 per cent.

H. S. Ellis once called this type of devaluation *ordinary* to distinguish it from *discriminatory devaluation* which results from the establishment of multiple exchange rates (*Exchange Control in Central Europe*, Cambridge, Mass.: Harvard University Press, 1941, p. 237). Most writers consider it unnecessary to state explicitly that a system of multiple exchange rates amounts to partial devaluation (or appreciation) coupled with discriminatory pricing. In fact, *devaluation* belongs to a family of policies any one of which can yield some or all of the effects of devaluation. For example, if a government has effectively pegged the international value of its monetary unit above its market value, removal of the props will allow this value to decline, thereby producing *de facto* devaluation; but this action would be hailed as a return to authentic pricing and not explicitly classed as devaluation. The existence of a black market is clearly equivalent to partial devaluation in fact, if not in name. Deflation (q.v.), though politically less acceptable than devaluation, tends to cheapen exports and to make imports more dear. Tariffs in conjunction with export subsidies can produce the same effects on international trade as devaluation, but no one would stretch the concept to cover this policy.

C. The purpose of devaluation is to encourage exports and increase receipts from them by reducing their prices to foreigners and to curtail purchase of foreign goods by making imports more costly. An act of devaluation may or may not attain these goals. (For interesting discussion of this matter, see: W. R. Allen, 'A Note on the Money Income Effects of Devaluation', *Kyklos*, vol. 9, 1956, pp. 372–80; S. S. Alexander, 'Effects of Devaluation on a Trade Balance', International Monetary Fund, *Staff Papers*, vol. 2, 1951–2, pp. 263–78; R. F. Mikesell, *Foreign Exchange in the Postwar World*, New York: Twentieth Century Fund, 1954, pp. 146–51; F. Machlup, 'Relative Prices and Aggregate Spending in the Analysis of Devaluation', *The American Economic Review*, vol. XLV, 1955, pp. 255–78; J. J. Polak & T. G. Chang, 'Effect of Exchange Depreciation on a Country's Export Price Level', International Monetary Fund, *Staff Papers*, vol. 1, 1950–1, pp. 49–53). Regardless of ex-post effectiveness, the intent is determining. Even, for example, when devaluation by one country is offset by depreciation by other countries of their monetary units, devaluation is said to have occurred, albeit ineffective.

D. A country may devalue either by changing the rate at which its currency exchanges for some other, or several other currencies, or by changing the rate at which it exchanges for gold.

William L. Miller

See also: CURRENCY REFORM
DEFLATION

Deviant Behaviour

A. *Deviant behaviour* is behaviour which departs from, or conflicts with, standards which are socially or culturally accepted within a social group or system.

B. 1. The idea of deviance derives from statistics—in one sense deviant behaviour is behaviour which diverges from the mean or standard position—behaviour which is atypical. More generally, however, the idea of deviance, like that of normality and related terms, gains its content from a consideration of the group cultural context within which the 'deviance' is gauged. Social and psychological research has placed increasing emphasis upon the multiplicity of social groups and upon multiple group-membership. Many studies have shown the extent to which what constitutes a typical or deviant behaviour varies with different societies and subcultures. Moreover, the significance attached to different forms of deviant behaviour varies with the social norms of the group. Behaviour is perceived as deviant behaviour by a group if it goes counter to the social norms established by that group. For the members of a teenage gang, for instance, law-abiding behaviour, expressions of respect for adult authority, may constitute deviant behaviour if they depart from the approved social norms of that group.

2. A definition of a kind which is increasingly employed is that offered by A. K. Cohen ('The Study of Social Disorganisation and Deviant Behavior', in *Sociology Today*, ed. by R. K. Merton, et al., New York: Basic Books, 1959, p. 462): 'behavior which violates institutionalised expectations—that is, expectations which are shared and recognised as legitimate within a social system'. Similar concern with the context of social systems is to be found in the formulation of W. J. H. Sprott (*Science and Social Action*, Glencoe, Ill.: The Free Press, 1956, p. 104) who argues that 'the concept of deviance implies the concept of order. We have at the back of our minds the notion of a social system with its normative regulations and deviance is the departure on the part of participants from culturally expected rules of conduct'. Sprott also raises the issue of deviance as a non-pathological ingredient of cumulative social change (ibid., p. 107).

C. 1. The extent to which such behaviour is disapproved of has been shown experimentally to vary with the cohesiveness of the group, the structure of the membership of the group (authoritarian v. democratic), and the actual or perceived threat to the group by outside forces. The more cohesive the group, the more authoritarian its structure, and the more threatened it feels, the stronger will be the demand for conforming behaviour and the greater the rejection of deviant members. Much experimental work has been carried out showing systematically that an increase of threat to the group increases the intolerance towards deviant behaviour or the expression of deviant views.

2. Much social research is devoted to the study of the aetiology of deviant behaviour, especially of deviant behaviour which is socially or clinically maladjusted: the behaviour of the delinquent, the mentally ill, the child from broken homes, the under-achiever, etc. Studies of deviant behaviour also attempt to evaluate the effectiveness of different types of remedial action, designed to reintegrate the individual into the group. It has been found that individuals who reject the norms of the larger group often form themselves into sub-groups of like deviants of which they become conforming members. Once such sub-groups are formed and prove satisfying to the individual, his reintegration into the larger group (which he may perceive as rejecting him) becomes more difficult than in the case of the 'lone deviant'.

3. It is important to bear in mind that the nature of deviant behaviour varies with the group to which the individual belongs and that this is seen in its most striking form in complex societies where each individual belongs to a variety of groups, each with its own set of social norms. Studies of social mobility have shown how the behaviour of an individual, while typical for the group from which he originates, may prove deviant and be disapproved of in the group to which he now belongs or aspires to belong. Stresses arise from conflicting group norms. It is also important to remember that deviant behaviour is differently evaluated and reacted against depending upon the structure of the groups, the relevance of the behaviour in question to its social norms, the tasks of the group and its relation to the wider society of which it forms a part.

H. Himmelweit

See also: ADJUSTMENT
CONFORMITY
NORM
SOCIAL DISORGANIZATION
SOCIAL INTEGRATION

Dialectic

1. The term *dialectic* denotes the investigation of truth by discussion; in earlier English use it is a synonym of *logic* as applied to formal rhetorical reasoning; it also refers to logical disputation (originally the art of disputation by question and answer, said to be first practised by Zeno of Elea, and developed by Plato.

2. It was applied by Kant to the study of the contradictions arising when principles of empirical knowledge are employed beyond the limits of experience and by Hegel to the process whereby such contradictions are resolved through their being absorbed in a more comprehensive system representing a higher plane of truth. This Hegelian process directs both individual thought and world-history according to the pattern—thesis, antithesis, and synthesis.

J. H. Warrender

Dialectical Materialism

This term denotes the philosophy underlying Marxism.

1. It is called dialectical because of its development from Hegelianism which it resembles (a) in regarding history as progressing through contradictions within a system, requiring periodically a more or less violent

Dictatorship

reorganization or synthesis and (b) in stressing unification of opposition, relativity of truth, etc.

2. Marx, however, rejected Hegel's idealism, and the historical role he accorded to heroes, nationalism, etc. For Marx, the evolution of human society is determined basically by economic factors outside or largely outside men's conscious control.

'My dialectic method is not only different from the Hegelian, but is its direct opposite. To Hegel, the life-process of the human brain ... is the demiurgos of the real world, and the real world is only the external, phenomenal form of "the Idea". With me, on the contrary, the ideal is nothing else than the material world reflected by the human mind, and translated into forms of thought. ... With him it [dialectic] is standing on its head. It must be turned right side up again, if you would discover the rational kernel within the mystical shell' (K. Marx, 'Preface' to 2nd German edn. of *Capital*. Marx/Engels, Selected Works, London: Lawrence & Wishart, 1950, vol. I, pp. 413–14).

On this view, underlying economic forces are responsible for the class-structure of society, and history is essentially the history of economic classes, their rise and fall, dominance and exploitation. Each period, however, contains the seeds of its own downfall. Capitalism, for example, for a time progressive, becomes economically restrictive; it is also forced to bring into existence an ever-growing property-less proletariat organized on a mass scale, which will eventually seize power and in turn dominate society. The process, however, is not endless. With the emancipation of the proletariat (q.v.), the lowest class in society, after a transitional period, a classless society will result.

Marx was concerned to differentiate his own theory from 'mechanistic materialism' and stressed the significance of evolution, flux, process in opposition to the mechanistic model of repetitive and reversible physical reaction.

J. H. Warrender

See also: CLASS CONSCIOUSNESS
CLASS STRUGGLE
DIALECTIC
SOCIAL CLASS

Dictatorship

1. In ancient Rome the *dictatura* was the institution of the *dictator*—the one man in whose hands, in times of exceptional stress, absolute power was vested for a period of six months—the incumbent being designated by one of the consuls. Thus the Roman dictatorship was a form of legitimate authority. Only towards the end of the republic was the title of dictator assumed by generals who seized power by illegal means.

2. Most commonly by *dictatorship* is meant the type of authority characterized by at least some of the following features: (a) Lack of laws or customs in virtue of which the ruler (or rulers) could be called upon to account for their actions or removed; (b) lack of limitations on the scope of authority; (c) acquisition of supreme authority by contravention of pre-existing laws; (d) absence of provision for orderly succession; (e) use of authority for the benefit of a restricted group only; (f) obedience of the subjects being due solely to fear; (g) concentration of power in the hands of one man; (h) employment of terror.

3. As the term *dictatorship* is indiscriminately applied to various incomplete combinations of these features, the question arises: which of them should we adopt as constitutive criteria? Even the case which is reputed to have been a dictatorship par excellence—that of Hitler's regime—fails to exhibit all of these features: for Hitler reached the headship of the state in a constitutional manner. Moreover, there are many borderline cases: usurpers of thrones, for instance, such as many of the Roman emperors, would have to be included among dictators if we adopted the third criterion above as decisive.

It seems that the most useful heuristically would be this definition: *dictatorship* is the type of government exhibiting the following features: (a) the supreme authority is absolute; (b) the headship of the state was acquired by conquest; that is to say not in virtue of pre-existing laws; (c) there is no rule of succession which can be regarded as established. Other features enumerated previously would then be regarded as contingent, including criterion (2) (g), so that we could speak of personal as well as collective dictatorships.

S. Andreski

See also: ABSOLUTISM
AUTHORITARIANISM
AUTOCRACY
DESPOTISM
TOTALITARIANISM
TYRANNY

Differentiation

A. *Differentiation* denotes (a) the process of becoming separate, distinct, specialized; the acquisition of specialized forms or functions; and (b) that which results from such a process.

B. 1. In biology the term means the process of becoming unlike by modification especially for a special function or purpose.

2. This biological usage was very influential in introducing the term into 19th-century 'evolutionary' sociology. The notions of *selection* and *specialization in growth and development* are illustrated by the following quotations from Herbert Spencer:

(a) 'It was not until Christian church-music had reached some development that music in parts was evolved; and then it came into existence through a very unobtrusive differentiation' (*First Principles*, 5th edn., 1884, p. 357);

(b) 'When a compound society has ... simultaneously differentiated somewhat its social ranks and industries, and proportionately developed its arts which all of them conduce in some way to better co-operation, the compound society becomes practically a single one' (*The Principles of Sociology*, London: Williams & Norgate, 3rd edn., 1885, vol. 1, p. 543).

3. When modern sociologists write about *social differentiation* they have in mind some, if not all, of these motifs. Social differentiation is a general term used to denote (a) the process whereby individuals or groups acquire more or less distinct and/or specialized roles and the accompanying statuses; and (b) the results of such a process. The classic work in this area is C. C. North, *Social Differentiation* (Chapel Hill: University of North Carolina Press, 1926). North argues (ibid., p. 5 et seq.) that 'the significant social differences ... fall into four types: namely differences of *function*, differences of *rank*, differences of *culture*, and differences of *interest*'. A full theory of social differentiation would explore the causes and dynamics of these (and other) social differences.

In recent years there has been a revived interest in the conceptual distinction between social differentiation and social stratification. Important analyses have appeared to define the latter concept in terms of the situation where 'the rights and perquisites of different positions in a society must be unequal' (K. Davis & W. E. Moore, 'Some Principles of Stratification', *American Sociological Review*, vol. 10, 1945, p. 243). Critics have argued in reply that this formula points to social differentiation and its results in the short run and not to *stratification* which more commonly implies ranked collectivities which '*continue through several generations*

to receive the same relative amounts of material ends, prestige and power' (W. Buckley, 'Social Stratification and the Functional Theory of Social Differentiation', *American Sociological Review*, vol. 23, 1958, p. 370).

C. In the economic theory of imperfect competition, when the product of one 'seller' is an *imperfect substitute* for the product of any other 'seller', the term differentiation may be used. Thus E. H. Chamberlin (*The Theory of Monopolistic Competition*, Cambridge, Mass.: Harvard University Press, 1935, p. 56) says 'A general class of product is differentiated if any significant basis exists for distinguishing the goods (or services) of one seller from those of another'; and 'With differentiation appears monopoly, and as it proceeds further the element of monopoly becomes greater' (ibid., p. 9).

J. Gould

See also: DIVISION OF LABOUR
             STRATIFICATION

Diffusion

A. *Diffusion* designates all the orderly processes which produce cultural similarities in various societies other than *invention*. It includes three distinct types of historical processes through which culture spreads.

1. The spread of culture sometimes occurs through the migration of its bearers, a process sometimes called *primary diffusion* or *cultural dispersion*. An example is the spread of the English system of Common Law over much of North America and Oceania.

2. On occasion, diffusion may occur through the direct borrowing or *secondary diffusion* of culture, including material traits, by one group from another, e.g. the spread of the horse complex among the Plains Indians of North America.

3. Sometimes it is sufficient for the idea alone to be suggested, a process A. L. Kroeber has called *stimulus diffusion* (*Anthropology*, New York: Harcourt, Brace, 1948, pp. 368–70).

B. The word *diffusion* in its broad sense has been generally used by anthropologists and sociologists, since its introduction by E. B. Tylor, to mean the spread of culture through borrowing, suggestion, or migration, alone or in combination (*Primitive Culture*, London: John Murray, 1871). The word has met the need for a term to refer to all the orderly processes which produce cultural similarities other than

Diminishing Returns

independent invention of similar traits to meet similar needs.

C. Although most anthropologists have employed *diffusion* in conjunction with *invention* in the explanation of cultural similarities there have been two schools of thought which have reduced invention to a minimally important level.

1. The English diffusionists, G. E. Smith and W. J. Perry, made Egypt the centre for cultural origins, and argued that borrowing explained almost all cultural similarities throughout the world (W. J. Perry, *The Children of the Sun*, London: Methuen, 1923).

2. The *kulturhistorische* school of F. Graebner and, later, of Father W. Schmidt (*The Culture Historical Method of Ethnology*, trans. S. A. Sieber, New York: Fortuny's, 1939) placed great emphasis on diffusion and the concept of the *Kulturkreis* (q.v.). Despite the greater sophistication of this group of anthropologists, as compared with the English diffusionists, its theories have not been accepted by the vast majority of English-speaking anthropologists.

Raoul Naroll

See also: INNOVATION

Diminishing Returns

A. The law of *diminishing returns* is frequently referred to in contemporary economic theory as the law of variable proportions. In general terms it is concerned with the effect on total product of using varying amounts of one productive service while holding the remaining services constant. 'As equal increments of one input are added, the inputs of other productive services being held constant, beyond a certain point the resulting increments of product will decrease, i.e. the marginal products will diminish' (G. J. Stigler, *The Theory of Price*, New York: The Macmillan Co., 1952, p. 111). Such a law is valid, of course, only within certain limitations, and is only one of two branches of the laws of return. The second branch of the laws of return deals with problems involving returns to scale of plant and thus describes the effects on total product of proportionate changes in the amounts of *all* productive services. Both branches of the laws of return are fundamental to the theory of production, for they determine the nature of the production function.

B. 1. Early economists wrote about the law of diminishing returns almost exclusively with respect to its application to problems of agricultural production. This applies, for example, to Turgot, who is generally credited with having been the first to provide an accurate statement of the law (J. A. Schumpeter, *Historic of Economic Analysis*, New York: Oxford University Press, 1954, pp. 259–61). Not until the latter half of the 19th century did economists begin to emphasize that the law of diminishing returns applies to all types of productive activity.

2. Another source of confusion during the classical period stemmed from a failure to distinguish carefully between *secular* diminishing returns and what is usually called the law of variable proportions. Starting with the assumption that the supply of land is permanently fixed, classical economists predicted that, in the long run, increased application of labour to land would inevitably result in secular diminishing returns. Such a proposition, however, permits sufficient time to elapse for major technological changes to occur. In fact, therefore, the classical prediction was upset and the basic nature of the problem is thus quite different from that posed by the law of variable proportions.

C. The definition of diminishing returns set forth in A. above requires further clarification if the concept is to be used with precision in economic analysis; no brief definition can adequately describe its full implications. Largely on the basis of the work of F. H. Knight and J. D. Black, J. M. Cassels ('On the Law of Variable Proportions', in *Exploration in Economics*, New York: McGraw-Hill, 1936, pp. 226–7) has suggested that the essential features of the law can be revealed most clearly by showing how the addition of successive equal increments of a variable factor to a fixed factor —or fixed combination of factors—would cause the *total physical output* to vary in magnitude through three distinct phases: (a) Throughout the first phase, total physical product '... would *increase* for a time at an increasing absolute rate and then at a decreasing absolute rate, but always at a percentage rate greater than the rate of increase of the variable factor'. The final point in this stage would be reached when the rate of increase in total product exactly equalled the rate of increase of the variable factor, i.e., when marginal physical product equalled average physical product. (b) In the second phase, total product would '... continue to *increase*, but at a decreasing absolute rate and at a percentage rate always less than that of the variable factor'. The final point of this phase would be reached when the maximum total product was obtained, and marginal physical product was reduced to zero. (c) In the last phase, total product '... would *decrease*, possibly for a time at an increasing absolute rate, but probably through most of this phase at a decreasing rate', until finally the total product was reduced to zero. Throughout this phase, marginal physical product would be negative.

Perhaps the greatest merit of the above 'phase' or 'stage' type of analysis is that it reveals the symmetrical nature of the law. Thus the third phase is merely the converse of the first. The so-called 'point' of diminishing returns is reached within the first phase when total product begins to increase at a decreasing rate, which is the equivalent of saying that the point of diminishing returns is where the marginal physical product is at a maximum.

D. Certain limiting features of the law of diminishing returns deserve emphasis. (a) In the first place, the law only purports to describe physical input-output relationships, and it is properly referred to, therefore, as a technological rather than an economic law. (b) Secondly, the law is essentially static, for it assumes there will be no improvement in the techniques of production as amounts of the variable factor are changed. (c) And finally, implicit in the law is the assumption that productive services held constant can be 'readapted' in form to the changing quantity of the variable service (G. J. Stigler, *The Theory of Price*, pp. 117–18).

Alfred F. Chalk

Diplomacy

A. There are three major usages of the term *diplomacy* in general usage and in political science:

1. In its broadest sense, diplomacy means the carrying on of relations between and among states. Some students of international politics discuss *diplomacy* in this sense as an *element* of national power (e.g. H. J. Morgenthau, *Politics Among Nations*, New York: Knopf, 1954, pp. 505–8). Others consider it only an *instrument* of national policy (e.g. N. D. Palmer & H. C. Perkins, *International Relations*, London: Stevens, 1954, pp. 155–8). From the latter grows the distinction often made between foreign policy as an end and purpose and diplomacy as a means and a method.

2. There is wide agreement on another usage of *diplomacy*—existing, actually, within the framework of the broader usage—namely, that diplomacy is synonomous with negotiation. Since negotiation aims at agreement, and agreement invariably means compromise, *diplomacy* may be defined as the art of making compromises in international political matters which promote rather than jeopardize the basic interests and security of a nation.

3. Finally, *diplomacy* is also used to refer both to the administrative machinery of international relations and to the personal qualities of persuasion on the part of those engaging in such relations.

B. One of the major questions in any attempt to define diplomacy is that of its relationship to war (q.v.). According to H. Nicolson, diplomacy '... is the agency through which foreign policy seeks to attain its purpose by agreement rather than war' (*The Congress of Vienna: A Study in Allied Unity*, London: Constable, 1945, p. 164). Both Nicolson and Morgenthau believe that the outbreak of war means the failure of diplomacy, while Palmer and Perkins, as well as others, feel that diplomacy can continue to be operative even during military operations (H. J. Morgenthau, *Politics Among Nations*, pp. 505–8; N. D. Palmer & H. C. Perkins, *International Relations*, pp. 157–8).

Q. Wright has said that '... where the possibility of war does not exist ... the term diplomacy is hardly applicable' (*The Study of International Relations*, New York: Appleton-Century, 1958, p. 185). In part, this position rests on the indisputable idea that the main function of diplomacy is to advance the interest of the nation engaging in it, and that this interest is more often than not gained at the expense of another nation, so that diplomacy has in the past even been used deliberately to provoke war. Furthermore, it is obvious that possession of military might is in itself a factor in diplomacy. Since the mid-1950s, however, some have come to believe that the interest of no nation can any longer be served by war, since war now involves the likelihood of universal destruction. Others still stress the possibilities of limited wars as an instrument of policy, and some concern themselves with first-strike strategies and capabilities.

C. Diplomacy has traditionally been carried on by diplomats accredited to foreign governments. Increasingly, however, it has come to be practised also by chiefs of governments and foreign secretaries themselves. In former years

Diseconomy

diplomacy was generally a bilateral affair, except for rare congresses of diplomats called to formulate a settlement after a war. With the advent of the League of Nations, however, diplomacy by conference came to be the rule rather than the exception. Whereas formerly diplomacy was carried on in secrecy, it has come, at least in part, to be practised in the glare of publicity and to involve popular opinion. Whereas in former years an ambassador was plenipotentiary and made many important decisions on his own, today he is able and expected to communicate directly with his foreign office at each step of the way. Simultaneously the reporting function of diplomacy has become more difficult, since the morale of the populace as well as what the governments are saying must be assessed. All this has led many critics to believe that modern diplomacy is severely handicapped in achieving its objective of reaching agreement by compromise.

Fred Warner Neal

See also: COMPROMISE
          INTERNATIONAL RELATIONS
          WAR

Discovery (See Innovation)

Discriminating Monopoly (See Monopoly)

Diseconomy

A. In the most general sense the word *diseconomy* refers to any unfavourable effects which result from the extension of an economic activity, whether in production or consumption. It is called an *internal* or an *external* diseconomy according to whether the unfavourable effect falls on the person responsible for the activity which causes them, or on another.

B. 1. Diseconomies may arise broadly in two ways, *either* (a) through direct effects, as in the case of a smoke nuisance, or river pollution, or ostentatious expenditure which raises the cost of 'keeping up with the Joneses' *or* (b) through the market mechanism, as in the case where increased purchases of a commodity by one person raises their price to himself or to another. These two categories are not too clearly distinct in all cases.

2. It should be noted that the expressions *internal* and *external economies* are used similarly; but in the specialized sense which will be considered in C. below the analysis of the causes of economies is not entirely symmetrical with that of the causes of diseconomies.

C. In the theory of competition the expressions internal and external diseconomies are used in a more specialized sense: There are external diseconomies of *expanding the production of the whole industry*, and internal diseconomies of scale *in a single firm*.

1. External diseconomies of expanding production are those factors contributing to rising per unit costs which lie beyond the control of any single firm in an industry. As industry output of a product expands, demand for resources used in the production of that product increases and, beyond some point, brings about rising resource prices. Rising resource prices in turn contribute to rising per unit costs of production. Those rising per unit costs, due to expanding industry demand for resources and not due to expanding demand of any individual firm for resources, are the result of external diseconomies.

The ultimate cause of rising resource prices and of external diseconomies as production of a product is expanded rests on the scarcity of particular resource supplies. As J. Robinson (*The Economics of Imperfect Competition*, London: Macmillan, 1933, p. 331) puts it, '... increasing cost for a particular commodity will arise whenever one of the factors of production ... is not in perfectly elastic supply to the industry producing that commodity'. Or, according to F. H. Knight (*The Ethics of Competition*, London: Allen & Unwin, 1935, p. 197), '... an increase in the production of any commodity means a transfer of productive resources into the industry and a decrease in the production of some other commodity. But, other things being equal, this decrease in the production of other goods will raise their prices and increase the strength of the competing attraction which they exert on productive resources against the industry in question in which output is being increased'.

2. Internal diseconomies of scale refer to those factors contributing to rising per unit costs of a firm which stem from the firm's own expansion of size and output. As the size and output of a firm increase from very small to very large, it is generally thought that costs per unit will fall in the early phases of expansion due to internal economies of scale, but that as expansion beyond some critical point occurs, costs per unit will increase due to internal diseconomies of scale.

Internal diseconomies have received neither extensive nor adequate treatment in economic literature, probably because they are not symmetrical with the more obvious internal economies of scale. Internal diseconomies are thought by some to occur because beyond some point the managerial resources of a firm cannot be increased in proportion to increases in the quantities of other resources; consequently, diminishing average returns to those other resources will cause costs per unit to rise. E. H. Chamberlin has pointed out that limitations of the managerial resource are unnecessary to explain internal diseconomies of scale. Borrowing from and adding to ideas of E. A. G. Robinson, he states that they occur 'because of the greater complexity of the producing unit as it grows in size, leading to increased difficulties of coordination and management' (E. H. Chamberlin, *The Theory of Monopolistic Competition*, London: Oxford University Press, 6th edn., 1949, p. 247). M. Kalecki cites as another cause of internal diseconomies the increasing costs of obtaining investment funds as expansion of the firm occurs ('The Principle of Increasing Risk', *Economica*, vol. IV, 1937, pp. 440-7).

Richard H. Leftwich

See also: COST

Discrimination

A. There are three major meanings of the term *discrimination*:

1. In its most general sense the term denotes the perceiving, noting, or making a distinction between things.

2. It is sometimes used to denote the differential treatment of categories of persons, either favourable or unfavourable, on grounds which have little or no relation to the actual behaviour of the persons so treated.

3. In its most usual contemporary sense, in both ordinary discourse and the social sciences, it denotes the *unfavourable* treatment of categories of persons on arbitrary grounds. In this usage it refers to a process or form of social control (q.v.) which serves to maintain social distance between two or more categories or groups by means of a set of practices more or less institutionalized and rationalized. The practices employed involve the arbitrary attribution of inferiority on grounds which have little to do with the actual behaviour of those discriminated against, and are frequently in conflict with accepted ideas of justice and fairness.

Such practices may include segregation (q.v.) but also include actions which go beyond it.

They may be seen as the objective parallel of prejudice (q.v.), as acts growing out of prejudiced attitudes.

B. Though it is recognized that there is discrimination favourable to the person or group toward whom it is directed, social science usage is almost wholly concerned with discrimination as denoting unfavourable treatment. One of the few neutral definitions encountered is that set out as a 'definition of the term' in a publication of the United Nations: 'Discrimination includes any conduct based on grounds of natural or social categories, which have no relation either to individual capacities or merits, or to the concrete behaviour of the individual person' (*The Main Types and Causes of Discrimination*, United Nations, 1949. XIV. 3, Lake Success, N.Y., 1949, p. 9). Types of advantageous discrimination are chivalrous treatment of women, or the aged; or family prerogatives which are hereditary.

B. Berry also offers a neutral definition of the term: 'Differential treatment accorded individuals who are considered as belonging in a particular category or group' (*Race and Ethnic Relations*, Boston: Houghton, Mifflin, 1958, p. 372). But he illustrates with negative treatment: 'Dominant peoples everywhere have resorted to various devices for restricting economically, politically, and socially the racial and ethnic groups over whom they have set themselves. The term commonly applied to such practices is discrimination (ibid., p. 432). Further, he comments: 'One of the functions of these discriminations is to isolate the dominant and subordinate groups and to limit contact and communication between them. Isolation and segregation, accordingly, help to preserve the *status quo*, impede the process of assimilation, and, in fact, serve to *dull the appetite for higher status on the part of the underprivileged group*. ... What is more important is the fact that discriminatory policies make it difficult for the oppressed group to acquire the knowledge, skills, and tools with which to improve their status' (ibid., p. 433).

The conception of discrimination as the overt manifestation of prejudice which 'comes about when we take steps to exclude members of an outgroup ...' is held by G. W. Allport (*The Nature of Prejudice*, Boston: Addison-Wesley, 1954, pp. 52-3). He also points out that separation of groups because of lack of congeniality, or of persons because of individual qualities

Displacement

cannot properly be classed as discrimination (ibid.).

Harry E. Moore

See also: Prejudice
        Race and Minority Group
           Relations
        Segregation

Displacement

A. *Displacement* refers either to (a) the transfer of feeling, ideas, or action from objects upon which the centring of such psychic phenomena is unacceptable to the ego, superego, or self-image of the agent to an object or objects upon which such centring is acceptable; or to (b) the transfer of feeling, idea, or action from one object to another because of the simple unavailability of the first object or because of similarity of the objects.

B. The primary usage of this term is as one of the technical words within the framework of psychoanalytic psychology. Both meanings of the term in A. above are found.

1. In the first sense *displacement* is a defence mechanism (q.v.), an affect which is related to one object is expressed toward another which is remote from or only superficially connected to the original object. This mechanism is especially important in obsessional neuroses. Freud also noted it in the analysis of what he called *dream-displacement* ('The Interpretation of Dreams', in *The Basic Writings of Sigmund Freud*, A. A. Brill (ed.), New York: Modern Library, 1938). In this process of changing the 'accent' of a dream, important ideas motivated by wish fulfilment tendencies are displaced by ideas only slightly related to the original ideas as a way of censoring or distorting the expression of the wishes so as to make them unrecognizable to the dreamer. In other behaviour, also, there occurs this defensive substitution of objects. For example, J. F. Brown and K. A. Menninger (*The Psychodynamics of Abnormal Behavior*, New York: McGraw-Hill, 1940, pp. 175–6) suggest that 'fiddling' with objects such as pencils is a masturbation substitute or displacement. This behaviour is defensive in that it prevents actual masturbation by substituting for it.

2. The second meaning simply denotes that process in which an impulse shifts from one object to another because the first is not available. Freud, since he postulated a series of instinctual goals as components of the sexual impulse, could conceive of displacement, or substitution of one sexual zone for another, as occurring because of simple environmental frustration. The nature of the unavailability is crucial here. If an object is unavailable for cathexis (q.v.) because the potential relationship to it on the part of the agent is unacceptable, then the first usage is indicated. If there is no obstacle to the relationship or if the object is simply absent, then displacement is being used in the second sense.

C. Some learning theorists use *displacement* primarily in the second meaning because they hold that the connection or association between the original object and the substituted object is one of similarity of stimuli presented to the agent by the objects. Thus, N. E. Miller ('Experiments Relating Freudian Displacement to Generalization Conditioning', *Psychological Bulletin*, vol. 36, 1939, p. 516) holds that displacement is only a form of stimulus generalization. He trained pairs of rats to fight each other and these rats would then fight a plastic doll when it was substituted for one rat of the pair. On the other hand R. R. Sears ('Experimental Analysis of Psychoanalytic Phenomena', in J. McV. Hunt (ed.), *Personality and the Behavior Disorders*, New York: Ronald Press, 1944, vol. 1, p. 317) believes that in displacement there is the diverting of affect from one object to another because of the fear of punishment. In this formulation there is apparent an effort to give 'behaviouristic' meaning to the first psychoanalytic usage of the term, but the element of punishment does not seem to be a sufficient behavioural correlate of ego, superego, and self-image disapproval to support such an attempt. Rather, experimental work concerning displacement within the learning theory framework seems to be limited to the second meaning of the term, in the one case where there is no obstacle with respect to the original object but displacement is produced by similarity of stimuli and in the second case where there is simple environmental frustration with respect to the first object in the form of punishment.

D. In social psychology the concept *displacement* has been used with respect to the hostility expressed toward minority groups. T. W. Adorno, E. Frenkel-Brunswik, et al. (*The Authoritarian Personality*, New York: Harper & Brothers, 1950, pp. 450ff.) use the concept to argue that hostility toward authoritarian parents can frequently not be expressed and as a consequence is displaced onto minority groups because they are vulnerable. Thus, the term is being used in its first meaning. G. W. Allport (*The Nature of Prejudice*, Cambridge, Mass.: Addison-Wesley, 1954, pp. 343–59), however, argues that while displacement is involved in prejudice toward minorities, it is a form of overgeneralization rather than a defence mechanism. Since it is the result of generalization on the basis of similarities, it is not adjustive, i.e. it does not drain aggression, but rather broadens aggression to include additional objects.

Thomas Ktsanes

See also: AGGRESSION
AMBIVALENCE
EGO
PROJECTION
SUPEREGO

Disposable Income (See **National Product**)

Diversification (See **Economic Integration**)

Divination

A. In its strict etymological sense, the term denotes inquiry of some sort of a *deity* about future events or matters, hidden or obscure, generally through attention to signs believed to have been sent by him or her. More widely, it refers to the process of obtaining knowledge of secret or future things by mechanical means or manipulative techniques—a process which may or may not include invoking the aid of non-empirical beings or powers, but does not include the empirical methods of science.

B. 1. In the analysis of pre-literate societies the term has reference (as distinct from *prophecy*) to a concern with the immediate problems and interests of individuals and sub-groups, and not with the destinies of nations. A good example may be found in S. F. Nadel's *Nupe Religion* (London: Routledge & Kegan Paul, 1954, p. 64). He calls the guidance it offers 'mechanical and of a case-to-case kind'. The diviner 'can discover and disentangle some of the hidden influences which are at work always and everywhere ... he cannot uncover any more embracing design'. Yet within its limits divination provides 'some of the certainty and guidance required for provident action'. Thus, though distinct from prophecy, divination denotes a whole series of techniques for revealing what is hidden and for forecasting events, especially 'good' or 'lucky' events.

2. Still further removed from prophecy is the reference of the term 'to the analysis of past events' especially untoward events; this analysis often includes the detection of guilt. Where such untoward events are attributed (as they are in most pre-literate and some literate societies) to sorcery (q.v.), and witchcraft the diviner has great freedom of judgement in detecting and determining guilt. Diviners are frequently consulted by victims' relatives, and show intuitive and deductive skill in discovering quarrels and grudges in their clients' kingroups. Social anthropologists find in their diagnoses useful clues to areas and sources of strain in the social structure, and to the character and strength of its supporting norms and values.

V. W. Turner

See also: MAGIC
SORCERY AND WITCHCRAFT

Divine Kingship

A. *Divine kingship* is an institution found in many societies lacking political centralization, but which nevertheless have what E. E. Evans-Pritchard calls 'moral density ... great enough for their segments to be represented by a common symbol in the kingship but not great enough to eliminate the powerful tendencies towards fission in the structure they compose' (*The Divine Kingship of the Shilluk of the Nilotic Sudan*, Cambridge: Cambridge University Press, 1948, p. 37).

It is also a system of ideas and beliefs centred upon the dogma that after his installation the incumbent becomes a vehicle or shrine of a god, royal ancestor, or culture hero. From this derive: (a) taboos separating the king from contact with profane persons, objects, relationships, and activities; (b) notions that the king's physical, moral, and ritual condition affect the welfare and fertility of society, land, and livestock; (c) the custom of regicide.

B. For J. G. Frazer (*The Golden Bough* (1890), London: Macmillan, abridged edn., 1933, p. 90 f.) divine kings or 'incarnate human deities' were transitional figures 'between the age of magic and the age of religion'. The king was the 'lineal successor of the magician' who tended 'gradually to exchange the practice of magic for the priestly function of prayer and sacrifice'. At this phase, 'the rift between the spiritual and the temporal sphere' had 'not yet widened' and exceptional men were 'supreme in civil as well as religious matters. In a word, they were kings as well as gods'.

Division of Labour

Frazer's formulation is highly ambiguous. Is the king a priest-magician, a priest, a god, or the temporary incarnation of a god? A. Hocart clarified matters considerably ('Deification', in E. R. A. Seligman (ed.), *Encyclopedia of the Social Sciences*, New York: Macmillan, 1931, vol. V, pp. 58–60) when he pointed out that a man had to undergo coronation or installation rites before he was regarded as a god. He also emphasized the king's role as controller over the weather and the universe generally. 'Through him a good food supply can be insured with consequent prosperity. This, and not ruling, is the essential function of primitive kings. If prosperity fails the people blame the king and in many cases depose or slay him. In rarer cases the king is put to death if his health fails, for his weakness is held to react upon the course of nature' (ibid., p. 60). Hocart, as opposed to Frazer, thus emphasizes the divinity of the kingship rather than the king, and the frailty rather than the power of the incumbent. He brought out also the antithesis between religious and political action.

E. E. Evans-Pritchard explains the institution in structural terms (*The Divine Kingship of the Shilluk of the Nilotic Sudan*, p. 37). He suggests that it is 'typical of, though doubtless not restricted to, societies with pronounced lineage systems in which the political segments are parts of a loosely organized structure without governmental functions. In societies of this kind the political organization takes a ritual or symbolic form which in polities with a higher degree of organization gives way, though never entirely, to centralized administration'. Regicide in such societies asserts the common interest of the society in the kingship at the expense of a morally or physically inadequate incumbent.

V. W. Turner

See also: Monarchy
          Segment

Division of Labour

A. The most general usage is expressed in the formulation of the *Oxford English Dictionary*: 'The division of a process or an employment into parts, each of which is performed by a separate person'. Though the term has not been invested with a *precise* scientific meaning, it should not be equated with *specialization*. In the latter case, usage extends over a wide range of phenomena—social, economic, biological, and technological. In sociological analysis, the term specialization may refer equally to the special characteristics of individuals, groups, economic enterprises, or social institutions. The division of labour, on the other hand, is usually concerned with the special *tasks* assigned to individuals and groups, and their social and economic consequences.

B. The importance of the division of labour in the analysis of social and economic organization has been generally recognized since the time of Adam Smith.

It is, however, useful to distinguish broadly between three successive phases in its usage:

1. With respect to the consequences of the division of labour in *economic systems*: 'It is the great multiplication of the productions of all the different arts, in consequence of the division of labour, which occasions, in a well-governed society, that universal opulence which extends itself to the lowest ranks of the people' (A. Smith, *The Wealth of Nations* (1st edn. 1776), London: Methuen, 1904, p. 12).

2. With respect to social evolution with special reference to the *differentiation of functions (and thus of roles) in a society*: E. Durkheim provides the best-known example of this use of the term, the principal emphasis of *De la division du travail sociale* (*The Division of Labor in Society*, trans. by G. Simpson, Glencoe, Ill.: The Free Press, 1947) being on the specialization of functions within society as a whole. His purpose was to give a causal explanation of the increasingly dominant role of the division of labour in social evolution, and to examine the effect on the conditions necessary for social cohesion. He excluded, however, an examination of the specific ways in which the division of labour had intensified; in consequence, throughout his theory, the division of labour remains a highly generalized factor in social change, associated with the break-up of 'segmental' social structures (a process characterized by an increase in the quality, intensity, and diversity of social relationships).

3. With respect to the *allocation of tasks* in a given system of production, including *the refinement and simplification of tasks (especially in machine production)*: in the past 30 years, and especially with the development of industrial sociology, increasing attention has been given to the impact of an intensifying division of labour on the nature and content of work, usually as part of a study of technical change (for an early U.S. example, see E. D. Smith, *Technology and Labor*, New Haven: Yale University Press, 1939; for a recent U.K. example see W. H. Scott et al., *Technical Change* *and Industrial Relations*, Liverpool: Liverpool University Press, 1956).

Recently G. Friedmann, in *Le Travail en Miettes* (Paris: Gallimard, 1957), has attempted to relate his own studies of the impact of machine production on the status and attitudes of the worker to Durkheim's general concept, but apart from this, the attention given to the refinement and simplification of tasks has remained a separate endeavour.

In such inquiries, there is a tendency to refer to the *result* of the division of labour in a given system of production as its *occupational structure* (see *Occupation*).

Recent interest in the social problems of economic growth in developing countries has renewed consideration of the role of an intensifying division of labour in social change (see, for example, B. F. Hoselitz, *Sociological Aspects of Economic Growth*, Glencoe, Ill.: The Free Press, 1960) and also of the international division of labour.

J. H. Smith

See also: OCCUPATION

Divorce

A. 1. *Divorce* means that the marriage bond has been ended.

2. It is sometimes used to denote a declaration of nullity, i.e. a recognition that the marriage has never existed.

3. It is also used to denote a physical separation of the spouses which does not otherwise alter the legal relations resulting from their marriage.

B. In law, in order to obtain a divorce, the plaintiff must first prove the marriage. If there be no legal marriage, there can be no divorce. In comparative sociology, the difficulty of defining marriage (q.v.) in the various cultures under investigation is itself too formidable for a strict notion of divorce to have been developed. Nonetheless, hypotheses have been advanced to account for differences in divorce rates; J. A. Barnes for example, when proposing a method of standardizing the statistics of divorce, leaves on one side the task of definition, by describing divorce (in simple societies) as a transitional stage between one marriage and the next. 'The more precisely we measure divorce frequency, the more necessary it is to know exactly what we mean by marriage and divorce. If we vary our definitions, we are likely to vary our frequency ... for purposes of this paper we assume we know what is a divorce' ('Measures

of Divorce Frequency in Simple Societies', *Journal of the Royal Anthropological Institute*, vol. LXXIX, 1949, pub. 1951, p. 39).

C. *Separation* is sometimes distinguished by sociologists from divorce. Barnes, taking as his criterion of divorce that the parties are free to make a new marriage, allows that 'In some societies it may be difficult to distinguish divorce from separation' (ibid., p. 39). D. N. Schneider follows closely the legal distinction between separation (or suspension, divorce from bed and board) and divorce. 'There is at times an implicit distinction between conjugal relations and certain of the jural relations which arise out of legal marriage. That is, the physical separation of the legally wedded couple does not in itself constitute a termination of the legal bonds between them, or the legal bonds which follow from their union, particularly with respect to the offspring of the woman ('A Note on Bridewealth and the Stability of Marriage', *Man*, vol. LIII, 1953, p. 55).

D. *Nullity* is not a term currently used much in sociology, but the idea is implied in many writings. 'There are also many peoples among whom true conjugal life does not begin before a child is born. ... The Igorrotes of Luzon consider no engagement binding until the woman has become pregnant ...' (E. Westermarck, *History of Human Marriage*, London: Macmillan, 1891, pp. 22–3). Many other more recent reports of the same kind could be cited. Among the Tallensi, 'a marriage is not properly consummated until coitus takes place between the partners. ... When a widow remarries ... if she has sexual relations with her new husband she becomes his wife, whether or not the formalities have been completed. If she succeeds in avoiding intercourse with him, she is not his wife, and may sleep with any other man without fear of being accused of adultery' (M. Fortes, *The Web of Kinship Among the Tallensi*, London: Oxford University Press, 1949, p. 106).

M. Douglas

See also: MARRIAGE

Domestic System (See Putting-Out System)

Domestication

A. *Domestication* denotes a social relation between men and animals, in which certain species of the latter are subjugated, kept and bred in captivity, and made dependent on the former.

Dominance

The term is also applied to similar relations between one animal and another (cf. the term *slavery* denoting the same relation of subjugation and dependence among human beings) and by analogy is also applied to cultivated plants.

B. The definition may be illustrated in terms of two important discussions and the issues raised.

1. F. E. Zeuner (in C. Singer, E. J. Holmyard, & A. R. Hall (eds.), *A History of Technology*, Oxford: at the Clarendon Press, 1954, vol. 1, ch. 13, p. 328 et seq.) distinguishes domestication from four comparable relationships:

(a) *Symbiosis* (q.v.) denotes all conditions of living together of two different species, provided both derive advantages therefrom.

(b) *Scavenging* denotes a relationship in which one species lives regularly on the food-debris or waste products of the other. Scavenging approaches true symbiosis when the removal of waste products benefits the producer.

(c) *Social Parasitism* occurs when scavengers prey on their hosts or on their progeny. The domestication by man of reindeer could be regarded as a case of social parasitism. Men control and exploit the tame reindeer, using them for decoy hunting of wild reindeer. Because of their adaptation to the habits of the reindeer, and because of their numerical inferiority, the Tungus and the Samoyed tribes live as social parasites of the animal.

(d) *Taming* occurs when one species whose social medium overlaps another's proceeds to limit the freedom of the latter. In place of the guest-host relationship, there is systematic compulsory incorporation into the social medium of the domesticator. The domestication of elephants has never passed the stage of taming for they are generally allowed to breed in freedom.

2. Evidence on the effects of selective breeding has led to the suggestion that civilized man is himself in a sense a 'domesticated animal'. J. B. S. Haldane bases his opposition to this view on the fact that domestic animals have become highly specialized, and have lost many of the characters of their wild ancestors as a result of artificial selection. 'From a purely animal point of view man is unspecialized in many important ways. No other animal can swim a mile, walk twenty miles, and then climb forty feet up a tree. Many civilized men can do this without much difficulty. If so it is rather silly to regard them as physically degenerate ... Perhaps the greatest difference between men and domestic animals is a very simple one ... as the result of domestication, they [domestic animals]

have ceased to a greater or less extent to communicate with members of their own species. ... In particular, with the abolition of mating choice, sexual communication, including the activities called courtship, has atrophied or been grossly simplified ... Whereas man has hypertrophied communication' (J. B. S. Haldane, 'The Argument from Animals to Men', Huxley Memorial Lecture, 1956, published in *Journal of the Royal Anthropological Institute*, 1956, vol. 86, pt. II, p. 5).

M. Douglas

Dominance

A. In urban ecology *dominance* denotes the coordinating and orienting influence exerted from a place, usually a central city or its central business district, over activities carried on in the surrounding area. Although the concept is used largely in a spatial context and, for the most part, without reference to the mechanics of dominance, it may also be used in analysis of social structures. In that event, dominance is an attribute of the function or class of functions that determine the conditions under which other functions must operate.

B. 1. This usage is drawn by analogy from two conceptions of 'dominance' found in other sciences. (a) According to one view, contributed by plant ecologists, the dominant is the species whose functions are such that they regulate the conditions essential to the functions of associated species (W. B. McDougall, *Plant Ecology*, Philadelphia: Lea & Febiger, 1931, pp. 78–92). (b) The second conception derives from physiological studies of organisms. That region of the organism is said to dominate which is most responsive to both internal and environmental stimuli and which, therefore, is able to maintain the integration of the organism essential to its survival in a given environment (C. M. Child, *Physiological Foundations of Behavior*, New York: Henry Holt, 1924, ch. X).

2. R. E. Park applied these two conceptions to the human community. The first, the dominance exercised by certain members of a population through their performance of a key function, is operative in the development of community structure. Once a structure is achieved, however, dominance assumes a form similar to that observed by physiologists, i.e. it becomes a property of the system rather than of individuals (*Human Communities*, Glencoe, Ill.: The Free Press, 1952, p. 161).

3. R. D. McKenzie's use of the term, following the analogy supplied by Child, referred to the relations of superordination-subordination among the parts of an organized area resulting from a territorial division of labour. Thus the central business district within the city, and the city within a metropolitan area, by virtue of their central office, financial, communication, and other mediating functions, exercise control or dominance over their adjacent, tributary areas ('The Concept of Dominance and World Organization', *American Journal of Sociology*, vol. 33, 1927–8, pp. 28–42). It is also observed that dominance diminishes in a gradient fashion with distance from a focal point (R. D. McKenzie, *The Metropolitan Community*, New York: McGraw-Hill, 1933, p. 312).

Amos H. Hawley

See also: ECOLOGY

Dominion

A. The word *dominion* means authority, power to rule, supremacy; as in such a phrase as 'dominion over' a particular territory. The usage moved from the *idea* of rule to the *territory* which was ruled: the object of rule became the dominion.

B. It is in designating the object of rule that the word has been given special significance in Britain.

1. Territories which the King ruled at home or overseas were his dominions. Then the Act declaring England to be a Commonwealth Government in 1649 referred to 'the people of England and of all the dominions and territories thereunto belonging'. In 1901 the words, 'the British Dominions beyond the Seas', to cover all British overseas territories, were added to the Royal Titles; since 1867 Canada had been known as the Dominion of Canada.

2. From 1907 onwards the word was reserved for *British colonies which were self-governing*. In that year the Imperial Conference directed that the phrase *self-governing Dominions* should be used to distinguish those parts of the British Empire which were fully self-governing in their domestic affairs. The phrase soon became shortened to *the Dominions*. *Dominion status* was said to be possessed by Canada, Australia, South Africa, New Zealand, and, from 1922, the Irish Free State. *Dominion status* was defined by the Imperial Conference in 1926 (see *Commonwealth*) and given legal effect by the *Statute of Westminster*, 1931 (a full discussion will be found in K. C. Wheare, *The Statute of Westminster and Do-*

minion Status, Oxford: The Clarendon Press, 1938 and subsequent editions). Briefly, a Dominion was understood to be a former British dependency which had attained equality of status with Britain, and which shared with Britain common allegiance to the Crown and membership of the British Commonwealth of Nations. It was distinguished from non-self-governing colonies, and from India.

3. Dominion status was conferred on India, Pakistan, and Ceylon in 1947. But since that latter date the term *Dominion* has fallen into disuse, except in Australia and New Zealand. In Canada, South Africa, India, Pakistan, and Ceylon it was held by many people to convey a sense of British supremacy which no longer fitted the facts. India, Pakistan, and South Africa have since become Republics. The term *Dominion* was not applied as a description in the Federation of Malaya Independence and Ghana Independence Acts of 1957—although in the second of these Ghana is described as 'part of Her Majesty's dominions'. *Dominion* is being replaced by *Member of the Commonwealth*.

J. D. B. Miller

See also: COMMONWEALTH

Double-Unilineal

A. *Double-unilineal* is a term used to describe descent systems in which both patrilineal and matrilineal descent groups are recognized as being corporate, at the same time and in respect of the same person. They are comparatively rare. Other terms used for double-unilineal descent are double descent, dual descent, and double unilateral descent. The terms bilateral, ambilateral, and ambilineal have also been used, but the first is now used almost invariably only for the recognition of kinship ties and the latter for non-unilineal descent groups, in which continuity through the generations is maintained by using male and female links without set order (see R. Firth, 'A Note on Descent Groups in Polynesia', *Man*, vol. LVII, 1957, pp. 2–8).

B. G. P. Murdock (*Social Structure*, New York: The Macmillan Co., 1949, p. 45) lists several different combinations of patrilineal and matrilineal descent, none of which are properly speaking double-unilineal, as in all of them there is merely an alternative rule of descent. He defines a system of double-unilineal descent (which he calls double descent) as one in which 'the society possesses both patrilineal and matrilineal kin groups, and a person is affiliated

Dream

at the same time with the patrilineal group of his father and the matrilineal group of his mother'. Murdock ignores the criterion of corporateness, which is, however, crucial. In many systems the submerged line of descent may be socially significant but does not form the basis of corporate groups; and these are not usually accepted as being double-unilineal systems.

J. Middleton

See also: LINEAL
MATRILINEAL
UNILINEAL

Dowry (See **Bride-Price**)

Dream
A. A *dream* ordinarily designates the remembered portion of the succession of images or fantastic ideas and associations presented, probably continuously, to the mind during sleep.

B. The dream, which we must suppose an universal human phenomenon, has been very widely regarded in human societies as a temporary glimpse into a higher or more basic metaphysical reality. For this reason the vision is accepted as a guide for life among American Indians, and spirit-possession in Asia and elsewhere as a source of religion, myth, and supernatural curing (R. Benedict, 'The Vision in Plains Culture', *American Anthropologist*, vol. 24, 1922, pp. 1–23). Dreaming was regarded by E. B. Tylor as one of the bases of animism (q.v.). A. F. C. Wallace has suggested that myths may so often resemble dreams in content and symbolism because they in fact once were dreams of a culture-hero or shaman ('Revitalization Movements', *American Anthropologist*, vol. 58, 1956, pp. 264–81).

C. Like the vision, spirit-possession, epilepsy, ecstasy, hallucination, hypnosis, and the mystical experience, to all of which it is related, dreaming is regarded in much of modern psychology as an activity of the mind in states of partial abeyance of functioning of the conscious ego and sensory reality-testing; the dream is therefore not a state of 'higher' consciousness of reality but of lower, i.e. apocopated or fragmentary. Since, from this perspective, dreams proceed not from outside empirical reality, but rather from deep within the wishful organism, temporarily unfettered from reality in sleep, the uses of dreaming for rationalization, solace, or cure of ills becomes readily understandable. This psychological insight is owed almost entirely to one of the most significant and revolutionary books of modern times, S. Freud's *The Interpretation of Dreams* (New York: The Macmillan Co., 1913; see also C. Abraham, *Dreams and Myths*, New York: The Journal of Nervous and Mental Disease Publishing Co., 1913).

D. In American anthropology, under the impetus of E. Sapir, field workers began to collect dreams from native tribes as part of total ethnography, but merely as documents and for interpretation by others. In England, on the other hand, the use of the newer psychological understanding of dreams began earlier with W. H. R. Rivers and C. G. Seligman. In recent years, however, particularly among American field anthropologists, there has been a tendency to do more than collect dreams passively as documents, and the beginning of a tendency to interpret dreams through the use of the field ethnographer's own knowledge and insights (G. Devereux, 'Dream Learning and Individual Ritual Differences in Mohave Shamanism', *American Anthropologist*, vol. 59, 1957, pp. 1036–45; A. F. C. Wallace, 'Dreams and the Wishes of the Soul: A Type of Psychoanalytic Theory Among the Seventeenth Century Iroquois', *American Anthropologist*, vol. 60, 1958, pp. 234–48; G. Roheim, *The Eternal Ones of the Dream*, New York: International Universities Press, 1945: G. Roheim, 'Technique of Dream Analysis and Field Work in Anthropology', *Psychoanalytic Quarterly*, vol. 18, 1949, pp. 471–9; D. Eggan, 'The Significance of Dreams for Anthropological Research', *American Anthropologist*, vol. 51, 1949, pp. 177–98, and 'The Manifest Content of Dreams: A Challenge to Social Science', *American Anthropologist*, vol. 54, 1952, pp. 469–85). The *major* works on the dream by anthropologists are those by W. H. R. Rivers and J. S. Lincoln (W. H. R. Rivers, *Dreams and Primitive Culture*, London: Longmans, Green, 1917–18; J. S. Lincoln, *The Dream in Primitive Cultures*, Baltimore, Md.: Williams & Wilkins, 1935).

Weston La Barre

See also: UNCONSCIOUS

Drive
A. *Drive* denotes the energy, particular to a class of purposive behaviour, that *drives* the

organism to satisfy a need. Examples are *sex drive*, *hunger drive*, or *drive for prestige*. Some writers prefer to limit the term to physiological needs. The third example would not then appear in their writings.

B. 1. The term was introduced as a technical term into psychology by R. S. Woodworth in *Dynamic Psychology* (New York: Columbia University Press, 1918, passim). Concerned as a functionalist with cause and effect in behaviour, but writing in opposition to W. McDougall, he wanted an omnibus term for motivation other than instinct. He chose the term, *drive*, and its complement, *mechanism*, taking them from machinery, on the grounds that, as they were used for answering 'why' and 'how' questions respectively about the working of a machine, so might they be used in psychological explanation. The distinction between drive and mechanism was not an absolute one. Any mechanism could become a drive. What this in effect meant was that learned activities could become drives if they aroused our interest. Drives then were conceived as specific and related to all the different activities we carried out in the course of daily behaviour. This was in contrast to explanation of motivation in terms of a few, genetically given instincts. Desires, emotions, sentiments, attitudes, motives, and mental set were all examples of drives in Woodworth's sense. The date of the introduction of the term relative to the date of the first translation of Freud's work is probably responsible for the German word *Trieb*, being translated as *instinct* instead of *drive*, which would have been more appropriate.

2. Woodworth's term won popularity as an alternative to McDougall's use of *instinct*, and as a way of expressing a theoretical standpoint opposed to McDougall's. But the dropping of its complement, *mechanism*, and the growth of interest in physiological researches on motivation led to a physiological specialization of *drive* for which there was already some justification in Woodworth's very catholic treatment. According to this, drive is considered to originate from some internal disturbance of the organism as a result of some deficit or some recurrent condition of the blood chemistry, and to manifest itself in (a) an increase in general activity, (b) in certain reactions preparatory to a consummatory one, and (c) in a lowered threshold to stimuli setting off the consummatory response, which then ends the activity from which the drive is inferred.

3. The more general sense of the word has come into favour again as a result of the influence of Hull's learning theory, in which drive is a key concept. A distinction is now made between *primary* and *secondary drives*. The first are inborn drives, largely concerned with vital bodily needs, and can be equated with the physiological specialization of *drive*. The second, known also as *acquired drives*, are derived by association with satisfaction of the first. *Acquired drives* are used by many social psychologists to account for the formation attitudes (q.v.).

W. H. N. Hotopf

See also: INSTINCT
NEED

Dual Organization (See **Moiety**)

Dualism

A. In general, *dualism* denotes a system which is founded on a double principle, or a twofold distinction.

B. 1. In philosophy it is any theory which considers the ultimate nature of the universe to consist of two mutually irreducible elements, such as mind and matter. Another kind of philosophical usage is given by J. W. Yolton ('The Dualism of Mind', *Journal of Philosophy*, vol. LI, 1954, p. 173), who concerns himself with two types of dualism in epistemological theory: '(1) epistemological dualism, which divides the knowing process into two factors, mental events and physical stimuli, with the former representing, in some fashion, the latter; and (2) ontological dualism, which divides the real into the mental and the physical'.

2. Varying usage in the social sciences may be illustrated by the following examples. (a) Reference is sometimes made to *ethical* dualism. It is pointed out, for example, that 'all tribal religions preach a dualism of ethics, one for the members of the tribe who are bound together by ties of kinship and by union to preserve existence; and the other, for the rest of the world' (E. A. Ross, *Social Control*, New York: The Macmillan Co., 1901, p. 72). (b) In the relationship between politics and economics, whereby the economic and political orders were considered to be co-ordinate, 'a new species of dualism was ... envisaged ...' (L. Lipson, *The Great Issues of Politics*, New York: Prentice-Hall, 1954, p. 186). (c) A dualism in social structure has been postulated: according to Professor Giddings, 'Civilized society affords four main

Due Process

sets of dualistic associations: political, juristic, economic, and cultural' (E. S. Bogardus, *A History of Social Thought*, Los Angeles: Jesse Ray Miller, 2nd edn., 1928, p. 479).

Oscar Svarlien

See also: MONISM
 PLURALISM

Due Process

A. *Due process* may be defined as legal action (legislative, judicial, or administrative) that accords with procedural forms sanctified by English and early American usage or with fundamental concepts of liberty and justice accepted by the English-speaking peoples. The substance of the legal action must avoid arbitrariness or other violation of the same fundamental concepts of liberty and justice, including freedom of speech, press, and religion, as they are provided for by the 1st Amendment to the Constitution of the United States.

B. 1. The concept of *due process of law*, deemed equivalent to the phrase 'by the law of the land', in Magna Carta, was part of the tradition of English liberties brought to North America by the colonists. It or its equivalent appears in many colonial charters and constitutional documents and in the Virginia Declaration of Rights, and in most American state constitutions. The 5th Amendment to the federal constitution (adopted immediately following the ratification of the Constitution itself), declares that 'no person shall be ... deprived of life, liberty, or property, without due process of law'. In 1868, following the Civil War, the 14th Amendment, using the same language, extended the limitation, which had heretofore applied only to the federal government, to the state governments as well.

2. Before the Civil War it was generally believed that the provision related only to procedural matters, to the way in which laws must be applied by courts or administrative officials, and not to the substance of laws (except as that might deal with matters of procedure). The first relevant decision by the United States Supreme Court dealt with procedure and assumed that the test of what was or was not according to due process was purely historical. The Court declared that, for a test, 'we must look to those settled usages and modes of proceeding existing in the common and statute law of England, before the emigration of our ancestors', and the suitability of which for American conditions they had confirmed

by 'acting on' them 'after the settlement of this country' (*Den ex dem. Murray v. Hoboken Land and Improvement Co.*, 1856, 18 How. 272, p. 374, sect. 277). But during the succeeding quarter of a century two important changes took place. The 14th Amendment made the clause applicable to state governments; and the rapid industrialization of the country gave rise to momentous economic and social problems, with the consequence that states enacted all manner of regulatory legislation, much of which was strongly opposed by business interests.

In 1884, the Supreme Court made a marked departure from the doctrine of the Murray case. While the grounds on which the decision was rested seemed in this case to enlarge the freedom of legislatures, permitting them to adopt new procedures as long as they respected the 'fundamental principles of liberty and justice which lie at the base of all our civil and political institutions' (*Hurtado v. California*, 1884, 110 U.S. 516, p. 238, sect. 535), the opinion also declared that the due process clause protected 'the very substance of individual rights to life, liberty, and property' (ibid., pp. 237, sect. 532).

3. In subsequent years the Court has had to apply the 'fundamental principles of liberty and justice' to a great many different procedural devices, but it has steadily refused to essay a definition, although it speaks of 'the concept of ordered liberty', and of 'those canons of decency and fairness which express the notions of justice of English-speaking people', and it has banned 'conduct that shocks the conscience'.

Specifically, it has been held that neither the common law jury nor the grand jury is essential to a fair trial. Nor are the privileges against self-incrimination or against double jeopardy essential to due process. On the other hand, it is essential, for instance, that a person accused of a crime be granted a fair trial by an unbiased court, an opportunity to know the charges made against him, to have competent counsel, and to be permitted to cross-examine opposing witnesses. Each form of action, criminal or civil, has its own standards of due process. Nor is due process limited to the actual process of adjudication; it includes the prohibition of unreasonable searches and seizures and of pretrial coercion to obtain confessions.

C. Once the idea of due process as 'fundamental principles of liberty and justice' came to prevail, it was soon extended to the substance of legislation. At an early date it became estab-

212

lished that rates charged by railroads or other public utilities must be 'reasonable', not 'confiscatory', and, more specifically, that they must permit the owner to earn a 'fair return' on the 'fair value' of his property engaged in the business (see *Minnesota Rate Cases*, 1890, 134 U.S. 418, p. 970 ff., and *Smyth v. Ames*, 1898, 169 U.S. 466, pp. 819 ff.).

D. The vagueness of the term *due process* and its identification with the idea of justice provided a back door through which the philosophies of natural law (q.v.) and natural rights (q.v.) were brought into American constitutional law. When *laissez-faire* theory, supported by ideas of natural rights to freedom of contract, choice of vocation, and the like, prevailed, the courts used the due process clause to strike down much legislation that offended against these notions. The high water mark was reached in the 1920s—long after the doctrine of *laissez-faire* had passed its peak—in decisions invalidating minimum wage legislation and laws extending the practice of rate-fixing beyond the rather limited category of 'businesses affected with a public interest'. In the early thirties, however, the Supreme Court radically revised its concept of what was 'reasonable'. Today it is very rare that a legislature will enact a statute affecting property rights or freedom of contract so arbitrarily that the courts invalidate it.

In another direction, however, the notion of substantive due process has in recent years been given a greatly enlarged interpretation. Particularly, the whole area of freedom of speech, press, and religion is now protected against state action through the due process clause of the 14th Amendment in precisely the same way that it is protected against the federal government by the 1st Amendment.

J. Roland Pennock

See also: Civil Liberties
Civil Rights

Duolocal (See **Residence**)

Duty
A. 1. *Duty* is sometimes used in a *very wide sense* to designate any actions (or even abstentions from action) which are enjoined by rules accepted as governing any important sphere of social life or co-operative enterprise.

2. Most often in common usage the word is used *more narrowly* to refer to the actions or services required of one who has some relatively enduring *role* or *function* to perform in a social group. Hence we speak of the *duties* of a husband, a citizen, a policeman, or of the umpire of a game. The word usually carries the implication that what is to be done is a matter of considerable importance, or involves some sacrifice. Hence what rules of etiquette or correct speech require is *not* thought or spoken of as a duty, and the contrast and conflict of *duty* and *interest* (q.v.) are commonplaces of the moralist.

B. 1. *Legal duties*: In modern Anglo-American legal usage, whenever legal rules require persons to do or to abstain from any action the word *duty* is appropriate. Distinctions have been drawn by jurists between the *relative* duties of the civil law (e.g. those arising under a contract or in the law of tort) which have as their correlatives legal rights vested in private individuals, and the *absolute* duties of the criminal laws to which there are no such correlative individual rights. Other schemes of classification distinguish between duties voluntarily assumed or created by contract and duties imposed by the law independently of the choice of those subject to them, to which category the duties of the criminal law and the law of tort belong. The principal controversies of legal theory over the concept of duty concern its analysis. One view shared by both the English 'Imperative' school of jurisprudence and the American 'Realists' defines the notion in terms of the *chance* or *likelihood* that if the action required to be done by law is not done, the person required to do it will suffer the punishment or sanction threatened by the law. This is most clearly expressed by Austin—and also by Holmes. 'But where there is the smallest chance of incurring the smallest evil, the expression of a wish amounts to a command, and, therefore, imposes a duty ... when I am talking *directly* of the chance of incurring the evil, ... I employ the term *duty*' (J. Austin, *The Province of Jurisprudence Determined: Lecture I*, London: John Murray, 2nd edn., 1861, pp. 8, 10; cf. also J. Bentham, *Fragment on Government*, Oxford: Clarendon Press, 1891, ch. v). 'A legal duty so called is nothing but a prediction that if a man does or omits certain things he will be made to suffer in this or that way by judgment of the court' (O. W. Holmes, *Collected Legal Papers*, New York: Harcourt Brace, 1920, p. 169).

The opposed view insists on the essentially normative character of statements of legal duty *and their independence of the probability of official action*. Thus 'The rule which a judge

Duty

applies in a concrete case does not tell the judge how he actually will decide, but how he ought to decide' (H. Kelsen, *General Theory of Law and State*, 20th Century Legal Philosophy Series, vol. I., Cambridge, Mass.: Harvard University Press, 1945, p. 168). Other theorists insist that duties may exist even where the legal system provides no sanction for them. Such duties are often called duties of imperfect obligation.

2. *Moral duty:* In much philosophical discussion the word *duty* is used in a wide sense (similar to the legal usage noted above) to refer to any action which a person has a moral reason for doing or not doing. Some object to this usage on the ground that 'morality' comprises many different types of reason for acting and conduct which is morally desirable simply on account of its consequences or is morally admirable as a 'work of supererogation' or heroism should be distinguished from duties which represent a moral *minimum* prescribed by well established rules essential for social life.

3. *Political duty:* This expression when not used merely to refer to the legal duties of state officials (legislative, judicial, or administrative) which arise under what is often called 'public' law, refers to the duty (or alleged duty) *of the citizen to obey the law*. This is a *moral* duty differing from others in that *the range of actions to be done or foreborne are specified indirectly by reference to the will of other persons who have authority to make law*. The duty is essentially one of obedience or *allegiance* (q.v.) to a *political authority*.

The central questions of European political philosophy have been concerned with (a) the manner in which and conditions under which such a duty arises and (b) the extent of this duty. For example, the early view that such a duty was imposed on man by God or nature: the various forms of the social contract theory to the effect that this duty could only arise through the promises expressed or tacit of those required to obey. Other theorists as diverse as Hume, John Stuart Mill, Hegel, and T. H. Green claimed that such a duty cannot be assimilated to the obligation voluntarily incurred by contract, but is explicable only in terms of the values which organized societies promote. The Utilitarian conception that there is no duty to obey the law as *such* but only to obey where obedience will *directly or indirectly* produce more good than evil is perhaps now acceptable to most ordinary men. It meets however with two objections. First, that in the outlook of many there is always some sphere of conduct (which in modern states includes matters of economic welfare and defence) where the individual is not morally free to make obedience conditional on his judgment of the consequences. Secondly, the duty of obedience is by many not conceived merely as a special case of maximizing good or minimizing harm for humanity indiscriminately but as something specially owed by the citizen to the members of his own society.

H. L. A. Hart

Dynamics (See Statics)

Dysfunction (See Function)

E

Ecology

A. The concept is borrowed from biology, where it means the study of relations between organisms and environment. In biological usage it includes relations between individual organisms and environment (autecology) and between groups and environment (synecology). In social science it is restricted to human synecology, that is, the study of relations between human groups (or populations) and their respective environments, especially their physical environments.

In the broadest sense, human ecology may be defined as the study of relations between human groups (or populations) and their environments. All definitions agree on this essential characteristic of the field. In addition, most definitions agree that human ecology includes the study of two aspects of group structure, both of which depend strongly on sustenance relations between man and physical environment, namely, spatial structure and the division of labour. Beyond this central core of agreement, definitions differ with respect to such matters as (a) degree of inclusiveness of the field, (b) selection of explanatory variables.

B. Among social scientists several differences in definition may be found, especially as related to degree of inclusiveness and criteria of identification of the field.

1. One point of view emphasizes the importance of obtaining complete descriptions of group adjustments to local physical environments. It makes this study embrace simultaneously all relevant features of man's organic body, the external physical environment, group culture, and interrelations among men, all of which operate to produce a distinctive kind of group life within a given territory (R. Mukerjee, *Man and His Habitation*, London: Longmans, Green, 1940).

2. A second point of view restricts human ecology in actual practice to the study of one limited aspect of the total complex, namely, the study of direct interrelations between human populations and their physical environments (C. L. White & G. T. Renner, *Geography: An Introduction to Human Ecology*, New York:

D. Appleton-Century, 1936); it looks for 'explanations' among differences in physical environments rather than interrelations among men.

3. A third point of view, illustrated by R. E. Park, emphasizes a subsocial type of interaction among men as the distinguishing feature of human ecology. This ecological interaction, which occurs indirectly merely through affecting limited parts of the physical environment on which participants depend, differs from truly human social interaction involving language. Human ecology, studies the impersonal, subsocial aspects of group structure that arise and operate through ecological interaction, as contrasted with those political and moral parts of group structure that depend principally on social interaction ('Human Ecology', *American Journal of Sociology*, vol. XLII, 1936–7, pp. 1–15).

4. A fourth point of view, represented by A. H. Hawley, also emphasizes various kinds of interrelations among men but ignores the distinction between ecological and social interaction as conceived by Park. According to Hawley, the human ecologist studies repetitive forms of human groups that arise in the course of symbiotic and commensal sustenance relations as the populations of human communities adjust to their physical environments (*Human Ecology*, New York: Ronald Press, 1950, pp. 66–7).

James A. Quinn

See also: COMMENSALISM
        DOMINANCE
        INVASION
        SUCCESSION
        ZONAL HYPOTHESIS

Econometrics (See Mathematical Economics)

Economic Competition

A. In economics *competition* (q.v.) has retained a meaning close to its general definition as a social process and includes elements of striving and/or rivalry with respect to scarce goods, of attempts at excellence or the excelling of another, of rationality as the actual or postulated psychological approach to the market

Economic Competition

situation, and of the effort to maximize the achievement of goals, in this case profit. Sub-forms of competition in economics are defined by the conditions of the market situation and by the dominance of striving or rivalry.

B. In the classical literature of political economy *competition* means open rivalry in the market between buyers or sellers of a good or service (A. Smith, *An Inquiry Into the Nature and Causes of the Wealth of Nations* (published 1776), New York: Random House, Modern Library edn., 1937, pp. 56-7). In the neo-classical literature this rivalry among dealers in the market—*free competition*—comes to connote rational behaviour whose consequence, under certain well-known assumptions, is the optimum allocation of resources (A. Marshall, *Principles of Economics*, London: Macmillan, 8th edn., 1920, p. 471). The conception of competition has become more complex in modern economic theory. The notion of competition as rivalry is retained in all those concepts which envisage the individual as having a policy with respect to his price, the character of his product, and his relations with his fellow competitors—*imperfect competition, monopolistic competition, oligopolistic or oligopsonistic competition, workable competition, non-price competition,* and *cut-throat* or *ruinous competition*. In addition, however, a set of concepts has evolved which envisage competition as a process which takes place in the market and to which the individual, given rationality and the desire to maximize income and conduct his enterprise as efficiently as possible, makes merely passive adaptations without any control on his part over either the price or the character of the product, and without any sense of rivalry with his fellow competitors. These concepts are those of *perfect* and *pure competition*. These latter concepts must be defined first, before those implying rivalry can be grasped.

1. In one usage *perfect competition* is said to take place in perfect markets, i.e. in markets where knowledge of all the data relevant to the bargain is perfectly available to all participants and where all resources are perfectly divisible and perfectly mobile. *Pure competition* is defined as competition among a group of sellers or buyers none of whom has any control over the price of the goods and services bought or sold in that market by virtue of his size, the character of his product, legal or extra-legal privilege conferred upon him, etc. If competition is pure, individual sellers or buyers face a hori-

zontal average revenue or cost curve; if pure and perfect the value of the marginal product of each factor of production is the same in every use. In another usage *perfect competition* would include *all* the phenomena described above (J. Robinson, *The Economics of Imperfect Competition*, London: Macmillan, 1938, pp. 88-9).

2. In one usage *imperfect competition* is the antithesis of perfect competition and *monopolistic competition* is the antithesis of pure competition, whereas in another usage *imperfect competition* is a more inclusive term antithetical to both perfect and pure competition, while *monopoly* would simply be a sub-form of imperfect competition (E. Chamberlin, *The Theory of Monopolistic Competition*, London: Oxford University Press, 6th edn., 1949, p. 69; J. Robinson, *The Economics of Imperfect Competition*, pp. 320-3). Individuals in imperfect or monopolistic competition as a rule face sloping average revenue or cost curves. *Oligopolistic—oligopsonistic* when applying to buyers rather than sellers—*competition*, which is a sub-class of monopolistic competition, is competion among sellers so few in number that each takes into account the effect of his tactics on the tactics of his rivals. Unless special assumptions are made concerning rivals' reactions, it is not possible to specify the average revenue curve which faces an oligopolist.

3. *Workable competition* is competition in a situation where there are handicaps to pure or perfect competition, but where it is regarded as sufficiently vigorous not to require public intervention to support it. Competition is said to be workable when in the market there is an adequate number of independent sources of supply or demand, reasonably free entry into the market, and a satisfactory rate of technological change. E. S. Mason writes as follows: 'Competition becomes unworkable if a firm or firms possess an "unreasonable" degree of market power. A major tenet of antitrust philosophy is that a policy of enforced competition is possible only if the rivalry of all firms in the market is such as to limit sharply the ability of each to earn more than [pure] competitive profit' (*Economic Concentration and the Monopoly Problem*, Cambridge, Mass.: Harvard University Press, 1957, p. 328).

4. *Non-price competition* is competition in the terms of sale or in the attributes of a product or service other than its price, for instance, in quality, packing, advertising, general surroundings, credit and shipment terms. Non-price competition is absent if competition is pure and perfect.

5. Colloquially in economic discussion *cutthroat* or *ruinous competition* is sometimes used to denote intense rivalry between few firms which drives prices below average costs of production of the low cost producers. It occurs in oligopolistic markets, especially where overhead costs are high and excess capacity is prevalent. *Unfair competition* is sometimes used by economic agents for any mode of competition that they dislike.

Stefan Stykolt

See also: COMPETITION
          PROCESS

Economic Determinism (See Cultural Determinism; Determinism)

Economic Equilibrium

A. The literal meaning of *equilibrium* is 'equal weights in the two arms of a balance'.

1. The use nearest to this literal sense occurs in connection with measurable quantities, such as income and expenditure in a budget, exports and imports in a trade balance, trade items and long-term capital transfers in a balance of payments. In these uses, *equilibrium* need have no analytical predictive, or evaluative connotation, although, in fact, it often has.

2. But economists attempt to do more than simply equate two sets of items, and introduce other economic variables considered relevant for a more significant definition. A system is then said to be in equilibrium when the forces acting in it are such that it has no tendency to change its condition. A book at rest on a table is in equilibrium relative to its surroundings. On the other hand, a book dropping through the air is not. Similarly in economics a price (quantity, firm, balance of payments, etc.) is in equilibrium if there are, on balance, no forces acting upon it which tend to change it.

3. In economics *equilibrium* is used more specifically of the state to which a system tends to return after being temporarily disturbed (see D. below, *stable equilibrium*).

B. From this general notion of equilibrium the following *particular* uses that have been made of the concept can be distinguished: the common element in all usages is the notion of a state in which certain selected interrelated variables are mutually compatible.

1. *Analytical:* The most fundamental use of *equilibrium* in economics is that of a device in abstract theory. It is employed to characterize a state of a model which contains interrelated variables and to analyse causal connections between events that have been conceptually isolated. It does not in this sense refer to an observed or described state (see (2) below) but to a mental construction or model in which there is no inherent tendency to change. The model and its interrelated variables are then said to be in equilibrium. The same observed state may be an equilibrium in relation to one model, a disequilibrium in relation to another. *Equilibrium* in this sense is ethically and politically neutral.

2. *Descriptive:* With reference to observable states and concrete economic situations it is used to characterize a historical situation as one that has lasted or will last for a relatively long time without significant change. But the transition from the analytical to the descriptive use is liable to give rise to confusion. Thus stability of equilibrium in sense (1) is fundamentally different from stability in sense (2).

3. *Normative:* Equilibrium here refers to a balance that is considered desirable. Social ideals are incorporated in the meaning of *equilibrium*. The normative meaning of *equilibrium* is found both in *positive economics* (where the values are often implicit, sometimes explicit) and in *welfare economics* (where *equilibrium* is identified with 'optimum' in relation to some value premises). Here again, the transition from use (1) to use (3) is not always logically tidy. Some authors attempt to make the concept serve all three purposes simultaneously.

Two comments must be made here in the light of these three particular usages: (a) The objection to the inclusion of social ideals in the definition of *equilibrium* is that the concept loses thereby some of its analytical power. Instead of discussing undesirable consequences as possible objections to achieving *equilibrium* (in the neutral sense), one is forced into a sterile dispute over the 'proper' definition of *equilibrium* (in the normative sense). (b) Confusion has arisen between sense (1) and sense (3), because it was suggested that a situation in which no one has opportunity and incentive to improve his position must be an optimum. But this is false, for equilibrium (in the analytical sense) is determined by the political, legal, and technological constraints in which it is reached and the kinds of competition that prevail. Although individuals are making the best of their situation, the situation may be bad. No value judgement enters. In the analytical sense, economists speak of under-employment equilibrium if no individual will find it to his advantage to do anything which will increase employment. On the other hand, in the normative sense, unemployment is often considered to be incompatible with *equilibrium.*

The normative use can be transformed into the analytical use if political action to achieve the social goals is built into the model as a dependent variable. Thus, instead of defining equilibrium so as to include full employment, it can be assumed that whenever unemployment occurs the Government takes action against it. Given the will and the ability of the state to achieve full employment, an inclusion of the state's behaviour into a model would make unemployment incompatible with equilibrium in the analytical, value-free sense.

C. 1. *Particular equilibrium* is the equilibrium of any part of the economic system: the individual is in equilibrium if, given his income and the prices he has to pay in the market, he spends his income in such a way as to get maximum satisfaction. The firm is in equilibrium if, given the costs it incurs from hiring factors and the proceeds it can raise from sales, it maximises its profits. The industry is in equilibrium if no new firms enter or leave, etc.

2. *General equilibrium* is the equilibrium of the system as a whole. The theory of general equilibrium investigates the conditions for the consistency of particular equilibrium positions. If the separate plans of different individuals and groups interact in such a way that desired change is not possible, and possible change is not desired, the economic system is said to be in equilibrium. Those with incentive must lack the opportunity and those with opportunity must lack incentive. The mutual determination of economic variables has been likened to the equilibrium position of three balls in a bowl. The ultimate equilibrium will depend on (a) the size and shape of the bowl, (b) the size, shape, and number of balls, and (c) the balance of the forces of gravity and of reaction. Similarly, economic equilibrium is determined by (a) the external obstacles to the satisfaction of wants, (b) the nature of the wants and resources of individuals and (c) the force that induces each individual to make the best use of his income.

D. A position of equilibrium will tend to perpetuate itself unless disturbed by forces outside the system. But this equilibrium may be either such that, once disturbed, forces will be set to work which will restore the initial position. We then speak of *stable* equilibrium. Or it may be such that, if disturbed, the system will move away from its initial position. We then speak of *unstable* equilibrium. Or it may be such that, after a disturbance, it settles down to a new equilibrium. We then speak of *neutral* equilibrium.

P. Streeten

See also: SOCIAL EQUILIBRIUM

Economic Geography

A. There are two related but somewhat distinct uses of the term *economic geography* to denote a field of investigation:

1. The first, earlier, definition starts from the notion that geography is best defined as 'earth description' and that economic geography is concerned solely with the study of the effect of the physical environment on man's economic activities or the relation of economic phenomena to the geographic distribution of resources. Since the discipline at one time was defined in this fashion, and since its development in recent years has been very rapid, the persistence of this older definition, particularly among those who are not themselves geographers, is readily understood.

2. Within the discipline of geography, economic geography is generally recognized as that group of studies whose purpose is to account for the location and arrangement of economic phenomena on the various portions of the earth's surface. In recent decades the scope of the discipline has been broadened to include all kinds of economic activities, the only restrictions being that they are readily identifiable and that their importance and position in earth-space be readily ascertainable. The phenomena of economic geography, therefore, appear to be identical with those of economics, *but the geographer's interest is confined to their analysis within a spatial frame of reference.*

In 1940, one introductory text defined the subject as 'the study of the distribution of economic activities and their relations to their physical environment' (L. E. Klim, O. P. Starkey, & N. F. Hall, *Introductory Economic Geography*, New York: Harcourt, Brace, 1940, p. 1); while another (E. Huntington, *Principles of Economic Geography*, New York: Wiley, 1940, pp. 1–2) stated that the main concern of economic geography is to 'discover ways in which the distribution of physical conditions influences the methods by which people satisfy their needs for food, clothing, shelter, tools, and other products'. By 1956, however, the third edition of the former text (with L. E. Klim, O. P. Starkey, J. A. Russell, & V. H. English as authors) stated simply, 'Economic geography describes and analyzes the distribution of man's economic activities'. In so far as these approaches step beyond the strictly economic aspects of human existence and concern themselves with the broader social features of spatial interaction, they are considered by the related field of *social geography*.

B. The approach to economic geography has been predominantly inductive, beginning, in nearly all cases with the identification and classification of the phenomena and proceeding with a description of its location, nearly always in the form of a map portraying its distribution. Lacking precedent in the use of a spatial frame of reference, economic geographers have devoted much time to the development of systems of classification that would facilitate description and analysis. These systems have done much to foster precise description, which is considered prerequisite to analysis.

In keeping with the inductive approach, the economic geographer normally begins his analyses with an attempt to discover the extent and kinds of order that appear within the spatial distributions he has described. After inspection has revealed the existence of certain patterns and arrangements, he is ready to 'lay bare the rationale' of those distributions (W. Smith, *Geography and the Location of Industry, an Inaugural Lecture*, 1951, Liverpool: The University Press, 1952, p. 3), primarily by formulating and testing hypotheses purporting to explain their existence.

Locational hypotheses for use in geographic analysis have been derived from a variety of sources and have employed divergent philosophies of science. Many of the earlier studies employed a determinism in which only physical factors were considered. That system of thought, known as 'environmental determinism', has long since been abandoned, and all economic geographers now appear to favour the use of hypotheses involving multiple factors, many of which are social and frequently historic in character. There is a considerable trend toward stating these hypotheses mathematically, as space-models, and toward testing them statistically.

C. Convergence between the fields of economics and geography is anticipated in that branch of economics known generally as *location theory*. Since scholars in this area are concerned primarily with discovering how various forces influence the ways in which man chooses locations for his economic activities, their approach has been essentially deductive. It is therefore productive of generalizations concerning the manner in which locational *processes* operate. Economic geography, on the other hand, typically starts with the presumed end-products of those processes. Under these circumstances it is understandable that a majority of the hypotheses used in economic geography are derived from economics; and that the most fertile source of material for refinement and enrichment of the body of location theory has been found in the researches of the economic geographers.

Harold McCarty

See also: ECOLOGY
ECONOMICS

Economic Goods

A. The word *good*, as used in economics, denotes anything which is capable of satisfying a human want. The term has no ethical connotation, however, for it may refer to something which is morally either good or bad. Moreover, it encompasses both material goods and intangible services.

Economists customarily divide goods into two broad categories: *free goods* and *economic goods*. The former are goods which either exist in such abundance that, at a given time and place, they may be obtained without cost, or else, though scarce enough to warrant a price, are in their nature incapable of being marketed (such as sunshine). Economic goods, on the other hand, are useful, scarce, and marketable, which is the equivalent of saying they have economic value. Such goods command a price in the market and they are the ones with which the discipline of economics is concerned.

B. Economic goods may be divided into two classes: (a) consumer goods and services, and (b) productive services or producers' goods and services.

1. Since consumer goods are those which are consumed in their final form, they are frequently referred to as *final products and services*. In other words, consumer goods are distinguished by the fact that they are used directly in the satisfaction of human wants.

2. Producers' goods and services satisfy wants indirectly, for they are used to produce

219

Economic Growth

consumer goods. Although the term *productive services* has been widely adopted to designate both producers' goods and services, economists occasionally use such synonyms as the following: factors of production, productive resources, and instruments of production.

During the last half of the 19th century, most economists attempted to draw sharp lines of distinction between the various 'types' of productive services. As a result, the well-known triad of 'factors' or 'agents' of production, i.e. land, labour (q.v.), and capital (q.v.), became widely used in economic literature. As J. A. Schumpeter (*History of Economic Analysis*, New York: Oxford University Press, 1954, p. 557) has observed, this system of classification still survives largely because it has been found useful in the teaching of elementary economics. Many modern economists are convinced, however, that from an analytical point of view such a division of productive services is frequently misleading. Thus F. H. Knight takes the position that *any* classification of productive services into distinct categories is unrealistic because 'the classes are not only indefinitely numerous, if one thinks of effectively homogeneous types whose units are really interchangeable, but shift their boundaries with the lapse of time' (*The Ethics of Competition*, London: Allen & Unwin, 1935, p. 173).

The fact of long-run interchangeability of productive services has led Knight to conclude that in a broad sense productive services 'are practically all capital' (ibid., p. 173). Although this position is regarded by some authors as extreme, the fact remains that the modern trend in economic theory has been to emphasize the homogeneous character of productive services over long periods of time and to recognize that the specialization of these services is largely, although not exclusively, a short-run problem.

Alfred F. Chalk

See also: CAPITAL
CAPITAL GOODS
COMMODITY
LABOUR
VALUE (Economics)

Economic Growth

A. *Economic growth* is commonly defined as a long-period increase in a country's national income in real terms. The theory of economic growth is concerned with analysing the process of economic growth, the forces responsible for it, and the accompanying structural changes in demand (q.v.) and supply (q.v.).

B. 1. 'A long-period increase' distinguishes economic growth from purely temporary variations in national income associated, for example, with good and bad harvests, or with the effects of the trade cycle. Cyclical changes in national income arise from changes in the degree of utilization of existing productive capacity; economic growth involves an expansion of productive capacity. 'In real terms' serves to distinguish economic growth from the situation in which an increase in the money value of the national income is the result of a rise in the general level of prices.

2. Sometimes, economic growth is restricted in its reference to situations in which there is an increase in some per-unit measure, such as real national income per head of population, or per head of labour force. An increase in aggregate national income, not accompanied by a rise in income per head, may then be called *economic expansion*. The use of per-unit measures directs attention to such matters as changes in productivity and in the ability of the economy to satisfy human needs. It can also be argued that fundamental changes in economic structure, which are of great interest for the theory of economic growth, are only likely to have taken place when there has been an increase in the per-unit measures. Writers who prefer to define economic growth in terms of a national aggregate, not reduced to a per-unit basis, suggest that an aggregate is 'a much safer single measure for comparisons of economic growth—safer in that it precludes the danger of omitting, from consideration of both causes and results of economic growth, a basic element—human population itself' (S. Kuznets, 'Problems in Comparisons of Economic Trends', in S. Kuznets, W. E. Moore, & J. J. Spengler (eds.), *Economic Growth: Brazil, India, Japan*, Durham, N.C.: Duke University Press, 1955, p. 12). It has also been said that for the more developed countries, where the main interest is not the raising of income per head but the maintenance of 'a steady growth in national income so as to avoid chronic deflation or inflation', the national aggregate provides the most satisfactory measure of economic growth (G. M. Meier & R. E. Baldwin, *Economic Development*, New York: Wiley, 1957, p. 5).

3. It has been pointed out that both aggregate and per-unit increases in national income are inadequate as indicators of economic growth because they say nothing about changes in the absolute extent of poverty—'the numbers of those living at the margin of subsistence ... may have grown steadily consistently with a rise in the average income of the population as a whole' (J. Viner, *International Trade and Economic Development*, Oxford: The Clarendon Press, 1953, pp. 99–100). This writer recognizes, however, that if he made the reduction of mass poverty the crucial test of economic growth he would be separating himself from the whole body of literature on the subject. Such measures also assume that growth of output implies or accompanies a rise in qualitative satisfaction—which may not necessarily be the case.

Similar qualifications to the significance of national income definitions and measures of economic growth are made on the grounds that they say nothing about the distribution of income, nor about the standard of living, nor about the 'cost' of increased income in terms of loss of leisure or of disruption of existing social patterns. Against this point of view it is argued that questions of distribution involve value judgements which are best precluded from a general definition of economic growth, and that it is unhelpful to define *economic growth* so that it is synonymous with an increase in economic welfare. On this view, an increase in national income, arising from an expansion of productive capacity, should be called economic growth whether it is devoted to increasing consumption, investment, or military power.

C. *Economic development* and *economic progress* are widely used synonymously with *economic growth*, although economic progress is sometimes used to mean an increase in economic welfare.

A. Hazlewood

See also: National Product

Economic History

A. *Economic history* is the study of the changing network of economic relationships, of the economic aspects of the social institutions of the past.

B. 1. Both it and social history (q.v.) are products of a reaction against narrowly defined political history, particularly the history of government and statecraft. Some of the first writers on the subject had practical interests in view—recommendations concerning contemporary economic policy—and they did not distinguish clearly between economic and social history. They treated *economy* not as an aspect of varied human activities but as a

particular department of human life. W. Cunningham, however, whose work began with a study of the activities of the state and the views of theorists, described economic history as 'not so much the study of a special class of facts as the study of all the facts of a nation's history from a special point of view' (*The Growth of English Industry and Commerce*, Cambridge: The University Press, 1882, p. 5).

2. The nature of the subject and the limits of its scope were matters of bitter controversy in 19th-century Germany, where economic history developed as an alternative to classical economic theory. W. Roscher, K. Knies, K. Bücher, and B. Hildebrand maintained the principle of historical relativism against the 'absolutism' of pure theory, queried the 'cosmopolitanism' of theoretical economists, and demanded a 'national' economic policy, stressed the limitations of deductive theory in economics, particularly reasoning based on the concept of the 'economic man', and used historical models of 'stages' of economic development, not mathematical models. Their aim, in Hildebrand's phrase, was 'to transform political economy into a theory of the laws of the economic development of nations' (B. Hildebrand, *Die Nationalökonomie der Gegenwart und Zukunft*, Frankfurt-am-Main: Literarische Anstalt, 1848, Introduction). The work of this early school of historical economists was carried further by G. Schmoller and W. Sombart. In 1883 Schmoller sharply criticized C. Menger's *Untersuchungen über die Methode der Sozialwissenschaften* (Leipzig: Duncker & Humblot, 1883), and was in turn rebuked by Menger, who attacked 'the erroneous assumption that political economy could be reformed simply by connecting it with historical knowledge' (C. Menger, *Die Irrtümer des Historismus in der deutschen Nationalökonomie*, Wien: Alfred Hölder, 1884). The confrontation of definitions and academic postures in this controversy was an important incident in the development of economic history. Although Sombart's substitution of 'economic systems' for historical 'stages' and M. Weber's use of 'ideal types' came later, the main issues had been stated.

The German controversy had many ripples outside Germany, but in England there was no major academic battle. English economic historians feared 'strangling with definitions' (J. E. Thorold Rogers, *The Economic Interpretation of History*, London: Unwin, 1909, Preface) and did not concern themselves even with boundary disputes. Sir John Clapham stressed 'the marked

Economic Integration

quantitative interests' of economic historians as the hinge of 'methodological distinctiveness', and argued that the four leading questions economic historians should ask in relation to any institution, policy, group, or movement, are: 'how large? how long? how often? how representative?' In his book *A Concise Economic History of Britain* (Cambridge: Cambridge University Press, 1949, Introduction), he related economic history to other branches of history as follows: 'Of all varieties of history the economic is the most fundamental. Not the most important: foundations exist to carry better things'.

3. The Marxist approach to economic history is different. Marx and Engels examined all economic questions in a historical context (see G. Lukács, *Geschichte und Klassenbewusstsein*, Berlin: Der Malik-Verlag, 1923). 'There is a continual movement of growth in productive forces, of destruction in social relations, of formation in ideas: the only immutable thing is the abstraction of movement' (K. Marx, *The Poverty of Philosophy*, (1847), London: Lawrence & Wishart, 1956, p. 122). This approach leads not only to a consistently historical approach to the economic and social sciences but to an interpretation of the whole history of economy and society as a history of class struggles (see under *Social History*). Economic and social history cannot be properly understood apart from each other.

C. Much recent work in economic history has been influenced more by theoretical economists than by historians or social philosophers, and there has been a marked tendency to choose subjects and to employ methods of analysis familiar to contemporary economists. Viewed narrowly as a territory explored by economists, the subject falls into sub-subjects parallel to the sub-divisions in economics itself—the study of prices, the study of fluctuations in income and employment, the study of growth, and the study of welfare. There are also parallels to the division in theoretical economics between macro-economics and micro-economics, some economic historians concerning themselves with quantitative aggregates, where they are available, others examining in detail the history of particular economic units—farms and firms, banks and transport services and enterprises. In dealing with long-term problems, however, economic historians cannot neglect either economic sociology or institutional factors, and in practice the borderline between economic and social history remains confused. (For

the use of economic history in a pragmatic economist's study of economic growth, see W. A. Lewis, *The Theory of Economic Growth*, London: Allen & Unwin, 1955).

A. Briggs

See also: SOCIAL HISTORY

Economic Integration

A. *Economic integration* denotes the unification or centralization of managerial control over two or more economic units.

B. 1. General use of the term *integration* to indicate the operation of more than one production or distribution unit under centralized managerial control is of fairly recent origin. In his presidential address to the Royal Economic Society in 1927, D. H. Macgregor ('Rationalization of Industry', *Economic Journal*, vol. XXXVII, 1927, pp. 521–50) discusses the concept of integration under the heading of rationalization. In the *Encyclopedia of the Social Sciences* (E. R. A. Seligman (ed.), New York: Macmillan, 1930, vol. III, pp. 664–74) integration is discussed by K. Wiedenfeld under the general heading of 'Industrial Combination'.

2. The term *integration* was apparently introduced in an attempt to distinguish between industrial combinations characterized by direct managerial control and operation of the component establishments and the looser form of combination—financial combination, bank control, interlocking directorates, and cartels— where the element of direct managerial control and operation was absent. This distinction was made quite clear by W. L. Thorp (*The Integration of Industrial Operation*, Census Monograph III, Washington: U.S. Government Printing Office, 1924) although he employed the terms *horizontal combination*—a combination of several establishments engaged in similar activities; *vertical combination*—a combination of establishments which operate at successive stages in the process necessary to prepare the final product for market; and *diagonal combination*—a combination including elements of both horizontal and vertical integration, to characterize the several forms of integration. In the Temporary National Economic Committee study of the *Structure of Industry* (TNEC Monograph No. 27, Washington: U.S. Government Printing Office, 1941), directed by W. L. Thorp, the terms *horizontal* and *vertical combination* were replaced by *horizontal* and *vertical integration*. Horizontal integration is the centralization of managerial control over

economic units producing the same products or performing the same function. Vertical integration centralizes the management of economic units engaged in successive stages of economic activity. Although a single economic organization may be organized along lines of both horizontal and vertical integration, such a situation is distinguished from a third form of expansion—diversification—where essentially unrelated lines of business are incorporated under centralized managerial control. In integration the control over the several economic units may be achieved through direct ownership or through contractual arrangements. The central criterion is the exercise of control rather than the formal arrangements by which control is achieved.

3. A good deal of early discussion centred around the question of whether the term *integration* should be applied to situations not characterized by direct technical or functional interdependence of industrial operations. L. K. Frank ('The Significance of Industrial Integration', *Journal of Political Economy*, vol. XXXIII, 1925, pp. 179-95) and F. A. Fetter (*The Masquerade of Monopoly*, New York: Harcourt, Brace, 1931) objected to the use of the term *integration* in reference to horizontal combinations 'where the relationships between the constituent plants and the objectives sought were principally pecuniary' (L. K. Frank, 'The Significance of Industrial Integration', p. 189).

As usage has developed, however, the emphasis on technical or functional interdependence has been replaced by criteria based on the exercise of centralized managerial control. F. Machlup (*The Political Economy of Monopoly*, Baltimore: Johns Hopkins, 1952, p. 110) for example points out that 'in its most common use the term denotes the unification of administrative functions; this may or may not include technological integration'.

Vernon W. Ruttan

See also: ECONOMIC ORGANIZATION

Economic Man

A. Because of the confusion and controversy concerning this term and because of its ideological as well as analytical importance, it is impossible to give a single definition of it. In general it may be said that *economic man* has been conceived in two ways.

1. Among classical economists, the hedonistic psychologists, and philosophers and psychologists of the 19th century, and certainly among the critics of these groups, *economic man* denoted a relatively low-level abstraction thought to be descriptive of human nature. This description stressed self-interestedness, the securing of pleasure and the avoidance of pain, and rational calculation based on excellent knowledge of market conditions.

2. Among modern economists, and perhaps to a greater degree than usually acknowledged, among classical economists, *economic man* denotes a highly abstract model of human action for analytical purposes only. Although in this model self-interest and the pleasure-pain calculus may be assumed, they need not be. In their place may be put the simple assumption that the ends of action are given for the purposes at hand. To this assumption may then be added the assumption of perfect rationality and perfect knowledge of market conditions. Thus it becomes possible to determine the rational allocation of scarce resources to the achievement of certain accepted ends (cf. L. Robbins, *An Essay on the Nature and Significance of Economic Science*, London: Macmillan, 1932, pp. 87-92).

B. The term *economic man* first assumed prominence in the works of critics of economic theory. During the 19th century a number of writers began to attack orthodox economics on the grounds that it was based upon an erroneous theory of human nature. More specifically, Adam Smith and other classical economists were accused of having grossly distorted the true nature of man by assuming that, in a capitalist system, virtually all economic activity must be motivated by purely selfish considerations. Early economists were ostensibly guilty of ignoring the 'higher' values of life and unduly emphasizing the 'baser' motives for human behaviour. In the concept of the economic man, therefore, critics in effect created a low-level abstraction, a prototype of the multitude of selfishly-motivated individuals. The economic man thus came to be used as a term of opprobrium; it became a symbol of discontent with orthodox economic theory.

1. There is no doubt that classical writers emphasized the importance of self-interest in the field of *economic* behaviour. Although Smith, for example, never gave blanket endorsement to the idea of the beneficence of self-interest, he was convinced that self-interest frequently played an essentially beneficent role in economic affairs, for in the pursuit of his own interests man on occasion was 'led by an invisible

Economic Man

hand to promote an end which was no part of his intention' (*An Inquiry into the Nature and Causes of Wealth of Nations* (1776), New York: Modern Library edn., 1937, p. 423), i.e. working within the framework of competition, the selfish individual would unwittingly promote the welfare of society despite his exclusive concern with furthering his own interests. Not only was this assumption of Smith's destined to occupy a central place in orthodox economic theory, but it was soon refined through the instrumentality of the hedonic psychology, which was accepted by many prominent 19th-century economists. The utilitarians, e.g. Bentham and his followers, viewed man as a highly rational creature who persistently endeavoured by means of the hedonic calculus, to maximize pleasure and minimize pain.

2. This alleged hyperrational behaviour came under attack during the last half of the 19th century, and critics began to use the term *economic man* to denote not only selfish behaviour but also to describe the behaviour of individuals who were rational to a degree that was exaggerated and unrealistic. The following is a brief list of representative critics and the works in which they devoted attention to the economic man concept: H. C. Carey, *Principles of Social Science* (Philadelphia: J. B. Lippincott, 1858); J. Ruskin, *Unto This Last* (Orpington: George Allen, 1882); W. Smart, *John Ruskin: His Life and Work* (Manchester: Abel Heywood, 1880); T. Veblen, *The Place of Science in Modern Civilization* (New York: Viking Press, 1919); and J. A. Hobson, *Wealth and Life* (London: Macmillan, 1929). Special mention should be made of the work of Veblen, who is probably the most widely known of the modern heterodox economists. Much of his critical effort was directed to what he regarded as the false psychological assumptions of neoclassical economic theory. In Veblen's eyes, the economic man of orthodox economics was a thoroughly hedonistic creature, a coldly calculating 'machine' that responded only to the stimulus of a desire for pleasure or the avoidance of pain. In a widely quoted passage from one of his essays, for example, he bitterly attacked the hedonistic man as 'a lightning calculator of pleasures and pains, who oscillates like a homogeneous globule of desire of happiness under the impulse of stimuli that shift him about the area but leave him intact' (*The Place of Science in Modern Civilization*, p. 73). He is frequently credited with having played an important part in forcing orthodox economists to re-examine their basic assumptions concerning the motivation for economic activity.

3. In defence against such criticism, more orthodox economists have insisted that the term *economic man* as used in the critical literature is a badly misleading caricature of the type of economic behaviour usually depicted in economic theory. Thus it is argued that the so-called economic man visualized by orthodox economists is merely 'a creature who chooses from among scarce alternative resources those which are best suited to produce certain accepted ends' (W. D. Grampp, 'Adam Smith and the Economic Man', *Journal of Political Economy*, vol. LVI, 1948, p. 315). Most economists take the position that economic theory, far from assuming that all behaviour is rational, only purports to describe what actions *would* be rational if certain ends or goals, e.g. the maximization of real income, were given data. The distinguishing feature of economic ends is that they are assumed to be quantitative and measurable in terms of money. In brief, all assumptions about the nature of economic ends are presumably made for purely analytical purposes and should never be construed as normative propositions. The economic man is therefore rational in the sense that he is assumed to use his means in the most efficient manner possible to attain given ends. In making such an assumption, however, economic theorists do not assert that men are *in fact* completely rational; on the contrary, the fictional economic man is used solely as an analytical device. Indeed, economists have emphasized that much economic behaviour is in fact irrational and does not, therefore, lend itself to scientific analysis, i.e. many problems cannot be reduced to the form of using given means to attain given ends (see F. Knight, 'The Limitations of Scientific Method in Economics', in his *The Ethics of Competition*, London: Allen & Unwin, 1935, pp. 105–47).

C. If one ignores the difference between the two levels of abstraction present in the use of the term *economic man* it may lead to considerable confusion in the analysis of social affairs. For example, it may be useful for many purposes to employ as an analytical assumption the old hedonistic conception of man as a 'disutility of labour' vs. 'utility of consumption' calculator. If on the other hand, this assumption is used at a low level of abstraction to describe man's total attitude toward work, it must result in ignoring the fact that men can and do get varying degrees of satisfaction through work itself. To employ the assumption on this level leads to the idea that if economic rewards are equal, people do not care which line they work in, and thus greatly minimizes the possibility of class struggle in socialist states. Marx himself was deeply confused on this issue for this very reason.

Alfred F. Chalk

See also: DECISION-MAKING
HEDONISM
RATIONALITY

Economic Organization
(and Economic System)

A. *Economic organization* denotes (a) the complex of institutions, the pattern of controls, by which a people uses its resources to attain its ends and through which priorities are established and decisions made concerning economic goods (q.v.); or (b) a unit of economic activity such as a corporation or labour union composed of the integrated activities of a number of persons, yet smaller than the total economy or economic system or than what might be called a sector of the economy. *Economic system* denotes (a) the same phenomena as *economic organization* in the first definition above; (b) the total web of economic interaction governed and regulated by the complex of economic institutions; or (c) in the plural, a subfield of economics constituted by the study of economic institutions and organized economic activities.

B. The major use of both *economic organization* and *economic system* as noted above is to denote the set of institutional arrangements, the framework for decision-making (q.v.) and priority-setting with regard to the economic life of a society or an international community. The functions of this set of institutions are to employ most efficiently scarce resources to meet the ends of the society. Its particular and distinctive functions, as stated definitively in the early 1930s by F. H. Knight are several: 'The first [function] is to decide what is to be done, that is, what goods and services are to be produced, and in what proportions. It is the function of setting standards, of establishing a social scale of values, or the function of social choice; the second is the function of organizing production, in the narrow sense, of getting done the things settled upon as most worth doing; third is distribution, the apportioning the product among the members of society; the fourth is

really a group of functions having to do with maintaining and improving the social structure, or promoting social progress (*Social Economic Organization*, University of Chicago Third Year Course in the Study of Contemporary Society —Selected Readings, Chicago: University of Chicago Bookstore, 10th edn., 1942, Sect. XV, p. 6). Knight also lists a fifth function: that of adjusting consumption to production within very short periods (ibid., pp. 12–13).

There is agreement, of course, that economic activity does require some system of organization and some tangible social control. Two reasons are cited: 'First, the scarcity of the means of production frequently leads to conflicts of interest among individuals and groups. The possession of these means (or their products) by any one person or group necessarily lessens the amount available to others. ... Second, efficient use of the means of production requires organized, coordinated, and cooperative action on the part of virtually all persons in society' (H. R. Bowen, *Toward Social Economy*, New York: Rinehart, 1948, pp. 6–7).

This is true regardless of the nature or the goals of the economic system. 'The actual existence of a unified economic organization with a central purpose is quite clear in a completely socialized country, where there is a government which places great emphasis on the fact and undertakes a sort of central management of all economic activity. But the organization is equally present in a private-enterprise society like our own, even though there is little or no central planning or management, and though the pattern of economic effort emerges from the activities of a large number of independent persons, each of whom is guided mainly by the pursuit of individual gain' (J. S. Bain, *Pricing, Distribution and Employment*, New York: Henry Holt, rev. edn., 1953, p. 1).

C. In recent years, there has been a great deal of interest in *economic organizations*, as units of economic activity. There has been particular concern with the importance and impact of the large organization as a unit in the economic life of the society. There is also a marked upsurge of interest in the rapidly developing field of organization theory. The impact of this interest may be reflected in a new concern with the actual behaviour of units and with their internal structure and functions.

D. *Economic system* is also frequently used to denote the web of economic interaction

Economic Theory

controlled and regulated by institutions. This meaning of the term, in a sense, includes the institutions themselves but also includes both the institutionalized behaviour and that behaviour which violates or goes beyond what is normatively called for. It is a more concrete and inclusive usage of the term.

E. In a certain sense, economics (q.v.) as a discipline centres upon the nature and functioning of economic systems. Thus, it is sometimes difficult to distinguish between the study of economic systems as a pervasive concern of the total discipline and as a distinct sub-field designated by the term *economic systems*. It is also difficult, perhaps increasingly difficult, to sharply distinguish the study of economic systems from the investigation of other types of systems. It has been urged that the economic system might well be studied from the vantage point of general systems analysis (K. E. Boulding, *The Image*, Ann Arbor: University of Michigan Press, 1956). It has also been suggested that economic systems merely constitute a sub-system of society and should be studied in terms of a general theory of the social system (T. Parsons & N. J. Smelser, *Economy and Society*, London: Routledge & Kegan Paul, 1936). Meanwhile, specific attempts are being made to integrate the study of economic systems with the examination of particular social and political systems.

Nevertheless, certain meanings are attached to this term in economics, and a sub-field does exist, although it is often ill-defined and its focus tends to shift from one period to another. As presently carried on, work in *economic systems* as a sub-field tends to focus upon one or more of the following particular matters: economic institutions, economic goals, comparative economic systems, changing economic systems, the evaluation of the performance of economic systems, and the study of particular economic systems.

C. Addison Hickman

See also: Decision-Making
Economic Goods
Economics
Institution
Social Control
Social System

Economic Statistics (See Mathematical Economics)

Economic Surplus (See Surplus)

Economic Theory

A. In its general sense *economic theory* is any systematic method or body of reasoning applied to economic data or problems. In the formulation of basic theory, economists seek to discover and state 'laws' or 'principles' which aid in the prediction and/or explanation of economic phenomena. In the application of such laws or principles economic theorists typically construct abstract 'models', i.e. simplified representations of the economic system or relevant portions thereof. After reaching tentative conclusions as to the behaviour of models in their simplest forms, economists then may attempt to relax the simplifying assumptions, with resulting modifications in their conclusions, until the model yields predictions which are capable, in principle at least, of being refuted by observation of the data.

For the great body of economists who have wished to use economics (q.v.) not only to predict and describe economic phenomena, but to prescribe economic policies, economic theory has been used to deduce from ethical premises norms of economic policy with particular respect to the allocation of scarce resources.

B. Because of the great complexity of economic institutions and phenomena, economic theory has always involved a high degree of abstraction from reality, with heavy reliance upon deductive reasoning. The resort to 'model building', as described above, has thus characterized economic theory from the days of Adam Smith to the present. This has been true both of the formulation of predictive-explanatory theory and in the application and use of theory for evaluation. The methodological device of ideal types, used by the historically minded Max Weber, the concept of *atomistic competition* developed by economists of the classical school, and the highly abstract conceptions of modern welfare theorists in economics, are all examples of the model-building technique.

Henry Oliver

See also: Economics
Ideal-type Analysis
Model

Economics

A. It is difficult indeed to find consensus on the definition of *economics*. Definitions range from the extremely broad to the extremely narrow: (a) 'Economics is a study of mankind in the ordinary business of life: it examines that part of individual and social action which is most closely connected with the attainment and with the use of the material requisites of well being' (A. Marshall, *Principles of Economics*, London: Macmillan, 8th edn., 1920, p. 1). (b) 'Economics is the science which studies human behaviour as a relationship between ends and scarce means which have alternate uses' (L. Robbins, *An Essay on the Nature and Significance of Economic Science*, London: Macmillan, 1932, p. 15). (c) 'Economics is the science that treats phenomena from the standpoint of price' (H. J. Davenport, *Economics of Enterprise*, New York: The Macmillan Co., 1929, p. 25).

A compromise definition may be attempted as follows: *Economics* is the study of human behaviour as it relates scarce means, which have alternative uses, to given ends, such as maximization of income, usually employing price data in the comparison. Choice among 'given' ends, however, often involves choice among social policies and values, as well as guesses concerning future growth—thus going beyond a mere hypothetical rational market.

B. The confusion in the definitions of economics is best explained by reference to an ebb and flow in what economists have tried and are trying to do.

1. The word began with the ancient use referring to household management. From there it developed into *political* economy—the study and practice of the management, first, of the government 'household' and then of the entire nation considered as a 'household'. In the last half of the 19th century economics split off from political economy, and became increasingly occupied with price (q.v.) and market (q.v.) behaviour, and less and less preoccupied with political theory.

2. Two forces are now pushing economics and economists back in the direction of 'political economy' and indeed even in the direction of a further merger with other social sciences.

(a) There is first the attempt to predict fluctuations of output (the study of unemployment and business cycles). In this study the previously dominant emphasis on study of the market was extended through the use of various concepts as the marginal efficiency of capital (q.v.) and the propensity to consume (q.v.). But it was soon discovered that these phenomena could not be deduced merely from statistical observation of past behaviour. They changed and often changed 'unpredictably'. Thus even the most 'scientific' economists

are now compelled to pay some attention to the social forces affecting consumer and business behaviour.

(b) Second, and of more recent importance, is the study of economic growth (q.v.) and the development of economically backward areas. In the study of these problems it becomes increasingly evident that men's religions and other cultural ideas and practices deeply affect the kind and degree of their economic development. Further, as government action to stabilize and stimulate economic development, the political-administrative element can no longer be disregarded.

3. While economics uses the results of other disciplines and vice versa, it remains a separate discipline. Manipulation of quantitative price and market models remains a major element in its procedure.

David McCord Wright

See also: MARKET
PRICE
RATIONALITY

Education

A. The most general usage of the term denotes bringing up (of the young); intellectual and moral training; the development of mental powers and character, especially through the provision of systematic instruction, e.g. in schools and other institutions of full-time education. By extension, it denotes similar instruction or training obtained in adult age.

It is sometimes extended to include the educative effect of all social arrangements.

B. It is not possible here to delineate all the historical and contemporary conflicts concerning education; but it is apparent that once one attempts to go beyond the definition in A. above difficulties ensue.

Conceptions of the nature and realm of truth, class and other interests, religious belief, etc., condition an individual's or group's ideas of the nature and function of education to a degree possibly greater than in the case of other areas of social life.

Differing definitions of education then result in differences concerning the methods and content of education. Under such circumstances the most general definition is probably most usable. Some of these issues are raised in the following attempts at definition.

1. E. Durkheim took the view that scientific usage should be more discriminating and proposed to reserve the term for 'the influence

Educational Sociology

exercised by adult generations on those that are not yet ready for social life', defining it succinctly as follows: 'Education consists of a methodical socialization of the young generation' (*Education and Sociology*, trans. by S. D. Fox, Glencoe, Ill.: The Free Press, 1956, p. 71). This definition follows from Durkheim's functional view of education as an institution serving to produce consensus (q.v.) and social integration (q.v.) through the fostering of appropriate personal qualities in oncoming generations: 'Society can survive only if there exists among its members a sufficient degree of homogeneity: education perpetuates and reinforces this homogeneity by fixing in the child, from the beginning, the essential similarities that collective life demands' (ibid., p. 70), and this is common ground among European sociologists, although some find the emphasis on 'generation' restrictive and confusing, since coevals may stand in an educational relationship.

2. M. Weber sketched, for the purposes of comparative study, a 'sociological typology of pedagogical ends and means', corollary to his typology of 'social structures of domination'. Every system of education aims at cultivating pupils for a particular 'conduct of life', characteristic of and suitable for the decisive status group in a particular structure of domination, identifiable at some point along the charismatic-rational bureaucratic continuum (*From Max Weber: Essays in Sociology*, trans. and ed. by H. H. Gerth & C. W. Mills, London: Kegan Paul, Trench, Trubner, 1947, pp. 243, 426–7).

3. K. Mannheim classed education among the *social techniques*—a general category of 'methods of influencing human behaviour so that it fits into the prevailing patterns of social interaction and organization (*Freedom, Power and Democratic Planning*, H. H. Gerth & E. K. Bramsted (eds.), London: Routledge & Kegan Paul, 1951, p. 6); but he was also much influenced by American usage, which, under the influence of John Dewey's pragmatism, has laid less emphasis on the conservative social functions of education and more on the part it has to play in social change.

Jean Floud

See also: ENCULTURATION
  SOCIALIZATION

Educational Sociology
(Also **Sociology of Education**)

A. Studies mainly described as *educational sociology* have flourished in the United States since 1918: their guiding assumption has been that education is merely another name for socialization in the broadest possible sense and that educational sociology is a branch of *applied* sociology, which should yield rational educational aims and methods and a body of knowledge and techniques for educators and educational research workers. Thus, F. J. Brown, quoting D. W. Dodson: 'Educational sociology is interested in the impact of the total cultural milieu in which and through which experience is acquired and organized. It is interested in the school, but recognizes it as a small part of the total. Educational sociology is particularly interested in finding out how to manipulate the educational process (social control) to achieve better personality development' (F. J. Brown, *Educational Sociology*, New York: Prentice-Hall, 1947, p. 36). It has been justly remarked of a standard work (E. G. Payne, *Principles of Educational Sociology*, New York: New York University Press, 1928) that 'educational sociology included anything in the field of sociology which could be related to the learning or socializing process and anything in education that was subject to sociological analysis' (W. B. Brookover, 'Sociology of Education: a Definition', *American Sociological Review*, vol. 14, 1949, pp. 407–15).

B. 1. Within the studies described above, and independently in Europe (particularly in Germany before 1939) there grew up a substantial body of work more rigorously linked to the concerns of the sociologist specializing in education. It is to such work that the label *sociology of education* has come to be attached. It has no normative intentions—but this does not mean that its findings are without practical relevance. The sociology of education is concerned with any instruction or training of individuals for which social provision is made, whether or not it is concentrated in the early years of life, undertaken through the agency of specialized institutions, directed generally to the promotion of consensus and integration through the inculcation of attitudes and values or the formation of personality, or specifically to vocational training. In short, its subject-matter is *the assimilation of individuals into a cultural tradition*.

2. Nevertheless, problems and methods must vary with differences in the stage of social development and structure.

(a) In more or less closed primitive societies, it is concerned *directly with the socialization process*—with relations between the generations wherever they occur, but especially in the family.

(b) In more developed societies, it concentrates on *the formal provision for instruction and training through specialized agencies and personnel*. Formative influences brought to bear on the individual informally or tacitly from other social sources are not ignored, insofar as these may promote or frustrate the implementation of educational policies or pedagogical aims; but they are not the primary focus of attention.

3. In pre-industrial societies what may be called the *structural problems* of education are either non-existent or relatively uncomplicated. It is when education becomes a formal institution, functioning in some measure as an independent part of a wider and changing social structure that these problems arise; and they present themselves in their most acute form in modern industrialized or industrializing societies. In these societies the educational system comes to occupy a strategic place as a central determinant of the economic, political, social, and cultural character of society. It plays a role, which must be analysed, in relation to all aspects of social structure—demographic, economic, political, and social, as well as ideological or spiritual. The educational or socializing functions of schools, colleges, and universities tend to be overshadowed, impeded, or transmuted by other latent or manifest social functions, and features of their organization such as bureaucratization, called into being by industrialism; they cannot be understood if this fact is not recognized and taken specifically into account in studying them.

The following problems which are characteristic arise in this context of advanced industrialism and may be grouped broadly under five main heads: (i) the social origins, determinants, and implications of educational ideas, theories, and policies; (ii) the relation of educational institutions, or of the educational system, to the wider social structure—e.g. to its demography (size and quality of the population), to the economy (supply and quality of man-power), to the political system (recruitment of the nation's leaders), to the system of social stratification (social selection and differentiation, sociology of the teaching profession); (iii) the structure and functioning of educational institutions (e.g. the school as community, as social system; the corporate life of universities; school and neighbourhood; transmission and inculcation of social values); (iv) the social relations inherent in, or arising out of educational activities—e.g. social psychology and sociometry of class-room and school (social distance, modes of authority, discipline, etc.), 'sociology of teaching'; (v) informal educational influences of the environment—material and spiritual factors promoting or hindering response to formal education (e.g. socio-economic situation, size and other characteristics of family environment; attitudes and values of social-class, ethnic, religious, age-group, or other sub-cultures).

4. A comprehensive review of the literature in Western Europe and the U.S. (*Current Sociology*, vol. VII, no. 3, 1958), showed that most work has been undertaken under heads (ii) and (v). Studies of the social distribution of educational opportunity in relation to that of ability, of the part played by education in social mobility (q.v.), and of the social determinants of educability, are not only intrinsically important for the understanding of modern industrial societies; they have flourished also because of their practical relevance to almost universal post-war attempts to democratize secondary and higher education. Work under (iii) and (iv) is most advanced in the U.S., where the study of institutions of higher education in particular has made rapid progress since 1950 (see A. H. Halsey, Jean Floud & C. A. Anderson (eds.), *Education, Economy and Society; a Reader in the Sociology of Education*, New York: The Free Press, 1962).

Jean Floud

See also: EDUCATION

Efficiency

A. The term, in its general usage, denotes effectiveness, efficient power, efficacy. In economics it is generally accepted that the concept relates to performance (and, in the view of many, comparisons of performance) by economic units or systems or personnel. More precise agreement or usage has not yet been reached.

B. Until the industrial revolution the term was used in a very general sense: it is only since the late 18th century that 'attempts have been made to find a basis for measuring industrial efficiency' (J. A. Scott, *The Measurement of Industrial Efficiency*, London: Pitman, 1950, p. 3).

First, in engineering and, later, in economics, attempts have been made to measure efficiency.

1. In engineering, a precise meaning can be given by defining the efficiency of a machine as the relation between the useful output (usually of energy) and that theoretically possible from the means employed. Thus, it would measure

Efficiency

the losses due to leakages of heat, friction and so on, e.g. when coal is burnt, we can compare the heat generated by the chemical reaction $C + O_2 = CO_2$ with the warmth given to a room —the difference being lost (mainly up the chimney).

2. Similar attempts in economics involve more precise definition of what exactly is being considered—and should therefore be measured—and also often a judgement about the use to which the measure is to be put, or, in other words, a judgement about the nature of the question to which the index of efficiency is supposed to provide an answer.

(a) The idea of efficiency is closely associated with the idea of productivity. Indeed, many writers appear to consider that the two terms have the same meaning. For example: G. Hutton, *We too can Prosper* (London: Allen & Unwin, 1953, p. 13) writes 'Productivity is the efficiency … of production'. The Organization for European Economic Co-operation Volume on the *Measurement of Productivity*, 1952, p. 16, speaks of 'the efficiency of the workman himself, that is to say, his degree of skill or the application with which he works'.

(b) Others differentiate the concepts, and P. S. Florence and A. J. Brown, for example, use the term *productivity* to mean the 'output from one particular factor of production or particular form of input' and the term *efficiency* 'to mean the output from the total inputs' (P. S. Florence writing in T. P. Davison and others, *Productivity and Economic Incentives*, London: Allen & Unwin, 1958, p. 21, fn. 1).

C. An alternative distinction is also current: Productivity is used to refer, *simpliciter*, to the ratio of output to input, whatever the measure or indicator of output or of input is used while efficiency implies a comparison of productivities and often the consideration of 'inefficiency' that is of lost potential in some sense. The possible measures or indicators of productivity are very numerous according to whether, for example, capital, power, raw materials, management or labour, for example, or all of these, are used as inputs. Each of these measures can be used to throw light on several distinct types of questions concerning efficiency.

D. M. Hall and C. Winsten, in an article entitled 'The Ambiguous Notion of Efficiency' (*Economic Journal*, vol. LXIX, 1959, pp. 71–86), have attempted to disentangle some of the various meanings of efficiency and to analyse how these will affect the statistical analysis of data.

All efficiency questions are concerned implicitly with decisions, or rather with providing material to assist in decisions. (Which plant to use? Which manager is better?—with the choice implied by such a question.) The following types of problem are given in illustration of different meanings of the term efficiency which are of very general interest.

1. The first type of problem is related simply to the determination of the efficiency of a productive unit in its present use. For example, if two mines, each with a similar labour force producing the same sort of coal with the same type and quantities of equipment, were being compared, the mine producing more coal would be called more efficient. The meaning of efficiency corresponds to the meaning given by P. S. Florence and A. J. Brown. But the term cannot be restricted to this use. This meaning is only one among many.

2. A different type of problem is that of managerial efficiency.

The broad distinction between these two types is that managerial efficiency judges the management but efficiency-in-use, as it might be called, judges the whole productive unit.

3. A third type of problem arises when a number of different production units are operating in a number of different environments. The question is how far the firm has to go to reach the best performance in its particular environment. This is measured efficiency on a scale, not merely a ranking. The question is how far the firm has to go to reach the best and not, as in the case of managerial efficiency, how difficult it is to get there. Nevertheless, there is always room for a difference of opinion about what is counted as best in a particular environment.

4. The rate of profit has frequently been used in making efficiency judgements. From the entrepreneur's point of view the most efficient use of capital is that which yields the highest rate of profit but the transfer of resources on this principle reduces the rate of profit until the most efficient allocation of resources from society's point of view is reached at minimum rate of profit levels. This concept has gained a far wider currency than is really justified because comparisons of returns, in this way, do not distinguish between the various types of efficiency question instanced above.

M. Hall
C. Winsten

See also: PRODUCTIVITY

230

Ego

A. In its broadest sense *ego* is synonomous with the broadest usage of *self* (q.v.), denoting the core of the personality system (q.v.) organized around its awareness of itself and its conscious and unconscious orientation toward its most vital interests and values, involving identity, status, commitment, and desire. In a narrower sense it is sometimes used, especially in psychoanalysis, to denote a sector of the personality system which mediates among the id (q.v.), the superego (q.v.), and reality.

B. Idealistic philosophy through its concern with the ego (or self), and pragmatism through its concern with the analysis of symbolism, are, in the main, the foundations of the social psychological conception of the ego (or self). In 1890 W. James wrote 'Every actually existing consciousness seems to itself at any rate to be a fighter for ends ...' (*Principles of Psychology*, New York: Henry Holt, 1890, vol. 1, p. 141). This sentence implies three significant things about the ego (or self). First, that it is conscious; second, that it is reflexively self-conscious; and, third, that it strives after goals with which it is seriously concerned.

1. For more than fifty years after this statement was uttered the concept of the ego (or self) practically disappeared from psychology proper. The concept of the self, however, remained alive in sociology and in sociological social psychology through the development of a powerful tradition stemming from James, C. S. Peirce, J. M. Baldwin, C. H. Cooley, and G. H. Mead, although in a form which gradually tended to narrow its meaning because of the stress placed on its social origins and its reflexive character.

2. In 1943 G. W. Allport called for a renewal of the use of ego (or self) as a central concept in social psychology ('The Ego in Contemporary Psychology', *Psychological Review*, vol. 50, 1943, pp. 451–78; reprinted in G. W. Allport, *Personality and Social Encounter*, Boston: Beacon Press, 1960, pp. 71–93). He opposed the narrowing of the concept in psychoanalysis to denote 'a passive organization of mental processes' (ibid., p. 75) and felt that it was not conceived in its full dynamics in the Gestalt psychology of K. Koffka (ibid., p. 76). Allport conceives the ego as a fighter for ends, deeply involved in many areas, but not all, of the functioning of the personality system. He expands the Jamesian definition to include parts of the unconscious as well as the conscious

sectors of personality. He retains the reflexive element of self-awareness, but not to the exclusion of other elements. He fails to give proper attention to G. H. Mead's social behaviourism, and so tends to underestimate the cognitive powers of the ego as these are derived from participation in the community.

C. 1. In Freudian psychoanalysis the structure of personality has three parts: the id, the superego, and the ego. Although each has its own functions with respect to behaviour, they always interact with each other. In this triad the ego is the organized, largely conscious subdivision of personality. The ego develops through the individual's experience in society, and its aim is to act on the basis of the reality principle (q.v.). In so doing it may modify but never nullify the pleasure principle (q.v.), although it strives to bring the individual into adjustment with the current situation. Thus the ego, acting on the basis of the reality principle, mediates among the warring forces of the imperious and unconscious demands of the id, the demands of society, and the exigencies of the physical world. The function of the ego is the defence of the individual, against others and against the unconscious impulses of the id which, unrestrained, could endanger the individual's life (see S. Freud, *The Ego and the Id*, trans. by J. Riviére, London: Hogarth Press, 1927; also S. Freud, *An Outline of Psychoanalysis*, trans. by J. Strachey, New York: W. W. Norton, 1949, pp. 15–18, 19–20, 109–23).

2. Not all psychoanalytic writers have continued to assign such passive functions to the ego. Some, such as H. Hartmann (*Ego Psychology and the Problem of Adaptation*, trans. by D. Rapaport, New York: International Universities Press, 1958), have, as G. W. Allport has pointed out, come to conceive the ego as a sector of personality which 'through its ideals reaches into the future, becomes an executive, a planner, a fighter' ('The Ego in Contemporary Psychology', in *Personality and Social Encounter*, p. 75). Others, however, such as A. Freud (*The Ego and the Mechanisms of Defence*, trans. by C. Baines, New York: International Universities Press, 1946) have continued to elaborate on the more passive functions of the ego.

Frank E. Hartung

See also: ID
PERSONALITY SYSTEM
SELF
SUPEREGO

Ego-Involvement

Ego-Involvement

A. *Ego-involvement* refers to the process (or the state which emerges from that process) by which the ego (q.v.) becomes identified with various objects, acts, attitudes, values, and so on to the extent that their fate becomes the fate of the ego —a threat to them threatens the ego, and their enhancement exalts the ego. This involvement of the ego leads to particularly intense, strongly motivated behaviour when such outside elements are seen as being pertinent to the action situation.

B. 1. Ego-involvement is a relatively new term in the vocabulary of social science. It became established largely through the publication of M. Sherif and H. Cantril's book, *The Psychology of Ego-Involvements* (New York: Wiley, 1947). The term grows out of the modern emphasis in social psychology on the importance of group membership and social relations in the personality development and behaviour of the individual. It focuses attention on the fact that an adequate understanding of the individual can be attained only through a knowledge of those referential frameworks (largely social in nature) in which his psychological processes (perception, memory, etc.) and behaviour take place.

The concept of ego employed here is that of general psychology and social psychology rather than that of psychiatry or psychoanalysis. It refers either to that same constellation of attitudes which is often designated 'the self' (q.v.) or to 'the self as something valued' (T. M. Newcomb, *Social Psychology*, New York: Dryden Press, 1950, p. 248). As Sherif and Cantril say (*The Psychology of Ego-Involvements*, p. 96): 'All attitudes that define a person's status or that give him some relative role with respect to other individuals, groups, or institutions are ego-involved'.

'In brief, the ego consists of many attitudes which from infancy on are related to the delimited, differentiated and accumulating "I", "me", "mine" experiences. These attitudes, which may be designated as ego-attitudes, are constituent components of the ego' (ibid., p. 4). When ego-attitudes are situationally aroused by some relevant object, person, event, task, situation, or group, the individual's experience and behaviour are characterized as *ego-involved* (M. Sherif & C. W. Sherif, *An Outline of Social Psychology*, New York: Harper & Brothers, 1956, p. 402).

2. The importance of ego-involvement in social behaviour has been widely recognized.

Thus, in their discussion of 'The Psychology of Voting' (G. Lindzey (ed.), *Handbook of Social Psychology*, Cambridge, Mass.: Addison-Wesley, 1954, p. 1163), S. Lipset, P. Lazarsfeld, A. Barton, and J. Linz indicate that: 'Acts may differ according to the degree of their ego-involvement, that is, the extent to which they are important for the person's self-respect and need for status. ... The large amount of non-voting which characterizes American elections, as compared with those in Europe, indicates a low ego-involvement on the part of a majority of voters'.

T. M. Newcomb (*Social Psychology*, p. 247–8) emphasizes the role of ego-involvement in attitude stability: 'When a person perceives an influence as a force opposed to some attitude of his which is ego-involved, he is apt to counter that force with other forces of supporting nature. ... When attitudes persist even in the face of opposed influences, it is altogether likely that they are ego-involved.'

Alan C. Kerckhoff

See also: Ego
        Self

Ego Structure (See **Character Structure**)

Elasticity

A. *Elasticity* as a concept in economics presupposes a *relationship between two variables*, such as the price of a commodity and the quantity of it demanded by a consumer, or the income of a consumer and the quantity he demands of a commodity, or the price of a commodity and the quantity of it supplied by a seller. Simply defined, the *elasticity* of a 'response' variable y with respect to a 'stimulus' variable x is approximately the number of percentage points by which y changes, in response to a 1 per cent increase in x, when relevant other things are held the same so that the change in x is the only thing that influences y. Thus if a 1 per cent increase in U.S. income brings about a 1·5 per cent increase in the quantity of tomato juice demanded, other things being equal, then the elasticity of demand for tomato juice with respect to income in the U.S. is approximately 1·5. The word 'approximately' must appear here because the formal definition below is stated in terms of infinitesimal changes in x, while this paragraph refers to changes of a fixed magnitude.

The formal definition is this: Suppose that a variable called y is a function of another variable called x, and that the relationship is denoted by $y = f(x)$. Then the elasticity of the function f(x) with respect to x is also a function of x: it is the derivative of f(x) with respect to x, multiplied by the ratio of x to y, thus:

$$\text{elasticity of f(x) with respect to } x = \frac{df(x)}{dx} \cdot \frac{x}{y}$$

If y is a function of several variables, $y = g(x_1, x_2, \ldots, x_n)$, then the elasticity of this function with respect to one of the variables, say x_i (where x_i is one of the variables

$$x, x_2, \ldots, x_n),$$

is the partial derivative of g with respect to x_i times the ratio of x_i to y, thus:

$$[\delta g(x_1, x_2, \ldots, x_n)/\delta x_i] x / y.$$

B. 1. The chief advantage of the elasticity concept, compared with the corresponding slope concept—given by the derivative $df(x)/dx$ alone—is that an elasticity is independent of the units in which x and y are measured. This makes it especially useful for comparing the degree of response in quite different kinds of commodities, e.g. tomatoes and motor cars.

2. Elasticities can be positive or negative. The elasticity of demand with respect to own price—usually called *price-elasticity of demand* for brevity—is negative for most commodities because as the price of the typical commodity rises the quantity of it demanded decreases. However, some writers define price elasticities of demand with the sign reversed, so that they will be positive for most commodities.

3. The terms *elastic* and *inelastic* refer respectively to relationships whose elasticities are *numerically* greater than and less than 1. *Perfectly elastic* and *perfectly inelastic* refer respectively to elasticities whose numerical values are infinite and zero. If the demand for a commodity is price-elastic, then if sellers lower the price they will get a larger total revenue for a larger quantity of the commodity. If the demand is price-inelastic, then if sellers lower the price they will get a smaller total revenue.

4. Relationships that have constant coefficients and are linear in the logarithms of the variables, have *constant* elasticities. Thus if $y = ax^b z^c$, so that $\log y = \log a + b \log x + c \log z$, then the elasticities of y with respect to x and z are respectively b and c.

C. Among the main elasticities used in economics are the following: elasticity of demand for a good with respect to (a) its price, (b) the price of another good, (c) income of the buyer(s); elasticity of supply of a good with respect to (d) its price, and (e) the price of another good; elasticity of output of a good with respect to (f) the quantity of input of another good, (g) the quantity of output of a related good; (h) the elasticity of the ratio of quantities of two goods required for some purpose with respect to the ratio of their prices—the elasticity of substitution. A large part of recent and current econometric research is devoted to the measurement of such elasticities as these, many of which are important for understanding the effects of private and public policy actions.

Carl F. Christ

Elasticity of Substitution (See **Substitution**)

Election

A. *Election* denotes a process whereby a number of persons choose one or more candidates to fill certain offices.

B. 1. If the number of candidates is greater than the number of places to be filled, and if the number of voters is large, or if it is desired that the voting shall be secret, the most satisfactory method is by ballot (q.v.). This is the method generally used at elections at which voters choose members of parliaments or other similar bodies.

At parliamentary elections, where very large numbers of people have to vote, it is usual for the voting process to be spread over a long period, generally not less than a whole day. The public authorities provide voting-places, often in schools or other public buildings, to which the voters come to record their votes. Each voter is provided with a ballot paper, on which to mark his preference in writing. He usually does this in a polling booth, which is screened so that no one can see how he marks the paper; having done this he places the paper, folded, in an urn. When the voting is completed, the ballot papers are counted, either by or in the presence of representatives of the candidates, who see that the counting is done correctly, and that no false ballot papers are inserted.

2. There are several types of election. Each voter may vote for only one of the candidates, or he may have several votes (assuming that there are several seats to be filled), or he may place the candidates in order of preference. In some totalitarian societies elections have taken place in which only one candidate's name appears on the ballot paper; in such cases the voter must either vote for that candidate or make his vote of no effect. In such a case the

Elite

election is not an election in the generally understood sense of the word.

3. In modern conditions the voters are usually choosing, really, between rival parties, rather than between individual candidates; this fact is sometimes recognized by indicating on the ballot paper the party allegiance of each candidate.

As most elections are dominated by parties, so that no candidate has any hope of being elected except as the candidate of a political party, the process whereby the party machines choose their candidates is an important preliminary to the formal election, at which the voters choose between the rival parties. In most countries the choice of candidates is regarded as a domestic affair, in which the party is engaged in an activity private to itself. In the U.S.A., however, the public importance of the choice of the candidates is recognized, and the parties hold primary elections. In most states the primaries are regulated by law, and even organized by the public authorities.

P. A. Bromhead

See also: BALLOT
PARTY
PLEBISCITE
PRIMARY
REFERENDUM
VOTING

Elective Office (See **Public Office**)

Elite

A. *Elite* in the most general sense, denotes a group of persons who in any society hold positions of eminence. More specifically, it denotes a group of persons who are eminent in a particular field—especially the governing minority and the circles from which the governing minority is recruited.

B. 1. The term began its career in French as 'the choice part or flower' of goods offered for sale, i.e. objects selected for sale because, on various criteria, they were worthy of *choice*. By the 18th century usage had widened to include 'distinction' in other contexts. Its modern use has entered other languages from French. In sociology and political science (under the influence of Pareto and others) the emphasis has moved away from 'choiceness' of objects or things toward 'eminence' of persons and groups.

2. As an analytical tool, the concept *elite* was popularized by V. Pareto: 'So let us make a class of the people who have the highest indices in their branch of activity and to that class give the name of elite. ... So we get two strata in a population: (1) A lower stratum, the *non-elite* ... (2) a higher stratum, *the elite*, which is divided into two: (a) a governing elite; (b) a non-governing elite' (*The Mind and Society*, ed. A. Livingston, trans. A. Bongiorno & A. Livingston, London; J. Cape, 1935, vol. 3, pp. 1423–4).

3. More recently H. D. Lasswell has defined *elite* as those with greatest access to and control of values: '... the holders of high positions in a given society. There are as many elites as there are values. Besides an elite of power (the political elite) there are elites of wealth, respect, knowledge (to name but a few). Since we need a term for persons who are elite in relation to several values we speak of "*the* elite" (the elite of society)' (H. D. Lasswell, D. Lerner, & C. E. Rothwell, *The Comparative Study of Elites*, Stanford, Calif.: Stanford University Press, 1952, p. 6).

Martin B. Travis, Jr.

See also: CIRCULATION OF ELITES

Emigration (See **Migration**)

Emotion

A. *Emotion* denotes, in general terms, an excited condition, involving a complex of feelings or sensations of internal origin, generally considered to be more than evanescent in duration, to be intense in character, and to have some reference to purpose and motivation.

B. 1. Within this broad, 'average' usage, there have been many different theories of *emotion*. When carefully examined, these theories may be seen to owe their truth to slight changes in the meaning of the term. Thus the theories of James and McDougall that emotion was the affective component of instinct (q.v.)—that is, of purposive behaviour—mean accepting that emotion can be a *mild* as well as an intense condition, depending on the strength of the motivation. On the other hand, those who, from Drever on, opposed McDougall's theory by stressing that emotion was only aroused when desires were obstructed, were those who tended to confine emotion to an intense affective condition. A modern version of this theory is that of emotion as 'disorganized response'. This also clearly involves a limitation on the range of application of the term, since it cannot apply to powerful feelings accompanying *integrated* responses.

Another theory which entailed a different meaning was the James-Lange theory of emotion. According to this, emotion was the feeling of the bodily changes that the external cause of the emotion occasioned in us. These changes were not limited to, for instance, visceral and similar changes of a preparatory kind, but included the actual actions we carried out in overt behaviour. As James wrote, 'We feel sorry because we cry, angry because we strike, afraid because we tremble' (*The Principles of Psychology*, London: Macmillan, 1890, vol. II, p. 450). Not only does this theory involve an extension in the sensations that characterize *emotion* for James and those who followed him, it also renders the term motivationally neutral. As opposed to those who use *emotion* in such a way as to include desires to do something, James's theory makes this redundant, because it holds that the emotion is the *consequence* of doing something. The action is the cause of the emotion and not the other way about. In this respect James's theory is similar to a version of learning theory according to which emotions are states which lead the organism to prolong or terminate them by carrying out appropriate behaviour, according to whether these states are pleasant or unpleasant. In such a theory, the desire to act appropriately to the emotion cannot be considered part of the emotion, else the theory would be circular.

2. Major philosophical disputes have also been the cause of differences in meaning in the word. Watson, in regarding emotion as 'implicit behaviour', was meaning by the word something different from those who regarded it as the *effects* of such behaviour in consciousness. Subsequently, in a spirit of cautious eclecticism, many psychologists have defined *emotion* as including both physical and mental events. Such a definition makes it impossible to formulate the James-Lange theory of emotion. In a neurological amendment to behaviourism, D. O. Hebb has recently defined *emotion* as 'the neural process that is inferred from and causes emotional behavior' (*The Organization of Behavior*, New York: Wiley, 1949, p. 148). This definition follows rejection of the idea that a mental state can be a cause of behaviour. Hebb, it seems, considered the word too valuable to be wasted on an epiphenomenon.

C. The extreme definitional lability of the word is no doubt due to the taking over from ordinary language of a word referring to a complex and relatively inaccessible condition by scientifically-minded psychologists. Habits of ordinary speech are no doubt responsible for the fact that usages have a good deal in common, despite the differences in the definitions.

W. H. N. Hotopf

See also: AFFECT
MOTIVATION

Empathy

A. *Empathy* denotes the understanding of the behaviour of another on the basis of one's own experience and behaviour.

B. The term *empathy* is a translation of the German *Einfühlung*, as that term was used by T. Lipps to denote a process in which one observes a gesture of another, imitates it, calls out through the imitation a previously experienced feeling, and then projects that feeling on to the other. *Einfühlung* or *empathy* entered the vocabulary of English-language social psychology through interest in the work, not of Lipps, but of M. Scheler, and generally the phenomenon denoted by the term is thought to be one of the forms of sympathy dealt with by Scheler. Actually Scheler uses the term to denote the phenomenon Lipps had dealt with, only to reject it as an explanation of the awareness on the part of one person of the feelings of another: 'It only needs to be emphasized that this acceptance and understanding does not come about as the conclusion to an "argument from analogy", nor by any projective "empathy" or "mimetic impulse" (Lipps). ... If this apprehension itself were only made possible (as Theodor Lipps believes), by a tendency to imitate and by the *reproduction*, thus evoked, of a previously experienced joy or fear (*plus* an empathic projection of what is reproduced into the other person), we should obviously be moving in a circle' (M. Scheler, *The Nature of Sympathy*, trans. by P. Heath from the 5th German edn. under the title *Wesen und Formen der Sympathie*, New Haven: Yale University Press, 1954, pp. 9–11).

C. Usage of the term following Scheler has sometimes centred on phenomena other than, or only a constituent part of, the phenomena that Scheler, following Lipps, intended it to denote.

1. H. Becker uses the term, in a free translation of part of Scheler's work to denote the *intuitive perception* of the emotional state on the part of one person by another ('Some Forms of Sympathy: A Phenomenological Analysis',

Empire

Journal of Abnormal and Social Psychology, vol. 26, 1931, p. 68). Actually the direct and primary perception of feeling in gesture, as perceiving shame in a blush or joy in laughter, is the process which Scheler opposes to empathy (M. Scheler, *The Nature of Sympathy*, p. 10).

2. For G. W. Allport, on the other hand, the term *empathy* is a fair translation for *Einfühlung* 'provided it is understood to mean only elementary motor mimicry and is not employed in the broad sense of "a gift of understanding people" as is sometimes the case today' ('The Historical Background of Modern Social Psychology', in G. Lindzey (ed.), *Handbook of Social Psychology*, Cambridge, Mass.: Addison-Wesley, 1954, vol. 1, p. 20). In one sense Allport is right, for Lipps and Scheler use the term in connection with (but not to denote) the imitation of gesture; but, as indicated in the earlier quotations from Scheler, the term is used not to denote the motor mimicry which in Lipp's theory underlies the reproduction of the feeling in one's self, but rather with respect to the projection of the feeling aroused in the self on to the other, and, by extension, to the total process of understanding the other in so far as that process is based on the ability to call out in one's self the response of the other through one's own experience and behaviour. D. L. S. Cottrell, Jr. and R. F. Dymond ('The Empathic Responses', *Psychiatry*, vol. 12, 1949, pp. 355–9) have used the term to denote the ability to understand others through being able to call out in oneself responses identical with or similar to the responses of the others, as that ability has been a central concept in the stream of social-psychological theory containing the works of C. H. Cooley, G. H. Mead, and H. S. Sullivan. Cottrell and Dymond call for empirical research into the nature and condition of empathy, because of its basic function in society in relation to sharing the attitudes and behaviour of others and to the therapy situation, where the psychotherapist must know how the patient is responding to him, by responding to himself in the same way.

T. H. Pear

See also: Imitation
           Internalization
           Sympathy
           Understanding

Empire

A. The term *empire* has been applied to states characterized (a) by their large magnitude in area, population, and power, including several nations, peoples, or states of different race or culture; (b) by their origin in the conquest of several of these peoples by a dominant tribe or nation which continues to dominate over the others and to treat them as inferior with the consequence that unity is maintained by compulsion rather than consent; (c) by their political structure vesting supreme authority in a single head (the *emperor*) from whose grant all local authority is derived; and frequently (d) by a theory of potential universality under a common religion, ideology, or law providing a political and moral structure which will eventually establish peace and harmony among all men. In the latter characteristic empires resemble modern conceptions of international organization and world federation which, however, differ in emphasizing the equality, autonomy, and consent of the component peoples, nations, or states. Every civilization, as pointed out by A. J. Toynbee (*A Study of History*, London: Oxford University Press, 1934, vol. I) has tended at some stage of its history to become united in a 'Universal State', usually taking the form of an empire. Each of the characteristics has been lacking in certain of the historic empires but a 'typical' empire would include them all, as did Ancient Rome at the height of its power.

B. Empires have arisen in human history whenever the idea and practice of territorial sovereignty (usually resting on settled agriculture) or of ideological sovereignty (usually resting on a crusading religion) has superseded the kinship or tribal basis of political authority which prevailed among primitive peoples and which militated against the expansion of political power through territorial or ideological conquest. The relative importance of the different characteristics of empire have, however, varied in history.

1. The empires of native African rulers were usually short-lived products of conquest, uniting similar tribes within relatively small areas. The same was largely true of the pre-Columbian empires in Mexico and Peru, though the Incas ruled a large area for a considerable time by effective administration and ideological propaganda.

2. The ancient empires of Egypt, Babylonia, Assyria, Persia, India (Asoka), China, and Japan were usually larger and more enduring, and went further in cementing union by religion, ideology, or law. These tendencies were further developed in the Greek empires of Athens and

Macedonia, and the Roman empire which lasted for several centuries through the vigour of Roman law and administration, and the general extension of Roman citizenship.

3. The medieval empires of the Arabs, Turks, and Moghuls, professing Islam, and of the Franks and Germans, professing Christianity, were unified by the bonds of religion; and the idea of a universal empire, destined to give peace to mankind, was asserted by both religions (M. Khadduri & H. J. Liebesny (eds.), *Law in the Middle East*, Washington: Middle East Institute, 1955, p. 350).

4. The modern empires have been of two kinds, maritime and land. Those of Portugal, Spain, Netherlands, France, Britain, and later, Germany, Italy, Belgium, the United States, and Japan resulted from overseas conquest and colonization, and were characterized by the cultural diversity and political inequality of the peoples they united. Some attempted to achieve political unity by spreading the civilization, law and economy of the central power throughout the empire, as in ancient Rome. Others permitted increasing cultural, economic, and political autonomy and 'self-determination' of the member peoples, hoping to maintain a moral solidarity even though the member states became politically independent. The latter tendency prevailed as the central power became democratic, as the colonies became modernized and nationalistic, and as international organization developed (Q. Wright, 'Recognition and Self-Determination', *Proceedings of the American Society of International Law*, Washington: American Society of International Law, 1954, pp. 23 ff.). The continental empires of France under Napoleon, of Russia under the Romanoffs and Communists, of Germany under the Hohenzollerns and Nazis, of Austria under the Hapsburgs, and of China under the Manchus and Communists, were composed of less diverse peoples, and sought to maintain unity through administrative efficiency, protected economies, the development of national or ideological solidarity, and the preservation of centralized and autocratic government.

Quincy Wright

See also: COMMONWEALTH

Empirical

A. In modern usage the adjective *empirical*, in its combinations with various nouns, appears to denote observations and propositions primarily based on sense experience and/or derived from such experience by methods of inductive logic, including mathematics and statistics. But 'the history of the use of the word "empirical" makes it evident that one cannot use the term clearly or precisely without antecedently stipulating its use' (A. Pierce, 'Empirical Propositions and Max Weber's *Verstehende Soziologie*, A Rejoinder', *American Sociological Review*, vol. 22, 1957, p. 224).

B. This adjective derives from the Greek ἔμπειρος, experienced, practised, or acquainted with. From this word stems the Greek ἐμπιρικός and the Latin *empiricus* which both mean experienced, belonging to experience, based on experience. Both the Latin and the Greek terms, however, also refer specifically to a physician belonging to a school which trusted in *practice only*, without reference to theory or science in any form. Even in present-day medical parlance *empirical* tends to be used and understood to mean based on trial and error without any rationale. In physics or chemistry, however, empirical is likely to mean factually true but theoretically unexplained.

Corresponding interpretations of the term also occur in social science contexts: Thus, according to P. H. Furfey, 'Empirical generalizations are based completely on experience. ... The mind sees no reason why this *must* be so; it sees merely that it *is* so' (*The Scope and Method of Sociology*, New York: Harper & Brothers, 1953, p. 76). C. C. Pratt distinguishes between causal and empirical laws, the former 'the formulation of observed correlations to which some form of the method of concomitant variation has been successfully applied', the latter also 'formulations of observed conditions, but in their case some of the antecedent terms are not subject to control or variation, or some of the items which unquestionably influence the correlations are inaccessible' (*The Logic of Modern Psychology*, New York: The Macmillan Co., 1939, pp. 157–8).

C. J. Dewey has pointed out two basic meanings of 'that ambiguous word', '... the word "empirical" is often set in opposition to the *rational*. ... The early meaning ... limited the application of the word to conclusions that rest upon an accumulation of past experiences to exclusion of insight into principles. ... when a scientific conclusion is said to be empirically established, no such exclusion of rationality or reasoning is involved. ... every conclusion scientifically reached as to matters of fact involves reasoning with and from principles usually mathematically

Empiricism

expressed. To say then that it is empirically established is to say the opposite of what is said when "empirical" means only observations and habitual response to what is observed' (*Logic: The Theory of Inquiry*, New York: Henry Holt, 1938, pp. 9, 37).

F. Kaufmann points to a different dichotomy: 'There are two levels of clarity in understanding the meaning of the methods of empirical science. The first is reached as soon as it is realised that knowledge of reality is acquired through systematic observations and their interpretations in terms of theoretical principles. The second is reached when the process of inquiry is freed of all interpretations that ascribe to its results an "absolute" validity transcending possible human experience' (*Methodology of the Social Sciences*, London: Oxford University Press, 1944, p. 13).

D. Current discussion tends to emphasize concrete characteristics required of whatever is to be called empirical: 'The term signifies not merely the inductive method of which the knowledge is obtained from experience; [it also implies] that hypotheses, however reached, must be verified by the facts of experience' (M. J. Adler & W. German (eds.), *The Great Ideas, A Syntopicon of Great Books of the Western World*, Chicago: Encyclopaedia Britannica, 1952, vol. I, p. 473). S. F. Barker calls statements empirical if they 'involve appeal to what has been seen or heard or felt or smelled or tasted: experience is involved' (*Induction and Hypothesis*, Ithaca, N.Y.: Cornell University Press, 1957, p. 2). B. Russell says of an empirical statement that 'empirical evidence may at any moment disprove it' and of empirical knowledge that it is 'dependent upon, or derived from perception' (*History of Western Philosophy*, London: Allen & Unwin, 1946, pp. 161, 171).

Franz Adler

See also: EMPIRICISM
NON-EMPIRICAL

Empiricism

A. *Empiricism* is the name of a doctrine or group of doctrines and is also the name of a disposition and of a manner of proceeding (be it in a science, an inquiry, or a practical activity). There is a close connection between the two senses, in that *empiricism* as a disposition or manner of acting is such that it is consonant with or would be approved by the doctrine of *empiricism*.

1. 'The thesis of empiricism found its clear elaboration in the philosophies of these men [Bacon, Locke, Hume]. The conception that perception is the source and the ultimate test of all knowledge is the eventual result of their work' (H. Reichenbach, *The Rise of Scientific Philosophy*, Los Angeles: University of California Press, 1951, p. 78).

2. '... empiricists firmly believe in [the] famous statement ..."There is nothing in the intellect that was not perceived before through the senses". Since the camera of the senses can photograph only sensory objects existing in space and time ... empiricists do not admit any supersensory reality ...' (P. A. Sorokin, *Fads and Foibles in Modern Sociology*, Chicago: Henry Regnery, 1956, p. 280).

B. 1. The doctrine of empiricism stresses either the importance or the exclusive importance of experience. It is in this sense that empiricism receives the approbation of a very substantial proportion of modern thinkers. The ultimate dependence of theories or principles on experience can be formulated in two ways, either genetically, or logically. The genetic formulation insists that every theory, abstraction, etc., has its origin or prototype in experience; the logical formulation leaves the question of origins open and merely insists that the final verdict concerning validity should be a matter of experience or experiment. The genetic formulation was more common in the past, whilst the logical one is more generally accepted at present.

Thus empiricism, as a theory of scientific method and of knowledge generally, may mean either (a) the doctrine that whilst theory is essential and desirable, it ultimately depends for its validity on observation and experiment; (b) a doctrine which asserts or recommends the absence of theory altogether.

It is in the former sense that *empiricism* receives the approbation of a very substantial proportion of modern thinkers. In the latter sense the term tends to be pejorative and to designate a state of affairs only tolerated when there is no alternative. The term is however also used in this latter sense, in which its meaning approximates something like 'trial and error without guiding idea', particularly in medicine but also outside it.

2. In the context of scientific methodology and the theory of knowledge, experience is opposed to *theory* (or, loosely, to 'ideas', hypotheses, etc.), which, according to empiricism, is either ultimately dependent on experience, or

238

altogether absent. In the context of morals, politics, and practical activity, experience is opposed to *principle* (of conduct, policy) or to 'plans', etc., rather than to theory. Empiricism then becomes the doctrine which insists that these principles are, or should be, ultimately based on experience, or be absent altogether.

E. A. Gellner

See also: EMPIRICAL

Enabling Act (See Appropriation)

Enculturation

A. *Enculturation* may be defined as conscious or unconscious conditioning occurring within that learning process whereby man, as child and adult, achieves competence in his culture.

B. The word, introduced into social science by M. J. Herskovits as recently as 1948, has not yet gained wide use. As Herskovits defines it, it overlaps with socialization (q.v.) and contrasts with acculturation (q.v.).

1. Herskovits defined *enculturation* as follows: 'The aspects of the learning experience which mark off man from other creatures, and by means of which, initially, and in later life, he achieves competence in his culture, may be called *enculturation*. This is in essence a process of conscious or unconscious conditioning, exercised within the limits sanctioned by a given body of custom' (*Man and His Works*, New York: Knopf, 1948, p. 39). According to Herskovits, the enculturative process is complex and lifelong, but it varies at different stages of the life cycle. For example, enculturation occurs as a somewhat arbitrarily imposed process in infancy, but as a person grows to adulthood he learns more consciously to accept or reject the values and preferences of his community. Although Herskovits does not specifically say so, his discussion implies the notion that each new-born child possesses a set of biologically inherited mechanisms, which he must somehow transform or control in conformity with his society's way of life. In this sense the function of enculturation is to convert each infant's biological responses to socially acceptable forms of cultural conduct. The result is what M. Titiev calls *biocultural behaviour* (*The Science of Man*, New York: Henry Holt, 1954).

2. *Enculturation* is basically synonymous with the more widely used term, *socialization*. Herskovits suggests that enculturation is the broader term in that '... not only is all adjustment to social living achieved, but also all those satisfactions that, though they are of course a part of social experience, derive from individual expression rather than association with others in the group' (*Man and His Works*, pp. 39–40). Contrariwise, if a limited definition of culture (q.v.) is used, socialization might well be regarded as the broader term.

3. *Enculturation* is to be contrasted with *acculturation* in that the latter refers to acquiring culture other than that of one's own society, and in general to the acquiring by one society of culture traits from another society.

Mischa Titiev

See also: ACCULTURATION
SOCIALIZATION

End (See Goal)

Endogamy (Also **Exogamy**)

A. *Endogamy* and *exogamy* are processes of marrying-in or of marrying-out, respectively, with reference to a specified social group. The terms can also be extended to mating-in and mating-out as determined by sexual taboos applying to relations within or without marriage; it has also been extended to mating-in and mating-out among sub-human primates.

B. *Endogamy* and *exogamy* are correlative terms, introduced into ethnology by J. F. McLennan (*Primitive Marriage*, Edinburgh: Adam & Charles Black, 1865, p. 48). Briefly, they mean, as their etymology would indicate 'marrying-in' and 'marrying-out' respectively. At the cost of violating their etymology they have been extended, on occasion, to cover sexual relations outside marriage as well. Endogamy and exogamy may be thought of as social processes, varying from mere tendencies to marry out or marry in to strict observance of explicit rules to do so. For example, E. C. Parsons, in describing the Tewa, points out that 'There is a tendency for the moieties to be endogamous ...' ('Tewa Kin, Clan, and Moiety', *American Anthropologist*, vol. 26, 1924, p. 337). At the other extreme, there are cultures in which marriage within one's own clan, or other specified group, may be prohibited by an explicit rule, violation of which is punishable with death.

C. The groups to which rules or tendencies to marry-out or marry-in refer vary: they include the family or an unnamed grouping of relatives to each of whom the incest taboo applies; the residents of a locality; the members of a lineage,

Entrepreneur

clan, moiety, or tribe; castes, aristocracies, races, members of a religious faith, occupational groups, or economic strata. 'Endogamy is found in local units. ... In India the basis of endogamy is caste ...' (F. Boas, 'Anthropology', in E. R. A. Seligman (ed.), *Encyclopedia of the Social Sciences*, New York: The Macmillan Co., 1930, vol. II, p. 86). 'Endogamy flourishes in stratified societies and is illustrated in the royal marriages of modern Europe and in the prevalent inbreeding of its aristocracies. The equivalent condition occurs in class conscious savage communities. Among the Masai of East Africa blacksmiths are pariahs; hence no Masai of good standing marries into a blacksmith's family' (R. H. Lowie, 'Marriage', *Encyclopedia of the Social Sciences*, 1933, vol. X, p. 146). It is sometimes said that this or that culture lacks exogamy or endogamy: '... the Andean region lacks ... exogamy' (R. H. Lowie, 'American Culture History', *American Anthropologist*, vol. 42, 1940, p. 412). '... both in cultures where exogamy is practiced and in those where there is no trace of the custom ...' (B. Z. Seligman, 'The Problem of Incest and Exogamy: A Restatement', *American Anthropologist*, vol. 52, 1950, p. 314). What is meant here, without doubt, is that there is no specific named group, such as a clan or a moiety, to which rules of exogamy or endogamy apply. But the processes of endogamy and exogamy are universal in human society. The universality of the incest taboo means the universality of marrying and mating out; and nowhere is magnitude of social distance between possible mates irrelevant to marriage.

It is sometimes thought that preliterate cultures are characterized by exogamy: '... among primitive people it [endogamy] is rare ...' (C. H. Wedgwood, 'Endogamy', *Encyclopaedia Britannica*, New York: Encyclopaedia Britannica, Inc., 14th edn., 1929, p. 436). Higher cultures are then thought to be marked by endogamy. It is true that most of the pertinent groups in preliterate cultures—family lineage, clan, or moiety—are defined in terms of exogamy although tribes are frequently endogamous; whereas the groupings in higher cultures tend to be defined in terms of endogamy: castes, aristocracies, religious faiths, etc. But the processes of marrying-out and marrying-in, though opposite, are inseparable and universal. A rule requiring one to marry out of one group is a rule requiring him to marry into another group if he is to marry at all. A rule prohibiting exogamy, such as a law against intermarriage

between Caucasians and Negroes, has the effect of making both groups endogamous, at least with reference to each other.

Leslie A. White

See also: MARRIAGE

Enterprise (See **Entrepreneur**)

Entrepreneur

A. The term *entrepreneur* denotes a person who exercises wholly or partly the functions of: (a) initiating, co-ordinating, controlling, and instituting major changes in a business enterprise and/or (b) bearing those risks of its operation which arise from the dynamic nature of society and imperfect knowledge of the future and which cannot be converted into certain costs through transfer, calculation, or elimination.

B. When the entrepreneur first was treated as distinct economic functionary rather than (as hitherto) as a particular kind of capitalist, his dual roles of co-ordinating and controlling the factors of production and of risk-bearing in business were recognized. Definitions and descriptions since have emphasized one or both these roles.

1. In those concepts of the entrepreneur emphasizing co-ordination and control, it has been pointed out that he initiates the enterprise, makes decisions on expansion and reduction of facilities, and establishes major policies on price and output (F. H. Knight, *Risk, Uncertainty, and Profit*, Boston: Houghton Mifflin, 1921, p. 271).

2. On the other hand, in portrayals of the entrepreneur as risk-bearer, stress is put on his shortage of knowledge concerning prices at which his product will sell and the exposure of his enterprise to other physical and economic hazards. This approach has been refined by showing that the entrepreneur exists only in a dynamic society and that he has responsibility for bearing residual risks which cannot be transferred to others and converted into money costs. Ultimately, because of these refinements, the entrepreneur came to be pictured as a bearer of uncertainty, which is not subject to transfer nor to exact estimation, rather than of risks, which are of calculable significance and in some cases are transferable. He was conceived as the responsible director of business enterprises under conditions of less than perfect knowledge of the future.

3. A functional approach not stressing risk-bearing while at the same time basing the entre-

240

preneur's role on the dynamic nature of economic life is that in which he is pictured as the innovator who employs in a practical way improvements of productive processes affecting demand for and costs of making the product of the firm (J. A. Schumpeter, *Business Cycles*, New York: McGraw-Hill, 1939, pp. 102–4).

C. In distinguishing the entrepreneur by the class of income he receives, it is usually indicated that acquisition of profits mark off his contribution from those by owners of other factors of production. Further, he is usually considered to be a residual income-recipient, who is compensated after rent, interest, and wages are paid. These latter three classes of income are described as basically contractual while that of the entrepreneur is non-contractual. Monopoly gains and windfall elements in entrepreneur income have also received attention.

D. One person may not only be an entrepreneur, however defined, but may also own other factors of production used in a particular business. Thus, he may receive an income which is a composite of profits and other elements. On the other hand, the growth in size of business units and particularly the increased use of limited liability companies means that in many firms there are groups of entrepreneurs rather than one and that there may be specialization of functions among them. It has also been pointed out that one need not be an owner of a business to be an entrepreneur; instead, an official of a corporation might qualify as entrepreneur if he exercises leadership and control and if its stockholders are inactive in the corporate management.

William H. Wesson

See also: PROFIT

RISK AND UNCERTAINTY

Environment

A. *Environment* may be defined as consisting of all external sources and factors to which a person or aggregate of persons is actually or potentially responsive.

B. An environment may be broken down into physical, social, and cultural elements, although the boundaries between these will vary according to the theoretical predilections of the observer. Thus, for example, if one regards tools and instruments as part of culture (q.v.) they will form part of the cultural environment, but if culture is restricted to shared symbolic-

ally communicated patterns governing action, tools will be part of the physical environment. In this respect it should also be pointed out that if the theoretical frame of reference (q.v.) employed stresses the point of view of the acting person, rather than that of the observer, an additional dimension of the environment must be added, viz. the realm of the non-empirical (q.v.) to which, imaginary or not, persons do respond.

C. The decision as to what is *external* will also depend upon the theoretical approach employed. In much social theory 'We think of our organisms as ourselves and environment as that which lies outside us' (R. M. MacIver & C. H. Page, *Society*, London: Macmillan, 1949, p. 74). In those theories which stress the concept of the self (q.v.) or the ego (q.v.) rather than that of the organism, the physical organism can be an object to the self and hence a part of the environment. Even the self itself so far as it can be an object to itself can be considered as a part of the environment (K. Davis, *Human Society*, New York: The Macmillan Co., 1949, p. 210).

D. Many of those who have used the idea of physical environment in the past have combined it with *heredity* (q.v.) to form a theoretical frame of reference for explaining social action (T. Parsons, *The Structure of Social Action*, New York: McGraw-Hill, 1937, pp. 112–13). Such people appear often to think of society (q.v.) as a biological system or at any rate a system of acts the normative and goal-directed aspects of which can be ignored or explained by the interaction of heredity and environment. Major difficulties have developed with such ideas, and recent theorists tend to argue that heredity and physical environment do not explain human behaviour or determine the content of normative culture (T. Parsons & E. A. Shils, et al., *Toward a General Theory of Action*, Cambridge, Mass.: Harvard University Press, 1951). Such writers do not abandon the idea of physical environment, although they are likely to discuss it under the terminology of 'physical objects in the situation' of the actor or the social system (q.v.) (ibid., pp. 98–105) and to treat it analytically as constituting part of the means and conditions of action (K. Davis, *Human Society*, pp. 125–7).

J. Mogey

See also: HEREDITY

SOCIAL SITUATION

Equality

Equality

A. In its social context the term denotes an 'ideal' arrangement of statuses and rights, the moral value of which derives from the extent to which (and the sense in which) 'what is common to all men is not *more* important but *infinitely more* important than the accidents by which men differ' (H. Belloc, *The French Revolution*, London: Williams & Norgate, 1925, p. 22).

B. The differing interpretations of the ideal are best assessed in the light of historically significant debates on the basic issues—i.e. (a) whether men can be *regarded* as equal in any particular, (b) whether they should be *treated* as equal, (c) the nature and source of 'inequality', i.e. failure to attain the 'ideal', observable social situations which fall short of the 'ideal' of equality and in terms of which the 'ideal' of equality itself is formulated. Thus:

1. Aristotle, writing at a time when substantial equality between Athenian citizens was one of the facts of political life, distinguished two sorts of equality in social treatment: numerical equality, which gave everyone the same rights; and proportionate equality, which gave men rights in accordance with their deserts. He considered that the second embodied justice, while the first did not. But he saw that, even when the principle of proportionate equality was established, men would still quarrel about its application. 'Some take the line that if men are equal in one respect, they may consider themselves equal in all; others take the line that if they are superior in one respect, they may claim superiority all round' (E. Barker (ed.), *The Politics of Aristotle*, London: Oxford University Press, 1948, p. 240).

2. The Stoic doctrine that men had all received the gift of *reason* enabled men to be viewed as fundamentally equal, both in nature and before the law. In Cicero's words, 'No single thing is so like another, so exactly its counterpart, as all of us are to one another. Nay, if bad habits and false beliefs did not twist the weaker minds and turn them in whatever direction they are inclined, no one would be so like his own self as all men would be like all others. And so, however we may define man, a single definition will apply to all. ... For those creatures who have received the gift of reason from Nature have also received right reason, and therefore they have also received the gift of Law, which is right reason applied to command and prohibition' (*De Legibus*, trans. by C. W. Keyes, Loeb Classical Library, London: Heinemann,

1951, vol. I, x, 29; xii, 33). The Roman jurists assumed an equality before the law, founded upon the common rationality of mankind.

3. Christian doctrine added to this a conception of equality amongst Christian believers and of common humanity in the possession of soul and free will. Equality in the eyes of God, however, did not mean equality of treatment on earth. The medieval conception of hierarchy gradually became accommodated to (but never entirely obscured) ideas of natural equality.

4. In the 17th and 18th centuries, Social Contract theory, in its various forms, revived the notion of a fundamental equality in order to explain the origins of society and government, and to combat the claims of hereditary monarchs and privileged aristocracies. Indeed, a contract theory presupposes some equality between those who are parties to a contract. Equality was treated in these ways:

(a) Hobbes asserted that in the state of nature men are equals: 'Nature hath made men so equal, in the faculties of the body and mind; as that though there be found one man sometimes manifestly stronger in body, or of quicker mind than another; yet when all is reckoned together, the difference between man and man, is not so considerable, as that one man can thereupon claim to himself any benefit, to which another may not pretend, as well as he' (*Leviathan*, pt. I, ch. XIII). Hobbes used this contention to explain why men in a state of nature are in a state of war (they are *equally capable of killing one another*, and equally subject to envy), and why men turn to an authority apart from themselves in order to have rest from the continual strife of war between equals.

(b) Locke also asserted that in the state of nature there was equality, but emphasized that it was essentially *equality of status*: 'there being nothing more evident than that creatures of the same species and rank, promiscuously born to all the same advantages of Nature, and the use of the same faculties, should also be equal one amongst another, without subordination or subjection, unless the lord and master of them all should, by any manifest declaration of his will, set one above another' (*Second Treatise*, ch. II, 4). Locke uses this equality to show that no man can claim supremacy over another, and that all have been commanded by the law of nature to respect one another's possessions. This forms part of his attack on arbitrary government and his view that men have a right to change their government if it offends against this law.

(c) Rousseau concentrates upon *inequality*, stating that it is of two kinds: 'Natural or physical', comprising differences of age, health, and strength, and qualities of the mind or soul; and 'moral or political', depending upon a kind of convention established or at least authorized by men, and comprising privileges in riches, honour, and power over others. Men come into society with certain natural inequalities, but these are accentuated, perpetuated, and increased by social convention and government. His conclusion is that 'moral inequality, authorised by positive right alone, clashes with natural right, whenever it is not proportionate to physical inequality' (*Discourse on the Origin of Inequality*, trans. by G. D. H. Cole (Everyman edn.), London: J. M. Dent, 1955, p. 221). Rousseau thus does not assert a natural equality, but does assert that society and government have created immense inequalities which must be eliminated or reduced. This has been the standpoint of most later advocates of equality.

5. The official doctrines of the American and French Revolutions were equalitarian and anti-hierarchical asserting that men were equal, in respect of their rights and in the eyes of the law.

6. Since the end of the 18th century, the doctrine of equality has proceeded on the assumption that, while there are natural inequalities (of mind, strength, etc.), this is no reason to accept artificial inequalities based on privilege. The kinds of equality demanded have varied with time and circumstances, depending upon the kinds of inequality encountered. There have been demands for equality of opportunity, equality of treatment by the state, equality of the franchise, equality between the sexes. In some cases the demand has been for *numerical equality* (the franchise), while in others it has been for *proportionate* (equality of opportunity, treatment at law). Today, when a man in Britain or the U.S.A. says he is in favour of equality, it usually means that he wishes to reduce the inequality between social classes. His belief, with R. H. Tawney, is that 'because men are men, social institutions—property rights, and the organisation of industry, and the system of public health and education—should be planned, as far as is possible, to emphasise and strengthen, not the class differences which divide, but the common humanity which unites them' (*Equality*, London: Allen & Unwin, 1952, p. 38). He will probably continue to make a distinction between numerical and proportionate equality. In particular, he is likely to argue for proportionate equality in fields where it is possible to distinguish between individuals without disturbing the pattern of social co-operation, e.g. in regard to earnings and to the application of social services. But in fields where groups of people are being treated as inferior on account of their race, colour, religion, or sex, he will probably argue for numerical equality, on the ground that these broad distinctions are irrelevant to the value to society of the individual human beings concerned, and should not be allowed to impose an artificial inequality upon them.

J. D. B. Miller

See also: STRATIFICATION

Error (See **Reliability**)

Estate (See **Social Class**)

Ethnic Group
A. The term denotes a social group which, within a larger cultural and social system, claims or is accorded a special status in terms of a complex of traits (*ethnic traits*) which it exhibits or is believed to exhibit. Such traits are diverse, and there is much variety in the complexes that they form. Prominent among them are those drawn from the religious and linguistic characteristics of the social group, the distinctive skin-pigmentation of its members, their national or geographic origins or those of their forebears.

B. 1. The term is most frequently applied to any group which differs in one or several aspects of its patterned, socially-transmitted way of life from other groups, or in the totality of that way of life or culture. Frequently, the group in question formerly enjoyed or still enjoys a separate political-national identity as well. Thus, various national-ethnic stocks in the United States would be considered as ethnic groups, e.g. Greeks, Poles, Italians, Swedes, etc. One of the dominant research interests is to discover the extent to which persons of these various origins still constitute active groups, with their common ethnic or 'old-world' culture traits still forming a focus of group integration, and with persisting ties to their co-ethnics abroad. A classic study in this vein was W. I. Thomas & F. Znaniecki, *The Polish Peasant in Europe and America* (Boston: Badger, 1918).

2. *Ethnic* as an adjective is often used interchangeably with *religious*, *racial*, *national*, *cultural*, and *sub-cultural*. Thus, in the U.S., the Negroes are more properly called an ethnic

Ethnic Group

rather than a racial group, as M. F. Ashley Montagu urges persuasively in his *Man's Most Dangerous Myth* (New York: Columbia University Press, 1942). Similarly, the Jewish population is sometimes treated as an ethnic group, sometimes, erroneously, as a racial group, sometimes as a sub-cultural group within the total American culture. A common coverall term which is used to refer to ethnic, national, racial, and cultural groups, etc. is *minority* or *minority group*. When so used in the U.S., the emphasis is upon the numerical dimensions of the group relative to the native-born white Protestant majority, though in fact the latter may contain numerous ethnic groups of diverse national origins within it.

3. European usage is very similar to the American, though other terms come to be applied, such as *colonials* to refer to citizens of Commonwealths or Federations who were born or reside in various of the present or former colonies of the major European powers. In the Soviet Union, *nationalities* is more frequently applied to the diverse national-ethnic units who make up the membership of the Union.

C. 1. R. E. Park and his students have done outstanding research work into the patterns of adjustment, accommodation, and assimilation of ethnic minorities, especially in the Chicago area in the 1920s and 1930s. The most recent focus of research in the United States has been upon the Puerto Ricans on the mainland who, enjoying equal citizenship, have tended to migrate from Puerto Rico in increasing numbers over the last decade (see, for example, N. Glazer & D. P. Moynihan, *Beyond the Melting Pot*, Cambridge, Mass.: Massachusetts Institute of Technology Press, 1963). A continuing body of anthropological research is directed at clarifying the processes of change among various American-Indian groups, with secondary interest in American-Mexicans in the Southwest, and American-Chinese and Japanese in the West and Southwest.

2. The interest of political scientists in ethnic groups has been confined largely to the role of such groups in the structure and function of urban political machines; their voting proclivities; and the relevance of ethnic origins for the political chances of various candidates for office. Here, religious, as well as national or ethnic origins and identities are taken into account.

D. A sharper contrast can be noted between usage in the last thirty years and that of earlier

portions of this century. The term *ethnic* has its derivation from the Greek *ethnos* meaning tribe or race, but *ethnic group* has come to be more closely associated with *ethos* or *custom* as the latter is now analysed and understood in terms of laws of social learning and social inheritance, as against former conceptions of biological and genetic determination of culture patterns. In current social science, the conjoining of race and culture, as in the earlier conceptions, is severely deplored and copious evidence of the independent variability of the two is available (see again, M. F. Ashley Montagu, *Man's Most Dangerous Myth*).

E. Modern social science literature recognizes that where religion, culture, and common biological origin are shared by a group, the bonds are mutually reinforcing. But studies in acculturation (q.v.) and assimilation (q.v.) amply document the uneven attrition in these three bonds, so that communities which formerly were bound on all three counts can be found at later times to possess many traditional cultural ties even though former religious ties have disappeared in greater degree and much marriage outside the groups has resulted in much more biological heterogeneity than before.

Study of the acculturation of Old World ethnic groups in New World cultures reveals the impact of changing social-class position on maintenance of former ethnic ties. As members of a group move up the class ladder, they come to resemble their class peers as much if not more than their co-ethnics. Some students suggest that there is a great concern among those desirous of upward mobility to discard their ethnic identification tags.

F. A major theoretical issue concerns the possibility of genuine ethnic or cultural pluralism (including pluralism of religious belief) within the framework of a democratic society. Formerly much of the concern with this issue centred on the strains arising from such pluralism; today attention is frequently paid to the difficulties of maintaining a pluralist society under the impact of mass society and culture.

Melvin M. Tumin

See also: ACCOMMODATION
ASSIMILATION
CONFLICT
GROUP
MINORITY GROUP
RACE AND MINORITY GROUP
RELATIONS

Ethnocentrism

A. *Ethnocentrism* may be defined as the '...view of things in which one's own group is the centre of everything, and all others are scaled and rated with reference to it' (W. G. Sumner, *Folkways*, Boston: Ginn, 1906, p. 13).

B. The denotation of ethnocentrism given above remains unchanged from the day of its introduction as a term in social science by W. G. Sumner in 1906. M. J. Herskovits presents ethnocentrism as '... the point of view that one's own way of life is to be preferred to all others' (*Man and His Works*, New York: Knopf, 1948, p. 68). Thus, the term includes the idea of identification by the individual with *his* group's culture, and the assumption on his part that his group's culture patterns are the best, and the right, ways of acting.

C. All other social sciences use the term in the same sense as does anthropology. Anthropologists tend to apply *ethnocentrism* to tribal groups, while sociologists and social psychologists more frequently extend the term to in-group attitudes exhibited by religious, economic, racial, caste and class groups *within* the larger social orders as well as between such orders. Thus G. W. Allport speaks of 'the ethnocentric pivots in culture' in correlating ethnocentrism to the problem of prejudice in modern society (*The Nature of Prejudice*, Cambridge, Mass.: Addison-Wesley, 1954, pp. 289–91).

D. In recent years, social science writing has treated *cultural relativity* (q.v.) as an antonym of ethnocentrism, with ethnocentrism being regarded as incompatible with the canons of social science. (See D. Bidney, 'The Concept of Value in Modern Anthropology', in A. L. Kroeber (ed.), *Anthropology Today*, Chicago: University of Chicago Press, 1953, pp. 682–99). A. L. Kroeber has indicated that there is no room in anthropology for a shred of ethnocentrism (*Anthropology*, New York: Harcourt, Brace, 1948, pp. 265–6). Similarly sociologists R. M. MacIver and C. Page have said, 'The student of social life must be on constant guard against ethnocentric bias in analyzing the ways of different groups; and to this extent he must follow the principle of cultural relativity in his sociological investigations' (*Society: An Introductory Analysis*, London: Macmillan, 1949, p. 167). In limiting the extent of following the principle of cultural relativity, MacIver and Page hint that at least a limited degree of ethnocentrism is inevitably present in the mind of the social scientist as a necessary condition for the authority which the values of his culture possess for him as for its other members and for the ability of such values to command attitudes of respect and loyalty.

E. Adamson Hoebel

See also: CULTURAL RELATIVITY

Ethnography (See Ethnology)

Ethnology (Also Ethnography)

A. 1. At the present time the term *ethnography* is fairly consistently used in anthropological literature to refer to *descriptive studies of human societies*, usually (though not necessarily) those so-called 'primitive' societies which are at a relatively simple level of political and economic development. Even descriptive studies must, however, imply some generalization, and since the theoretical framework employed in social anthropology (q.v.) has been greatly developed in the past half-century, much recent ethnographic writing (most of which is done by social anthropologists) is inevitably largely theoretical. The fact that modern social anthropologists are generally their own ethnographers (for a discussion of some of the implications of this see E. E. Evans-Pritchard, *Social Anthropology*, London: Cohen & West, 1951, ch. IV) has tended to blur the distinction between ethnography and social anthropology.

2. *Ethnology* has retained no such consistency of meaning, and in fact the broad field of enquiry which it originally designated is now shared between such separate disciplines as social, cultural, and physical anthropology. This depreciation in the value of what should be a most useful term is due partly to ethnology's claim to be explanatory, for fashions in explanation have changed and multiplied in the past century.

B. The terms first came into general anthropological use about the middle of the 19th century. Originally, ethnology appears to have been thought of as a kind of history, 'the history of nations termed ethnology' (J. C. Prichard, *The Natural History of Man*, London: Baillière, 1843, p. 132), in contradistinction to the descriptive study of ethnography, but by the end of the century the two subjects were rarely distinguished with any consistency or precision.

Thus in 1891 E. B. Tylor, while defining the

task of *ethnography* as 'the investigation of the causes which have produced the phenomena of culture, and the laws to which they are subordinate', a few pages later describes the development of culture as 'a branch of ethnological research' (*Primitive Culture*, London: Murray, 1871, vol. I, pp. 19, 23). A few writers did, however, attempt to maintain the original distinction. Thus A. H. Keane defined ethnography as being 'in correct language ... rather literature than science. It is purely descriptive, dealing with the characteristics, usages, social and political condition of peoples irrespective of their possible physical relations or affinities'. Its subjects are 'the various groups of peoples taken independently one of the other', in distinction from ethnology, which studies 'the same human groups regarded as so many correlated members of one or more primordial families' (*Ethnology*, Cambridge: Cambridge University Press, 1896, pp. 2, 3).

C. 1. Anthropological interests have shifted from a basic concern with *origin* (whether conceived in evolutionary or diffusionist terms) to the functional analysis of existing societies as integrated systems, by analogy (often overdrawn) with physical organisms. Thus social anthropology began to assume aims and methods different from those of the older ethnological anthropology, and the term *ethnology* came to be restricted by some writers to a *purely historical, or rather pre-historical, kind of inquiry*. Thus in 1936 Radcliffe-Brown defined it as 'the history of peoples', including 'the history of races, the history of languages and the history of cultures, whether derived from the study of living peoples or from archaeological remains' (*The Development of Social Anthropology*, Chicago: [Mimeograph], p. 30).

2. In America ethnology has usually been given a wider denotation, though it has been contrasted with social anthropology, which is said to be concerned with social structure rather than culture (cf. for example, D. Bidney, *Theoretical Anthropology*, New York: Columbia University Press, 1953, p. 101). A. L. Kroeber defines ethnology as 'the science of peoples and their cultures and life histories as groups, irrespective of their degree of advancement' (*Anthropology*, New York: Harcourt, Brace, 1948, p. 5), while Bidney simply equates it with cultural anthropology.

3. On the Continent of Europe ethnology is also used in a comprehensive sense. In France and Germany it is usually taken as comprising

the whole range of social and cultural (though not physical) studies of so-called 'primitive' or pre-literate peoples.

J. Beattie

See also: SOCIAL ANTHROPOLOGY

Ethos

A. *Ethos* is a rather general term designating the social and cultural character of a group or society. The term is very old, its meaning in Greek being habit or character,—*ethics* is a closely related term. It has come to refer to some kind of summing-up of all or certain customs of a people, the nature of the summing up depending on the purposes and categories of the observer.

B. For W. G. Sumner *ethos* designated '... the totality of characteristic traits by which a group is individualized and differentiated from others ...' (*Folkways*, Boston: Ginn, 1907, p. 70). Thus Sumner (ibid., p. 73) characterized the Chinese ethos as 'industrial and materialistic' in contrast to the 'militant' ethos of Japanese culture. Both descriptions were impressionistic and subjective.

C. Later use has become more conceptually sophisticated, though hardly less subjective. The observer tries to conceptualize the ethos by postulating a few covert states of motivation, a few values, implicit premises, or acquired drives. These are listed, and behaviour that seems to follow from, or to demonstrate, them is cited by way of illustration. *Ethos* can then be said to include cultural themes (q.v.), culture patterns (q.v.), and values (q.v.) (J. Gillin, 'Ethos Components in Modern Latin American Culture', *American Anthropologist*, vol. 57, 1955, p. 488–500).

1. G. Bateson defines *ethos* as '... the system of emotional attitudes which governs what value a community shall set upon the various satisfactions or dissatisfactions which the contexts of life may offer' (*Naven*, Cambridge: Cambridge University Press, 1936, p. 220). He also speaks of *ethos* as the 'tone of appropriate behaviour' and as 'a definite set of sentiments toward reality'.

2. For J. J. Honigmann *ethos* refers to the emotional quality which an observer perceives in cultural acts together with the motivations postulated to underlie that quality. Thus Kaska Indian ethos, for example, reveals the 'operation' of six basic motivations: egocentricity, utilitarianism, deference, flexibility, dependence, and emotional isolation (*Culture and Ethos of Kaska Society*, New Haven: Yale University Press, 1949).

3. J. Gillin includes the goals of a culture as part of its ethos; and thus uses the concept as referring to 'The constellation of acquired drives or motivations which are characteristic of a culture, plus the goals ... toward which cultural activities are directed or upon which high value is placed' ('Ethos and Cultural Aspects of Personality', in S. Tax (ed.), *Heritage of Conquest*, Glencoe, Ill.: The Free Press, 1952, p. 195).

4. A. L. Kroeber tends to identify *ethos* with the values of a culture. '... when we speak of the ethos of a culture, we ... refer not so much to the specific ethics or moral code of the culture as to its total quality, to what would constitute disposition or character in an individual; to the system of ideals and values that dominate the culture and so tend to control the type of behaviour of its members' (*Anthropology*, New York: Harcourt, Brace, 1948, p. 294).

John J. Honigmann

See also: Cultural Theme
Culture Pattern
Value

Evaluation (See **Value**)

Evolution

A. The core of the term's meaning is that of rolling out, unrolling, or unfolding, and thus the term comes to denote *movement of an orderly nature which is productive of change of a novel kind.* More specifically it denotes the process of change through which something new is produced in such a continuous way as not to violate the identity or individuality of the original entity.

B. In stricter usage, the term implies *organic evolution*, viz. the interaction of a living organism and its physical environment. In a rudimentary form the idea had its roots in classical times, e.g. Heraclitus; but before the hypothesis, now inseparably associated with the name of Darwin, could win general acceptance, certain conditions were necessary. It was necessary to supplant the conviction of the immutability of all organic species, based on the theological belief in an act of independent creation. The idea required for its conception, elaboration and verification an alliance between science and history. It was necessary both to construct a classificatory system of types, and to provide an historical explanation of the course of actual development.

Darwin elaborated his hypothesis in *On The Origin of Species* (London: John Murray, 1859), although he himself did not use the term *evolution*. Referring to 'the origin of species by means of natural selection', he argued (a) that the different forms of life had a common ancestry from which they had gradually evolved, and (b) that the survivors in the struggle for existence would be those best adapted to the task of obtaining nourishment and avoiding competitors' attacks.

C. The use of the term in sociology and anthropology is closely linked to philosophy of history, and derives from the work not only of the biologists but also from the writings of Comte, Spencer, Bagehot. Since evolution affects behaviour as well as structural changes, the concept is of especial relevance to man. The development of the capacity for ethical behaviour and the exercise of the higher mental faculties generally not only have obvious survival value, but introduce a hitherto unknown factor in evolution in the shape of conscious human choice and design.

Contemporary sociologists and anthropologists are cautious in their employment of the term, partly because of the speculative element inseparable from its employment as a predictive tool. In the past, for example, the concept has been employed to demonstrate such different hypotheses as the inevitability of religion and war (see B. Kidd, *Social Evolution*, London: Macmillan, 1894). Criticism of the work of earlier sociological evolutionists has been directed along the following channels: (a) The idea of a single, unvarying succession of stages through which all peoples have to pass, has been discredited. (b) Primitive institutional stages were liable to be explained by 'retrodictive' hypotheses, inadequately grounded empirically. (c) The idea that evolution was invariably a movement from the simple and undifferentiated to the complex was accepted uncritically.

R. V. Sampson

See also: Cultural Evolution

Exchange (Also **Exchange Economy**)

A. 1. In the social sciences (with the exception of economics) the term *exchange* has essentially the same meanings as in lay usage, applying in general to the mutual giving and receiving of

Exchange Rates

both material and non-material things. Thus it may refer to transfers of services, goods, money, rights, or benefits that are reciprocated by a transfer of something (whether similar or different) in return. In economic anthropology the term is used to refer to particular transactions as well as to define the nature of a system.

2. In economics the term *exchange* is commonly confined to transactions in which money is involved. Moreover, it is more often used as an adjective defining the nature of an economic system or organization than as a verb or noun in connection with a particular transaction.

B. There is at a minimum a sex division of labour in all societies, and this involves at least an informal, non-monetary 'exchange' of services within the family. However, subsistence economies (q.v.) in which exchange is virtually limited to such intra-family relations are commonly distinguished from all others which may be described, using the term very broadly, as *exchange economies*. More often the term *exchange economies* is used more narrowly to exclude *barter economies*. It then refers only to those economies in which exchange is predominantly carried out through the medium of money, and furthermore to economies in which some relatively large (though unspecified) proportion of production is 'for exchange'.

The phrase *exchange economy* is also used with a somewhat different connotation, to mean an economy in which the allocation of resources is determined through the action of market processes. In this sense it is often interpreted to be synonymous with *private profit economy*, *capitalistic private enterprise economy*, or *market economy*.

C. In a private profit economy most exchange is overt; it occurs in a 'market' and there is no ambiguity about transfer of ownership (legal-philosophical definitions of ownership coincide with the locus of immediate control over resource use). However, the development of modern organizational techniques, both of private business and in socialized or nationalized economies, diminishes the correlation between division of labour and market exchange. Moreover, the meaning of 'transfer of ownership' becomes blurred. This is especially important in Russia, where any analytical treatment of the concept of 'ownership' must recognize that it has many components and that 'ownership by the state' does not include them

all—or even many of the most important elements. Under these circumstances *concealed exchange* may be even more important than *overt exchange*; in fact, such transfers are recognized in the account-keeping of state enterprises, and where they are given such formal recognition the term *accounting exchange* may be more appropriate. Concealed or accounting exchange occurs when there are mutual transfers involving shifts in the locus of responsibility and control, but when no overt market transaction is involved and the formal legal 'ownership' remains unchanged. Economies characterized by a high degree of division of labour but minimal overt exchange may then still be termed *exchange economies* because of the importance of concealed exchange; a large part of production is for the use of others than the producers, and the latter will receive something in exchange for this—i.e. a large proportion of production is in this sense 'for exchange'.

Mary Jean Bowman

Exchange Rates

A. *Exchange rates* are simply prices quoted in one financial centre for monetary balances available in another; the monetary unit of one country is given in terms of those of others (J. B. Condliffe, *The Commerce of Nations*, New York: W. W. Norton, 1950, pp. 366, 385, 746; R. G. Hawtrey, *Currency and Credit*, London: Longmans, Green, 4th edn., 1950, pp. 102–27; L. Tarshis, *Introduction to International Trade and Finance*, New York: Wiley, 1955, p. 306). For example, the dollar-pound relationship, or exchange rate, is usually stated in this manner: £1 = $2.80, which is equivalent to saying that a dollar is worth 1/2·8 pounds. A change in the price from this level to £1 = $4 would mean that the pound has risen and that the dollar has fallen.

B. A given rate of exchange announced between two countries refers to a given type of transaction in a given market. To illustrate, *The Wall Street Journal* of 11 October, 1957, records the following information on the sterling-dollar rate in New York on 10 October:

Cables	$2·80 3/32
30-day Futures	2·79¼
90-day Futures	2·77 5/8
Transferable	2·78
Switch or Security	2·73

Each of these rates applies to a particular type of transaction. The first, cables, gives the price

248

in dollars of sterling balances delivered immediately. The second is the price to be paid in 30 days for sterling balances made available at that time (J. N. Behrman and W. E. Schmidt, *International Economics*, New York: Rinehart, 1957, pp. 278–80; J. P. Condliffe, *The Commerce of Nations*, pp. 380, 382, 389, 521; L. Tarshis, *Introduction to International Trade and Finance*, pp. 305–6).

Professor Condliffe cautions (*The Commerce of Nations*, p. 388, fn. 16): 'It is necessary to avoid confusing forward exchange with exchange which is sold spot for delivery in 30, 60, or 90 days. The exchange rate on bills or drafts falling due at a later date, is always the same as the rate for cables, or sight drafts, less the interest which is calculable for the time that elapses. ...

'The forward rate, for transactions which will become actual at a later date, may diverge rather widely from these spot rates if there is fear of currency depreciation or of interruption such as war or exchange control'.

Spot rates for future delivery are also called *time rates* (F. A. Southard, *Foreign Exchange Practice and Policy*, New York: McGraw-Hill, 1940, pp. 83–5).

Transferable rates apply to sterling balances acquired by countries in the sterling area which cannot legally be converted into dollars (A. I. Bloomfield, *Speculative and Flight Movements of Capital in Postwar International Finance*, Princeton Studies in International Finance, No. 3, Princeton: Princeton University Press, 1954, p. 38). 'Security sterling' is not subject to unrestricted repatriation (ibid., p. 13).

A practice, first used extensively by Germany in the 1930s, that of governmentally maintained multiple exchange rates, has been adopted by a number of countries—most of them in Latin America, Southeast Asia, and the Middle East (International Monetary Fund, *Eighth Annual Report on Exchange Restrictions*, Washington, 1957; see also IMF monthly publication *International Financial Statistics*). By *multiple exchange rates* is meant the establishment of different spot rates for immediate execution (R. F. Mikesell, *Foreign Exchange in the Postwar World*, New York: The Twentieth Century Fund, 1954, pp. 13, 165; L. Tarshis, *Introduction to International Trade and Finance*, pp. 307–8). Spain, for example, has an involved set of spot rates, 8 for sellers of dollars and 10 for buyers of dollars (International Monetary Fund, *Eighth Annual Report on Exchange Restrictions*, pp. 365–6). To repeat a few of these, a Spanish

exporter of fresh fish can get only 23,605 pesetas for a dollar, but, if the exporter sells books or ceramics, he may have 37,245 pesetas for a dollar. Dollars can be had in Spain at 11·22 pesetas for making governmental payments, 25·00 pesetas for importing liquid fuels, and 35·00 for bringing in aluminium oxide.

Multiple exchange rates provide a means for partial devaluation coupled with discriminatory pricing. Some exports are singled out for favourable treatment; some imports are to be discouraged more than others. Differences in elasticities of demand and supply can be exploited.

William L. Miller

See also: MONEY

Executive

A. 1. In political science the term *executive* may be defined in its broadest sense as including the total government bureaucracy, the politically responsible officials who direct it, and the chief of state. More restrictive definitions may be conveyed by reference to the *permanent executive*, the *political executive*, or the *titular executive*.

2. The term is also used in the sociology of formal organizations of any sort to designate the functions of deliberate control, management, supervision, and administration, the people who perform such functions, the positions they occupy, and the sector of the large organization in which they are found.

B. 1. Following the threefold classification formulated by Montesquieu, *the executive* as a functional part of a government has been distinguished from the legislative and judicial branches or agencies. It is generally agreed, however, that all government is a single process, that there is no function or power which by its quality or content is inherently 'executive', and that to label branches of various governments as 'executive' is simply to attach a convenient tag to branches which historically have come to acquire certain common characteristics. It is also recognized that while at one time the term may have accurately reflected the nature of the branch whose function it was to *execute* laws passed by the legislature, it no longer describes adequately the wide range of discretionary and policy-formulating functions entrusted to modern executives, many of which, under the orthodox threefold classification, might be labelled 'legislative' or 'judicial'.

Expectation

2. Usage differs as to the scope of the persons and agencies included. In its broadest sense, the executive branch includes the whole government bureaucracy, together with the politically responsible officials who direct and control it. Often, however, the term is used to refer only to what is sometimes described as the *political executive*. In this sense, the cabinet (or sometimes the more inclusive group known as the ministry) is seen to be the executive of a parliamentary government, the cabinet being a plural executive; while in the American system the Constitution places the executive power in a single President. Finally, in a parliamentary type government the executive is sometimes seen as including both the cabinet (or ministry) and the titular head, or chief of state.

3. American writers in public administration often distinguish *executive* from *administrative*. In the past this distinction has been closely associated with the attempt to draw the parallel distinction between politics and administration, a dichotomy which most students of administration now reject. It is still common, however, for textbooks to use the term *executive* to designate those persons at the top of the official hierarchy who participate in important policy determination—at the national level 'the President, the several hundred persons appointed by him, as well as the numerous career civil servants at the top of the federal pay scale' (J. M. Pfiffner & R. N. Presthus, *Public Administration*, New York: Ronald Press, 1953, p. 7)—while *administrative* is used in connection with officials lower in the hierarchy who, although they may influence policy, are entrusted with less discretionary power and are not involved with policy matters of a high level nature. Practice is not uniform, however, and the term *executive* is also frequently used to refer to any person who exercises leadership over an organizational unit regardless of its size, importance, or place in the hierarchy.

4. To the extent that British writers in public administration distinguish between *executive* and *administrative*, usage is frequently the opposite of American practice. Thus *administrative* suggests concern with high level policy formulation, as seen by the designation of the Administrative Class of the Civil Service, while *executive* is used in relation to those persons and functions somewhat lower in the hierarchy. In both countries, however, it is recognized that the terms are little more than convenient labels which suggest functions of greater or lesser importance, influence, and responsibility.

C. *Executive* has long been used in business to designate people and positions concerned with certain functions in large-scale business organizations. In the last twenty-five years these persons and their activities have been subjected to considerable observation by social scientists, particularly those concerned with the sociology of large-scale organizations. C. I. Barnard has written at length of *The Functions of the Executive* (Cambridge, Mass.: Harvard University Press, 1938), and his work has given rise to continued investigation. He uses the term *executive* as a noun to denote the occupant of positions which he terms *executive positions*, and these positions in turn are qualified by the adjective *executive* because they are concerned with the performance of *executive functions* and are found in that sector of the larger organization which Barnard describes as *executive organization*. The meaning of the term for Barnard is found in the *executive functions* which he describes as those of control, management, supervision, and administration. While much of the analysis of these functions has centred on business organization, there has been an increasing tendency to apply it to all large-scale formal organizations.

Howard Scarrow

See also: BUREAUCRACY
            JUDICIARY
            LEGISLATIVE BODY
            SOCIAL ORGANIZATION (Sociology)

Exogamy (See **Endogamy**)

Expectation

A. *Expectation* denotes a subjective state, deriving from an orientation within a time process, which may be described in non-behaviouristic approaches as the quality of experience which relates to the adjustment of the individual to anticipated future experiences.

B. 1. *Expectation* as a consciously present anticipation of a future event was included in the basic analyses of W. James: 'The knowledge of some other part of the stream [of consciousness], past or future, near or remote, is always mixed in with our knowledge of the present thing' (*The Principles of Psychology*, London: Macmillan, 1890, vol. I, p. 606). The subjective emphasis persisted in the *Dictionary of Psychology*, edited by H. C. Warren (Boston: Houghton Mifflin, 1934, p. 99) with the definition 'A mental attitude characterized by tension and characteristic of attention'. The shift toward objectivity may be seen in the definition by P. L. Harriman, 'a condition of readiness (or set) to make a certain type of response to a situation. ... The term usually connotes the emotional condition of preparedness for a given type of response. Titchener (1896) described it as an attitude based upon kinesthetic and organic sensations, usually accompanied by a feeling-tone' (*The New Dictionary of Psychology*, London: Vision Press, 1952, p. 129 f.). A more recent definition (H. B. English & A. C. English, *A Comprehensive Dictionary of Psychological and Psychoanalytical Terms*, New York: Longmans, Green, 1958, p. 193) shows the same shift: 'a tense and somewhat emotional attitude toward the prospect of a certain event-sign, *anticipation*, which emphasizes motor preparation; *foresight* or *forethought*, which emphasizes the intellectual aspect'.

2. With the development of relatively objective behaviouristic 'systems' in psychology, greater difficulty is encountered in dealing with this term. E. C. Tolman states 'An expectation is an immanent cognitive determinant [of behaviour] aroused by actually presented stimuli' (*Purposive Behavior in Animals and Men*, Berkeley: University of California Press, 1932, p. 444); with an 'immanent determinant' as inferred intervening variable (q.v.), and elaboration of the definitions requiring a restatement of the entire system. Efforts to avoid elaboration of inferences concerning subjective states and processes have caused behaviour theorists to develop 'operational' definitions such as: 'The goal object evokes a goal response. On successive trials stimuli in the immediate environment come to signal the occurrence of the goal object. Gradually, as the number of trials increases, stimuli which are more distant from the goal object acquire this property of signaling the occurrence of the goal object. Eventually the entire experimental apparatus will possess directive value for the organism. The directive properties which these stimuli acquire result from their relation with the goal object (incentive stimulus). It is this relationship between the incentive stimulus and other stimuli in the experimental situation that constitutes the expectancy' (R. A. Behan, 'Expectancies and Hullian Theory', *Psychological Review*, vol. 60, 1953, p. 252).

C. In the other social sciences where the term *expectation* is used, we find less concern with the precise psychological meaning of the term and greater stress on the function of expectations in social relations. Thus in economics it is held that economic decisions are to a considerable degree based on expectations of the future behaviour of others in the market. While in part such expectations are based on a rational calculation of what others will rationally do, there is also presupposed in economic behaviour the even more stable expectations based upon the shared norms of statuses and roles (C. A. Hickman & M. H. Kuhn, *Individuals, Groups and Economic Behavior*, New York: Dryden, 1956). It is this order producing function of reciprocal expectations as a part of institutionalized behaviour that is at the very heart of modern sociological theory (T. Parsons, *The Social System*, Glencoe, Ill.: The Free Press, 1951, pp. 38–40).

Eugene L. Hartley

See also: INSTITUTION
ROLE
STATUS

Experiment

A. 1. In science the purpose of an *experiment* is to observe invariant relations which obtain between a dependent and one or more independent variables (q.v.). Thus, an *experiment* denotes any process which may validly achieve this purpose. More specifically, an *experiment* is the observation of a joint variation of a dependent variable and one or more independent variables subject to the following conditions: (a) subjects to be observed comprise a homogeneous group; (b) rates of change in the independent variables during the experimental period are classified in mutually exclusive and exhaustive classes (thus including the class of no change); (c) subjects are assigned by a random process to one of these classes; (d) appropriate changes in the independent variable are effected for each class.

By this definition, it is irrelevant whether the experiment occurs in a laboratory or in a 'real life' situation. It is also immaterial whether or not variation in independent variables occurs as a direct result of some action on the part of the experimenter. So long as the experimenter is able to foresee events which will cause variation in some independent variable of theoretical importance and so long as he is able to assign subjects at random to the various rate of change classes prior to the occurrence of the event, and so long as he meets the rest of the conditions listed above, he is performing an experiment.

2. The term is also sometimes used loosely to denote deliberate innovation in any sphere of social life where there is the implication that the

Experiment

innovation is being introduced on a trial basis or in a limited area so that the results may be observed before general introduction of the innovation is made.

B. Four scientific uses of the term *experiment* are evident in the literature of social science. For convenience, these applications can be classified as statistical, laboratory, natural, and trial and error.

1. *Statistically*, an *experiment* is any act which yields at most a denumerable number of outcomes. An outcome can be either a non-decomposable event or one which can be analysed into more elementary events. Thus, the statistical experiment of tossing a single die yields any of six non-decomposable outcomes (the event of observing an ace, a deuce, etc.) or some decomposable outcome such as observing an even number. In the statistical sense of experiment, empirical observations often are of little interest. A statistician need not even own a die in order to chart an experiment consisting, say, of *n* tosses of a die and to assign an appropriate probability distribution to the outcomes.

2. A *laboratory experiment* is an activity which comprises three features: the observation of a dependent variable, either non-decomposable or otherwise, the manipulation of an independent variable, also possibly decomposable, and the control of all other relevant factors. In order to assure himself that all but the experimentally varied independent variables are held constant during the period of observation, the experimenter usually puts into effect some variant of the following steps: a sample is selected and each element is assigned at random to one of two or more groups one of which is a control group, the remainder of which are called experimental groups. Randomization implies that any differences in any relevant characteristics of the groups at the time of selection should themselves be random results of the selection process. Both sets of subjects, experimental and control, are subjected to constant conditions during the period of the experiment in so far as any variables are concerned which are possibly relevant to the dependent variable, with one exception: The experimental group is subjected to treatments which consist of the systematic introduction of variation in values of the independent variable. In a visual perception experiment, the independent variable might be light, in which case the control subjects would be given treatments consisting of constant light intensities while experimental subjects would be exposed to varying light intensities during the period of observation. If such a procedure is carried out, if changes are observed in the dependent variable in the experimental group, and if no such changes are observed in the control group, then it can be concluded within the limits of probability that the dependent and independent variables are not distributed independently.

3. The term *natural experiment* usually refers to the investigation of changes in some dependent variable after one or more independent variables have been altered as a result of circumstances beyond the immediate control of the investigator (cf. F. S. Chapin, *Experimental Designs in Sociological Research*, New York: Harper, rev. edn., 1955, pp. 1–3). To Chapin this constitutes, in fact, the most fruitful form of sociological investigation, the *ex post facto experiment*, in which a current set of conditions is analysed backwards through time in an attempt to isolate its relations to some previously acting factor. Some scholars have criticized the use of the term *experiment* in connection with such investigations as this. It is asserted by these critics that the so-called natural experiment cannot yield conclusions with the same logical status as those which were obtained from laboratory experimentation. It is argued that the random assignment of subjects and other controls which characterize the latter are partially or completely missing in the former (for a bibliography of such criticism see F. S. Chapin, *Experimental Designs in Sociological Research*, Appendix C).

4. *Trial and error experimentation* refers to the introduction of new behavioural forms, restrictions, or sanctions into some situation in an effort to achieve some specific goal. J. R. P. French observes that this form of experimentation '... seems to refer to all sorts of trials by laymen of new forms of social behavior' ('Experiments in Field Settings', in L. Festinger & D. Katz (eds.), *Research Methods in the Behavioral Sciences*, New York: Dryden, 1954, p. 99). Such investigation is characterized typically by the virtually complete lack of those features which make up a laboratory experiment except for the observation of some independent variable. Even this usually lacks the rigour associated with experimental observation.

C. Direct and indirect recourse to experiment at varying levels of subtlety is now an established technique of social research. Thus social scientists examine created as well as natural situations in order to test their hypotheses: 'Basically, in an experiment, whether it is natural or created, one is testing the tenability of an hypothesis' (M. Jahoda, M. Deutsch, & S. W. Cook, *Research Methods in Social Relations*, New York: Dryden Press, 1951, vol. 1, p. 59).

H. Hyman compares the experiment with the survey questionnaire: 'In the classic experiment, a stimulus variable is created in the laboratory setting, subjects are exposed, and the effects observed and measured. By analogy the questionnaire can be regarded not merely as an instrument to obtain answers, but as a method of exposing respondents to experimental, albeit verbal, stimuli (*Survey Design and Analysis*, Glencoe, Ill.: The Free Press, 1958, p. 210).

It has also been argued that the use of the comparative method (q.v.) is in effect a way of 'experimenting' with institutional and historical data to which the strict procedures of scientific experimentation cannot be applied.

D. The loose usage of *experiment* noted in A (2) above is sometimes employed by social scientists as well as by laymen. In this usage the idea of control is largely abandoned, so that all that is usually indicated is innovation and the observation of subsequent events without any ground for imputing invariant relations between the two.

Robert McGinnis

See also: VARIABLE

Experimental Anthropology (See Applied Anthropology)

Experimental Group (See Experiment)

Exports
A. In its most general sense *exports* denotes any social or cultural items transmitted from one social unit to another, the stress being placed on the social unit of origin. In its more technical, legal and economic meaning the term denotes either (a) economic goods transferred to a resident, business, institution, or government of a nation other than the nation of origin, or (b) any items centrally involved in a transaction which gives rise to a claim for payment by a domestic resident against a resident, business, institution, or government of a foreign nation.

B. 1. Officially, shipments of goods intended for a resident, business, institution, or the government of another country become exports when a Shippers Export Declaration is filed with the Collector of Customs at the port or point of exit. This declaration carries the name and address of the shipper; the place where the shipment originated; the name of the carrier; city and country of destination; and the itemized and total values of the goods at the port of exportation.

2. Credit entries are made in the international balance of payments for any transaction that gives rise to a claim for payment by a domestic resident against a resident, business, institution or the government of a foreign country. Under the current account, the first broad category in the balance of payments, the credit items listed include not only exports but also *commodity* and *service* exports. Service exports include travel expenditures by foreigners in the home country; shipping and freight services rendered by domestic vessels; insurance, banking and brokerage services rendered to foreigners by domestic institutions; expenditures by foreign governments in the home country for diplomatic, consular, and other functions; and interest and dividends received from abroad by domestic holders of foreign bonds, stocks, and other assets which yield interest or income. The capital account, the second category in the balance of payments, includes transactions that are representative of the flow of international money capital rather than of goods and services.

Hubert Bice
Bernard F. Sliger

See also: BALANCE OF PAYMENTS
         IMPORTS

Expressive Crowd (See Crowd)

Expropriation
A. The term denotes the action of the state in exercising its sovereign right of extinguishing title to specific goods or property and vesting both possession and ownership in the state itself.

B. *Expropriation* has a general, as distinguished from a precise and technical legal, meaning. It is similar to *eminent domain* but has broader connotations, e.g. it is more commonly used with reference to personal property as well as to real property. When expropriation occurs, title thus acquired is unquestionable and may be transferred to third parties. It has been argued by some that expropriation is accompanied by

Expropriation

the duty of making compensation for the property so acquired by the state. Others argue that while compensation is constitutionally required within many legal systems, and may be looked upon as a principle of right and justice, the sovereign right is nonetheless unlimited so far as national law is concerned. These people agree that the rule is otherwise at international law, which of course relates only to the expropriation by a state of property belonging to aliens. Here the 'international standard of justice' applies. A state may institute proceedings against a foreign state which has failed to compensate the protesting state's national for expropriated property.

Ralph Jones

Extended Family (See Family)

F

Fact

A. The more general usage of the term *fact* is such that anything described by an assertion which is *true* can be described as a *fact*: for instance, that Britain is an island, that there is no largest prime number, that sugar dissolves in water, that the population of the world is increasing, can all be described as facts.

B. There is no sharp opposition between the ordinary and the scientific use of the term. In ordinary usage facts are opposed to the untrue and to the surmised; in scientific usage, the opposition is rather between the *factual* and the *theoretical*, between facts and their *interpretation*, between 'given' facts and *constructions based on them*. (Nevertheless, one may speak of 'general facts' which are actually synoptic views of specific facts, or generalizations drawn from them.)

Anything can be described as a *fact*, but nevertheless some kinds of truths are more naturally so described, and may be a kind of paradigm case of what it is to be a *fact*. It is more natural to describe *concrete, individual, positive, observable, specific, and locally circumscribed situations* as facts, than it is to use this term for abstract, or social, or general, or negative, or unobservable, or indeterminate, or diffused states of affairs.

The philosophic problem which arises from this is the delimitation, identification, and classification of facts proper, and the explanation of the other, merely putative 'facts' in terms of the former. An alternative to such explanations or 'reductions' of putative facts in terms of real ones, is the possibility that the putative ones refer to nothing at all. Attempts have also been made to identify *atomic facts* from which (and from nothing else) the world is built up.

The kinds of fact whose existence or ultimacy have been contested are, for instance, negative facts, hypothetical facts, moral facts, social facts (q.v.).

The irreducible existence of social facts or, alternatively, their reducibility or illusoriness, are of particular interest to the social scientist.

E. A. Gellner

See also: Social Fact

Faction

A. The term *faction* is used in one of two senses.

1. Objectively, it may denote a certain condition or state of affairs, without implying a value judgement. This condition specifically occurs when a sub-group is formed from members of a larger group and they separate themselves from the rest. The components of a faction are: (a) definite personnel (the leaders, at least, should be identifiable, even if the boundaries of the membership are blurred); (b) enough organization to provide the sub-group with the rudiments of structure and cohesion; (c) a common interest which brings them together initially; (d) common objectives to keep them together for some time; (e) an awareness, by themselves and by others outside, that they are identified as having these relationships; and (f) an opponent or opponents (e.g. a rival faction) regarded as competitors.

2. *Faction* may also signify, in addition to the objective conditions set forth in (1), an attitude towards them. This attitude is unfavourable. It expresses, or implies, the feeling that forming factions is bad, that their existence leads to harmful results, and that they sacrifice the common good to partial interests. So conceived, factions put asunder those who ought to be united. Hence, all aspects of factions—their membership, aims, strategems, and tactics—fall under general condemnation.

B. The usage of the concept can best be illustrated by mentioning some of the historical situations to which it has been applied.

1. The first classic account of faction (and still one of the greatest on account of its psychological insight) was written by Thucydides (*History of the Pelopponesian War*, ed. & trans. by R. W. Livingstone, London: Oxford University Press, 1943, bk. III, p. 82) reflecting on the events in Corcyra and on similar strife in other cities. He uses the Greek word στάσις (stasis) as does Plato in the *Republic* (trans. by B. Jowett, Oxford: The University Press, 1922-7, e.g. 465 b, 556 d, 560 a) and Aristotle in the *Politics*, (trans. by B. Jowett, Oxford: The University Press, 1908, e.g. 1286 b, 1301 b). In the Roman Empire, the Latin *factio* was literally the name

Fad

for the companies which provided the teams of charioteers who competed at the circus. At Constantinople, in the Byzantine Empire, the supporters bet heavily on these factions and their partisanship led at times to bloodshed.

2. When governments were mostly monarchical, political factions consisted either of two groups vying for the royal favour or of the supporters of the king and his opponents. Under the latter circumstances, the faction opposing the Crown could not escape charges of disloyalty and risk the penalties of treason. These associations with discord and disloyalty still clung to the term after royal power had declined and legislatures were gaining in importance.

3. Eventually, it was out of factions that parties emerged. The two terms at first were used as synonyms and it has taken *party* a long time to rid itself of the connotations of *faction*. (Indeed, the dissociation is not complete, for the word party often retains a dishonourable meaning, though it has also acquired a respectable sense which faction never achieved.) Madison argued (in 1787) in the *Federalist* (no. X) 'Among the numerous advantages promised by a well-constructed Union, none deserves to be more accurately developed than its tendency to break and control the violence of faction. ... By a faction, I understand a number of citizens, whether amounting to a majority or minority of the whole, who are united and actuated by some common impulse of passion, or of interest, adverse to the rights of other citizens, or to the permanent and aggregate interests of the community' (*The Federalist*, ed. by M. Beloff, Oxford: Blackwell, 1948, pp. 41–2). Washington in the *Farewell Address* (1796) warned against the dangers of faction and alternated, with no change of meaning, between party and faction: 'Let me now take a more comprehensive view, and warn you in the most solemn manner against the baneful effects of the spirit of party, generally. ... The alternate domination of one faction over another, sharpened by the spirit of revenge, natural to party dissension, which in different ages and countries has perpetrated the most horrid enormities, is itself a frightful despotism'.

4. In modern times the term *faction* is employed more sparingly than it was in the 17th and 18th centuries. It is used today (a) in communities with well-developed party systems to refer to struggles over leadership and programmes that go on between sub-groups within the parties, and (b) in communities where the party system has not yet matured, to describe

clusters of persons and interests from which parties may develop later.

Leslie Lipson

See also: PARTY

Fad

A. A *fad* consists of markedly novel, trivial, and ephemeral behaviour which spreads rapidly through whatever portions of society choose to adopt it. Fad behaviour may involve crowd-like imitation directed toward momentary circumvention of folkways and mores; it may also provide substitute ways of expressing normatively thwarted emotions, such as status yearning and sexual drives.

B. 1. The most frequent usage of the term carries the following meaning: a rapid, sudden, and ephemeral collective adoption of novel behaviour which affects only superficial and trivial areas of life. Attention is sometimes called to the crowd-like character of fad behaviour, to the ways in which fads may meet psychological needs of participants, and to selective participation in terms of social class characteristics when fads occur in modern societies. Fads have been studied mostly by social psychologists and sociologists, but also by economists and anthropologists.

Illustrations of general usage are found in the works of L. L. Bernard (*An Introduction to Social Psychology*, New York: Henry Holt, 1926, p. 543) who states, 'A fad is some form of behavior which does not secure universal or continuous acceptance by the group, but is taken up by only a portion of the group and dies out in the course of a relatively short period of time because of lack of support'; and H. Bonner (*Social Psychology*, New York: American Book Co., 1953, p. 391) who observes, 'Faddist behavior is ephemeral and is not repeated in the same form. It must have novelty, for part of its hold upon people, both as performers and spectators, lies in its startling effect'.

2. Two aspects of the crowd-like character of fads are consistently noted in the writings which analyse fads as elementary collective behaviour. The first is the presence of suggestion and imitation. K. Young (*Social Psychology*, New York: Appleton-Century-Crofts, 1956, p. 327), for example, indicates that fads are 'really temporary crowd behavior without much structuring. Into these enter suggestion and imitation'. The second aspect of the crowd-like character of fads is indicated by R. Turner and L. Killian (*Collective Behavior*, Englewood

Cliffs, N.J.: Prentice-Hall, 1957, p. 208) who note, 'The fad may also exist as a *permission* [italics theirs] to act contrary to the folkways and mores, as in the example of college "panty raids" '.

3. Representative of those who consider psychological dimensions of fad behaviour are L. L. Bernard (*An Introduction to Social Psychology*, p. 543) who suggests 'its function seems to be that of calling attention to the one who adopts it'; H. Bonner (*Social Psychology*, p. 391) who states, 'it serves some compulsive need of the moment'; and L. Broom and P. Selznick (*Sociology*, Evanston, Ill.: Row, Peterson, 1955, p. 258) who point out, 'One of the underlying emotions seems to be *anxiety concerning social status* [italics theirs], which readily encourages taking cues from those "in the know" '.

4. Although it is generally conceded that fads, unlike fashions, may occur even in simple societies which have merely prototypical class systems, some mention of social class features of fads appears in discussions of modern society. For example, K. Young (*Social Psychology*, p. 327) indicates that 'by the top elite [the fad] is regarded as bizarre, and hence in poor taste'. Similarly, L. Broom and P. Selznick (*Sociology*, p. 258) report, 'Fads seem to spread primarily among individuals in similar social circumstances'.

Ray L. Gold

See also: COLLECTIVE BEHAVIOUR
FASHION

Family

A. The human *family* may be defined as an institutionalized bio-social group made up of adults (at least two of which, unrelated by blood and of the opposite sex, are married), and children, the offspring of the maritally related adults; the minimal functions of which are the providing of satisfactions and control of affectional needs, including sexual relations, and the provision of a sociocultural situation for the procreation, care, and socialization of offspring. The group constituted in such a way and performing such functions varies through several ranges of structure; and therefore any definition of *family* must include the definition of several types.

1. The universally human *biological family* consists of parents and their children; the *simple family* could include formally adopted children as well. This form has been called the *nuclear family*, the *natural family*, the *immediate* or *biological family*, the *primary family*, and the *restricted family* (in order, G. P. Murdock, *Social Structure*, New York: The Macmillan Co., 1949, ch. 1; E. B. Reuter & J. R. Runner, *The Family*, New York: McGraw-Hill, 1931, *passim*; E. D. Chapple & C. S. Coon, *Principles of Anthropology*, New York: Henry Holt, 1942, p. 277; R. L. Beals & H. Hoijer, *An Introduction to Anthropology*, New York: The Macmillan Co., 1953, p. 382; C. Lévi-Strauss, 'The Family', in H. L. Shapiro (ed.), *Man, Culture and Society*, New York: Oxford University Press, 1956, pp. 261–85, 273). These terms correspond to the *elementary family* of Radcliffe-Brown and other British scholars, and to the German *Kleinefamilie*. All authorities agree in regarding this minimal biologically based family unit as universal in all societies.

2. Because of incest taboos within the nuclear family, each individual ordinarily in his lifetime belongs to two different families: the *family of origin* or *orientation* into which he was born and the *family of procreation*, that formed by marriage within which he participates in the procreation of new individuals.

3. A concrete nuclear family always contains both the conjugal and the consanguine element. The child is related by blood to all other members of his family of origin, so that from his perspective it is a *consanguine family*. By contrast, the adults who join to form the nuclear family of procreation must not, by incest-definition, be related in blood, so that for them the nuclear family, created by marriage, is a *conjugal* family.

4. The nuclear family may have built upon it various forms of the *extended* family. An extended conjugal family may be formed by the addition of new spouses through *polygamous marriage*. While blood relatives may enter into the formation of an extended conjugal family, as brothers into fraternal *polyandry* (q.v.) and sisters into sororal *polygyny* this need not be the case, and, in any event, does not abrogate the rule that marriage partners cannot be related by blood. It is possible to extend the consanguineal family, in time, to include all the members living and dead of a *lineage* (q.v.). Strictly speaking, however, the lineage is not a family. It can, however, constitute the core of the *joint family*, that might also be called an *extended consanguine family*. The joint family may extend the nuclear family in two ways, since it grows primarily by adding consanguineal relatives together: either by adding together the conjugal families of siblings

Family

of one sex, or by adding the families of different generations in the lineage. Generally both principles are found in concrete joint families, so that in practice the distinction is artificial.

B. Social scientists have peculiar difficulty in dealing with the family because it so inextricably combines traits rooted in a universal human biology with other traits that are cultural, some of which are plainly variable and contingent.

1. R. M. MacIver writes that 'The family is a group defined by a sex relationship sufficiently precise and enduring to provide for the procreation and upbringing of children (*Society: A Textbook of Sociology*, New York: Farrar & Rinehart, 1937, p. 196). But this attempt to find a universally applicable definition, based primarily on the social relevance of a fundamentally biological function, ignores the vast number of cultural aspects inherent in the family.

2. While the MacIver definition stresses a largely biological element, it also hints at an approach which was historically dominant in sociology, the stress on the *institutionalization* of the family because of its important *societal* functions. While this is an important scientific approach to the study of the family, it cannot be used as the sole basis for definition, because it ignores many of the personal functions of the family.

3. Partly as a corrective to the institutional stress, and partly in response to a changing ethic of the family in the West, sociologists have more recently spoken of the family as being in transition from 'institution to companionship' and definable as a 'unity of interacting persons' (E. W. Burgess & H. J. Locke, *The Family*, New York: American Book Co., 2nd edn., 1953, p. vii). Here again the definition points to only one aspect of the family and to the way in which the ends of the family are conceived by many Americans, but it cannot genuinely encompass the family as a universal human group.

4. R. H. Lowie writes that 'The family is the social unit based on marriage' which makes of the family a purely cultural phenomenon, which it is not (*An Introduction to Cultural Anthropology*, New York: Farrar & Rinehart, 1934, p. 246). Again in a somewhat similar definition he says, 'The family is an association that corresponds to the institution of marriage, the socially approved form of sex relations' (*Social Organization*, New York: Rinehart, 1948, p. 215). Here he passes on the burden of definition to that of a cultural institution, marriage.

5. R. L. Beals and H. Hoijer describe the family as 'a social grouping the members of which are united by bonds of kinship' (*Introduction to Anthropology*, New York: The Macmillan Co., 1953, p. 382). This requires an atypical and special definition of *kinship* in order to include the husband and wife within the family, and the ignoring of the universal incest taboo.

C. Any adequate definition of the family must therefore take into account both its biological and cultural aspects, its institutional and more personal attributes. This can be done only by grappling with the following essential characteristics of the family.

1. Biologically the mammalian family consists in the biological mother and her offspring only, usually without the attendance of the male; ordinarily the breeding and nurturing behaviours alternate and are mutually exclusive. In some primates, notably the anthropoids, something like the human family emerges, viz. the quasi-permanent association of adults of both sexes for the protection and rearing of the young; but this depends upon the dominance, sexual drive, and strength of paramount individuals not upon cultural sanctions.

The increasing attendance of the male upon the older mother-offspring mammalian family in the sequence lemur-monkey-ape-man has been regarded by F. W. Jones as owing to the simultaneously increasing dependency of the young (*Arboreal Man*, New York: Arnold, 1926, p. 187). On the other hand W. La Barre regards the permanent, non-seasonal sexuality of man as the biological bond, universal in all human groups, which creates the family (*The Human Animal*, Chicago: University of Chicago Press, 1954, index entries under 'Family').

2. Since the nuclear family is universal in all known human groups past and present, and since the family depends by definition upon exclusiveness of sexual claims, the cultureless, or non-institutionalized 'cyclopean' family doubtless never existed. E. Westermarck has exhaustively refuted the theory of 'primitive promiscuity' postulated by the older cultural evolutionists as a universal stage preceding mother-right and father-right (*The History of Human Marriage*, New York: The Macmillan Co., 1925, 3 vols., vol. 1, chs. iii–ix). As M. J. Herskovits has pointed out, the family everywhere has a stability based on marriage (q.v.) (*Cultural Anthropology*, New York: Knopf, 1955, p. 171).

3. Within the context of the general bio-

logical and cultural nature of the human family, J. Gillin, among others, has pointed out its commonly encountered characteristics (*The Ways of Men*, New York: D. Appleton-Century, 1948, pp. 419–21).

(a) A marriage bond between two or more individuals always exists; this bond must exist between at least two members of the opposite sex and on occasion more, and sometimes between members of the same sex as in Kwakiutl man-marriage in the potlatch and West African woman-marriage, in both instances to serve economic ends (E. A. Hoebel, *Man in the Primitive World*, New York: McGraw-Hill, 1949, under 'Fictive Marriage', p. 213).

(b) There is a recognized, real or assumed, blood relationship on which kinship concepts, terms, and obligations are based.

(c) There is some form of residence (q.v.).

(d) There are numerous personal and societal functions performed. These include physical care, patterning of sexual activity, patterned transmission of culture, economic functions, social care, and in some cases familial control of occupation, and political, religious, and other activities.

All that such lists indicate is that the cultural and separable functions of the family must always, *in some local form or another*, subsume the necessary functions of reproduction, child protection and enculturation, economic co-operation, kinship structure and the patterning and control of affectional and sexual relations.

D. Once the factors that must enter into the definition of the family as such are formulated, and the family defined, it must be recognized that there is wide variation of function with respect to family sub-types. The nuclear family is of course universal and is found as a unit in all other family forms, and some variation of function with respect to family form can perhaps be treated best as variation in marriage. But it must be pointed out here that conjugal and consanguineal family structures tend to be involved with diverse functions. The conjugal family isolated as a unit from consanguine families and extended or non-extended, emphasizes the spouses and their mutual obligations; the consanguineal family, the kin. In this sense the conjugal family is a couple surrounded by their in-laws; the consanguineal, a child surrounded by relatives. If a society, such as ours, emphasizes the conjugal relationship and minimizes kinship, then romantic love, freedom, individuality, and distinctive personality may

all be encouraged. But since marriage is a man-made custom, the conjugal family may be brittle, easily annihilated in divorce, and the mobility of parents paid for in the security, economic or other, of the children. On the other hand, in the consanguineal family, such as the Chinese, conjugal love may be sacrificed to filial duty, sons and wives to fathers, and the security of kin relationships is bought at the price of inability to escape from them.

Weston La Barre

See also: Kinship and Kinship System
Marriage

Family Size (Also **Household Size**)

A. 1. In censuses (and some other types of statistical inquiries), the 'family' or 'household' is usually a group of persons who at a particular date live together. In some censuses (where a de facto count is taken) it is a group composed of those who are present together in the same dwelling at the enumeration.

2. In the study of fertility (q.v.), *family size* denotes the number of children born to an individual or couple up to a certain time.

B. 1. The idea of *family* or *household* used in censuses differs from the notions of family and household in ordinary usage or in anthropology or sociology. The word *family*, as used by all but statisticians, refers to a unit defined by relationships of longer duration than common residence at a particular date (let alone presence in the same dwelling on a particular night).

Confusion can easily arise from failure to understand this point. For example the number of families with one child recorded at a census will include families who have not yet had a second child and those where only one child out of a number is still at home. These two categories will usually outnumber the 'only children'. It is thus futile to use the number of families with one child as an indication of the number of 'only children'.

2. What persons are to be counted as living together? Three main types of concepts for 'census families' have been in use:

(a) The first type denotes those living together in the same 'dwelling unit'. This is the basic concept of censuses because it usually emerges as a by-product of the enumeration procedure. To count people it is necessary to find them. For this purpose a preliminary listing is generally made of all places (houses, flats, etc.) where people live. During the actual census

Fascism

the people in each such place (often termed a 'dwelling unit') have to be counted. Those who are counted together can then be treated as a family or household for the census tables.

(b) The second denotes those, within households of type (a), who have common housekeeping arrangements, e.g. take more than a certain number of meals together every week.

(c) The third denotes those, within households of types (a) or (b), who are related. Families may be distinguished in various ways on the basis of relationship. All relatives may be treated as one family. A second method is to regard only couples with their children as a family and treat others (e.g. grandparents) as separate families.

Types (b) and (c) are subdivisions of type (a), the *dwelling unit household*. Definitions which group together persons who are not in the same dwelling unit but may regard themselves as members of one household or family have not been applied in censuses. The growth of statistics in this field has occurred mainly in the 'developed' Western countries and the concepts used may be less appropriate elsewhere.

The variety of terminology adds to the possibilities of confusion. At the present time, in English-speaking countries units of type (a) or (b) are generally called *households*, those of type (c) *families*. In the older censuses the term *house* was used for dwelling unit, so that 'number of persons per house' means 'average size of household'. In the 1930 and 1940 U.S. censuses households of type (a) were called *families*. According to more recent U.S. terminology, a *family* is of type (c), distinctions being made between the *primary family* in a household (i.e. the head of the household and all his relatives) and *secondary families* (i.e. families of lodgers or resident servants). Within a primary family there may be a *subfamily* (i.e. a married couple, parent and child, etc.). As a second example of modern terminology, we may take the British Census of 1951. Here a *primary family unit* was distinguished in each household consisting of the head, his relatives (within certain degrees) and resident domestic servants. Members of a *household* outside the *primary family unit* were designated *remainder sections*; a *family nucleus* (where present in a remainder section) was separately treated.

Census definitions of households and families must also allow for persons not normally considered to live in families. Persons who do not belong to private households have to be allocated to institutional households or *quasi-*

households. Persons living alone become *single-person households* or *primary individuals* (U.S. terminology).

Other concepts of households and families than those used in population censuses occur in economic statistics, though in this field the chances of misunderstanding are nowadays reduced by such terms as *income units*, *saving units*, etc.

C. In the study of fertility the use of the term *family size* derives from the colloquial meaning of 'having a family'. In this sense the 'size of a family' is the number of children born to an individual or a couple up to a certain time. For example, one might consider the distribution by size of family after 5 years of marriage of those married in 1940. *Completed* size of family means the number of children born before a stage after which very few or no additional children can be expected, e.g. for women over 45 or marriages of more than 20 years' duration (see under *Fertility*).

J. Hajnal

See also: CENSUS
FERTILITY

Fascism

A. 1. The term *fascism* is derived from the Italian *Fascismo*, designating the principles of the Fascisti (a movement which was organized in March 1919, and assumed control of the government under Mussolini in October 1922). The ultimate derivation of the word is the Latin *fascis*, designating the bundles of elm or birch rods which were bound with a red cord and carried by the lictors (attendants of a magistrate) in ancient Rome, symbolizing the magistrate's right to enforce obedience.

2. *Fascism* denotes both (a) a political movement and (b) a doctrine seeking to justify such a movement, whose aim is the establishment of a dictatorial anti-parliamentary regime grounded in the glorification of the state and explicitly hostile to democracy, liberalism, and socialism. The movement and its attendant doctrine is Italian in origin but its ideology had supporters in many other countries. It cannot therefore be regarded as purely Italian in character.

3. The term and the adjective *fascist* have sometimes been loosely applied to denote other kinds of modern totalitarian movements, doctrines and regimes: but the analytical usefulness of such an application has been seriously questioned. More loosely still the terms have been used by some writers and politicians as pejorative blanket descriptions of political ideas or institutions of which they disapprove (e.g. the Communist critique of social democratic parties as instruments of 'social' fascism).

B. 1. Fascism, in Italy, was an activist political movement well before it was formulated by Mussolini and others in doctrinal terms. Indeed, as D. Mack Smith observes, 'Action, said Mussolini, was of primary importance, even when it was a blunder, and the theory and purpose behind action was largely irrelevant' (*Italy*, Ann Arbor: University of Michigan Press, 1959, p. 411). It is therefore, to some extent, misleading to construct a coherent statement of doctrine out of the patchwork of Fascist slogans and ideas, borrowed as they were from other forms of authoritarian anti-democratic ideology, past and present.

2. The most elaborate statement of principle made by Mussolini himself may be found in his contribution to the 14th edition of the *Encyclopedia Italiana* in 1932—translated by J. Soames, it appeared in English as *The Political and Social Doctrines of Fascism* (London: Hogarth Press, 1933). Mussolini's argument fell into two parts —one in which he set out the ideas to which Fascism stood opposed and another in which he offered some statements of what Fascism stood *for*.

(a) Fascism believed 'neither in the possibility nor the utility of perpetual peace'. Peace was a 'harmful postulate'.

(b) Fascism stood opposed to Marxism and other forms of socialist thought. All that remained of socialism, he argued, was 'the sentimental aspiration—as old as humanity itself—towards a social convention in which the sorrows and sufferings of the humblest shall be alleviated' (ibid., pp. 13–4). It likewise stood opposed to 'democratic ideology' (ibid., p. 14) both in theory and practice; and it combated liberalism, both in its political and in its economic forms.

(c) The bridge between his negative and positive statements was provided by his assertion that Fascism retained the elements which possess 'a living value in Liberal, Social and Democratic doctrines' (ibid., p. 19) and would carry such elements through into 'the century of collectivism and hence the century of the State'. For 'the foundation of Fascism is the conception of the State ... as an absolute in comparison with which all individuals or groups are relative, only to be conceived of in their relation to the State' (ibid., p. 21). The Fascist state was 'an

embodied will to power and government: the Roman tradition is here an ideal of force in action. ... For Fascism the growth of Empire was a manifestation of vitality and the opposite a sign of decadence' (ibid., p. 25).

C. The term *fascism* denotes a totalitarian political system which shares certain properties with other species of that genus, yet possesses certain features distinctive from them (C. J. Friedrich (ed.), *Totalitarianism*, Cambridge, Mass.: Harvard University Press, 1954, pp. 52–3; F. Neumann, *The Democratic and the Authoritarian State*, Glencoe, Ill.: The Free Press, 1957, p. 249). Among the basic elements which fascism shares with other types of totalitarianism (q.v.) are the subordination of all group life to that of the state, the use of terror, the maintenance of a one-party system and of state monopoly of the means of force and of communications (C. J. Friedrich, *Totalitarianism*, pp. 52–3; F. Neumann, *The Democratic and the Authoritarian State*, pp. 244–5). There has been much discussion on the resemblances which may be found between fascism and other kinds of modern totalitarianism. All such forms of totalitarianism do, in fact, rest upon basic affirmations of ideology: all totalitarian societies are, in their temper, 'ideological' societies —though it is important to note that such ideologies differ from each other, are *not* interchangeable, and do not have uniform (or unchanging) social functions.

D. By some authors the word *fascism* is used to include not only the socio-political system established by Mussolini in Italy but also the system of ideas and institutions of German National Socialism (nazism). Other authors, while conceding the generic relatedness of fascism and nazism, emphasize the differences between the two systems (W. M. McGovern, *From Luther to Hitler*, Boston: Houghton Mifflin, 1941, p. 617 ff.). In distinguishing fascism and nazism, some stress the syndicalist antecedents of fascism contrasted to the influence of state socialism upon the development of nazism (A. Cobban, *Dictatorship*, London: Jonathan Cape, 1939, p. 131). McGovern (*From Luther to Hitler*, p. 617 ff.) associates fascism with traditionalism and idealism stressing the anti-traditionalist nature of nazism and its emphasis upon the glorification of the *Volk* or nation instead of the glorification of the state. He finds a strong social Darwinist component in nazism which was not associated with

Fashion

Italian Fascism. In both movements the elements of irrationalism and unrationalized activism were strong. The two movements were different, however, in that while the Italian Fascists were committed to imperialism, it was the Nazis who sought a new world order.

E. There has been much discussion from many perspectives as to the origins and 'causes' of fascism. According to W. Y. Elliott both fascism and nazism were 'based upon an attack on rationalistic theories of the state' (*The Pragmatic Revolt in Politics*, New York: The Macmillan Co., 1928, p. 11). Both are interpreted as middle class revolutions against imperfect democratic institutions coupled with a malfunctioning capitalist economic system (Neumann, *The Democratic and the Authoritarian State*, p. 251). A recent important discussion 'Fascism—Right, Left and Center' by S. M. Lipset (in his book *Political Man*, New York: Doubleday, 1960, p. 130–76) discusses the growth of extremist movements in terms of status politics and the displacement of social classes. He presents data from a number of countries to show that 'classic fascism is a movement of the propertied middle classes, who for the most part normally support liberalism and that it is opposed by the conservative strata who have, however, at different times backed conservative, antiparliamentary regimes' (ibid., p. 174). He had earlier commented upon the opportunist character of Mussolini's appeals to diverse social strata and concluded that 'For much of its period in power, Italian Fascism represented a coalition between antidemocratic traditionalism and middle-class populist authoritarianism directed against the leftist revolutionary sectors of the urban and rural populations' (ibid., p. 164).

Cornelius P. Cotter

See also: Communism
Corporatism
Democracy
Dictatorship
Socialism
Totalitarianism

Fashion

A. *Fashion* may be defined as irrational and transitory items or patterns of behaviour which tend to recur in societies which have no fixed status symbols and whose members seek status recognition and self-expression through elite-oriented imitations. These imitations constitute channels for expressing collective tastes and dispositions, and may effect basic changes in both the subjective life of the people and their normative order.

B. Four primary usages of the term are found in sociology, social psychology, anthropology, and economics. First, *fashion* is described as a recurring cultural pattern, found in societies having open-ended class systems, which is intermediate in kind between fad and custom. Second, using the individual as the unit of analysis, *fashion* is depicted in terms of self-individualization made possible by reconciling the desires to conform and to be different. Third, using the group as the unit of analysis, *fashion* becomes a matter of imitation of higher by lower social classes in the common scramble for unstable and superficial status symbols. And fourth, *fashion* is conceived as an expressive social movement which provides a channel for collective change in people and hence for social change.

1. Considering fashion as a cultural pattern, K. Young (*Social Psychology*, New York: Appleton-Century-Crofts, 1956, p. 310) states, 'As a form of behavior fashion has to do with more or less current and accepted matters of dress, personal adornment, decoration, furniture, houses, and a wide variety of social manifestations'. Calling attention to the relation between fad and fashion at one end of the fad-fashion-custom continuum, L. L. Bernard notes (*An Introduction to Social Psychology*, New York: Henry Holt, 1926, p. 546), 'Fashions belong to the same order of instability and irrationality as fads, but their instability and ephemerality are not so marked'. Indicating the other end of the continuum, H. Blumer ('Collective Behavior', A. M. Lee (ed.), *New Outline of the Principles of Sociology*, New York: Barnes & Noble, 1946, p. 216) observes that, compared to fashion, custom is static. Pin-pointing fashion as a feature unique to societies having open-ended class systems, G. Simmel points out ('Fashion', *The American Journal of Sociology*, Chicago: University of Chicago Press, vol. LXII, 1956–7, p. 541), 'Fashion does not exist in tribal and classless societies. It concerns externals and superficialities where irrationality does no harm'. While many social scientists (the most notable example is A. L. Kroeber, *The Nature of Culture*, Chicago: University of Chicago Press, 1952) have taken the position that fashion has a cyclical character that operates almost independently as a cultural force beyond the control of such interested groups as clothing manufacturers, most would probably agree with the moderate position taken by H. Bonner (*Social Psychology*, New York: American Book Co., 1953, pp. 319–92): 'the term fashion applies not merely to clothes, but to *any recurring* activity which satisfies the interests of a large number of people' [italics not his].

2. Representative of those who analyse fashion from the viewpoint of the individual participant who seeks to balance self-demands with societal demands is R. Bierstedt's observation (*The Social Order*, New York: McGraw-Hill, 1957, p. 203): 'We have noticed that people like to be like their associates and friends. They also like to be different. One of the reasons they conform to the norms is that in doing so they identify themselves with their groups. But they also want to express their individuality. Fashion is a device beautifully suited to reconcile these opposing tendencies, the desire to conform on the one hand and the desire to be different on the other'.

3. Simmel's comments ('Fashion', pp. 541–58) concerning imitation in fashion as part of the process of social differentiation are in agreement with those of most students of this feature of fashion: 'Fashion is a form of imitation and so of social differentiation, but, paradoxically, in changing incessantly it differentiates one time from another and one social stratum from another. It unites those of a social class and segregates them from others. The elite initiates a fashion and, when the mass imitates it in an effort to obliterate the external distinctions of class, abandons it for a new mode. ... The very character of fashion demands that it should be exercised at one time by a portion of the given group, the great majority being merely on the road to adopting it. As soon as an example has been universally adopted ... we no longer speak of fashion. As fashion spreads, it gradually goes to its doom'.

4. The fourth dimension of fashion, which reveals it as an expressive social movement, takes into consideration the formation and expression of collective tastes and dispositions in the kind of society in which people are categorized according to external symbols. Here, as Blumer points out ('Collective Behavior', p. 218), fashion also plays a key role in changing the social order: 'In a changing society, such as is necessarily presupposed for the operation of fashion, people are continually having their subjective lives upset; they experience new dispositions and tastes which, however, are vague and ill-defined. It seems quite clear that fashion, by providing an opportunity for the expression of dispositions and tastes, serves to make them definite and to channelize them and, consequently, to fix and solidify them. ... In providing means for the expression of these dispositions and tastes, fashion acts, as suggested before, to shape and crystallize these tastes. In the long run fashion aids, in this manner, to construct a *Zeitgeist* or a common subjective life, and in doing so, helps to lay the foundation for a new social order'.

Ray L. Gold

See also: COLLECTIVE BEHAVIOUR
FAD

Fecundity
Fecundity denotes the capacity to have (live-born) children (this is the modern usage which has been firmly established only since about 1930). For the fecundity of a group the expression *reproductive capacity* is also used.

1. As applied to man or woman or a couple the term refers to the (a) capacity to have children. (It is the opposite of sterility or infecundity); (b) degree of capacity to have children. (One may speak of high fecundity as opposed to sub-fecundity).

2. As applied to a group, it refers to the maximum frequency of births that might occur, as opposed to the actual frequency (fertility): (a) in general terms, leaving unspecified the potential maximum envisaged; or (b) a physiological maximum, e.g. 'fecundity is measured by the number of ripe ova produced' (A. M. Carr-Saunders, *The Population Problem*, Oxford: The Clarendon Press, 1922, p. 51). (Fertility in any human society must remain considerably below fecundity as defined in such a way); (c) the fertility achieved in the absence of deliberate family limitation. (Fecundity in this sense may be studied either (i) by means of data relating to societies or groups where no significant family limitation is practised or (ii) by records of the fertility of couples in periods when no family limitation was attempted).

J. Hajnal

See also: FERTILITY

Federalism
A. *Federalism* denotes a political system (and the principles underlying such a system) which (a) provides for or recognizes the existence of a central government for the whole country and certain autonomous regional governments (states, provinces, länder, cantons) for the

Federalism

divisions of the entire territory; (b) divides the powers and functions of government between the central and regional governments; (c) gives to the regional constituents a special set of rights and duties; (d) authorizes both levels to legislate for, tax, and operate directly upon the people; and (e) provides various mechanisms and procedures for resolving conflicts and disputes between the central and the regional governments, and also between any two or more of the regional units.

B. No two federal systems closely approach an identity of institutions and arrangements upon the crucial question of making the division of powers effective and for making the dual system work. Furthermore, no two authorities emphasize the same points or use the same descriptive words.

1. A somewhat different formulation of the essential characteristics of a federal system from that here given is supplied by a well-known authority, A. W. Macmahon. In a recent work 'The Problems of Federalism: A Survey' (in A. W. Macmahon (ed.), *Federalism Mature and Emergent*, New York: Doubleday, 1955, pp. 4–5), he says that 'it is important to identify the salient characteristics of federalism but self-defeating not to allow for gradations. An exact classification would yield almost as many types as cases'. His own set of essential attributes of federalism is as follows: (a) 'a federal system distributes power between a common and constituent governments under an arrangement that cannot be changed by the ordinary process of central legislation ...'; (b) 'the matters entrusted to the constituent units ... must be substantial and not merely trivial'; (c) '[the] central organs are to some extent directly in contact with individuals, both to draw authority from them through elections and also for the purpose of exacting taxes and compliance with regulations ...'; (d) 'the member states have considerable leeway in devising and changing their forms of government and their procedures ...'; (e) 'A further essential is the equality of the constituent states, absolute as to legal status but at best relative as to such matters as size, population, and wealth.'

In an article written some twenty years before the one quoted above, Macmahon spoke of federalism as 'a protean but widely applicable principle'. 'The essential relationship,' he said 'involves a division of activities between the autonomous parts and the common or central organs of a composite whole. Arrangements

inherently so conditional do not foster an absolute nomenclature' ('Federalism' in E. R. A. Seligman (ed.), *Encyclopedia of the Social Sciences*, New York: The Macmillan Co., 1931, vol. VI, p. 173).

2. K. C. Wheare (*Federal Government*, London: Oxford University Press (1st edn. 1946) 3rd edn., 1953, pp. 1–15) discusses at some length 'What federal Government is'. Wheare recognizes the division of powers as the central issue but he formulates it differently and adds some conditions that are distinctly his own. He says: 'By the federal principle I mean the method of dividing powers so that the general and regional governments are each, within a sphere, coordinate and independent' (ibid., p. 11). Wheare's conditions seem to be rather rigid. In the United States, national and state powers do not appear as separate spheres but as overlapping and interlocking networks of power that are almost indescribably intermixed. Furthermore, the state powers are not coordinate with those of the federal government since the laws and treaties of the latter are, in the explicit words of the Constitution, 'the supreme law of the land, anything in the constitution or laws of any state to the contrary notwithstanding.' Finally, the states are not 'independent' of the national government, nor it of them, under a Constitution which in its development has come to bind them so closely together. The states have wide powers of autonomous action, but not independence. The same would appear to be true of the regional governments in the other generally recognized federal systems, e.g. Australia, Canada, the Federal Republic of Germany, Switzerland, the Federation of Rhodesia and Nyasaland, the now dissolved Caribbean Federation, and, more recently, Nigeria.

3. A sociological turn to the discussion of the subject is given by W. S. Livingston, who stresses that 'Federal Government is a device by which the federal qualities of the society are articulated and presented. ... If [the diversities] are grouped territorially, i.e. geographically, then the result may be a society that is federal. If they are not grouped territorially, then the society cannot be said to be federal' (*Federalism and Constitutional Change*, Oxford: The Clarendon Press, 1956, p. 2).

C. 1. Authorities agree that federal government and the principal ideas concerning federalism in the modern world stem from the constitution-making activities of the United States of

America since 1775. When thirteen English-speaking colonies along the Atlantic seaboard of North America revolted against British rule in 1775–6, they soon agreed to abide by certain 'Articles of Confederation and Perpetual Union' drawn up by their central revolutionary Congress. These articles made a sort of division of powers between the member states and the Congress in which all were represented. This division of powers followed rather closely that which had prevailed between the colonies and the British central government, but the Articles failed to create a strong central government with power to legislate directly for and to enforce its legislation upon the whole people. Given these deficiencies, the Articles fell short of establishing a federal system of government in the present sense of the term. At best the result was a confederal organization. The distinction between a federal and a *confederal* political structure has been discussed by C. J. Friedrich ('Federal Constitutional Theory and Emergent Proposals', in A. W. Macmahon (ed.), *Federalism Mature and Emergent*, esp. pp. 510–12).

When in 1787 a federal convention drew up a 'Constitution for the United States of America' (Preamble) to overcome the basic weaknesses of the system of government under the Articles, it provided in the Constitution for a complete central government to legislate for and operate directly upon the entire nation in accordance with a list of granted powers. They left the states in existence as autonomous units to exercise the residue of powers not conferred by the Constitution upon the central government. They also preserved the Union of the states, established by the Articles, and indeed tried to make it 'more perfect', but the Articles themselves were entirely superseded by the Constitution.

The proponents of the Constitution called themselves 'federalists' and the Constitution itself came to be called the 'federal Constitution' although the word 'federal' is not to be found in its text. The principles of this Constitution were expounded in a famous set of papers, 'The Federalist Papers' by A. Hamilton, J. Madison, and J. Jay. Likewise the central government so established was then and is still generally called the federal government, while the political party that emerged from the successful movement for the Constitution, and that in effect ruled the country for twelve years, became the Federalist Party, and its strongly nationalizing policy came to be designated as 'federalism'. Such in brief are the American origins of these terms.

2. After a number of other countries, notably Switzerland, Canada, and Australia, and, for certain periods, Germany, had acquired similar constitutions and dual forms of government, scholars felt the need for a general term to designate their governmental systems as a class. The abstract noun *federalism* began then to be used to denominate the type or principle of organization, while the more concrete terms *federation, federal republic, Bund*, and *Bundesstaat* were employed to designate the specific entities. More recently two other changes have occurred involving (a) the use of the term 'a federalism' to designate a particular country that operates under a federal type of constitution, and (b) the use of the plural term 'federalisms' to refer to two or more such actual governments or to the entire class of governments based on federal principles.

D. *Federalism* and a number of related terms have come to be used in the fields of church, labour and commercial organizations, and, indeed, in social affairs generally. But its main usage is with regard to the organization of systems of government.

William Anderson

See also: REGION
REGIONALISM (Political Science)
REGIONALISM (Sociology)

Fertility

A. 1. *Fertility* in modern demographic usage relates to the actual frequency of births and carries no overtones of ability to have children. For the latter concept *fecundity* (q.v.) or *reproductive capacity* are now used. In French (and other Latin languages) demographic usage has developed in the opposite direction; *fécondité* means fertility and *fertilité* means fecundity.

2. The demographer's use of *fertility* has, however, penetrated but little into non-specialist discussions of population questions. The word occurs in common usage in many contexts both literal and metaphorical (e.g. fertile soil, a fertile mind). In either case it may refer to actual output or to capacity, and it is frequently ambiguous.

3. In biology and medicine (especially in discussions of involuntary childlessness) *fertility* is generally used for capacity to bear children. *Fecundity* and *fertility* may nevertheless be distinguished also in medical works, e.g. fecundity may denote the capacity to liberate ova or spermatozoa, but not necessarily to produce a

Fetish

viable fetus. *Sterility* in medical literature always refers to involuntary childlessness and this is the customary meaning also in demography.

B. Several sub-varieties of the term's demographic usage may be noted.

1. As applied to an individual or a couple, fertility may be used to (a) denote the number of children produced (particularly in such phrases as 'planned fertility', 'intended fertility', etc.); or (b) denote the fact that at least one (live-born) child has been produced (especially in the phrases 'a fertile woman', 'a fertile marriage' as distinct from a childless one).

2. As applied to a group of people (nation, social class, marriages contracted in one year, etc.), fertility may be used (a) to denote the frequency of births in a general sense, often interchangeably with *birth rate*, e.g. 'Many writers have reflected upon the causes of variations in fertility. Opinions on the causes of changes in the birth rate have also been stated or implied in the policies designed to influence fertility which have been proposed or adopted in various countries' (United Nations, Population Division, *Determinants and Consequences of Population Trends*, Population Studies, no. 17, New York, 1953, p. 73). (b) It may also be used to denote the frequency of births as measured in some refined way, or the underlying variable which refined indices aim to measure. For example, data on birth order 'provide the only means of learning whether an increase in the number of births in a particular year is due to a real increase in fertility' (D. V. Glass & C. P. Blacker, *Population and Fertility*, London: The Population Investigation Committee, 1938, p. 46).

In particular, in the 1930s and early 1940s great stress was laid on age specific fertility rates of women and on reproduction rates. The view that 'The gross reproduction rate is the best single figure to convey a measure of fertility' (R. R. Kuczynski, *The Measurement of Population Growth*, London: Sidgwick & Jackson, 1935, p. 121) was widely accepted. The concept of fertility measured in this way is implied in such typical statements as 'nothing can arrest a continuous decline of the total population, unless something happens to increase fertility above its present level' (E. Charles, 'The Effect of Present Trends in Fertility and Mortality Upon the Future Population of Great Britain and Upon its Age Composition' in L. Hogben (ed.), *Political Arithmetic*, London: Allen & Unwin, 1938, p. 73).

The fluctuations in the numbers of births since the 1930s have caused a general revision of opinion on techniques of fertility analysis; many would no longer accept the assumption that there is some one 'best' method of fertility measurement. On this view phrases such as 'the present level of fertility' may have different equally justifiable meanings. (c) It may also be used in such expressions as *generality fertility*, *marital fertility*, *illegitimate fertility*, etc. to refer to the frequency of births in certain sections of the population or computed in a certain way. A variety of terms describe different indices, such as *total fertility rate*, *parity-specific fertility rates*, etc. For conventions governing the use of these terms technical works should be consulted (e.g. United Nations, *Multilingual Demographic Dictionary*, New York, 1958; M. Spiegelman, *Introduction to Demography*, Chicago: The Society of Actuaries, 1955). However, these conventions are by no means accepted by all authors, and the context should always be kept in mind. For the understanding of more general discussions, it may be useful to mention that *cohort fertility* and *generation fertility* refer to the fertility of a group of persons born at the same time or a group of marriages contracted at the same time. The term *family size* (q.v.) bears the same meaning. *Completed fertility* is the same as *completed family size*.

J. Hajnal

See also: Family Size and Household Size
Fecundity

Fetish (Also **Fetishism**)

A. The term *fetish* has been used by a variety of authorities to denote a cult object which is considered intrinsically potent and/or valuable on account of its symbolic and/or ritual associations without regard to its practical utility.

The use of the term ordinarily implies that the fetish is considered valuable for its own sake and not simply as a symbol but the distinction is largely theoretical; e.g., is a 'holy relic' valuable as 'a thing in itself' or as a 'symbol'?

B. 1. The basic usage of the term is in cultural anthropology in the analysis of primitive religion.

2. By analogy the term *erotic fetichism* was defined by H. Ellis (*Studies in the Psychology of Sex*, New York: Random House, 1936, vol. III, pt. 1, p. 2) as 'the tendency whereby sexual attraction is unduly exerted by some special part or peculiarity of the body, or by some inanimate object which has become associated with it'. He attributes the introduction of the term to Binet followed by Lombroso and Krafft-Ebing. This use of the term is still generally current in psychiatry.

3. In Marxist usage the concept of *commodity fetishism* is employed (as in *Das Kapital*, vol. I) to distinguish the culturally defined value of objects from their strictly utilitarian value. This terminology remains current among Marxist writers (e.g. P. M. Sweezy, *The Theory of Capitalist Development*, New York: Oxford University Press, 1942).

E. R. Leach

Feud

A. 1. The general sense of the term has always been *enduring enmity, hostility, or ill-will* (cf. *Oxford English Dictionary*, 1897), but for some centuries at least it has been used (often in the phrases *deadly feud* or *blood-feud*) to refer specifically to the state of lasting mutual hostility which exists between two groups when one party has suffered injury from the other (usually by homicide), and retaliation by means of reciprocal killing is sought.

2. Usage in sociology and anthropology follows the latter use above; the *feud* or blood-feud is a widespread social institution, known from many historical and contemporary societies. The term denotes actually or potentially homicidal relations of violent hostility between two of the component groups in a society, these relations being, none the less, subject to rule and terminable, at least ideally, by peaceful settlement. Where the hostilities are between whole societies and not merely between segments of a single society they are more conveniently described as *warfare*, and where, although the relationship is an inter-group one, no means for settlement exist or are resorted to, the continuous course of reciprocal killings which ensues is more properly called *vendetta*.

B. Characteristic features of the *feud* are these:
1. It is essentially an inter-group relationship, so a condition of it is a *high degree of group solidarity, typically (though not only) found where unilineal kinship forms the basis of territorial organization*. Thus according to L. T. Hobhouse (*Morals in Evolution*, London: Chapman & Hall, 1906, vol. I, p. 89) 'the blood feud is retribution exercised by a family upon a family; it rests upon the support which each individual can count upon from his own im-

mediate relations, possibly from his whole clan; it rests, in a word, upon the solidarity of the kindred'. Corollaries of this are (a) that individual responsibility is of little moment; though the victim of retaliation must be a member of the offending group he need not (though sometimes he may) be the original killer; and (b) that the feud cannot occur *within* the minimal effective group, for if it did it would destroy the very solidarity upon which the social structure and the possibility of the feud itself depend.

2. It is always *subject to some measure of social control:* 'the unmitigated feud was the negation of law' (W. Seagle, *The History of Law*, New York: Tudor Publishing Co., 1946, p. 36). Where there is no social limitation or restraint the conflict is best called *vendetta* or *war* (q.v.). This restraint customarily relates both to the conditions under which the feud may be initiated and carried out, and to the provision made for its termination. Typically, feud arises in consequence of homicide, and the retaliation sought should bear some proportion to the original offence, lex talionis being more or less rigorously applied. A reciprocal killing may conclude the blood-feud, being followed by a ceremony of reconciliation, but in many societies the feud may be 'nipped in the bud' by such expedients as the duel, the Australian 'expiatory encounter', or (where negotiable goods such as cattle are available) by the payment of compensation.

3. Recent scholars have stressed its significance as a means of maintaining social order in societies which lack any kind of centralized political or jural authority. When a central power above and outside the contending segments of the society emerges, the blood-feud either becomes permissive only or is proscribed altogether, and homicide becomes a crime or public delict, no longer the private concern merely of the local groups involved. Modern ethnographic research has exhibited the feud as a key political institution in those 'segmentary' societies in which it is found, for not only is the fear of incurring it a major social sanction for good behaviour, but by expressing and institutionalizing inter-group opposition while at the same time providing means for settlement it maintains the equilibrium between segments upon which the social structure depends. Thus E. E. Evans-Pritchard writes (*The Nuer*, Oxford: Oxford University Press, 1940, p. 159) that among the Nilotic Nuer tribe 'a feud has little significance unless there are social relations of some kind which can be broken off and resumed,

Feudalism

and, at the same time, these relations necessitate eventual settlement if there is not to be complete cleavage'. In societies of this type the feud is a regulated and politically significant mode of behaviour between communities within a tribe.

J. Beattie

See also: War

Feudalism

A. *Feudalism* denotes a socio-political system, based upon a rural economy, characterized by dispersal of power in a variety of semi-independent domains; the domains being styled as *fiefs* held on condition of the performance of service.

B. No arbitrary definition of this term is possible—as will be seen from the debates among historians both as to its meaning and as to its possible application to social systems other than the European social system to which this term has had especial reference. The problems involved may be gauged by a review of some among the most important criteria that have been employed in scholarly use of the term (and for its use as a term of opprobrium, implying the evils of inequality, exploitation, and traditionalism):

1. A general reference is made to the chasm between the rich and the poor. On this very broad interpretation, the denotation of feudalism would include all states or at least the great majority of them. This condition is too easily describable to merit a special term.

2. Stress may be put on the theme of a polity dominated by a hereditary group. This implies hereditary transmission of status. It would cover numerous polities, including Ireland at the time of St Patrick, as well as Venice in the 18th century. As such, a polity can be adequately described as aristocratic or nobiliary; it seems superfluous to call it feudal too.

3. Or emphasis may be on a polity dominated by the owners of large estates. As this type of society has been called latifundiarist, there is no point in wasting the word *feudal* on it. It can exist under an oligarchic republic as well as under an absolute monarchy.

4. Manorial economy. Taking the mode of production as the basis of classification, we might call feudal a polity whose economic foundation consists of manors (*manor* can be defined as a large estate, on the whole self-sufficient, the main part of which is cultivated for the benefit of its master by peasants, re-warded with strips of land the fruits of which they can retain in the main part). The first objection against this criterion is that it seems needless to qualify as feudal a type of society adequately described as manorial. Secondly, manorial economy can occur under different forms of top government. It co-existed with a fairly centralized bureaucratic administration in Byzantium, in Spanish America, and in Russia in the first half of the 19th century.

5. Seigneurial immunities may be taken as crucial. This means that full administrative, fiscal, and judicial authority over the inhabitants of a locality is vested in the same person (called seigneur) who has economic rights over this locality, and who is exempt in these respects from any supervision by higher authorities. Such an arrangement may underlie a hierarchy of nobles linked by bonds of enfeoffment (e.g. Western Europe) but may also occur without it (e.g. Poland). It may exist without manorial economy (e.g. Japan) and is even compatible with the bureaucratic type of top government (e.g. Byzantium). For these reasons it is preferable to call this type of structure seigneurial rather than feudal, if no other features are implied.

6. Crucial, too, might be the custom of rewarding administrative and military services by grants of land, held on condition of continuing the service. This custom is well nigh universal in agrarian states with undeveloped commerce. This criterion would exclude cases, like medieval and post-medieval Poland, where manorial economy and seigneurial immunities were accompanied by allodial land tenure.

7. To the sixth criterion may be added the point that feudal tenure arises from such grants only if a contract is involved—that is to say, if they cannot be withdrawn at will. This specification reduces the denotation radically by excluding most of the oriental states where benefices were unilaterally bestowed and withdrawn. Indeed, the fully developed procedure of enfeoffment can be found only in Western Europe and in Japan. It might therefore be advisable not to insist on formal contract (enfeoffment) and to call feudal any type of tenure under which land (called fief) is held on condition of performing service; provided that there is some regularity in the procedure, and it is not just a matter of whimsical gifts. So we could distinguish strict (or contractual) feudalism as a species of feudalism in the broader sense. Compare M. Weber's distinction between *Pfründenfeudalismus* and *Lehenfeudal-*

isimus (M. Weber, *Theory of Social and Economic Organization*, ed. by T. Parsons, New York: Oxford University Press, 1947, p. 373). A more primitive variant of feudalism in this sense appears where herds and pastures are assigned in this way (e.g. Hamitic kingdoms in East Africa, Turkish khanates in Central Asia).

A clear distinction must be made between: (a) a real conclusion of a contract, and (b) a merely ceremonial enfeoffment celebrating de facto inheritance. Contrary to what is sometimes said, feudal land tenure is incompatible with generalized automatic inheritance of positions, though it is compatible with hereditary restrictions on the entry into the circle of aspirants to fiefs. It thus appears that as soon as western European feudalism crystallized, it began to turn into a corporative regime of estates, where only purely ceremonial enfeoffment was practised. Feudal tenure does not imply seigneurial immunities, though it is likely to lead to them. Fiefs may or may not consist of manors; the Japanese *sho* and Islamic *iqta* were composed of strips of land cultivated independently by the peasants from whom dues in kind (or sometimes even in money) were collected.

8. Emphasis may also be put on the domination of the polity by a class of warriors. This would exclude, for instance, Ancient Egypt and Manchu China, where the priests and the mandarins were respectively the most powerful classes. This criterion does not imply the preceding: the ruling warriors may not form a hereditary body—e.g. the Mamluks who were recruited by purchase on slave markets, or Mughal jagirdars, recruited among adventurers and frequently demoted. On the other hand, Sparta, Europe at the beginning of the present millenium, Ankole kingdom and many other cases satisfy No. (8) as well as (9). But they do not necessarily fit the other criteria: Sparta, for instance, had neither manors nor feudal land tenure.

9. The following characteristics of political structure may be stressed together: (a) the existence of a definite hierarchy comprising the entire polity; (b) lack of functional divisions in the hierarchy—that is to say, fusion of military, judicial and fiscal and general administrative kinds of authority; (c) complete decentralization—that is to say, such a state of affairs that a position of authority bestows the right to make decisions on all matters concerning the subordinates, and neither they have a right of appeal, nor the overlord the right of revision. It must be noted that whereas (c) requires (b), (b) is possible without (c). (Whereas (b) is fully realizable, (a) and (c) are rather in the nature of idealized extremes.)

On this interpretation feudalism could be said to have been very common, and could be found, for instance, in numerous African as well as in early Slav and Germanic kingdoms. So it could be stated that 'feudalism is a transition zone between the extreme poles of political organization—centralized bureaucracy and the multitude of semi-independent domains ...' (S. Andrzejewski, *Military Organization and Society*, London: Routledge & Kegan Paul, 1954, p. 144). It follows that feudalism could come into existence through either political disintegration or incomplete subjugation.

10. To this constellation may be added the following traits: (a) the incumbents of positions in the hierarchy are appointed in some manner—they are not, say, hereditary tribal chiefs or virtually independent dynasts merely rendering homage and paying tribute; (b) they are rewarded with lands held under feudal tenure (fiefs). The conjunction of these criteria seems to provide the most useful definition of feudalism. 'Feudalism is primarily a method of government, not an economic or a social system, though it obviously modifies and is modified by the social and economic environment' (J. R. Strayer & R. Coulborn, 'The Idea of Feudalism' in R. Coulborn (ed.), *Feudalism in History*, Princeton: Princeton University Press, 1956, p. 4).

C. A number of features not included in these criteria (for the sake of economy) are in fact necessary correlates of those which are. Thus, so long as war is endemic, the lack of functional divisions of authority inevitably gives a hierarchy a predominantly military character. Seigneurial jurisdiction is also a necessary concomitant of feudalism as here defined, though it can appear separately. But although differentiation of a class of warriors and its dominant position are usual in agrarian states, a feudal structure is possible without them: for example, some nomad khanates in Central Asia where all men were warriors.

Considerable diagnostic difficulties stem from two complications. First, often the central region is governed with the aid of patrimonial bureaucracy (e.g. the area around Paris under the Capetians or the area around Delhi under the Mughals), while the provinces are held by a feudal hierarchy. Second, feudal relations can

Field Theory

be inserted as a part of the lower reaches of a bureaucratic structure (e.g. Byzantine stratiotai under the Heraclean dynasty), or a hierarchy may have a feudal character only on its upper rungs, and patrimonial lower down (e.g. Chou China).

Among the conditions favouring the development of feudalism the following are the most important: rudimentary means of transport, the state of the military art favouring defence of small regions, undeveloped commerce and monetary circulation, widespread illiteracy and low level of administrative technique, a large territory in relation to the means of administration.

S. Andreski

See also: DESPOTISM
MILITARISM

Fief (See **Feudalism**)

Field Theory

A. *Field theory* is a term used by psychologists to describe approaches to the study of behaviour which view it as a resultant of a pattern of forces operating in a space analogous to that employed in *physical* field theory.

B. 1. The concept of *field* in physics is employed to show that 'it is not the charges nor the particles but the field in the spaces between the charges and the particles which is essential for the description of physical phenomena' (A. Einstein & L. Infeld, *The Evolution of Physics*, New York: Simon & Schuster, 1938, p. 259).

2. In the social sciences (especially psychology) the concept of *field theory* is chiefly associated with the work of Lewin, but stems from Gestalt psychology, in which the idea of psychological events as systems of energy is an essential element. Although a *gestalt* in general might be considered a kind of field, according to K. Koffka (*Principles of Gestalt Psychology*, New York: Harcourt, Brace, 1935, pp. 66–7) the field concept as specifically used by gestalt psychologists refers to organized conscious behaviour accompanied by a physiological energy pattern and forming a part of a larger physiological system. W. Köhler also referred to the concept of this psycho-physical system as a 'field theory' (*Gestalt Psychology*, New York: Liveright, 1947, p. 359).

3. Lewin's conception of *field theory* lacks entirely the physiological element of the gestaltists and introduces other qualifications which restrict the definition. It is, however, the *field*

theory ordinarily connoted by this term and has become almost exclusively associated with his name through his broad use of the approach in psychology, particularly in the study of social motivation. According to Lewin, field theory is a method of approaching psychological phenomena; it states that an individual's behaviour at a given time results from a constellation of psychological forces which can be located in a mathematically constructed life space.

The relationship between physical and Lewinian field theory is a very general one and refers essentially to the attempt to represent mental events as fields of force analogous to those of the physical world. Lewin did not present his field theory as a formal theoretical system but as a 'method of analyzing causal relations and of building scientific constructs. This method of analyzing causal relations can be expressed in the form of certain general statements about the "nature" of the conditions of change' (K. Lewin, *Field Theory in Social Science, Selected Theoretical Papers*, ed. by D. Cartwright, New York: Harper & Brothers, 1951, p. 45). The principal attributes of field theory are: 'the use of a constructive rather than classificatory method; an interest in the dynamic aspects of events; a psychological rather than physical approach; an analysis which starts with the situation as a whole; a distinction between systematic and historical problems; a mathematical representation of the field' (ibid., p. 60).

By a classificatory method Lewin meant the classification of scientific data for explanatory purposes. For example, behavioural data might be classified into 'traits' such as intelligence, rigidity, etc., and specific actions explained as the outcome of these traits. In contrast, the 'constructive method' views behaviour as the outcome of a constellation of elements in the psychological space, such field elements as 'position', 'forces', etc. Scientific laws based on relationships of such elements would deal with the underlying forces of behaviour, hence the term *dynamic*.

Especially specific to field theory, Lewin considered, were the conditions: (a) that analysis should begin with a consideration of the entire situation in which behaviour is to occur; and (b) that this situation is as it exists for the person rather than a physical stimulus described by the experimenter. In Lewinian field theory all facts are psychological and the interest of gestalt psychologists in neural energy fields accompanying mental events is not present. Field theory also deals only with the *present* situation as causative of behaviour. Past events have influence indirectly as the origins of the present field, but they have ceased to exist and thus cannot be considered as active in the situation under study. The coexisting parts of the individual's immediate experience of the situation are seen by Lewin as structured or having positions relative to each other and therefore as occupying a type of space, the *life space*. For the analysis of this space Lewin attempted to develop from topological and dynamic concepts a non-metric geometry which would represent positional relationships, direction, distance, and force in psychological space. The resulting representation he called *hodological space* (ibid., p. 151).

Joan Criswell

See also: GESTALT

Filiation

In anthropology a distinction is sometimes made between *descent* (q.v.) and *filiation* such that the first term covers the rules governing membership of a kinship group and the second term the rules governing the attachment of children to their parents. Rules of filiation determine under what conditions A may be said to be the child of B (by birth socially recognized or by adoption) and what social consequences are to follow from this ascription.

In societies organized on the basis of unilineal kinship the nature of the tie of filiation with the father must differ from that of the corresponding tie with the mother, for in one case filiation carries with it membership in a descent group. The compound term *complementary filiation* is sometimes used for the tie to the parent (and through him or her to his or her kin) through whom descent in a unilineal system is not traced.

Maurice Freedman

See also: DESCENT

Fiscal Policy

A. *Fiscal policy* denotes a national policy of varying taxing and spending to maintain national economic stability.

B. 1. In its broadest usage fiscal policy is the name given to a national government's programmes with respect to taxing, spending, and borrowing. An example of such usage is the following: 'Anything the Federal government does to affect the level or direction of public spending, the level of tax rates or the kinds of taxes, the relation of taxing to spending, or the

management of the debt comes under the heading of fiscal policy' (K. E. Poole, *Fiscal Policies and the American Economy*, New York: Prentice-Hall, 1951, p. 2).

2. Since the early 1930s the term has taken on a narrower meaning. In this context it refers to the 'purposeful manipulation of public expenditures and taxes ... to modify the aggregate demand for the goods and services of society, upon which the levels of output and employment depend' (J. A. Estey, *Business Cycles*, New York: Prentice-Hall, 2nd edn., 1950, pp. 394–5). During depression periods the government spends more than its current tax income, financing the deficit by borrowing. This stimulates upward total spending, the demand for goods and services, total employment, and probably the general price level. During inflationary periods the opposite policy is followed. Tax collections exceed current government expenditures, reducing private spendable income if a surplus is maintained, but not if the excess tax receipts are used to retire an amount of debt. A. H. Hansen implies that fiscal policy is synonymous with a government financial policy directed toward full employment (*Monetary Theory and Fiscal Policy*, New York: McGraw-Hill, 1949, p. 167). P. A. Samuelson says 'by a positive fiscal policy, we mean the process of shaping public *taxation* and public *expenditure* so as (1) to help dampen down the swings of the business cycle and (2) to contribute toward the maintenance of a progressive, high employment economy free from excessive inflation or deflation' (*Economics: An Introductory Analysis*, New York: McGraw-Hill, 4th edn., 1958, p. 344).

3. Fiscal policy is often linked with monetary policy as both are directed towards the maintenance of full employment with price stability. Monetary policy tries to reach this objective by making credit easy in order to stimulate borrowing, buying, production and employment when the economy is at less than full employment; when inflation threatens in a full employment economy, credit is tightened to curb borrowing, and excessive demand for goods and services. Monetary policy can be co-ordinated with fiscal policy in an effort to attain full employment.

Norman J. Wood

See also: PUBLIC DEBT
        TAX

Fixed Capital (See **Capital**)

Fixed Cost (See **Cost**)

Folk Culture

Folk Culture

A. A *folk culture*, defined as an ideal type, is a culture in which behaviour is highly conventionalized, personal, based on kinship, and controlled informally, traditionally, and through the 'sacred' (q.v.). Such a culture is homogeneous, itself strongly 'sacred', and the moral order (q.v.) is paramount. It rests upon oral heritage, is relatively static, and develops indigenously. It is especially found among the so-called primitive (q.v.) peoples, but persists among peasant and enclaved groups.

B. During the 19th century in the social sciences a tremendous effort was made to grasp at the level of 'whole' societies the meaning of the industrial and urban revolution among urban peoples through the development of polar typologies of society. Maine's concepts of *status* and *contract*, Morgan's stages of savagery, barbarism, and civilization, Durkheim's conceptions of mechanical and organic solidarity and, perhaps most important for later social theory, Tönnies' analysis of *Gemeinschaft* (q.v.) and *Gesellschaft* (q.v.), were all efforts to compare what appeared to be the relatively simple, unchanging life of the small society with the rush of modern change. This continued in the 20th century with such typologies as Becker's sacred and secular societies (q.v.), Sorokin's concepts of idealistic, ideational, and sensate, etc. In anthropology the most important effort was that of R. Redfield, who in applying the terms *folk society* and *folk culture* to 'primitive' societies succeeded in making concrete what was frequently only general and abstract.

C. Redfield's first important formulation of the idea was informally expressed in his book, *Tepoztlan* (Chicago: University of Chicago Press, 1930). During the 1930s Redfield developed this point of view in his teaching and in 1938 gave it more formal expression in his book, *The Folk Culture of Yucatan*, Chicago: University of Chicago Press, 1941, using four specific societies as the base for his analysis. The most important and specific formulation of his ideas came later in 'The Folk Society' (*American Journal of Sociology*, vol. LII, 1946–47, pp. 293–308). He thought of the folk society as one least like our own and explained that he chose the word folk because, 'Neither the term "primitive" nor any other is denotative, and none has sufficient generally accepted precise meaning to allow us to know in just what

characteristics of a society to discover the degree to which it is or is not "primitive", "simple", or whatever' (ibid., p. 293 fn.). His decision to use the term *folk*, despite its own imprecision, came from the fact that 'it suggests the inclusion in our comparisons of peasant and rustic peoples who are not wholly independent of cities and because in its compounds, "folklore" and "folksongs", it points in a rough way to the presence of folklore and folksongs ...' (ibid., p. 293 fn.).

While Redfield sometimes used folklore and folksongs as indices of folk culture, he did not use the former to define the latter. Rather he always stressed the fact that the folk culture is an ideal type, a mental construction, never found in pure form, but most closely approximated by those cultures which have formed the chief interest of the anthropologist. Rather than folklore or folksong being the most crucial indices of folk culture, their most important characteristic is that they belong to such small, scattered, isolated groups. Because folk societies are small and isolated, personal relationships predominate, especially in the form of kinship relations, and the individual is subordinated. Sacred values outweigh secular values. The moral order is very strong resulting in a relatively static society, which develops indigenously, in so far as it does change. Social control (q.v.) is informal, traditional, and sacred, as might be expected where the transmission of culture is largely oral and by example. In contrast to urban culture and urban society the culture of the folk society is an integrated whole which 'provides for all the recurrent needs of the individual from birth to death and of the society through the seasons and the years' and which is the result of 'long intercommunication within the group in the face of these problems' (ibid., p. 298).

D. The folk culture concept has gained in currency but has also encountered criticism. One critic has been Redfield's colleague, S. Tax, who suggested that his own research in Guatemala indicated that impersonal relations and economic values could be strong in an otherwise folk culture ('Culture and Civilization in Guatemalan Societies', *Scientific Monthly*, vol. 48, 1939, pp. 463–7). Another critic has been O. Lewis, whose restudy of Tepoztlan convinced him that this community at least was not as folk-like as Redfield had reported (*Life in a Mexican Village: Tepoztlan Restudied*, Urbana: University of Illinois Press, 1951).

But perhaps the strongest criticism has been that the peasant way of life is not adequately categorized as being of the folk type. Tax in 1945 made a mild modification of Redfield's construct when he attempted to define the peasant situation as 'essentially one in which otherwise folk-like communities have lost their isolation but not their identity', (' "Revolutions" and the Process of Civilization', in *Human Origins, Selected Readings*, Series II, 1945, mimeo). Redfield himself showed cognizance of his critic's suggestions and took steps to isolate the peasant culture as one which 'has developed in very important respects indeed away from the ideal type of folk society' (*The Primitive World and Its Transformations*, Ithaca, N.Y.: Cornell University Press, 1953, p. 39). He later wrote a whole book in which he elaborated on this view (*Peasant Society and Culture*, Chicago: University of Chicago Press, 1956). Despite these and other changes, his description of the folk culture has remained virtually what it was in the beginning.

W. A. Lessa

See also: FOLKLORE
GEMEINSCHAFT
PEASANT SOCIETY
SACRED
SACRED SOCIETY

Folk Society (See Folk Culture)

Folklore

A. Anthropologists use the term *folklore* to mean unwritten literature or traditional narrative as expressed in folktales, incantations, proverbs, riddles, songs, prayers, and the like. The term is also used to designate an anthropological discipline which studies such materials in the same way that any ethnographic data is treated.

B. Ambrose Merton (William John Thoms), an English antiquarian, coined the word *folklore* more than a century ago, when he wrote, 'What we in England designate as Popular Antiquities, or Popular Literature (though ... it ... would be most aptly described by a good Saxon compound, Folk-Lore,—*the Lore of the People*)' (*The Athenaeum*, 22 August, 1846, p. 862). Since his time the word has been adopted by practically every European language, but its meaning has undergone alteration.

C. While some scholars have tended to adhere to the original meaning as developed in Europe, viewing folklore as peasant or folk culture (q.v.) as expressed in beliefs, customs, and narratives, social scientists generally have considerably narrowed the meaning of the word. They feel that to have it encompass the whole of the culture of rustic or primitive peoples is going too far; they limit it to what has come to be called unwritten literature, i.e. myths, folktales, spells, riddles, proverbs, prayers, songs, and the like. They omit such things as festival rites, traditional games, arts, and crafts. In short, they view folklore as a special segment of folk culture. This difference in definition is shown in the twenty-odd definitions of folklore given by the leading folklorists in the United States in the definitive *Standard Dictionary of Folklore* (M. Leach (ed.), *Standard Dictionary of Folklore, Mythology and Legend*, New York: Funk & Wagnall, 1949–1950, vol. 1, pp. 398–403).

D. Folklore is not only a certain aspect of culture but is also the discipline based on the study of such culture. In some instances the students in this discipline are interested in viewing its materials in the perspective of culture history (q.v.) and in stating particular fact rather than general fact. In other instances they have analytic and generalizing goals. In the latter approach emphasis has fallen either on analysis of the function of folklore, as in myth and its relation to ritual, or upon the testing or advancing of psychological hypotheses, sometimes, but not mostly, of the psychoanalytic variety.

W. A. Lessa

See also: FOLK CULTURE
MYTH
RITUAL

Folkways (Also Mores)

A. *Folkways* are the learned shared behaviour common to a people. *Mores* are such of these ways as are regarded as being of such social concern that their violation produces shock, horror, moral revulsion or indignation, and justifies the use of sanctions against the violator.

B. These terms have had very wide American but hardly any British usage. In 1906 W. G. Sumner published a work bearing the title *Folkways* (Boston: Ginn). He coined the word to symbolize behaviour common to a people. In this stress upon common usage and tradition he was following the work of a number of pre-

Foreign and Comparative Government

decessors, among whom Spencer was probably the most famous. Sumner sought to designate more precisely the difference between the habits of the individual adjusting directly through exploratory movement and those learnt from others as appropriate to the situation. Such of the folkways as become verbalized and violation of which calls for socially approved sanction directed against the violator he called *mores*. Subsequent attempts to sharpen or clarify the meaning of these terms have not modified their meaning greatly. Analysis of recent American texts in Introductory Sociology confirms that the terms are still given their original meaning.

C. G. Myrdal (with R. Sterner and A. Rose) has criticized these concepts for (a) relating to 'a bias in social science against induced changes and especially against all attempts to intervene in the social process by legislation', (b) erroneously presenting commonly held valuations in the form of 'a homogeneous, unproblematic, fairly static, social entity', (c) being an inadequate tool for the analysis of 'a modern western society in process of rapid industrialization' (*An American Dilemma*, New York: Harper & Brothers, 1944, pp. 1031–2).

Fred Cottrell

Force (See Coercion)

Foreign and Comparative Government

A. The phrase *foreign and comparative government* denotes, in America, a field of political science comprised of the study of governments other than that of the United States. Although the phrase implies comparison of these governments with one another (and with that of the United States), the method of study in actuality may or may not be comparative, and even the study of a single foreign government may be considered by some to be part of this field. The phrase implies a study not only of formal governmental institutions but also of broader aspects of foreign societies as they relate to politics.

B. 1. *Foreign and comparative government* is one of the major fields of study in American political science. There is no precise definition of what it must include, but generally as a minimum it involves study of the governments of Great Britain, France, Germany, and the Soviet Union. In recent years there has been a tendency to examine other governments as well, both European and Asiatic, but emphasis remains on the four cited above. Although study of several governments is implied, more concentrated and detailed studies or courses concerned with single foreign governments are also considered to be a part of the field.

There is sometimes an endeavour to make genuine comparisons between the governments of various nations, but the more usual academic practice is to take up in text or course the government of first one nation, then another. This is often, but by no means always, followed by an attempt at comparison through synthesis. When comparisons are made, reference is occasionally also made to American governmental institutions.

2. The purpose of the study and comparison of foreign governments is held to be both the better understanding of the governmental process generally as well as knowledge of the particular governments studied. At the same time such study aims at promoting understanding of the main social and political currents of other societies and as such furnishes a necessary basis for the study of international politics.

3. The study of foreign and comparative government implies more, therefore, than merely a study of formal political institutions. An attempt is usually made to distinguish between the state and its governmental mechanisms and the nation, comprising the people and their ways of life. Invariably there is involved a survey of the history of the countries in question, although the trend seems to be to shorten this aspect, a look at the geography and natural settings of the nations; an analysis of social and economic conditions; and an examination of philosophical and ideological elements as well as general cultural development. Some students hold that the field is broad enough to encompass area studies, in which a country or area is examined from the viewpoint of a number of scholarly disciplines. There is no question, however, but that stress in most studies in the field is placed on political institutions and processes, although even here the increasing use of the methods and techniques of the behavioural sciences brings into play types of analyses and data utilized formerly for the most part by sociologists, social psychologists, and cultural anthropologists.

The elements normally receiving greatest stress in studies in the field include political parties and elections, organization and practice of the executive and legislative mechanisms, and the legal system. Foreign policy is usually treated in an abbreviated manner, although

274

there is a tendency now to place increasing emphasis on this sphere. Foreign policies, of course, are sometimes made the object of study independent of this field and are also included in the study of international relations (q.v.).

Fred Warner Neal

See also: INTERNATIONAL RELATIONS

Frame of Reference

A. *Frame of reference* is used as a technical term in methodology to denote a set of basic assumptions necessary to delimit and determine the subject matter of a science or a theory.

B. This use is clarified by E. W. Hobson (*The Domain of Natural Science*, Cambridge: At the University Press, 1923). He distinguishes between two kinds of concepts in science, those that have direct perceptual counterparts and those that do not. These latter concepts 'are formed by an effort of constructive imagination, for the purposes of the representative scheme' (ibid., p. 32). They function as components of a frame of reference. Such frames of reference as a whole cannot be inferred from experience but are necessary to make meaningful observations. They determine upon which aspects of reality the scientist directs his attention (for instance, the frame of reference of Newtonian physics). H. Becker (*Systematic Sociology on the Basis of the Beziehungslehre and Gebildelehre of Leopold von Wiese*, New York: Wiley, 1932, p. 39) uses the term in Hobson's sense when he says: 'Scientific sociology regards human beings as pieces on the giant chessboard of life; with each succeeding move (social occurrence) they draw closer together, separate, or converge in certain respects and diverge in others. ... Such approach and avoidance constitute the basis of the sociological frame of reference'. The same use is made of the term by T. Parsons and E. A. Shils (*Toward a General Theory of Action*, Cambridge, Mass.: Harvard University Press, 1951, p. 56), even though they differ as to the content of their frame of reference. They state: 'The frame of reference of the theory of action involves actors, a situation of action, and the orientation of the actor to that situation'. In methodology, then, frame of reference means a set of basic assumptions necessary to determine the subject matter to be studied and the orientation toward such study.

Burkart Holzner

See also: MODEL

Franchise (See **Voting**)

Free Association (See **Psychotherapy**)

Free Capital (See **Capital**)

Free Goods (See **Economic Goods**)

Free Trade (See **Multilateralism**)

Freedom

A. In its most general sense the term denotes the state of being free or at liberty, of not being under the control of another; of being unimpeded, unrestrained, or unburdened.

B. 1. The history of the concept records a variety of definitions; some have followed the normal meaning of the word (as above); others have departed from it, asserting e.g. that freedom means the presence of those conditions or opportunities deemed essential for the development of one's capacities. Nazi and Fascist philosophers took up this argument in support of Hitler and Mussolini (see Sir Isaiah Berlin's *Two Concepts of Liberty*, Oxford University Press, 1958). Among those who have treated the concept of freedom in its normal sense are Hobbes and J. S. Mill. Thus Hobbes: 'A free man is he that in those things, which by his strength and wit he is able to do, is not hindered to do what he has a will to' (*Leviathan*, ed. by M. Oakeshott, Oxford: Basil Blackwell, 1957, ch. XXI, p. 137).

2. On the other hand it has been persistently represented as a particular way of living, i.e. doing what conforms to the moral law or to reason. Thus Epictetus holds that no wicked man is free (*The Discourses and Manual*, trans. by P. E. Matheson, London: Oxford University Press, 1916, vol. II, Book IV, i) and Carlyle that 'the true liberty of a man ... consists in his finding out the right path, and to walk thereon' (*Past and Present*, Works, London: Chapman & Hall, 1899, vol. X, p. 212). The same idea lies behind Milton's distinction between liberty and licence: '*Licence they mean when they cry Liberty. For who loves that must first be good and wise*'.

3. Elsewhere, for example, in the works of T. H. Green and Hegel, this concept of freedom forms part of an elaborate political philosophy. Moral freedom, says Green, is the determination of the will by reason; for the individual it consists 'in the realization of an idea of perfection in and by himself' (*Principles of Political Obligation*, London: Longmans, Green, 1913,

Frustration

pp. 26–7). Hegel goes further still: for he maintains that the standard of goodness or reason, the observance of which constitutes *freedom*, is to be found in the state; 'the state in and by itself is the ethical whole, the actualization of freedom' (Hegel, *Philosophy of Right*, trans. by T. M. Knox, Oxford: At the Clarendon Press, 1942, p. 279). It has been argued that, since the individual finds his true self in the service of the state, he can, in the case of disobedience, be forced to be free.

C. 1. In view of the many diverse ways in which freedom can be curtailed, it is necessary to distinguish various kinds of *liberty*. 'There is no *one* freedom but many freedoms; and they are as various as are constraints, impediments and burdens' (M. Cranston, *Freedom*, London: Longmans, Green, 1953, p. 6). However, in each case of its normal usage the elements present have been commonly thought to comprise: (a) a desire to do something; (b) the ability (real or supposed) to do it; and (c) prevention by some other person(s), group(s) or institution(s). Thus D. Fosdick: 'The claim for liberty ... is a demand for conditions under which one is not prevented from doing what one has desire, competence and means to do' (*What is Liberty?*, New York: Harper & Brothers, 1938, p. 7).

The context assumed here is one where a *demand* for freedom is made in order to *do* something positive. It does not cover the occasions when one desires to be rid of a burden or a responsibility rather than to perform a specific action, to be released from onerous ties or obligations or from a sense of guilt. Moreover, it does seem appropriate to say that a person lacks freedom if, even though he has no present desire to do something, he *would* be restrained should he want to do it. Thus we need to distinguish freedom to do only what the state allows, when no one desires to do otherwise, from a condition in which 'all present and potential alternatives of choice' are still open (see ibid., chap. I).

2. It has been argued that freedom cannot be identified with the fulfilment of one's moral capacity or with obedience to the commands of the state. Freedom, as K. J. Scott argues, is a non-moral state ('Liberty, Licence and Not Being Free' in *Political Studies*, vol. IV, 1956, pp. 176–85). Licence is merely a special case of liberty, i.e. the sort of liberty (freedom) of which the speaker (writer) disapproves. 'Licence' carries unfavourable, 'freedom' ('liberty'), favourable, associations.

Furthermore, although freedom has 'a strong laudatory emotive meaning' (see Cranston, *Freedom*, p. 21), it is not always good in itself; it depends on what one is free to do. Being one of several values, freedom has sometimes to give way to other claims, e.g. equality, justice or security. Thus freedom of economic enterprise and of bequest have, with general approval, been much curtailed in recent decades for the sake of other ends. The existence of a social order as such rests on the imposition of some restraints. Law is not necessarily the enemy of everyone's freedom; 'freedom for the pike is death for the minnows' (R. H. Tawney, *Equality*, London: Allen & Unwin, 3rd edn., 1938, p. 208.

J. C. Rees

Frustration

A. *Frustration* denotes the obstruction or thwarting of a (felt) need and/or the feelings that result from such obstruction.

B. 1. The term is widely used, and its technical usage does not differ very markedly from its connotation in popular speech. It should be clear that the need obstructed can be *any* need, be it the attainment of a specific goal or object, the expression of an emotion or habit, the desire to think of oneself or others in certain ways, etc. The need can be wholly obstructed, or only partly, and the obstruction or barrier can be external or internal, material or social, personal or impersonal. The frustration may be temporary or more permanent, in which case it may be linked with gastric ulcers and other psychosomatic illnesses. The term is commonly applied both to humans and animals.

2. It has often been suggested that a person's response to frustration becomes habituated. Thus we have the concept of the *frustration threshold* or 'frustratability' and, more generally, various typologies of reactions to frustration. Perhaps the best known is that by S. Rosenzweig ('The Experimental Measurement of Types of Reaction to Frustration', in H. A. Murray et al., *Explorations in Personality*, New York: Oxford University Press, 1938, pp. 585–99) who describes extrapunitive, intropunitive, and impunitive styles of reaction.

3. In psychoanalytic terms, the tension and anxiety set up by the ungratified need bring various defence mechanisms (q.v.) into play Frustration can be dealt with by sublimation (q.v.) or substitute gratification, by repression, (q.v.), regression (q.v.), displacement (q.v.), projections (q.v.), etc. and these processes may be conscious or otherwise, and can be linked to various forms of psycho-pathology. Moreover the entire process of socialization (q.v.) can be seen as a series of frustrations and the individual's modes of reaction to these, which constitute adaptation. Freud himself, and several of the neo-Freudians, have proposed typologies of adaptation and these, in turn, have been of interest to cultural anthropologists and sociologists (cf. R. K. Merton, *Social Theory and Social Structure*, Glencoe, Ill.: The Free Press, 1957, pp. 139–57).

Frustration may sometimes be followed by displaced aggression (q.v.), i.e. by aggression which is not directed against the outside source or agent of the frustration. This has led to the popular phrase 'scapegoatism' and to the *frustration-aggression hypothesis* as a way of explaining racial prejudice. (This hypothesis has been most clearly formulated by J. Dollard et al., *Frustration and Aggression*, New Haven: Yale University Press, 1939).

4. Frustration, because it produces tension within the individual, is sometimes artificially induced in experiments on learning, perception, conflict, and phantasy. It is important in such cases to ascertain that an inner state of frustration has been produced, and not to infer the existence of frustration from the objective situations alone.

H. T. Himmelweit

See also: AGGRESSION
DEFENCE MECHANISM

Function

A. A *function* is a *consequence* of some kind of the *existence and/or action (or motion) of persons or things*, including here intangible items such as culture patterns, group structures, attitudes. In the general context of social science the consequences of the existence and action or motion of persons or things are viewed with special reference to their effects upon the social arrangements or the structuring and patterning of a situation or of a system and ultimately upon the social acts, or the course of interaction, of human actors. The consequences need not be intended or even recognized by the actors themselves; and they need not necessarily satisfy some end(s) or requirement(s) given in nature or 'chosen' or otherwise effected by human actors. Functions, or functional relations, are described non-mathematically as well as mathematically.

B. The concept of function appears to have been introduced originally into social science by Spencer primarily from physiology. It has also been used by social scientists in the more limited sense in which mathematicians from Leibnitz on have used it when they speak of Y as a function of X, or of X_1 as a function of $X_2, X_3, \ldots X_n$, in simple and in multiple regression and correlation equations.

C. 1. In the most general sense in which it is used in social science, function appears to refer to a *consequence* of some sort, either theoretically statable and expected and/or empirically observable, or inferable, and observed or inferred. The critical question is whether or not the consequence in question is regarded merely as a development which may be *anticipated* and may even be, on theoretic grounds, logically *necessary* or whether it is assumed to meet, discharge, fulfil, in an instrumental way, or to 'express' or 'embody' some known (or theoretically posed) condition, need, requirement, end or purpose. In the case of the second of these alternatives it is essential to know whether the conditions, etc. are assumed to be laid down by nature or whether they are assumed to be 'chosen' or otherwise determined by human actors and action or, possibly, whether they are assumed to be established in some other way not specified here.

2. In order to identify more precisely the different denotations of the word *function*, it appears to be necessary to know what the assumptions of the user are concerning (a) the possibility and/or the desirability of specifying theoretically (and of actually describing) what *all* or what only *some* of 'the consequences' will be, (b) whether the consequences specified are *necessary* or only probable or possible ones, and (c) whether this specification can or should be done in quantitative or in non-quantitative terms or in both. Still other questions concern the assumptions, or postulates, of the user concerning the variability or degrees of unity, universality, and indispensability of the functioning items in the context in which they are viewed (on this last point, see R. K. Merton, *Social Theory and Social Structure*, Glencoe, Ill.: Free Press, rev. edn., 1957).

3. In general, those social scientists who emphasize (a) operational definitions, (b) precise and detailed verifiability of every statement of fact (and of every statement of presumed relationship among facts), (c) quantification of variables and attributes, and (d)

Function

reduction of 'problems' to hypotheses concerning expected or probable relationships among two or more variables have used function in the sense of necessary consequence *without* reference to human intention or to intended goals or purposes and also without either implicitly assuming or theoretically positing some more or less complete set of conditions (and the needs or requirements which follow from these) which must be met if a system, structure, organism, group, or whatever, is to survive, or remain in static or in moving equilibrium, or maintain some form, pattern, configuration, or design. (Examples of this usage are found in the work of T. C. McCormick, S. A. Stouffer, G. A. Lundberg, and others.)

D. The problems that arise may best be illustrated by examples of usage.

1. Some anthropologists (R. Linton, for example) use the concept of function without raising any explicit questions concerning any conditions for survival (or other given ends) which may have to be met. Thus Linton, for example, says, 'the function of a trait-complex is the sum total of its contribution toward the perpetuation of the social-cultural configuration' (*The Study of Man*, New York: Appleton-Century, 1936, p. 404). 'The functional view', according to M. J. Herskovits, 'attempts to study the interrelation between the various elements, small and large, in a culture. Its object is essentially to achieve some expression of the unities in culture by indicating how trait and complex and pattern, however separate they may be, intermesh, as the gears of some machine to constitute a smoothly running, effectively functioning whole' (*Man and His Works*, New York: Knopf, 1948, p. 215). Usually where the concept of *integration* is introduced, something more than mere maintenance of consistent design or of total form or arrangement is implied—namely, that the integration serves some given end or fills some necessary set of conditions or otherwise enhances or maximizes the chances of survival of the culture and of the society that practises it or of the social system that embraces both.

2. For A. R. Radcliffe-Brown, function is 'the contribution which a partial activity makes to the total activity of which it is a part. The function of a particular social usage is the contribution it makes to the total social life as the functioning of the total social system ...' ('On the Concept of Function in Social Science', *American Anthropologist*, vol. 37, 1935, p. 397).

In another article, Radcliffe-Brown writes, 'I would define the social function of a socially standardized mode of activity, or mode of thought, as its relation to the social structure, to the existence and continuity of which it makes some contribution' ('On Social Structure', *Journal of the Royal Anthropological Institute*, vol. LXX, 1940, p. 10). Radcliffe-Brown traces his own interpretation of function to Durkheim who defined as the function of a social institution the correspondence between it and the needs (*besoins*) of the social organism.

3. Although Malinowski was specifically interested in the contributions which the culture patterns, institutional organizations, and practices made to the emotional and other psychological needs of individual persons and of groups, he also was concerned with the ways in which culture might be used to meet 'needs' generally imposed by the conditions of social life and of physical environment. Functional theory, he explains, 'aims at the explanation of anthropological facts at all levels of development by the part which they play within the integral system of culture, by the manner in which they are related to each other within the system, and by the manner in which this system is related to the physical surroundings' ('Anthropology', in *Encyclopaedia Britannica*, 13th edn., 1926, 1st suppl. vol., p. 132).

4. Sociologists, in contrast to most anthropologists, seek to employ the concept of function not so exclusively with reference to *culture patterns* (q.v.) but to on-going processes, social actions, group structures, and a somewhat wider range of phenomena, including some which are not culturally patterned. Not all sociologists who utilize the concept of function regard themselves as working within the somewhat limited 'structural-functional' mode of analysis.

Sociologists who do use this mode generally regard it as necessary to posit theoretically some (or all) of the conditions for maintenance, survival, etc. in a given state of a given society, group, social system, etc. (or of any of these in their most general form) and the *probable* and/or *necessary* existent items, or objects, actions, motions, etc. which must or will be present and operative if the conditions are to be met, the needs or requisites filled. In this context, T. Parsons regards the concept of function as 'all-important. ... Its crucial role is to provide criteria of the *importance* of dynamic factors and processes within the system. ... A process or set of conditions either "contributes" to the maintenance (or development) of the system or it is "dysfunctional" in that it detracts from the integration, effectiveness, etc. of the system' and he goes on to add, 'the functional reference of all particular conditions and processes to the state of the total system as a going concern provides the logical equivalent of simultaneous equations in a fully developed system of analytic theory. [Functional interpretation] appears to be the only way in which dynamic interdependence of variable factors in a system can be explicitly analyzed without the technical tools of mathematics and the operational and empirical pre-requisites of their employment' (*Essays in Sociological Theory*, Glencoe, Ill.: The Free Press, rev. edn., 1954, p. 217).

5. The concept of function has been refined somewhat in structural-functional theory to the point where distinctions are made between consequences which are 'intended and recognized by participants in the system' (i.e. *manifest functions*) and those which are 'neither intended nor recognized' (i.e. *latent functions*) (R. K. Merton, *Social Theory and Social Structure*, p. 51). This leaves in abeyance such questions as (a) whether or not the consequences are to be regarded as fixed in the nature of things, i.e. prescribed and in this sense 'determined' in some naturally established way or whether human action (and especially 'choice' consciously or unconsciously made) governs *the setting up of the conditions in any way*, (b) how any or all of these are to be 'known' and (c) whether functions can be recognized reliably by non-participant analyst-observers.

Allan W. Eister

See also: SOCIAL STRUCTURE

Functional Rationality (See **Rationality**)

G

Game Theory

A. *Game theory* denotes a set of mathematical operations designed to provide a solution to a situation in which a participant endeavours to guarantee himself a certain minimum success by his course of action even though his actions can only influence, without completely determining, the outcome of an event.

B. The mathematical theory denoted by the term was first conceived by J. von Neumann. It attempts to provide a mathematical solution to the problem of selecting the optimum strategy for a 'player' considering the possible actions of his opponent or opponents. Where there is more than one opponent, a possible strategy is coalition provided this is not prohibited by the rules of the game.

While the theory may be used for the analysis of purely recreational games such as poker, its interest for social scientists lies in the similarity between recreational games involving strategy and many real-life situations studied by social scientists. The economic problems of pricing under conditions of imperfect competition of consumer choice and demand, and of collective bargaining are all of this type (cf. J. von Neumann & O. Morgenstern, *Theory of Games and Economic Behavior*, Princeton: Princeton University Press, 1947).

The word *game* as used in game theory refers to a set of rules and conventions for playing, not to the actual play, which is a meaning often given in popular terminology.

C. The forms which game theory has taken are too complex to permit a detailed summary here. Distinctions, both simple and complex, have been successively made within the overall framework of the theory—distinctions, e.g. as to the number of 'players', their 'rationality', and the balance of losses and gains to the different parties. But in essentials the term *game theory* has continued to denote an approach to model-building aimed at clarifying the outcome of conflict situations. Thus R. D. Luce and H. Raiffa offer as a 'compact summary' the view that 'game theory is a model for situations of conflict among several people in which the principal modes of resolution are collusion and conciliation' (*Games and Decisions*, New York: Wiley, 1957, p. 10). Another authority has recently pointed out that 'game theory provides us with tools to construct useful models of competitive situations' (M. Shubik, *Strategy and Market Structures*, New York: Wiley, 1959, p. 18); he earlier asserted that 'With the word *game* we can associate *rules, players, moves, strategies, pay-offs*, some concepts of *competition or co-operation*, and some usually ill-defined notions about the nature and importance of *information* as it is manifested in bidding in bridge or bluffing in poker' (ibid., p. 4). In this sentence are contained many of the key terms employed in game theoretical work.

D. This approach to problems of conflict and strategy has been, for obvious reasons, much employed in theoretical discussions of international policy and military planning. There is no clear agreement on the practical usefulness of the approach: criticism has been levelled at the assumptions which are generally built in to the abstract and mathematical models characteristic of game theory. The sociologist M. Janowitz, recently writing on the role of the American military, has summarized the key notion in game theory as 'that by taking into consideration our own reactions to our opponent's response to our moves, we can evolve a strategy designed to make him involuntarily choose a course of action favorable to us' (*The Professional Soldier*, Glencoe, Ill.: The Free Press, 1960, p. 434), but insists that 'a social science theory of international relations based upon game theory appears to be an unfulfilled promise for it has not produced hypotheses and understanding beyond commonsense' (ibid., pp. 434, 441–2).

Royall Brandis

See also: Cognition
Cybernetics
Decision-Making
Risk (Also Uncertainty)

Gang

A. *Gang* is a term which sociologists have borrowed from general parlance and have tried, with some success, to use as a technical term.

In general usage, the term *gang* may be used to refer to people who are organized to work together, travel together, or play together. This usage of the term connotes closeness of friendship ties, and has little or no reference to delinquent or criminal activities.

The usage from which gang as a sociological term most directly comes, probably, is applied to a voluntary, informal group of 'friends', usually young people.

In sociology the term has been applied to an organization of people who have committed delinquency or crime, or are considered likely to do so. The term usually connotes a considerable degree of solidarity or cohesiveness of the group, but there is no yardstick of group characteristics which can be used to distinguish a gang from other kinds of groups.

B. Its main use in sociology is in the study of juvenile delinquency (F. M. Thrasher, *The Gang*, Chicago: University of Chicago Press, 1936). Attention has been called to the importance of *association* among delinquents as a causal factor in crime by E. H. Sutherland, in what is now known as the 'theory of differential association' (*Principles of Criminology*, Chicago: Lippincott, 1947, pp. 6–8; W. C. Reckless & M. Smith, *Juvenile Delinquency*, New York: McGraw-Hill, 1932, pp. 143–8). Statistical data were collected showing that only 10 per cent or less of delinquent acts are done by a single youth operating alone; the vast majority are done by two or more working together. The term gang has been extensively applied to the pal or friendship groups formed. Authors frequently point out that a gang need not be delinquent, but *gang*, as a technical term, is seldom applied to youth groups except in juvenile delinquency studies.

Sociologists have not made much progress in formulating a concise definition of the term *gang* in terms of this usage. Such groups differ in size, in length of life, in the degree to which they have a closed membership, in the formality of their organization, in the degree of control they exercise over their members, etc. Sociologists have not evolved a formula to say how much a group must have of any of these to be a gang. Thus the dividing line between a clique or a play group and a gang is by no means clear and in practice such a group is whatever the researcher chooses to call it.

Harlan W. Gilmore

See also: CRIMINOLOGY

Gemeinschaft

A. *Gemeinschaft* is an ideal-type concept, and as such is most correctly applied in describing or analyzing social systems in its adjectival form, *Gemeinschaft*-like. *Gemeinschaft*-like social systems are those in which *Wesenwille* (natural or essential will) has primacy. Natural will has primacy when association is based upon relationships which have one or more of the following characteristics: they are ends in and of themselves, are spontaneous and affective, and are the outcome of interaction between status-roles such as mother and child or siblings which traditionally or out of habit provide these qualities. Thus families, friendship groups, clans, peasant neighbourhoods, and religious sects may be said to be *Gemeinschaft*-like.

B. The term was given its specific meaning in systematic sociological analysis by F. Tönnies (1855–1936).

1. As a conceptual tool it refers to an ideal type of social structure and value orientation which does not exist as such in the empirical world. When it, or its opposite, *Gesellschaft*, has been used as a classifactory type rather than an ideal type, misinterpretation has resulted. F. Tönnies wrote of both *Gemeinschaft* and *Gesellschaft* and their respective social psychological or motivational components, natural will and rational will, as follows: 'I call them normal concepts. What they represent are ideal types, and they should serve as standards by which reality may be recognized and described ... these concepts signify the model qualities of the essence and the tendencies of being bound together ... both names are in the present context stripped of their connotation as designating social entities or groups, or even collective or artificial persons; the essence of both *Gemeinschaft* and *Gesellschaft* is found interwoven in all kinds of associations' (*Community and Society—Gemeinschaft und Gesellschaft*, trans. and supplemented by C. P. Loomis, East Lansing, Mich.: Michigan State University Press, 2nd edn., 1957, pp. 248–9).

Historical stages are not to be called *Gemeinschaft*, or its opposite *Gesellschaft*, thus reifying the ideal types. Tönnies (ibid., p. 197) recognized that, although stages with primacy of *Gemeinschaft*-like relations usually precede stages in which there is a primacy of *Gesellschaft*-like relations, the order of development may be reversed.

Although Tönnies (ibid., pp. 2–3) has been accused of favouring *Gemeinschaft*, he has

Genealogy

written that the process by which *Gemeinschaft*-like societies were 'freed' and became the subject of rational will, and consequently more *Gesellschaft*-like, is 'healthy' and 'normal'.

2. An understanding of *Gemeinschaft* and its 'opposite', *Gesellschaft*, requires an understanding of the motivational concept of will as Tönnies and his followers have used it. As R. Heberle (F. Tönnies, *Community and Society, Gemeinschaft und Gesellschaft*, Preface, p. xii) says: 'Social relationships were to him [Tönnies] "willed" relationships, wanted and maintained by the more or less instinctive or purposive-rational volition of the related persons. The "will" of a social relationship between, let us say, two friends or two business partners, is expressed in rules of conduct in essentially the same sense in which customs, ethics, laws, and public opinion can be perceived to express the will of larger collective groups.' Thus will as used by Tönnies includes within its meaning values and some aspects of such elements of the value system as ends, norms, beliefs, and the bases or standards for social rank. He states (F. Tönnies, *Einführung in die Soziologie*, Stuttgart: Ferdinand Enke, 1931, p. 6) that Max Weber's more recent concepts, *affektuell*, *traditionell*, and *wertrational* action provide the motivation for *Gemeinschaft* and are generally comparable to his concept *Wesenwille*.

3. 'The creative, formative, and artistic ability and works in the spirit of genius' as described by Tönnies (*Community and Society*, p. 249) represents expressive behaviour characteristic of *Gemeinschaft*. In *Gemeinschaft* sentiments are expressed spontaneously and not for an ulterior effect. Thus T. Parsons, et al. (*Working Papers in the Theory of Action*, Glencoe, Ill.: The Free Press, 1953, pp. 207–8) write that 'attention may be particularly called to the combinations involved in what are here called the instrumental and the system-integrative norms, which very closely characterize what in much sociological literature have been thought of as polar types of institutional structure, the best known version of which perhaps has been the *Gemeinschaft-Gesellschaft* dichotomy of Tönnies'. Status-roles which are illustrative of *Gemeinschaft*-like sentiments and actions, for Tönnies, are those of mother interacting with her child, faithful servant with master, and friends, in which responsibilities are functionally diffuse, and the relationships are ends in and of themselves. In *Gemeinschaft*-like societies rank is stratified in estates (*Stände*), membership in which is usually determined by birth and occupation. Many facilities such as land in *Gemeinschaft*-like society may be in part at least sacred. Communication is dominated by personal relations and marked by its informality and spontaneity. Boundary maintenance is strong and the status-role of stranger is so structured as to protect against disruption of the value system from outside.

Charles P. Loomis

See also: GESELLSCHAFT
PEASANT SOCIETY

Genealogy

A. A *genealogy* is a statement (written or unwritten) of the accepted ancestry of a person or group.

B. It is now generally understood that genealogies (especially unwritten ones) are not always historically accurate statements, but may be changed in order to provide support for, and validation of, actual present-day relationships between the persons who feature in them. In most societies a knowledge of genealogies is essential to an understanding of the kinship systems (especially with regard to succession, inheritance and the regulation of marriage). An account of methods of collecting genealogies, with the usually accepted symbols for genealogical data, is given in *Notes and Queries in Anthropology* (London: Routledge & Kegan Paul, 6th edn., 1951, pp. 50–5).

J. Middleton

See also: DESCENT
KINSHIP
LINEAGE

General Will

A. The doctrine of the *general will* is at bottom a theory about the relations of the individual and the state which purports (on the basis of differing ideas concerning the state) to set out both what those relations ought to be and to some extent they always are. Anyone holding seriously to the doctrine means to assert (a) that it is as a member of the state that man becomes a moral person; (b) that he is, as a moral person, necessarily his own critic, preferring some of his desires to others because they accord better with his idea of how he should live; and (c) that therefore the better the state and the more adequate his understanding, the more inclined he will be to see in the state's discipline a liberating influence helping him to live up to his own ideals.

B. This is clearly shown in the earlier systematic usage, i.e. by Rousseau. In 'Of the Political Economy' an article published in 1755 in the great French Encyclopaedia, Rousseau says: 'The body politic is thus also a moral being having a will; and this general will, which tends always to the preservation and well-being of the whole and of each part, and which is the source of the laws, is ... the rule of what is just and unjust' (C. E. Vaughan (ed.), *The Political Writings of Jean-Jacques Rousseau*, Cambridge: Cambridge University Press, 1915, vol. I, pp. 241–2). Rousseau then says that this will, though general in relation to the citizens, is not general in relation to foreigners, and also that every smaller society within the state has its general will. Any group of men deliberating in common are, he says, disposed to give expression to the general will, unless some of them have agreed separately to push their particular interest against the common interest; and the general will 'is always for the common good'. In *Du Contrat Social* (Amsterdam 1762, ch. vii, bk. I), Rousseau distinguishes between a man's 'particular' will and his 'general' will as a citizen, saying that when he is constrained to obey the general will, he is forced to be free.

C. Since Rousseau's time the idea of a general will (though not always by that name) has been central to several political philosophies, even when those philosophies have not been democratic.

1. Hegel, in para. 257 of *The Philosophy of Right*, praises Rousseau for holding that 'will' is the 'principle of the state' but blames him for putting it forward as a 'general will' finding expression in the decisions of a popular assembly; and in a passage added to para. 268, (*The Philosophy of Right*, trans. by T. M. Knox, Oxford: Oxford University Press, 1942, p. 282) he says that 'commonplace thinking often has the impression that force holds the state together, but in fact its only bond is the fundamental sense of order which everybody possesses'. The state, for Hegel, is literally a mind or will greater than the minds or wills of its citizens, but existing only in them and in the institutions which make an enduring community of them. Whatever draws citizens to the state he calls the 'rational' or 'universal' element in their wills.

2. T. H. Green, in his *Lectures on the Principles of Political Obligation* (London: Longmans, Green, 1913, p. 98), calls the general will 'that impalpable congeries of the hopes and fears of a people, bound together by common interests and sympathy'.

3. B. Bosanquet, in *The Philosophical Theory of the State* (London: Macmillan, 1899), is more elaborate and clear, and also closer to both Hegel and Rousseau. He holds that man is free when he controls himself in the pursuit of ends giving him lasting satisfaction and that the state is a social order making it possible for him to conceive of such ends and providing the discipline which helps him to pursue them. Man needs that discipline to become what he 'really' wants to be; and his 'real will' is identical with the 'general will' embodied in the laws. Bosanquet, like Rousseau, uses the doctrine of the general will to answer the question: How can man be free when he is forced to obey the laws?

J. P. Plamenatz

Generalized Other

A. The *generalized other* is a role abstracted from the common elements of the attitudes and actions of those with whom the individual interacts. It is this role through which the individual develops consistency in his awareness of himself, broadens his perspective concerning the network of self-other relationships, internalizes the shared attitudes of others, and exercises self-control within the framework of the normative order with which he identifies. Taking the role of the generalized other makes possible the growth of complex and integrated personalities, just as it does the development of 'complex co-operative processes and activities and institutional functionings of organized human society' (G. H. Mead, *Mind, Self, and Society*, Chicago: University of Chicago Press, 1934, p. 155).

B. To date, the only thorough discussion of the concept *generalized other* to appear in a book is G. H. Mead's original introduction (ibid., pp. 154–63). One is hard pressed to find as many as a dozen volumes which have subsequently devoted as much as a full page to the concept. Mead's provocative analysis of the generalized other remains largely an intuitively acceptable one, because systematic investigations of the generalized other in the empirical world have yet to be published.

C. It is useful to place discussions of the generalized other into four analytical categories.

1. The first presents the generalized other as an organization of social activity or expectations which the individual internalizes through co-operative participation in group life. It is the

Generation

individual's abstraction of interrelations of the several roles of those with whom he participates, directly or ideationally, in collective endeavour. As Mead points out (ibid., p. 154), 'The organized community or social group which gives to the individual his unity of self may be called "the generalized other". The attitude of the generalized other is the attitude of the whole community. Thus, for example, in the case of such a social group as a ball team, the team is the generalized other in so far as it enters—as an organized process or social activity—into the experience of any one of the individual members of it'. Similarly, A. Rose indicates (*Sociology: The Study of Human Relations*, New York: Knopf, 1956, p. 31), 'The nature of communication changes as the group ... gets larger. The communication changes from the direct, face-to-face kind to an indirect communication through one or more intermediaries or through a set of rules written down for all to read or to be taught by specialist teachers. The other whose role is being taken is not a single "other" or even a team of "others" but rather a "generalized other", as Mead calls it'.

2. The second analytical category presents the generalized other as a key element in the final stage of the development of self. Here, *generalized other* is defined to show an interdependent relation between social organization and self-organization. More succinctly, R. Faris states (*Social Psychology*, New York: Ronald Press, 1952, p. 152), 'The set of responses which a person gets from his participation in organized social relations also become generalized into a self, which has unity corresponding to the organization in the social groups'.

3. The third aspect of *generalized other* is defined as a process of internalization of the attitudes of others through taking the roles of others which makes possible the internal conversation of gestures and symbols that constitute thinking. Thinking is a vital aspect of the individual's ability to share meanings with others with whom he interacts—that is, with whom he participates in the social process.

4. The fourth dimension of *generalized other* is defined to show how it relates social control to self-control. Social norms represented by generalized others are utilized by the individual to govern his own conduct. Self-control is exercised with reference to internalized generalized others of the groups to which he feels he belongs. It is then also possible for him to establish colleague relationships with others who consider

themselves members of the same groups, for they govern their conduct by using essentially the same symbols and norms. Referring to this dimension of the generalized other, A. Lindesmith and A. Strauss (*Social Psychology*, New York: Dryden Press, 1956, p. 394) state, 'The term "generalized" other does not refer to an actual group of people; but rather to a conception or an interpretation which a person derives from his experiences. He then regulates his behavior in terms of these supposed opinions and attitudes of others. He imagines what "people" would say "if they knew" or what they will say "when they know". The term "people" may not have any specific reference to actual persons, but may merely represent his conception of abstract moral standards. These standards widen as role playing becomes more generalized'.

Ray L. Gold

See also: ATTITUDE
      INTERNALIZATION
      ROLE
      SELF
      SELF-CONCEPTION
      SOCIAL INTERACTION
      SOCIALIZATION
      SYMBOL

Generation

A. *Generation*, as it is employed by social scientists, may be given four definitions:

1. A generation comprises all those members of a society whose behaviour towards each other and towards members of other generations is based on the fact that they are contemporaries, or that they are descended by the same number of degrees from a common ancestor.

2. A generation comprises the offspring of the same parent or parents and is counted as a single degree or step in reckoning the descent of a person or family from a more distant ancestor.

3. A generation comprises all those members of a society who were born at approximately the same time, whether or not they are related by blood.

4. A generation is the time segment between the birth of those members of a society born at the same time and the birth of their offspring, statistically assumed by the social scientist to be a certain period, usually thirty years.

B. Anthropological usage, as it refers to *kinship terminology* (q.v.) and behaviour, has been described thus by A. Goldenweiser: 'From the standpoint of the mature men and women, they themselves represent the present generation, below this is the generation of their children, and below this the incipient generation of the grand-children. Above the present generation is that of the mothers and fathers, and above this the waning generation of the grandparents' (*Anthropology*, New York: F. S. Crofts, 1937, p. 316). Whether *generation* in this context is used to refer to contemporaries or to those descended by the same number of degrees from a common ancestor depends on the usage of the people whose culture is described, since the anthropologist is concerned with the behaviour and beliefs of the members of the society studied. Thus, in some societies, members of a generation constitute those who are approximately the same age; in others, where careful genealogical records are kept, there may be a considerable age span among the members of a generation, since they are defined as being descended by the same number of degrees from a common ancestor. Where membership in a generation is fixed by family genealogical records, it is based on actual or adoptive kinship. In many societies, however, whether or not there are genealogical records, behaviour toward contemporaries or toward members of older or younger generations is modelled on that expected between kin, even though the individuals are unrelated. Any man of the father's generation, for example, is addressed as 'uncle' and given the deference due an uncle.

C. Anthropologists follow genealogists and lawyers in employing *generation* to denote a step in the line of descent from an ancestor. An individual is said to be *x* generations removed from a particular ancestor, and two branches of a family or tribal group are related through descent from a common ancestor *x* generations back.

D. Social scientists frequently use *generation* to *designate* those born at approximately the same time, whether or not they are related by blood. In this usage it is usually accompanied by an effort to explain the behaviour of the members of the generation by the conditions peculiar to their time. Thus the generation itself may be described as being the 'lost generation', 'the post-war generation', etc.

E. *Generation* is employed by historians, anthropologists, and sociologists to designate the time severed by a segment of the lives of contemporaries: 'In reckoning historically by "generations", the word is taken to mean the interval of time between the birth of the parents and that of their children, usually computed at thirty years, or three generations to a century' (*The Oxford English Dictionary*, Oxford: University Press, 1933). It is employed in this meaning by anthropologists when they use genealogies to calculate the dates of traditional historical events, and by sociologists when they use *generation* as a time segment in the analysis of population statistics.

Elizabeth E. Bacon

See also: DESCENT

Generational Terminology (See **Kinship Terminology**)

Gens

A. *Gens* has two definitions in social science.

1. Historians, students of jurisprudence, and other social scientists define *gens* in the Roman sense as a patrilineal descent group, distinguished by a name and associated with a locality, which in Early Rome had social, economic, political, and religious functions; in a later period it came to mean little more than 'family name'.

2. In American anthropological usage *gens* normally refers to a group of individuals, larger than an extended *family* (q.v.), who believe themselves to be descended in the paternal line from a common ancestor, and who share a common name.

B. 1. L. H. Morgan in 1877 introduced the term into Anglo-American anthropological usage in place of the term *clan* (q.v.) then current. He assumed (a) that the Roman gens represented an advanced stage in the evolution of the social structure of the period of Barbarism, which differed from the kin organization of the archaic stage only in being patrilineal rather than matrilineal in descent; and (b) that all societies passed through these stages (*Ancient Society*, New York: Henry Holt, 1877, pp. 61-8 368-80). He defined the *gens* as 'a body of consanguinei descend from the same common ancestor, distinguished by a gentile name, and bound together by affinities of blood' (ibid., p. 63). He held exogamy to be a regular attribute of the gens, and explained kin marriage, such as was practised by the ancient Hebrews, as evidence of an archaic matrilineal form (ibid., pp. 365-70).

2. Later American anthropologists reserved

Gesellschaft

gens for patrilineal descent groups in contrast to *clan* which they applied to matrilineal groups. This second usage was followed until very recently. R. H. Lowie, seeking a single term for unilinear descent groups, introduced *sib* (q.v.), and proposed 'father-sib' and 'mother-sib' as alternatives to *gens* and *clan* (*Primitive Society*, London: Routledge, 1921, pp. 111–12). Although *sib* was adopted by many American anthropologists, the British use of *clan* as referring to unilinear descent groups in general also came to be widely followed in the United States, and the term 'patrilineal clan' was more commonly used as an alternative to *gens* than was 'father-sib'. G. P. Murdock proposed 'patri-sib', a modification of Lowie's 'father-sib', and this appears to have been adopted by many American and British anthropologists (*Social Structure*, New York: The Macmillan Co., 1949, p. 47). American anthropological textbooks continue to explain *gens*, usually characterizing it as a patrilineal *sib* or *clan*, but the term appears to have been largely superseded by the other terms. Where it is still used it is applied somewhat loosely to refer to any group having patrilineal descent, whatever its other characteristics may be.

Elizabeth E. Bacon

See also: CLAN
        SIB

Geographical Mobility (See **Mobility**)

Gerrymander (See **Constituency**)

Gesellschaft

A. *Gesellschaft* is an ideal-type concept and as such is most correctly applied in its adjectival form, *Gesellschaft*-like, in describing or analysing social systems. *Gesellschaft*-like social systems are those in which rational will (*Kürwille*) has primacy. Rational will prevails when social relations and facilities become means to ends which are sharply differentiated so that the relationships and facilities as means are chosen and employed in conformity with norms of rationality and efficiency in both the technical and economic sense. Thus modern governmental bureaucracies and manufacturing concerns may be said to be *Gesellschaft*-like.

B. The term was used variously by a number of writers but was given its specific meaning in systematic sociological analysis by F. Tönnies (1855–1936) who states that he was influenced by H. Maine's concepts, status and contract. He also states that his own concept, rational will (*Kürwille*), which provides the social psychological underpinning for *Gesellschaft*, is not unlike Weber's concept *zweck-rational* developed much later. 'The end under consideration requires that the means be as suitable to it as possible, and that no means or segment thereof be used which is not conditioned by the end, but that the means most suitable be chosen and used. This implies a definite divorce and differentiation of end and means which, therefore, permits no consideration of means other than that of their perfect suitability for the attaining of the end' (F. Tönnies, *Community and Society— Gemeinschaft und Gesellschaft*, trans. and supplemented by C. P. Loomis, East Lansing, Mich.: Michigan State University Press, 2nd edn., 1957, p. 248). Although the concept *Kürwille* is most frequently translated into English as rational will, H. P. Becker (L. von Wiese, *Systematic Sociology*, adapted and amplified by H. P. Becker, New York: Wiley, 1932, p. 478) translates it as arbitrary will.

C. In *Gesellschaft*, beliefs must submit to such critical, objective, and universalistic standards as employed in logic, mathematics and science in general. The norms for the expressing of sentiments follow the model of the 'calculating scheming person' (F. Tönnies, *Community and Society*, p. 130) e.g. 'Honesty is the best policy' under the *Gesellschaft* only if it pays dividends in terms of the goal (or ends) to be honest, not because of any intrinsic morality in honesty. Behaviour in the market place is taken as the model and those who find difficulty in conforming to the norms of affective neutrality but nevertheless are 'despising or disavowing such feelings' as sympathy 'Sometimes ... find their satisfaction in bravado and arrogance ...' (ibid., p. 248). Obligations in relationships are functionally specific (ibid., pp. 177, 194, *278*, and 279, fn. 22) and affectively neutral (ibid., pp. 75, 90, 129, 141, 156, and 157). The status-role most frequently mentioned as conforming to the norms of *Gesellschaft* is that of merchant symbolizing the economic man. In fact one of the first if not the first usages of role playing as a concept in social science literature is Tönnies's description of 'deliberate acting of roles' (ibid., p. 131). Army leaders and other bureaucratic figures are mentioned and a recognition of the necessity for legitimation of such status-roles as doctor, lawyer and judge is given (ibid., p. 241). Motivation in *Gesellschaft* is dominated by those who 'hatch plots', 'set traps', and 'mould plans' (ibid., p. 147). Power may be pyramided as in the army or relatively evenly divided as in fellowships. The model of the *Gesellschaft*-like hierarchically organized social system is the state. Employee-employer relationships of the capitalistic society are frequently mentioned as illustrative of *Gesellschaft*. Stratification in the *Gesellschaft*-like society results in social classes.

Charles P. Loomis

See also: GEMEINSCHAFT
URBAN SOCIOLOGY
URBANISM

Gestalt

A. A *gestalt* is an organized entity or whole in which the parts, though distinguishable, are interdependent; they have certain characteristics produced by their inclusion in the whole, and the whole has some characteristics belonging to none of the parts. The gestalt thus constitutes a 'unit segregated from its surroundings' (W. Köhler, *Gestalt Psychology*, New York: Liveright, 1947, p. 137), behaving according to certain laws of energy distribution. It is found throughout human behaviour as well as in physiological and physical events and is thus a fundamental aspect of scientific data.

B. The term *gestalt* is principally associated with the names of M. Wertheimer, K. Koffka, and W. Kohler and their followers. Their distinctive emphasis upon the dynamic properties of 'wholes' (as distinct from 'parts') in human experience has led some to speak of a Gestalt school of psychology.

1. Köhler reports that von Ehrenfels first called attention to *Gestaltqualitäten* or characteristics of sensory fields which 'are generically different from the sensations of traditional theory' (ibid., p. 173). An example of such a quality is 'dimness or fuzziness which appears as a quality of things seen in a dark corner. Again no local impression, examined separately, shows any fuzziness; but some extended areas do' (ibid., p. 174).

For von Ehrenfels these form-qualities 're-presented experiences added to "the sensations" when these have been first established' (ibid., p. 176). But for the Gestalt psychologists these characteristics are not simply added to the sensations but are the products of organization, the characteristics of a *gestalt* or whole, which are traceable to none of its parts. M. Wertheimer says, 'The fundamental "formula" of Gestalt theory might be expressed in this way:

there are wholes, the behavior of which is not determined by their individual elements, but where the part-processes are themselves determined by the intrinsic nature of the whole' ('Gestalt Theory' in W. D. Ellis (ed.), *A Source Book of Gestalt Psychology*, New York: Harcourt, Brace, 1939, p. 2). Köhler emphasizes that gestalt refers to 'a specific object and to organization' (*Gestalt Psychology*, p. 178). He states further that gestalt 'has the meaning of a concrete individual and characteristic entity, existing as something detached and having a shape or form as one of its attributes' (see K. Koffka, *Principles of Gestalt Psychology*, New York: Harcourt, Brace, 1935, p. 682).

Gestalts are of different strengths according to their degree of organization. Koffka says, 'The strength of the Gestalt character is defined by Köhler by the degree of interdependence of the parts. The stronger the Gestalt, the more will each of its parts depend on all the others, and the more will this dependence affect every aspect of the parts' (ibid., p. 650). A gestalt is also a dynamic whole, with its order the outcome of a self-distribution of processes. When the balance of forces is disturbed, the pattern tends to return to its previous state. 'Dynamic self-distribution in this sense is the kind of function which Gestalt Psychology believes to be essential in neurological and psychological theory. ... From this point of view, a stationary visual field corresponds to a balanced distribution of underlying processes. When conditions change, resulting developments will always be in the direction of balance' (W. Köhler, *Gestalt Psychology*, p. 133).

2. Although first used in relation to sensory experience, the term *gestalt* is in its most general definition extended to 'the processes of learning, of recall, of striving, of emotional attitude, of thinking, of acting, and so forth' (ibid., p. 179). Koffka extends the term to personality and to social groups (*Principles of Gestalt Psychology*, pp. 677, 649).

The concept is thus made the basis of a general approach to human behaviour. The continuity of psychology with biological and physical science is often mentioned. One evidence of this unity is the correspondence considered to exist between organizations in the brain and in the mind; 'the physiological organization is the same as the mental organization' (W. Köhler, *Gestalt Psychology*, p. 238). The existence of purely physical gestalten is also pointed out: 'and yet nature *does* exhibit numerous instances of physical wholes in which

Gesture

part events are determined by the inner structure of the whole' (M. Wertheimer, 'Gestalt Theory', p. 7). 'In physics, a molecule constitutes a larger functional whole which contains several atoms as subordinate wholes; but in this unit they do not altogether lose their individuality' (W. Köhler, *Gestalt Psychology*, p. 144).

This general approach to natural phenomena as implied by the word *gestalt* is expressed by Koffka who says of the term: 'It carried in its connotation the *chaos-kosmos* alternative; to say that a process, or the product of a process, is a gestalt means that it cannot be explained by mere chaos, the mere blind combination of essentially unconnected causes; but that its essence is the reason of its existence, to use metaphysical language for an idea which has been presented so many times in this book in notions as free from metaphysics as any science can be' (*Principles of Gestalt Psychology*, p. 683).

Joan Criswell

See also: FIELD THEORY

Gesture

A. *Gesture* denotes verbal and other bodily configurations which man utilizes to engage in the meaningful interactions necessary for organized social activity. Gestures tend to be culturally defined, but may also be uniquely situational or idiosyncratic in meaning, or may even be of the spontaneous, animal-like kind that is characteristic of homo sapiens. Like man, many sub-human species employ gestures in stimulus-response fashion. However, man is singular in adding and sharing meanings of ideas which lie behind his gestures. Thus man alone employs significant gestures, or language.

B. 1. Biological conceptions of gesture usually incorporate an evolutionary point of view which calls attention to primitive means of communication which homo sapiens has retained despite his socio-cultural advances. As F. Boas observes (*General Anthropology*, New York: D. C. Heath, 1938, p. 126), 'Gestures and cries like those of animals still survive. They are immediate reactions to situations replete with emotion, like cries of pain, pleasure, anger, or fear'.

2. A considerable literature discusses bodily, or non-verbal, gestures in terms of interaction between biological and cultural determinants of behaviour. Because such discussion usually places this interaction in a context of socialization, or social learning, it may appropriately be called social usage of the concept. Most widely cited is the work by D. Efron, which points out

(*Gesture and Environment*, New York: King's Crown Press, 1941) that gestural behaviour, like other forms of interaction, can be explained much more adequately as a social, than as a biological, phenomenon. In this view, gesture is depicted as essentially another item in a group's stock of meaningful behaviours, which are therefore subject to learning, unlearning, and relearning.

3. Gesture is also used to show that some aspects of behaviour are basically matters of stimulus-response, and therefore do not involve the exchange of ideas. This usage calls attention to the dimension of reaction in gestural actions. Using a dog-fight to illustrate this conception of gesture, G. H. Mead states (*Mind, Self, and Society*, Chicago: University of Chicago Press, 1934, pp. 42–3), 'The act of each dog becomes the stimulus to the other dog for his response. There is then a relationship between these two; and as the act is responded to by the other dog, it, in turn, undergoes change. The very fact that the dog is ready to attack another becomes a stimulus to the other dog to change his own position or his own attitude. He has no sooner done this than the change of attitude in the second dog in turn causes the first dog to change his attitude. We have here a conversation of gestures. They are not, however, gestures in the sense that they are significant. We do not assume that the dog says to himself, "If the animal comes from this direction he is going to spring at my throat and I will turn in such a way". What does take place is an actual change in his own position due to the direction of the approach of the other dog'.

C. Usages of gesture in the theory of symbolic interaction relate it to social acts. Here gesture is viewed as the very stuff out of which role-taking and role-playing activities are developed. G. H. Mead (ibid., pp. 45–7) distinguishes between significant gestures (or symbols) which do, and non-significant gestures which do not, involve self-conscious role-taking and role-playing. Meaningful interaction, according to Mead, is that in which people designate to themselves and to each other the affective and cognitive meanings which lie behind their gesture. Along with Mead and others, R. E. L. Faris notes (*Social Psychology*, New York: Ronald Press, 1952, p. 109) that a basic function of symbolic gestures (i.e. language) is to make possible complex, co-operative social activity: 'The function of the gesture is to make adjustment possible among the individuals implicated in any given social act with references to the object or objects with which that act is concerned; and the significant gesture or significant symbol affords far greater facilities for such adjustment and readjustment than does the non-significant gesture ...'

Ray L. Gold

See also: COMMUNICATION
SOCIAL INTERACTION
SYMBOL

Ghost Dance (See **Nativism**)

Ghost Marriage (See **Levirate**)

Gift
1. The more general meaning of *gift* is that given by the *Oxford English Dictionary* as 'something the property in which is voluntarily transferred to another without the expectation or receipt of an equivalent'.
2. In social anthropology the term (both as itself and as a translation of the French *le don*) is most often used with reference to the exchange of goods or services which, although regarded as voluntary by the people involved, is in all societies a part of the behaviour expected of persons in specific social relationships. Such 'gifts' (whatever the element of voluntary 'kindness' which may or may not accompany them) are normally given with a clear expectation that some return will be made, sometimes in a specified form and quantity. For example, B. Malinowski, in his analysis of giving in the Trobriand Islands (*Argonauts of the Western Pacific*, London: Routledge, 1922, pp. 167, 191-4, showed that gifts are always in a special sense part of social relationships, and that they carry symbolic meanings; and M. Mauss (*Essai sur le don* (1925), trans. by I. Cunnison as *The Gift*, London: Cohen & West, 1954, pp. 1, 11) shows that very commonly the initial gift, its acceptance and a due return are all compulsory.

A. P. Stirling

See also: PRESTATION

Glottochronology
A. In its primary sense *glottochronology* is the study of types and rates of change in language over time. Applied to a particular genetic group of languages—family, stock, or phylum—it is the study of the time sequence, and rate of divergence, of the several branches and members as reflected in the linguistic differences found among the languages. The term is also used as an abbreviation of *lexico-statistic glottochronology*, meaning the practice of determining the time relationship of genetically related languages from the percentage of cognates (i.e. words of common origin going back to the common period of related languages) they share in diagnostic word lists.

B. *Glottochronology* was introduced by M. Swadesh in 1949, with reference to research and conclusions as to the rate of change in 'basic' vocabulary and the possibilities of comparing 'diagnostic vocabularies' so as to estimate the time that separates two stages of a single language or the time since two distinct languages, which have diverged from an earlier common form, became separate (M. Swadesh, 'Salish Internal Relationships', *International Journal of American Linguistics*, vol. 16, 1950, pp. 157-67). Because of its use of vocabulary comparison as a measuring device, this type of study has also been called lexico-statistics or *lexico-statistic glottochronology*. The latter may be regarded as the most apt designation and the other two as abbreviated expressions.
1. The 'diagnostic' wordlists used in lexico-statistic glottochronology, consist of standardized sets of meanings expressed in any convenient language, depending upon the investigator and the part of the world in which he is working. The everyday equivalents of each item are obtained in each of the language entities—each a particular language as spoken in a particular place in a particular period of time—being studied. The lists are compared item by item and the percentage of *cognates*—elements of common origin whose presence is due to their common history and original identity and not to borrowing—determined. The percentage is related to the time that separates the two samples to determine the rate of change or the rate of non-change, called the rate of persistence, provided the two belong to a single linguistic line and their dates are known. Such cases of known time separation serve as control cases for establishing an index of retention, which may then be used to estimate intervening time between two stages of the same language when the dates are unknown or minimum separation time in the case of languages which have diverged from a common earlier tongue.
2. Lexico-statistic glottochronology is based on the finding that 'Over relatively long periods of time, the rate of shift of items in what we may call the Basic Lexicon of a language is approximately constant' (C. F. Hockett,

Goal

'Linguistic Time-Perspective and its Anthropological Uses', *International Journal of American Linguistics*, vol. 19, 1953, p. 148). In estimating the time of separation of once-identical languages, this fact is complicated by the *separation factor*. The divergence between the two languages as measured by the comparison of cognates will be directly related to the passage of time *only* if the languages have developed in complete isolation from each other, and they will have diverged more slowly in proportion to the degree of contact. Consequently any estimate of time derived from linguistic divergence can only relate to the minimum possible period, and in many instances the estimate falls far short of actual time since the first movement apart, thus giving a range of probabilities (ibid., pp. 146–52; see also M. Swadesh, 'Comment', *International Journal of American Linguistics*, vol. 19, 1953, pp. 152–3).

3. The relative effectiveness of the method depends on the fact that it recognizes the influence of culture contact and changing content upon the use of words, and therefore operates with that part of the vocabulary which is least affected by such influences. At the same time, it has been used for measuring more accurately the rate of change in specific items of vocabulary and it is anticipated that it may eventually give rise to the comparative study of rate of change in various types of vocabulary (M. Swadesh, 'Towards Greater Accuracy in Lexicostatistic Dating', *International Journal of American Linguistics*, vol. 21, 1955, pp. 121–37).

Morris Swadesh

See also: LINGUISTICS

Goal (Psychology)

A. *Goal* in psychology and in some social psychology has come increasingly to denote an end result of an act or series of acts whether or not it can be said to be intended by the organism acting.

B. The term *purpose* is becoming to be more and more discarded in both psychology and philosophy, and as *goal* is largely used, in modern psychology in connection with animals, it is inappropriate to equate altogether goal and purpose. The emphasis on purposive behaviour and the related phenomena of goal-seeking was sponsored probably first of all by W. McDougall (1871–1938) who pointed out that organisms have certain goal-seeking tendencies, a point of view which was taken up in a behaviouristic framework in E. C. Tolman's book *Purposive Behaviour in Animals and Men* (New York: D. Appleton-Century, 1932). As used with animals, or with the predominantly physiological activities of humans, *goal* has been regarded as an end result linked with the need for food, drink, sex, rest, and sometimes activity. The theoretical importance of the term has turned very much on what was regarded as an innate need. What is of note is not of course the nature of the goal, be it so much food pellets for the rat or a female for the male organism, as the whole cycle of events which is initiated by a need and cessated by the acquirement of the end result. The three elements of need, striving activity, and goal are linked together in a regulative cycle which is homeostatic in character. Such a cycle can be demonstrated to be present in quite automatic systems; hence it is unnecessary to postulate the 'consciously purposive' aspect of goal.

W. H. N. Hotopf

See also: DRIVE
GOAL (Sociology)
MOTIVATION

Goal (Sociology)

A. In sociology—and in much of anthropology, economics, political science, and social psychology—the term *goal* denotes any change in a situation which a person or a group intends to bring about through his or its action. It is a concept designating one of the *subjective* elements of action, i.e. elements internal to the personalities of those participating in the action. Synonyms of goal are *end*, *objective*, and *purpose*. *Motive* is sometimes used as a synonym, but usually covers a wider range of phenomena.

B. Usage of these concepts in social anthropology and sociology ranges from those who make an expressed effort to avoid the words to those who use them explicitly. Thus, as representative of the latter, T. Parsons ('A Revised Analytical Approach to the Theory of Social Stratification', in R. Bendix & S. M. Lipset (eds.), *Class, Status and Power—a Reader in Social Stratification*, Glencoe, Ill.: The Free Press, 1953, p. 93) writes, 'We conceive action to be oriented to the attainment of goals, and hence to involve selective processes relative to goals'. P. Sorokin (*Society, Culture, and Personality*, New York: Harper & Brothers, 1947, p. 44) after differentiating purposive and non-purposive actions writes 'In purposive actions ... there is always an idea of the future goal, or end, and of the means of its attainment'. R. E. Park and E. W. Burgess (*Introduction to the Science of Sociology*, Chicago: University of Chicago Press, 1933, p. 42) state 'We may apply the term social to any group of individuals which is capable of consistent ·action, that is to say, action, consciously or unconsciously, directed to a common goal'. This usage implies that the categories of the means-end schema (q.v.) apply to unconscious motives as well as conscious ones.

As Parsons (*The Structure of Social Action*, New York: McGraw-Hill, 1937, p. 79) has shown, in positivistic thinking 'ends may disappear from analytical significance altogether, the concrete "end" becoming a prediction, correct or erroneous, of the future trends of the situation'. Thus, E. D. Chapple and C. S. Coon (*Principles of Anthropology*, New York: Henry Holt, 1942), among others, have followed in this tradition attempting to study human relations by avoiding such 'subjective' and 'non-operational' terms as *purpose*, *ends*, or *goals*.

C. C. P. Loomis and J. A. Beegle (*Rural Sociology—The Strategy of Change*, Englewood Cliffs, N.J.: Prentice-Hall, 1957, p. 3) make ends or objectives one of the elements of *the social system* (q.v.), or organization viewed as a 'going concern'. In this context R. K. Merton (*Social Theory and Social Structure*, Glencoe, Ill.: The Free Press, 1957, p. 155) indicates the importance of the conceptualization, and the conceptual separation of norms or rules from ends or goals by the following: 'Adherence to the rules, originally conceived as a means, becomes transformed into an end-in-itself ... whereby "an instrumental value becomes a terminal value" '. F. Tönnies (*Community and Society*, trans. and ed. by C. P. Loomis, East Lansing, Mich.: Michigan State University Press, 1957) makes an important distinction between those groups or social systems which he characterizes as *Gemeinschaft*-like, in which relationships are primarily ends-in-and-of themselves, and those groups or social systems which he characterizes as *Gesellschaft*-like, in which relationships are primarily means to ends subscribed to by members of the social system. M. Weber (*The Theory of Social and Economic Organization*, trans. by A. M. Henderson & T. Parsons, New York: Oxford University Press, 1947, p. 115) develops four types of social action, *zweckrational*, *wertrational*, *affektuell*, and *traditionell* which relate to the use of the concept of goal, end, motive, and purpose. The

first is *Gesellschaft*-like in Tönnies's sense that it is characterized by a rational orientation to a system of discrete individual ends (*rational*), that is, through expectations as to the behaviour of objects in the external situation and of other human individuals, it makes use of these expectations as 'conditions' or 'means' for the successful attainment of the actor's ends.

D. R. K. Merton (*Social Theory and Social Structure*, pp. 50–1) has called attention to the difficulties arising when 'concepts of subjective dispositions (motives, purposes)' and 'concepts of objective consequences (functions, dysfunctions)' are confused. Any comprehensive analysis whether involving social systems or personalities, requires that *manifest functions* which Merton states are 'those objective consequences ... which are intended and recognized by participants' and *latent functions* which are not intended or recognized be distinguished.

Charles P. Loomis

See also: Function
GOAL (Psychology)
MEANS-END SCHEMA
MOTIVATION
RATIONALITY

Gold Standard

A. In its narrowest sense, the term *gold standard* is used in the classic sense of a monetary mechanism in which the unit of value is kept equal to a fixed quantity of gold, the value of gold being determined in a free international market. In its broader connotations the term is often used, particularly in recent years, to refer to situations in which somewhat different arrangements govern the relation of the unit of value to gold. Although wide variations have occurred in practice, the central features of the recent variants of the *gold standard* are that the monetary unit is defined in terms of gold, and that gold or its equivalent is used to settle international balances.

B. 1. What may be regarded as the gold standard in its 'classic' or 'full' form was defined by E. W. Kemmerer (*Gold and the Gold Standard*, New York: McGraw-Hill, 1944, pp. 134, 138) in the following terms: 'This standard may be briefly defined as a monetary system where the unit of value, in terms of which prices, wages, and debts are customarily expressed and paid, consists of the value of a fixed quantity of gold in a large international market which is substantially free ... the

Gold Standard

supreme test of the existence of the gold standard is the answer to the question whether or not the money of the country is actually kept at a parity with the value of the gold monetary unit comprising it, in the outside free international gold market, assuming, of course, that such a market of reasonable size actually exists'. The devices through which the gold standard in this sense was maintained usually included (a) the definition of the monetary unit in terms of a weight of gold, (b) the free and unlimited coinage of gold, (c) the redeemability of all non-gold moneys in gold, and (d) the absence of restrictions upon the import and export of gold.

2. However, it was generally recognized that actual coinage was not essential for adherence to the gold standard. If there was coinage, a *gold coin standard* was said to exist. Many supporters of the classic gold standard from the time of Ricardo to the present have advocated a *gold bullion standard* under which gold would not actually be coined, but would be freely exchanged—for both residents and non-residents—at the mint at fixed buying and selling prices. Some would restrict the quantity of money to the amount of gold, thus making the circulating media consist in effect of warehouse receipts for gold. More would permit commercial and central banks to create additional money on the basis of centrally held gold reserves. In this case the possibility of the demand for gold by domestic or foreign holders of the created money would provide a check on the expansion of the money supply. Another form of the gold standard that conformed in essence to the classic requirements was the *gold exchange standard*. The characteristic of this arrangement, found chiefly in colonial or underdeveloped countries, is that the reserves for domestic circulating media consist not of gold but of the money of some centre country, such as Great Britain or the United States, which maintains gold convertibility.

C. However, the mere description of institutional arrangements relating to gold cannot convey an understanding of the gold standard; the functions that it is supposed to perform must also be set forth. Internally, the maintenance of the gold standard tends to limit the creation of money. This is regarded as a boon by those who, fearing the tendency of governments to encourage inflation by the creation of too much money, prefer automaticity in monetary arrangements. It is regarded as a weakness by those who argue that a nation should be free to manage its money supply to promote price stability, full employment, economic growth, or other national objectives that are deemed important. For the community of nations, the gold standard provides a stable link between the currencies and price structures of the various members of the gold standard system. Since each currency is defined in terms of a common substance, gold, the relative values (exchange rates) of the currencies are automatically established. The stability of exchange rates is generally believed to encourage international flows of trade and capital. Currency convertibility in gold makes it possible, some argue, for automatic forces to maintain or to restore equilibrium in trade among the countries. The nature of this equilibrating mechanism has formed the basis for a substantial literature, which cannot be recapitulated here (for a recapitulation and bibliography, see G. Haberler, *A Survey of International Trade Theory*, Special Papers in International Economics, no. 1, September 1955, Princeton, N.J.: Princeton University). Suffice to say that the adjustments to disturbances in equilibrium are conceived as being achieved through international flows of short-term capital and, less frequently, by the international movement of gold, and through the price and income changes that follow from these shifts. The widely publicized 'rules of the game' of the 1920s held that countries participating in the international gold standard were supposed to allow the expansionary or deflationary forces to work out the adjustments rather than to adopt counteracting monetary policies that would maintain domestic stability. In practice, however, central banks, concerned with maintaining stable prices and incomes, often did adopt offsetting policies that tended to hamper the speed and efficiency of international adjustments.

Since the functions of the gold standard are the key to an understanding of what it is, analytical definitions or descriptions are frequently given. For example, W. A. Brown, Jr., in his classic study *The International Gold Standard Reinterpreted* (New York: National Bureau of Economic Research, 1940, vol. II, p. 774) says: 'The most striking single feature of the pre-war gold standard was the highly integrated world banking structure centered in London and operating on the basis of the strong international creditor position of Great Britain. This system of banking provided for efficient and rational distribution of long and short term credit and gold on a world-wide scale. It provided a common medium of payment for the financing of world trade, just as a national banking system provides a domestic currency for the financing of domestic trade. It was also the center of a system of international clearance which resulted in the same sort of banking economies that intra- and interbank clearances provide in any banking system.'

D. In the strictest sense, the classic form of the gold standard may be regarded as having ended with World War I. Until recently the United States has been sufficiently rich and powerful to affect or even control the price of gold. For this and other reasons, there has been for gold no 'large international market which is substantially free', to return to Kemmerer's language. Despite this, the currencies of most Western countries have been linked to gold in important respects.

The international currency arrangements established by the free world at the end of World War II, organized through the International Monetary Fund (I.M.F.), may be interpreted as an adaptation of the gold standard. They resemble the gold standard in that (a) currencies are defined in terms of gold and pars of exchange among the currencies follow from this; and (b) gold (or U.S. dollars which are redeemable in gold for international transactions) is used to settle international balances. The deviations from the classic international gold standard described above are: (i) There is no large free international market in gold. (ii) In most countries, including the United States and Great Britain, residents may acquire gold only for the settlement of foreign balances or for uses in industry or the arts; money is not convertible into gold for domestic hoarding. (iii) Although the I.M.F. is designed to promote stable exchange rates, the arrangements clearly contemplate circumstances—viz. the existence of a fundamental disequilibrium—under which a nation may change its currency's gold par (i.e. appreciate or depreciate its currency). (iv) The automatic adjustment features of the gold standard have been given up in favour of domestic policies designed to promote stability, full employment, and economic growth. In fact, no nation can remain indifferent to adverse developments in the balance of payments. In most cases, after limited losses of gold, nations have imposed increased restrictions on payments or imports so as to force the restoration of a balance of payments position which is compatible with the maintenance of inter-

national reserves. Following D. H. Robertson, we might say that we choose to regard these arrangements as representing a variant of the gold standard but '... a truer impression of the state of the world's monetary affairs would be given by saying that America is on an arbitrary standard, while the rest of the world has climbed back painfully on to a dollar standard' (*Money*, London: Nisbet, 1948, p. 81). This has not precluded independent movements by important countries such as England and France.

Irving B. Kravis

See also: BALANCE OF PAYMENTS
MONEY

Good Offices (See **Mediation**)

Government

1. *Government* may denote *the activity or process of governing*; i.e. the exercising of control over others; the inducing of certain others to behave in specified ways, as required.

This activity has to be understood as lasting through a period of time in such a manner as to establish a stable relationship between participants in the process: an isolated incident in which one man (or state) compels another to do his will *might* be described as 'an act of government', but language would be strained. Yet, on the other hand, a continuous succession of such incidents through time could fairly be described as a situation of the one man (or state) 'governing' the other; and equally this relationship could be described as the 'government' of one man (or state) by the other.

It used to be customary to confine the term in this usage to the relationship between a state and its subjects; but there is no reason why it should not apply to the exercise of control inside private associations or between private associations.

Where persons amongst whom control is exercised form a stable group, and where this exercise of control has become institutionalized, the definition can be widened into: 'the process or activity of prescribing rules for and enforcing them upon a specific group of persons'.

The group in question may be that territorial association known as 'the state', and it is in respect to the state that the term 'government' has been used par excellence.

2. *Government* may denote the state of affairs in which this activity or process is found: i.e. ordered rule. This is a special use of the term, common in the 18th century. Locke, and the Federalists, often use it in this sense, thus John

Gratification

Locke's argument in his *Second Treatise*: 'He that will not give just occasion to think that all Government in the World is the product of Force and Violence ... must of necessity find out another rise of Government, another Original of Political Power'. Here 'government' is equated with 'political power' which is equated with: 'A Right of making Laws with Penalties of Death and consequently all less Penalties, for the Regulating and Preserving of Property and of employing the force of the Community, in the Execution of such Laws ... etc., etc.'.

A late instance of this usage is J. Bentham, *The Book of Fallacies* (London, 1824, pt. II, ch. IV), where, commenting on the phrase 'Attack us (i.e. the Government), you attack Government', Bentham explains that the fallacy consists precisely in the confusion of two senses of the word 'government', viz. as a group of people (see below) and also as 'ordered rule'.

This 18th-century sense of the term was the contemporary equivalent of the Latin *imperium civile* or *potestas civilis* and in modern French is translateable as *le pouvoir civil* or even as *le pouvoir*.

3. *Government* may denote *those who govern*, and more specifically and usually, the 'executive' (q.v.) branch of these.

In Britain (as also in France) *Government* may mean all the Ministers collectively (as opposed to the Conseil de Ministres or Cabinet, which are more restricted bodies).

J. J. Rousseau was one of the first to popularize 'government' in the sense of 'the executive'. 'What, then is Government? It is an intermediary body set up to serve as a means of communication between subjects and sovereign, and it is charged with the creation of the laws and the maintenance of liberty, both civil and political' (*Contrat Social*, bk. III, ch. 1; see *Social Contract*, ed. E. Barker (World Classics), London: Oxford University Press, 1956, p. 316).

A usage allied to the above (stemming from what was originally a specifically English usage which dates from the end of the 18th century and the beginning of the 19th century) is that by which *Government* designates the body of Ministers in power in contradistinction to the 'alternative government' (i.e. the body of men who, by constitutional usage and convention, are to be expected to replace the existing ministers by some recognized constitutional process). Here 'the government' is used as one of a brace of antitheses, viz.: 'Government' and 'Opposition'.

4. Government may denote a particular system or form of government, i.e. the constitution (q.v.) and more often the 'working' as opposed to the 'formal' constitution of a State (e.g. W. R. Sharp: '*The Government of the French Republic*', New York: Van Nostrand, 1938) or of a private association (e.g. J. Goldstein, *The Government of British Trade Unions*, London: Allen & Unwin, 1952). Hence its use, adjectivally qualified (as in 'Parliamentary Government', 'Presidential Government', or 'Cabinet Government') in classifying the *forms* in which government is carried out.

Montesquieu and Rousseau both use the term 'government' in this sense (e.g. *Esprit des lois*, Paris, bk. V, ch. X): 'Monarchial Government has a great advantage over the republican'; while Rousseau (*Contrat Social*, bk. III, ch. 2) has a chapter on 'The Different Forms of Government'. But the corresponding terms in Hobbes and in Locke is *Commonwealth* (cf. J. Locke, *Second Treatise*, ch. X, 'Of the forms of a Commonwealth'): and 'Commonwealth' was the contemporary equivalent of 'civitas' or 'respublica'.

S. E. Finer

See also: Law
Politician
Politics
State

Graft (See **Corruption**)

Gratification

A. *Gratification* denotes the process of satisfying or the state of satisfaction of the organism which accompanies action in accord with its impulses or the achievement of its goals.

B. 1. Psychoanalysts speak of gratification (as opposed to inhibition, frustration, or deprivation for impulses of the id and also of the ego. '... dreams of pain and anxiety', according to Freud ('Interpretation of Dreams' in *The Basic Writings of Sigmund Freud*, trans. and ed. by A. A. Brill, New York: The Modern Library, 1938, p. 503) 'are, in accordance with our theory, just as much wish-fulfillments as are the straightforward dreams of gratification'. In psychoanalytic theory: '... the accumulation of excitation ... is felt as pain and sets the apparatus in operation in order to bring about again a state of gratification in which the diminution of excitation is perceived as pleasure' (ibid., p. 533).

2. O. H. Mowrer in *Learning Theory and Personality Dynamics* (New York: Ronald

Press, 1950, p. 85) uses *gratification* as synonymous with *goal attainment, problem solution, pleasure, success, satisfaction, adjustment, reestablishment of equilibrium, motivation reduction, consummation*, and *reward* as a state of affairs favourable to learning. It is used in much the same way throughout T. Parsons's *The Social System* (Glencoe, Ill.: The Free Press, 1951).

Goodwin Watson

See also: FRUSTRATION
NEED

Gresham's Law

A. *Gresham's Law* in its simplest possible form may be stated as follows: money overvalued at the mint tends to drive out of circulation money undervalued at the mint (cf. R. M. Robertson, *History of the American Economy*, New York: Harcourt, Brace, 1955, p. 129).

B. The 'law' takes its name from Sir Thomas Gresham (1519(?)–79), English merchant and financier, who advised Queen Elizabeth I on financial matters. Gresham's Law, cryptically expressed in the statement 'bad money drives out good', was apparently first attributed to Gresham by H. D. MacLeod in his *Elements of Political Economy*, published in 1858. MacLeod later (see his *Bimetalism*, 1894) said that Copernicus, thirty-two years before Gresham, and Oresme, 162 years before Gresham, had demonstrated the principle. J. L. Laughlin, in *A New Exposition of Money, Credit and Prices* (Chicago: The University of Chicago Press, 1931), quotes a passage from Aristophanes to suggest that the law was known to the ancients. Writing in the *Encyclopedia of the Social Sciences* (E. R. A. Seligman (ed.), New York: The Macmillan Co., 1932, vol. 7, p. 169), J. F. Rees has remarked that it was well known before Gresham's time and that there is no evidence of a theoretical statement by him of its working.

C. R. G. Thomas in *Our Modern Banking and Monetary System* (New York: Prentice-Hall, 2nd edn., 1950, p. 30), states Gresham's Law as follows: 'Given a sufficient supply of bad or overvalued standard money with the characteristic of general acceptability, the good or undervalued standard money may be displaced by the lighter or overvalued money. Bad money or overvalued money is that which contains less bullion value for a stated face value than the good or undervalued money'. Thomas lays stress on the importance of Gresham's Law as an aid to understanding monetary problems under bimetallism, pointing out that as late as the 1930s supporters of a bimetallic standard were urging its adoption in the United States. G. N. Halm in his *Monetary Theory* (Philadelphia: Blakiston, 2nd edn., 1946) gives a more abstract discussion of the problem. He remarks that 'If two metals can be coined freely as standard money and if the ratio between the value of the two metals in terms of the unit of account is fixed by law, so that there is only one standard unit and only one system of prices, then we have a bimetallic standard or double standard. This system works as long as the legally fixed ratio coincides with the real ratio between the international market values of the metals' (ibid., pp. 108–9). When, however, the mint ratio and the international market ratio diverge (and only in transitory periods are they the same), it becomes profitable to bring one metal to the mint and to export the other to countries where it has a higher value. Gold will flow to the country where it is more valuable in terms of silver and silver to the country where it is more valuable in terms of gold. 'This process of arbitrage in the metals, as the formulation known as Gresham's Law asserts, results in the displacement of the dearer metal by the cheaper one in the monetary circulation unless it is arrested by corrective changes in the respective mint ratios' (ibid., p. 109).

Ross M. Robertson

See also: MONEY

Gross National Product (See **National Product**)

Gross Reproduction Rate
(See **Rates of Reproduction**)

Gross Revenue (See **Revenue**)

Group

A. The definition of the term *group* is based on the following criteria:

1. In order to have utility for sociological analysis, a definition of group must refer to an integrated social structure rather than a mere category of individuals.

2. There is need for a generic concept of group devoid of limitations in membership size; the size factor can be treated adequately as an additional variable.

3. The prevailing sociological conception of

Group

a group as the structural aspect of some sort of integrative ties among persons suggests, as a logical implication, that not only the strength of such ties but also their structural manifestation be seen as a matter of degree.

4. Sociological definitions of the group differ in their respective stress on communicative, normative, or functional ties among its members. Such differences in definition appear as mutually complementary in the light of a generic conception of social integration (q.v.), within which one may distinguish between communicative, normative, and functional integration as special types.

The preceding considerations suggest the following definition: A number of persons constitute a group in so far as a specified type of integration occurs among them, and to the degree of such integration.

B. The only generally shared element in the definition of *group* is that this concept refers to more than one person. Beyond this, the use of the term *group* shows the following major variations:

1. While most contemporary sociologists limit the concept to an integrated entity or whole made up of several persons, some writers have applied it to a mere plurality of persons. This broader use may be found in early sociology as well as in current social psychology. Among sociologists, the older view is represented by A. W. Small, for whom 'the "group" is the most general and colorless term used in sociology for combinations of persons' (*General Sociology*, Chicago: University of Chicago Press, 1905, p. 495). Social psychologists have designated as *reference group* (q.v.) not only integrated collectivities but also simple pluralities of persons who fall under such categories as 'overseas combat troops', 'married civilians', or persons on a given status level (R. K. Merton & A. S. Kitt, 'Contributions to the Theory of Reference Group Behavior', in R. K. Merton & P. F. Lazarsfeld (eds.), *Continuities in Social Research: Studies in the Scope and Method of 'The American Soldier'*, Glencoe, Ill.: The Free Press, 1950, pp. 62 ff.).

2. The most common definitions of *group* are those which place emphasis on some sort of social ties by which the group is held together. There seems to be disagreement, however, as to the nature of these ties. A major point of view, focusing on the integrative function of communication, is represented by E. E. Eubank for whom a group 'exists wherever two or more human beings reciprocally influence one another through mental contact' (*The Concepts of Sociology*, Boston: D. C. Heath, 1932, p. 159). Others have stressed the importance of shared social norms as binding elements in a group (for example, E. T. Hiller, *Social Relations and Structures*, New York: Harper & Brothers 1947, p. 286).

3. There seems to be agreement that the minimum number of persons in a group may be as small as two. Some maximum in size is implied in an occasional usage which distinguishes between groups and larger collectivities, such as societies or communities. An upper limit is set, in effect, by G. C. Homans who defines a group as 'a number of persons who communicate with all others not at second hand through other people but face-to-face' (*The Human Group*, New York: Harcourt, Brace, 1950, p. 1). More commonly, however, the concept is defined without specification of maximum size.

4. Thus far, most sociologists have employed the concept of *group* as a qualitative classification, yielding a dichotomous distinction between groups and non-groups. A few writers, however, have attempted to give the concept a quantitative meaning. From this point of view, a number of persons may constitute a group in varying degrees, or it may possess specified group properties to a greater or lesser extent. Thus, E. F. Borgatta and L. S. Cottrell propose to shift the question 'from whether an aggregate is a group or not to one concerning the degree to which such an aggregate is characterized by a specified complex of variables assumed to be components of "groupness"' ('On the Classification of Groups', *Sociometry*, vol. 18, 1955, p. 409).

C. 1. Among concepts referring to special types of groups, that of *primary group* has been prominent, both with regard to the extent of its use and the diversity of its denotations. The term was coined by C. H. Cooley who specified the following characteristics of a primary group: '(1) Face-to-face association; (2) the unspecialized character of that association; (3) relative permanence; (4) the small number of persons involved; (5) the relative intimacy among the participants' (C. H. Cooley, R. C. Angell & L. J. Carr, *Introductory Sociology*, New York: Charles Scribner's Sons, 1933, p. 55). Although Cooley himself never designated groups lacking in these characteristics as *secondary groups*, the latter term has also come into widespread use (see R. E. Park & E. W. Burgess, *Introduction to the Science of Sociology*, Chicago: University of Chicago Press, 2nd edn., 1924, p. 50).

In contrast to the multiplicity of elements in Cooley's conception of the primary group, some later writers sought to formulate a definition in terms of a single criterion. E. Faris rejected the criterion of face-to-face association as not essential for the existence of primary groups. Instead, he chose to identify a primary group as being characterized by intimate relationships among its members, manifested by group consciousness, esprit de corps, and a feeling of 'we'. Face-to-face relationships may lack this property (E. Faris, *The Nature of Human Nature*, New York: McGraw-Hill, 1937, ch. 4). E. A. Shils, on the other hand, treated the concept of *primary group* as synonymous with that of *informal group*, thus allowing the inclusion of ephemeral gatherings of little intimacy, while excluding formally organized groups strong in esprit de corps ('Primary Groups in the American Army, in R. K. Merton & P. F. Lazarsfeld (eds.), *Continuities in Social Research*, p. 16 ff.).

There seems, indeed, an advantage in employing a unidimensional definition of primary group and thus avoiding the difficulty that diverse criteria comprised in a single definition may yield inconsistent results. Among the various items contained in Cooley's own formulation the most strategic one would seem that which points to the unspecialized character of primary groups, particularly if the relative absence of specialization is treated as a matter of degree. This variable is a probable source of derivation of other phenomena which vary in interest to different students of primary groups. Accordingly, a group may be said to be a *primary group* to the degree to which the activities of the group are unspecialized.

2. The suggested definition of primary group would make it possible to treat its relationship to phenomena designated by other qualifications of the group concept as a series of empirical problems. One of these concepts is that of *peer group* which commonly refers to a group of homogeneous age composition. There is no reason, however, why this term cannot be applied to a group whose members are equal in some respect other than age. Thus it becomes a researchable question to ask whether groups which are homogeneous in a given respect show a higher degree of primary group quality than do less homogeneous groups.

3. For either primary groups or peer groups,

similar problems can be posed regarding their relationship to a third group phenomenon designated by W. G. Sumner's concept *in-group* (*Folkways*, Boston: Ginn, 1906, p. 12). Sumner describes this type of group as characterized by 'we'-feelings, loyalty to the group, sacrifice for it, and comradeship among its members. Thus, a group is an in-group to the extent to which it is an object of self-identification for its members. Conceivably, a group may possess this quality to a high degree while lacking primary group character to any significant extent. Sumner's corollary concept of *out-group* refers to an aspect of inter-group relations. No group is an out-group in and by itself but only if it is viewed as such by another group. In relation to the latter, a group functions as an out-group or others-group in so far as it is perceived in stereotyped terms of 'they' or 'the others' and is an object of hostility or contempt.

Merton and Kitt ('Contributions to the Theory of Reference Group Behavior', pp. 86–7, fn. 42) have further refined the concepts of in-group and out-group by indicating the relativity of the distinction. While for Sumner, basing his observations on 'primitive society', in-groups and out-groups were mutually exclusive collectivities, Merton and Kitt show that in a complex society the boundary between an in-group and an out-group may fluctuate. Within one context, a given sub-group of a larger group may constitute an in-group and perceive another sub-group as an out-group; within another context, both sub-groups may jointly form a single in-group.

Werner S. Landecker

See also: COMMUNITY
  REFERENCE GROUP
  SOCIAL INTEGRATION
  SOCIETY

Group Dynamics

A. *Group dynamics* denotes the study of (a) the structure and functioning of groups (q.v.), notably the psychological aspects of 'small groups', with especial reference to the changing pattern of intra-group adjustment, tension, conflict, and cohesion; and (b) the shifts in relationships of one group with another.

B. The approach of K. Lewin (e.g. *Field Theory in Social Science*, ed. by D. Cartwright, New York: Harper & Brothers, 1951), one of the major influences on studies in this field, was

Guilt

both important and constructive; but as M. Deutsch points out, despite his emphasis on 'theoretical analysis and experimental study of the dynamic problems of changing group life ... referred to by the title *group dynamics* ...' Lewin actually wrote very little on the theory of group dynamics (M. Deutsch, 'Field Theory in Social Psychology', in G. Lindzey (ed.), *Handbook of Social Psychology*, Cambridge, Mass.: Addison-Wesley, 1954, vol. I, pp. 213–4). It does not diminish the importance of Lewin's origination of the term to point out that many of the problems raised in group dynamics had been treated by earlier writers such as Simmel and Cooley and studied in the context of the formulations of J. L. Moreno; nor to indicate that the techniques and concepts of group dynamics have been sharpened by post-Lewinian research, especially by the experimental research of A. Bavelas, R. F. Bales, D. Cartwright, L. Festinger, A. Zander, and others.

C. M. Deutsch (ibid., p. 215) discusses his own and other writers' depiction of cohesiveness as a central concept in interpreting the dynamic influence of groups over their membership. Likewise P. Lazarsfeld ('Problems in Methodology', in R. K. Merton, L. Broom & L. S. Cottrell (eds.) *Sociology Today*, New York: Basic Books, 1959, pp. 56–7) stresses the place of *cohesion* in contemporary group dynamics: 'in a variety of experiments the group dynamics people show how cohesion ... is related to opinion, to efficiency, to amount of communication and so on'.

Other concepts could be mentioned, but it is perhaps unnecessary to specify the full range of concepts and topics upon which group dynamics has operated or with which it is concerned. It is obvious that in theory and in practice it overlaps with a wide range of psychological and sociological concerns (see, for example, *sociometry*). An important recent survey (A. W. Eister, 'Basic Continuities in the Study of Small Groups', in H. Becker & A. Boskoff (eds.), *Modern Sociological Theory in Continuity and Change*, New York: Dryden Press, 1957, pp. 305 ff.) discusses a variety of such areas and techniques used in their exploration (see also H. Bonner, *Group Dynamics*, New York: Ronald Press, 1959, pp. 3–30).

D. A critical discussion of the popularized application of group dynamics, especially in business organizations, may be found in W. H.

Whyte, Jr., *The Organization Man* (New York: Simon & Schuster, 1956, p. 46 ff.).

Eugene L. Hartley

See also: Field Theory
Group
Social Interaction

Group Marriage (See **Marriage**)

Guilt

A. The term *guilt* denotes a condition of recognized departure from fixed or generally recognized serious norms of conduct, for which departure a penalty is exacted. This usage involves three points: (a) the violation of prescribed norms of conduct; (b) the idea of responsibility for such violation; and (c) the idea of penalty which may be imposed by the state, society, or by the conscience of the individual.

B. 1. In legal usage an act entailing individual criminal liability is one involving personal *guilt*. In American and British criminal procedure, the accused is brought into court to be arraigned, a proceeding in which he is asked to plead guilty or not guilty to the charges which are embodied in the indictment or the information which has been returned against him. 'Where the accused pleads guilty to the crime as charged, the reason presumably is that the evidence is so strong against him that he has no hope of escaping conviction but hopes by saving the time of the court and prosecutor ... he may earn leniency in sentence ...' (L. Mayers, *The American Legal System*, New York: Harper & Brothers, 1955, p. 150).

2. Another form of legal usage comprehends the idea of *guilt by association* or guilt attaching to an individual through his relation or connection with a group of persons who are charged with violation of a legally established line of conduct. In this sense the term involves *collective responsibility*. The Charter annexed to the London Agreement of 8 August 1945 provides in Article 6, defining the jurisdiction of the International Military Tribunal at Nuremberg: 'Leaders, organizers, instigators, and accomplices participating in the formulation or execution of a Common Plan or Conspiracy to commit any of the foregoing crimes are responsible for all acts performed by any persons in execution of such plan' (*Trial of the Major War Criminals before the International Military Tribunal*, Nuremberg, 42 vols (1947–9), vol. I, p. 11).

The ideas of *collective* and *associative guilt*

have socio-political implications, especially where a line of conduct is popularly interpreted as constituting an attack upon the established order, the nature of the state, or the organization of government, and where 'association' is defined to include irrelevant relationships. The scope of popular or legal condemnation may be far-reaching. As the late Z. Chafee, Jr., put it: 'The doctrine of guilt by association is abhorrent enough in the criminal and deportation fields without being extended into the relation between lawyer and client' (*Free Speech in the United States*, Cambridge, Mass.: Harvard University Press, 1941, p. 359).

3. In sociological usage, the term *guilt* extends to the violation of serious group norms, non-legal as well as legal. The individual during his childhood is indoctrinated with or conditioned to a certain socially shared norm of conduct which in adulthood may be modified, criticized, or repudiated, resulting in censure or punishment by the group and guilt feelings (q.v.) on the part of the norm violator. Such violation of social norms can be individual or collective and the problems of collective guilt and guilt by association may well be present.

Alona E. Evans

See also: CRIME
           GUILT FEELINGS
           TRIAL

Guilt Feelings

A. In its most general use the term denotes a painful emotional state, the mental content of which is a sense of having done wrong in the light of either personal or social ethical standards. The common content of all guilt feelings or qualms of conscience is 'I have done wrong'; a painful judgement about some past occurrence, having the character of remorse—'I should not have done wrong'. They may be distinguished from other expressions of conscience (q.v.) which do not judge the past but the future: e.g. 'I should do this, should not do that', etc.

This usage is carried over into psychological writings: Thus, H. C. Warren (*Dictionary of Psychology*, Boston: Houghton Mifflin, 1934) defines the 'sense of guilt' as 'an emotional state, in which the individual is dominated by the belief or knowledge that he has contravened some social custom, ethical principle, or legal regulation'.

B. 1. *Guilt feelings* have been rarely studied in general and social psychology, where they are usually treated, together with shame and re-morse, within the broader group of anxiety and insecurity states. P. T. Young, however, in his *Emotion in Man and Animal* (New York: Wiley, 1943, p. 369) differentiates shame, remorse, and the sense of guilt from shyness and stage-fright, and considers them together as 'those forms of embarrassment which arise when an individual has carried out some act contrary to the standards of his group or in violation of his personal principles'.

2. In psychoanalysis, however, guilt feelings have been the subject of much detailed study, and the concept of 'unconscious guilt' has been introduced to link many phenomena which superficially may not appear to be related to guilt feelings. In psychoanalysis (and in clinical psychology and psychiatry of a psychoanalytic viewpoint) three types of guilt are described:

(a) There are those guilt feelings of conscious origin, and consciously felt: these are forms of social anxiety, and their reference point is either external authority or its internal representative, the conscience. (It may be noted that, in psychology generally, objective moral guilt is not used in any metaphysical sense).

(b) Second, there are guilt feelings of unconscious origin, but consciously felt: these are signs of neurotic anxiety, the origin of which has been repressed from consciousness. The person experiencing this form of guilt is conscious of a sense of wrong-doing, denigrates himself, and often seeks some punishment to relieve his sense of sin, despite the fact that he does not know its origin. The self-reproaches of the melancholic and the impaired self-regard associated with inferiority feelings may result from such guilt. Rationalizations are often used to make such guilt plausible, leading to the occurrence of excessive self-punitive reactions for apparently minor social transgressions. Freud showed that the origin of such guilt feelings lay in infantile phantasies, especially those of an aggressive nature, which had been repressed through exaggerated fear of imagined consequences. The impulses, though inhibited from outward expression, are discharged against the self, producing the painful, self-attacking experience of guilt. Paradoxically, it is those who behave in a most scrupulous way who may suffer this form of guilt most intensely.

(c) Finally, there is guilt of unconscious origin felt as the need for punishment or reparation: some persons do not have strong conscious feelings of guilt, but act as if they feel they should. They seek punishment (e.g. some types of accident-proneness fall into this category), have

Guilt Feelings

forebodings of disaster, find success intolerable, or make exaggerated attempts to atone for some unknown sin (e.g. in self-sacrificing helpfulness or excessive generosity). In such cases, there is ignorance both of the sense of guilt and of its origin, but action is taken *as if* wrong had been done. Sometimes the sufferer from this form of unconscious guilt may even commit a real crime in order to justify it. It will be seen that this third meaning is a conceptual rather than descriptive use of the term.

C. de Monchaux

See also: CONSCIENCE
GUILT

Guttman Scale (See **Scaling**)

H

Habit

A. *Habit* denotes any regularly repeated action on the part of an individual that is learnt and that is observable to others. Though the mechanisms involved are necessarily different, the analogy with custom (q.v.) is very close: habits are to individuals as customs are to societies, or other collectivities. The controversies in which the term has been involved have had to do with the essential conditions under which such regularities come about and persist or change, rather than with the basic meaning of the term.

B. 1. In its technical sense, the term is primarily, if not exclusively, a psychological one. It was the British 19th-century associationists who first gave systematic attention to habit, as a psychological problem, and in particular A. Bain, who, according to E. G. Boring (*A History of Experimental Psychology*, New York: The Century Co., 1929, pp. 226–7), 'represented the culmination of associationism and the beginning of its absorption into physiological psychology'. Bain described the acquisition of habit 'in terms of (1) random movements, (2) retention of acts which bring pleasant results, with elimination of those bringing unpleasant results, (3) fixation through repetition' (G. Murphy, *Historical Introduction to Modern Psychology*, London: Kegan Paul, Trench, Trubner, 1932, p. 111).

2. W. James is perhaps best remembered for his famous chapter on 'Habit' (*Principles of Psychology*, 2 vols., New York: Henry Holt, 1890), though the chapter itself is doubtless remembered more for its eloquent persuasiveness than for its original contributions to psychological theory. For James, the tyranny of habit was rooted in neurology, but the neurological facts available to him were limited. James was in revolt against British associationism, while at the same time being indebted to it, and perhaps the most important contribution of his famous chapter was to shift the emphasis from mental to neurological and motor associationism.

3. J. Dewey, in a little book that has probably influenced sociologists more than psychologists (*Human Nature and Conduct*, New York: Henry Holt, 1922), is more faithful to the then contemporary 'functional school' of psychology than (in a literal sense, at least) to James, his former teacher, in rejecting mechanistic and merely repetitive notions of habit. 'Repetition is in no sense the essence of habit', he wrote. 'The essence of habit is an acquired predisposition to *ways* or modes of response ... Habit means special sensitiveness or accessibility to certain classes of stimuli, standing predilections and aversions, rather than bare recurrence of specific acts' (ibid., p. 42). This, of course, sounds very much like today's definition of attitude (q.v.).

C. In recent years technical usage of the term *habit* has become virtually restricted to the behavioural school of psychologists. Thus E. R. Hilgard writes, 'The stimulus-response theorist and the cognitive theorist come up with different answers to the question, What is learned? The answer of the former is "habits"; the answer of the latter is "cognitive structures" ' (*Theories of Learning*, New York: Appleton-Century-Crofts, 2nd edn., 1956, p. 10). No concept is more central to the systematic formulation of the principles of learning by C. L. Hull (cf. *Essentials of Behavior*, New Haven: Yale University Press, 1951) than the concept of *habit strength*, which may be defined as 'the tendency for a stimulus trace to evoke an associated response' (E. R. Hilgard, *Theories of Learning*, p. 131), and which is postulated as varying directly as a function of the number of reinforcements, other things equal. Thus reinforcement becomes the primary condition for habit formation. In Tolman's theory—the major present competitor of Hull's—'cognitive structures' or 'expectancies' are 'confirmed' rather than 'habits' being 'reinforced', though the phenomena that both are trying to account for, via their differing terminologies, are pretty much the same (E. C. Tolman, *Purposive Behavior in Animals and Men*, New York: The Century Co., 1932).

Theodore M. Newcomb

See also: ATTITUDE
　　　　　CONDITIONING
　　　　　CUSTOM
　　　　　EXPECTATION
　　　　　LEARNING
　　　　　REINFORCEMENT

Habitat

Habitat

In order of frequency of usage, *habitat* has the following meanings:

1. It denotes the physical environment in its totality (e.g. E. Huntington, *The Human Habitat*, London: Chapman & Hall, 1928).

2. More narrowly, it denotes 'the physical and chemical conditions that distinguish one unit of occupied space from another' (A. H. Hawley, *Human Ecology*, New York: Ronald Press, 1950, p. 42).

3. Very broadly, it denotes both the social and the physical environment. In this usage it is sometimes employed as an alternative word for the 'natural region' of the geographer and for the *culture area* (q.v.) of the anthropologist.

J. Mogey

See also: ENVIRONMENT

Head of State

1. Traditionally in Europe the *Head of State* was a Monarch to whom ambassadors were accredited and formal State communications addressed. The Head of State was also the head of Government, being personally responsible for foreign and domestic policy and appointments throughout the public service. There is usually a similar arrangement in modern dictatorships.

2. (a) In *parliamentary monarchies*, the Executive is divided into (i) a Head of State, the Monarch, to whom ambassadors are accredited and who acts on behalf of the State on formal occasions; and (ii) a Government with whom real political power (except, on occasion, the appointment of a Prime Minister) rests. In the latter power is still exercised, however, on behalf of the Crown (q.v.).

(b) In *parliamentary republics*, the Executive is also divided into (i) a Head of State, who is a President usually elected by the Legislature; and (ii) a Government, headed by a Prime Minister or, in the Federal German Republic, a Chancellor.

The President's powers vary from the mainly formal, as in the German Democratic Republic (East Germany) until 1960, to active participation in policy, as in Finland.

(c) In *presidential systems*, for example the U.S.A., the President is elected by the people to be both head of Executive and Head of State.

(d) In some other countries there is no place for an individual Head of State. In certain Communist countries, notably the U.S.S.R., supreme power rests with the Supreme Soviet and, between sessions, its Presidium. Constitutionally the Presidium acts as Head of State (Article 49 of the Soviet Constitution). In practice the Presi-dent of the Presidium *acts on its behalf* as Head of State on formal State occasions.

D. V. Verney

See also: MONARCHY
PRESIDENCY

Health

A. *Health* is a loose concept, well understood and applied in practice over a wide area of human behaviour but neither unitary nor well-bounded: i.e. the criteria used in defining bodily health and mental health are not necessarily uniform nor is there a uniform mode of distinguishing health from other human conditions, e.g. illness or disease; changes in the area of human knowledge have prompted changing usage of the concept. Usage of the term varies according to whether it is defined in terms of (a) negative and positive criteria; (b) conceptions of 'the normal'; (c) adaptation to the environment.

B. Depending upon the criteria used in definition, the concept may be defined in either negative or positive terms.

1. Negatively, health has been taken to consist in *freedom from any subjective feelings of discomfort or disability and from any objective disturbances of function*. 'Health is the absence of disease' (J. Bentham, *An Introduction to the Principles of Morals and Legislation*, Oxford: Clarendon Press (1st edn. 1789), 1876, p. 45).

It should be noted that:

(a) This view was consistent with human knowledge prior to the minute study of bodily pathology and its relation to symptoms and signs of disease.

(b) In the light of such pathology the distinction between bodily and mental illness was sharpened.

(c) In the light of such pathology the bounds between health and illness became more difficult to draw because of those pathological changes which may be present in the body for a long time without *producing discomfort or objective disturbances of function*.

(d) There is a third state between illness and health having some of the characteristics of both, e.g. states of defectiveness (mental or physical) exhibited since birth but stationary and not manifestly shortening life: certain departures from average structure and function which do not entail gross impairment of physical or mental efficiency (e.g. certain metabolic deficiencies: changes incident to the ageing process).

2. Positively, according to the Constitution of the World Health Organization 'Health is a state of complete physical, mental and social well-being, and not merely the absence of disease or infirmity' (*The First Ten Years of the World Health Organisation*, Geneva: W.H.O., 1958, p. 459). This is an implicit way of saying that no one can be healthy. In its insistence on an unattainable ideal, it is consonant with much that is written on the concept of mental health.

C. *Healthy* and *normal* are sometimes used as if they were synonyms. This leads to confusion because of the two meanings of *normal*. Health may be considered a form of normality determined by a value-judgement involving once again positive and negative criteria. What is normal (in the other widespread usage of the term) may be decided statistically for a given population, irrespective of whether it is favourable to survival and well-being. Dental caries may be normal, in this sense, but they are not healthy; extreme strength or intelligence may be abnormal, but need not be incompatible with physical and mental health.

D. Physical (and mental) health is often defined in terms of adaptation to the environment and internal equipoise. Most attempts at defining mental health relate it to the cultural environment. Clearly there are some 'environments' in which the stresses and demands upon the individual must warp him and may induce mental illness, no matter how healthy he would have been in a happier environment: this is on all fours with the relation of physical health to environment, but it is easy and misleading to incorporate this into a social and often moral assessment into which the medical concept of health hardly enters. This difficulty is most conspicuous when the concept of health is applied to personality. Thus *psychopathic personality* is commonly regarded as a description appropriate to those who are not mentally ill with a recognizable disorder but whose personality is deformed, as judged by their behaviour, particularly by their lack of conformity to the social requirements of their environment.

Sir Aubrey Lewis

See also: NORMAL

Hearing (See **Trial**)

Hedonism

A. *Hedonism* denotes a theory of value (q.v.) and motivation (q.v.) which holds that the ultimate values and motives of human action lie in the pleasure produced for the individual or the community, and in the avoidance of pain.

B. 1. The concept of hedonism is found, in some form and degree, in many of the social sciences. As a theory of conduct it is at least as old in philosophy as the Cyrenaics of Ancient Greece. Hobbes revived it in the 17th century, adding an ethical conception to the older pschological hedonism. He thought that pleasure was to be obtained, and pain avoided, within the institutions of the state. The state assists in the realization of one's desires, and makes correlative demands in the form of duties.

2. Hedonism was the leading psychological principle of classical economics, until the school of marginal utility was developed in the 19th century. The 'economic man' was held to make his calculations in the market in terms of the gains that he would derive from the transaction or the effort or loss that it might cost him. Veblen said that the economic man became 'a lightning calculator of pleasures and pains'.

3. Hedonism was extended to the philosophy of law by the classical school of criminology, the best example of which is Beccaria's *Essay on Crimes and Punishments* which appeared in 1764 (English trans., London: F. Newbery, 2nd edn., 1769). The *Essay*, based on the rationalism of the Enlightenment, argued from the premises of the greatest good of the greatest number and that crime is an injury to society. Hence the only rational measure of a crime was the extent of that injury. Since men calculated pleasures and pains in advance of their actions, each crime was to carry a specific sanction that would just outweigh its derived pleasure; the sanctions were to be published so that the cost of the crime would be known; and they were to apply equally to all: young and old, commoner, nobility, and clergy. Thus punishment was justified in terms of its deterrent quality. The application of this conception had enormous consequences for jurisprudence, especially for the Anglo-American system. Although exceptions have been made, it is still the dominant basis of this legal system.

4. Utilitarianism (q.v.) in the works of Bentham and Mill continued Beccaria's extension of hedonism to the general problems of social change that resulted from the Industrial Revolution.

C. All these expressions of hedonism were based on an individualistic psychology. Even when man was placed in 'society' he was conceived of as a separate particle and 'society' as an aggregation of these; and pleasure and pain as the psychical units of discrete men.

Heredity

1. Hedonism as an assumption of contemporary psychiatry, psychoanalysis, and social work perpetuates this conception. In much social work practice, man is assumed to be a pleasure-seeking and tension-discharging organism, with pleasure-pain being the dominant principle and encompassing much, if not most, of, human behaviour. This is derived from the Freudian postulate of the unconscious, which is held to be the source of impulses to action that are uncontrollable by the individual. The principle of pleasure-pain can be regarded as a working hypothesis in psychiatry. It is held, for example, that there must be some psychical gain in hysterical paralysis, that martyrs must possess some degree of masochism in order to endure their lot, and that a modicum of masochism may assist in survival, as among the Jews in Germany during the Nazi period.

2. Hedonism has not taken as complete a hold in social psychology and sociology. The pleasure-pain principle is regarded by many as 'an overly simple, superficial statement of human conduct' (G. H. Mead, *Movements of Thought in the Nineteenth Century*, Chicago: University of Chicago Press, 1936, pp. 199–214). Its psychology is questioned because it is individualistic and voluntaristic, and 'assumes freedom of the will in a manner which gives little or no possibility of further investigation of the causes of crime or of efforts to prevent crime' (E. H. Sutherland & D. R. Cressey, *Principles of Criminology*, Chicago: Lippincott, 5th edn., 1955, p. 53). Furthermore, the ends that we pursue are not subjective ends. 'The great things of life are objective . . . The greatest things are those for which we sacrifice ourselves and thus realize ourselves. That phase of human endeavour the utilitarians could not present' (G. H. Mead, *Movements of Thought in the Nineteenth Century*, p. 209). Deliberation is no mere algebraic sum of pleasures and pains. The office of deliberation is 'to resolve entanglements in existing activity, restore continuity . . . and redirect habit,' and its conclusion is the choice of some course of action (J. Dewey, *Human Nature and Conduct*, New York: Henry Holt, 1922, p. 199). Nevertheless hedonism is to be found as a strand of modern sociological theory from Sumner's statement in 1906 that 'The ability to distinguish pleasure and pain is the only psychical power which is to be assumed' to T. Parsons's statement in current writing that '*By definition*, in the theory of action it does not make sense for an actor to seek deprivation and avoid gratification' (W. G. Sumner, *Folkways*, Boston: Ginn, 1906, p. 2; T. Parsons, *The Social System*, Glencoe, Ill.: The Free Press, 1951, p. 497).

Frank E. Hartung

See also: MOTIVATION
UTILITARIANISM
VALUE

Henotheism (See Monotheism)

Heredity

A. Heredity may be defined as a biological process and as a cultural process.

1. Biological heredity is the process of transmission of discrete units of inheritance, genes, from parents to offspring. It is accomplished through the process of organic development consequent upon the union of sex cells at fertilization. Biological heredity may also be defined as self-reproduction for an essential feature of heredity lies in the ability of each unit to replicate itself (E. W. Sinnott, L. C. Dunn, & T. Dobzhansky, *Principles of Genetics*, New York: McGraw-Hill, 5th edn., 1958). While biological heredity is sometimes defined as the tendency of like to beget like, or the transmission of similarities, similarities are not inherited as such but rather the genetic capacities for their expression. Genes determine processes and they interact with the environment in which they are placed.

2. Cultural heredity transmits acquired cultural characteristics, by teaching and learning in each generation, rather than by means of genes.

B. Concern with heredity, biological and cultural, has been reflected in the redefinition of culture as a biological adaptation with non-genetic modes of transmission (*The Nature and Transmission of the Genetic and Cultural Characteristics of Human Populations*, New York: Millbank Memorial Fund, 1957; J. N. Spuhler, 'Somatic Paths to Culture', *Human Biology*, vol. 31, 1959, pp. 1–13). An important nexus between biological and cultural heredity lies in genealogical relationships. It was recognized early in the study of man (G. W. Marshall, 'Remarks on Genealogy in Connexion with Anthropology', *Memoirs, Anthropological Society of London*, vol. II, 1866, pp. 68–73), that the genealogical method provided a common point of departure for the study of the two great aspects of man, physical and intellectual. This is reflected in Galton's law of ancestral inheritance which, apart from Mendelian theory enunciated in 1865, represents the best-known attempt to formulate a law of biological heredity applicable to humans. Use of biological and social concepts pertinent to this area is illustrated in C. Kluckhohn & Z. Griffith ('Population Genetics and Social Anthropology', *Cold Spring Harbor Symposia on Quantitative Biology*, vol. XV, 1950, pp. 401–9). The scientific study of genetic transmission of characteristics has resulted in redefinition of the respective roles of heredity and environment, including cultural as well as physical environment, so that studies are increasingly concerned with the relative contributions of heredity and environment to the expression of physical traits and behaviour rather than with dividing traits that are hereditary from those that are environmentally produced (L. C. Dunn, *Heredity and Evolution in Human Populations*, Cambridge, Mass.: Harvard University Press, 1959).

William S. Laughlin

See also: CULTURE
INHERITANCE
PHYSICAL ANTHROPOLOGY
SOCIALIZATION

Hierarchy

1. *Hierarchy* as used in the social sciences denotes any graded, ranked body of persons and/or their relationships as reflecting differences, e.g. of power, authority, and prestige.

This principal usage is illustrated by the following: 'Whenever persons join or otherwise enter into a plurality pattern they almost invariably take their places in an implicit or explicit hierarchy, and consciously or unconsciously expect the fact that there are ranks above and below them' (L. von Wiese & H. Becker, *Systematic Sociology*, New York: Wiley, 1932, p. 355). It is also illustrated by this statement: 'This hierarchy, like any other, is a social order in which human relations are determined by the degree of authority exercised by one group over another' (J. Meyer, 'Hierarchy and Stratification in the Shop', *Social Research*, vol. XIV, 1947, p. 165).

2. The notion of a hierarchy is also applied to subjects, sciences, and principles. Here it implies arrangement or classification in ascending/descending orders, of generality or complexity—for example, Comte's idea of a classification of sciences each of which was deemed to depend on those below it and to be more 'complex' than them.

J. Gould

See also: BUREAUCRACY
DIFFERENTIATION
STRATIFICATION

Historical Linguistics (See **Linguistics**)

Historicism

The word *historicism* has been principally used in English in two very different senses.

1. The older of these usages is that to be found in Germany in such writings as F. Meinecke's *Die Entstehung des Historismus* (Munich & Berlin: R. Oldenbourg, 1936) or in the post-war works of G. Barraclough. In this sense historicism can be traced back at least to the 18th century, possibly to Vico, certainly to Voltaire. It can be defined as the attempt to see all the categories of social life and of the experience of the individual as belonging essentially to the domain of history which penetrates, whether we will it or not, into all acts.

Those who hold this view argue that (a) to understand the present, knowledge of the past is essential, and all science and knowledge are historically coloured; (b) this past can best be investigated by the process of 'scientific history' developed in Germany by Ranke and his school; (c) work which tries to break away from the categories of 'scientific history'—whether successfully or not—in the direction of comparative studies is therefore to be described, as G. Barraclough (*History in a Changing World*, Oxford: Basil Blackwell, 1955, p. 16) does the work of Toynbee, as anti-historicist.

2. The word has more recently been used in English in an almost opposite sense. According to K. R. Popper (*The Open Society and its Enemies*, London: Routledge & Kegan Paul, 1952, vol. I, pp. 3–8), historicism implies *the attempt to subsume all the social sciences under history and to take as their principal object the prediction of the future through the assertion of universal historical laws.* Ultimately, in this sense, historicism is a theory of social predestination. It is very doubtful whether there are any actual examples of historicism in this special meaning, though no doubt certain writers have approximated to it.

D. G. MacRae

See also: CULTURE HISTORY

Home Rule (See **Local Government**)

Homeostasis (See **Social Equilibrium**)

Horde

A. The common elements of most usages are united in the definition of the *horde* as a local group in a nomadic society, laying claim to exclusive rights of hunting, gathering, and/or grazing over delimited tracts of land.

Human Nature

B. 1. An adaptation of the Turki *orda*, passing into English through Russian and Polish, *horde* originally referred to tribal units among Tartar or related Asiatic pastoral nomads. By transfer of meaning, it came to be used more vaguely and eventually denoted, in common usage, a large, undefined group or gang of supposedly savage and undisciplined people or even animals. A similar usage was adopted by evolutionists in reconstructing early forms of human society (e.g. Cunow's theory of the 'horde' as 'the initial stage of society', as discussed in A. Lang, *Social Origins*, London: Longmans, Green, 1903, p. 114).

2. Anthropologists have subsequently attempted to restore to *horde* its formerly more precise meaning, but without any exact agreement as to the unit of society to which it could refer. Present-day technical usage tends to gather about two different referents: one being a large non-kin-based political unit of importance in defence and aggression (such as formerly among the Tartar or the Kazak), and the other being a fairly small local group. The second, more frequent usage of *horde* is found particularly in analyses of Australian aboriginal societies. It has been used in this context to mean a local group defined by matrilineal (q.v.) descent (e.g. A. W. Howitt, *The Native Tribes of South-East Australia*, London: Macmillan, 1904), a local group defined by patrilineal descent (e.g. A. R. Radcliffe-Brown, *The Social Organization of Australian Tribes*, London: Macmillan, 1931), and as a local group defined by kinship for part of the year only (e.g. W. L. Warner, *A Black Civilization*, New York: Harper & Brothers, 1937, p. 138: 'The horde is an unstable economic group whose membership and size are regulated by the seasonal cycle').

L. F. Baric

See also: TRIBE

Horizontal Mobility (See Mobility)

Horticulture (See Agriculture and Horticulture)

Human Ecology (See Ecology)

Human Nature

A. *Human nature*, in general terms, denotes the nature of man, with more especial reference to his personality and/or character as acquired in the course of socialization (q.v.) and often with further reference to aspects of human potential and powers of development.

B. The phrase *human nature* is defined and used in various ways in all social science fields, ranging from psychiatry to anthropology. Amid the diversity three types of definition are recurrent.

1. The first, emphasizing physiological needs and unlearned impulses, is the organic or biological approach. B. Malinowski is a good example: 'We can define the term "human nature" by the fact that all men have to eat, they have to breathe, to sleep, to procreate and to eliminate waste matter from their organisms wherever they live and whatever type of civilization they practice' (*A Scientific Theory of Culture and Other Essays*, Chapel Hill, N.C.: University of North Carolina Press, 1944, p. 75). Similarly, the Sherifs distinguish between biogenic and sociogenic motives, with the former being 'human nature' in the form of 'the biological endowment of the organism' (M. Sherif & C. W. Sherif, *An Outline of Social Psychology*, New York: Harper & Brothers, rev. edn. 1956, p. 385). Curiously enough, this type of formulation contains nothing which is *distinctively human*.

2. A second type of definition emphasizes the social aspects of human nature, the classic statement being found in C. H. Cooley: 'By human nature . . . we may understand those sentiments and impulses that are human in being superior to those of lower animals, and also in the sense that they belong to mankind at large, and not to any particular race or time. It means, particularly, sympathy and the innumerable sentiments into which sympathy enters, such as love, resentment, ambition, vanity, hero-worship, and the feeling of social right or wrong' (*Social Organization*, New York: Charles Scribner's Sons, 1909, p. 28). Further: '... the view here maintained is that human nature is not something existing separately in the individual but a *group nature* or *primary phase of society*. ... It is the nature which is developed and expressed in those simple, face-to-face groups that are somewhat alike in all societies; groups of the family, the playground, and the neighborhood ... In these, everywhere, human nature comes into existence. ... What else can human nature be than a trait of primary groups?' (ibid., pp. 29–30).

It has been suggested (R. T. LaPiere & P. R. Farnsworth, *Social Psychology*, New York: McGraw-Hill, 3rd edn., 1949, p. 221) that the meaning of the concept has shifted from Cooley's to the 'typical personality attributes of the members of a particular group'. This is found for example, in the statement that each group and society has its own 'characteristic needs and demands and other characteristic ways of expressing and satisfying them ... Looked at in this way, there is not one human nature, but many—as many as there are cultures, societies, and social groups' (D. Krech & R. S. Crutchfield, *Theory and Problems of Social Psychology*, New York: McGraw-Hill, 1948, p. 47).

There are other variations in this second type of formulation, emphasizing the social aspects of human nature. W. Coutu, who states that his is not a 'standard' definition, refers to human nature as 'the ability to communicate on the symbolic level or conceptual level', thus denying it to all infants, and to those who are born of woman but who either lack the potential for such communication, or who fail to develop the capacity (*Emergent Human Nature*, New York: Knopf, 1949, p. 65). Another usage distinguishes between *human-social nature* and *human-cultural nature*, the former deriving from experience in primary groups, the latter from experience in secondary groups and institutions (J. B. Gittler, *Social Dynamics*, New York: McGraw-Hill, 1952, p. 1).

3. The third type of formulation seems to emphasize the dynamic potential of man, independently of biology, on one hand, or social and cultural influences, on the other. Thus, E. Fromm writes: 'Human nature is neither a biologically fixed and innate sum total of drives nor is it a lifeless shadow of cultural patterns. ...' It 'has a dynamism of its own that constitutes an active factor in the evolution of the social process. Even if we are not yet able to state clearly in psychological terms what the exact nature of this human dynamism is, we must recognize its existence' (*The Fear of Freedom*, London: Kegan Paul, Trench, Trubner, 1942, pp. 17, 247). Similar viewpoints are expressed in D. Bidney, 'Human Nature and the Cultural Process' (*American Anthropologist*, vol. 49, 1947, pp. 375–99); and A. H. Maslow, *Motivation and Personality* (New York: Harper & Brothers, 1954, esp. ch. 18).

C. The principal controversies surrounding *human nature* are the following: Is it shared with other animals or is it specifically human? Is it present at birth or something developed in primary interaction? Is it a substantive concept, i.e. containing specific elements, or a generalized potential? Is it fixed or variable? Given such problems (not to mention the confusion arising from the 'common sense' usage of the phrase) it is not surprising that several scholars have

suggested dropping it from the scientific vocabulary (R. T. LaPiere & P. R. Farnsworth, *Social Psychology*, p. 221; J. F. Brown, *Psychology and the Social Order*, New York: McGraw-Hill, 1936, p. 259; M. J. Herskovits, *Man and His Works*, New York: Knopf, 1949, pp. 617–18).

Two solutions are possible. One is found in T. M. Newcomb, who surveys the problem and concludes: 'The most inclusive statement that can be made about distinctive human nature is that humans have an enormous capacity for acquiring motives' (*Social Psychology*, New York: Dryden Press, 1950, p. 144). The other is found in L. Wilson and W. L. Kolb, who distinguish between *original nature* and *human nature*. The former consists of 'the totality of characteristics possessed by the organism at birth plus those which later develop through the process of biological maturation'; the latter is essentially individual personality because 'apart from society original nature cannot become human nature. The elements of original nature are necessary conditions of personality ... but they are not the sufficient conditions, for without the process of socialization they must remain unrealized potentialities' (L. Wilson & W. L. Kolb, *Sociological Analysis*, New York: Harcourt, Brace, 1949, pp. 157, 160).

Edmund H. Volkart

See also: MAN
ORIGINAL NATURE

Hunting, Fishing, and Gathering Economy

This term denotes the type of economy based on obtaining food and other supplies by fishing, hunting game, and collecting (or foraging for) wild vegetable and animal products.

It is often referred to briefly as *food-gathering*. 'Food-gatherers display great diversity, both in the combination of techniques, and in the degree of specialization on particular means and natural resources ... we shall seek in vain for pure gleaners, or pure fishers. The Tasmanians, with the most meagre equipment of all recent peoples, were collectors of wild roots, fruits and shore molluscs, but they also organized small drives for game. The Arctic Eskimos, specialized as hunters and fishers, also gather vegetable foods in summer' (C. Daryll Forde, 'Foraging, Hunting and Fishing', in C. Singer, E. J. Holmyard & A. R. Hall (eds.), *History of Technology*, London:, Oxford University Press, 1954; vol. I, p. 183).

M. Douglas

See also: AGRICULTURE
SUBSISTENCE ECONOMY

Hypergamy

Hypergamy

A. *Hypergamy* denotes that form of marriage in which a woman of lower status is married to a man of higher status. Hypergamy is not to be understood as a fundamental sociological category in itself, nor merely as a form of marriage, but in relation to a theory of social stratification.

B. 1. Hypergamous marriages are found in many parts of the world, but the discussion which follows concerns India, where a highly developed ranking system lends a peculiar interest to this institution (examples of hypergamous marriages are to be found in Bengal, Kerala, Gujerat, Rajputana, and elsewhere in India). Hypergamous marriages in India are called *anuloma* ('with the hair') in contrast to hypogamous unions, which occur when the groom is of lower status than the bride: the latter are *pratiloma* marriages ('against the hair').

2. Hypergamous unions may take place within castes between ranked descent groups or local groups; or between sub-castes; or between different castes.

In Bengal the Rarhi Brahmins are divided into a number of status categories, the higher of which will take brides from the lower but will not give their daughters in return. In a typical case the father of the girl is wealthy and he pays a heavy bridegroom-price to a poorer family of higher status. The transaction has the effect of increasing the prestige of the family into which the bride was born. The system makes it difficult for girls of the highest category to obtain bridegrooms, and grooms in this category are in much greater demand than are brides. A groom of high status may make a business of going through many formal marriages (*Kulinism*). It has also been suggested that the practice of marrying off girls when they are children is connected with competition between fathers to find grooms for their daughters.

In Gujerat, within the Patidar caste, hypergamy is practised between ranked descent groups, which are also local groups. The ranking is expressed somewhat in the idiom of caste purity, lower groups, for example, allowing widow remarriage, while higher groups do not.

In the case of the Rajputs, as in that of the Patidars, the units concerned in hypergamous marriages are not castes or sub-castes, but descent groups. These are exogamous clans within the Rajput caste. The clans differ in status, and those which belong farther west rank higher than those in the eastern part of the country. In an approved marriage, therefore, the groom comes from the western part of the country, and the bride from the east. The functions of this form of marriage among the Rajputs remain obscure. One may conjecture that it had political correlates, but there can be no certainty about this until the relation between rank and political power in traditional Rajputana has been more systematically explored.

On the other hand, the political functions of Nayar hypergamy in Kerala before the period of British rule have been well described by E. J. Miller ('Caste and Territory in Malabar', *American Anthropologist*, vol. 56, 1954, pp. 410–20). The Nayars were divided into a number of ranked sub-castes, and Nayar women married either into their own sub-caste or into a higher sub-caste. These sub-castes were ranked in accordance with political office. Nayar women might also marry into royal castes (Ksattriya and Samantan) or into Nambudiri Brahmin castes. Bride and groom commonly belonged to one political unit, and the effect of the system was to keep relationships within that unit, and so isolate it from other similar units. Had caste endogamy been observed then a small royal lineage, or a small Nambudiri lineage, given the rule of lineage exogamy, would have had to go outside the political unit in order to find brides. Hypergamous unions between Nambudiri younger sons and Nayar women, whose children were matrilineally descended and therefore Nayars, helped to preserve intact Nambudiri estates: only the eldest son in a Nambudiri family could marry within caste and father Nambudiri descendants.

C. The institution of hypergamy has given rise to a number of speculations and explanations, but no coherent and authoritative theory has emerged. Firstly, there appears to be no satisfactory structural explanation for the fact that hypergamous unions are countenanced and approved, while hypogamous unions are almost universally (in India) condemned. Secondly, H. Risley (*The People of India*, London: W. Thacher, 1915, p. 178 ff.) and others have used hypergamy to explain the origin of the caste system, on the assumption that invading groups, when they first arrived, contracted hypergamous unions with the indigenous population and later forbade such unions. Theories of this kind are not part of current social thinking, and objections to them will not be considered here. (For a discussion see J. H. Hutton, *Caste in India*, Cambridge: Cambridge University Press, 1946).

D. The four examples quoted clearly do not have the same structural significance. Probably in the case of the Rajputs and the Patidars, and certainly in the case of the Nayars, a structural explanation of the institution is to be found in its political correlates. Bengal hypergamy, on the other hand, does not seem to be a patterning of relationships between groups which are politically significant (at least so far as our information goes). Rather it is to be seen as an institution which introduced a mechanism of elasticity into the theoretically rigid framework of caste: a means by which wealthy people were able to raise their own prestige and the status of some of their descendants, by contracting valid marriages with persons in higher sub-castes. On the other hand, Nayar hypergamy, while it resolved political difficulties which could have arisen from narrow caste endogamy, did nothing to break down the exclusiveness of castes, since hypergamous marriages did not lead to kinship links across caste boundaries. Matrilineal descent and the virtually complete elimination of the rights and duties of fatherhood, ensured that children born of hypergamous unions belonged exclusively to the mother's group. It will be clear from this example also that the significance of hypergamy as a mechanism which allows kinship relationships to cross caste or sub-caste boundaries, will depend on the nature and intensity of the relationships which persist between the bridegroom's group and the bride's group after the marriage, and also between the children of the union and their maternal kin.

F. G. Bailey

See also: CASTE
ENDOGAMY
MARRIAGE

Hypogamy (See **Hypergamy**)

Hypothesis

A. As used in philosophy and the social sciences (including statistics) its strict usage denotes a testable assertion, statement, or proposition about the relationships between two or more phenomena in the field of inquiry.

B. In logic and philosophy, hypotheses are distinguished both from *laws* and from self-evident undemonstrable *axioms*. They are part of *theories* and/or deducible from *theories* and/or *sources* of further deductions. (In some contexts they are themselves described as *theories*).

Some of the criteria specified in usage may be seen in the following:

1. 'In the first place the hypothesis must be formulated in such a manner that deductions can be made from it and that consequently a decision can be reached as to whether it does or does not explain the facts considered' (M. R. Cohen & E. Nagel, *Logic and Scientific Method*, London: Routledge, 1934, p. 207).

2. 'The propositions which serve as starting points of deductions in modern science ... are *hypotheses* and we do not know whether the hypothesis is true or false, probable or improbable, *before* having deduced consequences from it' (A. Pap, *Elements of Analytic Philosophy*, New York: The Macmillan Co., 1949, p. 154).

3. 'Empirical propositions are one and all hypotheses which may be confirmed or discredited in actual sense experience' (A. J. Ayer, *Language, Truth and Logic*, London: Gollancz, 1936, p. 132).

C. In empirical research, an hypothesis is an assertion about some property of elements in the field of study. The hypothesis is deemed true or false depending upon whether or not the asserted property actually characterizes the elements.

1. There is disagreement among social scientists as to whether an empirical hypothesis should be formulated so as to be immediately testable or whether it is permissible to make use of relatively abstract constructs in the formulation. J. F. Brown, for example, states that abstract constructs are admissible to empirical hypotheses so long as the hypotheses yield predictions '... which may be tested in experiment. The constructs ... must be capable of operational definition' ('Topology and Hodological Space', in M. H. Marx (ed.), *Psychological Theory*, New York: The Macmillan Co., 1951, p. 236). Others believe that any assertion the constructs of which are too abstract to test directly is properly classified as an element of theory rather than as an empirical hypothesis. Thus, the assertion that intra-family tension varies inversely with social class level would comprise an empirical hypothesis, according to one viewpoint, but not according to the other.

2. C. A. Moser (*Survey Methods in Social Investigation*, London: Heinemann, 1958, p. 4) argues that 'in the narrower sense, implying the testing of a postulated relationship between two or more variables, the formulation of hypotheses is irrelevant to—and impossible for— many fact-collecting enquiries'.

D. In statistics the usual definition of an hypothesis is consistent with that found in the

Hypothesis

empirical sciences, although it is ordinarily employed in a somewhat more restricted manner. A statistical hypothesis is an assertion about one or more parameters of an empirical distribution function. Thus M. G. Kendall and A. Stuart (*The Advanced Theory of Statistics*, London: Griffin, 1958, vol. I, p. 202), 'Suppose (as is nearly always the case with statistical work) that the hypotheses with which we are concerned assert something about the numerical value of the parameter'.

Robert McGinnis

See also: EXPERIMENT

I

Id

A. *Id* is a term used in the study of the dynamics of personality and may be defined as a classificatory concept (or construct), or as a category comprehending all of those forms of behaviour or functions which are unconscious, undifferentiated, instinctive, infantile, primitive, unverbalized, a-moral, a-logical, not subject to rational control and those impulses which demand immediate gratification. The other two categories of functions or behaviour which make up the whole of the dynamics of personality are the ego and the superego.

B. 1. This term is primarily associated with psychoanalytic theory. Freud followed the example of Nietzsche and Groddeck (S. Freud, *The Ego and the Id*, trans. by J. Riviere, London: Hogarth Press, 1927, from the original, *Das Ich und das Es*, Vienna: Internationaler Psychoanalytischer Verlag, 1923) in his choice of the term *id*. He proposed that there were three provinces or agencies which constitute the psychical apparatus, i.e. the id, the ego, and the superego. The id is the oldest of these agencies, phylogenetically and ontogenetically; it is the great 'reservoir of libido', the container of all that is inherited or instinctive or fixed in the constitution of man. It is described as unconscious, primitive, infantile, undifferentiated, a-moral, a-logical, unaware of contradictions; as constituting the primary process (instinctual and physiological as contrasted with the secondary process of the ego); as operating on the pleasure principle (in contrast to the ego's reality principle); as containing repressed impulses; as a place where Eros and the death instinct struggle. The infant at birth is an id organism. For Freud and the orthodox psychoanalysts, ego develops out of id, under the influence of the external world through the processes of learning and socialization. In their literature id is referred to figuratively as a place or province, an entity, a storehouse, a foundation on which ego rests, a force. Always, however, it is an essentially dynamic concept as is indicated in the phrases, 'the power of the id', 'id impulses', the id as 'a cauldron of seething excitement', 'the cathexes (of the id) seeking discharge', 'the psychical processes of the id', 'the instincts of the id press for immediate satisfaction'.

2. Many social scientists and neo-Freudian psychoanalysts have avoided the use of the term while making constant references to those behaviours which are held by Freud to be functions of the id. This avoidance is due probably to a fear that the term breeds reification; that it has a mystical, or mythical, non-scientific aura; that it is too easily used with a pseudo-etiological reference. Others use the term with a consistent reference to functions, as 'id functions', 'id behaviours', 'id impulses'. J. B. Rotter (*Social Learning and Clinical Psychology*, New York: Prentice-Hall, 1954, p. 38) says, 'Terms such as *life instinct, the Id*, and *psychic energy*, since they are not directly observable or measurable, can never be satisfactorily defined unless they are accepted as constructs and not as endogenous entities'. The term is also used as a nosological label.

Dorothy W. Seago

See also: EGO
            SUPEREGO

Ideal-type Analysis

A. *Ideal-type analysis* denotes a method of sociological analysis the development of which is associated with the name of M. Weber (whose major methodological and sociological works have been partially translated as *The Methodology of the Social Sciences* by E. A. Shils & H. A. Finch, Glencoe, Ill.: The Free Press, 1949, and as *The Theory of Social and Economic Organisation* by A. R. Henderson and T. Parsons, ed. by T. Parsons, London: Hodge, 1947). Building on the foundations laid down by Dilthey and Rickert, ideal-type analysis as developed by Weber represents an extension of the basic methodology of analytical economics to sociology, and is comparable, though not exactly equivalent to the conception of '*exacte*' *Wirtschaftswissenschaft* advocated by C. Menger in his polemic against the historical school of economics (*Untersuchungen über die Methode der Sozialwissenschaften*, Leipzig: Verlag von Duncker & Humblot, 1883). The major charac-

311

Ideal-type Analysis

teristics of ideal-type analysis in the Weberian sense are as follows:

1. An ideal type is not ideal in an ethical sense; nor does it correspond to an 'average' type either in a statistical sense or in the sense of a common denominator of a number of empirical phenomena.

2. It is rather ideal in a logical sense. It is a freely created mental construct (*phantasie-massige Konstruktion*) by means of which an attempt is made to 'order' reality by isolating, accentuating, and articulating the elements of a recurrent social phenomenon (e.g. bureaucracy) into an internally consistent system of relationships.

3. One mode of accentuation (*Steigerung*) is the construction of a purely rational course of action (e.g. *homo oeconomicus*). But it is also possible to develop ideal types of less rational behaviour (e.g. *charismatic authority*).

4. By definition, ideal-type constructs (among which Weber listed the so-called 'materialistic conception of history') do not exhaust empirical reality; to think that they do is to be guilty of conceptual realism. Any given phenomenon (e.g. capitalism) permits of a multiplicity of ideal types depending on which elements are brought into focus.

5. An ideal-type construct performs two basic functions:

(a) It provides a limiting case with which concrete phenomena may be contrasted; an unambiguous concept by which classification and comparison is facilitated.

(b) As such, it constitutes a framework for the development of type generalizations (*Generelle Regeln des Geschehens, generelle Erfahrungsregeln*) which, in turn, serve the ultimate purpose of ideal-type analysis: the causal explanation of historical events.

6. Ideal types and type generalizations, though abstract and referring to social phenomena, must (a) be 'objectively possible', in the sense that concrete phenomena approximate more or less to the theoretically conceived pure type; (b) be 'subjectively meaningful' in the sense that the type of social action is understandable in terms of individual motivation.

Only ideal-type explanation that satisfies these two conditions can be considered adequate (on the level of causation and on the level of meaning).

B. Although there has been much criticism based on a misunderstanding of the method, A. von Schelting has drawn attention to one confusion in the Weberian usage ('Die logische Theorie der historischen Kulturwissenschaft von Max Weber und im besonderen sein Begriff des Idealtypus', *Archiv für Sozialwissenschaft*, vol. 49, 1922, pp. 623–752; *Max Webers Wissenschaftslehre*, Tübingen: J. C. B. Mohr (Paul Siebeck), 1934). He argues that Weber's ordinary usage of the term implies: (a) a one-sided exaggeration or accentuation of the elements of a phenomenon; (b) an abstract general conceptualization.

Both conditions are satisfied in the case of ideal types such as '*Charisma*', '*traditionalistische Wirtschaft*', '*Sekte*', '*Kirche*', '*Bureaukratie*'. They are supra-historical types in the sense that they refer to phenomena which recur in a variety of historical contexts. They are sociological or 'generalizing' concepts. But Weber also uses the term ideal type in connection with concepts such as '*mittelalterliche Stadtwirtschaft*', '*Urchristentum*', '*protestantische Wirtschaftsethik*', and '*antike Poliswirtschaft*'. These are not genuine ideal types since the abstract general quality is lacking. They are historical or 'individualizing' concepts in the sense that they sharpen our awareness of the uniqueness of the phenomena. They are historically relative types of 'historical individuals'. Therefore, von Schelting would confine the term *ideal type* to the first class of concepts.

The same difficulty arises in connection with Weber's use of the term *ideal-typical* to describe the construction of purely rational modes of action for the explanation of ad hoc situations (e.g. the course of a battle). Such 'ideal types' again lack the abstract general quality which is present, for example, in economic theory where similar models of rationalized action are employed in the analysis of *recurrent* situations (e.g. pricing) which are subsumable under types and type generalizations (see L. Robbins, *An Essay on the Nature and Significance of Economic Science*, London: Macmillan, 1932).

C. Usages similar to the Weberian *ideal type* have recently been worked out by (a) H. Becker who has advocated the use of the term *constructed type* in preference to that of *ideal type*. ('Constructive Typology in the Social Sciences', in *Contemporary Social Theory*, ed. by H. E. Barnes, H. Becker, & F. B. Becker, New York: Appleton-Century, 1940, pp. 17–46. See also the entry *Constructs* in this dictionary); and by (b) K. R. Popper, whose concept of *methodological individualism* (as opposed to methodological holism) is entirely in accordance with Weber's idea of a *verstehende Soziologie* (*The Poverty of Historicism*, London: Routledge & Kegan Paul, 1957).

D. The difficulties and ambiguities in the use of the term reflect methodological rather than terminological issues. In particular they have their origin in the problem of the logical status and function of concept formation in generalizing and historical disciplines. H. Rickert (*Die Grenzen der naturwissenschaftlichen Begriffsbildung*, (1902) Tübingen: Verlag von J. C. B. Mohr (Paul Siebeck), 1929), and T. Parsons (*The Structure of Social Action*, New York: McGraw-Hill, 1937), attempt to formulate from different points of view the wider context into which the Weberian usage (the development of which was dictated always by primarily heuristic considerations) fits.

D. Lockwood

See also: CONSTRUCTS

Idealism

A. *Idealism* can be sketched only against its background of positive inheritance and of controversy. The empiricist doctrine that the sole source of knowledge is passively accepted singular ideas which represent external things had collapsed before Hume's scepticism: if it were true we could never know it. Modern idealism starts with Kant (1724–1804), whose rejoinder to Hume effected the greatest revolution in the history of philosophy. Kant denied both that the mind accepts empirical ideas passively, and that such ideas are its sole source of knowledge. He held that, in knowing, the mind (the 'understanding') actively judges, i.e. determines, the empirically given as an object, and does so by virtue of certain necessary, universal, and a priori principles. These it knows because they constitute the structure at once of the mind and of its objective world. These principles are: (a) the identity of the self as the same subject in all its actual and possible experiences, (b) the categories, of which the most important is causation, and (c) the forms of space and time.

Without them there could be no coherent experience at all. But human knowledge is strictly limited, because our world of objects is not real and unconditioned but phenomenal and mechanically conditioned: each of its structural principles—space, time, causation, and the rest—begets an indefinite regress if you think it out. The knowable world is one, but it is not a genuine unity. It is only the appearance which the

unconditioned thing-in-itself, reality as it really is, somehow produces in our minds through our empirical sensations. It is the world par excellence of mathematical and physical knowledge.

How do we know that our objects are appearances of things-in-themselves? We do not know it, says Kant, but we inevitably think it. Besides our understanding with its constitutive categories we have reason, and reason possesses us with ideas of the unconditioned and with an ideal of it as a real unity. These indispensably regulate our understanding and its object-world, enabling us to recognize our limitations; but they constitute no object of knowledge.

Kant, having thus justified mathematics and physics, proceeded to develop this obviously ambiguous position in ethical and aesthetic systems, in a discussion of teleological concepts in biology and, late in life, in a theory of religion. His topic is everywhere reason. He never quite relinquishes the view that reason is purely regulative, but his new and profound treatment of all the main fields of human experience made an epoch in philosophy.

B. The supreme exponent of idealism was G. W. F. Hegel (1770–1830). His criticism of Kant provides the least misleading clue to his complex system: an idea or ideal which regulates without in any sense constituting is an absurdity. In some sense to recognize a limit is to know what is beyond it. Moreover, if the universal and necessary a priori forms constitute both the experiencing mind and the world of objects, the former must be something more than the mere singular finite mind which Kant had still assumed it to be. In knowing it as a mere singular, we must really be knowing it, as we know objects, only as appearance. If the phenomenal object implies an unconditioned thing-in-itself, equally the finite subject must imply a mind-in-itself. Since, too, finite mind and its object are a unity, unconditioned—or, as Hegel prefers to call it, absolute—mind and its absolute, unconditioned object are a unity, and the problem of knowledge, which Kant had treated as a problem of consciousness, is really a problem of self-consciousness.

Thus Hegel, as against Kant, holds that we have rational knowledge of intrinsic values, and that the ultimate criterion of all values is the Kantian 'unconditioned' reinterpreted as absolute mind manifesting itself, not merely as the quasi-unity of the indefinitely regressive scientific world (which is one only of its appearances), but as the coherent self-conditioning activity which

Identification

is the single theme differentiated in all the fields of human experience.

Philosophy will thus display the progress of finite mind rising to a fuller and fuller experience of this absolute activity, and display it as the development of human self-consciousness. But since, on the other side, absolute mind constitutes itself in and through the progressive expansion of finite mind, philosophy must present this progress primarily as the activity of absolute mind's self-manifestation. To solve this obviously difficult problem of presentation, Hegel began his system with a logic of categories, which he conceives, not with Kant as principles constituting merely finite mind and its scientific object-world, but as self-definitions in terms of pure thought of absolute mind embracing its object within itself. Hence among them there appear reconstructed not only Kant's categories but also his ideas of reason, and also many other principles drawn from all the great western philosophies of the past from Plato onwards. Hegel is almost as much an Aristotelian as a Kantian. His scholarship was wide and deep, and he claims to have included and developed the thought of all his important predecessors in his own system. It must at least be admitted that he has studied them profoundly and offered his own interpretation of them all.

This expansion of Kant's categories clearly entails a corresponding expansion and reinterpretation of the whole relation in Kant of a priori to empirical. Hegel in effect states it thus. Absolute mind, as the relatively abstract totality of pure thought in which logic culminates, manifests itself progressively—Hegel again presents its activity as dialectical—first in Nature from space and time to organism, and then as human experience from mere feeling and sensation to philosophy. In human experience the theme is the expansion of man's mind from singular individual through social and political life and 'world-history', and finally through aesthetic, religious, and philosophical experience, to a self-consciousness which is no longer merely finite-centred.

C. Hegel's successors borrowed very variously from the immense riches of his system, and there is space to mention only a few. The British idealists of the 19th and early 20th century (T. H. Green, F. H. Bradley, B. Bosanquet) battled with temporary success against native empiricism. In Germany and France the Hegelian idealists produced little of major importance. The main contribution of Italian

idealism, which still flourishes, was B. Croce's new and fruitful aesthetic doctrine and his identification of philosophy and history.

In an era of rapid social change it was natural that interest should concentrate on Hegel's conception of the spiritual reality of social and political institutions and on his world-history. In particular, his theory of the state as organic, largely inspired by Plato and Aristotle, has been a continual topic of controversy. It was in part a reaction against the atomic individualism of liberal thinkers, though certainly not its polar opposite—the theme of Hegel's world-history is the development of freedom—and Hegel has been charged with begetting Fascism and Nazism. On the other side, Marx absurdly caricatured Hegel's dialectic to bolster a determinist doctrine of social revolution, and some have tried to father communism on Hegel. In both cases he would have denied paternity with horror.

G. R. G. Mure

See also: EMPIRICISM

Identification

A. *Identification* denotes the tendency to imitate and/or the process of imitating the behaviour of an object. It may also denote the process of merging emotionally, or the state of having so merged, with the same object.

B. The term was introduced into psychology by S. Freud in 1899. At this stage Freud stated that '… identification is not simple imitation but *assimilation* on the basis of a similar aetiological pretension; it expresses a resemblance and is derived from a common element which remains in the unconscious' (*The Interpretation of Dreams*, trans. by J. Strachey, London: Allen & Unwin, 1954, p. 150). By similar and unconscious 'aetiological pretension' he meant that at least some identifications, i.e. the hysterical kind, are prompted by neuroses similar to those of the model. Later, in his *Group Psychology and the Analysis of the Ego* (1921), he proceeded to give a more comprehensive treatment to this subject. Here he speaks of three kinds or levels of identification, 'First, identification is the original form of emotional tie with an object; secondly, in a regressive way it becomes a substitute for a libidinal tie, as it were by means of the introjection of the object into the ego; and thirdly, it may arise with every new perception of a common quality shared with some other person who is not an object of the sexual instinct' (*Group Psychology and the Analysis of the Ego*, trans. by J. Strachey, London:

The International Psycho-Analytical Press, 1922, p. 65). N. Sanford tried to effect separation of the concepts of identification and imitation (q.v.) by calling the first an unconscious and the second a conscious process ('The Dynamics of Identification', *Psychological Review*, vol. 62, 1955, pp. 106–18), while J. P. Seward reunited the two concepts by defining identification 'as a generalized disposition to imitate the behaviour of a model. ...' ('Learning Theory and Identification', *Journal of Genetic Psychology*, vol. 84, 1954, p. 202).

It seems that the term's fluidity is even greater than this: 'The term is broad and ill-defined,' writes G. W. Allport, 'but it serves to convey the sense of emotional merging of oneself with others. One form of identification is indistinguishable from love and affection' (*The Nature of Prejudice*, Cambridge, Mass.: Addison-Wesley, 1954, p. 293). M. Scheler speaks of *idiopathic* and *heteropathic identification*; in the former, identification comes about 'through the total eclipse and absorption of another self by one's own ...' and in the latter the identifier 'is overwhelmed and hypnotically bound' by the model (*The Nature of Sympathy*, London: Routledge & Kegan Paul, 1954, pp. 18–19). The four prototypes of identification in psychoanalytical literature are these: (a) boy with father; (b) boy with mother; (c) girl with mother; (d) girl with father. According to S. Isaacs, 'The broad pattern, whether for the boy or girl, is laid down by heterosexual preferences' (*Social Development in Young Children*, London: Routledge, 1933, p. 303). In social psychology identification is sometimes used in a sense not directly connected with these prototypes, e.g. identification with the in-group, the dominant group, the oppressed group, and so on.

C. P. Halmos calls Freud's three types of identifications primary, secondary, and tertiary (*Solitude and Privacy*, London: Routledge & Kegan Paul, 1952, p. 4), and observes that there should be no difficulty in construing secondary and tertiary identifications as defence mechanisms which the Freudians have, in fact, done. But, in Freud's own showing, primary identification is pre-Oedipal: 'We may well ask, why should the son admire and imitate his father *before* the Oedipal phase? What imperative does the son obey when he attempts to model himself after his father? Unless the "sexual libido" is taken to mean a simple but comprehensive "life force" primary identification cannot be made to fit into the libido theory. Of course if such a meaning

was intended, the adjective "sexual" would not only become meaningless but also misleading' (ibid., p. 4). In the light of this we must distinguish *two* principal variants of identification: the *first* is an instrument, a mechanism of goal-seeking behaviour, i.e. a mechanism which ensures that the apparently successful goal-seeking behaviour of others will be unconsciously adopted, the *second* is an identification the goal of which is identification itself, the experience of merging, of communion through identity. In the latter sense *identification* may well be considered as a superfluous addition to our vocabulary for here identification is nothing but the social and cohesive function of life.

D. By extension the term has come to denote certain relationships of a person to social roles and social groups: 'One is said to identify with a social *role* if one not only internalizes the role but adopts it as one's own, striving to attain the necessary skills and to conform with the role norms. One is said to identify with a social *group* if one internalizes the role system of the group and considers oneself a member of it' (H. M. Johnson, *Sociology: A Systematic Introduction*, New York: Harcourt, Brace, 1960, p. 128).

P. Halmos

See also: IMITATION
INTERNALIZATION
INTROJECTION
SOCIALIZATION

Ideology

A. *Ideology* is a pattern of beliefs and concepts (both factual and normative) which purport to explain complex social phenomena with a view to directing and simplifying socio-political choices facing individuals and groups.

B. Such a general description does not pretend to explicate the many nuances of the term or to specify the variety of intellectual systems which have been styled ideologies, the different modes in which they have been legitimized, the internal balance between the ethical and factual components, etc. Some of the issues which arise may be gauged from attention both to the historical development of the term and some questions now current in sociology.

1. The term first appears to have been used in its basic sense of 'the study of ideas' by the Comte de Tracy at the very end of the 18th century. This usage as A. Lalande shows (*Vocabulaire technique et critique de la philosophie*, Paris: Felix Alcan, 1926, vol. I, p. 336)

315

Ideology

survived to be found in various French 19th-century writers. But almost at once the word acquired a pejorative meaning ('abstract and misleading ideas'). Thus Napoleon (in a speech in 1812 quoted in De Sade, *Lexicon politique*, Paris, 1837, vol. II, p. 95) contrasts the 'dark metaphysic' which is ideology with the 'knowledge of the heart and the lessons of history'. In so far as the term has a common persisting usage it is this pejorative one. Such a nuance is clearly what M. Oakeshott had in mind in his celebrated inaugural lecture 'Political Education' (reprinted in *Rationalism in Politics*, London: Methuen, 1962): 'A political ideology purports to be an abstract principle, or set of related abstract principles, which has been independently premeditated. It supplies in advance of the activity of attending to the arrangements of a society a formulated end to be pursued, and in so doing, it provides a means of distinguishing those ideas which ought to be encouraged and those which ought to be suppressed or redirected' (ibid., p. 116).

2. The term came to be used by Marxists—but with more than a tinge of ambiguity. The usage adopted by Marx and Engels is in the main governed by their concern with 'false consciousness'. They view ideologies as forms of false consciousness, i.e. as systems of distorted and misleading ideas based upon illusions—as contrasted with a 'scientific' theory or view. Thus Marx writes that ideology is consciousness of reality wherein 'men and their circumstances appear upside down as in a *camera obscura* ...' (K. Marx & F. Engels, *The German Ideology*, pts. I and III, ed. by R. Pascal, New York: International Publishers, 1939, p. 14).

Such systems may be the rules which govern or are built into e.g. moral behaviour, the work of a church, or a political or legal structure. They may also be thoughts or theories on such subjects or assessments of social situations or statements about social structure. They may also be belief systems which buttress such assessments or statements, and, as Marxists would put it, 'superstructures' i.e. class-determined or class-regulated 'mental' phenomena such as language or morals.

Marxist views on the 'scientific' quality of their theories imply that Marxist thought is not an ideology and does not give rise to ideologies in the above senses. The Marxist implies that the partisan, sectional character of Marxism will recede as Marxist anticipations are realized. Since it will, then, in a classless society, become universal in scope and acceptance, it already is a unique product of the mind—something which is both 'science' and 'ideology'.

Thus, latter-day Marxists, especially in the U.S.S.R. and the Soviet orbit, speak of e.g. 'improving the quality of ideological work', with, of course, no pejorative suggestions of 'false consciousness'.

3. This ambiguity in Marxist usage is reflected in the usage of the term *ideology* by K. Mannheim. In his *Ideology and Utopia* (London: Kegan Paul, Trench, Trubner, 1936, pp. 238–9) he writes, 'the study of ideologies has made it its task to unmask the more or less conscious deceptions and disguises of human interest groups ...' and goes on to discuss two types of falsity in observation and statement: (a) those which 'taking place on a psychological level structurally resemble lies' (these are what he calls 'particular ideologies'); (b) perspectives or 'total ideologies'—'mental structures in their totality', a man's 'whole mood of conceiving things as determined by his historical and social setting'.

Thus, as D. G. MacRae has observed, the most frequent sense of *ideology* has come to be 'both the distortion of thought by interest—public or private, consciously or unconsciously known—and the study of such distortion ... non-ideological thinking is thought to be impossible' (*Ideology and Society*, London: Heinemann, 1961, p. 64). Macrae goes on to comment upon the problems of objectivity which this notion of distortion provokes and to discuss Mannheim's further distinction between ideology and utopia. 'For myself I believe that under certain not uncommon circumstances judgments which are in no important sense ideologically distorted are perfectly possible—and, indeed, frequent' (ibid., p. 65).

4. Of interest too is the use of the word by H. Arendt, i.e. 'Ideologies aimed at total explanation ... by the application of a single idea to the various realms of reality' (*Totalitarianism*, ed. by C. J. Friedrich, Cambridge, Mass.: Harvard University Press, 1954, p. 133). In an earlier paper ('Ideology and Terror: A Novel Form of Government', in *Review of Politics*, vol. XV, 1953, p. 303) Miss Arendt emphasized not only the element of 'falsity' and the 'normative element' in ideologies but also the 'explanatory' function assigned to them within certain abstract and deductive systems of social thought.

C. Political sociologists and theorists have of late been debating what has been called 'the end of ideology' in advanced industrial societies. The target has been the belief patterns which have supported extremist and totalitarian political movements. The aim has been to trace the decline of enthusiasm for such patterns among intellectuals against the background of economic growth and social change (see E. Shils, 'The End of Ideology?' *Encounter*, vol. V, Nov. 1955, p. 52, et seq., especially p. 57; S. M. Lipset, *Political Man*, London: Heinemann, 1960, p. 403, et seq.; D. Bell, *The End of Ideology*, Glencoe, Ill.: The Free Press, 1960, passim). Thus Shils warns against the construction of 'new ideologies, as rigid, as eager for consistency and for universal observance as those which have been now transcended' ('The End of Ideology?', p. 57); Bell observes that 'we have witnessed an exhaustion of the nineteenth century ideologies, particularly Marxism, as intellectual systems that could claim *truth* for their views of the world' (*The End of Ideology*, p. 16).

Critics of this approach have been quick to impute 'conservatism' to its authors. This is as firmly denied. Bell argues that 'a repudiation of ideology, to be meaningful, must mean not only a criticism of the utopian order but of existing society as well' (ibid., p. 16). And answering his critics, S. M. Lipset explicitly states that he does not 'favor a decline in political interest or in reform movements' (*Political Man*, New York: Anchor Books edn., 1963). Indeed, both Lipset and Shils expressly point to the functions of existing ideological movements in new states. Their critique is reserved for political extremism and messianism in advanced societies. It is against this context that the view of M. Ginsberg may be set. Commenting on the theme of 'the end of ideology' he urges a distinction between what he calls 'open' and 'closed' ideologies. By 'closed' ideologies he has in mind 'self-contained systems demanding all or none commitment, of the kind demanded by, for example, Bolshevist communism'. He denies that 'the ideas underlying liberalism, conservatism, socialism in its non-Marxist varieties' form ideologies in this sense. They are 'open' in that 'they are often criticised from within and that they also learn from each other. If, as a result, they recognize their onesidedness, and discover areas of agreement this may indicate not exhaustion but healthy advance' ('Facts and Values', *The Advancement of Science*, vol. XIX, 1962, p. 12).

J. Gould

See also: CLASS-CONSCIOUSNESS

Illiterate (See Nonliterate)

Imitation

A. Paraphrasing and amplifying the definition of E. G. Boring, H. S. Langfeld, and H. P. Weld (*Introduction to Psychology*, New York: Wiley, 1939, pp. 12–13), *imitation* may be said to denote the conscious or unconscious attempt of an individual to reproduce in his thought or behaviour the same pattern of thought or behaviour that he has perceived in another individual, and the outcome of the attempt, successful or unsuccessful.

B. Imitation has an important place in the history of social-psychological thought, since, together with suggestion (q.v.), it serves as the basic concept during the transition from stress on instinct (q.v.) as the source of human behaviour to learning (q.v.) and culture (q.v.) as the source of such behaviour. Today, however, the concept has been largely replaced by such ideas as socialization (q.v.), acculturation (q.v.), and internalization (q.v.). It remains, however, as a term designating a process of behaviour much more limited in scope and significance, a process that is important only as it serves as *one* of the bases for the more inclusive and central processes which bring the individual into membership in the social group.

The original significance of *imitation* as a concept linking the individual on the one hand and society and culture on the other, and its gradually diminishing importance may be briefly traced in the works of such writers as G. Tarde, J. M. Baldwin, and G. H. Mead (cf. G. W. Allport, 'The Historical Background of Modern Social Psychology', in G. Lindzey (ed.), *Handbook of Social Psychology*, Cambridge, Mass.: Addison-Wesley, 1954, vol. 1, pp. 21–3). For Tarde, imitation, together with *opposition* and *adaptation*, was the key to social life (*The Laws of Imitation* (1st Fr. edn., 1890), trans. by E. C. Parons, New York: Henry Holt, 1903). In the case of Baldwin the situation is somewhat more complex. Imitation is for him the '*true type of social function*', but its significance for social life cannot be understood without knowing what it is that is susceptible to imitation so that it is fixed as social habit and progressively modified so as to constitute social progress (*Social and Ethical Interpretations in Mental Development*, New York: The Macmillan Company, 3rd edn., 1902, pp. 495–7). The 'matter' of imitation, in Baldwin, is thought, and thought has its origin not in imitation, but in the situation of the thinker; and of thought that which is socially most important is the person's thought

Imperialism

about himself and others in a social situation (ibid., pp. 506–9). In this formulation, attention is shifted from the process of imitation to the interaction of participants in a social situation as this interaction relates to the increasingly shared and situationally modified thoughts of self-and-other: 'Objective social relationships are the objective manifestations to the on-looker of a common self-thought-situation in the different individuals, together with the movements of its growth in each as the imme-diate situation calls it out' (ibid., p. 511). This transition completes itself in the work of G. H. Mead who concentrates his attention on the de-velopment of the self (q.v.) in the social situation and who speaks of role-taking and role-playing as the primary processes of internalization, rather than imitation. In Mead's thought imita-tion is extremely reduced in its significance (*Mind, Self, and Society*, Chicago: University of Chicago Press, 1934, pp. 58–9).

C. According to G. W. Allport, at least five mechanisms may be involved in imitation: (a) motor mimicry or empathy, (b) classical condi-tioning, (c) instrumental conditioning, (d) cog-nitive structuring, including deliberate copying and insightful reproduction, and (e) identifica-tion ('The Historical Background of Modern Social Psychology', p. 25). It is interesting to note that this understanding of imitation itself reflects the shift from instinct to learning, for at least four of these five mechanisms involve learning, not only as the outgrowth of imitation but as the basis of imitation (cf. N. E. Miller & J. Dollard, *Social Learning and Imitation*, New Haven: Yale University Press, 1941).

From this it may be said that imitation de-notes *any* attempt to be like, or behave or appear like, a particular other person (model) in some specific respect or in all respects, *and* the out-come of such attempts regardless of their suc-cess or failure. Thus imitation is a broader con-cept than that of copying, since imitation does not necessarily reproduce a replica of the ori-ginal. Further, while it sometimes stems from identification, it need not do so, since identifica-tion suggests an emotional relationship with the model and a desire to take in its standards and become like it because of that emotional rela-tionship. The outcome of the process of imita-tion need not be successful, because so much de-pends on perception and on the individual's own abilities and resources. Since, therefore, imita-tion is not always recognizable as such, and

since the model is not always present or obvious, perhaps imitation should be seen essentially as an inner state, i.e. as the attempt to take over some feature of thought or behaviour of another person.

Whereas the behaviour of the model usually has some purpose or reward other than that of functioning as a model, the imitator's gratifica-tion frequently comes from a sense of achieve-ment and of coming closer to the admired model, from whom he may receive praise or reward. In these cases, only later will the new learning be purposefully employed. By then, the behaviour or attitude is no longer imitative, but has become part of the person's own repertoire: thus, since imitation is part of the social learning process, when learning has become mastery, we no longer speak of imitation.

A. N. Oppenheim

See also: ACCULTURATION
INTERNALIZATION
LEARNING
ROLE
SELF
SOCIALIZATION
SUGGESTION

Immigration (See Migration)

Immunity (See Privilege)

**Imperfect Competition
(See Economic Competition)**

Imperialism

A. It is possible to distinguish five uses of the word, which follow one another in historical sequence and are broadly connected:

1. Its basic usage is to describe the rule of an emperor, especially when despotic or arbitrary. In this sense we might speak of imperialism as the system of government of the Roman Em-pire, or, in modern times, the French, Austro-Hungarian, and German Empires.

2. In the 1870s and 1880s, the word gained currency in Britain and the self-governing col-onies to describe the policy of preserving the interests of the British Empire. An Imperialist was a man who approved of the British Empire and of its extension, and who wished to see it more united. In his view, there was a distinction between other empires, past and present, which were essentially authoritarian and exploitative, and the British Empire, which was beneficent and spread political freedom. This usage—the only one in which the term *imperialist* was used in self-description—lingered well into the 20th century but is hardly ever encountered today.

3. However, at about the same time, the word came to be used to describe the general extension of European territorial control in Africa and Asia which took place in the 1880s and 1890s, whether that control was British, French, or German, and the extension of American control into Latin-American states and the Philippines. Imperialism in this sense was often held to be occasioned by economic motives; but J. A. Hobson, whose *Imperialism* (London: Nisbet, 1902) was an influential expression of this view, recognized that the 'three Ps'—Pride, Pugnacity, and Prestige—also had their place as motive-forces.

4. A more recent, and perhaps the most influential, use of the word is in communist phraseology. Here the use dates from V. I. Lenin's *Imperialism, the Highest Stage of Capitalism* (1916). Lenin gave the word a special technical meaning, fitting it into the scheme of Marxist thought. Imperialism to him was 'the monopoly stage of capitalism', with five basic features: '(1) The concentration of production and capital, developed to such a high stage that it had created monopolies which play a decisive role in economic life. (2) The merging of bank capital with industrial capital and the creation, on the basis of this "finance-capital", of a financial oligarchy. (3) The export of capital, as distinguished from the export of commodities, becomes of particularly great importance. (4) International monopoly combines of capitalists are formed which divide up the world. (5) The territorial division of the world by the greatest capitalist powers is completed' (New York: International Publishers, 1933, p. 81). It will be seen that Lenin made the territorial division of the world by the great powers the *last* of his five features, although other writers on imperialism had seen it as the most notable feature of the process; to Lenin this aspect was not so important as the fact (to him) that imperialism was the moribund stage of capitalism. In this stage, he considered, capitalism was temporarily able to sustain itself by plundering foreign lands, through either political control or economic domination. It was able to buy off some working-class leaders by a falsely high standard of living, based upon exploitation of peoples; but the situation would inevitably lead to war between the capitalist powers, as the division of the world became complete. Imperialism as an historical phenomenon is thus seen to be wholly economic. Its essence is not the seizure of territory but the extension of the power of finance-capital. Later communist writers have identified as 'imperialist' every country hostile to the Soviet Union.

5. The most recent use is to apply the word very generally to the control of one state by another. For example, it is sometimes said that Russian control of East European countries is 'Russian imperialism', or that 'Chinese imperialism' has been extended over Tibet. This is a return to uses (1) and (3) above. When used against Communist Russia and China, it can be regarded as an attempt at a tu quoque, in order to combat the propaganda effect of the Communist usage when applied to such countries as Britain or the U.S.A.

B. Imperialism is now a discredited word and a term of abuse. Hardly anyone would now call *himself* an imperialist, although the late 19th-century use described in (3) above, lingered well into the 20th century. If a Communist says that Britain and the U.S.A. are practising imperialism, he means that, as monopoly capitalist countries, they are fulfilling their nature by subduing foreign countries to their control. When an Indian or an Indonesian speaks of British or Dutch imperialism, he may mean much the same (since diluted Leninism provided much of the theoretical background for anti-imperialist movements between the wars); but he will probably be thinking more of territorial control than of economic penetration, and he is more likely now to use the term *colonialism* (*q.v.*). When an Englishman or American speaks of imperialism, he means the process of a country imposing its will on other countries; he may say that it was something which his own country did in the past, but he would not consider it to be a feasible or proper policy now.

J. D. B. Miller

See also: Colonialism
　　　　　 Empire

Impersonal

The term *impersonal* is rarely specifically defined, but appears in many combinations as a qualifying adjective. It is used most characteristically in the description and analysis of secondary groups and relations, associations, and mass phenomena, and is frequently associated with such adjectives as *formal, secular* (*q.v.*), *rational, specialized, casual*, and the like. Its core meaning may be deduced from its use in such contexts.

The primary reference of the term is to social

Imports

phenomena and relationships that do not attach uniquely to a particular individual and in which, therefore, the individual is easily replaceable. K. Davis says, 'One party may be substituted for another without affecting the relationship' (*Human Society*, New York: The Macmillan Co., 1949, p. 302). This core meaning has three correlated referents:

1. *Impersonal* refers to social relations that are unusually devoid of emotion and in which only a segment or fraction of the personality of the participant is involved. Some writers see the result of such relations to be a failure to become human, e.g. E. Faris writes, 'The more completely, the relations are mechanized, the more fractional the contacts become and the less effective in generating the sentiments which are distinctly human' ('The Primary Group: Essence and Accident', *American Journal of Sociology*, vol. XXXVIII, 1932–3, p. 46).

2. *Impersonal* refers to social relations that maximize the treatment of persons as means rather than ends. K. Davis states, 'Such contacts do not necessarily imply any identity of ends between the parties concerned, any interest in the other party as an end in himself, any conception of the relationship as an end in itself, or any sentiment whatever attaching to the contact' (*Human Society*, p. 302).

3. *Impersonal* refers to social relations that are formal, indirectly mediated or briefly face-to-face, and specialized; E. Chinoy notes that some 'relationships ... tend to be formal and impersonal ... with clearly formulated rules frequently governing the behaviour of members' (*Sociological Perspective*, New York: Random House, 1954, pp. 34–5), while H. Bonner believes that 'impersonality and specialization isolate man from his fellows and heighten his insecurity' (*Social Psychology*, New York: American Book Co., 1953, p. 379).

Joseph S. Himes

See also: GROUP
       PERSONAL

Implicit Cost (See Cost)

Implicit Culture (See Covert Culture)

Imports
A. 1. In its oldest meaning the term denotes tangible products brought into a country from abroad. This definition has been refined, however, because of the need of the Customs administrator who is concerned largely with the question of *which* of the goods brought into a country really become imports, and *when* they become imports. As used in the tabulations made by the U.S. Bureau of the Census and by comparable agencies in many other countries, 'merchandise imports' are regarded as being synonymous with *general imports*, which include goods intended for immediate consumption plus entries into bonded warehouses. The statistics of such imports are usually derived from the declarations of valuations or appraisals of merchandise coming into the country. Much less accurate, of course, are the records relating to such 'less visible' items as payments for freight and shipping, travel expenditures, remittances to friends and relatives, and interest and dividends.

Various port authorities and related organizations consider, as do the governmental agencies, import by vessel as representing *general imports*, that is, the total of imports for immediate consumption plus entries into Customs bonded storage and manufacturing warehouses. Usually, however, they do not include in their import figures the incoming shipments on vessels *owned* and *operated* by the armed forces. Import shipments on vessels *chartered* by these organizations are included. Not included are the arrivals of cargo in transit under bond to a third country.

2. A more extensive meaning of the term follows the viewpoint of the student of international economics whose primary regard for imports and exports concerns their relation to the international balance of payments defined as the summary of the money value of all exchanges and transfers of goods, services, and evidences of debt or ownership between a nation and the rest of the world for a given period of time.

Debit entries are made in the balance of payments for any transactions that give rise to claims for payment, during the time for which the balance is drawn up, against a resident, business, institution, or the government of the country by anyone outside the country.

(a) Two classes of these debit items are specifically designated as imports: *commodity imports* and *service imports*. *Service imports* include, prominently, payments for tourist expenditures; shipping and freight services rendered by foreign vessels; insurance, banking, and brokerage services received from foreign concerns; expenditures abroad by governmental agencies for diplomatic, consular, and other functions; and interest and dividend payments to foreign holders of domestic bonds, stocks, or other assets which yield interest or income.

(b) Gold is also regarded as an import whether brought into a country as an industrial raw material or as a medium of international payment. Irrespective of its function or purpose, an inflow of gold, like any other import, is a debit transaction in the balance of payments.

(c) Not so clearly identified with imports is an important group of debit transactions associated with the purchase of evidences of debt or ownership from foreigners, although at the time the purchases are made such transactions are, of themselves, debit transactions. Nevertheless, they are primarily representative of the flow of international money capital rather than of the flow of goods and services. This differentiation is concretely provided for by the first two of the major categories of the balance of payments: the current account and the capital account. Such a distinction is of course consonant with the increased interest in capital flow as a 'sustainer' of international trade.

B. In a day when the balance of payments condition of most countries is such a crucial determinant of trade and economic relations, both in the national and international spheres, there is a markedly increased tendency to view imports with an eye towards accentuating their balance of payments importance (definitions and classifications from this perspective are set forth by P. T. Ellsworth, *The International Economy*, New York: Macmillan, 1958; D. A. Snider, *Introduction to International Economics*, Homewood, Ill.: Irwin, 1958; and other writers in the field of international economics). The character of a country's balance of payments is determined to a much larger extent by the status of the service items than by movements of merchandise. The service items fluctuate from year to year and respond to the varying economic conditions and stimuli in a given country, whereas the merchandise pattern is less flexible. This further favours the definition of imports in such a way as to include *service imports* as well as *merchandise* or *commodity imports*, and their separate designations as such, in view of the traditional meaning attached to the general term, *imports*.

Similarly, with respect to imports as regarded by Customs authorities and other agencies interested in practical distinctions which serve the purpose of quantitative measurement of amounts of imports and their valuation, specific designa-

tions appear to be unavoidable if not thoroughly supportable. The development of specific designations calls for the use of such descriptive terms as *general imports*, *consumption imports*, and *bonded imports*.

Bernard F. Sliger
Hubert Bice

See also: BALANCE OF PAYMENTS
EXPORTS

Incentive

A. The term is a synonym for reward (q.v.), motivation (q.v.), goal (q.v.). In general it tends to be used, in all the social sciences except economics, less frequently than the other terms and also to be used more loosely. In a manner similar to *motivation* but not the other terms cited above, it can be used to denote the goal or end of action or the drive or tendency to act aroused by that goal or both in relation to one another.

B. The word is encountered more frequently in economics and sometimes in political thinking related to economic phenomena than it is in the other social sciences. It tends to be used as a synonym for motivation to do work, and is used particularly to denote the motivation of entrepreneurs and of workers. In both cases, historically, *the incentive* was assumed to be material reward: in the one case profit in the other wages (cf. C. A. Hickman & M. H. Kuhn, *Individuals, Groups, and Economic Behavior*, New York: Dryden, 1956). Social science research has shown that this is an oversimplified conception of incentive; that profit can hardly be a motive at all, but rather is an institutionalized imperative of important but not unlimited significance for the business enterprise; that modern managers can be motivated by a great range of incentives; and that workers are probably more motivated by factors other than increases in monetary income. That such shifts in theories of economic motivation do not necessarily destroy all arguments for a market economy is shown by the work of H. C. Wallich (*The Cost of Freedom: A New Look at Capitalism*, New York: Harper & Brothers, 1960) who combines a sophisticated analysis of incentives with an argument for a competitive economy as the cost of freedom.

William L. Kolb

See also: GOAL
MOTIVATION
PUNISHMENT
REWARD

Incest

Incest

A. *Incest* may be defined as heterosexual relations between members of the nuclear family and, by extension, between family members beyond the nuclear family.

1. In sociology and psychology the term is confined to heterosexual relations between members of the nuclear family. In anthropology alone a wider definition has been attempted, one which either conforms with local custom within a particular group, or one which is variable depending on local custom. Although it is true that psychoanalytic psychology and sociology tend to deal primarily with western European culture, where the definition of incest is customarily narrow, there are other reasons why such a definition may have special utility or disutility in terms of the specific problems dealt with by sociologist and psychologist. There can be no arbitrary resolution of this difference on a priori grounds.

2. There can be, however, a useful separation within the definition of incest such as will permit the articulation of sociological, psychological, and anthropological endeavour. This has been attempted in the definition set forth. By use of this definition, extensions can be treated separately from incest among nuclear family members until it is demonstrated in fact that these are of the same or different order of phenomena.

3. One special question which arises from this and other definitions usually employed is their specification or implicit reference to *heterosexual* relations. There appears to be insufficient evidence available at present to rule *homosexual* relations outside the definition of incest, or to consider it as of the same order as heterosexual relations. But the problem remains to be considered and must not be arbitrarily included or excluded by definition alone.

B. 1. In psychoanalytic psychology incest tends to be treated primarily in terms of its role as a wish which each growing child must cope with and learn to control, and the persistence of this wish in the unconscious. Specifically, the wish is directed by the child towards its parent or sibling of the opposite sex. It is on the basis of the Oedipus complex, allegedly universal sexual desire of the son for the mother and his sexual conflict with the father figure, that Freud has erected a theory of culture and religion. From being considered this fundamental creative and destructive force in orthodox psychoanalytic theory, the incestuous wish ranges down to the point of being one among other important problems with which the maturing child must grapple.

2. In sociology, the concern is rather with the actual occurrences of sexual relations than with the wish and is generally viewed against the background or normative family regulations which prohibit this activity. Its occurrence can then be taken as an index of family disorganization, or it can be examined to discover the conditions under which it tends to occur (S. Riemer, 'A Research Note on Incest', *American Journal of Sociology*, vol. XLV, 1939–40, pp. 566–75). Here, as in psychoanalytic psychology, it tends to be defined as sexual relations between opposite-sexed members of the nuclear family.

3. In anthropology, the definition of incest has tended to vary both as a reflection of the very different types of societies dealt with and in terms of the very different types of problems of concern to the anthropologist. The primary concern of the anthropologist has been with the *incest taboo*—the prohibition of sexual relations among members of the consanguine family, lineage (q.v.), or other kinship group—and with attempts to explain it.

(a) The earliest concern with incest came with the observation that exogamy rules were frequently, though not invariably, supported by the sanction of the prohibition against incest. The incest taboo was seen, by E. B. Tylor, for instance, to have played a critical role in the evolution of culture, for until in-group marriage was prohibited there could be no development of a wider society through alliances created by affinality ('On a Method of Investigating the Development of Institutions', *Journal of the Royal Anthropological Institue*, vol. 18, 1889, pp. 264–9). The prohibition on incestuous marriage was thus seen essentially in the context of exogamy, and the boundary of the exogamous group was seen as co-terminous with the group within which the incest taboo operated. In this context incest could be defined as '... illicit sexual relationship between persons within the degrees of consanguinity excluded from such relationship by socially determined regulations' (R. Fortune, 'Incest', in E. R. A. Seligman (ed.), *Encyclopedia of the Social Sciences*, New York: The Macmillan Co., 1932, vol. 7, p. 620).

(b) Although most anthropologists agree with the importance of the incest taboo in its relation to exogamy, theoretical explanations of this relationship have varied widely.

(i). One of the oldest theories, espoused, for

example, by L. H. Morgan, was that the taboo grew out of the effort to prevent biological deterioration (*Ancient Society*, New York: Henry Holt, 1877, pp. 69, 378, 424). Closely related to Morgan's theory and equally dubious is that of E. Westermarck who also saw incest as biologically harmful and prevented by the development of instinctive aversion based on familiarity (*The History of Human Marriage*, London: Macmillan, 1921, ch. 20). (ii). A group of theories stress the potentialities of internal disruption of the family through incest. Among the older theories together with that of Freud, are those of B. Z. Seligman and R. Briffault, the former stressing prohibitions established by both father and mother, the latter, prohibitions established by the mother (B. Z. Seligman, 'Incest and Descent, Their Influence on Social Organization', *Journal of the Royal Anthropological Institute*, vol. 59, 1929, pp. 231–72; R. Briffault, *The Mothers*, London: Allen & Unwin, 1927, 3 vols.). Still important is the functional theory of B. Malinowski, which realizes the importance of extended kinship relations but simultaneously stresses the disruptive possibilities of intra-family sexuality ('Culture', in *Encyclopedia of the Social Sciences*, 1935, vol. 4, p. 630). Finally, W. La Barre has used Freudian theory to explain both the incest taboo and exogamy (*The Human Animal*, Chicago: University of Chicago Press, 1954).

David M. Schneider

See also: ENDOGAMY
TABOO

Incest Taboo (See **Incest**)

Income (See **National Product**)

Independent Variable (See **Variable**)

Index

A. An *index* is a measure or sign of a concept, based on a set of observations. The index is often stated as a number (e.g. a ratio or a weighted average). Webster's *New International Dictionary* (1956) sums up much current usage by defining index as a 'ratio or other number derived from a series of observations and used as an indicator or measure of a certain condition'.

B. More than half a century ago, E. Durkheim, noting that a particular concept (social solidar-ity) which he wished to measure 'does not lend itself to exact observation nor indeed to measurement', says, 'we must substitute for this internal fact which escapes us an external index which symbolizes it and study the former in the light of the latter'; he chooses law as 'this visible symbol' (*The Division of Labor in Society*, trans. by G. Simpson, New York: The Macmillan Co., 1933, p. 64). R. K. Merton, following this classic formulation, defines *index* as a 'sign of the conceptualized item', which 'stands ideally in a one-to-one correlation with what it signifies' (*Social Theory and Social Structure*, Glencoe, Ill.: The Free Press, rev. edn., 1957, p. 115). And C. F. Schmid refers to an *index* as 'a relatively simple and readily observable phenomenon that is used to measure relatively complex and less readily observable phenomena. The things that are used as measures of the characteristic are either part of the characteristic or things that have some consistent relation to it' (in P. V. Young, *Scientific Social Surveys and Research*, Englewood Cliffs, N.J.: Prentice-Hall, 1956, p. 425). In this generic sense the term has been widely used in the social sciences, often intended as closely similar to such other words as *measure*, *score*, or *scale*.

C. Many writers underscore the distinction between direct and indirect measurement, employing the term *index* or *indicant* only for the latter. S. S. Stevens, for example, defines *indicant* as 'a presumed effect or correlate bearing an unknown ... relation to some underlying phenomenon', as distinct from 'a scaled value of the phenomenon itself' ('Mathematics, Measurement, and Psychophysics', *Handbook of Experimental Psychology*, ed. by S. S. Stevens, New York: Wiley, 1951, p. 48). The textbook by M. J. Hagood and D. O. Price, emphasizing that an index measures '*indirectly* the incidence of a characteristic that is not directly measurable', cites the number of rooms in a dwelling as an index of the occupant's economic status (*Statistics for Sociologists*, New York: Henry Holt, 1952, p. 138). The distinction between direct and indirect measures does not seem water-tight, however, since, as J. P. Guilford early pointed out, 'all measurements [including physical measurements] are indirect in one sense or another' (*Psychometric Methods*, New York: McGraw-Hill, 1936, p. 3).

D. A distinction is also commonly made between *simple indexes* which employ a single item or observation, and *composite indexes*, which use

Indifference Curve

multiple items that, on combination, yield the total measure, P. F. Lazarsfeld and M. Rosenberg call the single observation an *indicator*, reserving *index* for the combination of several indicators in one measurement. 'This means', they say, 'that we think of each indicator as a dimension in geometrical space. Each "element" is a point in this space. An index then is a rule according to which various points will be considered equivalent' (*The Language of Social Research*, Glencoe, Ill.: The Free Press, 1955, p. 16). When several indicators (or items) are combined, some authors apply the term *index* exclusively to arbitrary procedures for combining the items, using some other term (e.g. *scaling* (q.v.) for methods which involve a test for internal consistency of the items. L. Guttman, for example, speaks of the assignment of 'arbitrary weights' and the addition of 'these weights to obtain a total score which can be called an *index* ('Relation of Scalogram Analysis to Other Techniques', in S. A. Stouffer et al. (eds.), *Measurement and Prediction*, Princeton, N.J.: Princeton University Press, 1950, p. 174).

E. The term *index number*, as widely used in economics, is defined in *A Dictionary of Economics* (ed. by H. S. Sloan & A. J. Zurcher, New York: Barnes & Noble, 1949) as 'a figure which discloses the relative change, if any, of prices, costs, or some similar phenomena between one period of time and some other period of time selected as the base period. The latter period is usually assigned the index number 100'. Index numbers have been applied to commodity prices, wages, interest rates, business activity, industrial and agricultural production, etc.

Several authorities stress the difference between a *relative* or *variation*, which refers to a term in a single time series, and an *index number* as 'an average of relatives or variations'. F. C. Mills says, 'Though the term index number has been applied to such relatives it is better practice to reserve the term for figures which represent the combination of a number of series'. As an example, he cites the construction of an index number representing fuel consumption in a given year by averaging the relative representing coal consumption with the relative representing oil consumption (*Statistical Methods*, New York: Henry Holt, 1924, pp. 162–3).

Matilda White Riley

See also: SCALING
      VARIABLE

Index Number (See **Index**)

324

Indifference Curve

A. The term *indifference curve* was coined by F. Y. Edgeworth (*Mathematical Psychics*, London: Kegan Paul, 1881, pp. 21, 29) and used in the field of economics to indicate the geometrical locus of points representing collections of goods and services that are equally desirable to an individual consumer. It has been employed infrequently but with the same meaning by psychologists.

B. 1. The indifference curve as the geometrical counterpoint of collections of goods and services yielding equal satisfactions to a consumer is derived from the assumption that the consumer can distinguish and compare satisfactions arising from different collections of goods and services. He is thus able to rank the various collections of goods and services within his purview in the order of their desirability, and it is an easy inference that the consumer can recognize equally desirable collections of goods and services.

The formulation giving rise to indifference curves can be envisioned by imagining a three-dimensional axis system with the quantities of two goods measured on the axes in the horizontal plane, and utility measured on the vertical axis. This space is occupied by a utility surface, rising from the origin, whose height at any point indicates the utility of the corresponding point in the horizontal plane. If the utility surface is cut in such a way that each point on the cut has the same height or utility as any other point on the cut, the points directly below each point on the cut and in the horizontal plane represen collections of goods that are equally satisfactory to the consumer. The curve traced out in the horizontal plane by equally satisfactory collections of goods is called an indifference curve. Hence by using projections of such cuts in the horizontal plane, it is possible to abandon the three-dimensional diagram in favour of the two-dimensional horizontal plane or indifference map. Since the utility surface can be cut at any height, every point in the indifference map belongs to an indifference curve (cf. J. R. Hicks, *Value and Capital*, Oxford: Clarendon Press, 1939, pp. 17–18).

In a more general case, we postulate a utility or preference equation, $U = U(x_1, ..., x_n)$, where U represents the preference level or satisfaction and the xs represent the various goods. This equation corresponds to the utility surface. Then by setting the equation equal to a constant, we obtain values of the xs representing equally satisfactory collections of goods and services.

2. An important property of indifference curves is that they do not rely on measurable utility but only on the consumer's ranking of the various collections of goods and services. Thus the utility surface can be stretched or contracted without distributing the rankings of the collections and the preference function can be transformed monotonically without disturbing the rankings of the collections. Hence, no particular utility scale is necessary; 'Literally nothing is implied for empirical price behavior by the choice of any particular utility index' (P. A. Samuelson, *Foundations of Economic Analysis*, Cambridge, Mass.: Harvard University Press, 1947, p. 104).

R. W. Pfouts

See also: UTILITY

Individual

A. The noun *individual* is a synonym for *person* or *human being*. As an adjective, *individual* denotes that the object modified is single, separate, distinguishable, as in *the individual human being*.

B. 1. In social science literature the word *individual* has lost its original meaning of 'indivisible', and is used as a synonym for *person* or *single human being*. As L. Von Wiese and H. Becker point out (*Systematic Sociology*, New York: Wiley, 1932, p. 83), 'We do not wish to assert that the single human being is indivisible, but rather that he is unique or singular; we should, therefore, really say "singular" instead of "individual" '. It is as an equivalent of *singularity* that *individual* is used by almost every social psychologist and sociologist, K. Young (*Social Psychology*, New York: Appleton-Century-Crofts, 1956) clearly equates 'individual' to 'single human being' and to 'person', e.g. 'older, more powerful, wiser individual ...', and 'older, wiser, and more powerful person'. The same use is made of the term by nearly all other writers in the field.

2. A slight departure from this use is found in R. E. Park & E. W. Burgess, *Introduction to the Science of Sociology* (Chicago: University of Chicago Press, 1922, p. 55), who write that 'The person is an individual who has status. We come into this world as individuals. We acquire status, and become persons'. However, in the following paragraph and elsewhere in the book, the term *individual* is used as a synonym for *person*. Similar to this use is H. D. Lasswell's 'Person, Personality, Group, Culture' (in P. Mullahy (ed.), *A Study of Interpersonal Relations*, New York: Hermitage Press, 1949, p. 319), 'A person is an individual who identifies himself with others'. But here, as in the case of the Park–Burgess use of the term, Lasswell uses *person* synonymously with *individual* throughout the remainder of the article.

Richard Dewey

See also: PERSONALITY SYSTEM

Individualism

A. *Individualism* denotes (a) a political theory which, by emphasizing property rights as a necessary condition of liberty, seeks to set definite and circumscribed limits to the regulatory powers vested in the Government over social and economic processes; (b) the belief that the individual is an end in himself, and as such ought to realize his 'self' and cultivate his own judgement, notwithstanding the weight of pervasive social pressures in the direction of conformity.

B. The term was used by St. Simonians, and appears to have been first introduced into English by H. Reeve's translation of de Tocqueville's *De la démocratie en Amérique* (1835). While de Tocqueville distinguishes individualism from egotism, his distinction is essentially one of degree. '... individualism, at first, only saps the virtues of public life; but, in the long run, it attacks and destroys all others, and is at length absorbed in downright egotism' (*Democracy in America*, World's Classics abridgement of trans. by H. Reeve, London: Oxford University Press, 1946, p. 367).

The roots of individualism go back much further, i.e. to classical times. In its modern form, however, it stems from the Reformation, a movement which, in a society predominantly directed by tradition, affirmed the right to the individual's judgement to challenge important beliefs and institutions. Furthermore, Puritan individualism differed from classical individualism in its Christian emphasis on the individual's obligation to transcend the merely secular to include the service not of the self but of God.

Historical usage of the term has been mainly pejorative, i.e. it has implied that individualism might prove a virtue more conducive to power and prosperity than to individual awareness of social obligation. But more recently, conservative writers, claiming to represent the true liberal tradition in contradistinction to socialism, have sought to repudiate the pejorative undertones. In such writings individualism has been contrasted with economic and social planning,

Industrial Revolution

condemned as 'totalitarian', e.g. 'Individualism has a bad name today and the term has come to be connected with egotism and selfishness. But the individualism of which we speak in contrast to socialism and all other forms of collectivism has no necessary connection with these' (F. A. Hayek, *The Road to Serfdom*, Chicago: University of Chicago Press, 1944, p. 14). It has also been contrasted with egalitarianism, e.g. 'While individualism is profoundly opposed to all prescriptive privilege, to all protection, by law or force, of any rights not based on rules equally applicable to all persons, it also denies government the right to limit what the able or fortunate may achieve' (F. A. Hayek, *Individualism: true and false*, Dublin: Hodges, Figgis, 1946, p. 31).

The term has also been used by political theorists to express the view that the individual is a self-determined whole, a complete autonomous being in himself capable of being considered in isolation from society. This atomistic view of the individual is inseparable from such a theory of political obligation as was held by Hobbes, for example; and indeed lies at the root of other social contract theories of the state. In this context, *individualism* is used to contrast with those theories which, if they do not necessarily insist that society is more than the aggregate of the individuals who make it up, do insist that Law is not simply a necessary curb on the anarchical impulses of men but embodies some notion of common weal.

Finally, there is a current usage where the term is given a predominantly psychological significance with a favourable connotation. Sociologists like Fromm and Riesman, for example, in attacking what they consider to be an increasing trend towards cultural conformity, reaffirm the tradition of Protestant individualism. They contrast with conformist types of character, the self-reliant, inner-directed individual who brings evidence to the bar of his own personal judgement or conscience. True *individualism* in this context presupposes a capacity on the part of the individual to discover and realize his own spontaneous self. 'It follows from this premise that the realization of positive freedom and individualism is also bound up with economic and social changes that will permit the individual to become free in terms of the realization of his self' (E. Fromm, *The Fear of Freedom*, London: Kegan Paul, Trench, Trubner, 1946, p. 234).

R. V. Sampson

See also: COLLECTIVISM
FREEDOM

326

Industrial Revolution

A. The term *industrial revolution* denotes the sum total of those comparatively rapid changes —economic, technical, social, and intellectual— which first launched the industrialized society into existence in Great Britain between 1760 and 1860; this was followed by similar, though not identical, industrial revolutions which have brought industrialization to other countries.

B. A definition of this kind is bound to fall within certain ranges of disagreement which are the price of brevity. Economic historians have argued, and will doubtless continue to argue, about the dating, character, speed, and scope of the British and later industrial revolutions. Precision of definition may well be precluded by the complexity of these historical phenomena.

1. The term originated in France during the early years of the 19th century, being the obvious vehicle for a comparison between the French Revolution and the striking economic and technical changes which were then occurring in Great Britain. It passed into common academic usage after the publication of A. Toynbee's *Lectures on the Industrial Revolution in England* (London: Rivingtons, 1884) and fairly rapidly into popular usage, especially in Britain, in the present century.

2. Its principal modern usages are two:

(a) Initially, the term was used to characterize the comparatively rapid series of changes which, between roughly 1760 and 1860, swept across many parts of the British economy. These changes were primarily associated with the introduction into many, though not all, branches of manufacturing industry of new machinery and new processes, some of them being dependent on contemporary scientific advances; the use therein of power and especially of steam-power; and notable improvements in transport and communications, particularly the introduction of railways. In economic terms the notion signifies the capital investment in plant—factories, iron-works, textile mills, etc.—which these innovations necessitated and which in turn made possible great increases in output and in productivity, as well as corresponding falls in the prices of goods thus affected. The term is also seen as comprehending the attendant demographic, social, and intellectual changes which were part cause, part consequence of the economic and technical transformations.

(b) From this primary use, the term has come to be applied to very similar, though not identical, phases in the economic development of other countries. The U.S.A. and Germany, for example, are spoken of as having undergone industrial revolutions, beginning in the 1860s and 1870s. It should be added that some countries have been said to industrialize without the rapid phase of 'revolution'. For example, J. H. Clapham writes that: 'In the course of the nineteenth century most French industries were remodelled, but it might be said that France never went through an industrial revolution' (*The Economic Development of France and Germany, 1815-1914*, Cambridge: Cambridge University Press, 4th edn., 1936, p. 53).

In both these main uses the term implies the comparatively rapid and far-reaching set of changes which launch an economy from a predominantly agrarian nature (though often with much trade and industry of a pre-mechanized sort) into the shape of the modern industrialized society. It marks, in W. W. Rostow's phraseology, the 'take-off' into industrialization (q.v.) (*The Process of Economic Growth*, New York: W. W. Norton, 1952, p. 102).

3. The term has also been used in other ways:

(a) In one usage it serves to describe some major innovation, usually technical in nature, which is regarded as radically transforming an industry and as having far-reaching results (cf. its use regarding the introduction into the medieval English cloth industry of the fulling mill, in E. M. Carus-Wilson, 'An Industrial Revolution of the Thirteenth Century', *Economic History Review*, vol. XI, 1941, pp. 39–60).

(b) In another it describes any cluster of economic and technical innovations in an economy, within a given period, which results in some marked increase in industrial development (cf. its use to describe an 'early English industrial revolution', seen as taking place between 1540 and 1640, in J. U. Nef, 'The Progress of Technology and the Growth of Large-scale Industry in Great Britain, 1540–1640', *Economic History Review*, vol. V, 1934, pp. 3–24). More recently the term has been popularly used in this way to draw attention to the advent of automation and nuclear power (for discussion of these and other uses, cf. D. C. Coleman, 'Industrial Growth and Industrial Revolutions', *Economica*, vol. XXIII, 1956, pp. 1–22).

D. C. Coleman

See also: INDUSTRIALIZATION

Industrial Sociology

A. *Industrial sociology* denotes that sub-field of sociology which deals with some of the social aspects of the behaviour of people who, within industrial societies, are engaged in making, transporting, and distributing goods and providing some types of services. It is concerned both with the social structure of industrial organizations and with the relations between such organizations and the total social structure of which they are part. More specifically it comprises the study of the systematic relationships which arise from the work-situation and of the social factors which affect such relationships. The field covered is also known as *sociology of work*.

B. The term *industrial sociology* is of fairly recent origin in the United States and even more recent is its use elsewhere—though the subject matter it includes has had extensive study. In the United States the title is used to cover a considerable range of phenomena. For W. E. Moore (*Industrial Relations and the Social Order*, New York: The Macmillan Co., 1951, p. 3) industrial sociology 'attempts a systematic dissection and analysis of the industrial system as a social organization and of the industrial way of life'. In this work Moore concerns himself largely with the factory so that in a sense he identifies *industrial* with *factory-using* systems. D. C. Miller and W. Y. Form (*Industrial Sociology*, New York: Harper, 1951, p. 16) decry such limitations. They define the field as being that of the study of '(1) work groups and work relations, (2) the role the worker plays in work groups, and (3) the social organisation of work plant society'. In reviewing this work for the *American Sociological Review* (vol. 16, 1951, pp. 420–1) D. E. Wray widens the scope of the field still further and would include under the rubric *industrial sociology* the work of all those who have studied economic organization as a social phenomenon, including such men as Marx, Tawney, Max Weber, and Durkheim. On the other hand E. V. Schneider says that in his work (*Industrial Sociology*, New York: McGraw-Hill, 1957, p. 1) he deals only with 'the industrial institutions of the United States'. In a recent appraisal of the field of industrial sociology as it has developed in many countries, J. H. Smith discusses a number of definitions that have appeared in the literature and concludes that the subject is 'concerned with industry (or any form of work organization) as a social system, including those factors (technical, economic, political) which affect the structure, the functions and the changes in that system' (J. H. Smith, *Industrial Sociology*, Paris: Unesco, 1961, p. 31).

Most of what is called industrial sociology

Industrialization

investigates areas which are also claimed by other disciplines such as labour economics, institutional economics, applied anthropology, industrial relations, and industrial psychology. The methods of investigation, the theoretical orientation, and the special competence of the scholar seem to have more to do with the results secured than does the phenomenon investigated. So industrial sociologists find themselves at variance with each other but also with those from other disciplines who are attempting to outline a field of knowledge.

Fred Cottrell

See also: LABOUR ECONOMICS

Industrialization

A. *Industrialization* is a term covering in general terms (and without reference to any specific industrial revolution) the growth, in a society hitherto mainly agrarian, of modern industry, with all its attendant circumstances and problems, economic and social.

B. Though not as widely known as its more famous parent—industrial revolution (q.v.)—the term has come into use mainly during the past thirty years or so, in order to meet certain needs of classification for which the older term seemed unsatisfactory.

Two main usages may be distinguished:

1. It describes in general terms, the growth of a society in which a major role is played by manufacturing industry of the modern type, i.e. characterized by heavy, fixed-capital investment in plant and buildings, by the application of science to industrial techniques, and by mainly large-scale, standardized production. In this usage the term is distinct from the specific industrial revolution which may or may not have set in motion the still continuing process of industrialization, e.g.: 'In northern Italy, in parts of the Hapsburg Empire (especially Bohemia), in Russia, and in Japan, the beginnings of industrialization were evident, but the economic life of these areas had been far less completely transformed' (W. Ashworth, *A Short History of the International Economy, 1850–1950*, London: Longmans, Green, 1952, p. 33).

Just as the term *industrial revolution* has come to cover a range of economic, social, and other changes, as constituents of the idea, so the process of industrialization may denote characteristic changes in various branches of society, e.g.: 'The best general test of the industrialization of a nation's life under modern conditions is the rate and character of the growth of its towns'

(J. H. Clapham, *The Economic Development of France and Germany, 1815–1914*, Cambridge: Cambridge University Press, 4th edn., 1936, p. 53). 'Throughout the second half of the nineteenth century ... the use of steam became the most characteristic feature of industrialization wherever it took place' (W. Ashworth, *A Short History of the International Economy, 1850–1950*, p. 34).

On the other hand, the term may be specifically and deliberately limited, e.g.: 'In the Council's discussion the term "industrialization" was used in its restricted sense to designate the growth of manufacturing industry. ... In the light of this narrow connotation, industrialization is conceived of as a part—but no more than a part—of the much broader process of economic development. ...' (*Processes and Problems of Industrialization in Under-developed Countries*, United Nations, New York: Department of Economic and Social Affairs, 1955, p. 2).

2. With or without this limitation, in the use given above industrialization is considered in terms of the type of industry introduced by the British industrial revolution or its successors elsewhere (cf. 'The feasible rate of industrialization is thus not governed merely by the problems associated with the erection of *factories* [my italics]; it is a function of an organic type of growth in which the essential feature is the mutual dependence of the various sectors that are involved' (*Processes and Problems of Industrialization in Under-developed Countries*, p. 10). But the term is sometimes also used by historians to signify the growth of any form of industry as opposed to agriculture. This may mean industry organized on a handicraft or putting-out basis on a large scale or a small, on capitalist or other lines, e.g.: 'For Tuscany ... industrialization would appear to be a wholly medieval phenomenon' (*Cambridge Economic History of Europe*, Cambridge: Cambridge University Press, 1952, vol. II, p. 393).

This use is generally less common than that given in (1) above.

D. C. Coleman

See also: INDUSTRIAL REVOLUTION
UNDERDEVELOPED AREAS

Industry

A. An *industry* is comprised of a number of producing organizations, such as establishments or business firms, that are grouped together for analytical or policy-making purposes according to certain criteria. This technical meaning of the term, which will be emphasized in the following discussion, is to be distinguished from its use either as roughly synonymous with manufacturing or as contrasted with transport, trade, finance, agriculture, etc.

B. 1. Traditionally the customary criterion for industry grouping was the characteristics of the product(s) offered by producing organizations. Thus, in the manner of Alfred Marshall, if a number of firms turned out products that in the minds of potential buyers were either perfect or close substitutes for one another, then all these producing units would be classified as belonging in the same industry. If only one producer accounted for the total output of a product, defined as separated in buyers' minds by a significant gap from other products in the chain of possible substitute goods, then that producer was a monopolist who encompassed the whole industry.

2. It will be apparent upon a moment's reflection, however, that defining an industry in terms of products exclusively can be either too broad or too narrow, according to varying empirical considerations. It might be too broad in the realistic case of a wide range of substitutes, such as automobiles of different brands and styles. It might be too narrow in the case of a product like copper, for which there are a number of substitutes of differing degree of closeness in the viewpoint of potential demanders. It was the development of the theories of *monopolistic* or *imperfect competition*, with their recognition of real-world product heterogeneity, that properly complicated a classification problem previously made too simple by the Marshallian world of industries conceived in terms of firms producing identical products. On the basis of these later doctrines, unfortunately, it became conceivable to classify as an industry the single, branded commodity produced by only one firm, even though the commodity has many close substitutes.

3. It is now customary to emphasize the notion that industry classifications, like nomenclature systems in all sciences, must, with due consideration for accepted usage, be in the first instance adapted to the purposes of a specific analysis. Within this approach economists, industrial geographers, and others now usually employ the close-substitute-products requirement plus certain other criteria when delineating an industry.

Additional criteria may include the following: (a) All firms organized into a trade association, such as lumber producers, may be grouped together. (b) Use of a single raw material, as in cottonseed oil processing, may provide a basis for grouping producers into an industry (E. A. G. Robinson, *The Structure of Competitive Industry*, Chicago: University of Chicago Press, 1962, p. 8). (c) Another criterion might invoke any group of producing organizations ' . . . whose techniques of production are sufficiently alike for it to make sense to conceive of one as being able to do the business of another' (J. Downie, *The Competitive Process*, London: Duckworth, 1958, p. 31). Equally broad criteria have been employed by other authorities including, in addition to the last named, (d) similarity in technological data confronting a group of concerns, and (e) similarity in other kinds of decision-making data, such as market data on either the buying or selling side and even common organization problems (A. G. Papandreou & J. T. Wheeler, *Competition and Its Regulation*, New York: Prentice-Hall, 1954, pp. 55–61 passim).

4. Since most large producing organizations are multiproduct as well as multiplant concerns, the assignment of a firm or even a plant to any given industry does not preclude its actual participation in other industries. The *Standard Industrial Classification Manual* of the United States Bureau of the Budget, for example, in relying primarily upon the close-substitute-products criterion for the classification of manufacturing establishments (not firms) into appropriate industries, emphasizes that a plant is assigned to an industry only if its output of the selected product or product group exceeds in value its production of any other product group. (In some instances, similarity of processes employed is also invoked). This method obviously permits enormous discrepancies, due to the high frequency of multiproduct establishments, between 'industry' production or shipment totals and the totals for value added and other plant-wide magnitudes in any particular aggregate of plants allocated to an industry so defined.

5. Some authorities, faced by such formidable haziness in any industry definition, have despaired of employing the industry concept. K. Boulding illustrates this attitude when he declares, ' . . . what we have in reality is a mass of firms rather than a collection of "industries", each firm entering into complex competitive relationships with other firms in increasing circles of diminishing intensity' (*Economic Analysis*, New York: Harper & Brothers, 3rd edn., 1955, p. 629). However, the notion of an *industry* con-

Inflation

tinues to lead a robust life, invigorated not only by common sense but also by its widespread application in the business world, its undeniable analytic usefulness for understanding a great range of theoretical problems, and its high relevance to many public policy decisions.

Harold G. Vatter

See also: DEMAND
ECONOMIC COMPETITION
INDUSTRIAL REVOLUTION
INDUSTRIALIZATION
MARKET
MONOPOLISTIC COMPETITION
PRICE SYSTEM
SUPPLY

Inflation

A. *Inflation* denotes a situation in which the money demand for output grows relatively to output, the situation being manifested, in the absence of effective controls, in the form of rising prices per unit of output. Such a definition is neutral with respect to possible causes or initial sources of inflation. No confusion need arise in applying the term in a more specific way (e.g. inflation of the money supply) or with modifying adjectives and prefixes. Definitions which depart from common usage must be specified in detail in any case.

B. Most of the problems and inequities of what is called inflation stem from increases in the general level of prices, as measured by some representative wholesale or retail price index. Such price behaviour is also implied or explicitly denoted in popular discussion and understanding of the term, as well as in the prevailing usage among economists. Accordingly, it seems most appropriate to cast a general definition in terms which at least associate the concept with rising prices. It is further desirable to conform to the well-established usage of applying the term to one or more of the variables which determine general price levels. The definition in A. above meets these requirements.

C. Despite the absence of an agreed definition among economists, *inflation* is usually associated with an actual or potential rise in the general level of prices, which is to say, a decline in the purchasing power of the monetary unit. Occasionally, it is associated with a failure of the general price level to fall to the extent warranted by increases in the productivity of economic agents and processes.

1. Many writers identify inflation with a rising price level per se. Thus, observes A. J. Brown (*The Great Inflation, 1939–1951*, London: Oxford University Press, 1955, p. 2), 'inflation as ordinarily understood has something to do with an inordinate rise of prices'. A. G. Hart (*Money, Debt and Economic Activity*, New York: Prentice-Hall, 2nd edn., 1954, p. 256) is more general in defining the term as an 'upward movement of price levels'. Brown (*The Great Inflation*, p. 2) comments upon the varied contexts in which the word *inflation* is used in a rather wider sense—thus in addition to 'price inflation meaning an inordinate rise in the general level of prices' we speak of *income-inflation*, *cost-inflation*, or *currency-inflation*—and the tendencies denoted by these terms do not necessarily move in the same direction nor have the same consequences.

The balance of opinion would probably accept the view of W. L. Thorp and R. E. Quandt (*The New Inflation*, New York: McGraw-Hill, 1959, p. 9) that, concerned as it is with prices, 'inflation is not a matter of individual prices but of the general price level'. Even in this general sense the word is often prefixed in some way, e.g. *cost-push inflation*—but here the prefix indicates less a sector of the economy within which inflation occurs and more a set of 'causes' to which the inflation may be attributed. Indeed definitions of inflation—even at a very general level—tend to incorporate some discussion of 'causes'. Thus there is the view of those who hold to some variant of the quantity theory of the value of money, that inflation pertains directly to the money supply. The latter is 'inflated', that is, expanded relatively to the demand for money as a medium of exchange and store of value, and a rise in general prices follows as a consequence. Such a view—that a large and sustained rise in the general price level is the *result* of inflation (of the money supply)—is held by C. Bresciani-Turroni (*The Economics of Inflation: A Study of Currency Depreciation in Postwar Germany, 1919–1923*, London: Allen & Unwin, 1937, esp. pp. 42–82). Finally, there are those who, taking the income-expenditure approach to the value of money, would describe as 'inflationary' the volume of expenditure which results in higher price levels. Seen thus, inflation is 'a situation in which the flow of purchasing power is increasing faster than the flow of goods and services—with consequent price increases' (A. Smithies, 'The Control of Inflation', *Review of Economics and Statistics*, vol. XXXIX, 1957, p. 272). A variation on this theme is provided by L. V. Chandler (*Inflation in the United States, 1940–1948*, New York: Harrap, 1951) who, although giving no precise definition, employs *inflation* in the sense of an increase in the general level of prices growing out of an enlargement of expenditure relative to goods available for purchase. Those economists who are less concerned with monetary than with physical features of the economy nonetheless define inflation with reference to price movements. Thus M. Kalecki discussing deficit finance as a way to full employment observes that inflation, 'i.e. a vicious spiral of prices and wages' will come about 'only if effective demand increases so much that a general scarcity of labour or equipment (or both) arises' ('Three Ways to Full Employment', in Oxford University Institute of Statistics, *The Economics of Full Employment*, Oxford: Blackwell, 1946, p. 43).

2. There are so many difficulties in defining *inflation* so as to embrace all its possible manifestations, and yet to retain a satisfactory degree of precision, that a modifying adjective or prefix is commonly employed with the term. Thus secular (long-term) inflation may be distinguished from cyclical and sporadic increases in prices. J. M. Keynes (*The General Theory of Employment, Interest and Money*, London: Macmillan, 1936, pp. 301–3) sought to distinguish between *semi-inflation* and *absolute*, or true, *inflation*. The former results when in a cyclical recovery increase in the money demand for goods spends itself partly in increasing employment and real output of goods, and partly in raising unit production costs and prices. The latter results when 'increase in the quantity of effective demand produces no further increase in output and entirely spends itself on an increase in the cost-unit fully proportionate to the increase in effective demand' (ibid., p. 303). Another distinction associated with Keynes relates to effects upon inducements to alter the rate of output. *Income inflation* is defined as a rise in money earnings of productive factors relative to real output (*A Treatise on Money*, London: Macmillan, 1930, vol. I, pp. 138, 155). *Profit inflation* is a rise in entrepreneurial incomes above the 'normal' level, i.e. above the level which would provide just sufficient inducement to maintain the rate of output unchanged (ibid., pp. 125, 155). The former, per se, has no effect upon output, while the latter, by definition, does. Similar implications are contained in the distinction between *excess-demand inflation* and *cost-push inflation* (A. G. Hart, *Defense* *Without Inflation*, New York: Twentieth Century Fund, 1951, p. 59), although the latter terms more obviously connote initial sources of general price increases. *Cost-push* is most commonly equated with an advance of unit labour costs, but it may also result from growing inefficiencies in production or artificial scarcities, such as may arise in war, mounting capital costs, rising prices of imports, and falling exchange rates.

3. Often it is found useful to convey a degree or rate of inflation. Thus, *hyperinflation* (sometimes *runaway inflation*) is the term applied to such experiences as that of Germany in 1919–23. J. Robinson defines *hyperinflation* as a situation which exists 'when continuously rising prices set up the expectation of further rises, so that a scramble for goods sets in which ends in a complete collapse of the currency' (*Collected Economic Papers*, Oxford: Blackwell, 1951, p. 89). In hyperinflation the velocity of circulation plays a major role, mounting to such levels that the monetary unit ceases to function first as a store of value and finally as a standard of value and medium of exchange. *Creeping inflation*, on the other hand, describes a gradual but steady advance of costs and prices, more or less restrained by monetary-fiscal policy and not involving a general loss of confidence in the monetary unit, but perpetuated by the repeated efforts of wage-earners and entrepreneurs to get and keep larger advances in real income than increasing productivity permits (cf. D. H. Robertson, *Economic Commentaries*, London: Staples Press, 1956, pp. 117–20).

4. Experience with emergency controls, usually during war and its immediate aftermath, has led to a distinction between *repressed (or suppressed)* and *open inflation*. Thus: 'Repressed inflation is characterized by the fact that prices, and possibly wages, are fixed by the institution of direct controls; whereas such controls are not in operation under open inflation' (B. Hansen, *A Study in the Theory of Inflation*, London: Allen & Unwin, 1951, p. 3).

D. Although most economists take an actual or potential increase in the general price level to be a criterion of inflation, whatever the precise definition or alleged causal sequence, A. C. Pigou among others (notably F. A. Hayek, F. Machlup, L. von Mises, and the whole Austrian school) is an exception. In his view, 'inflation is taking place when money income is expanding relatively to the output of work— not the output of goods and services (real

Influence

income)—by productive agents, for which it is the payment ...' (A. C. Pigou, *The Veil of Money*, London: Macmillan, 1949, p. 14). Following this definition, it is possible to have 'inflation' and falling prices at the same time, due to advances in productivity which exceed concurrent increases in money incomes; or to have rising prices without 'inflation'—even with 'deflation'—as a consequence of decreasing productivity and less than proportionate concurrent reduction in rates of pay for effort.

Stephen L. McDonald

See also: DEFLATION
           MONEY

Influence

A. Useful definitions of *influence* come close to the commonsense and 'lay' usage of the term. In its most general sense *influence* denotes whatever causes in any social, and especially political context, individuals or groups to deviate from a predicted path of behaviour. More specifically the term is used to denote changes in behaviour of a person or group due to anticipation of the responses of others. In this sense the term connotes the outwardly quiet and possibly gradual exertion of power and persuasion rather than the more demanding legal or overt exercise of power connected with formal authority.

B. 1. Elements common to definitions of influence in various fields of social sciences are (a) that influence will lead to a change or reversal of previous (or predicted) decisions, policies, or behaviour; (b) that the 'exercise of influence (influence process) consists in affecting policies of others than the self' (H. D. Lasswell & A. Kaplan, *Power and Society*, New Haven: Yale University Press, 1950, p. 71). If social scientists speak of the influence of A over B they note the difference between the way in which B actually behaves and the way he would have behaved if A had not entered into relations with him, or simply did not exist.

2. Psychologists, including social psychologists, generally do not go beyond describing influence as causal relation. The definition in H. C. Warren's *Dictionary of Psychology* (Boston: Houghton Mifflin, 1934) appears typical of this appoach: 'Any prior condition which in explaining the temporal succession of events is considered as a factor in determining or leading to the later conditions'. Similarly, a political scientist beleives that 'any statement of influence ... can just as easily be formulated in terms of causality' (J. G. March, 'An Introduction to the

Theory and Measurement of Influence', *American Political Science Review*, vol. XLIX, 1955, p. 437).

3. There is also fairly wide, though not complete, agreement that influence involves an interpersonal and asymmetrical relationship between people, either as individuals or members of a group. 'Influence is not an abstract attribute of a person, it is a process implicating two or more people' (R. K. Merton, 'Patterns of Influence', in P. F. Lazarsfeld & F. Stanton (eds.), *Communications Research, 1948-9*, New York: Harpers, 1949, p. 208).

C. 1. Differences between the sociologists' and political scientists' definitions, albeit not always in evidence, seem to evolve around the question as to how to differentiate *influence* from *power*. For Merton ('Patterns of Influence', p. 217 and *passim*) the two concepts are closely related but not identical, since power, prestige, position in a hierarchy, etc., may contribute to the potential for interpersonal influence, but do not determine the extent to which influence actually occurs. On the other hand, H. A. Simon in his widely quoted article, 'Notes on the Observation and Measurement of Political Power' (*Journal of Politics*, vol. 15, 1953, p. 501) explicitly uses the terms *influence* and *power* as synonyms. H. D. Lasswell, who often moves within categories which Weber established in his discussions of politics and power, unequivocally states that 'The study of politics is the study of influence and the influential' (*Politics, Who Gets What, When, How*, New York: McGraw-Hill, 1936, p. 3). In a chapter on 'Elite', the same author describes the influential as those who get most of what there is to get. Elsewhere the political scientist Lasswell, joining efforts with a philosopher, Kaplan, defines influence as the 'value position and potential of a person or a group' and insists that the study of influence (i.e. of politics) comprises values more than power (*Power and Society*, pp. 55, 60). If one adopts, however, such a concise definition of power as another philosopher, B. Russell, has proposed, when he calls power 'the production of intended effects' (*Power*, New York: Norton, 1938, p. 35) then the terms *influence* and *power* become indeed identical.

2. In discussions concerned with the basis on which influence rests, the forms in which it is exercised, and the methods by which to gauge it, some slight definitional and descriptive differences between the two concepts, power and influence, emerge. Influence, rather than power, is noted where the change in behaviour of the influenced is due to advice, manipulation, imitation, and the like, instead of coercion or the exercise of formal authority. While the values of deference may serve both the influential and the powerful, sanctions are generally less severe where one speaks of influence.

At least sociologists are reluctant to use the term influence where changes in attitudes are brought about by mass media or through the 'market', and will reserve the word to the greater intimacy of personal relationships, although the latter may affect political decisions and administrative behaviour.

3. The 'rule of anticipated reaction' which C. J. Friedrich has developed to describe and define influence as a 'very evasive' form of power has found wide acceptance. To him influence is 'apart from power ... probably the most important basic concept of political science'. But because 'the person or group which is being influenced *anticipates the reactions* of him or those who exercise the influence,' influence operates most of the time 'by changing the conduct of people without any outward appearance of change' (*Constitutional Government and Democracy*, Boston: Ginn, 1946, p. 589). Such an analysis of influence does not deny that an asymmetrical relationship is involved wherever influence is exercised. But the behaviour described by Friedrich will frequently obfuscate the distribution of values between the influencer and the influenced. The more accurate the predictions or expectations of participants concerning their mutual reactions, the more difficult it becomes to observe and even to define influence.

4. Accounts of the role of pressure groups (q.v.) in the political process use the term *influence* fairly broadly as a synonym for *access*. Access or influence involve relationships between groups and such individuals who by their position are able to bring about mutations of governmental institutions (see D. B. Truman, *The Governmental Process*, New York: Knopf, 1951, pp. 65, 288 and passim), also in such discussions the relationship between power, whether political or economic, and influence is never entirely clarified, except occasionally as to the form in which it is exercised.

D. In general there may be reason to regret with March ('An Introduction to the Theory and Measurement of Influence', p. 450) that the formalization of the concept of influence has proceeded in an '*ad hoc* fashion, with little communication either between the "theorists" and

the "empiricists" or between the several practitioners within each class of that dichotomy'. In the absence of an inclusive theory of influence elaborate attempts at measuring what is difficult to define do not promise early results.

Henry W. Ehrmann

See also: AUTHORITY
LOBBY
POWER
PRESSURE GROUP

Information Theory (See Cybernetics)

In-Group (See Group)

Inhibition

A. *Inhibition* denotes a condition in which the presence of one stimulus renders another one ineffective at the same time through a final 'common path', the neural locus at which simultaneous stimuli converge in producing a response. It is a constant feature of activity in the nervous system. Even a simple activity like walking requires for its performance the co-ordinated inhibition of certain muscle groups in the body. Any drive which facilitates some behaviour inhibits other behaviour. It is through this (facilitation-inhibition process) that directed or organized learning takes place. Normal inhibition must be distinguished from neurotic inhibition. Normal inhibition is characterized by discrimination of response, whereas neurotic or defensive inhibition is indiscriminate, as seen when a panic-stricken person for whom threats are 'free-floating' instead of localized performs senseless acts.

1. Inhibition differs from repression (q.v. with which it is not infrequently confused. Repression is the exclusion of thoughts, wishes, or feelings from consciousness. Inhibition is the blocking of impulses from overt or motor expression.

2. Inhibition, because it is commonly considered as a restraining force, is often conceived as a passive process. This is a mistake. Except in neurotic inhibition, where there is a hyperintensity of response to undiscriminated stimuli, and which therefore differs primarily in intensity rather than in kind, inhibition is a positive process. To use the example of L. F. Shaffer and E. J. Shoben (*The Psychology of Adjustment*, Boston: Houghton Mifflin, 2nd edn., 1956, p. 74), when a dog has learned *not* to react to a discriminated stimulus this not-responding is not a 'passive loss' but a positive or active restraining process.

333

Inhibition

3. In neurotic or defensive inhibition the operating mechanism is the same as in normal inhibition. A state of continuous conflict, however, demands a constant control and inhibition of impulses. This leaves the individual in a persistent state of tension which impairs his capacity to adjust himself productively to conditions of daily living. Excessive inhibition narrows his range of interest and emotional responsiveness. The net result is a restricted or constricted personality. The common feature of all inhibitions is that the 'executive activity' as A. Kardiner calls it (*The Individual and His Society*, New York: Columbia University Press, 1939, p. 71), is not accessible; i.e. the individual's resources for dealing with his problems are either absent, only partly exercised, or unused because of a fear of jeopardizing other interests.

B. This concept has a long history in learning theory and in dynamic psychology. In recent years the two lines of development have been converging, with the result that inhibition is increasingly described in a learning-motivation framework. A good instance of this convergence is found in the researches of J. Dollard and N. E. Miller (*Personality and Psychotherapy*, New York: McGraw-Hill, 1950).

In its widest meaning *inhibition* denotes the blocking of the expression of an impulse. In its elementary form it is induced by simple conditioning. In a learning-motivation complex it is brought about by a competing factor which weakens the strength of a response tendency. The competing element is an inhibitory factor the strength of which is a function of such conditions as the degree of blocking of the response, the degree of non-reinforcement, and the amount of habituation in working toward a goal.

1. Experimental psychologists have long investigated the phenomenon of inhibition in learning, forgetting, and transfer of training. Their investigations have centred around two important problems: (a) pro-active inhibition, and (b) retroactive inhibition.

(a) *Pro-active inhibition* denotes the phenomenon in learning where the first item in a list is learned more easily than the second, the second more easily than the third, and so on (R. Stagner & T. F. Karwoski, *Psychology*, New York: McGraw-Hill, 1952, p. 260).

(b) *Retroactive inhibition* refers to the process in which later items in a list tend to interfere with the recall of preceding items (ibid., p. 261). After we have learnt something our activity, as C. T. Morgan points out (*Introduc-*

tion to Psychology, New York: McGraw-Hill, 1956, p. 130), works backward to block memories of what we have learnt. Such inhibition is a case of *negative transfer* and is the most important factor in forgetting. We forget, says Morgan (ibid., p. 131), because '*what we do inhibits retroactively what we have learned*'.

2. Clinically the term *inhibition* is used extensively to denote certain traumatic neuroses. *Defensive inhibition*, which is the fundamental mechanism of all traumatic neuroses, serves as a protective device in the face of acute danger. Defensive inhibition differs from normal inhibition, such as that operating in retroactive learning phenomena, in that it functions in a very indiscriminate fashion. A soldier in battle, for instance, to use an example of A. Kardiner's ('The Neuroses of War', in S. S. Tomkins (ed.), *Contemporary Psychopathology*, Cambridge, Mass.: Harvard University Press, 1943, pp. 194–201), will get paralysed legs because he was running at the time of the trauma. It is also characteristic of defensive inhibition that it irradiates and functions in all threat situations which are construed as overwhelming by an individual and the facing of which would produce unbearable anxiety. Its function is, clearly, to enable the individual, as K. Horney (*The Neurotic Personality of Our Time*, London: Kegan Paul, Trench, Trubner, 1937, p. 53) has indicated, 'to avoid the anxiety which would arise if the person attempted to do, feel, or think' certain things. Thus in the sexual sphere it will produce frigidity and impotence; in the mental sphere, difficulty in concentration; in the social sphere, fear of forming or expressing opinions or of making contacts with people, etc. (ibid., p. 54). Some writers extend the clinical meaning of inhibition even farther, and consider it as a generalization of a basic defensive process. Thus A. Freud (*The Ego and the Mechanism of Defence*, London: The Hogarth Press, 1937, pp. 167–72) ascribes the asceticism of many adolescents, during which normal pleasures like eating, the enjoyment of comfort, music, and dancing are renounced, to a defence against their sexual needs and impulses. This is no doubt an extension of S. Freud's (*Three Contributions to the Theory of Sex*, Washington, D.C.: Nervous and Mental Disease Publishing Company, 1930) concept of sublimation, or the inhibition of sexual impulses during the latency period. This *generalized inhibition*, as R. W. White (*The Abnormal Personality*, New York: Ronald Press, 2nd edn., 1956, p. 256) calls it, is carried so far by some individuals as to cause them to experience any strong impulse or deep feeling as a danger signal in the face of which they must rigidly control themselves.

Hubert Bonner

See also: REPRESSION
SUBLIMATION

Initiation

A. *Initiation* refers to the rituals which celebrate the passage of an individual into jural adulthood, a fraternity or secret society, or a special and frequently religious occupation.

B. M. Eliade (*Birth and Rebirth: The Religious Meanings of Initiation in Human Culture*, New York: Harper & Brothers, 1958, p. 2) distinguishes three categories of initiations: (1) 'the collective rituals whose function is to effect the transition from childhood or adolescence to adulthood'; (2) those which mark the entry into a fraternity or secret society; and (3) the rites involved in assuming a 'mystical vocation'.

In his classic work A. van Gennep (*The Rites of Passage*, trans. by M. Vizedom & G. Caffee, London: Routledge & Kegan Paul, 1960) treats all of these categories. He objects to the common identification of the first category with puberty rites, since the transition to adulthood may begin before and continue long after puberty. His point cannot be disputed, but *puberty rites* may still serve as a convenient label for the first category of initiations. M. Fortes ('Introduction', in J. Goody (ed.), *The Developmental Cycle in Domestic Groups*, Cambridge Papers in Social Anthropology, No. 1, Cambridge: Cambridge University Press, 1958) views the deprivations and ordeals of this type of initiation as shock tactics which are necessary to separate the individual from the domestic domain and introduce him to the politico-jural domain.

H. Webster (*Primitive Secret Societies*, New York: Macmillan, 1908) considers puberty rites the basic type of initiation and maintains that they often survive in the ceremonies of secret societies. Eliade suggests that initiations into secret societies and into religious vocations might be regarded as varieties within a single category, but he prefers to distinguish them because of the ecstatic element usually involved in the latter type.

Frank Miller

See also: CEREMONY
RITUAL

Initiative

The *initiative* is a political device—used widely in Switzerland and in state and local governments in the United States—through which the electorate may by petition propose a statute or an amendment to a constitution. It is put into operation through a petition, which must be signed by the number of qualified voters that is required by the constitution. A measure so initiated may go first to the legislature (*indirect initiative*) for its consideration and possible adoption, with the further provision that should the legislature fail to adopt the proposal it will be submitted to the people for approval or rejection at a forthcoming election. Constitutions frequently provide that a measure so proposed by petition may be referred directly to the voters without prior consideration by the legislature (*direct initiative*). In rare cases the initiative may be used as a device solely to obtain an expression of opinion by the electorate on an important question of policy. However, it is employed more frequently as a protection against an unrepresentative legislative or party system. The initiative quite often is coupled with the *referendum* (consult J. T. Shotwell (ed.), *Governments of Continental Europe*, New York: The Macmillan Co., 1952; C. J. Friedrich, *Constitutional Government and Democracy*, Boston: Little, Brown & Co., 1941; and, for the experience of an American state, V. O. Key, Jr. & W. W. Crouch, *The Initiative and the Referendum in California*, Publications of the University of California at Los Angeles in Social Sciences, vol. 6, no. 4, Berkeley, Cal.: University of California Press, 1939).

Charles Aikin

See also: REFERENDUM

Inner-Directed (See Conformity)

Innovation (Also Discovery and Invention)

Innovation denotes 'any thought, behaviour, or thing that is new because it is qualitatively different from existing forms' (H. G. Barnett, *Innovation*, New York: McGraw-Hill, 1953, p. 7). Barnett to a limited extent uses *invention* and *innovation* synonymously, but is aware that in this he differs from accepted usage: 'For most people an invention is a thing, and the label seems inappropriate when applied to novel behavior patterns, theories and social relations' (ibid., p. 8). He therefore brings his usage into line with popular practice by using *invention* to designate only technological innovations.

It is customary to distinguish *invention* from *discovery*. R. B. Dixon distinguishes them on the basis of presence or absence of purpose: 'Discovery would then be limited to the unpremedi-

Insecurity

tated finding of something new, whereas invention might be defined as purposeful discovery' *The Building of Cultures*, New York: Charles Scribner's Sons, 1928, p. 34). Compare again: 'Discovery is a revelation of the unpredictable' (H. S. Harrison, 'Opportunism and the Factors of Invention', *American Anthropologist*, vol. 32, 1930, p. 108). Harrison, who regards *invention* as any new application of a discovery, protests against the tendency to apply it to such complex processes as agriculture, pointing out that any complex human activity evolves slowly, and that it is necessary to distinguish the different stages at which real invention occurs. It is only important to define invention precisely in the context of the controversy about the possibility of independent invention which was waged between cultural historians at the turn of the century. Apart from that context it may be maintained, with Barnett, that no rigorous and meaningful distinction can be established between invention and discovery, or between basic and secondary inventions.

M. Douglas

See also: DIFFUSION

Input (See **Productivity**)

Insecurity

A. *Insecurity* is an emotional state which, if chronic, determines: (a) pathological reactions such as fears, obsessions, and phobias; (b) a specific character structure in the individual; (c) a specific group organization.

Loosely it designates the state of mind of an individual facing an actual or potential threat. As such it is opposed to the feeling of ease. It is often applied indirectly to external circumstances of life, such as, for instance, 'financial insecurity' denoting precarious economic conditions.

B. 1. In psychology *insecurity* tends to become a technical term connoting a chronic mental condition which generates some forms of abnormal behaviour. In this sense it is closely related to anxiety (q.v.) as this has been defined by psychoanalysis. The Freudian concept of 'free-floating anxiety' is particularly suggestive in this respect. A specific feeling of fear detached by a strong repression from its object may continue to operate from the unconscious mind as an irrational or generalized fear. This is a neurotic condition which includes a general state of insecurity among its symptoms.

2. *The insecurity syndrome* is a term used by A. H. Maslow designating the totality of symptoms associated with chronic insecurity. The term can be regarded (a) genetically, and (b) descriptively.

(a) The mother-child relations are often considered of paramount importance for the satisfaction of the individual's basic need for emotional security. On these early experiences depends whether the individual suffers later in life from chronic insecurity or not.

(b) Maslow describes fourteen symptoms of chronic insecurity of which the most important are as follows: (i) feelings of rejection; (ii) feelings of not belonging, and isolation; (iii) attitudes of alarm towards life; (iv) feelings of suspiciousness, jealousy, and hatred; (v) guilt feelings; (vi) loss of self-esteem; (vii) feelings of unworthiness ('The Dynamics of Psychological Security-Insecurity', *Character and Personality*, vol. 10, 1942, pp. 331–44).

3. Insecurity is sometimes defined in a socio-cultural context. Thus, K. Horney (*New Ways in Psychoanalysis*, New York: Norton, 1939) speaks about 'inner insecurity' created in the individual by competitive social relations. The typical way in which this basic insecurity is acted out determines the character structure of the individual. Insecurity is sometimes considered as a dynamic factor determining not only the individual's personality but also the structure of the social group. Security–insecurity serves as a criterion of discrimination at the motivational level between democratic and authoritarian groups. According to this view political dictatorship is a symptom of group adjustment to conditions of stress and insecurity (see E. Fromm, *The Fear of Freedom*, London: Kegan Paul, 1942; G. M. Gilbert, *The Psychology of Dictatorship*, New York: The Ronald Press, 1950; N. Cohn, *The Pursuit of the Millennium*, London: Secker & Warburg, 1957, especially p. 308).

Z. Barbu

See also: ANXIETY
GUILT FEELINGS
ISOLATION

Instinct

A. The term *instinct* as employed in the context of biology refers to those recurring sequences of animal experience and behaviour together with their underlying neuro-physiological conditions which (a) appear to terminate in specific consequences; (b) are functionally beneficial to both the individual and the species; (c) are well adapted to the normal environmental circumstances of the species (though they are often 'blind' and maladapted to unusual conditions); (d) are common to all the individual members of the species (though their particular manifestations may vary from individual to individual); (e) emerge with a definite order and regularity in the life of the individual in close relation to the process of growth and maturation; and (f) are not learnt on the basis of individual experience (though they may emerge in the context of learning, and though learning may take place in relation to them).

Controversies on the meaning and utility of the term have been fierce and detailed so that any attempt to impose a completely agreed usage would be unwarranted.

B. Instincts are held to be established by heredity (i.e. genetically transmitted from parent to offspring) in the same way as anatomical structures are. They are just as universal in the members of a species as are anatomical features, and (as is the case with these physical characteristics) their existence and nature are accounted for by the theory of evolution.

There is much disagreement as to the existence of distinguishable instincts in man. Those who do believe that instincts play an important part in human experience and behaviour do not attribute the same degree of rigidity of inherited mechanisms to man as to other animal species, but regard the instincts as inherited *impulses*, sometimes lacking appropriate inbuilt behavioural automatisms, but which, nonetheless comprise important, ineradicable conative forces in human experience. There is much disagreement, too, as to the *number* of instincts to be postulated in any species, but much of this disagreement can be traced to the employment of different principles of classification.

C. 1. The scientific use of the term begins essentially in the context of biology, and emerges in the attempt to account for those recurrent sequences of animal experience and behaviour which appear to be established by heredity and evolution, and which cannot be explained in terms of learning. Thus C. Darwin says, 'An action, which we ourselves should require experience to enable us to perform, when performed by an animal, more especially by a very young one, without any experience, and when performed by many individuals in the same way, without their knowing for what purpose it is performed, is usually said to be instinctive' (*On the Origin of Species* (1859), London: Watts, 1950, p. 178).

2. There has been much controversy as to whether elements of *experience* (e.g. perception, conation, cognition, etc.) can legitimately be included in the concept of instinct. W. MacDougall, for example, defined instinct in such a way as to emphasize elements of subjective experience. An instinct is '... an inherited or innate psycho-physical disposition which determines its possessor to perceive, and to pay attention to, objects of a certain class, to experience an emotional excitement of a particular quality upon perceiving such an object, and to act in regard to it in a particular manner, or, at least, to experience an impulse to such action' (*An Introduction to Social Psychology*, London: Methuen, 1928, p. 25).

Other British psychologists, though criticizing and qualifying MacDougall's approach, continued to give a place to subjective experience in the concept of instinct.

3. J. B. Watson—concerned to rule elements of subjective experience out of the sphere of psychology, because they could not be dealt with 'objectively' or 'scientifically'—insisted on the attempt to define instinct in a completely physiological way. For him an instinct is '... an hereditary pattern reaction, the separate elements of which are movements principally of the striped muscles. It might otherwise be expressed as a combination of explicit congenital responses unfolding serially under appropriate stimulation' (*Psychology from the Standpoint of a Behaviorist*, Philadelphia: Lippincott, 1924, pp. 262–3).

This concentration on the inherited physiological components of behaviour and their subsequent 'conditioning' led Watson, later, to reject the concept of instinct altogether as having no utility in psychology, and this behaviourist rejection has since been the dominant attitude in America. Other definitions have been offered, however, of those experiential components which the earlier psychologists included in the term *instinct* (e.g. *drive* (q.v.), *need* (q.v.)), but the emphasis here has been to the effect that not all human drives, or needs, are inherited, but that many stem from diverse and complex patterns of learnt social experience.

4. A recent school of zoologists (Comparative Ethology = the scientific study of animal behaviour) has undertaken a detailed study of instinct in a way completely consistent with earlier usage. In this view an instinct is '... a hierarchical organised nervous mechanism

Institution

which is susceptible to certain priming, releasing, and directing impulses of internal as well as of external origin, and which responds to these impulses by co-ordinated movements that contribute to the maintenance of the individual and the species' (N. Tinbergen, *The Study of Instinct*, Oxford: at the Clarendon Press, 1951, p. 112).

This definition stresses the physiological approach, but other ethologists (e.g. Thorpe) think that their study of instinct does not exclude the psychological approach, 'but makes clear where it is useful, indeed essential' (W. H. Thorpe, 'The Modern Concept of Instinctive Behaviour', *Bulletin of Animal Behaviour*, 1948, no. 7, p. 7).

5. Psychoanalysis also lays much stress upon the instinctual aspects of human nature. Freud defines instinct as an inescapable, constantly recurring stimulus to the mind stemming from sources within the organism ('Instincts and their Vicissitudes', 1915, *Collected Papers*, trans. J. Riviere, London: L. & V. Woolf, 1925, vol. IV, pp. 60–83). His usage is therefore consistent with other scientific usage, though some of his elaborate speculations (e.g. on the Life and Death instincts) are not.

Ronald Fletcher

See also: DRIVE
        NEED

Institution

A. The term denotes an aspect of social life in which distinctive value-orientations and interests, centring upon large and important social concerns (e.g. education, marriage, property) generate or are accompanied by distinctive modes of social interaction. Its use emphasizes 'important' social phenomena, relationships of 'strategic structural significance'.

B. Usage is extensive as well as appreciably variant. Citations must therefore be restricted, but those that follow are of representative works.
1. W. G. Sumner (*Folkways*, Boston: Ginn (1906), 1940, p. 53) asserts that 'an institution consists of a concept (idea, notion, doctrine, interest) and a structure'. Both 'concept' and 'structure' are very broadly, not to say vaguely, conceived by him. Thus: 'The structure is a framework, or apparatus, or perhaps only a number of functionaries. ... [It] holds the concept and furnishes instrumentalities for bringing it into the world of facts and action ...' Sumner and A. G. Keller (*The Science of Society*, New Haven: Yale University Press, 1927, vol. I, p. 89) aver that 'mores gather ... about

interests, and develop, where the interests are salient, into institutions'.
2. L. T. Hobhouse argues that the term 'covers (1) recognized and established usages governing certain relations of men, (2) an entire complex of such usages and the principles governing it, and (3) the organisation (if such exists) supporting such a complex' (*Social Development*, London: Allen & Unwin, 1924, p. 49).
3. R. M. MacIver and C. H. Page (*Society*, New York: Rinehart, 1949, p. 15) understand by institutions 'the *established forms or conditions of procedure* characteristic of group activity'. Associations (q.v.) in their conception are groups organized to pursue one or more interests, while institutions may be said in general to represent the modi operandi of the associations. In an illustrative charting of associations, characteristic institutions, and interests, these writers list marriage, the home, and inheritance as institutions proper to the association known as the family; collective bargaining, the strike, and picketing as proper to the trade union; constitution, legal code, and forms of government as proper to the state. The general view of institutions suggested by MacIver and Page is also held by Hobhouse (see above), and by later British writers such as M. Ginsberg (e.g. in *Sociology*, London: Oxford University Press, 1934, p. 42) and W. J. H. Sprott (*Sociology*, London: Hutchinson's University Library, n.d., p. 41, where MacIver and Ginsberg are quoted).
4. The influential view of T. Parsons may be rendered as follows: Human agents internalize values and norms, and conformity to these thereby has personal significance for them. In so far as there is *sharing*, i.e. in so far as particular others have internalized the same values, so that conformity is both personally satisfying and a necessity for evoking 'favourable' reactions from others, a value pattern is 'institutionalized'. An 'institution', as such, becomes then 'a complex of institutionalized role integrates [or, alternatively, says Parsons, "status-relationships"] which is of strategic structural significance in the social system ...' (*The Social System*, Glencoe, Ill.: The Free Press, 1951, p. 39).

C. A definition may usefully concentrate on three main points. First, the term might well be reserved for 'important' social phenomena, as 'salient interests' (Sumner) or reference to relationships of 'strategic structural significance'

(Parsons) would suggest. Second, a central component or set of components in institutions is still intimated by Sumner's old and rather indefinite term, 'concept'. Here it seems advisable to give stress to 'value-patterns', norms, and standards; and there is no need to exclude 'interests' even if in the MacIver-Page categories interest is distinguished from both association and institutions, and Parsons is primarily concerned with values. Sumner's term 'structure' points to the third element: modes of social interaction, *as conditioned by value-patterns and interests*, may be said to comprise the element of 'structure'.

The tying together of value patterns and interests on the one hand with modes of social interaction may be suggested as particularly important, as indicated above. The following illustrative material may be helpful in this regard: an 'authoritarian' type of school, run under the conviction that its teachers are transmitting an imperishably true heritage, involves *particular kinds of interaction* between teachers and students; whereas a 'liberal' school, run under the conviction that there is indeed something worth while to transmit but with an inclination towards a certain tentativeness and towards receptivity to students' own ideas, will involve *different kinds of interaction* between teachers and students. Thus, different basic value-orientations and interests will differently condition the character of interaction. We deal with institutions, then, where distinctive value-orientations and interests, centring upon large and important social concerns (e.g. education, marriage, property), generate or are accompanied by distinctive modes of social interaction. In the present state of usage of the term, no more can be expected than that a roughly synthetic definition of this kind will appeal to some social scientists.

Louis Schneider

See also: SOCIAL STRUCTURE
VALUE

Integral Nationalism (See Nationalism)

Integration (See Social Integration)

Intellectual (See Intelligentsia)

Intelligence
A. In common use the term denotes (a) the capacity of organisms to learn by experience and make adaptive responses to new situations, as contrasted with instinctive or reflex responses; (b) the faculty of understanding, intellect; that is, the cognitive aspect of mental functioning and in particular the higher thought processes and conceptual activities, and the grasping of relationships; (c) a measurement of the common element or factor underlying successful performance at varied mental tasks such as those included in intelligence tests (e.g. the intelligence quotient).

B. The above three types of definition reflect the different approaches of biologists, psychologists, and statisticians during the late 19th and early 20th centuries—approaches which are still incompletely reconciled.

1. *Biological.* Spencer and Darwin drew attention to the progressive increase, with evolution, in the flexibility of behaviour, associated with the increasing size and complexity of the higher brain centres. Intelligence, in Spencer's view, gradually differentiates into a hierarchy of more specialized capacities ranging from the simple sensory to the most complex relational thinking abilities. The same kind of growth is characteristic of the development of the human individual from baby- to adulthood.

To Gestalt psychologists such as W. Köhler (*The Mentality of Apes*, trans. from the 2nd rev. edn. by E. Winter, New York: Harcourt, Brace, 1925) adaptation by trial and error or by the acquisition of conditioned reflexes is less significant than 'insight'—that is the capacity shown by apes and other higher species to restructure a situation, or to solve a problem by grasping its interrelationships. Moreover the current work of comparative psychologists such as N. Tinbergen (*Social Behavior in Animals*, New York: Wiley, 1953) tends to break down the distinction between instinct and learning.

2. *Statistical.* Galton's *Hereditary Genius* (New York: Appleton, 1871) represents the earliest approach to the study of individual differences in intelligence, which he regarded as distributed among the population, much as differences in height are distributed, according to the normal curve. With K. Pearson he developed the technique of correlation, which was applied by Spearman for investigating how far abilities are specific, or dependent on a single general intelligence, or organized into separate faculties. C. E. Spearman claimed to show, in 1904, that every ability depends partly on a common factor, 'g', and partly on 's'—a wholly

Intelligentsia

specific element (cf. *The Abilities of Man*, London: The Macmillan Co., 1927). This approach seemed to justify the attempts of Binet and his followers to measure intelligence by summing a child's performances on a series of varied intellectual problems. However C. L. Burt and others showed that additional sub-types of ability—verbal, numerical, practical, etc., could be distinguished in specialized fields, over and above 'g' (C. L. Burt, *The Factors of the Mind*, London: University of London Press, 1940; and 'The Structure of the Mind: a Review of the Results of Factor Analysis', *British Journal of Educational Psychology*, vol. 19, pp. 100–11, 176–99). American writers also, such as Thorndike and Thurstone, doubted the generality of intelligence: and currently they prefer to distinguish and measure a considerable number of more specialized abilities or mental factors— verbal, reasoning, rote memory, number, spatial, etc., though the extent of their independence is still a matter of controversy (E. L. Thorndike and others, *Measurement of Intelligence*, New York: Bureau of Publications, Teachers College, Columbia University, 1927; L. L. Thurstone, *The Nature of Intelligence*, New York: Harcourt, Brace, 1924).

3. *Psychological.* Little agreement has ever been reached by psychologists in their theoretical discussions of the nature of intelligence. Some, like Burt, emphasize that it is general or all-round cognitive ability, and that it is innately determined by multiple genes; although, when we try to measure it, our test results are affected to a minor extent by upbringing and environment. A. Binet committed himself only to a rough definition: '... to judge well, to comprehend well, to reason well, these are the essentials of intelligence' (*The Development of Intelligence in Children*, trans. by E. S. Kite, Baltimore: Williams & Wilkins, 1916, p. 43). Following Spencer and Galton, he based his choice of tests largely on those mental functions which seemed to show the most striking development among children with age. Others have tried to identify the essence of intelligence as reasoning, problem-solving, abstract thinking, foresight, etc., C. E. Spearman, however, repudiated the term as too unscientific to be useful, and was concerned rather with the common factor 'g', underlying all cognitive functions. This he interpreted as 'general mental energy', and considered that it emerged in purest form in tests involving abstraction and 'the eduction of relations and correlates' (*The Abilities of Man*, pp. 75 ff.). American psychologists in particular

have questioned the genetic determination of intelligence, and provided much evidence of its dependence on environmental and social-class influences.

C. The views of J. Piaget (*The Psychology of Intelligence*, trans. by M. Piercy & D. E. Berlyne, New York: Harcourt, Brace, 1950) and D. O. Hebb (*The Organization of Behavior*, New York: Wiley, 1949) appear to offer promise of an acceptable reconciliation. According to Piaget the behaviour of lower organisms and of young infants is more directly and immediately determined by innate neural or biochemical mechanisms, and by external stimulation to which they become conditioned; whereas at higher levels, intervening processes occur to a greater extent in the central nervous system, between stimulus and response. Mental development is regarded as the cumulative building up of 'schemata' (which Hebb attributes to 'assemblies of neurones' and 'phase sequences' in the association areas of the brain (ibid., p. xix and ch. 6) as a result of interaction between the organism and its environment. Such schemata underly the simpler sensory-motor adaptations, then the perceptual and later the autonomous conceptual functions. Thus intelligence is the product of genetic potentiality for the formation of schemata, and of experience or stimulation by the environment, and though present at all stages it is most fully manifested in the higher thinking capacities. From the point of view of the mental tester, intelligence is a fluid collection of overlapping abilities, rather than any single identifiable faculty. And, while tests which would differentiate abilities along different lines would be of great value, the predominant influence of the overall level of intellectual development reached by an individual should be recognized.

P. E. Vernon

See also: MIND
REASON

Intelligentsia

A. 1. In Western societies the word is currently used mainly to denote a *small inner elite*, or *self-styled elite, of writers and cultural dignitaries*. That such bodies have an identity of their own, and even possess at times some social and political influence, cannot be denied, e.g. the *Quartier latin*, Bloomsbury. But though it may have more or less prestige in one Western society than in another, this group is not sharply differentiated from other sections of the pro-

340

fessional classes, nor are these rigidly separated from the middle classes as a whole. Although frequently critical of the common ethos which it shares with other middle-class groups, such an elite grows up with its society as a whole.

2. In 'underdeveloped societies (a term which here includes 19th-century Russia as an outstanding early example), the modern intellectual elite did not grow with the society as a whole, and was linked by no common ethos with the other middle-class groups. The intelligentsia was artificially created as a result of external forces, either in imitation of Western society, in order to acquire Western skills and compete with Western military and economic power (as in Russia and Japan), or through Western conquest and the imposition of Western political and educational patterns (as in India and Indo-China). The distinctive and modern culture which such an intelligentsia enjoys separates its members from the rest of society. This sense of isolation, and the vast contrast between the realities of its own society and the modern ideas with which its education has made it familiar, are powerful factors leading first towards uncritical acceptance of revolutionary ideas, and later to leadership and organization of revolutionary action.

3. In Soviet society the phrase 'toiling intelligentsia' has been used simply to describe *all who are not workers or peasants*. In the 1950s there were reckoned to be about 15 million of them, and with family dependants this figure should certainly be more than doubled. So large a group includes, of course, far more than the intellectual elite or than the intellectual professions. It denotes the *whole upper stratum*, and the word *intelligentsia* has been chosen for it because it has 'progressive' historical associations, and so is preferable to such names as *ruling class, bureaucracy, state capitalist class*, or *state bourgeoisie*, which would more accurately describe the phenomenon. Its use can also partly be explained by the fact that many of those who now belong to the upper stratum originate from the old professional classes.

B. The term comes from the Russian *intelligentsia* and was first used in the mid-19th century. In its most general usage it described the small but growing cultural elite, which had received an education of the contemporary West European type, either at one of the newly created Russian universities or in study abroad.

1. At first the word was chiefly used for what may be called *the cream of this elite*—the writers, literary critics, scientists, and university professors.

2. During the century it came to be extended to the professional classes in a wider sense—to the law, teaching, and medicine in particular.

3. Owing to the autocratic system of government, which until 1905 denied any expression to political opposition, the word acquired a further notion of more or less *radical rejection of the whole political and social system of Russia*. It is hardly an exaggeration that the whole intelligentsia was against the regime, and that a well-educated man who supported the regime (and there were, of course, many such in government service) could not by definition be considered a member of the intelligentsia.

4. From Russia the word spread also to other countries. West European nations and non-European nations in 'underdeveloped societies' subject to European influence, contain social groups that are described as *intelligentsia*. But in the U.S.S.R., the term, as noted above, denotes the *whole upper stratum* of society.

G. H. N. Seton-Watson

See also: SOCIOLOGY OF KNOWLEDGE

Interaction (See Social Interaction)

Interest (Economics)

A. *Interest* denotes the price, or rent, paid in money in exchange for the use of a sum of money, 'the premium obtained on current cash over deferred cash' (J. M. Keynes, 'The Theory of the Rate of Interest', *The Lessons of Monetary Experience: Essays in Honour of Irving Fisher*, ed. by A. D. Gayer, London: Allen & Unwin, 1937, p. 145; A. Marshall, *Money, Credit and Commerce*, London: Macmillan, 1923, p. 73; B. Ohlin, 'Some Notes on the Stockholm Theory of Savings and Investment', *The Economic Journal*, vol. XLVII, 1937, pp. 221–40; D. H. Robertson, *Essays in Monetary Theory*, London: P. S. King, 1940, pp. 1–2).

B. Economists have commonly not been much interested in this commonplace definition and have asked why interest must be paid and why the borrower is willing to pay it.

1. Economists first answered that interest must be paid, so that enough saving will be done to permit desirable progress from capital accumulation. While it is generally agreed that some saving would be done at zero interest, the amount would be undesirably small. Positive

Interest

interest has been looked upon as a necessary bribe to get recipients of income to consume less than they might. N. W. Senior, one of the first to be clear-cut in his explanation, declared that interest compensated for the pains of abstinence (*An Outline of the Science of Political Economy* (1st edn., 1836) London: Charles Griffin, 6th edn., 1872, pp. 58–60; see also M. Bowley, *Nassau Senior and Classical Economics*, London: Allen & Unwin, 1937, pp. 137–66).

2. Socialists poured scorn upon the notion that interest is a reward for the pains of abstinence. If abstinence involves pain, they said, then the Rothschilds and other rich must have suffered monumentally. Senior, of course, could have admitted that saving by the rich involved no obvious or even hidden pain but then have argued that without interest an insufficient amount of abstaining from consumption would be supplied. Marx himself argued that the capitalist wished to consume and at the same time to acquire power through accumulation of property. Of course marginal analysis clears up the difficulty by viewing interest merely as the opportunity cost of the marginal unit of saving. Where small savers represent marginal supply real 'pain' appears.

3. Socialist criticism, nevertheless, left economists uncomfortable. Help came through a shift in emphasis which converted abstinence into time preference. The time preference theory of interest had its early development in the work of W. S. Jevons and the Austrians, particularly E. von Böhm-Bawerk (*The Positive Theory of Capital*, trans. by W. Smart, London: Macmillan, 1891, pp. 285–424; W. S. Jevons, *The Theory of Political Economy* (1st edn., 1871), London: Macmillan, 4th edn., 1911, pp. 71–4). This theory has been criticized and refined by J. A. Schumpeter, I. Fisher, F. A. Fetter, F. A. Hayek, and others. Böhm-Bawerk imputed to man a 'perspective undervaluation of future wants'. For many people this undervaluation explains the preference for present goods over those available in the future, but the presence of this element is not a necessary ingredient of the time preference theory except in a stationary society. 'All that is required in a progressive society for the existence of interest is that its members should feel some *reluctance to postpone* consumption of present income in order to increase future income beyond the present level at more than a limited rate' (F. A. Hayek, *The Pure Theory of Capital*. London: Routledge & Kegan Paul, 1941, p. 420). Few economists

today deny the importance of time preference, but many of them do think that the schedule of saving, in which the quantity of saving is presented as a function of the rate of interest, has little elasticity through much of its length.

4. In 1936 J. M. Keynes emphasized liquidity preference as necessitating the payment of interest (*The General Theory of Employment, Interest, and Money*, London: Macmillan, 1936, pp. 136–7, 145–6, 166–74, 202). Interest must be paid because people and institutions have the alternative of hoarding their monetary savings. Lord Keynes thought that a decline in interest set up expectation of a return to a higher level. The lower the rate of interest, the stronger the incentive to accumulate hoards, for every fall in the interest rate 'reduces the current earnings from illiquidity, which are available as a sort of insurance premium to offset the risk of loss on capital account, by an amount equal to the difference between the squares of the old rate of interest and the new' (ibid., p. 202). As Sir Dennis Robertson was prompt to point out, Lord Keynes came near to saying that interest exists because it is expected to differ in magnitude from what it is (D. H. Robertson, *Essays in Monetary Theory*, p. 25). An improved statement of the liquidity theory of interest is that interest cannot decline below a minimum because of the alternative of hoarding but that any rate above this minimum is adequate to induce dishoarding if higher future rates are not anticipated and if other circumstances are favourable. With justice Sir Dennis scolded Lord Keynes for failing to note that the rate of interest must in equilibrium satisfy both the 'marginal convenience of holding money' and the 'marginal inconvenience of refraining from consumption'. Sir Roy Harrod noted that the borrower 'will have to pay the price necessary to satisfy the lender in his capacity of waiter or the price necessary to satisfy him in his capacity of parter with liquidity, whichever is higher. There seems to be the assumption in Keynes that the second will be the higher' (*Towards a Dynamic Economics*, London: Macmillan, 1948, p. 70).

C. Regardless of the emphasis in their theory of interest, all economists recognize productivity or yield of capital as a determinant of interest. Much confusion however results from the intermingling of static and dynamic analysis. Both Schumpeter and Böhm-Bawerk pointed out that it was *value* productivity, not physical productivity that mattered. Schumpeter, in his

Theory of Economic Development (Cambridge, Mass.: Harvard University Press, 1934), pointed out that if there were no new technical changes or disturbance, and the process of capital accumulation continued uninterruptedly, the prospect of a marginal value product would disappear. He denied that there would be any reason for time preference in the resulting risk-less equilibrium or 'stationary state'. F. H. Knight also maintained that without continual growth and change there would be no reason for Böhm-Bawerk's time preference; thus he said Böhm-Bawerk, despite his frantic denials, *had* a productivity theory. Knight, however, argued that Schumpeter's stationary state was an impossibility, in theory anyhow, as there are no 'limits on the use of capital' (see F. H. Knight, 'Interest' in E. R. A. Seligman (ed.), *Encyclopedia of the Social Sciences*, New York: The Macmillan Co., 1932, vol. VIII, p. 134). Any actual stationary society would be the result of 'non-economic' or sociological forces (F. H. Knight, 'Capital, Time and the Interest Rate', *Economica*, vol. I, new series, 1934, pp. 257–86; 'The Quantity of Capital and the Rate of Interest', *The Journal of Political Economy*, vol. XLIV, 1936, pp. 433–53, 612–42).

Productivity theories of interest thus reflect the fact that in a free enterprise economy the motive for borrowing is in anticipation of return from investment. While a socialist state might figure costs differently, and have different value scales it also would need to consider returns for rational planning. But those who presented the cases for time preference and liquidity preference did great service for they showed that a simple productivity theory was never complete in itself.

Fewer and fewer economists now subscribe to any one of the extreme positions represented by Böhm-Bawerk, Keynes, or Schumpeter. On an empirical level one recognizes the influence of at least three dimensions: profit prospects from technical change, etc., liquidity preference, planned saving. To this may be added time preference. D. McC. Wright in an article approved by Keynes, pointed out that the 'marginal efficiency of capital' did affect the rate of interest via induced variations in L, demand for liquidity ('The Future of Keynesian Economics', *American Economic Review*, vol. XXV, 1945, pp. 292–3; also D. McC. Wright, *The Keynesian System*, New York: Fordham University Press, 1962). The majority conclusion is thus apt to be substantially that of D. Patinkin, 'that interest exerts its influence in all markets and that, in particular, it operates simultaneously on the "threefold margin" of time preference (consumption decisions), marginal productivity of capital (investment decisions), and liquidity preference ...' (*Money, Interest, and Prices*, Evanston, Ill.: Row, Peterson, 1956, p. 267).

William L. Miller

See also: PROFIT
RENT
SAVING
WAGES

Interest (Political Science)

A. An *interest* may mean (a) a claim worthy of consideration; (b) a right to a share of something; (c) a right to take part in an activity; (d) whatever is profitable to a person or group, because it gives him or them what he or they want or will find satisfactory; (e) a group who have an interest in common in the sense defined under (d); and (f) any object so important to those who pursue it that it helps to determine the rules of conduct they are required to obey and the value-judgements they make.

B. 1. A man's interest is whatever is profitable to him, whatever helps him get what he wants or what will satisfy him. In this sense, a man may not know his own interest or others may know it better than he does. What is profitable to more than one person is an interest common to those who profit by it. It can be our interest not to get what we want, if our getting it prevents our getting other things we want more or makes us want what we cannot get. Hence a distinction between wants and interests, and also between immediate and long-term interests. Interests, in this sense, are always related to wants, actual or potential. If we give a man what we think is good for him, regardless of what he wants or may come to want, we do not promote his interest. Though a man's interest is often called his *good*, just as *common good* (q.v.) and *common interest* are often synonymous, good in these cases is used in the sense of 'most satisfying on the whole'.

2. To have an interest is to have a claim on other persons in respect of something. This claim, moral or legal, need not be valid; it may, after investigation, be dismissed as ill-founded. But it must be plausible, it must be worth considering. Thus, to have an interest in some matter is, at the very least, to have a right to be heard by those whose right it is to decide. To have an interest in something can also mean to

Interest

have a share or part in it, as when a man puts money into a business, thus acquiring a right to a share of the profits, or takes part in managing it. These two uses, which are still common, are among the oldest.

3. By an interest we sometimes mean a number of persons having, or supposed to have, a common interest, as when we speak of an 'agricultural interest' or a 'Catholic interest'. By a 'sinister interest' Bentham meant a privileged group or profession pursuing, under pretence of serving the community, an interest incompatible with the interest of the whole community.

4. To take an interest in something is to be curious or concerned about it, but this sense of the word has nothing special to do with the social sciences.

5. Two important schools of thought have treated interests as prior to morals. The Utilitarians, believing that everyone desires pleasure and is averse to pain (whether his own only or also other people's) said that it is always the common interest to encourage types of behaviour which usually increase pleasure and diminish pain and to discourage types which usually do the opposite, and that the function of moral rules is to promote the common interest.

Marxists treat morality as a function of *class interest*, saying that the dominant moral code in a class society serves the interest of the exploiting class, the exploited acquiring a moral code of their own only when they become aware of their 'objective' class interests. Thus, Marxists distinguish between the 'objective' or 'true' interests of a class and their actual wants; their 'objective' interests are what they would want if they understood the position of their class in the course of social evolution. This does not mean that classes never pursue their 'true' interests unless they have this understanding. Marxists, though they believe that only their theory correctly describes the course of social evolution, admit that classes often pursued their 'true' interests before that theory emerged. Nevertheless, to ascertain what are the 'true' interests of a class, we must have this understanding.

6. Since the 18th century it has been quite usual to explain social institutions as if their function were to protect and reconcile interests rather than rights. For example, democracy is often described as a system allowing any group who believe they have common interests to collaborate the better to pursue them, the essential business of government being to reconcile as many interests as possible. This type of explanation need not assume, as Bentham and Marx do, that interests are prior to rights.

J. P. Plamenatz

See also: INTEREST (Economic)
VALUE

Interest (Social Psychology)

A. *Interest* in its most general sense refers to a subject–object relationship in which a person (or group of persons) persists in attending to and exerting effort toward some object because of its attractiveness. In this general context *interest* may designate either the object of attention and effort or the attitude (q.v.) and feeling directed toward the object.

B. Interests are closely related to, but not totally dependent upon the ability of the relevant objects and activities to offer consummatory value in satisfying needs; for interest involves not merely the objective possibility of tension reduction, but also the subjective structuring of a field in terms of individual and cultural interest patterns. This latter characteristic links the social-psychological definition of interest with that of sociologists and anthropologists who have generally treated interests as shared among the members of a group. Thus R. Linton (*The Study of Man*, New York: Appleton-Century, 1937, p. 422) writes, 'No matter how numerous or how intense any individual associations with a particular thing are, this does not make the thing an interest as long as these associations are exclusively his own'.

C. Although social psychologists, sociologists, and anthropologists sometimes use the political definitions of interest organized around conceptions of objective advantage and the holding of claims in a particular situation, such definitions are relevant to the definition given above only when an objective economic or political interest is made the object of sustained attention and effort. This may occur simply as the result of desire and need, or it may be the result of normative attitudes. Thus the social-psychological definition of interest is related to objective economic interest if we accept the proposition that 'the conceptual ideal of economic behavior is ..., at least within limits, also a normative ideal, that men in general, and within limits, wish to behave economically, to make their activities and their organization "efficient" rather than wasteful' (F. H. Knight, 'Deduction and Induction in Economics', in

M. Herskovits (ed.), *Economic Anthropology*, New York: Knopf, 1952, p. 510).

Kurt Lang

See also: INTEREST (Political Science)

Interest Group (See Pressure Group)

Intergroup Relations (See Race and Minority Group Relations)

Internalization

A. The word *internalization* is given at least three meanings in the social sciences. The first equates it with learning (q.v.). The second makes it synonymous with symbolization. Since there are precise and common technical terms already existing for these two uses, it seems desirable to reserve *internalization* for the third, or psycho-analytic, usage, i.e. learning (or the state of having learnt) in cases where the learner is unaware of the conditions which have impelled, influenced, or motivated him.

B. 1. A somewhat casual use equates internalizing with learning. Thus one might speak of a dog learning or internalizing the connection between a ringing bell and the subsequent experience of an electric shock.

2. In the works of some social psychologists, especially the symbolic-interaction school, *internalization* has had the more limited meaning of acquiring a sign which subjectively replicates or stands for an experience and which can be the object of self-conscious attention. In this use of the term, social psychologists sometimes speak of the individual's internalization of a social role. The assumption is that the individual has acquired symbols which represent his relationships to others, his family, for example, with the result that these relationships now have a continuing presence in the covert aspects of his behaviour.

3. A third meaning of *internalization* appears most frequently in works influenced by psychoanalytic ideas. In this third sense, *internalization* is the process of learning, or the resultant state of having learnt, when the learner is unaware of the conditions which motivated his engaging in this learning. This lack of awareness may be due to the learner's inability to perceive the motivating conditions when they occurred. Thus E. Schachtel ('On Memory and Childhood Amnesia', *Psychiatry*, vol. 10, 1947, pp. 1–27) accounts for the individual's inability to recall events from the first year of his life as the result of his not having symbols which might re-present such events in memory. A different, and more common, explanation is to say that self-conscious awareness is absent as a result of the individual's having repressed his knowledge of the conditions which motivated his learning.

In its psychoanalytic meaning, *internalization* plays an especially useful role in designating the special variety of learning which is considered common to the acquiring of all of the super-ego's contents, e.g. moral norms and conscience. It thus refers to a process shared by many other terms common in psychoanalysis (e.g. identification, introjection, and incorporation).

Guy E. Swanson

See also: ENCULTURATION
LEARNING
SOCIALIZATION

International Economics

A. *International economics*, as a sub-field of economics, denotes economic behaviour, and economic phenomena of all kinds that transcend the boundaries of a region or of a nation.

B. 1. Strictly, as the term suggests, the focus is upon the international aspects of economics, but except in monetary and policy matters, little distinction is made between principles that apply to relations between regions and those that are relevant to relations between nations. It has long been a major sub-field of economics, as well as an important part of what is frequently termed international relations. Any summary survey of recent literature in the field would reveal some of the following particular focal points: historic trends, trade theory, capital movements and investment, labour movements and migration, monetary relations, payments problems, equilibrium and disequilibrium, economic development and growth, trade restrictions and controls, national trade policies, international co-operation, and problems occasioned by past wars, by the 'cold war', and by preparation for possible future wars. The sub-field is inescapably sprawling, as are the complex and ramified phenomena upon which it centres.

2. Interest in certain aspects of international economics, notably trade, trade theory, and trade policy, goes back to the earliest era of economics as a discipline. Indeed, emphasis upon this phase of economic life pre-dates formal economics, as evidenced by mercantilist writing and policy prescriptions. In recent decades, however, the scope and emphasis of international economics have undergone a

International Law

marked change. The international aspects of economic activity and behaviour are treated with increasing frequency as being of one piece with the rest of economic life. Rather than a water-tight compartment, treated as something distinct, different, and apart, international economics is now merely the study of economic phenomena that happen to extend beyond the boundaries of a single region or nation. Thus, the boundaries that have set international economics apart from other sub-fields of economics, and from the main body of economic thought, have tended to shift and, in the process, to become blurred. It is widely recognized that what goes on within a national economy almost invariably has international repercussions, and vice versa. Trade, factor movements, growth, and even policy are essentially all of one piece, whether the focus is domestic or international.

Even so, international economics has a particular focus that sets it somewhat apart in the division of labour within economics. It confronts special problems, or at least special aspects of general problems. The special aspects of exchange between two or more different currencies, and more important, between two or more different countries with independent monetary and fiscal policies give rise to much of the work in this field. The international institutions to which these economic problems have given rise are critical in the study of international economics. It operates against the background of a continually changing institutional setting, and it comes constantly in contact with the many-faceted relations between nations. Thus, international economics today can still be examined as a sub-field, despite its essential merger with the main body of economics.

C. Addison Hickman

See also: ECONOMICS
INTERNATIONAL RELATIONS

International Law

A. The following definition deserves to be considered as the starting point of any discussion of the nature of international law. 'International law governs relations between independent States. The rules of law binding upon States therefore emanate from their own free will as expressed in conventions or by usages generally accepted as expressing principles of law and established in order to regulate the relations between these co-existing independent communities or with a view to the achievement of common aims. Restrictions upon the independence of States cannot therefore be presumed' (*Lotus* case between France and Turkey, 1927, P.C.I.J., Series A, no. 9, p. 18).

B. The problems which arise from such a definition concern the scope of the rules of international law and the sources of (and obligations entailed by) those rules.

1. While relations between independent states form the most important part of international law, they do not constitute the whole of it. States that are not fully independent (e.g. protected states) are not completely outside the scope of international law. Mandated territories under the League of Nations system of mandates (the only remaining one is South-West Africa) and trust territories under the international trusteeship system of the United Nations also possess a limited status under international law. The Holy See has for centuries been regarded as an 'international person', thus proving that it is not necessary to be a state at all in order to be a subject of international law. It has been stated by the International Court of Justice that the United Nations is 'an international person' and 'a subject of international law and capable of possessing international rights and duties'. Explaining this conclusion the Court said that 'the progressive increase in the collective activities of States has already given rise to instances of action upon the international plane by certain entities which are not States' (*I.C.J. Reports* 1949, pp. 178, 179). The principle that organizations created by states (such as the United Nations and the specialized agencies) are, no less than the states themselves, subjects of international law is now generally accepted. Acceptance of this principle, however, does not mean that the organizations are regarded as the equals, let alone as the superiors, of states. As the Court explained, 'The subjects of law in any legal system are not necessarily identical in their nature or in the extent of their rights, and their nature depends upon the needs of the community' (ibid., p. 178). Thus the view should be accepted that international law is concerned, not merely with relations between independent states, but also with the constitutions and procedures of international organizations, with the relations of these organizations with each other and with their member states, and even with the relations between such organizations and individual members of the staffs who work for them.

2. It is inherent in a legal system that its rules are binding upon its subjects. This remains true even if, as in the case of international law, its rules cannot always be enforced. There is general agreement that the rules of international law are binding on so-called 'sovereign states', even if there is much controversy as to how the rules come into existence, why they are binding and, in some cases, what they are. According to one view, which finds some support in the passage from the Judgement of the Permanent Court of International Justice quoted above, the rules are binding upon states because they were voluntarily made by states. This view is unsatisfactory, however, because it does not explain why the entire corpus of international law should be binding, as in fact it is, upon a new state which has played no part in its creation; nor does it explain why even older states, which may have played a part in the creation of the rules, are not free to disavow them. Others base the binding character of the rules of international law not so much on the will of states as on the notion of international solidarity or on the needs of the world community. The most authoritative text is the first paragraph of Article 38 of the Statute of the International Court of Justice. This provides that 'The Court, whose function is to decide in accordance with international law such disputes as are submitted to it, shall apply: (a) international conventions, whether general or particular, establishing rules expressly recognized by the contesting states; (b) international custom, as evidence of a general practice accepted as law; (c) the general principles of law recognized by civilized nations; (d) subject to the provisions of Article 59 [this Article provides that 'The decision of the Court has no binding force except between the parties and in respect of that particular case'] judicial decisions and the teachings of the most highly qualified publicists of the various nations, as subsidiary means for the determination of rules of law' (I.C.J., *Acts and Documents Concerning the Organisation of the Court*, May 1947, pp. 46, 49).

D. H. N. Johnson

See also: INTERNATIONAL RELATIONS
LAW

International Organization

A. Three sources of ambiguity giving rise to different meanings can be distinguished, arising respectively from the prefix *inter*, the adjective *national*, and the noun *organization*.

1. *Inter* can imply either relation or location between. *International* applied to an organization may thus mean either: (a) that an organization links together a number of participant nations, *international* referring to the relationship between them, e.g. the United Nations Organization; or (b) that the organization operates among and parallel to nations, not being itself a nation, e.g. the international commercial agencies in which nationals of more than one nation participate as for example, Royal-Dutch Shell, the Suez Canal Company.

2. *National* can comprehend both the government of a nation state, or a private agency claiming to represent the national interest in spheres of activity not universally reserved to the government. In this sense, *International* applied to an organization can, e.g. refer to (a) the United Nations; (b) the Olympics organization, Rotary International, the Second International, the International Federation of Free Trades Unions, the International Union of Students, etc.

3. *Organization* can comprehend both organized bodies and procedures. In this sense *international organization* can, e.g. refer to (a) the United Nations; or (b) diplomacy, treaty negotiation, international customary law, etc.

B. 1. The term is often used loosely to mean *inter-state* organizations and thus applied to schemes such as Henri IV of France's 'Grand Design', (1604), or Gustavus Adolphus of Sweden's 'Corpus Evangelicorum', (1632). The development of centralized autocratic states in the 15th–16th centuries directed interest to the problems of relations between them, giving rise on the one hand to early writings on international law, on the other to development of techniques of diplomacy, subversion and espionage.

2. The term properly defined should not be applied to any inter-state organization before the emergence, in the 19th century, of the nation-state, the diversion of nationalist interests to the status of the nation in the eyes of other nations, and the consequent identification of the property and interests of the national citizen living abroad with those of the nation as a whole. It then came to be applied to a number of procedures and institutions which developed in the latter half of the 19th century to supply to one nation the co-operation of its fellows, and to avoid every minor conflict of interests becoming a cause of major embitterment.

International Relations

C. 1. The application of the term to 'procedures' (A3b above) is becoming less frequent and could well be abandoned, especially as the procedures defined really cover *inter-state* rather than *inter-national* relations.

2. The exclusion from the scope of the term, of the non-governmental organizations (A2b) advocated by some writers, on the grounds that they are *cosmopolitan* rather than *inter-national* seems difficult to justify generally and in many specific cases is clearly impossible to maintain.

3. The exclusion from the scope of the term, of international relationships of a non-corporate kind, such as alliances and associations, advocated by other writers, seems permissible. Currently most such alliances and associations tend to set up institutional frameworks.

4. The inclusion of 'immediate and completely voluntary co-operation between nations' advocated by P. B. Potter in the essay, 'International Organization (in E. R. A. Seligman (ed.) *Encyclopedia of Social Sciences*, New York: The Macmillan Co., 1932, vol. VIII, p. 178) would seem illegitimate.

5. The problem of the non-national international organization (A1b above), can only be noted. Extreme nationalism is tending to reduce their numbers though they are unlikely to disappear entirely.

D. C. Watt

See also: ALLIANCE
DIPLOMACY
INTERNATIONAL LAW
INTERNATIONAL RELATIONS
INTERNATIONALISM

International Relations

A. There is general agreement that the term *international relations* denotes the contacts of peoples and states across national frontiers (F. H. Hartmann, *The Relations of Nations*, New York: The Macmillan Co., 1962, p. 5). The predominant emphasis in *international relations* as a field of political science is on describing and explaining the contacts of states in terms of their interacting national interests. The nature of national policies and interests is such that the contacts described are necessarily a mixture of conflict (q.v.), competition (q.v.), and co-operation (q.v.), involving both peace and war, friendship and enmity.

B. Any definition of this field of study raises questions and difficulties. Writers frequently offer initially useful but broad formulations, e.g. 'International relations as the totality of social phenomena transcending national boun-

daries . . .' (H. J. Morgenthau, 'The Nature and Limits of a Theory of International Relations', in W. T. R. Fox (ed.), *Theoretical Aspects of International Relations*, Notre Dame, Ind.: University of Notre Dame Press, 1959, p. 15). But, as Morgenthau elsewhere makes plain, the very word 'international' is ambiguous—and the interests of the inquiry frequently place the focus of attention upon only one of the variety of social phenomena encountered, e.g. the political or the economic. This is no new problem. In 1935 P. Mantoux, pleading for 'a narrow definition of international studies', observed: 'One can without doubt call international any phenomenon because it belongs to all countries ... From this point of view, seasickness is an international fact. ... Yet the question remains outside our field of enquiry until one concerns oneself with the conclusion of an international convention obligating vessels to equip themselves with certain medicines which are recognized as necessary for the protection against seasickness' (quoted in H. J. Morgenthau, *Dilemmas of Politics*, Chicago: University of Chicago Press, 1958, p. 90). More recently S. Hoffman discusses the view of the subject which emphasizes 'the relations between states' and shows how it 'glosses over the fact that states are not monolithic blocs and that within them and often side by side with them, individuals and ideological or interest groups are the real decision-makers' ('International Relations as a Discipline', in S. Hoffman (ed.), *Contemporary Theory in International Relations*, Englewood Cliffs, N.J.: Prentice-Hall, 1960, p. 5). Hoffman goes on to consider other views —including that which stresses the *power* of states—and he notes the difficulty there is in deciding 'whether a certain activity involves the power of states or not'. He also examines, in the political focus of the subject, the opinion that 'international politics is concerned with the relations between *all* groups in so far as they affect international society but *only* with those relations among groups which are indeed important for world society'. But what, he asks, is 'world society'? (ibid.).

H. and M. Sprout in *Foundations of International Politics* (Princeton: D. Van Nostrand, 1962, p. 74) point out that 'the complex of activities' which are 'transnational in the sense that they cut across the boundaries of jurisdiction of national states is loosely called international relations', but argue that in addition the term 'is also used to denote only transactions involving the organised political communities variously called nation states, nations or states. The term ... suffers from further ambiguity in that it is sometimes used to denote all interstate transactions; and again only those which exhibit some conflict of purpose or interest. For transactions of the latter type we favor the term *international politics*'.

An alternative emphasis has been stressed by the British scholar, C. A. W. Manning, 'Political Science, at least as heretofore developed, has centred essentially upon the governmental process. International Relations (alias Diplomatics) its neighbour discipline, presupposes indeed a quasi-social co-existence of "governed" countries. But its own peculiar concern is with the special nature of one special mode of social co-existence, marked by the absence, even in principle, of any inclusive system of governmental arrangements, any overarching framework, that is, of formal authority' (*The Nature of International Society*, London: Bell, 1962, p. 182).

C. From a functional point of view and in terms of usage, the study of international relations can be, and often is, subdivided into such areas as international politics, international law (q.v.), international economics, international organization (q.v.), foreign policy, and military relations. When such divisions are made, the types of contacts emphasized vary, of course, tremendously. Of these subdivisions, *international politics* is frequently used as synonymous with *international relations*. Where this occurs it is not an indication that the other subdivisions are excluded from consideration, but rather that non-political contacts will be discussed from the point of view of the political considerations involved. Where this is done there is frequently a great emphasis on the rival or hostile contacts of states.

While the preceding remarks are particularly relevant to American writing, it is worth noting that they are also generally applicable to English, French, and German literature as well. The French and German terms for international relations are exact equivalents of the English words: *relations internationales* and *internationale Beziehungen*.

D. The term *international relations* has wide application in four other fields besides political science: history, economics, sociology, and psychology. In these fields, differences in definition from those of political science are primarily matters of emphasis. Historians are more concerned with the historical description of events of international importance. Economists are more concerned with transnational trade and finance. Sociologists and psychologists are more concerned with the development of social changes and psychological attitudes. Since social changes vary from country to country and mass attitudes are difficult to describe, sociologists and psychologists tend to restrict their academic investigations to individuals and to national communities. When they extend their investigations to the international community, they tend to de-emphasize the state as the main actor.

E. In the last fifteen years there has been a noticeable increase of emphasis on the theoretical and systematic aspects of the study of international relations. W. T. R. Fox in his preface to a book specifically concerned with such aspects (*Theoretical Aspects of International Relations*, pp. xi–xii) notes that such students of international relations as Q. Wright, D. Fosdick, L. J. Halle, G. F. Kennan, C. B. Marshall, J. Herz, G. Liska, M. Kaplan, E. Haas, and A. Whiting have been attempting to state the philosophical assumptions underlying and the theoretical concepts informing this field of investigation. A good example of such efforts to systematize the study of international relations is to be found in an article by P. H. Nitze ('Necessary and Sufficient Elements of a General Theory of International Relations', in W. T. R. Fox (ed.), *Theoretical Aspects of International Relations*, pp. 1–14). In this article he suggests that a theoretical system composed of a few fundamental elements would be both more elegant and more useful than one composed of several hundred conceptual elements. He therefore proposes that 'a general theory of international relations needs to deal with the relationships between at least three fundamental concepts. These are structure, purpose, and situation' (ibid., p. 2). In turn 'Power, and restraints on power, will be considered as subsidiary concepts within the system suggested by the three fundamental concepts' (ibid.).

Frederick H. Hartmann
Heyward Moore

See also: INTERNATIONAL LAW
INTERNATIONAL ORGANIZATION

Internationalism

A. The word is a vague one with a number of overlapping usages—all of them denoting the

Interpersonal Relations

beliefs and policies of those who emphasize the *common* interests of different nations and peoples: a reaction against strident and aggressive nationalism, and a conviction that peaceful means of co-operation are possible between all peoples, if not all states.

B. 1. An early and now defunct usage, by which internationalism was identified with support for the International Working Men's Association and its successor, the Second International, survived until at least the 1880s.

2. More recently and commonly there are two usages—the first in self-description by 'internationalists', the second a derogatory usage by those who oppose them.

(a) Thus L. L. Lorwin characterizes *internationalism* as 'an ideal, a policy, or a method. In any case, its characteristic feature is emphasis on the common interests of nations, on the political and economic interdependence of all peoples, on goodwill and co-operation as opposed to wars and national conflicts' (*Labour and Internationalism*, London: Allen & Unwin, 1929, p. 1). In this sense an internationalist at the start of the 20th century was one who approved of such international bodies as the Postal Union and the Union for Hygiene, and wished to see the extension of the principles espoused by the Hague Conferences of 1899 and 1907. Such persons (nearly all of whom, in Britain and the U.S.A., would have thought of themselves as liberals in domestic politics) were later in favour of the League of Nations. They would have been inclined to say, with C. R. Buxton: 'More and more, as occasion offers, we must assert the principle of internationalism. There is no other line of advance. The right attitude ... is that which frankly accepts the idea of a "Great Society", to which the sovereign state must subordinate itself. An effective League of Nations, whether to arbitrate, to develop, or to protect, is more needed than ever before in the world's history' ('Intercontinental Peace', in L. Woolf (ed.), *The Intelligent Man's Way to Prevent War*, London: Gollancz, 1933, p. 232).

(b) Internationalism describes any system of thought which seems to nationalists to imply a neglect of national security, or to 'realistic' political thinkers to imply a failure to recognize the facts of international life. Thus 'The internationalist ... has no direct contact with the international scene. His thought, if it is sufficiently general, can roam over the globe without ever risking collision with the stark facts of politics' (H. J. Morgenthau, *Scientific Man vs.* *Power Politics*, London: Latimer House, 1947, p. 88).

J. D. B. Miller

See also: ISOLATIONISM

Interpersonal Relations

A. *Interpersonal relations* refers to everything that 'goes on' between one person and another (or others) by way of perception, evaluation, understanding, and mode of reaction.

B. This 'felicitous phrase' is encountered most frequently in modern American psychiatry and is usually associated with the name of H. S. Sullivan. In large measure Sullivan was reacting against a mode of thought which tended to see individuals as isolated, self-contained entities rather than in their relationships to other people.

Following this line of thought, and clearly influenced by such social psychologists as Mead and Cooley, Sullivan was led to define psychiatry as 'the study of the phenomena that occur in interpersonal situations, in configurations made up of two or more people, all but one of whom may be more or less completely illusory' ('Psychiatry: Introduction to the Study of Interpersonal Relations', in P. Mullahy (ed.), *A Study of Interpersonal Relations*, New York: Hermitage Press, 1949, p. 99). In brief, Sullivan was arguing that a particular person cannot be understood, either in health or illness, apart from the way he relates to others and they, in turn, relate to him.

One consequence of this formulation was to lead psychiatry from an overwhelming pre-occupation with physical, intra-psychic and constitutional factors in personality toward a concern with such matters as self-image, role taking, and empathy (q.v.).

Conversely, the more academic disciplines have taken over the word *interpersonal* as applying to many of their own concerns. Thus, T. M. Newcomb speaks of 'interpersonal influence' and 'interpersonal attitudes' as being the core of social psychology (*Social Psychology*, New York: The Dryden Press, 1950, pp. 34–5). Similarly, G. Lundberg, et al., have written: 'Interpersonal relations form various social networks that make a group a dynamic sociological phenomenon rather than a mere collection of individuals. Sociologists are interested, therefore, in determining the kind, degree, direction, and duration of interpersonal relations' (*Sociology*, New York: Harper & Brothers, 1954, p. 412).

Measurement of interpersonal phenomena is

found in sociometry by studying choice or preference behaviour, the attraction and repulsion patterns among individuals of a group, etc. In more behavioural terms, the phrase *interpersonal mechanisms* has been used as a means of describing the public level of personality: 'The rater or observer ... asks the following question: What is the subject of the activity, i.e. the individual whose behaviour is being rated, doing to the object or objects of the activity? The answer, e.g. he is aggressing against him or them, affiliating with them, teaching him etc., is the interpersonal mechanism' (M. B. Freedman, T. F. Leary, A. G. Ossorio, & H. S. Coffey, 'The Interpersonal Dimension of Personality', *Journal of Personality*, vol. 20, 1951, p. 149).

Edmund H. Volkart

See also: Empathy
Group
Role
Self
Self-Conception
Social Interaction
Social Object

Interstitial Area

A. An *interstitial area* refers to a break in the social and spatial organization of a community which permits, or results from, the intrusion from without, or development from within, of a group with deviant and disapproved values and behaviour.

B. The concept was introduced by F. M. Thrasher in his study of juvenile gangs in Chicago. 'Gangland represents a geographically and socially interstitial area in the city'. Interstitial areas are 'fissures and breaks in the structure of the social organization. The gang may be regarded as an interstitial element in the framework of society, and gangland as an interstitial region in the layout of the city' (*The Gang, a Study of 1313 Gangs in Chicago*, Chicago: University of Chicago Press, 1927, p. 22).

The main spatial interstitial area in the city is the zone in transition resulting from the invasion (q.v.) of residential neighbourhoods by business and industry, and its social correlate constituted by the intrusion of prostitution and the emergence of crime and juvenile delinquency into this spatial area.

J. A. Quinn (*Human Ecology*, New York: Prentice-Hall, 1950, p. 483) has questioned the usefulness and validity of the concept of interstitial area as developed by Thrasher, at least as

applied to gangs. He asserts that inspection of the latter's map data seems to show concentration of gangs within the little social world of immigrant groups rather than in the interstices between them. Thrasher, however, points out that interstitial areas are 'the borderlands and boundary lines between residential and manufacturing or business areas, between immigrant or racial colonies, between city and county or city and suburb, and between contiguous towns' (*The Gang*, p. 23).

Ernest W. Burgess

See also: Natural Area
Zonal Hypothesis

Interval Scale (See **Scaling**)

Intervening Variable

A. *Intervening variable* denotes (a) an abstraction of an empirical set of operations, preferably but not necessarily experimental in nature, which does not require any assumptions about the existence of presently unobservable entities; (b) an hypothetical construct, i.e. an abstraction of empirical relationships that involves the introduction of at least one entity which is not observable with available instruments; or (c) a test factor, i.e. a concrete, empirically measurable variable which intervenes in a relationship and which can be employed as an interpretation of that relationship.

B. 1. Virtually without exception, social scientists define *intervening variables* as constructs or concepts devised for the interpretation of functional relationships among variables. Intervening variables are used because of scientific dissatisfaction with the explanatory power of purely functional descriptions of relations. An example from psychology will illustrate this point. It is well known that the percentage of rewarded turns observed among rats familiar with a maze situation can be expressed fairly accurately as a function of time since last feeding. Few experimental psychologists, however, would say that time is the cause of the phenomenon. Rather, they would interpret the empirical relationship by introducing an intervening variable, presumably hunger or demand in this instance.

2. Beyond this, there is disagreement as to what is or is not an appropriate and scientifically fruitful intervening variable. Probably the greatest contention arises over the question of how much abstraction from empirical fact is permissible and to what extent, if any, these

Introjection

abstractions should be conceived as entities rather than as more or less convenient labels for the relationship. An obviously related question concerns the extent to which intervening variables which are thought of as entities should be measurable directly. These disagreements have led to three principal uses of the term intervening variable in the social sciences: (a) as a label for a completely specified set of operations; (b) as a generic term for observable entities which intervene causally between *independent* and *dependent variables*; (c) in reference to empirically measurable concrete factors.

C. 1. E. C. Tolman, generally credited with introducing the term, originally believed that an intervening variable should refer to nothing more than a completely specified set of empirical operations. In this sense, Tolman has asserted that 'mental processes ... figure only in the guise of objectively definable *intervening variables* ... a set of intermediating functional processes which interconnect between the initiating causes of behavior, on the one hand, and the final resulting behavior itself, on the other' ('The Intervening Variable', in M. H. Marx (ed.), *Psychological Theory*, New York: The Macmillan Co., 1951, pp. 87–102). In this paper, Tolman makes it clear that to him intervening variables are merely convenient labels for observed relationships and, moreover, that they are to be arrived at by means of 'standard experimental setups' exclusive of introspection.

2. Other social scientists, notably the Hullian group in psychology and the various psychoanalytic schools are far more willing than Tolman was originally to imbue intervening variables with properties of structure and process and, presumably, to bury them somewhere within the organism. An outstanding example of this tendency is afforded by those psychoanalysts who use the term *libido* and who invest it with certain physical, especially hydraulic, properties. In light of this tendency K. Mac Corquodale and P. E. Meehl have suggested a two-fold reclassification of the term into *intervening variable* and *hypothetical construct*. The authors propose that *intervening variable* '... be restricted to the original use implied by Tolman's definition ... simply a quantity obtained by a specified manipulation of the values of empirical variables; it will involve no hypothesis as to the existence of nonobserved entities or the occurrence of unobserved processes' ('On a Distinction between Hypothetical Constructs and Intervening Variables', *Psycho-*logical Review*, vol. 55, 1948, p. 103). Alternatively, they propose that the term hypothetical construct be used to denote '... theoretical concepts [that] involve terms which are not wholly reducible to empirical terms' (ibid., p. 104). The authors point to Allport's *biophysical traits* and Murray's *regnancies* as illustrations of hypothetical constructs.

In this way it is possible to distinguish between interpretations which cannot be incorrect unless the empirical observations themselves are wrong and those which have a non-zero probability of being false, whether or not the probability value can be assessed at any given time. As Mac Corquodale and Meehl clearly recognize, their dichotomous classification is less than wholly satisfactory. The extent to which an intervening variable takes on the properties of an hypothetical construct varies considerably with individual usage.

3. Other social scientists use the term *intervening variable* neither in Tolman's sense nor in the sense of *hypothetical construct*. In this third sense, an *intervening variable* is synonymous with a *test factor*, a real variable which is directly measurable. Given the concrete nature of test factors, the following paradigm of interpretation is useful: '... we expect that when the population is stratified according to different values of the test factor, the partial relationships between the two original variables will vanish' (P. L. Kendall & P. F. Lazarsfeld, 'Problems of Survey Analysis', in R. K. Merton & P. F. Lazarsfeld (eds.), *Continuities in Social Research*, Glencoe, Ill.: The Free Press, 1950, pp. 133–96). Stated somewhat more formally, if a relationship, R, between a dependent variable, y, and one or more temporally preceding independent variables, x, is such that $P_{yx} \neq 0$, a test factor, z, which intervenes temporally between x and y is an interpretation of R if and only if $P_{yx \cdot z} \longrightarrow 0$ and $P_{yx \cdot z'} \longrightarrow P_{yx}$, where P is a measure of correlation and z' is any alternate test factor.

Robert McGinnis

See also: VARIABLE

Introjection

A. The term *introjection* appeared for the first time in S. Ferenczi's paper on 'Introjection and Transference' (*Jahrbuch für Psychoanalytische Forschungen*, vol. I, 1909, pp. 422–57). 'Whereas', he wrote, 'the paranoiac expels from his ego the impulses that have become unpleasant, the neurotic helps himself by taking into the ego a large part of the outer world making it the object of unconscious phantasies. ... One might give to this process, in contrast to *projection*, the name *Introjection*' (*First Contributions to Psychoanalysis*, London: Hogarth Press, 1953, p. 47).

B. Ever since its first appearance this term became hopelessly confused with *identification* (q.v.). This is obvious in a good deal of psychoanalytical writing of which the following passage from Freud is representative: 'One ego becomes like another, one which results in the first ego behaving itself in certain respects in the same way as the second; it imitates it, and as it were takes it into itself. This identification has been not inappropriately compared with the oral cannibalistic incorporation of another person' (*New Introductory Lectures on Psychoanalysis*, London: Hogarth Press, 1949, p. 86). In addition to identification, *imitation* (q.v.) too is included, and the precise meaning of each becomes more elusive than ever. It was only later that the character of introjection became more specifically described. After the work of M. Klein this concept has been brought into close relationship with the oral functions of infantile life. She writes, 'From the beginning the ego introjects objects "good" and "bad", for both of which the mother's breast is the prototype—for good objects when the child obtains it, for bad ones when it fails him' (*Contributions to Psycho-Analysis 1921–1945*, London: Hogarth Press, 1948, p. 282). Then, '... The child's fear of its introjected objects urges it to displace that fear into the external world' (M. Klein, *The Psycho-Analysis of Children*, London: Hogarth Press, 1951, p. 207). S. Isaacs, one of Klein's followers, explains its oral origin by saying that introjection '... is simply the mental function which is built upon the pattern of actual bodily experiences in the oral phase of development, namely, taking the outer world, and primarily, of course, the parents into the internal mental life. Descriptively one could say ... that the child comes to behave towards himself as if he were a parent' (*Social Development in Young Children*, New York: Harcourt, Brace, 1933, p. 304). Introjection in this sense is incorporation, mastication, and ingestion, therefore a mode of *destruction*; whereas identification allows the model to survive, introjection cannibalizes him. This is well recognized by N. Sanford who, in his article, 'The Dynamics of Identification', sums up the difference thus, '... in introjection the object "disappears inside" as it were, whereas in identification proper a continuing relationship with the external object is a distinctive

feature ...' (*Psychological Review*, vol. 62, 1955, p. 115).

C. It is difficult to see how Sanford's distinction can protect us from confusion altogether. It is plausible or at any rate conceivable that the fantasied oral cannibalistic incorporation leads to an equally fantasied end of the object; but even in the case of the infant the denial of the reality-situation, i.e. of the continued existence of the object, must be ineffectual. And so there will be a continuing relationship with the external object in any circumstances. Furthermore 'internalizations' go on during later life and these too do not take away from the reality of the object from which they are derived. Indeed it is questionable whether there is, in fact, a distinct concept here. It is more probable that as a result of the powerful oral medium of the initial object-relations, identification may assume a more or less oral-cannibalistic, incorporative, and therefore introjective terminology. In this view introjection is identification couched in an oral language (cf. P. Halmos, *Solitude and Privacy*, London: Routledge & Kegan Paul, 1952, p. 5).

P. Halmos

See also: IDENTIFICATION
INTERNALIZATION

Invasion

Within the broad field of social science, three somewhat different meanings may be distinguished.

1. In history and political science *invasion* often refers to the organized entrance of persons from one group into the territory occupied or claimed by another, against the wishes of the latter, and often with hostile intent. For example, one state sends armed troops into the territory of another, without its consent, and for the purpose of exercising unwanted control.

2. The term is occasionally used to refer to the process occurring when within a society or a community, one segment of the population encroaches on certain rights enjoyed by another segment, against the wishes of the latter. For example, a king may invade the traditional rights of his subjects.

3. Finally the term may be used to denote the process which occurs when one kind of population begins to occupy a territory (or an occupational niche) already occupied by another, or it increases its rate of occupancy. For example, stores are built in a formerly exclusive residential area, or women take a

Investment

higher proportion of jobs in an occupation generally restricted to males. In human ecology *invasion* is restricted to this third meaning. It does not imply either organized societal or community planning or deliberate control. Instead, human ecologists conceive the process as involving changes in the position of a number of population units, each acting individually on its own initiative, but with the result that the combined effect of these separate actions brings changes in the population composition of a local area or an occupational niche or in the spatial boundaries of a natural area. Usually, but not necessarily, the already established population regards the in-movement as undesirable.

(a) Territorially, invasion refers to the movement into an occupied area of individual members of a population who are different from the former residents. It includes as sub-types such instances as the following: the movement into a locality of individuals from a non-contiguous area, as when immigrants from a distant land displace residents of a different cultural background within an urban neighbourhood; the building of new stores or factories in a residential neighbourhood; or the gradual encroachment, possibly through expansion, of one type of area into an adjacent area of a different kind so that the spatial boundaries of both areas are altered.

(b) Occupationally, invasion means that a specialized job position which traditionally has been occupied by one segment of the population, is now being entered by individuals of a different segment, either initially or in increasing proportion.

James A. Quinn

See also: ECOLOGY
SUCCESSION (Sociology)

Invention (See Innovation)

Investment

A. In the social sciences *investment* may denote (a) the act of investing in the sense of furnishing a person or group with power, privilege, or authority; or (b) the act of investing in the sense of exchanging one asset for another which is expected to produce a greater return over a longer period of time; or (c) either the asset invested or the asset acquired as the result of the act of investing in sense (b).

1. While investment is used frequently in the social sciences in sense (a) it has not acquired in that usage a highly technical character, and nothing more need be said about it.

2. When the term is used in senses (b) and (c), but the term *asset* defined broadly, then *investment* may be used in many social science disciplines. Thus, for example, the social psychologist may speak of the investment of one's emotions in another person with the expectation of emotional response as a return. Here again usage tends to be broad and general, and need not be further discussed.

3. In economics *investment* in senses (b) and (c) is restricted to assets which can be valued in terms of a money price, and most of the investment which is studied is the actual investment of money, although the latter must be seen as a means of exchange for other assets. Even here the form of investment which has the greatest significance for economic theory has been restricted to the investment which characterizes the economy as a whole which is made possible only by domestic production that exceeds current consumption or by foreign trade.

B. 1. The growth of a technical, industrial economy has been known since the time of Adam Smith to be dependent upon the investment of the excess of production over consumption or assets gained from foreign trade into capital goods. In the history of capitalism this has been investment by private business men, and has been regarded by economists as the central motor of the development of the capitalist economy. In the 20th century among the developing societies the accumulation of capital and its investment in capital goods for purposes of economic growth has become a function of the state, and hence, at least in part, a matter of public rather than private investment.

2. If the investment of the excess of production over consumption is the force primarily responsible for the growth of an industrial economy, it is also the force that keeps the economy expanding rather than contracting. '... When a major change in the rate of investment occurs, a turn in the cycle can be expected. It is a commonplace matter for business analysts and investment counsellors to keep a close eye on prospective changes in any of the component parts of gross investment. What is happening to new construction, to expenditures on producers' equipment, to inventory accumulation, and to net foreign investment throws light on how business activity, employment, and income are likely to unfold' (A. H. Hansen, *Business Cycles and National Income*, New York: Norton, 1951, p. 122). Based on the empirical fact that in the early years of the industrial economy savings and investment had been linked in that those who were able to save were also those who invested in capital goods, etc. and upon the theory that a decline of investment of this sort would bring about an accumulation of savings, thus lowering interest rates and stimulating investment, savings and investment had been equated: '... Provided it is agreed that income is equal to the value of current output, that current investment is equal to that part of current output which is not consumed, and that saving is equal to the excess of income over consumption—all of which is conformable both to commonsense and to the traditional usage of the great majority of economists—the equality of savings and investment necessarily follows' (J. M. Keynes, *The General Theory of Employment, Interest, and Money*, New York: Harcourt, Brace, 1936, p. 63).

This linkage is deceptive, however, for when saving and investing are done by different groups of people, the investors may not invest what the savers have saved, and with the resultant contraction of the economy incomes fall as do savings so that there is not an accumulation of savings at a low rate of interest to encourage investment. Thus the economy may remain at a low level of activity. Here again activity on the part of the state may occur. It may attempt to lower interest rates, it may engage in public investment to stimulate the economy, or it may lower taxes to stimulate private investment by making additional private income available.

3. In recent years there has been a tendency on the part of some economists to broaden the conception of investment as it contributes to the growth and the expansion of the economy. Thus J. K. Galbraith holds that investment in the education of individuals is as important for the growth and expansion of the economy as investment in material capital goods: 'Investment in individuals is in the public domain; this investment has become increasingly essential with the advance of science and technology; and there is no machinery for automatically allocating resources as between material and human investment' (*The Affluent Society*, Boston: Houghton Mifflin, 1958, p. 274).

Richard V. Clemence

See also: Capital
        Capital Goods
        National Product
        Saving

Irrationality (See Rationality)

Isolation

A. The central meaning of *isolation* is that of 'separation', and it may be applied in such different contexts as the intra-psychic, the relation of person to group, and the relation of groups to other groups. Within this broad area of agreement there are different emphases relating to the extent to which it is a conscious feeling, a necessary part of social structure, an inferential or descriptive concept, an explanatory concept, and how it is to be measured.

B. The essential meaning of this concept is retained in all social science fields, although it is used at different levels of analysis and is attached to different entities.

1. It is used in psychoanalysis to refer to a defence mechanism (q.v.) whereby unfavourable or ego-alien experiences are 'blocked' from full conscious awareness. This refers to an intra-psychic process in individuals and is usually found in compulsively neurotic patients (S. Freud, *The Problem of Anxiety*, trans. by A. Strachey, London: Hogarth Press, 1936, p. 74; F. Alexander, 'Development of the Fundamental Concepts of Psychoanalysis', in F. Alexander & H. Ross (eds.), *Dynamic Psychiatry*, Chicago: University of Chicago Press, 1952, p. 14).

2. (a) One sociological usage emphasizes the relative lack of participation on the part of the individual in group affairs. Here, one type of formulation purports to be merely descriptive, as when R. T. LaPiere defines *isolation* as 'a failure of the individual, through inability, preference, or whatever, to establish and maintain communications with those about him' (*A Theory of Social Control*, New York: McGraw-Hill, 1954, p. 330). Similarly K. Davis equates 'the absence of social relationships' with 'isolation' (*Human Society*, New York: The Macmillan Co., 1949, p. 149). In a different context, isolation is regarded as one of the dynamic variables in the failure to acquire personality (K. Davis, 'Final Note on a Case of Extreme Isolation', *American Journal of Sociology*, vol. LII, 1946–7, pp. 432–7) and as a predisposing or precipitating factor in mental illness, particularly schizophrenia (R. E. L. Faris, 'Cultural Isolation and the Schizophrenic Personality', *American Journal of Sociology*, vol. XL, 1935–6, p. 157). On this point S. K. Weinberg asserts that it is not isolation, per se, but 'the meaning and reaction to isolation' which bears most significantly on 'eventual schizophrenic behavior' ('A Sociological Analysis of a

Isolationism

Schizophrenic Type', *American Sociological Review*, vol. 15, 150, p. 609).

(b) A second sociological usage is that of E. G. Jaco who defines *social isolation* as 'the cutting off or minimizing of contact and communication with others' and attempts to measure it in populations by such indices as anonymity, spatial mobility, location of friends, frequency of participation in groups, etc. ('The Social Isolation Hypothesis and Schizophrenia', *American Sociological Review*, vol. 19, 1954, pp. 567-77). K. Davis suggests that the type of isolation sociologists are most interested in is 'that [which] is integrated with other social relationships', and which has normative elements. 'When isolation from mutual contact becomes a prescribed rule affecting only sectors of relationship, we see that it then forms a basic principle of social organization. Social distance as well as social nearness is therefore a structural principle in society' (*Human Society*, New York: The Macmillan Co., 1949, pp. 151, 155).

(c) Finally, the concept of *isolation* is used by sociologists to refer to groups or societies in their relationships with other groups or societies. Thus: 'The folk society is an isolated society ... made up of people who have little communication with outsiders' (R. Redfield, 'The Folk Society', *American Journal of Sociology*, vol. LII, 1946-7, p. 296). H. Becker, in dealing with sacred and secular societies, refers to the 'isolation' and 'accessibility' of societies, and emphasizes three distinguishable aspects: vicinal (physical separation), social (in physical contact but with barriers to interaction) and mental (in interaction, but without genuine communication) ('Current Sacred-Secular Theory and its Development', in H. Becker & A. Boskoff (eds.), *Modern Sociological Theory in Continuity and Change*, New York: Dryden Press, 1957, pp. 164-5). The term *isolationism* (q.v.) is used by political scientists, and economists to refer to the advocacy, or practice of political or economic isolation of one society from other societies.

C. Indeed, the term *isolate*, first introduced by G. Simmel ('The Number of Persons as Determining the Form of the Group', reprinted in E. F. Borgatta & H. J. Meyer (eds.), *Sociological Theory*, New York: Knopf, 1956, pp. 126-58) is being used more and more to apply to a person who feels isolated, or separated, from others in physical proximity. '... there is decided significance in the well-known psychological fact that the feeling of loneliness seldom occurs so decidedly ... as when one is conscious of being a stranger and without attachments among many physically quite adjacent people' (ibid., p. 138). In sociometry, 'The *isolate* is the individual who receives no choices and makes no choices (or receives no choices and rejections and makes none)' (G. Lindzey & E. F. Borgatta, 'Sociometric Measurement', in G. Lindzey (ed.), *Handbook of Social Psychology*, Cambridge, Mass.: Addison-Wesley, 1954, p. 411).

Edmund H. Volkart

See also: ISOLATIONISM

Isolationism

A. *Isolationism* denotes a policy or the advocacy of a policy based on the belief that the interests of a nation are best served by withdrawal from close connections with other states. While complete isolation can be advocated or sought, it is rare that a state can achieve it or put it in practice. For example, Japan once did so, while the United States and Great Britain never did. The point which distinguishes varying usages of the term is the varying degree of isolation advocated, sought, or achieved.

B. The word *isolation* took on political meaning in the 1890s with the characterization of British policy as one of 'splendid isolation' from the affairs of Europe. Speaking in the Canadian House of Commons on 16 January 1896, G. E. Foster said: 'In these troublous days the great Mother Empire stands splendidly isolated in Europe'. The phrase was widely publicized. It meant that Britain, in contrast to the other great powers was free from any obligations of alliance. She was party to neither the Triple Alliance nor the Franco-Russian Alliance. It did not mean, however, that Britain was prepared to follow a policy of withdrawal from concern with world political developments.

C. The term *isolationism* came into use in the 20th century to describe certain aspects of American foreign policy and the ideas and attitudes of certain groups about American foreign policy. Following World War I, American participation in international affairs was characterized by considerable withdrawal from responsibility. The term, itself, however, first gained wide acceptance as a broadly descriptive category for the ideas and policies of all those who, as World War II approached, opposed the 'interventionists' and a more active role in the affairs of Europe. Since the range of ideas and policies was rather wide, the meaning of the term is somewhat imprecise, including not only what *isolation* has meant for the British (no alliances but continued activity in world affairs), but also much more complete forms of withdrawal. It is for this reason that *unilateralism* is now used to mean 'no alliances' while *isolationism* is more often used to mean an attitude of withdrawal.

Frederick H. Hartmann
Heyward Moore

See also: INTERNATIONALISM

Issues

A. *Issues* are matters of policy (q.v.) on which people disagree. Specifically they are questions (*questions at issue*) on which candidates and voters at election time tend to be divided, e.g. full employment policy, farm subsidies, the cost of living. Thus '... the main electoral arguments ... were found to a large extent in the party manifestos, but there were also fresh issues over which controversy developed as the battle advanced' (D. E. Butler, *The British General Election of* 1951, London: Macmillan, 1952, p. 105).

B. The term is commonly used in election analysis to distinguish one factor—the party programmes and points of genuine controversy —from others which influence voters' behaviour, e.g. traditional loyalty to a party or response to the personal attractions of a candidate. Hence analysts regard issues as but one of many important aspects. 'We have attempted to identify the major components that make up the total matrix of forces influencing the individual vote' (A. Campbell, G. Gurin & W. E. Miller, *The Voter Decides*, Evanston, Ill.: Row, Peterson, 1954, p. 8).

Recent studies have begun to analyse the type of issues over which a campaign is fought, for example, *position* (or material) and *style* (or *ideal*) issues (B. R. Berelson, P. F. Lazarsfeld & W. N. McPhee, *Voting*, Chicago: University of Chicago Press, 1954, p. 182).

C. Issues are emphasized less today than in the 19th century, when political scientists were tempted to discuss politics predominantly in rational terms. W. Bagehot (*Physics and Politics*, London: King, 1873) never subscribed to this view which was also challenged in G. Wallas's *Human Nature in Politics* (London: Constable, 1908). Nevertheless, there are still students of politics who think that 'This is to explain society as an irrational structure and therefore not to explain society at all' (E. Barker, *Political Thought in England 1848–1914*, London: Thornton Butterworth, 1928, p. 150).

Thanks in large measure to the influence of sociologists and social psychologists election analyses have supported Wallas's conjectures (see M. Benney, A. P. Gray & R. H. Pear, *How People Vote*, London: Routledge & Kegan Paul, 1956, p. 5 ff. and D. E. Butler, *The British General Election of* 1951, p. 3 ff.). Today, issues are regarded as of importance but not as *the* key to the understanding of the political process (B. Berelson et al., *Voting*, p. 182).

D. V. Verney

See also: PARTY PLATFORM
        VOTING

J

Joint Family (See **Family**)

Joking Relationship

A *joking relationship* is a relationship between two persons (sometimes between two groups) in which one is by custom permitted (and in some cases obliged) to tease or make fun of the other, who must take no offence. Sometimes the joking is reciprocal. The actual form of the joking varies considerably, but obscenity, which is at other times prohibited, and the taking of property are common forms. The relation is a combination of friendliness and antagonism, and is found in situations which contain the possibility of conflict yet require the avoidance of strife. Such an ambivalent relationship can be given a stable form either by maintenance of extreme respect and limitation of direct contact (avoidance) or by permitted mutual disrespect and licence. (See A. R. Radcliffe-Brown, *Structure and Function in Primitive Society*, London: Cohen & West, 1952, pp. 90–104.) M. Griaule ("L'alliance cathartique", *Africa*, vol. XVIII, 1948, pp. 242–58) suggests that the exchange of insults is cathartic, dispelling hostility, and that the most important function of the relationship is to provide 'purification'.

J. Middleton

Judgemental Sampling (See **Sampling**)

Judicial Review

A. *Judicial review* denotes the institutional arrangements whereby courts exercise the power to invalidate or nullify the acts of legislatures, chief executives, and administrative officials when they find these acts to be in conflict with a written constitution or other superior body of law.

B. 1. The term originated in the United States to designate the institutional arrangements whereby courts may pass upon the constitutional validity of acts of their co-ordinate legislatures. Although in the strict sense it still refers primarily to such arrangements, it has been extended to cover review of executive and administrative actions and is sometimes even loosely used to apply to such review when those actions are being judged by statutory rather than constitutional standards. In this sense, which will not be further discussed here, the institution is in force in England and other countries where courts do not enjoy the power to interpret and apply provisions of a constitution.

The roots of judicial review are to be found in English legal history. The doctrine of a body of 'fundamental law', superior to king and government was generally accepted in the medieval period. Characteristically, however, the courts lacked power to enforce this law against any other branch of the government. But the ideas of fundamental or 'higher' law were in no small measure identified with parts of the common law and with the historically recognized rights of Englishmen. Not unnaturally, the courts, whose business it was to interpret and apply the common law, came to be thought of as protectors of the fundamental (or 'natural') rights of the people. Indeed, the Lord Chief Justice of England, Sir Edward Coke, went so far as to declare, by way of dictum, in *Bonham's Case*, that 'it appears in our books, that in many cases, the common law will control acts of Parliament, and sometimes adjudge them to be utterly void; for when an act of Parliament is against common right and reason, or repugnant, or impossible to be performed, the common law will control it and adjudge such act to be void' (8 Co. 118a, 1610).

2. This doctrine did not come to prevail in England; it gave way to the idea of legislative sovereignty. Before this development, however, many Englishmen who had come to think of courts as peculiarly the defenders of the people's rights, settled in America. And during the years just preceding the American Revolution the colonists found it convenient to assert that Parliament was subject to legal limitations.

It is true that the American Constitution made no express provision for judicial review. Nor was it provided for or regularly practised by the state constitutions in the years before the Constitutional Convention (1787), although a few instances may be cited in which courts claimed they had the power and in one case (unknown to the framers of the Constitution) a state court successfully exercised it.

What the framers of the Constitution intended when they provided for a federal judicial system and vested it with 'the judicial power' has been the subject of much debate. The weight of scholarly authority seems to favour the belief that at least the majority of the framers who gave the matter any thought believed the courts would have the power to invalidate unconstitutional acts of Congress. However that may be, Chief Justice Marshall, in the celebrated case of *Marbury* v. *Madison* (1 Cranch 137, 1803), soon settled the matter, for practical purposes, by declaring a provision of the Judiciary Act void and of no effect, as being in conflict with a provision of the Constitution.

Once this fundamental power of the federal courts had been vindicated it was not seriously disputed that they could also invalidate acts of administrative officials and even of the Chief Executive. The further power of the courts to declare acts of state governments void for conflict with the federal constitution was established at an early date. Likewise, state constitutions were generally interpreted as granting the power of judicial review to their own courts.

It is important to note that, in exercising the power of judicial review, influenced by the doctrine of the separation of powers (q.v.), the courts restrict themselves to the exercise of 'judicial power' as that phrase had been understood at common law. They pass on constitutional questions only as they find it necessary to do so in carrying on their regular business of adjudicating cases or controversies involving the asserted rights of individuals. The federal courts will not render 'advisory' opinions, although the practice is permitted in certain states. They will not answer abstract questions. They will act only at the instance of a party whose interests are at stake, and who is engaged in a legal struggle with someone (which may be the government itself) whose legally recognized interests are adverse to his. And they will resolve the legal issues without raising and deciding constitutional questions, if it is possible to do so while still allowing the constitution to prevail.

C. 1. Since the development of the institution of judicial review in the United States, it has been adopted in many other countries. Federal states generally provide for judicial review as a means of resolving controversies regarding the extent of the powers of their constituent units. For this purpose it is not necessary to go beyond allowing the federal courts to invalidate laws of the constituent states. But judicial review in the stricter sense of the power to invalidate the acts

of national legislatures is now also provided for in a considerable number of constitutions. Nowhere, however, has it assumed anything like the importance it has enjoyed in the United States. Often, too, the manner of exercise of the power is quite different.

2. The term is now used more centrally than hitherto in English legal writings—following upon the increased importance of administrative law. In 1959 there appeared the first work to be written by an English author on the theme of the judicial review of administrative action (S. A. De Smith, *The Judicial Review of Administrative Action*, London: Stevens, 1959). De Smith argues that the term is 'not a term of art', and goes on to say that 'it is sometimes used to mean judicial scrutiny and determination of the legal validity of instruments, acts and decisions. Here we have chosen to give it a wider meaning, which cannot be neatly defined in a phrase but which is broad enough to include, for example, the many-sided jurisdiction exercised by the award of declaratory orders to and against administrative bodies, and the jurisdiction to scrutinize administrative determinations for errors of law and other defects which render them voidable but not invalid' (ibid., p. 16).

J. Roland Pennock

See also: CONSTITUTION
        CONSTITUTIONALISM
        DUE PROCESS
        JUDICIARY
        LAW
        SEPARATION OF POWERS

Judiciary

A. The term *judiciary* designates a judicial system, comprehending structure and jurisdiction of courts, appointment and tenure of judges, and judicial proceedings.

B. In current usage the term *judiciary* specifically refers to the function of the judge in the judicial process. The independence of the judiciary from political influence and control is an important principle in the constitutional systems of Great Britain and the United States. The rationale for independence is the assurance of the impartiality of the judge in the exercise of his function, that is, the assurance to the individual that justice will not be arbitrarily administered. 'This means that a judiciary as independent from interference by the executive as is possible, given the interlocking of State functions and the human factor in the judicial function, is an essential of the democratic ideal

Jurisdiction

of justice' (W. Friedmann, *Law and Social Change in Contemporary Britain*, London: Stevens, 1951, p. 283). In the United States, a Justice of the Supreme Court writes: 'The judiciary is in a high sense the guardian of the conscience of the people as well as of the law of the land' (W. O. Douglas, *We the Judges*, New York: Doubleday, 1956, p. 445). The American practice of judicial review (q.v.) affords the judiciary an opportunity to assert a control (albeit a temporary control) over activities of the political branch of government which may have important political repercussions. As D. B. Truman puts it: 'The judiciary is inevitably a part of the political process' (*The Governmental Process*, New York: Knopf, 1951, p. 498). The concepts of independence and impartiality as criteria of juridical practice, however, establish a limit on the political function of the judiciary, for '... Western democracy has never held strongly to the idea that the judiciary should respond easily to the currents of public attitude made apparent by political representation' (F. G. Wilson, *The Elements of Modern Politics*, New York: McGraw-Hill, 1936, p. 341).

The concept of the judiciary as an independent and impartial agency is well enough accepted that it may be taken as a standard of conduct for other governmental institutions. T. Parsons, for example, in discussing the role of the propaganda agency in the modern state, urges that such an agency '... should avoid involvement in any of the internal struggles for power of partisan groups; both in its constitution and publicly conspicuous personnel it should be as close as possible to the ideal of an impartial judiciary' (*Essays in Sociological Theory*, Glencoe, Ill: The Free Press, rev. edn., 1954, p. 174).

Alona E. Evans

See also: JUDICIAL REVIEW

Jurisdiction

A. The term *jurisdiction* denotes the sphere of authority exercised by a state, agency of the state, international juridical or administrative organization, or a non-governmental association, over places, persons, or things. In international law it includes the general authority recognized as belonging to a state or to an international agency, and the particular authority recognized in national law as belonging to an agency of government or to a statutory or voluntary non-governmental association.

B. For purposes of analysis, the different kinds of jurisdiction may be considered to fall into two categories: the jurisdiction of the state as an international entity, and the jurisdiction of agencies of government, international juridical or administrative agencies, or non-governmental associations.

1. The *territorial jurisdiction* of a state denotes the assertion of its authority, as recognized by other states, over a given land area, the sea adjacent, if it is a coastal state, the air space over its territory, and '... to the air space over the territorial sea as well as to its bed and subsoil' (Convention on the Territorial Sea and the Contiguous Zone, April 29, 1958, Article 2, U.N. Doc. A/CONF. 13/38 (Sales No. 58. V.4, vol. II), p. 132). Although in the practice of states, '... there seems to be little reason for attempting to distinguish between civil and criminal cases in determining jurisdiction' (P. C. Jessup, *Transnational Law*, Storrs Lectures on Jurisprudence, New Haven: Yale University Press, 1956, p. 64), for purposes of definition the distinction may be made. *Civil jurisdiction* may be defined as '... the power of a state to create interests which under the principles of the common law will be recognized as valid in other states' (American Law Institute, *Restatement of the Law of Conflict of Laws*, St. Paul: American Law Institute, 1934, ch. 3, section 42). *Penal jurisdiction* comprehends the state's '... competence under international law to prosecute and punish for crime' (Draft Convention on *Jurisdiction* with Respect to Crime, Supplement to the *American Journal of International Law*, Washington: American Society of International Law, 1935, vol. 29, p. 467).

'The jurisdiction of the nation within its own territory is necessarily exclusive and absolute' (*The Schooner Exchange* v. *Mcfaddon*, 11 *United States Supreme Court Reports*, 7 Cranch, 116, 136, 1812), as to persons and things including aliens present in the state; thus aliens '... are often under two concurrent jurisdictions' (L. Oppenheim, *International Law, A Treatise*, 2 vols., London: Longmans, Green, 8th edn., 1955, vol. I, p. 330), that is, the jurisdictions of the state to which they owe allegiance and the state in which they are present. 'Any exclusion or limitation of territorial jurisdiction runs counter to the presumption against the limitation of sovereignty, may not be presumed and must be interpreted restrictively. Such restrictions may result from international customary law or treaties or general principles of law recognised by civilised states' (G. Schwarzenberger, *International Law*, 3 vols., London: Stevens, 3rd edn.,

360

1957, vol. I, p. 192). A state may permit another state to exercise *extra-territorial jurisdiction* within its territory. A member state of the North Atlantic Treaty Organization, for example, may exercise 'criminal and disciplinary jurisdiction', with certain restrictions, over its own armed forces stationed in the territory of another member state (Agreement between the Parties to the North Atlantic Treaty Regarding the Status of Their Forces, Art. VII, *United Nations Treaty Series*, 1951, vol. 199, pp. 67, 76).

2. (a) The second category of jurisdiction concerns entities or associations the scope of whose authority is more limited than that of the state. 'The exercise of jurisdiction requires the establishment of courts of justice as well as of a system of judicial procedure by means of which the general decision of the territorial sovereign concerning both the lawfulness and unlawfulness of acts committed within places subject to its control, and the respect to be paid to lawful or unlawful acts committed abroad, may be enforced' (C. C. Hyde, *International Law*, 3 vols., Boston: Little, Brown, 2nd rev. edn., 1945, vol. I, p. 728). In Great Britain one hierarchy of courts exercises *criminal jurisdiction* while another exercises *civil jurisdiction*, the latter includes the Chancery Division of the High Court of Justice which exercises *equity jurisdiction* in cases involving the application of equitable rules rather than general common law rules. There is little or no differentiation as to civil, criminal, or equity jurisdiction in the organization of American courts. A case is instituted in a court of first instance or a court having *original jurisdiction*; where an appeal is made to a higher court, the case comes before that court in its *appellate jurisdiction*. In the United States only the original jurisdiction of the Supreme Court is defined in the Constitution; Congress determines the classes of cases which may fall within the jurisdiction of federal courts and may confer '... jurisdiction in such cases on the federal courts *concurrently* with the state courts' (L. Mayers, *The American Legal System*, New York: Harper, 1955, p. 10).

The jurisdiction of the International Court of Justice is also more limited than that of the state. Its jurisdiction '... comprises all cases which the parties refer to it and all matters specially provided for in the Charter of the United Nations or in treaties and conventions in force' (Statute of International Court of Justice, Art. 36, para. 1). The Court also has an 'advisory jurisdiction' (ibid., Art 65). The jurisdiction of the Court is based upon the consent of the states party to the Statute. 'Where the consent refers to a future class of disputes, and a dispute within the class has then arisen, the jurisdiction is said to be "compulsory"; when it is only *ad hoc* after the dispute has arisen, it is said to be "voluntary" ' (J. Stone, *Legal Controls of International Conflict*, London: Stevens, 1954, p. 123). But a state may restrict its submission to the Court's 'compulsory jurisdiction' by declaring that a given dispute involves '... a matter which is essentially within its domestic jurisdiction', a sphere of jurisdiction which is also outside the purview of the United Nations (H. Kelsen, *The Law of the United Nations*, London: Stevens, 1950, pp. 529, 772).

(b) The term *jurisdiction* may also be applied to the scope of authority of non-governmental organizations. In discussing the effect of the depression upon employment in American railroads, S. H. Slichter points out that 'the staff reductions at small points raised jurisdictional controversies between the unions' with respect to spreading available work among remaining personnel (*Union Policies and Industrial Management*, Washington: Brookings Institution, 1941, p. 499). The 'jurisdictional dispute' has been particularly evident where rival unions have sought to organize a given group of workers or a shop. Such a difference arose when the American automobile industry was being organized: 'It involved jurisdiction—whether the automobile workers were to be marshalled into craft or industrial unions' (P. Taft, *The Structure and Government of Labor Unions*, Cambridge, Mass.: Harvard University Press, 1954, p. 218).

Alona E. Evans

See also: Authority

Jurisprudence

A. The word *jurisprudence* is used in the English-speaking countries to denote the analysis of the nature and application of legal rules and concepts: i.e. generalized reflection on legal questions. The exact nature of that generality can only be suggested by illustration.

The following may be suggested as examples of the legal topics discussed in this field of systematic study: (a) the uses of the terms *law* and *jurisprudence* themselves; (b) the use and application of the concepts occurring within the rules of a legal system; (c) the comparison of rules or concepts occurring in one legal system or branch of law with the rules and concepts occurring in another legal system or branch of law in the same system; (d) the working and purposes of legal machinery and the judicial

Jury

process; (e) the boundaries or connections between legal studies and other disciplines; (f) the historical development of legal ideas or institutions; (g) the relation between legal and moral rules.

B. 1. The Roman jurists appear to have applied the term to the knowledge of all forms of law, divine and human. 'To them jurisprudence was philosophy and all philosophy' (*Imperatoris Iustiniani Institutionum*, ed. by J. B. Moyle, Oxford: at the Clarendon Press, 1912, p. 62).

2. At the other extreme the term acquired a number of uses in English, some of them far removed from philosophy—as in *medical jurisprudence* or *equity jurisprudence*, connoting merely a technical exposition of the law relating to a particular topic or branch of law. In French and certain other languages 'la jurisprudence' and its etymological equivalents means judicial doctrine or case law.

3. In the sense of 'legal theory' the word has served, since the efforts of Bentham and Austin to 'delimit' and 'determine' its scope, as a focus of dispute for jurists with differing philosophies of law. Austin in *The Province of Jurisprudence Determined* in 1832 (J. Austin, *The Province of Jurisprudence Determined* and *The Uses of the Study of Jurisprudence*, ed. by H. L. A. Hart, London: Weidenfeld & Nicolson, 1954, p. 126) spoke of the subject matter of jurisprudence as positive laws 'considered without regard to their goodness or badness', while in *The Uses of the Study of Jurisprudence* in 1863 (and the word 'Uses' may be important) he defined *jurisprudence* as 'the science of what is essential to law, combined with the science of what it ought to be' (ibid., p. 372). A succession of writers has derived from Austin both a method of approach (analysis of concepts) and a delimitation of subject matter (positive law) as characteristic features of the study of jurisprudence. It is clear that these characteristics have no necessary connection. It is also clear that Austin's second definition of jurisprudence is compatible with its covering the criticism of the content of positive law.

4. In the late 19th and 20th centuries, topics, methods, and approaches have been classified in a number of ways. Austin distinguished *general* and *particular jurisprudence*. The principal classifications to be found in legal writing include:—*analytical jurisprudence, historical jurisprudence, philosophical jurisprudence, psychological jurisprudence, sociological jurispru-*

dence, comparative jurisprudence. Another type of classification is in terms of allegiance to particular theories about (a) the nature of moral rules and their relation to the concept of law, and (b) the nature of the process of judicial decision. Thus *positivist jurisprudence* has been a term applied to theorists denying the necessity of incorporating any reference to moral rules as an element in the definition of *law*; and *realist jurisprudence* to writers aiming to analyse the application of legal rules in terms of judicial motives and the sociological facts relevant to judicial discretion. The term *realist jurisprudence* has been applied to developments from both these attitudes, in particular in the United States and in Scandinavia. J. Stone (*The Province and Function of Law*, Sydney: Associated General Publications, 1946, ch. 1) has suggested that all forms of jurisprudence may be brought within the threefold classification (a) analytical jurisprudence, (b) sociological (or functional) jurisprudence, and (c) theories of justice (critical, censorial or ethical jurisprudence). Stone adds (and the comment is just) that the term today denotes 'a chaos of approaches to a chaos of topics, chaotically delimited' (ibid., p. 16).

G. Marshall

See also: LAW

Jury

A. A *jury* is a legal institution consisting of a selected group of persons who have sworn to render a true answer or verdict regarding a question or questions of fact submitted to them in a judicial proceeding.

B. The term *jury* is often broadly used to designate any selected group of persons called upon to examine a matter and to present a conclusion on the basis of that examination (for example, an art jury selecting works for exhibition). But its common application is to the juridical institution which came into use in England after the Norman Conquest. According to F. Pollock and F. W. Maitland: 'The essence of the jury ... seems to be this: a body of neighbours is summoned by some public officer to give upon oath a true answer to some question ...' (*The History of English Law before the Time of Edward I*, Cambridge: The University Press, 2nd edn., 1898, 2 vols., vol. I, p. 138). As English law developed, 'one of the most important instruments of the royal power was the inquisition held under the supervision of a royal judge by means of a jury' (W. S. Holdsworth, *A History of English*

Law, London: Methuen, 3rd edn., 1922, 3 vols., vol. I, p. 316). In an age of customary law, the 'jury of recognition' would be called upon to determine '… whether an alleged custom did in fact exist in popular practice, and, if so, what was its precise nature and extent' (C. K. Allen, *Law in the Making*, Oxford: The Clarendon Press, 6th edn., 1958, p. 125). The task of the jury gradually became differentiated as to the accusatory or investigative function and the trial function.

C. The *grand jury* has a preliminary, accusatory, or investigative function. Criminal proceedings in felony cases are instituted in American federal courts and in many state courts by indictment by grand jury, a procedure which in Great Britain, and in some states in the United States, has been replaced by accusation by an information. The *coroner's jury* is an investigatory body of six or more persons who may be summoned to hear evidence at a coroner's inquest into a death which has occurred under suspicious circumstances. The jury is required to render a verdict as to the apparent cause of death.

D. In civil and criminal procedure, trial by jury developed from the principle '… that if in any action the litigants by their pleadings come to an issue of fact, they may agree to be bound by the verdict of a jury and will be bound accordingly' (F. Pollock & F. W. Maitland, *The History of English Law Before the Time of Edward I*, vol. I, p. 149). In England in the Middle Ages, trial by jury came to replace trial by battle or by ordeal. The jury used in civil or criminal proceedings is known as a *petit* (or *petty*) *jury*, usually a body of twelve persons selected from a panel representing a cross-section of the community. In the United States 'the civil jury however may now be regarded as having entered a period of decline—a decline presaged by its abandonment, almost to the point of extinction, in England itself' (L. Mayers, *The American Legal System*, New York: Harper & Brothers, 1955, p. 276). The use of the *petit jury* in criminal proceedings is still common although in some jurisdictions it is possible to waive trial by jury. The *petit jury* is sworn to render a unanimous verdict concerning the facts under dispute as determined by the evidence presented to them. The judge fixes sentence on the basis of the jury's verdict. A 'special jury' or 'blue ribbon' jury is one chosen subject to more stringent requirements as to the

type of membership than would be true of an ordinary jury.

Alona E. Evans

See also: JUDICIARY

Justice

A. The word has been chiefly used in two senses: (a) 'giving every man his due', and (b) 'the setting right of wrong', either by compensating the victim of wrong or by punishing the doer of it.

B. 1. The second sense is narrower than the first and derives from it; it is the doing of justice to the victim or doer of injustice by giving him what becomes his due only because injustice has been done. Justice, in the first sense, is respect for whatever rules prescribe how men shall behave towards one another, or in other words, for rights and duties. Though these two perennial senses were first systematically discussed in Book V of Aristotle's *Ethics* (in *The Works of Aristotle*, ed. by W. D. Ross, Oxford: Clarendon Press, 1925, vol. IX), there is nothing specifically Greek about them.

2. Boldly by Plato, and more uncertainly by Aristotle, there is a distinction made between law (in the wide sense which includes custom) as it is and as it ought to be. In the *Statesman* (trans. by B. Jowett, in *The Dialogues of Plato*, Oxford: Clarendon Press, 3rd edn., 1892, p. 497), Plato argues that it is better that the wise should rule rather than the law, because 'the law does not perfectly comprehend what is noblest and most just for all and therefore cannot enforce what is best'. In this dialogue and in the *Republic*, Plato conceives of a justice perfectly adapted to man's nature and which can be discovered by the use of reason. In the *Ethics*, Aristotle distinguishes between natural and conventional justice, of which the first is universal and the second is peculiar to individual states, but he does not say that conventional justice, when it conflicts with natural, must give way to it.

3. In the *Republic*, Plato treats justice as one of the four principal virtues, the other three being temperance, wisdom, and courage. Justice is the controlling or architectonic virtue; the just man is the self-disciplined man whose passions are controlled by reason. Plato argued that since some men are deficient in this virtue they should be placed 'under a rule like that of the best and be servants of the best, in whom the Divine [i.e. reason] rules' (*The Republic of Plato*, trans. by B. Jowett, Oxford:

Juvenile Delinquency

Clarendon Press, 3rd edn., 1922, vol. IX, p. 590B).

4. For the Stoics, as for Plato, justice was discoverable by reason and superior to positive law and custom. It is natural in the sense that man, merely by reflecting on his nature as a rational being, can see how he ought to behave. Natural law or justice, *ius naturale*, is therefore the conduct proper to man merely as a rational being living among other beings like himself. It is divine and immutable and the same for all men, and positive law, to be worthy of the name of law, must conform to it. Thus the natural law or justice of the Stoics treats all men as equals, as Plato's justice does not. It consists, not of the rules actually common to all peoples, but of rules that derive from the essential nature of man. The Roman jurists absorbed this conception into their accounts of law, and in Justinian's *Institutes* there is a clear distinction made between *ius naturale*, the law prescribed by reason, and *ius gentium*, the law common to all peoples. Thus an institution (e.g. slavery) universal in the world known to the Romans might be everywhere tolerated and yet admitted to be contrary to natural justice. This idea of natural justice was taken over by the Christian Fathers and survives among European peoples to this day.

5. Hobbes puts forward yet another conception of justice. 'But when a covenant is made, then to break it is Unjust: And the definition of Injustice, is no other than *the not Performance of Covenant*. And whatsoever is not Unjust, is *Just*' (*Leviathan* (1651), Everyman's Library, London: Dent, 1914, p. 74). But there is no obligation, says Hobbes, to keep covenants if there is more to be lost than gained by keeping them, which there ordinarily will be unless there is a coercive power strong enough to enforce them. Thus Hobbes also treats justice as obedience to a superior who has the power to make himself obeyed. Though Hobbes's account of justice has never been widely accepted, it has had negatively a great influence, because many have agreed with him that there is no natural justice superior to positive law in the sense of the long tradition which begins with the Stoics.

6. Hume calls justice an 'artificial virtue', meaning thereby that sympathy with others is not enough to cause men to practise it. It consists in the keeping of rules which men would never have imagined, let alone approved, had experience not taught them that they were in the common interest. They are not rules discoverable by reflecting on man's nature as a rational being, nor do they arise from covenants. 'It has been asserted by some, that justice arises from Human Conventions. ... If by *convention* be here meant a *promise* ... nothing can be more absurd. ... But if by convention be meant a sense of common interest ...; it must be owned that, in this sense, justice arises from human conventions' (D. Hume, *An Enquiry Concerning the Principles of Morals* (1751), ed. by L. A. Selby-Bigge, Oxford: Clarendon Press, 2nd edn., 1902, p. 306). The Utilitarians commonly used the word justice in much the same way, but were also disposed to say that no rule of justice is properly so called unless there is a sanction attached to it, unless the breaker of it incurs some penalty. 'The idea of justice supposes two things: a rule of conduct, and a sentiment which sanctions the rule ..., a desire that punishment may be suffered by those who infringe the rule' (J. S. Mill, *Utilitarianism* (1861), Everyman's Library, London: Dent, 1910, p. 49).

C. *Justice* is still commonly used in the two primary senses, of giving every man his due, and of the setting right of wrong. If it is supposed that what is due to a man is so merely because he is a man, then the justice in question may be called natural, even though it is admitted that no rule of conduct can be derived logically from man's nature as a rational being. If what is due to him is so in virtue of some rule which happens to be generally accepted in his community, then the justice is *conventional*. If it is due to him in virtue of a rule the breach of which makes the breaker answerable for his action (or inaction) to some public authority, then the justice is *legal*.

J. P. Plamenatz

Juvenile Delinquency

A. The core reference of the term is to those social acts (usually socially learnt) of juveniles that are prohibited by law or socially disapproved. The term *juvenile*, although defined differently by the various jurisdictions, generally includes most of the years of childhood and adolescence. Moreover, the specific social acts designated as juvenile delinquencies vary markedly from one jurisdiction to another. In addition to those offences (exclusive of capital crimes and those punishable by life imprisonment) which when committed by adults are punishable as felonies and misdemeanours, the list generally includes certain acts peculiar to childhood and adolescence.

364

Juvenile Delinquency

The phrase *juvenile delinquency* is so overlaid with legal, normative, and moral implications that there is a wealth of ad hoc definitions. Its core reference in social science seems to be to social acts of juveniles that are demarcated and evaluated as deviant or antisocial by relevant legal or social norms, and that are usually, though not always, socially learnt. A crucial problem of definition rests in whether the standards applied are the object of legal norms which are rigid and narrow or of more flexible, diffuse, and variable social norms.

B. In the phrase *juvenile delinquency* each word contributes to the composite meaning.

1. The term *juvenile* refers (a) chronologically to a proximate age period defined legally as extending from six to ten as a minimum, to sixteen to twenty-one as a maximum, and socially as including the years between infancy and adulthood, generally called childhood and adolescence; (b) functionally, to individual characteristics, capabilities, and responsibility greater than those of infancy but less than those of maturity.

2. The term *delinquency* is often used loosely to describe what are sometimes also called *crimes* or *offences*. This is the more likely to be the case where the laws of the land themselves employ the term. The White House Conference on Child Health and Protection (*The Delinquent Child*, New York: Century, 1932, p. 23) states that '*delinquency is any such juvenile misconduct as might be dealt with under the law*'. M. H. Neumeyer (*Juvenile Delinquency in Modern Society*, New York: Van Nostrand, 1949, p. 16) stresses law violation 'as well as patterns of behavior that are peculiar to childhood, princi-

pally truancy, waywardness, and incorrigibility'. The *Children's Court Act* for New York City (ch. 482, 1933) in addition to violations of federal, state, and local laws, names the following as delinquencies: (a) incorrigible, ungovernable, and habitually disobedient behaviour, (b) habitual truancy, (c) desertion of home, (d) engaging in illegal occupation, (e) association with immoral or vicious persons, (f) frequenting unlawful places, (g) habitual use of obscene or profane language, and (h) wilful endangering of the morals or health of self or others.

3. In Great Britain the legislation does not use the term at all. The category of 'juvenile' is broken down into those of 'children', i.e. persons between 8 and 14 years of age, and 'young persons', i.e. those who have reached the age of 14 but are under the age of 17 (Childrens and Young Persons Acts 1933 to 1958).

4. There is much to be said for the procedure followed by O. Nyquist in his comparative study of juvenile justice in California and Scandinavia. He observes that he uses 'the term "juvenile offender" ... exclusively for a juvenile (under 21 years of age) who has committed *crime*. For all forms of criminal or non-criminal anti-social conduct on the part of juveniles which society for one reason or the other does not accept, we use the term "delinquency" and "juvenile delinquent". A juvenile offender, accordingly, is always a juvenile delinquent too, while a juvenile delinquent is not necessarily a juvenile offender' (*Juvenile Justice*, London: Macmillan, 1960, p. 1 fn.).

Joseph S. Himes

See also: Crime (and Criminal Law)
Criminology and Penology

K

Kinship and Kinship System

A. In contemporary English (in Great Britain) *kinsman* is an aristocratic word for relative. *Kinship* in its technical sense follows naturally from the common understanding of words containing the element *kin* (*kindred*, *kinsman*, *kinsfolk*). The ordinary expression 'kith and kin', acquaintance and kinsfolk, sums up the world of intimate relationships. A *kinship system* is usually taken to refer to the complex of rules in any one society (or section of a society) which, by governing descent, succession, inheritance, marriage, extra-marital sexual relations, and residence, determines the status of individuals and groups in respect of their ties of consanguinity and marriage.

B. 1. Two people are kin(smen) when they share a common ancestor or one is descended from the other. The word 'ancestor' here means somebody standing in the social position of a father who had a child who had a child until the present generation is reached; or somebody standing in the social position of a mother, etc. An ancestor is not necessarily a forbear or progenitor in a biological sense, and the tracing of kinship links by genealogies (which are statements about social relationships) is a process different from that of the tracing of blood relationships by the geneticist. The facts of procreation provide men-in-society with certain elements which they use for the expression of social relations. Different societies perceive the facts of procreation differently (in a sense the facts differ); but even if the facts are perceived in the same way they may well be put to different social use. In their eagerness to dispel the wrong notion that the study of kinship is the study of blood relationships, anthropologists sometimes fall into the error of denying any connexion between the two things. The procreation and rearing of children form a kernel around which a particular society evolves its own system of allocating rights and duties. Biology does not explain why any particular kinship system exists, but the engendering of children is the natural key to the elaborate social edifice known as kinship.

2. Kinship relations are sometimes called relations of *consanguinity* (q.v.), a term which, shorn of its biological implications, is a satisfactory way of showing that kinship is concerned with descent. The relationships which flow through marriage are relationships of *affinity* (q.v.). And because kinship and affinity are closely linked the first term is often used to cover the second. Some anthropologists regard the expression *affinal kin* as a solecism; it may well be, but it is impossible to speak of a kinship system without including marriage and its consequent relationships.

3. In many industrial societies the range over which kinship spreads, both in regard to functions and individuals covered, is (or is commonly thought to be) so narrow that the terms family (q.v.) and kinship tend to merge. But in fact the family is a crucially distinct area of kinship. It is in the family that society reproduces itself. The family supplies members to kinship and other groups. The basic elements in the family are ties of filiation (that is, the linkage between two adjacent generations), even though a particular form of the family (*extended*, *joint*, etc.) may contain several generations.

The constitution of the family is a reflex of the wider *kinship system*. This system determines, by its rules of marriage, and descent, who may marry whom and the differences in the rights and duties which will accrue to children vis-à-vis their parents and their kinsfolk through these parents.

C. In formal analysis a primary distinction is made between *unilineal* and *non-unilineal kinship*.

1. The first is a kind of kinship in which the tracing of descent in one line (either through males exclusively or through females exclusively) to a common ancestor is an entitlement to membership of a discrete group (clan, lineage, etc.). Such a group is accordingly either *patrilineal* or *matrilineal*. In some societies both groups exist, so that an individual is at once a member of his father's patrilineal group and his mother's matrilineal group (*double unilineal*— sometimes called *dual* or *double descent* systems). Unilineal descent does not of course exhaust kinship; in a patrilineally organized

366

society a man must also have kinship relations through his mother, and mutatis mutandis in a matrilineally organized society. In a double unilineal system, while both parents are severally members of the same group as their child, he has kinsmen (e.g. his father's sister's son or mother's brother's son) who are not members of either of his unilineal groups.

2. In societies lacking unilineal organization we may find what some anthropologists call *descent groups* (*bilateral descent groups* and *ramages*). If an individual traces descent from an ancestor through any link and forms a group with other people descended from the same ancestor, he may be a member of several such groups; and these groups taken together will have overlapping membership (bilateral descent groups). If there are groups in which an individual may claim membership through different kinds of kinship tie, but he is at the same time forced to choose only one of these groups, we find a kind of discrete (non-overlapping) descent group which in certain respects resembles a unilineally constructed group (ramage). On the other hand, in some societies we find no descent principle at all. In such cases kinship is organized exclusively on the basis of a circle of relatives traced outwards from an individual (*kindred*). A formalized kindred is definable in terms of the degree of cousinship to which it is traced. A kindred which is bounded by third cousins, for example, will include an individual's eight sets of great-great-grandparents and their descendants. No two individuals, unless they are full siblings, can have exactly the same kindred. This kind of grouping is not a descent group because the members of it as a whole fail to share a common ancestor. My cousin on my mother's side, for example, does not have ancestry in common with my cousin on my father's side (unless certain marriages have occurred). Kindreds of this kind have a symmetry which springs from the reckoning of relationship by degrees of distance, no account being taken of the sex of the individuals through whom a relationship is traced. Sex for sex, a relative on my mother's side is structurally equivalent to one occupying a similar position on my father's side. It is for this reason that such a system can be easily described in the language of English kinship— uncle, aunt, and cousin denote positions which are balanced on either side of a given individual.

Because in a kindred an individual traces relationship through both parents, a kinship system which has no groupings other than the kindred is sometimes called *bilateral* or *cognatic*. But the terms are unfortunate because all kinship is bilateral (or cognatic) whatever the nature of the descent system. Moreover, formalized kindreds may be found in unilineally organized societies.

The terms *multilineal* and *omnilineal* are sometimes used for systems of kinship which are not unilineal, but these words, by implying the existence of lines, suggest too much. There are no lines in a kinship system which knows no formal grouping other than the kindred.

D. Formal analysis is merely a first step in the understanding of kinship systems.

The qualities of any one system can be judged only in terms of, first, the extent to which kinship relationships and alignments correspond to other forms of relationships and alignments, and, second, the nature of the rights and duties by which particular kinship relations are defined. For example, two societies may be classified formally as having patrilineal systems, but while in one of them patriliny may define the framework of groups on which the society as a whole rests (so that political, economic, and religious activities are closely interwoven with kinship, patriliny permeating society in toto), in the other case patrilineal groups may be confined to local organization, the wider institutions of society being based on non-kinship criteria. Certain parts of pre-Communist China showed localized large-scale patrilineages of a kind which resemble patrilineages in a number of primitive societies, but the study of kinship in China cannot by itself take us very far in understanding the political, legal, economic, and religious framework of Chinese society as a whole.

Again, the rights and duties between an individual and a specific relative are not likely to be exactly the same even in systems which formally resemble one another closely. A man's relationship with his mother's brother in matrilineal society A may well differ in some significant respects from the corresponding relationship in matrilineal society B.

The nature of a particular kinship system can be comprehended only when what is implied in kinship is measured against what is implied in other modes of organization in the same society. The study of descent, rules of incest and exogamy, kinship terminology, residence rules, rules of succession and inheritance, and preferential and prescriptive marriage allow us to characterize a kinship system as an internally

Kinship Terminology

consistent entity; we have then to move out of this system to gauge how far it is significant in placing people in their society, in shaping the relations between them, and in affecting their modes of activity (political, legal, economic, and religious).

In studying works on kinship written at different times during the last century the reader must grasp their underlying theoretical preoccupations. Much of the earlier work is concerned with the evolutionary sequence of forms of kinship and marriage, great reliance being placed upon kinship terminology. Contemporary interests in the subject and modern systems of analysis are exemplified in A. R. Radcliffe-Brown, 'Introduction' to A. R. Radcliffe-Brown & D. Forde, *African Systems of Kinship and Marriage* (London: Oxford University Press, 1950); C. Lévi-Strauss, *Les Structures élémentaires de la parenté* (Paris: Presses Universitaires de France, 1949); G. P. Murdock, *Social Structure* (New York: The Macmillan Co., 1949) and E. R. Leach, *Rethinking Anthropology* (London: Athlone Press, 1961).

Maurice Freedman

See also: CONSANGUINITY
DESCENT
FAMILY
MARRIAGE
RESIDENCE

Kinship Terminology

A. *Kinship terminology* consists of terms which designate, in the first instance, social relationships—or persons occupying such relationships—established by marriage and parenthood, and which are subsequently extended to relationships formed in other ways.

1. Parenthood establishes the relationships which comprise the nuclear family (q.v.), namely, father, mother, son, daughter, brother, and sister.

2. Extension of the same kind of relationships outward from the nuclear family will give such terms as *grandparent*, *uncle*, *aunt*, *nephew*, *niece*, and *grandchild*.

3. Marriage (q.v.) establishes primarily a relationship between two persons, husband and wife, and secondarily with an indefinite number of affinal relatives or 'in-laws'.

4. Kinship terms are mutually correlative or reciprocal; the use of one term always implies the use of another or of the same term. Thus *father* implies *son* or *daughter* and vice-versa; *brother* requires the correlative *sister* or the reciprocal *brother*.

B. The range of usage of kinship terms is wide indeed. They are applied to (a) persons whose genealogical relationship to the speaker is known, e.g. my mother's mother's brother's daughter's daughter; (b) persons who are unquestionably related, through parenthood and by marriage, but whose precise genealogical relationship to the person speaking is not known, e.g. to members of a clan (q.v.), moiety (q.v.), tribe (q.v.), or an endogamous folk community; (c) persons related to the speaker by social ritual such as adoptors, god-parents, etc.; (d) members of social groupings not based upon ties established by parenthood or marriage, such as fraternities, sororities, secret societies, church congregations, monastic orders, guilds, labour unions, and socialist parties; (e) heads, or officers, of political or ecclesiastical organizations, such as village chiefs, heads of churches—e.g. Pope, from Greek πάππας—father, and kings—*sire*; (f) nations: mother country, the fatherland, and universities: alma mater; (g) deities; and (h) natural phenomena: mother earth, sun father. And, in addition to the designation of social relationships, kinship terms are used metaphorically: 'Sleep and his brother, Death'.

C. The usages of kinship terms are interrelated, constituting a system. Systems vary widely in structure and they may exhibit varying degrees of integration and internal consistency. A number of classifications of systems of kinship terminology have been proposed, but none is wholly satisfactory.

1. L. H. Morgan, who founded the science of kinship, classified all systems into two major groups, the *classificatory* and the *descriptive* (*Systems of Consanguinity and Affinity of the Human Family*, Washington: The Smithsonian Institution, 1871). The *classificatory* system is characterized by the terminological merging of lineal and collateral kindred at certain points— e.g. calling father's brother 'father'; mother's brother's son, 'son'— and by the absence of compound and secondary terms such as grandparent and second cousin. In the descriptive system, each term designates only one kind of relationship—cousin, for example, is not a classificatory term as many have assumed, since it labels but one kind of relationship, viz. the child of a sibling of a parent.

2. W. H. R. Rivers proposed a threefold classification: a 'clan system'—Morgan's classificatory system; a 'family system'—Morgan's descriptive; and a 'kindred system' (*Kinship and*

368

Social Organization, London: Constable, 1914, pp. 71, 77, 80).

3. R. H. Lowie offers a fourfold classification: (a) *generation* systems of kinship terminology, in which 'collateral lines are wholly merged in the lineal within a particular generation'; (b) *bifurcate merging* systems of kinship terminology in which 'each generation is bisected so that only half the collateral kin are merged in the lineal', e.g. parents merged with their siblings of the same sex but distinguished from those of the opposite sex; (c) *bifurcate collateral* systems of kinship terminology, in which 'the immediate collateral lines are distinguished from the lineal *and from each other*'; (d) *lineal* systems of kinship terminology, in which 'collateral lines are distinguished from the lineal but *not from each other*' ('Relationship Terms', in *Encyclopaedia Britannica*, New York: Encyclopaedia Britannica, 14th edn., 1929, vol. 19, p. 84).

4. P. Kirchhoff, working independently of Lowie, produced essentially the same type of classification ('Verwandtschaftsbezeichnungen und Verwandtenheirat', *Zeitschrift für Ethnologie*, vol. 64, 1932, pp. 41–71).

D. Despite the organization of kinship terms into systems, and the efforts to classify systems, there is almost infinite variety in kinship terminologies. Use of a term may depend upon the sex of the speaker or of the person spoken to, or both; upon the relative ages of speaker and person spoken to; or upon the sex of the person through whom speaker and person spoken to are related. Terms of reference may differ from terms of direct address. In some systems father's sister may be called 'father'; in others, mother's brother may be called 'mother'. In classificatory systems one may have many 'fathers' and 'mothers' and they may be found on several generation levels. Some systems have no 'cousin' terms; others have no term for brother or sister but have terms for sibling of the same and of the opposite sex.

E. A kinship terminology is not the result of the operation of a single factor, such as a form of marriage and the family, as Morgan and Rivers were inclined to believe. On the contrary, many factors are involved in addition to form of marriage: customs of residence (q.v.), descent reckoning, tenure and inheritance of property, exogamous and endogamous kinship groups such as clans and moieties influence and shape terminologies (see G. P. Murdock, *Social*

Structure, New York: The Macmillan Co., 1949, pp. 113–83). Kinship terminologies tend faithfully to reflect their social determinants, but social relations may change faster than terminologies so that a lag between the two is produced and the terminology no longer fits the social system. Social disorganization, too, finds expression in incoherence of terminology. But the lag between terminology and social system may make it possible to reconstruct the history of social relations. Thus a nomenclature in which mother's brother and father-in-law are called by the same term points definitely to cross-cousin marriage as a common practice of the past, even though it is no longer observed.

As socio-cultural conditions change so will kinship terminologies change. A few historical studies of kinship terminologies have been made, such as those by F. Eggan and A. Spoehr (F. Eggan, 'Historical Changes in the Choctaw Kinship System', *American Anthropologist*, vol. 39, 1937, pp. 34–52; A. Spoehr, 'Changing Kinship Systems', *Anthropological Series*, Field Museum of Natural History, vol. 33, no. 4, 1947, pp. 153–235).

Leslie A. White

See also: KINSHIP AND KINSHIP SYSTEM

Kulturkreis

A. The term *Kulturkreis* refers to the central concept of the German culture-historical school, which uses a limited number of cultural trait clusters or *Kulturkreise* (each assumed to have originated in a temporal sequence in a different area of the world) as the basis of a system of classification of the world's cultures. Since the term is unique to the anthropological school which created it, it can also be used to designate that school.

B. 1. In reaction to the unilinear evolutionary theories of classical evolutionism, there developed in Germany under the leadership first of F. Graebner and later of W. Schmidt a theory of world cultural growth through the process of diffusion (q.v.). The essence of this theory was that all cultures, including those of the modern world, were the result of the diffusion of clusters of cultural material which had originated at different times and different places in the world. Each culture studied by the modern ethnographer could be classified by its relation to these streams of historical diffusion—some clearly revealing the historical past through the existence of obvious cultural strata, others

Kulturkreis

presenting more complex problems for analysis. The theory has been known both as the *Kulturkreis* theory and as the *culture historical* method. Because of the ambiguous relation of the latter term to the Anglo-American *culture history* (q.v.), it is probably preferable to use only *Kulturkreis*.

2. The *Kulturkreis* group has been recognized as more important than other diffusionist schools because of the carefulness of their method of tracing historical connection. Thus M. J. Herskovits, while critical of Father Schmidt's claim that empathy and *verstehen* can be used to reconstruct the earlier *Kulturkreise* which then yield clues for the historical reconstruction of the contacts of modern cultures, is convinced of the importance of Graebner's stress upon 'form' and 'quantity' as guides to the existence of historical contact between cultures (*Man and His Works*, New York: Knopf, 1948, pp. 509–14). Outside the United States and Great Britain the *Kulturkreis* group is of considerable importance. It can be said to have carried out a half century of significant work in Germany. Its continuing influence in Germany can be likened to that of Durkheim on French anthropology. Moreover the method is taught widely by Catholic anthropologists in Austria, South America, and India.

3. Nevertheless the location, time, and even existence of the original *Kulturkreise* have been severely questioned by anthropologists. Even one of the members of the group, W. Koppers, has stated that he and his associates now reject the earlier *Kulturkreise* as being inadequate and unnecessary for the use of their historical method (R. L. Beals & H. Hoijer, *An Introduction to Anthropology*, New York: Macmillan, 1953, pp. 616–17).

Bert Gerow

See also: Culture History
Diffusion

L

Labour (Economics)

A. The term has a variety of related usages and applications stemming from its general meaning of *work* or *effort*, often in the sense of painful or heavy toil (cf. 'laborious' meaning costing much effort and needing much endurance rather than skill). As a verb *to labour* has the same general sense, meaning *to work* or, more simply, *to endeavour*. Thus in economics labour has several meanings:

1. As a collective noun it denotes those who work as employees—but commonly only manual workers. The noun *labourer* means an unskilled man, or as in 'farm labourer', one who has at least no industrial proficiency. When qualified by an adjective, *labour* denotes all workers of a specified kind, e.g. juvenile labour, skilled labour, migrant labour. In this use it carries no connotation of roughness, but it is commonly used only for manual workers (thus 'medical manpower' would be more usual than 'medical labour').

2. As a general term it denotes the exertion of effort as in the phrase 'the marginal disutility of labour'.

3. It is sometimes used to denote one of the three basic factors of production—land, labour, and capital. As such it comprehends all forms of human effort, at whatever level of skill and remuneration, and includes employers equally with employed. Similarly in such a concept as 'the share of labour in the national income' labour may refer to the aggregate income of the first of the following groups alone or to the first two or all three: (a) wage earners (b) other employees (c) employers and self-employed, so far as their incomes do not accrue in respect of their property.

B. It is also important to note three important adjectival uses of *labour* in economic writings.

1. *Labour economics* is the study mainly of the forces governing the deployment of the working population between different jobs; the determination of the rates of pay and numbers employed in those jobs; the movements of the general level of pay, monetary and real; and the efficiency and well-being of the human factor in production. In each case the institutions and procedures concerned are also studied.

2. *Labour relations* denotes the relations between employers and employed, both directly between managers and workpeople at the place of work, and between employers or employers' associations and trade unions.

3. Labour, as an adjective, may mean 'concerning employees', as a whole, or mainly those who are wage-earners or otherwise in subordinate or lower-paid positions, e.g. in such phrases as *labour statistics, labour unions, labour disputes*.

E. H. Phelps Brown

See also: Labour (Economics)
Labour (Political Science)
Labour Theory of Value

Labour (Political Science) (Also **Labour Movement**)

A. The word *labour*, in English political writings since about 1800, is used in five different senses, of which the chronological development can be clearly traced.

1. It was simply a synonym for *work*.

2. During the second quarter of the 19th century, it came to be used as a figure of speech, the personification of an act, in phrases like 'the rights of labour', the 'product of labour', 'the value of labour', and so on.

3. The precise moment when this personification (together with its antonym *capital* (q.v.)) gave way to the notion of *a collective entity* cannot be fixed. W. Thompson, in *Labour Rewarded* (London: Hunt & Clarke, 1827) appears to be using the personification; J. F. Bray in *Labour's Wrongs and Labour's Remedy* (London: David Green, 1839) is clearly referring to a collective entity and expects to be understood. In any case, its meaning at that time and when it is used in the same way later is adequately covered by the New English Dictionary definition: 'the general body of labourers and operatives, viewed in its relation to the body of capitalists, with regard to its political interests and claims'. In this sense, then, labour denotes the *self-conscious working class in politics*. The *Pall Mall Gazette* was

Labour Economics

clearly using the word in the same sense when, in 1884, it referred to the trade union M.P.s in the British House of Commons as 'the new Labour Party', and the word still had essentially the same meaning when it was used in the title of the Labour Representation Committee of 1900.

4. *Labour* took on its fourth meaning in Great Britain from 1906 when the M.P.s sponsored by the L.R.C. decided to call *themselves* the 'Labour Party', and still more so from 1918, when the party adopted a Socialist programme. The usage of the term in the British context may be briefly stated as follows. It can mean the Labour Party or its Parliamentary mouthpiece, or those who vote for it or (more rarely) the whole Labour movement (see B. below). The main practical and theoretical interest of the term derives from special characteristics of the British Labour Party, both as to its structure and its position on matters of doctrine. The part played by affiliated trade unions in the *structure* of the Labour Party has led to certain gradualist assumptions from which the term *labour* develops its fourth meaning, i.e. the assumption that accumulated reforms can lead to Socialism and that Socialism achieved in this way will be acceptable to many (including some members of the Labour Party itself) who would not otherwise accept it.

5. When the term is exported it acquires what is, in effect, a fifth meaning. The assumptions described above about doctrine or programme, together with some form of organic association between trade unions, Socialist and others, have characterized, in different degrees and different ways, left-wing parties in other countries which have used the term *labour* or an equivalent. This is true, for instance, of the Australian and New Zealand Labour Parties, of the Norwegian Labour Party (*Arbeider Partiet*) and Dutch Labour Party (*Partij van der Arbeid*) today, and was true of the Belgian Labour Party (*Parti Ouvrier Belge*) before World War II. Something similar is in the minds of French politicians who speak of creating *un travaillisme français*. In all these cases, a distinction is made between *labour* and *socialist*, the latter term implying a purely socialist objective and a membership limited to socialists.

B. *Labour movement* is more widely used normally to describe the *whole body* (sometimes brought together in a single unit, as in Britain in the National Council of Labour) or *organizations, industrial, political or commercial* (e.g. consumers' and producers' co-operatives) in which wage-workers are or are intended to be predominant, or which claim to serve predominantly the interests of the working class, whether these interests are 'socialist' or not.

W. Pickles

See also: LABOUR (Economics)
SOCIALISM

Labour Economics

A. *Labour economics* is a special branch of economics which analyses relationships in the labour market and evaluates existing and proposed labour policies. It examines specific issues dealing with the level of employment, collective bargaining, and labour standards and wages.

B. 1. Labour economics has developed out of a division of labour within the discipline of economics. It is characterized by a heavy emphasis upon policy, focusing attention upon the interrelationships among workers, unions, and management in the labour market. It deals with specific issues most of which are associated with the level of employment, collective bargaining, and labour standards and wages (S. C. Sufrin & R. C. Sedgwick, *Labor Economics and Problems at Mid-century*, New York: Knopf, 1956, p. 6). A major purpose of labour economics is to achieve an understanding which would aid in correcting maladjustments and resolving problems occurring in the labour market.

Most general treatises in this field stress 'problems' or conflicts. C. R. Daugherty's classical text, for example, gave attention 'to almost all the main areas of human maladjustment ... found in American industry' and 'to the chief existing and proposed attempts to bring about adjustment and harmony' (*Labor Problems in American Industry*, Boston: Houghton Mifflin, 5th edn., 1941, p. vii). Other writers, however, argue that although 'there are many problems peculiar to labor and labor relations... they can be best understood within a framework of economic analysis rather than approached as pathological phenomena' (F. Peterson, *Survey of Labor Economics*, New York: Harper & Brothers, 1947, p. xviii).

2. Although labour economics is concerned almost exclusively with questions involving *workers*, the interests of management, stockholders, unions, government and the general public are recognized and explored. The term *workers* includes both hand and brain workers, but is confined to persons who are 'bossed' or directed on the job. As F. Baerwald states (*Fundamentals of Labor Economics*, New York:

Fordham University Press, 1947, p. 5), 'While general economic analysis deals with labor as a factor, the economics of labor deals with the problems and conditions that arise because the factor "labor" is embodied in human beings'.

3. The scope and content of labour economics have reflected changes in the labour market and in economic analysis. The early concentration upon the history of the labour movement has been followed by study of labour laws and of the problems of the individual worker. Labour economists have attempted to integrate new developments in distribution and employment theory into their analysis of the labour market to unify theory and fact. The growth of labour unions has led to an emphasis upon collective bargaining. Attention also has been directed to the varied interrelationships within the plant and office societies. More recently, stress has been laid upon labour market research which tests the basic assumptions and conclusions of general economics in the field of employment.

4. In their attempts to analyse the labour market, labour economists have sought assistance not only from economic theory but from other social sciences. Not only are there borderline issues which might be analysed from the standpoint of various disciplines, but many individual questions which cannot be resolved by a single discipline. Labour problems have become a 'centre of gravity' for such social sciences as economics, sociology, anthropology, psychology, history, politics, law and even philosophy. Some writers avowedly approach labour problems as 'social scientists' rather than as economists (C. E. Dankert, *An Introduction to Labor*, New York: Prentice-Hall, 1954, p. vi). Others stress the economic aspects of labour problems, even though they recognize non-economic variables, because they believe that '... many a noneconomic element derives, directly or otherwise, from some economic force' (J. Shister, *Economics of the Labor Market*, Chicago: Lippincott, 1949, p. vii).

H. Ellsworth Steele

See also: INDUSTRIAL SOCIOLOGY
LABOUR (Economics)
LABOUR (Political Science)

Labour Force

A. *Labour force* denotes the body of workers of all grades and occupations available or engaged in a certain region, industry, or undertaking.

1. The term is used where writers are concerned with an enumeration of the manpower within specified limits: the force is the strength or number at work or available for work. Usage prescribes no particular delimitation.

2. The labour force of a whole economy is usually called the total working population or the occupied population, though these terms commonly include some who were not working at the time of the count. Statistics of the labour force in this sense are usually prepared by an agency of central government, in whose publications information must be sought in detail on the coverage of the figures provided. There are many points at which the drawing of the boundary line calls for decisions, and some of these may affect the numerical results substantially, e.g. whether to include those who work as members of families and not under a contract of employment.

E. H. Phelps Brown

See also: LABOUR (Economics)
OCCUPATION

Labour Market

A. The term serves as a metaphorical description of the interplay between the supply of, and demand for, labour in particular employments and in the aggregate.

B. 1. A market is an institution which enables each of a number of potential buyers and sellers of a class of commodity to get into touch with any of the others, and so make his own transactions on the most beneficial terms open to anyone at the time. Out of the interchange of offers to sell and bids to buy there emerges a going price, at which current selling orders are balanced by current buying orders; if the flow of these orders changes so as to alter the balance, the price will change, but at any one time all the transactions of a given kind will be made at approximately the same price. These functions of a market are most fully provided for when all orders pass through a limited number of dealers who meet face to face, as in a wheat pit or stock exchange. But the term *market* is extended to cover any group of dealers in a class of commodity who are able to keep in touch with one another even though they do not all meet.

2. It is in this sense that economists use the term *labour market* (a) to cover all the agencies and procedures by which those who have jobs to offer and those who are looking for jobs get into touch and arrive at terms of engagement with one another; or, more abstractly, (b) to denote

373

Labour Theory of Value

the interplay of the supply and demand for employees of particular kinds and all kinds. But because the labour market is commonly an imperfect counterpart to the produce market, it does not fully discharge that market's functions of protecting each dealer by making the going rate available to him irrespective of his personal circumstances, and of balancing supply and demand: so the treatment of the labour market may stress its differences from other markets rather than its similarities—e.g. A. Marshall offers an 'explanation of much of that instinctive objection which the working classes have felt to the habit of some economists, particularly those of the employer class, of treating labour simply as a commodity and regarding the labour market as like every other market; whereas in fact the differences between the two cases, though not fundamental from the point of view of theory, are yet clearly marked, and in practice often very important' (*Principles of Economics*, London: Macmillan, 8th edn., 1920, bk. V, ch. II, p. 336, see further bk. VI, chs. IV, V).

E. H. Phelps Brown

See also: LABOUR (Economics)

Labour Theory of Value

A. The *labour theory of value* is a theory which purports to show that economic value is composed of or created by or determined by 'labour'. Especially in Marxist writings the theory is taken to have a special explanatory function in analysing 'capitalist' systems of economy.

B. The labour theory has been used in four senses.

1. In the first approach labour is treated as creating a positive substance called value. 'If we decide to regard the labour used to produce a commodity not only as the source of its value but also as constituting the very *substance* of its value, so that the commodity is looked upon as a sort of mass of "congealed" or "crystallized" attractive power, we are nearer a solution' (R. L. Meek, *Studies in the Labour Theory of Value*, London: Lawrence & Wishart, 1956, p. 63).

2. In the second sense labour is regarded as the determinant of *relative* values. 'Marx had found in ... Aristotle the idea that "exchange cannot exist without equality, and equality cannot exist without commensurability"' (E. von Böhm-Bawerk, *Karl Marx and the Close of His System*, P. M. Sweezy (ed.), New York: Kelley, 1949, p. 68). 'Possessing utility, commodities

derive their exchangeable value from two sources: from their scarcity and from the quantity of labour required to obtain them' (D. Ricardo, *Principles of Political Economy and Taxation*, P. Sraffa (ed.), Cambridge: Cambridge University Press, 1951, vol. I, p. 12). 'If among a nation of hunters ... it usually costs twice the labour to kill a beaver which it does to kill a deer, one beaver should naturally exchange for, or be worth two deer' (A. Smith, *The Wealth of Nations*, Cannan (ed.), London: Macmillan, 5th edn., 1930, vol. 1, p. 49).

3. The third sense of the *labour theory of value* is as a theory of 'natural right', 'concerned not with actual but with ideal prices', 'primarily interested in what a man ought to get in reward for his labour' (A. D. Lindsay, *Karl Marx's 'Capital'*, London: Oxford University Press, 1925, p. 61).

4. Finally the theory is treated as a statement of the 'laws of motion for a definite type of social organization' (capitalism) (R. Hilferding, *Böhm-Bawerk's Criticism of Marx*, P. M. Sweezy (ed.), New York: Kelley, 1949, p. 186).

C. 1. As a theory explaining actual prices and market price behaviour for the modern world, the labour theory has been long abandoned even by numerous Marxists. Marx's attempt to explain the difference between 'values' and 'prices' is treated as 'tautology' (Böhm-Bawerk, *Karl Marx and the Close of His System*, p. 35), an 'incantation' (J. Robinson, *An Essay on Marxian Economics*, London: Macmillan, 1947, p. 22).

2. The theory is much more alive as an explanation of the 'laws of motion' of capitalist society, and of 'natural right' or 'exploitation' (see B.3 and B.4 above). Here orthodox and Marxian theory run side by side—up to a point. For Marx's statement that 'constant revolutionizing of the means of production' is essential to capitalism can be interpreted to mean little more than the familiar orthodox doctrine that, without growth and technical change, profits and interest will fall to a 'minimum' (much below the usual capitalist figure) or 'zero', depending on the author. Marx, thus, is sometimes praised for superior emphasis upon the dynamic nature of capitalism.

In the sense of natural right or 'exploitation', Marxian and orthodox theorists remain far apart. The essential *scientific* point is Marx's insistence that capital is only 'canned' labour and can add no greater 'value' than the labour going in to it. From this point he regards technical change as raising profits only by reducing the bargaining power of labour through actual or threatened unemployment. Profits cannot rise unless wages fall.

The mistake here is the failure to evolve a *consistently* dynamic approach to distribution. *Novel* capital instruments are not merely canned labour but vehicles embodying the creative power of a novel technical combination, combinations often so productive they can raise the absolute income of labour *and* capital *simultaneously*. Reducing the value of the new combination to the 'labour cost' of *thinking* would be tautology. True, the impact of each new combination upon the profit and interest rate eventually dies down (J. A. Schumpeter, *The Theory of Economic Development*, Cambridge, Mass.: Harvard University Press, 1951). But if development continues, new ones emerge. The essential feature is not unemployment, but willingness to accept new methods. Instead of saying the constant revolutionizing of production is essential to capitalism, Marx should have said it was essential to growth in any system.

David McCord Wright

See also: VALUE (Economics)

Labour Union (See Trade Union)

Laissez-Faire

A. *Laissez-faire* denotes non-intervention by the state in the economic activities of individuals, sometimes stated as an infinitive—*laisser-faire*—sometimes as an imperative—*laissez-faire* or *laissez nous faire*, leave us alone.

B. 1. The phrase was in common usage in mercantile and industrial circles during the 19th century. 'They have learnt a few words of French', it was said of the British factory owners in 1833, 'and each parrot from his perch, as he keeps swinging himself to and fro in his glittering cage, ejaculates "Laissez nous faire" ' (*Blackwoods' Edinburgh Magazine*, Edinburgh: Blackwood: vol. 33, 1833, p. 423).

2. The term is a popular rather than a scientific concept. The British classical economists did not regularly employ the phrase until John Stuart Mill pronounced it a rule of general practice in 1848. They did not share one single set of attitudes towards government, and they believed that the *agenda* of government would vary from country to country and from time to time.

3. The phrase appears to have been used in print for the first time in April 1751 in the *Journal Oeconomique* in Paris. An anonymous writer, later identified as the Marquis d'Argenson (1694–1757), stated the case for greater liberty of trade and quoted the following story. 'It is reported of Colbert that, when he convened several deputies of Commerce at his house, and asked what he could do for the benefit of trade, the most sensible and plainest spoken among them replied in one phrase, "Laissez nous faire". Have we ever sufficiently pondered on the good sense of that short answer?' D'Argenson himself used the phrase as a maxim on other occasions; he approached laissez-faire as a claim for personal freedom in industry and as a demand for a change in public policy not on the philosophical grounds of belief in a 'natural order'. By contrast the Physiocrats based their economics on their view of nature, and usually wrote of 'l'entière liberté du commerce'—the full freedom of commerce—rather than of laissez-faire. Turgot, the distinguished Physiocrat, attributed the popularity of the maxim (in the form 'laissez-faire, laissez-passer') not to an author but to Jacques C. M. Vincent de Gournay (1712–59), a businessman and later an official. He added that the merchant who made the celebrated retort to Colbert was called 'Le Gendre'.

4. During the course of the 19th century the phrase was used in all parts of the world, frequently as a shorthand expression to express a belief in the freedom of industry from state interference. Originally a radical phrase, used by opponents of the cumbrous machinery of social and political control, it became a conservative phrase, used by supporters of powerful private interests. During the middle years of the century after John Stuart Mill in his *Principles of Political Economy* (London: Parker, 1848) had argued that the 'burden of proof' always lay with the supporters of public interference, who had to demonstrate that there was a 'strong case' for government action, some writers draw a distinction between laissez-faire in economic matters and laissez-faire in social matters. In 1870 J. E. Cairnes ('Political Economy and Laissez Faire', introductory lecture delivered at University College, London, 1870, quoted by J. M. Keynes, *The End of Laissez-Faire*, London: L. & V. Woolf, 1926, p. 26) claimed that 'the maxim of laissez-faire has no scientific basis whatever, but is at best a mere handy rule of practice'.

5. The phrase has not been in general use in the 20th century, except in relation to previous periods of history, but J. M. Keynes's essay *The End of Laissez-Faire* summed up a tradition, while refusing altogether to take the phrase as a test of economic policy. 'The most important

Land Tenure

Agenda of the State relate not to those activities which private individuals are already fulfilling, but ... to those decisions which are made by *no one* if the State does not make them' (ibid., p. 46). In other words, as D. H. Macgregor has written, 'the end of laissez-faire is "Laissez-faire L'Etat"; the principle is ... buried in dishonour and raised in glory' (*Economic Thought and Policy*, London: Oxford University Press, 1949, p. 69).

A. Briggs

See also: INDIVIDUALISM

Land Tenure

A. *Land tenure* denotes the rules and regulations governing rights of holding, disposing, and using land.

B. 1. The most general usage by social anthropologists today of the term and the concepts involved in it may be summarized by the following quotations from *Notes and Queries on Anthropology*: 'The concepts of property and ownership are closely linked. Ownership is best defined as the sum total of rights which various persons or groups of persons have over things: the things owned are property' (*Notes and Queries on Anthropology*, London: Routledge & Kegan Paul, 6th edn., 1951, p. 148). Land is only one form of property and 'land tenure may best be understood in terms of the *rights* of persons and groups in land' (ibid., p. 154).

Usage has varied little since social anthropologists first began to concern themselves with primitive legal and economic systems. As land is the principal source of wealth and therefore the main form of property in most primitive societies, in any description of a land tenure system all types of land right must be distinguished, together with the manner in which they are held and exercised in and conditioned by a particular social system, its technology, and the physical environment in which it is found.

2. In discussing land tenure, social anthropologists have always relied on legal theory, although their usages are not always identical with those of jurists. The term *property* (q.v.) used by lawyers to mean rights or interests in things protected by law, possesses a wide range of application. It may imply all rights of any kind vested in an individual or, more usually, the rights he holds in material things or corporeal property, such as land or chattels. Land tenure therefore denotes rights in connexion with only one form of property.

The ambiguity of the term *right* has always occupied the attention of legal writers. Most anthropologists, however, use the term in a wider and looser sense than do jurists. H. S. Maine, summarizing legal theory in the last century, wrote: 'A law ... is addressed by political superiors or sovereigns to political inferiors or subjects; it imposes on those subjects an obligation or duty and threatens a penalty [or *sanction*] in the event of disobedience. The power vested in a particular member of the community of drawing down the sanction on neglects or breaches of the duty is called a Right' (*Village-Communities*, London: Murray, 5th edn., 1887, p. 67). A modern legal author amplifies the usage thus: 'There must be distinguished a *legal* right, of which the test is a simple one—is the right recognized and protected by the legal system itself?' (G. W. Paton, *A Textbook of Jurisprudence*, Oxford: The Clarendon Press, 2nd edn., 1951, p. 218). Maine, however, was especially concerned with the application of legal concepts to primitive land tenure. He observed that land interests embodied in archaic or primitive forms of tenure were not necessarily enforceable by organized political and legal sanctions, and that in the sense of analytical jurists such interests were therefore not rights. Nevertheless, this did not imply that they were uncertain or unprotected, although the sanctions, as anthropologists now call them, would only be considered as custom or morality by lawyers.

3. Today few anthropologists would limit the term *right* as narrowly as do the jurists. In general A. R. Radcliffe-Brown followed legal usage closely. He wrote: 'The field of law will ... be regarded as co-terminous with that of organized legal sanctions' (*Structure and Function in Primitive Society*, London: Cohen & West, 1952, p. 212). He defined a sanction as 'a reaction on the part of society or a considerable number of its members to a mode of behaviour which is thereby approved [positive sanctions] or disapproved [negative sanctions]' (ibid., p. 205). This definition involved him in distinguishing legal from customary, religious, and other types of sanction; it also compelled him to distinguish legal from other kinds of right—a distinction he did not always in practice observe.

By their nature, rights, legal or other, are subject to ownership, which 'in its most comprehensive significance denotes the relationship between a person and any right that is vested in him' (G. Williams, *Salmond on Jurisprudence*, London: Sweet & Maxwell, 11th edn., 1957, p. 300). In its widest connotation, therefore, the ownership of land 'is the right to the entirety of the lawful uses of a corporeal thing' (ibid., p. 302). Full ownership of this sort may be limited by other kinds of rights held by encumbrancers; and in primitive systems of land tenure various encumbrances, such, for example, as a limited right to usufruct, can assume so much importance that the legal concept of full ownership may have little application. Legal authors have often treated ownership as if it were 'a bundle of rights' (G. W. Paton, *A Text-book of Jurisprudence*, p. 413); and in doing so have been followed by social anthropologists, who mostly regard all interests in land as a collection of rights (in their extended sense) distributed by the formal rules of land tenure. These rights may be vested in one or many different persons either severally or jointly.

4. The allocation of such rights will always be conditioned by a particular social system. M. Herskovits writes: 'Anthropological interest in the institution of property has been ... largely dictated by its close relationship to the social structure under which it exists' (*The Economic Life of Primitive Peoples*, New York: Knopf, 1940, p. 274). This close relation between property rights, especially those in land, and the wider social system is particularly conspicuous in the inheritance of rights, which in pre-literate communities is mainly governed by the principles of kinship prevalent in the society.

H. S. Morris

See also: PROPERTY

Language

A. *Language* may be defined as a distinctively human system of communication based on oral symbols. *A language*, characteristic of a speech community, definable in various ways, is a structured system of communication by means of oral symbols, hence by means of sound, not necessarily writing, used by a human group in order to describe, classify, and catalogue experiences, concepts, and objects.

B. While language has been the object of attention of several disciplines outside the social sciences, and to some degree of each of the social sciences, only anthropology among the social sciences has subjected language and linguistic phenomena to the closest scrutiny. Even in this field, however, *language*, like culture (q.v.), has been variously defined.

1. Foreshadowed by men like von Humboldt, Tylor, and Boas who were interested in language as a universal cultural phenomenon, E. Sapir was the first anthropologist to be drawn into the problem of defining language as a pan-human development, a behavioural aspect of the human being which serves as a point of differentiation from other animal forms (*Language*, New York: Harcourt, Brace, 1921; 'Language', in E. R. A. Seligman (ed.), *Encyclopedia of the Social Sciences*, New York: The Macmillan Co., 1933, vol. 9, pp. 155–68). Sapir thus conceives *language* to be '... a purely human and non-instinctive method of communicating ideas, emotions, and desires by means of a system of voluntarily produced symbols' (*Language*, p. 7). This definition has come to be, at least implicitly, normative for the social sciences, ruling out as it does the apparently instinctive methods of communication apparent among lower animals, notably the social insects; although it does not rule out some continuity of such modes of communication, as in the case, for example, of phatic communication (q.v.).

2. While Sapir's definition serves to delimit language as an abstract feature of human behaviour, it does not aim at the definition of *a language* as a delimiting characteristic of a speech community. For much empirical research in the social sciences, however, the concept of *speech community* is directly related to the delimitation of *individual languages*. Here again anthropology is deeply involved, especially in delimiting community or local culture, since one of the deepest impulses toward community solidarity derives from the element of mutual intelligibility obtainable through a common language (cf. E. Durkheim, *The Rules of Sociological Method*, trans. by S. A. Solovay & J. H. Mueller, Chicago: University of Chicago Press, 1938; French edn., Paris: Alcan, 1895). As has been demonstrated by H. A. Gleason, Jr., however, *a language* is defined with the greatest difficulty (*An Introduction to Descriptive Linguistics*, New York: Henry Holt, 1955). While the general meaning of *a language* as a structured system of oral communication used by a human group seems clear enough, the vaguely definable areas where dialect shades off from language or one system diverges from another create a series of problems which require individual solution.

Robert F. Spencer

See also: COMMUNICATION
LINGUISTICS
SEMANTICS
SYMBOL

Latent Function (See Function)

Law

Law

A. A *law* may be defined as a rule of human conduct that the bulk of the members of a given political community recognize as binding upon all its members—this recognition being induced by certain factors such as general obedience to the rule, the organization of sanctions for its enforcement and of procedures for its interpretation and application, and a general conviction of the rightness of the rule (or of the end it is apparently designed to promote), especially when this conviction is reinforced by the knowledge that others believe it right or at least act in accordance with it. *Law* without the article denotes a body or system of such rules.

B. The word *law* signifies a kind of rule; it implies regularity. Beyond this point one must distinguish between *descriptive laws* and *prescriptive laws*.

1. The former refer to some believed invariant relationship, such as that, if the temperature is kept constant, the volume of a gas varies in inverse proportion to the pressure (Boyle's law). Social sciences as well as natural sciences aim at descriptive laws, although they are usually less precise.

2. In the prescriptive sense, the primary and commonest use of the term *law* refers, as indicated in A, to a rule of human conduct thought of as in some sense binding. In the original usage it applies to the rules or customs by which members of a political community are governed. By extension one speaks of laws of God and the laws (or by-laws) of private organizations.

C. When it comes to more precise definition, agreement on all its components is elusive, and the relative weight to be attached to each is often a matter of dispute. To the element of regularity must be added factors of 'rightness', or correspondence to a standard of justice, and of 'authority'. The latter in turn implies ingredients both of command and of recognition or acceptance of the legitimacy of the source of the command.

Much confusion has arisen out of the fact that in Latin, French, German, Italian, and Spanish the word for *law* (jus, Recht, droit, diritto, and derecho) includes a larger area than does 'law'. These words also stand for what an English-speaking person would render as *just law*, *right law*, or *justice*. Nor is it simply that Europeans have used the same word in two senses. Even when applying the term to law as it is, they tend to add a larger admixture of *right-ness* than is commonly accepted in modern English usage. This concept leads easily to the notion that a particular law that is not in accord with justice and right reason is not true law, or not a law at all.

1. This way of viewing the matter—importing the concept of justice into the word *law* itself—has its root in the notion of Natural Law (q.v.). This idea finds classic expression in Cicero's contention that justice inheres in the very definition of law, and prevailed throughout the Roman and medieval periods. Although both Roman and canon lawyers for centuries made a distinction between Natural Law (jus naturale) and Human Law (such as the jus gentium and the jus civile), the latter was always thought of as dependent for its validity upon some correspondence with the former. St. Thomas Aquinas (c. 1226–74) defined human law (lex) as 'an ordinance of reason for the common good, made by him who has the care of the community, and promulgated' (*Summa Theologica*, pt. II, Q.xc, art. 4, London: Burns Oates & Washbourne, 1915, vol. 8, p. 8). He gave equal stress to four essential elements: rationality, relevance to the common good, promulgation to the public, and formulation by someone acting on behalf of the people, and declared 'a tyrannical law, not being according to reason, is not, absolutely speaking, a law ...' (*Aquinas Ethicus*, ed. J. Rickaby, London: Burns & Oates, 1892, vol. I, p. 272).

2. While the Stoic-Christian tradition stressed the *content* or *substance* of law, particularly the element of reason, feudalism looked to the *source* of law, specifically custom or practice. Law was created bit by bit over long periods of time by the practice of the people. As altered conditions increasingly required revision of the law, however, the idea and practice of legislation replaced the notion that all law was established by custom. Moreover, as a strong state developed to carry out such changes the idea grew that law was essentially what the organs of the state commanded.

3. What has come to be known as the positivist definition of law was first set forth clearly by Hobbes (1588–1679). 'Law in general', he declared, 'is not counsel, but command ...' (*Leviathan* (1651), ed. by M. Oakeshott, Oxford: Basil Blackwell, 1957, ch. XXVI, p. 172). Civil law, he continues, consists of the rules laid down as to what is right and what is wrong by the sovereign power in any commonwealth. Nearly two centuries later John Austin (1790–1859) elaborated the notion, stressing the elements of command supported by a sanction provided by a sovereign power.

Austin's emphasis on sanctions has been criticized by some for his neglect of the substance of the law, and by others who insist that it exaggerates the element of force. But it has dominated the field of jurisprudence, especially Anglo-American jurisprudence, to the extent that rival definitions have tended to do no more than modify it.

Stage by stage, however, these modifications have led to quite different concepts. Two lines of evolution are to be noted.

(a) In common-law countries, where judge-made law is of primary importance, the tendency has been to find the essence of law in judicial decisions. Courts tend to replace the 'sovereign' as the organ that gives legal validity to rules of conduct. Thus J. Salmond defined law as 'the rules recognized and acted on by Courts of Justice' (*Jurisprudence*, London: Sweet & Maxwell, 8th edn., 1930, p. 39). Subsequent 'realists' eliminated even the notion of rules. Professor (later Judge) J. Frank, in what he advanced as a 'rough definition', declared that 'For any particular lay person, the law, with respect to any particular set of facts, is a decision of a court with respect to those facts so far as that decision affects that particular person' (*Law and the Modern Mind*, New York: Brentano's, 1930, p. 46).

(b) Meanwhile, continental European students of jurisprudence (especially the Neo-Kantian or Vienna School) took a different line. Emphasizing the element of rules and of system (as is natural in countries whose law is codified and where court decisions are not considered as making or changing the law), they sought to 'purify' Austin's definition by eliminating the factors of obedience and enforcement. Law, in their view, consists in a system of rules or norms all interrelated by common derivation from a single fundamental norm. The latter, the 'Grundnorm' or 'initial hypothesis', would be something like 'All rules laid down for the governance of a given society by "X", or by persons with authority delegated by "X" and in accordance with procedures determined by him, shall be laws, and as such, obligatory upon the members of the society'. 'X' might be a group or assemblage of people or numerous people acting in accordance with a defined and perhaps quite complicated procedure (as in the case of the Constitution of the United States). The rules are part of a 'coercive order'; the system as a whole must be 'efficacious'. The requirement of efficacy is the only point at which this 'pure theory

of law', as set forth by its foremost expositor, H. Kelsen, deals with the actual facts of human behaviour (see his *General Theory of Law and State*, Cambridge, Mass.: Harvard University Press, 1945).

4. At no time has either type of positivist theory described above prevailed to the exclusion of those that insist on definitions including reference to other than purely formal elements. Catholic theory, for instance, has continued to insist that law that contains no element of reason or justice is not true law. Many non-Catholics as well, especially in recent times, have felt uncomfortable about an ethically neutral concept of law. Others, e.g. the Dutch jurist H. Krabbe (1857–1936), insist that the most essential element in *law* is correspondence to the sense of right of the community (*The Modern Idea of the State*, trans. by G. H. Sabine & W. J. Shepard, New York: Appleton-Century, 1930).

5. Sociologically oriented students of jurisprudence, while agreeing with Austin in stressing general obedience, often minimize the element of command and sanction. When they seek careful definition, however, they generally distinguish law from other social rules by reference to something like the sense of right. Thus L. T. Duguit (1859–1928) argued that law consists of the rules recognized by the community as supporting the principles of social solidarity. In America essentially the same idea was advocated by J. C. Carter (1827–1905).

D. While most of the theorists discussed above have been trying to discover what they would call the 'essence' of law, others deny this 'essentialist' presupposition. They assert that definition is an arbitrary matter. At the same time some of them claim that the formalistic definitions do less than justice to general usage in that they do not include phenomena like primitive law and international law (q.v.) which are not the product of societies formally organized to provide effective sanctions.

Perhaps the most effective answer to the latter objection has been advanced by the Scandinavian school of jurisprudence. Members of this school have combined hard-headed realism with a continuation and refinement of the line of thought represented by Carter, Duguit, and Krabbe. They hold that law is best defined as a set of rules backed by force and concerning the use of force, and binding upon the community. Then this binding quality is a psychological phenomenon arising partly from fear of compulsion and partly from various other conditioning

Leadership

factors. Typical statements of this view are to be found in K. Olivecrona's *Law as Fact* (London: Oxford University Press, 1939) and A. Ross's *Towards a Realistic Jurisprudence* (trans. by A. I. Fausboll, Copenhagen: Munksgaard, 1946).

J. Roland Pennock

See also: NATURAL LAW
SOCIOLOGY OF LAW

Leadership

A. *Leadership* denotes the occupancy of a status (q.v.) and the active performance of a role that mobilizes more or less organized collective and voluntary effort toward the attainment of shared goals and objectives. This is well summed in C. I. Barnard's rather general formulation that leadership 'refers to the quality of the behavior of individuals whereby they guide people or their activities in organized effort' (*Organization and Management*, Cambridge, Mass.: Harvard University Press, 1948, p. 83). Leadership shades, on one side, into other informal types of influence lacking central importance for collective effort. On the other side, leadership shades into domination and formal authority. Any concrete leadership situation will, of course, involve elements of informal influence, emotional dominance, and authority.

B. In recent usage the idea that leadership might be reducible to some specific competence or to a list of personal attributes has been almost completely abandoned. The quality of leadership inheres not in an individual but in a role that is played within some specified social system. A summary of studies attempting to define the personal traits of leadership concludes that leadership is 'a relation that exists between persons in a social situation, and that persons who are leaders in one situation may not necessarily be leaders in other situations' (R. M. Stogdill, 'Personal Factors Associated with Leadership: A Survey of the Literature', *The Journal of Psychology*, vol. XXV, 1948, p. 65). The concept of leadership so defined entails four elements, on which writers place stress in varying degrees; namely (a) role performance, (b) whose influence is (c) central with regard to (d) collective action.

1. Leadership is always effective action, not mere prestige, attainment, or competence. Thus H. D. Lasswell and A. Kaplan state that leadership 'has reference to both formal and effective power. ... Where the latter [is] present but little effective power is actually exercised, we speak of formalistic authority and not leadership' (*Power*

and Society, New Haven: Yale University Press, 1950, p. 152).

2. Leadership, moreover, involves social interaction (q.v.). The manifestation of leadership behaviour can be observed only in relation to other persons who act in response to the leader and who are collectively referred to as the *following*. But in so far as leadership usually arouses opposition as well, this following is not coextensive with some organized group and therefore leadership is not always integrative. A. W. Gouldner (*Studies in Leadership*, New York: Harper & Brothers, 1950, p. 17) emphasizes this point in considering the 'leader as any individual whose behavior stimulates patterning of the behavior in some group' who constitute his following but not necessarily the group as previously constituted.

3. The third element in usage is the requirement that the leader occupy a position of 'centrality' in the sense that he is the focal point for the activity of his group. The leader frequently initiates action for the group without waiting for the suggestions of his followers. An example is W. F. Whyte's finding that 'a follower may originate action for the leader in a pair event [which takes place between two people] but he does not originate action for the leader and other followers at the same time—that is, he does not initiate action in a set event [for two or more others] which includes the leader' (*Street Corner Society*, Chicago: University of Chicago Press, 1943, p. 262).

4. Finally, the central influence of leadership must be related to collective action. This last requirement is exemplified in Lasswell and Kaplan's proposition that 'the rank and file identifies with the leader and adopts his perspectives' (*Power and Society*, p. 156).

C. It is important to differentiate clearly between leadership and other forms of influence. Efforts to define the concept of leadership in terms of group syntality (referring to factors derived from measured group performance) or personal influence (designating 'opinion leadership') reduce leadership to influence, as illustrated by R. B. Cattell's statement that 'every group member is ... in some degree a leader' ('New Concepts for Measuring Leadership in Terms of Group Syntality', *Human Relations*, vol. IV, 1951, p. 182).

Efforts have also been made to distinguish between the leader and a central person on whom primarily emotional relationships centre. If the dominant individual's position 'rests upon nothing more than his capacity to appeal to the members of the group through stimulating their emotions and offering suggestions to their instincts, he is to be classed as an agitator or as a demagogue (in the derogatory sense of this term), acting upon a mob in which individuals virtually cease to be independent agents' (R. Schmidt, 'Leadership', in E. R. A. Seligman (ed.), *Encyclopedia of the Social Sciences*, New York: The Macmillan Co., 1933, vol. IX, p. 282).

Kurt Lang

See also: AUTHORITY
INFLUENCE

Learning

A. Following E. R. Hilgard, *learning* can be said to denote 'the process by which an activity originates or is changed through reacting to an encountered situation, provided that the characteristics of the change in activity cannot be explained on the basis of native response tendencies, maturation, or temporary states of the organism (e.g. fatigue, drugs, etc.)' (*Theories of Learning*, New York: Appleton-Century-Crofts, 2nd edn., 1956, p. 3).

B. G. A. Kimble (*Hilgard and Marquis' Conditioning and Learning*, revised by G. A. Kimble, New York: Appleton-Century-Crofts, 2nd edn., 1961, pp. 2–4) describes this kind of definition as a factual definition which treats *learning* as an intervening variable between such things as practice on the one hand and changes in behaviour on the other. Hilgard (*Theories of Learning*, p. 6) indicates that this kind of definition will find agreement among different kinds of theorists, but then goes on to point out that there are in psychology two major families of learning theories, stimulus-response and cognitive; and that some theorists do not belong in either family. Thus he names Tolman, the Gestalt psychologists, and Lewin as belonging to the cognitive family; Thorndike, Guthrie, Skinner, and Hull as belonging to the stimulus-response groups; and functionalism, psychodynamics, and the probabilistic theories of the model-builders as not classifiable in either (ibid., pp. 7–8). With respect to some issues such as series of muscular responses as opposed to central brain processes; habits vs. cognitive structures; and trial and error vs. insight, the lines are clear between the schools. With respect to other issues like association vs. reinforcement, intervening variables of a purely mathematically functional nature vs. hypothetical constructs which point to palpable processes

and structures, and one kind of learning vs. several, the families do not divide so easily.

Nevertheless, issues like these, both those that differentiate the families of theory and those which do not, according to the Kimble revision (*Hilgard and Marquis' Conditioning and Learning*, pp. 8–10) result in conflicting theoretical definitions. Among those he cites, for example, are the following: 'Learning is a reorganization of the cognitive field' (D. Krech & R. S. Crutchfield, *Theory and Problems of Social Psychology*, New York: McGraw-Hill, 1948, p. 112n). 'Learning is the process of the formation of relatively permanent neural circuits through the simultaneous activity of the elements of the circuits-to-be; such activity is of the nature of change in cell structures through growth in such a manner as to facilitate the arousal of the entire circuit when a component element is aroused or activated' (B. R. Bugelski, *The Psychology of Learning*, New York: Holt, 1956, p. 120).

C. The different theoretical definitions of learning, together with the shared factual definition, have carried over into social psychology, particularly among those trained in psychology departments rather than sociology departments. Even sociologically trained social psychologists must have some theoretical conception of learning, but most of these have depended upon psychologists who fall outside the families described above. Thus Parsons, for example, relies heavily on a modification of Freudian theory (T. Parsons & F. Bales, *Family, Socialization and Interaction Process*, Glencoe, Ill.: The Free Press, 1955), while many other American social psychologists rely on the social behaviourism of G. H. Mead. What characterizes this sociological social psychology in its conception of learning, however, is the stress on symbolic social interaction as constituting the main context for learning. The psychological mechanisms of learning, whatever they may be, are not considered as important as the fact that human learning is a social process. Therefore, frequently in social psychology, there is a rather careless use of such precise psychological concepts as conditioning.

William L. Kolb

See also: CONDITIONING
REINFORCEMENT

Left and Right (Current meanings):

A. *Current meanings* **1.** In their most general sense, *left* and *right* are each used to characterize

Left and Right

three main tendencies of socio-political thought and action. Thus the *left* possesses (a) belief in a greater rather than a lesser degree of educability in the human race; (b) a greater faith in the power of institutions to influence or determine human conduct; (c) the recognition of many social rights and social needs, either as essential to the preservation of individual rights and needs, or as superior to those of the individual, whenever conflict occurs, whereas the *right* is characterized by (a) acceptance of the value of established authorities in controlling irrational and only limitedly educable human beings; (b) acceptance of evolved institutions only; (c) emphasis on individual rather than social needs and rights, except where individual needs appear to be more fully satisfied within those of traditionally valued and over-riding authorities, like Church and State.

2. Further light on the content of these tendencies may be afforded by reference to the following notions, necessarily imprecise, which in different countries and at different times, have entered into them.

Characteristic of the *left* are (a) desire for change (more change, most change, rapid change, more or most rapid change); (b) acceptance of or belief in the inevitability of violence, as compared with evolution or with parliamentary action, as a method of change; (c) objection to Church participation in political action and decision, and in particular in control of education; (d) belief in State responsibility for some part or the whole of individual welfare; (e) belief in the necessity or desirability of State intervention in, or partial or total control of the processes of production, distribution and exchange; (f) belief in individual liberty, including freedom from State interference in economic activities; (g) belief in the equality of all in political rights and before the law; (h) belief in the right of ethnic and sometimes linguistic (but rarely cultural or religious) minorities to independent self-government; rejection in all other cases of national or nationalist sentiments in favour of international organization and co-operation, or of federal, functional-federal, or simply unitary supra-national authorities, as manifestations of a belief in the common heritage and destiny of all men; (i) belief in the need to protect advanced and especially socialist societies from corrupting contact with less advanced or less socialist societies; (j) rejection of respect for tradition, in favour of reason, as the basis of political judgement, and often in its turn, rejection of reason in favour of certain emo-

tions, like desire to help the weak, or trust in the people; (k) sometimes rejection of religion in favour of humanism; (l) emphasis on the element of 'consent' in the belief in 'government by consent'.

Characteristic of the *right* are (a) belief in a minimum of change, or in caution, or in stability, or in a return to past forms of government; (b) belief in religion, or in Church influence, as stabilizing and moralizing factors in political life, and especially in education; (c) belief in the limitation of State activities to the maintenance of law and order, internal and external, or only in such extensions of it as are suggested by current experience; (d) belief in State intervention in economic life largely or exclusively by means of tariffs, where overall national interest appears to justify such intervention; (e) belief in individual freedom; (f) distrust of free individuals; (g) scepticism regarding any projects for creating new independent States and sacrificing any of the rights of existing States, except in so far as some merging of national rights with those of similarly-minded States may be expected to preserve something of a particular national tradition against a powerful external threat; (h) acceptance of human inequalities as natural and capable of modification only within narrow limits; (i) belief in the guidance offered by a limited number of basic emotions, like patriotism and love of family and kin, and in religion and tradition as guides to political behaviour; (j) emphasis on the element of 'government' in the belief in 'government by consent'.

B. *Origin.* **1.** *Left* and *Right* were first used as political terms in France during the Revolution, but the precise circumstances of the origin of this usage are obscure. The commonest explanation is that at the first joint meeting of the States-General on May 5, 1789, or at its second, the *séance royale* of June 23, the Nobility took the place of honour, on the right hand of the King (who sat in the middle of one of the long sides of a flattened ellipse) and the Third Estate went to the King's left.

There are, however, other versions and all accounts must be accepted with reserve. What is certain is that within a very short time, the more revolutionary Deputies were sitting on the left of the National Assembly and the more conservative on the right. The modern (feminine) French forms *la droite* and *la gauche* (presumably for *la partie droite*) occur as early as 1791, and soon became the accepted forms.

382

At this stage, the meanings of the two terms were simpler and more precise than they have been at any time before or since. To be on the left was to be for the Revolution, that is, in its gradations, to be in favour of change, or more change, or most change; to be on the right was to desire no change, or some return, or a total return to the past.

2. The terms and the conflict which they expressed were revived after 1815. For the next century, at least, *left* and *right* in France continued to describe, in the first place, attitudes to the Revolution—not to a possible, future revolution, but to the Revolution of 1789. As late as 1930, A. Siegfried (*Tableau des Partis en France*, Paris: Grasset, 1930, p. 57) claimed that 'acceptance of the spirit of 1789 is the essential demarcation between right and left'. By then, however, two new elements had been added to the content of the terms. To be *left* was (from about 1852 onwards) also to be *anti-clerical*, while to be *right* was to proclaim, in effect, one's acceptance of *clericalism* by denying the existence of a clerical problem.

About the same time, or a little earlier, the rise of the Socialist movement brought to the semantic content of *left* and *right* a third element, namely, an attitude to the idea of State intervention in economic life. Here, again, there were gradations, maximum *leftness* implying a desire for total State control of industry (though often not of agriculture) and maximum *rightness* a lip-service to the idea of complete economic freedom, which, however, was not normally incompatible with a belief in protective tariffs. In the first half of the 20th century in France, therefore, the *left* was composed of those parties whose adherents believed, in varying degrees, in the spirit of 1789 as defined above, in anti-clericalism and in State intervention, while *rightness*—a more negative and often defensive attitude—implied a rejection of all three.

3. Since World War II, various factors have combined to blur the earlier distinction between the two terms in the country of their origin, and to make them less useful. The Communists' belief in dictatorship has led increasing numbers (though still a minority) to class them with the *right* (a proposal that the Communist group in the National Assembly should sit on the extreme right was defeated in 1951). The role of right-wing leaders like M. Marin, M. Laniel, M. Mutter, M. Jacqinot and others in the war-time resistance movement and therefore in the defence of the Republic blurred the old distinction at its roots, and the acceptance by right-wing leaders like M. Pinay of 'supra-nationalism' and 'Europeanism', that is, of some of the internationalism which had been a *left* attitude, continued the process. The emergence of a strong left Catholic movement, the M.R.P., and the increasing Radical dislike of any further extension of State economic activity helped to take away much of the meaning of the other principal criteria of *leftness*, so that it can now be and often is convincingly argued in France that the two terms have lost all useful meaning and function.

C. Although the influence of French revolutionary ideas and practices gave the terms currency in many continental countries, they never acquired either the emotional aura or the sporadically cohesive force that they had in France.

In English-speaking countries their acceptance was even slower, and most 19th-century uses refer to France. The word *left* was used in England from the 1920s onwards, sometimes to describe the Communists, sometimes covering Communists and Socialists and sometimes Liberals as well. But in all European countries outside France in recent years, both *left* and *right* are more commonly used to describe *internal party divisions*. Thus in Britain the *left* of the Conservative party meant (and probably still means) those Conservatives who were ready to accept something of concepts like economic planning, redistributive taxation, social services and colonial freedom, and the *right* those who opposed these things. For a long time, the *left* of the British Labour Party meant either those who believed in socialism or those who wanted a more rapid approach to socialism, and the *right* those who were either non-socialist or whose concept of socialism was more evolutionary.

The term *right* is most commonly (though not exclusively) used as a pejorative term, by those who believe themselves to be on the left.

In the U.S.A., on the other hand, it is *left* which most often has a pejorative sense. Both *right* and *left* are used, though less commonly than in Britain, to describe loosely-conceived wings of the Republican and Democratic parties. The *left*, in its wider connotation, means in the U.S.A. an unorganized but self-recognizing minority, composed mainly of intellectuals, whose *leftness* is characterized by ideas ranging from a desire for governmental assistance in the area of medical service to the belief that the Russian and even Chinese Communist States are

Legend

realities of the 20th century that cannot be met simply by blind opposition.

W. Pickles

See also: COMMUNISM
CONSERVATISM
LIBERALISM
RADICALISM
SOCIALISM

Legend

A. A minimal definition of *legend* is that it is a folktale with a simple narrative motif purporting to relate the experiences of real individuals or happenings in the past, the actors in which can be human, supernatural, or both.

B. The systematic and restricted use of *legend* came into being with the development of modern folklore (q.v.) studies. An early definition in this scholarly tradition was given by J. G. Frazer: 'By legends I understand traditions, whether oral or written, which relate the fortunes of real people in the past, or which describe events, not necessarily human, that are said to have occurred at real places' ('Introduction', *Apollodorus, The Library*, New York: G. P. Putnam's Sons, 1921, vol. I, pp. xxviii–xxix).

C. Contemporary usage is suggested by the following:

1. B. Malinowski ('Myth in Primitive Psychology', *Magic, Science and Religion*, Glencoe, Ill.: The Free Press, 1948, pp. 80–4) suggested that the groups within which myths and legends are found themselves distinguish among the forms of tale which they tell. He distinguished among three major groups of which myth (q.v.) and fairy tales are two. The third group more serious than fairy tales and less associated with religion and ceremony than myth, he divides into three sub-groups: historical accounts in which the teller is assumed to have been a direct witness; legends in which the teller was not present but which refer to ordinary experience; and hearsay tales relating to real but remote events, places, and people. Actually, *legend* might well be used for the entire category in which the three sub-groups fall.

2. S. Thompson (*The Folktale*, New York: Dryden Press, 1946, pp. 7–10) using several categories for classifying folk-tales but stressing the German *Märchen* (inadequately translated by the English fairy-tale), myth, and a third category designated by the German *Sage* identifies legend with the latter, particularly in the form of the *migratory* and *local* legend. These modifying adjectives indicate the fact that the tale '...

may recount a legend of something which happened in ancient times at a particular place—a legend which has attached itself to that locality, but which will probably also be told with equal conviction of many other places, even in remote parts of the world' (ibid., p. 8). The legends which cluster around the Old Testament flood myth, for example, find their parallels in other cultures, just as the myth itself does. Thompson also indicates that such terms as local tradition and *tradition populaire* find much in common with *Sage* and *legend*.

D. Legends have been treated to the same psychoanalytical, culture-history, and functional types of analysis as myth.

Arden R. King

See also: FOLKLORE
MYTH

Legislation

A. *Legislation* is the process of making rules considered binding upon the persons to whom they are applicable, or the rules resulting from that process. In the more narrow and common usage it denotes the function of making general law on behalf of the state, or the body of the law so made. In its strictest sense, particularly in the United States, it is the function of a legislative body in enacting statute law, or the resulting statute law itself.

All accepted definitions thus contain two common factors: (a) legislation is or results in *law*, considered binding where applicable; and (b) the process involved is that of *making* new law, not finding or applying law already existing. In definitions in political science and law, a third factor is universal: the acting agency (usually, though not always, a representative assembly) speaks for the state.

B. 1. The strictest sense (in A. above) follows closely the term's origin, in that 'lex'—as defined by H. F. Jolowicz, in his treatment on 'Roman Law' (*Encyclopaedia Britannica*, Chicago: Encyclopaedia Britannica, 1959, vol. 19, p. 448) 'is properly an enactment of one of the assemblies of the whole Roman people', as distinguished from *ius non scriptum*, or custom, on the one hand and imperial and magisterial edicts on the other. Judicial usage in the United States, where national and state constitutions give legal status to the principle of separation of powers (q.v.) often follows this strict course, and American court decisions have frequently distinguished *legislation* in this sense from constitutional enactment, from executive or administrative rule-making, or from judicial interpretation of law; as G. W. Paton says, 'In countries where there is a written constitution the precise distinction between legislative, judicial, and administrative powers may be of great practical importance, for the exercise of each power may be surrounded by safeguarding conditions' (*A Text-book of Jurisprudence*, Oxford: The Clarendon Press, 2nd edn., 1951, p. 264). In those American States employing the initiative (q.v.) and referendum (q.v.) to create statute law, *legislation* (usually in the form *direct legislation*) covers the process and products involved under the legal dictum that the people when so acting form a 'coordinate legislative body' with the legislature (*Straw* v. *Harris*, 54 Or. 424, 430, 1910). Legislation as action by a legislative body normally establishes general law, but the terms *special legislation* and *private legislation* refer to statutes affecting a specific, single situation.

2. Commonly today, *legislation* is used to refer to 'the act of giving or enacting laws' (*Black's Law Dictionary*, St. Paul: West Publishing Co., 4th edn., 1951, p. 1045), whether involving constituent assembly, legislative body, executive or administrative agency, or court. H. Walker thus contrasts '*legislation* by rule' with 'statute lawmaking' (*The Legislative Process*, New York: Ronald Press, 1948, p. 417), and Mr. Justice Cardozo contends that a judge interpreting law is 'legislating within the limits of his competence' (*The Nature of the Judicial Process*, New Haven: Yale University Press, 1921, p. 113). Used in this sense, legislation is distinguished from natural or divine law (e.g. by A. V. Dicey, *Introduction to the Study of the Constitution*, London: Macmillan, 3rd edn., 1889, pp. 58–60), and from the common law and equity, which under legal fiction are 'found' rather than 'made'; Maine thus speaks of legislation as an instrumentality 'ameliorating' the effects of 'found' law and defines it as 'the enactments of a legislature which, whether it take the form of an autocratic prince or of a parliamentary assembly, is the assumed organ of the entire society' (Sir Henry Maine, *Ancient Law*, London: John Murray, 2nd edn., 1863, p. 29). This usage has somewhat more significance in England and the Dominions than in the United States in view of larger English dependence on the executive ordinance power (as in the 'statutory rules and orders in council'); and even greater importance attaches to it among other western European countries. In the United States it is common to accept general rules with the force of law emanating from other than a legislative body as part of the total law but to identify them for precise use by such expressions as *constituent legislation, administrative legislation*, or *judicial legislation*; to meet constitutional requirements, general rules issued in pursuance of legislatively granted authority, are *delegated legislation* or *subordinate legislation* (J. Hart, *An Introduction to Administrative Law*, New York: Appleton-Century-Crofts, 1950, p. 113), or the term itself, in the words of Mr Justice Holmes, is 'softened by a quasi'.

3. In yet a broader, though less common, and certainly less accepted, usage, 'legislation embraces the totality of general rules of law binding upon the community ...' (J. W. Garner, in the *Encyclopedia Americana*, New York: Americana Corporation, 1956 edn., vol. XVII, p. 211). In this sense it may be brought to include even the rules of the common law and equity—the 'unwritten law'—in addition to the 'written law' and decrees issued in pursuance of it.

4. In sociology and related fields, *legislation* is sometimes applied to the function and products of rule-making by any agency, governmental or private, the rules of which are normally accepted by the persons to whom they apply. Pluralists like L. Duguit (in *Law in the Modern State*, New York: B. W. Huebsch, 1919) and H. J. Laski (as in *Foundations of Sovereignty*, New York: Harcourt, Brace, 1921) argue for the pragmatic force of legislation prescribed by and for voluntary associations. A somewhat related usage, in that acceptance is largely voluntary, is generally accepted today to cover the function of rule-making in international law; *International Legislation* is the title of M. O. Hudson's standard work (Washington: Carnegie Endowment for International Peace, 1931), and the term appears in the titles of numbers of articles by international lawyers and political scientists on the subject.

John M. Swarthout

See also: LAW
          LEGISLATIVE BODY

Legislative Body

A. The term denotes a group of persons, elected or appointed, which has the power of making or altering the laws.

B. Two main questions have occupied commentators: (a) the relation of this power to other powers; and (b) the composition and procedure of a body possessed of such formidable power.

1. The doctrine of separation of powers (q.v.)

Legitimacy

was that in a government which has liberty for its object, no one person or body of persons ought to be allowed to control the legislative, executive, and judicial power or any two of them. Madison ('The Particular Structure of the New Government and the Distribution of Power Among Its Different Parts', *The Federalist*, no. xlvii (1788), New York: Heritage Press, 1945, p. 323) pointed out that 'on the slightest view of the British constitution, we must perceive that the legislative, executive, and judiciary departments, are by no means totally separate and distinct from each other', and on the basis of this and other arguments defended the American constitution even though separation of powers under it was not absolute and complete. It simply is not the case that the functions assigned to each power are performed exclusively by that power. A distinction must be drawn between functions and bodies, so that legislative bodies, for example, can delegate legislative powers to executive bodies.

2. F. Frankfurter and J. M. Landis (*The Business of the Supreme Court*, New York: Macmillan, 1927, p. 312) wrote that 'The duty of ascertaining the need for corrective legislation is the essential function of legislature'. H. A. Simon, noting that 'law making' as distinct from 'law-finding' is a relatively recent development, goes further: 'Human rationality, then, gets its higher goals and integrations from the institutional setting in which it operates and by which it is moulded. In our democratic culture, legislation is the principal designer and arbiter of these institutions' (*Administrative Behavior*, New York: Macmillan, 1951, p. 101). Legislation itself, however, develops within an institutional framework: 'A legislature takes action in a prescribed fashion within a predetermined organization, which is not the same as individual legislators taking unrelated and independent action on their own' (R. Young, *The American Congress*, New York: Harper & Bros., 1958, p. 9).

K. B. Smellie

See also: Assembly
Bicameral
Bill
Cabinet Government
Checks and Balances
Constituency
Executive
Legislation
Party
Party Responsibility
Presidency
Referendum

Legislature (See **Legislative Body**)

Legitimacy

A. *Legitimacy* denotes (a) the condition of being a child presumably lawfully begotten or born in wedlock, having or involving full filial rights and obligations; or (b) a condition of positive valuation, validity, and acceptance enjoyed by individual rulers, political institutions and movements, and by systems of authority, by reason of the accordance of such rulers, institutions, movements, and systems of authority with some law, principle, or source of authorization.

B. 1. Virtually all societies distinguish between legitimacy and illegitimacy of birth and apply sanctions to the parents and in many instances to children. There is a large literature on the legal aspects of illegitimacy in various countries and in various periods of history, but no problem of definition.

2. In political science a second range of meanings predominates. Thus *legitimacy* may denote an important act of the title of a sovereign: the condition of being in accordance with law or principle requiring acceptance of the claims of sovereign power. Sometimes the legitimacy of government is narrowly construed as when it is held to be legitimate only if it is constitutional, when 'the succession to power is predetermined under a fundamental law which the acceding government does not make or break' (R. M. MacIver, *The Web of Government*, New York: The Macmillan Co., 1947, pp. 225–6). More narrowly still *legitimacy* may denote a condition (generally that of individual rulers) which is based on hereditary right. In this latter narrower sense the meaning of legitimacy is closely linked with the meaning in B.1 above.

One of the most important discussions of principles of legitimacy in their wider implications (both for systems of authority in general rather than governmental authority in particular, and for the extension of the nature of the principles of legitimacy themselves from constitutionality and inheritance to others such as speaking in the name of a greater power than oneself) may be found in M. Weber's discussion of the social and ideological bases of systems of authority. In a recent book on Weber, R. Bendix stresses Weber's view that 'beliefs in the legitimacy of a system of domination ... can contribute to the stability of an authority relationship. ... Like all others who enjoy advantages over their fellows, men in power want to see their position as "legitimate" and their advantages as "deserved", and to interpret the subordination of the many as the "just fate" of those on whom it falls' (*Max Weber: An Intellectual Portrait*, London: Heinemann, 1960, p. 297). In the light of differing principles of legitimacy Weber distinguished three pure types of legitimate authority:

(a) *Rational-legal authority* rests 'on a belief in the "legality" of patterns of normative rules and the right of those elevated to authority under such rules to issue commands' (M. Weber, *The Theory of Social and Economic Organization*, trans. by A. M. Henderson & T. Parsons, New York: Oxford University Press, 1947, p. 328). (b) *Traditional authority* rests 'on an established belief in the sanctity of immemorial traditions and the legitimacy of the status of those exercising authority under them ...' (ibid.). (c) *Charismatic authority* rests 'on devotion to the specific and exceptional sanctity, heroism or exemplary character of an individual person, and of the normative pattern or order revealed or ordained by him ...' (ibid.).

More recently, and in the tradition of Weber, *legitimacy* has been defined as 'the degree to which institutions are valued for themselves and considered right and proper' (S. M. Lipset, *Political Man*, New York: Doubleday, 1960, p. 46) and as involving 'the capacity of the system to engender and maintain the belief that the existing political institutions are the most appropriate ones for the society' (ibid., p. 76).

Robert Bierstedt

See also: AUTHORITY
CHARISMA
CONSTITUTIONALISM

Leisure Class (See **Conspicuous Consumption**)

Level of Achievement (See **Level of Aspiration**)

Level of Aspiration
A. *Level of aspiration* denotes the goals or standards that an individual sets himself.

B. 1. Psychiatrists use the term in a wide sense to describe the ambitions or hopes of an individual. Usage in psychology has been limited in recent years to the discussion of objective measures of the deviation between performance of given tasks and prediction of future performance. The emphasis has shifted from the *wish* to the question, 'What do you *think* you will do next time?' The following illustrates this:

'The subject is given some motor task; after a few trials, sufficient to familiarize him with the difficulties of the task, he is asked to estimate how well he will perform on a subsequent trial. The discrepancy between the estimated future score and the actual performance score of the preceding trial is taken as a measure of the subject's level of aspiration' (H. T. Himmelweit, 'Personality Tests as Research Tool', in C. A. Mace & P. E. Vernon (eds.), *Current Trends in British Psychology*, London: Methuen, 1953, p. 197).

Wide variations in the ability to predict accurately one's future performance have been noted.

2. K. Lewin and his school have carried out numerous studies to define the concept by isolating the factors involved. According to K. Lewin, T. Dembo, L. Festinger, and P. S. Sears, the valence or attractiveness of a given level of difficulty for an individual is equal to the sum of the need (or valence) to succeed times the subjective probability of success minus the need to avoid failure times the subjective probability of such failure. The valence of success of any given level of difficulty is in part a function of the reference scales the subject employs. Where he is told, or thinks, that the level of difficulty has been successfully reached by individuals or groups whom he considers less skilled than himself, the need to succeed increases and with it the individual's level of aspiration. Past experience determines his perception of the likelihood of success ('Level of Aspiration' in J. McV. Hunt (ed.), *Personality and the Behavior Disorders*, New York: Ronald Press, 1944, vol. 1, pp. 333–78).

3. In the last few years, attention has also focused on tests of level of aspiration as measures of personality adjustment. It has been found, for instance, that anxious and depressed individuals have unusually high levels of aspiration. Characteristic of this type of individual is the rigidity with which a given goal is adhered to almost irrespective of the actual level of achievement or the probability of success.

4. The concept is an important one both in clinical and social psychology. Methods of measuring levels of aspiration have been devised and studies are being carried out into the personality dynamics and social factors relating to differences in the size of the goals set.

H. Himmelweit

See also: GOAL

Level of Living (See **Standard of Living**)

Levirate

Levirate

A. The term (derived from the Latin *levir*, brother-in-law) denotes the custom of marrying the widow of the elder brother: it is used to distinguish inheritance of widows by brother-in-laws from inheritance by sons or by nephews. 'Filial inheritance ... can co-exist with the competing principles of the levirate and nepotic inheritance'(R.H. Lowie, *Social Organization*, London: Routledge & Kegan Paul, 1950, p. 103).

B. 1. In such a marriage the first husband's rights and duties in the marriage are not extinguished by his death. His right to affiliate the future offspring of the woman to his own line of descent, and his duties towards her and her children continue as if he still lived. One of his surviving brothers acts as proxy-husband on his behalf, but no new marriage is contracted with the widow, since her original marriage is not dissolved. For example, among the Nuer, 'In leviratic marriage the legal husband has performed these actions [the rites of marriage] himself, and the brother merely enters as pro-husband a family already in being. The widow is always referred to as the wife of the dead man and not as the pro-husband's wife ... Moreover, the children clearly regard themselves as members of a legal family to which the brother of their pater does not belong, although he is their foster-father, and may also be their genitor' (E. E. Evans-Pritchard, *Kinship and Marriage Among the Nuer*, London: Oxford University Press, 1951, p. 113).

2. The term *levirate* has been used to cover fraternal polyandry, on the grounds that the latter is also a case of marriage with the brother-in-law (G. P. Murdock, *Social Structure*, New York: The Macmillan Co., 1949, p. 29). This extension of meaning is not traditional, and whether the term *brother-in-law* applies at all in institutions of fraternal polyandry is dubious.

3. The practice of levirate differs from (a) *widow inheritance*: where the man who marries the wife of his deceased brother acquires full legal status as her husband, and as the legal father of her subsequent children; (b) *ghost marriage*: the custom of marrying a girl to the name of a dead brother or other relative. Several instances of this vicarious marriage for the sake of raising seed to the name of a dead man can be quoted from Africa.

M. Douglas

See also: MARRIAGE
POLYANDRY
SORORATE

Liberalism

A. *Liberalism*, as a term of political thought has had many denotations, but is never entirely separated from its derivation from the Latin word *liber*, free. It denotes the view or policies of those whose primary concern in politics and government is to gain or maintain some degree of freedom from control or direction by the state or by other agencies which may be deemed unfriendly to human liberty.

B. 1. Liberalism has been traditionally a movement to secure that the people as a whole are not subjected to arbitrary government but are protected in their private life by the rule of law (q.v.) and in public affairs can control the executive government through a freely elected legislative body. Liberals have traced the struggle for political freedom back through history to the opposition of the English Barons to the King, notably in the signing of the Great Charter in 1215, and in the realm of pure theory have tended to follow the philosopher Locke in his belief in a state and law of nature by which it was recognized that no one ought to harm another in his health, life, liberty, and possessions. The American colonists, revolting against the British government, claimed that men are endowed with certain inalienable rights, life, liberty, and the pursuit of happiness. In spite of the marked differences in the political institutions of Great Britain and the United States the belief in the need for a rule of law and a control upon the government is common to both and constant in the faith in which it is held.

The development of the British Commonwealth and Empire has caused the English conception of liberalism to spread through many parts of the world where the doctrine is consciously applied and adapted to local circumstances.

2. In the 19th century the influence of utilitarian thought gave a particular emphasis to the concept of the individual, as the individual alone could be regarded as the sole centre of experience and his desires and needs the only test of utility and happiness. Liberalism thus became a belief in the importance of the individual as opposed to a collective entity whether that was the state or the mass of the people. Bentham's conception of the 'greatest happiness of the greatest number' as developed by later thinkers gave scope for the growth of liberal collectivism, and 20th-century liberalism has been able to march to some considerable length with social democracy.

3. In economic thought liberalism implied resistance to the state control of economic life and more particularly to restriction of trade by import duties, to all forms of monopoly and to unnecessary and vexatious interference by government in the production and distribution of wealth. The extreme assertion of individual economic liberalism was seen about the middle of the 19th century when liberals would even oppose the regulation by law of labour in factories. Since then liberalism has accepted and promoted many measures of state control for the general benefit such as health and social insurance. It has favoured the growth of trade-unions as a means of protecting the interests of workers but has always been suspicious of any tendency by unions to monopolize power and coerce fellow workers.

4. British Liberalism during the latter half of the 19th century was embodied in the Liberal Party appealing to the generality of the people as against the aristocracy and privileged groups and liberalism has never lost this popular and democratic sentiment. It was also an anti-military and pacific force but never went to the length of pure pacifism or non-resistance.

In the 20th century liberalism in Britain as an organized force has declined with the decline of the Liberal Party but it may be said that its general principles have spread to the two other parties, Conservative and Labour. In the United States liberalism never gave rise to a single political party, but found its way as one of many strands of thought and influence in the two major parties.

5. In the face of the dangers posed by fascism and communism to its concept of freedom, many elements of liberal belief have been revised, e.g. in Britain military measures including compulsory service have been accepted where previously they had been repugnant. The use of force by states however was always seen purely as a means of defence and not of imperial expansion and was thought only to be justifiable if it should lead to an international organization for the preservation of peace such as the League of Nations *or* the present United Nations.

6. In religious thought liberalism has implied a belief in the right of men to worship in whatever manner and form their consciences dictated and this includes the right not to worship. In the 19th century most free-thinkers or agnostics in England and America would be on the liberal side but most liberals were Christians and believed that their political creed was conformable with Christianity and indeed a necessary product of Christianity. In Britain and the United States

therefore liberalism, for the most part, never had the anti-Christian or anti-religious connotation it came to have in some of the countries of Europe especially the Catholic countries.

7. The association between liberalism and extreme nationalism which was common in Western Europe was not evident in British or American liberalism although the national aspirations of countries such as Italy and Greece aroused much enthusiasm amongst English liberals. English liberals became the patrons of national aspirations elsewhere and favoured the development of full self-government throughout the British Commonwealth, in Ireland, India, and elsewhere. To British nationalism or imperialism however they were bitterly opposed, holding that the Empire was already too large and fearing and detesting national and imperial pride as a radical political vice, whether it took the form of aristocratic arrogance or popular frenzy.

R. B. McCallum

See also: CONSERVATISM
DEMOCRACY
FREEDOM
INDIVIDUALISM

Liberal Nationalism (See Nationalism)

Liberty (See Freedom)

Libido
A. *Libido* denotes the energy of the broadly sexual and creative instincts, in Freud's theory of personality.

B. 1. *Libido* is a term first used in psychological theory by Freud, founder of psychoanalysis, as the name for a store of energy within a person, expressed through drives or instincts (*Triebe*). His ideas on the nature of the instincts underwent several important changes. In Freud's earlier writings (*Three Contributions to the Theory of Sex* (1905), in *The Basic Writings of Sigmund Freud*, trans. and ed. by A. A. Brill, New York: Random House, 1938, pp. 553–629), he distinguished the sexual instincts of the libido from the ego instincts, whose purpose was self-preservation. This distinction allowed him to account for the energies used in neurotic illnesses to combat erotic impulses, by means such as anxiety or guilt. This division was dropped when it became apparent that the energy used in caring for oneself could be accounted for as of the same nature as energy used in loving

Life-Chances

others. In this formulation there is only one type of instinct: the libidinal or broadly sexual. The last form of Freud's theory of the instinct or drives (*An Outline of Psychoanalysis*, trans. by J. Strachey, New York: Norton, 1949, pp. 219–24), was a proposal that besides the libidinal instincts there was also a death instinct or destructive drive. This formulation had the purpose of accounting for the existence of aggression. This last theory of the death instinct has not been so generally accepted in psychoanalysis as has the theory of the sexual instincts.

2. 'Sexual instincts' in Freudian theory does not refer to genital activity only but rather to a developmental sequence in infancy and childhood of psycho-physical needs and gratifications, together with typical forms of perceiving the self and of relating to other people. The major stages are oral, anal, phallic, latency, and genital. The culmination of development, if all goes well, is psychological maturity, and the creation of and preservation of 'ever greater unities' (ibid., p. 20).

3. The libidinal and aggressive instincts are capable of great diversity in aim (satisfying activity) and object (the means of satisfaction). Thus, any activity, no matter how mature, how trivial, or how important, can be traced through clinical study of the individual back to the instincts which supply its energy. Sarcasm, for example, may be an altered form of the infant's desire to bite. The study of motivation is therefore the study of the outlets, modifications, and blockings of instinctual energy as these are shaped by the ego and its defences.

C. Except for psychoanalytically oriented writers *libido* as a term is not used in psychological theory. However, most psychological theories, even the most experimental, refer in some way to a store of energy in the organism and to inner directing forces of action. 'Even parsimonious behaviorists had to admit innate pushes of some sort, variously called "tissue changes", "prepotent reflexes", or "primary drives" ' (G. W. Allport, 'The Historical Background of Modern Social Psychology', in G. Lindzey (ed.), *The Handbook of Social Psychology*, Cambridge, Mass.: Addison-Wesley, 1954, p. 42).

Dorrian Apple Sweetser

See also: AGGRESSION
EGO
ID
SUPEREGO

390

Life-Chances (Lebenschancen)

A. This is a term used by M. Weber in his attempt to formulate a precise definition of class (see *From Max Weber: Essays in Sociology*, H. H. Gerth and C. W. Mills (eds.), New York: Oxford University Press, 1916, ch. VII; also M. Weber, *Wirtschaft und Gesellschaft*, Tübingen: Mohr, 4th edn., 1956, pt. I, ch. 4). In its general connotation *life-chances* comprises 'supply of goods, external living conditions and personal life-experiences'.

Weber did not intend to equate class with standard of living, however broadly conceived. Only if the typical life-chances of a group of people can be shown to be determined by their typical power in the commodity or labour markets do they constitute a class in Weber's sense. The class-structure of a society represents the social distribution of the power to dispose of goods or skills for the sake of income, and the determining factor is property. Under pure market conditions the distribution of property is responsible for the differentiation of class-situations—i.e. for creating the specific life-chances which characterize the different classes: ' "property" and "lack of property" are the basic categories of all class situations' (ibid., p. 182). The mechanism whereby typical 'life-chances' result from a particular manifestation of economic power *as rooted in the distribution of property* has a central place in Weber's origination of the term. But, notwithstanding its theoretical importance, *how* the result was attained was nowhere demonstrated.

B. That there are persistent and consistent differences in the typical life-chances of socio-economic groups in modern industrial societies is a well-established fact. Thus, by way of illustration, we can tell from a child's social origins as judged by the grading of his father's occupation, whether he is more or less likely to be born prematurely, to survive the first month or year of life, to have numerous brothers and sisters or to be the only child, to live in conditions of overcrowding, to score well in intelligence tests, to remain at school beyond the age of compulsory attendance, to go to a university and to maintain or improve on his father's occupational status, to succumb to various diseases and to enjoy a longer or shorter life. But it is another matter to relate these probabilities directly to the influence of the distribution of property on the market-situation of these different socio-economic groups in such a way as to enable us to identify *classes* as postulated by Weber. It is possible as a theoretical exercise to elucidate the role of property and power in the theory of distribution (cf. E. Preiser, 'Besitz und Macht in der Distributions Theorie', in *Festgabe für Alfred Weber*, Heidelberg: Lambert Schneider, 1949, pp. 331–58) and eventually to relate differences in life-chances to the outcome of the analysis. But the task becomes unmanageable if account has to be taken of forms of property other than land, of changes in modern industrial societies in the character of ownership and the distribution of wealth, of the growth of types of economic power which do not have their origins in ownership, and of state intervention to change the conditions or terms of economic competition. The life-chances of social groups in these societies are a complex function of all these phenomena and it does not help to revise Weber's dictum concerning the precise significance of property. It is still the case that ' "Economic power" and "lack of economic power" are the basic categories of all class-situations'; but the market-situation of social groups and their characteristic life-chances are no longer, if indeed they ever were, *simple functions of the distribution of property*. This thesis is well illustrated by C. W. Mills (*White Collar*, New York: Oxford University Press, 1951).

Jean Floud

See also: SOCIAL CLASS
STRATIFICATION

Limited Monarchy (See Monarchy)

Lineage

A. A *lineage* a group consisting of persons who trace descent (q.v.) in a single line of descent (patrilineal or matrilineal) from a common ancestor. It is not merely a line of descent. Irregularities apart, no one can belong to more than one lineage at a time, but everyone has kin in other lineages.

B. Accounts of unilineal descent groups today called lineages have been common since W. R. Smith's *Kinship and Marriage in Early Arabia* (Cambridge: University Press, 1885); the term as used in modern anthropology first appeared in Gifford's account of the Miwok ('Miwok Moities', *University of California Publications in American Archaeology and Ethnology*, vol. 12, no. 4, 1916, pp. 134–94. Since then the term has been applied by various writers to several different types of descent group. The usually accepted characteristics include: (a) A group of kin emphasize their unilineal linkage in a putative genealogy. (b) The group has corporateness, which is expressed in joint secular rights and ritual activities from which other kin are excluded. (c) The corporate group recognizes its identity and unity in contrast both to other like groups and also to other kin of its own members, and is recognized as a distinct unit by these other groups and kin. (d) The rights and obligations of the members of the group are distinguished from other rights and duties of kinship, although the two may overlap. (e) The group is assumed to be permanent, although its actual personnel may change through birth, marriage and death. (f) The group includes both living and dead members (the term *lineage group* usually being used for the living members only).

C. 1. Lineages are found in many types of society, and emerge as a response to many different factors. Among these are the existence of heritable wealth and status and a reasonable degree of stability of settlement and density of population (they are discussed by C. Daryll Forde, *The Anthropological Approach in Social Science*, in *The Advancement of Science*, vol. IV, no. 15, 1947). Lineages may or may not coincide with residential groups. Wealth and status are normally inherited with them.

2. Lineages vary in size with genealogical depth. Thus two or more small lineages may form part of a larger lineage, if their founders are believed to be descended from a common ancestor. At each step in a genealogy, it is formally possible to repeat this arrangement, forming what are known as 'segmentary lineage systems'. What is a segment of a lineage is also in its own right a smaller lineage of lower order.

Some of these societies with systems of this type lack centralized political authority. In these, people think of local groups as being formed around lineages, and the relations between the local groups can then be conceived in terms of the relations between the lineages, that is of the kin relationships between the apical ancestors who founded the lineages.

Lineage organization then reflects that of territorial groups.

The lineage relationships may be seen as unchanging, and by this means relations between the local groups, which may vary in size and locality over time, can none the less be seen as persistent and relatively stable. In this case lineages may compose a total structure or system, the lineage structure or the lineage system. This is an abstraction, a concept used by the members to express certain relations between

Lineal

local groups. There has been much recent discussion of the nature of segmentary lineage systems (see, for example, M. Fortes & E. E. Evans-Pritchard (eds.), *African Political Systems*, London: Oxford University Press, 1940; E. E. Evans-Pritchard, *The Nuer*, Oxford: Clarendon Press, 1947; M. Fortes, 'The Structure of Unilineal Descent Groups', *American Anthropologist*, vol. 55, 1953, pp. 17–41; M. G. Smith, 'On Segmentary Lineage systems', *Journal of the Royal Anthropological Institute*, vol. 86, pt. II, 1956, pp. 39–48; R. Firth, 'A note on descent groups in Polynesia', *Man*, vol. LVII, Art. 2, January, 1957; M. H. Fried, 'The Classification of Corporate Unilineal Descent Groups', *Journal of the Royal Anthropological Institute*, vol. 87, pt. I, 1957, pp. 1–29; J. Middleton & D. Tait (eds.), *Tribes without Rulers*, London: Routledge & Kegan Paul, 1958).

J. Middleton

See also: AGNATION
DESCENT
MATRILINEAL
SEGMENT
UNILINEAL

Lineal

A. *Lineal* is used to denote a direct line of descent (q.v.), succession (q.v.), or inheritance from parent to child as contrasted with that traced through collateral relatives—the descendants of siblings of paternal or maternal ancestors. 'Consanguinity, which is the relation of persons descended from the same ancestor, is ... of two kinds, lineal and collateral. Lineal consanguinity is the connection which subsists among persons of whom one is descended from the other. Collateral consanguinity is the connection which exists among persons who are descended from a common ancestor, but not from each other' (L. H. Morgan, *Systems of Consanguinity and Affinity of the Human Family*, Washington: The Smithsonian Institution, 1871, p. 17). This definition offered by L. H. Morgan has been accepted by modern anthropologists, both English and American (e.g. A. R. Radcliffe-Brown, 'Introduction', in A. R. Radcliffe-Brown & D. Forde (eds.), *African Systems of Kinship and Marriage*, London: Oxford University Press, 1950, p. 8; J. Gillin, *The Ways of Men*, New York: Appleton-Century, 1948, pp. 428–9).

B. The term *lineal* appears in several compound adjectives. Normally the line is traced through either males—patrilineal—or females—matri-

lineal—and in the past the anthropological use of the term has been based on the assumption that descent and inheritance were regularly unilineal (q.v.), except when they were *bilateral* (q.v.). Recently three new compounds have been introduced, which together with the introduction of double-unilineal (q.v.), suggests a current re-evaluation of the concepts pertaining to the social processes of descent.

1. G. P. Murdock has used the term *bilinear* in referring to the intricate social structure characteristic of the Australian aborigines: '... a bilinear kin group is composed of persons who are affiliated with one another by both patrilineal and matrilineal ties ... Excluded from one's own group will be all persons who are related only patrilineally or only matrilineally to Ego, as well as those who are not connected in either line' (*Social Structure*, New York: The Macmillan Co., 1949, p. 51).

2. T. Parsons noted that in the United States an individual traces descent through both parents and through both the paternal and maternal ancestors of these; and proposed the term *multi-lineal* to describe this kind of descent ('The Kinship System of the Contemporary United States', *American Anthropologist*, vol. 45, 1943, pp. 25–6).

3. E. E. Bacon employed the term *asymmetrically ambilineal* to denote a practice in which descent is normally traced through one line—either paternal or maternal—but in which a subordinate weighting is given to the other line of descent (*Obok: A Study of Social Structure in Eurasia*, New York: Wenner-Gren Foundation for Anthropological Research, Viking Fund Publications in Anthropology, no. 25, 1958, pp. 65, 74–75, 193).

Elizabeth E. Bacon

See also: DESCENT
KINSHIP AND KINSHIP SYSTEM
MATRILINEAL
UNILINEAL

Lineal Terminology (See **Kinship Terminology**)

Linguistics

A. *Linguistics* is that science of language which views language as an autonomous system subject to formal variation.

B. Historically *linguistics* developed out of the humanities as well as out of the social sciences, developing rapidly in the 19th century (O. Jespersen, *Language: Its Nature, Development, and*

Origin, New York: Henry Holt, 1922, pp. 19–99). Today many linguists are found in other than the social sciences, and a considerable number of linguists consider the discipline completely autonomous. Nevertheless, although members of other fields work in the discipline, common usage in American social science makes linguistics one of the sub-disciplines of anthropology.

C. Linguistics must be regarded separately from the interest in communication (q.v.) developed by several social sciences. Linguistics, as a scientific discipline, is primarily concerned with the 'linguistic codes' or languages themselves, i.e. the nature of the language, its sounds, structure, and syntax. Treating language as an objective phenomenon, it has no interest in language learning nor yet with specific semantic categories except as these relate to the internalized structure of the given language (cf. J. B. Carroll, *The Study of Language*, Cambridge, Mass.: Harvard University Press, 1953).

D. One of the two major fields of linguistics, a highly specialized discipline, is that of *historical* linguistics.

1. Once known as *philology*, it treats questions of connections between languages in the same families and sub-families, such as the divisions and relationships of the major Indo-European speech phylum or the affinities of the languages of native America.

2. Similarly, it is concerned with the distributions of various languages and language families and with the changes through time of the patterns of sound, structure, and meaning (see, e.g. L. Bloomfield, *Language*, New York: Henry Holt, 1933; C. F. Voegelin, 'Relative Chronology of North American Linguistic Types', *American Anthropologist*, vol. 47, 1945, pp. 232–4; C. F. Voegelin, 'Map of North American Indian Languages', *Publications of the American Ethnological Society*, no. 20, 1941).

3. Of more recent development in this field is the theory of glottochronology (q.v.), a method developed by M. Swadesh for inferring the time depth of linguistic change.

E. The second major field of linguistics is constituted by the analysis and description of various units in structural terms. This pursuit arose both as a pedagogical and a research method and owes its existence in part to the necessity for applying linguistic techniques which came with World War II.

1. Linguistic description has as its primary aim the analysis of a language in holistic terms, the implication being that a language, regardless of its historical antecedents, may be treated as a total patterned configuration. On this level, the analogy to the concept of the culture pattern (q.v.) of a total culture is clear. Description is thus designed to encompass the entire structure of a given language (cf. J. B. Carroll, *The Study of Language*; H. A. Gleason, Jr., *An Introduction to Descriptive Linguistics*, New York: Henry Holt, 1955; Z. S. Harris, *Methods in Structural Linguistics*, Chicago: University of Chicago Press, 1951; C. F. Hockett, *A Course in Modern Linguistics*, New York: The Macmillan Co., 1958; and E. H. Sturtevant, *An Introduction to Linguistic Science*, New Haven: Yale University Press, 1947). Pioneer efforts in the direction of structural approaches to language were made by E. Sapir (*Language*, New York: Harcourt, Brace, 1921).

2. Structural analysis and description conventionally require the treatment of a language under the headings of phonology, morphology, and syntax.

(a) *Phonology* treats the sound patterns of a given language both phonetically, i.e. a description of the array of acoustical properties in the language—phonetic (q.v.), and phonemically, i.e. relating to the idiosyncratic patterning of its sounds—the use of the phoneme (q.v.) (R. Jakobson & M. Halle, *Fundamentals of Language*, 's-Gravenhage: Mouton, 1956).

(b) *Morphology* treats the structural basis of utterance units, i.e. words, or forms compounded in numerous ways which create meaningful units (cf. E. A. Nida, *Morphology: The Descriptive Analysis of Words*, Ann Arbor: University of Michigan Press, 1949).

(c) *Syntax* in turn refers to the interrelations between morphological units on the level of the phrase or sentence.

3. Cultural anthropologists working in this sub-field are addressing themselves to such problems as the interrelations between language as a structure reflecting definitions of the universe, time, action, etc., and the cultural premises of the group speaking a given language. In the main, the study of the interaction of language and culture, usually designated by the term *metalinguistics*, while foreshadowed by Boas and Sapir, has been suggested by the late B. L. Whorf, whose concern with the kinds of categories developed in a given language led to a realization of the mutual influencing of language and socio-cultural behaviour (*Language*,

Lobby

Thought, and Reality, New York: Wiley & Massachusetts Institute of Technology, 1956). H. Hoijer, among others, has opposed Whorf's tendency to assign the primacy in the relationship to language ('The Relation of Language to Culture', in A. L. Kroeber (ed.), *Anthropology Today*, Chicago: University of Chicago Press, 1953, pp. 554–73; see also, H. Hoijer (ed.), *Language in Culture*, Chicago: University of Chicago Press, 1954, which has articles by Hoijer, C. F. Hockett, C. F. Voegelin, et al.).

Robert F. Spencer

See also: LANGUAGE

Lobby

A. As a noun the term *lobby* refers to those persons and organizations outside of the legislature who seek to influence legislation. It includes both those who are regularly employed to do such work, and those who on occasion attempt to influence the passage or defeat of legislation.

As a verb *lobby* means the efforts and acts of those attempting to influence legislation.

B. 1. There is reasonably general agreement among social scientists in the use of *lobby*, *lobbyist*, and *lobbying*. A lobby refers to a group or interest attempting to secure the enactment of certain legislation, or the defeat or modification of it. There may be a farm lobby, a labour lobby, an oil lobby and so on. A lobbyist is a person engaged in such activity either full-time or part-time, salaried or non-salaried. Party officials and members of the executive branch of the government who attempt to influence legislation have in a general way been regarded as lobbyists.

2. Lobbying includes a great diversity of activity such as personal contacts with legislators, presenting testimony and information to legislators and legislative committees, sending communications to legislators or getting other persons to do so, rendering campaign assistance to candidates presumably favourable to legislative interests of the lobby. The *social lobby* as a technique consists in providing entertainment, parties and the like for members of the legislature and their families with the purpose of cultivating personal friendship with those in the legislature.

Originally lobbying referred to direct contact between legislator and lobbyist. The expansion of suffrage and the great development of mass communications media led the lobbyist to use indirect pressure on the legislature. Lobbyists more and more attempt to mobilize public opinion 'back home'. The opinion from constituents presumably will be communicated to the lawmakers. Public relations programmes are employed by the large interest groups to win large segments to its point of view and to build up 'goodwill'.

3. The Federal Regulation of Lobbying Act (1946) in the United States requires any person or organization soliciting or receiving money to be used 'principally to aid', 'or the principal purpose' of which person or organization is to aid, the passage or defeat of legislation before Congress, to register with the Clerk of the United States House of Representatives. This application of the term is far more restricted than used by social scientists. Some highly important lobbying is done by certain members of the administrative branch and by officials of multi-purpose interest groups who give less than half of their time or of the organization's money to legislative objectives. These persons do not fall under the provisions of the law.

4. E. P. Herring ('Lobby', in E. R. A. Seligman (ed.), *Encyclopedia of the Social Sciences*, New York: The Macmillan Co., 1933, vol. 9, pp. 565–8) notes the unfavourable connotation of the term, because *lobby* has frequently been associated with the efforts of unscrupulous persons and organizations to secure legislation for selfish ends. The lobby has sometimes been called the 'invisible government' or 'third house'. At one time bribery and other unethical means were associated as general lobbying techniques. Few of these means are used today as both the lobbyist and law-makers are wary of them. Social scientists have not accepted the view that lobbying is inherently bad and have, indeed, recognized that this form of group representation may be useful provided the public interest is protected. As the term has generally been used it does not refer to pressure or influence on government in general but only on the legislative branch. Interest groups often work within and on the executive bureaucracy to win favourable decisions or sympathetic administration. This has been occasionally termed 'lobbying on administrators'. General usage of the word, however, has not extended to pressures on the administrative branch.

Hugh A. Bone

See also: INFLUENCE
PRESSURE GROUP

Local Government

A. The definition of *local government* presents difficulties. The simplest way to go about it is to follow W. E. & W. O. Hart (*Introduction to the Law of Local Government and Administration*, London: Butterworth, 6th edn., 1957), i.e. to say that it is the government carried out by local authorities. But these themselves are a matter of conjecture, in Britain at any rate; and in any case there is always the temptation to define them normatively as does G. L. Gomme ('Lectures on the Principles of Local Government', London, 1897). He drew a distinction between *local* and *quasi-local* authorities, the former being the type of authority he liked, the second the type he disliked.

E. Jenks (*An Outline of English Local Government* (1894), London: Methuen, 7th edn., 1930, p. 1) says that 'the various governing bodies and individuals' found in 'every civilized state of any importance' are 'either *central*, that is, exercised by persons whose jurisdiction extends over the whole area ruled by the State, or *local*, that is, exercised by persons whose authority is limited to some special portion of the State's territory' (ibid., p. 1). This definition sharply raises the two difficulties inherent in the concept of 'local government'. For:

(i) The definition would apply to the individual states, Länder, provinces etc., forming constituent parts of *Federations*. These are not commonly styled 'local authorities', nor is their system of administration styled 'local government'.

The reason would appear to lie in the notion that in true Federations the individual states are coeval or at least of legally co-equal status with the Federal authority, neither deriving their powers from it nor being, within their own sphere of functions, subordinate to it. A 'local authority', on the other hand, as commonly thought of, tends to derive its powers, or at least, to continue to hold these powers, at the discretion of the central government.

(ii) The definition would also apply to the field services of departments of the central government; e.g. a central government 'Region' (as it is styled in Britain) would be a 'local authority', and the government carried out in such regions would be styled 'local government'. This too, would strain our usual conception of 'local government'.

The reason for this is that 'local government' usually implies that the local inhabitants enjoy *some* discretion to decide on some at least of the matters with which they are entrusted.

Local Government may thus be defined as: 'The government of restricted territories of a state in so far as it is carried out, under the general jurisdiction of the government of the whole territory, by authorities representative of their localities and enjoying a measure of discretion in the execution of their powers and duties.'

This itself has difficulties; for the Government of Northern Ireland could be described in these terms, yet it is usually styled as an example of 'Home Rule', or 'Regional Devolution'. But this difficulty could be met by recognizing 'Home Rule' or 'Regional Devolution' as a *type* of local government, in which the territories controlled, the functions exercised, and the degree of autonomy enjoyed, are all, alike, greater than is usual in what is commonly styled 'local government'.

B. It is difficult to set a precise date for the introduction of this term. 'Local Act', 'Local Revenues', 'the local administration of justice' are common in the late 18th century. E. Chadwick used the term 'Local administration' in a general sense, meaning the whole *system* of such administration as early as 1836, and again in the Report on the Sanitary Conditions of the Labouring Classes, 1842 (cf. S. E. Finer, *The Life and Times of Sir Edwin Chadwick*, London: Methuen, 1952, pp. 91–2, 319–20). The term was in all likelihood popularized by Toulmin Smith (*Local Self-Government and Centralization*, London, 1851). Its first statutory mention in Great Britain is in the *Local Government Act* 1858. Thereafter the term becomes common.

S. E. Finer

See also: GOVERNMENT

Logical Positivism (See Positivism)

Long Ballot (See Ballot)

Love

A. The term *love* has been and is used to denote a wide range of strong, positive emotional attachments to any object, animate or inanimate. Elements of hate, aggression, or dislike which may render the relationship ambivalent are frequently conceptualized as part of the attachment.

B. Historically, controversy about the nature of love has revolved around two conceptions: the Greek *eros* and the Biblical *agape*. Eros designates an emotional striving to attach the self to an object because of a need, or a lack, in the self or the organism that is striving. *Agape* denotes an emotionally charged striving to serve the object that transcends the needs or

Loyalty

interests of the self or organism. If it is insisted that these two modes of attachment are mutually exclusive, the tendency is to deny the existence of one or the other or to place them in absolute opposition. Generally those who have espoused eros have denied the existence of agape, while those who have stressed agape have been forced to recognize the reality of eros and have stressed agape as an extreme of self-lessness to the point where even affection and liking have been emptied from agape love. Thus in the former case, P. Rieff reads Freud so that 'All loves are unmasked as self-satisfactions: from the love of the child for the parent-provider, to the love of spouses which reincarnates these parent-images, to the parent's "narcissistic" love for his own children. ... That love must serve the self or the self will shrink from it, that the self may chase love round an object back to itself again—this is Freud's brilliant and true insight ...' (*Freud: the Mind of the Moralist*, New York: Viking Press, 1959, p. 158). And in the latter case A. Nygren has defined *agape* so that it does not concern the emotions (*Agape and Eros*, trans. by P. F. Watson, London: S.P.C.K., 1953).

Such opposition between agape and eros is not found in all definitions, however. *Agape* may be defined as the exercise of care, responsibility, respect and knowledge for an object (E. Fromm, *Man for Himself*, New York: Rinehart, 1947, p. 98). Fromm calls such an emotional attachment 'productive love', but it will be seen below that this corresponds to some theologians' conception of agape. Such an exercise may express a need for relatedness and be possible only under conditions in which one is one's self loved, but it does not exist primarily in order that the self be loved or served in some other way. In such a conception agape may be viewed as eros transcending itself. According to E. La B. Cherbonnier (*Hardness of Heart*, Garden City, N.Y.: Doubleday, 1955) such a view is not incompatible with the Biblical tradition for in the Judaic-Christian conception agape is not possible for man except for God's love of man. 'Herein is love, not that we loved God, but that he first loved us. We love, because he first loved us' (John iv. 10, 19). Moreover, God's love for man is not fulfilled unless it is returned (*Hardness of Heart*, p. 52).

C. 1. Whatever the validity of these two approaches to agape and eros sociologists and social psychologists have tended to embrace the first approach of opposing eros and agape and

have denied then the reality of agape. Generally speaking they have abandoned the tragic—or perhaps better, pathetic—dimensions of Freud's analysis of the human self, but they have accepted his view that the self's primary concern in loving is with its own needs. Thus a typical recent definition of love reads as follows: '... we view love as a positive emotion which one person feels in relation to another and which is based upon the former's experience of having had his needs gratified by the latter, or the expectation, or at least a hope or fantasy, that the latter will gratify the needs of the former' (R. F. Winch, *The Modern Family*, New York: Henry Holt, 1952, p. 316). Using this or a similar definition they are willing to approve those forms of love where the expectations are realistic as for example *companionship love*; to accept those where the expectations are unrealistic but not too disruptive, as for example *nostalgia*, the love for a remembered place or time in which it is the feeling itself that gives satisfaction; and to disapprove those where the expectations are unrealistic and disruptive of established relations, as, for example, *romantic love* which has been defined as 'that complex of attitudes and sentiments which regards the marriage relation as one exclusively of response' (E. R. Mowrer, *Family Disorganization*, Chicago: University of Chicago Press, 1927, p. 160).

2. A recent attempt to set out the significance of 'the concepts of understanding and responsible love, or *agape*, in the daily practice of social work ...' may be found in T. S. Simey, *The Concept of Love in Child Care* (London: Oxford University Press, 1961, p. 38 et seq.).

William L. Kolb

See also: AGGRESSION (Social Psychology)
GRATIFICATION
LIBIDO
NEED

Loyalty

A. 1. In its more general use *loyalty* has had no precise meaning, but has been used to denote emotional ties to persons, institutions, political ideas and symbols, and also (a literary usage) to suggest a willing uncomplaining and devoted service of an idea, person, or institution.

2. It has long been used to express attachment either to a nation, or to a political concept for which a nation or a country is the intellectual and emotional rallying-point.

3. This usage (2) has carried over into the labelling of political movements. Thus, some of those who did not side with the American Colonists in their revolutionary struggles called themselves 'Loyalists' while at the present time a group of ultra-conservative political activists in Britain today are called the 'League of Empire Loyalists'—their programme is to stop any further break-up of the British Empire.

B. In the United States since the end of World War II, *loyalty* has been an important issue in politics, not least because a precise definition has been lacking. It is interesting that, although since the end of World War II *loyalty* has been a concept of considerable importance and concern for social scientists, it was not included in the pre-war *Encyclopedia of the Social Sciences* (E. R. A. Seligman (ed.), New York: The Macmillan Co., 1930–35). Similarly, it is significant that while under President Truman (see Executive Order 9835, March 21, 1947, 12 Fed. Reg. 1935) and President Eisenhower there was an elaborate *procedure* for determining the 'loyalty' of servants of the U.S. government, there was nowhere to be found a definition of 'loyalty'. It remained, even at that high level, a matter of opinion and judgment. In England, where similar provisions are in force for preventing subversive elements from gaining access (through civil service employment) to state secrets, the test is not of loyalty but of *reliability*.

C. From the social science literature of the post-war period it is clear that the main effort to clarify the concept has centred upon (a) the procedures designed to allow examination of the subject's activities, associations, etc.; (b) the entities to which the attachment styled 'loyalty' is most appropriately directed. It has not proved easy to avoid the two extremes of very *narrow* and very *wide* application. Thus governments have tended to stress a concept of loyalty which is concerned with *state security*; many other persons were equally concerned to attempt a practical definition in terms of political, social and scientific values—and even such wider ideas as truth and freedom. Thus the recent works of W. Gellhorn, A. Barth, & M. M. Grodzins, all attempt to show that loyalty can be and in some cases ought to be directed towards principles and practices which transcend the temporary demands of the government (W. Gellhorn, *Security, Loyalty, and Science*, New York: Cornell University Press, 1950; A. Barth, *The Loyalty of Free Men*, New York: Viking Press, 1951; M. M. Grodzins, *The Loyal and the Disloyal*, Chicago: University of Chicago Press, 1956).

R. H. Pear

See also: ALLEGIANCE

M

Machine

A. The term *machine* is used in a general sense to describe an organization, usually hierarchical in form, or a combination of persons which distributes its functions, pursues its purposes, and acts with a degree of precision and predictability so as to suggest the automatic functioning of a machine in the mechanical sense. Illustrations of this usage include governmental machine, social machine, legislative machine, and party machine.

B. The term is more commonly used in descriptions of American political parties, but is not confined to describing U.S. practice. Variations in meaning range broadly between *machine* as a neutral synonym for party organization and as a term of reproach for 'perverted' party organization.

1. Usage of *machine* as a synonym for party organization may be illustrated by T. Bryce. In chapters on 'The Machine', Bryce describes and discusses party organization—the array of committees and conventions at all levels of government concerned with party business (*The American Commonwealth*, New York: The Macmillan Co., 1914, vol. II, chs. LX–LXII). Bryce employed the terms 'Rings' and 'Bosses' to describe perverted party organizations.

Some contemporary authorities follow in the tradition of Bryce. Using *party* in a broad sense to include all who regard themselves as 'members', V. O. Key, Jr. describes the 'party machine or organization' as the 'inner core of the party', the 'more or less cohesive group held together by the ambition to gain power' (*Politics, Parties, and Pressure Groups*, New York: Crowell, 1952, p. 337). What the machine does with the power it gains by control of nominations and elections—whether its purposes are wholly selfish or mixed with motives of advancing the community's welfare—is secondary in the usage. The machine may coincide with the official party organization or it may be an unofficial core of professionals that runs party affairs. It may be corrupt or clean. Those who use the term in this neutral sense usually apply it to the better organized and more efficient party cores, composed of professional politi-

cians, at the state and local levels of government.

2. Usage of *machine* to describe perverted party organization may be illustrated by M. Ostrogorski. Primarily referring to the situation at the city and state levels in the more populous parts of the United States in the latter part of the 19th century, Ostrogorski described a party organization 'captured' by 'mercenary' politicians. The organization thereby became 'The Machine', 'that is to say an aggregation of individuals stretching out hierarchically from top to bottom, bound to one another by personal devotion, but mercenary, and bent solely on satisfying their appetites by exploiting the resources of a political party' (*Democracy and the Organization of Political Parties*, London: Macmillan, 1902, vol. II, p. 371). To him, 'an honest Machine is not in the course of nature ...' (ibid., 422).

The odious nature of a party machine as thus described dominates usage of the term in contemporary writing, but it is usually noted that *machine* may also be employed in a neutral sense.

Holbert N. Carroll

See also: PARTY
 POLITICAL BOSS

Magic

A. The term *magic* denotes a complex of belief and action on the basis and by means of which persons and groups may attempt to control their environment in such a way as to achieve their ends, the efficacy of such control being untested and in some cases untestable by the methods of empirical science. The core of the magical act is that it rests on empirically untested belief and that it is an effort at control. The first aspect distinguishes it from science, the second from religion.

B. 1. Medieval writers tended to class all the arts of learned scholars as magic in contrast to the common crafts of artisans. Magical knowledge was the secret possession of the learned (i.e. of magicians). William of Auvergne (13th century) distinguishes Magi who work 'natural magic' for beneficial ends and others who work evil magic with the aid of demons. The content of 'natural magic' was based on tradition not verified experiment but included much that has since been shown to be true in a scientific sense. Alchemy was magic in this sense (L. Thorndike, *A History of Magic and Experimental Science*, New York: Columbia University Press, 1923–1958.).

2. Developments in European philosophy since the 16th century have created a category distinction between (a) scientific knowledge—which is actually or potentially verifiable by research, and (b) dogmatic knowledge—the truth of which is asserted without regard to empirical verification. Dogmatic knowledge may be further distinguished as between (i) that which is intrinsically unverifiable—e.g. religious beliefs concerning the supernatural, and (ii) that which if put to an empirical test would prove to be false. This epistemological triad was popularized by J. G. Frazer (*The Golden Bough*, London: Macmillan 1890) in the form (a) science, (b.i) religion, (b.ii) magic. Magic was defined as a 'pretended art'', 'a bastard science'. The emphasis here is on falsity, rather than secrecy. This distinction between magic and religion is dubious, since magic may involve supernatural beings. Magic is the use of 'dogmatic knowledge' for control, religion, the worship or propitiation of beings known dogmatically. Further, it is not a matter so much of empirically testable dogmatic knowledge being false, if tested, as it is the simple fact that it has not been tested.

3. A category distinction of the medieval type, as between the *secret* knowledge of specialists and the *common* knowledge of ordinary men, is found in many societies. B. Malinowski (*Argonauts of the Western Pacific*, New York: Dutton, 1953, pp. 392 ff. and elsewhere) virtually equated this with the distinction between the supernatural and the natural. On the one hand, magico-religious behaviour is concerned with the control of what is dangerous, abnormal, and uncertain; on the other, rational technical behaviour operates in the field of common knowledge concerning natural facts. Magico-religious action is not false science but an effective mode of relieving anxiety. Malinowski regarded the utterance of verbal formulae (spells) as the central feature of such magical action, but general ethnography does not support this view. It is clear that in Malinowski's terminology technical and magical behaviours may be present in the same performance. All activities which are carried out in accordance with set formulae (e.g. cooking) are

likely to contain non-rational elements, though such elements are much more obvious in religious than in secular contexts.

H. Hubert and M. Mauss ('Esquisse d'une théorie générale de la magie', *L'Année Sociologique*, Paris: Alcan, 1902–3, vol. VII, pp. 1–146) also stress the secrecy as opposed to the falsity of magic. Magic to be effective must be performed in a special secret way by an actor who is in a special ritual condition. This links the power of magicians with the power of other ritual specialists, e.g. priests and kings.

4. Psychoanalytical writers following S. Freud (*Totem and Taboo*, London: Routledge & Kegan Paul, 1950, pp. 78–85) would agree with Malinowski that magic is effective because it is psychologically cathartic. Where Frazer regarded the symbolism of magic as indicating a 'false' association of ideas, the psychoanalysts consider such symbols to be meaningful because they correspond to 'repressed' feelings of the magician and his audience.

Current anthropological usage generally puts the emphasis upon the unconscious expressive symbolism of magic as distinct from either secrecy or falsity. This broadens the concept.

Frazer considered that magic ('bastard science') must always be superseded by true science. Hence magic was a 'primitive' not a 'civilized' characteristic. But if magic is expressively symbolic rather than false, magical elements may be present in all types of ritualized behaviour in all types of society.

E. R. Leach

See also: RELIGION
RITUAL

Majority

A. The term is most frequently used in connection with voting, both in the sense of *plurality*, or the number by which the highest vote exceeds the next highest, and in the *absolute* sense of more than half the number of potential or actual voters. In legislative bodies, *majority* is sometimes applied as a proper noun to the party or coalition of party leaders controlling the agenda, calendar and organization of the Chamber.

B. 1. Rules—legal or conventional—are required if a collective body of persons, such as an electorate, legislature, or board of directors is to arrive at a binding decision. In the absence of specific constitutional or legislative definition, Anglo-American courts have generally held in disputed cases that the majority shall be computed upon the basis of the total number of valid votes in the electoral unit or deliberative body cast by those actually voting. Unless the recognized source of authority (statute, by-laws, or formal rules of procedure) explicitly requires an absolute or extraordinary majority, the candidate or formal question that receives the highest number of votes will be declared elected or adopted. An *extraordinary* majority is a mandatory requirement that more than an absolute majority, e.g. two-thirds or three-fourths, of those eligible or actually voting, shall be necessary to a favourable decision, the effect being to give a defined minority a legal veto over the preferences of the majority. It should be noted that there is an important ambiguity in the referment of the term *majority* whenever the electoral unit is not prescribed or agreed upon in advance of the vote (see *Apportionment*; *Plebiscite*).

2. An important distinction is that between the *numerical* majority and the *concurrent* majority—turning upon the extent to which action on the part of, or on behalf of, a numerical majority anticipates 'the sense of the whole' among the multiplicity of affected and involved interests (q.v.) in the political community. Here one is concerned less with the principles for determining a valid vote than with guiding principles of political decision. The notion of a *concurrent* majority connotes the balance of consensual agreement among the influential minority groupings to whom decision-makers feel themselves formally or informally accountable, and whost tacit or explicit concurrence is a de facto condition of the acceptability (viability) of the numerical majority's decision. The concurrent majority, conceived as a hypothetical distribution of influential opinion emerging as a product of controversial discussion over time (see Public Opinion), is not to be confused with consensus (q.v.), which denotes the predominant sentiment among the members of a group or community who adhere sincerely and unquestioningly to certain norms of belief and conduct held to be above controversy.

3. Political philosophers disagree on the appropriate meaning of majority rule as a moral *criterion for categorizing political systems*. The 'absolute majoritarian' position asserts that majority rule exists in any political system where a decision taken with the support of more than 50 per cent of the members, voters or representatives is presumed to be a right and proper rule of public policy and legal coercion, on the formal ground that any other criterion

by definition implies minority rule. The 'limited, or constitutional-majoritarian' position restricts application of majority rule to those political systems which exclude certain basic individual rights from abridgment or deprivation by government acting in the name of the majority, and which prescribe certain preconditions (e.g. 'free elections', freedom of speech, press, political association and opposition) to the process of determining the formal majority before its decision acquires legitimacy.

Such differences of opinion make explicit the normative implications inherent in the usages of the term as discussed above. They relate to the issue of whether or not the formal criterion of an absolute majority carries with it the presumption of its ethical rightness or moral superiority. The point here is whether one prefers (values) a political system of majority rule more highly than a system of minority rule. If so, one is logically (formally) required to presume that the majority is more likely to be right than the minority, even though as a matter of fact the presumption may be erroneous. It involves no necessary contradiction, however, also to assume that the majority is not fixed or unchanging, and hence, that individuals and minorities shall be protected by government in their rights to associate, communicate, and attempt to transform themselves within the limits of the system into proponents of a freely-recreated majority.

Avery Leiserson

See also: Civil Liberties
           Consensus
           Voting

Majority Rule (See **Majority**)

Maladjustment (See **Adjustment**)

Man

A. *Man* is generically any hominid anthropoid, specifically a sapient one, possessing culture (q.v.).

B. As a technical biological term, *man* describes a type of animal set off from other types with a remarkable degree of hesitation and uncertainty.

1. Doubtless the vast majority of specialists tend at least to equate the term with Homo sapiens in the binomial taxonomy of biology, but while this is a reasonably clear synonym for the contemporary scene, students of primate history often prefer to use *man* for all members of the genus Homo, or even, somewhat more equivocally, of other hominid genera. Thus 'Neanderthal man', 'Rhodesian man', 'Heidelberg man', or the apologetic 'South African man-apes', or the 'Java ape-men', are commonplace expressions in anthropological literature (e.g. C. S. Coon, *The Story of Man*, New York: Knopf, 1954).

2. No great precision has been attained in these matters by attempts to describe the animal, for the detailed differentia are complex and debated. They are usually matters of degree. The size and complexity of the brain have usually been accorded heavy emphasis in the differentiation of man from the non-human primates, and even here the complexity is generally considered more important than mere size. The very great difficulty of interpreting the complexity of the brain from fragmentary and fossilized crania, and the even greater difficulty of relating this to other implicit attributes, have limited the utility of a purely anatomical approach to human speciation, although the epigrammatic definition of man as a 'featherless biped' has both cogency and wit, and erect posture is still widely accepted as a definitional criterion of great importance. Many taxonomically important physiological features, such as the interfertility of members of a species, the extended helplessness of the human infant, or the aperiodic sexuality of man, remain, of course, only indirectly relevant to interpreting the fossil record. A particularly comprehensive statement of the physical characteristics of man is given by E. A. Hooton: 'Man differs physically from the anthropoid apes and the lower primates in the great absolute and relative size of his brain; his supporting, non-prehensile foot with its massive, non-opposable great toe; the reduced size and lessened protrusion of his jaws; the development of a positive chin eminence and the absence of projecting, interlocking canine teeth; the possession of a lumbar curve and a basin shaped, tilted pelvis modified for the functions of balancing and supporting the body in the erect posture; greatly hypertrophied and elongated lower limbs adapted for biped gait; shortened and refined upper limbs with broad hands provided with long and perfectly opposable thumbs and short fingers; a prominent nose with well developed tip and wings; complete absence of tactile hairs or feelers together with a marked sparsity of secondary body hair except on the head, in the pubic and axillary regions and on the face of adult males; and the presence of full, everted membranous lips'

('Man', in E. R. A. Seligman (ed.), *The Encyclopedia of the Social Sciences*, New York: The Macmillan Co., 1933, vol. 10, p. 71).

C. Inevitably anthropologists, who, as students of man, are under some obligation to define the object of their study, have been forced to seek definitions emphasizing the behavioural and material consequences and correlates of a specifically human body; this involves an effort to define man in terms of the culture he creates and which creates him. In many respects human heredity seems to offer a wide range of plastic possibilities capable of shaping a life adapted to varying natural environments, and perhaps permitting within the limitations of those environments ways of life that are either the result of choice or of some internal psychological determination (T. Dobzhansky, 'The Concept of Heredity as It Applies to Man', *Columbia University Forum*, vol. 1, 1957, pp. 24–7). Hence the detailed elements in these definitions—the possession of language and of fire, the use of tools, the institution of the family and the incest taboo, the command of extended realms of empirical knowledge, the presence of myth, ritual, and religion—are by general agreement subordinated to the general definition that man is *a* and probably *the* culture-bearing animal. Neither in general nor in its specifics does this definition resolve the taxonomic difficulties. The cultural history of man in the Pleistocene involves at least as much complexity and obscurity as does the biological, and the implied correlation between physical and cultural features remains ambiguous and vague. Self-domestication as a uniquely human attribute pointedly poses this ambiguity on an important plane, raising the question of whether man is cause or result, creature or creator of his cultural possessions, a question rendered all the thornier by the almost universal concern with the human unconscious brought about by psychoanalytic psychology. The question of the determinism or freedom of the human condition is perhaps rather more the concern of a meta-anthropology than of the empirical sciences of man.

D. A cultural definition, however, does make possible the explication of some of the implicit attributes mentioned earlier.

1. The search for cultural universals (q.v.) or for the functional prerequisities of specifically human society cannot but be directly relevant and contributory to the definitional problem.

401

Mana

2. And while *soul* no longer has for the social scientist the defining property that it once had for humanists and theologians, and *mind* has tended to be relegated to a similar unresearchable status, modern psychologists continue to wrestle, if obscurely, with the problems of a specifically human nature (q.v.) and psychology. Recent research has tended to focus attention afresh on the symbolic character of cultural phenomena and on the correlated self-aware character of human consciousness; it has also offered new definitional possibilities emphasizing systematics—patterns, structures, and configurations—as a contrast to the flexibility and imprecision of non-cultural organic nature.

Munro S. Edmonson

See also: CULTURE
HUMAN NATURE
MIND
PERSONALITY SYSTEM
SOCIETY

Mana

A. This is an Oceanic term—a generalized 'power' concept associated with notions of effectiveness achieved by more than ordinary human physical means.

B. 1. Locally the term *mana* was widely known in many Oceanic languages before it attracted anthropological attention as a technical term. The first dictionary reference to *mana* in Polynesia seems to have been by L. Andrews, who translated it as 'power, might, supernatural power, divine power' (*A Vocabulary of Words in the Hawaiian Language*, Lahainaluna: Press of the High School, 1836). The critical definition was provided by R. H. Codrington. As equivalents for *mana*, he used 'spiritual power', 'magical power', 'supernatural power or influence'. But in what became a classical text he described *mana* as 'A power or influence, not physical, and in a way supernatural; but it shews itself in physical force, or in any kind of power or excellence which a man possesses. ... All Melanesian religion consists, in fact, in getting this *mana* for one's self or getting it used for one's benefit'. He also emphasized that this power was transmissible and was widely diffused, being 'present in the atmosphere of life' (R. H. Codrington, *The Melanesians: Studies in their Anthropology and Folk-Lore*, Oxford: Clarendon Press, 1891, pp. 118–9).

2. On the basis of this description R. R. Marett, H. Hubert, and M. Mauss and many others attempted to generalize the concept into that of a basic element in magic and religion. *Mana* was regarded as 'the element which magic and religion have in common ... the unity consisting in wonder-working power and the difference in the social or anti-social use to which it was put by the rival systems' (R. R. Marett, in J. Hastings (ed.), *Encyclopaedia of Religion and Ethics*, Edinburgh: T. & T. Clark, 1915, vol. VIII, p. 379). Analogies with *mana* were found in a range of terms in other areas—*orenda, wakan, manitou*, among American Indians, *arungquiltha* among the Aranda of Australia, etc. Mana was conceived as non-personal in its nature, anonymous and diffused, a 'vague and impersonal fluid', hence a notion characteristic of a pre-animistic phase of religion. It thus provided a minimum definition of the magicoreligious. Mana was regarded as being the positive aspect of the occult, and complementary to taboo, which was the negative aspect. It was identified with a wide range of ideas—divine force (Handy); totemic principle (Durkheim); truth (Hocart). It has been compared with holiness (Snaith); luck (Hogbin, Herskovits); and even more figuratively the ether, electricity, and radio-activity (Driberg).

3. Difficulties in using *mana* as a term representing a basic conception in the origin of religion and magic were pointed out by B. Malinowski. Such conceptions 'are simply an example of an early generalization of a crude metaphysical concept ... extremely important for our knowledge of primitive mentality but, as far as our present data go, opening only a problem as to the relation between the early concepts of "force", "the supernatural" and "the virtue of magic".' With the information available the relation between the concepts of physical force and supernatural efficiency in mana or between mana and religious or magical cult and belief was not at all clear (*Magic, Science and Religion*, Glencoe, Ill.: The Free Press, 1948, p. 58).

4. More empirical evidence from the Western Pacific by Hogbin (1936) and R. Firth (1940) brought out the concrete aspect of the *mana* concept, its continual reference to material results. Mana represented achievement, success at a level of efficacy more than normal; this was obtained or promoted by control of spiritual powers. Socially mana tended to be associated with persons of influence.

5. A philosopher's view of the concept of *mana* has been given by D. Emmet. 'It is a word the fortunes of whose interpretation bear witness to a felt need for a power concept which, like the notion of blessing, brings out the importance both of considerations of status in the social structure and of the question of whether some people should be thought of as having an exceptional inner strength which makes them effective. ... Our own term "power" has a multiple range of meaning, so why should we expect the word *mana* to have a single precise meaning? It might bear interpretations as causal efficacy, creative energy, impressiveness (such as prestige or charismatic leadership) and ritual power. We need more evidence from field studies on this' (*Function, Purpose and Powers*, London: Macmillan, 1958, p. 229).

R. W. Firth

See also: ANIMISM
MAGIC
RELIGION

Management

A. *Management* denotes the process of formulating and executing business or industrial policy through the functional activities of planning, organization, direction, co-ordination and control. It also denotes the hierarchy of persons who assume, or are entrusted with, such tasks. In the economic theory of distribution, management is often treated as synonymous with *entrepreneurship* and *enterprise*, i.e. the contribution of the entrepreneur to the productive process; some writers, such as Schumpeter, sharply distinguish between management and entrepreneurship.

B. Business literature contains definitions and usages applying the term to a process, to a group of functions, to a type of human ability and skill, to a class of personnel in business, and to other categories.

1. O. Sheldon's definition of management is frequently cited; he explained it as the function in industry concerned in the execution of policy, within the limits set up by administration, and the employment of the organization for the particular objects before it ('Management', in E. R. A. Seligman (ed.), *Encyclopedia of the Social Sciences*, New York: The Macmillan Co., vol. X, 1933, pp. 76–80). Sheldon distinguished *administration*, as largely concerned with determination of policy, from *organization*, as basically the process of combining work of individuals with facilities. Other definitions, however, have not distinguished administration and have included determination of policy within the bounds of management.

Similarly, F. W. Taylor conceived management as discovering how tasks should be performed and seeing that they were performed in the most economical way. This would be considered today, at most, as only a small part of the management process or functions.

2. Numerous definitions or descriptions of management have named its component functions, with some of the following occurring in most lists: forecasting and planning, organization, directing or commanding, co-ordination, control, and staffing. Increasingly, definitions have appeared which stress the concern of management with people rather than with physical objects. For example, M. Koontz and C. O'Donnell describe management as '... the function of getting things done through others' (*Principles of Management*, New York: McGraw-Hill, 1955, p. 3). Sometimes this approach embodies quite explicit judgements as in the view that 'Reduced to its essentials *good management means getting effective results with people*' (P. Pigors & C. A. Myers, *Personnel Administration*, New York: McGraw-Hill, 4th edn., 1961, p. 11).

3. When management denotes those who manage it is often necessary to distinguish the levels of the enterprise at which they operate and explore the patterns of relationships between the different levels (e.g. the use of terms such as *top management* or *middle management*). But this kind of distinction is not universally adopted. Thus M. Dalton notes in his book (*Men Who Manage*, New York: Wiley, 1959) that the term *management* is employed loosely 'for all members of management—executives and foremen, staff specialists and supervisors' (ibid., p. 1, fn.).

C. It could be argued that the term has, in many branches of the literature, been implicitly reserved for the conduct of enterprises for profit and not applied to analogous processes in government, i.e. public administration. Such a distinction is hardly tenable analytically— especially in societies where some or all of industrial activity is under various forms of governmental sponsorship or control. Indeed, of recent years, fruitful attempts have been made by economists and sociologists to employ the term in comparative study of socio-economic change and development. Thus C. Kerr, J. T. Dunlop, F. H. Harbison, and C. A. Myers observe that 'Management is more than the mere sum of its members. It is an integrated hierarchy of people with differentiated functions whose activities must be co-ordinated to achieve specific objectives'. They then go on to

Mandate

distinguish patrimonial, political and professional forms of management and to classify managerial approaches as (a) dictatorial, (b) paternalistic, (c) constitutional, and (d) consultative/participative (C. Kerr et al., *Industrialism and Industrial Man*, Cambridge, Mass.: Harvard University Press, 1960, pp. 146–7).

William H. Wesson

See also: ADMINISTRATION
ENTREPRENEUR
EXECUTIVE

Mandate

A. The term (the general implication of which is 'command') is used in the theory of democratic politics in a special sense—to describe the things which electors have told their elected representatives to do.

B. The word cannot be satisfactorily applied to political practice, and is in fact interpreted in differing and conflicting ways.

1. In the conditions of British politics, a government as a whole (rarely individual members of Parliament) is said to 'have a mandate'. Thus if a meeting of electors in a constituency, or even of the Conservative Party members of the constituency, passed a resolution calling upon their Conservative M.P. to vote for 'equal pay for women', we would not normally say that he had a mandate from his electors to do this, although in its natural sense this is just what the word apparently *should* mean. It is rather said of a Government, which has been returned to power through the operation of the electoral system, that it has, by virtue of its electoral success, a mandate *to do certain things*. Unfortunately, we can never be quite clear what these things are, or precisely what is meant by the term *mandate* in this sense. Active politicians sometimes find it helpful to their arguments to claim that they have themselves a mandate for a certain policy, or that their opponents are doing things without a mandate.

2. If a general election is fought on a single issue, in such a way that the whole election seems to turn on the question whether or not a particular policy should be adopted, the victorious party can meaningfully claim that it has a mandate to follow its known policy in that particular matter. Thus we say that the Liberal Party received a mandate in 1910 to restrict the power of the House of Lords; and that Baldwin in 1923 failed to get a mandate for a policy of tariffs, when he asked for it.

Familiarity with these cases in which mandates seemed clearly to be given by the electors has led many to seek to define all policies in terms of the mandate doctrine. It is sometimes argued that a party in power has a mandate to do all the things that it has said, in its election programme, that it will do, but no other things. It should be remembered, however, that the programme must always include many items which are unrelated to each other, and that most of those who vote for a party dislike some of its policies.

It is perhaps more sensible to say that a party has a mandate to do the things which were in its programme, than to say that it has no mandate to do other things; but even so, it is unwise to press this claim too far. The word is perhaps best used in a very general sense—a mandate to deal with events as they arise in a way which accords with what might have been expected in the light of the party's programme and record.

It is significant that the equivalent word *mandat* is used in French in quite another sense—to describe merely the fact of being elected.

C. There is also another political usage of the term *mandate*. After the 1914–18 war, the government of some territories (former German and Turkish possessions) was entrusted by the League of Nations to individual countries, which were to report annually to the League on their administration. Some such regimes still exist. A territory governed under such a system of trusteeship is said to be *mandated*.

P. A. Bromhead

See also: ELECTION

Manifest Function (See **Function**)

Manor (See **Feudalism**)

Marginal Analysis

A. *Marginal analysis* has several meanings in contemporary economics—some broader than others. It sometimes means casting an economic problem into mathematical or quasi-mathematical form and finding a maximum or a minimum. Sometimes it connotes any *incremental* analysis, as distinguished from one dealing with average or total magnitudes. A more general reference which encompasses the others, is to economic analysis which focuses on borders or limiting areas rather than on the entire range of phenomena being studied.

Marginal Analysis

B. 1. The *New Oxford English Dictionary* defines *marginal*, in economics, as 'on the "margin", or close to the limit, below or beyond which something ceases to be possible or desirable', citing A. Marshall (*Principles of Economics* (1890), London: Macmillan, 8th edn., 1922). The core characteristic of the marginal analysis, as this definition implies, is its focusing on certain areas or 'boundaries' that appear to be of special importance. The objective may be to discover conditions of equilibrium or disequilibrium or processes of change (see Statics and Dynamics), and the method may be mathematical, statistical or descriptive.

2. In economic theory the term is sometimes more narrowly equated with *incremental* quantitative analysis, as, for example, in focusing on the incremental or 'extra' (marginal) cost of producing one unit of a commodity rather than on the total or average cost of producing a stock thereof.

3. A still narrower meaning is the handling of economic matters as mathematical or quasi-mathematical problems of finding a *maximum* (sometimes a minimum), as in maximizing profit or utility (or minimizing costs). This involves the notion of objective or subjective mathematical functions, and focuses on their derivatives, the solutions being found by the differential calculus when the first derivatives are zero and hence the functions are at maxima (or minima) (see Mathematical Economics).

C. 1. The marginal method of analysis represented a great forward step in economics. Ricardo (1772–1823) (*Principles of Political Economy and Taxation*, London: John Murray, 1817), although much abused by later marginal theorists, was in fact the first economist to employ it systematically. This he did in his analysis of the rising (marginal) cost of foodstuffs with more extensive and intensive margins of cultivation of land, and his derivative theories of land rent and of secular changes in income distribution. Ricardo's general theory of value, however, was based on relative labour requirements without general reference to the marginal principle.

For this he and other classical economists were severely criticized by those who set afoot, about 1870, the so-called 'marginal revolution' in economic theory (see Utility and Value). Initially this consisted in turning from the cost to the demand side of the value equation, and explaining economic value by the *marginal* or incremental utility of *one* unit of a stock of a commodity. If a good were plentiful, this marginal value would be low; if scarce, it would be high (see Scarcity). It was unnecessary, therefore, it was argued, to evoke costs of production to explain value. This marginal demand principle was extended, between 1870 and 1890, to factors of production or resources in what came to be known as the marginal productivity theory of distribution.

2. A. Marshall, 1890, (ibid.) combined marginal demand analysis with generalized marginal cost analysis to construct a rounded marginal analysis of value and distribution. Broadly speaking, his is the prototype of the marginal analysis of these problems which has continued down to this day.

3. During the 20th century marginal analysis has been much further elaborated. The economy of the individual firm has been carefully scrutinized along marginal lines: on the one side leading to sharper analysis of cost behaviour under varying conditions, short-run and long, and on the other stimulating the rise of monopolistic or imperfect competition theory. The marginal analysis of welfare problems, which Marshall (ibid.) and others (e.g. L. Walras, *Eléments d'économie politique pure*, 1874) had begun in the late 19th century, has been carried much further (see A. C. Pigou, *The Economics of Welfare* (1920), London: Macmillan, 4th edn., 1932; and for a recent treatment T. Scitovsky, *Welfare and Competition: the Economics of a Fully Employed Economy*, London: Allen & Unwin, 1952).

These developments had the effect of casting more of economic theory into the form of finding maxima and minima. In some quarters economic behaviour and almost the whole of economic theory came to be identified with maximization along marginalist lines. For example, F. H. Knight ('Immutable Law in Economics: Its Reality and Limitations', *American Economic Review*, Proceedings, vol. XXXVI, no. 2, 1946, pp. 93–111) has written, 'The first and primary economic law ... is the (abstractly) fairly simple mathematical formula for maximizing a function of a number of variables (so related as to yield a maximum)' (ibid., p. 97).

D. Marginal analysis has always had its critics. The earlier of these, notably the Institutionalists, held the analysis was superficial, particularly in not dealing with causal-genetic factors in the economy. Recently there has raged the so-called 'marginalist controversy', with the

Marginal Efficiency of Capital

anti-marginalists claiming: (a) that consumers and business firms do not in fact behave in a maximizing manner; and (b) that the conditions of divisibility and continuity required for the strict application of marginal analysis typically do not exist in the real world. Recent developments, such as the theory of games and mathematical programming, have departed somewhat from the classical conditions of maximization analysis, but have maintained the rigour of mathematical treatment.

James S. Earley

See also: UTILITY
VALUE (Economics)

Marginal Cost (See Cost)

Marginal Efficiency of Capital

A. *Marginal efficiency of capital* denotes a schedule of the expected marginal rate of return over cost for different possible flows of investment over a given period of time and under a given set of conditions.

B. 1. The term was invented by J. M. Keynes and defined by him as follows: 'I define the marginal efficiency of capital as being equal to that rate of discount which would make the present value of the series of annuities given by the returns expected from the capital asset during its life just equal to its supply price. This gives us the marginal efficiency of particular types of capital assets ... for each type of capital we can build up a schedule, showing how much investment in it will have to increase within the period, in order that its marginal efficiency should fall to any given figure. We can then aggregate these schedules. ... We call this the investment-demand schedule, or alternatively, the schedule of the marginal efficiency of capital' (*The General Theory of Employment, Interest, and Money*, London: Macmillan, 1936, pp. 135–6).

2. Keynes's definition, only part of which is given, has been much criticized for ambiguity. (a) Putting it in more simple terms, the marginal efficiency of capital is the *expected* rate of return over cost on a capital instrument *about* to be created. Profits being earned on capital assets already built must not be confused with the marginal efficiency of capital. Indeed A. Lerner suggests that 'marginal efficiency of investment' would be a much less ambiguous term. (b) It is, in the aggregate sense, not a single rate, but a *schedule* reflecting the marginal

rates of return that would be expected on various sized flows of investment, within a given time interval, other things being equal. (c) The rate of return is expressed not in physical but in value terms, but opinions differ as to how far the business man takes account of inflation. (d) Since the emphasis is on expectation, the schedule is subject to all sorts of sudden shifts, due to shifts in 'confidence', as Keynes points out (*The General Theory of Employment, Interest, and Money*, p. 162).

3. One may distinguish between a long-run marginal efficiency of capital schedule which deals with the expected marginal yield of a significantly changing total capital stock over time, and the short-run schedule referring to the marginal rate of return of alternative possible investment flows over a short period of time.

There has been much discussion concerning whether it is legitimate to speak of the schedule as falling, or downward sloping either in its long-term or short-term form. Since the schedule is, in a dynamic society, largely a short-hand description of possible flows of *change*, innovation, and development, ordinary ceteris paribus logic can not be applied. Most economists, however, feel on balance, that for any given period the schedule tends to slope downward. But, since, in reality, it is constantly being shifted by new inventions and other dynamic forces, we must distinguish between the theoretical short period, in which the schedule is assumed, other things being equal, to slope downward, and an actual historical period in which almost anything can happen.

4. Perhaps the two most important errors often implicit in the use of the concept are (a) the assumption that the schedule generally depends unilaterally upon the level of consumption, and (b) confusion of the idea of a schedule with the idea of a single fixed rate. Both these errors can be found in the writing of Keynes himself (notably in ch. 8, p. 105, and ch. 14, pp. 182, 184 of the *General Theory*).

David McCord Wright

See also: CAPITAL
INVESTMENT

Marginal Man

A. *Marginal man* may be defined in broadest terms as any individual who is simultaneously a member (by ascription, self-reference, or achievement) of two or more groups whose social definitions and cultural norms are distinct from each other. The extent or range of this marginality depends on (a) how much difference exists between the cultural norms of the different groups; (b) the prevalent social definition of this actual difference; (c) the differential treatment which results from (b); (d) the differential participation in two or more spheres as affected by (c); (e) the differential awareness of (c) and (d); (f) the definition of factors (a) to (d) by the *marginal man* in terms of unique personality elements, and the responses arising therefrom, his aspirations and goal-directed activities.

. **1.** This term originated with the work of R. E. Park (*Race and Culture*, Glencoe, Ill.: The Free Press, 1950) who first used it in 1928 to refer to the cultural hybrid sharing the life and traditions of two distinct peoples as the result of migration ('Human Migration and the Marginal Man', *American Journal of Sociology*, vol. XXXIII, 1927–8, p. 892). Later Park, while still focusing on cultural duality, referred to the person of mixed racial inheritance as the 'typical' marginal ('Personality and Cultural Conflict', *Publication of the American Sociological Society*, vol. XXV, 1931, pp. 95–110). Park emphasized the disorganizing effects of marginality. 'The marginal man ... is one whom fate has condemned to live in two societies and in two, not merely different but antagonistic cultures' (Introduction to E. V. Stonequist, *The Marginal Man*, New York: Charles Scribner's Sons, 1937, p. xv).

2. Stonequist elaborated Park's seminal but undeveloped concept by devoting a whole work to the exposition and illustration of four marginal types: the migrant foreigner, the second generation, the Jew emancipated from the ghetto, and the mixed blood (*The Marginal Man*, p. 3). He mentions other types of marginality—the parvenu, the déclassé, the migrant from country to city, and women in a changed role, but fails to give them further attention (ibid., pp. 5–6). He tends to treat maladjustment as characteristic of marginality (cf. esp. ibid., p. 201) in spite of theoretical recognition that it may not occur (ibid., p. 4).

3. In following years sociologists wrote of the second generation immigrants as the most distinctively marginal group, measured by their relatively high index of crime, family disorganization, and emotional disturbances. Much of the impetus here came from W. I. Thomas and F. Znaniecki (*The Polish Peasant in Europe and America*, Boston: Badger, 1918). Marginality has in the past been associated with ethnic and racial situations where subordination is undisguised. It has, however, no intrinsic connection

with these situations. Thus D. I. Golovensky takes exception to the evaluative connotations of marginality and the restriction of the term to ethnic groups when societal pluralism involves other types ('The Marginal Man Concept, An Analysis and Critique', *Social Forces*, vol. 30, 1951–2, pp. 333–9) and A. W. Green shows that internal analysis reveals variables neglected by Stonequist—amount of culture conflict, striving to leave the ethnic group, and situational factors of rejection ('A Re-examination of the Marginal Man Concept', *Social Forces*, vol. 26, 1947–8, pp. 167–71).

4. More recently marginality has been extended to multiple group and status membership of all kinds as in E. C. Hughes ('Social Change and Status Protest', *Phylon*, vol. 10, 1949, pp. 59–65) and D. Riesman who further distinguishes 'secret' marginality where there are 'people who subjectively fail to feel the identities expected of them' (*Individualism Reconsidered and Other Essays*, Glencoe, Ill.: The Free Press, 1954, p. 154).

R. A. Schermerhorn

Marginal Propensity to Consume (See **Propensity to Consume**)

Marginal Propensity to Save (See **Propensity to Consume**)

Marginal Rate of Substitution (See **Substitution**)

Marginal Revenue (See **Revenue**)

Market

A. A *market* is typically an institution that brings all sellers and buyers into communication with one another for the purpose of exchanging economic goods and money for current or future delivery. The interaction of sellers and buyers determines the unit prices and the quantities transacted. Thus markets are an essential component of the price system (q.v.), and their effective functioning determines in considerable part the smooth functioning of the latter.

1. There may be any number of persons on either the selling or the buying side of a market. Similarly, there may be any number of products typically traded in a given market. For example, wheat and leaf-tobacco markets are each organized to affect the exchange of one product, whereas retail grocery markets may accomplish the exchange of thousands of products.

2. Markets also vary greatly in the degree to

Market

which they function continuously to accommodate the flow of output and have formal organization and established rules. The securities markets, where bonds and shares are exchanged, are both highly organized and continuous. Continuity in this case, however, involves primarily the exchange of *existing stocks* rather than of *output flows*. House-to-house solicitation, on the other hand, represents a type of market that is loose-knit and often intermittent.

3. Markets have a spatial dimension that in some cases sets them apart from other markets by virtue of transportation costs or other distance influences. There are thus more or less competitively insulated local markets for tonsorial or laundry service, regional and national markets for trucking service, international markets for sugar. With many products, such as steel, these spatial dimensions overlap. Distance influences are the more important, the more homogeneous is the product in the view of potential buyers. But it is noteworthy that the reference of the term *market* is by no means necessarily limited to a particular place. The overriding requirement is communication among sellers and buyers. With respect to time, markets may be episodic, intermittent, casual, seasonal, or continuous, but in advanced economies they tend to be continuous, although technological change may alter the type and amount of goods available from sellers, and changes in tastes the type and amount of goods wanted by buyers.

B. Economists have usually classified markets according to the type of good or service transacted. Perhaps the most widespread classification of this kind used in economic analysis is the distinction between the *factor market*, where land, labour, or capital goods are exchanged between producing organizations, on the one hand, and the somewhat clumsily labelled *product market*, on the other hand. In the latter type of market, final goods of the consumer variety are sold by producing organizations to households.

Many other less important classifications of discrete market types based upon the item exchanged or the location of trading partners are also used, such as *capital markets* for long term funds, *export* and *import markets*, and *regional markets*. The term *industrial market* is widely employed to identify markets for manufactured products at their point of origin.

C. From the demand side, in a business economy, a market takes shape to the degree that the prices of a number of close substitute products tend towards equality. This tendency is likely to be the case where products are close substitutes because the price quoted on a close substitute product of one seller will affect the quantity demanded from another seller. In this regard, the meaning of *market* and of one prominent conception of an *industry* (q.v.) are almost synonymous, for producing organizations turning out a number of close substitutes at nearly uniform prices are usually lumped together as a group of sellers comprising an industry. Prices need not attain complete equality, however, where productive factors or consumer goods are moderately differentiated, for in such markets sellers are endowed with the power to set deviant prices without a consequent substantial variation in quantity sold (see Monopolistic Competition).

D. An economy in which the bulk of the output is typically produced for exchange rather than for the absorption of the immediate producers is termed an *exchange*, or *market economy*. The market economy has been traditionally identified with private capitalism, or, alternatively, with *laissez-faire* (q.v.) capitalism. Particular markets in the capitalistic economy are connected into a system of price and production decisions through time on the basis of the interplay of sellers' and buyers' influences, with mutual interdependence among such sellers and buyers recognized in varying degree. However, socialistic planned and mixed capitalistic economies have also developed institutions formally approximating the arrangements of market capitalism, albeit with public agencies on one or both sides of the exchange.

When viewed in the aggregate, the differences between the predominantly private market economy and the socialist public ownership system become decisive. In the former, the multitude of particular markets are linked together through the pricing and distribution system of many individual decisions having the objective of maximizing gain for the individual or the organization with which he is affiliated. In the latter, the web of particular markets are coordinated under an overall plan encompassing price, quantity, and income distribution targets. Between the extremes of this spectrum in the contemporary real world lie many variations, including the mixed capitalistic economies with administered markets and national economic budgets, as well as quasi-socialistic arrangements in which private markets function in the context of far-reaching central government development plans.

Harold G. Vatter

See also: DEMAND
ECONOMIC COMPETITION
EXCHANGE
INDUSTRY
MONOPOLISTIC COMPETITION
PRICE SYSTEM
SUPPLY

Market Economy (See Exchange)

Marriage

A. *Marriage* denotes *mating arrangements* approved in society with special reference to the institutionalized relationships of husband and wife; also the *ceremonies* which establish such relationships. In ordinary usage *marriage* includes two distinct ideas: (a) that a man and a woman cohabit, generally with the intention of founding a family; (b) that some distinction can be drawn between marriage and other forms of sexual union, qualifiable as *pre-marital, extra-marital, adulterous*, etc. This distinction is sometimes held to be essential to the definition of marriage: 'A mere casual commerce, without the intention of co-habitation, and bringing up children, would not constitute marriage under any supposition' ('Marriage', in R. Burrows (ed.), *Words and Phrases Judicially Defined*, London: Butterworth, 1944, vol. 3, p. 331).

B. In the analysis of advanced modern societies usage in general follows the above—but mating arrangements in societies studied by social anthropologists display so much diversity that it is impossible to find a comprehensive definition that is not tautologous. For this reason current practice is to leave the word marriage undefined, and use it merely as a pointer-term, indicating a number of characteristics found in varying combinations in different societies. On this approach marriage may have all, or only some of the following functions: (a) of establishing the legal status of the children of the parties to the marriage; (b) of transferring rights to each of the parties: (i) domiciliary; (ii) in the sexuality of the other; (iii) in the labour and domestic services of the other; (iv) in the property of the other; (c) of establishing a joint fund of property (for the benefit of the children of the marriage); (d) of establishing an alliance or relation of affinity between the kinsmen of the parties; (e) of giving public recognition to the relationship.

C. Some of the problems of definition are more fully illustrated by the following considerations.

1. Some writers have attempted to follow ordinary usage, e.g. E. Westermarck who took *marriage* as being 'A more or less durable connection between male and female lasting beyond the act of propagation till after the birth of offspring'. The formula was intended to be broad enough to give a basis for comparison, and yet to be 'narrow enough to exclude those wholly loose connections which by usage are never honoured by the name of marriage' (*History of Human Marriage*, London: Macmillan, 1901, p. 19).

Broad though this may seem, it does not cover all the usage of the term. Although it is usual to find the institution of marriage concerned with the procreation and rearing of children, this is not always the case, nor is it always possible to distinguish between marriage and casual temporary unions.

2. In some cases, as in some Eskimo and scattered American Indian groups, the family unit itself is so vaguely defined that the status of husband, and of wife, is not distinguishable from other temporary forms of sexual union, and no recognizable difference between marriage and concubinage (q.v.) may exist. This is important for a definition of marriage, as a number of words, which derive their meaning from this distinction, would have no significance for such a society: e.g. divorce, nullity, validity of marriage, etc.

3. In other cases, the approved forms of mating may be unconnected with the establishment of the family or rearing of children. To some extent this was the case among the Nayar of Malabar, S. India, where the girl used to undergo a pre-pubertal 'marriage' rite, with a man from whom she was 'divorced' at the end of the ceremony. Then she was free to enter into sexual unions with any number of men from appropriate castes. Although these unions are generally called 'polyandrous', implying a type of marriage with plural husbands, there is only a sexual relationship, no living together, no recognition of paternity, no responsibility beyond that of making small gifts at annual festivals, and a small contribution to the expenses of pregnancy (see K. Gough, 'Changing Kinship Usages among the Nayars of Malabar', *Journal of the Royal Anthropological Institute*, vol. LXXXII, pt. I, 1952). As they recognize no conjugal family, no status of husband, wife or father, any definition of marriage which is based

Marriage and the Family

upon the founding of a family would seem to exclude the customary sexual unions of the Nayars. This clearly conflicts with the general formula of R. M. MacIver and C. H. Page (*Society*, London: Macmillan, 1950, p. 238): 'The family is a group defined by a sex relationship sufficiently precise and enduring to provide for the procreation and upbringing of children'.

4. A comprehensive definition would also have to allow for the fact that in some societies *more than one form* of sexual relationship may be considered as marriage. M. J. Herskovits discerned seven types of marriage among the Dahomeans (*Dahomey*, New York: J. J. Augustin, 1938, p. 300f.).

5. Careful distinction between the functions of marriage is required in certain specialized cases: (a) In some societies the physical separation of the husband and wife does not in itself end the legal relations arising from their marriage, and in which the physiological father is not necessarily expected to be the same person as the legal husband of the mother. Among the Nuer conjugal relations may be broken if a man's wife runs off and leaves him, but the jural bonds of his marriage are fixed because he cannot get a divorce (see 'A Note on Bride-wealth and the Stability of Marriage', by D. M. Schneider, *Man*, April, 1953, No. 75, pp. 55–7). (b) The institution of 'woman-to-woman' marriage has been noted: the legal roles of husband and wife are set up between two women, while the conjugal relations of husband and wife are established between one of the women and a man approved by the 'legal husband'. In Dahomey, for example, a wealthy woman 'may "marry" several girls and give them to men to breed children for her, so that her compound may become more and more populous' (M. J. Herskovits, *Dahomey*, New York: J. J. Augustin, 1938, vol. I, p. 320).

M. Douglas

See also: Concubinage
Family
Monogamy
Polyandry
Polygamy

Marriage and the Family

A. The phrase denotes a sub-field of social science whose content ranges from studies of marriage, family, and kinship patterns as institutional elements of culture and society the world over to applied studies concerned with preparation for marriage and family life in specific cultures.

B. Historically the study of marriage and the family was first developed by social anthropologists who provided descriptions and analyses of the origin and evolution of these institutions (e.g. E. A. Westermarck, *The History of Human Marriage*, New York: The Macmillan Co., 1921, 3 vols.). This mode of study developed into descriptive and comparative studies of marriage and kinship studies of various pre-literate societies (cf. R. H. Lowie, *Primitive Society*, New York: Boni & Liveright, 1925, chs. 2–8). The emphasis was mainly on the structural aspects of the family, and little attention was paid to family interaction.

In the early 1920s sociologists undertook to devote themselves systematically to the study of the family, particularly as it existed in American culture. They were initially concerned with family problems and disorganization (e.g. E. R. Groves & W. F. Ogburn, *American Marriage and Family Relationships*, New York: Henry Holt, 1928). Later they turned to institutional analysis and to the study of variations in family patterns according to socio-economic, urban-rural, and ethnic factors (see, for example, M. C. Elmer, *The Sociology of the Family*, Boston: Ginn, 1945; E. R. Mowrer, *The Family: Its Organization and Disorganization*, Chicago: University of Chicago Press, 1932; E. Franklin Frazier, *The Negro Family in the United States*, Chicago: University of Chicago Press, 1939). This approach continued to the present day and gradually expanded to include cross-cultural comparisons (N. W. Bell & E. F. Vogel, *A Modern Introduction to the Family*, Glencoe, Ill.: The Free Press, 1960). Following the lead of E. W. Burgess (see E. W. Burgess & H. J. Locke, *The Family: From Institution to Companionship*, New York: American Book Company, 2nd edn., 1953), who called attention to the family as an interaction of personalities, other sociologists developed an interest in the social psychological aspects of the family, analysing it in terms of the pattern of roles assumed by the members, and the interaction among them.

Beginning in the late 1920s a new type of interest in the factors that make for marital happiness or unhappiness began to evolve. Many so-called functional courses in marriage and the family have been established with the practical intent of preparing students for marriage. Simultaneously the profession of marriage counselling developed, utilizing the insights of sociology.

410

social psychology, psychiatry, and biology. It may be said, however, that both the courses and the counselling came into being in advance of the knowledge they required. They doubtless provided powerful motivation for the extensive research into the interpersonal aspects of marriage and family life of the last two decades (E. W. Burgess & L. S. Cottrell, Jr., *Predicting Success or Failure in Marriage*, New York: Prentice-Hall, 1939; L. M. Terman et al., *Psychological Factors in Marital Happiness*, New York: McGraw-Hill, 1938; E. W. Burgess & P.Wallin, *Engagement and Marriage*, Philadelphia: Lippincott, 1953).

C. The most interesting recent developments in the study of marriage and the family have to do with (a) the search for new criteria for marital success other than the criterion of adjustment; (b) the effort to study the nuclear family in terms of the stages of its development and change from marriage to dissolution through the death of one of the partners; (c) the renewal of the study of kinship in modern urban societies.

1. N. N. Foote and L. S. Cottrell, Jr., drew on an accumulative body of literature critical of the older criteria of marital success to formulate an approach which placed stress on growth, identity, and interpersonal competence as the central concepts for family research (*Identity and Interpersonal Competence: A New Direction in Family Research*, Chicago: University of Chicago Press, 1955). While older criteria probably still prevail, this book has opened up new possibilities in the determination of what constitutes successful marriage.

2. E. M. Duvall, in her *Family Development* (Philadelphia: Lippincott, 1957), has brought together much of the theoretical and empirical work done on the stages of the family life cycle. R. Hill, who has also been much concerned with this approach does not regard this method of study as a competing framework 'since it is really an attempt to transcend the boundaries of present approaches through incorporation of the compatible sections of several approaches into one unified scheme' ('Sociology of Marriage and Family Behaviour, 1945–1956', *Current Sociology*, vol. 7, 1958, p. 18).

3. The renewed interest in kinship systems has grown both out of the application of anthropological methods of research to modern cities and out of the realization that the nuclear family of the modern city may not as be isolated as it was once thought to be. Some of the most interesting work in this area has been done in England (see, for example, M. Young & P. Willmott, *Family and Kinship in East London*, London: Routledge & Kegan Paul, 1957).

Meyer F. Nimkoff

See also: FAMILY
MARRIAGE

Marriage Payments (See **Bride-Price**)

Marxism (See **Dialectical Materialism**)

Mass Culture

A. *Mass culture* denotes, broadly, the cultural correlate of mass society (q.v.), especially characteristic of modern urban and industrial civilization but found in varying extents also in societies on the way to industrialization. Description and interpretation of mass culture take many forms but the implication is that the *masses* consume or enjoy a *culture* which differs significantly from that enjoyed, either now or in the past, by *elite* elements in social structure; that such differences are differences both of content and quality; that *mass* cultural objects are transmitted and diffused through the modern *mass media of communication*; and that they are, in important respects, affected by this, by their *marketability*, and by the size of the *market* which enjoys them.

B. Use of the term has been much debated especially of late by social scientists and by literary critics (for a recent collection of essays see N. Jacobs (ed.), *Culture for the Millions*, Princeton: Van Nostrand, 1961). The debate has been quite varied but has centred upon certain key questions, e.g. (a) the causal factors which have brought mass culture to the fore; (b) the consequences for social and moral order; (c) the validity of the cross-cultural and historical comparisons in terms of which mass culture has been praised or denounced; (d) the ambiguities, both explicit and latent, in words like *mass* and *culture*; (e) the assessment and 'improvement' of the standards exhibited by mass culture, the comparison of those standards with those attained by other cultural forms, the quality of the interaction between *mass* and other standards, and the coexistence within a pluralistic setting of diverse, conflicting and overlapping cultural levels and standards. No short summary can attempt to cover the complexity of the debate but some of the contrasting viewpoints may be briefly illustrated.

1. According to D. Macdonald ('A Theory of Mass Culture', in B. Rosenberg & D. M. White (eds.), *Mass Culture*, Glencoe, Ill.: The Free

Mass Media

Press, 1957, pp. 57–73), mass culture came into being when 'Political democracy and popular education broke down the old upper-class monopoly of culture ... For about a century, Western culture has really been two cultures: the traditional kind—let us call it "High Culture"—that is chronicled in the textbooks, and a "Mass Culture" manufactured wholesale for the market'. C. Greenberg ('Avant-Garde and Kitsch', in *Mass Culture*, pp. 98–107) states that mass culture—which he calls *Kitsch*—'is a product of the industrial revolution which urbanized the masses of Western Europe and America and established what is called universal literacy ... Losing ... their taste for the folk-culture whose background was the countryside, and discovering a new capacity for boredom at the same time, the new urban masses set up a pressure on society to provide them with a culture fit for their own consumption. To fill the demand of the new market a new commodity was devised: Ersatz culture, *kitsch*, destined for those who, insensible to the values of genuine culture, are hungry nevertheless for the diversion that only culture of some sort can provide'. E. Van den Haag ('Of Happiness and of Despair We Have No Measure' in *Mass Culture*, pp. 504–36) writes: ' "Folk" and "high" cultures flowered simultaneously in different strata of many past societies. But popular culture [here used as a synonym of mass culture] when fully developed penetrates all strata about equally and without significant variations of its main qualities. As society becomes fully industrialized, popular culture becomes the most universally shared type of culture and colors most aspects of individual and social life'.

The authors cited so far seem agreed in the main to regard mass culture as peculiar to modern urbanized and industrialized societies, as being oriented toward marketability, as parasitic, spurious, mass produced and appealing to the lowest common denominator in its audience. Others, both in America and in Britain, have taken a more hopeful stance.

2. J. W. Bennett and M. M. Tumin (*Social Life*, New York: Knopf, 1948, p. 609) focus upon the integrating functions of mass culture: 'Mass culture is composed of a set of patterns of thought and action which are common to the subcultures of a heterogeneous society. These patterns have common meanings and values for all or most of the members of the society and serve as points of mutual identification and recognition for these members. The mass culture thus can be seen as a kind of least common denominator, or as the overall configuration, or as a kind of film hiding the diversity beneath'. E. A. Shils, though not satisfied that the concept of mass culture is an adequate one, has been notable among those who have rejected the 'parasitic' view of the phenomenon and has sought to identify the sources of the 'parasitic' view (see, for example, his discussion of modern culture in terms of the categories 'superior', 'mediocre', and 'brutal' culture in 'Mass Society and Its Culture' in N. Jacobs (ed.), *Culture For the Millions*, p. 1 et seq.; also his 'Daydreams and Nightmares', *Sewanee Review*, vol. 65, 1957, p. 587 et seq.).

In Great Britain, R. Wollheim has recently surveyed the extension of the American discussion to the British situation. The old middle-class 'literary' culture is now challenged by 'a new culture, which in its entry requirements and in its general characteristics, stands in marked contrast ... For whereas the old culture is primarily literary, the new culture is a leisure culture. Where the old culture is highly critical, the new culture is based on acceptance. Where the old culture is modest and unobtrusive, the new culture is ostentatious and essentially bound up with high consumption. And while the old culture is a class culture, the new culture is classless. The new culture is generally referred to as Mass Culture' (*Socialism and Culture*, London: Fabian Society, 1961, p. 7). Wollheim goes on to meet some of the objections which British writers (e.g. R. Williams) have levelled at the concept, e.g. that the use of the word *mass* is patronizing or antidemocratic. Wollheim agrees that 'the word "mass" does not merely describe people: it also describes a certain attitude adopted towards people'. 'But ... what is called a "mass-culture" is a characteristic product of those who do adopt just this attitude towards others, and it is this fact that makes the expression useful' (ibid., p. 8).

Lewis A. Coser

See also: Mass Media
         Mass Society

Mass Media

A. *Mass media* (broadly defined in a way which does not specify the audience's precise characteristics) are all the impersonal means of communication by which visual and/or auditory messages are transmitted directly to audiences. Included among the mass media are television, radio, motion pictures, newspapers, magazines, books, and billboards. It must be kept in mind, however, that there are variations among the mass media and that radio, motion pictures, television, and the popular press are likely to have larger and more heterogeneous audiences.

B. *Mass media* is a shortened form of the phrase *media of mass communication*. Two features are cited in definition, one relating to the technical means of transmission and the other to the audience.

1. According to some social scientists, the first feature is adequate in itself. J. T. Klapper (*The Effects of Mass Media*, New York: Columbia University Bureau of Applied Social Research, 1949, p. 3) says, 'the term connotes all mass media of communication in which a mechanism of impersonal reproduction intervenes between speaker and audience. By this criterion radio, screen, books and any other media of impersonal communication would be classified as mass media'. With this definition, *mass media* excludes only such communications as the drama, personal conversation, and public address.

2. When the specific meaning of *mass* (i.e. the audience which receives the communication) is brought into the definition, the range of the mass media is variously delineated.

(a) G. D. Wiebe ('Mass Communications', in E. L. Hartley & R. E. Hartley, *Fundamentals of Social Psychology*, New York: Knopf, 1952, pp. 164–5) writes, 'The two essential characteristics of mass media are: (i) their product is easily available—in a physical sense—to most of the public, including a sizeable number of people in all major sub-groups; and (ii) their cost is so small to the individual that they are generally available to these same people in a financial sense'. By this criterion, *mass media* excludes not only personal communications but also such media as the special interest magazine, hard-cover book, and educational film.

(b) M. Sherif and C. W. Sherif (*An Outline of Social Psychology*, New York: Harper & Bros., rev. edn., 1956, p. 562) also imply that a large audience is necessary for the proper usage of *mass media* and introduce a further time dimension. The mass media, they say, 'reach millions of people simultaneously or within very brief periods of time'.

(c) According to another conception of *mass* the members are not only numerous and heterogeneous, they also respond to the communication as separate individuals. L. Wirth ('Consensus and Mass Communication', *American Sociological Review*, vol. 13, 1948, p. 10) says that the mass media of communication transcend 'the peculiar interests and preoccupations of the special and segmental organized groups and direct their appeal to the mass'. This conception of *mass media* also excludes those communications directed to selected or specialized groups.

C. A British writer has recently claimed that the techniques referred to by the phrase *mass media* are marked by 'a steady growth of ... *multiple transmission*' (R. Williams, *Culture and Society, 1780–1950*, London: Chatto & Windus, 1958, p. 302) but criticizes the normative and policy assumptions latent in the use of *mass* to denote the audience in this context. 'If ... our purpose is manipulation—the persuasion of a large number of people to act, feel, think, know in certain ways—the convenient formula will be that of the masses' (ibid., p. 303).

Frederick Elkin

See also: Mass Culture
Mass Society

Mass Society

A. 1. This term denotes a *society* which is *a mass* and/or taken to be characterized in some respects by the *mass* or *masses* of individuals which it contains.

Such a society is characterized variously by features of increased mobility and social differentiation, and the loss of traditional roots, values, or attachments.

Usage of the term is normative and political as well as analytical; and its significance in different contexts depends upon the sense(s) of *mass* which is (are) being employed.

2. Some attempt has been made to use the term with a less normative flavour to denote a society in which individuals respond independently, but more or less similarly, to the same object of attention.

B. 1. Commenting upon the pejorative use of the word *mass* as *mob*, R. Williams argues that 'the traditional characteristics of the mob were retained in its significance-gullibility, fickleness, herd-prejudice, lowness of taste and habit' (*Culture and Society, 1780–1850*, London: Chatto & Windus, 1958, p. 298).

2. D. Bell sketches 'five different and sometimes contradictory usages' of the term *mass* as influencing the criteria of mass society. These are mass as undifferentiated number; the judgement of incompetent persons; the mechanized society; the bureaucratized society; and, finally,

Material Culture

the mass as mob characterized by 'uniformity, aimlessness, alienation, failure of integration' (*The End of Ideology*, Glencoe, Ill.: The Free Press, 1960, pp. 22–24).

Some of these senses of *mass* enter into the meaning of *mass society* as sketched by leading European theorists. Thus J. Ortega y Gasset regards a mass society as one in which power in public life is held by the mass of people in distinction from a selected elite. 'Society is always a dynamic unity of two component factors: minorities and masses. The minorities ... are specially qualified. The mass is the assemblage of persons not specially qualified ... a characteristic of our time is the predominance ... of the mass and the vulgar' (*Revolt of the Masses*, New York: Norton, 1932, pp. 13, 16). K. Mannheim describes *mass society* as producing 'all the irrationalities and emotional outbreaks which are characteristic of amorphous human agglomerations' (*Man and Society in an Age of Reconstruction*, New York: Harcourt, Brace, 1940, pp. 44, 61). Another usage regards the quality of mass society as being conducive to totalitarianism. E. Lederer, speaking of the mass-state, writes, 'modern political leaders, prospective dictators, have ... institutionalized the masses, making them a political and social steam roller, crushing social groups of every kind ... The totalitarian state is the state of the masses' (*State of the Masses*, New York: Norton, 1940, p. 45).

C. There are other usages which are less political and normative, emphasizing aspects of communication, structure, culture, and response.

1. K. Young defines mass societies as 'modern populations which are chiefly characterized by secondary group contacts, by high specialization of role and status, by anonymity, high mobility, and impersonal relationships generally' (*Social Psychology*, New York: F. S. Crofts, 2nd edn., 1944, p. 562).

2. L. Wirth adds dimensions of democracy and complexity. He writes, 'mass societies ... are the product of the division of labour, of mass communication and a more or less democratically achieved consensus ... mass democratic society [is] enormous in scope and intricate in structure' ('Consensus and Mass Communication', *American Sociological Review*, vol. 13, 1948, pp. 2, 4).

3. R. H. Turner and L. M. Killian define *mass* in the context of mass society as a 'number of separate individuals each responding independently to the same stimulus in the same

way' (*Collective Behavior*, Englewood Cliffs, N.J.: Prentice-Hall, 1957, p. 167).

These attempts are never fully successful. The aspects stressed retain a normative content and may become incorporated in political analysis. For example, C. W. Mills (contrasting the mass society with the public (q.v.)) asserts that the mass has the following characteristics, 'far fewer people express opinions than receive them ... the communications that prevail are so organized that it is difficult or impossible for the individual to answer back ... the realization of opinion in action is controlled by authorities who organize and control the channels of such action ... agents of authorized institutions penetrate this mass, reducing any autonomy it may have in the formation of opinion by discussion' (*The Power Elite*, New York: Oxford University Press, 1956, p. 304).

Frederick Elkin

See also: MASS CULTURE
MASS MEDIA

Material Culture

A. The earliest usage of this term was to denote techniques and artifacts as elements of culture (q.v.). But in the light of more recent criticism a more appropriate definition of the term might be offered as follows: *material culture* denotes those aspects of culture which govern the production and use of artifacts.

B. The points at issue are more clearly illustrated by the following:

1. 'A distinction often made between material and nonmaterial culture is mentioned here only as probably having no first rank significance. The literal difference is of course obvious: physical objects as against institutions and ideas. But do they stand for something basically different? Do they function with significant difference in culture? The answer seems No. What counts is not the physical axe or coat or wheat, but the idea of them, and the knowledge how to produce and use them, their place in life. It is this knowledge, concept, and function that get themselves handed down through the generations, or diffused into other cultures, while the objects themselves are quickly worn out or consumed. ... Accordingly, we may forget about this distinction between material and nonmaterial culture, except as a literal difference that it is sometimes of practical convenience to observe' (A. L. Kroeber, *Anthropology*, New York: Harcourt, Brace, 1948, pp. 295–6).

414

2. R. Linton makes the same point: 'Early in the development of anthropological studies the term *material culture* was coined to refer to such artifacts. However, the present tendency among anthropologists is to exclude the objects themselves from the culture concept, but to include what might be termed the patterns for objects. Thus, a stone axe itself is not regarded as a culture element, but the shape, size, finish, materials and so forth characteristic of the axes made and used by a particular society are considered culture elements' (*The Tree of Culture*, New York: Knopf, 1955, pp. 36–7).

3. ' "Material culture", though it is a useful label for one of the many aspects of our study, is in itself a contradiction in terms, since culture, scientifically viewed, consists of abstract and therefore immaterial relationships' (R. Piddington, *Introduction to Social Anthropology*, Edinburgh: Oliver & Boyd, 1957, vol. 2, pp. 521–2).

M. Douglas

See also: CULTURE

Mathematical Economics
(Also Econometrics)

A. 1. In its broadest sense *mathematical economics* refers to the use of mathematical logic or any mathematical method in economic theory. Consequently, in this sense economic theory in which demand curves, indifference curves, or other elementary geometrical constructions represent the chief method of reasoning is *mathematical economics* since graphs are a mathematical device.

2. Ordinarily, a somewhat different meaning is ascribed to *mathematical economics*. The use of graphs has become so commonplace that mathematical economics is usually distinguished by the use of symbols and the development of propositions in economic theory by symbolic methods of reasoning. *Econometrics* joins mathematical economics with empirical data by means of statistical methodology. That is, equations adapted from the theories of mathematical economics form the basis of models in which actual estimates of parameters are made.

B. 1. Although occasional references are encountered that explicitly state that graphical or diagrammatic devices are included within the scope of mathematical economics, this usage appears to be dying out. While such devices are used frequently in mathematical economics, they are hardly a distinguishing feature. This may be realized by recalling that modern elementary textbooks ordinarily make extensive use of diagrammatic methods, yet few economists would refer to these works as mathematical economics.

2. The restriction of the term *mathematical economics* to economic reasoning by means of symbols brings out the essentially methodological aspect of mathematical economics. Mathematical economics is not a branch of economic theory co-ordinate with price and value theory, monetary theory, or any other segment of economic theory; rather it is a methodology of thought capable, at least conceptually, of being applied in any part of economic theory. The mathematical theorems and techniques applied in economic theory range from the most elementary algebraic manipulations to topics in advanced calculus, modern algebra, analysis, topology, symbolic logic, and game theory.

C. 1. Two related, but distinguishable, aspects of mathematical economics should be pointed out. The first of these is the symbolic logic or language aspect of the mathematical approach in economics; the second is the quantitative aspect of mathematical economics. Historically, the former aspect of mathematical economics has been the primary advantage of the mathematical method, but in recent years the quantitative aspect has assumed increasing importance because the development of econometrics has been thought by some to have lessened the space between mathematical economics and the realities of empirical data.

The symbolic logic or language aspect of mathematical economics refers to the formulation and development of abstract topics in economic theory by symbolic reasoning. Through the use of mathematical methods, a precision and brevity in the statement of the assumptions made, the reasoning process employed and the conclusions reached is obtained that is not possible with non-mathematical methods. In addition a power of thought is obtained through the rigour of the reasoning process that is difficult to obtain by other means.

2. The particularly quantitative aspect of mathematical economics arises from the use of mathematical apparatus which itself is quantitative in form. This quantitative form suggests the need for careful definition of the variables to be considered and this in turn suggests the need for defining variables in such a way that they are operationally and empirically meaningful. In other words, the writing in equation form of an

415

Matriarchy

economic process leads rather naturally to a speculation as to how similar equations with empirical coefficients would compare with the theoretical formulation. Thus econometrics is a natural outgrowth of mathematical economics.

D. 1. The equations used in econometrics are derived or adapted from mathematical economics. Statistical methods are applied to empirical data to obtain estimates of the coefficients in the equations. Consequently, econometrics unites mathematical economics with reality. In view of the theoretical structure behind econometric models, this discipline should be distinguished from economic statistics which lacks the rigorous economic background. That is, economic statistics is the application of statistical methods to economic data without a clearly defined economic model being contemplated by the investigator.

2. Because systems of simultaneous equations are often used in econometrics, special problems of the calculation of regression coefficients and of other statistics arise. These problems have led and are leading to the development of statistical methods peculiar to the field of econometrics.

3. Finally, it should be noted that findings made in the field of econometrics suggest modifications of economic theories as well as provide means of testing economic theories. Thus an important interplay between theory and reality is established that is similar to the interplay between theory and experimentation in the physical and biological sciences.

R. W. Pfouts

See also: ECONOMICS

Matriarchal (See **Matriarchy**)

Matriarchate (See **Matriarchy**)

Matriarchy

A. The term *matriarchy* was used in the 19th century to designate the hypothetical form of society in which women were the leaders and rulers. Anthropologists now agree that there is no evidence to substantiate the claim that any society has ever been under such control. A few anthropologists have attempted redefinitions, but none of these has gained general acceptance.

B. The closely related terms *matriarchy*, *matriarchate*, and *matriarchal*, as well as the complementary terms, *patriarchy* (q.v.), *patriarchate*, and *patriarchal* were part of the 19th-century terminology in anthropology. R. Lowie states that the concept of *matriarchy* was originally Bachofen's, who viewed it as including not only matrilineal (q.v.) transmission of group membership, but also 'rule of the family by the mother, not the father; control of government by women, not men; and the supremacy of a female deity, the moon, not of the male sun' (*Social Organization*, London: Routledge & Kegan Paul, 1950, p. 262).

C. Today these terms have been discarded by most anthropologists. M. Jacobs and B. J. Stern express the present-day view concerning matriarchy when they define it as implying 'the improbable hypothesis that there were socio-economic systems characterized by preponderantly feminine property ownership and economic control, governmental management, and cultural leadership' (M. Jacobs & B. J. Stern, *Outline of Anthropology*, Cambridge: Heffer, 1947, p. 309).

D. In an attempt to increase the utility of these 19th-century concepts, anthropologists and others, in very different ways, have redefined *matriarchy* and *matriarchate*.

1. One rather loose usage in anthropology and sociology defines *matriarchy* simply as 'rule by women' (R. L. Beals & H. Hoijer, *An Introduction to Anthropology*, New York: The Macmillan Co., 1959, p. 466; G. A. Reichard, 'Social Life', in F. Boas (ed.), *General Anthropology*, New York: Heath, 1938, p. 416; R. H. Lowie, *Social Organization*, p. 35). Closely similar is C. B. Richards's suggestion that matriarchy be equated with the ability of women to make 'key decisions' (C. B. Richards, 'Matriarchy or Mistake', in V. F. Ray (ed.), *Cultural Stability and Cultural Change*, Seattle: American Ethnological Society, 1957, p. 36).

2. The psychoanalyst E. Jones gives another variant when he writes: 'The term "matriarchy" should be limited to the other cases where there is true mother-rule, i.e. where the mother is the head of the household and disposes of the final authority over the children' ('Mother-right and the Sexual Ignorance of Savages', *The International Journal of Psycho-analysis*, vol. 6, 1925, p. 112). In qualifying this discussion Jones explicitly excludes from this category societies with the avunculate (q.v.) and those in which descent is matrilineal but the father has the final authority over the children.

3. A. R. Radcliffe-Brown in his definition of

matriarchy restricts its meaning to include approximately the same phenomena as does the term *matrilineal descent*. On one occasion, he states that 'matriarchy ... implies an emphasis on unilineal descent through females' ('Introduction', to A. R. Radcliffe-Brown & D. Forde (eds.), *African Systems of Kinship and Marriage*, London: Oxford University Press, 1950, p. 18). Elsewhere he writes: 'A society can be called matriarchal when descent, inheritance, and succession are in the female line, marriage is matrilocal ..., and when the authority over the children is wielded by the mother's relatives' (*Structure and Function in Primitive Society*, London: Cohen & West, 1952, p. 22). R. R. Marett also holds this view (*Anthropology*, New York: Henry Holt, 1912, p. 165).

Arnold R. Pilling

See also: MATRILINEAL
PATRIARCHY

Matrilateral

Matrilateral is sometimes used as a synonym for *matrilineal* (q.v.); that is, it describes a kinship system in which descent is traced only through females.

It is more usual nowadays to use *matrilateral* for relationships traced through the mother in a patrilineal system (these relationships are not lineal but are on the mother's side); or for relatives on the mother's side in a non-unilineal kinship system.

Maurice Freedman

See also: DESCENT
KINSHIP AND KINSHIP SYSTEM
PATRILATERAL

Matrilineal

A. The term denotes a method of tracing descent (q.v.) by the recognition of relationships based upon descent from a common ancestor or ancestress through women only. Men may be matrilineal kin of each other, but matrilineal kin may not be linked through a male.

B. Some writers have linked matrilineal descent with matriarchy (q.v.), a system in which authority is vested in the mother; but they must be distinguished. In almost all matrilineal systems of organization authority is vested in men; in this case formal authority may be exercised over a man by his mother's brother, and inheritance and succession are from a man to his sister's son (see A. R. Radcliffe-Brown, 'The Mother's Brother in South Africa' and 'Patrilineal and Matrilineal Succession', in his *Structure and Function in Primitive Society*, London: Cohen & West, 1952, pp. 15–48).

C. Matrilineal descent is found not only with matrilocal (uxorilocal) residence, but also with patrilocal and virilocal residence (see G. P. Murdock, *Social Structure*, New York: The Macmillan Co., 1949, ch. 8).

D. Many early anthropologists considered that matrilineal descent was found prior to the recognition of patrilineal descent (J. J. Bachofen, *Das Mutterrecht* (1861) Basel: Benno Schwabe, 1897; L. H. Morgan, *Ancient Society*, New York: Henry Holt, 1877, and others); but this hypothesis has been exploded. W. H. R. Rivers (*Social Organization*, London: Kegan Paul, Trench, Trubner, 1926, pp. 85–99) showed that descent refers to group membership, not to the recognition of kinship as such. As Murdock points out, the fact that certain Australian tribes which are ignorant of physical paternity nevertheless recognize patrilineal descent is conclusive. Descent is a social phenomenon, not a biological one. A summary of this controversy is given by G. P. Murdock (*Social Structure*, pp. 184 ff.) and R. H. Lowie (*A History of Ethnological Theory*, New York: Farrar & Rinehart, 1937, pp. 40 ff.).

J. Middleton

See also: PATRILINEAL

Matrilocal (See **Residence**)

Matrimoiety (See **Moiety**)

Maturation

A. *Maturation* denotes inferred growth processes that result in orderly changes in behaviour. While an environment within the range needed to sustain life and development is assumed, the behaviour-changes, although partly learnt, retain their sequential order and their rate of appearance in time within a wide range of environmental stimulation, and hence can be distinguished from changes due primarily to learning.

B. 1. The word has been used chiefly within psychology and education to refer to certain features of individual growth and development not to be attributed exclusively to learning. The term came to prominence in the late 1920s and

Meaning

early 1930s as a consequence of several converging trends: (a) the anti-instinct tendencies of the times, which diverted those previously interested in instinct into species-specific processes under new rubrics such as *drive* (e.g. maternal drive replacing maternal instinct) and *maturation* (e.g. sexual behaviour as a maturing function rather than as an instinctual one) (C. P. Stone, 'Maturation and "Instinctive" Functions', in F. A. Moss (ed.), *Comparative Psychology*, 1934, pp. 37–72); (b) a then-current interest in longitudinal studies of child development, with the need for some concept to describe the orderly sequences of changes (A. Gesell, 'Maturation and the Patterning of Behavior', *Psychological Review*, vol. 36, 1929, pp. 307–19); (c) new leads coming from experimental embryologists as to a possible anatomical basis for orderly behavioural development (G. Coghill, *Anatomy and the Problem of Behavior*, New York: The Macmillan Co., 1929).

The concept of maturation thus saved something of hereditary potential at a time of extreme environmentalism, because maturation suggested some kind of internal regulation characteristic of the organism to supplement learning under the impact of the environment. While there were many attempts to refine the distinction between learning and maturation (e.g. D. Marquis, 'The Criterion of Innate Behavior', *Psychological Review*, vol. 37, 1930, pp. 334–49; L. Carmichael, 'A Re-evaluation of the Concepts of Maturation and Learning as Applied to the Early Development of Behavior', *Psychological Review*, vol. 43, 1936, pp. 450–70), for the most part there was little polemic, and the topic suggested many careful studies of pre-natal and post-natal development.

2. The descriptive and explanatory uses of the term have often been confused, and the two meanings are hard to disentangle. On the one hand, we may refer descriptively to behaviour that matures by noting only the orderly sequences (e.g. the infant's crawling before walking), without reference to any specific underlying growth process. On the other hand, we may infer a specific regulatory mechanism, so that one might say that particular behavioural changes, rather than being themselves what we mean by maturation, are 'due to' maturation:

'Growth is a process so intricate and so sensitive there must be powerful stabilizing factors, intrinsic rather than extrinsic, which preserve the balance of the total pattern and the direction of the growth trend. Maturation is, in a sense, a name for this regulatory mechanism' (A. Gesell,

'Maturation and the Patterning of Behavior', in C. Murchison (ed.), *A Handbook of Child Psychology*, Worcester, Mass.: Clark University Press, rev. 1933, p. 232).

Some related concepts include *readiness* (as in reading readiness), and *imprinting*, because the time when imprinting can occur is regulated by intra-organismic factors (N. Tinbergen, *The Study of Instinct*, Toronto: Oxford University Press, 1951).

Ernest R. Hilgard

See also: DRIVE
        INSTINCT
        LEARNING

Meaning

A. In its broadest sense the *meaning* of an object is its position of relatedness to all other objects with which it is associated in the experience of the individual (or group) in question. Although social scientists have been concerned with the philosophical controversies concerning meaning, with particular reference to the meaning of various types of propositions set forth in the social sciences and to the distinction between empirically verifiable statements and those which are not verifiable, their contributions to the definition of meaning have been concerned with the cultural, psychological, and social dimensions of the concept.

B. 'There is perhaps no more bewildering and controversial problem than "the meaning of meaning" ' (E. Cassirer, *An Essay on Man*, New Haven: Yale University Press, 1944, p. 112). Concern with this bewildering and controversial problem was once restricted to philosophers, but more recently anthropologists, psychologists, and sociologists have also dealt with the issue. Although there is a common core of similarity in all the approaches to this problem, they are sufficiently different to necessitate separate exposition.

1. In anthropology the concept of meaning has assumed importance because of the inability of the naïve observer to determine the significance of behaviour traits in another culture without a knowledge of the cultural context within which they occur. R. Linton (*The Study of Man*, New York: Appleton-Century-Crofts, 1936), for instance, notes: 'The meaning of a [culture] trait complex consists of the associations which any society attaches to it. Such associations are subjective and frequently unconscious. They find only indirect expression in behavior ... '(ibid., p 403) 'Many elements of culture have multiple uses, but nearly all of them have multiple meanings. We are not referring, of course, to individual associations based upon accidents of experience but to the associations which are a regular part of the culture configurations and which are transmitted and shared like any of its other elements' (ibid., p. 410).

Another anthropologist, H. G. Barnett, (*Innovation: The Basis of Cultural Change*, New York: McGraw-Hill, 1953), emphasizes the individual's need to attach meaning to new experiences and the role of this 'need for meaning' in the selective adoption of innovations: 'Meaning is the insight which comes when the idea of the presented thing is referable to the idea of some past experience ... In so far as unfamiliar experiences are concerned, meaning is evoked if some familiar configuration is aroused either directly or indirectly, either spontaneously or by search and effort' (ibid., pp. 334–5).

2. This emphasis on the significance of a new experience to the individual is, of course, the usual emphasis of the psychologist. As with the anthropologist, the psychologist normally finds the meaning of any given event in the total set of events with which it is (or has been) associated. The difference is the locus of these associations, the anthropologist usually finding them in the realm of culture configurations, the psychologist finding them in the realm of the individual's personal experience. G. A. Miller ('Psycholinguistics', in G. Lindzey (ed.) *Handbook of Social Psychology*, Cambridge, Mass.: Addison-Wesley, 1954, pp. 706–7) defines the problem of the psychologist with reference to meaning as the attempt to consider how: '... a complex matrix of symbolic behavior depends upon the whole linguistic history of the talker, upon his motivation, his audience, his past experience with the topic he is discussing, his present perception of the situation he is in, his intraverbal associations with other words immediately preceding, etc.' '... to provide an analysis of meaning that is scientifically realistic and adequate to the great complexities of psycho-linguistics, the psychologist must learn how these many psychological dimensions influence the statistical parameters that are used to describe verbal behavior'.

This suggests that psychologists have been more concerned with the problem of the meaning of language symbols than with the more general problem of the meaning of all signs (q.v.). Although this more general problem of signs cannot be ignored, most social scientists have focused on the more limited problem of the meaning of verbal symbols. The concern here has varied from some psychologists' interest in conceptualizing the process that takes place within the human organism when an experience 'has meaning' (cf. C. Morris, *Signs, Language and Behavior*, New York: Prentice-Hall, 1946, or C. E. Osgood, *Method and Theory in Experimental Psychology*, Oxford: Oxford University Press, 1953) to the social psychologists' interest in the function of the interpersonal context within which verbal behaviour occurs.

3. Most sociologists who have concerned themselves in any way with the problem of meaning have emphasized the latter of these two concerns. As A. R. Lindesmith and A. L. Strauss (*Social Psychology*, New York: Dryden Press, 1949, p. 54) have put it: '... Meaning is often thought of as a metaphysical essence which resides in symbols, or in a person's brain, or in objects themselves. ... *The meaning of an object or word is determined by the responses that are made to it: that is, meaning is a relationship,* not an essence'.

This approach to the question of meaning is in the tradition of the social behaviourism of G. H. Mead (*Mind, Self and Society*, Chicago: University of Chicago Press, 1934) who noted that: 'Meaning arises and lies within the field of the relation between the gesture of a given human organism and the subsequent behavior of this organism as indicated to another human organism by that gesture. If that gesture does so indicate to another organism the subsequent (or resultant) behavior of the given organism, then it has meaning' (ibid., pp. 75–6).

All of the above uses of the term *meaning* emphasize the function of the pattern of relationships between the object, symbol, etc. in question and other objects with which it is in some way associated. This emphasis on a pattern of relationships is perhaps the central core in all the definitions. S. K. Langer (*Philosophy in a New Key*, Cambridge, Mass.: Harvard University Press, 1942, p. 55) emphasized this aspect of meaning when she stated: 'There is in fact no quality of meaning; its essence lies in the realm of logic, where one does not deal with qualities, but only with relations. ... It is better, perhaps to say: "Meaning is not a quality, but a *function* of a term." A function is a *pattern* viewed with reference to one special term round which it centers: this pattern emerges when we look at the given term *in its total relation to the other terms about it*. The total may be quite complicated.

Means-End Schema

... The meaning ... rests on a pattern, in which the term itself holds the key-position'.

Alan C. Kerckhoff

See also: COMMUNICATION
GESTURE
LANGUAGE
SIGN
SYMBOL

Means-End Schema

A. The *means-end schema* involves a teleological rather than a mechanistic approach to the description and explanation of social phenomena. Its datum is *action* rather than *behaviour*. In its broadest sense the means-end schema is a representation of human activities, in their temporal aspect, as a sequence of nearer and remoter states of affairs, all purposively coordinated in the minds of human agents.

B. The means-end schema is a set of categories for the description of concrete human acts and for the explanation of certain relationships among different properties of those acts. The schema is a formalization of a long tradition in European social thought, culminating in Pareto and Weber, in which the behaviour of human agents is conceived in a teleological, purposive sense rather than in a mechanistic, causal sense —aiming at ends rather than impelled by causes. In R. M. MacIver's words, 'There is another type of chain that ... lies outside the strict causal category, viz. the free schema of means-ends leading to some goal. We seek D in order to get C, and we seek C in order to get B, and we seek B for the sake of A. A value relation links A to D, and at each step it enters into a process of teleological causation' (*Social Causation*, Boston: Ginn, 1942, p. 185).

C. 1. In its systematization by T. Parsons (*The Structure of Social Action*, New York: McGraw-Hill, 1937), the means-end schema consists of these elements: (a) an agent or actor; (b) an end to intended future state of affairs; (c) an objective situation, part of which is controllable by the actor (means) and part of which is not controllable by the actor (conditions); and (d) a normative relationship among these elements. Two broad classes of analytical problems can be formulated in terms of this schema: (i) the technological, in which interest centres on the most efficient means for achieving a given end, and (ii) the economic, in which interest centres on the best allocation of given means to alternative ends. Cutting across this distinction is another

one: that between rational, non-rational, and irrational action, the differentiating criterion being the scope of cognition, affect, and ignorance in the choice of means to ends.

2. Formulations of the means-end schema vary in: (a) the number of elements which are considered to be minimal; (b) the empirical relationships held to obtain among the referents of these elements; and (c) the correspondence of these elements to mechanistic concepts of cause and effect. Thus: (i) The distinction between means and ends is sometimes explicitly eliminated. F. W. Znaniecki writes: '... purpose includes both the end in the sense of the anticipated final result of the action which the agent expects to achieve and the means in the sense of the anticipated changes in existing data by which he expects to achieve it' (*Cultural Sciences*, Urbana: University of Illinois Press, 1952, pp. 198–9).

(ii) The empirical relationships obtaining between means and ends are always empirically problematical. R. K. Merton notes that: 'To say, moreover, that cultural goals and institutionalized norms operate jointly to shape prevailing practices is not to say that they bear a constant relation to one another. The cultural emphasis placed upon certain goals varies independently of the degree of emphasis upon institutionalized means' (*Social Theory and Social Structure*, Glencoe, Ill.: The Free Press, 1949, p. 127).

(iii) Means and ends are sometimes made correlative with cause and effect. According to S. F. Nadel '... we can readily visualize the double relationship of means-and-ends and cause-and-effect as a gradual process in which, step by step, one becomes adjusted to the other; that is, an end is anticipated, however vaguely; causal effects are observed which suggest a suitable means, until the means has been fully tested and fitted to the desired end' (*Foundations of Social Anthropology*, London: Cohen & West, 1951, pp. 286–7).

Walter Firey

Measurement (See **Science**)

Mechanism

A. A *mechanism* may be defined as any arrangement or structure and/or sequence of acts, responses, attitudes, culture patterns, social positions or other units that facilitates or makes possible the accomplishment, fulfilment or performance of given ends, functions, needs, or processes regardless of whether these are considered to be 'established in the nature of things'

420

or chosen, in a proximate sense, by human actors, or theoretically identified and specified by an observer.

B. 1. The concept of *mechanism* is used in a figurative rather than in a literal sense in social science, designating, generally, the arrangement (natural or constructed) of parts and of processes by means of which (or as a result of the operation of which) specified goals or ends are achieved, functions performed, needs met, and wants, or desires, gratified, consciously or unconsciously, intentionally or unintentionally. Variations in use to which the concept is put can perhaps best be pointed out in relation to certain questions which focus attention on possible differences in denotation—viz. of what kind(s) of elements is a mechanism considered to be composed? how is it activated and kept in motion? what ends (if any) does it 'serve' or what consequences does it have? are these chosen, and, if so, by whom? can or do mechanisms operate independent of human volition or choice and/or of human consciousness?

In current usage, teleological questions tend to be avoided completely and the word is used to designate any operative arrangement of parts or elements (whether these be acts or other responses, culture patterns, including institutions, group structures, or, in some other contexts, cells or other simpler or more complex, organic or inorganic units).

2. In psychology, as in anthropology and in sociology, *mechanism* is used to refer to some arrangement of parts which *functions* or operates to meet or fill some theoretically (or otherwise) specified ends, needs, goals, purposes or has some other predictable consequences. In a still more basic sense, *mechanism* may refer to any structure or arrangement which is the vehicle for, or which makes *possible* any of these effects. Thus, (a) a social psychologist may write a paper entitled 'Physiological Mechanisms of Motivation' (C. T. Morgan, in M. R. Jones (ed.), *Nebraska Symposium on Motivation*, Lincoln: University of Nebraska Press, 1957, pp. 1–35) or can say that 'mechanisms can so function as to bring about the *conditions for the appearance of new needs and demands*' (D. Krech & R. S. Crutchfield, *Theory and Problems of Social Psychology*, New York: McGraw-Hill, 1948, p. 45).

In psychiatric usage, as well as in social psychology, frequent reference is made to compensatory mechanisms, defence mechanisms and escape mechanisms, among others. (b) In anthropological usage, attention focuses on culture patterns (single traits, complexes, institutions) which function (or can be, and are, used) in ways that are instrumental to the achievement of some given end, or goal or simply to some expected consequence, as, for example, the use of money vs. barter as mechanisms for facilitating the exchange of goods and services in a culture. (c) In sociological analysis, all of the above usages are found, with additional, and particular, emphasis given to the arrangement of positions (or statuses and roles) in various types of social structures (and the possibilities for social action which are thus implied) as the mechanism of most immediate or direct relevance. A recent example is R. K. Merton's discussion of 'social mechanisms articulating role-sets' ('The Role-Set: Problems in Sociological Theory', *British Journal of Sociology*, vol. 8, 1957, pp. 106–20).

Allan W. Eister

See also: DEFENCE MECHANISM
FUNCTION

Mediation

A. When two or more parties are unable to compose their differences between themselves, they may appeal for mediation, that is, the intervention by some other party or group of parties with the object of proposing a compromise (q.v.). Thus *mediation* has been defined as the 'direct conduct of negotiations between parties at issue on the basis of proposals made by the mediator' (L. Oppenheim, *International Law*, vii, 7th edn., by Lauterpacht, London: Longmans, Green, 1952, p. 10).

B. Mediation implies (a) actual participation in the negotiation by the mediator and is to be distinguished from the tendering of *good offices*, which is merely confined to urging the parties to begin or resume negotiation: 'Whereas in offering "good offices" the third party confines himself to calling negotiations between the conflicting states into existence, in "mediation" the third party goes further and not only brings negotiations into existence, but actually brings them into existence on the basis of proposals made by him' (E. M. Satow, *A Guide to Diplomatic Practice*, 4th edn., by Sir Nevile Bland, 1957, p. 438); (b) a concern with something more than *legal* rights and interests; (c) a resort to flexible and pragmatic methods, ranging from friendly pressure on both parties to yield or to continue their search for a formula, to the

Memory

proposing of new terms which neither party has yet considered; (d) voluntary acceptance of the proposed settlement, otherwise the process is *arbitration*. If successful, the mediator may become a party to, or even guarantee, the resulting agreement, or his name may simply be mentioned in the agreement. A state may be more willing to accept a mediator's proposals if he is likely to underwrite them.

C. 1. In diplomatic practice it is usual for the mediator to be another state or government and sometimes a head of state or government. But it is not unknown for persons of great repute or dignity to be called upon to serve. Pope Leo XIII thus intervened as mediator in 1885 during the dispute between Germany and Spain over the Caroline Islands. In recent times it has been customary for conflicting states to apply for mediation by some international body of which they may be members, e.g. the League of Nations (by Article 11 of its Covenant); similarly, under Article 36 of the United Nations Charter, the Security Council is authorized to recommend terms of settlement to disputing states and to non-members of the Organization on their application to the Council; by Article 14 a similar function is entrusted, on certain conditions, to the General Assembly. These international bodies are usually entitled themselves to mediate collectively or to call upon some state or person to act on their behalf. A striking development in this respect has been the way in which the Secretary-General of the United Nations, in contrast with his predecessor in the League of Nations, has acted on several occasions in a mediatory or quasi-mediatory capacity.

2. In 1856 the Declaration of Paris expressed the wish that 'states between which any misunderstanding might arise, before appealing to arms, [would] have recourse as far as circumstances might allow, to the good offices of a friendly Power'. At the Hague Peace Conference of 1899 and 1907 it was laid down that any Power could by law offer its good offices to other states, which should not be regarded as an unfriendly act. In these declarations the expression *good offices* was understood to cover mediation. In Article 33 (1) of the United Nations Charter it is more imperatively stated that Members must settle their disputes by any peaceful means of their own choice, mediation being then mentioned as one possible means.

D. In this century, particularly in the United States, the term has been extended in the social sciences to designate a process similar to that practised in diplomacy but occurring in the area of industrial disputes and bargaining. Again the process is voluntary with the respect to any settlement proposed by the mediating service, and the term *arbitration* is used where the decision of the third party must be accepted.

F. S. Northedge

See also: BARGAINING
COMPROMISE
CONCILIATION

Memory

A. *Memory* is a generic term denoting the conscious recurrence, totally or in part, of a function or an experience learned or undergone in the past. It is one of those substantive terms which have come to be less frequently used in modern psychology, terms which denote a faculty of the mind. Today it is more usual to speak of *remembering* or *retention*, with the sub-types of *recall* and *recognition*. By extension *memory* can also refer to the specific content of the recurring function or experience.

B. Memory is obviously connected with learning (q.v.) and its theoretical interpretation in psychology is bound to turn on the suggested mechanisms underlying it. The conception that memory is somewhat like a recording machine has been mostly discarded in modern psychology, although there are variant and opposing theories concerning it which are not of direct relevance to social psychology. In the latter discipline interest is much more likely to be focused on the determinants of the content of memory and the relations of such content to culturally determined interests and to repression (q.v.) as in the following examples:

1. The work of F. C. Bartlett (*Remembering*, Cambridge: At the University Press, 1932) has demonstrated that the content of what has been previously acquired in ordinary experience may be radically altered when remembered, although form is fairly well retained. It is his argument that the individual tends to incorporate new items into a mental 'schema' so that remembering is 'an imaginative reconstruction, or construction, built out of the relation of our attitude towards a whole active mass of organized past reactions or experience, and to a little outstanding detail which commonly appears in image or in language form' (ibid., p. 213). These reconstructions tend to centre on certain interests of the person.

2. Accuracy of memory is likely to be sharpest where the interest on which memory is focused is strong. A. R. Lindesmith and A. L. Strauss (*Social Psychology*, New York: Dryden Press, 1949, pp. 81–3), use as examples Bartlett's analysis of the excellent memory of Swazi of South Africa with respect to cattle and cattle raising which was a central concern of Swazi society, together with Mark Twain's description of the phenomenal memories of Mississippi River pilots with respect to thousands of items concerning the river.

3. Where the focus of interest is not an adaptive sector of social life, but rather an integrative one in which common symbols, values, and memories serve as a basis of consensus, the element of accuracy is subordinate to the integrative function of the shared schema. Details of history, for example, are woven into a fabric of maximum emotion producing power in the interests of group solidarity (see, for example, W. L. Warner, *The Living and the Dead*, New Haven: Yale University Press, 1959, pp. 101–225).

4. The requirements of group life frequently result in the shaping of memory through repression as well as through the focusing of memory in certain spheres of interest and through the assembling of solidarity producing patterns. In the case of B. (3) above, some details of history may simply be forgotten, but others are deliberately or non-deliberately repressed. Similarly the person in his ordinary rounds of life is required to repress much of what he might remember. Thus Freud writes 'Memory very often produces in dreams impressions from the dreamer's early childhood of which we can definitely assert not only that they had been forgotten but that they had become unconscious owing to repression' (*An Outline of Psychoanalysis*, trans. by J. Strachey, New York: Norton, 1949, p. 49).

D. R. Price-Williams

See also: LEARNING

Mentality

A. In the most common usage, *mentality* refers to the specific manifestation of mind in any organism, having regard to the differences in quality and degree of mental organization within and between species.

B. The word has nearly always been used to denote the totality of all the characteristics distinctive of mind whether in animal or man. For example, A. R. Wallace spoke of 'an insect's very limited mentality' (*Nature*, vol. 42, 1890, p. 291), and a book by W. Köhler is entitled *The Mentality of Apes* (London: Kegan Paul, 1925). Sometimes the word is employed in a sense equivalent to 'mental capacity' (J. Drever, *A Dictionary of Psychology*, Harmondsworth: Penguin Books, 1952). A rare usage restricts the word to the purely intellectual aspects of mind 'Pope ... has an excess of mentality' (G. Santayana, *Interpretations of Poetry and Religion*, New York: Charles Scribner's Sons, 1900, p. 258).

According to C. G. Jung (*Psychology and Religion: East and West*, trans. by R. F. C. Hull, London: Routledge & Kegan Paul, 1958, pp. 479–80), in the West *mentality* means the mind of an individual whereas corresponding expressions in the East refer to cosmic mind which is 'the very essence of existence'.

J. Cohen

See also: LEARNING
MIND
REASON

Mercantilism

A. The term *mercantilism* denotes the principles of the mercantile system, sometimes understood as the identification of wealth with money; but more generally, the belief that the economic welfare of the state can only be secured by government regulation of a nationalist character.

B. 1. The term is of comparatively recent usage in English, though the phrase from which it derives—the mercantile system—is of 18th-century origin. First used by the Physiocrats it was popularized by Adam Smith in *The Wealth of Nations*, in which 'the Commercial or Mercantile System' is compared with 'the system of agriculture' as a means of 'enriching the people'. The system was in general represented as a conspiracy of merchants and manufacturers devised for their own ends. It victimized one section of the community for the benefit of another and regarded production rather than consumption as the object of economic activity. This system of 'mercantile' regulations had passed through two phases, according to Adam Smith. (a) In the first, the accumulation of bullion had been sought through direct prohibitions on its export. (b) In the second, largely under the influence of Thomas Mun, regulation had applied to the balance of trade, which was believed to control the flow of money. Both types were equally fruitless, for bullion did not possess the virtues it was credited with, and lack

Metaanthropology

of it was not the fundamental cause of trade depression.

2. These unfavourable opinions were generally shared by later British economists. In the later 19th century, the German school of 'historical economists', G. Schmoller especially, took a more favourable view, holding that mercantilism was not merely economic policy-making but 'state-making' in the larger sense. Only the state could provide the people with the necessary backing of power demanded by a successful economy. States which had done this had taken the lead in the struggle (G. Schmoller, *The Mercantile System*, (1884), New York: Peter Smith, 1931). Such views influenced not only German thought and policy but English scholars like W. Cunningham whose *Growth of English Industry and Commerce* (Cambridge: University Press, 1882) emphasized the element of power in mercantilism.

3. The most important recent study is *Mercantilism* by E. Heckscher (trans. by M. Shapiro, London: Allen & Unwin, rev. 2nd edn., 1955). His study did much to popularize the use of a term hitherto mainly of Germanic usage (*Merkantilismus*) but less to clarify its meaning, which it tended to divorce from the mercantile context where it originated. Heckscher regarded mercantilism as a uniform body of doctrine which could be considered under five heads: (a) national unification; (b) state power; (c) protectionist policies; (d) monetary theory; (e) social ideas. Heckscher found little to approve in an ideology which he thought aimed at power rather than economic welfare.

C. Writers have differed widely on the merits of mercantilism but there has been general agreement that the practical mechanism of the system consisted (as Adam Smith said) of the 'two great engines' of regulation designed to promote manufactured exports and to discourage all but essential imports. The system was completed in England in the 17th century by the construction of the Navigation Laws which aimed at strategic as well as economic power and survived till after the Napoleonic Wars, being finally dismantled only by Gladstone. In France the writings of Bodin, de Laffemas and Monchretien bear witness to the growth of similar ideas, finally embodied in Colbert's system, though Colbert placed more emphasis on industrial regulation and was less explicit on balance of trade theory. 18th-century writers, following Josiah Child, John Cary, and others, generally paid more attention to the volume of employment as a criterion of the efficacy of regulation and less to the net gain of bullion. This 'social' phase of mercantilism had great influence in the less developed economies of Europe—Uztariz in Spain, Genovesi in Italy, and the Cameralists in Germany being especially impressed by the employment argument.

Recent inquiries have centred less on the abstract merits or otherwise of mercantilism and more on the relationship of its ideas and policies (especially on monetary matters) to contemporary economic conditions.

C. Wilson

Merit System (See **Civil Service**)

Metaanthropology

A. *Metaanthropology* is the philosophical and historical study of the philosophical presuppositions and postulates of scientific anthropology in general and cultural anthropology in particular.

B. The term *metaanthropology* was introduced by D. Bidney to indicate a sphere of interest in anthropology which deals especially with the philosophical presuppositions of scientific anthropology, particularly cultural anthropology (D. Bidney, *Theoretical Anthropology*, New York: Columbia University Press, 1953, pp. 156–82). Just as the editor of Aristotle's works used the term *metaphysics* to refer to that work which came after the *Physics* and was concerned with the ultimate concepts and principles presupposed or postulated in his physical theories, so the term *metaanthropology* is used to refer to the analysis of the foundations or presuppositions of anthropological theory. Thus the term is not merely another name for anthropological theory; it refers to a special kind of theory, namely, the theory concerned with such problems as the nature of the reality of culture, cultural causality, and the significance of cultural determinism and its bearing on the modes of human experience and evaluation. The metaanthropologist seeks to show the relation of anthropology to the philosophy of science in general and to indicate how the general theories and approaches developed in the philosophy of science may apply or may be uncritically assumed in anthropology and the other social sciences as well.

C. It is merely an accident of history that the term *metaphysics* has come to take over the whole sphere of ontological thought, thereby obscuring the fact that ontological postulates

Methodology

constitute an indispensable element in the philosophy of *each* of the sciences. Thus the prefix *meta*, if joined with the name of any one of the social sciences, could serve usefully to refer to the philosophy of the given science, i.e. to the analysis of problems concerning the relation of the phenomena and processes of a given science to the mind of the knower and to reality as it exists independent of the knower. As against the positivistic view that the prefix *meta* indicates a pre-scientific state of a discipline, it may be claimed that the prefix can be legitimately used, as in the case of metaanthropology, to designate the theoretically postulated aspect of each science and that the discipline so designated deals with those ontological and epistemological postulates necessary to render the theory and method of the science intelligible. Thus there are legitimate areas of investigation that might well be entitled *metasociology, metapsychology*, etc.

David Bidney

See also: SCIENCE
SOCIAL ANTHROPOLOGY

Metalinguistics (See Semantics)

Methodology

A. *Methodology* is the systematic and logical study of the principles guiding scientific investigation. It must not be confused with (a) substantive theory since it is only interested in the general grounds for the validity of theories, not in their content; (b) research procedures (general modes of investigation) and techniques (specific fact-finding or manipulating operations) themselves, since the methodologist evaluates procedures and techniques as to their ability to provide us with certain knowledge. Finally, methodology as a normative discipline differs sharply from the factual study of scientists at work as conducted e.g. by the sociology of knowledge, history of science.

B. 1. The term *methodology* in its original and proper usage refers to the systematic study of principles guiding scientific and philosophical investigation. Traditionally this discipline was seen as a branch of philosophy, more particularly as a branch of logic. Since philosophical methodology failed to answer many questions of practical importance to social scientists, they tended to become their own methodologists. As a consequence methodology in the social sciences came to be seen by many as a 'bent of mind' (P. F. Lazarsfeld & M. Rosenberg (eds.), *The Language*

of Social Research, Glencoe, Ill.: The Free Press, 1955, p. 4) rather than an independent discipline, and the term came to be applied by some in a loose fashion to *anything having to do with procedures or techniques of investigation*. Today it is sometimes applied in a colloquial sense to the totality of investigative procedures and techniques customary in a specific science (an informal plural of 'method') or the set of research techniques used in one piece of research. In this second, informal sense the term *methodology* refers to the subject matter of *methodology* used in the original sense.

2. The definition of methodology emerging from the work of German post-Kantian philosophers exercised considerable influence on contemporary usage through M. Weber, A. von Schelting, and T. Parsons. Methodology is seen as a separate discipline studying the different methods of gaining scientific knowledge. It differs, however, from other approaches to the study of science in that it does not concern itself with the actual processes involved in scientific research, as the psychology of cognition or the sociology of knowledge might do. Instead the methodologist examines systematically and logically the aptness of all research tools, varying from basic assumptions to special research techniques, for the scientific purpose. Methodology is in this sense a normative discipline. Yet it does not impose values on empirical science from without but discovers its inherent norm. F. Kaufmann (*Methodology of the Social Sciences*, London: Oxford University Press, 1944, p. 240) expresses this point in modern terms: 'Methodology does not speak "about" empirical science in the same sense as empirical science speaks about the world; it rather clarifies the meaning of "empirical science" '.

3. Within this concept of methodology some writers emphasize strongly the general, more philosophical pole, others the pole of special problems of actual investigation. T. Parsons tends toward the philosophical pole when he says that methodology does not refer 'primarily to "methods" of empirical research such as statistics, case study, interview, and the like. These latter it is preferable to call research techniques. Methodology is the consideration of the general grounds for the validity of scientific procedures and systems of them. It is as such neither a strictly scientific nor a strictly philosophical discipline' (*The Structure of Social Action*, New York: McGraw-Hill, 1937, pp. 23–4).

A similar view is held by J. C. McKinney who states: 'The methodologist makes certain

425

Metropolitan Area

necessary assumptions about the world and then proceeds to structure the inquiry concerning it. On the other hand, the philosopher, the logician, and the epistemologist focus upon and wrestle with the assumptions themselves' ('Methodology, Procedures, and Techniques in Sociology', in H. P. Becker & A. Boskoff (eds.), *Modern Sociological Theory in Continuity and Change*, New York: Dryden Press, 1957, p. 187). McKinney seems to include in the concept *methodology* what R. K. Merton (*Social Theory and Social Structure*, Glencoe, Ill.: The Free Press, 1957, pp. 87–9) excludes as 'general sociological orientations', i.e. broad postulates which are for Merton the beginning of a substantive theory. The difference is, however, more apparent than real. Basic postulates have of course both theoretical and methodological consequences. Compared to the usage of *methodology* in the writings of Parsons, McKinney, Merton and especially F. Znaniecki (*The Method of Sociology*, New York: Farrar & Rinehart, 1934), there is a different emphasis in, for example, Lazarsfeld's and Rosenberg's work, '... the methodologist codifies ongoing research practices to bring out what is consistent about them and deserves to be taken into account the next time' (*The Language of Social Research*, p. 4). Clearly, they use the same overall definition of *methodology* as, for example, Weber and von Schelting. Yet within this definition they place more emphasis on the analysis of concrete research procedures and techniques than, for example, Parsons, who focuses more on the basic, or general methodological problems.

Burkart Holzner

See also: SCIENCE

Metropolitan Area
(Also **Standard Metropolitan Area**)

A. This term is used in a number of ways although each usage shares the idea that the *metropolitan area* is a territorial space related to a metropolitan centre or centres.

B. 1. The earliest widespread use of this term in social science is that of the human ecologists such as N. S. B. Gras, R. D. McKenzie, A. Hawley, and D. Bogue. These ecologists defined the *metropolitan area* in the sense of a metropolitan community with a centre of dominance (q.v.).

2. The metropolitan area also is a concept in the censuses of many western countries, but definition varies from country to country and census to census. In the United States, for example, the 1940 Census defined a metropolitan district as an area with a central city of 50,000 or more population and all contiguous land with a population density of 150 or more per square mile. The 1950 Census worked with the constructs of urbanized area and standard metropolitan area (SMA), the latter concept becoming the Standard Metropolitan Statistical Area (SMSA) for the 1960 Census. Urbanized areas correspond to what are called conurbations (q.v.) in some other countries. The Census of Population for 1960 gives the following definition for an SMSA: 'Except in New England, an SMSA is a county or group of contiguous counties which contains at least one city of 50,000 inhabitants or more or "twin cities" with a combined population of at least 50,000. In addition to the county, or counties, contiguous counties are included in an SMSA if, according to certain criteria, they are essentially metropolitan in character and are socially and economically integrated with the central city' (U.S. Bureau of the Census, *U.S. Census of Population: 1960. Number of Inhabitants, United States Summary*. Final Report PC (1)–1A. Washington, D.C.: U.S. Government Printing Office, 1961, p. xxiv). The criteria followed by the U.S. Bureau of the Census to delineate SMSAs relate to a city, or cities, of sufficient size to constitute the central city and to the economic and social relationships with counties that are metropolitan in character (ibid.). In 1960 there were 212 Standard Metropolitan Statistical Areas in the U.S.A., containing a population of 112,885,178.

Albert J. Reiss, Jr.

See also: CONURBATION

Middle Class

A. *Middle class* denotes, broadly, that stratum within a social structure that is deemed 'intermediate' between the 'upper class' and the 'working class'. The lines of demarcation, however, are not precise and are dependent upon a number of varying and ambiguous criteria. The most frequently adopted criterion relates to occupation. Developments within the occupational structure of advanced societies create conceptual as well as practical difficulties in attempts to draw clear boundaries for the middle class: the core of the class membership being more readily located in occupational terms. It should be noted, also, that a shift in occupational status does not of itself create more than the conditions for a shift in class orientation, attitudes, interests, or loyalties. The notion of the middle class (or classes) is to an inevitable extent coloured by the social and political history of the societies in which it is an element: and within any one society (as well as within societies of comparable type) its meaning develops over time—the most significant development being the line of distinction, noted by social scientists, between the old and the new middle classes.

B. The concept of the 'middle ranks' of society is a very old one—being advanced, with varying precision, from Greco-Roman times. In the 18th century in England and Scotland the term *rank* was widely used in the context of what is now called social stratification (e.g. J. Millar, *Observations concerning the Distinction of Ranks in Society*, London: J. Murray, 1771). In the same century the term *middle ranks*, as intermediate between the nobility and the common people, was used increasingly to describe the new groups that were profiting from the great English expansion of trade and commerce. With the development of steam technology and the further impetus that this gave to economic growth, the image of society which had postulated an hierarchical ranking within an ordered continuum came under slow but intensive review. The manufacturing 'interest' developed a sense of its own distinctiveness in terms of its real or potential contribution to the society. Its spokesmen came to emphasize its utility to the disparagement of that of the 'landed interest'. Indeed the term *middle class* seems to have gained currency as a term of self-praise. For a time, in the early 1840s, such self-praise assumed and encouraged a homogeneity of interest and attitude that had no lasting reality. To some extent this homogeneity was incorporated into the classical attributes of the 'capitalist' or 'bourgeois' class in Marxist writings in the same period and it became both source and conclusion of many a Marxist argument. Later in the 19th century, some Marxist writers were to comment upon the 'aristocratic' bias of the British bourgeoisie in the 'most bourgeois of nations'. Throughout the 19th century the place of the 'liberal professions' was located within this middle class—though the sources of their income differed greatly from case to case, though they were not engaged in productive industry, and though they were far from homogeneous in their outlooks.

The size of this class in 19th-century England is difficult to ascertain. P. Laslett argues that the numbers of the so-called 'solid middle class' were much inflated by widespread social mi-

mesis among aspirants to such status: and that this class 'consisted at most of about a seventeenth' of a total population of nearly forty million people ('The Solid Middle Classes', *The Listener*, 4 January 1962, pp. 13–14). (On the origins of the 'middle class' see A. Briggs. 'The Language of Class in Early Nineteenth Century England', in A. Briggs & J. Saville (eds.), *Essays in Labour History*, London: Macmillan 1960, p. 43 et seq.).

C. In its more recent usage the focus of the term has widened—and the norm of a solid homogeneous grouping has become still less plausible or acceptable. The divergence from the norm has been sharpened by new trends, both technological and managerial, which have brought into being the *new middle class* (cf. E. Lederer & J. Marschak, 'Der Neue Mittelstand', in *Grundriss der Sozialökonomik*, Sect. IX, pt. I, 1926) and which have introduced a further 'blur' into the boundaries between 'middle' and 'inferior' classes. Thus, to take one example from many, C. W. Mills notes the following strata in 'Central City' in 1945: (1) 'Big Business and Executives', (2) Small Business and Free Professionals', (3) 'Higher White Collar' and (4) 'Lower White Collar' and adds that 'these strata fall objectively into the "old" (1 and 2) and the "new" middle classes (3 and 4). Both these classes, however, are definitely split by income, and this split ... is also true of other variables' ('*The Middle Classes in Middle Sized Cities*', *American Sociological Review*, 1946, vol. 11, p. 521). More recently, especially in political sociology, American writers have explored the political orientations of the various segments of the middle class. Thus D. Bell speaks of 'the dispossessed' among the 'old' American middle class ('The Dispossessed', in D. Bell (ed.), *The Radical Right*, New York: Doubleday, 1963, p. 25) and D. Riesman and N. Glazer describe 'a new middle class' as 'former masses' ('The Intellectuals and the Discontented Classes', in Bell, op cit., p. 90).

In the American situation special features have attended the whole discussion, both by social scientists and others, on the issue of class. In a celebrated survey in 1959 in which Americans were asked 'To what social class do you feel you belong?' 88 per cent replied 'middle class'. Commenting upon this response, L. Reissman (*Class in American Society*, London: Routledge & Kegan Paul, 1960, p. 12) relates it acutely to the general American concern with 'equality' and notes that 'the psychological

Migration

emphasis is upon the word "middle" and not upon the word "class".'

D. T. H. Marshall, in a survey of the subject at the Third World Congress of Sociology in 1956, concluded that 'most Western societies have been developing an enormous middle class (with relatively little above and below it)' ('Change in Social Stratification', in T. H. Marshall, *Sociology at the Crossroads*, London: Heinemann, 1963, p. 148). To the extent that this is so, the term may be said to lose both analytic and descriptive value. There is indeed some tendency to use the term pejoratively—to describe qualities or developments deemed inimical to a real or imaginary working-class culture. But there is no unanimity among social scientists that, in all Western societies, entry into the 'middle class' has been as widespread as it sometimes appears. Nor is it agreed that, by crossing certain occupational lines or acquiring new improved levels of living, the former 'working-class' members also acquire, or aspire to, 'middle-class' standing in their society.

J. Gould

See also: SOCIAL CLASS
WORKING CLASS

Migrant (See **Migration**)

Migration

A. The term as used in the social sciences refers to geographical movements of individuals or groups. In specialized literature types of migration are distinguished, e.g. internal and external; voluntary and involuntary; primary and secondary; complete and incomplete; conservative or innovating; short term or long term.

B. 1. International agencies have endeavoured to provide a definition in order to make possible the preparation of comparable statistics of emigration and immigration. Thus the International Labour Office suggested that 'Statistics of permanent migration should cover every person passing from one country to another for more than a year, whatever the reason for their removal … The statistics of temporary migration should cover every person who passes from one country to another for more than a month and not more than a year, for the purpose of carrying on an occupation' (I.L.O., Studies and Reports, Series N. (Statistics) no. 18. *Statistics of Migration*, Geneva, 1932, p. 28).

In the light of discussion between statistical experts in this field and of current usage, both common and technical, the U.N. Department of Social Affairs (*Problems of Migration Statistics*, United Nations: New York, 1949, pp. 3–4) placed within the category of migrants those travellers who are not (a) tourists, businessmen, students, transit passengers; (b) residents in frontier areas engaging in frequent 'frontier traffic'; (c) refugees, displaced persons, transferred populations. The two important groups which remain are (a) those who come seeking employment either permanent or seasonal or temporary; and (b) dependents of such persons. These latter groups constitute the *migrants;* and their movements constitute *migration.*

2. R. G. Latham in tracing the main movements of populations throughout the world, distinguished between *primary* and *secondary migrations*. The former meant occupation of hitherto uninhabited territories while the latter involved contact with an indigenous population and consequent social adaptation. 'Secondary migrations … differ from primary in many respects. They are slower, because the resistance is that of Humanity to Humanity; and they are violent because dispossession is the object. They are partial, abortive, followed by fusion of different populations; or followed by their extermination as the case may be' (*Man and His Migrations*, London, 1851, pp. 155–6).

3. R. Mayo-Smith distinguished between *internal* and *external migration*. The former took place within the limits of a single nation-state and the latter crossed international boundaries giving rise to *emigration* and *immigration* (*Emigration and Immigration*, London: Fisher Unwin, 1890; and 'Migration' in the *Encyclopaedia Britannica*, 11th edn., vol. XVIII, pp. 427–33). Other writers such as A. M. Carr-Saunders made a further distinction between *intra-continental* and *inter-continental migration*. The latter also drew attention to the difficulty in giving a precise definition to the term *migrant* for statistical purposes: 'Who is a migrant? One who leaves a country in order to take up permanent residence in another country, it may be replied. Yes, but intention is not enough. The migrants must fulfil it, and then the question arises how long he must live in a new country in order to be considered a resident' (*World Population*, Oxford: Clarendon Press, 1936, p. 15).

4. Most migrations are a voluntary response to an expectation that removal will lead to an increase in overall gratification or a diminution of deprivation. But there are also the forced migrations of those who are expelled by invaders, taken as slaves, involved in compulsory transfers of population or who are refugees from religious or political persecution. Having been coerced into emigrating the latter sometimes find themselves unable to complete the process by becoming acceptable immigrants in another country. They are then compelled to remain in camps for displaced persons under international supervision. In this respect emigration and immigration are not merely the same phenomenon seen from different points of view, but may involve 'incomplete migration' (J. Isaac, *Economics of Migration*, London: Kegan Paul, Trench & Trubner, 1947, pp. 2–4).

5. A distinction has been made between *conservative* migration, which aims to preserve a way of life, and *innovating*, which involves radical change. It has been pointed out also that some international migration is part of the process of urbanization, and the crossing of national boundaries merely incidental to it (W. Petersen, 'A General Typology of Migration', *American Sociological Review*, 1958, vol. 23, pp. 256–66). Studies of international migration since the second world war have also recognized that an increasing number of people, while fulfilling international definitions of migrants, are only short-term residents in the receiving country. They either remigrate or return to their former country, not because they are dissatisfied or maladjusted, but because this was their original intention having achieved their particular goals (J. Isaac, 'British Post-War Migration', National Institute of Economic and Social Research, *Occasional Paper XVII*, Cambridge University Press, 1954).

A. H. Richmond

Milieu (See Environment)

Militarism

A. *Militarism* may be defined as the compound of militancy, preponderance of the army in the state, adulation of military virtues, and militarization. Where all four components are present to a high degree (e.g. Japan under Tojo), we have a clear case of militarism. Where only two or three are in evidence we might speak of partial militarism. Different types of militarism could be distinguished in accordance with the relative strength of the components.

B. Militarism is used in several distinct senses.

1. It is sometimes taken to mean militancy or aggressive foreign policy involving the readiness to resort to war. It does not seem profitable to adopt this usage as the words *militancy* and *combativeness* adequately describe these features.

2. In other contexts *militarism* means preponderance of the military in the state.

(a) Such a preponderance implies a differentiation of civil and military spheres of authority, and of civil and military administrative personnel. It would be improper, therefore, to apply the term *militarism* in this sense to situations where such differentiations are absent, as was the case in all primitive states such as, for instance, the Zulu and Ankole kingdoms in Africa, or the Polish kingdom under early Piasts, or even the enormous empire of Genghis Khan. Whereas the differentiation of the roles of the chief priest and of the war leader occurs even in small tribes, the first trace of a distinction between military and civil (to be exact—financial) spheres of authority, exercised over the same subjects, appears in the Persian Empire in the 5th century B.C. Although some American Indian tribes had war chiefs as well as peace chiefs, this arrangement constituted neither a division of authority over the same persons nor an allocation of the population to permanent units; it could be best described as alternation of types of authority.

(b) An important feature distinguishing different kinds of preponderance of the military is the extent to which the rank and file share the privileges of those at the top of the hierarchy. Variations in this respect depend on the military participation ratio, which has been defined as 'the proportion of militarily utilized individuals in the total population [of the state]' (S. Andrzejewski, *Military Organization and Society*, London: Routledge & Kegan Paul, 1954, p. 33). Obviously, if the military participation ratio is very high the privileges of the rank and file have to be diluted to the point of non-existence. Germany under Wilhelm II and Poland under Pilsudski exemplify a variant where political preponderance and economic favours were restricted to the officer corps. The late Roman Empire, on the other hand, is an instance of the more inclusive variant, the distinctive feature of which is the inclusion of all soldiers in the privileged body. The connection between the preponderance of the military and bureaucracy depends on the type of military organization.

Contrary to widespread opinion, this preponderance is not necessarily accompanied by external militancy: Tokugawa Shogunate in Japan, as well as a number of Latin American military dictatorships are examples to the point.

Mind

3. *Militarism* can also be interpreted as connoting the extensive control by the military over social life, coupled with the subservience of the whole society to the needs of the army. This leads usually to a recasting of various parts of the social life in accordance with the pattern of military organization. It seems, however, that we might reduce the danger of ambiguity if we use the term *militarization* instead of *militarism* to describe this phenomenon. Militarization can occur without the preponderance of the military as can be seen from the examples of Britain and the U.S. during the Second World War; nevertheless it seems that this can be so only in the short run. On the other hand many cases show— a number of Latin American dictatorships, for instance—that preponderance of the army can endure without producing a wholesale militarization.

4. It has been proposed by some writers that by *militarism* we should mean the pointless, or even harmful from the point of view of efficiency, addiction to drill and ceremonies, and adulation of trappings. But the tendency towards a shift of valuation from ends to means, and from content to form, is a ubiquitous social phenomenon; and *militarism* in this sense is thus merely a manifestation of this tendency in the military field. This usage seems to be unprofitably restricted.

5. Sometimes the word *militarism* is used to refer not to an institutional arrangement but to an ideology propagating military ideals. Such an ideology often accompanies preponderance of the army (e.g. Germany under the Hohenzollerns, Japan under Tojo). Yet the latter can occur without it (e.g. Cuba under Batista, where the soldiers ruled but were rather despised than admired). Furthermore an ideology extolling the soldier and the military virtues may flourish even where the army is weak (e.g. Germany at the time of the Weimar Republic). For the sake of clarity it would be better to speak of *militaristic ideology* than of *militarism* in this sense.

6. There is an interesting phenomenon which, however, it would be inappropriate to call *militarism*: namely, the inclination to imitate military demeanour and paraphernalia in the walks of life entirely unconnected with war. The example of the Salvation Army shows that such a practice can flourish even where militarism is not prominent.

S. Andreski

Militarization (See **Militarism**)

430

Mind

A. In the most general sense *mind* denotes (a) the organized totality of psychical structures and processes, conscious and unconscious; (b) the total activity of a man or animal in responding to internal or external stimulation in relation to experience in the past and expectancy of the future; (c) (metaphysical) the entity or substratum underlying psychical structures and processes (J. Royce, 'Mind', in J. Hastings (ed.), *Encyclopaedia of Religion and Ethics*, New York: Charles Scribner's Sons, vol. 8, 1915) *or* a substance which pervades individual minds and which contrasts with material substance.

B. First among the modern British thinkers to adopt an empirical conception of *mind* were Hobbes and Locke, but use of the term and shifts in emphasis (even if we confine attention to English practice) are suffused with a variety of religious and cosmological overtones drawn from Christian and pre-Christian ideas about the 'psyche' or soul. In more recent times, some writers have gone so far as to say that the word *mind* is devoid of meaning: 'Psychology is supposed to be the study of mind, but since no one knows what is meant by mind, it is impossible to define psychology' (C. C. Pratt, *The Logic of Modern Psychology*, New York: The Macmillan Co., 1939, p. viii). He continues: 'There is no such thing as mind—at least not with a capital "m" … for all scientific intents and purposes the concept has already outlived its usefulness (ibid., p. 26). Nonetheless the term is more than a historical curiosity and the following points are designed to indicate briefly some of the problems of, and development in, usage.

1. *Passive or active nature of mind.* Locke, while repudiating the belief in innate ideas and declaring that knowledge and ideas are developed in the course of individual experience, retained a passive notion of mind. It was not until Mill that the active principle, 'mental chemistry', was introduced into British thought.

2. *Mind as organization.* The *organized* quality of all mental processes has been emphasized by the Gestalt psychologists in their attack on the 'atomism' of the associationists, although in Gestalt theory the mind is as passive as it is in associationism.

3. *Mind as dynamic structure.* The conception of mind as a dynamic structure, shaped genetically, of inter-related conscious and unconscious agencies is a contribution of Freudian theory. C. G. Jung, in addition, attaches considerable importance to archetypes of the collective unconscious.

4. *Mind-body problem.* Views on this vary from the common-sense position of psychophysical interactionism to the extremes of (a) idealist or dualist view of mind, as a world of psychical processes subject to its own causal principles sui generis; (b) materialist or Marxist viewpoint, which regards the word *mind* as denoting at best an epiphenomenon or metaphysical entity, and, at worst, a mere ghost in the machine.

5. *Individual or group mind.* Those who find the word *mind* useful normally mean by it a property of *individual* man, as Sir Charles Sherrington insisted: 'mind, always, as we know it, finite and individual, is individually insulated and devoid of direct liaison with other minds' (*Man on his Nature*, London: Cambridge University Press, 1951, p. 206). But it is not uncommon to find references to a *group mind* (MacDougall, Lewin), and to the 'minds' of animals. Such Western usage in which *mind* signifies a 'phenomenon' contrasts strikingly with Eastern religious psychology where a connexion is assumed between individual 'mind' and a hypothetical Universal Mind (C. G. Jung, *Psychology and Religion: West and East*, trans. by R. F. C. Hull, London: Routledge & Kegan Paul, 1958, pp. 475–6). The Eastern view is only encountered in Western mystics such as M. Eckhart.

J. Cohen

C. *Mind* is not, at the present time, a definitive concept in American social sciences. It rarely appears in the indexes of books, and is even absent from some dictionaries. As each field has turned from philosophical interests to the behaviouristic, quantitative approaches, *mind* is rarely used and is even less frequently discussed or defined.

1. There is some degree of truth in G. Allport's (*Personality*, New York: Henry Holt, 1946, p. 238) observation that 'Mind is capable of being all things to all psychologists, according to their personal lines of interest'. To him, however, '... the most essential characteristics of mind [are] locus, organic quality, reciprocal action of parts, and self-consciousness' (ibid., p. 5). D. O. Hebb (*Organization of Behaviour*, London: Chapman & Hall, 1949, p. xiv) holds that 'Mind can only be regarded, for scientific purposes, as the activity of the brain, ...' Here, as with certain other writers, the reader may draw the inference that mind and some organic entity such as the brain are akin, and perhaps identical.

2. In contrast to those who locate the mind in the body are the social scientists who see mind as process or activity involving more than the organism. W. Coutu (*Emergent Human Nature*, New York: Knopf, 1949, pp. 302, 303, 308) states that 'Mind is emergent behavior; it is a social phenomenon. ... Mind occurs rather than exists. ... Its locus is between people; it is interactional, not spatial'. In the same trend is G. H. Mead (*Mind, Self and Society*, Chicago: The University of Chicago Press, 1934, pp. 118–33), whose influence upon Coutu is well known. Mead writes: 'What I suggested as characteristic of the mind is the reflective intelligence of the human animal. ... We speak of a human being thinking a thing out, or having a mind. ... This is the point at which mind appears, or if you like emerges, [i.e.] ... When the organism is able to point out meanings to others and to himself ... mind is essentially a social phenomenon ...'.

To some, not only is mind not 'inner', but it is also more than cognitive or intellectual in nature. They see mind as involving non-cognitive learning and impulses as well. C. H. Cooley (*Social Process*, New York: Charles Scribner's Sons, 1922, p. 357) alludes to mind as something greater than intelligence, speaking of intelligent and unintelligent minds, and stating that 'Intelligence, in the fullest sense, is wisdom, and wisdom draws upon every resource of the mind'. Cooley further indicates the more-than-intellectual nature of mind by observing that 'The obscure impulses that pass from man to man ... have quite as much to do with the building of the collective mind as has explicit reasoning' (ibid.). E. Jordan (*Forms of Individuality*, Indianapolis, Ind.: Lane, 1927, pp. 142, 154) carries this point further with the statement 'It is therefore the mind that sees, feels, hears, imagines, thinks, etc., and the mind in its entirety in each case. ... The mind is then not a hodge-podge of severable functions of sensation, perception, reason, etc., but as a whole acts in one connection as sensation and in other connections as perception, memory, imagination, etc. It takes all the mind I have to see, perceive, imagine, think, etc.'

Richard Dewey

See also: LEARNING
MENTALITY
REASON

Minister

A. In the United Kingdom there are two political uses of minister, both fairly clear. The term refers to (a) diplomatic representative, and (more

Ministry

common) (b) members of the House of Commons or House of Lords who (with the exception of Ministers without Portfolio) are political heads of government departments or charged with other special responsibilities placing them in the Cabinet or associating them with it.

B. In the plural the term may be used to refer to these alone or it may refer both to these and to their parliamentary assistants. When the latter are referred to separately they are called *junior ministers*. Ministers in the narrower sense include both office holders with the actual title of Minister (e.g. Minister of Health) and with other titles (e.g. Secretary of State for Scotland). No junior ministers have 'minister' in their titles: most of them are called parliamentary secretaries (to chiefs entitled Minister) or parliamentary under-secretaries (to Secretaries of State). The more comprehensive use in the plural is the distributive equivalent of the collective Ministry (q.v.), a term covering both members of the Cabinet and non-Cabinet Ministers. Ministers actually in the Cabinet should strictly be called *Cabinet Ministers*.

C. The English usage of the term has moved from the generalized sense of any kind of servant or agent acting for a principal (with the latter of which is associated the use of the verb 'to minister to'—i.e. to look after the wants of) to two main senses (a) ecclesiastical—certain kinds of Protestant clergymen, (b) political and constitutional—a high officer of state. Until the early 19th century the second use was imprecise and was liable to include types of official that would today be called civil servants.

Wilfrid Harrison

See also: Cabinet
 Government
 Ministry

Ministry

A. In British constitutional and political use *ministry* may denote:

1. The Ministers of the Crown collectively in their role as the heads of the Government of the day (cf. the use of *administration* (q.v.) in this sense). Sometimes this means Ministers actually in the Cabinet; on other occasions it refers both to these and to Ministers not in the Cabinet.

2. A government department presided over by a minister actually so called (e.g. a department such as the Ministry of Labour under the Minister of Labour, as distinct from one such as the Foreign Office under the Secretary of State for Foreign Affairs or the Board of Trade under its President).

3. More loosely (a) the building in which a Ministry under a Minister is housed; (b) any department of State. (The plural is commonly used to refer to departments of State collectively—a synonymous use is 'Whitehall' derived from the street in London which has housed a number of government departments; (c) any building of any department, or any regional or local office of any department.

It may also refer (in any of the above senses) to such features of another political system which seems to be a counterpart of a like institution in the United Kingdom.

Uses in Northern Ireland and the Irish Republic and in the countries of the British Commonwealth are similar.

B. In political and constitutional contexts the usages perhaps most common are A. (2) and A. (3) (b) above. They probably have the merit that they indicate that the departments referred to differ from other forms of British administrative organization (e.g. Public Corporations, or Local Authorities) in that these departments will be staffed by Civil Servants, and will be directly under Ministers and, therefore, come clearly within the scope of ministerial responsibility, treasury control, the comptroller and auditor-general and the Public Accounts Committee. The other uses are, in general, not very precise, and it is generally best to substitute another term if one is available, e.g. for A. (1) the *Cabinet* or *Ministers;* for A. (3) (a) the title of the department or a more distinctive description of its address; for A. (3) (c) e.g. 'the regional office of the Ministry of X'; and for political systems other than the British, the actual use current in the country in question (see A. above).

Wilfrid Harrison

See also: Minister

Minority (Political Science) (See **Majority**)

Minority: Minority Group

A. The term *minority group*, sometimes *minority*, is often used as a synonym for ethnic, racial, and religious groups. There appears to be a tendency to utilize the term *ethnic group* when invidious distinctions are not under consideration and to use the term *minority group* to imply invidious distinctions. Both terms have physical, religious, racial, and other cultural characteristics or referents. It would appear that a modification of R. A. Schermerhorn's discussion (see B. below) would cover the essential characteristics of minority groups as observed both in American and non-American societies: Minorities are sub-groups within a culture which are distinguishable from the dominant group in power by reason of differences in physical feature, language, customs or cultural patterns (including any one or combination of these factors). Such sub-groups are regarded (or regard themselves) as inherently different from the dominant power group; for this reason they withdraw from or are consciously or unconsciously excluded from full participation in the life of the culture. Such a definition would include groups with secessionist, pluralist, or assimilationist orientations as defined by L. Wirth (see B. below).

B. The use of the term *minority group* has been confused by uncertainties as to the characteristics which may properly be said to centre *minority* status on a group. These include statistical or numerical size, power distribution (social or political), homogeneous physical or cultural traits, and differential treatment or status. The latter can be further subdivided as to whether or not the differential treatment is self-imposed and whether or not there is a collective awareness of differential treatment on the part of the members of the minority group. There is a wide consensus among sociologists that the term should not be regarded as a statistical concept. The classical definition is that of L. Wirth who said: 'We may define a minority as a group of people who, because of their physical or cultural characteristics, are singled out from the others in the society in which they live for differential and unequal treatment, and who therefore regard themselves as objects of collective discrimination ... Minority status carries with it the exclusion from full participation in the life of the society' ('The Problem of Minority Groups', in R. Linton (ed.), *The Science of Man in the World Crisis*, New York: Columbia University Press, 1945, p. 347).

While Wirth placed the minority group in opposition to the majority group, A. M. and C. B. Rose, rejecting any purely numerical definition, give special emphasis to this opposition in their definition: 'The mere fact of being generally hated and being hated because of religious, racial or national background is what defines a minority group' (*America Divided*, New York: Knopf, 1948, p. 3).

Unlike Wirth and Rose, R. A. Schermerhorn gives a definition of minority group which does not require a conscious application of differential treatment of the minority group on the part of the dominant or majority group. Schermerhorn says, 'Minorities are sub-groups within a culture which are distinguished from the dominant group by reason of differences in physiognomy, language, customs or cultural patterns (including any combination of these factors). Such sub-groups are regarded as inherently different and "Not belonging" to the dominant group; for this reason they are consciously or unconsciously excluded from full participation in the life of the culture' (*These Our People*, Boston: Heath, 1949, p. 5).

Preston Valien

See also: RACE AND MINORITY GROUP
RELATIONS

Mob

A. *Mob* denotes an active collectivity akin to or analogous with *crowd* (q.v.). The minimal requirements of a sociological definition are spatial contiguity, instability, and collective action under the influence of a common emotional impulse rather than oriented to institutionalized roles and statuses. An inclusive definition of this sort has, moreover, the advantage of allowing subclassification along any one of several dimensions. Thus the classification into aggressive, escape, expressive, and acquisitive mob draws on the substance and meaning of the behaviour; it is equally possible to classify mobs on the basis of their forms of organization by distinguishing the mob that acts in concert, from that which acts competitively, and that which exists primarily in parallel actions, and so forth.

The characteristics imputed to the mob-mind and the nature of suggestion as well as its effects on individual thought process are not essential to the above definition.

B. Initially *mob* was not employed as a rigorously defined sociological category with a clearly delineated form. The psychological crowd or mob, it was recognized, formed more easily when members were physically present, but it was not necessarily a physical contact group. Writers influenced by the collective psychology of Sighele, Tarde, and Le Bon have emphasized the irrationality and excesses of which people are capable when acting under the influence of the 'mob mind'. In line with this tradition, E. A. Ross insists that 'mental touch is no longer bound up with physical proximity' and that with rapid communication 'remote people are brought, as it were, into one another's presence'

Mobility

(*Social Psychology*, New York: The Macmillan Co., 1908, p. 63). Writers governed by this usage have drawn attention to the intellectual inferiority of large numbers, regardless of setting, as long as they act under the impulse of a common emotion. A good illustration of this usage, which is still common, is E. A. Strecker's explicit premise that one should think of the 'crowd and the mob and even the highly emotionalized permanent group as concerted and massive attempts to evade reality' (*Beyond the Clinical Frontier*, London: Chapman & Hall, 1940, p. 61).

C. Three main characteristics are commonly used to differentiate between the mob and related categories of formal sociology, irrespective of whether the mob is contrasted to the crowd or defined as one of its subspecies.

1. The first is activity. H. D. Lasswell and A. Kaplan consider the mob as 'a crowd in action' (*Power and Society*, New Haven: Yale University Press, 1950, p. 40). A similar notion underlies R. W. Brown's classification of crowds (cf. 'Mass Phenomena', in G. Lindzey (ed.), *Handbook of Social Psychology*, Cambridge, Mass.: Addison-Wesley, 1954, p. 841). He makes a basic distinction between the active, mobile, kinetic mob and the passive and receptive audience (q.v.). The term *mob* is applied to four kinds of crowd phenomena: (a) aggressive mobs as in lynchings, terrorizations, and riots; (b) escape mobs exemplified by panics; (c) acquisitive mobs like those in bank runs or food-hoarding stampedes; and (d) expressive mobs which give vent to common emotions.

2. A second characteristic results in a more restricted usage which confines the term *mob* to a crowd 'that has a defined objective toward which the members act cooperatively or in concert' (E. B. Reuter, *Handbook of Sociology*, New York: Dryden Press, 1941, p. 136). The key requirement here is not merely action or motion but the existence of a common objective around which action is centred. Accordingly usage is confined to only one category within Brown's schema, namely the *aggressive mob* (ibid.). H. Blumer indicates that the '*acting*, aggressive crowd, [is] best represented by a revolutionary crowd or a lynching mob' ('Collective Behavior', in A. M. Lee (ed.), *New Outline of the Principles of Sociology*, New York: Barnes & Noble, 1946, p. 178), and R. T. LaPiere prefers to 'restrict the term "mob" to the members of a rebellious situation' (*Collective Behavior*, New York: McGraw-Hill, 1938, p. 526).

3. A third characteristic used in differentiating a mob from other types of crowds emphasizes the absence of clear foci of interaction rather than a common objective. Though there is some kind of spontaneous leadership in every mob, interaction tends to be of an each-to-everyone character, without clear polarization between a 'leader' (or speaker) and the crowd following. Instead there is a strengthening of ties among the participants, some kind of emotional rapport, and increased suggestibility and facilitation at the expense of the members' susceptibility to reasoned discourse. 'Strong interrelation among members of the mass forms the first and primary characteristic of the mob' (M. Bentley, 'A Preface to Social Psychology', in *Studies in Social and General Psychology from the University of Illinois*, vol. XXI, 1916, p. 22).

Kurt Lang

See also: AUDIENCE
          COLLECTIVE BEHAVIOUR
          CROWD

Mobility

A. In its most general sense, *mobility* denotes movement or the capacity to move. In the social sciences it denotes movement through physical space, sometimes called *physical mobility* or *geographic mobility*; or movement within the system of stratification (q.v.). If this latter movement represents a change of status and role, particularly in the occupational realm, without a change in social class position, it is called *horizontal mobility*. If such a change in status and role does involve a change in social class position it is called *vertical mobility*, with the sub-classes of *upward mobility* and *downward mobility*.

B. The primary scientific questions in recent years about mobility have been those of measuring it and accounting for it.

1. The measurement of geographic mobility is primarily a problem in demography, and that of physical mobility in other senses one of traffic-counting, etc. We have developed over the years, through the use of census questions and other methods, some rather clear pictures of the amount and direction of geographical mobility in Western societies. While horizontal mobility has been defined, it has not for the most part been an object of study, except as a residual category accompanying studies of vertical mobility. The problems of determining the amount, direction, and areas of location in the system of social stratification of mobility are extremely complex. From such studies, however, have emerged recent conclusions that the amount of mobility in the past was not as great as previously assumed; that there has not been a great decline in mobility, although here the question of what area of the system of stratification is being studied is relevant; and that industrial societies with strong open-class ideologies do not necessarily have greater mobility than industrial societies without such ideologies (cf. N. Rogoff, *Recent Trends in Occupational Mobility*, Glencoe, Ill.: Free Press, 1953; S. M. Lipset & R. Bendix, *Social Mobility in Industrial Societies*, Berkeley, Cal.: University of California Press, 1959; D. V. Glass, *Social Mobility in Britain*, London: Routledge & Kegan Paul, 1954; and S. M. Miller, 'Comparative Social Mobility', *Current Sociology*, vol. IX, no. 1, 1960).

2. Theoretical efforts and studies to account for mobility have been fewer than studies of the incidence and amount of mobility. One of the few serious theoretical and empirical efforts to explain certain aspects of geographic mobility is S. Stouffer's 'Intervening Opportunities: A Theory Relating Mobility and Distance' (*American Sociological Review*, vol. 5, 1940, pp. 845–68). In this study an effort was made to test the hypothesis that 'the number of people going a given distance is directly proportional to the number of opportunities at that distance and inversely proportional to the number of intervening opportunities' (ibid., p. 846).

Studies of the determinants of mobility within the system of social stratification have for the most part centred on the nature of the institutional structure of the system, including both the value elements and the actual expansion or contraction of the number of positions located at various points within the system. In recent years some attention has been paid to the motivational elements of such mobility (see, for example, J. A. Kahl, 'Educational and Occupational Aspirations of "Common Man" Boys', *Harvard Educational Review*, vol. 23, 1953, pp. 186–203).

William L. Kolb

See also: SOCIAL CLASS
STRATIFICATION

Modal Personality (See Basic Personality Structure)

Model (Theoretical Model)

The term *model* or *theoretical model* is an expression occurring within the sciences and in accounts of the working of the sciences. It designates any one of a range of things which form a kind of continuum:

1. It may denote an actual physical model, i.e. an artifact such that its parts, their relations, and its working are suitably analogous to some other system, so that by observing the artifact, by producing changes in it and seeing their consequences, inferences can be made about the system of which the artifact is a 'model'.

2. It may denote a merely conceptual model, i.e. the envisaging or the specification in words of an artifact as described in (1) without actually building it.

3. It may denote the envisaging or the specification in words of a system simpler in various ways than some other system of which it is a model, simpler but not otherwise dissimilar. It may be simpler, for instance, in there being fewer variables and their values being known with precision. A model in this sense is similar to the kinds described under (1) and (2) in that simplification and greater determinateness are generally involved, but it differs from them in that the relations of the real system are *not* so to speak *reproduced in some other medium*, either in reality or in the imagination. A model in this sense is merely the indication of a simpler and more accurately determinable state of affairs, with the intention of facilitating deduction of further consequences which can then be tentatively reapplied to the more complex and elusive real system. By describing a system by means of definite postulates which specify the properties of the model, and thus in a way give rise to it, it becomes possible to deduce further consequences *from* the postulates and about the model by rigorous deduction.

4. There is a tendency to call any theory whatever a model, in as far as *any* theory tends to possess at least unwittingly the features intended to characterize models in the sense (3).

5. By a similar argument, it has been maintained that any proposition whatever, whether theoretical or not, either is or represents a *model*.

There is no sharp line in the transition from (1) to (5): merely imaginary models may subsequently have artifacts built for them, unselfconscious theories may lead to deliberate simplifications for purposes of analysis or vice versa, propositions may become theories, and so on. Nevertheless, it is probably more useful to restrict the expression to the first three kinds of *theoretical model*.

E. A. Gellner

See also: FRAME OF REFERENCE

Moiety

Moiety

A. *Moiety* denotes (a) a social group which is one of two divisions within a society or (b) a sub-type of this broader category. The strictest definition includes only social units which are one of a total of two mutually exclusive divisions within a society, membership in which passes through males—*patrimoiety*—or through females—*matrimoiety*; marriage between members of such a group is disapproved if not totally forbidden upon penalty of death.

B. The term *moiety* as used in the social sciences was first employed by A. W. Howitt in 1888 to describe a unilineal descent group present among Aboriginal tribes in eastern Australia ('Further Notes on the Australian Class Systems', *Journal of the Anthropological Institute*, vol. XVIII, 1888, p. 39). This social unit discussed by Howitt had the essential characteristics of the moiety as that term is now applied in both the United States and England when scholars are using the strictest and most precise definition. As R. H. Lowie has written: 'A moiety is one of two exogamous clans in a tribe. Hence, neither a unit that forces members to marry among themselves nor a unit without a definite rule of descent belongs in the same category' (*An Introduction to Cultural Anthropology*, New York: Farrar & Rinehart, 1934, p. 262). E. W. Gifford has pointed out that total exogamy is not an essential characteristic of the moiety; for instance, the relatives of a Miwok couple about to marry endogamously 'merely objected and pointed out the impropriety of such marriages' ('Miwok Moieties', *University of California Publications in American Archaeology and Ethnology*, vol. 12, Berkeley: University of California Press, 1916, p. 141). Moieties may, but need not, contain sub-divisions such as phratries (q.v.) and clans (q.v.).

Moieties under the above definition are common in Australia, Melanesia, and North America (R. H. Lowie, 'Social Organisation', in E. R. A. Seligman (ed.), *Encyclopedia of the Social Sciences*, New York: The Macmillan Co., 1934, vol. XIV, p. 143). In Africa they are restricted to the Galla (A. R. Radcliffe-Brown, 'Introduction', to A. R. Radcliffe-Brown & D. Forde (eds.), *African Systems of Kinship and Marriage*, London: Oxford University Press, 1950, p. 39).

C. Anthropologists, including Lowie, have used *moiety* with another more generalized meaning of a social unit which is one of two divisions of a society, without regard to the means of recruitment and/or without reference to the presence of a rule of exogamy.

1. This loose definition of the term seems to have resulted from the application of the term to social groups which bisect certain societies. For instance, the Canella of Brazil, as described by C. Nimuendajú and R. H. Lowie, have at least four different but contemporaneous pairs of such groups ('The Dual Organizations of the Ramkókamekra [Canella] of Northern Brazil', *American Anthropologist*, vol. 39, 1937, pp. 565–82). One of these has matrilineal descent and a rule of exogamy, but membership in the others is determined by either the personal name given an individual by his mother's brother, the period when his male age-mates are initiated, or the names bestowed upon him by one of the Canella social clubs. G. P. Murdock has proposed the term *pseudo-moiety* for such divisions of a village or society into two without reference to descent groups (*Social Structure*, New York: The Macmillan Co., 1949, p. 47).

2. R. Linton defines *moiety* so as to restrict it to unilineal descent groups, but applies the term without reference to marriage regulation (*The Study of Man*, New York: Appleton-Century, 1936, p. 207). With apparently the same meaning Murdock writes of *non-exogamous moieties* (*Social Structure*, p. 47). A. R. Radcliffe-Brown applies the term *moiety* to social units formerly found among the Aborigines of the York Peninsula, South Australia, who condoned endogamy within such a grouping ('The Social Organization of Australian Tribes', *Oceania*, vol. 1, 1930–1, p. 221). R. H. Lowie describes the non-exogamous Hidasta unilineal descent groups as *moieties* (*Primitive Society*, London: Routledge, 1921, p. 126). The non-exogamous divisions of the Toda have also been called *moieties* by Lowie, E. A. Hoebel, and G. A. Reichard (R. H. Lowie, *Social Organization*, London: Routledge & Kegan Paul, 1950, p. 240; E. A. Hoebel, *Man in the Primitive World*, New York: McGraw-Hill, 1949, p. 264; G. A. Reichard, 'Social Life', in F. Boas (ed.), *General Anthropology*, New York: Heath, 1938, p. 431).

D. Certain other terms are closely related to the concept *moiety* as used in anthropology.

1. *Dual organization* has been used as a synonym in both Britain and the United States (Committee of the Royal Anthropological Institute, *Notes and Queries on Anthropology*, London: Routledge & Kegan Paul, 6th edn., 1951, p. 79;

436

R. H. Lowie, *An Introduction to Cultural Anthropology*, p. 260).

2. The terms *matrimoiety* for a moiety with matrilineal descent and *patrimoiety* for one with patrilineal descent are now in common use (G. P. Murdock, *Social Structure*, pp. 166, 241).

Arnold R. Pilling

See also: DESCENT
UNILINEAL

Monarchy

A. *Monarchy* primarily denotes a form of government in which the Head of State and/or Government is entitled King or Queen (or their equivalents), and to whom there is attached a special religious and/or symbolic significance. It also refers to (a) a particular institution within the form of government, and (b) a state possessing such a form or such an institution.

B. The following will concentrate upon the primary usages, the others being derivations therefrom.

1. For Aristotle the term meant 'one-man rule', in the forms both of 'kingship' and of its perversion 'tyranny' (*Politics*, B.C. 336–22, especially bks. III and V). The term has since been largely reserved for the former. Filmer also held that 'a monarchy is the government of one alone' (*The Anarchy of a Limited or Mixed Monarchy* (1648), ed. by P. Laslett, Oxford: Blackwell, 1949, p. 281) but refers to the 'one' as a King who, if legitimate, rules in virtue of Divine Right as the Father of his People (*Patriarcha* (1680), ed. by P. Laslett, Oxford: Blackwell, 1949).

2. In modern usage such unlimited rule is called *absolute monarchy*, as opposed to *limited* or *constitutional monarchy*. The latter phrases refer to a system in which the Head of State is a Monarch, but one who, while possessing important formal and ceremonial functions, plays a governmental role only in certain clearly and narrowly defined circumstances—e.g. in selecting a Prime Minister under a system of Cabinet Government. This is the sense intended by statements like: 'though India ... will have an elected President, he will in fact be a constitutional monarch' (I. Jennings, *The Commonwealth in Asia*, Oxford: The Clarendon Press, 1951, p. 92).

3. In drawing the distinction between monarchical and republican government three main points are commonly made:

(a) The distinction 'means little more than that where the head of a state is a president, then that state is a republic, and where the head of the state is a king (or queen, or any comparable title), that state is a monarchy or kingdom' (K. C. Wheare, *Modern Constitutions*, London: Oxford University Press, 1951, p. 41).

(b) Hereditary succession is often said to distinguish monarchy. But 'hereditary right is only one of four staircases by which the throne may be ascended, the others being election, nomination by predecessor and selection by divination or lot' (H. J. T. Johnson, 'Monarchy in Eclipse', *The Cambridge Journal*, vol. I, 1948, p. 268).

(c) Monarchy is distinguished from all non-royal institutions by the presence of one or both of two factors: (i) a magical and/or religious significance, usually marked by special coronation rites. Thus W. Bagehot wrote of 'the mystic reverence, the religious allegiance, which are essential to a true monarchy' (*The English Constitution*, London: Chapman & Hall, 1867, ch. 1); and Frazer has illustrated this theme anthropologically (*The Golden Bough*, London: Macmillan, 1890–1915; and *Lectures on the Early History of Kingship*, London: Macmillan, 1905; (ii) a special symbolic function (see, for example, the official statement that 'the Kabaka ... shall continue to be the symbol of unity of the people of Buganda and of continuity between their past, present, and future' (S. A. de Smith, 'Constitutional Monarchy in Buganda', *Political Quarterly*, 1955, p. 12).

G. C. Moodie

See also: HEAD OF STATE
PRESIDENCY
REPUBLIC

Monetary Reform (See Currency Reform)

Money

A. *Money* may be defined as anything that can at all times, within a particular national system of markets, be used as a medium of exchange. It has sometimes been defined in terms of other functions, but such categories are neither inclusive of everything that is termed money nor exclusive of everything that is not money.

B. 1. American writers have traditionally defined *money* by listing its so-called 'functions'. Thus, an official Federal Reserve publication states that 'money is defined in terms of one or more of its three main functions: (1) as a medium of exchange; (2) as a store of purchasing power; and (3) as a standard of value' ('The

Money

Monetary System of the United States', *Federal Reserve Bulletin*, February, 1953, p. 98). This is a customary textbook approach. R. P. Kent (*Money and Banking*, New York: Rinehart, 3rd edn., 1956, p. 4) writes that we may regard money as 'anything which is commonly used and generally accepted as a medium of exchange or as a standard of value'. L. V. Chandler speaks of four functions of money: it serves as (a) a unit of value, (b) a medium of exchange, (c) a standard of deferred payments, and (d) a store of value. The first two, according to Chandler, are *primary* functions and the last two *derivative* functions (*The Economics of Money and Banking*, New York: Harper & Brothers, 1948, p. 7).

2. British economists place less emphasis on a variety of monetary functions. A. C. L. Day conceptualizes money, and 'several of the other kinds' of wealth, as a 'claim'. Two levels ('one of which is relatively superficial while the other is fundamental') are distinguished. 'At one level, some kinds of money are expressed in the form of a claim to other kinds of money. At the more important level, the real significance of money is that it is a claim which can be used by its owner to buy anything. Money is the most convenient way of laying certain claims to such goods and services as one wishes to buy' (*Outline of Monetary Economics*, Oxford: Clarendon Press, 1957, p. 4). E. H. Phelps Brown (*The Framework of the Pricing System*, London: Chapman & Hall, 1936, p. 190) takes as money 'whatever at a given time is generally acceptable for the discharge of debts'. D. H. Robertson (*Money*, London: Nisbet, 1948, p. 2) writes that the term may be used to denote 'anything which is widely accepted in payment for goods, or in discharge of other kinds of business obligation'. Robertson (ibid.) makes the further point that whatever is used as a medium of exchange need not itself be also a standard of value, but must only 'be expressed in terms of something which is a standard of value'. E. S. Shaw (*Money, Income, and Monetary Policy*, Chicago: Irwin, 1950, p. 3) emphasizes the same point when he asserts that the 'money-of-account is the germ cell of any monetary system ... Prices can be quoted and debt incurred in terms of this accounting unit even though it has no physical counterpart in money proper'. A. G. Hart feels that usual discussions of the 'functions' of money are confusing because they are not coordinate. Thus, 'The unit of account, not money, is the standard of value; debt, not money, is the ordinary medium of exchange; all wealth, not only money, is a store of value' (*Money, Debt and Economic Activity*, New York: Prentice-Hall, 1948, p. 18).

Lord Keynes attributed 'peculiar significance' to the money rate of interest because of two characteristics of money—its very small (usually zero) elasticity of production and equally small elasticity of substitution (*The General Theory of Employment, Interest and Money*, London: Macmillan, 1936, pp. 230–1). Money, that is, cannot be produced by private entrepreneurs as its price rises in terms of the wage unit, and as its exchange value rises there can be no substitution of some other factor for it.

C. Whatever conceptual disagreements persist, there is substantial agreement among most writers as to what constitutes the *money supply*. It consists of coins, paper bills (in modern times issued by the treasury of a sovereign government or by a central bank), and the demand deposit liabilities of the joint-stock or commercial banking system (see A. C. Pigou, *The Veil of Money*, London: Macmillan, 1949, p. 6). A few writers insist upon including time deposits of commercial banks in the money stock, but a large majority prefer to consider time deposits in the category of *near-money*, along with deposits in mutual savings banks, savings and loan association shares, and short-term government securities owned by individuals and business firms.

For purposes of economic analysis, however, it is advantageous to distinguish clearly, even if somewhat arbitrarily, between *money* on the one hand and a *security* on the other. Money is anything that can at all times and *without conversion* be used to remove any obligation whatsoever. Money can only be created and destroyed by the government or, within permissive limits, by the central bank and the commercial banking system. A security, on the other hand, must invariably be converted into money before effecting a payment (this is true even of a time deposit in a commercial bank) and can *only* be created by the issuing intermediary in exchange for money—i.e. in exchange for either currency or a check drawn on a demand deposit.

It is apparent, of course, that any set of assets will possess a spectrum of 'moneyness'. But much harm and little good is done by attributing to financial intermediaries the power of creating money. Like every other nonbank institution, savings and loan associations, mutual savings banks, life insurance companies, and the like, must keep accounts with commercial banks; and they can create liabilities against themselves *only* when money is brought to them for the purpose.

Ross M. Robertson

See also: CURRENCY REFORM
DEPRECIATION
DEVALUATION
MONEY AND BANKING

Money and Banking

A. *Money and banking*, as a sub-field of economics, is concerned most directly with (a) the nature, history, and functioning of money-creating institutions including devices developed for their control and (b) interrelations between monetary, value, and employment theories.

B. 1. The combination of the two words *money* and *banking* calls attention to the fact that commercial or joint stock banks create deposits which serve as money. As R. S. Sayers points out (*Modern Banking*, Oxford: Clarendon Press, 1958, p. 1), 'banks are not merely traders in money but also in an important sense *manufacturers* of money'. There is, therefore, sound logic in joining together the study of the functions of money *and* the institutional organization of the monetary and banking system (i.e. the central bank as well as the commercial banks).

2. It should be observed that this sub-field of economics, like other sub-fields, cannot profitably be studied except within the broader framework of economic theory. Nor, in the light of the economic institutions and phenomena with which it is concerned, can it be studied in abstraction for other sub-fields (e.g. public finance).

C. The American Economic Association set out the following sub-divisions of this area of study: (a) monetary theory and policy, (b) commercial banking and other short-term credit, and (c) consumer finance and mortgage credit. According to a statement by a committee consisting of Professors F. W. Fetter, F. Machlup, H. S. Ellis, and J. W. Bell, 'Economists specializing in this branch study the nature and functions of money and banks, the means by which banks create purchasing power, and devices used to regulate amount of bank lending. They study forms of credit and credit instruments, and the relationship of money purchasing power to

levels of economic activity' ('The Profession of Economist', *The American Economic Review*, vol. 39, 1949, p. 341).

William L. Miller

See also: FISCAL POLICY
MONEY
PUBLIC FINANCE

Money Cost (See Cost)

Money Supply (See Money)

Monism

A. *Monism* in its most general sense denotes a theory or interpretation which is developed in terms of one principle.

1. Thus in metaphysics reality would be *reduced* to some single ultimate substance or principle.

2. In history or sociology some one factor is considered the basic *cause* which determines all behaviour and institutions or all history. This same factor may also become the basis for a causal theory describing the present or predicting the future.

3. In political science *monism* refers to the idea that the state is the supreme power or body in society and only through the state can order or unity in society be obtained. This concept may be basically a legal one in which event sovereignty would be emphasized or it may be a functional one emphasizing the operations or activities of the state as a social group. In international law the monists are those who believe that international and municipal law are both parts of a *single* system of law.

B. 1. In metaphysics the doctrine of monism holds that all reality may be reduced to one ultimate substance or principle, such as mind (idealism), or matter (materialism), or something that is neither mind nor matter but the ground of both. This usage is to be found in various social philosophies.

2. It is also used to describe theories which claim that one single factor is the basic cause of all other social and historical phenomena. In this sense some one factor in a given field or discipline—for example, history, economics, psychology, geography, anthropology, sociology, political science, or any of the various combinations of these—is singled out as *the* basic factor which determines all behaviour and institutions—indeed all culture, civilization, or history. This usage may take the form either of a

Monogamy

philosophy of history or of a causal theory which describes or explains the present and possibly offers the basis for predictions.

C. Political scientists use the term in two important contexts.

1. *Monism* is the notion (in origin a legal concept) that in any society there must be one supreme power or authority and this must be lodged in the state (for an excellent discussion of this usage, see F. W. Coker, *Recent Political Thought*, New York: Appleton-Century, 1934, pp. 497–520. Coker's analysis is in ch. XVIII, 'The Pluralists' Attack on State Sovereignty', which is actually a critical analysis of the debate between the monists and pluralists). As a result of possessing this supreme legal power and/or authority the state was said to be sovereign both in its relation to other groups in its area (internal sovereignty) and in its relation to other areas (external sovereignty). This type of approach was characteristic of political theorists such as Bodin, Hobbes, Bentham, Austin, and the analytical school of jurisprudence generally. In contrast, pluralists such as Laski, Figgis, Duguit, MacIver, and others maintained that no one group, not even the state, possessed such complete or absolute power and/or authority even in law, much less in political or social or economic fact; instead this power or authority was divided among various groups and this in effect limited the omnicompetence of the state. The pluralists based their approach upon social, economic, and political factors, and questioned the whole concept of legal sovereignty.

This argument has had an important effect on usage of the idea by political scientists so that the current debate over monism usually is not conceived in the same terms as the older one. For example, L. Lipson, after a sociological analysis of the origins of the state as one group in society, argues that the issue of monism vs. pluralism inevitably arises and must be settled one way or the other (*The Great Issue of Politics*, New York: Prentice-Hall, 1954, ch. 7 especially, but also chs. 4, 8, 15). Either the state is to be *the* unifying agency in society, and its functions therefore are not to be limited by any other group, or the state is to be one among various groups in society, its functions limited by these other groups, in which event he does not see how unity can be obtained. He thus concludes in favour of monism. Perhaps it should be added that although Lipson's analysis is not conceived in terms of sovereignty, there are some, C. E.

Merriam for example, who would claim that in effect this is what such theorists are talking about and they might as well admit it (*Systematic Politics*, Chicago: University of Chicago Press, 1945, pp. 35–45). Be this as it may, it is nevertheless probably true that contemporary users of the term *monism* in this sense are not as legalistically oriented as their predecessors. Moreover, some of these users would not even think of monism in terms of the state; instead they would think in terms of government or 'the political system', e.g. the system providing in D. Easton's terms for 'the authoritative allocation of values for a society', as the focal point for their monistic theories.

2. The second usage is unquestionably a legal one found primarily in international law. In this sense the monists are those who believe that international law and municipal or national law are parts of a single system of law. Perhaps the best known of this group is H. Kelsen who argues for a single legal order with a hierarchy of norms and places international law at the top of the pyramid (see, for example, Kelsen's *Principles of International Law*, New York: Rinehart, 1952, especially pt. V). Although most monists seem to place international law above municipal law, there are some who do the opposite—for example, A. Zorn and M. Wenzel. In contrast to the monists, the dualists or pluralists would regard international law and municipal law as different and co-ordinate systems of law. It is interesting to note that it is possible to be a monist in this sense, thus conceiving of international law and municipal law as parts of the same legal system, and yet not be a monist in the sense referred to under the first political usage, thus refusing to grant legal sovereignty to the state or to think of it as the unifying agency in society. This seems to be the position of Duguit who was referred to as a pluralist in the first sense but is considered a monist in the second.

Warren Roberts

See also: PLURALISM

Monogamy

Monogamy denotes the rule or principle which regards marriage as an exclusive union of one man to one woman, at least at one time. A married person, where monogamous institutions prevail, is restrained from contracting a second marriage.

Monogamous marriage is sometimes loosely used to describe the marriage of one man to one woman when it occurs in a polygamous system, e.g. 'enforced monogamy, where polygamy is the ideal'.

M. Douglas

See also: MARRIAGE
POLYANDRY
POLYGAMY

Monolatry (See Monotheism)

Monopolistic Competition

A. *Monopolistic competition* denotes a condition of partial market control due to the exclusive possession of the trade in some commodity on the part of a seller and limited by the fact that one commodity may be substituted for another with varying degrees of ease.

B. Prior to the 1930s emphasis was placed on *pure monopoly* even though it was thought to be a rare and isolated phenomenon. The work of E. H. Chamberlin (*The Theory of Monopolistic Competition*, London: Oxford University Press, 6th edn., 1949) and J. Robinson (*The Economics of Imperfect Competition*, London: Macmillan, 1938) completely changed this attitude, as it did in the case of competition. Pure monopoly—the exclusive possession of the trade in some commodity for which there is no substitute whatever—was seen to be virtually impossible, and pure competition—a complete lack of market control—very nearly so.

Instead the economic system came to be viewed as a set of overlapping markets in all of which greater or lesser concentration of market power exist depending upon the ease of substituting one commodity for another. These concentrations of market power may lead to higher profits, but may lead merely to higher costs.

Pure monopoly is thus virtually impossible. What exists is nearly always *monopolistic competition*. How large an area of market control is to be tolerated involves consideration of a wide range of social, political, and economic values. These considerations must include the probability that without some degree of market power and control on the part of an economic enterprise, there can be no incentive toward further expansion. They must also include recognition of the fact that many of the wastes and instabilities of a developing economy are the results not of monopoly or monopolistic competition, but of inherent 'imperfections' in the competitive process, e.g. lack of perfect knowledge, lack of complete mobility, at least partially beyond the power of any social system to remedy.

It is due to this change in attitude that in a recent British work on economic competition (J. Downie, *The Competitive Process*, London: G. Duckworth, 1958) no mention is made of monopoly, and oligopoly is not mentioned in its own right but is cross-referenced in the index to *concentration*.

David McCord Wright

See also: ECONOMIC COMPETITION
MONOPOLY

Monopolization (See Monopoly)

Monopoly

A. *Monopoly* denotes a condition of market control due to the exclusive possession of the trade in some commodity on the part of a seller (*monopsony*, in the case of a buyer; *oligopoly* if control is concentrated in a few enterprises).

B. *Monopoly* is defined as the 'exclusive possession of the trade in some commodity' by the *Shorter Oxford Dictionary* (Oxford: Clarendon Press, 1933). Similarly, T. Scitovsky (*Welfare and Competition*, London: Allen & Unwin, 1952, p. 377) defines it as a condition in which '... a firm or person ... is all alone on his side of the market, or ..., if not alone, controls the market behavior of his competitors'.

Monopoly may be conferred upon a seller (monopsony, if he is a buyer) by the state as in the case of the great English trading companies of the 16th, 17th, and 18th centuries, and in the case of charters of public utility companies and of grants of patent or copyright privilege today. Monopoly may be the inevitable consequence of indivisibilities of factors of production (e.g. a railroad joining two cities) or, less frequently, of internal economies of large-scale production (e.g. the telephone system in a single city), in which case it is known as a *natural monopoly*. Finally, it may be the result of deliberate efforts to eliminate competition on the part of one or more competitors (e.g. monopolies or near-monopolies created by the merger movement in the United States between 1879 and 1904, of which the United States Steel Corporation, the Standard Oil Company, the Consolidated Tobacco Company, the American Smelting and Refining Company, and the United Shoe Machinery Company were the most important). *Monopolization* is the name given to such deliberate efforts which are illegal at the present time in a number of countries, among which are the United States and Canada.

Monotheism

C. In the literature of political economy monopoly is unfavourably contrasted with competition since it results in a poorer allocation of resources in all those cases where competition is a realistic alternative.

Thus A. Smith (*The Wealth of Nations* (1776), New York: Random House, 1937, pp. 61, 147): 'The monopolists, by keeping the market constantly understocked, by never fully supplying the effectual demand, sell their commodities much above the natural price, and raise their emoluments, whether they consist in wages or profit, greatly above their natural rate'. 'The price of monopoly is upon every occasion the highest which can be got. The natural price, or the price of free competition, on the contrary is the lowest which can be taken, not upon every occasion indeed but for any considerable time together'. 'Monopoly, besides, is a great enemy to good management which can never be universally established but in consequence of that free and universal competition which forces everybody to have recourse to it for the sake of self-defence'.

And, in the same vein, A. Marshall (*Principles of Economics*, London: Macmillan, 8th edn., 1920, p. 477): 'It has never been supposed that the monopolist in seeking his own advantage is naturally guided in that course which is most conducive to the well-being of society regarded as a whole. ... The doctrine of Maximum Satisfaction has never been applied to the demand for, and the supply of, monopolized commodities'.

Monopoly *power* is the power which enables the seller to set his price for the commodity he sells. The extent of this power varies inversely with the availability of substitutes to the buyers. *Pure* monopoly is the limiting and unrealistic case of the exclusive possession of the trade in a commodity for which there is no substitute whatsoever. In the real world, however, monopoly is the condition of a seller for whose commodity imperfect substitutes exist (i.e. his average revenue curve is less than perfectly elastic). Monopoly price is in excess of marginal cost.

Monopoly profits are the fruits of monopoly power (F. H. Knight, *Risk, Uncertainty, and Profit*, Boston: Houghton, Mifflin, 1921 [italics added] p. 189): 'Monopoly is impossible except on the basis of some control over an element essential in the production of a commodity, *and the extra product is rightly imputed to this essential element, or to the condition which makes control possible*, if separable from the rest of the situation'.

D. 1. A *discriminating monopoly* makes '... sales of technically similar products at prices which are not proportional to marginal costs' (G. J. Stigler, *The Theory of Price*, New York: The Macmillan Co., 1952, p. 215); a discriminating monopoly can exist only if it sells in two or more markets which are separate.

2. A *bilateral monopoly* is a situation in which a buyer faces a seller and neither has good alternative sources of supply and demand respectively (e.g. a newsprint mill facing a hydroelectric power company in an isolated company town in Canada).

3. *Monopoly capitalism* in Marxist terminology is the stage of capitalism in which control over means of production and distribution has become highly concentrated in the hands of a small group of capitalists.

Stefan Stykolt

See also: Economic Competition
Monopolistic Competition

Monopoly Capitalism (See **Monopoly**)

Monopsony (See **Monopoly**)

Monotheism

A. *Monotheism* denotes the belief that there is only one god.

B. 1. Defined in these terms the concept is usually restricted to the higher theistic religions —Zoroastrianism, Judaism, Islam, and Christianity—in which a single transcendent deity who is the sole creator of the universe and source of all existence alone is worshipped. Among the higher theisms, Zoroastrian monotheism rapidly became a dualism in Mazdaeism when the forces of good and evil were regarded as opposed divine principles. Post-exilic Judaism, since the 6th century B.C., can be described as a genuine monotheism, and it exercised a powerful influence on the subsequent monotheistic faiths of Christianity and Islam. In the case of Christianity the claim to be a monotheistic faith is based on the belief that the Godhead is essentially a unity in tripersonality.

2. It is also used sometimes to include the worship of one particular god in a tribe or nation, as in the case of Yahweh among the early Hebrews, who was regarded as the jealous god of Israel who forbade his people to worship the gods of the surrounding nations without denying their existence. This deviation, however, is perhaps more accurately described as *monolatry* (Greek, *latreia*: worship + *mono*), while the doctrine that ascribes supreme power to one of several gods in a pantheon or in a region is sometimes called *henotheism* (Greek, *heis* (*hen–*), one + *theos*).

3. In primitive society the widespread recognition of a supreme being as a high god or tribal all-father, often located in the sky, has been interpreted as a primeval monotheism (cf. W. Schmidt, *Der Ursprung der Gottesidee*, Münster: Aschendorff, 1912–49, 9 vols., trans. and abridged by H. J. Rose, *The Origin and Growth of Religion*, London: Methuen, 1931).

This view was elaborated in the work of W. Koppers. An anthropological discussion of 'monotheistic tendencies' in primitive religion may be found in P. Radin's book *Primitive Man as Philosopher* (New York: Appleton, 1927). Radin observes that '… explicit monotheism, it is true, is rare among primitive peoples but it is possibly not quite so uncommon as the literal reading of the facts might seem to indicate' (ibid., p. 371). The balance of later views would classify the conception of deity among primitives as monolatry or henotheism, since a number of other divinities are recognized, albeit on a lower plane than the supreme being. Thus E. F. Evans-Pritchard points out that among the Nuer in the Sudan 'at no level of thought and experience is Spirit thought of as something altogether different from god', but it includes belief in a number of lesser beings having divine status as his children. Consequently, he concludes that 'on one level Nuer religion may be regarded as monotheistic, at another level as polytheistic; and it can also be regarded at other levels as totemistic or fetishistic' (*Nuer Religion*, Oxford: Clarendon Press, 1956, p. 316).

C. While monotheism is primarily the belief that there is but one transcendent deity, monolatry and henotheism are so very closely allied to this doctrine that they may be said to fall within the scope of the definition in its wider applications and references.

E. O. James

See also: ANIMISM
POLYTHEISM
RELIGION

Moral Order (or Normative Order)

A. *Moral* or *normative order* is a term used to denote (a) the system of values (q.v.) and norms which govern social behaviour in a group or society and/or (b) the behaviour so governed or the order discoverable in the behaviour so governed, insofar as that behaviour or order conforms to and is to some degree the product of the system of norms and values.

B. Perhaps no term in the vocabulary of sociology shows more clearly than *moral order* the continuing interest sociologists have had in norms and values since the time of Comte. R. E. Park (*Society*, Glencoe, Ill.: The Free Press, 1955, pp. 16, 214, 261, 285) sees the moral order as the distinguishing characteristic of human interaction at the level of conscious communication. R. C. Angell, following Park, defines *moral order* as 'how oughtness is organized' (*Free Society and Moral Crisis*, Ann Arbor: University of Michigan Press, 1958, p. 16). He includes values, norms, law, and institutions in the 'anatomy of the moral order' (ibid., p. 17).

C. In some recent social theory the term *normative order* has been substituted, but the meaning remains the same. T. Parsons uses the term to denote the behaviour (and the order in the behaviour) which is governed by norms. 'Normative order … is always relative to a given system of norms or normative elements, whether ends, rules, or other norms. Order in this sense means that … [action] … takes place in conformity with the paths laid down in the normative system' (*The Structure of Social Action*, New York: McGraw-Hill, 1937, p. 91). K. Davis, on the other hand, uses *normative order* to refer to the system of norms which governs social behaviour: 'a normative system embodying what *ought* to be, and … a factual order embodying what is. … The normative order acts for example as a determinant … of the factual order'. 'The normative order makes the factual order of human society possible' (*Human Society*, New York: The Macmillan Co., 1949, pp. 52, 53).

William L. Kolb

See also: NORM
SOCIAL INTEGRATION
VALUE

Morale

A. In its most general usage *morale* denotes a favourable attitude on the part of a member or members of a group towards that group, in particular toward its goals and leadership. The possibility remains that this may not always be a uni-dimensional attitude—people may like the goals but dislike the leadership. The same people

Morale

will have a different degree of morale depending upon whether they are considered as members of one or another primary group, social organization, etc.

B. 1. The term was at one time used to refer to individuals apart from their relations with groups, and is still in popular use in this sense. An individual was said to have high morale if he was (a) well-adjusted, or (b) confident in the future, or (c) highly motivated. S. A. Stouffer et al. distinguish between *morale* as an aspect of group behaviour and *adjustment* as a characteristic of individuals, i.e. not in relation to any particular group membership (*The American Soldier*, Princeton, N.J.: Princeton University Press, 1949, p. 83). Although *morale* is a measure applied to an individual or number of individuals, it is not now used except in relation to some social group or organization.

2. (a) The morale of small groups is sometimes equated with the 'cohesiveness' or friendliness of the group. This can be measured by the percentage of in-group sociometric choices, or some similar index (for an example of this see the description of J. G. Jenkins's study of Air Force Squadrons, in D. Krech & R. S. Crutchfield, *Theory and Problems of Social Psychology*, New York: McGraw-Hill, 1948, pp. 405–7).

(b) Various attitudes of the members may be used as measures of morale—for example pride in the group, or confidence in attaining group goals.

(c) There is as yet no agreed conceptual meaning, or connotation, for the morale of small groups, though a variety of operational indices have been used. Furthermore, the empirical research has not been carried out which would determine the precise empirical functional relations between the variables. In some cases, research suggests that the whole concept of morale leads to misleading over-simplifications: for example cohesive work groups do have a higher output if they are engaged on joint work, but they have a *lower* output than other groups if their work prevents interaction between them (cf. M. Argyle, *The Scientific Study of Social Behaviour*, London: Methuen, 1957, ch. 6).

3. (a) Management generally uses the term in a general sense to include both high individual (or group) output or efficiency, and high job satisfaction, believing these two variables to be highly correlated. A number of studies show that there is in fact no significant correlation between satisfaction and output (A. H. Brayfield

& W. H. Crockett, 'Employee Attitudes and Employee Performance', *Psychological Bulletin*, vol. 52, 1955, pp. 396–424). In this case the combination of the two variables to form a third, called 'morale', is unwarranted from a scientific point of view.

(b) Many industrial psychologists use the term to mean a generally favourable attitude towards the organization as a whole, including its goals and leadership. Thus the morale of workers may be considered in relation to the factory and management organization, or in relation to the trade union—the attitude scales for measuring it would, of course, be different in the two cases. Various attitude scales have been devised for assessing worker morale. R. S. Uhrbrock devised a Thurstone-type scale, of which some of the items are:

Scale Value

10.4 I think this company treats its employees better than any other company does.

5.1 The workers put as much over on the company as the company puts over on them.

2.5 I think the company goes outside to fill good jobs instead of promoting men who are there.

'Attitudes of 4,430 Employees', *Journal of Social Psychology*, vol. 5, 1934, pp. 365–77).

(c) Some American industrial psychologists use the term in a sense closely allied to *job satisfaction*. D. Katz et al., for example, use four indices of morale (*Productivity, Supervision and Morale in an Office Situation*, Ann Arbor: University of Michigan Press, 1950): (i) pride in work group, (ii) intrinsic job satisfaction, (iii) involvement in the company, and (iv) financial and job status satisfaction. Of these, (iii) is the same as 3 (b) above, while (i) is the same as the morale of small groups, considered previously; (iii) and (iv) are straight job satisfaction.

4. (a) Military morale is usually taken in much the same sense as the second usage 3(b) of industrial morale, save that the component attitudes are different. As A. M. Rose says: 'The many components of military morale can probably best be defined through enumeration: Identification with the war effort, confidence in training, confidence in equipment, hatred of the enemy, confidence in officers, acceptance of the military reward system, confidence in rear echelons, a belief that the unit is well managed, a feeling that headquarters understands one's problems, and many other factors make up military morale' (A. M. Rose, 'Factors in Mental

Breakdown in Combat', in A. M. Rose (ed.), *Mental Health and Mental Disorder*, New York: Norton, 1955, p. 307).

(b) In military circles, *morale* is sometimes used in the sense of efficiency, especially as persistence in the face of opposition. There are, however, advantages in using the term to refer to an attitude which is empirically associated with such behaviour measures.

Michael Argyle

See also: ADJUSTMENT

Morbidity

A. *Morbidity* denotes the incidence of illness or disability in a population. In very many conditions there is no clear-cut line between the healthy and the ill. Some arbitrary criterion must be adopted, or, better, several degrees of severity distinguished. Frequently suitable criteria are provided by the effects of the illness upon everyday life. This is the only possible approach to aggregating *morbidity rates* from all conditions. Two types of criteria may be broadly distinguished: (a) those which emphasize conditions which are often temporary, and (b) those which stress more permanent defects. Roughly, criteria of type (a) demarcate the *ill* from the *healthy*; those of type (b) the *disabled* from the *fit*. Under (a) one may consider diseases which cause the patient to (i) complain of illness, (ii) stay away from work, (iii) go to bed, (iv) consult a doctor, (v) go to hospital. Examples of (b) are disabilities severe enough to disqualify from: (i) entry into the army, (ii) driving a motor vehicle, (iii) the type of work previously engaged in (for old people), (iv) normal schooling (for children), etc.

The main uses of morbidity statistics relate to the study of particular conditions, public health work, the economic aspects of illness, the cost of medical care or social security systems. However, morbidity statistics have also been employed as a measure of the absence of health conceived in a general sense as a state of adequate functioning and well-being for an individual or for a society as a whole.

B. 1. Ideas of disease have varied through the ages (changing conceptions of mental illness furnish a striking example). The statistical study of disease, after a few earlier beginnings, developed rapidly in the 18th and 19th centuries (notably studies of occupational diseases). Some of the 19th-century pioneers of health services, such as W. Farr and F. Nightingale, expected great benefits from the general study of all morbidity, i.e. schemes for reporting all illness or all hospital cases.

In fact the statistics of disease have developed piecemeal. Today the study of morbidity is not so much a topic on its own, as an aspect of many widely different subjects. Information on morbid conditions is, of course, important in most branches of medicine. However, it is easy to enumerate studies of more than specialized interest, such as the effects of malnutrition or over-crowding, the genetic basis of diseases and defects, mental illness, the disabilities of old age. Other examples are mentioned below; these may suffice to suggest why concepts and techniques differ in various fields of application, and generalizations are difficult.

Since World War II, there has been a rapid expansion in many types of morbidity statistics. References to the work done in various countries may be found in several publications of the World Health Organization's Technical Reports Series (notably no. 53, Geneva: 1952, and no. 137, Geneva: 1957).

2. Morbidity is a more complex subject to summarize in statistics than mortality. Disease, unlike death, is not a clearly defined event which happens to each person once only at a single instant. It is of many kinds and degrees; the time of its onset and termination is often vague. The manifestations, upon which the reporting of most conditions depends, vary with subjective reactions, changing conventions, and institutional arrangements. The significance of changing medical practice and knowledge scarcely needs to be pointed out.

Because of the complexity of the subject as well as the lack of an accepted terminology no description will be given here of the statistical indices used in morbidity studies. Two common confusions may be mentioned. (a) Morbidity statistics may refer either to the number of diseased *persons* or the number of *illnesses*. (b) Secondly, it is important to distinguish between *prevalence* rates, which measure the proportion of persons affected by a given condition at a point of time (or in a period), and *inception* or *attack* rates which measure the proportion of persons who begin to suffer from a condition in a given period. The term *incidence rate* normally means inception rates, but is sometimes used for prevalence rates or generally for rates of either type. (Successful treatment, such as insulin therapy for diabetes, which keeps alive victims of a disease who would otherwise have died, will *increase* the prevalence rates, but not the inception rates of the disease concerned). A

Morpheme

variety of measures relate to the duration of diseases or their outcome, e.g. *case fatality rates* measure the proportion of cases resulting in death.

3. Whereas the meaning of a death-rate can be understood without knowledge of the process by which deaths are registered, this is not so for morbidity rates. The definitions used make a great deal of difference to the figures and some understanding of the administrative procedures by which the data are collected is essential for their interpretation. This applies even to conditions which are well understood. Indeed, the variability even of data collected by means of a single 'objective' diagnostic test, such as miniature mass X-ray for tuberculosis, has been amply demonstrated in recent studies. For conditions whose nature is not clearly understood, such as the rheumatic diseases, the problems are even more serious.

The only kinds of morbidity data which are sufficiently well-developed to permit some comparisons over long periods of time and between countries are statistics of death by cause and, to a lesser extent, the reporting of infectious diseases. These sources would, even if the data were perfect, throw light on very limited aspects of disease; in particular chronic non-infectious conditions which kill only rarely or only after many years' duration, are not covered, though they may cause much suffering and disability.

Most morbidity data derive from administrative records of various institutions (often of agencies concerned with medical care). Examples are: hospitals, social security systems, life insurance companies, pension funds, school medical inspection, special clinics (tuberculosis, venereal diseases, etc.), recruitment records of Armed Forces, etc. Data collected in this way have all the usual limitations of administration records as sources of statistics. Attempts have been made in some countries to set up unified reporting systems, e.g. for all hospitals or all centres treating certain conditions (cancer registration schemes may be specially noted).

It is obvious that much illness escapes reporting in any administrative system. Reports of all illness of which the sufferer is aware can, at any rate in principle, be obtained in Sickness Surveys, i.e. surveys at which a sample of individuals or households are visited and questions concerning illness are asked. National sample surveys of this kind have been conducted in a number of countries since the war. More intensive information can be obtained in inquiries of smaller scale (relating to a single city, a sample of old people, a single group of diseases, etc.), where thorough questioning, examination by trained personnel, X-ray or laboratory tests may be employed. Surveys at which repeated visits to the same households are made, or continuing surveys at which one group of people is kept under observation for a number of years are important refinements.

J. Hajnal

See also: HEALTH

Mores (See Folkways)

Morpheme

A. The European and American definitions of the term are somewhat different.

1. In its European usage, a *morpheme* is an affix or a set of phonetically similar affix forms having a single meaning, constituting or considered to constitute a single speech element. It is particularly used of elements of inflective or other grammatical meaning.

2. In its American usage, a *morpheme* is any unitary meaningful element of language, whether root or affix, characterized by a single phonetic form, or a set of phonetically similar forms, constituting or considered as constituting a single speech element.

B. Usage varies in the matter of alternant or variant forms with the same meaning but occurring in different formations, as past tense *-d* in freed and *-t* in kept. For some, these are two morphemes which make up a *morpheme set*, while for others they are *morphs* or *morpheme variants* making up a single morpheme. 'A single shape of a morpheme is a *morph*; the various morphs which are the shapes or *representations* of one and the same morpheme are its *allomorphs*' (C. F. Hockett, 'Two Models of Grammatical Description', *Word*, vol. 10, 1954, pp. 210–31).

C. For some scholars the morpheme has to be *continuous*, others recognize the possibility of *discontinuous* morphemes. For example, one way of identifying the root of sing-sang-sung is to set it up as s . . ng, that is the consonants alone, while considering the vowels to be infixes that express the tense; in this case the parts of the root are discontinuous. However, there are other ways of handling the problem, for example, setting up a form si$_v$ng, in which i$_v$ represents a variable vowel as against wi$_f$nk with fixed

446

vowel in which case the *morpheme* is continuous. In French, the negative is expressed by two parts, *ne* before the verb and *pas* after it, e.g. *je ne vais pas* — I do not go —; some would call this a discontinuous morpheme, *ne . . . pas* (but note that *point, rien, personne, jamais* may also complete the negation).

D. Although the morpheme is held to be an unanalysable unit, there are many ambiguous cases. English *dead* seems to be a simple unit entirely parallel with *live, well, good, bad, red,* etc.; but it has something in common in meaning and form with *die*, and is evidently an irregular derivative from this verb. Similarly *kitten* is connected with *cat*; and *flame, flicker, flush, flare* seem to have some connection with each other. Such cases are sometimes fossilized formations, once normal in a very ancient form of the language, or again they may be potential new formations based on accidental similarities among words of different origins. However, whatever may have been their past status or the possibilities of development in the future, such vaguely existent morphemes are at the moment *marginal*. In a morphological analysis they may be either disregarded or set down as *marginal morphemes*.

E. Even among full-fledged or normal morphemes there is the matter of the morpheme's degree of freedom. For example, the ending *-ness* can be added to almost any adjective in English and is therefore called a *free morpheme*. The ending *-th* occurs in a fair number of words, like *warmth, width, breadth, stealth, wealth,* and *health*, but is not freely used; it is a *limited morpheme*. The suffix *-tion* is used with a great many verb roots, mainly of Latin origin, but cannot possibly be used with others of Germanic origin; it is definitely limited although not as much as *-th*. When the usage narrows down to one or a very few combinations, we have *bound morphemes*, as *huckle(berry), (re)peat, (re)hearse, chest(nut), (kit)ten*. The characteristic of these formations is that one part of the combination is more or less identifiable with an otherwise-occurring free element, while the other is limited to the special case. The *bound* element is either an old one which has lost its currency in all but the special combination, e.g. *repeat* from Latin *re-petere* meaning *to strike again*, or is an accidental residue of some sort as *chestnut* from Old French *chastagnier*—Latin *castanerius*—, in which the last part has been modified to resemble an English word.

F. The variants of a meaningful element are often related to the different complexes in which it is used, but in other cases a variation of meaning is involved independent of the context, as for example plural *men* to singular *man*, but such a case may be handled by assuming an infixed element of plural number which contracts with the stem vowel; or, in view of the normal suffix formation of plurals in English, by assuming a *zero* suffix with a transforming effect upon the stem vowel. The idea of a *zero morpheme*, this time without any effect on the stem vowel, may also be used in a case like singular *sheep*, plural *sheep*.

Morris Swadesh

See also: Linguistics
Phoneme

Morphology (See Linguistics)

Mortality

In its most general sense the term denotes the fact of being mortal, i.e. subject to death. In social and demographic analysis it denotes the frequency of death in a population, with meanings analogous to those given under *fertility* (q.v.).

1. It may refer to frequency of death in a general sense.

2. Or it may refer to frequency of death as measured in a refined way, usually in contrast to crude *death rate* (q.v.). Generally age specific rates or some index derived from them, such as expectation of life, are meant.

3. Finally, it may refer to frequency of death in various expressions referring to special aspects of the subject or special rates, e.g. infant mortality rate, maternal mortality rate, etc. 'Rate of mortality (at age x)' and 'Force of mortality (at age x)' are technical actuarial terms connected with life tables; the former measures the risk of death within one year after the xth birthday, the latter the risk in the immediate neighbourhood of the xth birthday.

J. Hajnal

See also: Death Rate
Fertility

Motivation

A. The term *motivation* refers to any organismic state that mobilizes activity which is in some sense selective, or directive, with respect to the environment. Since a great deal of human behaviour that is obviously *motivated*, in this sense, cannot be directly associated with any specific, discriminable organismic states, it is

Multilateralism

necessary to distinguish one motive from another in terms of the goals (q.v.) toward which behaviour is directed, if the term is to have a constant meaning regardless of whether or not the motive in question corresponds to a specific, known physiologic state. Thus careful usage requires not 'the hunger motive', but the *hunger drive*, and the *food motive*. Exactly the same usage permits the *achievement motive*, for example; indeed, with respect to humans, any object or state of affairs may be regarded as motivating, provided only that there is independent evidence that behaviour is in fact directed toward that object or state of affairs.

B. The several variants of this term, in their technical senses, are taken from psychology, and careful usage by other social scientists recognizes them as such. The concept *motivation* in a strict sense applies only to individuals. Such phrases as 'group motivation' must therefore be regarded, at the conceptual level, as loose analogies, like 'social organism', though in a specific research context they may be given very precise operational meaning.

Though different psychologists use the term in different senses, their common theme is unmistakable: a state of the organism that is activity-arousing. No psychologist, however, would consider all such organismic states as motivational in nature; those which eventuate in reflex-like activities like hiccoughing, for example, are commonly excepted. The exception is instructive, for it points to an essential limitation in the nature of the activity that is aroused: the activity must in some way be *selective* with respect to the environment, as reflex behaviour is not.

Analysis of the motivational components of behaviour, particularly in the case of humans, becomes complex because of the differential contributions of intra- and extra-organismic factors to variations in motivation, and because the two sets of factors interact. It can be shown that certain dimensions of behaviour on the part of laboratory animals vary in orderly ways with changes of such bodily states as hunger and thirst, which are commonly referred to as *drives*, though some psychologists use that term interchangeably with *motive*. But the behaviour of even the rat, and, a fortiori, of humans, varies also with environmental conditions, an important class of which is referred to as *goals*, or *incentives*.

The theoretical problems of motivation thus have to do with the interrelationships of drive and incentive. Many behaviours of many species of organisms are outcomes of 'built in' relationships of this kind, and are often labelled *instinctive*. In all but the simplest organisms, however, there are learnt relationships between drive conditions and incentive conditions. Hence there is no topic more central to the psychology of motivation than that of the conditions under which stimuli acquire reward value —i.e. the problem of secondary reinforcement. (cf. J. Olds, *The Growth and Structure of Motives*, Glencoe, Ill.: The Free Press, 1956).

Theodore M. Newcomb

See also: DRIVE
GOAL (Psychology)
GOAL (Sociology)
INTERVENING VARIABLE
NEED

Motive (See **Motivation**)

Multilateralism
A. *Multilateralism* in economics, denotes a pattern of trade between three or more countries, resting upon free convertibility of currencies. Where currencies are freely convertible, trade debts between any pair of countries may be settled through the transfer of a credit balance which the debtor has accumulated in some third country. Multilateral trade can best be understood as the converse of the conditions which exist under bilateral trade.

B. 1. Under bilateral trade a country attempts to balance its accounts individually with each of the countries with which it trades. If country A buys more from country B than it sells to country B, the difference represents a loan from B to A. There is no means under bilateral trade through which A can settle its debt to B by transferring exchange assets accumulated in some third country C. This means that the currency of country C is not freely convertible into that of country B.

2. The presence or absence of multilateral trade affects the degree of specialization which can occur in international trade. If currency A is not convertible into currency B, then foreigners who earn currency A and residents of A cannot use it to buy B's goods, even though they may be cheaper. Foreigners and residents of A may be forced to buy these goods in A, thus diverting resources in A from uses to which they might otherwise be put. Likewise resources in B must find other employment.

3. In the absence of free convertibility of

currencies, trade relations tend to break down into sectors connected by bilateral trade. The European Payments Union represents an example of a core of countries conducting multilateral trade with each other. Some of these countries are connected through bilateral trade with other trading regions. The bilateral connection exists because of limitations on the convertibility of the currencies of the countries within the multilateral trading area.

4. Multilateral trade is a necessary condition for *free trade*, but it is not sufficient. *Free trade* implies not only the convertibility of currencies but also the absence of tariffs, import quotas, and import licences. It is therefore possible to have multilateral trade among a group of countries without having *free trade*.

George H. Borts

See also: CURRENCY
TRADE

Multiplier

A. The term denotes the process (or the index, or coefficient, measuring such a process) whereby initial changes within economic systems (e.g. changes in the levels of investment) have cumulative and, in principle, measurable effects upon the system, its components and its equilibrium.

B. Its use dates from Keynes's formulation in his *General Theory of Employment, Interest and Money*. 'The conception of the multiplier was first introduced into economic theory by Mr R. F. Kahn in his article on "The Relation of Home Investment to Unemployment" (*Economic Journal*, June 1931). His argument in this article depended on the fundamental notion that, if the propensity to consume in various hypothetical circumstances is (together with certain other conditions) taken as given and we conceive the monetary or other public authority to take steps to stimulate or to retard investment, the change in the amount of employment will be a function of the net change in the amount of investment; and it aimed at laying down general principles by which to estimate the actual quantitative relationship between an increment of net investment and the increment of aggregate employment which will be associated with it' (J. M. Keynes, *The General Theory of Employment, Interest and Money*, London: Macmillan, 1936, pp. 113–4).

'Let us call k the *investment multiplier*. It tells us that, when there is an increment of aggregate investment, income will increase by an amount which is k times the increment of investment.

'Mr Kahn's multiplier is a little different from this, being what we may call the *employment multiplier* ...' (ibid., p. 115).

The fact that an initial increase in the incomes of members of an economy would give rise to further increases through a chain of respending had been obvious for several centuries before R. F. Kahn explored the nature of the relationships involved, and with the aid of simple assumptions formulated them precisely.

C. Usage has, with trivial exceptions, followed Keynes from the beginning. More recent examples indicate current usage.

1. P. A. Samuelson describes it as 'the numerical co-efficient showing how great an increase in income results from each increase in investment' (*Economics*, New York: McGraw-Hill, 4th edn., 1958, p. 232).

2. A. C. L. Day observes that the 'theory of the multiplier' states the relationships between changes in the volume of investment and an 'equilibrium level of income'. A simple example assumes that 'a rise of 100 in investment leads to a ten-fold rise in the equilibrium level of income' in a system where the marginal propensity to save is 0·10 (*Outline of Monetary Economics*, Oxford: Clarendon Press, 1957, p. 62). The changes (rises or falls) in such an example are governed by a multiplier of 10, i.e. the *inverse of the marginal propensity to save*.

3. Economic literature uses the term *foreign trade multiplier* in analysing the effect of changes in exports-cum-investment upon equilibrium levels of income. This is basically an extension of the 'closed economy' multiplier, based upon a number of possible assumptions concerning the variables in an international balance of trade.

4. For an account of the distinction between the *static* and *dynamic* multiplier in macroeconomic models see R. G. D. Allen, *Mathematical Economics*, London: Macmillan, 1955, p. 42, et seq.; also R. Turvey, 'Some Notes on Multiplier Theory', *American Economic Review*, vol. 43, 1953, pp. 275–95.

D. The bulk of the discussion turns upon the notion of equilibrium levels of income within economic systems—whether they are *closed* or *open*. To some extent, therefore, the formal precision of the theory as often set out is either post hoc or definitional—and the qualifications of the theory expressed by Keynes himself are not always remembered.

Richard V. Clemence

Myth

Myth

A. In anthropology there is general agreement that a *myth* is a narrative tale concerned with the gods and the nature and meaning of the universe and man. In political science and sociology the meaning of the term is sometimes extended to include the whole world picture held by a social group, and the value system anchored in that picture.

B. Interest in the anthropological use of the term to denote a narrative tale has followed two paths.

1. Anthropologists interested primarily in the history and diffusion of culture tend to confine themselves to the obvious meaning of a myth and to view it as a part of culture to be described at the surface level or to be traced from one culture to another. There is likely to be present an underlying attitude which takes myth to be 'false' and the product of 'superstition'.

2. Anthropologists who make a functionalist interpretation of myth stress the idea that a group's literal belief in its own myths helps the group to express basic human feelings toward the world and to safeguard its rituals and moral values. 'Myth fulfils in primitive culture an indispensable function: it expresses, enchances, and codifies belief; it safeguards and enforces morality; it vouches for the efficiency of ritual and contains the practical rules for the guidance of man' (B. Malinowski, 'Myth in Primitive Psychology', in his *Magic, Science and Religion and Other Essays*, Glencoe, Ill.: The Free Press, 1948, p. 79). The question of the truth of *myth* in functional theory is somewhat ambiguous, but because of the emphasis on function it is likely to receive less attention.

C. Some sociologists and political scientists have extended the meaning of the term to include the whole realm of world view, religion, and values. R. M. MacIver, for example, has used *myth* to denote this area of human creativity as distinct from such empirically grounded aspects of culture as science and technology which he designates as *technique* (*The Web of Government*, New York: The Macmillan Co., 1947, pp. 3–12). The most famous use of the term in this sense is that of G. Sorel. E. A. Shils has described Sorel's usage as designating 'a complex of remote goals, tense moral moods, and expectations of apocalyptic success ... a value system and picture of the world' which inspires and guides rulers or aspirants to rule ('Georges Sorel: Introduction to the American Edition', in G. Sorel, *Reflections on Violence*, trans. by T. E. Hulme & J. Roth, Glencoe, Ill.: The Free Press, 1950, pp. 20–1).

Arden R. King

See also: COSMOLOGY (Also COSMOGONY)
RELIGION
RITUAL

450

N

Nation

A. A *nation* may be defined as the largest society (q.v.) of people united by a common culture and consciousness. While a nation occupies a common territory so that its members have common interests of place and land, the vital binding force of the nation is variously derived from a strong sense of its own history, its special religion, or its unique culture, including language. A *nation* may exist as an historical community and a cultural nexus without political autonomy or statehood.

B. Early usage of the word *nation* to indicate tribes or peoples, such as the European groups encountered in Julius Caesar's *Commentaries*, or the Arabs, or the six 'nations' of the Iroquois Indians in America has yielded to more specific psychological and political identification. The classic definition by E. Renan ('Qu'est-ce qu'une nation?', *Œuvres Complètes*, Tome 1, Paris: Calmann-Lévy, 1882, p. 903), 'A nation is a soul, a spiritual principle. Two things which are really one and the same make up this soul ... One is the possession in common of a rich heritage of memories; and the other is actual agreement, the desire to live together, and the will to make the most of the joint inheritance', stresses the motivation of a felt community of interests. The fact that a nation possesses mental homogeneity has been emphasized by E. Barker (*National Character and the Factors in its Formation*, London: Methuen, 1927, p. 17) in that a nation is comprised by people '... inhabiting a definite territory, who ... possess a common stock of thoughts and feelings acquired ... during the course of a common history ...'.

J. Stalin (*Marxism and the National & Colonial Question*, English edn. A. Fineberg, London: Lawrence, 1935, p. 8) framed the Communist definition of nation, slightly dissimilar in its emphasis on historical evolution and materialism, as 'A nation is a historically evolved, stable community of language, territory, economic life, and psychological make-up manifested in a community of culture'.

In all the social sciences factors such as the individuality of a people due to stable geographic contiguity, an historical and cultural tradition and an economic interest are taken into consideration in defining a nation. But self-consciousness due to some transcending idea—such as a unique heritage, a religion, liberty, or independence—brings about the ultimate synthesis characteristic of a nation. G. Schwarzenberger (*Power Politics*, New York: Praeger, 1951, p. 56), alluding to the dynamic nature of the nation, states, 'It is a collective consciousness of fellowship and a sentiment of a particular kind. Its essential characteristics are exclusiveness and emotionalism'. Popular usage of the word *nation* for other social science concepts should not blur its real meanings. As Q. Wright (*The Study of International Relations*, New York: Appleton-Century-Crofts, 1955, p. 4) observes, 'The words *nation, state, government* and *people* are sometimes used interchangeably, but each has a distinct connotation. The word *nation* suggests a considerable group of people, united by common culture, values, standards, and political aspirations, usually occupying a definite territory ...'.

The problem of definition has a more than theoretical importance in the context in which the idea of nation has recently been developed—the context of emergent states and nations. R. Emerson in his recent study *From Empire to Nation* (Cambridge, Mass.: Harvard University Press, 1960) observes that the peoples of Asia and Africa have tended to apply concepts of nation and nationalism which had been generalized from European experience: 'the ideal model of a nation towards which the European precedents pointed, even though no such nation existed in total purity, is a single people, traditionally fixed on a well-defined territory, speaking the same language and preferably a language all its own, possessing a distinctive culture, and shaped to a common mold by many generations of shared historical experience' (ibid., p. 103). He goes on to say that this model 'was frequently out of line for peoples outside the European orbit' (ibid., p. 104). It is interesting that Emerson stresses the difficulty there has been in securing water-tight definitions of nation—and how this has intensified problems of discussing the nationhood properties of the peoples of emergent states. But despite the absence of

National Income and Social Accounting

reliable criteria he offers the view that 'The nation is a community of people who feel that they belong together in the double sense that they share deeply significant elements of a common heritage and that they have a common destiny for the future' (ibid., p. 95); and further that 'the simplest statement that can be made about a nation is that they are a body of people who feel that they are a nation' (ibid., p. 102). He adds, significantly, that 'it may be that when all the fine spun analysis is concluded this will be the ultimate statement as well' (ibid.).

Gerard J. Mangone

See also: NATIONALISM
SOCIETY
STATE
TRIBE

National Character (See **Basic Personality Structure**)

National Debt (See **Public Debt**)

National Expenditure (See **National Product**)

National Income (See **National Income and Social Accounting; National Product**)

National Income and Social Accounting

A. The phrase denotes a sub-field of economics, the focus of which is the summation of the economic and financial data of a country's individual economic units (persons, business firms, governmental units, etc.) into consolidated accounts from which it is possible to develop general purpose statements for the nation. Because social accounting in modern times was first associated with national income accounts the sub-field was designated frequently as *national income and social accounting*. In recent years, however, other accounts have been included so that it is probably more proper to speak simply of *social accounting*.

B. The statements prepared in social accounting serve the same purposes as the related statements of business firms. There are *status statements* analogous to the corporate balance sheet which show the amount of present wealth; there are *flow statements* which describe and summarize the economic transactions for a period of time; and there are *single significant measure statements* analogous to corporate statements of profit or loss which indicate the volume of production and the interrelations among the parts of the total economic structure during a particular time period. Within this framework five types of social accounts have been developed:

1. *National balance sheets* are consolidated statements of the total assets, liabilities, and net worth of all economic units, public and private, within the nation.

2. *Balance of payments accounts* are summary statements of all economic transactions during some time period between the residents of the nation and the residents of all other nations.

3. *Flow of funds accounts* present a consolidated statement of the flow of funds through financial channels and encompass all transactions in the economy that are affected by the transfer of credit and/or money. The economy is divided into sectors such as consumers, corporate business, banks, farms, Federal government, etc., and the account for each sector shows the sources and uses of its funds and the changes in its monetary balances.

4. *Input–output tables* show the interrelations among the major industry groups of the economy. The economy is divided into a number of sectors or industries, sometimes several hundred, and, using these sectors, tables or matrices are constructed which show the goods-and-services inputs and outputs of each on a 'from-whom to whom' basis.

5. *National income accounts* are essentially statements showing for a definite time period the nation's net total production of goods and services, and the incomes arising out of and the expenditures on that production.

C. The term *national income* is used in a generic sense to refer to the net value of all economic goods and services produced by a nation during a particular time, usually a calendar year (see *National Product*). In a more specific sense *national income* is the title given to a particular measure in the system of social accounts. In this sense it denotes the aggregate of all income payments accruing to the factors of production; these payments take the form of employee compensation, rent, interest, and profit. In the system of social accounts this conception of *national income* is to be distinguished from the generic conception, which is given the title *gross national product*. There are two specific reasons why *national income* in the *generic* sense (gross national product) is not equal to *national income* in the *specific* sense. First, producers do not receive from the sale of products the full market price that consumers pay. In most cases the market price includes indirect business taxes such as the excises on whisky and many other commodities. These taxes accrue to the government and that part of price cannot be distributed

452

as factor payments. Second, productive activity causes the wearing out or depreciation of capital equipment, and therefore a part of output must be used to repair and replace the nation's equipment. This part cannot be distributed as factor payments.

Paul G. Craig

See also: BALANCE OF PAYMENTS
NATIONAL PRODUCT

National Product

A. *National product* refers to the money value of all the goods and services produced in a nation during some stated period of time, typically a year. Thus it is a rate of flow, and is usually expressed in units such as dollars per year, pounds per year, francs per year, or the like. *National income* refers to the total money value of incomes earned in production in a nation during a period. *National expenditure* refers to the total money value of expenditure in a nation during a period. National income and expenditure, like product, are expressed as flows of money value per period. National expenditure is typically regarded as the sum of consumption plus investment expenditure.

B. 1. There is wide agreement among economists that, for any nation and any period, national product, national income, and national expenditure are all equal by definition, provided that for all three the same prices are used to value goods and services produced and purchased, and the same degree of grossness or netness is used (see below for an explanation of these two terms). This amounts to saying that whenever goods and services are *produced*, the factors of production that co-operated to produce them receive jointly as *income* the value of the goods and services produced, and the buyers of them (who may be either the producers or others) expend for them an amount equal to their value.

2. Because of the definitional identity of the three magnitudes, it is possible to measure any one of them in either of three ways: by adding up all incomes earned in production in the economy, or all expenditures, or all products. (In practice no two of the three totals agree exactly, because of errors in estimating them.) In adding up such a total, it is essential to avoid double counting. For example, in adding up incomes, one must not count both the wages paid by a firm and the total value of products sold by the firm, because then the amount of the wages would be counted as income twice, once when

received by the firm from its customers, and again when paid to the employees. Instead, one should count the wages, and the profits of the firm *after* paying wages (and of course after paying other costs too). Similarly, in adding up products, one should not count both the total value of steel produced and the total value of automobiles produced, because some of the steel is used in automobiles and would be counted twice. Instead, one should count for each enterprise only the *value added* by that enterprise to the materials that it buys from other enterprises. Similarly, in adding up expenditures, one should count only expenditures for products by their final users, not expenditures for raw materials by firms that process the materials and sell them again.

C. 1. In defining national product or income or expenditure, one has a choice about whether or not to subtract from the total an allowance for the depreciation of capital goods that occurs during the period. If one makes no such subtraction, the results are called *gross* national product, income, and expenditure. If one does make such a subtraction, the results are called *net* national product, income, and expenditure. Thus gross national product measures the total value of goods and services produced in a period, *including* whatever amount of production is required to replace capital goods used up during the period. And net national product measures the value of goods and services produced, *after setting aside* whatever is required to maintain the stock of capital goods as it was at the beginning of the period. Similar interpretations apply to gross and net national income and expenditure,

2. One has a choice also about what prices to use for valuing the goods and services. The two important alternatives are known as *market prices*, which means the prices paid for the products by buyers in the market, *inclusive* of any excise taxes that may be levied, and *factor costs*, meaning the prices received for the products by the sellers of the factors of production that co-operated to produce the output, *exclusive* of any excise taxes that may be levied. The essential difference between national product (or income or expenditure) valued at market prices and valued at factor costs lies in the fact that the former includes excise tax receipts of government and the latter does not.

3. *Personal income* is the total of net incomes received by persons (as opposed to firms and government) in a period. According to its usual

National Product

definition, its magnitude can be obtained from net national product at factor cost by subtracting the income tax and social insurance tax liabilities of corporations or limited companies, and the undistributed profits of such companies, and then adding transfer payments. *Disposable income* (sometimes called *disposable personal income*) usually means personal income after payment of personal income taxes.

D. In practice, only those products that pass through the market are counted in national product, income, and expenditure, with a few conspicuous exceptions. This is because it is difficult to measure the value added in products that are produced by individuals for themselves at home, such as meals, clothing, furniture, household repairs, etc. This creates some strange anomalies. For instance, if a bachelor marries his housekeeper and stops paying wages to her, but she continues to perform the same housekeeping duties as before, the national product, income, and expenditure as measured will decline, because her product no longer passes through the market but is now produced at home instead. The national accounts of Norway did at one time include an estimate of the value of the services of housewives. Important exceptions usually made to the rule about including only products that pass through the market are the services of owner-occupied housing, and the value of food produced and consumed on farms.

E. For many purposes it is essential to separate changes in national income or product or expenditure into two parts, one representing changes in the level of prices, and the other representing changes in the quantity of goods and services produced. This can be done approximately by means of index numbers. If a series of national product estimates for several years is divided by a price index, each year's national product being divided by the price index for that year, the resulting series is known as *deflated* or *real* national product, or national product *in real terms* or *in constant dollars*. The so-called constant dollars in which this real national product is measured will be dollars whose purchasing power is equal to that enjoyed by a dollar in the comparison-base year of the price index, i.e. the year when the value of the price index was 1·00.

F. Although there is wide agreement among economists on the conceptual basis and technique of national accounts, there are some im-

portant unsettled questions, centring mainly around the problem of the extent to which national income and product and expenditure statistics succeed in measuring national welfare. Some of these questions concern the process of deflating money values to get real values, as mentioned in the foregoing paragraph: clearly it is changes in the real values, not in the money values, that one wants in order to assess changes in national welfare. Other questions concern the extent to which taxes, or government expenditures, should be included as part of national income. These and other questions inspire a good deal of current research in the national accounting field. Current work is also directed toward the preparation of national wealth accounts as well as national income accounts, and toward the integration of these with input-output studies (sometimes called interindustry relation studies) and with flow-of-funds accounts (sometimes called money-flows accounts).

G. 1. According to the usage of the U.S. Department of Commerce, which prepares and publishes annual and quarterly estimates of national income and expenditure statistics for the U.S., *gross* and *net national product* always refer to totals valued at market prices, and *national income* always refers to net national income at factor cost; the terms 'at market prices' and 'at factor cost' are not used at all. This usage has become fairly general in the U.S. It is described fully, and the estimation methods and the U.S. estimates themselves for 1929–53 are presented, in *National Income* (supplement to *Survey of Current Business*, Washington: United States Department of Commerce, 1954 edn). Current estimates appear in the *Survey of Current Business*.

2. British usage conforms to that described initially, using the terms 'at market prices' or 'at factor cost' to identify the valuation method used. United Kingdom estimates of national income and expenditure statistics for 1938 and annually since 1946 are prepared by the U.K. Central Statistical Office and presented annually in the so-called National Income 'Blue Books', entitled *National Income and Expenditure*. They are described in *National Income Statistics: Sources and Methods* (London: H.M.S.O., 1956).

3. Many other governments prepare and publish national income and expenditure estimates for their countries, using various modifications of the basic definitions. In addition, such statistics for many countries are assembled in various publications of the United Nations, the International Monetary Fund, and the Organization for European Economic Cooperation. Soviet concepts of national product and income are rather different from those described here.

Carl F. Christ

See also: INCOME
NATIONAL INCOME AND SOCIAL ACCOUNTING

National Security (See **Security**)

Nationalism

A. 1. *Nationalism* denotes a form of group consciousness, i.e. consciousness of membership in, or attachment to, a nation (q.v.). Such consciousness is often called consciousness of *nationality* and it identifies the fortunes of group members with that of a nation-state, desired or achieved.

2. *Nationalism* also denotes ideologies seeking to justify the nation-state as the ideal form of political organization. Nationalists desire membership in a nation-state-to-be, or they are devoted to an existing one, with which they identify themselves.

3. *Nationalism* also denotes the modern historical process whereby nations have been established as independent political units.

B. 1. As group consciousness *nationalism* implies a cohesiveness, a sense of unity, or of community that identifies the individual with an existing political state, or with the desire for one. It has been variously described as a 'state of mind', a 'feeling', as 'common sympathies', as a 'corporate sentiment', and as 'certain affinities', prevalent among groups of human beings (E. M. Sait, *Political Institutions: A Preface*, New York: Appleton-Century, 1938, pp. 341–51).

Often cited are certain objective and subjective factors that produce the group awareness necessary for nationalism. The following are representative examples: common language, value systems, religion, and literature; common economic and political creeds; common government, historical traditions, symbols, and experiences; conflict and common enemies; the growth of communications systems. Which of these factors will be present in any particular instance, in what strength and in what combinations, is a matter for empirical observation.

2. H. H. Gerth and C. W. Mills refer to *nationalism* as the 'justifying ideology of the nation-state' (*Character and Social Structure*, New York: Harcourt, Brace, 1953, p. 198). It is a system of 'symbols of justification for the acts of a state ... [or] ... symbols by which ... the state-organized cohesiveness of a nation is advanced and justified (ibid., pp. 198, 199).

Nationalism is characterized by numerous fictions and myths in its ideological content, but at least four may be used as a point of departure. These are: (a) an independent nation-state, (b) national progress, (c) a national mission, and (d) supreme loyalty to the nation-state.

(a) Devotion to the ideal of achieving an independent nation-state and the preservation of its freedom of action once that status is attained is a uniform trait of nationalism. H. Kohn points out that nationalism is a 'state of mind ... which recognized the nation-state as the ideal form of political organization' (*Nationalism: Its Meaning and History*, Princeton: Van Nostrand, 1955, p. 10). B. C. Shafer points out that nationalists are characterized by a desire for a 'common independent or sovereign government (type does not matter) ... . The "principle" that each nationality should be separate and independent ...'. (*Nationalism: Myth and Reality*, London: Gollancz, 1955, pp. 7–8).

(b) Nationalism dictates that goals of economic, social, cultural, and political progress, however they may be defined, can only be accomplished through the framework of national independence and national effort and energy. Kohn asserts that the nationalist belief system insists that the nationality 'is the source of all creative cultural energy and economic well-being' (*Nationalism*, p. 10). This is manifest in the nationalist's devotion to his own literature, history, philosophy, culture, economic creed, etc., as superior to those of alien nations.

(c) Committed to the ideal that progress is by definition a national phenomenon, some nationalists also assume a superiority which implies a responsibility to spread the true faith to other national groups. This is conceptualized as a 'national mission'. Historical illustrations are abundant—the Jacobin mission of spreading Liberty, Equality, and Fraternity, Russian Pan-Slavism, a British sense of the 'white man's burden', or an American devotion to spreading democracy.

(d) Nationalism in its ideological content delineates a priority of loyalties. Within the framework of nationalist beliefs C. J. H. Hayes states that 'the individual is commonly disposed, in case of conflict, to sacrifice one loyalty after another, loyalty to person, places and ideas, loyalty even to family, to the paramount call of

Nationality

nationality and the nation-state' (*Essays on Nationalism*, New York: The Macmillan Co., 1926, p. 94–5).

Loyalty to the nation-state, however, may not be merely negative. Pride in the nation's accomplishments, veneration of its historical greatness, devotion to its cultural achievements, an esteem for fellow nationals, may be held necessary to fulfil a creed of loyalty.

The intensity of nationalism as an ideology, with its baggage of emotion-laden symbols, is explicit in the writings of those who treat nationalism as a 'secular religion' (W. Sulzbach, *National Consciousness*, Washington: American Council on Public Affairs, 1943, and C. J. H. Hayes, *Essays on Nationalism*). These writers point to parades, processions, pilgrimages, holy days, saints, temples, icons, etc., as evidence of a *mystique* of nationalism that has religious overtones.

Other writers in defining nationalism as an ideology, contrast liberal with integral nationalism. *Liberal nationalism* stresses political democracy, humanitarian values, the rights of man, and individual freedom. It can be symbolized in the career of such a leader as Mazzini. On the other hand, *integral nationalism* stresses that the individual exists to serve the state, glorifies the organic conception of the state, rejects political democracy, and values aggressive international behaviour as a positive good (H. Kohn, *Nationalism*).

3. Finally, some writers treat nationalism primarily as a historical process. C. J. H. Hayes says that 'nationalism ... stands ... for an actual historical process, that of establishing nationalities as political units, of building out of tribes and empires the modern institution of the national state' (*Essays on Nationalism*, p. 5). The key word in such an approach is *modern*. Although some writers such as Kohn find the historical roots of nationalism in the Hebrew-Greek civilizations, they see nationalism as essentially a modern phenomenon which rose out of a set of historical circumstances in the middle of the 18th century (H. Kohn, *Nationalism*).

Charles P. Schleicher

See also: NATION
 STATE
 SELF-DETERMINATION

Nationality

A. *Nationality* has been defined by the International Court of Justice as 'a legal bond having as its basis a social fact of attachment, a genuine connection of existence, interests and sentiments, together with the existence of reciprocal rights and duties'. This definition was made in the second phase of the *Nottebohm* case between Liechtenstein and Guatemala (*I.C.J. Reports*, Leyden: Sijthoff's, p. 23) in which the Court also said that nationality constitutes 'the juridical expression of the fact that the individual upon whom it is conferred ... is in fact more closely connected with the population of the State conferring nationality than with that of any other State'. According to this definition the grant of nationality depends upon the existence of certain criteria of a social character. This conception of nationality is not easy to reconcile with the traditional rule, also confirmed by the Court in the same case, that 'international law leaves it to each State to lay down rules governing the grant of its own nationality'. The position, however, appears to be that, while it is for each state to determine who are its nationals under its own law, other states are not necessarily bound under international law to accept that determination.

B. 1. An individual is not a subject of international law, but through the possession of a nationality he comes within the ambit of that system. Thus, while an individual has no rights under international law which he can enforce directly against a foreign state, his own state may require of that state that he be treated according to the rules of international law. For this reason an individual who has no nationality, known as a 'stateless' person, suffers from many disadvantages, although these have been mitigated to some extent by international agreements.

2. The normal way in which nationality is acquired is through birth. Most states now combine the principle of *jus soli*, under which children born in their territory acquire their nationality, with the principle of *jus sanguinia*, under which children of their nationals acquire their nationality wherever they are born. Nationality may also be granted to a person who is originally foreign or stateless. This process is known as naturalization. When a change in the sovereignty over territory takes place, it is normal for the inhabitants to acquire the nationality of the new sovereign and to lose that of the old. It is possible for a person to possess two or more nationalities, or to possess none (i.e. 'stateless' person).

3. Article 15 of the Universal Declaration of Human Rights 1948 (United Nations Department of Public Information, 1949), provides '(1) Everyone has the right to a nationality', and '(2) No one shall be arbitrarily deprived of his nationality nor denied the right to change his nationality'. These principles, however, have not yet been adopted by states as legally binding rules.

In addition to linking individuals with international law, nationality performs a similar function in regard to companies, aircraft, and ships. These entities too are regarded as having national character and come under the protection of the state whose nationality they possess. Although a number of tests are applied, the most reliable is to consider a company as having the nationality of the state in which it is incorporated. In Article 17 of the Chicago Convention on International Civil Aviation, 1944, it is provided that 'Aircraft have the nationality of the State in which they are registered' (see *United States Aviation Reports*, Baltimore, 1945, p. 250). Similarly, in Article 5 (1) of the Geneva Convention on the High Seas, 1958, (*The Law of the Sea, The Final Act and Annexes of the United Nations Conference on the Law of the Sea*, Geneva, 1958, London: The Society of Comparative Legislation and International Law, 1958, p. 12) it is provided that 'Each State shall fix the conditions for the grant of its nationality to ships, for the registration of ships in its territory, and for the right to fly its flag. Ships have the nationality of the State whose flag they are entitled to fly. There must exist a genuine link between the State and the ship; in particular, the State must effectively exercise its jurisdiction and control in administrative, technical and social matters over ships flying its flag'. Although these provisions are somewhat obscure, their intention seems to be to apply to ships the same sort of criteria that were applied to an individual in the *Nottebohm* case.

D. H. N. Johnson

See also: CITIZENSHIP
NATION

Nationalization

A. 1. The term was first used at the beginning of the 19th century, and is occasionally still so employed, *to mean the action or process of rendering national in character*; e.g. 'Preeminently it [1860-77] was the period of nationalization in the American labor movement. Back of it all lay the nationalization of the economic life of the country' (J. R. Commons, *History of Labor in the United States*, New York: Macmillan, 1918, vol. II, p. 3).

2. A further usage, now rare, has the meaning of the *process of becoming a nation*; e.g. 'There is a distinct period in the history of our race, which may be aptly called the period of nationalization. Tribes, fragments, separate political societies, are united into nations, and politically they appear more and more as states' (F. Lieber, *On Civil Liberty* (1853), New York: Lippincott, 1875, p. 47).

3. Closely related to this is the use, still current in sociology, meaning the process of absorption or assimilation of an alien group into a nation and the now obsolete use as a synonym for *naturalization*.

4. The most common usage, however, which dates from about 1870, denotes the action of vesting the ownership and/or control of property, such as land and industries, in the nation. In this sense, the word is one of a group of cognate terms, including *socialization, public ownership, state ownership, common ownership* and *social ownership*, all of which are employed to designate one of the principal objects of modern socialist parties. No consistent usage has emerged and the meaning of *nationalization* remains vague. The predominant meaning of *nationalization* has been national ownership, as distinct from municipal or co-operative ownership.

B. Much of the ambiguity associated with usage (4) above stems from the distinction frequently drawn between ownership, on the one hand, and control and management, on the other. Strictly, nationalization might be said to entail *both ownership and control* by the state, but the term has been used to cover diverse schemes, ranging from ownership by the state with direct control by its officials to ownership or partial ownership by the state and control by independent or quasi-independent bodies, including workers' unions. It has also been used to describe measures taken by governments to control industries in the national interest, ownership remaining in private hands.

1. In recent years there has been a tendency, especially in Britain, to restrict the use of the term to the meaning of the taking over by the state of a *complete* industry. Nationalization is then seen as a form of public ownership; e.g. '... *nationalization* ... is generally understood to mean the taking over by the State of a complete industry so that it is owned by and managed and controlled for the Community, and *public ownership* ... strictly speaking means the ownership by the community of any property whether

Nativism

individual or not, whether embracing the whole of an industry or only part of it' (H. Gaitskell, *Socialism and Nationalization*, Fabian Tract 300, London: Fabian Society, 1956, p. 6).

2. There has also been a tendency to distinguish between *nationalization* and *socialization*, the latter signifying, in this context, a more democratic type of nationalization, e.g. 'The infusion of the public corporations by a genuine spirit of democracy is what people have in mind when they speak of the conversion of nationalization to socialization' (W. A. Robson, *Problems of Nationalized Industry*, London: Allen & Unwin, 1952, p. 346).

G. N. Ostergaard

See also: SOCIALISM

Nativism

Nativism is the movement of societies toward the reaffirmation of native tribal cultures in reaction to the stress of acculturation (q.v.). The term is owed to R. Linton ('Nativistic Movements', *American Anthropologist*, vol. 45, 1943, pp. 230–40). Related terms are *fundamentalism, reformation, reform movements, religious revival, messianic movements, utopianism, sect formation, mass movement, social movement, social revolution, grass roots movement*, or *charismatic movement* to the extent that these are seen as occurring under conditions of acculturation. Thus nativism is not an unusual phenomenon, but is recurrent in human history whenever conditions of acculturation threaten the tribal culture and create what G. Murray (*Five Stages of Greek Religion*, Oxford: Oxford University Press, 2nd edn., 1925, pp. 153–209) describes as 'Hellenistic despair' or the 'failure of nerve'. Sometimes it has been of great historical importance. Examples of nativism would include peyotism (q.v.) and cargo cults (q.v.). Another example is the Ghost Dance of the American Indians in which many Plains, Plateau, Great Basin, and formerly Eastern Woodlands tribes believed that the Whites and all their works and ways would be destroyed in a universal cataclysm, after which a new world would arrive containing the buffalo and the ghosts of the dead (J. Mooney, *The Ghost Dance Religion and the Sioux Outbreak of* 1890, 14th Annual Report of the Bureau of American Ethnology, Washington: Bureau of American Ethnology, 1896, pp. 653–1004).

Weston La Barre

See also: REVITALIZATION MOVEMENT

Natural Area

A. A *natural area* is a territorial unit whose distinctive characteristics—physical, economic, and cultural—are the result of the unplanned operation of ecological and social processes. Accordingly, its boundaries are determined by barriers to movement and communication. Natural areas stand in contrast with administrative areas which are arbitrarily delimited to serve some special purpose. Natural areas have been characterized in empirical studies by such terms as cultural, delinquency, gang, family, immigrant, industrial, residential, rural, suburban, trade, and vice areas. The term, introduced into anthropology by F. Ratzel, was borrowed and redefined by sociologists.

B. In sociological research the concept of natural area has been used as a frame of reference (a) for identifying and describing neighbourhoods, local communities, and regions, (b) for the spotting, assembling, and interpretation of population distribution data, (c) for the analysis of the functional interrelations of local communities in a larger unit such as the metropolitan region.

Ernest W. Burgess

See also: ECOLOGY
INTERSTITIAL AREA
METROPOLITAN AREA

Natural Increase

A. The term denotes that increase in the size of a population that is due to a surplus of births over deaths. A decline in the size of a population due to a surplus of deaths over births would be a *natural decrease*, although this term is seldom encountered simply because there have not been very many empirical situations to which it is applicable in the modern world.

B. Populations can increase or decrease in size only through two processes of which one is natural increase or decrease, the other is migration. In the analysis of the population of the world only the former is relevant, but in almost all contemporary tribes or nations the increase or decrease is due to a combination of the two processes.

William L. Kolb

See also: BIRTH RATE
DEATH RATE
FERTILITY
MIGRATION
MORTALITY
RATES OF REPRODUCTION

Natural Law

A. *Natural law* refers to a body of principles and rules believed to be uniquely fitting for and binding upon a community of rational beings. Sometimes thought of as applying only to a primitive society or, again, to an ideal society, it is generally believed to have some relevance to the governance of existing societies and usually is related directly as ideal, standard, or guide for the positive laws of existing societies.

B. In the social sciences the terms *natural law* and *law of nature* are prescriptive; that is they relate to some concept of what rules ought to prevail. It is often held, however, that there is a close relationship between natural human laws and natural physical laws. Although the latter are purely 'descriptive', they may be thought of as 'regulating' the phenomena to which they apply. At the same time, the prescriptive laws of nature held binding upon human conduct are often believed to derive from a general body of laws of the universe that includes the laws of physical nature as well. According to this view, some laws of nature govern the movements of the planets and others govern the conduct of men; but they are of the same general kind.

Ever since the dawn of political and legal theorizing, natural law doctrine has played an important role in political and legal philosophy. Adopted from the Stoics by the Roman lawyers, it played a key role in the formation and spread of Roman law, in two epochs of history, over most of the civilized world. In the medieval period the Church took it up and gave it currency and prestige, while in the 17th and 18th centuries a secularized version, expounded first by Grotius, not only served as the foundation for the developing law of nations but also absorbed the whole body of theory of law, state, and society. Today utilitarianism and positivism have greatly loosened its hold on the modern mind. Yet, adhered to by the Catholic Church, and recurrently finding new sources of support, especially as a reaction to the doctrines of totalitarianism, natural law can by no means be written off as a dead dogma.

C. The set of ideas that attach themselves to the term can best be portrayed by a series of antinomies.

1. There is the opposition between *natural* and *artificial*. Artificial law is law that is the product of deliberation and will; and conversely natural law is spontaneous and uncontrived, a product of the continuous flow of life.

2. Natural law is *rational* as opposed to *empirical*; it is the product of reason and conforms to reason as contrasted with rules of conduct that lack such correspondence or that are accepted as binding merely because they are generally obeyed or because they are commanded by recognized authority.

3. A third antinomy, between the *ideal* and the *real*, is perhaps the most basic of all, at least for modern usage. But the point at which the ideal applies varies. Some writers have considered natural law as the law that would be ideal for (and perhaps would prevail in) a primitive society. Others have spoken of it as the law that would be proper for an ideal society. But the most common notion is that of an ideal for existing society.

4. Finally, one must note the twin antinomies of the *immutable* and the *changing* and the *eternal* and the *temporary*. Throughout all concepts of natural law runs the thread of universality and eternity. Even those modern notions that speak of 'natural law with changing content' retain the idea of a central core, though it be a matter of form rather than substance that is eternal.

D. Natural law may also be defined, or at least explained, in terms of its source, nature, or foundation. How is natural law discovered or made known to man?

1. A widely acceptable answer would be that natural law is the law peculiar to rational beings and is made evident to them by their reason. How reason discovers natural law is a more difficult question. Some hold with Plato that reason in its highest form includes the faculty of perceiving a priori truth, of direct insight into the eternal verities. Many who speak of the principles of natural law as self-evident to rational beings have this sense in mind. This concept of natural law may be referred to as *transcendental*. Most writers, however, would hold that only the most general principles of natural law (e.g. that one should not do harm to others) could be known in this fashion. Other principles and rules can be derived from these by reasoning and experience.

2. Another way in which it is held that natural law may be found out by reason is by deriving it from the physical and psychological nature of man and especially from observed *tendencies* of human nature. Just as it is the nature of an acorn to become an oak tree, so it is the nature of man to develop wisdom and virtue, and those things that are natural and right may be discovered by observing the tendencies inherent in man and essential to him. This *immanent* view of natural law is characteristically Aristotelian. Some modern writers who reject any idea of 'essence' nonetheless hold that it is possible to discover, empirically, certain rules of conduct that lead to the most satisfactory life, or the most happy and harmonious society, or something of the sort. This notion of *empirical* natural law provides yet another category.

3. For centuries Churchmen tended to identify natural law with the law of God. Although St. Thomas kept the two distinct, no less an authority than Gratian identified natural law with the law of the Scriptures and the Gospel, and more particularly with the golden rule. For supporters of this view the source of natural law is revelation.

4. In recent times many writers have sought to avoid difficulties regarding the foundations of right and justice by defining natural law simply as those principles of morality that could appropriately be enacted into positive law; or, alternatively, as that portion of morality that finds support in the popular 'sense of right'.

E. However defined, natural law may be thought of as serving various functions; and the way it is viewed will in turn affect the role it plays in society.

1. For instance, it may be considered as the basis of all human (positive) law, the latter being only an extension and application of its principles. This view, generally combined, as with Aristotle and Aquinas, with the contention that the state is natural, tends to be conservative, because it is then presumed that the laws of the state partake of the quality of natural law.

2. Again, natural law may be considered as a standard by which to judge positive laws and the actions of the rulers who make and administer those laws. Such a critical notion is conducive, as generally in the medieval period, to the thought that the acts of tyrants who defy natural law are not binding and may even justify violent resistance. While the notion of resistance was generally minimized during this period, post-Reformation philosophers, who started with man's natural freedom and thought of the state as an artificial device for the protection of that freedom and of other rights derived from natural law, were easily led to more radical doctrines. Thus Locke and Paine

used natural law, and its derivative natural rights, to justify individual claims against the state and ultimately the right to revolt. While this point of view has been characteristic of the post-Reformation world, it should be stressed that this individualistic approach is by no means necessarily anti-social. Burlamaqui was typical of many 18th-century writers in defining natural law as 'that which so necessarily agrees with the nature and state of man that, without observing its maxims, neither the individuals nor society can maintain themselves in an honest and comportable state' (*The Principles of Natural and Politic Law*, 2 vols., trans. by T. Nugent, London: Nourse, 3rd edn., 1784, vol. 1, pt. 1, ch. X, par. 15, p. 110).

3. Finally, natural law may also play a role in the more limited sphere of the judicial process, providing a standard for judges in interpreting laws and constitutions, in filling in gaps in the law, and even (in the most extreme application of the theory) for declaring laws null and void as contrary to the law of nature (see *Judicial Review*). In this application the theory may be conservative, reformist, or neutral.

F. As to the content of natural law there is much disagreement. If we confine ourselves to the most general rules and principles, however, there is probably more agreement as to the substance of the rules than as to their origin or authority. Almost any list of such rules would include the following propositions: human life is to be protected and forwarded; no one should injure another. Perhaps more subject to dispute, yet very widely held, are the propositions that all men are born free and equal. Modern analysis tends to reduce this age-old formula to the contention that there is a presumption in favour of freedom, and likewise of equality. In other words, any infringement on man's freedom or equality must be justified.

J. Roland Pennock

See also: CULTURAL RELATIVITY
NATURAL RIGHT

Natural Monopoly (See **Monopoly**)

Natural Right

A. A *natural right* may be defined as a liberty or immunity that ought to be protected or a service or enablement that ought to be provided for all men at all times and under all conditions.

B. Although it has an ancient lineage, the term *natural right* came into general use in the 17th and 18th centuries, with regard to assertions of liberties, immunities, or enablements assigned to individual men by natural law (q.v.). By definition natural rights must be unconditional, immutable, and inalienable, and it is usually claimed that they are the same for all men. They were thought of as those rights that man enjoyed in a 'state of nature' before the establishment of civil society; or rights that *would* pertain to man in the absence of government. The most commonly asserted natural rights were those of life, liberty, and equality—generally stated without further definition.

C. 1. Natural rights were widely believed to be self-evident. When justification was attempted, especially in earlier periods, it was generally in terms of one or another of the lines of reasoning discussed in this volume under *Natural Law*. Especially in England, natural rights were often identified with particular legal rights alleged to have been recognized and guaranteed in the past. As such they provided a potent rallying cry for revolutionaries seeking the re-establishment of old rights that had been infringed upon or, sometimes, seeking the establishment of new rights under the guise that they were old. The Puritan Revolution and the Revolution of 1688 in England and the American Revolution all provided examples of this kind of use.

2. More philosophically minded attempts at justification were made by Hobbes, Locke, and by the French philosophers of the Enlightenment. T. Hobbes (1588–1679) would have nothing of self-evident or rationally apprehended truth. Rights, he reasoned, are liberties to do what is not prohibited by law. Since in the state of nature there is no law, 'nature hath given to every one a right to all' (*De Cive or The Citizen*, ed. S. P. Lamprecht, New York: Appleton-Century-Crofts, 1949, p. 27). But with the coming of society, even so much as is involved by the family, man enters into various engagements that limit his natural rights; and according to the social contract, by which civil society is established, man gives up all his natural rights except the right to that which is necessary to preserve his life against attack, and certain matters believed incident or equivalent thereto.

Locke (1632–1704) held the view, more typical both of his own age and of the natural law tradition from which it was derived, that it was self-evident that certain rights pertained to man as man. They existed in the state of nature and they

continued in civil society. On entering the state man gave up only his right to enforce his natural rights; this he transferred to the state. These rights included the rights of life, liberty (freedom from arbitrary rule), and equality. Property, by a process of derivation from principles believed to be self-evident, was added to the list.

It is the Lockean doctrine that has been historically more important, providing the foundation both for alleged rights of revolution (a use to which Locke himself put the notion and which was applied by Jefferson in formulating the American Declaration of Independence) and for bills of rights as frequently embodied in constitutions (as in the case of the French Declaration of the Rights of Man and Citizen and the American Bill of Rights).

D. In England, a century after Locke, both Burke and Bentham, so unlike in most ways, united in condemning the doctrine. They would have agreed with the remark of the American Supreme Court Justice Holmes, who declared that the word 'rights' was 'a constant solicitation to fallacy'. Bentham himself considered talk of rights as 'nonsense', while natural rights to his way of thinking were 'nonsense on stilts'. But, especially in the United States, the doctrine long retained its vigour and is even today not without force. Courts not infrequently have made use of the concept in declaring certain laws invalid, and especially in interpreting the vague constitutional provision regarding due process of law (q.v.). While nowadays the doctrine is generally conservative rather than revolutionary, being invoked in support of vested interests, it is also used to justify certain procedural liberties essential to individual freedom and justice, such as the right to a fair trial.

E. Philosophers long since came to realize that the notion of a right implies the existence of others against whom the right is claimed, and that therefore it makes no sense to talk of rights in a pre-social condition. It remains possible, however, to speak of natural rights as those claims of liberty, immunity, or enablement that ought to be given legal sanction in an ideal society, or, alternatively, as those moral rights that exist in all societies and at all times. Today as in the past most assertions of natural right are qualified by the limitation that the natural rights of each person are limited as much as is necessary to secure the like rights for all others. Whether any such rights can be validated is a matter of dispute among philosophers. The

Need

tendency among those who accept the notion as valid is to define the asserted natural rights much more carefully than was the practice of earlier theorists and to narrow their range, sometimes to a single natural right, as for instance the right to equal freedom.

J. Roland Pennock

See also: CULTURAL RELATIVITY
NATURAL LAW

Need (Psychology)

A. In psychology the term denotes whatever is required for the health or well-being of a person. If this is lacking, there is set up an internal disturbance which occasions a drive (q.v.). Examples are the need for oxygen, for food, for stimulation, or for love. A wider use of this term is sometimes found in personality theory, where it refers to anything a person wants with sufficient consistency over time for this to be treated as a feature of his personality.

B. The use of this term in psychology is not generally a technical one, since it is the same as used in ordinary language. The word is generally used as a complement to *drive* and therefore may be associated with the reaction against instinct theory. Most psychologists, however, use the word *drive* in preference to *need*, when referring to the particular objects of the drive or need, such as food, sex or prestige. An important exception is H. A. Murray, who in his system of personality description uses the word *need* rather than *drive*. Hence it is in terms of need rather than of drive that productions in the T.A.T. projection test are generally analysed. In Murray's scheme, however, *need* includes personality traits such as dominance, exhibitionism, affiliation, etc., conceived as purposeful behavioural and neurological entities (*need* in the wider sense referred to under A. above). Not all traits, according to this scheme, are needs. Examples of ones that are not are anxiety, creativity, and endurance. That Murray has technicalized the word is suggested by his definition 'A need is a construct ... which stands for a force ... in the brain region, a force which organizes perception, apperception, intellection, conation and action in such a way as to transform in a certain direction an existing, unsatisfying situation. A need is sometimes provoked directly by internal processes of a certain kind (viscerogenic, endocrinogenic, thalamicogenic) arising in the course of vital sequences but, more frequently (when in a state of readiness) by the occurrence of one of a few commonly effective press (or by anticipatory images of such press). Thus, it manifests itself by leading the organism to search for or to avoid encountering or, when encountered, to attend and respond to certain kinds of press ... Each need is characteristically accompanied by a particular feeling or emotion and tends to use certain modes (sub-needs and actones) to further its trend' (*Explorations in Personality*, New York: Oxford University Press, 1938, pp. 123–4). Barring the fact that nothing is said about genetic aspects. Murray's conception of need is not dissimilar from McDougall's of instinct.

W. H. N. Hotopf

See also: DRIVE
MOTIVATION
NEED (Sociology and Anthropology)

Need (Sociology and Anthropology)

A. 1. The use of the term *need* in sociology and anthropology is frequently the same as that found in psychology (see *Need (Psychology)*) and in social psychology derived from individual psychology: the denotation of whatever is required for physical well-being, or what if lacking, will lead to internal disturbance that sets off a drive.

2. Such usage is not universal, however. Rather the term may be used to denote requirements of which the person becomes aware when he acquires values (q.v.) that demand he should strive for a certain end or comport himself in a given fashion in a given situation. This usage is found in sociology and anthropology and in social psychology which is rooted in sociology and anthropology.

B. Usage A. (1) results in the denigration of the cultural and social sources of human conduct, because social needs are held to be secondary needs derived from basic or biological needs. The ultimate basis of human or sociocultural behaviour is thus some constitutional or hereditary ground. Usage A. (2), in contrast, distinguishes between the physical requirements necessary for life and the sociocultural principles of human conduct. Physiological processes contribute to human motivation by generating an unspecific restlessness and a few undefined sensations that can have no meaning and result in no co-ordinated activity until there has been some learning of symbols (q.v.).

Symbols provide one with the means of interpreting to oneself the meaning of the sensations one believes one is experiencing. It is through symbolic interaction that the sociocultural takes precedence over the biological in human behaviour. Human beings in interaction with one another create values and these values having been created are learnt in the community and guide and control behaviour. Values not only determine the form of the fulfilment of the biological necessities, but also whether or not they will be fulfilled at all. Thus religious convictions (values) may determine that one will starve when food is available (dietary rules), or remain celibate (the priesthood), or die (martyrdom). Needs, in this context, arise when a person acquires values that demand that he should strive for a certain end or comport himself in a given fashion generally or in a given situation (cf. D. Lee, 'Are Basic Needs Ultimate?', in D. Lee, *Freedom and Culture*, New York: Prentice-Hall, 1959, pp. 70–7).

Thus when need is used in this manner it is understood that *human* needs are not homologous with the hierarchy of needs that have been established for animals. One's human needs, being derived from sociocultural experience, are qualitatively different in three respects from the organic necessities for physical existence. First, the locus of existence of human needs is the culture and society in which the person lives. Second, the person develops needs that are appropriate to the general values by which he lives. Third, the person is able to have needs because he becomes able to think through the use of symbols. Through symbols he can organize and comprehend his experience, and through the use of language can infer the existence of his needs or motives, and learn to interpret certain situations as calling for the expression of a certain kind and degree of action and perhaps also of emotion.

Frank E. Hartung

See also: NEED (Psychology)
  SOCIAL INTERACTION
  SYMBOL
  SYMBOLISM
  VALUE

Negotiation

A. The term *negotiation* denotes discussions between representatives of two or more sovereign states initiated with the object of settling differences between them or concluding an agreement on matters of mutual concern.

B. Negotiation is to be distinguished from (a) resort to armed force; (b) judicial methods for the settlement of contentious issues, such as international courts of justice and arbitral tribunals; (c) an application by the states concerned to third parties who are asked to use their good offices or to mediate; (d) the diplomatic 'exchange of views', the latter being simply informal conversations between diplomatic agents seeking to clarify the positions of their respective governments; (e) imposed or dictated settlements, such as the Treaty of Versailles (1919), which was first negotiated between the Allied and Associated Powers themselves and then presented to Germany for signature. In this last distinction there is a certain artificiality, however, as in practically all negotiated agreements there is an element of coercion on one side or the other, and most states to whom settlements are dictated at a peace conference have consented to that condition by freely laying down their arms. Negotiated and dictated treaties are equally binding in law.

C. Negotiation is not necessarily bilateral, that is, between two states only. Most of the great peace settlements in modern history, as for instance the Peace of Utrecht (1714), Paris (1763), Vienna (1815), Versailles (1919), have been negotiated between all the great Powers of the day with a more or less subordinate role accorded to smaller states. With the creation of permanent international institutions such as the League of Nations and the United Nations the practice has grown of widening the basis of negotiation, on political as well as technical questions, so as to embrace more and more states, together with the obligation to register all negotiated settlements with the secretariat of the institution. Such institutions also often impose the obligation of Members, as under Article 33 (1) of the United Nations Charter, to settle their disputes by peaceful means, including negotiation. The entrusting of negotiation to these multilateral bodies, however, sometimes called 'diplomacy by conference', has been objected to on three grounds: first, because it tends to destroy the essentially confidential character of negotiation; secondly, because it may give a voice in negotiation to states other than those directly concerned and hence may weaken the durability of the ultimate settlement; and thirdly, because it serves to place negotiation in the hands of principals, that is, Heads of Government and Ministers, rather than in those of diplomats with special training and experience

Neighbourhood

in negotiation. But these institutions have never superseded private negotiation between states.

F. S. Northedge

See also: CONCILIATION
DIPLOMACY
MEDIATION

Neighbourhood

A. *Neighbourhood* denotes one or more of the following: (a) a small inhabited area; (b) the inhabitants of such an area; (c) the relations which exist between the inhabitants: the fact or quality of their nearness to each other; (d) friendly relations between the inhabitants.

B. 1. There is no doubt that the scientific use of the term was much influenced by C. H. Cooley who (in his book *Social Organization*, New York: Scribners, 1909, and elsewhere), placed stress upon spontaneous, primary group relationships and their appearance in the 'neighbourhood'. Nonetheless, as is clear from the *Oxford English Dictionary*, there are 17th- and 18th-century usages of the word in the sense of community. Indeed, Steele, in *Spectator*, vol. 9, writes 'those little communities which we call by the word neighbourhoods', and this clearly foreshadows the more technical use of the word as found in the 20th-century sociological and town-planning literature.

2. In modern usage the term neighbourhood is used to refer to a small inhabited area considered, so to say, 'on its own'. 'The neighbourhood which in early times was virtually identical with the village community, is in modern times also practically synonymous with crossroad and open country population groupings which have not yet attained the status of villages' (N. Carpenter in E. R. A. Seligman (ed.), *Encyclopedia of the Social Sciences*, New York: The Macmillan Co., vol. XI, 1933, p. 356). It is more commonly used in urban sociology, to refer to a small segment of a larger inhabited area—territorial groups within the town that are more or less distinguishable on physical and socio-economic criteria. To the notion of the neighbourhood as a 'geographical expression' is added the idea that those who dwell in such a segment enjoy (or are capable of enjoying) frequent 'primary' or 'face-to-face' contacts with each others. Thus the University of Liverpool Social Science Department said that 'It must be emphasized that the essence of a neighbourhood from the point of view of the planner and sociologist alike, is the opportunity it provides for people to meet together, to share the burdens of daily life, and to co-operate in an endeavour to overcome their common problems' (*Social Aspects of a Town Development Plan*, Liverpool: University Press, 1951). So also E. R. R. Power claims that 'Neighbourhood arises out of the impact of locality on society but it does not arise inevitably or automatically. Individuals may be neighbours in physical fact without being neighbours in social fact. It implies something more than mere contact. It implies common interest' ('Social Structure of an English County Town', *Sociological Review*, vol. 29, 1927, p. 401).

C. Much use has been made of the conception of *neighbourhood unit*. As used by administrators and sociologists this principle is two-fold: 'This idea involves not simply a grouping of people in a unit convenient for certain local services and amenities—for which perhaps it may be eminently practical—but also a social objective—a unit small enough to encourage a neighbourhood spirit and at the same time large enough to be relatively self-contained' (D. V. Glass, 'The Application of Social Research', *British Journal of Sociology*, vol. 1, 1950, p. 20). It is also made to imply, in important cases, the need for a 'balanced' heterogeneous social composition: 'Instead of accepting administrative efficiency as the objective, the aim has rather been to create a "balanced community" in each Neighbourhood, by giving all classes and all kinds of individuals an appropriate place and an appropriate function in it' (University of Liverpool Social Science Department, *Social Aspects of a Town Development Plan*, pp. 26–7); on aspects of this requirement see D. V. Glass, 'The Application of Social Research', and J. Westergaard & R. Glass, 'A Profile of Lansbury' (*Town Planning Review*, vol. XXV, 1954, pp. 50–1).

J. Gould

See also: COMMUNITY
GROUP

Neighbourhood Unit (See Neighbourhood)

Neolocal (See Residence)

Nepotism

A. *Nepotism* is the practice whereby a public officer appoints one or more close relatives to the public service or confers on them other favours in order to promote the family's prestige or augment the family's income or to assist in building up a political machine, rather than for the promotion of the public welfare. The family relationship distinguishes *nepotism* from the broader but closely related terms, *patronage* (q.v.) and *spoils*.

B. The term may have been used originally 'to describe the distribution of power and principalities by the pope to his natural sons, euphemistically termed nephews, and to his other relatives' (L. D. White, 'Spoils System' in E. R. A. Seligman (ed.), *Encyclopedia of the Social Sciences*, New York: The Macmillan Co., 1934, vol. XIV, p. 302). Nepotism is not a phenomenon of government restricted to any single period in history. In modern democracies this practice often is associated with the spoils system. Nepotism is a word of scorn when it is applied to the practice of a public officer who places relatives on the public payroll in order to promote the family's prestige, to augment the family's income, or to assist in building up a political machine. It is less justly applied to the responsible official who appoints his spouse, a son, or other near relative to serve as his personal and confidential assistant or adviser. The term *nepotism* is not commonly applied to the well-established practice of business men of appointing relatives to positions in business under their management. Nor is it applied to the practice, common in some nations, of selecting public officers from the dominant social class closely knit by family and friendship ties, thereby assisting in the development of a closely knit governing class of narrow social outlook.

Charles Aikin

See also: PATRONAGE

Net National Product (See **National Product**)

Net Reproduction Rate (See **Rates of Reproduction**)

Net Revenue (See **Revenue**)

Net Worth
A. *Net worth* is an accounting concept, the chief usage of which is in the record-keeping of business firms. In this usage it denotes the excess of the *book value* of all assets over liabilities to outsiders. Thus it is an indication of the interests of the owner(s) in a business enterprise; in the case of a corporation it would represent the interests of the stockholders; in a sole proprietorship, the proprietor's equity in the business. Defined in this manner, net worth is the

equivalent of the capital investment in a business.

B. The chief purpose of early bookkeeping was to determine the gain or loss from the operation of an enterprise during a period of time and to show the net wealth or assets of the enterprise at a point in time. Thus the predecessors of the present-day balance sheet were essentially statements of profit or loss in which the assets as of the beginning and end of an accounting period were derived and stated. Early treatises on accounting practice reflect this purpose and show that several different expressions were used interchangeably to mean *owner's interest or wealth*. E. Peragallo (*Origin and Evolution of Double Entry Bookkeeping*, New York: American Institute, 1938) cites examples showing that early Italians used the Italian equivalents of *balance to our credit*, *net worth*, and *capital* as synonyms. A. C. Littleton (*Accounting Evolution to 1900*, New York: American Institute, 1933) gives evidence that the English accountants from the 16th century on followed 'after the Italian manner' but showed a preference for such terminology as *stocks*, *net capital*, *capital*, or *capital stocks*.

C. Historically, the net worth or capital account was intended to show two things, the share or interest of the owner(s) in the assets of the enterprise and the value or worth of that interest. Therefore, the expression *net worth* was particularly descriptive of the purpose of the account so named. However, as accounting matured it became obvious that the book value of net worth was an estimate derived from historical records based on the conventions of accounting practice and policy decisions within the firm. For this reason, the *book value* may or may not equal the true *economic value* at the time of the statement. For example, a piece of machinery or a building is typically recorded in the books at the price paid for it at the time of purchase minus any depreciation charged against it. If price levels change or if the method of charging depreciation is in error, the accounts will not state the true market value of the asset. Hence, net worth in a statement of accounts is properly interpreted only as an indication of ownership claims against the total assets of the business entity *as they are recorded*.

Because of this realization, the expression *net worth* is becoming obsolete. The British now frequently use the expression *total equity*. E. L. Kohler (*A Dictionary for Accountants*,

Neurosis

Englewood Cliffs, N.J.: Prentice-Hall, 1952, p. 71) lists *stockholders' equity* as recognized American terminology, and the Committee on Accounting Concepts and Standards of the American Accounting Association (*Accounting and Reporting Standards for Corporate Financial Statements and Preceding Statements and Supplements*, Columbus, O.: American Accounting Association, 1957, p. 16) uses *stockholders' interest*. Although the newer terminology is more precise and less likely to mislead, it highlights the fact that accounting records do not provide a measure of the economic value or market value of the owner(s)' capital invested in an enterprise. This makes most difficult the economists' attempts to measure the profitability of an enterprise or the rate of return on capital in various industries. Such analysis must rely on other estimates of capital at work in an enterprise.

Paul G. Craig

See also: CAPITAL

Neurosis

A. *Neurosis* denotes a psychological disorder, of varying degree of severity, which arises defensively to ward off, by inhibiting or acting-out behaviour, anxiety-ridden conflicts. In basic form it is incurred in early life, but can also be acquired in later life, depending upon the severity of the critical experience. It varies in content and sometimes in form with the culture and the social organization.

B. 1. There is controversy over the dynamics, classification, and causation of neuroses. From the orthodox psychoanalytic view, according to E. Jones, 'A neurosis essentially means that the patient is unconsciously clinging to various infantile pleasurable longings and phantasies ... and that his symptoms constitute a compromise-formation by means of which he vicariously obtains a gratification of these' (*Papers on Psychoanalysis*, London: Baillière, Tindall & Cox, 3rd edn., 1932, p. 317). W. Healy, A. F. Bronner, and A. M. Bowers (*The Structure and Meaning of Psychoanalysis*, New York: Knopf, 1930, p. 409) note Walder's definition of neurosis as 'the automatisation of anxiety reaction' and the unresolved question of 'why some people fall victim to this automatisation ... and the rest of mankind manage to escape this fate to a degree sufficient for practical purposes'.

2. Equally important are the points of view concerning cultural factors implicit in analysis of the deviations from customary behaviour on the basis of which neuroses are imputed (see K. Horney, *The Neurotic Personality of Our Time*, London: Routledge & Kegan Paul, 1953, p. 14 et seq.).

3. There are related controversies about whether or not neurosis (a) is a defensive reaction to avert anxiety, (b) has acting-out as well as inhibiting symptoms, (c) can be acquired from frustrations in later life as well as in early life, (d) is a psychological and not a constitutional disorder, and (e) pertains to a similar category of disorder in the case of both animals and humans.

(a) The prevalent conception of neurosis is that it is a defensive reaction which is aroused by anxiety and is oriented towards averting the recurrence of anxiety. The key defensive reaction is repression (q.v.) in which the afflicted individual forgets, denies, or cannot face the experiences which aroused the anxiety. The multitude of neurotic reactions incapacitate the individual by compelling him to avoid the problems arousing the anxiety. Hysteria, obsession-compulsion, and phobic reactions, as broad categories of neurotic defences, tend to restrict the scope of the neurotic's behaviour, are repetitious, and by averting the basic personal conflicts compel the afflicted individual to suffer. Another view of neurosis does not regard anxiety as the core of neurosis, but as a symptom parallel to other neurotic symptoms. The neurosis itself then becomes a conscious escape from conflicts, but this latter view does not clarify the basis of personal conflicts nor does it relate these conflicts to self-esteem and to unconscious attitudes and impulses.

(b) Although frequently considered inhibited behaviour, and hence prevalent among middle-class urbanized persons, neurosis also can include acting-out behaviour. Thus fighting, destruction, and antisocial behaviour become defensive recourses to quiet anxiety and are considered neurotic reactions, just as excessive fears and aversions are. This inclusive view would resolve the divergent views of neurosis as either the repression of intense impulses or as the expression of immature impulses. From this position both types of defences would be divergent expressions of neurosis for different personality types. This inclusive view of neurosis does not, however, include psychoses (q.v.) such as schizophrenia.

(c) Neurosis has been regarded as a basic disorder, the predispositions for which occur in early life, but the neurotic breakdowns of relatively stable soldiers during combat were demonstrable exceptions. The disorders of these stable soldiers were diagnosed as neurotic reactions distinct from basic neurosis. Neuroses which are acquired in later life, are less ingrained than basic neuroses which are acquired in early life but are more responsive to treatment.

(d) Neurosis has been described as a psychological disorder which arises from critical stresses. This view is opposed by another emphasis which regards the constitution as exerting the chief predisposing influences. For example, R. Linton (*Culture and Mental Disorders*, Springfield, Ill.: Thomas, 1956, p. 100) maintains that 'even the limited data available at present suggests that in neurosis, as in psychosis, there may be an underlying constitutional factor, since in all societies many individuals undergo experiences which make only some people neurotic but leave the majority who also had such experiences, non-neurotic'. It is doubtful, however, that neurotics and normal persons have had meaningfully similar developmental and precipitating stress situations. Furthermore the separation of neurotics from normals is quite difficult without direct clinical examinations.

(e) The conception of neurosis as an emergent of anxiety emphasizes its symbolic and complicated character. For this reason human neuroses must be differentiated from the simple, non-symbolic, neurotic-like 'startles', 'shocks', and 'failures to behave' among animals.

S. Kirson Weinberg

See also: ANXIETY
         DEFENCE MECHANISM
         PSYCHOSIS

Neutralism

A. The term *neutralism* has entered into international currency, especially since World War II, to indicate the position of those who wish to avoid being politically or diplomatically committed to either side in the struggle between the Communist and non-Communist worlds.

B. 1. This position has taken, or takes, a variety of forms (e.g. in Western Europe, in Asia, in Yugoslavia) dependent upon the politics and geographical situation of the countries concerned.

2. It differs from traditional neutrality (q.v.) (though the two expressions are sometimes used synonymously) in three major respects.

(a) It refers to the mental attitudes of individuals and groups as well as to the foreign policies of states. *Neutrality*, on the other hand, is the legal condition of impartiality which states alone may adopt in conflicts between other states. Hence neutralism covers a diversity of positions, extending from isolationism at one extreme to active effort to lessen international tension at the other, whereas the implications of neutrality are specified by the uniform provisions of international law.

(b) Neutralism usually implies a relatively coherent political philosophy, involving either the acceptance of principles intermediate between those of the rival powers or the outright rejection of the principles of both groups, and possibly also a distinct conception of international relations, as for instance the repudiation of force, the balance of power, etc. By contrast neutrality necessitates no general political outlook of this kind. Certain neutrals in the past have defended their actions in moral terms, but traditionally neutrality has been adopted in the national interest and as occasion served without any conscious need for such justification.

(c) Although states such as Sweden, Holland and the United States have sometimes been described as 'permanent neutrals', neutrality refers to non-participation in a state of war, whereas neutralism expresses detachment in relation, not to war or peace as historically understood, but to conflict, peaceful or violent, between two organized power groupings.

C. Neutralism entails refusal to join military pacts, to receive arms or military aid from either side or provide military bases for either side, and to commit oneself, either by treaty or more informally, to uphold one or other of the contemporary world ideologies. This negative aspect of neutralism is sometimes called non-alignment, non-involvement, or the pursuit of an 'independent' foreign policy, its devotees being described as the uncommitted peoples. Since a suggestion of moral indifference or selfishness may seem to inhere in such an attitude, neutralism commonly has a more positive side, taking the form of attempts to reconcile or mediate between the rival groups or to promote international peace through disarmament or disengagement and, above all, by support for the method of interpreting each issue as it arises 'on its merits', rather than in terms of rigid, preempted ideological categories. This aspect is sometimes called *positive neutralism* or the promotion of a 'regime of peace'.

F. S. Northedge

See also: NEUTRALITY

Neutrality

Neutrality

A. *Neutrality* denotes the condition of impartiality or non-belligerence in war or the rights and duties of states enjoying such a condition. There has always been some argument regarding the substantive content of neutrality rules between belligerents and neutrals, with the former claiming limited neutral rights and extended neutral duties and the latter taking the reverse stand. It seems that the root of the disagreement may be the fact that those who speak of the destruction of neutrality emphasize specific rights and duties, the content, while those who argue that it exists emphasize neutrality as an attitude, or a claim to a certain status.

B. Two world wars followed by two attempts to establish systems of collective security have led writers in the field of international law to be concerned more with the question of the existence of neutrality than with its meaning.

'Neutrality, in popular thought, means keeping out of war. It is the condition of those who remain at peace while others are fighting. In this sense, the problem of neutrality is as old as war itself. From a more technical point of view, this is scarcely true because in its modern meaning "neutrality" is a legal status involving certain rights and duties' (P. C. Jessup, *Neutrality: Its History, Economics and Law*, New York: Columbia University Press, 1936, vol. 4, p. 3).

The substantive content of the law of neutrality (the rights and duties referred to above) has been a developing body of rules, but basic among the rights and duties of neutral states are the inviolability of territory and the obligation of impartiality and non-participation in war (Harvard Research, 'Rights and Duties of Neutral States in Naval and Aerial War', *American Journal of International Law*, Supplement 33, 1939, pp. 232, 334). Specific content can only be sampled here. The Declaration of Paris (1856) reasserted the maxim of 'free ships, free goods'; the so-called Washington rules (1871) prohibited a neutral from allowing the fitting of a vessel in its territory for participation in war; the Hague Convention Concerning the Rights and Duties of Neutral Powers and Persons in Case of War on Land (1907) obligated a neutral to intern troops belonging to a belligerent army.

Following the violations of neutrality during the world wars and the establishment of collective security systems which appeared to diminish the possibility of neutrality, interest in substantive content declined to the point that one editor of a standard text on international law 'drastically cut' materials on the subject and suggested that his readers rely on the bibliographical references he supplies (H. W. Briggs (ed.), *The Law of Nations*, London: Stevens, 1953, p. 1038). C. Eagleton asserts that the law of neutrality was 'destroyed' in the past wars and now that 'it is an obsolete status' (*International Government*, New York: Ronald Press, 1957, p. 16). P. B. Potter asserts that the 'term, as known prior to 1945, was abolished for all signatory states within the limits of the Charter. For issues and conflicts not covered by that instrument neutrality could still exist or be maintained and practised' ('Neutrality, 1955', *American Journal of International Law*, vol. 50, 1956, p. 102). The implication from Eagleton is that the violations of neutrality in wars resulted in its destruction; from Potter, that neutrality is incompatible with a system of collective security. On the other hand, P. C. Jessup wrote in 1936 that 'governments still insist on talking in terms of neutrality' (*Neutrality: Its History, Economics and Law*, vol. 4). More recently, J. Stone took a similar view, saying that it is 'regrettably clear that the law of neutrality (as distinct from its particular rules) is not visibly more obsolete in the mid-twentieth century than it was in the ill-fated League of Nations' (*Legal Controls of International Conflict*, London: Stevens, 1954, p. 382).

John M. Howell

See also: NEUTRALISM
NEUTRALIZATION

Neutralization

A. *Neutralization* is the process by which a group of powers agree by treaty to respect the neutrality of a particular state or portion of territory or of an international amenity such as a canal or strait.

B. 1. The conditions in which neutralization is resorted to are generally those in which the signatory powers are willing and able to uphold the neutralization treaty and have a vital interest in seeing that it is respected. To this should be added the fact that states or territories selected for neutralization have often been situated outside the conflicts of the major powers or have constituted such valuable acquisitions for any single power that there is a common interest in maintaining their neutrality. Where a state forms a considerable element in the balance of power in its own right, however, as for instance divided Germany at present, doubt has been genuinely raised whether neutralization is a feasible solution.

2. The treaty normally indicates in a negative and positive sense the form neutralization is to take in the given instance. Negatively the powers may undertake never to violate the neutrality of the state or territory by crossing its frontiers with armed force or by the despatch into it of naval vessels or by committing acts of war within it. Positively they may bind themselves either severally or collectively to ensure that these provisions are observed by themselves and by third parties. The neutralized state on its side agrees never to depart from neutrality, that is, strict impartiality as between belligerents and never to use armed force save in self-defence.

3. A distinction may be drawn between neutralization and *demilitarization*, that is, the mere prohibition of armed force within a territory. By Article XI of the Treaty of Paris (1856) the Black Sea was 'interdicted to the Flag of War' of any power; it was also neutralized 'in perpetuity'. The German Rhineland was demilitarized by the Treaty of Versailles in 1919, though this provision was broken by Germany in 1936 when she reoccupied the territory with her military forces. The shores of the Bosphorus and Dardanelles Straits were demilitarized by the Treaty of Lausanne in 1923; this treaty was revised at Montreux in 1936 when Turkey was permitted to fortify them again.

4. The condition of *neutralization* differs from that of *neutrality* in that a *neutral* state can only rely on the customary rules of international law for the respect for its neutrality which it expects from others. A neutralized state has the signed undertakings of the powers as well. Nevertheless, some states have found neutralization to be irksome as it may place the neutralized state in a disadvantageous position on the outbreak of hostilities in its neighbourhood. The creation of organs for collective security has also raised the question whether membership in these bodies is compatible with neutralization. Hence the neutralization of Belgium and Luxembourg was revoked in 1919. Both countries are members of the United Nations, their international status now being the same as that of other states. Switzerland remains outside the U.N.

F. S. Northedge

See also: NEUTRALITY

Nihilism

A. *Nihilism*, in its most general sense, denotes an attitude of total rejection of current morality codified into an ideology which makes the propagation of negativism itself a moral duty.

B. 1. The term's earliest usage denoted an extreme form of philosophical scepticism involving the denial of all existence. Such a denial clearly has profound and complex moral implications—it comes to involve, by extension, the total destruction of current moral and religious beliefs, and, usually, the substitution of negative doctrines advocating their destruction. What this means has been aptly set out by A. Camus in his discussion of Dostoievsky's book *The Brothers Karamazov*. In that book Ivan acts on the premise that 'everything is permitted'. 'With this "everything is permitted" the history of contemporary nihilism really begins. . . . Ivan compelled himself to do evil so as to be coherent. He would not allow himself to be good. Nihilism is not only despair and negation, but, above all, the desire to despair and negate' (*The Rebel*, trans. by A. Bower, New York: Vintage Books, 1956, pp. 57–8).

2. The term has a narrower reference to the 19th-century Russian anarchists—and was first applied to them by Turgenev in his novel *Fathers and Sons* (1862). The central figure of anarchism during its nihilist phase was M. A. Bakunin (1814–76) of whom it has been said that he 'rejected not only the idea of a constitutional order, but of any order, even that of a revolutionary dictatorship. He saw salvation in the overthrow and destruction of existing society . . .' (L. B. Schapiro, *The Communist Party of the Soviet Union*, London: Eyre & Spottiswoode, 1960, p. 5). His ideology contained three central doctrines: (a) propagation of atheism, (b) destruction of the state, (c) rejection of political action in favour of insurrection. While this ideology penetrated deeply in some industrially backward countries with a large oppressed peasantry—such as Russia, Italy, Spain—the nihilist phase turned out, historically, to have been an aberrant interlude in the philosophic evolution of anarchism begun by Proudhon and resumed by Kropotkin.

C. 1. Recent analyses which have used the term often emphasize the destructiveness implicit in nihilism. H. Arendt, for example, writes of 'a philosophy of power' which 'became the philosophy of the elite who quickly discovered and were quite ready to admit that the thirst for

Nomination

power could be quenched only by destruction. This was the essential cause of their nihilism (especially conspicuous in France at the turn, and in Germany in the twenties, of this century) ...' (*The Burden of Our Time*, London: Secker & Warburg, 1951, p. 144). For another discussion of contemporary relevance, see J. Monnerot, *Sociology and Psychology of Communism* (trans. by J. Degras & R. Rees, London: Allen & Unwin, 1953, p. 287 et seq.).

2. A noteworthy link of nihilism with current social science comes through its conception of modal personality among political revolutionaries. The Nihilist newspaper *Le Révolté* (Geneva and Paris, 1879–94) supplied the name and the concept which are still echoed in current studies by Camus of *L'homme révolté* (Paris: Gallimard, 1951), and by Anglo-Americans of the 'alienated intellectual'. Among professional social scientists, H. D. Lasswell has studied the process of 'displacement' from primary to secondary symbols which produces alienated types of political personality in his *Psychopathology and Politics* (Chicago: University of Chicago Press, 1930) and *Power and Personality* (New York: Norton, 1948). Related work is reported in T. W. Adorno et al., *The Authoritarian Personality* (New York: Harper & Bros., 1950).

Daniel Lerner

See also: ANARCHISM
          SYNDICALISM

Nobility (See **Aristocracy**)

Nomadism (See **Transhumance**)

Nominal Scale (See **Scaling**)

Nomination

A. *Nomination* denotes the designation by name of an individual as a candidate for a public office, such candidacy to be formally ratified or rejected by whatever agency or system the law prescribes.

B. In Britain, during the period when the monarch actually governed, nomination by the Crown was synonymous with appointment. Thus, when Henry VIII or Elizabeth I named an individual to be Secretary of State, or Judge, or Bishop, this completed the appointment, since there was no further authority with power to ratify or reject the selection of the Crown.

C. The achievement of parliamentary supremacy in Britain, and of a republican form of government in the United States and elsewhere, produced a change in the procedure of filling offices which was consonant with less authoritarian, and more democratic, principles. The change was marked by a clear division between two stages in the process. The first of these consisted in the selection of a person as a candidate for an office; while the second was his being formally approved as the office-holder. The separation between the two stages is enforced by the fact that they are conducted by different persons or agencies.

1. Thus, in modern Britain the holders of high executive and judicial offices, of Archbishoprics and Bishoprics in the Church of England, of certain military commands and other special public positions, are still in law appointed by the Crown, but in practice only after nomination by the Government of the day. The Crown, in fact, no longer has the choice either to propose or to reject a nominee. In the case of elections to the House of Commons, nomination is the system whereby the constituency party organizations—or ten registered voters—designate an individual as their candidate for a seat at Westminster.

2. American constitutional usage has from the beginning drawn a perfectly clear distinction between nomination and appointment, and the political practice and the terminology have been correspondingly well demarcated. Thus, in Article II, section 2, the Constitution of the United States provides that the President 'shall nominate, and by and with the advice and consent of the Senate, shall appoint ambassadors, other public ministers and consuls, judges of the Supreme Court, and all other officers of the United States, whose appointments are not herein otherwise provided for, and which shall be established by law'. The nature of this distinction, and the arguments justifying it, were fully explained by A. Hamilton in *The Federalist* (nos. LXXVI and LXXVII (1788), ed. by M. Beloff, Oxford: Blackwell, 1948).

However, the offices of which the Constitution makes mention are specifically executive or judicial. Political practice has further extended the same basic principle—of having one system for choosing a candidate, and a later one for formally approving him—by applying it to contests for legislative office and for the highest positions of executive leadership, i.e. the Presidency, governorships, and mayoralties. The nomination of candidates to contest these posts is inextricably connected with the evolution of the party (q.v.) system and the structuring of party organization. In chronological order, the caucus (q.v.) meeting of legislators of a given party, the convention (q.v.) of delegates chosen to assemble for this specific purpose, and finally the preliminary election by the voters within a party (the direct primary), have all been employed to nominate party candidates. In some cases, e.g. some Southern states, nomination as the result of the primary is tantamount to election. Today, in current usage, the term *national nominating convention* is regularly used to describe the assembly of delegates in the United States which meets every four years in federal politics to pick the men who will later compete for the Presidency and Vice-Presidency in the November election. In these cases it is the majority within the party (as determined by a mixture of the direct primary and delegate-convention systems) which selects the candidate whom the majority in the nation (as modified by the voting mechanics of the electoral college) will subsequently adopt or reject.

Leslie Lipson

See also: CAUCUS
CONVENTION
PRIMARY

Non-conformity (See Conformity)

Non-Empirical

A. The term *non-empirical* can be defined residually to the term *empirical* (q.v.). However, it has acquired a sufficiently stable range of uses to justify an effort to state them specifically.

1. Methodologically the term is used to describe all methods of acquiring belief other than those of positive science or its rough equivalents in everyday life.

2. Substantively it is used to describe the philosophical, religious, or ideological beliefs gained by other than scientific methods as well as the realms and objects to which actors relate themselves through such beliefs. Such beliefs and relations are frequently regarded as functionally necessary components of every social order.

B. According to T. Parsons, non-empirical methods of acquiring belief and the beliefs themselves are not to be equated with ignorance and error for they are 'beliefs which fall *outside* the scope of scientific applicability' (*The Social System*, Glencoe, Ill.: The Free Press, 1951, p. 359). Nor are the realms to which they point necessarily to be regarded as non-real since

'non-empirical beliefs [concern] subjects which are defined as beyond the reach of the methodology of empirical science or its equivalents in the culture in question' (ibid., p. 329).

Walter Firey

See also: EMPIRICAL

Nonliterate

A. *Nonliterate* is a term used to designate people without a written language, that attempts to avoid a commitment to a sequential view of culture development, implied by the terms *preliterate* and *primitive* (q.v.).

B. Terms such as *preliterate, early, savage*, and *primitive* have been used by anthropologists and others to denote those societies outside the range of higher civilizations, with the term *higher civilization* sometimes reserved for those civilizations definitely dependent upon a script, at other times inclusive of societies like that of the ancient Incas, without a script but with a form of social organization and mnemonic devices which to some extent took its place. The term *preliterate* has served the purpose of describing those peoples who neither have a script themselves nor live in a *folk society*, in which they are a part of a larger unit dependent upon a script. *Nonliterate* has been preferred to *preliterate* by those who feel that the term *preliterate* implies an evolutionary sequence rather than a description of all societies from a given position in history. M. J. Herskovits, for example, says: ' "Preliterate" has found more favour, but here the objection is that the prefix *pre-*, derived from the contemporary ancestor concept, implies that peoples without written languages are at a stage antecedent to the one in which, presumably, they will devise, or at least acquire writing … "non-literate" simply describes the fact that these people do not have written language' (*Cultural Anthropology*, New York: Knopf, 1955, p. 363).

C. E. Dozier ('The Concepts of "Primitive" and "Native" in Anthropology', in W. L. Thomas Jr. (ed.), *Current Anthropology*, Chicago: University of Chicago Press, 1955, pp. 187–202) has noted the absence of literacy in the groups studied by contemporary ethnological field methods, and discussed the strategy involved in the use of terms that will not offend the sensibilities of people recently classifiable as nonliterate. The term preliterate implies certain definite

Norm

characteristics of the people so described, of isolation from contact with high civilization and of possession of a smaller body of culturally transmitted knowledge from one generation to another in the absence of a script for the preservation of such knowledge. If the term *nonliterate* is simply substituted for preliterate, these same characteristics would be implied. Thus the present preference for *nonliterate* is primarily to fight outworn battles about evolution, or else a very partial attempt to avoid the type of ethnocentricity involved in the use of Christian dating or of such terms as the *paleolithic*. Only if we consistently develop a terminology which does not invoke known historical sequences, is such a procedure necessary.

D. It would be valuable to distinguish between those people who have no experience of a written language at a period of history when such knowledge is available and who may be expected to respond to script (although not necessarily by using it when they encounter it), and those peoples who lived in a period before writing was invented and were, therefore, not potentially accessible to diffusion. If the evolutionary and invidious considerations could be forgotten, *preliterate* (with *pre-* used in its typical sense of *just before*) could be used to designate the first category of people and *nonliterate* the second. We could, then, reserve *illiterate* for members of a society within which persons of a given social status are expected to be able to read and write who cannot do so; and *unliterate* for individuals or groups to whom reading and writing have been taught but by whom they are not used—a frequent transitional phase between *preliteracy* and true *literacy*.

Margaret Mead

See also: PRIMITIVE

Non-partisan Primary (See **Primary**)

Norm

A. The term *norm* denotes (a) a statistical standard of comparison constituted by what is in some sense the average or modal value of the variable on which the items in a population are being compared; (b) the average or modal, i.e. most typical, behaviour, attitude, opinion, or perception found in a social group; (c) a standard shared by the members of a social group to which the members are expected to conform, and conformity to which is enforced by positive and negative sanctions.

B. 1. The purely statistical usage of *norm* may be illustrated by the following: If the mean, median, or modal rate of murders known to the police for cities of more than 100,000 population is 6.5 murders per 100,000 population per year; and if the standard deviation from the mean, median, or mode is small, i.e. if there is genuine clustering of the rates; then 6.5 can serve as the norm to which the rate for any particular city can be significantly compared.

2. If there is found to be a genuine clustering of the modal or average perceptions, attitudes, opinions, or acts of the members of a social group, there is no reason why norm in the statistical sense should not be used to denote this clustering. By applying it to social groups, however, something very interesting emerged, namely, that there is a process of norm formation. Thus M. Sherif (*The Psychology of Social Norms*, New York: Harper & Brothers, 1938) found that when groups of people face together an ambiguous perceptual situation their initial interpretations of an event may be widely divergent, but then gradually converge. In the beginning it would be difficult to speak of a norm because the various estimates of the event are too widely scattered for a mean, mode, or median to be meaningful. But a norm finally arises because of the process of convergence. In this original work Sherif seemed to mean by a norm simply this concentrated average or modal perception, but in his later work (M. Sherif & C. W. Sherif, *An Outline of Social Psychology*, New York: Harper & Brothers, 1948) he suggests that there is an element of social constraint. Thus norm as applied to the clustering of group perceptions, etc., ceases to be purely a statistical concept and begins to take on the characteristics of an enforced standard.

3. Whatever the causal connection between the process of statistical norm formation with respect to the tendency toward convergence in the direction of such a norm on the part of the perceptions, etc. of the members of a social group on the one hand and the element of constraint characteristic of an enforced standard as norm on the other (this relationship has still to be sharply conceptualized and analysed), the usage of *norm* to denote an enforced standard is *logically* independent of its usage as a comparative statistical standard. In this latter usage 'A norm, then, is an idea in the minds of members of a group, an idea that can be put in the form of a statement specifying what the members or other men should do, ought to do, are expected to do, under given circumstances' (G. C. Homans, *The Human Group*, New York: Harcourt, Brace, 1950, p. 123). Its only statistical reference in this context is when the *shared* character of such norms is stressed, so that there is implied the average or modal idea of what ought or ought not be done.

The norms of a group in this sense can be assessed in three ways: (a) individual members can be interviewed to discover their conscious ideas about what ought to be done (if stress is placed purely on 'oughtness' rather than on the shared and sanctioned quality of such ideas, norm could mean simply *any* idea of what ought to be done, even one held only by a single individual); (b) observation of the group can disclose when sanctions are exerted; (c) written rules can be observed and interpreted.

Such norms are not the same as (a) what is in fact done—although there is obviously some relationship—or (b) what is believed to be done. Rather they are standards to which people are obligated and expected to conform, frequently because they are believed to be functional for the group in question. The clearest type is the moral norm—'Thou shalt not kill'; but cognitive norms like the rules of logic, aesthetic norms, and technical norms are all models held up to life.

William L. Kolb

See also: Folkways
Law
Moral Order
Mores
Value

Normal (See **Abnormal**)

Normal Value (See **Scarcity**)

Nuclear Family (See **Family**)

O

Objectivity (See **Science**)

Obsolescence (See **Depreciation**)

Occupation (Also **Occupational Structure**)
A. The principal usage in the social sciences (e.g. in the preparation of census data and in the study of the labour market) follows closely the common usages which take an *occupation* to denote an employment, business, or calling. 'The occupation is the kind of work performed by the individual, regardless of the industry in which this work is performed and of the status of employment of the individual' (*International Standard Classification of Occupations, 1949*, Geneva: International Labour Office, 1949, p. 14).

B. 1. The British 1951 Census of Population used the classification of occupations compiled in 1950 in which the term *occupation* is defined as follows: 'The occupation of any person is the kind of work which he or she performs, due regard being paid to the conditions under which it is performed; and those alone determine the particular group in an occupation classification to which the person is assigned. The nature of the factory, business or service in which a person is employed has no bearing upon the classification of his occupation, except to the extent that it enables the nature of his duties to be more clearly defined. This will perhaps be made clearer by an example. A crane driver may be employed in a shipyard, an engineering works or in a building and construction, but this has no bearing upon his occupation and all crane drivers should be classified to the same occupational group' (General Register Office, 'Classification of Occupations, 1950', London: H.M.S.O., 1951, p. i).
    2. Usage is illuminated by M. Jeffreys' distinction between job change ('when a man changed from one employment to another') and occupation change, to be found in his *Mobility in the Labour Market* (London: Routledge & Kegan Paul, 1954, pp. 9–11). '... no occupational change was recorded if a bricklayer moved from a site where he was building new houses to a job as maintenance bricklayer

in a factory, since neither the essentials of his occupation, the laying of bricks, nor the tools which he handled had changed' (ibid., p. 9). It should be noted that occupations are classified not only on a titular basis, but also in terms of the degree of skill demanded, e.g. skilled, semi-skilled, unskilled.

C. The term *occupational structure* has come into use in recent years, especially with the development of industrial sociology (q.v.). By it is meant the categories of occupation which are found in a particular industry or service, or within a given enterprise; though it may also be used with respect to society as a whole, as in examinations of the relation between the educational system and occupational structure. Occupational structure may be analysed simply in terms of kinds of occupation, or also (as is common in studies of technical change) in terms of quality of skill demanded. In the latter case, the relative proportions of skilled, semi-skilled, and unskilled occupations are measured and the effects of technical change assessed by recording shifts in these proportions. The analysis of occupational structure is also utilized in the study of levels of economic and social development. The term *occupational sociology* may also be encountered; it is used to describe the study of the social characteristics of occupations.

J. H. Smith

Occupational Sociology (See **Occupation**)

Occupational Structure (See **Occupation**)

Oedipus Complex (See **Incest**)

Office
A. *Office* denotes a status and role which is well defined, authoritatively sanctioned, and recognized as being separable from the persons occupying and performing it.

B. The widest use of the term in the United States apparently stems from the work of M. Weber for whom an office consists of a

474

status created and sanctioned by authority. Thus a person occupying such a status must act only within the limits authoritatively set in rules, laws, or administrative regulations. Any behaviour other than this is not considered to be that of the officer but that of the person acting in some other capacity. The concept is basic to Weber's concept of bureaucracy (q.v.) and is necessarily treated as an integral part of it by those who use the Weberian analysis. For K. Davis, *office* 'designate[s] a position in a deliberately created organization, governed by specific and limited rules in a limited group, more generally achieved than ascribed' (*Human Society*, New York: The Macmillan Co., 1949, p. 88–9).

Fred Cottrell

See also: BUREAUCRACY

Oligarchy

A. *Oligarchy* is a word that has pejorative connotations: it means not only rule of a small group, but rule of a small group that is not responsible to the many, that is corrupt, or that has otherwise excited disapprobation.

B. *Oligarchy* may refer to the rule of the few not only in the context of government as such, but to rule by a coterie or small group in any association, whether a church, labour union, or any other. In the political sense it has been contrasted ever since Plato with rule of the one —monarchy—and rule of the many—democracy. Oligarchy for Plato, however, is a degenerate form of government, the corruption of aristocracy, just as tyranny is the corruption of monarchy and mob rule the corruption of democracy. Plato's classification has persisted, though it has not been without its critics, as for example, T. Hobbes, who remarked 'They that are displeased with Aristocracy, call it Oligarchy' (*Leviathan* (1651), Oxford: Blackwell, 1955, vol. II, ch. XIX, p. 121).

In our own day the concept of oligarchy has been subjected to criticism also on the ground that all government is, of necessity, oligarchical. Thus R. M. MacIver says, 'In the strict sense we cannot classify states by asking whether one man rules or a few or the many. The many, or the people, never *rule*—the actual business of ruling is always in the hands of the few. The constitutional question concerns the relation of the one to the few but above all the relation of the few who rule to the many who are ruled. Are the few not responsible to the many in this sense? Then it is oligarchy' (*The Web of Government*, New York: The Macmillan Co., 1947, p. 149).

The rule of the few, MacIver goes on to say, is the rule of a class, clique, party, or group, and it is the structure of this group that gives us monarchy, empire, dictatorship, theocracy, or some other, rarer, form of government (see his entire discussion, and classification of the forms of government, ibid., pp. 151–62).

Similarly, D. Spitz says that it is not the fact of small group rule, the inevitable existence of an elite, that is the important distinction between democracy and oligarchy. 'The central point at issue is the fact of responsibility: whether the leadership derives its power from the freely given assent of the people and whether the policies pursued by the leadership conform to the changing tides of public opinion. These, the components of political responsibility, and not the mere fact of minority leadership, are the essential criteria of forms of government' (*Patterns of Anti-Democratic Thought*, New York: The Macmillan Co., 1949, p. 74).

Robert Bierstedt

See also: ARISTOCRACY
ELITE

Oligopolistic Competition (See Economic Competition)

Oligopoly (See Monopoly)

Open Primary (See Primary)

Operating Revenue (See Revenue)

Operationism (Also Operationalism)

A. If *operationism* or *operationalism* is to be defined as a phenomenon distinct from other currents in scientific method or philosophy, it should be defined in terms of the original intentions of P. W. Bridgman and his more radical followers. *Operationism* or *operationalism* is, then, the insistence upon the use of operational definitions in science whenever the meaning of a term in quantitative discourse is to be understood. A mathematical formula indicating a relationship among variables holds true only if these variables are measured in a definite manner. Thus *only definitions in terms of operations of measurement or of production and control should be referred to as operational definitions* (cf. F. Adler, 'Operational Definitions in Sociology', *American Journal of Sociology*,

Operationism

vol. LII, 1946–47, pp. 438–44). Other definitions may be empirical or demonstrable, but they are not operational in the strictest sense.

B. Use of the term dates from the publication of P. W. Bridgman's *The Logic of Modern Physics* (New York: The Macmillan Co., 1927). Bridgman, however, rejects the term 'which seems to imply a dogma, or at least a thesis of some kind ... an attitude or a point of view' ('Remarks on the Present State of Operationalism', *The Scientific Monthly*, vol. LXXIX, 1954, p. 224). He prefers to refer to 'Operational Analysis' as a method which is characterized by 'the demand that the concepts or terms used in the description of experience be framed in terms of operations which can be unequivocally performed' ('Operational Analysis', *Philosophy of Science*, vol. 5, 1938, p. 119).

Other writers see in operationism more than a method. H. Margenau sees in it an attitude 'that emphasizes the need of recourse, wherever feasible, to instrumental procedures when meanings are to be established' ('On Interpretations and Misinterpretations of Operationalism', *Scientific Monthly*, vol. LXXIX, 1954, p. 209). S. S. Stevens defines it as a theory of meaning: 'Operational doctrine makes explicit recognition of the fact that a concept, or proposition, has empirical meaning only if it stands for definite, concrete operations capable of execution by normal human beings' ('The Operational Definition of Psychological Concepts', *Psychological Review*, vol. XLII, 1935, p. 517). G. Boas and A. E. Blumberg believe that 'for a term to have meaning its definition must formulate operations which enable us to determine the truth or falsity of the propositions in which the term occurs' ('Some Remarks in Defense of the Operational Theory of Meaning', *Journal of Philosophy*, vol. XXVIII, 1931, pp. 544–5). These more ambitious intentions in the use of the term are discounted by C. G. Hempel: 'The central ideas of operational analysis ... are so vague that they constitute not a theory concerning the nature of scientific concepts but rather a program for the development of such a theory' ('A Logical Appraisal of Operationism', *The Scientific Monthly*, vol. LXXIX, 1954, p. 216). C. C. Pratt adds: 'Operationism is no panacea ... [It] is the manner in which the present generation utters the familiar cry of science, "Be careful" ' (*The Logic of Modern Psychology*, New York: The Macmillan Co., 1939, p. 81).

C. Even if operationism is to be understood as a method, its meaning remains vague due to the uncertainty of what does or does not constitute an appropriate operation and an adequate operational definition. S. S. Stevens makes the definition of an operation sound simple: '[It] is the performance which we execute in order to make known a concept' ('The Operational Basis of Psychology', *American Journal of Psychology*, vol. XLVII, 1935, p. 323), without clarifying whether the concept is to be made known by observation to oneself or by communication to others. F. S. C. Northrop, on the other hand, contends that 'few words are more ambiguous than the word "operation". There is the denotatively given, immediately apprehended operation. There is also the theoretically conceived operation ... Those who have formulated and defended the operational theory have shifted back and forth surreptitiously between these two meanings ...' (*The Logic of the Sciences and the Humanities*, New York: The Macmillan Co., 1947, p. 126). A. C. Benjamin discovers two distinct meanings of the term *operation* in Bridgman's own writings, 'one specific or narrow ... [which] restricts the work to physical operations, and even at times to metrical operations. [Another] general use allows mental, verbal and "pencil and paper" operations ...' (*Operationism*, Springfield, Ill.: Thomas, 1955, p. 5). H. E. Israel points to another ambiguity: 'According to one [meaning of the term], a set of operations is a rigidly invariable series of unique operational items, but according to the other, it is a purposive activity directed toward obtaining a certain result with the allowance of variation in the component operations' ('Two Difficulties in Operational Thinking', *Psychological Review*, vol. LII, 1945, p. 261).

D. Concerning operational definitions, Bridgman originally specified that 'the concept is synonymous with the corresponding set of operations' (*The Logic of Modern Physics*, p. 5). S. C. Dodd attempted to define an operational definition operationally: 'A definition is an operational definition to the extent that the definer (a) specifies the procedure (including materials used) for identifying or generating the definiendum, and (b) finds high reliability for his definition' ('Operational Definitions Operationally Defined', *American Journal of Sociology*, vol. XLVIII, 1942–43, p. 482). H. Feigl sees in operationism 'a critical standard'. This is expressed in the following requirements for

476

definitions: 'Concepts ... must be definable by operations which are (1) logically consistent; (2) sufficiently definite (if possible quantitatively precise); (3) empirically rooted, i.e. by procedural and, finally, ostensive links with the observable; (4) naturally and, preferably, technically possible; (5) intersubjective and repeatable; (6) aimed at the creation of concepts which will function in laws or theories of greater predictiveness' ('Operationism and Scientific Method', *Psychological Review*, vol. LII, 1945, p. 258). Present-day operationists including Bridgman himself have moved away from earlier orthodoxy. 'The operational aspect is not by any means the only aspect of meaning' (P. W. Bridgman, 'The Nature of Some of our Physical Concepts', *British Journal of the Philosophy of Science*, vol. I, 1950–1, p. 257). Thus the operational point of view if that is to be more than 'just another formulation of the empiricist requirements of testability ...' (C. G. Hempel, 'Fundamentals of Concept Formation in Empirical Science', *International Encyclopedia of Unified Science*, Chicago: University of Chicago Press, 1952, vol. II, p. 43) is actually abandoned.

Franz Adler

Opinion

A. An *opinion* is a judgement, conviction, view, or belief held by a person on some issue. It may be expressed or covert, based on value judgements or on any kind of reasoning or evidence, and to the individual his opinion on some issue may be important or unimportant in varying degrees. Opinions have many attributes; for instance, we distinguish degrees of clarity in an opinion, degrees of strength or emphasis, degrees of salience and of ego-involvement. Above all, we tend to order opinions along a pro-con continuum with regard to their object. However, it is often mistakenly assumed that a person has an opinion on some issue when in fact he has none.

B. It is useful to distinguish opinions from the broader attitudes (q.v.) and value systems on which they are based. Opinions are generally expressed on fairly narrow and specific points, and a number of expressed opinions may allow us to infer the existence of an underlying, more general, attitude. Thus, while opinions are relatively superficial, changeable, and limited, they often have their roots in attitude systems which are more enduring, less changeable, with wider scope and with closer links to the individual's personality. It is not often that one finds an opinion which is isolated and not connected with, and an expression of, some underlying attitude or trait.

It is clear from the foregoing that attempts at changing opinions are often misdirected unless they take into account the underlying attitudes. It is thought that attitudes and their related opinions have a function in maintaining the individual's emotional balance; for this reason, opinion change may be particularly difficult and impermanent. One of the most effective ways of changing attitudes and opinions is by bringing about a change in the norms of the individual's reference group (q.v.), or by causing him to change his reference group. Other methods of changing opinions include lectures, prestige suggestion, and the use of media of mass communication (see K. Lewin, 'Group Decision and Social Change', in T. M. Newcomb & E. L. Hartley (eds.), *Readings in Social Psychology*, New York: Henry Holt, 1947, pp. 330–44). New opinions are generally acquired in these ways, i.e. by coming into contact with the opinions of other people or, more rarely, by arriving at certain conclusions and judgements of one's own.

Sometimes a collective opinion is required, e.g. the opinion of a jury. *Public opinion* is a nebulous concept; it is not the simple aggregate of the opinions of members of a public, but depends on the society's power structure, the mass media, channels of influence, etc.

C. If an opinion exists, it can generally be measured, and various scaling techniques have been developed for this purpose. Usually, the opinions of large numbers of people are collected, e.g. in the so-called public opinion polls. This involves numerous complex sampling problems, and opinion scales, attitude statements, projective techniques, and various other questionnaire techniques may be used. The stress on verbal response in opinion research has led some scholars to define opinion in such terms. Thus C. I. Hovland, I. L. Janis, and H. H. Kelley (*Communication and Persuasion*, New Haven: Yale University Press, 1953, p. 6) say 'Operationally speaking, opinions are viewed as verbal "answers" that an individual gives in response to stimulus situations in which some general "question" is raised.'

A. N. Oppenheim

See also: ATTITUDE
PUBLIC
PUBLIC OPINION

Opposition

Opportunity Cost (See Cost)

Opposition

A. In the special political sense of the term, *The Opposition* normally means a coherent group of people, regularly acting together, and able to present themselves collectively to the electorate as an alternative government with an alternative policy.

B. One of the main features of types of government which are commonly regarded as *democratic* is the provision they make for people to oppose those who have power for the time being. Not only do they allow people to criticize the holders of executive power; they also provide machinery whereby the opposers may press their criticisms and attempt to persuade the voters to eject the existing government at a future election.

1. The role of an opposition is most clearly seen in a country where the political scene is normally dominated by two parties. Thus in Great Britain, at any given time, one of the parties is in power, while the other is both 'His (Her) Majesty's Opposition' and an alternative government, with a reasonable chance of finding itself in power without a great deal of delay. In Parliament the Opposition members criticize the Government's bills and administration, and try to persuade it to modify its policies. The force of modern party discipline usually ensures that when the Opposition leaders decide to vote against the Government, they are faithfully supported by their followers; but as the Government is no less faithfully supported by its own followers, who are more numerous, the hostile vote of the Opposition is no more than the registration of a protest. All the time the Opposition is trying to persuade the electorate of the superiority of its policies as compared with those of the Government, in the hope of finding itself returned with a majority at the next election.

2. Where there are several major parties, and a government is made up of a coalition, or of one party supported by others, the term *opposition* has not quite the same meaning. Parties outside the majority may be said to be in opposition, but they are often opposed not only to the government but also to each other, and so cannot be called collectively 'the Opposition' except in a rather general sense.

P. A. Bromhead

See also: DEMOCRACY

Ordinal Scale (See Scaling)

Organism

A. *Organism* may be defined as a living system of mutually adapted parts which function together to maintain a unitary whole. By analogy, only, a society (q.v.) may be viewed as a system *organically* structured in accordance with the patterns and dynamics of its culture.

B. The term *organism* comes from the discipline of biology where it is a concept so fundamental and accepted that it is difficult to find it defined explicitly or in any detail. In general it can be said that an organism is regarded in biology as the minimum protoplasmic unit potentially able to carry out all the life processes: reproduction, growth, metabolization, response to stimuli, and adaptation. Organization is the touchstone of the living organism. The component parts, when not integrated into a whole, represent merely complex but lifeless matter.

C. *Organism* is used in two major senses in the social sciences. The first of these is the direct application of the biological definition to individual men and the generic *man*. Psychology, social psychology, and anthropology use this concept as a fundamental starting-point for theory and investigation. Thus K. Young, in writing of personality development, proposes 'there is first ... the biological organism which comes into the world from the previous generation, with its potentials for development, with the general predisposition for physical growth, with a set of characteristics it has inherited from its ancestors. This physical organism, with its roots in the animal world, possesses the essential structures and functions from which eventuate the human personality' (*Social Psychology: An Analysis of Social Behavior*, New York: Crofts, 1930, p. 14). Social scientists are primarily interested in the unity, capability for response, and the adaptive qualities of the organism, characteristics which lend themselves to social development.

1. *Organism* implies an entity made up of integral parts interacting in unity. 'In this ... [unity] ... ', R. M. MacIver and C. H. Page say, 'we interpret the cells and organs and the various systems that these compose—circulatory, glandular, nervous, and so forth—as deriving their significance *solely* from their utility to the life of the organism as a whole' (*Society: An Introductory Analysis*, New York: Rinehart, 1949, p. 49). The following statement from a contemporary

work on political theory reflects the general view held by social scientists about the unitary character of biological organisms: 'An organism is something animate which is a compound of parts serving one another, and serving thereby the whole which they collectively constitute, as instruments for the attainment of a common purpose; it is a composite living structure, in which the parts are "organs" or tools, mutually instrumental to one another and collectively instrumental to the life-purpose of the whole' (E. Barker, *Principles of Social and Political Theory*, Oxford: Oxford University Press, 1951, pp. 127–8).

2. While the concept of life-purpose may be too teleological for some, it must be remembered that it is usually reduced to stress on continued existence of the organism through the adaptability of response to stimuli—e.g. 'all living organisms, in short, respond to the environmental stimuli to which they are sensitive, and these responses are said to be adaptive if they have the effect of continuing the survival of the individual or the species or of both' (J. L. Gillin & J. P. Gillin, *An Introduction to Sociology*, New York: The Macmillan Co., 1942, p. 69). Adaptation (q.v.) is thus a key concept in organic evolution providing as it does, a major clue to the processes of structural change.

D. The second contemporary use of the concept *organism* in the social sciences is to be found in its analogic application to social systems (q.v.). Earlier writers as far back as Aristotle have from time to time viewed society as a greater organism possessed of the same general patterns of organization, and subject to the same laws, as are the biological organisms, and even possessing its own mind and consciousness. The overwhelmingly prevalent view today, however, is that expressed by E. Barker: '... the term "social organism" is a metaphor, and only a metaphor: it is not a description or a definition. The question before us, therefore, is not whether the term "social organism" is an accurate definition: it is a question whether the term is a useful metaphor' (*Principles of Social and Political Theory*, p. 127). While the level of human cultural and social life transcends the biological level as is indicated by the frequent use in social science of the term *superorganic* (q.v.), in many respects the problems posed for biological science and social science are fundamentally analagous: (a) problems of the structure and functions of organic and social systems and (b) problems of the origin and

development of organic and social systems—biological and cultural evolution (q.v.).

E. Adamson Hoebel

See also: ADAPTATION
CULTURAL EVOLUTION
EVOLUTION
FUNCTION
MAN
ORIGINAL NATURE
SOCIAL SYSTEM
SOCIETY

Original Nature
A. *Original nature* refers to those residues of widespread or tenacious uniformity in the behaviour of individuals and groups which cannot be attributed to the influence of group membership or social experience.

B. The phrase implies the existence of an object to which it refers, but identification of the object (like that of the related concept *human nature*) in this case has been exceptionally difficult. The difficulties suggest that the analytic value of these concepts is somewhat limited.

1. Throughout the century since Darwin published his *Origin of Species and the Descent of Man*, if not longer, the question of which tendencies in human behaviour are given *from the outset* has agitated many minds. A classification of the points of controversy furnishes perhaps the broadest view of the matter, although some partisans would hold that to term the matter controversial is itself to take a stand.

(a) There are numerous formulations as to the correct *point of origin* to be emphasized: when the world was created, when man as a species emerged from more primitive species, or when the infant is born into the world.

(b) Formulations differ as to the source from which the human nature manifested at its origin derives, whether from a divine act, from genetic constitution, or from historical or biographical experience.

(c) The views of authors range from those which uphold the existence of a universal nature found in all human beings, those which are concerned to distinguish the fundamental dispositions of large groupings of humanity from those of other large groups, and those which are principally concerned to explain differences in the behaviour of individuals by reference to differing constitutional endowments. Any credence given to opposing viewpoints precipitates the unresolved problem of sorting out original from acquired traits.

Ortho-Cousin

All three of these sets of formulations, however, share the metaphysical postulate of some permanent thread of fixed traits or identity 'underlying' human behaviour and explaining the similarities among men or within men over time. Although the nominalist-realist controversy is ancient in philosophy, the most recent chapter in the treatment of human nature by the post-Darwinian social sciences conceives it as not original at all, and neither universal nor individual, but as the continuous product of group interaction. One attributes a continuing nature to another in order to act categorically toward him. The old fires of argument between theology and science, and among scientists over heredity *versus* environment, have died down, at least for the present, but more recently and quietly further reformulations have ensued.

Sociologists in the main have depended heavily on anthropologists for comparative formulations. C. H. Cooley in *Human Nature and the Social Order* (New York: Charles Scribner's Sons, 1902) produced the highly original hypothesis that the recognizable similarities of all human beings in the organization of their intimate interpersonal ('primary group') relations is not the consequence of hereditary endowment; it is learnt; but since it is learnt under universally recurrent conditions—socialization of children within family and neighbourhood—near-uniformity in essentials is the consequence. The course of world history, he went on to claim, shows despite many backward moves the steady infusion of primary-group attitudes into secondary-group relations. After scepticism, neglect, and such contrary evidence as the rise of Nazism, formulations like Cooley's enjoy revived interest, at least among some sociologists. Among economists and political scientists, the idea that some systems of government and industrial organization are more congenial to human nature than other systems, hence possess more survival power, is regarded more as a forlorn hope than a reasonable hypothesis.

2. The idea of *original nature* overlaps with that of *human nature*. Psychologists and social psychologists have been the most concerned to discern what distinguishes human behaviour from animal behaviour. It would be somewhat unfair to say they have been more successful in observing human-like capacities among animals than in identifying those concrete aspects of human behaviour which cannot be found, at least in simple form, among animals. Play, deception, shame, memory, insight, and learning, for example, all appear in animals. Only certain powers of speech and creativity seem entirely lacking, but these of course represent potentialities for the most varied outcomes, yet outcomes extremely patterned culturally. Like anthropology, experimental education and abnormal psychology have repeatedly widened scientific awareness of the social and cultural origins of patterns of behaviour previously deemed of constitutional origin. As a consequence of noting how much human behaviour is structured by learning and how fruitless it has been to identify any instincts which issue in specific uniform responses by human beings, many social psychologists have come to treat the most durable tendencies in the behaviour of individuals and groups as expressions of *commitments* made more or less unconsciously by individuals as a consequence of their particular group memberships and experience; they do not postulate any uniformity beyond the degrees of similarity to be empirically observed. As put in most extreme form by the existentialist philosophers, man has not a nature but a history.

Nelson N. Foote

See also: HEREDITY
HUMAN NATURE

Ortho-Cousin

This term is little used nowadays, but has been employed either as a synonym for parallel cousin (q.v.) or, more commonly, for that parallel cousin who is a member of the same unilineal descent group as the person in reference (i.e. a man's father's brother's child in a patrilineal system and his mother's sister's child in a matrilineal system). Cf. the definition given in *Notes and Queries in Anthropology* (London: Royal Anthropological Institute, 5th edn., 1929, p. 57): 'The children of two brothers when descent is patrilineal, of two sisters when it is matrilineal ...'.

Maurice Freedman

See also: CROSS-COUSINS
PARALLEL COUSIN

Other-Directed (See **Conformity**)

Out-Group (See **Group**)

Outlay (See **Cost**)

Output (See **Productivity**)

Ownership (See **Proprietorship**)

P

Pacifism

A. The most general reference of *pacifism* (and of *pacifist*) is to the love of peace and repugnance for the use of armed force, especially in the relations between nations. From the period of World War I several more specific usages came into prominence.

1. The first refers to the beliefs and conduct of those who believed that war could and should be eliminated by appropriate institutional procedures. President Wilson and other advocates of a League of Nations in 1916–19 were called *pacifists* for holding that war, besides being immoral, was destructive of civilization. Yet they did not eschew the use of force against militarism or unprovoked aggression. They wished to 'collectivize' force by removing it from individual nations and placing it at the service of the international community. Hence they should be called *internationalists* rather than *pacifists*.

2. A second usage refers to the beliefs and conduct of those who refuse under any condition to take part in the employment of armed force against another nation. This may be described as *personal* (or *religious*) *pacifism* and has its origins primarily in religious teachings such as those of Jesus, in particular the Sermon on the Mount, and, in the East, in the Buddhistic, Confucian, and Hinduistic teachings which exalt compassion and submission and urge love and reconciliation as the basis of human relations.

3. Finally, a third usage refers to the beliefs and conduct of those who renounce armed conflict mainly on the ground that it allegedly leaves the contestants in a far worse position than they were before, and hold that to change an opponent's will one must advance tolerance and charity, while seeking actively to remove his grievances.

This may be designated *political* or *rationalist pacifism* as expounded in the inter-war period by such writers as A. Huxley, H. M. Swanwick, M. Murry, V. Woolf, R. Macaulay, and G. Heard. While in some cases it has had a religious colouring and has tended to fuse with religious pacifism (as in the case of the Peace Pledge Union), it is logically and empirically independent of any religious teaching or theology.

B. Pacifism has never yet been adopted as official policy by any state, but it received powerful support in the English-speaking world generally and in western and northern Europe in the period between the two world wars. It encouraged many who were themselves without strong religious faith to oppose policies of re-armament and armed resistance to unsatisfied states. The supporters of the League of Nations tended to be divided between opponents of wars of every kind, League wars included, and those who wished to limit national armed force to causes approved by the League. The latter have argued subsequently that the unsuccess of collective security before 1939 was largely due to absolute pacifists acting in unconscious alliance with nationalists and isolationists. Personal pacifism tended to decline with World War II and conscientious objection to military service was less frequent in states which legalized it than it had been in 1914–18. The invention of nuclear weapons, however, revived the pacifist argument and advocacy of the unilateral renunciation of nuclear armaments began to come from many who had raised no objection to conventional warfare.

F. S. Northedge

See also: INTERNATIONALISM
ISOLATIONISM
NEUTRALISM

Parallel Cousin

The term means that first cousin who is either father's brother's child or mother's sister's child; cousins are *parallel* when the parental siblings through whom they are related are of the same sex.

Maurice Freedman

See also: CROSS-COUSINS
ORTHO-COUSIN

Parallelism (See Cultural Parallelism)

Parliament (See Legislative Body)

Parliamentary Government

Parliamentary Government (Also
Parliamentarism, Parliamentarianism)
A. The term is used in two main senses:

1. Broadly, it denotes all political systems where there exists an assembly of elected representatives which, in theory or in practice, has considerable responsibility for affairs, especially in finance and legislation. Thus the U.S.A. and the U.S.S.R. are among the members of the Inter-Parliamentary Union.

2. More specifically it denotes a system of which Britain ('The Mother of Parliaments') provides the model, best described by contrasting it with the presidential form common in North and South America. It is particularly popular where monarchies have become constitutional, e.g. members of the Commonwealth, and Scandinavia; but is also found in republics, e.g. France, Germany, Italy, and India.

B. 1. *Parliamentary government* is the usual English expression for the British form of government and others like it. Many modern writers, especially in other countries, prefer the term *parliamentarism* or *parliamentarianism*.

2. The parliamentary system is one where the Assembly is transformed into a Parliament where the Government as well as the other elected representatives of the people are to be found. In a presidential system such as the American, the President (whose office is referred to as the *Executive* or *Administration* rather than as *Government*) remains outside the legislature, which is not, therefore, a Parliament. The parliamentary Executive is divided into a *Head of State* (q.v.) (monarch or president) and a *Government* whose head, usually called *Prime Minister* (in the Federal German Republic, *Chancellor*) is appointed by the Head of State. The Prime Minister in turn nominates his colleagues in the Ministry which is collectively responsible to Parliament, of which Ministers are usually members. By contrast the President in a presidential system is both Head of State and Head of Government and is solely responsible for the Executive branch. Moreover he is not responsible to the Assembly but to the Constitution and the people who elected him.

3. Parliamentary government is not to be confused with Convention or Assembly government where supreme power is vested in the Assembly, which elects such government as there is. There are Convention characteristics in many Communist constitutions as well as those of the French Third and Fourth Republics.

4. A distinctive characteristic of parliament-

arism is the power of the Government to dissolve Parliament. Under the presidential separation of powers there is no dissolution of the Assembly; in convention government the Assembly may dissolve Parliament, a power it must possess as a counterpart to the adverse vote which the Assembly may give the Government policies.

C. In practice the balance of forces between Government and Parliament varies considerably. At one extreme is strong Cabinet Government as in the U.K. where the Ministry acts on behalf of the Crown. In France, owing to the leanings towards convention government, power tended to lie with the National Assembly during the Third and Fourth Republics.

D. V. Verney

See also: LEGISLATIVE BODY
PRESIDENCY
REPRESENTATION

Party

A. A definition embracing all phenomena that are regularly called *party* in this age is a difficult task unless it be reduced to its most general form, i.e. a *party* is a group framing general issues and putting forward candidates in elections.

B. 1. *Factions, cliques, gangs, cabals, private armies, lobbies, pressure groups, special interests, clubs,* and *caucuses* are terms which, like *party*, denote voluntary associations to influence government. Party and faction were synonymous in Rome. In the early United States the terms were used interchangeably. Today they are rarely used to mean the same thing. Party has come to have a special and important connotation in the last century and a half. It refers to that paramount private association that is privileged to compete for control of a government. Government by legislature occasioned the emergence of modern parties. The word began to be used during the English Restoration period in something like its present sense. 'On the whole, the development of parties seems bound up with that of democracy, that is to say with the extension of popular suffrage and parliamentary prerogatives' (M. Duverger, *Political Parties*, London: Methuen, 1954, p. xxiii). A strong monarchy, predicated on traditional principles, sees no purpose in parties. A rationalistic ethos justifies a competitive struggle of parties for control of the government. Burke was less the champion of traditionalism than the instrument of the dawning rationalistic, competitive theory of government when he produced his famous definition: 'party is a body of men united, for promoting by their joint endeavours the national interest, upon some particular principle in which they are all agreed' (*The Works of Edmund Burke*, London: Oxford University Press, 1930, vol. II, p. 82) Burke's definition cannot be used in objective political discourse. Like so many other early definitions of key terms in politics, it begs the major questions it has to attack: whether parties are indeed devoted to principle, are united in order to promote anything, or have any relation to a national interest, whatever that may be. E. Burke himself could be most realistic, of course: 'Party divisions, whether on the whole operating for good or evil, are things inseparable from free government' (*Observations on a Late State of the Nation*, London: Dodsley, 1769, p. 1). Or, as Jefferson put it, 'in every free and deliberating society, there must ... be opposite parties, and violent dissensions and discords; and one of these, for the most part, must prevail over the other for a longer or shorter time' (To J. Taylor, 1798, in *Memoirs, Correspondence and Private Papers of Thomas Jefferson*, London: Colburn & Bentley, 1829, vol. III, p. 400). Yet Jefferson, like most writers, continued to assert the function of seeking the national interest in partial contradiction of reality and in lieu of other obviously important functions.

2. Beginning with the studies of M. Ostrogorski (*Democracy and the Organization of Political Parties*, London: Macmillan, 1902) a realistic and analytic approach to party study is manifest, and party definitions show the result. M. Weber wrote (*Theory of Social and Economic Organization*, trans. by A. R. Henderson & T. Parsons, London: Hodge, 1947, pp. 373–4) that 'the term "party" will be employed to designate an associative type of social relationship, membership in which rests on formally free recruitment. The end to which its activity is devoted is to secure power within a corporate group for its leaders in order to attain ideal or material advantages for its active members. These advantages may consist in the realization of certain objective policies or the attainment of personal advantages or both. ... By definition a party can exist only *within* a corporate group, in order to influence its policy or gain control of it'.

3. Some modern definitions stress the fact of the power drive of parties. Thus C. E. Merriam and H. F. Gosnell: 'The party may be looked upon as a type of social group, primarily concerned with social control as exercised through the government. ... The party system may be regarded as an institution, supplementary to the government, aiding the electorate in the selection of official personnel and in the determination of public policies, and in the larger task of operating or criticising the government' (*American Party System*, New York: The Macmillan Co., 3rd edn., 1949, p. 464). Also C. J. Friedrich (*Constitutional Government and Politics*, New York: Harper & Brothers, 1937, p. 297) says: 'A group of human beings, stably organized for the purpose of securing or maintaining the control of a corporate body ...'. Others focus on elections. Thus H. D. Lasswell and A. Kaplan say 'a party (political) is a group formulating comprehensive issues and submitting candidates in elections' (*Power and Society*, New Haven: Yale University Press, 1950, p. 169). D. B. Truman (*The Governmental Process*, New York: Knopf, 1951, pp. 270–1) writes similarly that 'the political party has come to be thought of as the instrumentality through which choices are made among aspirants for office. ... Whatever else it may be or may not be, the political party in the United States most commonly is a device for mobilizing votes ...'. The difference between the two types of definition is not large. Perhaps both forms may be used, depending upon circumstances. Thus rephrasing the broader (yet very specific) Weberian statement it may be said that 'a political party is a voluntary society of propaganda and agitation, seeking to acquire power in order to procure chances for its active adherents to realize objective aims, personal advantages, or both'; and rephrasing the more contemporary and simpler definitions that 'a political party is a group publicly organized to capture, through elections, the control of the government'. However, it should be appreciated that definitions stressing elections have difficulty in including totalitarian or 'elite' parties such as the German National Socialist (Nazi) and Communist parties, whose methods, besides propaganda and agitation, and whose medium, besides elections, include physical coercion. Such parties reject the idea of remaining a 'part' of politics and see violence as an adjunct to propaganda and agitation.

Alfred de Grazia

See also: FACTION
PARTY PLATFORM
PARTY RESPONSIBILITY

Party Platform

Party Platform

A. A *party platform* is a general statement of principles, policies, and issues, and a programme of promises which the party pledges to enact into legislation.

B. In the vocabulary of politics and political science, a party platform is a statement of the general principles which presumably bind the party together, a statement of policies which the party members expect to follow, and promises of programme which the party will attempt to put into legislation if elected. Because the major national parties in the United States do not possess the discipline or cohesion of European parties, the platforms of the national parties are not manifestos nor documents of firm doctrine, but are couched in broad and often ambiguous language, with appeals to a multiplicity of groups whose support is sought in the ensuing presidential campaign.

The party platforms are prepared at the quadrennial conventions of the national parties under the nominal auspices of the Committee on Resolutions, which holds 'hearings' at which spokesmen for many groups of special interest present arguments for the inclusion of policy and programme statements that will work to their benefit. The actual writing of the platform is in the hands of a few professional leaders of the party and it becomes, in their hands, an instrument for stating the minimum consensus on policy and programme that will bind the greatest diversity of interests in a coalition for the purpose of contesting the national campaign under the same doctrinal cover. In the campaign of 1956, for example, the Democratic Party platform contained a civil rights plank designed to harmonize the different factions in the party which had divided on the issue of segregation. It rejected 'all proposals for the use of force to interfere with the orderly determination of these matters by the courts'. A move on the floor of the convention by Northern liberals to substitute a stronger statement in favour of desegregation was voted down.

Although the Democratic convention of 1840 is usually credited with having written the first comprehensive party platform in American political history, there were antecedents. Before the party convention became the device for nominating presidential candidates—in the election of 1828—nominations were generally made by a caucus of party leaders in the Congress. In the election of 1800, the party of Thomas Jefferson in the House of Representa-

tives adopted a series of short resolutions which may be regarded as the forerunner of the party platform. And until the election of 1840, the national party conventions customarily adopted resolutions of policy.

The party platform is adopted before the candidates for President and Vice-President are nominated and although the platform is sometimes made in consultation with a leader who eventually secures the nomination, it can happen that the candidate and the platform disagree in important particulars. Thus, in the campaign of 1928, the Democratic platform bound the candidates of the party to an 'honest effort to enforce the Eighteenth Amendment' which prohibited the sale, manufacture, and transportation of intoxicating beverages. The Democratic candidate Alfred E. Smith, ran instead on the issue, among others, that the Eighteenth Amendment should be repealed.

Earl Latham

See also: CONVENTION
PARTY
PARTY RESPONSIBILITY

Party Responsibility

A. The idea of *party responsibility*, as operative in British government and as a reform doctrine in America, aims at facilitating the practice of majoritarian democracy by concentrating authority over the political organs of government in the political party, and then holding the party accountable to the voters, through such devices as periodic elections and an institutionalized opposition party, for the results produced during its period of governmental control (cf. A. Ranney, *The Doctrine of Responsible Party Government: Its Origins and Present State*, Urbana: University of Illinois Press, 1954).

B. The uniformity in British and American usage of the term is due to the fact that the practice of party responsibility in Britain is adopted as a 'model' by reformers critical of the American party system. The essence of party responsibility involves a joining of political *authority* (q.v.) and *responsibility* within the limits, of course, of the larger context of overall institutional arrangements of government, social structure, and belief system.

1. In Britain, party responsibility involves control of the political functions of government by one or two disciplined and policy-oriented parties, the responsibility of elected office-holders to support positions adopted by their party, the responsibility of the opposition to criticize constructively, to present alternatives of action, and to be ready to undertake control of government, and the responsibility of the parties to the voters for policies advocated and actions taken. The final requirement of such a system is that the electorate perceive and react to politics in the frame of reference provided by party responsibility.

2. Advocates of a responsible party system for America urge, in effect, that within the limits of its radically different setting American national politics should be conducted in a manner approximating that of British government. The doctrine of party responsibility, in this broad view, is merely one version of the general criticism of the diffusion of power in American politics and government and of the common reform goal of centralizing political controls. The political party is selected as the most appropriate vehicle for centralization because of its adaptability and its capacity to alter the operation of political institutions without the necessity of formal revision of the Constitution.

(a) The descriptive details of a potential American responsible party system vary somewhat from writer to writer (see Committee on Political Parties of the American Political Science Association, *Toward a More Responsible Two-Party System*, New York: Rinehart, 1950, for the most elaborated version), but a reasonably representative outline may be suggested. (i) The socio-economic composition of voting support for each of two competing national parties would tend toward greater homogeneity within each party and toward greater differentiation between the parties, a development both reflecting and contributing to a new predominant concern with policies by parties and voters. (ii) Building upon its new potential for high cohesion, each party would centralize its organization, with the result that party control would be heightened over the nomination of candidates bearing the party label and over the conduct in office of elected partisans. (iii) As the elements of a responsible party system interacted in a cumulative fashion, national legislators and the President would be harnessed together in patterns of co-operation, the claims of pressure groups would be integrated into systematic national policies, and state party organizations would more closely approach the status of branch affiliates of the national party apparatus.

(b) Differences among American proponents of centralized, disciplined, cohesive, and pro-grammatic parties are apparent on a number of important sub-topics, such as: (i) the extent to which a revamped party system can function as intended without extensive changes in institutional forms and in the underlying belief system and social structure; (ii) the extent of ideological realignment of the parties deemed desirable, possible, or necessary; (iii) the extent to which there are forces at work capable of producing such a new party system; and (iv) the extent to which the requirements of democracy are met by the existence of competition between elite-controlled parties in the absence of internal democracy within each party.

(c) Defenders of the American party system (see E. P. Herring, *The Politics of Democracy*, New York: Norton, 1940) reject the premises and the goals of the party responsibility school. Their position is that the diversity of groups and interests in America creates as the primary objective of government the fostering of consensus and unity, an objective which can be achieved only by the practice of limited majoritarianism. The argument is further developed to suggest that either responsible parties cannot be developed in the American context or, if they are developed, the effects are likely to be unanticipated and detrimental. In addition, criticisms of British government have claimed that the capacity of a responsible party system to produce clear alternatives of policy for electoral choice, to resist the claims of pressure groups, to protect minority interests, and to maximize popular control over government may be greater in theory than in practice.

Allan P. Sindler

See also: DEMOCRACY
MAJORITY
PARTY

Patriarchal (See **Patriarchy**)

Patriarchate (See **Patriarchy**)

Patriarchy (Also **Patriarchate, Patriarchal**)
A. The terms *patriarchy*, *patriarchate*, and *patriarchal* have now nearly disappeared from the vocabulary of the social scientist. They formerly referred most commonly to the governing of a family group by an elderly male, although there were other slightly different usages.

B. Writers such as H. Maine and L. H. Morgan originally gave *patriarchy* a special place in the social sciences (H. Maine, *Lectures on the Early*

Patrilateral

History of Institutions, London: Murray, 1875, p. 116; L. H. Morgan, *Ancient Society*, London: Macmillan, 1877, p. 465). The modern lack of popularity of the use of *patriarchy*, due to the decline of classical evolutionism in which patriarchy was regarded as an important stage of development, is explained by E. A. Hoebel when he writes: 'The patriarchal tyrant of the primitive horde is nothing but a figment of nineteenth-century speculation' (*The Law of Primitive Man*, Cambridge, Mass.: Harvard University Press, 1954, p. 294). Formerly, *patriarchy* was used to refer to that type of family government in which the father or male heir of his choice ruled the household. R. L. Beals and H. Hoijer give a somewhat broader definition of 'absolute rule by men' and propose that it is an 'exceedingly rare' extreme (*An Introduction to Anthropology*, New York: The Macmillan Co., 1953, p. 407). Webster's *New International Dictionary* (Springfield: Merriam, 1952) states that patriarchy not only refers to the presence of *androcracy*—physical or social supremacy of men in primitive society—but also requires *father right* or *patrilineal descent*.

C. The closely related term *patriarchate* has been defined by M. Jacobs and B. J. Stern as 'any society in which the feminine sex has lower status' (*General Anthropology*, New York: Barnes & Noble, 1952, p. 319). G. Reichard designates as examples of the *patriarchate* either 'tribes having patrilineal descent' or those groups of 'people over which some old and powerful leader or sib head, the patriarch, has final control' ('Social Life', in F. Boas (ed.), *General Anthropology*, New York: Heath, 1938, p. 416).

D. The adjectival form *patriarchal*, especially as applied to the family, likewise has had various, but similar, definitions. For instance, A. R. Radcliffe-Brown gives the term one of its most precise definitions when he writes: 'A society may be called patriarchal when descent is patrilineal (i.e. the children belong to the group of the father), marriage is patrilocal (i.e. the wife removes to the local group of the husband), inheritance (of property) and succession (to rank) are in the male line, and the family is patripotestal (i.e. the authority over the members of the family is in the hands of the father or his relatives)' (*Structure and Function in Primitive Society*, London: Cohen & West, 1952, p. 22). If the term has any promise of retaining usage in anthropology it will be with

respect to this clustering of *patrilineal* (q.v.)—*patrilocal* (q.v.)—*patripotestal* modes of social organization as the dominant form of *non-literate* (q.v.) social life (G. C. Homans & D. M. Schneider, *Marriage, Authority, and Final Causes*, Glencoe, Ill.: The Free Press, 1955). B. Malinowski, however, uses *patriarchal* to refer to *patria potestas* alone (*Sex and Repression in Savage Society*, London: Kegan Paul, Trench, Trubner, 1927, p. 169).

Psychoanalysts, including S. Freud and E. Jones, have also employed *patriarchal* (S. Freud, *Totem and Taboo*, trans. by A. A. Brill, London: Kegan Paul, Trench, Trubner, n.d., p. 248; E. Jones, 'Mother-Right and the Sexual Ignorance of Savages', *International Journal of Psychoanalysis*, vol. 6, 1925, p. 130). While it is central to much of their theory of culture as the product of repression, they have not attempted to give it a special definition, but have tended to use the 19th-century picture of the primal horde.

Arnold R. Pilling

See also: Matriarchy

Patrilateral

Patrilateral is sometimes used as a synonym for *patrilineal*; that is, it describes a kinship system in which descent is traced only through males.

It is more usual nowadays to use the term for relationships traced through the father in a matrilineal system (these relationships are not lineal but are on the father's side); or for relatives on the father's side in a non-unilineal kinship system.

Maurice Freedman

See also: Descent
Kinship and Kinship System
Matrilateral

Patrilocal (See **Residence**)

Patrimoiety (See **Moiety**)

Patronage

A. *Patronage* is the right vested in a person, official, or political party to appoint persons to offices and positions, to award contracts, and to dispose of emoluments and other favours. The person or organization holding the right to appoint or to bestow favours is not exclusively moved by considerations of the merits or competence of the appointee. Although the term is most widely used to denote the giving of jobs or other rewards in politics, it is also used colloquially with regard to business and other spheres of social life.

B. 1. Political patronage was widespread in England during Walpole's administration (the end of the 17th century and the beginning of the 18th century) a period in which it was 'more and more ... becoming the decisive factor in political life' (J. H. Plumb, *Sir Robert Walpole*, London: Cresset Press, 1956, p. 64). Thus we find that 'patronage and diplomacy were the most important' preoccupations of the King's Ministers, and Walpole himself had to learn to cajole and control patronage (ibid., pp. 52, 72, 112). On the local level the Lord Lieutenant commanded patronage, the best example being the Duke of Newcastle, who was Lord Lieutenant throughout most of his life (ibid., p. 43), and who 'controlled more borough patronage than any other nobleman' (ibid., p. 363). Patronage was also to be found in the army (ibid., p. 159) and in the universities (G. M. Trevelyan, *England Under the Stuarts*, London: Methuen, 1930, p. 19).

From the 19th century onwards recourse to 'patronage methods' and *nepotism* (q.v.) diminished. The term *patronage* is still used, however, in some contexts. Thus, even today, in Great Britain, the Government 'Chief Whip is also often referred to as the Patronage Secretary, even though he has little if anything to do with the departmental business of the Treasury. The term Patronage Secretary comes from the days when the Chief Whip exercised a material influence on numerous Government appointments' (H. Morrison, *Government and Parliament*, London: Oxford University Press, 1959, p. 101). Morrison also talks about the 'Prime Minister's power of patronage' which accrues to him through his responsibility 'for a number of specific things including proposals to the Sovereign for the appointment or transfer of Ministers, recommendations for honours and ecclesiastical patronage' (ibid., pp. 37, 350). Furthermore, in so far as the meaning of the term is 'a right of nomination' (*The Oxford English Dictionary*), whether this be vested in one person or a group of persons, *patronage* must still exist in most walks of life. In the sense in which it was practised, however, in earlier days, especially in the field of public administration, it is true to say with E. N. Gladden that there has been an 'elimination of nepotism and other forms of patronage' (*An Introduction to Public Administration*, London: Staples Press, 1952, p. 77).

2. In the U.S. *patronage* has had a derogatory connotation. Thus, L. D. White uses *patronage* and *spoils* synonymously and designates both as 'the practice of making appointments to public office not on the basis of merit or fitness but on that of party or factional affiliations or personal gain' ('Spoils System', in E. R. A. Seligman (ed.), *Encyclopedia of the Social Sciences*, New York: The Macmillan Co., 1934, vol. 14, p. 301).

Patronage practices appeared in the American states as early as 1800 and spread into the Federal service during the 19th century. The civil service and merit systems were designed to curb what were believed to be the excesses of patronage.

There have been two general purposes behind the giving of political patronage. First, jobs, positions, contracts, and various other favours are given to persons to help strengthen the political organization and apparatus of the political party. Recipients are thus placed under obligation to work for the party, support its candidates at the next election, make financial contributions, and render other services. Second, jobs and contracts may be given as rewards for faithful party service and to fulfil promises made by successful candidates or the party hierarchy. Appointments are made upon the basis of party services rather than upon the qualifications of the applicants for the office. The word *spoils* is widely used to describe the method of filling public positions. *Spoils* as a term is attributed to Senator W. L. Marcy when in 1832, he remarked, 'To the victor belong the spoils of the enemy'. Another type of patronage is *nepotism* (q.v.) which refers to the bestowing of jobs in consideration of family connections rather than on the basis of party services or merit.

C. *Patronage* is also used in an ecclesiastical sense to mean the right vested in a church body or a layman to appoint a properly qualified person to a church position. Patronage of this type goes back far into the Middle Ages.

Hugh A. Bone

See also: NEPOTISM

Pattern Variables

A. The *pattern variables* are the dichotomous courses of action from each of which *any* actor must select explicitly or implicitly in order to formulate a choice among the alternatives open to him in *any* relationship. Each of these variables is defined in the discussion below.

Pattern Variables

B. This term was introduced by T. Parsons and E. A. Shils (*Toward a General Theory of Action*, Cambridge, Mass.: Harvard University Press, 1951) and later elaborated by T. Parsons, R. F. Bales, and E. A. Shils (*Working Papers in the Theory of Action*, Glencoe, Ill.: The Free Press, 1953). Its meaning is rooted in the theory of action proposed by Parsons and Shils. Something of that theory must be presented before the pattern variables can be defined.

Action is behaviour involving a choice among alternatives and the use of criteria derived from past experience to make that choice. The choice must be oriented to the attainment of goals. It may or may not be made self-consciously.

To choose is to select from among alternatives. Parsons and Shils emphasize that, while some of the alternatives present at the time of choice are peculiar to a given situation, certain alternatives appear in *all* situations involving choice. What are these universally present alternatives?

There are two broad considerations involved in *all* instances of choosing and pursuing a chosen alternative. First, the actor will be sensitive to the possible rewards or deprivations which a situation may provide for his needs. Parsons and Shils speak of these aspects of the actor's orientation to his situation as his 'motivational orientation'. Second, the actor's choice takes into account expectations acquired from past experience concerning the criteria which are appropriately used in deciding among alternatives. Parsons and Shils speak of these aspects of the actor's orientation as his 'value-orientation'.

There are three forms or 'modes' of motivational orientation. The *cognitive mode* consists of those behaviours by which an actor *perceives* the existence of situations and discriminates their characteristics and their consequences for the gratification or deprivation of his needs. The *cathectic mode* consists of those behaviours by which an actor *responds* to a situation in accordance with its consequences for his needs. The *evaluative mode* consists of those behaviours by which an actor 'allocates his energy among the various actions with respect to various cathected objects in an attempt to optimize gratification' (T. Parsons & E. A. Shils, *Toward a General Theory of Action*, p. 59). While all of these modes of motivational orientation may be involved in any given instance of behaviour, it is typical that the actor gives primary attention first to one and then to another in the order stated above.

In the course of perceiving the features of situations, responding to those features, and allocating energy to various actions relevant to those features, the actor employs what are variously called norms, standards, and criteria. These are the acquired expectations concerning appropriate methods of choosing among alternatives—the value orientations. There is a mode of value orientation corresponding to each mode of motivational orientation. Thus the '*cognitive* mode of value orientation involves the various commitments to standards by which the validity of cognitive judgments is established' (ibid., p. 60). Next, the '*appreciative* mode ... involves the various commitments to standards by which the appropriateness or consistency of the cathexis of an object or class of objects is assessed' (ibid.). Finally, the '*moral* mode of value orientation involves the various commitments to standards by which certain consequences of particular actions and types of action may be assessed with respect to their effects upon systems of action' (ibid.), that is, upon personality systems or social systems.

When a choice is made in a situation involving social objects, by which Parsons and Shils mean other actors (individual or collective), the actor-subject may bring two further orientations to bear. First, he may judge social objects significant for his action in terms of the complexes of qualities which they embody or in terms of the acts they perform. Thus a mother whose behaviour toward her son is determined by the fact that he is her child, not by how he behaves, is oriented to a *quality* of the boy. In contrast, a mother who acts toward her child in terms of what he does is oriented to his *performance*. These alternatives comprise the *quality-performance* classification.

Second, actors orient to social objects according to 'the scope of significance distinction: In the first place, social objects may have such a broad and undefined significance for the actor-subject that he feels obliged to grant them any demand they make of him, so long as the granting of the demand does not force him to fail in other obligations higher on a priority scale of values. In this case we may say the object has for the actor ... a broad scope of significance. Its significance is *diffuse*' (ibid., pp. 57–8). The alternative is that social objects 'may have such a narrow and clearly defined significance for the actor-subject that ... [he] does not feel obliged to grant them anything that is not clearly called for in the definition of the relationship which obtains between them.

488

In this case we say the scope of significance of the object for the actor-subject is *specific*' (ibid., p. 58).

C. It is from among these universal and inherent types of motivational and value orientations and of orientations to social objects that Parsons and Shils declare actors must select when they choose in *any* social situation. 'Specifically, we maintain, the actor must make five specific dichotomous choices before any situation will have a determinate meaning. The five dichotomies which formulate these choice alternatives are called the *pattern variables* because any specific orientation (and consequently any action) is characterized by a pattern of the five choices' (ibid., p. 76).

The five pairs of choices which comprise the pattern variables are:

1. *Affectivity and Affective Neutrality:* To choose affectively means to give immediate gratification to impulses without regard to the later consequences of such action. Affective neutrality means holding up such immediate gratification in the interests of evaluating the consequences of action. This pair of choices derives from deciding between expressing the cognitive and cathectic modes of motivational orientation or expressing the evaluative mode.

2. *Self-Orientation and Collectivity-Orientation:* In applying the moral mode of value-orientation, the actor must choose between action for private goals (self-orientation) and action on behalf of collective goals (collectivity-orientation).

3. *Universalism and Particularism:* In applying the cognitive and appreciative modes of value orientation, the actor must choose one as having primacy. He may decide 'to treat the objects in the situation in accordance with a general norm covering *all* objects in that class' (ibid., p. 81). That is a universalistic choice. He may decide to be particularistic, treating them 'in accordance with their standing in some particular relationship to him or his collectivity, independently of the objects' subsumibility under a general norm' (ibid., p. 81).

4. *Quality and Performance* (this was called Achievement-Ascription in *Toward a General Theory of Action* and T. Parsons, *The Social System*, Glencoe, Ill.: The Free Press, 1951. The terms were changed in the *Working Papers in the Theory of Action*): When dealing with social objects, the actor must decide to act toward them in terms of what they are (their quality) or in terms of what they do (their performance).

5. *Diffuseness and Specificity:* When dealing with social objects, the actor must decide to act toward them 'by accepting no inherent or prior limitation of the scope of the actor's "concern" with the object, either as an object of interest or of obligations [diffuseness], or by according only a limited and specific type of significance to the object in his system of orientation [specificity]' (T. Parsons & E. A. Shils, *Toward a General Theory of Action*, p. 83).

D. When an actor formulates a course of action in relationship to physical objects, it may be presumed that some of these pattern variables will be modified or will become unavailable. It might be expected, for example, that a collectivity-orientation is not a possible choice in relation to a physical object. Whether quality-performance and diffuseness-specificity are available alternatives in such situations is a matter for further theoretical development.

Because the five dichotomies are drawn from what was believed to be an exhaustive and highly general statement of the elementary components of action, they are not presented as an arbitrary catalogue. A recently published rationale for their meaning and interrelations appears in T. Parsons, et al., *Working Papers in the Theory of Action*, pp. 63–109, 163–269). Within the basic argument of that rationale, it seems possible that further dichotomies can be generated.

Guy E. Swanson

See also: SOCIAL ACT
SYSTEM OF ORIENTATION

Peace

A. *Peace* is primarily a term of international relations. It may refer (a) to the ending of specific hostilities, as the Peace of Westphalia, the Peace of Versailles. In a more general sense it may refer (b) to the absence of hostilities, (c) to active friendship, or (d) to certain institutions which have successfully maintained order in the relations of two or more states or of states in general. St Augustine distinguished the second from the third and fourth definitions saying that 'true' peace was not merely the absence of active hostilities but 'tranquillity in order' (*De Civitate Dei*, bk. XIX, ch. 13, quoted by Q. Wright, *A Study of War*, Chicago: University of Chicago Press, 1942, pp. 10 fn., 431 fn., 864). This distinction has been recognized in recent times by the terms *peaceful co-existence*, which in most cases implies latent hostility, and *peaceful co-operation* which implies active efforts to realize common goals

Peasant Society

and settle differences justly. The same distinction is implied by the paradox of a *cold war peace*, i.e. a prolonged absence of active hostility among states which however are so suspicious and antagonistic to each other that they continuously engage in hostile activities short of actual war.

Confusion between the concrete and the general meaning of peace (definitions A.(a) above and A.(c) above) has led to such paradoxical expressions as 'a peace to end peace' and 'a war to end war'. The first of these expressions refers to a peace treaty ending specific hostilities but with such injustice that it ends the possibility of genuine and co-operative peace among the parties. The expression 'peace at any price' suggests the same distinction. 'A war to end war' similarly refers to hostilities in the concrete sense undertaken with the object of remedying injustice (a 'just war') or of establishing peace-preserving institutions (definition (d)) and so preventing the occurrence of war in the general sense in the future.

The fourth connotation of peace (A.(d) above) is implied by such terms as the Pax Romana of the Antonine Caesars, the Pax Ecclesiae of the Middle Ages, and the Pax Britannica of the 19th century. The League of Nations and the United Nations have been designed with the aim of organizing such a peace in the 20th century. Some would call such an absence of overt hostilities *order* unless it was accomplished by a willing acceptance of rules rather than by imposition.

Analogous to this conception is the usage of the term *peace* in relation to the internal affairs of a state, as 'the King's peace' or 'domestic peace' implying a condition of order and justice maintained by law and suitable political organization (this usage will hereinafter be lettered (e) following on usages (a), (b), (c), (d). The term 'breach of the peace' implies a violation of such a law defining peace. The close relation of this usage to the preceding one is indicated by the difficulty of distinguishing breaches of the peace by insurrection within a federation or confederation as in the American Civil War from breaches of the peace by aggression within an international organization, as in Article 39 of the United Nations Charter.

More metaphorical are the usages of the term *peace* in a sociological sense as harmony, concord, and amity in family, group, or industrial relations (hereinafter (f)); in a psychological sense as a condition of mind or personality free from agitation, fear, passion, or moral conflict (hereinafter (g)); and in a physical sense as quiet, silence, absence of noise (hereinafter (h)).

B. These different connotations of the term have each been made the basis for an approach to practical action to maintain peace. Diplomats usually aim at peace in the first (a) or second (b) sense i.e. the ending of a particular war or the peaceful solution of disputes likely to lead to war. International organizations usually aim at peace in the third (c) or fourth (d) sense i.e. promoting of international co-operation or the establishment of institutions for preventing war and solving disputes justly. Advocates of world government or federation think of peace in the fifth (e) sense and attempt to establish authoritative institutions to administer law preventing violence. Pacifists and non-resisters, though often appearing to emphasize the mere absence of war, or 'peace at any price', in contrast to the internationalists who are prepared to use military sanctions against aggression, actually think of peace in the sixth (f) or seventh (g) sense i.e. the maintenance of human minds at peace internally and friendly with all people. The final conception (h) is perhaps implied by certain religious concepts such as Nirvana i.e. elimination of all individual antagonisms and conflicts in a universal spirit of harmony and tranquillity (ibid., p. 1089 ff.).

Quincy Wright

See also: BALANCE OF POWER
WAR

Peasant Society

A. Taking the most commonly cited traits, modern *peasant society* may be defined as a subsociety of a large stratified society which is either pre-industrial or only partly industrialized. It is further characterized by most or all of the following traits: rural residence; familial agriculture on self-owned small land holdings or other simple rural occupations providing a modest or subsistence livelihood; the family as the centrally important social unit; low social status; economic interdependence in varying degree with urban centres; simple culture; and attachment to the soil, the local community, and tradition. As a societal type, peasant society occupies a position between tribal society and industrial, urban society, sharing in some degree characteristics of both.

The term *peasant society* has long referred to Europe, changing in meaning as the industrial revolution has brought about changes in

European life. Usage of the term, often without explicit definition, has recently been extended to native populations of much of the world, especially as formerly primitive societies have come to resemble the old European peasantry. This use is most common in anthropology, economic geography, and writings on colonial affairs.

B. Modern concern with peasant society as a sharply defined ideal or constructed type has been chiefly confined to anthropology and sociology.

1. In the 19th century the German sociologist F. Tönnies was particularly interested in peasant society as the source of his description of *Gemeinschaft* (q.v.).

2. In 1918 W. I. Thomas and F. Znaniecki published their classic *The Polish Peasant in Europe and America* (New York: Knopf, 1927), describing many of the characteristics of peasant society in Poland.

3. R. Redfield, who in his earlier writings employed folk culture (q.v.) to include what others have called peasant society, later distinguished *peasant society* as intermediate between the two extremes of a folk-urban continuum embracing all societies from the simplest primitive to the most complex urban (*Peasant Society and Culture*, Chicago: University of Chicago Press, 1956). G. M. Foster presents a view of folk culture which excludes primitive society and deliberately includes Redfield's peasant society ('What is Folk Culture?', *American Anthropologist*, vol. 55, 1953, pp. 159–73). Other American anthropologists have followed one or another of these usages and, as primitive societies have become acculturated, have tended increasingly to employ the term *peasant society*.

4. Anthropologists writing in England, e.g. R. Firth (*Elements of Social Organization*, London: Watts, 1951), interpret *peasant society* essentially in accordance with the definition given in A. above.

C. Contemporary peasant society is generally viewed as an element of pre-industrial or only partially industrialized nations.

1. As Firth notes (*Elements of Social Organization*, p. 87), the term *peasant* 'has primarily an economic referent'; i.e. livelihood is provided by small-scale, technologically simple agriculture engaged in by family groups. Firth and others would, however, also include simple fishing and rural crafts.

2. Concrete peasant societies—as opposed to the ideal type—are frequently interlocked with the institutions of feudalism (q.v.) in varying degrees. Or they may be interlocked with a plantation agricultural system in which production is extensive and centrally managed (A. Pim, *Colonial Agricultural Production*, London: Oxford University Press, 1946, pp. 1–12).

D. As circumstances have changed, older views placing emphasis on the self-sufficiency and isolation of peasant society are being supplanted by a conception of the modern peasant society as an integral part of a larger, stratified social whole. Sub-types of peasant society, independent of each other, may also exist within the single large society. The peasant element is in symbiotic economic relation with its towns and cities, providing them with agricultural products and receiving in turn money for the purchase of goods. In other respects the peasant element is also a part of the greater society; although culturally simple and clinging more firmly to tradition than other elements, it assimilates in considerable measure national traits and institutions derived from contact with towns and cities.

Edward Norbeck

See also: FOLK CULTURE
SUBSISTENCE ECONOMY

Peer Group (See **Group**)

Penal Jurisdiction (See **Jurisdiction**)

Perception

A. *Perception* denotes sensory experience which has gained meaning or significance. When, as the result of learning experiences, one understands the relationships of objects which were previously merely raw, undifferentiated sensory experiences, he is said to perceive these objects. The non-sensory learning experience which is essential to transforming meaningless sensory experiences into perceptions involves the development of concepts or ideas about the sensory experiences.

B. *Perception* has been a central concept in modern psychology since what many take to be the discipline's beginning in the philosophy of Descartes (E. G. Boring, *A History of Experimental Psychology*, New York: Appleton-Century-Crofts, 1950, pp. 160–5). Moreover, the central theoretical issue concerning the concept has remained the same since that time: the relationship between mind and the objective

Personal

world in the generation of sensation and idea and their manner of intertwining in perception. The world may be related to mind through innate categories of space, time, and motion (Descartes, Kant); it may be generated by mind if the ideas formed through experience are taken as the reality (Berkeley) or conversely mind may be generated by the world if stress is placed on sensations as the real in contrast to ideas (Locke); or mind and the significant world may be generated by man interacting with his environment in the process of adaptation as suggested by more recent philosophers (Dewey, Mead). Whatever the answer, the problem of *esse* and *percipi* is still alive and reflected in the varying conceptions of *perception*.

C. Despite the continuing question, there is, for all practical purposes, general agreement in contemporary psychology and sociology upon the meaning of *perception*. The word denotes the changed relationship between organism and external world of objects which is brought about by the assignment of meanings to the previously raw and undefined sensory experiences. Despite occasional protests that the sensation-perception distinction is artificial (see H. Bartley, *Principles of Perception*, New York: Harper & Brothers, 1958, p. 7), almost without exception the word is used to indicate those relations of man and his environment which lie midway between the *sensations* of classical psychophysics and the cognitive processes which are usually subsumed under the heading of *concepts*. 'Perception occupies an intermediate position between simple and complex behavior, or as sometimes called, lower and higher functions' (H. Werner, 'Introductory Remarks', in J. S. Bruner & D. Krech (eds.), *Perception and Personality*, Durham, N.C.: Duke University Press, 1949, p. 3).

1. E. L. and R. E. Hartley (*Fundamentals of Social Psychology*, New York: Knopf, 1952, p. 228) write that perception is not '... mere sensation that results from exposing the eye to complicated patterns of light waves, but ... the process by which we register what is in the field of view in a way that is meaningful'. They add that the sensory experiences become percepts or perceptions when they are interpreted '... according to our concepts of the external world'. D. O. Hebb (*The Organization of Behavior*, New York: Wiley, 1949, p. 91) argues from the neuropsychological viewpoint that 'each perception would thus involve a conceptual activity (an activity, i.e. not *directly* con-

trolled by sensory processes)'. H. Blumer ('Science Without Concepts', *American Journal of Sociology*, vol. XXXVI, 1931, pp. 515–33) elaborates upon the relation of perception to conception, but does not make explicit the relationships to sensation per se, as do H. Gerth and C. W. Mills (*Character and Social Structure*, New York: Harcourt, Brace, 1953, p. 20): 'For sensation (the physical and organic event, for example, of light waves impinging upon a certain kind of eye) to become perception, (the seeing of the object as a red light) certain meanings must be added'.

2. Some writers stress the subjective aspects of perception. Bartley (*Principles of Perception*, p. 22), for example, states that 'Hence, in studying perception, we are studying what it is that the organism experiences; not what the physical world contains, or is made up of'. G. Allport (*Theories of Perception and the Concept of Structure*, New York: Wiley, 1955, p. 14) argues similarly, that although perception involves, to some degree, an understanding awareness of objects, 'It is the way things look, to us, or the way they sound, feel, taste, or smell'.

3. Still others emphasize the aspects of perception which carry beyond the purely cognitive nature of perception, indicating that what is perceived is a function of the autonomic nervous system as well as of the higher mental functions. Such an approach is found in H. Werner and S. Wapner, 'Sensory Tonic Field Theory of Perception' (in J. Bruner & D. Krech, *Perception and Personality*, pp. 88–107). Even more inclusive is the statement of M. and C. W. Sherif (*An Outline of Social Psychology*, New York: Harper & Brothers, 1956, p. 79): 'Perceptual structuring is not only a "cognitive" affair. It is jointly determined by the totality of functionally related external factors and internal factors coming into the structuring process at a given time'.

Richard Dewey

See also: Cognition
Learning
Mind

Perfect Competition
(See **Economic Competition**)

Personal

A. The term *personal* is a qualifying adjective that is used in combination with various substantive concepts or with one of several possible prefixes or suffixes. It is most commonly employed in the description or analysis of primary groups and primary relations. Although the context and combinations in which the term is used vary widely, all seem to indicate that *personal* refers to social phenomena that relate to one particular person and hence cannot be transferred, duplicated, or replaced. Such phenomena are therefore inclusive, spontaneous, direct, and tend to escape in some measure from the formal confines of culture.

B. The term is seldom defined specifically in social science literature. It seems to have its most significant use in the social sciences in the description and analysis of primary groups and primary relations. The core meaning of the term can be deduced from its use in context and seems to have several correlated referents.

1. In its core meaning *personal* designates social phenomena and relations that are decisively unique, unduplicated, and non-transferable. 'The most obvious and inevitable quality of a personal relationship is that it is *not transferable*. It attaches to determinate individuals who cannot be duplicated nor replaced' (R. C. & F. W. Binkley, *What is Right with Marriage?*, New York: Appleton, 1929, pp. 31–2).

2. One logical correlate of this meaning is recognition that personal phenomena and relations are inclusive. Inclusive in this sense has both a lateral dimension, comprehending all segments of the self and personality, and an intensive dimension, being intimate, pervasive, and sentimental. A. Green writes: 'the total self is involved. One shares with others not aspects of the self but its core. The barriers are down, and it is the intensive personalness of the primary group which makes betrayal of any of its members an extremely serious matter' (*Sociology*, New York: McGraw-Hill, 1956, p. 43). Intensity of inclusiveness is evidenced by the feeling component of *personal*.

3. A second correlate of the basic meaning is the recognition that personal phenomena and relations often, though not necessarily, seem to escape from the confines of cultural forms. K. Young defines 'personal-social' relations as 'social interaction which is not predetermined by culturalized habits and attitudes but which grows out of more or less natural interrelations of persons' (*Social Psychology*, New York: Crofts, 1944, p. 563). In further comment Young stresses the culture-free character of personal phenomena, stating that 'the roots lie in the very essential interaction of mother and child in the first months of life and of later

primary-group contacts that have not been established in the culture' (ibid., p. 9).

4. It follows that since personal phenomena and relations tend to transcend cultural forms they may be highly fluid and variable. This fact is expressed in such associated terms as spontaneity, informality, and voluntariness. Thus K. Davis observes that 'as a consequence, the personal relationship which depends always on the will of either party at any point in the interaction, is voluntary in a more complete sense; and as mentioned before, it therefore implies the greatest spontaneity on the part of the participants' (*Human Society*, New York: The Macmillan Co., 1949, p. 298).

Joseph S. Himes

See also: IMPERSONAL

Personal Income (See **National Product**)

Personality (See **Personality System**)

Personality Integration

A. *Personality integration* denotes the process by which, the state in which, and the degree to which (a) in a particular situation, single courses of action emerge from the predispositions competing for expression, and/or (b) over time, consistency of choice emerges in consecutive situations.

B. The observations to which the concept of *personality integration* is addressed may be stated as follows: (a) The choices which individuals make among alternative behaviours show a considerable consistency from one situation to another; (b) choices which individuals make in particular situations are limited or facilitated by dispositions which they have to make certain choices in other situations; (c) despite the individual's desire to undertake many courses of behaviour, he is able to enact only a limited number of these at any given time and must assign other times as appropriate for the remainder.

1. In short, we find that the individual is, to some degree, master in his own house, determining which dispositions will be enacted and when and how they will become overt. The choices which he made in the past and which he hopes to make in the future guide those made in the present, and there is a discernible consistency from one time to another in the choices which he makes. In any case, there is the conception that personality is an organization of some more

Personality System

elementary units, and that, to be integrated, this organization must exhibit the three features just listed.

2. The notion which appears central to personality integration is simply that the elementary units of personality are functionally dependent on one another and, in many cases, 'competing' with one another for expression, or for expression at a particular time. By some means, these units must be sorted, and priorities assigned to the expression of each in any given situation. A personality is integrated to the extent that such sorting and assignment are possible. Integration implies that the individual has criteria and processes which enable the selection and assignment of priorities among competing predispositions.

3. These considerations lead to another. A personality may be integrated in one situation, less integrated in a second, and unintegrated—that is, incapable of producing a single course of action—in a third. Thus we must distinguish between the idea of a personality's being integrated in a particular situation and being integrated over several consecutive situations.

C. At times, the idea of an integrated personality has been identified with mental health or some other desirable state. Again, personalities which are highly integrated may be spoken of as 'rigid'. Neither of these connotations is intrinsic to the idea of personality integration. They refer, rather, to such matters as the appropriateness of the individual's choices, or the speed with which he can make choices in particular situations.

Guy E. Swanson

See also: PERSONALITY SYSTEM
SOCIAL INTEGRATION

Personality System (Also **Personality**)

A. In its broadest psychological sense *personality system* or *personality* denotes the organization of all the behaviour of an individual organism and the resulting organized behaviour itself. Sociologists and social psychologists have limited this definition by restricting it either to (a) behaviour developed through social experience or (b) behaviour involving choice, ends, and norms based on past experience.

B. The term *personality system*, or, more commonly, *personality*, has had a wide variety of meanings in common speech and in such fields as theology, biology, psychology, and sociology. G. W. Allport surveyed most of these

in his book *Personality* (New York: Henry Holt, 1937). In recent years, however, there has been a growing convergence in the use of this term by social scientists. Three meanings are common. The first is familiar to psychologists and many sociologists; the second and third to sociologists.

1. Allport's (ibid., p. 48) definition contains the elements usually found in the psychological meaning. He says, 'Personality is the dynamic organization within the individual of those psychophysical systems that determine his unique adjustments to his environment'. Several characteristics of this definition may be noted.

(a) It speaks of an organization of psychophysical elements. In amplifying his words, Allport indicates that such systems include habits, attitudes, sentiments, and 'dispositions of other orders'. Each of these is a type of predisposition to relate in some fashion to the environment. It is not clear whether he wants to construe environment narrowly and rule out the internal processes of the individual or whether relations with one's self would be included. Further, we are not told whether 'relating' may refer to autonomic neural processes (e.g. the processes controlling heartbeats or eye blinks) or the secretion of the ductless glands (e.g. the flow of adrenalin or of saliva) as well as to behaviours involving learning and choice. Some psychologists certainly do intend that personality shall refer to the organization of all aspects of an individual's behaviour. D. C. McClelland (*Personality*, New York: Sloane, 1951, p. 69), for example, defines it as '... the most adequate conceptualization of a person's behavior in all its detail that the scientist can give at a moment in time'.

(b) Another feature of Allport's usage specifies that personality is the organization, or state of interrelatedness, among predispositions.

(c) It is a dynamic organization—an organization in which some of the predispositions are limiting, facilitating, or activating one another at all times.

(d) The predispositions, themselves, are organized into 'systems'. Personality is the organization of these systems of predispositions.

(e) Each personality is somewhat different from any other personality. This is Allport's way of emphasizing the individuality of the person.

(f) Finally, Allport wants us to consider 'adjustments' to the environment as including the individual's efforts to master his world as well as his more passive adaptations to it.

2. The meaning of personality when employed by sociologists is sometimes more limited than the common psychological usage. The limitations are set by a prior distinction between the individual and the person. Following R. E. Park and E. W. Burgess (*Introduction to the Science of Sociology*, Chicago: University of Chicago Press, 1924, p. 55), the individual (q.v.) is equated with the organization of the behaviour of the human biological organism. The person is the individual as he comes to be shaped in the course of interacting with others. Personality then refers to the organization of the person. It is in this framework that H. Blumer ('Social Psychology' in E. P. Schmidt, *Man and Society*, New York: Prentice-Hall, 1937, p. 176) says, 'Personality represents the organization of tendencies to act that are developed by an individual in the course of his interaction with others'. One finds evidence both of this sociological tradition and that of psychology in K. Young's view that personality represents 'the more or less integrated body of habits, attitudes, traits, and ideas of an individual as these are organized externally into specific and general roles and statuses and internally around self-consciousness and the concept of the self, and around the ideas, values, and purposes which are related to motives, roles and status' (*Social Psychology*, New York: Crofts, 2nd edn., 1944, p. 120).

3. Another kind of narrowing is found in the meaning given to *personality system* by T. Parsons and E. A. Shils (*Toward a General Theory of Action*, Cambridge, Mass.: Harvard University Press, 1951). They refer to personality system as '... a relatively specific, definite, and consistent system of need-dispositions operating as selective reactions to the alternatives which are presented to him by his object situation or which he organizes for himself by seeking out new object situations and formulating new goals' (ibid., p. 18). Expanding this conception, they note certain of its characteristics: '(1) It is the system comprising the interconnections of the actions of an individual actor. (2) The actor's actions are organized by a structure of need-dispositions. (3) ... the actions of the single actor must have a determinate organization of compatibility or integration ... the goals or norms involved in a single action of one actor will be affected and limited by one another and by other goals and norms of the same actor' (ibid., p. 55). Thus, like Allport's, their conception refers to an organization of dispositions which, in turn, determine the individual's relations with his environment. In their conception of 'need-dispositions', they, like Allport, have in mind a dynamic organization, and, as their later discussion shows, they assume that these dispositions are organized into systems subsidiary to the total personality.

The distinctive features of Parsons and Shils's treatment are produced by their speaking of 'action'. To this term they give the technical meaning of behaviour which is 'oriented to the attainment of ends in situations, by means of the normatively regulated expenditure of energy' (ibid., p. 53). This rules out autonomic reflexive behaviours or any items of conduct which are not founded on past experience (in their words 'normatively regulated') and which do not involve the actor in making a choice among alternatives.

Guy E. Swanson

See also: ATTITUDE
EGO
INTERNALIZATION
PERSONALITY INTEGRATION
SOCIALIZATION

Personality Trait

A. *Personality trait* denotes, generally, a distinguishing and enduring characteristic, element, or quality of the human personality. This definition makes trait a purely descriptive term which focuses on the behavioural regularities of the individual actor rather than on any particular conceptual explanation of these regularities.

B. *Trait* is widely used by psychologists with rather variable conceptual connotations. Probably the broadest definition in current use is that which G. Murphy offers in *Personality* (New York: Harper & Brothers, 1947, p. 999): 'Anything by means of which one person may be distinguished from another'. Few other writers have been willing to accept such a general definition, and the limitations they impose have led to some notable disagreements.

1. G. W. Allport (*Personality: a Psychological Interpretation*, New York: Henry Holt, 1937, p. 295) defines *trait* as a 'generalized and focalized neuropsychic system (peculiar to the individual), with the capacity to render many stimuli functionally equivalent, and to initiate and guide consistent (equivalent) forms of adaptive and expressive behavior'.

He goes on to argue that *traits* 'are always biophysical in nature, concrete and personal in their organization, contemporaneous in their

Petition

effect, capable of functional autonomy, but not structurally independent of one another; they are generalized (to the extent that the effective stimuli are equivalent, and to the extent that the resultant responses are equivalent). They are *modi vivendi*, ultimately deriving their significance from the role they play in advancing adaptation within, and mastery of, the personal environment' (ibid., p. 342).

2. Although Allport's definition of the term is probably as widely accepted by psychologists as any, there are numerous points of disagreement. R. B. Cattell (*Personality: A Systematic Theoretical and Factual Study*, New York: McGraw-Hill, 1950) bases his use of the term on the findings of factor analysis and thus contradicts Allport's notion of the uniqueness and structural interdependence of all personality traits. Cattell speaks of a correlation cluster as a 'surface trait' which is made up of 'trait-elements' or 'trait-indicators' ('lesser, narrower traits or behavior fragments'). 'A surface trait is in any case simply a collection of trait-elements, of greater or lesser width of representation, which obviously "go together" in many different individuals and circumstances' (ibid., p. 21). Thus a factor, or a 'source trait', '*may be* considered an *underlying influence among* or *cause of* the observed correlations among trait-elements' (ibid., p. 27). Cattell agrees with Allport to the extent of acknowledging that there are both 'unique and common' traits, only the latter being present to some degree in all (or most) individuals.

3. D. McClelland takes issue with aspects of both Cattell's and Allport's definitions. He uses the terms 'schema' and 'motive' to include some of the aspects of trait as used by Allport and Cattell. 'It is the person's schema or schematic system which determines whether situations are reacted to as equivalent and to some extent it is the person's motives which guide and direct consistent responses. The trait then must be the consistent response system itself which occurs when situations are viewed as similar and when the subject is similarly motivated' ('Personality: An Integrative View', in J. L. McCary (ed.), *Psychology of Personality*, New York: Logos Press, 1956, p. 357).

This same emphasis on behaviour seems to be in the minds of R. Dewey and W. J. Humber when they state: 'In a sense, attitudes are the ways in which we define a situation, and traits are the ways in which we actually behave in response to our definition, which definition, of course, always involves the immediate condi-

tions' (*The Development of Human Behavior*, New York: The Macmillan Co., 1951, p. 211). However, this particular relationship between trait and attitude is not widely accepted.

C. Dewey and Humber's inclusion of the 'conditions' of the action situation in their discussion brings to the fore the most serious criticism levelled at the concept of trait by sociologists, social psychologists, and Gestalt psychologists, i.e. that the use of the term places too much emphasis on the individual person as the locus of behavioural uniformities with inadequate emphasis on the situational and cultural bases of uniformity. This specific criticism has been expressed in the literature for at least twenty-five years (cf. J. M. Reinhardt, 'Personality Traits and the Situation', *American Sociological Review*, vol. 2, 1937, pp. 492–500; K. Young, *Personality and Problems of Adjustment*, London: Kegan Paul, Trench, Trubner, 1947, pp. 106–7, 277–83).

The more recent development of the concept of role (q.v.) has given some sociologists a sharper conceptual weapon in their attack on theories built around the concept of trait. For instance, A. R. Lindesmith and A. L. Strauss in their discussion of the characteristics of the taxi-dancer state: 'Her traits should not be viewed as "inside" her but as consistent modes of response organized around a role' (*Social Psychology*, New York: Dryden Press, 1949, p. 274). Their emphasis here is on the fact that behaviour within a particular role may be quite consistent, but the same person playing another role may behave very differently.

Alan C. Kerckhoff

See also: PERSONALITY INTEGRATION
PERSONALITY SYSTEM
ROLE

Petit Jury (See **Jury**)

Petition
A. *Petition* may be defined as a plea from a private individual or organization to an official or agency of government requesting that some wrong suffered by an individual be righted or that some general grievance be remedied.

B. Petition is an old and familiar word in the language of politics and has been regularly employed in substantially the same sense since the Middle Ages. Only in the field of modern Anglo-American law has petition survived in a specialized, technical connotation—though that itself is a derivation of a political relationship long since discarded on both sides of the Atlantic.

1. The general meaning of *petition* denotes a plea or request addressed by an individual, group, or organization to a particular public official or to some agency of government. The content of the petition is normally devoted to calling attention to a situation where, in the petitioner's view, an injustice exists or a wrong has been committed. The official or agency has the legal power to remedy the situation, but cannot be compelled to do so. The petitioner, therefore, makes an appeal that right be done.

Much of the basic work of medieval government (including functions that were later differentiated under the headings of legislative, executive, and judicial) originated by the process of petition. The English Parliament owes its birth, or rebirth, to the need for a national forum where petitions could be brought from the localities to the King. Legislation often originated in the attempt of a Parliament to generalize from a number of separate complaints and seek a common form under which future abuses might be prevented; and the request for such legislation was itself, initially, a petition from Parliament to the King who alone could sanction it. Later on, as Parliament itself acquired political power and, with it, legal authority in its own right, petitions were presented to the Parliament as the agency from which redress might be obtained. Indeed, in order to avoid being overawed by mob demonstrations, Parliament found it necessary in 1662 to enact a statute against 'tumultuous petitioning'.

For so long was petition the approved channel of communication from subjects to sovereign that its exercise has come to be asserted as a basic right and one that is fundamental to the liberties of a free people. The term *petition* acquired specific meaning in the very title of the Petition of Right to which Charles I assented in 1625. Likewise, the Bill of Rights (1689) enumerated 'that it is the right of the subjects to petition the King, and all commitments and prosecutions for such petitioning are illegal' (E. Dumbauld, *The Bill of Rights and What it Means Today*, Norman: University of Oklahoma Press, 1957, p. 168).

Both the practice, and the same use of the same term, have been continued in the American tradition. The Declaration of Independence listed this among its complaints against George III: 'In every state of these oppressions we have petitioned for redress in the most humble terms; our repeated petitions have been answered only by repeated injury' (E. Dumbauld, *The Declaration of Independence and What it Means Today*, Norman: University of Oklahoma Press, 1950, p. 160). Fifteen years later, when the Bill of Rights was adopted as a series of amendments to the Constitution of the United States, the First Amendment included, after the rights to freedom of religion, of speech, of the press, and of assembly, 'the right of the people —to petition the government for a redress of grievances' (in E. Dumbauld, *The Bill of Rights*, p. 220). Throughout its history, the Congress has been the recipient of numberless petitions from individuals and organizations exercising this right.

2. In the Anglo-American court system, a special terminology that derives from old practices still lingers on. The Crown, being the source of law, was considered above the law. Legally, the King could do no wrong and could not be sued in his own courts. When a wrong was therefore committed by him or by his servants acting in his name, a subject who sought judicial restitution had first to petition the Crown to allow a suit to be brought. Furthermore, there were found to be some situations which the common law did not cover and with which the established courts were not empowered to deal. A petition to the King, pleading for justice, would be referred to a branch of the royal administration which would determine the merits of the case on the basis, not of law, but of equity. The distinction between law and equity, in the U.K. and the U.S.A., has long outgrown the circumstances of its origin. But terminology still enshrines that distinction in the sense that those who bring a suit under equity procedure are still called petitioners.

Leslie Lipson

Peyotism

A. *Peyotism* is an inter-tribal nativistic religious cult (q.v.) of the American Indian in which the remnants and debris of areal culture in various tribal cultures reinforce one another in a vision quest in response to acculturation (q.v.) with respect to American culture. Central in the meetings of members of the cult is the eating of the 'peyote button'.

B. In historic times, largely since the abeyance of the 1890 Ghost Dance, *peyotism* has become the major religion of the Indians of the United States, from Texas to southern Canada and from the Eastern Woodlands to east-central

Phatic Communication

California. The Indians eat the 'peyote-buttons' in an all-night meeting in a tipi, sitting around variously-shaped ground altars and a central fire, while a water-drum, sacred gourd, and staff are passed around clockwise as each man sings four special peyote songs. The meeting is punctuated by smoking, censing with cedar and sage at the opening, by eagle-bone-whistling at the compass points at midnight, and by the 'early morning songs' all led by the road-chief or officiating shaman; and ends with a ritual day-break meal of boneless meat, fruit, and parched corn in sugar-water which goes back to Mexican first-fruits ceremonies.

Peyotism has been studied comparatively by W. La Barre (*The Peyote Cult*, Yale University Publications in Anthropology, no. 19, New Haven: Yale University Press, 1938). The religion involves, unimportantly, some Christian elements; it is chiefly an accommodative, pan-Indian movement, with the common denominators of Indian cultures—especially the vision quest—in various tribes mutually reinforcing one another. Repeated legal attempts, both state and federal, to suppress peyotism have almost uniformly failed, since it is not 'simple drug addiction' as many missionaries allege—none of the peyote alkaloids has been proven addictive—but a bona fide cult of nativism (q.v.). An early, and still model, study of peyotism in a single tribe is by A. L. Kroeber (*The Arapaho*, American Museum of Natural History, Bulletin 18, New York: American Museum of Natural History, 1907, pp. 398–410). For the life history of a peyotist, see P. Radin (ed.), *Crashing Thunder: The Autobiography of an American Indian* (New York: Appleton, 1926).

C. Peyote, from the Nahuatl word *peyotl*—something white, shining and silky, like a cocoon, spiderweb or the pericardium, in Aztekan usage—is a small, spineless, carrot-shaped cactus, bearing short tufts of whitish flocculence, somewhat like artists' camel's hair brushes, in spaced medial lines on the puffy portions between the curved radial depressions on the top surface of the plant; in the top centre is a larger spot of matted fuzz. From these silky tufts, peyote derives its botanical name, '*Lophophora* ("*bearing crests*") *williamsii* (Lemaire) Coulter'; peyote is the unique member of its genus, formerly designated *Anhalonium*. The greyish-green, cushiony portion of the plant appearing above ground is cut off horizontally and eaten either green or, more usually, dried,

as the 'peyote-button'; sometimes it is taken in an infusion with water. Peyote contains nine narcotic alkaloids of the isoquiniline series—an unusual number even for the *Cactaceae*—ranging from morphine-like to strychnine-like in their physiological effects. Mescaline is the alkaloid chiefly responsible for the visual hallucinations in brilliant colours—along with kinaesthetic and auditory hallucinations—which have led to peyote's use by prehistoric Mexican natives as a source of supernatural 'power', and by modern mystics.

Weston La Barre

See also: ACCOMMODATION
        ACCULTURATION
        NATIVISM
        REVITALIZATION MOVEMENT

Phatic Communication
(Phatic Communion)

A. *Phatic communication*—sometimes *phatic communion*—is that process of communication (q.v.) by vocalization, speech, or other form of symbolization in which precise meaning is not communicated, but rather states of feeling which serve to create common attitudes and social solidarity.

B. The term *phatic* was first used by B. Malinowski ('The Problem of Meaning in Primitive Languages', in C. K. Ogden & I. A. Richards, *The Meaning of Meaning*, London: Kegan Paul, Trench, Trubner, 3rd edn., 1930, pp. 296–336). Malinowski applied the term to the emotive or non-denotative language described by Ogden and Richards. Phatic communication '... serves to harmonize [primitives'] behaviour towards other men'; it '... creates new bonds and sentiments by the emotional appeal of the words', '... an atmosphere of sociability ... convivial gregariousness' (ibid., pp. 311, 313, 315). He describes such use of language as follows: 'In its primitive uses, language functions as a link in concerted human activity, as a piece of human behaviour. It is a mode of action and not an instrument of reflection. ... There can be no doubt that we have here a new type of linguistic use—phatic communion I am tempted to call it, actuated by the demon of terminological invention—a type of speech in which ties of union are created by a mere exchange of words. ... Are words in Phatic Communion used primarily to convey meaning, the meaning which is symbolically theirs? Certainly not! They fulfil a social function and that is their principal aim, but they are neither the result of intellectual reflection, nor do they necessarily arouse reflection in the listener. Once again we may say that language does not function here as a means of transmission of thought' (ibid., pp. 312, 315).

C. In the opinion of modern linguists and others, Malinowski was undoubtedly mistaken in his cultural evolutionist notion that '... such and no other is the nature of primitive speech' (ibid., p. 315). So called primitives, of course, have every whit as much articulate semantic speech as civilized men, although they do have phatic communication. As Malinowski also observed, it must be noted that much of the alleged semantic communication of civilized men is in fact phatic communication (ibid., pp. 315–6).

Thus modern students of communication use the term to refer to that use of symbols in both primitive and civilized societies which communicates attitudes and creates solidarity. C. F. Hockett, for example, says: 'The term *phatic communion* has been proposed for this sort of minimal communicative activity which has no obvious consequences save to inform all concerned that the channels are in good working order for the transmission of more "important" messages' (*A Course in Modern Linguistics*, New York: The Macmillan Co., 1958, p. 585). He also calls attention to the fact that much of the communication in art and music is of this order (ibid., p. 585). W. Breed has indicated that 'What Malinowski called "phatic communion" can thus also be found in formal mass communications' ('Mass Communication and Socio-Cultural Integration', *Social Forces*, vol. 37, 1958–9, p. 116).

D. W. La Barre (*The Human Animal*, Chicago: University of Chicago Press, 1955, pp. 57–8, 166–7) has used *phatic* to apply to primate 'vocalization', and considers that human semantic speech arose from primate phatic communication in a new biosocial context, viz.: prolonged dependent infancy, a brain large in association areas, absence of instinct, close organic-phatic ties of an intensified mammalian nature, and long continued association of specific adult and juvenile individuals. For human speech to arise from primate vocalization, meanings based on repeated 'familiar' experiences must become stabilized as the common coinage of a larger society, lest they embody only private phatic associations of the individuals in a nuclear family and perish

with them. Only the universal human incest taboo procures this circulation of individuals from family of origin to family of procreation, with new phatic ties as intense as the old ones; hence, as man is the only animal with the requisite socio-biological traits, he alone possesses true semantic language.

Weston La Barre

See also: COMMUNICATION
SIGN
SYMBOL

Phoneme

A. In its most common use in scientific linguistics, a *phoneme* is a minimal unit speech sound or well-defined complex of phonetic features in the phonetic system of a given language or dialect. It is typically, though not always, less in extent than a syllable. It shows variation within a larger or smaller range, definable in each phonetic context for each phoneme of each language, but normally always showing contrast with other comparable phonemes of the same language.

B. The general non-professional meaning of *phoneme*—any unit or segment of speech sound whether long or short, complex or simple—has largely been lost in modern professional usage. Instead, it is now generally understood as the fundamental or minimal unit of sound in human speech. To identify it in common-sense terms, it is a simple speech sound, commonly though not always represented by a single letter in alphabetical writing. Syllables in some languages occasionally consist of a single phoneme, but many languages need at least two, a consonant and a vowel. Words, being made up normally of at least one syllable, only exceptionally are as short as a single phoneme.

C. The scientifically accurate determination of the phoneme presents problems because of two circumstances, (a) the complete joining of sounds in undivided sequences—syllable, word, etc.—in speech, and (b) the variability of all the sequences, with many differences of detail in each language. Because speech utterances involve a continuous sequence of movements of the several speech organs—lips, tongue, soft palate, pharyngeal muscles, the 'vocal cords'—and of correspondingly fluctuating sound waves, it is not always clear where the boundary should be drawn between one phoneme and the next. And because no two acts of speech are exactly alike, there may be questions of identifying the

Phonetics

sounds of one utterance with those of another, e.g. if the sibilant in *see* is pronounced a bit thickly, does that make it the *sh* of *she* or is it to be classed as an intermediate, independent sound? Practical and theoretical difficulties in handling these problems have given rise to considerable variation in the definitions and explanations of the phoneme by different scholars. The following quotations are intended both to clarify the problems and to show the variety of solutions which have been proposed.

1. 'The immense, practically unlimited number of sounds and sound-variations in every language appears to be a manifestation ... of a definite and strictly limited number of phonemes' (J. Vachek, 'What is Phonology?' *English Studies*, Amsterdam: Swets & Zeitlinger, 1933, vol. 15, p. 83).

2. 'Part of the gross acoustic features are indifferent (*non-distinctive*), and only a part are connected with meanings and essential to communication (*distinctive*). The difference between distinctive and non-distinctive features of sound lies entirely in the habit of the speakers. A feature that is distinctive in one language, may be non-distinctive in another language' (L. Bloomfield, *Language*, New York: Henry Holt, 1933, p. 77).

3. '... a functionally significant unit in the rigidly defined pattern or configuration of sounds peculiar to a language' (E. Sapir, *Selected Writings in Language, Culture, and Personality*, ed. by D. G. Mandelbaum, Berkeley: University of California Press, 1949, p. 46).

4. 'The phoneme is the smallest potential unit of difference between similar words recognizable as different to the native' (M. Swadesh, 'The Phonemic Principle', *Language*, Baltimore: Waverly Press, 1934, vol. 10, p. 118).

5. 'The term of any minimum phonological difference among forms is called a *micro-phoneme*. ... The sum of all similarly ordered terms (micro-phonemes) of similar minimum phonological differences among forms is called a *macro-phoneme*. A phoneme, accordingly, does not occur; it "exists" in the somewhat peculiar sense of existence that a brother, *qua* brother, "exists"—as a term of a relation' (W. F. Twaddell, 'On Defining the Phoneme', *Language Monograph 16*, 1935, pp. 44–9).

D. Complicating the difficulties of phoneme determination and definition, are the theoretical differences among scholars. Some hold or imply that the division of the stream of speech into phonemes is purely a convenience

for scholars, and that any procedure of division and classification is more or less arbitrary. Others consider that the complexes of sound in each language make up a system, and that the scholar's task is to discover that system; they usually do not deny that there may be an element of arbitrariness in choosing the best manner of presenting or 'interpreting' the system. Some seem to believe that the variations of phonemes represent partially unsuccessful attempts of the speakers to produce a single model; but it is probably more common to see them as primarily a matter of custom in the speech community, to be explained in ways that hold in general for all social norms. The mental side of the phoneme is considered by some to be all-important, by others to be inaccessible to study and therefore of no concern to science, and by still others to be a legitimate parallel interest. The physical characteristics of the phoneme are minimized by some, either because they regard the abstraction of contrast with reference to other phonemes in the same language as the only thing that counts or because they consider the mental side primary.

E. For all the differences in theoretical conception, there is at least fairly general agreement on some principal points: (a) that phonemes do not occur in isolation but in complexes constituting the stream of speech; (b) that phonemic analysis is essential to the scientific study of each language and of the general properties of language in general; (c) that the phoneme is basically a unit in the phonetic differentiation of speech elements and that it is not in itself meaningful; (d) that what is true in the phonemics of one language need not apply to other languages.

Morris Swadesh

See also: Linguistics
Morpheme
Phonetics

Phonemics (See Phonetics)

Phonetics

A. *Phonetics* refers to the section of linguistics (q.v.) which deals with the production of sounds, the representation of sounds in symbols, and the acoustical properties associated with sounds. *Phonetics* reflects the inventory of sounds of a given language, although it does not show their phonemic distinctiveness or patterning, and does not deal with such secondary characteristics of speech as stress, juncture, tonality, etc., these latter elements being investigated by the student of *phonemics* who examines all aspects of the phoneme (q.v.).

B. Phonetics has been chiefly studied by anthropological linguists and by linguists in the humanities. Further, because phonetics relates to the acoustical properties of language, special attention has been given by the phonetician of whatever background to the speech organs of the human being. Phonetics thus has a physiological side.

C. Phonetics has been used comparatively and historically by linguists, philologists, and others concerned with the development of languages and linguistic change through time, e.g. in the work of J. Grimm, whose laws relating to the nature of phonetic change in the Indo-European speech family have become a methodological model for the determination of linguistic relationships (cf. O. Jespersen, *Language: Its Nature, Development, and Origin*, New York: Henry Holt, 1922, pp. 19–99). This method was applied by J. W. Powell to the analysis of relationships among American Indian languages ('On the evolution of language, as exhibited in the Specialization of the grammatic processes, the differentiation of the parts of speech, and the Integration of the Sentence, from a Study of Indian languages', *Bureau of American Ethnology Annual Report* 1, Washington: U.S. Bureau of American Ethnology, Smithsonian Institution, 1880). In general, however, other techniques than those founded in comparative and historical phonetics have been developed for analyses of language relationships. Methods based solely on phonetic analysis reflect the linguistic preoccupations of the past century.

D. While concepts of phonetics—the sounds of language and their production—have been employed in pedagogy and research both with regard to the field of speech and in respect to the teaching of certain modern languages, notably French and Portuguese, most linguists recognize that phonetic analysis alone is not an adequate point of entry to a given language. Structural linguistics requires more attention to the patterning of sound and a treatment of the positional variations of individual sounds. This approach reflecting the concept of the *phoneme* (q.v.) has proved more fundamental in approaching the phonologic system of a given language (Z. S. Harris, *Methods in Structural Linguistics*, Chicago: University of Chicago

Press, 1951; H. A. Gleason, Jr., *An Introduction to Descriptive Linguistics*, New York: Henry Holt, 1955). The concept *phonetics* has thus come to be employed solely in relation to acoustical phenomena without necessary reference to more formalized aspects of linguistic structure (cf. E. A. Nida, *Morphology: The Descriptive Analysis of Words*, Ann Arbor: University of Michigan Press, 1949).

E. Phonetic systems are required in the transcribing of various languages and special orthographic symbols have been developed in line with the needs for transcription. 'Such a set of symbols is a *phonetic alphabet* ...' (L. Bloomfield, *Language*, New York: Henry Holt, 1933, p. 85). *Phonetic* symbols, however, are not given proper value if seen outside the context of a *phonemic* system.

Robert F. Spencer

See also: LINGUISTICS
PHONEME

Phonology (See Linguistics)

Phratry
A. *Phratry* has two meanings in modern scholarship.

1. It is used to refer to the Greek φρατρία. This appears originally to have been a synonym for *genos*, a patrilineal descent group; as the tribal structure became more rigid, phratria came to be applied to a group in the segmented lineage structure which was a major segment of the tribe, more extensive than the *genos*.

2. In anthropological usage, the *phratry* is a cluster of common descent groups—sibs (q.v.)—which are linked together by ceremonial functions and a feeling of common unilinear descent which may be the source of the ceremonial affiliation or derivative from it.

B. *Phratry* is employed by scholars of various disciplines in referring to the Greek *phratria*. In addition, it has sometimes been applied by Western European anthropologists to some segment or other of the extensive segmented lineage structure of Central Asian tribes. In the United States, L. H. Morgan in 1877 introduced the term with the definition of '... an assemblage of related gentes united in a higher association for certain common objects' (*Ancient Society*, New York: Henry Holt, 1877, p. 66). It has since been employed by Anglo-American anthropologists to designate clusters of unilinear descent groups which were associated either by belief in a distant common ancestor or

Physical Anthropology

by reciprocal ceremonial functions. Usually the term *phratry* has been applied to any such cluster, whether there were two or more clusters in the society. There has been a recent tendency, however, to reserve *phratry* for those societies having three or more clusters, with *moiety* (q.v.) replacing *phratry* where a dual division exists (E. A. Hoebel, *Man in the Primitive World*, New York: McGraw-Hill, 1949, pp. 264–5). American anthropologists apply *phratry* both to groups of which the member sibs are envisaged as segmented offshoots of a parent sib, as among the Tlingit, Haida, and Aztecs; and to those, such as the Hopi and Zuñi, where unrelated sibs have, by banding together, acquired attributes usually associated with common descent groups, such as ceremonial functions and exogamy. *Phratry* is applied to linked sibs whether the descent be patrilineal or matrilineal.

Elizabeth E. Bacon

See also: Lineage
Moiety
Segment
Sib

Physical Anthropology

A. The wide variety of objectives sought by workers in this field makes it difficult to arrive at one definition that would satisfy everybody. Without exception, however, physical anthropologists deal with those manifestations of the human body that develop from genetic materials that each offspring inherits from its parents at the moment of conception. Their aim is to interpret human biological variation and its relation to primate evolution. These materials may be subject to a degree of change in the form of mutations, or else they may fail to be transmitted because of environmental, strictly biological, or social pressures, but in all cases the physical anthropologist deals only with the products that originate from heritable substances that are passed on from one generation to another through sexual reproduction. This is what binds together the work of all physical anthropologists, whether they specialize in problems of biological evolution; comparative anatomy as between races, or as between members of *Homo sapiens* and various infrahuman animals; blood groups; genetics; interbreeding populations; disease and its resistance; growth patterns; sex and age differences; or the complex relations of body structures to behaviour. Physical anthropology must and often does maintain close relations with the

502

other branches of anthropology. Archaeology (q.v.) is closely tied in with physical anthropology's interest in fossil men, particularly at the point where findings show the early emergence of human culture together with the physical structures of early man. Linguistics (q.v.) is concerned with the biological correlates of human speech not only in the limited sense of concern with the speech organs, but also with the relation of biological traits to the nature of the human social grouping in which speech and language (q.v.) emerge and are used. *Cultural* and *social* anthropology are greatly concerned with the biological foundations of group life and culture, and with the continuing role that these play in human society and culture. In all these sub-fields the recent break-throughs in the areas of human genetics and analysis of functional biological complexes, have raised among *some* the hope that the gap in logic and knowledge between the biological animal man (q.v.) and the sociocultural human being may be bridged and even, perhaps, that theories of human culture stressing its biological base may be restored to respectability.

B. *Physical anthropology* grew out of the 19th-century recognition that *man* is an animal and has developed his bodily structure and functions through the processes of biological evolution (L. Eiseley, *Darwin's Century*, New York: Doubleday, 1958). In its beginnings and for many years it was a science of physical measurement and classification, for while it saw man as the product of evolution the general ignorance of genetics prevented the thorough analysis of the processes of evolution with respect to the human body and of the problems of interbreeding populations, racial characteristics, and the relations of body structures to behaviour (cf. S. L. Washburn, 'The New Physical Anthropology', *Transactions of the New York Academy of Sciences*, vol. 13, 1951, pp. 298–304). With the development of modern genetics, physical anthropology has come to emphasize increasingly heredity, genetic process, and structural anatomy. In this renewal physical anthropology has been able not only to take material from genetics but to offer insight and data to genetics, particularly with respect to migration, selection, and genetic drift.

C. Among social scientists, only the anthropologists make a special effort to study and understand the subject matter of physical anthropology, which deals with all manifestations of the human body. Hence the usages and definitions employed by other social sciences are apt to strike anthropologists as incomplete or limited. Many handbooks and textbooks in sociology—and sometimes in anthropology—either omit physical anthropology, or else define it in the very restricted manner of S. Graham, who has written: 'Physical Anthropology is closely related to biology in that it is concerned with, for example, the physical characteristics of man. It studies the body of man, the differences in shape of skull and skeletal structure of man of different races, and at different periods of man's evolution' (*American Culture*, New York: Harper & Bros., 1957, p. 19). Such a definition plays down the large-scale efforts of modern physical anthropologists to study the soft parts of human bodies, as well as their bony components, and omits the present emphasis on body fluids, especially blood, as well as on human genes. Again, P. L. Harriman defines physical anthropology as dealing with '... similarities and differences in morphology among men and animals, as well as among human races' ('Physical Anthropology', in P. L. Harriman (ed.), *The New Dictionary of Psychology*, Toronto: McLeod, 1947, p. 28). This definition provides little or no clue to contemporary interests in the breeding habits of human populations, genetic analysis, patterns of growth, differences between the sexes, and the intricate relationships that are thought to exist between various body types and such behavioural factors as temperament, personality, and a host of related topics.

Mischa Titiev

See also: MAN
           ORGANISM
           RACE

Pilot Study

A. The term is used, with special reference to field investigations, to denote an exploratory stage of investigation.

In quantitative survey work, the pilot stage (or stages) forms the final trial before a large-scale enquiry is begun. Such a stage comes between the stage of general planning and the more extensive application of the techniques of enquiry.

In this sense it has four principal objects: (a) to collect information on the availability, variability, and adequacy of the material; (b) to test different forms of the instruments to be used in the enquiry (e.g. the questionnaire) and to test the administration of the proposed study; (c) to obtain an estimate of time taken so that costs can be calculated; (d) to determine, in the light of these objects, the feasibility of the proposed study.

B. The term *pilot study* is reserved for a *general* 'final' stage in survey-planning, one that is carried out after the basic plan of enquiry has been determined. The term *pre-test* is used to designate probes into *parts* of the plan which are (a) smaller in scope and (b) applied at a still earlier stage. But, as C. A. Moser points out, it is difficult 'to state definitely which functions belong to the pretest and which to the pilot survey, since much will depend on the circumstances of the enquiry, (*Survey Methods in Social Investigation*, London: Heinemann, 1958, p. 45 fn.).

J. Mogey

See also: SOCIAL SURVEY

Plan (See **Planning**)

Planning

A. *Planning* is generally regarded as a method for delineating goals and ways of achieving them. There is no agreement, however, as to the precise nature of the method. One attempt at partial synthesis (developed by this writer in M. Meyerson & E. C. Banfield, *Politics, Planning and the Public Interest*, Glencoe, Ill.: The Free Press, 1955, pp. 312–22) defines a plan as 'a course of action which can be carried into effect, which can be expected to lead to the attainment of ends sought, and which someone intends to carry into effect' (ibid., p. 312). 'Efficient' planning is then described in terms of a widely-used model of rational decision-making (ibid., p. 314). The advantage of this approach is that it employs concepts which are analytically relevant in social science.

B. The term is used in a bewildering variety of ways, being equated with socialism, budgeting, measures to control the business cycle, regional resource development schemes like TVA, scientific management or 'Taylorism', the physical design and layout of cities or of structures, city management, and so on. C. Landauer (*The Theory of National Economic Planning*, Berkeley: University of California Press, 1947, pp. 12–13) defines it as 'coordination through a conscious effort' by a communal organ. Probably all definitions agree on this much. There is decided disagreement, however, as to the nature of the effort. Even in economics the term has no technical meaning, but there is a tendency to equate planning with any interference with the price system. Thus Sir Henry Clay says that planning is 'the opposite of reliance on a market economy' ('Planning and the Market Economy', *American Economics Review*, vol. XL, 1950, p. 3). More positively, according to P. S. Florence, 'National planning is an intention to promote the public interests by the more or less visible hand of the State. In its fully-fledged form it is an acknowledgement of intention embodied in prearranged tasks, based on knowledge of existing conditions and controlled or carried on by an organized structure' (*The Logic of British and American Industry*, London: Routledge & Kegan Paul, 1953, pp. 267–8).

R. G. Tugwell, writing in the tradition of the scientific management movement, describes planning as a process by which a team of technicians assembles and reduces to reciprocal relatedness the materials furnished by the ordinary techniques of political science, economics, sociology, anthropology, engineering, and architecture, and by which it projects (in maps, budgets, and related documents) a view of the requirements of the social organism which serves as a basis for present co-ordination and direction of it ('The Study of Planning as a Scientific Endeavor', *Fiftieth Annual Report of the Michigan Academy of Science, Arts, and Letters*, Ann Arbor: University of Michigan Press, 1948, p. 41).

For K. Mannheim, planning is a 'mode of thought' which 'not only changes individual links in the causal chain and adds new ones but also tries to grasp the whole complex of events from the *key position* which exists in every situation' (*Man and Society in an Age of Reconstruction*, London: Kegan Paul, Trench, Trubner, 1940, p. 153). L. Mumford says 'planning involves the job of coordinating specialisms, focusing them in common fields of knowledge, and canalizing them in appropriate channels of common action. ... In every department of art and practical activity' he says, 'we must learn to deal not with specialized interests and atomic elements but with elements in association and generalized interests; we must deal with organism, function and environment, with place, work, and people, with political, economic, cultural, and esthetic life. ... A good plan is, in essence, an attempt to put such an integration in a graphic or dramatic form' ('Foreword', in F. Mackenzie (ed.), *Planned Society*, New York: Prentice-Hall, 1937, pp. vii-viii).

A specialist in public administration, J. Millett, says 'the job of planning, reduced perhaps to its most elementary aspect, is the constant task of "defining and sharpening the objectives" ' (*The Process and Organization of Government Planning*, New York: Columbia University Press, 1947, p. 33). He distinguishes 'operational' planning, which involves carrying out policies decided upon by others at a higher level of administration, from 'central' planning, which may be involved in the making of those policies. G. Galloway, a political scientist, defines planning as 'a process of coordination, a technique of adapting means to ends, a method of bridging the gap between fact-finding and policy-making' (*Planning for America*, New York: Henry Holt, 1941, p. 5).

E. C. Banfield

See also: MEANS-END SCHEMA
RATIONALITY

Pleasure Principle

A. *Pleasure principle* denotes a tendency, characteristic of all infants, and, to differing degrees, of children and adults, to discharge tensions as they arise and thus to attain pleasure irrespective of the consequences of such pleasure-directed behaviour.

B. Freudian psychology deals explicitly with the rise and the dissipation of (instinctual) energy. The concepts of the pleasure principle and the reality principle (q.v.) concern the manner in which such energy (or tension) is released or dissipated.

To Freud pleasure 'is in some way connected with lessening, lowering, or extinguishing the amount of stimulation present in the mental apparatus'. Conversely, pain involves heightening the degree of stimulation (S. Freud, *A General Introduction to Psychoanalysis*, New York: Permabooks, 1953, p. 365). Then the 'ruling tendency of psychic life, perhaps of nerve life altogether, is the struggle for reduction, keeping at a constant level, or removal of the inner stimulus tension' (S. Freud, *Beyond the Pleasure Principle*, London; The International Psycho-Analytical Press, 1922, p. 71).

In infancy and through the first few years of life a human being is disposed to discharge tensions as they arise. In early life such tensions are largely associated with the primary drives (hunger, thirst, excretion, etc.), and the id is said to be in control of the psychic apparatus. Behaviour which provides an immediate discharge of tension, i.e. without regard for or perhaps even awareness of the consequences, is said to be in accordance with the pleasure principle. The normal expectation is that with time the young child begins to take account of the consequences of his behaviour and to begin to inhibit the expression of some impulses and to delay the expression of others until the setting is appropriate (e.g. waiting until dinner-time to gratify the hunger drive). In Freud's phrasing, 'restraint of motor discharge ...[is] provided ... by means of thought' ('Formulations Regarding the Two Principles in Mental Functioning', *Collected Papers*, London: Hogarth Press, 1925, vol. IV, p. 16). What constitutes an appropriate setting for the expression of a specific impulse varies of course from one cultural setting to another: in some societies it is bad form to defecate in public; in others to eat in public. To the degree that the individual delays tension reduction until the setting is appropriate his behaviour is said to be in accordance with the reality principle.

C. It is evident that the pleasure principle involves the assumption that man's original nature is hedonic. Moreover, the recurring cycles of building up and discharging tension may be conceived as akin to the concept of homeostasis (W. B. Cannon, *The Wisdom of the Body*, London: Kegan Paul, Trench, Trubner, 1932) as that concept has been figuratively introduced into psychological discussion. And finally, J. Dollard and N. E. Miller (*Personality and Psychotherapy*, New York: McGraw-Hill, 1950, p. 9), have proposed the principle of reinforcement as the behaviouristic equivalent of Freud's pleasure principle, but it may be objected that whereas Dollard and Miller define reinforcement in terms of the strengthening of a stimulus-response connection (ibid., p. 39), Freud had no such instrumental conception of the pleasure principle.

Robert F. Winch

See also: HEDONISM
REALITY PRINCIPLE

Plebiscite

A. Broadly defined a *plebiscite* is a popular referendum (q.v.) on any question. Its modern usage has followed this broad definition—but the term has also been used, more particularly, to denote a referendum concerning changes in sovereignty (q.v.) (S. Wambaugh, *Plebiscites Since The World War: With A Collection of Official Documents*, Washington: Carnegie Endowment For International Peace, 1933).

B. 1. The use of plebiscites as a mode of determining the 'will of the people' was legitimized by the ideology of 'popular sovereignty' which was so influential in the French Revolutionary period. Writing of this period J. L. Talmon points out that '... plebiscitary, direct democracy is the preliminary of dictatorship. ... It is an invitation to a totalitarian party in opposition to whip up agitation, to "organize" the discontent or the will of the people by engineering mass petitions, manifestations, and pressure from below' (*The Rise of Totalitarian Democracy*, Boston: Beacon Press, 1952, p. 207). In the Napoleonic era plebiscites were employed on three occasions—public support being sought in 1800 for the ratification of a new constitution, in 1802 for the conferment upon Napoleon of the title of Life Consul and in 1804 for confirming Napoleon in his title of Emperor of the French. The idea of recourse to plebiscite was revived in the revolutionary ferment of 1848 but its most recent marked use in internal politics was by Hitler in the early years of his rule in Germany.

2. Use of the plebiscite as a referendum concerning changes in sovereignty was an essential part of the position taken up by President Wilson at the Peace Conference of 1919. He asserted that 'no right anywhere exists to hand peoples about from sovereignty to sovereignty as if they were property' and he included in his Fourteen Points the principle 'that in determining all such questions of sovereignty, the interests of the populations concerned must have equal weight with the equitable claims of the government whose title is to be determined' (in H. Rudin, *Armistice 1918*, New Haven: Yale University Press, 1944, p. 414). The treaties of 1919 provided for nine popular referenda in Europe which involved changes in sovereignty. The Saar plebiscite of 1935, considered by many to be the most successful, was the only one conducted by the League of Nations; the others were administered by international commissions. Two international plebiscites have been held since World War II: the Saar plebiscite of 1955 was administered within the framework of the Western European Union, and the 1956 plebiscite in Togoland was conducted by the British under provisions of a United Nations General Assembly resolution (*Plebiscites Held Since 1920 under the Control or Supervision of International Organizations*, United Nations General Assembly, 11th Session, 4th Committee, A/C.4/351, 20 Feb. 1957).

Plural Society

C. Support of the plebiscite thus came from the liberal nationalism of French and Italian writers, and from Wilsonian principles: given the proper division of people into political units based upon considerations of nationality, it was argued, democracy would grow internally, and would be expressed internationally with the development of tolerance and co-operation. Criticism of plebiscites has come from writers stressing the role of power in international relations. They claim that plebiscites disregard the balance of power, permitting the exigencies of a popular vote to upset a stable distribution of world power (F. H. Simonds and B. Emeny, *The Great Powers in World Politics*, New York: American Book Co., 1939). Others have noted that a plebiscite 'embitters national feeling, creates temptations to bribery, coercion, and terrorism on both sides, and offers no assurance that the voters will record their permanent national preferences rather than their fears, prejudices, and economic interests of the moment' (F. L. Schuman, *International Politics*, New York: McGraw-Hill, 6th edn., 1958, p. 292). Q. Wright has written that cultural nationality, even more than legal nationality is subject to continuous change, and is a consequence of agitation and poor administration. 'The results of plebiscites are influenced by the selection of the voting area, by the policing of the area, and by efficiency in propaganda' (*A Study of War*, Chicago: University of Chicago Press, 1942, vol. II, p. 997). Contemporary internationalists have recognized that national self-determination will not in itself induce natural harmony of free peoples, co-operating voluntarily through an international organization; alerted to the difficulties involved in the effective administration of plebiscites and to the limited areas in which beneficial results may be expected, they have turned their attention to strengthening international organizations for the purpose of guaranteeing human rights, preventing aggression, and fostering international economic, social, and political co-operation.

D. Plebiscites have been classified legally by the degree to which they have been subjected to international control. Informal and unilateral plebiscites have been held without agreement between the two parties in interest; formal plebiscites have been conducted under provisions established in bilateral or multilateral treaties. As a device for applying the principle of self-determination to certain areas where there is no obvious line of cleavage in national sentiment, formal plebiscites are more likely to guarantee adequate measures of neutral control or supervision. Successful plebiscites must be based on some form of agreement to which both of the contending countries are parties. The conditions of plebiscite, particularly those regarding the removal of partisan troops and officials, should be clearly set forth to avoid later disagreement. Immediately upon signature of the agreement, the area should be put under neutral control or supervision, and the make-up of the plebiscite commission should balance partisans with third parties. The commission should have at its disposal a sufficient number of neutral troops to police both urban and rural regions. Powers of the commission over the political administration of the area must be absolute. In this sense, plebiscites would prove a useful tool for securing a stable settlement of certain boundary questions and would provide an important indication of the strength of independent sentiment in colonial areas.

Martin B. Travis, Jr.

See also: BALLOT
REFERENDUM
SOVEREIGNTY
VOTING

Plural Society

A. There is a sense in which every society is *plural* in that it contains divergent elements with differing interests and it may even be said that every society is *plural* in character since it contains a plurality of individuals. But the current meaning of *plural society* was developed by J. S. Furnivall to help in his investigation of the country which is now Indonesia. To him, a plural society was 'a society comprising two or more elements or social orders which live side by side, yet without mingling, in one political unit' (*Netherlands India*, Cambridge: The University Press, 1939, p. 446).

B. 1. 'The most obvious feature is already indicated in the name; in a plural society there is no common will except, possibly, in matters of supreme importance, such as resistance to aggression from outside. In its political aspect a plural society resembles a confederation of allied provinces, united by treaty or within the limits of a formal constitution, merely for certain ends common to the constituent units and, in matters outside the terms of union, each living its own life. But it differs from a confederation in that the constituent elements are not segregated each within its own territorial limits. In a confederation secession is at least possible without the total disruption of all social bonds, whereas in a plural society the elements are so intermingled that secession is identical with anarchy. Thus a plural society has the instability of a confederation, but without the remedy which is open to a confederation if the yoke of common union should become intolerable' (ibid., p. 447).

2. A plural society is one in which communalism (q.v.) is likely to appear. The most obvious examples in recent years have been Palestine under the British Mandate, undivided India, Cyprus, Kenya, Algeria, and the Federation of Rhodesia and Nyasaland. In all these cases the failure to develop a common will has frustrated the smooth working of political institutions. It was Furnivall's view that 'in a plural society the community tends to be organized for production rather than for social life; social demand is sectionalized, and within each section ... the members are debarred from leading the full life of a citizen in a homogeneous community; finally, the reaction against these abnormal conditions, taking in each section the form of Nationalism, sets one community against the other so as to emphasize the plural character of the society and aggravate its instability, thereby enhancing the need for it to be held together by some force exerted from outside' (ibid., p. 459). Although there is presumably no inevitability about this development, events since 1939, when his book was published, suggest that Furnivall was broadly correct in his assessment of the political fate of plural societies.

J. D. B. Miller

See also: COMMUNALISM
PLURALISM

Pluralism

A. The term has the following meanings:

1. It denotes the views which hold that political, cultural, and social systems may (or should) (a) be conceived as being constituted from a multiplicity of autonomous but interdependent groups or (b) be interpreted in terms of a multiplicity of factors.

2. It also denotes the views which claim that the multiplicity and autonomy of social groups are morally valuable or that by reason of these qualities such groups together constitute a significant form of moral order.

3. Sometimes by extension it denotes the situation, actual or desired, which the holders of such views specify, admire, or value.

B. In philosophy pluralism is a system of thought which, as opposed to monism (q.v.), recognizes more than one ultimate principle of Being (see, for example, W. James, *A Pluralistic Universe*, London: Longmans, 1909). Political pluralism is the name applied to those political doctrines, ranging from extreme to modest claims on behalf of group interests in society, which assert that certain groups (e.g. family, church, union, local government) embody important social values prior to and independent of their authorization or approval by the state. The scope of pluralism is not usually interpreted as including anarchism or revolutionary syndicalism because, unlike such theories, most pluralists retain for government the functional responsibilities of compulsory citizenship and taxation, and admit the necessity for an inclusive governmental authority transcending group associations to regulate, direct, or co-ordinate, inter alia, the domestic economy, personal liberties, national security, and foreign affairs (see F. W. Coker, *Recent Political Thought*, New York: Appleton-Century, 1934).

1. The principal impact of pluralistic theories has been to dramatize the limited utility of the formal concept of legal sovereignty as a working, analytical model of the political process. On the positive side, the results of political pluralism have been less impressive. The pluralist emphasis upon the roots of politics in personality and social structure, and the values of a vigorous, many-sided, voluntary associational life in the commonwealth, is quite compatible with Hegelian and idealistic monism (see B. Bosanquet, *The Philosophic Theory of the State*, London: Macmillan, 1899; M. P. Follett, *The New State*, New York: Longmans, 1918). Most pluralistic doctrines fail: (a) to recognize explicitly and elucidate adequately the requirements of unity and co-ordination, as well as diversity, in their models of political organization and behaviour; (b) to distinguish the analysis of the personal and group bases of politics from hopes and preferences for a different social order or different mechanism of political representation (see W. Y. Elliott, *The Pragmatic Revolt in Politics*, New York: The Macmillan Co., 1928; E. Latham, *The Group Basis of Politics*, Ithaca, N.Y.: Cornell University Press, 1952); (c) to distinguish political processes as analytically separable from other group-based social processes.

The failure of the pluralists to develop a systematic political theory comparable to the classical theory of the state was probably connected with

Police Power

their general rejection of or antipathy to politics as such. Notwithstanding this tendency to substitute social organization for political structure and process, political pluralism helped to destroy the hegemony of legal formalism and ideological absolutism in political theory, and prepared the way for the realistic study of politics upon an interdisciplinary and comparative basis.

2. Political pluralism focuses upon the relationships of geography and social organization to governmental structure and processes of policy formation. The scope of pluralistic studies thus includes the various forms of institutional federalism, the functioning of party systems, formal devices for group representation and decentralization in electoral apportionment, legislative organization, the administrative machinery of government, and informal processes of group pressure and influences upon public opinion formation, elections, legislatures, chief executives, administrative agencies, and courts (see F. W. Coker, 'The Technique of the Pluralistic State', *American Political Science Review*, vol. 15, 1921, p. 186; A. de Grazia, *Public and Republic*, New York: Knopf, 1951; D. B. Truman, *The Governmental Process*, New York: Knopf, 1951). Pluralistic doctrines, which had their principal vogue between 1895 and 1920, stimulated an extensive empirical and descriptive literature during the following thirty years about the structure and functioning of all types of political groups. During the 1950s this began to crystallize around a more systematic approach to the interactions between party politics, group politics, and bureaucratic politics in the comparative analysis of political systems (see S. J. Eldersveld, 'American Interest Groups: A Survey of Research and Some Implications for Theory and Method', in H. W. Ehrmann (ed.), *Interest Groups in Four Continents*, Pittsburgh: University of Pittsburgh Press, 1958, pp. 173–196; G. A. Almond, 'A Comparative Study of Interest Groups and the Political Process', *American Political Science Review*, vol. LII, 1958, pp. 270–82; S. H. Beer, 'The Representation of Interests in British Government: The Historical Background', *American Political Science Review*, vol. LI, 1957, pp. 613–50).

3. The linkages between liberalism and pluralism have been a significant feature of recent usage of the term. Thus E. A. Shils discussing what he calls 'the pluralist society' observes that 'Liberalism is a system of pluralism. It is a system of many centers of power, many areas of privacy and a strong internal impulse towards the mutual adaptation of the spheres, rather than of the dominance or the submission of any one to the others' (*The Torment of Secrecy*, London: Heinemann, 1956, p. 154). More recently still H. S. Kariel has proposed a reconsideration of pluralism to meet the changed environment of 'big organization' and has criticized the explicit and tacit liberalism of social scientists insofar as they hold 'the tenet of a normative pluralism, the identification of the common good with the struggle of groups for power ...' (*The Decline of American Pluralism*, Stanford, Cal.: Stanford University Press, 1961, p. 137). A useful attempt to wed liberal-pluralist ideas to the consideration of research methods will be found in the article by N. W. Polsby, 'How to Study Community Power: The Pluralist Alternative' (*Journal of Politics*, vol. 22, 1960, p. 474 et seq.). He criticizes the 'various disabilities of the stratification approach to the study of community power' (ibid., p. 475), and sets out the criteria for a pluralist approach, stressing inter alia the diversity and fluidity of leadership roles. He argues (ibid., fn.) that 'all varieties of pluralist theory contrast effectively with stratification theory'.

C. It is, of course, possible to discuss other types of pluralism than the political forms. The term, for example, is used to denote diversities found in the study of religious and ethnic groups. An important notion in the United States has been that of *cultural pluralism* 'a state of affairs in which each ethnic group maintains in large measure, a separate way of life, with its own customs, its own supplementary schools, its special organizations and periodicals, and perhaps even its favored secondary languages' (N. Glazer, *American Judaism*, Chicago: University of Chicago Press, 1957, p. 8). This term was introduced by H. M. Kallen (see his *Cultural Pluralism and the American Idea*, Philadelphia: University of Pennsylvania Press, 1956), although the concept had existed for a long time prior to the term.

Avery Leiserson

See also: LIBERALISM
MONISM

Police Power

A. *Police power* may be defined as the broad and elastic power of government, especially of one of the states of the United States, to restrict, control, regulate, and restrain individuals and groups in the use of their liberty and property in order to protect and promote the health, safety, morals, convenience, peace, order, and general welfare of other individuals and the public generally.

B. While W. Blackstone (*Commentaries on the Laws of England*, London: Murray, 1862 edn., bk. IV, ch. XIII), referred to offences against the 'public police and economy' and discussed many actions that subsequently were classified as exercises of the police power, the addition of the word 'power' to 'police' and the description of a category of governmental power called *police power* has been the work of American jurists, primarily since the last quarter of the 19th century. Usage of the phrase in the social sciences conforms to the definitions of jurists. The phrase is used primarily in one of three senses and a social scientist normally employs qualifying adjectives to distinguish the sense he wishes to convey.

1. Using the less common plural form, 'police powers', Chief Justice R. Taney expressed the comprehensive meaning of the phrase. 'They are nothing more than the powers inherent in every sovereignty to the extent of its dominions. And whether a State passes a quarantine law, or a law to punish offences, or to establish courts of justice, or requiring certain instruments to be recorded, or to regulate commerce within its limits, in every case it exercises the same powers; that is to say, the powers of sovereignty, the power to govern men and things within the limits of its dominion' (Licence Cases, Howard, vol. 5, 1847, pp. 504, 582). As thus broadly defined, the police power includes virtually all functions of government and almost all legislation. Social scientists rarely use the phrase in this sense except to indicate how comprehensively courts may define it to justify exercise of the power.

2. Most commonly the phrase is employed in the more limited but still quite broad sense of meaning 'the power of promoting the public welfare by restraining and regulating the use of liberty and property' (E. Freund, *The Police Power, Public Policy and Constitutional Rights*, Chicago: Callaghan, 1904, p. iii). It is the power of government to 'see to it that the individual in the use of his freedom of action, of contract, or of property, does not unduly prejudice the interests of others or society at large' (W. W. Willoughby, *Constitutional Law of the United States*, New York: Baker, Voorhis, 1910, vol. II, p. 1230). As political scientists, following the lead of jurists, add content to this usage they list exercises of power to suppress public nuisances, to prevent fraud, and to protect and

promote the public health, safety, morals and convenience.

While violations of a law enacted under the police power as thus defined may technically be a crime, legislation punishing intrinsically vicious acts—infamous crimes—is usually excluded '... the province of the police power is the enforcement of merely conventional restraints, so that in the absence of positive legislative action, there would be no possible offense' (E. Freund, *The Police Power*, pp. 21–2). Police power, in this sense, is also usually described as an 'elastic' or 'dynamic' power which can never be precisely defined but has the capacity of accommodating to changing community demands and needs. Finally, it is most commonly regarded as a reserved power of one of the states of the United States, although it is conceded by most political scientists that some exercises by Congress of its enumerated powers may take on the character of exercises of the police power.

3. A third sense of the phrase is occasionally employed by social scientists, usually with appropriate qualifications that it is the popular, man-in-the-street and narrow, rather than the exact, usage of the phrase. This is to equate the exercise of police power with the activities of the policeman and, even more broadly, to include all exercises of power by the police, courts, and legislatures directed to 'the prevention of what we regard as evil conduct' (C. B. Swisher, *The Theory and Practice of American National Government*, Boston: Houghton, Mifflin, 1951, p.21).

Holbert N. Carroll

See also: SOVEREIGNTY

Policy

A. The most common social and political usage of the term *policy* refers to a course of action or intended course of action conceived as deliberately adopted, after a review of possible alternatives, and pursued, or intended to be pursued. Thus H. D. Lasswell and A. Kaplan (*Power and Society*, New Haven: Yale University Press, 1950, p. 71) write '*policy* is a projected program of goal values and practices: the *policy process* is the formulation, promulgation and application of identifications, demands and expectations'. This sense goes back to the 15th century and may be used both of individuals and organizations. So used the term appears to be peculiar to the English language (see B. Leoni, 'The Meaning of "Political" in Political Decisions', *Political Studies*, vol. V, 1957, p. 226).

B. There is some ambiguity in current usage. The term may indicate the existence of a

Political Behaviour

considered intention, plan or programme (as in 'the Labour Party's housing policy'); but it is often used rather to refer to a course of action in some field where a plan or programme may exist but does not necessarily exist (as in 'Lord Palmerston's foreign policy', which could be used simply to refer to what Lord Palmerston did in the field of foreign affairs). It is also used very compendiously (as in the book title *The Cambridge History of British Foreign Policy*) to refer to a series of policies rather than one policy.

Current interest centres on such questions as the nature of policy decisions. A question so far unanswered is how far the field of policy and policy decisions is separated from other fields of activity. Policy decisions are contrasted, for instance, with judicial decisions by reference to the relatively greater freedom of choice in the former. Judicial decisions are conceived as arrived at, at least in part, by reference to standards internal to a legal system, whereas policy decisions are thought of as being subject to no limitations other than such as arise from considerations of e.g. prudence or morals. On this basis the legislative rather than the judicial process tends to be thought of as being the process that turns policy into law.

This kind of distinction can be questioned. Thus, e.g. J. Stone (*The Province and Function of Law*, Sydney: Maitland Publications, 1950, p. 300) says: 'The Court's power to invoke public policy in new situations is no other than its duty, where a clear view of law has not emerged for the situation at bar, to adjust the conflicting interests by the creation of a rule of law with its attendant rights'. Attempts to separate the fields of policy on the one hand and administration on the other are similarly questioned.

Wilfrid Harrison

See also: ADJUDICATION
ADMINISTRATION

Political Behaviour

A. 1. In the narrowest and perhaps the oldest sense *political behaviour* refers exclusively to the behaviour of voters (H. L. Tingsten, *Political Behaviour: Studies in Election Statistics*, London: P. S. King, 1937). This is the most common usage in sociology and social psychology. For example, the first sentence in the report by P. F. Lazarsfeld and others, on the 1940 Presidential election states, 'This is a report on modern American political behavior' (*The People's Choice*, New York: Columbia University Press, 1944, p. 1). Some within these disciplines by implication also restrict the coverage of the term to voting behaviour as manifested in data on individuals, 'psychological' data rather than on aggregate data such as election returns.

2. The broader scope of the term in the usage of most political scientists is implied in the title of a collection of H. D. Lasswell's papers covering a wide range of topics (*The Analysis of Political Behaviour*, London: Kegan Paul, Trench, Trubner, 1948). Similarly broad in scope is the conception in the report of a Social Science Research Council seminar, which views the study of 'political behavior' as involving an interdisciplinary approach which attempts to understand 'government as a process made up of the actions and interactions of men and groups of men' through empirical research deriving from and contributing to 'the formulation of concepts, hypotheses, and explanations in systematic terms' ('Research in Political Behavior', *American Political Science Review*, vol. XLVI, 1952, pp. 1004–5).

Its scope probably should be understood as encompassing the whole range of political phenomena, within which electoral behaviour is one category. Its distinctive concern is with empirically focused conceptualization and theory, based upon and leading to systematic empirical research in which the units of analysis are men and groups rather than elements of the formal political structure.

B. In the light of these usages, while *political behaviour* has come to be regarded as a subfield, within the social sciences, including political science, there are, at least by inference, divergent views on the range of subject matter referred to by the term, and whether it should be treated as a sub-field.

1. Many political scientists who stress *political behaviour* argue that the term properly points to an 'approach' that 'aims at broadening and recasting the traditional fields' of political science 'so that (a) existing principles and empirical generalizations can be stated in behavioral rather than normative terms, and (b) emphasis in research will be placed upon explicit formulation of assumptions and hypotheses, to the end that empirical investigations can be made ... systematic, quantitative, and cumulative' (A. Leiserson, 'Problems of Methodology in Political Research', *Political Science Quarterly*, vol. LXVIII, 1953, p. 567).

2. Perhaps largely because of the novelty or unfamiliarity of the concepts and techniques employed in this approach, the characteristic preoccupations of its adherents have been regarded by others, and in some cases by themselves, as a 'field'. This seems to be more a reflection of administrative convenience than a necessary consequence of deliberate and logical organization within the discipline. In recent years the programme of the American Political Science Association has contained one section on *political behaviour*, although the papers assigned to this section have not been consistently different in substance or method from many of those classified under such headings as national government, international relations, comparative government, and other conventional fields. On the other hand, D. Waldo's Unesco trend report on political science in the United States treats *political behaviour* as an area involving an approach constituting one aspect of an interdisciplinary movement (*Political Science in the United States of America*, Documentation in the Social Sciences, Paris: Unesco, 1956, pp. 22 ff).

David B. Truman

See also: EMPIRICAL
POLITICAL THEORY

Political Boss

A. The term *political boss* (sometimes simply *boss*) denotes a person who controls a political machine (q.v.).

B. The terms *political boss* and *political machine*, referring to peculiarly American phenomena, are closely interrelated in usage. Since one of the essential elements of bossism is leadership of an elaborated organization dubbed a 'machine', and since other characteristics of bossism are applied jointly to the boss and his machine, it is difficult to distinguish significantly in the usage of the two terms. Both terms, reflecting the values held by most American commentators, are derogatory judgements indicating a perversion, respectively, of leadership and organization. Although the criteria employed to distinguish bosses from acceptable forms of leadership are more explicit than in the case of demagogues, the problems in usage that arise are quite similar.

The combination of characteristics that is held to differentiate bossism from leadership is indicated by E. M. Sait ('Machine, Political', in E. R. A. Seligman (ed.), *Encyclopedia of the Social Sciences*, New York: The Macmillan Co., 1933, vol. IX, p. 657), in defining a 'political machine' as 'a group composed mainly of professional politicians who gain and hold power by secret and often corrupt methods—although with a show of popular sanction—who dictate party nominations and appointments to public office and who set personal advantage over that of the party or the community'. To Sait's conclusion (ibid.) that 'the test is one of motive and method' may be added a third standard implicit in the foregoing quotation, namely 'irresponsible power'.

1. The standard of *motivation* or *purpose* is frequently used. D. D. McKean (*Party and Pressure Politics*, Boston: Houghton Mifflin, 1949, p. 269) applies the term *boss* to 'political leaders who are chiefly interested in politics and political power as a business and whose interest, if any, in issues of public policy is incidental'. D. W. Brogan (*An Introduction to American Politics*, London: Hamilton, 1954, p. 123) makes the same point: 'the true character of the machine is its political indifferentism'.

2. Not only is the boss held to pursue selfish goals of a non-policy sort, but it is asserted that he attempts to achieve his purposes by adopting certain characteristic political methods and techniques. As put by C. E. Merriam and H. F. Gosnell (*The American Party System*, New York: The Macmillan Co., 4th edn., 1949, p. 204), 'the boss is a political leader, local or state in range, who uses chiefly the weapons of patronage and spoils'. The standard of 'method' also is implied, at least in part, in the judgement that the tactical core of bossism lies in the control of party machinery and of the nominating process.

3. *Irresponsible power* constitutes a third dimension of bossism that in one sense is independent of the preceding criteria and in another sense is a broad restatement of them. E. E. Schattschneider (*Party Government*, New York: Farrar & Rinehart, 1942, p. 172) states, 'the American local boss is remarkable for his success in exercising power for which he is accountable to no one'. What is meant is no surface distinction between leaders who hold elective office and those who do not, but an irresponsibility of ruler to ruled based upon the fact, as D. D. McKean (The American Assembly Reports, *The Forty-Eight States*, Harriman, N.Y.: Graduate School of Business, Columbia University, Participants' Edition, 1955, p. 79) puts it, 'a real boss governs through his control of the machinery of his party, and that he governs beyond the office, if any, that he holds'.

C. Most writers on bossism, including those cited above, concede the limited utility of such

Political Leadership

a typology of bosses and leaders when applied empirically. Many politicians not commonly designated as bosses have been motivated by self-interest to a high degree, many have engaged in methods deemed to be appropriate to bossism, and many have been influential beyond the powers possessed by virtue of office. Conversely, the evidence pertaining to those frequently adjudged to be bosses defies their neat classification in terms of the three factors discussed. Similarly, at least in so far as the available skimpy systematic evidence is concerned, there can be no simple delineation of a distinctive personality type or life history associated with bosses in contrast to leaders.

Usage of *bossism* thus suggests that a high degree of subjective judgement underlies an inadequate boss/leader typology. The observation of a reputed 'boss', E. J. Flynn (*You're the Boss*, New York: Viking Press, 1947, pp. 231–2) pointedly refers to subjectiveness of judgement and perhaps implicitly suggests that the attempt to construct such a typology is not likely to be fruitful: 'It is only the "leader" you don't like who is a "boss", and the "organization" you don't like that is a "machine" '. Thus, while the term *boss* may be of limited use in suggesting one type of leadership clustered at one end of a continuum of leadership, a reliance upon imprecise and subjective notions of bossism, however, may commit the analyst to the erroneous position that the fact of organization or that of minority control of an organization is equivalent to bossism and is incompatible with 'good' leadership.

Allan P. Sindler

See also: MACHINE
PARTY
PATRONAGE

Political Leadership

A. *Political leadership* denotes that activity which is constituted by the origination, guidance, and control of voluntary and joint effort toward the attainment of common goals in the arena of politics (q.v.).

B. 1. Political leadership in a society is provided by one or more persons who lead others, the followers, who are led. Leadership depends on the acceptance by the followers of the role of the leaders and may be distinguished from authority (q.v.) whereby followers become subordinates, and from demagogy acting on a mob in which individuals cease to be separate

agents. 'Strictly speaking the relation of political leadership arises only where a group follows an individual from free choice ... and ... on positive and more or less rational grounds (R. Schmidt, 'Leadership', in E. R. A. Seligman (ed.), *Encyclopedia of the Social Sciences*, New York: The Macmillan Co., 1933, vol. IX, p. 282).

2. Political leadership may be attained in various ways, e.g. by election, inheritance, appointment, co-option by existing leaders, and force. Often there is a combination of factors: a man may start as a scion of an important family (heredity); set himself up as a party boss (force); be elected to the legislature (election); and subsequently be appointed a member of the Government (co-option). Liberal-democratic and, especially, radical theory has stressed the importance of leadership dependent on election. Thus many hereditary monarchies which have claimed more than titular leadership have been abolished, while dictators reinforce their position by plebiscites (q.v.). There is even an occasional demand for the election of Ministers instead of their appointment by the Head of State (q.v.), e.g. in Australia and in the British Labour Party in the 1930s.

3. Nowadays it is agreed that all types of leadership usually depend on some measure of acceptance by the led; on respect as well as power (see H. D. Lasswell & A. Kaplan, *Power and Society*, New Haven: Yale University Press, 1950, pp. 153–61).

D. V. Verney

See also: AUTHORITY
ELECTION
LEADERSHIP
LEGITIMACY
POLITICAL BOSS
POLITICS
POWER

Political Power (See **Power**)

Political Process (See **Process**)

Political Realism

A. *Political realism* refers to a system of ideas or a criterion of motivation which emphasizes the value of that which is objective and necessary in contrast to that which is merely apparent, nominal, or illusory. It not only postulates power relationships between men, groups, or nations as a distinctive, independent variable (necessary for its own sake) in politics, but also recognizes that power is sought instrumentally for the sake of other goal-values: hence both the quest and the exercise of power are modified by alternative values actively maintained by the power-seeker, and by those persons upon whom his power depends (C. E. Merriam, *Political Power*, New York: McGraw-Hill, 1934; H. D. Lasswell & A. Kaplan, *Power and Society*, New Haven: Yale University Press, 1950).

B. 1. As a system of ideas political realism is closely connected with philosophic realism, which postulates the necessity of discriminating between certain fundamental antinomies: (a) *normative statements* of personal preference and ultimate conviction v. *descriptive statements* of objective, publicly-verifiable fact (see M. R. Cohen, *Reason and Nature*, New York: Harcourt, Brace, 1931; M. R. Cohen, *Introduction to Logic and Scientific Method*, New York: Harcourt, Brace, 1934; G. H. Sabine, *History of Political Theory*, New York: Henry Holt, 1937; George Santayana, *Realms of Being*, New York: C. Scribner's Sons, 1940); (b) propositions of *formally-necessary*, *logical implication* v. hypothetical estimates of *probable variation under specified contingencies* (J. Dewey, *The Quest for Certainty*, New York: Minton, Balch, 1929; C. K. Ogden & I. A. Richards, *The Meaning of Meaning*, New York: Harcourt, Brace, 1926; A. J. Ayer, *Language, Truth and Logic*, London: Gollancz, 1936); (c) decisions on the basis of *priorities determined in advance* among selected values (authoritative planning) v. *calculated adjustments* among effective, opposing pressures in concrete situations so as to maximize net social advantage (utilitarian expediency) (C. E. Merriam, *The Role of Politics in Social Change*, New York: New York University Press, 1936; W. A. Leys, *Ethics for Policy Decision*, New York: Prentice-Hall, 1952).

The realistic postulate underlying these antinomies of thought does not imply that the categories are rigid and absolute, but rather that they are polar concepts which provide a basis for creative theoretical inquiry and analysis.

2. (a) As a criterion of motivation political realism refers to the capacity of a political agent to calculate the consequences and make his decisions in terms of enhancing the power position of the political interest (q.v.) with which the individual agent identifies himself. The theoretical problem here arises partly from the defects of the traditional model, which confronts the individual, singly or en masse, with the Leviathan state, and partly from the ambiguity of the index of interest. Some persons conceive realism to be the maximization of individual self-interest, others as the interest of a political

group or party, still others as the public interest, i.e. the security, prosperity, continuity or equilibrium of the inclusive political system in which individual political actors are implicated.

(b) The label of political realism has also attached to the work of thinkers who regard the state as an abstraction and the formal machinery of government as a façade, or tool for the 'real' interests of individuals, groups, or a ruling elite. Such theorizing fails to produce a satisfactory analysis of the problem of power. The superficiality of pure materialist-empirical theorists is revealed by the naïve assumption that power is somehow more legitimate when used to promote the interests of private individuals and non-governmental groups than for public purposes, and by the uncritical inference that public officials either cannot or will not act for the common good or general welfare. Outstanding examples are the nihilo-anarchist conception of government as organized exploitation, and the Marxian idea that the state will 'wither away' when the right kind of social order has been achieved.

C. As indicated in the definition (A. above) political realism consists in visualizing the problem of power naturalistically rather than compulsively. Individuals, organized groups, and the policy-making structure of government each constitute, on different levels, interacting centres of authority and responsibility for the adjustment of conflicts of interest and power. Important conflicts occur within the individual, others between symbolic and organized groupings in society, others between individuals, groups and agencies of government. These complex decision-making processes, though discrete, are connected, and it is unrealistic to assume that individual group and government are mutually exclusive and necessarily in opposition to each other (O. Garceau, 'Research in the Political Process', *American Political Science Review*, vol. 45, 1951, p. 69). Realistic political statesmanship is concerned with the calculation of adjustments between those conflicting interests which require determination in terms of the security, prosperity and survival of the political community, conceived not as a revealed, absolute standard of value but as a vital symbol of human unity and interdependence, whose meaning the community has continually to rediscover in controversial situations where powerful groups and well-meaning individuals sincerely differ (J. Dewey, *The Public and Its Problems*, New York: The Macmillan Co.,

Political Theory

1927). Thus, realistic political science is concerned with the comparative analysis of systems for allocating authority and responsibility between individual, private-group, and public-official processes of decision. Aristotle's *Politics*, Machiavelli's *Discourses*, Montesquieu's *Spirit of the Laws*, Hamilton and Madison's *Federalist Papers* are in the main line of the realistic tradition, utilizing both rational and empirical methods, while maintaining a central focus upon the consequences of alternative modes of allocating and transferring power between individuals, groups, and government in varying types of political regimes and value systems.

Avery Leiserson

See also: AUTHORITY
POWER

Political Theory

A. *Political theory* may be defined as a sub-field of political science in which the term *theory* is loosely interpreted to embrace a wide range of intellectual activities. Substantively, four major areas of investigation fall within the sub-field of political theory, the first two also being called political philosophy: (a) the moral theory of politics; (b) the historical study of political ideas; (c) the linguistic analysis of political ideas; (d) the discovery and systematic development of generalizations about political behaviour.

B. Historically the earliest and predominant usage of the term has been to designate that branch of political science which is theoretical in the sense that it invokes speculation at the highest level of generality about the nature of the good life and the political institutions appropriate for realizing this life. R. M. MacIver exemplifies this usage when he says: 'To what ends should it [the state] be directed? How should it be constituted to advance these ends? ... How should its activity be related to all other activities in the whole swirl of society? These are the questions of political philosophy ...' (*The Web of Government*, New York: The Macmillan Co., 1947, p. 403).

1. In this area of political science, the primary objectives are to set forth the moral criteria that ought to be used to judge the ethical worth of a political system and its institutions and to propose alternative political arrangements and practices likely to meet these ethical standards.

2. Stress upon the task of constructing moral theories of government, does not necessarily involve a neglect of history. In this context the history of political ideas is employed as a means

for scrutinizing the ideas of earlier political philosophers in order to determine their meaning, logical consistency, timelessness, and implications for action, as well as for their relationship to the broader philosophical assumptions about the nature of the universe and society, and man's place in them.

C. Closely related to the definition of political theory as a study of the moral significance of politics is that of its definition as the study of the history of political ideas. Because throughout most of Western history the empirical and moral elements of political ideas have not been separated, and because the former have been subordinated to the latter, the history of political thought is largely the history of political philosophy. Although the history of political ideas can itself be ethically centred, this need not be the case. Increasingly such history has become the investigation of the reciprocal influences of social structure and processes, culture, and personality on the one side, and all types of political ideas on the other. This kind of historical research has occupied by far the largest part of the efforts of political theory in this century.

D. Growing out of political philosophy and the history of political ideas as a subtle and highly refined mode of analysis has been that branch of investigation which would identify political theory with the analysis of the language of politics. In this usage political theory would not contribute to our substantive knowledge about morals, political behaviour, or the place of political ideas in history. Rather it would '... expose and elucidate linguistic muddles; it has done its job when it has revealed the confusions which have occurred and are likely to recur in inquiries into matters of fact because the structure and use of language are what they are' (T. D. Weldon, 'Political Principles', in P. Laslett (ed.), *Philosophy, Politics and Society*, Oxford: Blackwell, 1956, p. 23).

E. Perhaps the most recent and most rapidly growing usage of *political theory* is that which identifies it as the task of formulating and systematizing the concepts of a science of political behaviour in which emphasis is placed on empirical research rather than moral philosophy. In this sense theory is a branch of the scientific enterprise, together with methodology and concrete research. The task of the theorist is to construct, clarify and criticize systems of concepts which have empirical relevance to political

514

behaviour. Such bodies of theory consist 'first, of a set of concepts, corresponding to the important political variables and, second, of statements about the relations among these concepts. Systematic (or general) theory corresponds at the level of thought to the concrete empirical political system of daily life' (D. Easton, *The Political System*, New York: Knopf, 1953, p. 98). The purpose of such theoretical activity, and the accompanying work in methodology and research, is the establishment of generalizations that can ultimately be used for the purpose of prediction and application to social problems.

David Easton

See also: POLITICAL BEHAVIOUR
POLITICAL REALISM

Politician

A. The term *politician* is most commonly used to refer to a person actively engaged in the struggle for governmental power and/or office, whose success largely depends upon the favour of others and who, to achieve success, must therefore be skilled in the arts of persuasion, negotiation, and compromise. In any given society, according to the prevailing methods adopted in the struggle, and to the use normally made of power and/or office when once achieved, politician will or will not be generally used in a pejorative sense.

B. Basically, the term means 'a person who, whatever his motive or purpose, is actively engaged in the struggle for governmental power and office'; but to this have been attached certain important glosses.

(a) The term does not normally apply to professional full-time administrators. 'Seats in Parliament made these civil servants to some extent politicians; but to some extent only, for again, . . . one must remember that they were civil servants' (L. B. Namier, *The Structure of Politics at the Accession of George III*, London: Macmillan, 2nd edn., 1957, p. 38).

(b) It does not apply to those who, for all their concern with political power, are neither members of a governing body nor openly aspiring to such office. Thus, delegates to the British Trades Union Congress often refer to their allies in the Labour Party as 'the politicians' in the movement (for example, *Manchester Guardian*, 6 Sept. 1957, p. 1, col. 1).

(c) A special, but strictly analogous usage of the term is adopted by the 'Namier School' of British 18th-century historians. It is used by them to distinguish that group in Parliament who were neither 'placemen' nor 'country gentlemen' but members of the political factions whose leaders and orators 'were the men who played for the highest prizes, for Cabinet posts and the conduct of the king's business in administration and parliament' (L. B. Namier, *Monarchy and the Party System*, Oxford: Clarendon Press, 1952, p. 19).

(d) In general the term acquires much of its colour from the nature of the political system in whose context it is used. In the United Kingdom the struggle in which the politician is engaged is *openly* competitive, and victory finally depends on the ability to persuade some other person or body (Monarch, Parliament, Party, or electorate) to accept his claims. To call someone a 'politician' therefore often implies the attribution of a skill in manipulating people and opinions which, at its lowest evaluation, is regarded as mere wiliness, albeit effective: see, 'a politician, . . . one that would circumvent God' (Shakespeare, *Hamlet*, V.i.). Associated with this view is the idea that the politician is essentially fickle, concerned with short-term considerations, with immediate popularity, and hardly at all with principle. Adam Smith thus distinguished between 'a legislator, whose deliberations ought to be governed by general principles . . . [and] . . . that insidious and crafty animal, vulgarly called a statesman or politician, whose councils are directed by the momentary fluctuations of affairs' (*Wealth of Nations* 2 v., London: W. Strahan & T. Cadell, 1776, vol. 2, bk. IV, p. 51). Later usage, which continues to the present, elevates the statesman to the level of Smith's legislator, as in, for example, 'the world is wearied of statesmen, whom democracy has degraded into politicians' (B. Disraeli, *Lothair*, London, 1870, ch. 17). This pejorative usage of politician is more or less common to the degree that principles play a less or more obviously important part in current political divisions. It is therefore less common in modern Britain than it was 150 years ago or than it is in contemporary America.

G. C. Moodie

See also: POLITICAL BOSS
POLITICS

Politics

A. *Politics* denotes those processes of human action by which conflict concerning on the one hand the common good and on the other hand the interests (q.v.) of groups is carried on or

Politics

settled, always involving the use of, or struggle for, power (q.v.).

1. The term is sometimes restricted to denote these processes only as they occur within the institutional framework of the state (q.v.).

2. It is used by some to denote these processes as they occur within any human grouping.

3. The term may be used broadly to include non-institutionalized violence as a means of carrying on or settling conflict; or it may be restricted to conflict carried on by institutionally controlled patterns, voting, lobbying, etc.

4. By extension, the term is sometimes used to denote the *study* of these processes.

B. Although one may accept Aristotle's conception that politics is constituted by the striving for the good life by a society or community, modern definitions of politics recognize that the core of politics is the conflict about the nature of the good life and the relation of group interests to it. Conflict, power and policy are the central analytical elements in defining politics.

1. The analytical element most often stressed is power. 'A political act is one performed in power perspectives', according to H. D. Lasswell and A. Kaplan (*Power and Society*, New Haven: Yale University Press, 1950, p. 240; see also H. D. Lasswell, *Politics, Who Gets What, When, How*, New York: McGraw-Hill, 1936). If the definition stopped here, practically all interpersonal relations would be to some extent political.

2. This general meaning of politics is sometimes made more specific by restricting the term so that it denotes power-oriented behaviour *with respect to the process of government* within the framework of the state. Thus V.O. Key, Jr. says politics 'deals with human relationships of superordination and subordination, of dominance and submission, of the governors and the governed. The study of politics is the study of these relationships of political power; the concern of practising politicians is the acquisition and retention of political power' (*Politics, Parties, and Pressure Groups*, New York: Crowell, 1955, pp. 4–5).

Similarly C. E. Merriam, while stressing the central place of the concept *power* and acknowledging that 'there is little room for clear lines of distinction' lists certain 'marks of distinction' between political and other groups. The latter, he says, have a territorial basis, a generality of purpose, a 'peculiar and indefinable integrating quality', and wider latitude in the assignment of sanctions (*Political Power*, New York: McGraw-

Hill, 1934, pp. 7–13). Neither of these writers would regard a struggle for power within a club or an office, for example, as a political matter; for them politics is power relations when (and only when) the *state* is actually or potentially involved.

3. Some political scientists have put other analytical elements in place of power while retaining the association with government and the state. D. Easton (*The Political System*, New York: Knopf, 1953, p. 128), for example, observes that 'the central theme of a political problem is as much the kind of policy at stake as the means used to influence that policy'. For him politics is pre-eminently the making of *policy* but it is not the making of policy in *any* kind of group (e.g. a club or office). 'Political life,' he says, 'concerns all those varieties of activity that influence significantly the kind of authoritative policy adopted for a society and the way it is put into practice' (ibid.). It will be seen that the words 'authoritative' and 'for a society' link the analytical criterion (policy) with the concrete one (governmental things).

D. B. Truman makes a similar linkage, but using the analytical concept *conflict* (*The Governmental Process*, New York: Knopf, 1951, pp. 502–3). For him the activities of interest groups and the process by which conflict among interests is adjusted are the central phenomena of politics. In this view he follows A. F. Bentley (*The Process of Government*, Bloomington, Ind.: The Principia Press, 1908).

4. A definition which deliberately avoids the association of politics with the state ('we want a conception of politics which will apply as well to "office" politics as to national politics') is that of E. C. Banfield (in M. Meyerson & E. C. Banfield, *Politics, Planning, and the Public Interest*, Glencoe, Ill.: The Free Press, 1955, pp. 303–12). For him, '*Politics* is the activity (negotiation, argument, discussion, application of force, persuasion, etc.) by which an issue is agitated or settled'.

The concept of *political decision* and *political structure* in a recent work of P. Diesing (*Reason in Society*, Urbana: University of Illinois Press, 1962) are relevant in this context. He says that 'the political structure of a group is the organization of forces which determines how its decisions are made ...' All decisions, he says, occur within a decision structure of some sort, but *political* decisions in addition have decision structures as their special subject matter. Political decisions are necessary, therefore, whenever there is a deficiency in a decision structure (e.g. it is slow

516

to admit error or shuts out novelty) and in a political decision 'action never is based on the merits of a proposal but always on who makes it and who opposes it' (compromise being essential for the well functioning of decision structures, the maintenance and improvement of which is the task of political rationality and the sine qua non of all rationality) (ibid., pp. 170, 198, 204).

E. C. Banfield

See also: CONFLICT
  GOVERNMENT
  POLITICAL BEHAVIOUR
  POLITICAL THEORY
  POLITICIAN
  STATE

Poll

A. Poll denotes (1) the casting of votes in an election; (2) the canvas of opinions, prior to an election, by simple or complex interviewing.

B. 1. The basic meaning of the word is 'head' and is still evidenced in the phrase 'poll-tax' i.e. a levy the payment of which, in some societies, qualifies an individual to become a voter. By extension it came to mean enumeration—and then the processes whereby a population elects its representatives or officials. Thus we speak of 'going to the polls' and 'polling districts'. In the U.S.A. the term is used also in respect of primary elections.

2. The term has come to denote the 'unofficial' assessment of a population's preferences—mainly, if not exclusively, its political preferences. The earliest such usage is American. M. Ostrogorski pointed out that party organizations conduct 'a sort of political and social survey ... for each locality' (*Democracy and the Organization of Political Parties*, trans. by F. Clarke, London: Macmillan, 1902, vol. II, p. 306) and that in states where 'the issue of the contest is always uncertain ... each elector is asked what his views are on three separate occasions, ninety, sixty and thirty days before the election ...' (op. cit., p. 307). American journals also sought, in a variety of ways, to elicit 'public opinion' on electoral and other political choices—culminating in the forecasts offered from 1916 onwards by the *Literary Digest* through the distribution, at times, of up to 20 million 'polling' poll cards. The history and claims to accuracy of such *straw polls* are examined by C. E. Robinson in *Straw Votes* (New York: Columbia University Press, 1932, esp. pp. 40–144).

3. Subsequent developments of research tech-nique, notably in commercial market research, have led to considerable refinement in the planning and execution of these 'private' polls. Thus, as W. Albig observes: 'the representative sampling procedure in public opinion surveying is now called polling' (*Public Opinion*, New York: McGraw-Hill, 1956, p. 177). Political bodies, both in Britain and America, now make continuing use of the professional services of private 'polling' agencies—thus contributing to the emergence of what has been called 'market politics'. On the British trends see M. Abrams, 'Public Opinion Polls and Political Parties' (*Public Opinion Quarterly*, vol. XXVII, Spring, 1963).

J. Gould

See also: VOTING

Polyandry

A. The term denotes the marriage of one woman to several men.

B. 1. If the plural husbands are brothers, it is called *adelphic* or *fraternal* polyandry. In this form the children may be reckoned to be descended from the eldest brother, or from all the brothers equally. When the husbands are not brothers, and the wife cohabits with each in turn, a special ceremony may be performed to establish the social paternity of the offspring, as among the Todas. The custom of loaning or sharing a wife temporarily is not polyandry.

2. *Secondary marriage* has been used for a form of marriage with plural husbands, which is defined by M. G. Smith as 'marriage of a wife during the lifetime of her primary husband which neither follows nor precedes divorce or annulment of pre-existing marriages', and he distinguishes it thus from polyandry: 'Whereas in polyandry the woman participates in multiple cohabitations and marriages simultaneously, under conditions of secondary marriage she participates in only one cohabitation at any time, though she remains a partner to several marriages simultaneously' ('Secondary Marriage in Northern Nigeria', *Africa*, vol. XXIII, 1953, pp. 312, 322). Her secondary husbands are, equally with her first husband, legal husbands, not lovers.

M. Douglas

See also: MARRIAGE
  POLYGAMY

Polygamy (Also Polygyny)

A. This term denotes the type of marriage in which more than one legal spouse is permitted.

517

Polytheism

The etymology does not imply plural spouses of one sex rather than the other, but historically the word has always been used for the commonest form of marriage with plural spouses, i.e. with two or more wives. 'Large polygamous households, of four wives or more, were met with only among the chiefs … Under modern conditions, polygamy is obviously declining' (I. Schapera, *A Handbook of Tswana Law and Custom*, London: Oxford University Press, 1938, p. 13).

B. Recognizing a source of ambiguity in the fact that polyandry is, in a literal sense, also a form of polygamy, anthropologists now tend to use *polygyny* whenever marriage with two or more wives is intended. Except where the context requires a clear distinction between marriage with plural wives and with plural husbands, the use of polygyny might seem to be pedantic, and many writers, where there is no danger of ambiguity, prefer to use polygamy for the former sense. However, *Notes and Queries* is unequivocal: 'Polygamy must be distinguished as either polygyny (plural wives) or polyandry (plural husbands)' (*Notes and Queries in Anthropology*, British Association for the Advancement of Science, London: Routledge & Kegan Paul, 6th edn., 1951, p. 112).

M. Douglas

See Also: MARRIAGE
POLYANDRY

Polygyny (See Polygamy)

Polytheism

A. *Polytheism* denotes the belief in, or worship of, more gods than one.

B. 1. In general use the term has been employed to describe the deification of natural phenomena—the sun, moon and stars, the winds and clouds, rivers, trees, and mountains—conceived as individualized independent gods, together with ancestors, culture heroes, outstanding benefactors, rulers, and ritual experts who have been raised to divine rank after their death, unless they were gods in their own right from the beginning.

2. Since it is used to designate primarily the more organized and departmentalized deities, it is distinguished from that belief in less clearly defined spiritual beings commonly called *animism* (q.v.).

3. While monolatry and henotheism (cf. *monotheism*) fall within the scope of the term, usually they are differentiated from polytheism

as being more akin to a monotheistic belief in and worship of a single god, as the first syllables of the words suggest (e.g. *monos*, single; *hen*, one). Nevertheless, the fact remains that the exaltation of one god to a superior or unique status in a particular tribe, nation, or pantheon does not exclude the existence of other gods. On the contrary, it implies a number of lesser or rival deities.

4. In a normal polytheistic system, however, it is a difference of degree rather than of kind which distinguishes the various members of an assembly of gods. Thus, the status of the local gods of a city or of a city-state often has been determined by political events. In Mesopotamia, for instance, when Babylon became the capital its god Marduk rose to supremacy supplanting Enlil the god of Nippur as the central figure. Yahweh in Israel, on the other hand, being a monolatrous deity, retained the exclusive allegiance of his people throughout the period of their exile in the 6th century B.C.

5. Universal polytheistic sky-gods like Dyaus Pitar in Vedic India (the prototype of the Greek Zeus and the Roman Jupiter) have tended to become such shadowy and remote figures that they have been in great measure displaced by the more dominant nature gods (e.g. Indra the god of storms and the Rudra the mountain-god). Zeus, however, originally the god of the bright sky, the rain, thunder and lightning, and chief of the gods on Mount Olympus, in later Greek thought became the name assigned by poets and philosophers to the supreme power in the universe, of whom the gods were only manifestations.

E. O. James

See also: ANIMISM
MONOTHEISM
RELIGION

Population

A. 1. The *Oxford English Dictionary* defines population as 'the state of a country with respect to numbers of people, the degree to which a place is inhabited, hence *the total number of persons inhabiting a country, town or other area, the body of inhabitants*'. In the social sciences the term is generally used in its last two senses, which have been italicized. A population is always defined with reference to a particular area or locality, but by a process of extension, it is frequently applied to a group of people who have certain common characteristics: biological, legal, social, or economic, e.g. the female population, the married population, the Roman

Catholic population, the gainfully occupied population, etc. Such groups are properly sub-populations of the wider body.

2. Very occasionally the term may be used as being equivalent to the process of peopling a territory, but this is becoming out of date. The term *depopulation*, however, is still used for the reverse process, i.e. for the reduction of the number of inhabitants of a given area.

3. Where the term is used adjectivally, as in population statistics, population studies, etc., it is generally regarded as a synonym for *demographic* (see *demography*).

B. Normally, the term *population* when used without further qualification refers to human populations, thus Malthus's famous essay was called 'An Essay on the Principle of Population'. Gradually, however, the word came to be used for collections of other objects, at first animals, and later inanimate objects. Thus, we speak of the pig population of the United Kingdom, the motor car population of the U.S.A., etc.

C. The word has been used in statistics, where it has gradually acquired a technical meaning. A *population* refers to an aggregate of objects about which information is desired, but from which a sample only is chosen for investigation (e.g. W. G. Cochran, *Sampling Techniques*, New York: Wiley, 1953, p. 3: 'The word *population* will be used to denote the aggregate from which the sample is chosen'). Here a population may again be a finite collection of objects within a particular area, e.g. the population of non-farm households in the United States, but the term is also used in a more abstract sense, where an infinite population, such as the population of all possible throws of a die is postulated, and the results of a particular experiment, such as the actual throws of a die are regarded as samples from that population. 'The idea of an infinite parent population is a mathematical abstraction of the same kind as the idea that a given random experiment might be repeated an infinite number of times. We may consider this as a limiting case of a finite population, when the number N of individuals increases indefinitely' (H. Cramer, *Mathematical Methods of Statistics*, Princeton: Princeton University Press, 1946, p. 144).

E. Grebenik

See also: DEMOGRAPHY

Population Density

A. The term denotes the number of people occupying a unit of area. It is usually used to denote the *average* number of people occupying a unit of area (usually a square mile) within a larger area constituting the physical location of a society or community.

B. *Population density* has been one of the more important demographic variables in the development of social theory. Generally speaking it has been held that certain levels of institutional complexity and certain characteristics of social interaction develop only when population density has reached a certain level (usually not quantitatively specified). Thus in the theory of urbanism and the ecological theory of the division of labour the concentration of large numbers of people in a small area of space over a considerable period of time is regarded as the most important variable in creating the characteristics of urban life and a complex division of labour. Because of the recognition that this concentration is not a sufficient cause, some ecologists have held, with Durkheim, that what is needed is a concept of *dynamic* or *social density* which includes the instrumentalities of communication which together with population density then account for the intensity of social interaction (A. H. Hawley, *Human Ecology*, New York: Ronald Press, 1950, p. 196).

The concept is also useful as a way of expressing the relationship between living-space and other natural resources and population. Thus conservationists can deplore the threat of the population explosion for the use of natural resources by speaking of densities which are extremely high, and city planners can criticize the low residential density brought about by the American ideal of a house on a plot of land.

William L. Kolb

See also: DIVISION OF LABOUR
          URBANISM

Population Optimum

A. In its most general sense *population optimum* denotes that value of population size and/or density at which the value of some other normatively selected variable is maximized (P. M. Hauser & O. D. Duncan, 'Demography as a Body of Knowledge', in P. M. Hauser & O. D. Duncan (eds.), *The Study of Population*, Chicago: University of Chicago Press, 1959, p. 91). Historically, and more specifically, the normatively selected variable has been the variable of per capita real income or some closely related variable.

Positivism

B. 1. According to W. Petersen (*Population*, New York: The Macmillan Co., 1961, pp. 526–7) the concept of population optimum derives from Malthus's principle that population tends to press against the means of subsistence, and involves three modifications. First, the Malthusian principle can be restated in terms of the law of diminishing returns (q.v.) in that if to a fixed amount of land more labour is added the result will be a declining per capita return. Second, it is possible to posit underpopulation as well as overpopulation. Third, it is possible to analyse industry as well as agriculture in the same way, so that land is only one resource that can be depleted by growing numbers.

M. Gottlieb ('The Theory of Optimum Population for a Closed Economy', in J. J. Spengler & O. D. Duncan (eds.), *Population Theory and Policy*, Glencoe, Ill.: The Free Press, 1956, pp. 160–1) believes that an economic population optimum is the outcome of a 'law' of increasing returns in manufacturing in that larger population brings an enlarged market, a finer division of labour, and a heightened industrial efficiency as well as of the law of diminishing returns applied to resources. He also believes that the most precise formulation of the concept should use the variable of man-hour productivity rather than per capita productivity because variation in hours of work will affect the former. Thus he indicates that 'in a closed modern economy the size of the population and average man-hour productivity—with all the other factors held constant—will have a functional relationship with such properties that a given size of population ("optimum") will result in a maximum man-hour productivity' (ibid., p. 161).

2. Perhaps more than most concepts the idea of economic population optimum has been vigorously attacked for its 'static' quality which grows out of its ceteris paribus assumptions, as indicated, for example, by Gottlieb's 'with all the other factors held constant' in B.1 above. As might be expected with such assumptions the concept has been criticized because (a) the functional relationship between population size and economic productivity cannot be directly empirically established because as population size varies so also do other variables such as technology and social organization and the degree of dependence and interdependence of this complex of variables is not known; and (b) the optimum itself will vary as these other conditions change, thus being highly 'volatile' (P.M. Hauser & O. D. Duncan, 'Demography as a Body of Knowledge', pp. 92–3). In this respect, however, *population optimum* as a concept appears no worse off than most social science concepts. At the present time there are very few situations in social science in which there is the possibility of handling all the relevant variables as they vary simultaneously in the actual world. For the time being the answer to the problems posed by this fact in the case of population optimum is to be found as it has been found in the case of other concepts, namely, by using it in those cases which are significant and in which the other variables can be presumed to be at least relatively constant, by allowing other variables to vary insofar as they can be conceptually handled, and by using it imaginatively in various kinds of typological constructions.

A related but not identical criticism is that the concentration of attention on population optima neglects the possibility that the age and sex composition of a population, particularly during a period of transition may not be economically productive even though size and density are, and further, that the consequences of population *changes* may be overwhelmingly more significant than the state toward which the population is changing. Proponents of the use of the concept argue that its opponents overstress the probability of composition change and the importance of the consequences of the processes of change (M. Gottlieb, 'The Theory of Optimum Population for a Closed Economy', pp. 168–9).

C. Despite the desire of those who use the concept of population optimum to restrict it to economic criteria (cf. W. Petersen, *Population*, pp. 529–30) there is nothing inherently impossible about extending it to relate to almost any sort of normative criterion (P. M. Hauser & O. D. Duncan, 'Demography as a Body of Knowledge', p. 91). Among such criteria that have been used are conservation of natural resources, military power, and the maximum distribution of knowledge and culture among a people (W. Petersen, *Population*, p. 529).

William L. Kolb

See also: Birth Rate
Death Rate
Population Density

Positivism

A. This term denotes a philosophical approach, theory, or system based on the view that in the social as well as in the natural sciences sense experiences and their logical and mathematical treatment are the exclusive source of all worthwhile information. Introspective and intuitional attempts to gain knowledge are rejected. The main significance of the term today in social science contexts is epistemological and methodological.

B. 1. The French *positif*, which served as the basis of Comte's coining of the term for the purposes of his philosophy, signifies 'based on facts or experience'. 'By this word Comte indicated his rejection of all philosophers in the theological or metaphysical sense' (M. De Grange, *The Nature and Elements of Sociology*, New Haven: Yale University Press, 1953, p. 152).

Comte never specifically defined the term he had created. He made it quite clear, however, that he intended a twofold meaning for it, one philosophical, the other political, one 'to generalize our scientific conceptions', the other 'to systematize the art of social life' (*A General View of Positivism* (1848), trans. by J. M. Bridges, London: Reeves & Turner, 2nd edn., 1880, p. 2).

This philosophical view of Comte was summed up by J. S. Mill (*Auguste Comte and Positivism*, London: N. Trubner & Co., 1865, p. 6): 'We have no knowledge of anything but Phaenomena; and our knowledge of phaenomena is relative, not absolute. We know not the essence, nor the real mode of production, of any fact, but only its relation to other facts in the way of succession or similitude. These relations are constant; that is always the same in the same circumstances. The constant resemblances which link phaenomena together, and the constant sequences which unite them as antecedent and consequent, are termed their laws. The laws of phaenomena are all we know respecting them. Their essential nature, and their ultimate causes, either efficient or final, are unknown and inscrutable to us'.

This definition of positivism applies both to Comte's social theory (his Law of The Three Stages) or to his Positivist Religion of Humanity.

2. A naïve view held by some positivists, but often attributed to all of them, is described as covering 'the whole tendency to discuss human behaviour in terms of analogies drawn from natural science' (H. S. Hughes, *Consciousness and Society*, London: MacGibbon & Kee, 1959, p. 37). L. von Mises similarly defines *positivism* as 'the substitution of an illusory social science which should adopt the logical structure and pattern of Newtonian mechanics' (*Human Action, A Treatise on Economics*, London: Hodge, 1949, p. 4).

3. The most recent form of positivism is *logical positivism* as it was developed by the Vienna Circle (G. Bergmann, R. Carnap, H. Feigl, P. Frank, O. Neurath, M. Schlick, and others). In spite of some differences among the views of the proponents of this doctrine—sometimes also referred to as *neo-positivism*—it can be defined either in terms of its principal aims which are 'to provide a secure foundation for the sciences ... [and] to demonstrate the meaninglessness of all meta-physics ... [by the method of] the logical analysis of all concepts and propositions' or in terms of its fundamental doctrines which state that 'propositions of existential import have an exclusively empirical reference and ... this empirical reference can be conclusively shown by logical analysis' (J. R. Weinberg, *An Examination of Logical Positivism*, London: Kegan Paul, Trench, Trubner, 1936, p. 1).

Some of the definitional difficulties arise from the conflicts between the positivism of Comte and his followers and that of the Vienna Circle. 'The only direct connection between the older and the contemporary positivism is the insistence on empirical method as the sole source of truth' (ibid., p. 7). The tendency among social scientists who consider themselves positivists to stand in their thinking somewhere between the old and the new schools of thought contributes to the uncertainty.

4. In the field of ethics, modern positivism, contrary to Comte's, asserts the impossibility of discovering absolutely valid ultimate values, but ascertains the capability of sense experience and scientific method to furnish means for the achievement of chosen goals.

5. In legal theory, the term *positivism* has acquired a special meaning: '... such a theory has to derive its concepts exclusively from the contents of positive legal norms ... [it] is directed at a structural analysis of positive law rather than at a psychological or economic explanation of its conditions, or a moral or political evaluation of its ends' (H. Kelsen, trans. by A. Wedberg, *General Theory of Law and State*, Cambridge, Mass.: Harvard University Press, 1945, pp. xiii, xiv. Some, like G. Gurvitch (*Sociology of Law*, London: Kegan Paul, Trench, Trubner, 1947, p. 4), feel that positivism in jurisprudence has nothing in common with *sociological positivism* which relates law to social forces and groups. This seems to be an erroneous distinction. The legal theory of positivism (as contained in writings setting forth the 'pure theory of law' or 'analytical jurisprudence') engages in

Postulate

distinguishing law from non-law by investigating whether or not a given norm was created in agreement with the ways prescribed for the creation of such a norm in the basic norm of the country and other norms derived from it. The 'basic norm' is one 'the validity of which cannot be derived from a superior norm. [It] ... establishes a certain authority, which may ... [delegate] norm-creating power. [It] ... is nothing but the fundamental rule according to which the various norms of the [legal] order are to be created' (H. Kelsen, *General Theory of Law and State*, pp. 111, 113, 114). The sociologist has to accept this formal and legalistic definition of what the given law is at the given place and time: 'Only by referring the human behaviour to law as a system of [legally] valid norms ... is it possible to distinguish sociologically between ... legal and illegal behaviour ...' (ibid., p. 177). Only when law is distinguished from non-law can its enforcement or non-enforcement, its relation to institutions, movements, ways of thought, etc., be studied scientifically in agreement with the tenets of general positivism as defined above.

Legal positivism, then, is the view that only that norm is to be considered as law which has been created in the manner prescribed by and is consistent with the basic norm of the country in question.

Franz Adler

See also: OPERATIONISM
SCIENCE

Positivist Jurisprudence (See **Jurisprudence**)

Postulate

A. *A postulate* is a proposition we ask others to 'take for granted', or at least for purposes of further discussion. We assume it as a basis for reasonable discussion, as being so self-evident, or axiomatic, that no formal proof is possible or necessary. It is a fundamental assertion or predication which is accepted as a prerequisite for logical analysis, even though it is undemonstrated and probably undemonstrable; a hypothetical assumption; a primitive hypothesis which, if accepted, will generate other logically or empirically provable hypotheses. From this it follows that communication is impossible without implicit or explicit postulates.

B. Most postulates employed by students of social phenomena have been and are implicit. Social theorists and researchers have not devoted the care and criticism to their postulates

that has been characteristic of mathematicians from Euclid to Gauss, Lobachewski, Riemann, and Einstein. Postulates must be revised as new empirical facts and theoretical principles are developed. J. Dewey and A. F. Bentley (*Knowing and the Known*, Boston: The Beacon Press, 1949; A. F. Bentley, *Behaviour, Knowledge, Fact*, London: Williams & Norgate, 1936; and A. F. Bentley, *Inquiry into Inquiries*, Boston: The Beacon Press, 1954) say that *postulation* is a better word than *postulate* because '... postulations arise out of the field of inquiry and maintain themselves strictly subject to the needs of that field' (J. Dewey & A. F. Bentley, *Knowing and the Known*, p. 81).

For scientific purposes, a postulate or postulation is a proposition tentatively stated to guide inquiry in a specific field open to sensory experience aided by instruments whenever possible and subject to revision as the inquiry proceeds. Useful postulations usually are multiple. While this greatly increases the difficulty of constructing a logically coherent set, or system, a single postulation is usually too inclusive, and therefore too vague to be useful.

Read Bain

Potlatch

A. In the widest meaning of the term, a *potlatch* was a complex of activities, including feasts, dances, dramatic displays, public announcements, and the lending, giving, and destroying of property, found among the Indian tribes inhabiting the northwest coast of North America from the State of Washington to Southern Alaska. The core and climax of the activities, however, was the distribution of goods amassed by the host for the occasion through saving, donation, and borrowing. With the possible exception of the southern Kwakiutl, the distributed items were in part gifts and in part nominal payments for luxury services, *given to support a declaration of status by the host*, apportioned to acknowledge the social placement of the recipients, and entailing reciprocation on the same principles and at the discretion of the donor.

There have been a few attempts to extend the term to comparable institutions elsewhere. M. Mauss (*The Gift: Forms and Functions of Exchange in Archaic Societies*, trans. by I. Cunnison, Glencoe, Ill.: The Free Press, 1954, p. 30), for example, finds the potlatch in Melanesia and Papua. Anthropologists are wary of using the term beyond the range of Northwest Coast culture, although they recognize features in common with institutions involving property exchange in other societies, including our own.

B. Potlatching was the indispensable means of gaining and maintaining political influence and social position among the rank-conscious Indians of the North Pacific Coast. Its distinctive feature was the distribution of various types of material goods, including food, to formally invited guests assembled to witness their host's announcement of his assumption of a new status. Births, deaths, marriages, claims of power and privilege, and initiations into ceremonial orders and secret societies all had to be proclaimed and validated in this fashion. The host and his immediate relatives benefited directly from the publicity, and the guests were thereby officially informed. The potlatch donor and his proteges spoke, danced, sang, etc. with an implied or expressed claim on the social distinction traditionally associated with their actions. Such claims were commonly embodied in historic names or titles, so that assuming such titles was tantamount to asserting certain rights and benefits. The announcement or reaffirmation of these claims was in all cases the justification for the potlatch, and no potlatch lacked them, although in many instances they appear to be incidental rather than central to the occasion. Conversely, so firm was the association that no acknowledgment could be expected without a distribution of goods.

C. Some potlatches, called *face-saving*, were given to *regain* status. If, for example, a person were humiliated by an accident which made him appear ridiculous, or if he were taken in war and made a slave, he or his relatives must *potlatch* in his name in order to reinstate him in public esteem. A more spectacular turn was given to the custom when two rivals 'fought with property' to avenge insults or to establish superiority in rank. On these occasions the contestants strove to excel in the amount of property they gave to each other or destroyed with a challenge to the rival to duplicate the waste.

D. Potlatching demanded reciprocity, a guest on one occasion acting as host at some later time; and a host allocated his goods with reference both to what he had previously received from his guests and their ratings relative to each other. The total amount expended by the donor was expressive of his own self-regard and his social potentialities; the relative amounts that he bestowed were indicative of his estimate of the social worth of his guests. A recipient felt obliged to return at least the equivalent of the goods he had received, and important men always gave more.

Students of the subject disagree on the character and the amount of the potlatch return:

1. Some have interpreted it as interest on a loan, commonly at the rate of 100%. F. Boas (*The Social Organization and the Secret Societies of the Kwakiutl Indians*, U.S. National Museum Report for 1895, Washington: Smithsonian Institution, 1897, p. 341), an early investigator among the Kwakiutl, declared that, 'This custom has been described often, but it has been thoroughly misunderstood by most observers. The underlying principle is that of the interest-bearing investment of property'. R. Benedict, relying on Boas's data, appears to accept this interpretation, as does H. Codere (R. Benedict, *Patterns of Culture*, Boston: Houghton Mifflin, 1934, p. 184; H. Codere, *Fighting with Property*, American Ethnological Society Monograph 18, New York: American Ethnological Society, J. J. Augustin Publisher, 1950, pp. 69–76).

2. Other students, on the basis of their own investigations, insist that potlatch goods are gifts in the same sense that Christmas presents are. According to E. S. Curtis (*The Kwakiutl* in his *The North American Indian*, Norwood, Mass.: The Plimpton Press, 1915, vol. 10, p. 143), 'The potlatch and the lending of property at interest are two entirely distinct proceedings. Property distributed at a potlatch is freely given, bears no interest, cannot be collected on demand, and need not be repaid at all if the one who received it does not for any reason wish to requite the gift'. H. G. Barnett reaches the same conclusion and assembles other data in support of it: 'It is also clear that the sums given to guests are not loans. Some confusion has arisen over this point, for the institution of the loan with interest, quite comparable to our own, flourished among the Kwakiutl and is known, at least, to some Salish, Haida, and Tsimshian. The significant fact is that lending and repayment form no part of the potlatch distribution. They are preliminary to it, and are engaged in for the purpose of accumulating the amounts necessary for the distribution. Dawson recognized this and more recently Curtis and Murdock have verified it in print' ('The Nature of the Potlatch', *American Anthropologist*, vol. 40, 1938, p. 353).

3. Real differences in interpretation have arisen largely as a result of the contrast which southern Kwakiutl potlatching presents when it is compared with forms and practices among other northwest coast tribes. It was mainly the

Power

southern Kwakiutl who engaged in the destructive contests, 'fighting with property' to an extent and for reasons seldom appreciated by their neighbours. And if Boas's analysis is correct, they were the only group who treated their presentations as loans.

H. G. Barnett

See also: GIFT
PRESTATION

Power

A. *Power* in its most general sense denotes (a) the ability (exercised or not) to produce a certain occurrence; or (b) the influence (q.v.) exerted by a man or group, through whatever means, over the conduct of others in intended ways (a man or group, in this sense, merely because he or it *could* influence their conduct, i.e. has the 'power' in sense (a) to do so, for such power in sense (a) must actually be employed to be power in sense (b)). While H. D. Lasswell and A. Kaplan (*Power and Society*, New Haven: Yale University Press, 1950, pp. 84, 98) would use *influence* as the general term and restrict *power* to the case where conduct is influenced by promising relatively 'severe deprivation or indulgences', ordinary usage does not, in this context, very sharply distinguish between power and influence.

B. Rights under a set of rules, when they are of a certain kind, are called *powers*. Thus under rules of law, X may have (a) a right to alter, by a prescribed procedure, the rights, duties, etc., under those rules, of himself or others, or (b) a right to take action of a certain kind. A right of type (a) is commonly called a *power*, even where X is not a state organ. A right of type (b) is commonly called a *power* in the case, at least, where X is a state organ. We can evidently speak similarly of power (a) under non-legal constitutional rules: 'Where should that power [the power to dissolve] reside? I see no effective alternative to its residence in the Cabinet' (H. J. Laski, *An Introduction to Politics*, London: Allen & Unwin, 1931, p. 77).

C. Power is sometimes used as a synonym for *political power* which in turn may denote (a) political authority in the sense of (i) the legal powers of state organs (with any conventional powers possessed by them) and/or (ii) political rights, i.e. the legal rights of individuals to appoint to, and be appointed to, state organs; (b) political influence, i.e. influence (power in sense A. (b) above) over the decisions of those possessing political authority; or (c) influence based on political authority.

D. In cases B. and C. above, certain usages of *power* have been explained only in connection with the state. But as every organization has rules, each of these usages of *power* has an analogue for organizations other than the state.

E. 1. The existence of political authority logically implies no more than is logically implied in the 'operation' of a system of law. Thus it logically implies, at some point, a *power* (sense A. (a) above) to apply the sanction; but it does not logically imply power (sense A. (b) above)—though empirically, we expect that those possessing political authority will thereby have some power in this sense (see H. Kelsen, *General Theory of Law and State*, Cambridge, Mass.: Harvard University Press, 1945, pp. 61–2; S. I. Benn, 'The Uses of "Sovereignty"', *Political Studies*, vol. III, 1955, p. 115).

2. Authority is frequently defined as 'a recognized *right* to power', or similarly. This is unsatisfactory, if what is meant is (as in H. D. Lasswell & A. Kaplan, *Power and Society*, p. 133) a right to power in sense A. (b) above. Briefly, there can be a right to be obeyed, or a right to punish, or a right to use force, but a right to have influence is strictly unintelligible.

F. Analogous to the colloquial usage 'He is a power in the land' (i.e. someone who enjoys power in either sense A. (a)) is the usage 'The Powers' to refer to two or more Nation States.

J. M. Brown

See also: AUTHORITY
COERCION
INFLUENCE

Practical Anthropology (See **Applied Anthropology**)

Precedent

A. The term is used to mean either (a) an earlier example of something under consideration; or (b) an earlier example which, for some reason, is believed to provide a model for subsequent instances. The precise denotation will vary with the context.

B. 1. Both usages occur in discussions of constitutional conventions: 'A single precedent with a good reason may be enough to establish the rule. A whole string of precedents without such reason will be of no avail, unless it is perfectly certain that the persons concerned regarded them as bound by it' (W. I. Jennings, *The Law and the Constitution*, London: University of London Press, 3rd edn., 1943, p. 131). The 'reason' will normally consist of arguments from political necessity or desirability.

2. In administrative organizations, official caution frequently induces a respect for past decisions quite apart from any specific instructions. If an action, taken before, was sanctioned (explicitly or implicitly) by superior officials, and/or did not arouse political opposition, an official will tend to regard it as a good model. The action will therefore be cited as 'a precedent' which justifies or requires its repetition in similar circumstances.

3. In Anglo-American law 'a case decided is called a precedent; and is an authority, which, under many circumstances, binds a court to the same decision in a future similar case' (J. Ram, *The Sciences of Legal Judgement*, London: Maxwell, 1834, p. 112). In contemporary English law the decisions of the highest courts in the strict judicial hierarchy are binding under virtually all circumstances: 'when a space has once been closed by a precedent, then no further development is possible' (A. L. Goodhart, 'Precedent in English and Continental Law', *Law Quarterly Review*, vol. L, 1934, p. 50). The U.S. Supreme Court, however, is prepared on occasion to overrule a previous decision. But a case is a precedent only to the extent that the rule of law it establishes is clear, and only for future cases where the material (i.e. relevant) facts are the same. On both points there may be room for argument. Given that all previous decided cases are precedents, the judge must therefore distinguish between them in deciding which one, if any, is binding in a particular subsequent one.

In modern Civil Law systems a series of similar earlier decisions will normally be followed in subsequent cases. It is not a single precedent, but a stream of precedents, which establishes a rule of law.

G. C. Moodie

Prediction

A. The term *prediction* refers to the act of stating beforehand the outcome of a course of change that must or may be expected to occur. At least three elements are involved: (a) the process of change upon which the prediction is based; (b) a set of conditions under which change occurs; (c) the estimate of the probability (q.v.) that the anticipated outcome will occur. The act of pre-

diction constitutes a judgement based on the combination and organization of these elements. Distinctions of accuracy in the predictive process are made in terms of the degree of measurement and/or control of these elements.

1. *Inferential* prediction consists of stating probable outcomes as inferences or projections from observations of change or probability samples often by means of extrapolating statistical curves. Thus P. F. Lazarsfeld and R. H. Franzen ('Prediction of Political Behavior in America', *American Sociological Review*, vol. X, 1945, p. 261) state: 'When people think of predicting elections they usually have in mind the popular public opinion polls where inferences are made from the vote intention of a cross-section of the population to the actual returns of the total population on election day'.

2. *Scientific prediction* states outcomes of change as calculated probabilities after the role and relationship of key factors have been subjected to precise measurement. Lazarsfeld and Franzen (ibid., p. 261) add: 'But, in social research, the term prediction is used in still another way. We predict marriage success or parole success by studying the correlations between all sorts of data and the main criterion of interest'.

B. Prediction in science is a controlled logical process involving the construction of an actual or mental experiment and the exercise of judgement. Thus T. Parsons (*The Structure of Social Action*, New York: McGraw-Hill, 1937, p. 612) observes: 'It is clear that this is nothing, in principle, but the logic of experiment. Where practical difficulties make it impossible actually to reproduce the initial situation, and alter the factor in question and then see what would happen, recourse must be had to a mental experiment, the construction of an objectively possible course of events'. Scientific prediction seems to involve at least three basic steps: (a) accurate empirical knowledge of the process of change within a theoretical frame of reference (q.v.); (b) control of key factors in the process; and (c) statement of logically expected probable next steps of change.

Prehistory

A. *Prehistory*, in its present application, denotes the diachronic study of the material culture of preliterate peoples.

B. 1. The term has been current for a little over one hundred years and appears to have been first applied to the study of the tribes and

Prehistory

peoples peripheral to the classical world and to the study of the Roman Empire.

2. Today the interpretations of the prehistorians attempt to reconstruct human behaviour and the thoughts which underlay this behaviour. The development of this programme of investigation has led to the realization that it is not sufficient to study human artifacts, whether these be tools or monuments: the ambit of the prehistorian's research must be extended to include all changes in the material world that have been brought about by human activity. This vast extension has been accompanied by an equally large extension of time-scale with the realization that human activity, so far from being a matter of some 6,000 years, has occurred over some 600,000 years, and that, for all except perhaps the last 5,000 of these, such activities have been the work of pre-literate societies.

C. The development of prehistoric archaeology was much affected by palaeontology and glaciology, and the association of tools and extinct animal remains had already been remarked 250 years ago. But it was not until Boucher de Perthes's conclusions about his researches in the Somme Valley (published in 1847) had been supported by Evans, Falconer, and Prestwich in 1859, the same year as the publication of *The Origin of Species*, that the existence of Pleistocene man was accepted.

1. C. J. Thomsen, who had been appointed Curator of the Copenhagen Museum in 1816, had already proposed a classification of antiquities, following a Lucretian pattern, into Stone, Bronze, and Iron. This was a purely archaeological classification based upon the material from which the principal tools and weapons were manufactured. Its chronological value was, however, limited, since although it was believed that the three stages were inevitable, it was clear that they were by no means universally coeval. De Mortillet therefore proposed a system of sub-divisions which were based on a geological system in so far as their identification was dependent upon the existence of 'type-fossil' tools in different strata, the strata being named after sites in which the 'fossils' were well represented. The system had considerable merit, but its application, especially by its innovator, was complicated and confused by the representation of each stage as a phase through which every society must pass. (This complication remained a part of Soviet prehistoric theory until 1950.)

2. The next development was the realization, in part due to de Mortillet, that an assemblage might indicate not only a distinct period but also a distinct human group. To such assemblages the German prehistorians applied the term *Kulturen*. The logical conclusion to these developments was furnished by Kossinna who wrote: 'Sharply defined archaeological culture-provinces coincide at all times with quite definite peoples or tribes; cultural regions are ethnic regions, culture groups are peoples.'

D. 1. The analysis of material culture by function, chronology, and chorology underlies the whole of prehistory and has yielded profitable results. But the subsequent synthesis, in the attempt to establish behaviour and thoughts has always been handicapped by the imperfect survival of the records of ancient human activities, the uncertain chronology and the inadequacy of functional identifications. It was long believed that analogies from more recent societies in an unsophisticated stage of development could help to fill the gaps in the record, but the conclusions of social anthropologists as to the validity of earlier attempts at comparative ethnology and ethnography have thrown considerable doubt on the propriety of this method.

2. More intensive techniques of excavation and investigation with minute attention to the collection of data which throw light upon the environment of the sites under study have helped to increase the total amount of material available for analysis. In addition the physical sciences have been called upon, not only to assist in the study of the material collected, but also to establish absolute systems of chronology. These developments, which have intensified considerably within the past fifteen years, have now reached the point at which, if there is a conflict between the date determined by the scientist and that held by the archaeologist on traditional grounds, then the archaeologist must abandon his traditional view.

The contributions from the physical sciences include dendrochronology (a method of dating based upon tree-ring counts); pollen analysis, which affords valuable data upon climatic conditions in the past; fluorine analysis (offering a method of differentiating the date of fossil material from an apparently similar horizon); potassium analysis, still in an experimental stage, which seems likely to provide absolute dating for pleistocene material (or rather the horizons in which such material is found). Of paramount importance at present is radiocarbon dating, discovered by W. Libby, which depends upon the determination of the quantity of C^{14}, a radio-active isotope of C^{12}, present in organic material from archaeological sites. These developments, and their application to prehistoric archaeology, have introduced a new element of scientific precision into the subject, a precision which is further increased by the improvement in the techniques and application of physical analysis to the artifacts which are the principal data upon which the prehistorian depends for his research. Other promising developments are in the fields of palaeomagnetic studies and in the use of electro-magnetic surveying methods in the detection of buried artifacts and structures. The use of modern skin-diving equipment has also introduced the possibility of underwater investigations with some reasonable degree of controlled recovery of objects. The use of aerial photography not only to detect sites but also as a tool of analysis in the study of, for example, ancient field or irrigation systems, or the mapping of defensive systems, has provided another tool for the prehistorian.

E. The combination of these new techniques and methods with improved methods of excavation and field study has revolutionized our knowledge of man's early history, although their application has been largely in those areas which were already best known as the result of previous work. Very large areas of Asia and almost the whole of Africa remain *terrae incognitae*. Much work of synthesis has yet to be undertaken, even in the best studied areas. It must be admitted that much evidence for the study of prehistory has been irretrievably lost, either through natural causes or as the result of subsequent human activities, a cause whose effects are ever-increasing with the rapid development of hitherto undisturbed regions and the increasing use of large-scale earth-moving machinery. Methods of attempting the reconstruction of past social phenomena which will be acceptable to the social scientists have still to be evolved. Studies in prehistoric economics and technology are clearly capable of considerable expansion, especially in tropical areas, where the poor survival rate of such substances as bamboo is a complicating factor. Prehistory has undergone a technical revolution as a result of the contributions of the physical sciences: the theoretical and interpretative revolutions which should follow upon this are only now beginning to take shape.　　　　A. H. Christie

See also: ARCHAEOLOGY
CULTURE HISTORY

1. Empirical observation provides data on the basis of which prediction may be made. The frame of reference makes it possible to identify key elements and to determine the weight or value of each element as it relates to the others under varying conditions. Such theory, according to R. K. Merton (*Social Theory and Social Structure*, Glencoe, Ill.: The Free Press, 1957, p. 98), 'by providing a rationale, ... introduces a *ground for prediction* which is more secure than mere empirical extrapolation from previously observed trends'.

2. Prediction rests upon ability to control the key factors in a process of change. In experimental situations it may be possible actually to manipulate key factors. In actual social situations, however, the behaviour of key factors under a variety of specific conditions in the process of change must be observed and if possible measured, and stated quantitatively. One mode of stating such measured behaviour of key factors is the actuarial-type of expectancy tables employed in population, marriage, and parole prediction (see E. W. Burgess & P. Wallin, *Courtship, Engagement and Marriage*, Chicago: Lippincott, 1953; and S. S. & E. T. Glueck, *500 Criminal Careers*, New York: Knopf, 1930).

3. The act of predicting consists of stating in advance the outcome of the change process in which control over key factors has been established. In experimental situations, the anticipated outcome may be stated as a certainty before manipulation of appropriate key factors has been initiated. In social situations anticipated outcomes must be stated as probabilities after the observed behaviour of key factors under specific conditions is matched with the behaviour of similar factors under similar conditions.

In scientific prediction this matching operation is best achieved by the use of measures of correlation. The resultant coefficients not only state the anticipated outcome as a class of possible outcomes; they also indicate the degree of probability that the stated outcome will actually occur.

Joseph S. Himes

See also: EXPERIMENT
PROBABILITY

Prejudice

A. *Prejudice* is a negative, unfavourable attitude toward a group or its individual members; it is characterized by stereotyped beliefs; the attitude results from processes within the bearer of the

Prerogative

attitude rather than from reality testing of the attributes of the group in question.

Sociological definitions of the term go beyond the above in stipulating that the content of the attitude must violate existing social norms.

B. In the social sciences the term *prejudice* is used almost exclusively in relation to ethnic groups. Within this limitation there is widespread consensus on some elements in the definition of the term: prejudice is an 'unfavourable' attitude toward an ethnic group (or individual members of that group).

Differences arise over the question whether these necessary aspects are also sufficient. An affirmative answer is embodied in the definition 'prejudice is simply an unfavorable ethnic attitude' (J. Harding, B. Kutner, H. Proshansky & I. Chein, 'Prejudice and Ethnic Relations', in *Handbook of Social Psychology*, G. Lindzey (ed.), Cambridge, Mass.: Addison-Wesley, 1954, vol. II, p. 1022).

C. All other usages of the term narrow its meaning further, sociologists by reference to aspects of the society in which the attitude occurs, psychologists by reference to the individual bearer of the attitude.

1. Thus, R. M. Williams, Jr., speaks of prejudice as 'a negative attitude which violates some important norms or values nominally accepted in the culture' (*The Reduction of Intergroup Tensions*, New York: Social Science Research Council, Bulletin 57, 1947, p. 37). According to this usage anti-Semitism in Hitler's Germany was not prejudice because it was in keeping with social norms.

2. Psychologists, as a rule, refer to an attitude as prejudice when it is not in keeping with or not based on adequate *reality testing* of the qualities of the group against whom the attitude is directed. In line with the term's etymology some authors stipulate specific aspects of the cognitive processes in the attitude. G. W. Allport, e.g., speaks of prejudice only when the ethnic attitude is 'based upon a faulty and inflexible generalization' (*The Nature of Prejudice*, Cambridge, Mass: Addison-Wesley, 1954, p. 9). In other words, he distinguishes from prejudice unfavourable ethnic attitudes arrived at by proper inductive reasoning and unfavourable ethnic attitudes which are based on faulty reasoning but are correctable. However, when the error in judgement is impervious to factual correction, that is, when the belief about the

ethnic group is a stereotype, the attitude constitutes prejudice.

3. Psychoanalytically oriented authors suggest that inadequate reality-testing or stereotypical beliefs about an ethnic group must be understood as serving an irrational function within the psychic economy of the holder of the attitude. Otherwise, inflexibility would not occur. Accordingly, prejudice is conceived of as an ethnic attitude which 'fulfills a specific irrational function for its bearer' (N. W. Ackerman & M. Jahoda, *Anti-Semitism and Emotional Disorder*, New York: Harper & Brothers, 1950, p. 4). The distinction of this functional use of the term from Allport's emphasis on the cognitive process corresponds to that between the underlying theories of personality. The two usages are not necessarily incompatible.

4. The introduction of the term *prejudice* into systematic social science has occasionally been criticized on the ground that its use opens the door to value judgements of the user. The most extreme conclusion drawn from this alleged danger holds that 'the very use of the term "prejudice" as a scientific concept in connection with social attitudes should automatically disqualify the user as a social scientist' (R. B. Cattell, 'Ethics and the Social Sciences', *American Psychologist*, vol. 3, 1948, p. 195). While this opinion is not widely held, it is a useful reminder of the importance of clear definitions in this area to which implicit value judgements could indeed be easily introduced.

Marie Jahoda

See also: DISCRIMINATION
STEREOTYPE

Preliterate (See **Nonliterate**)

Prerogative

A. *Prerogative* usually refers to (a) some special or prior right, power, or privilege; or more particularly, (b) the discretionary power acknowledged, in law, to belong to a government or part thereof, and, most frequently, the discretionary power belonging to the executive branch of government. Such discretion normally is exclusive, and hence also, in some sense, a privilege.

B. British Constitutional Law provides the most precise usage of the term. 'By the word prerogative we usually understand that special pre-eminence, which the king hath, over and above all other persons, and out of the ordinary course

528

of the common law, in right of his regal dignity. It signifies, in its etymology, ... something that is required or demanded before, or in preference to, all others ... it can only be applied to those rights and capacities which the king enjoys alone' (W. Blackstone, *Commentaries on the Laws of England*, Oxford: The Clarendon Press, 1765, p. 232).

However, its exact significance has varied with different historical periods.

1. 'On the rare occasions when mediaeval lawyers had applied it [the term] to the powers rather than the property rights of the King, it denoted the whole sum of authority inherent in and peculiar to him, whatever the mode of its exercise' (D. L. Keir & F. H. Lawson, *Cases in Constitutional Law*, Oxford: The Clarendon Press, 4th edn., 1954, p. 45). By the 17th century the distinction was established between the ordinary and absolute powers of the king. The former referred to his powers to execute civil justice through the ordinary courts, and the latter to his powers in 'Policy and Government'. Increasingly, the term became reserved for his absolute powers, whose extent and nature formed the central point of constitutional dispute and conflict at that time. The Stuart attempt permanently to widen the scope of the prerogative having failed, it was established that 'the King hath no prerogative, but that which the law of the land allows him' (Sir Edward Coke, *Case of Proclamations*, 1611, XII *Reports* 76, London: H. Twyford & T. Dring, 1656).

2. The term is now used to refer to the 'residue of discretionary or arbitrary authority ... legally left in the hands of the Crown' (A. V. Dicey, *The Law of the Constitution*, London: Macmillan, 9th edn., 1939, p. 424) and derived from the Common Law, not from Statute. Legislation can abolish or limit the prerogative, yet 'for the exercise of a prerogative power the prior authority of Parliament is not required' (E. C. S. Wade and G. G. Phillips, *Constitutional Law*, London: Longmans, Green, 5th edn., 1955, p. 141), nor can the Courts challenge its exercise, although they may have to determine its nature and extent.

3. Since the prerogative powers are now exercised on the responsibility of Ministers, rather than the Monarch, their use is subject to direct political control. 'There are, however, certain prerogative powers which he [the Monarch] exercises on his own responsibility, and which may fitly be called "the personal prerogatives" ' (W. I. Jennings, *Cabinet Government*, Cambridge: at the University Press, 2nd edn., 1951,

p. 368)—e.g. the power to dissolve Parliament, subject to the relevant constitutional conventions.

C. 1. The term is also used with respect to other countries. The 'autonomous executive power' vested in the President by the Constitution of the U.S.A. is sometimes referred to as his 'prerogative' (E. S. Corwin, *The President: Office and Powers*, New York: New York University Press, 3rd edn., 1948, pp. 3, 15–16, 367). See also discussion of the French President's 'prerogatives' to veto legislation or dissolve the Chamber of Deputies (A. Esmein, *Eléments de Droit Constitutionnel*, Paris: Recueil Sirey, 1928, vol. II, pp. 73–5).

2. 'This power to act according to discretion for the public good, without the prescription of the law, and sometimes even against it, is that which is called prerogative' (J. Locke, *The Second Treatise of Civil Government*, ed. by J. W. Gough, Oxford: Blackwell, 1946, para. 160). Compare, for example, the concept of *actes de gouvernement*, which is essentially an extra-legal action (L. Duguit, *Traité de Droit Constitutionnel*, Paris: Ancienne Librairie, Fontemoing & Cie, Editeurs, E. de Boccard, Successeur, vol. III, 1923, pp. 685, et. seq.).

3. Less technically, the term is often used as a virtual synonym for 'privilege' or 'special preserve' (for example, in J. L. de Lolme, *The Constitution of England*, London: G. Robinson & J. Murray, 1793, ch. 1).

G. C. Moodie

See also: AUTHORITY
                POWER

Presidency

A. The term *presidency* is used most frequently in political science to designate the office and/or functions of a president, i.e. the elective head of a constitutional republic. However, the term is sometimes also used to specify the incumbency or administration of a particular president.

B. 1. In political terminology the most important meaning of *presidency* is that which designates the office of an elective head of state or government or both. As a result of American constitutional usage since 1789, *presidency* has been used most frequently to connote the chief executive or chief of state of a constitutional republic, and this usage in turn has been extended to designate inter alia the principal office of joint stock companies, eleemosynary

Pressure Group

corporations, functional group organizations, and learned societies.

2. When used to designate the office of a head of state or head of government, the term *presidency* has two meanings, depending upon the nature of the presidential function. In the United States of America and the Latin American Republics, the functions of head of state and active head of government are combined in the presidency. In other countries, e.g. the Federal Republic of Germany, India, the Irish Free State, and other republics, only the function of head of state is vested in the president, and the active direction of government is vested in a cabinet headed by a premier, chancellor, or prime minister. In addition to this differentiation of presidential functions, two other major differences exist between the government of the two types of republics which give rise to the distinction between presidential and parliamentary government. In the United States and Central and South America the executive is single and is independent of the legislature and serves for a fixed term; in parliamentary government the executive or cabinet is chosen from the legislature and holds tenure only so long as it enjoys the confidence of a majority of parliament.

C. The term *presidency* had a specialized meaning in British imperial administration as the designation of administrative districts, e.g. the three great administrative units of the Indian Empire, Bengal, Bombay, and Madras.

Robert J. Harris

See also: CABINET GOVERNMENT
HEAD OF STATE
PARLIAMENTARY GOVERNMENT

Presidential Primary (See Primary)

Pressure Group

A. A *pressure group* may be defined as any combination of persons, bound together by shared goals and attitudes, who attempt to obtain decisions favourable to their preferred values by all means at their disposal but especially by gaining access to the governmental process.

B. 1. The term is almost certainly American in origin: even during the heydays of pluralism in British political theory it does not seem to have been in use. The first American political scientist to pay much attention to the phenomenon describes it in original fashion but uses only the term *interest group* though speaking about the various 'pressures' exercised by such groups (see A. F. Bentley, *The Process of Government*, Chicago: The University of Chicago Press, 1st edn., 1908). The term *pressure group* appears then in the United States 'as normal usage without apology or definition' in scholarly writings of the late 1920s (see W. J. M. Mackenzie, 'Pressure Groups: The "Conceptual Framework"', *Political Studies*, vol. III, 1955, p. 249). It appears likely that it was first coined by American journalists during the post-war years when the influence of organized interests on legislatures, both federal and state, was widely noted and critically discussed.

2. Political scientists now use the terms *pressure group* and *interest group* interchangeably, preferring of late the latter to the former, obviously because of the pejorative connotation of 'pressure'. D. B. Truman, whose book, *The Governmental Process* (New York: Knopf, 1951) follows in the tradition of Bentley, defines it (ibid., p. 33) in a fashion typical of many others: 'any group that, on the basis of one or more shared attitudes makes certain claims upon other groups in the society for the establishment, maintenance, or enhancement of forms of behavior that are implied by the shared attitudes'.

C. 1. Distinctions between pressure or interest groups and lobbies (q.v.) (a term that has been in use far longer) are sometimes difficult to draw. But the description by A. de Grazia (*The Elements of Political Science*, New York: Knopf, 1952, p. 216) seems to be generally accepted: 'The pressure group is simply any organized social group that seeks to influence the behavior of political officers without seeking formal control of the government. The lobby is one type of pressure group whose agents apply whatever influence they may command directly upon the legislators'. In Great Britain one of the foremost observers of pressure groups, S. E. Finer, uses lobby as the broader term embracing (a) interest groups proper, (b) promotional (or propaganda) groups. He reserves the term *pressure* for those activities of both categories which amount to the 'application, or threatened application of a sanction should a demand be refused' (see his 'Interest Groups and the Political Process in Great Britain' in H. W. Ehrmann (ed.), *Interest Groups on Four Continents*, Pittsburgh: University of Pittsburgh Press, 1958, pp. 117–18).

2. Many of the current usages of the term gain in precision when the writers seek to differentiate between pressure groups and political parties. D. D. McKean (*Party and Pressure Politics*, Boston: Houghton, Mifflin 1949, p. 16), speaks of pressure groups as of 'organizations interested primarily in policy which do not ordinarily nominate candidates', and P. Odegard states that they are formed 'without regard for party opinion or other matters ... (they) carry on agitation for or against projects deemed favorable or prejudicial to their interests' (*Pressure Politics: The Story of the Anti-Saloon League*, New York: Columbia University Press, 1928, p. vii).

That such differences between parties and pressure groups do not deprive the latter of their political character has been particularly stressed by V. O. Key, Jr., who in his *Politics, Parties, and Pressure Groups* (New York: Crowell, 2nd edn., 1947, pp. 15–16) insists: 'such groups while they may call themselves non-political are engaged in politics; theirs is a politics of policy in the main ... In contrast political parties, in order to win elections, have to cater to all kinds and classes of people ... Theirs is a politics chiefly of place and position'. In refutation of the Marxian idea that the 'class struggle' (q.v.) is the sole source of pressure groups, D. McC. Wright in his *Capitalism* (New York: McGraw-Hill, 1951) and other writing has elaborately developed the non-economic and altruistic sources of pressure group conflicts.

D. There seems to remain a significant difference in the usage of the term by political scientists and by sociologists. R. M. MacIver (in his article on 'Pressures, Social' in E. R. A. Seligman (ed.), *Encyclopedia of the Social Sciences*, London: Macmillan, 1934, vol. XII, p. 347) includes such phenomena as fascist movements in his definitional analysis of pressure groups. He acknowledges as 'serviceable' the use of the term *pressure groups* as denoting 'any aggregate, organized or unorganized, which applies pressure tactics'. But then the author draws a distinction between pressure groups and interest groups. To him the exercise of pressure is not inherent in the concept of an interest group. 'Social pressures, in a word, constitute a particular method of achieving results—one of the many methods which interest groups may adopt'.

On the other hand political scientists have, especially of late, developed in connection with the concept of pressure group that of 'access' to the organs of decision-making. They thereby emphasize the relationship between groups and the political process. All pressure groups 'must devise means for gaining access to and influencing those who are constitutionally empowered to make, administer, or otherwise define the law' (O. Garceau & C. Silverman, 'A Pressure Group and the Pressured', *American Political Science Review*, vol. XLVIII, 1954, p. 672).

Henry W. Ehrmann

See also: INFLUENCE
INTEREST (Political Science)
LOBBY
POLITICS

Prestation

Prestation, from the French *prestation*, denotes the transfer of any right to goods or services, or any service rendered, to another. This term has been borrowed from the French by some English and American writers in their search for a term which covers all forms of transfer of rights to goods or services, or any service rendered by a person (or group) to another person (or group).

A. P. Stirling

See also: GIFT

Prestige

A. *Prestige* denotes in general the influence, (high or low) exercised by individuals, groups, institutions, pursuits, and artifacts, and/or the standing (high or low) enjoyed by such individuals, groups, etc.

B. The shifts of meaning will emerge from a review of historical and scientific usage.

1. Until the end of the 18th century, *prestige* in English and German, as in the French from which it was derived, was used exclusively in the sense of the original Latin: an extraordinary effect achieved by means of a trick. The plural form is often used.

2. Usage by metaphor was extended to artistic and literary effects (e.g. by Diderot). The further metaphorical extension from this use to mean a *blinding or dazzling influence* or the glamour of a person cast over others appears to be associated quite specifically with contemporary reactions to Napoleon. It is so used by his admirers as well as enemies.

3. Thereafter the word came into more frequent use, and denoted (in England) qualities possessed by institutions, nations, pursuits, and artifacts as well as by individuals.

4. Later in the century, political usage (i.e.

Price

with respect to nations, national leaders) became dominant, referring to the influence over others, and especially the regard in which one was held, derived from achievements or moral character or, pejoratively, from display or pretension, as against that based on military or economic power.

5. Sociological usage of *prestige* has denoted an influence cast over others either legitimately by the demonstration of superior attainments, or illegitimately by a parade of attainments (or powers, or possessions) not actually possessed. M. Weber writes of the *feeling* of prestige conferred by the possession of talents even when they are unused (*Gesammelte Aufsätze zur Wissenschaftslehre*, Tübingen: Mohr, 1951, p. 491) and of the prestige *interests* of different orders of society being furthered by fashion and conventions (ibid., p. 557). The word is currently used much more widely with a looser meaning of the social standing of persons or classes in a stratified society. Issues relevant to the legitimacy or illegitimacy of prestige have tended to disappear from the technical meaning, and with it the meaning of *prestige* as influence over others. In recent and current literature, it denotes the evaluation accorded to persons, groups, or classes in so far as they are ranked invidiously by each other and by society at large:

(a) 'The bases on which various people raise prestige claims, and the reasons others honor these claims, include property and birth, occupation and education, income and power—in fact almost anything that may invidiously distinguish one person from another. In the status system of a society, these claims are organized as rules and expectations which regulate who successfully claims prestige, from whom, in what ways, and on what basis. The level of self-esteem enjoyed by given individuals is more or less set by this status system' (C. W. Mills, *White Collar*, New York: Oxford University Press, 1951, p. 239). (b) 'This hierarchical ordering we may call *prestige*, which is the relative esteem in which an individual is held in an ordered total system of differentiated evaluation' (T. Parsons, *The Social System*, Glencoe, Ill.: The Free Press, 1951, p. 132). (c) 'What we wish to do is to compile a standard framework which would enable us to build up an index to the classification of the more common occupations according to the *social prestige accorded to each by the public in general*' (letter addressed to 'a number of people occupying prominent positions in their several professions or in industry'). 'We should like to know in what order, *as to their social standing*, you would grade the occupations in the list given by you' (instructions addressed to members of adult education classes, in J. Hall & D. C. Jones 'Social Grading of Occupations' —Appendix, *British Journal of Sociology*, vol. I. pp. 50, 51.

Tom Burns

See also: SOCIAL CLASS
STATUS
STRATIFICATION

Pre-test (See **Pilot Project**)

Price

A. A *price* is a measure, in terms of money, or some other widely accepted commodity, of the exchange value of a good or a service. The word is also used in a looser, almost figurative, sense as in 'the price of savings is the goods and services given up because the individual does not spend his entire income'. The word is used as a verb as in pricing goods in the sense of fixing a price. Finally it may be used in the sense of supply price as for example the 'price of effort'.

B. Fundamentally a price is a ratio indicating the terms on which goods and services are exchanged. Thus in a primitive society two knives might exchange for one calf. Often one good is singled out to serve as a *numeraire* or common measure for other goods, thus precious metals serve both as a good wanted for particular purposes and as a unit of value and exchange. When a homogeneous commodity such as gold, or silver or iron is adopted as money, a system of money prices is established. In advanced economies, money, including credit, is not usually wanted for the particular uses to which it can itself be put, but only for the goods and services for which it can be exchanged.

C. Use of the word as a verb, meaning to establish a price, sometimes refers to *administered prices*, i.e. prices that are not completely determined by the interplay of demand and supply in the market, but which may be set within limits, by the selling firm. The range within which a firm can and will 'administer' prices is limited by the demand situation that it faces and by its own objective, e.g. maximizing profits, increasing market share, etc.

R. W. Pfouts

See also: MONEY
PRICE SYSTEM

Price System

A. The term *price system* is used to denote a form of economic organization in which the allocation of economic resources among various possible uses is determined by price. Hence, it connotes a system of rationing in which the chief guides to choice and action are prices

B. 1. In a general sense any economic system in which market prices play some part in guiding the allocation of economic resources makes use of a price system. 'In order to show that price is a phenomenon incident to all forms of organization of society and to economic action in general, it is sufficient to look upon it as a coefficient of choice' (J. A. Schumpeter, 'The Nature and Necessity of a Price System', in *Economic Reconstruction*, New York: Columbia University Press, 1934, p. 171). For an interesting example of the development of a price system in a prisoner-of-war camp, see R. A. Radford, 'The Economic Organization of a P.O.W. Camp', *Economica*, N.S., vol. XII, 1945, pp. 189-201).

2. The operation of a price system may be understood by considering a case in which consumers' preference for good increases. Inasmuch as this implies that consumers are now willing to buy more at the existing price—and the same amount at a higher price—there will be profitable opportunities for expanding output, initially through an increase in the output of the existing firms, ultimately, perhaps, by an increase in the number of firms.

3. The demand for factors by production is derived from the demand for consumers' goods. An increase in the demand for a particular good entails an increase in demand for the factors engaged in its manufacture, and any ultimate rise in the price of a finished good relative to other goods is generally reflected in a rise in the price of those factors which are used in greater proportion in that good than in other goods.

4. The actual operation of a price system, is, of course, more complex than the simple case outlined above. Complexities arise from many sources. For example, the existence of stocks of goods which might have to be reduced in some amount before additional resources were guided to the favoured good were ignored. Another important complexity is found in demand relationships between goods, i.e. the existence of relationships of complementarity and substitutability between goods. As a consequence of these relationships, a change in the price of one good affects the quantities of related goods that are sold as well as its own sales. Interrelated and complex networks of demands exist and in fact are common. Similarly, interrelationships of the supply of goods exist, e.g. joint products. Other complications that tend to delay the working of a price system include imperfect knowledge of market operations on the part of buyers and sellers, immobility of factors of production, absence of freedom of entry of producers and sellers to an industry, etc.

The price system is essentially an institution whose functioning guides economic resources into uses that meet the expressed wants of consumers as exhibited through their willingness and their ability to buy, that is through their demands. Incidental to and in conjunction with, its allocative function, the market determines the distribution among the population of the aggregate products of industry through its attribution of prices to the various factors of production.

One line of criticism would have it, to be sure, that the price system is undesirable because it subordinates 'quality' to 'mass taste'. Defenders of the pricing system reply that it is itself neutral, and the problem of 'mass taste' is merely one aspect of the whole problem of non-coercive progress under democratic values.

C. 1. Though it is frequently implied by liberal economists that the price system is a feature peculiar to private enterprise, some socialist writers claim that the use of prices as guides to the allocation of economic resources is quite compatible with a socialist economy. '... the leading writers of the Marxist school were and are quite aware of the necessity of the price system in a socialist economy' (O. Lange & F. M. Taylor, *On the Economic Theory of Socialism*, Minneapolis: University of Minnesota Press, 1938, p. 141).

2. In a socialist economy the operation of a price system clearly parallels that of a capitalist economy except in the question of how the state-owned factors of production are to be priced in the absence of a market for such factors. Socialist economic theory holds that the Central Planning Board can establish prices for such factors on a historical basis. If these prices are incorrect under current conditions this difficulty will be manifested by either a surplus or a deficit of availability of these factors according to whether the price is too high or too low for current conditions. Thus a guide for correcting prices and for allocating state-owned factors

Primary

that is based on the price system and the demands of consumers is possible in a socialist economy.

R. W. Pfouts

See also: ALLOCATION OF RESOURCES
PRICE

Primary

A. A *primary* is a method of nominating candidates for election to public office in the United States by act of the party membership at large, which makes its choices by ballot in a public poll much like the procedure of a final election.

B. *Primary* in the vocabularies of politics and political science refers to the process of nominating a party's candidates who will (where party competition exists) compete with each other in a final election for public office.

1. The political primary requires the direct participation by voters in the nomination of candidates who will run for public office, and was invented as a device for democratizing the political process by taking the power of nomination from oligarchies of professional politicians, skilled in manipulating the business of nominating conventions. Although the rise of the direct primary is often associated with the reform movements agitated first by the Populists in the 1890s and then by the Progressives in 1912, it started much earlier: 'As early as 1842 the direct primary was employed by the Democratic Party in Crawford County, Pennsylvania; other counties in Pennsylvania soon adopted the system' (V. O. Key, Jr., *Politics, Parties, and Pressure Groups*, New York: Crowell, 3rd edn., 1952, p. 409). Key further observes '... for nomination of party candidates for state and local offices, and for United States Senators and Representatives the direct primary is the predominating method' (ibid., p. 411). It should be borne in mind, however, that neither the laws which govern the primaries nor the procedures employed are uniform throughout the states. There are also 'exceptions', e.g. 'In six Southern states ... parties are permitted to employ conventions if they choose ...' (F. A. Ogg & P. O. Ray, *Essentials of American Government*, New York: Appleton-Century-Crofts, 1952, p. 161 fn.).

2. A distinction is usually made between the *open primary* and the *closed primary*. In the first, any qualified voter may come to the polls on primary day and ask for the ballot of either the Republican or Democratic party without establishing his party membership in any other way. In the closed primary, only those are permitted to vote the ballot of their choice who have already established their party identification in some other way, usually by declaring their party identification at the time of registering to vote. The open primary makes it possible for the voter to keep his party identification secret, but it has the disadvantage of permitting the members of one party to influence the nominations of the opposition by voting the ballots of the opposition.

3. Until 1941, some primaries were held by the Supreme Court to be purely party affairs, like social clubs, without official characteristics. It was on this theory that the Supreme Court permitted parties in the South to exclude Negroes. Because the primary in one-party states is the equivalent of final election, the Court's conception of the southern primary changed. So far as basic voting rights are concerned, primaries in such one-party states are held to be public and not private affairs.

4. In the effort to reduce the preponderant influence of party officials in public elections, some communities use what is called the *nonpartisan primary*, one in which voters, without distinction as to party, participate. The winners of the highest vote and the next highest vote are declared to be the candidates in the final election that follows. One variation on this method allows the winner of an absolute majority of primary votes to be declared the winner of the office contested, without a final election. Nonpartisan primaries are generally confined to local contests.

C. Candidates for the Presidency and Vice-Presidency were originally chosen by caucuses of Congressmen. Since the national election of 1828 candidates for these offices have been nominated by conventions of party members. Choice by convention has been very often preceded by the so-called *presidential primary*. In the election year 1956, eighteen states conducted presidential primaries for the purpose of determining which presidential possibility should receive the support of delegates to the national party convention. The choice of the presidential primary is usually only moderately binding upon the delegates who, after an interval, are free to cast their votes in convention for other candidates if the choice of the primary is out of the running. The presidential primary is not strictly therefore a device for nominating presidential candidates, but is more in the nature of a popularity poll.

Since 1916 the movement towards presidential primaries has lost impetus (see J. P. Harris, 'Presidential Primaries', in H. A. Turner (ed.), *Politics in the United States*, New York: McGraw-Hill, 1955, p. 330).

Earl Latham

See also: BALLOT
CONVENTION
ELECTION
NOMINATION

Primary Group (See **Group**)

Primitive

A. There are two uses of *primitive* in the social sciences.

1. One is modelled on usage in evolutionary biology from which it takes the meaning of ancestral, and, by extension, early in time, simple in form, and arrested in development, sometimes with the additional connotation of moral, aesthetic, or other inferiority.

2. The second usage eschews these meanings and attempts to delineate an area of reference or a class of phenomena through the application of a non-evaluative criterion, such as the group's being nonliterate (q.v.).

B. Most of the historical usages of *primitive* in anthropology have stressed the reference of the term as pointing to some early state of man either long past or, more frequently, surviving in the groups studied by the anthropologist.

1. One sense in which this term has been used is to designate an ancestral form or state. This is the meaning which is stressed by those who seek to know the origins and the developmental stages of artifacts, institutions, and man himself. Thus, 'By comparing the various stages of civilization among races known to history, with the aid of archaeological inference from the remains of pre-historic tribes, it seems possible to judge in a rough way of an early general condition of man, which from our point of view is to be regarded as a primitive condition, whatever yet earlier state may in reality have lain behind it' (E. B. Tyler, *Primitive Culture*, London: John Murray, 5th edn., 1913, vol. I, p. 21).

2. Closely allied with this usage, but with an added meaning, is the suggestion that an ancestral form has persisted relatively unchanged into modern times. It is structurally ancient but temporally present; it is a survival (q.v.). Elements of culture and whole groups of mankind have been interpreted in this way. The latter are preserved stages of human progress (L. H. Morgan, *Ancient Society*, London: Macmillan, 1877, p. vi). It is a culture, 'primitive' in this sense, (i.e. the aboriginal Australian) that E. A. Hooton had in mind when observing 'Meanwhile it behooves the social anthropologist to study and comprehend this fossilized society, the psychologist to investigate the mental processes of those exiguous brains, and the physical anthropologist to measure and observe the fleshly forms of these "contemporary ancestors" and carefully to preserve their bones' (*Up from the Ape*, New York: The Macmillan Co., 1931, p. 553).

3. Another historical connotation of *primitive* is that which is simple, uncomplicated or undifferentiated in structure or process—a usage which translates the meaning of *logical primitive*, any simple, underived element of thought, into culture history. The social evolutionists, by a process of eliminating the arts and customs of existing peoples, arrived at a postulated earliest logical state of mankind, without any contemporary representation. It was a phase of existence close to that of sub-human forms, lacking institutionalized behaviour, with the possible exception of language, amorphous, indiscriminate, and homogeneous (L. H. Morgan, *Ancient Society*, p. 20). While not necessarily adopting an evolutionary explanation of the phenomenon, many anthropologists and sociologists today hold the view that primitive societies are less complicated than the civilizations of the West or Far East. 'It is one of the philosophical justifications for the study of primitive peoples that the facts of simpler cultures may make clear social facts that are otherwise baffling and not open to demonstration' (R. Benedict, *Patterns of Culture*, Boston: Houghton Mifflin, 1934, p. 55).

4. *Primitive* has also meant pristine and uncorrupted. Thus Rousseau pictured the unfolding of human history as a regression from a state of individual freedom and equality to one of dominance by the rich who, fearing for their safety, conspired to defraud the poor by imposing on them laws which they did not comprehend. Other writers, including some non-evolutionary anthropologists, more sophisticated and with more data at hand, have maintained that some particular aspect of culture has degenerated from some primordial form through losses and adulterations.

5. For some theorists, *primitive* is a property of an elementary mentality which is qualitatively different from that of the mature, realistic,

Privilege

and rational individual. For Freud, the mind of primitive man has much in common with that of infants and neurotics in our own society (*Totem and Taboo*, London: Kegan Paul, Trench, Trubner, n.d., pp. 1–2). For L. Lévy-Bruhl, primitive mentality is dominated by 'collective representations' which are a-logical in that they typically disregard distinctions in time, place, state, and being (*The 'Soul' of the Primitive*, trans. by L. A. Clare, London: Allen & Unwin, 1928, pp. 15–55).

6. Among students of society in the past, and among laymen at present, a common referent of *primitive* is any state, attribute, or behaviour that is regarded as rude, coarse, vulgar, or inferior. Thus, Morgan viewed the stage of savagery, the earliest, according to him, in man's history as follows: 'The inferiority of savage man in the mental and moral scale, undeveloped, inexperienced, and held down by his low animal appetites and passions, though reluctantly recognized, is, nevertheless, substantially demonstrated by the remains of ancient art in flint stone and bone implements, by his cave life in certain areas, and by his osteological remains' (*Ancient Society*, p. 41).

C. A reaction to all these 'evaluational' uses of the term is evident at the present time in the social scientists' qualification of the term, as in the phrase, '*so-called primitive*'; or in their re-definition of it in some operational or neutral way: 'The Aztecs and Incas, for instance, are primitive only in the sense that they are usually studied by the anthropologist rather than by the historian and the sociologist' (G. P. Murdock, *Our Primitive Contemporaries*, New York: The Macmillan Co., 1934, p. viii). A common neutral definition hinges upon the use of writing: primitive societies are those whose members are nonliterate (q.v.). Another substitutes *tribal* in contexts where expressions such as *primitive cultures* otherwise appear. Yet another attempt at neutrality is evident in the use of the term *folk culture* (q.v.). Thus R. Redfield writes, 'I shall use "primitive" and "preliterate" interchangeably. I shall also use the phrase "folk society" ' (*The Primitive World and Its Transformations*, Ithaca, N. Y.: Cornell University Press, 1953, p. xi).

H. G. Barnett

See also: NONLITERATE

Principle of Limited Possibilities (See **Cultural Convergence**; **Cultural Parallelism**)

Principle of Substitution
(See **Substitution**)

Privilege

A. In general a *privilege* is a benefit or right enjoyed by a particular person or class of persons not shared with or available to the generality of persons. In the social sciences it denotes a special right, benefit, exemption, or immunity (legal, economic, or social) conferred by law or custom on a particular group, office, or class.

B. 1. The term, when used in political controversy, generally carries a pejorative implication that advantages derived from hereditary position or wealth are being enjoyed without regard to any principle of equity, e.g. 'Ours is still a class-conscious society in which class distinction is based largely on educational privilege' ('Personal Freedom', *Labour's Policy for the Individual and Society*, London: The Labour Party, Transport House, 1956, p. 7). There may, however, be an honorific implication when *privilege* is used as equivalent to *right* or *liberty*, e.g. 'By a constitutional policy working after the pattern of nature, we receive, we hold, we transmit our government and our privileges, in the same manner in which we enjoy and transmit our property and our lives' (E. Burke, *Reflections on the Revolution in France*, in *Works*, London: Rivington, 1852, vol. iv, p. 178). In this sense, the implication of discrimination remains only in the unstated assumption that all the members of a group or nation share some advantage not accorded (perhaps justly) to other groups or nations.

2. The term *privileges* occurs in a number of branches of the law. The following are examples: (a) the *absolute* or *qualified* privilege or protection from the legal consequences of defamatory statements made on certain occasions and for certain purposes (thus statements made in a legal judgement or by witnesses or counsel, or in the course of Parliamentary proceedings are absolutely privileged; a statement made in good faith in the course of a testimonial may enjoy qualified privilege); (b) the privilege of withholding certain categories of evidence, as, for example, of matters which tend to self incrimination, or of information transmitted from client to solicitor; (c) Crown privilege (a subcategory of (b))—the right of the Crown (in the United Kingdom) and therefore of government departments to withhold evidence on the ground that its publication would be inimical to the

public interest or the proper working of the public service.

In jurisprudence a special significance was given to the term *privilege* in W. N. Hohfeld's *Fundamental Legal Conceptions* (ed. by W. W. Cook, New Haven: Yale University Press, 1923, pp. 5–7) Hohfeld's scheme contains eight concepts in terms of which legal situations may be analysed, namely *privilege*, *duty*, *right*, *no-right*, *power*, *disability*, *immunity*, and *liability*. The essence of a privilege, according to Hohfeld, is the absence of duty on the part of its possessor. It is the freedom from the right or claim of another. Unlike the term *right* it does not assert the existence of a positive claim on or the possession of a correlative duty by another. Thus (it is argued) many things loosely described as *rights* ought properly to be called *privileges*.

In ordinary language, however, the existence of any legal privilege depends upon the existence of a legal rule which defines the way in which conflicting *rights* or *claims* may be reconciled and imposes a duty to refrain from acting in any way inconsistent with its provisions.

3. *Parliamentary privilege* in the United Kingdom implies both the possession of certain honorific traditional rights and liberties and the freedom of members of parliament from the legal consequences of certain actions. One of these has already been referred to above (immunity of parliamentary statements from actions for defamation). Other immunities or rights are the general right to freedom of speech in Parliament, the right to punish any action of an outside body which is adjudged by either House to constitute a contempt of its proceedings, and the right to determine the constitution of each House and the qualifications of its members. T. E. May (*Parliamentary Practice*, ed. by Sir E. Fellowes, T. B. Cocks, London: Butterworth, 16th edn., 1950, p. 42) defines Parliamentary privilege as: 'The sum of the peculiar rights enjoyed by each House collectively as a constituent part of the High Court of Parliament, and by members of each House individually, without which they could not discharge their functions, and which exceed those possessed by other bodies or individuals'. Thus privilege, it is added, 'though part of the law of the land, is to a certain extent an exemption from the ordinary law' (ibid). Most written constitutions provide for an analogous category of Parliamentary *immunities*.

G. Marshall

See also: CIVIL RIGHTS
            NATURAL RIGHT

Probability

A. The term *probability* refers to the estimation of likelihood incorporating a degree of belief in a probable or likely outcome. Actual estimates form a continuum of values, more or less precisely calculated, whose zero limit is impossibility, and which extends through bare possibility, high improbability, etc., to certainty. Two types of likelihood can be identified: (a) likelihood of the recurrence of an event in a series of occurrences, and (b) likelihood of the confirmation of a proposition by less than complete data.

B. 1. The term has a long history in philosophy and has been most used in philosophical and mathematical discussions of induction. Bishop Butler observed 'To me probability is the very guide of life', denoting a way of reasoning from which probable, as distinct from certain, conclusions emerge (J. Butler, *The Analogy of Religion*, London: Knapton, 1736, p. iii).

2. *Probability* is used in two different ways in sociological literature.

(a) First is *classical probability* which P. H. Furfey (*The Scope and Method of Sociology*, New York: Harper & Bros., 1953, p. 65) defines as 'the ratio of the number of times an event occurs in a given way to the total number of occurrences'. Two sub-forms can be identified. *Chance* or *intuitive probability* may be illustrated by the proposition: The probability that an unbiased coin when tossed will show heads is 0.5. *Actuarial* or *calculated probability* is illustrated by the proposition: The probability that a white male, just twenty years old, will die within a year is 0.00212.

(b) Second, *inferential probability* refers to the degree of confirmation of a proposition by less than complete empirical data.

(i) Referring to Weber's work, T. Parsons says 'When it is necessary to make a very complex judgment of causal imputation, as in the relation of the Protestant ethic to modern capitalism, the historical individual concerned must be analysed into a larger number of type-units. Each of these must be subjected to judgments of probability as to its line of development under the relevant circumstances ... the judgment can be only one of probability ... "Probability" here means only an expression of our failure to attain completely accurate empirical knowledge' (*The Structure of Social Action*, Glencoe, Ill.: The Free Press, 1949, pp. 629–30).

(ii) One tool in probability inference is the *probability sample* which M. L. Mark (*Statistics*

537

Process

in the Making, Columbus: Ohio State University Bureau of Business Research, 1958, p. 102) says 'leads to inference as to the nature of the parent universe rather than to exact description of it; to the indirect knowledge derived by induction rather than the direct knowledge derived from exhaustive observation and measurement'.

Joseph S. Himes

See also: PREDICTION
SAMPLING

Probability Sampling (See **Sampling**)

Process
A. 1. In sociology the term is usually prefaced by the word *social*. *Social process*, though often used, is unfortunately one of the most vague terms in sociology. At one extreme it is a general term which can denote almost *any* aspect of social interaction (q.v.). At the other extreme it can denote a continuous sequence of social activities rigorously defined on the basis of empirical research. In its most frequent use the term means a transition or series of transitions between one social condition and another. Among some sociologists a distinction is made between *the social process* and the *social processes*. *The* social process is seen by them to be social interaction and is the prerequisite for social activity of any sort. All of the other so-called social processes are only more specific forms of interaction. In the 1920s and 30s standard American sociology texts devoted up to one third of their total content to the social processes while by the late 1950s many introductory texts made no mention of the term. Interesting in this respect is one widely used text which in its various editions devotes decreasing space to the concept until the third edition uses it not at all (W. F. Ogburn & M. F. Nimkoff, *Sociology*, Boston: Houghton Mifflin, 1st edn., 1940; 2nd edn., 1950; 3rd edn., 1958).

2. The biological heritage of sociology is clearly reflected in its use of the concept. In the late 19th century the idea that biological structures change by means of definite processes led social scientists to hunt for these same processes in social structure. The work of Gumplowicz is basic in regard to this aspect of social process theory. He believed that the natural process involves the reciprocal interaction of diverse elements. Things that are identical and have no separate existence do not interact. Where there is no interaction there is no process. The two essential factors in any natural process, therefore, are diverse elements and mutual interaction (F. N. House, *Development of Sociology*, New York: McGraw-Hill, 1936, ch. XIV).

3. Gumplowicz's primary emphasis was on the social processes of conflict (q.v.) and competition (q.v.), but later theorists, such as Kropotkin, emphasized the importance of the concept of co-operation. As the concept of the social processes matured in the early 20th century, these two fundamentally different kinds of relationship became the base for a dichotomous classification of social processes, those which are associative or conjunctive and those which are dissociative or disjunctive. The former included such processes as co-operation (q.v.), accommodation (q.v.), and assimilation (q.v.) while the latter included the processes of competition, contravention, and conflict. While some classifications embody only two categories, the associative and dissociative, others go into minute classification, and under contravention, for example, would further include rebuffing, repulsing, restraining, disparaging, deprecating, circumventing, harassing, and numerous other terms.

Although the associative and dissociative were conceived as being fundamentally different types of process, social relations were thought to shift from one to the other as when two groups which have been in conflict decide to accommodate themselves to one another, then co-operate, and then may become assimilated or amalgamated. Also present, although rarely explicit, in process theory is some idea of equilibrium or homeostasis. Dissociative processes tend to break down the internal equilibrium of a group or of groups in contact while the associative processes tend to restore equilibrium, usually a new equilibrium related to but unlike that existing before a particular process occurred.

4. In its fundamental aspects social process is a concept of movement, change, flux. One of its most important functions in the development of social theory has been to stimulate a sense of time sequence. Social process theory thus represents an important reaction against static theories and theories of structure. It was the dynamic aspect of process theory which most attracted adherents at the University of Chicago where it became highly systematized and even institutionalized. Seen from the point of view of the sociology of knowledge it is perhaps no accident that process theory was developed by men who were living and working in the centre of a dynamic and changing city in the centre of

538

a new society. Social process theory is characteristically opposed to the conception of society as structure, or society as a formal or static arrangement of blocks of material. It views society as a succession of frames on a movie film rather than a single snapshot. While the Chicago school of social process theory furnished an important antidote to undue emphasis on structure, it has not been fruitful as an experimental tool of analysis. Exceptions to this statement would be E. W. Burgess's theory of invasion (q.v.) and succession (q.v.) in urban ecology and R. E. Park's theory of the race relations cycle. Burgess notes four steps in ecological succession: initial movement into an area, reaction on the part of occupants, general influx of newcomers and climax ('Residential Segregation in American Cities', *Annals of the American Academy of Political and Social Science*, vol. 140, 1928, p. 112). The important processes here are competition and conflict for scarce space. Park saw in the race relations situation competition, accommodation, assimilation, and amalgamation recurring in an almost inevitable cycle (*Race and Culture*, Glencoe, Ill.: The Free Press, 1950).

5. Perhaps the reason why social process theory has not been more productive of solid experimental findings is because it has been employed mainly at the macroscopic level where rigorous methodological procedures are difficult. One outstanding attempt to apply social process theory at the microscopic level is R. F. Bales's 'interaction process analysis'. Using highly rigorous research techniques, Bales has found social process patterns in experimental problem-solving small groups (*Interaction Process Analysis: A Method for the Study of Small Groups*, Cambridge, Mass.: Addison-Wesley, 1950). Bales's system implies competition for scarce resources in the group (control of outcome, freedom of control from others, and time) and the solution of the problem also involves accommodation and co-operation. The problem is solved when equilibrium is re-established in the group.

B. Among anthropologists, the study of social process has been concentrated in two areas, (a) acculturation, and (b) cultural emphasis on particular social processes. The acculturation studies of anthropologists are not unlike the concern of the Chicago school with assimilation and amalgamation. The anthropologists have investigated the conditions of interaction and the re-establishment of equilibrium of cultures

in contact (Social Science Research Seminar on Acculturation, 'Acculturation: An Exploratory Formulation', *American Anthropologist*, vol. 56, 1954, pp. 973–1000). R. Benedict, M. Mead, and others have shown that a particular culture will emphasize one social process, such as competition, in its characteristic problem-solving patterns while another culture will emphasize some other social process (M. Mead (ed.), *Co-operation and Competition among Primitive Peoples*, New York: McGraw-Hill, 1937).

An important article by E. Z. Vogt calls attention to the neglect of social process in anthropology and presents a theory of social process in terms of tension or conflict between the elements of a society ('On the Concepts of Structure and Process in Cultural Anthropology', *American Anthropologist*, vol. 62, 1960, pp. 18–33).

C. The term *political process* has been much used in the literature of political science (see A. F. Bentley, *The Process of Government*, Chicago: University of Chicago Press, 1908; and D. B. Truman, *The Governmental Process*, New York: Knopf, 1951). A recent paper by Professor W. Harrison distinguishes three main senses of the term ('Political Processes', *Political Studies*, vol. VI, 1958, pp. 234–52).

1. The term reflects a way of talking about politics current among those who are highly preoccupied with 'movement and change' as the sole aspect of significance in politics.

2. In other writers the use of the term is linked to, and is part of, the wider notion that 'constantly repeated patterns of change are bound to be found universally in politics because politics are bound to be governed by *process* laws'. Such an analogy with natural science represents 'aspiration, and possibly misguided aspiration'.

3. The third use centres upon the notion of 'procedure' as in such phrases as 'legislative process' and the 'nominating process', i.e. it refers to an 'isolable complex of interactions between procedural rules, individual statuses and activities and attitudes, and the internal and external relations of various kinds of social groups'. Professor Harrison comments that (a) not all areas of political analysis operate in accordance with rules of procedure; (b) 'processes', even in this linkage with 'procedures' are not marked off from each other by clear and definite boundaries and thus do not form distinct units of political research; (c) to describe certain general aspects

Productivity

of political process (e.g. legislative process) is to invite the risk of undue abstraction and possible misuse in cross-national comparative study.

Russell L. Langworthy

See also: Accommodation
Assimilation
Competition
Conflict
Co-operation
Invasion
Social
Social Interaction
Succession

Producers' Capital (See **Capital**)

Producers' Surplus (See **Surplus**)

Productivity

A. *Productivity* in its broadest sense denotes the ratio of useful results obtained to the resources expended in obtaining them. The resources expended (the input) and the results obtained (the output) are generally expressed in terms of physical quantities, but output may be measured either in physical quantities or in value units. The most commonly used application of this definition relates output to labour time input, usually calculating output per man-hour.

B. The term includes a family of concepts each involving some comparison of output with its related input. Both output and input are measured in specified physical or value units. The specific meaning assigned to the broad concept of *productivity* depends upon the purposes of its measurement which vary from one inquiry to another. As B. Gold (*Foundations of Productivity Analysis*, Pittsburgh: University of Pittsburgh Press, 1955, p. 10) contends, '... no single measure of productivity adjustments can serve effectively in making the appraisals needed for a variety of dissimilar purposes'.

1. Productivity studies may be 'input centred' or 'output centred'. This specific meaning of *productivity* will vary accordingly. (a) Input studies may be 'resource oriented' and analyse the extent of utilization of productive factors, or they may be 'user oriented' and deal with the input requirements necessary to achieve output goals. (b) Output studies may be 'producer oriented' and face the problems of increasing output with given inputs, or they may be 'buyer oriented' and focus upon the volume and price

of goods and services made available. The economic level at which analysis is to take place also influences the definition of *productivity* used. Comparisons of input and output may be made at the job, department, plant, company, industry, group of industry, regional, national, and international levels. The broader the economic scope of the investigation, the more difficult it is to utilize physical measurements, particularly of output.

2. Productivity definitions may relate output to a wide variety of inputs. Such inputs may be: persons in the population, workers, man-hours, units of capital, machine-hours, acres of land, kilowatt hours of electricity, gallons of gasoline, square feet of store floor-space and others. The most common measures of *productivity* compare output with the amount of labour expended in its production. Labour time is usually measured in man-hours to avoid the errors involved in gauging productive effort by the number of workers employed. Even when it is decided to use man-hours to define productivity, definitional questions remain concerning the inclusion of supervisory, maintenance, clerical, and other indirect labour and the use of man-hours paid for as against the actual man-hours worked.

3. 'When the term *productivity* is used without other qualification, labor productivity is ordinarily meant ...' (W. D. Evans, in W. S. Woytinsky and Associates, *Employment and Wages in the United States*, New York: The Twentieth Century Fund, 1953, p. 63) even though 'labour efficiency' or 'physical output per man-hour' would more accurately describe most of these ratios. P. O. Steiner and W. Goldner defend the use of labour time as the unit of input because, '... first, it is present in all production; second, because we are a society of men, not machines, we are especially interested in how man's efforts are used; third, better statistical records exist for employment and hours worked than for most other factors that serve as inputs' (*Productivity*, Berkeley, Cal.: Institute of Industrial Relations, 1953, p. 6). Furthermore, labour time data are usually presumed to be homogeneous, although actually skill and effort vary.

4. Definitions of *productivity* which measure inputs solely by the labour time expended may lead to distortions. They tend to confuse *labour productivity* with 'labourers' productivity'. They may also understate or overstate the actual change in output relative to input because comparative quantities or qualities of inputs other than labour may change during the

540

period under examination. Thus, it is more accurate to state with P. F. Drucker (*The Practice of Management*, London: Heinemann, 1955, p. 33) that 'Productivity means that balance between *all* factors of production that will give the greatest output for the smallest effort'. 'Only by relating output to all tangible inputs can it be determined whether there has been a *net* saving in real costs per unit of output, or conversely, a gain in productivity' (J. W. Kendrick, 'Productivity Trends: Capital and Labor', *Review of Economics and Statistics*, vol. XXXVIII, 1956, p. 248). Thus in a later discussion J. W. Kendrick specifies the role of indices of (a) *capital productivity* (an output capital ratio) which indicate 'economies achieved over time in the use of capital per unit of output' and (b) *total factor productivity* which is based on capital as well as labour input ('Productivity Costs and Prices: Concepts and Measures', in American Assembly, *Wages, Prices, Profits and Productivity*, New York: The American Assembly, Columbia University, 1959, p. 45).

Use of all-inclusive definitions of input makes it necessary to select a common denominator in which to express the various inputs and to develop a system of weighting to reflect their relative importance. To meet this need, measurement of inputs by their embodied labour content or by their costs at constant prices have been suggested, but each of these approaches has its difficulties (*Summary of Proceedings of Conference on Productivity*, Washington, D.C.: U.S. Govt. Printing Office, 1946, p. 11). Such broad definitions also emphasize the limitations of purely physical measures of productivity for '... it must be recognized', according to Gold, 'that every change in physical relationships takes place within a particular valuational context; that any such change might not take place if the valuational context were different ...' (B. Gold, *Foundations of Productivity Analysis*, p. 11).

5. Output as well as input may be stated in either physical or value terms in productivity ratios. The problems stemming from multiple products and quality changes make it increasingly difficult to use physical measures if the level of analysis of productivity is raised from the job to the industry and to the nation. For some sectors of the economy, including the service and trade industries, government and military, there appears to be no definable unit of output, hence, no workable definitions of productivity can be constructed for them.

To solve problems of distribution and employment, theoretical economics seeks to determine the 'contribution' attributable to each factor of production. Here, *productivity* ultimately must be measured in value units. In this context, as S. Fabricant states, '... productivity may be the relation between the total output and input of a period, or it may be the relation between the increment in output associated with the addition of one unit of a given factor of production; that is, it may be "average" or "marginal" ...' (*Summary of Proceedings of Conference on Productivity*, p. 2).

6. Many factors affect *productivity*. Most definitions accent the influence of: quality of manpower, state of labour relations, employee morale, quality of capital resources, quality and kinds of materials, availability of power, availability of supplies, production processes, production organization, and weather. Physical measures, however, have difficulty in coping with changes in the proportions of either inputs or outputs, new product designs or changed demand. Furthermore, some writers plead for a sharp distinction between increases and decreases in productivity caused by changes in the degree of plant utilization, *volume productivity*, and increases caused by improvements of production or organization, *real productivity* (J. Hirsch, 'Productivity in War and Peace', *American Economic Review*, vol. 37, 1947, p. 402).

7. For extended discussion of the conceptual problems involved, see L. Rostás, *Comparative Productivity in British and American Industry* (Cambridge: University Press, 1948, esp. pp. 1–25); and J. W. Kendrick 'Productivity Trends, Capital and Labor'; (*Occasional Paper* 53, Washington: National Bureau of Economic Research, 1956).

H. Ellsworth Steele

Profane

A. In general use *profane* is that which is unholy, irreverent, blasphemous, defiled, or opposed to the religious. It is also that which is ordinary, common, unconsecrated, temporal, or outside the religious. Thus to profane is to treat the religious with irreverence or contempt or to cause the unholy to be defiled or desecrated by improper contact with the ordinary and unconsecrated.

B. In the social sciences the term mainly means the ordinary and non-religious. In this sense whatever is not religious is profane. When B. Malinowski observes that the 'collective effervescence' of Melanesians at work is 'entirely profane ('Magic, Science and Religion',

Professions

in J. Needham (ed.), *Science, Religion and Reality*, London: Sheldon Press, 1925, p. 55), he is not saying that it is wicked or irreligious. He means only that it is non-religious. E. Durkheim was applying a similar meaning when he wrote: 'The division of the world into two domains, the one containing all that is sacred, the other all that is profane, is the distinctive trait of religious thought ...' (*The Elementary Forms of the Religious Life*, trans by J. W. Swain, London: Allen & Unwin, 1915, p. 37). K. Davis is quite definite in including both the ordinary and the unholy, the irreligious and the non-religious in his use of profane: 'When the term "profane" occurs, it is used to embrace both the ordinary and the unholy. This usage is followed because the unholy generally consists of an unauthorized contact between the ordinary and the holy' (*Human Society*, New York: The Macmillan Co., 1948, p. 520).

Luke Ebersole

See also: SACRED

Professions

A. In its more general application the term denotes occupations which demand a highly specialized knowledge and skill acquired at least in part by courses of a more or less theoretical nature and not by practice alone, tested by some form of examination either at a university or some other authorized institution, and conveying to the persons who possess them considerable authority in relation to 'clients'.

Such authority is carefully maintained and often deliberately heightened by guildlike associations of the practitioners (*professional associations*) which lay down rules of entry, training, and behaviour in relation to the public (*professional ethics*), see to it that the standard of knowledge and skill of the practitioners is not lowered, defend the level of their professional remuneration, try to prevent competing groups from encroaching upon the boundaries of their professional activities, and watch over the preservation of their professional status.

At present the term usually denotes certain occupations whose members give service rather than engage in the production and distribution of goods: those occupations are normally *excluded* whose members sell goods over the counter (or openly) for profit, or do manual work, except in cases, such as surgeons, pharmacists, or some groups of engineers, in which selling or manual work demand forms of knowledge and skill which can only be acquired by means of a scientific training.

B. It is important, historically, to distinguish narrower and wider usages as follows:

1. In the narrower and older sense the term refers to the professions of divinity, law and medicine, the first occupations that gave to people not living on unearned income a chance to make a living which did not involve trade or manual work. It has been extended to include the army and the naval profession.

2. In the wider and more recent sense it refers to all people with an academic training and degree or its equivalent, such as scientists, teachers, sociologists, civil servants, or architects.

3. In accordance with a strong trend in the development of industrial societies the meaning of the term has been still further extended to include occupations that require some scientific training and knowledge, though not necessarily of university standard, and a diploma or certificate, usually based on examinations, for the exercise of their specific occupational skills (*minor profession, professional auxiliaries*).

N. Elias

See also: OCCUPATION

Profit

A. The summary given here refers to prevalent modern usage only.

1. The broadest theoretical definition may be stated as follows: *Profits* are the income (positive or negative) that arises because the economy is dynamic—i.e. because there is change, foresight is imperfect, and there are lags and frictions in adaptation to change.

2. The pure uncertainty definitions identify profits (positive or negative) as residual, non-functional incomes reflecting luck or chance. There are profits of this kind in all actual incomes received in a dynamic society. In some theories an institutional compromise is introduced, excluding from the definition any components of contractual incomes.

3. Focusing on those functions that arise because a society is dynamic, profits (positive or negative) are defined as returns to the exercise of these functions, called *entrepreneurial functions*. The nature of the functions perceived and included varies from one theory to another, and they may be in part 'socially disfunctional'. The uncertainty component is generally viewed as inseparable from the exercise of entrepreneurial functions, though not necessarily the reverse, unless *passive* 'uncertainty bearing' is defined as an entrepreneurial function. Functional profits constitute an element in all those incomes, contractual as well as non-contractual, that accrue in part in payment for performance of entrepreneurial functions. However, contractual entrepreneurial incomes are usually visualized as components of incomes of business executives only, and passive 'uncertainty-bearing' is recognized as an 'entrepreneurial function' (if at all) only when it involves owners of capital in some form.

4. Profits are defined as the difference between the gross revenues of an enterprise and all costs, including as costs imputed interest and wages of management. This is essentially the text-book model used in treatment of profits in the theory of the firm. It differs from accounting profits primarily in the exclusion of imputed interest and imputed wages of management. It is also the definition most amenable to statistical analysis, though arbitrary estimates for imputed costs are required. In this definition *profits* include not only returns that reflect the dynamic nature of the economy, but also permanent *monopoly profits*, more properly termed *monopoly rents*.

5. Profits are defined as the net revenue of an enterprise (as in (4) but excluding monopoly rent and quasi-rents. There are several variants, depending upon the treatment of quasi-rents and the nature of the ex ante (or cost) base with which ex post returns are compared. Moreover, either functional or non-functional interpretations of the nature of profits may be involved. This definition may therefore break down into either (2) or (3), but with the exclusion of all components of contractual incomes.

B. No special technical meaning is attached to the term *profit* in any of the social sciences except economics—where it is usually used in the plural, as *profits*. Within economics, profit concepts may be roughly grouped into three (overlapping) main types: (a) *profits* as incomes accruing to institutionally identified categories of income receivers, (b) *profits* (positive or negative) as a theoretically abstracted, residual, non-functional income, (c) *profits* as returns (positive or negative) for the performance of entrepreneurial functions. One of the major arenas in which the battles over profit concepts, and the compromises in these battles, have occurred is thus the no-man's and every-man's land between concepts (a) and (b) above. The other arena is where the proponents of functionalism, disfunctionalism, and non-functionalism meet.

1. In classical economics *profits* were the income accruing to the business class, or *capitalists*. In their attempt to analyse the incomes of the three major socio-economic groups—landlords, labourers, and capitalists—classical economists viewed profits as a residual after payments for wages and rents. Marx dropped the distinction between land and capital, defining profits as all non-labour income. This definition occasionally appears in modern writing, by non-Marxians as well as Marxians, although it is remote from the main streams of thought. The modern variant of strict institutionalism more often defines profits as they appear in business accounting or on tax returns, identifying profits with business net income (gross before and net after taxes), which vary in content with shifting provisions of tax laws, business accounting practices, etc.

2. The refinement and elaboration of analytical components of the classical profit concept, the exclusion of some of them from profits, and the addition of newly perceived analytical elements mark the transition from a strictly institutional toward a more theoretical approach. The English classicists themselves took the first step; although they did not separate these components out as distinct theoretical types of income, they nevertheless recognized three: wages of management, interest, and a premium for risk. Meanwhile, J. B. Say in France distinguished interest from profits, regarding profits as a special kind of wage (and hence a complex, but functional, income). And von Thünen in Germany (1826) defined profits as a residual after deducting interest, insurance for risk, and wages of management. Modern economists, even those closest to an institutional approach, exclude both contractual and imputed interest and 'wages of management'; i.e. payment for strictly managerial as distinct from entrepreneurial functions.

At the other extreme from institutional approaches, Walras made a major, if negative, contribution by defining the characteristics of a general static competitive equilibrium system—in which there would be no *profit* income. Stemming essentially from this approach, modern theories are concerned with incomes that accrue because the economy is not static. While some include monopoly incomes that would accrue in a static economy which was not purely competitive throughout, such permanent *monopoly profits* are more properly termed *monopoly rent* and will not be discussed further here.

Progress

3. Given the Walrasian theory, the basic theoretical problem became one of identifying and analysing those components of income attributable to economic change, imperfect foresight, and the frictions or lags in adjustment to change. Identifying the components of non-static income raises the further question as to which of these are *profits*.

Those who view profits as a non-functional residual rather than payment for some economic function emphasize the elements of luck or chance. The first essential step was to distinguish between those risks or uncertainties that are insurable or otherwise transformable into determinate ex post or predictable costs, and those that are not. *Pure* or *windfall profits* are then defined as residual incomes accruing because of non-insurable, non-transformable uncertainties and the frictions or time lags in adjustment to unanticipated or incorrectly anticipated change. They have no functional meaning.

The functional view of profits first identifies those functions that arise only because the economy is dynamic. Windfall or uncertainty elements in profits are then seen as inseparable from the performance of these functions, though in some cases 'uncertainty bearing' may itself be regarded as a 'function'.

4. Knight's concept constitutes a significant bridge from the pure uncertainty definitions toward the functionalist concepts. Pointing out that uncertainty is associated fundamentally with economic change, he then considered the special kinds of ability required in the entrepreneurial role of bearing the uncertainty and making the decisions involved in responding to and introducing change. Thus, profit became a payment for the functions necessitated by change: a reward for uncertainty-bearing and decision-making jointly.

Subsequent writers who define profits in this way have argued at length as to what the *entrepreneurial function* is. On the one hand there is forecasting of and adaptation to external change. On the other, entrepreneurs may initiate change. Broadly, two types are often distinguished: innovative change and manipulations for monopolistic market position. This distinction is not clear-cut, since an innovator obtains temporary monopolistic advantage. But, whether to the benefit or detriment of society as a whole, all of these entrepreneurial activities are *functional* in that they are directed to the obtaining of net income—i.e. profits.

5. The *innovation* theory has a special place in profit theory because of Schumpeter's emphasis on it. Defining innovation so broadly as to make it almost synonymous with initiating change, he saw returns to innovation as the dominant element in profits. This is one of the few profit theories interwoven with a theory of economic growth and fluctuation. Schumpeter attributed the first definite formulation of an innovation theory of profits to J. B. Clark, and pointed out that both Ricardo and Marx occasionally mentioned returns to innovation as an element in classical profits.

6. As noted, those incomes derived from permanent monopoly advantage are more properly termed monopoly rent than monopoly profit. Logically this would exclude all monopolistic returns essentially static in nature. But in a dynamic society there is a continuous juggling for market position and for monopolistic advantage. Some modern writers focus on this as *the* true cause of profits. There is usually a polemical element in such theories, which attack *functional* concepts on the grounds that they ignore behaviour that is essentially restrictive, predatory, and socially disfunctional. Note the implication of a social (rather than a private gain) interpretation of *functional*. Instead of the old Marxian profits of exploitation, resting on a labour theory of value, these modern theories find the chief source of profits in monopolistic efforts that set one businessman apart from another.

Mary Jean Bowman

See also: Entrepreneur
Interest (Economics)
Rent
Risk and Uncertainty

Progress

A. The term *progress* is commonly used to signify any movement in a desired direction. In the field of politics the idea of progress implies *specific* values. Thus if we are to judge whether or not progress has occurred in society, we must be apprised not only of the period of time over which the measurement is to take place but of the *standard of value* to be applied.

B. Historical and scientific usage follow the sense outlined above and in essence the meaning has changed little since the 18th century, although those who employ the term today tend to evince a more cautious confidence.

1. Given the strong ethical connotation, the

544

term generally implies an *egalitarian* norm or at any rate a conception of justice which embraces equality as well as equity. 'I believe that the eighteenth-century thinkers were right in regarding progress as a movement towards "reason and justice" and in laying stress on equality as the core of justice' (M. Ginsberg, *The Idea of Progress: a Revaluation*, London: Methuen, 1953, p. 68).

2. Necessary conditions for the growth of belief in the idea of human progress were (a) the elimination of the medieval belief that the world was destined to end in a proximate future, (b) the discoveries of the Renaissance and the revolutionary advances in scientific enquiry which confirmed men's faith in the power of reason to control nature, (c) the development of faith in the tendency of the human mind to become more reasonable.

3. (a) In the 19th century the belief came to embody the conviction (e.g. Hegel and Marx) that natural laws at work within the *historical process* guaranteed progress. This belief seemed to many to receive confirmation from the theory of evolution (q.v.) propounded by the biologists. The belief in progress was, moreover, attuned to the confidence of the 19th century; and for long progress consisted largely of the faith that *technological changes would probably continue indefinitely to enrich human society by advancing prosperity, improving communications, and generally making people happier.* The superficial elements in this idea made it peculiarly vulnerable to the major setbacks sustained by Western society in the great wars and genocide campaigns of the 20th century.

(b) In current usage, it is unusual except in Marxist writings for the term to carry with it any suggestion of inevitable historical law. It remains an important concept embodying the *moral aspirations of those who feel impatience with things as they are.* Critics of the idea point to its vagueness as a general criterion or maintain that historical evidence provides no warrant for any supposition other than that man 'has seen all that has been and shall be'.

4. Although logically, *progress* cannot be said to be the opposite of *tradition* since the possibility of progress depends on the ability of each generation to assimilate its predecessor's stock of knowledge, *progress* is frequently contrasted with *tradition*. A belief in progress is likely to stem from rational principles in the light of which existent reality is measured and found wanting. *Progress* thus contrasts with *tradition*

as conceived by those who suspect abstract rational principle and mistrust change.

R. V. Sampson

See also: CIVILIZATION
　　　　　CULTURAL EVOLUTION
　　　　　EVOLUTION
　　　　　TRADITION

Projection

A. In its widest sense *projection* refers to the attribution of traits or motives by partners in a situation involving interaction. These attributions are ones on which there would be broad consensus among the partners. If psychoanalytic defining criteria are added: (a) the motives attributed must be only 'bad'; (b) in the perception of 'self' and 'other' a shift must occur in which a trait formerly conceived as belonging to the 'self' is ascribed to the 'other' but consensus is missing; and (c) the process must provide some psychological gain, expression of an impulse, or temporary reduction of anxiety, i.e. it must be a defence mechanism.

B. 1. The original usage of this concept is the psychoanalytic one in which it is one of the defence mechanisms (q.v.) against anxiety. In this sense, unacceptable wishes and impulses, the recognition of which in the self might cause discomfort, are ascribed to others. Freud ('Psychoanalytic Notes Upon an Autobiographical Account of a Case of Paranoia', in *Collected Papers*, London: Hogarth Press, 1925, vol. III) first delineated the mechanism in relating paranoia and homosexuality. He held that homosexual impulses are first denied, then changed to hatred by reaction formation, and finally projected, i.e. perceived as hatred and persecution by others.

2. R. R. Sears ('Experimental Analysis of Psychoanalytic Phenomena', in J. McV. Hunt (ed.), *Personality and the Behavior Disorders*, New York: Ronald Press, 1944, vol. I, pp. 324–7) states that of all the technical terms of psychoanalysis *projection* has been the least adequately defined. Hence it has been used in a variety of ways among which Sears (ibid.) attempts to distinguish. Only a few of these will be mentioned here. Speaking of the 'attribution of traits', he notes that some researchers have held an 'ideas of reference' interpretation. In this, projection of feelings of self-criticism results in 'ideas of reference'. He finds a relationship between them in his own research, although he is not certain that feelings of self-criticism are

Projection

temporally prior. Although feelings of self-criticism are hardly socially reprehensible, they might cause considerable anxiety and require a defence. In this sense this usage also is much like the primary one noted above.

Another usage mentioned by Sears (ibid.) does depart from the one above. That is the usage referring in a general way to any motivationally determined perception. This is the sense in which projection is used in the concept of projective tests. In such tests, perception is considered to be a function of the needs and motives of the personality. Since there is no attribution of motives in an interpersonal situation except in a very indirect sense in the case of the T.A.T., and since there is none of the aspect of defence mechanism and the reduction of anxiety about this usage, it can hardly be called projection at all.

C. A second important usage has its theoretical roots in the analysis of interaction and communication. Projection is seen as part of a general 'anticipatory response' (K. Young, *Personality and Problems of Adjustment*, London: Kegan Paul, Trench, Trubner, 1947, pp. 118–9) involving perception and assessment of another's gestures in guiding one's own actions. Anticipating the possible reactions of others involves taking 'the role of the other' which requires people to 'project themselves into each other's points of view' according to A. R. Lindesmith and A. L. Strauss (*Social Psychology*, New York: Dryden Press, 1949, p. 310). This is possible only when interaction becomes defined in terms of abstract categories mediated by language. From the point of view of the individual actor there is projection here in two senses. In the first place there is projection in the attribution to the 'other' of some abstract motive or expectancy of behaviour appropriate to a role. In the second place there is projection of the 'self' into the point of view of the 'other' in the sense that the actor understands the content of the attributed role or motive. Motives and role definitions attributed can be either 'good' or 'bad' but are always appropriate for various actions since being derived from language they have already been subjected to consensual validation. In this sense of 'taking the role of the other' projection is made almost synonymous with empathy (q.v.).

Although this usage also implies the attribution of motives, it is not identical with the psychoanalytic usage. There is an emphasis on the general social definition of any situation involving interaction while in the psychoanalytic usage there is emphasis on the distortion of consensus by an idiosyncratic view of the 'self' and the 'other' and stress upon the reduction of intra-psychic conflict.

D. A third important usage of the concept represents an attempt to apply the psychoanalytic meaning to explain certain social phenomena. In this usage unwanted traits in the self are attributed to members of a group, a racial or minority group. Thus the laziness of the Negro and the greed of the Jew are but reflections of the greed and sloth of the attributers. G. W. Allport (*The Nature of Prejudice*, Cambridge, Mass.: Addison-Wesley, 1954, pp. 382–92) distinguishes between direct projection, mote-beam projection, and complementary projection.

The distinction between direct projection and mote-beam projection is one of degree. In direct projection the trait or motive attributed is not at all characteristic of the person to whom it is attributed, while in mote-beam projection the trait attributed is possessed by the person to whom attributed but not to the degree indicated. The distinction does not seem too crucial. In complementary projection, also distinguished by H. A. Murray ('The Effect of Fear upon Estimates of the Maliciousness of other Personalities', *Journal of Social Psychology*, vol. IV, 1933, pp. 310–29) the person doing the attributing does not have the trait being attributed but rather possesses a trait which requires the one being attributed in order to complete or 'complement' the projector's trait and make it understandable and reasonable. Thus the fearful person has to find reasons for his fear by seeing menacing behaviour in others. This would seem to be a form of rationalization (q.v.) rather than of projection. The two of Allport's usages which are clearly projection seem to fall within the primary usage above.

T. W. Adorno, E. Frenkel-Brunswik, et al. (*The Authoritarian Personality*, New York: Harper & Brothers, 1950) using projection in the same sense, argue that in highly prejudiced persons problems in the area of authority cause hostility toward authority which is projected on to minority groups.

Thomas Ktsanes

See also: DEFENCE MECHANISM
EMPATHY
RATIONALIZATION (Social Psychology)
REPRESSION

Proletariat

A. *Proletariat* in the most general sense means the lowest class of the community, however this is conceived. In a widely used (but more specific sense) it denotes a poor industrial class of manual workers, owning no significant capital and forced to sell their labour in order to subsist. This latter sense, however, has been subject to considerable extension under changed conditions and has become more confused, as poverty, lack of capital, manual work, etc., have been variously used as the distinguishing factor(s).

B. 1. In Ancient Rome the *proletarii* were the lowest class of the community, regarded as contributing nothing to the state but children.
2. In Europe right up to the 19th century the term was applied loosely, and generally contemptuously, to an alleged lowest class of the community. The meaning varies with what is regarded as socially 'low', the test(s) being in different degrees poverty, squalor, idleness, manual labour, ignorance, criminality, etc.

C. 1. More modern usage follows B. (2) above and is blended with the Marxist usage which is discussed below—with the latter usage tending to be dominant. The class of persons indicated normally has one or more of the following marks: (a) industrial occupation, (b) manual labour, (c) poverty, (d) absence of capital ownership. Thus the most precise use is for a class of *poor industrial manual workers who have no capital*, with extensions freely made according to which mark is insisted upon or ignored. Hence, 'proletarianization of the white-collar workers' refers mainly at present to their relative decrease in income; whereas 'proletarianization of the peasantry' refers to their exchange of private ownership of land for communal ownership, though perhaps increasing their income. If manual workers command higher wages, or wealthy citizens live from labour (manual or otherwise) rather than capital; or if there are poor landlords or shareholders, the attributes give conflicting results and extensions of the term are proportionately obscure. Largely owing to Marxist influence *proletariat* is no longer automatically pejorative.
2. In Marxist usage the term is extended to include both industrial wage-earners and agricultural labourers (sometimes these are distinguished as the *industrial proletariat* and *agricultural proletariat*); and in its widest meaning—to include anyone who owns little or no capital and must live from work.

Though poverty is clearly implied, the most persistent element in Marxist usages is absence of capital and, however poor, classes owning capital (such as the peasantry) are normally kept distinct (see K. Marx & F. Engels, *Manifesto of the Communist Party*, in *Selected Works*, London: Lawrence & Wishart, 1953, vol. I, p. 42).
3. Since 1937 official Soviet usage has not applied the term to the working class of 'socialist societies'.

J. H. Warrender

See also: COMMUNISM
WORKING CLASS

Propaganda

A. *Propaganda* denotes (a) the techniques and methods of influencing or controlling the attitudes, opinions, and behaviour of men by the use of words and other symbols; (b) the statements or impressions issuing from the use of such techniques or methods and sometimes also deeds or actions which, mediated through publicity, are primarily 'propagandist' in function or purpose.

B. 1. It seems to be generally accepted that *propaganda* describes modes of influencing conduct where there exists controversy or an issue to be resolved. Thus R. S. Lambert thinks of it as an instrument of conflict or 'war' used in ideological, economic, and physical conflicts (*Propaganda*, London: Nelson, 1938, p. 18 ff.); also D. B. Truman considers propaganda as 'any attempt, by the manipulation of words and word substitutes, to control the attitudes and consequently the behavior of a number of individuals concerning a controversial matter' (*The Governmental Process*, New York: Knopf, 1951, p. 223).
2. Attempts have been made to distinguish propaganda from other techniques of influencing attitudes or conduct (such as bribery or violence). A classic definition in these terms is that of H. D. Lasswell 'Propaganda in the broadest sense is the technique of influencing human action by the manipulation of representations' ('Propaganda', in E. R. A. Seligman (ed.), *The Encyclopedia of the Social Sciences*, New York: The Macmillan Co., 1933, vol. XII, p. 521).

C. In the U.S.S.R. and in other societies under Communist rule propaganda denotes the intensive analysis of Marxist works and 'of the

Propensity to Consume

history of the Bolshevik Party and its task' (G. F. Alexandrov, V. Galyanov & N. Rubenstein, *Political Dictionary*, Moscow: State Publishing House, 1950). Communist usage also follows the distinction between propaganda and agitation (q.v.) first set out by Plekhanov and later developed by Lenin in *What is to be Done?* (New York: International Publishers, 1931). Lenin (ibid., p. 65) cites with approval Plekhanov's dictum that 'A propagandist presents many ideas to one or a few persons; an agitator presents only one or a few ideas, but he presents them to a mass of people'. He goes on to describe the different kinds of political persuasion and to argue that 'the propagandist operates chiefly by means of the *printed* word; the agitator operates with the *living* word'.

D. 1. The concept of propaganda as a technique is a relatively recent development which in effect broadens the meaning of the term and includes earlier more narrow meanings. In Lambert's opinion the term was originally applied to an organization—in particular to the various Catholic organizations for propaganda purposes; then later to a doctrine—i.e. to that which was being spread; and now is used to refer to the 'methods employed in spreading'. With regard to that which is being spread, many now think that this includes not only words or word substitutes such as pictures or other symbols but also actions or events consciously or unconsciously designed to influence attitudes and behaviour.

2. There is considerable difference of opinion as to whether propaganda should be regarded as bad, or good, or either bad or good depending upon certain criteria, or as morally neutral—i.e. as in itself neither bad nor good. Many take a position similar to that of the man-in-the-street and regard it as essentially bad. For example, F. C. Irion defines it as a 'one sided effort to present information, usually by secret or undercover method, which the author knows to be at least partially false' (*Public Opinion and Propaganda*, New York: Crowell, 1950, p. 9). This group may emphasize the use of such devices as the concealed source; distortion, suppression, or fabrication; and non-rational appeals—i.e. appeals to the emotions or to the affections rather than to reason. Others attempt to judge the morality of propaganda in terms of the purposes to which it is directed—sometimes arguing that the techniques of persuasion are themselves 'neutral'. Often the criterion of morally justifiable propaganda

is taken to be the truth content of the case that is being argued—or the degree and form which techniques described as 'manipulative' assume in given cases. Clearly no absolute standards are likely to be applicable in evaluating persuasive activities which, whatever the 'controversies' (see B. (1) above) in which they are weapons, have such close affinities with advertising and education.

Warren Roberts

See also: AGITATION

Propensity to Consume
(Also **Propensity to Save**)

A. The *average propensity to consume* may be defined either as the amount that is expended or as the amount that will be expended at a given level of income. The *marginal propensity to consume* is the amount expended out of an *additional increment* of income. The *average propensity to save* may be defined as the amount saved at a given level of income. The *marginal propensity to save* is the amount saved from an *additional increment* of income. All these concepts are attempts to relate income, expenditure, and saving under the condition of ceteris paribus, attempts which require at the theoretical, historical, and predictive levels the formulation of *consumption* and *savings functions* manifested in propensity to consume and propensity to save schedules containing various levels of income. Reflecting as they do the extent to which consumers reacted in the past to changes in income, the forecasting value of these terms generally necessitates, like so many other analytical devices, heroic assumptions with regard to the extrapolation of past experience into the future and with regard to the ability to hold factors other than income constant. Thus prediction may vary widely from what actually occurs. The concepts may be used at the macro-economic or micro-economic levels of analysis.

B. Though referred to obliquely by Lauderdale, Malthus, and other classical economists of the 19th century, the terms *propensity to consume* and *propensity to save* did not attain prominence until the publication of J. M. Keynes's *General Theory of Employment, Interest and Money* (New York: Harcourt, Brace, 1936). Keynes gave greatest stress to the *propensity to consume* because of the importance he attached to it as a determinant of the level of national income. The *propensity to consume* was defined by Keynes as '... the functional

548

relationship ... between ... a given level of income ... and ... the expenditure on consumption out of that level of income' (ibid., p. 90). This concept, perhaps better termed the *average propensity to consume*, has as its first derivative the *marginal propensity to consume*. The *marginal propensity to consume* was defined as the expenditure or consumption out of each additional *increment* of income, thereby indicating, according to Keynes, '... how the next increment of output will have to be divided between consumption and investment' (ibid., p. 115). In this context the *propensity to save*— or better, the *average propensity to save*—is the complement to the *average propensity to consume* or the amount saved or that will be saved out of a given level of income; and the *marginal propensity to save* is the complement to the *marginal propensity to consume* or the amount saved or that will be saved out of *each additional increment* of income.

Robert Ferber

See also: CONSUMPTION
CONSUMPTION FUNCTION
SAVING

Propensity to Save (See Propensity to Consume)

Property

A. *Property* in its most general usage denotes ownership or the thing owned. But this is of relatively recent origin, roughly coterminous with the rise of the modern institution of private property. The word *ownership* begins to come into use only in the 16th century, and the word *property* in its English form only in the 18th century.

An extreme statement of the norm of private property which underlies common usage in modern Western societies is contained in Blackstone's definition: 'that sole and despotic dominion which one man claims and exercises over the external things of the world, in total exclusion of the right of any other individual in the universe' (*Commentaries on the Laws of England* (1765), Oxford: Clarendon Press, 5th edn., 1773, bk. II, p. 2).

B. Legal usage on the Continent, following Roman law, embodies the same notion of property. Thus, Article 544 of the French Civil Code: 'Property is the right to enjoy and dispose of things in the most absolute manner, provided that no use is made thereof which is forbidden by law or by rules'.

Anglo-American law does not define property as such, but the encroachments upon a man's right to possession which enable him to set in motion the machinery of the courts. Moreover, the courts recognize as property the possession not merely of tangible objects, but also of immaterial entities such as stocks and shares, patents and copyrights. This Common Law notion of property as a bundle of powers or a constellation of rights in any source of economic utility is closer than the Roman and Continental notions to the needs of sociological usage.

C. Sociological usage encompasses a wide range of attributes varying according to (a) the nature and extent of property rights; (b) the objects of property; and (c) the forms of property.

1. Property rights are, in effect, protected powers of very varying extent and significance to make decisions about the disposal of valuables (alienation by gift or sale, destruction or bequest, of movable objects, including livestock; land and water; and immaterial entities such as shares, leases, copyrights, etc.).

It is usual to reserve the term *property* to those of such powers listed above as survive the individual lifetime and are inheritable, either by testament or by automatic rule of succession, by individual heirs or by social units such as corporate bodies, holders of offices, etc.; and it is also usual to distinguish degrees of property and ownership. Thus, *complete property* is defined by the American Law Institute in its *Restatement of the Law of Property* (St. Paul: American Law Institute, 1936, vol. I, p. 11) as: 'the totality of rights, privileges, powers and immunities which it is legally possible for a person to have with regard to a given piece of land or thing other than land, that are other than those which all members of society have as such'; and it is noted that 'this totality varies from time to time, and place to place' but that 'at any one time and place, however, there is a maximum combination of rights, privileges, powers and immunities in the land that is legally possible and which constitutes complete property'.

2. Objects of property vary according to the nature of the society concerned.

(a) Among primitive peoples there is a bewildering variety of co-existing individual, family, and community rights in land (cf. L. T. Hobhouse, G. C. Wheeler & M. Ginsberg, *The Material Culture and Social Institutions of*

Property

the Simpler Peoples, London: University of London, 1930, p. 243 ff.).

(b) In feudal societies proprietary and political notions are fused (cf. F. W. Maitland's description of *dominium* in feudal England): 'It stands for ownership, lordship, sovereignty, suzerainty ... it has to cover both proprietary rights and many kinds of political power' *Domesday Book and Beyond*, Cambridge: Cambridge University Press, 1921, p. 344).

(c) In modern industrial societies the dominant part in economic life is played by property in capital funds and other immaterial entities rather than in material objects, and property is predominantly corporate in character (cf. A. A. Berle & G. Means, *The Modern Corporation and Private Property*, New York: The Macmillan Co., 1936).

(d) For the purposes of comparative study of the institution, M. Ginsberg (*Sociology*, London: Home University Library, 1934, pp. 181–2) offers the kind of comprehensive definition required: 'As an institution, property may be described as the set of rights and obligations which define the relations between individuals or groups in respect of their control over material things (or persons treated as things)'. Weber's definition encourages a functional as well as comparative analysis. Property relations appear among his 'sociological categories of economic action' as 'forms of appropriation' of rights in sources of economic utility—forms of appropriation which vary widely with the functional needs of different types of economy and with the different sources of utility characteristic of them at various levels of technical development (*Theory of Social and Economic Organisation*, trans. by A. M. Henderson & T. Parsons, London: Hodge, 1947, p. 234 ff.).

3. The nature of the body in which property rights are vested distinguishes the various forms of property or systems of ownership: individual or private, common or communal corporate, and public ownership.

D. 1. *Corporate property* denotes the vesting of ownership in a group regarded as a single entity—e.g. medieval ecclesiastical, municipal, and craft corporations. In its influential modern form, however, it presents special difficulties of analysis and is accurately to be described as *incorporated joint stock*, being not a group, but a capital fund (cf. C. A. Cooke, *Corporation, Trust and Company*, Manchester: Manchester University Press, 1950).

2. The modern business corporation or joint stock company originated in the 18th century and must be distinguished both from its medieval ancestors and from its predecessor the great trading company of the 16th century operating a joint stock fund. It is not a group of individuals given an artificial legal framework because of the identity of certain of their interests and holding property for their benefit; it is *a capital fund*, incorporated joint stock, a legal entity *which is itself the object of property*. '...the property comprised in the company is not the material wealth it has amassed, but a sort of goodwill in the corporate personality—in its own existence as a living enterprise—as well as in the material assets and trading goodwill it may own' (ibid., pp. 17, 18). 'What is called tangible property has come to be, in most great enterprises, but the embodiment, physically, of an underlying life—a life that, in its contribution to success, is immeasurably more effective than the mere physical embodiment' (Mr Justice Grosscup, quoted by J. R. Commons, *Legal Foundations of Capitalism*, New York: The Macmillan Co., 1924, p. 18). This 'underlying life' of the modern business corporation is itself a sociological phenomenon of considerable interest and has become the subject of an extensive literature.

Thus, shareholders do not own a share in the property of the company but a 'share in the legal entity which is the corporate company' (C. A. Cooke, *Corporation, Trust and Company*, p. 18). They are not members of a common enterprise but contributors to a capital fund. Neither individually, nor collectively, do they own any part of the assets of the corporation. As individuals, they are, of course, property owners; but they possess, not physical assets, but transferable rights to a share in profits accompanied by varying rights of control over the manipulation of the fund.

With the growth in the scale of enterprise, however, their ownership has suffered a radical change of character. When investors are numerous and holdings small, ownership is increasingly divorced from control and management of the company and its activities. The legal right of shareholders to vote at general meetings is without effect on the company's policy, which passes into the control of directors and/or salaried executives. With this development, the concept of a 'share' changes; it ceases to represent a pro rata share in an asset fund or a continuing pro rata participation in earnings. Legally the underlying assets, and the participation in earnings are supposed to measure the legal right of a shareholder—but the fact is that it is the appraisal of the open market as to the shareholder's expectations of the fulfilment of the legal rights and participations that gives his property value (A. A. Berle & G. C. Means, *The Modern Corporation and Private Property*, New York: The Macmillan Co., 1933, pp. 286, 287).

Jean Floud

See also: PUBLIC ENTERPRISE

Proportional Representation

A. *Proportional representation* is a name given to systems of voting (q.v.) which are deliberately designed to ensure that as far as practicable the different shades of opinion in a country all receive a fair representation in the elected Assembly, i.e. a representation proportionate to their relative strength.

B. 1. The term is normally used to describe systems providing for large constituencies, each returning several members to Parliament. As a general rule, it can be said that the larger the constituencies the more nearly the system can attain its aim of representing the different shades of opinion. Usually, proportional representation is based on constituencies returning from five to ten members each.

2. If each constituency (q.v.) returns one member only—the one who receives most votes —the balance of political feeling in the country as a whole tends to be distorted. The distortion may be corrected, to some extent, by allowing the voters to place candidates in order of preference, and by taking account of the voters' second preferences. This system goes only a little way towards achieving *proportional representation*.

C. Such systems fall into two main types, one based on party lists and the other not.

1. The *party list* system, in various forms, has been and is widely used on the continent of Europe. Each party competing in a constituency enters a list of its own candidates. The simplest arrangement is for each voter to be entitled to vote for one party list. When all the votes are counted, and it is seen what proportion each party has obtained of the total number of votes cast, the seats are distributed among the parties accordingly. Two special problems inevitably arise, and various solutions are possible.

(a) Suppose that ten seats are to be filled, and that there are 10,000 voters. To begin with, each party gets one seat for every 1,000 votes that it receives. But as the parties do not in fact receive precisely 2,000 or 3,000 votes each, provision must be made for allocating the seats still left over after each party has received its entitlement. This may be done by the 'rule of the largest average'—often called the D'Hondt rule—or by the 'rule of the largest remainder'.

(b) In some places voters who vote for a particular party's list are given an opportunity for influencing the allocation of the party's seats among its candidates; in some they are not. Or, again, if each voter has as many votes as there are seats to be filled, he may, or may not, be allowed to vote for candidates of different lists.

2. The second main type of proportional representation, the single transferable vote, is used in Ireland and some parts of the Commonwealth. It does not require party lists. It is simple enough for the voter to vote by this system, but not so simple to understand how the system works. All the candidates' names are printed in a single list, and the voters show their order of preference. Any candidate who receives the necessary quota of first preferences is elected. (If there are 6,000 voters and 5 seats to be filled, the quota is $\frac{6,000}{5} + 1$). The surplus votes, or votes in excess of the quota, are distributed according to the second preferences indicated.

D. Any system of proportional representation tends to cause more than two parties to flourish. Although proportional representation is in a sense more 'fair' than plurality voting, it tends, sometimes, to produce a parliamentary assembly in which it is difficult for any government to have a stable majority. This danger is often exaggerated in political discussion in Britain.

P. A. Bromhead

See also: BALLOT
VOTING

Proprietorship

A. *Proprietorship* denotes a form of business organization in which one person owns the business, manages it, and is responsible for the results of his management. In the abstract, proprietorship refers to the residual equity of the owner(s) in the assets of a business.

B. The term *proprietorship* is used generally as a synonym of *ownership*, but in the social sciences, particularly economics, it also possesses somewhat special meanings. It is used in two senses, one concrete and the other abstract.

Protectorate

1. Concretely, it is used to designate one of the forms of business organization: the type in which a single individual is the owner. The proprietor may delegate management functions, but he assumes ultimate responsibility for the operation of the business. Usually this form is referred to as a *single proprietorship*, *individual proprietorship*, or *sole proprietorship*, but the word *proprietorship* standing alone is also used (e.g. C. L. Harriss, *The American Economy*, Homewood, Ill.: Irwin, 1956, pp. 88 ff.; A. E. Burns, A. C. Neal, & D. S. Watson, *Modern Economics*, New York: Harcourt, Brace, 1953, pp. 425 ff.; B. Mitchell, et al., *Economics: Experience and Analysis*, New York: Sloane, 1950, p. 214).

2. In the abstract sense, the term is used to refer to the residual equity or claim of the owners of a business in its assets. Proprietorship (owners' equity) is the difference between the assets and the liabilities (creditors' equity) if any, of a business; in other words, it is synonymous with *capital* or *net worth*, as these terms are employed by accountants. In the single proprietorship and partnership (multiple proprietorship) the owners' equity is represented on the balance sheet by *capital* accounts, while in the corporation it is customarily represented by two accounts: *capital stock* and *surplus*. These accounts are referred to in the case of the single proprietorship, partnership, and corporation, as the proprietor's equity, partners' equity, and stockholders' equity, respectively. Technically, in the last situation the corporation as a separate legal entity is the legal owner of the assets.

Charles E. Ratliff, Jr.

See also: ENTREPRENEUR

Protectorate

A. *Protectorate* in international law or politics, denotes a territory (and its inhabitants) when controlled by (or in varying degrees subordinated to) a 'protecting' power or powers.

A *protectorate* usually means the entity protected (or controlled), but it sometimes refers to the relationship between the protector and the protected.

B. Any one of three different relationships or entities is called a protectorate.

1. In the first, sometimes termed the *true protectorate*—e.g. Morocco, formerly under French control—the 'protected' power retains some control, in form at least, of a part of its foreign relations, remains a subject of international law, and is thus a 'statelike community'.

2. The second conception is that of an entity that may continue to be called a state, but which is wholly subject to another state at least as far as its international relations are concerned. It is no longer sovereign in the usual sense of that term, and is therefore not a state. It is sometimes said that it has *internal sovereignty*, by which is meant it has control of its internal affairs. The former Malay States are usually said to have fallen into this category. In reality though, their internal affairs were, or legally could, with few exceptions, be controlled by Great Britain. If these entities possessed no international personality it would seem that their rights were those of national rather than international law.

3. The third situation to which the term applies varies only in degree from the second. The 'protected' are usually peoples not organized into states; the so-called treaties were, therefore, not real treaties in the international law sense. The *colonial protectorate* is a thin disguise for the usual colonial relationship.

C. Most writers hold that a protectorate originates from a treaty between two parties, and that the treaty defines their respective powers and rights. 'The extent of the powers of a protecting state in a territory of a protected state depends, first, upon the treaties between the protecting state and the protected state establishing the Protectorate, and secondly, upon the conditions under which the Protectorate has been recognized by third Powers as against whom there is an intention to rely on the provisions of these treaties' (*Tunis-Morocco Nationality Decrees*, Permanent Court of International Justice, Leyden: Sijthoff, 1923, P.C.I.J., Series B. No. 4, p. 27).

D. The greatest difficulty in defining the term grows out of the divergence of views with respect to (a) the extent of the authority which the protector may exercise for the relationship and/or the protected to remain a protectorate; (b) the status of the protected under international law. In what are called protectorates by various writers, the authority varies from control over a part to all of the foreign affairs of the protected, and it may even extend to a part of all of its internal affairs.

H. Kelsen contends that if a state maintains a part of its competence in international matters it is a 'statelike community', but if it surrenders them all it disappears completely from the sphere of international relations and cannot be considered a subject of international law (*Principles of International Law*, New York: Rinehart, 1952, pp. 161–2). He appears to regard even the latter as a protectorate. On the other hand, H. Oppenheim maintains that it is characteristic of a 'protected state' that it retains for some purposes a position as an 'International Person'. He points out, however, that the status of some of the British protectorates in Asia is not clear, and that the African tribal 'protectorates' possess no international status whatsoever (*International Law*, ed. by H. Lauterpacht, London: Longmans, Green, 8th edn., 1955, vol. 1, pp. 192–6).

Although 'colonial protectorate' is sometimes used to designate entities without international personality, the reality is merely a mask for colonial administration. 'Virtually colonies; constitutionally foreign soil—that is the definition of "protectorates": juridical monsters' (T. Baty, 'Protectorates and Mandates', *The British Yearbook of International Law*, 1921–2, London: Henry Frowde and Hodder & Stoughton, 1921, p. 114). If protectorates in the two latter categories possess international personality it would appear to arise from conventional international law, such as Chapter XI of the Charter of the United Nations.

Charles P. Schleicher

See also: COLONY
       MANDATE

Protestant Ethic

A. 1. *Protestant* is the name given to those European Christian Churches which originated in the break with Papal authority in the 16th century—the first such 'Protestants' did not so term themselves but used the term 'Evangelical'; in its earliest usage *Protestant* referred to the political protest to the Holy Roman Emperor in 1529 by those of his German subject Princes and cities who refused to renounce the new doctrines.

2. The term *Protestant Ethic* was given its current significance by M. Weber (1864–1920) who in 1904–5 published in the *Archiv f. Sozialwissenschaft* his extended essay, *The Protestant Ethic and the Spirit of Capitalism* (trans. by T. Parsons, New York: Charles Scribner's Sons, 1930). Weber's concern was with the conditions under which capitalism (q.v.)—in its later form based upon the *enterprise* as distinct from the *household*—had developed in Europe. He was thus led to trace a

link between this development and the special psychological properties of the Protestant personality—with a special reference to the Calvinistic development of Luther's theme of the calling, the specifically Protestant attitude to worldly work as a religious vocation.

Thus the theory of the 'Protestant Ethic' argues that the ethic and theology of Calvinism were the anvils upon which the Protestant personality was forged.

(a) The typical Calvinist was concerned with ultimate election or damnation by an arbitrary God; desperately he sought for signs of election.

(b) In the 17th century in particular, the Calvinists began to interpret success in the world as such a sign: they were so anxious about salvation that success impelled them to work harder still to prove their elect status to themselves. Their religion in general imposed great psychological demands on the individual, denied him the relief of the confessional and promoted him to that virtuoso religious role previously allocated only to priests. Further, it exiled magic from the world, which became a neutral sphere in which the believer was enjoined to work for the greater glory of God, *ad maiorem Dei gloriam*.

(c) Calvinism stressed the notion that a man exercised stewardship over his goods instead of having the right to use them to further his pleasures.

(d) Its political derivatives, a repugnance for the worship of the flesh and (usually) a rejection of the absolute authority of state over conscience, played their part in creating the conditions under which capitalism could develop.

(e) Thus the disciplined and rational organization of work, the ascetic devotion to the enterprise, which marked the early capitalist spirit, were consequences—mainly unintended—of Calvinist theology.

B. The chief critic of Weber's thesis is R. H. Tawney (*Religion and the Rise of Capitalism*, London: John Murray, 1926) who holds that the Calvinist attitude towards work and wealth was modified not by immanent theological developments and their psychological consequences but by economic and political pressures arising from the objective social position and interests of the Calvinists. The discussion has been surveyed by E. Fischoff ('The Protestant Ethic and the Spirit of Capitalism', *Social Research*, vol. 11, 1944, pp. 53–77) and a recent study of the origins of Calvinism in the Zurich Reformation shows that capitalism appeared to have preceded it (N. Birnbaum, 'The Zwinglian Reformation in Zurich', *Past and Present*, no. 15, 1959, pp. 27–47). More recently still H. R. Trevor-Roper has reviewed the problems in 'Religion, the Reformation and Social Change' (*Historical Studies*, vol. IV, 1963, pp. 18–44).

C. The notion of a specific ideological and psychological complex associated with the Protestant Ethic has been carried into the general literature of sociology. Weber himself held that the Protestant Ethic had become detached from its historical base, to spread throughout the industrial world ('The Puritan wanted to work at his calling but we are forced to do so'). A comparable notion is found, again, in D. Riesman's inner-directed personality (*The Lonely Crowd*, New Haven: Yale University Press, 1950), and in W. H. Whyte's contrast of the pattern of conscientious individuality (the *Protestant Ethic*) with the conformist pattern (the *Social Ethic*) of those who work in, or are influenced by, large bureaucratic structures (*The Organization Man*, New York: Simon & Schuster, 1956, pp. 4–22).

N. Birnbaum

See also: CAPITALISM

Psephology

A. The term as used in Great Britain denotes the study of voting (from the Greek ψῆφος —the pebble which the Athenians dropped into an urn when voting). It covers what is elsewhere designated *electoral sociology*.

B. The invention of the term is attributed to R. B. McCallum, Master of Pembroke College, Oxford, and joint author of the first Nuffield study of the British General Elections (see D. E. Butler, *The British General Election of 1951*, London: Macmillan, 1952, p. 1). Butler explains (*The British General Election of 1955*, London: Macmillan, pp. 1, 2) that it was 'invented as ... an academic jest' and adds that it is perhaps unfortunate that a term suggesting 'some occult mystery' should have begun to obtain fairly widespread usage in Britain. *Psephology* is no more than an attempt to apply statistical analysis, the technique of opinion polling, and the writing of contemporary history to the study of elections.

R. T. McKenzie

Psychic Unity (See **Cultural Parallelism**)

Psychoanalysis (See **Psychotherapy**)

Psychopathology

A. *Psychopathology* in a broad sense is the study of psychological abnormalities and their origins. Today, through the influence of psychoanalytic theory, it is frequently understood as the study of unconscious psychological origins of any kind of abnormality in mind, body, or society.

B. The term *psychopathology* gained currency in German psychiatry during the second half of the 19th century. In its widest sense it denoted the *science of the diseased mind*.

Like all scientific disciplines, the science of the diseased mind has a descriptive and an explanatory aspect. Descriptively it deals with psychological abnormalities, their classification and grouping into putative disease categories. In its explanatory aspect it tries to establish links between abnormal clinical phenomena and possible noxious causes that have been either observed or theoretically postulated.

In the 19th century the term pathology acquired strong anatomical connotations. It tended to be used, in its descriptive sense as an abbreviation for *anatomical pathology* or, in its explanatory sense, as a synonym for *anatomical pathogenesis* which attempts to interpret clinical phenomena by reference to underlying pathologic anatomical changes.

Because of these anatomical connotations the term psychopathology came to imply that there was an—as yet unknown—anatomical pathology of the brain which—when discovered—would explain many observed phenomena of psychological pathology. It was in this sense that the term first appeared in a book title, viz. Krafft-Ebing's *Lehrbuch der Gerichtlichen Psychopathologie* (Stuttgart: F. Enke, 1875). Krafft-Ebing stated in his introduction to the book that he had used the term 'forensic psychopathology' instead of the customary term 'forensic psychology' because he wanted to emphasize that it was part of the psychiatrist's task to look for 'all discoverable signs of an abnormal condition of the brain' (ibid., p. vi).

Krafft-Ebing's book gave rise to the first English definition of psychopathology. In D. H. Tuke's (ed.), *Dictionary of Psychological Medicine* (London: Churchill, 1892, 2 vols.), it was defined in its forensic sense as the 'science which treats of the legal aspect of insanity, i.e. the rights and responsibilities of lunatics'.

In the beginning of the 20th century it became increasingly clear that the anatomical interpretation of psychopathology was largely built on hopes which remained unfulfilled, especially in the case of the so-called functional psychoses (manic-depressive insanity and schizophrenia) and the psychoneuroses. Anatomical speculation began to be regarded as 'brain mythology' and went out of favour.

Psychological speculation took its place. Under the influence of Freud's psychoanalytic theory the term psychopathology began to lose its descriptive connotations. They were replaced by psychoanalytic concepts of the unconscious origin of mental symptoms. This presumed origin is today often referred to by the term *unconscious or dynamic psychopathology*. The novel usage of the term was initiated by Freud in his book *The Psychopathology of Everyday Life* ((1904), trans. by A. A. Brill, London: Benn, 1914). In it psychopathology was used in an explanatory sense; abnormal psychological phenomena in the form of inadvertent lapses in purposive actions were interpreted as due to conflicts between unconscious mental forces.

This psychoanalytic psychopathology has since been employed to explain, not only the ills of individuals, but also those of societies; not only mental symptoms but also the physical lesions of so-called psychosomatic diseases; not only disease but also the traits and quirks of normal or deviant personalities.

F. Kräupl Taylor

See also: NEUROSIS
PSYCHOSIS
PSYCHOTHERAPY

Psychosis

A. *Psychosis* may be defined as a severe personality disorder, whether caused by organic or developmental sources, resulting in the lack or marked lessening of role-taking, of communication, of self-control, and in extreme cases of self-care. It leads to private versions of the culture and the self, to a decline of rational and integrative behaviour and to distorted emotionality. It results in deviant and bizarre behaviour which in many societies necessitates hospital commitment or supervised care. Psychoses are categorized broadly into the organic and the so-called functional types. In the former, organic pathology is present; in the latter organic pathology is not evident.

B. Definitions of psychosis vary because of different approaches to, as well as methods of studying, this disorder.

1. First, *psychosis* has been defined in its most limited way as a form of severe abnormality necessitating the hospitalized commitment of the afflicted person. Since what is considered abnormal varies culturally, what might be *psychosis* in one society would be considered normal in another society which accepted the particular bizarre behaviour. This usage of *psychosis* which is generally regarded as only one dimension of disordered behaviour, namely its cultural recognition and evaluation, does not consider the inner personality pathology that prompted the bizarre behaviour.

2. Second, the operational usage of *psychosis* as a psychiatric diagnostic classification is that of a variable denoting a hospitalized condition and does not have an explicit verbal definition of the disorder. This operational approach does not inquire into the personality dynamics of the disorder but uses it as a correlate for study with social variables such as community location, social class, ethnic group, age and sex.

3. The third or dynamic definition of *psychosis* emphasizes it as a severe personality disorder resulting in loss of contact with reality and in relative incapacitation and lack of self-care of the afflicted person. Since reality consists of the shared attitudes of a group, the psychotic (a) lacks a role-taking capacity to share the perspectives of other persons (N. Cameron, *The Psychology of Behavior Disorders*, Boston: Houghton Mifflin, 1947, pp. 347–8); (b) acquires private meaning, unique words (or neologisms) and practices; (c) becomes disoriented (delusional) or has a private version of aspects of the culture and of himself; and (d) from the viewpoint of social position frequently is socially isolated.

4. From the viewpoint of action, *psychosis* is defined as the inability to respond in an organized way to objects in accord with social expectations. And from the viewpoint of the self, psychosis results in an aberrant identity which varies from the stark self-condemnation of the depressive to the disorganized sense of identity of some types of the schizophrenic.

C. One misconception arises from designating societies or groups as 'psychotic'. This reference is analogous rather than analytic because individual members in a so-called 'psychotic' society are ordered. For example, the characterization of the Kwakiutl as megalomanic or the Germans as paranoid does not mean that the individual members have these personality traits. It refers to the cultural pattern to which the members conform, so that their capacity for

Psychotherapy

communication and self-control expresses their ordered personality condition (see S. K. Weinberg, *Society and Personality Disorders*, New York: Prentice-Hall, 1952, pp. 97–9). However, in certain fanatical sects or cults, the leaders may be psychotic, especially paranoid, and by their authoritative position, force their followers to sanction their delusions and bizarre practices.

These functional psychoses, such as schizophrenia, manic-depression, and paranoid behaviour, are regarded by some as constitutional disorders and by others as psychological disorders. One derivative inference from the constitutional approach is that psychoses are biological and hence exist in all cultures (A. Kardiner, *The Psychological Frontiers of Society*, New York: Columbia University Press, 1945, p. 431). The opposite inference from the psychological approach is that the psychoses would be absent or minimum in simple homogeneous societies with minimum stress (R. E. L. Faris, 'Some Observations on the Incidence of Schizophrenia in Primitive Society', *Journal of Abnormal and Social Psychology*, vol. XXIX, 1934, pp. 30, 31). A third and perhaps most plausible inference maintains that while schizophrenia arises in even the simplest social settlement, it is influenced both by the person's constitutional endowments and by the varied interpersonal stresses in his development. The bases for this inference are that the simplicity of social structure does not necessarily minimize inter-personal stress and that homogeneity of culture does not eliminate the idiosyncratic hostile and ambivalent relations of individuals even though these inter-personal relations are manifested within the range of the cultural norms.

S. Kirson Weinberg

See also: ANXIETY
DEVIANT BEHAVIOUR
NEUROSIS

Psychotherapy

A. *Psychotherapy* was originally understood as the treatment of the mind itself by whatever means (physical, chemical, or psychological) that could improve its functioning, remove symptoms, or reduce predispositions towards mental illness. Today a narrower interpretation is prevalent which stipulates that the means employed should be psychological, i.e. consist in the communication of thought and feeling between doctor and patient. This communication is a two-way traffic in psychoanalytically oriented treatments, but is a one-way doctor-to-patient process in all suggestive, educative, counselling, and training procedures.

B. 1. *Psychic therapy* was occasionally mentioned in the beginning of the 19th century, e.g. by J. C. Reil (*Rhapsodien über die Anwendung der psychischen Cur-methode* [i.e. method of psychic therapy] *auf Geisteszerrüttungen*, Halle, 1803). The term *psychic or moral therapy* referred to a variety of therapeutic methods presumed to have a direct effect on the mind itself, as opposed to the methods of physical therapy which were thought of as primarily affecting the body and only secondarily the mind.

Among the main methods employed in psychic or moral treatment were (a) correction of disordered behaviour and thought by physical coercion, discomfort, and pain; (b) encouragement of healthy responses by kindness, sympathy, and personal interest; (c) appeal to the patient's reason and spiritual beliefs; (d) incitement of strong emotions, especially those of fear, anger, and nausea by physical or chemical means; (e) education of the patient's abilities and training in occupational and social activities; (f) the use of artifice and drama to remove or modify insane delusions.

2. In the second half of the 19th century the coining of compound terms became fashionable in scientific literature. *Psychic therapy* became *psychotherapy*. The term appeared for the first time in Bernheim's well-known book *Hypnotisme, Suggestion, Psychotherapie, Etudes Nouvelles* (Paris: Doin, 1891).

Psychotherapy in Bernheim's sense was, however, distinct from the 'psychic' or 'moral' therapy of the early 19th century; it was not merely therapy of the psyche, but *therapy of the psyche by psychological means*, such as hypnosis, suggestion, and kindred procedures. It was not applied by asylum doctors to *lunatics*, but by doctors in private practice to *hysterical* and *neurasthenic* patients who had physical symptoms for which there was no apparent physical basis. These patients were presumed to suffer from morbid ideas. Psychotherapy aimed at cleansing their minds of these ideas and at implanting new and salutary ideas in their stead.

3. Freud translated Bernheim's book into German in 1892 and used the term *psychotherapy* to describe his and Breuer's therapeutic technique in their joint book ('Studies on Hysteria' (1895), trans. J. Strachey, in *The Complete Psychological Works of Sigmund Freud*, London: Hogarth Press, 1955, vol. II). He asserted that the morbid ideas of his patients were unconscious memories of traumatic sexual seductions. His psychotherapy at that time consisted in uncovering such unconscious memories through hypnosis and suggestion, and in fostering the discharge of emotions which had been harmfully linked with them.

In 1896 Freud coined the term *psycho-analysis* to characterize his therapeutic search for morbid unconscious memories. He gradually relinquished hypnosis and suggestion, and replaced them by a technical innovation of far-reaching consequence. He induced his patients to disclose their thoughts without censorship, allowing ideas to enter their minds in undirected *free association*.

This device of free association, coupled with Freud's interest in the vicissitudes of his patients' sexual instincts in earlier life, encouraged the confession of guilt-charged incidents, desires, and fantasies. The age-old psychotherapeutic medium of the confessional was thus re-established, but with the doctor in place of the priest.

Of even greater significance was the alteration in the therapeutic role of the doctor which Freud's new technique brought about. From a busy and active fighter against disease, the doctor changed into a mainly passive listener who put the onus of therapeutic effort on the patient. A new dimension was thus added to psychotherapy: the permissive-tolerant approach. Today psychotherapeutic techniques range from active, suggestive, 'inspirational' methods through educative, persuasive, counselling activities to the analytical procedures of Jung, Adler, Freud, and others which combine permissiveness with the communication of 'insight' into unconscious processes, and ultimately to the most passive, 'non-directive' and 'client-centred' approach of C. Rogers.

Freud's permissive approach led him to the discovery that the doctor-patient relationship is affected by unconscious conflicts in the patient's mind so that unwarranted feelings intrude themselves which are 'transferred' from a forgotten past into the therapeutic present. With this discovery Freud's aim in treatment gradually changed from a search for specific unconscious memories, responsible for particular symptoms only, to the interpretation and modification of 'transference feelings' and their underlying unconscious conflicts which were thought to be at the core of the patients' neurotic predispositions.

This concept of transference feelings has been extended by other therapists to apply to inter-personal relations outside the treatment situation. The existentialist school of psychotherapy, which bases itself on the metaphysical doctrines of Heidegger and has established itself since the war, especially in Switzerland, seeks to interpret and modify a patient's total life situation, his 'being-in-the-world', in the light of his past life experiences.

The techniques and teachings of Freud have emphasized that the essence of psychotherapeutic activity is the communication of thought and feeling between doctor and patient; i.e. the communication of psychological phenomena.

4. There have been many attempts to find psychotherapeutic shortcuts as alternatives to the exacting and time-consuming demands of psychoanalysis. One of the most popular time-saving methods consists in the simultaneous treatment of a small number of patients in therapeutic groups. Some brief forms of psychotherapy have made use of hypnosis or drugs to speed up some partial—and perhaps obsolete—psychoanalytic aim, such as the uncovering of specific unconscious memories or the discharge of strong emotions.

5. Other psychotherapists of today have revived in modified form, and with the rationale of modern theories, still other methods that constituted the 'moral treatment' of the early 19th century. Some forms of treatment through 'conditioning', for example, which derive their theoretical justification from the teaching of the great Russian physiologist Pavlov, try to remove symptoms, that have become damaging habits, by means of mild discomforts; such as slight electric shocks whenever a sufferer from writer's cramp squeezes or jerks his pen; or nausea induced when an alcoholic, undergoing aversion therapy, is given a drink.

Occupational and social activities are as popular psychotherapeutic tools today as 150 years ago. The salutary effect of acting has been rediscovered in Moreno's psychodrama.

F. Kräupl Taylor

See also: Neurosis
          Psychopathology
          Psychosis

Public

A. Because the usage is so varied and vague, at least two tentative definitions must be attempted.

1. *Public* in its general usage is an adjective which indicates the supposed common interests and objectives of all or at least a majority of the people in a political unit, as in public agencies, public opinion, public welfare, public interest,

Public Administration

public works, public buildings, public domain, public services, etc. In this usage *the public* refers to the membership of the political unit.

2. *A public* as the term is used by social scientists refers to an amorphous social structure whose members share a community-of-interest which has been produced by impersonal communication and contact.

B. Usage in social psychology and sociology is quite similar. Scholars in these fields are more likely to speak of 'publics' than 'the public'. Thus G. A. Lundberg, C. C. Schrag, and O. N. Larsen (*Sociology*, New York: Harper & Brothers, 1954, p. 491) say, 'One may belong to as many publics as one has interests; further, a public may or may not coincide with physical, geographical, or political units …'.

C. At least two classes of publics as defined in A.2 may be observed.

1. *An appreciative public* is one whose members have a common interest in some specific kind of social behaviour such as music, literature, or sports. Each artist or cricket star has his 'public'—'fans', or admirers. Thus there are millions of publics and each person usually is a member of many. The modern newspaper does not serve 'the public' but a large number of publics. Each 'department' serves a public, and often many, as in the case of music, sports, columns, advertising, 'comics'.

2. *Action publics* are 'pressure groups' (note the misuse of *group*) or rather classes of people who want some specific things to be done. Most citizens are members of several such publics which may range from promoting the interests of learned societies to providing shelters for homeless dogs.

D. All publics have one thing in common: they are not formally organized (though they frequently give rise to formal organizations) and the members are not in personal contact with each other, though they may gather in an audience to satisfy their interest. They are not *groups* (q.v.) but they are more structured than those who may be placed together in an *aggregate* (q.v.). When the members of a public meet each other or communicate in writing or by telephone, they have a 'fellow feeling' and 'talk each other's language'. This is what makes them a social structure, though obviously a very amorphous one, rather than a logical category or term in a classification.

Read Bain

See also: PUBLIC OPINION

Public Administration

A. *Public administration* has been used in two senses: (a) to indicate that sector of administration (q.v.) which is particularly associated with government or the state—'the process or activity … of administrating public affairs' (D. Waldo, *The Study of Public Administration*, New York: Garden City, Doubleday, 1955, p. 3); (b) to indicate the systematic study of this field (see the divisions of Political Science set out in *Contemporary Political Science* (Paris: Unesco, 1950, p. 4). This double use has been pointed out by L. D. White's article, 'Administration, Public' (in E. R. A. Seligman (ed.), *Encyclopedia of the Social Sciences*, New York: The Macmillan Co., 1930, vol. I, p. 440); and also by D. Waldo, *The Study of Public Administration*, and others.

B. 1. The expression seems to have become current in the early years of the present century, although it was used by Woodrow Wilson in 1887 in a famous article ('The Study of Administration', *Political Science Quarterly*, vol. II, 1887, pp. 197–222)—'Public administration is [the] detailed and systematic execution of public law' (ibid., p. 212).

2. Both the senses set out in A. (a) and (b) above have undergone developments in the course of the past quarter of a century as interpretation has moved (as with *administration* (q.v.)) from concentration on formal aspects towards greater emphasis on the informal. Explanation exclusively by reference to the relation to the State (or law, as in Wilson's definition) has become relatively rarer.

C. 1. Views have varied as to exactly how large a field of practice is covered by the term.

(a) It may be used for all 'the activities of the Executive Branch of our national government and of the comparable areas of state, local and other governments' (H. Stein, *Public Administration and Policy Development*, New York: Harcourt, Brace, 1952, p. x). But a narrower interpretation has also been attempted. 'Sometimes the term *Executive* which strictly means an Authority which puts the laws in force, is opposed to the term *Administrative*, which implies the performance of every other sort of immediate Governmental act …' (S. Amos, *The Science of Politics*, London: Kegan, Paul, Trench, 1883, p. 99). 'The chief executive [should] be given all the duties and powers of a general manager and be made in fact, as well as in theory, the head of the administration'

(W. F. Willoughby, *Principles of Public Administration*, Washington: The Brookings Institution, 1927, p. 36). H. Walker (*Public Administration in the United States*, New York: Farrar & Rinehart, 1937, p. 1) argues that 'The classical trinity of governmental powers, legislative, executive, and judicial, is loudly challenged by the use of administrative power ... it is more satisfactory to add administration ... with a resulting recognition of four classes of government power'.

These variations of use connect with variations of ideas about the relations between administrative activity and policy formulation (see H. Stein's reference in *Public Administration and Policy Development* to 'Public Administration as Politics', pp. xiv–xvii, which represents the newer trend as against F. J. Goodnow's statement in *Principles of the Administrative Law of the United States*, New York: G. P. Putnam's Sons, 1905, p. 6, 'Politics has to do with policies or expressions of the state will. Administration has to do with the execution of these policies'. See also the discussion of this under *Administration*).

2. A further variation arises on whether, if at all, any clear line can be drawn between *public* and *business* administration. Thus 'It has been customary in this country [U.S.A.] to make a sharp distinction between governmental and non-governmental administration. ... Actually, the distinction is much too sharp to fit the facts' (H. A. Simon, D. W. Smithburg & V. A. Thompson, *Public Administration*, New York: Knopf, 1950, p. 8). Likewise W. J. M. Mackenzie claims that 'the distinction between public administration and private administration is now quite secondary' ('The Study of Public Administration in the United States', *Public Administration*, vol. XXIX, 1951, p. 136). D. Waldo (*The Study of Public Administration*, p. 11) suggests an approach in terms of 'structural-functional analysis and culture' which will 'help us to understand why public administration has some general or generic aspects, but also why the line between public and private is drawn in different places and with differing results, why public does not have precisely the same meaning in any two cultural contexts'. Simon, Smithburg and Thompson (*Public Administration*, pp. 9–16), however, do set out similarities and difference between public and private administration and the differences indicated are those usually accepted—'the duties and responsibilities of the public administrator will usually be described by law in much greater detail', 'there will usually be greater possibility for holding him accountable', 'the private administrator is often given much more latitude in interpreting the relationship between his organization and the general welfare ... [the public administrator] is expected to serve the public interests'.

D. These variations in the interpretation of the field have affected conceptions of how widely the subject should range. The conception of the subject has also varied in accordance with whether it has been held to involve simply description (and if so, whether of a framework or an art) or the promulgation of principles and if so whether these have any 'scientific' basis. Thus L. D. White (*Introduction to the Study of Public Administration*, New York: The Macmillan Co., 4th edn., 1955, p. 2): 'the art of administration is the direction, co-ordination and control of many persons to achieve some purpose or objective'; O. Tead (*The Art of Administration*, New York: McGraw-Hill, 1951, p. 6): 'Administration is ... a fine art because it summons an imposing body of special talents on behalf of a collaborative creation which is integral to the conduct of civilized living today'; finally, D. Waldo (*The Administrative State*, New York: Ronald Press, 1948, pp. 206-7): '... the notion that the work of government is divisible in two parts, decisions and execution, and that execution (administration) is, or could be made a "science" ... the notion that there are "principles" scientifically and ethically valid that can be uncovered by scientific study is also still an orthodox tenet'.

Wilfrid Harrison

See also: ADMINISTRATION

Public Debt

A. The *public debt* of a nation is the sum total of all the financial obligations resulting from borrowing of all its government units—national, regional, and local. It does not include those financial obligations of government which are not the result of borrowing, e.g. gold certificates, currency, or contractual obligations for goods and services; nor does it include the private debts of persons and corporations.

B. The significance of deficit spending by which debt is incurred and of debt management for the economy of a society is generally treated today under the head of public finance (q.v.).

Public Enterprise

Popular and political controversy still occurs with respect to the idea that a sizeable public debt is bad and that it constitutes a burden either on the present or on future generations; but there is considerable consensus concerning these matters among economists, although they may disagree concerning the timing and amount of deficit spending as a part of fiscal policy. *External public debt*, owed to governments or citizens of other countries, of course, does involve a mortgaging of future income and productive powers (G. L. S. Shackle, *Economics for Pleasure*, Cambridge: At the University Press, 1959, p. 226). But *internal public debt*, owed by government to its own citizens, does not create so great a burden on the economy as a whole because it involves transfer between those owning government securities and the taxpayers (D. McC. Wright, *The Creation of Purchasing Power*, Cambridge, Mass.: Harvard University Press, 1942, p. 136). At the same time it is recognized that real costs may be imposed on the community if it needs high taxes to meet the interest charges on the public debt as the result of the following possible frictions: (a) unwillingness to impose taxes for public services, if there is already a high tax for the purpose of interest payments; (b) disproportionate taxation on a particular field, discouraging development in that field; (c) difficulty in adjusting taxes to foster saving or consumption because of high taxes for interest payments; (d) fear of inflation; and (e) the rigidity which the need to meet large annual interest charges imposes on the economy in the form of a reluctance to permit a decline in money income which would result in increased percentage of income transferred by taxes (ibid., pp. 136–7). The seriousness of these frictions, of course, is in each case not related to the capital amount of the public debt, since this is always fundable. Rather it is related to the interest charges and the taxes levied to meet them. Even here, however, the frictions are relative to the size and rate of growth of the gross national product and national income, so that as the economy grows the amount of absolute interest paid—and hence in most cases the capital amount—may also increase, without increasing the frictions described, provided the citizens of the country are aware of the situation and respond to it rationally.

Norman J. Wood

See also: NATIONAL PRODUCT
PUBLIC FINANCE

Public Enterprise

A. The term is used to denote enterprises which are *public*, i.e. not entirely operated by private individuals or groups. It applies to enterprises under state direction at national level, and in its broadest sense includes those controlled by regional and local bodies also. It denotes public services which are economic *enterprises*, i.e. which may be expected to pay for themselves. Education, the armed forces, and the judiciary are public services which do not pay for themselves and are not, therefore, economic enterprises.

B. 1. The definition and classification of public enterprises is still at an early stage (see D. N. Chester, 'Public Corporations and the Classification of Administrative Bodies', *Political Studies*, No. 1, 1953). A short and able analysis of current usage and trends is to be found in *Some Problems in the Organisation and Administration of Public Enterprises in the Industrial Field* (New York: United Nations II H, Technical Assistance Administration, 1954, vol. 1, especially ch. I). This short study assumes, however, that public enterprises fall into one of three categories: public corporations, government departments, and mixed undertakings.

2. (a) Some public enterprises are operated as part of the Civil Service, their employees being Civil Servants: (i) the earliest in many countries was the *Government Department*, e.g. the Post Office; (ii) in certain countries, e.g. Sweden and Germany, special *Civil Service Agencies* were set up separate from the departmental structure.

(b) Local authorities often control their own public utilities, e.g. transport, water, electricity services, as *municipal enterprises*.

(c) Others are fashioned after the pattern of the joint-stock company: (i) numerous *mixed undertakings* exist in which the share capital is owned half by the state and half by private persons. (Since control is not explicitly vested in the state by this arrangement—indeed it has often been adopted to make the enterprises free from state interference—these are often excluded from classifications of public enterprise); (ii) it is increasingly common, however, for the state to set up or take over companies in which it owns all or most of the shares. (These *state companies* are frowned upon in certain quarters for not seeming to be what they really are.)

(d) The most popular form today appears to be the *public corporation*, developed in Britain before and after World War I (e.g. Port of London Authority, British Broadcasting Corporation and London Passenger Transport Board). It has been widely adopted since 1945 in many countries though in Britain itself it is not certain how far the nationalized industries are of the same genre as their smaller predecessors. The corporation has the attraction of being neither a department of the Civil Service nor a limited company governed by company law. It is especially created by the Government and has a peculiar relationship to the state (see W. A. Robson (ed.), *Problems of Nationalised Industry*, London: Allen & Unwin, 1952). Owing to the considerable variation between particular enterprises its precise nature is not clear. It seems doubtful whether the term can properly be used outside countries which have inherited the Anglo-Saxon common law tradition (see W. Friedmann (ed.), *The Public Corporation: a Comparative Symposium*, London: Stevens, 1954; and A. H. Hanson (ed.), *Public Enterprise*, Brussels: International Institute of Administrative Sciences, 1955).

C. The main problem of public enterprises remains their public accountability. This is particularly manifest in the United Kingdom but is to be found increasingly discussed elsewhere (see, for example, D. V. Verney, *Public Enterprise in Sweden*, Liverpool: University Press, 1959). The need for special bodies (e.g. Committees of the Legislature) to control or supervise public enterprise, the method of their finance, and the degree of autonomy from the Government and/or Legislature which should be granted to monopolies are all current topics of debate and are important criteria in deciding whether a particular institution is a public enterprise or not.

D. V. Verney

See also: BUSINESS ENTERPRISE

Public Finance

A. *Public finance* denotes the financial methods, principles, and procedures whereby governments (whether federal, national, state, or local) discharge their functions. It, therefore, has a primary concern with the pattern and channels of public spending and tax collection. The term also denotes that sub-field of economics wherein the financial operations of governments and the impact of such operations upon the level of consumption, investment, production, employment, etc. are studied.

B. From this definition it will be clear that the scope of public finance is dependent upon the role of the state in the economic life of nations (which has grown sharply in recent decades—not least in certain countries with the growth of state concern over social welfare provisions). The development of *mixed* economies and *public enterprise* (q.v.) presents problems of demarcation between *private* and *public* finance. U. K. Hicks, arguing that 'the main content of public finance consists ... of the examination and appraisal of the methods by which governing bodies provide for the collective satisfaction of wants and secure the necessary funds to carry out their purpose' goes on to point out that public finance 'when we are concerned with the broader aspects of policy ...' must 'take into account not only the activities of governing bodies but also of all organizations whose policy is subject to some degree of public control' (*Public Finance*, London: Pitman, 1947, pp. 6–7). Thus two broad approaches to the field of public finance can be discerned.

1. The classical approach, which assumed a rather limited role for the state in a nation's economic life, studied merely the collection and expenditure of public funds. Since an unbalanced budget was frowned upon, this approach considered as the main objective of the treasury to raise no more and no less in taxes than are to be spent. For instance, Adam Smith strongly opposed unbalanced budgets. One of his major objections was that it amounted to government borrowing from industry and commerce, thus depriving a capital-poor society of revenue which could have been productively reinvested.

2. The second approach, which is almost universally accepted by contemporary economists, gives public finance a much broader scope.

(a) The Keynesian attack (J. M. Keynes, *The General Theory of Interest, Employment and Money*, London: Macmillan, 1936) on the classical principles of public finance was a logical outgrowth of his view that the economy does not tend to equilibrium at full employment. If there were unemployed resources which the private sector did not use, they might be employed by the state. The additional public expenditures need not be matched by new taxes. Instead, deficit financing might be relied upon to stimulate the economy so that it will move towards full employment.

(b) A. H. Hansen (*Fiscal Policy and Business Cycles*, New York: Norton, 1941), taking Keynes's propositions as a point of departure,

Public Office

is perhaps most directly responsible for the now prevailing approach to public finance. Hansen showed that public finance, because of political necessity, had to be broadened to include those aspects of public spending, taxation, borrowing and debt management, which affect employment and the level and distribution of income. He cast aside the traditional budgetary policy and suggested reliance upon a compensatory fiscal policy which would view the expenditures and receipts of government in relation to the overall level of economic activity.

(c) Hansen's ideas were elaborated upon by A. P. Lerner ('Functional Finance and Federal Debt', *Social Research*, vol. 10, 1943, pp. 38–51). According to Lerner, modern public finance views government expenditure, revenue, borrowing and debt management as means to control aggregate community expenditures and thus assure generally agreed upon employment and income objectives. From this viewpoint, expenditures and taxes are increased or reduced to affect the community's rate of spending; debt instruments are sold to the public to absorb their idle balances and reduce liquidity in times of inflation, and redeemed to increase liquidity in times of depression.

C. As the role of the state in the economic life of nations has grown over the years, the scope of public finance, too, has been broadened. Its main areas of present concern are: (a) determination of how much is to be spent for specific government services, and in total; (b) effective rendering of government services; (c) search for an appropriate tax system and tax structure together with the establishment of a proper tax level and efficient tax collection system; (d) public borrowing; (e) management of the public debt; (f) study and formulation of a fiscal policy which relies upon public spending, taxation, public borrowing and debt management to insure full employment at high levels of income; (g) inter-government fiscal relations, and certain problems that are unique to state and local governments.

D. 'Public finance is one of those subjects which lie on the borderline between economics and politics' (H. Dalton, *Public Finance*, London: Routledge, 1929, p. 3). Both economics and public finance deal with problems of scarce resources and of value and wealth relationships of individuals. At the same time, both political science and public finance deal with government activities and the relation of the individual to the state.

Werner Z. Hirsch

See also: PUBLIC DEBT

Public Law (See Administrative Law)

Public Office

A. *Public office* refers to any position established by law to which certain duties or services are attached, and which the incumbent officer, the holder of the position, is duty-bound to perform. The duties in question being public, they involve the exercise by the incumbent of some governmental or at least quasi-governmental authority.

B. A *public office* is a position established and defined by law—whether the law be a constitution, a statute, or a charter—and attached to or made a part of the organization of some unit of government. The position is normally described in the laws by (a) a certain title, (b) its allocation to the unit of government concerned, (c) a designated method of election or appointment of the person or persons who are to fill the position, and (d) a list of powers, duties, restrictions, emoluments, terms and conditions, that attach to and distinguish the office from other offices. Thus the office of county clerk will be designated in the laws by the title (county clerk) indicating an attachment to a governmental unit (the county), and will be further defined as to the powers, duties, emoluments, mode of election or appointment, etc., attached by law thereto.

C. The concept of *public office* is not entirely clear, partly because of certain confusions and ambiguities in the statutes and in judicial decisions, and partly because there are many types of positions in the public service that have some but not all the characteristics of an office. Many persons perform public services without becoming public officers. A few examples are: a contractor building a public school; any one of his workmen; a convict used to repair the roads; and an employee like a typist, a street-sweeper, etc., who works under an officer but has no authority of his own to act for the public. Every public officer is in a broad and loose sense a public employee, but not every employee is an officer. One difference between an officer and a mere employee is that an officer can, within the range of the powers granted to him, bind the public authority or governmental unit that he serves, subject to being overruled by higher authorities in many cases; while a mere employee has as a rule no such power. His functions are entirely ministerial or almost so, and involve no power to make decisions for the public.

D. The law defines how the office shall be filled. In democratic countries people are usually either elected to office by popular vote or appointed thereto by the governing body or by some commission, board, committee, or officer having the legal power to make the appointment. Hence the short-cut expressions *appointive office* and *elective office*.

There are, of course, other ways to acquire public office even in democratic countries; by legislative designation of certain officers as entitled to hold other offices ex officio, for example. In the past there have been cases of private property in public offices, with attendant provisions for the inheritance, sale, and purchase of such offices. These are generally relics of the past if they exist at all.

Whether a public office is elective or appointive depends on the provisions of the applicable laws, and is not a matter of principle. In general the distinction is so clearly made in the statutes that there can be no question. It is true, however, that, under many statutes, offices that are ordinarily filled by popular election may be filled by appointment by some public officer or agency to fill vacancies for short terms or until an election can be held.

The distinction between *elective* and *appointive* offices is not one that goes to the nature of the office or its duties. In the United States it has been partly a matter of chance whether a particular office has come to be filled by election or appointment. Some minor and relatively unimportant offices in local government are filled by election, while highly important ones like Attorney General of the United States or Commissioner of Finance in a state are filled by appointment. If the members of legislative bodies be left to one side, as being only dubiously entitled to be called officers, then in general the national government has very few elective offices, the typical state government has more, and many counties and cities have proportionately more still. Conversely the national government has thousands of appointive officers, the average state or large city or county has a considerable number, while many small local governments have very few.

William Anderson

See also: OFFICE

Public Opinion

A. *Public opinion* is usually defined functionally as the opinion(s) of a *public* (q.v.), i.e. a group whose membership is defined only by a shared concern for the subject of the opinion(s).

Controversy turns on (a) the degree to which given opinion(s) must be common to the *public*; (b) the degree to which given opinion(s) must be voiced, i.e. 'made public'.

The divisions on (a) and (b) can be roughly classified as being between advocates of a monistic, organic view and holders of a pluralistic, numerical theory of *public opinion*.

1. Monists prefer to include not only voiced expressions but also opinions for whose voicing no occasion has arisen. They include under *opinion* general preference, inclinations, attitudes, customs, mores, and 'the reservoir of accepted beliefs'. Expressions of disagreement are excluded. Politically, public opinion is regarded by the monists as simply the manifested general will (q.v.).

2. Pluralists define opinion in terms of controversy and the expression of ideas in controversy. They tend to stress the existence of publics rather than the public and to see the makers of policy as distinct from the publics which manifest public opinion on the issues (q.v.) at stake.

B. 1. In the past, 'No one used the words "public opinion" but the concept was so familiar to them that they worked with it as with something self evident' (W. Bauer, *Die öffentliche Meinung und ihre geschichtlichen Grundlagen*, Tübingen: Mohr, 1914, p. 16). Separate aspects of public opinion appear in classical concepts: *fama, public reputation, rumor, vox populi, consensus populi, consensus gentium*, this last as public opinion the basis of legal and political sovereignty.

The idea of *opinion* as the origin of authority was a product of the post-Renaissance secularization of the state, voiced by Machiavelli in the 16th century, Sir William Temple in the 17th century, Pascal and the *Philosophes* in the 18th century. Rousseau distinguished *la volonté générale* from *l'opinion publique*. Necker, financier and minister of Louis XV, took from experience of the public credit of the state the idea of public opinion as a check on absolutist government. Bentham found a moral sanction, one of four sources of pleasure or pain, in public opinion, and also developed the concept of public opinion as a tribunal, and as a system of laws emanating from people. Nineteenth-

Public Utility

century liberal theorists studied the interaction between popular opinion and governmental policy.

2. In the late 19th and in the present century there was the development of study of social aspects of public opinion, the process of its formation, together with an emphasis on non-rational emotional elements, and the analysis of the idea of the 'public'.

The alleged role public opinion and its manipulation played in events preceding and during World War I developed analysis in three directions, (a) into content and motivation (social psychologists), (b) into definition and formation (sociologists), and (c) into its political role (historians and political scientists).

Further development came in the 1930s, through commercially-motivated market research, and American liberals' urge for direct democracy; the emphasis was on statistical analysis of opinions, news, and attitudes by polls and questionnaires.

Thus the peculiarly modern study of public opinion began in those years (B. Berelson, 'The Study of Public Opinion', in L. D. White (ed.), *The State of the Social Sciences*, Chicago: University of Chicago Press, 1956, p. 300). Research activity in the study of public opinion has expanded tremendously since that time. According to B. Berelson (ibid., p. 304), this research now has several characteristics which public opinion research did not have in the beginning, in that it is (a) primarily American; (b) academic; (c) the result of team research; (d) topical, empirical, and limited rather than broadly theoretical; (e) technical; (f) quantitative; (g) specialized; and (h) focused on public opinion per se rather than on some larger concern. For a recent critical British discussion see D. E. G. Plowman ('Public Opinion and the Polls', *British Journal of Sociology*, vol. XIII, 1962, p. 331 et seq.).

C. Two problems seem common to all discussion:

1. The first is the question of the scope of the term *opinion* in the definition; this turns on the definition of a *public*. To include any random selection of individuals is to render the concept nugatory. Meaningful discussion must assume the members of a 'public' to have in common attitudes, customs, mores etc. If these last are to be included as *opinions*, then for the purposes of political sociologists, political scientists, and historians, distinction must be made between those matters on which members of a group may

disagree and remain members, and those where disagreement implies self-exclusion.

2. The second is the question: when can an opinion be termed *public*? The problem arises from an opinion being only attributable to an individual. This being so, the question of whether it can be said to be *public* has two aspects:

(a) The first is whether it is made public: *public opinion* is 'what someone says to a stranger, e.g. an interviewer' and is 'only a part of private opinion and that part which . . . dare show itself at any moment' (T. Harrison, 'What is Public Opinion?', *Political Quarterly*, vol. XI, 1940, pp. 368–83).

(b) The second is whether it is shared by others, members of the *public*. Here valid distinctions can be made between (i) *public* and *private* opinions, i.e. those which an individual will express publicly (his admission being governed by a desire to remain a member of the 'public') and those which he will keep to himself or his intimate circle; (ii) *public* and *publicly-expressed* opinions, i.e. those expressed as a member of the 'public', and those expressed as an individual, *before* members of the 'public'; (iii) public opinions publicly expressed and those for which at the moment of investigation no occasion for expression has arisen. It should be noted that the act of investigation itself makes opinions public, just as the venue of the investigation may effect the formulation of those opinions; (iv) public opinion(s) and the attitudes etc. of the public.

D. C. Watt

See also: POLL
           PSEPHOLOGY
           PUBLIC

Public Regulation of Business (See Social Control of Industry)

Public Revenue (See Revenue)

Public Utility

A. The term *public utility* is applied to certain industries—gas, electricity, telephone services, railways, tramways, and others—which require for their operations special wayleaves or other rights over the use of land, often including compulsory powers, which the legislature is willing to give to only one operator at a time in any one place.

B. 1. The exclusive rights conferred by law create a legal monopoly, though in many cases the technical character of the operations tend in any case to give rise to a 'natural' monopoly. The degree of monopoly power depends on the availability of substitutes which varies from one industry to another, from time to time, and from place to place.

2. In return for the grant of exclusive powers the legislature imposes various restrictions on the operator designed to protect the public interest. Works on public utilities usually list some further alleged characteristics of these industries, e.g. that they produce necessities, that their products cannot be stored, that they have a high ratio of capital cost, etc.; but even if particular public utilities have these characteristics, they are shared with many other industries and are clearly not central to the concept.

C. Public utilities may be subjected to many restrictions; for instance they may be obliged to supply people in a certain area on given terms, to keep prices below fixed levels, to refrain from discriminatory charging, or to limit their profits or dividends. Broadly speaking there are three main methods of regulation.

1. The first, which is generally used in the U.S., is to appoint regulatory commissions which exercise continuous supervision over the industries, and vary the details of the restrictions imposed on them from time to time. The main disadvantage of this approach is that the flexibility of management is reduced and that a quasi-judicial process is set up; therefore justice must be done and be seen to be done, and legal rules are developed which in course of time may become increasingly removed from the underlying economic aims of the legislation.

2. The second method which was widely but not exclusively used in Great Britain in the 19th century, is to enact some basic rules of conduct and formulae for the control of prices, dividends, or profits at the time when privileges are first granted to the utility, and to revise these rules and formulae only when new privileges are sought. The principal disadvantages of this approach are that the controls tend to become obsolete, owing to unforeseen changes such as technical innovations, changes in prices of raw materials, or general inflation, and that intelligent managements can often find some administrative or financial devices which effectively nullify the controls.

3. The third method is nationalization (q.v.) which to some extent eliminates the conflict between the profit motive and the aims of government policy, but creates new problems of supervision instead.

D. In the economic literature on public utilities interest has centred on the problem of finding a formula for determining the socially ideal prices and outputs of regulated industries—and indeed of industries generally. The suggestion that output should be adjusted so that price and marginal cost are equated has given rise to a controversy which has now lasted for more than a century. It has become clear that the problem is incapable of general solution in the abstract, partly because the aims of policy may vary, partly because of differing conditions in parts of the economy other than the industry under consideration.

L. P. Foldes

See also: MONOPOLY
SOCIAL CONTROL OF INDUSTRY

Public Welfare (See **Common Good**)

Punishment

A. *Punishment* in psychology denotes any aversive stimulus which has the immediate but temporary effect of reducing in strength (or in probability of occurrence) the response upon which it was contingent. It is a painful stimulation received by the organism for doing something, the punishment being an incentive to stop or suppress that response.

B. The term *punishment* is best understood by seeing its relation to the term *reward*. It is *not* simply the opposite of reward in its effect upon an individual. Whereas reward *permanently* increases the probability of occurrence of a particular response, punishment has only a *temporary* repressive effect upon a particular response.

According to B. F. Skinner, punishment is the presentation of a negative reinforcer (an aversive stimulus) or the withdrawal of a positive reinforcer. 'The most important effect of punishment, then, is to establish aversive conditions which are avoided ...'. But he goes on to say that punishment cannot permanently extinguish behaviour. 'If punishment is repeatedly avoided, the conditioned negative reinforcer undergoes extinction. Incompatible behavior is then less and less strongly reinforced, and the punished behavior eventually emerges. ... If punishment is discontinued, the behavior may emerge in full strength' (*Science and*

Purge

Human Behavior, New York: The Macmillan Co., 1953, p. 189).

C. 1. The social psychologist uses the term in a broad sense as 'the imposition of any unpleasant consequences [other than non-reward] for an act' (I. L. Child, 'Socialization', in G. Lindzey (ed.), *Handbook of Social Psychology*, Cambridge, Mass.: Addison-Wesley, 1954, p. 685).

2. The psychoanalytic writers add the notion of self-inflicted or internal punishment. Thus G. H. J. Pearson (*Psychoanalysis and the Education of the Child*, New York: Norton, 1954, p. 275) says 'It [the superego] warns the ego with guilt and loss of self-esteem. ... I do not like this action. If you do I will punish [by guilt and shame]'. O. Fenichel asks what does punishment really mean and answers, 'Inner punishment performed by the superego is felt as an extremely painful decrease in self-esteem and in extreme cases as a feeling of annihilation' (*The Psychoanalytical Theory of Neurosis*, New York: Norton, 1945, p. 105).

Robert J. Havighurst

See also: REWARD
        SANCTION

Pure Competition (See Economic Competition)

Purge

A. The term *purge* denotes exclusion from political party, government, or other institution, with or without arrest, of elements hostile or objectionable to leadership. It is also sometimes applied to mass arrest and imprisonment or execution of categories of population held to be 'socially dangerous'. In this sense it has been considered by some authors to be an essential feature of totalitarian regimes (e.g. H. Arendt, *The Origins of Totalitarianism*, New York: Harcourt, Brace, 1951; Z. K. Brzezinski, *The Permanent Purge*, Cambridge, Mass.: Harvard University Press, 1956).

B. 1. While mainly used with respect to modern totalitarian parties and systems of government, especially Communist, there are earlier examples of use, e.g. 'Pride's Purge', Col. Pride's exclusion from the Long Parliament in 1648 of members suspected of Royalist or Presbyterian leanings.

2. (a) The National-Socialist regime in Germany provided a classic case in the 'Night of the Long Knives', the destruction on 30 June 1934 of radical leaders of the S.A. and other Nazis whose policy was at variance with Hitler's,

followed by a rigorous screening of the whole party membership.

(b) A purge of the Italian Fascist Party immediately after the assumption of power led to at least 150,000 expulsions, and there was a further wave of expulsions in 1925–6).

(c) In the U.S.S.R. *purging* (*chistka*) is defined as 'cleansing the communist party of class-alien and hostile elements which have penetrated its ranks, of double-dealers, degenerates, careerists, self-seekers, bureaucrats, morally corrupt persons and violators of party and state discipline' (*Large Soviet Encyclopedia*, Moscow: 2nd edn., vol. 47, p. 398).

The first official purge of the Soviet Communist Party was launched in 1921. However, as early as 1919, in connection with the mobilization of communists for the Civil War, a re-registration of Party members was ordered, with the object of weeding out 'careerist elements' and 'hangers-on'; this reduced the size of the Party by about half.

The purge of 1921–4 involved the expulsion of about a quarter million or one third of the membership. Official figures covering about half those expelled indicated the most common offences to be 'passivity' (34 per cent), 'careerism', drunkenness, bourgeois mode of life, etc. (25 per cent), bribe-taking, extortion, etc. (9 per cent) and 'refusing to carry out Party directions' (11 per cent). Although the leadership claimed the purge would not be used to victimize groups who had opposed official policies, many oppositionists were evidently included in this last category.

In 1924–5 there was a further check of administrative and educational cells, involving about a quarter of the Party membership, and 6 per cent of those checked were expelled. This was followed in 1926 by a check of Party cells in the villages.

In April 1929 a purge was ordered of 'bureaucratic elements' and members of 'anti-party groups', including Trotskyists, which resulted in 130,500 exclusions. The second massive general purge took place in 1933–5, followed in 1936 by a further screening accompanying the issue of new membership cards. These operations led on in 1936–9 to the mass arrest as 'enemies of the people' of some millions of Party members and others (actual figures never published) on charges now stated to have been fabricated. The Party's size fell from $3\frac{1}{2}$ millions in 1933 to under 2 millions in January, 1938; thereafter renewed recruitment concealed the scale of further expulsions and arrests.

The Eighteenth Party Congress in 1939 resolved that further mass purges would be unnecessary. Since then cleansing the party of 'class-alien and hostile elements' has been treated as a continuous process rather than a series of campaigns and the few large-scale purges have been local in character. In some cases, notably the Leningrad purge of 1949–50 and the Georgian purges of 1951–3, these have been accompanied by mass arrests on fabricated charges, as in the general purges of the thirties. The arbitrary and repressive features of Stalin's purges have been condemned by his successors as aberrations of the dictator's personality. It should be noted, however, that similar methods were employed by them in removing the supporters of L. P. Beria from the police apparatus and Transcaucasian Party organizations in 1953–4.

(d) Communist parties in power in other countries have been subject to waves of expulsion and arrest of members considered unreliable or followers of defeated factions in the leadership, e.g. in Eastern Europe in 1949 and 1950, following Yugoslavia's break with the Soviet bloc. Comprehensive checking and sifting of the whole party membership, on the earlier Soviet model, has been rarer. Perhaps the most extensive of the several purges in Communist China was the 'rectification campaign' launched in the summer of 1957 and directed mainly at intellectuals and administrators.

Purges have been undertaken by Communist parties not in power only in exceptional circumstances, e.g. the removal of 'Trotskyists' during the twenties, especially from the German Communist Party, as a reflection of the inner-party struggle in the U.S.S.R.

T. H. R. Rigby

Purpose (See **Goal**)

Putting-Out System

A. *Putting-out system* denotes one of the stages in the economic evolution of the factory system whereby a merchant or a 'putter out' assigned raw materials and sometimes tools out to labourers who 'worked up' the raw materials into semi-finished or finished products at home at rates or payments agreed upon. The merchant or 'putter out' marketed the product, and assumed all the functions of the modern middlemen.

B. The term is used by economic historians to denote one of the phases of the economic evolution of the development of the factory system. *Putting-out system* was once considered to be synonymous with the term *domestic system*; as a result, in Germany the system was called *Hausindustrie* and in France, *industrie à domicile*. However, since domestic production characterizes *all* the stages in the development of the factory system, save the factory system itself, the term domestic system is perhaps not quite specific enough to be an accurate synonym for the putting-out system. In the case of the system of production under consideration, though the production was carried out in the home, such production was for the market. Hence English writers like W. J. Ashley (*The Economic Organisation of England*, London: Longmans, Green, 1914) came to prefer the use of the term *putting-out system* to that of *the domestic system*. D. H. Robertson (*The Controls of Industry*, Cambridge: At the University Press, 1955) uses the term *merchanting system*.

C. It is thought that the putting-out system originated in Italy and the Low Countries about the same time as the craft guilds, and became in time a serious competitor of the latter. The system spread to Northern Europe and the Rhineland region and was introduced into England in the 15th century, becoming entrenched in the industrial life of that country by the 16th century. Under the putting-out system a merchant called the 'putter out' (and in the textile industry, a clothier) owned the raw materials and sometimes the tools and assigned them to labourers who 'worked up' the raw materials into semi-finished or finished products in their own homes at rates or payments agreed upon.

D. H. Robertson best describes the putting-out system under the term *merchanting system*: '... under the merchanting system this division of function between those who plan and those who toil assumes a new importance. The craftsman still works in his own house, under his own supervision, and sometimes with his own tools; but he works to the order of a merchant, and his status is, in some respects, but little removed from that of a wage-earner' (ibid., p. 11).

One of the earliest records extant of the use of the putting-out system is that of Jehan Boine Broke at Douai. The putting-out system was most fully developed in the textile industries and was used to some extent in the cutlery, leather, and iron industries. The system exists today in the countries of the Orient and in the Middle East. In the countries of the Western

Putting-Out System

World there are semblances of the putting-out system in the clothing and needlework trades located in the large cities like London and New York.

The putting-out system is characterized by *sweat shop* conditions such as woman and child labour, long hours, and low wages. Those who have written on the putting-out system have devoted more attention to these conditions than to the system itself.

Kathleen E. Dunlop

See also: INDUSTRY

Quantification (See Measurement)

Quota Sampling (See Sampling)

R

Race

A. A *race* is a subdivision of a species, individual members of which display with some frequency a number of hereditary attributes that have become associated with one another in some measure through a considerable degree of in-breeding among the ancestors of the group during a substantial part of their recent evolution.

B. At the level of popular usage there is a remarkable international consensus that *race* implies common descent, matched by an enormous confusion at both popular and professional levels about what common descent implies. The popular controversy, expressed in an almost unparalleled polemical literature from virtually all parts of the world, reflects the social movements of the last hundred years from colonialism to Nazism and from American *integration* and *segregation* to South African *apartheid*. Perhaps no other single concept has been surrounded with such bitter conflict or subjected to such distortion. This conflict is, however, primarily a matter of race relations and racism (q.v.) rather than of race as such. It may be noted that the term *social race* is used with increasing frequency to refer to socially visible or institutional racial or quasi-racial distinctions in this area.

C. The scientific confusion reflects a continuing partial division between scholars concerned with the marks of common descent—the overt physical characteristics by which races are classified—and those concerned with the process of descent itself—the genetic mechanisms of inheritance.

1. Some definitions still current in anthropology are not easily related to those current in genetics. E. A. Hooton, for example, defined a race as '... a great division of mankind, the members of which, though individually varying, are characterized as a group by a certain combination of morphological and metrical features, principally non-adaptive, which have been derived from their common descent' (*Up From the Ape*, New York: The Macmillan Co., 2nd edn., 1946, p. 448).

2. Even before Hooton set forth his defini-

tion, an important and partially conflicting view was expressed in genetics by T. Dobzhansky: 'The fundamental units of racial variability are populations and genes, not complexes of characters which connote in the popular mind a racial distinction' (*Genetics and the Origin of Species*, New York: Columbia University Press, 2nd rev. edn., 1941, p. 78). Later L. C. Dunn and T. Dobzhansky defined races as '... populations which differ in the relative commonness of some gene or genes' (*Heredity, Race and Society*, New York: Penguin Books, 1946, p. 101). This admirable and much-quoted definition requires some taxonomic qualification, since as it stands we could justifiably refer to a 'male race', clearly not a usage traditional nor useful to the concept. As V. V. Bunak says, 'In zoological systematics, the term race corresponds in meaning to the term sub-species' ('Race as a Historical Concept', in E. W. Count (ed.), *This is Race*, New York: Schuman, 1950, p. 573). It should be noted that there are differences of opinion about whether human racial divisions are as general as sub-species distinctions, or whether perhaps they are comparable to sub-sub-species in other animals. Such a stricture must certainly be noted in relation to the relatively small populations sometimes called sub-races, but elevated to the status of full races by C. S. Coon and H. V. Vallois (C. S. Coon, *The Races of Europe*, New York: The Macmillan Co., 1939; H. V. Vallois, 'Race', in A. L. Kroeber (ed.), *Anthropology Today*, Chicago: University of Chicago Press, 1953, pp. 145–62).

3. M. Krogman combines several of these considerations in a somewhat discursive definition which reflects many of the modern problems in this field: 'A race is a sub-group of peoples possessing a definite combination of physical characters, of genetic origin; this combination serves, in varying degree, to distinguish the sub-group from the other sub-groups of mankind, and the combination is transmitted in descent, providing all conditions which originally gave rise to the definite combination remain relatively unaltered; as a rule the sub-group inhabits, or did inhabit, a more or less restricted geographic region' ('What We Do Not Know About Race', *Scientific Monthly*, vol. 57, 1943,

Race and Minority Group Relations

pp. 97–104, quoted in his 'The Concept of Race', in R. Linton (ed.), *The Science of Man in the World Crisis*, New York: Columbia University Press, 1945, p. 49).

4. Recent research on heredity and disease calls into question the non-adaptive character of some, possibly of many racial characteristics. This element in Hooton's definition may therefore be abandoned in a modern definition, while leaving the question open for further research on specific traits, as Hooton himself has noted (*Up From the Ape*, pp. 452 ff).

5. Increasing application of genetic principles and continuing new discoveries about human genetics further underscore the essentially statistical character of any useful modern definition, weakening or destroying the bases for the taxonomic clarity of Hooton's 'divisions of mankind'. The ability of the sub-species of man to cross breed (and their de facto interbreeding) throughout the history of the species is continuously documented by studies both in genetics and in physical anthropology. In other species, where breeding processes can be subjected to rigorous experimental control, where reproduction is asexual, or where the habitat range of various sub-species may be more restricted than is the case in man, 'racial' classification becomes somewhat easier, but other terms—strain, variety, sub-species, population, geotype, ecotype, clone, biotype, and the like—are commonly employed for these more precisely definable concepts. With expanding modern knowledge of the cultural basis of many phenomena formerly thought to be racial, other concepts have emerged for referring to the cultural and social units which also operate as more or less transitory breeding groups—*a* culture, ethnic group, nationality, community, clan— each with its particular bearing on mating and descent. Some of these groupings may come to have a close relationship to such concepts as sub-race, strain, breed, or gene pool.

Munro S. Edmonson

See also: RACE AND MINORITY GROUP
RELATIONS
RACISM

Race and Minority Group Relations

A. The field of *race and minority group relations* is constituted by the study of social contact, conflict, and accommodation among racial, nationality, religious, and language groups with particular reference to prejudice and discrimination and their causes and consequences.

B. Race (q.v.) is a concept that comes from biology and physical anthropology, and refers to a subdivision of a species. The sociological use of the term is only partly related to this biological use: because of extensive amalgamation, what are called racial groups by sociologists— who partly follow popular usage—seldom possess a high degree of biological relatedness. Some sociologists even follow popular usage so far as to include relations between language, nationality, and religious groups, as well as mixed racial groups, when speaking of 'race relations'.

Largely to avoid this difficulty, the term *minority group relations* has come into currency among sociologists in the past few decades. The term had its origin in reference to the so-called 'national minorities' of Europe, which were relatively small enclaves of people of one nationality living among a larger number of people of a different nationality. In more heterogeneous countries without a single numerically dominant nationality—like the United States— the term *minority group* has come to refer to any racial, nationality, religious, or language group (whether pure or mixed) who face certain special situations, who are subject to certain discriminations, and who are the objects of prejudice from most other peoples. In these countries, there is no one numerical 'majority group' with a distinctive history and a special claim to the territory. The term *majority group* is there used as a residual term, to refer to those who are not in the minorities under consideration, and with the implication that they have certain privileges, advantages, and powers in contrast with the minorities.

Since 1945, some sociologists have avoided both the terms *race relations* and *minority group relations* as misleading, and have referred to the same phenomena as *intergroup relations*. But whatever term is used, those who study in this field attempt 'to describe and analyse the phenomena which arise when groups of people who differ racially or culturally come into contact with one another' (B. Berry, *Race and Ethnic Relations*, Boston: Houghton Mifflin, 1958, p. vii).

C. There are two distinct foci of interest in this field of study and each of these subdivides the field in different ways.

1. The first concentrates on the different patterns of relationship that have developed in various parts of the world when people of different racial or cultural background come into contact with each other. The interest here is in social organization and cultural products. Processes of competition, conflict, accommodation and assimilation (to use R. E. Park's terms) are described and analysed, as are characteristic minority institutions (such as the immigrant press). Some writers in this tradition (like A. Locke & B. J. Stern (eds.), *When Peoples Meet*, New York: Progressive Education Association, 1942) are almost exclusively descriptive. Those who employ an analytic scheme usually refer to some form of a *natural history*, such as Park's sequence.

2. The other category of students in this field take a *social problems* (q.v.) approach and concentrate on the behaviour of discrimination, the attitude of prejudice, and the consequences for the minority and majority groups of both of these. A. M. Rose, for example, says 'A group is a minority group if it is the object of prejudice and discrimination from the dominant groups, and if the members think of themselves as a minority. It is not a minority *because* its members have a distinctive racial or nationality background, or *because* its members adopt a certain religion or language, although minority status ... is attached to at least one of these four characteristics' (*Race Prejudice and Discrimination*, New York: Knopf, 1951, p. 5). The usual topics dealt with under this approach are (following G. Myrdal, *An American Dilemma*, New York: Harper, 1944): economic, political, legal, and social discriminations; race prejudice; minority group reactions (accommodation and protest) and institutional adjustments to discrimination and prejudice; minority group solidarity.

Arnold M. Rose

See also: ACCOMMODATION
CONFLICT
DISCRIMINATION
ETHNIC GROUP
MINORITY
PREJUDICE
RACE
RACISM
SEGREGATION

Racism

A. *Racism* is the doctrine that there is a connection between racial and cultural traits, and that some races are inherently superior to others. Racism indiscriminately includes such non-biological groupings as religious sects, nations, linguistic groups, and cultural groups under its concept of race, and hence can be regarded as a particularly virulent form of ethnocentrism (q.v.).

B. *Racism* is a newer term for the word *racialism*, which was used extensively in the recent past by most writers dealing with the problem, e.g. L. L. Snyder (*Race: A History of Modern Ethnic Theories*, New York: Alliance, 1939).

The disagreement among scholars as to the word *race* (q.v.) does not extend to its derivative *racism*; there is virtual agreement that it refers to a doctrine of racial supremacy. R. Benedict has defined *racism* as '... the dogma that one ethnic group is condemned by Nature to hereditary inferiority and another group is destined to hereditary superiority' (*Race, Science and Politics*, New York: Viking Press, 1943, p. 98). Racism is more than race prejudice. It is a formal doctrine whose contemporary intellectual notions are derived from A. de Gobineau's *Essai sur l'inégalité des races humaines*, published in 1853. Most prominent perhaps in carrying the doctrine into the 20th century was H. S. Chamberlain the English-born German publicist (1855–1927).

C. Racism fuses national, ethnic, linguistic, religious, and racial groups into an amalgam, the alleged inferiorities of which are spuriously attributed to race alone. J. Comas writes, 'Racism is quite different from a mere acceptance or scientific and objective study of the fact of race and the fact of the present inequality of human groups. Racism involves the assertion that inequality is absolute and unconditional, i.e. that a race is inherently and by its very nature superior or inferior to others quite independently of the physical conditions of its habitat and of social factors' ('Racial Myths', in *The Race Question in Modern Science*, Paris: Unesco and Sidgwick & Jackson, 1956, pp. 52–3). It has played an important part in domestic and world politics of many nations in the 20th century as in the internal treatment of Jewish populations and the justifications for world conquest on the part of the Nazi regime in Germany, the present struggle over civil rights in the United States, and the Apartheid policy of South Africa.

W. A. Lessa

See also: DISCRIMINATION
ETHNIC GROUP
MINORITY
PREJUDICE
RACE
RACE AND MINORITY GROUP
RELATIONS
SEGREGATION

Radicalism

Radicalism

A. *Radicalism* denotes political and social action and thought calling for drastic and immediate change in existing institutions.

B. 1. For the most part the term (and the adjective *radical*) has been used in describing extreme leftwing political action and thought—both Marxist and non-Marxist. It has also been used pejoratively in critiques of quite moderate proposals for gradual reform. 'Those who take an overprotective attitude toward existing social structures frequently become disturbed and classify all ameliorists as "left-wingers" or "reds" or "radicals" ' (A. M. & E. B. Lee (eds.), *Social Problems in America*, Henry Holt, 1949, p. 672). More scientifically, of course, radicalism designates social ideas which purport to go to the root of things and therefore call for drastic and sweeping changes in existing institutions.

2. Radicalism is sometimes thought of as being at the far left end of a 'political spectrum'. Liberals, seeking slower, less drastic change, come next, followed by conservatives, opposed to conscious effort at basic change. At the extreme right end of such a spectrum are reactionaries, desiring a return to previously-existing institutions and practices. In recent years political sociologists, in analysis of the American scene, have noted the emergence of a 'radical right'. Thus D. Bell speaks of 'the group that S. M. Lipset has dubbed the "radical right"—radical because it opposes traditional conservatism, with its respect for individual rights, and because it sought to impose new patterns in American life' (*The End of Ideology*, Glencoe, Ill.: The Free Press, 1960, p. 100; see also S. M. Lipset, 'The Sources of the Radical Right', in D. Bell (ed.), *The New American Right*, New York: Criterion Books, 1956, pp. 210–12).

C. 1. The term *radicalism* was first used in Great Britain in connection with opponents of the Reform Bill of 1832 and later applied to J. Bentham and his followers, who were called philosophical radicals. As a general political movement in the sense it is now understood, radicalism may be said to have begun with French syndicalism.

2. In the United States, radicalism first took the form of utopianism, which in various forms had many proponents in the 19th century. In the sense of advocacy of extreme political action, it embraced the abolitionists. Modern radicalism in America, however, is more often thought of as having its roots in the Populist movement and

coming into full fruition with the I.W.W. and the Socialists at the beginning of the 20th century. The character of this native American radicalism was altered somewhat with the split among left-wing groups over the advent of Bolshevism in Russia.

Since the 1920s, radicalism has come more and more to involve acceptance of Marxism. The radical movement on the Left was most influenced by Stalinism, although certain forms of non-Stalinist radicalism remained, as, for example, the left wing of the Socialist Party and the Socialist Workers Party. Radicalism was contrasted with modern American liberalism of the sort which underpinned the New Deal of F. D. Roosevelt. During the days of the 'popular front' in the 1930s, common opposition to European fascism drew the Marxist radicals and many liberals together. The liaison was given a severe jolt by the Nazi-Soviet pact, but it received new life when the Soviet Union entered World War II. For many years after World War II, non-Marxist 'radicalism of the Left' was virtually non-existent in the United States. This was an index not only of rejection of Communism at home and abroad but also of a generally diminished concern with ideology in a context of growing affluence.

Fred Warner Neal

See also: COMMUNISM
     FASCISM
     LEFT AND RIGHT
     SOCIALISM

Ramage (See Kinship and Kinship System)

Random Sampling (See Sampling)

Rates of Reproduction

A. The phrase denotes the *gross reproduction rate* and the *net reproduction rate*.

1. The gross reproduction rate is found by summing the age-specific fertility rates (constituted by the number of births in a given year per 1,000 women in a particular age-group usually covering a five-year span) for the age-groups composing the span of child-bearing years in a particular society; multiplying the sum by the number of years in each age-group (usually five) to relate the rate to the age of the women by single years; multiplying the product by the percentage of females at birth; and multiplying that product by ·001 to reduce the rate to that for one woman. Thus W. Petersen (*Population*, New York: Macmillan, 1961, pp. 624–5) presents the following for the United States in 1950:

Age-group	Age-specific fertility rate
15–19	80·0
20–24	192·5
25–29	163·0
30–34	101·5
35–39	51·2
40–44	14·6
45–49	1·1
	603·9

Gross Reproduction Rate $= 603·9 \times 5 \times ·487$ (percentage of women at birth) $\times ·001 = 1·47$.

2. The net reproduction rate is calculated in exactly the same way, except that before the age-specific fertility rates are summed each is multiplied by the proportion that would survive on the basis of current age-specific death rates from birth to the mid-point of that age-group.

B. According to Petersen (ibid., p. 278) 'A *gross reproduction rate* is the ratio of female births in two successive generations, assuming no change in the age-specific birth rates and no deaths before the end of the childbearing period. A *net reproduction rate* is the ratio of female births in two successive generations, assuming no change in the age-specific birth and death rates'.

Thus assuming that the age-specific fertility rates (e.g. of 1950) in the United States have not changed and will not change for a long period of time, it would be possible to say that an average cohort of 1,000 American women, born in 1935 and surviving until the end of their childbearing period in 1985, will have produced a total of 1,470 daughters, or 1·47 daughters per woman, by the latter date. If the age-specific death rates (e.g. of 1950) are also introduced and assumed to remain unchanged, then this same cohort will have produced 1,410 girls or 1·41 daughters per woman, by 1985.

Now, even if these assumptions were valid, the rates of reproduction would not be a great improvement over the crude rates of birth and of natural increase, unless the proportion of fecund females varied greatly from time to time (cf. ibid., pp. 625–6). But the assumptions are obviously not valid, for age-specific fertility rates and age-specific death rates do change, so that the rates of reproduction have not been as great an improvement for purposes of population projection as had been hoped (cf. P. H. Landis, *Population Problems*, New York: American Book Co., 2nd edn., prepared by P. K. Hatt, 1954, pp. xxviii–xxix (appendix)).

William L. Kolb

See also: BIRTH RATE
DEATH RATE

Ratio Scale (See Scaling)

Rationality

A. In a broad sense, *rationality* denotes a style or behaviour (a) that is appropriate to the achievement of given goals, (b) within the limits imposed by given conditions and constraints.

B. In particular contexts, terms (a) and (b) of the definition may receive more exact specification. Some of the more important of these specialized uses are:

1. The goal may be assumed to take the form of maximizing (or, in game theory, minimaxing) the expected value, over some time interval, of a utility function. Further, the existence of the utility function may be derived from postulates about the ordering and consistency of the choosing organism's preferences. Thus, the rational consumer of formal economic theory maximizes his expected utility, and the rational entrepreneur maximizes his expected profit. If a distinction is wanted between this very strict species of rationality and more general forms, the former may be termed *optimality*, the latter *adaptiveness* or *functionality*.

2. The goal may be assumed to consist of criteria to be satisfied in an all-or-none way (e.g. attainment of the level of aspiration).

3. The conditions and constraints referred to in the general definition may be *objective characteristics* of the environment external to the choosing organism, they may be *perceived characteristics*, or they may be *characteristics of the organism itself* that it takes as fixed and not subject to its own control. The line between the first case and the other two is sometimes drawn by distinguishing *objective rationality*, on the one hand, from *subjective* or *bounded rationality*, on the other.

4. The goals referred to in the definition may be goals of the choosing organism, goals of a social system to which he belongs, or goals imputed by the observer.

5. An unambiguous use of the term *rationality* requires the user to specify what assumptions he is making about both goals and conditions.

C. *Rationality* and its synonyms were important in the vocabulary of philosophy and ethics before the social sciences emerged as independent

Rationalization

disciplines. The modern usage of rationality is very close to Aristotle's concept of calculative or deliberative intellectual virtue. In this sense, the rationality of an action involves its derivation by logical processes from valid premises. Rationality sometimes refers to processes of choice that employ the intellective faculty; sometimes to the choices themselves. The former emphasis is typical of earlier usage in psychology, logic, and ethics; the latter emphasis predominates in economics and sociology.

1. Thus, W. James (*Principles of Psychology*, New York: Holt, 1890, ch. 22) uses rationality as synonymous with 'the peculiar thinking process called reasoning'. In this view, the rationality of a choice depends on the process of making it. Correspondingly, *irrationality* in psychological literature denotes domination of choice by affective mechanisms (emotion, drive, instinct, impulse) rather than intellective mechanisms (G. Allport, 'The Historical Background of Modern Social Psychology', in G. Lindzey (ed.), *Handbook of Social Psychology*, Cambridge, Mass.: Addison-Wesley, 1954, pp. 15–18). Because of this historical identification of rationality with the doctrine of *rationalism*, recent psychological writing tends to prefer terms like *cognitive process* (J. S. Bruner, J. V. Goodnow, & G. A. Austin, *A Study of Thinking*, New York: J. Wiley, 1956, p. viii) or *intellective process*. Hence, *rationality*, in reference to the process of choice, appears to be disappearing from social science literature.

2. Economists have generally used *rationality* to denote an attribute of an action selected by a choice process, rather than an attribute of the process. Thus R. A. Dahl and C. E. Lindblom (*Politics, Economics, and Welfare*, New York: Harper & Brothers, 1953, p. 38) say: 'An action is rational to the extent that it is "correctly" designed to maximize goal achievement, given the goal in question and the real world as it exists'. In sociology, similar definitions can be found in M. Weber (*The Theory of Social and Economic Organization*, trans. by A. M. Henderson & T. Parsons, New York: Oxford University Press, 1947, p. 117), K. Mannheim (*Man and Society in an Age of Reconstruction*, London: Kegan Paul, Trench, Trubner, 1940, pp. 51–7), and T. Parsons (*The Social System*, Glencoe, Ill.: The Free Press, 1951, pp. 549–50). (Pareto prefers the term *logical* to *rational*.) The term is used rather loosely in sociology, while in mathematical economics and statistical decision theory it has received exact axiomatic treatment (see B. above).

3. There is a somewhat distinct usage of *rational* in the writing of Weber (*The Theory of Social and Economic Organization*, pp. 329–41) and others on bureaucracy. In the ideal type of 'rational legal authority', rationality means the conscious adaptation of the organization to goals, and its operation through the impersonal application of rules without deflection by the personal goals of the functionaries. An approximate synonym is Mannheim's phrase, *functional rationality* (*Man and Society in an Age of Reconstruction*, p. 53).

Herbert A. Simon

See also: COGNITION
MIND
RATIONALIZATION
REASON

Rationalization (Economics and Sociology)
A. This term has a number of meanings in several social sciences. They all relate to a varying extent to the common usage of the term denoting (a) the activity of making something reasonable, intelligible, simple; and/or (b) the result(s) of such activity.

B. In economic writings, the term in its German form (*Razionalisierung*) arose in the context of German reconstruction in the early 1920s. The term was subsequently taken over and used in various ways in Germany and in Great Britain and in the United States in the 1920s and 1930s. The word itself does not now appear at the centre of discussions of industrial questions with anything like the same frequency.

1. The most general emphasis of this term is upon 'reducing waste and inefficiency' in financial, commercial, and industrial organization. The term implies increased resort at levels of planning and control, to rational, simplifying, utilitarian criteria. Industry is to be so organized, or reorganized that engineering, financial and 'welfare' optima are simultaneously secured. Rationalization thus designates an *end* which, in principle, is separable from the *methods* of attainment, such as, e.g. industrial concentration, 'scientific management', etc. The following represent such usage: 'Rationalization means that instead of traditional processes, especially routine, empirical rules and improvisation, use is made of methods that are the fruit of patient scientific study and aim at the optimum adjustment of means to ends, thus securing that every effort produces a maximum result' (International Labour Organization, *Social Aspects of Rationalization*, Geneva: International Labour Office, 1951, p. 1). 'Improved planning and

574

mechanical power, accelerated labour, better organization of business personnel and better marketing arrangements are the main factors in rationalization' (J. A. Hobson, *Rationalization and Unemployment*, London: Allen, 1930, p. 62).

2. Some writers use the term to denote a species of amalgamation in industry: '... a method of removing some of the disadvantages of imperfect competition. By rationalization is meant action taken by the State or by the majority of producers in a particular industry to bring the industry under single control. Such action will remove many of the wastes ...' (J. E. Meade, *An Introduction to Economic Analysis and Policy*, London: Oxford University Press, p. 174).

3. Some industrialists have used the term in a very loose way: 'Basically rationalization is simply rational control of industry to ensure that as far as possible you do not produce more than the market can absorb' (Lord Melchett, quoted in Hobson, *Rationalization and Unemployment*, p. 65). The trouble with this line of thought is that the size of the market is itself partly shaped by the amount of production. Thus, cutting production may further cut the market resulting in a vicious circle. It may also divert attention from needed innovation by too much attention to mere economy.

C. Sociologists, especially in Germany, have sometimes conceived of this process as part of a wider process—that of the more general acceptance of certain standards and/or methods deemed rational. For such writers, the term implies emphasis upon, or increased recourse to, the methods which reputedly characterize the activities of e.g. (a) economic theorists; (b) accountants, bookkeepers and those concerned with, in general, the calculation of quantities—more especially economic quantities; (c) applied science. Thus Weber argues that 'In the last resort the factor which produced capitalism is the rational permanent enterprise, rational accounting, rational technology, and rational law, but, again, not these alone. Necessary complementary factors were the rational spirit, the rationalization of the conduct of life in general, and a rationalist economic ethic' (*General Economic History*, trans. by F. H. Knight, Glencoe, Ill.: The Free Press, 1950, p. 354).

J. Gould

See also: RATIONALIZATION (Social
    Psychology)
  RATIONALITY
  REASON

Rationalization (Social Psychology)

A. The most general sense of this term is the act of making rational or intelligible; in a somewhat narrower usage in psychological and psychoanalytical writings it denotes the process of devising reasons for acts and ideas which have their origin in motives which the rationalizer seeks to conceal from himself and others.

B. 1. An example of Freudian usage is given by E. Jones (Glossary to *Papers on Psycho-analysis*, London: Baillière, Tyndall & Cox, 5th edn., 1948), who defines rationalization as 'the inventing of a reason for an attitude or action the motive of which is not recognized'.

Elsewhere 'Rationalization in Everyday Life', in *Papers on Psycho-analysis*, London: Baillière, Tindall & Cox, 3rd edn., 1923, p. 13) Jones notes that those who deliberately perform irrational acts distort 'the mental processes concerned' and provide 'a false explanation that has a plausible ring of rationality'.

Thus, acts of rationalization are the result of the repression of thought from consciousness. A distasteful emotion or intention is concealed from the self, and replaced by a more acceptable substitute. This rationalized version of the concealed idea serves both to hide the act of concealment itself, and to camouflage the content of what is concealed, thereby reinforcing the repression (q.v.). It is important to note that in the psychoanalytic use of the term, the process of rationalization is understood to be an *unconscious* one. For example, the obsessional neurotic may rationalize his compulsion to wash over-frequently by the idea of the danger of infection. Subjects of post-hypnotic suggestion typically rationalize their behaviour, e.g. a hypnotic subject is ordered to pick up an umbrella and open it—when asked to explain his behaviour, he gives as a reason: 'because it is raining' when in fact it is not.

The choice of social goals for action may serve as a rationalization for personal motives, e.g. stubbornness may be rationalized as a 'fight for a good cause', or personal paranoid delusions may be rationalized through joining a group likely to be persecuted.

Freud also described a version of rationalization which plays a part in dream formation. By 'secondary revision' of the dream thoughts, the dream is made plausible to the dreamer, and its latent unconscious content is disguised. Sharp contrasts between dream elements may be reconciled, gaps filled in, and the whole dream glossed to give a more logical appearance.

Reality Principle

2. Usage in general psychology follows that in psychoanalysis. Thus G. Allport (*Personality*, New York, Henry Holt, 1937, p. 172) discusses rationalization as one of many 'techniques of self-deception', and contrasts it with reason: 'Reason fits one's impulses and beliefs to the world of reality; rationalization fits one's conception of reality to one's impulses and beliefs'. The positive function of rationalization has been noted by some social psychologists. Thus G. Murphy, L. B. Murphy, & T. M. Newcomb, in *Experimental Social Psychology* (New York: Harper & Brothers, 1937, p. 373) say 'The development of rationalizations and forgetfulness of sources of attitudes may be a step in this process of organization and integration ... [of social behaviour].

C. de Monchaux

See also: REASON
        REPRESSION

Real Cost (See **Cost**)

Realist Jurisprudence (See **Jurisprudence**)

Reality Principle
A. *Reality principle* denotes a learnt tendency to defer the immediate gratification of an impulse or even to undergo pain in the present for the purpose of maximizing future pleasure and/or minimizing future pain.

B. According to Freud, the infant normally seeks to discharge tensions as they arise, and the discharge of tensions is pleasurable. Thus the infant behaves in accordance with the pleasure principle (q.v.) which tends to render 'the psychic apparatus as a whole free from any excitation, or to keep the amount of excitation constant or as low as possible' (*Beyond the Pleasure Principle*, London: The International Psycho-Analytical Press, 1922, p. 81). With the passage of time, however, the external world, as represented by parents, older siblings, et al. begins to demand of the child that he forego some immediate gratification. Such demands take the form of rewarding the young child when the discharge of tension (e.g. defecation) occurs in an appropriate setting and not rewarding and perhaps punishing the child when his behaviour is in accordance with the pleasure principle. In Freudian language the ego and superego are beginning to emerge, and among the functions of the ego is that of 'discovering the most favourable and least perilous method of obtaining satisfaction, taking the external

world into account' (S. Freud, *An Outline of Psycho-Analysis*, trans. by J. Strachey, London: The Hogarth Press, 1949, p. 5). In addition to such social learning, some physiologic maturation is a necessary condition for the child to achieve control over the discharge of his tensions.

To the degree that the individual delays tension reduction until the setting is appropriate, his behaviour is said to be in accordance with the reality principle. Thus the reality principle designates a willingness to forego immediate pleasure and even to undergo immediate pain in the interest of the long-run maximization of pleasure and minimization of pain. It should be emphasized that when behaviour is in accordance with the reality principle, pleasure remains the objective, but the instrumental acts become more roundabout in the course of avoiding the now foreseen undesirable and painful consequences of immediate gratification. In Freud's words, 'The reality-principle is only continuing the work of the pleasure-principle in a more effectual way, gratification being the aim of both and their opposition only a secondary fact' (E. Jones, *Sigmund Freud: Life and Work*, vol. 2, *Years of Maturity, 1901–1919*, London: The Hogarth Press, 1955, p. 502). Freud did believe, however, that the reality principle not only delayed but also diminished pleasure (*A General Introduction to Psychoanalysis*, New York: Perma Books, 1953, p. 365) and that fantasy was one mode of thought which 'was kept free from reality-testing and remained subordinated to the pleasure-principle alone' ('Formulations Regarding the Two Principles in Mental Functioning', *Collected Papers*, London: Hogarth Press, 1925, vol. IV, pp. 16–17).

C. 1. The transition from pleasure principle behaviour to reality principle behaviour constitutes a form of socialization which has interested many social scientists, some of whom rejected the corpus of psychoanalytic theory. Thus W. I. Thomas saw the human adult engaging in labour only reluctantly and as reverting to more pleasurable activity as soon as the pressure was off: 'Tramps and criminals represent a repudiation of [labor], and the rich man's son often shows how superficial are the race habits of industry, failing when the pressure is withdrawn' ('The Gaming Instinct', *American Journal of Sociology*, vol. VI, 1901, p. 757). And again: 'From this standpoint our problem is not so much to account for the gambler as to account for the business-man' (ibid., p. 760).

Dewey's conception of intelligence is somewhat akin to Freud's reality principle. Although Dewey rejected the notion of a hedonistic calculus, he saw intelligence functioning in the service of impulse (*Human Nature and Conduct*, New York: Henry Holt, 1922, pp. 203–6, 255).

2. Poor performance in school and improvidence among the lower classes have been attributed to pleasure principle behaviour and the absence in the lower social strata of adequate and sufficiently consistent rewards to produce reality principle behaviour (J. Dollard & N. E. Miller, *Personality and Psychotherapy*, New York: McGraw-Hill, 1950, p. 45; A. Davis, 'Child Rearing in the Class Structure of American Society', in *The Family in a Democratic Society: Anniversary Papers of the Community Service Society of New York*, New York: Columbia University Press, 1949, pp. 56–69). Another phrasing for the same phenomenon imputes a pattern of 'deferred gratification' to middle-class people (B. Barber, *Social Stratification*, New York: Harcourt, Brace, 1957, pp. 315–17).

3. In the history of Western Europe the Protestant Reformation has been interpreted as a sort of analogue of the transition from pleasure to reality principle behaviour. Weber has pointed out that in Calvinism there was 'no place for the very human Catholic cycle of sin, repentance, atonement, release, followed by renewed sin' (*The Protestant Ethic and the Spirit of Capitalism*, trans. by T. Parsons, New York: Charles Scribner's Sons, 1958, p. 117). Rather Calvinism 'gave the broader groups of religiously inclined people a positive incentive to asceticism' (ibid., p. 121) because the Calvinist created the conviction of his own salvation through 'a systematic self-control which at every moment stands before the inexorable alternative, chosen or damned' (ibid., p. 115). And A. Kardiner differentiates Calvinism from Catholicism on the ground that the former involves the 'internalization of conscience' (*The Psychological Frontiers of Society*, New York: Columbia University Press, 1945, pp. 439–40).

Robert F. Winch

See also: PLEASURE PRINCIPLE

Reason

A. From the strict usage, denoting the activity of ratiocination or logical deduction of necessary truth, the term *reason* comes to denote, more generally, the power of intellect to formulate concepts and establish logical relations in such a way as to draw a correct conclusion from a given premise or to make an objectively valid judgement about empirical phenomena. By extension it has also come to mean a logical and valid explanation or justification for an event or relationship; and by still further extension any cause or motive.

B. As analysis of the term *reason* has constituted the central subject of Western philosophical thought for more than two thousand years, it is necessary here to illustrate its meaning in the light of changing historical usage.

1. Plato conceived of reason as that *instrument whereby man has access to genuine knowledge, the apprehension of unchanging forms or essences*, as contrasted with mere opinions based on sense perception of the changing world of physical bodies. This provided an epistemological basis for a belief in right reason which dominated European political thought down to the 18th century. Reason, in this somewhat exalted sense, was a *special intuitive faculty* possessed by human beings as distinct from other animals, which enabled them directly to apprehend universal truths or principles which governed the workings of a universe considered to be rational.

2. Two factors have combined to produce a climate of opinion in which the term *reason* is either avoided altogether or approached with a great deal of caution by many contemporary writers. One is the discrediting of the traditional 'faculty' psychology which thought of *reason* as *a power inherent in a specific organ*. And the other is the revolution in modern professional philosophy which is characterized by a high degree of self-consciousness concerning the logic of linguistic usage.

These trends, however, have not eliminated the need for some term to denote the *purposeful activity of regulating means and ends in a way characteristic of human beings*. Thus the usage of reason as a name for all satisfactory, rich, or full human living, which is to be found in writers as far removed as Aristotle and Spinoza, recurs in one as modern as Santayana. 'Reason is as old as man and as prevalent as human nature; for we should not recognize an animal to be human unless his instincts were to some degree conscious of their ends and rendered his ideas in that measure relevant to conduct' (*The Life of Reason*, New York: Charles Scribner's Sons, 1905, vol. 1, p. 4).

3. Reference should also be made to that employment of the term which emphasizes the contrast between reason and passion. Reason, in this sense, when embodied in human character

Recall

produces the man of sagacity and prudence as distinct from the man who is 'passion's slave'. Reason in this context, carries a strong suggestion of *freedom from bias, consistency, uniform application of rules, and an absence of doctrinaire or fanatical adherence to rules regardless of circumstance*. In a post-Freudian epoch, there may well also be a suggestion of *freedom from unconscious conflict* so that objective judgement may not be distorted by the compulsive concentration of the imagination on impulses, congenial but not spontaneous. Thus J. Dewey writes, ' "Reason" as a noun signifies the happy co-operation of a multitude of dispositions, such as sympathy, curiosity, exploration, experimentation, frankness, pursuit—to follow things through—circumspection, to look about at the context, etc., etc.' (*Human Nature and Conduct*, New York: Henry Holt, 1922, p. 196).

4. A characteristic contemporary approach to the problem of defining reason would consist of an attempt to find an answer to the question of what we in fact do when we are said to employ reason. Reason in this sense would embrace a *number of methods of procedure in seeking the truth concerning empirical phenomena*. It would be concerned with such techniques as observing, measuring, comparing, experimenting, formulating hypotheses, verifying, formulation of concepts, logical analysis of meanings and linguistic grammar. Thus ' "Reason" in such a context will be looked on not as some kind of pure faculty, but as attempts on the part of human beings to use and improve their tools of concepts and language so as to make logical connections and to advance knowledge' (D. Emmet, ' "Reason" in Recent Theological Discussion', *Political Quarterly*, vol. 26, 1955, p. 282). On the other hand, it must be emphasized that there are those who would wish to confine the term reason more strictly, i.e. to ratiocination or mathematical demonstration whereby necessary truth is deduced (see A. above).

R. V. Sampson

C. The word *reason* is rarely found in the indexes of works in social science. As in the case of many other words, it has ceased to be a technical term for social psychology and sociology, and has become a lay term for most writers. Some see it as a form of thinking. W. Coutu, in his *Emergent Human Nature* (New York: Knopf, 1949, p. 159) states that 'In the present setting reasoning is not a type of activity different from thinking; it is merely more restricted by some logic or conceptual system and

therefore more controlled by the structure of that system and therefore more accurate'. Other writers, either explicitly or implicitly, distinguish between mere reflective thinking, which may be random and seemingly without definite purpose, and reason as the capacity to think logically and purposefully. G. Allport (*Personality*, New York: Henry Holt, 1937, p. 172) argues that 'Reason may be defined as one's capacity to shape one's belief and conduct to accord with one's knowledge of the world, and if one's knowledge is insufficient, the capacity to set out to acquire more knowledge pertinent to the issue at hand'. It is just this equating of reason to rationality, this faith in man's ability to discover a rational and moral social order, that R. Bendix (*Social Science and the Distrust of Reason*, Berkeley: University of California Press, 1951) argues has been lost in modern social science, and for which has been substituted a faith in fact-finding techniques in the hands of an intellectual elite who avoid questions concerning the significance of knowledge.

Reason is related intimately to logic by most writers. In addition to being used in the sense of capacity to think logically, reason denotes logical and sound explanations for situations, as, for example, in 'It will be useful to examine the reasons for this ...' A few writers (e.g. W. Coutu, *Emergent Human Nature*, p. 159) hold that 'All reason is relative to some conceptual system in terms of which its validity is determined', whereas others argue that if the thinking is syllogistic, reason and hence reasons occur only when there are valid inferences drawn from true premises. Allport (*Personality*, p. 172) writes that 'Reason fits one's impulses and beliefs to the world of reality; rationalization fits one's conception of reality to one's impulses and beliefs'. By extension, however, reason has also come to be used as a synonym for cause or motive.

Richard Dewey

See also: Cognition
Mind
Motivation
Rationality

Recall

A. In political science *recall* denotes a device or procedure by which a public official's tenure in office may be terminated by popular vote. Thus, the recall should be considered in relation to impeachment, address by the legislature, *quo-warranto*, executive removal, and ouster through judicial proceedings. The recall differs from the others in that the removal is effected through popular electoral decision, and is in this way similar to the referendum (q.v.).

B. 1. The difficulty of keeping representatives continuously responsible to the general public has persisted throughout historic times. In the Athenian democracy, banishment or *ostracism* was developed as an instrument for protecting the citizenry from wilful and ambitious officers. These dangerous individuals could be banished for a period of ten years by a vote of the citizenry (A. F. Hattersley, *A Short History of Democracy*, Cambridge: At the University Press, 1930, pp. 37, 38). Short terms of office in Republican Rome obviated most of the necessity for removal devices, but the emergence of modern forms of representative government in Europe brought with it the problem of keeping the representative continuously responsible. Impeachment was widely used in England against irresponsible officialdom until the system of responsible cabinet government began to develop.

Implementing the doctrines of Rousseau, some Swiss cantons established the right to force a dissolution of the legislative body by a popular election. But agitation for the recall of individual officers by popular vote began in the United States during the age of Populism in the last two decades of the 19th century. Thus Los Angeles adopted the recall for its municipal officials in 1903. The state of Oregon followed in 1906. Twelve states of the United States and about a thousand American municipalities now possess recall provisions in their constitutions and charters.

2. In the United States recall is used almost exclusively in local government areas; only Oregon and North Dakota have recalled statewide elected officers. Elected executive and administrative officers are most commonly eligible for recall, but some systems provide for recall of judicial and legislative officers. Some also provide for the recall of appointed officials.

3. The operation of the recall procedure is reasonably simple. A private citizen or group of citizens drafts a petition (q.v.) stating the reason for seeking an officer's removal, secures the signatures of eligible voters upon the petition, and files the petition with the proper official (usually the secretary of state for state officers and the county or city clerk for local officers).

The minimum number of signatures is not uniform among the various recall systems, though 25 per cent of the total vote in the last election is the most common figure. A designated official checks the signatures for authenticity and, if he finds the number of valid signatures sufficient, he certifies to the sufficiency of the petition. Thereafter, the executive authority sets the date for the recall election. In most systems the challenged officer is a candidate for the position. The opposition nominates one or more candidates by petition. In the election a voter votes upon two questions: (a) Shall the officer be removed? and (b) Who shall fill the office for the remainder of the term if the officer is recalled? A majority vote is necessary to recall the officer, though most systems permit a plurality vote to fill the vacancy. A few systems provide that these two issues shall be decided in separate elections.

Some of the statutes protect an officer by making him immune from recall charges during the first six months and/or the last six months of his term.

Of the many thousand officers subject to recall in the United States, the average annual number of recall attempts was only six in the first quarter-century of the recall's operation (F. L. Bird & F. M. Ryan, *The Recall of Public Officers*, New York: The Macmillan Co., 1930, p. 20).

Cortez A. M. Ewing

See also: INITIATIVE
           PETITION
           REFERENDUM

Reductionism

A. The term *reductionism* when used in science denotes the effort or the advocacy of the effort to simplify methods of research, analysis of causal relations, or the formulation of hypotheses, theories, and laws, by assuming that the methods, causes, or laws adequate for the interpretation of one range or kind of phenomena are also adequate for another, apparently different, range or kind of phenomena. It implies an identity or complete correlation of some sort between the two kinds or ranges of phenomena concerned.

B. While the term is usually used pejoratively, this need not be the case, since whether reductionism is legitimate or not depends upon whether or not it yields the results intended.

1. Attempts have been made to *explain* social phenomena through the laws of physics. Such efforts usually imply that social phenomena are *nothing but* special cases of physical phenomena. The results of such efforts seem to justify P. A. Sorokin's conclusion that 'we are still very far from being able to reduce social phenomena and their mechanics to the simple laws of physical mechanics. For this reason we should be modest in our desire to make such a reduction' (*Contemporary Sociological Theories*, New York: Harper & Bros., 1928, p. 36).

2. Frequent efforts have been made to explain one kind of social phenomena as being determined completely by another kind of social phenomena. Thus religious behaviour may be said to be caused in every instance by economic interests. Whether, in this case, religious phenomena may be said to be a special case of economic behaviour or a set of non-economic variables totally dependent upon a set of economic variables is a fine point probably dependent upon the scientific vocabulary one uses. In any event there is considerable consensus that such efforts at single-factor explanations have failed.

3. Arguments concerning methods of research in social science have been much more diffuse, and the charge of illegitimate reductionism sometimes levelled against those who advocate the use of 'natural science methods' in the social sciences contains many ambiguities.

(a) There have been those, e.g. W. Dilthey, who have argued that human actions are so unique and free that any effort to generalize about them or to find causal relations is a form of illegitimate reductionism.

(b) Others, e.g. most modern sociologists, have argued that 'subjective' categories such as motive, attitude, value orientation, etc. are applicable to human actions as they are not to other phenomena, but that this does not militate against observation, generalization, and inference. Illegitimate reductionism, for these sociologists, consists in the effort to ignore the phenomena placed in such 'subjective' categories.

(c) Some 'positivists' have argued that the investigation of human 'actions' or behaviour requires the use only of categories which refer directly to overt behaviour.

Joseph H. Fichter

See also: DETERMINISM
SOCIAL CAUSATION

Reference Group

A. The term denotes a social group with which an individual feels identified and to which he aspires to relate his identity. A person derives from his reference groups his norms, attitudes and values and the social objects these create. He also derives significant social categories, both the ones to which he is assigned and the ones with which he is, in one way or another, contrasted.

B. In the early writing of C. H. Cooley and in the later writing of G. H. Mead, much is made of the 'other' and of 'taking the role of the other' in interpreting the actor's self-conception and in understanding his social behaviour. H. S. Sullivan refined the idea by discussing the 'significant' other, which pointed to some kind of *selectivity* in identification with those 'others' with whom the actor comes in contact. It has only been recently, however, that an attempt has been made to delineate the differential lines of influence and social control over the acting individual by the introduction of the concept of *reference group* as distinguished from *membership group*.

H. Hyman introduced the term *reference group*. He speaks of variables being 'mediated through an individual who acts selectively in his choice of reference group ... whose conceptualization of a reference group may be different from its actual character, who is not affected by all aspects of the culture nor by all references in the environment. ... we cannot deal with these variables independent of their meaning to individuals' ('The Psychology of Status', *Archives of Psychology*, no. 269, 1942, p. 80). These groups are regarded as the source of an individual's basic attitudes and values.

Other writers stress the function of self-evaluation: 'In general ... reference group theory aims to systematize the determinants and consequences of those processes of evaluation and self-appraisal in which the individual takes the values or standards of other individuals and groups as a comparative frame of reference' (R. K. Merton & A. Kitt, 'Contributions to the Theory of Reference Group Behavior', in *Continuities in Social Research: Studies in the Scope and Method of 'The American Soldier'*, R. K. Merton & P. Lazarsfeld (eds.), Glencoe, Ill.: The Free Press, 1950, pp. 50–1).

Still others have stressed the characteristic of wishing to belong or to continue as member: '... *reference groups*: the groups in which [the individual] aspires to attain or maintain membership. ... membership groups and reference groups may or may not be identical' (A. E. & S. Siegel, 'Reference Groups, Membership Groups, and Attitude Change', *Journal of Abnormal and Social Psychology*, vol. 55, 1957, p. 360).

C. It is apparent that while there may be some

common content of meaning, the expressions, 'to relate to', 'to identify with', 'to assume one shares norms with', 'to aspire to attain or maintain membership in', and so on, are not all equivalent in reference, and it is understandable that some issues have therefore been raised in connection with this concept. It has been suggested by one writer that *reference groups*, as cited in the literature, serve two distinguishable functions and hence are of two distinguishable varieties: 'The first of these is that of setting and enforcing standards for the person ... The second of these functions is that of *serving as* or *being* a standard or comparison point against which the person can evaluate himself and others' (H. H. Kelley, 'Two Functions of Reference Groups', in *Readings in Social Psychology*, G. E. Swanson, T. Newcomb, & E. L. Hartley (eds.), New York: Henry Holt, rev. edn., 1952, pp. 410–14). The author calls these the normative and comparison functions of reference groups and he asks that reference groups be so distinguished in future research.

Another issue has arisen, in this case over the question of the propriety of distinguishing between *positive* and *negative reference groups*, such as Newcomb and some others have done. The Sherifs, who suggest renaming reference groups, 'anchoring groups', take issue with the idea of a 'negative' reference group, saying 'Nothing is to be gained by calling every group in relation to which the individual has formed an attitude a reference group ...' (H. and C. Sherif, *Groups in Harmony and Tension*, New York: Harper & Brothers, 1953, p. 168).

Both of these issues appear to have arisen from failure to make, in dealing with reference relations, the usual distinction between *group* and *category* or classification. A *group* is generally considered as a number of persons interacting in terms of consensually held norms, while a *category* is simply any sort of classification—by income, say, or colour, or level of education. The term *reference group* has been used promiscuously to apply to either, even in the otherwise excellent paper by Merton and Kitt. Only reference *groups* can conceivably be the *source* of attitudes and norms; such groups create meaningful *classifications* of social objects (q.v.) and assign identifying members to such classifications.

Manford Kuhn

See also: CATEGORY
          GENERALIZED OTHER
          GROUP
          IDENTIFICATION

Referendum

A. The term *referendum* denotes a device by which an organization's constituent membership may approve or veto a policy proposed by the leaders or representatives. Through the referendum, a particular public (q.v.) may protect itself from injurious or unpopular legislation.

B. 1. The referendum was initially utilized for the ratification of written constitutions. Massachusetts voters in 1778 rejected a constitution proposed by the general court (legislative body). The constitutions of Massachusetts (1780) and of New Hampshire (1783) were the first popularly ratified constitutions (C. S. Lobingier, *The People's Law: or Popular Participation in Law-Making*, London: Macmillan, 1910, pp. 169–76, 180–7).

2. The referendum was applied to ordinary (as distinguished from constitutional) enactments of representative assemblies by the Swiss canton of St. Gall in 1831 (H. D. Lloyd, *The Swiss Democracy: The Study of a Sovereign People*, London: T. Fisher Unwin, pp. 62, 63). Thereafter, the legislative referendum was adopted by other Swiss cantons, by twenty-one member-states of the United States federation (1898–1957), and by a few other national states.

3. When applied to proposed 'constitutional' or 'ordinary' legislation the referendum is actually a potential popular veto upon the judgement of a representative body. Beginning in the Swiss cantons before the middle of the 17th century (Vaud, 1845; and Aargau, 1852), the referendum was applied to measures initiated outside the legislative halls—the popular initiative (see *Initiative*). Provisions for the initiative were added to the constitutions of all but three of the Swiss cantons, of nineteen member-states of the United States federation, and to the charters of many municipalities.

C. There are two specific types of referenda— (1) compulsory and (2) optional.

1. The *compulsory referendum* applies generally to the ratification of new constitutions and to proposed amendments of existing written constitutions. (The Constitution of the United States is a notable exception.) It is equally applicable to certain types of ordinary legislation, viz. proposals to increase the public debt. In the field of municipal government, charter amendments, granting franchises to privately owned public utility companies, and proposals for the public purchase of privately owned utilities must usually be submitted to popular referenda.

2. The *optional referendum* may be employed in submitting laws, not coming within the purview of the compulsory referendum, to popular decision. The legislative body may exercise the option of referring to the electorate a controversial measure, such as prohibition of alcoholic beverages.

The scope of the optional referendum is limited by the emergency clauses of some written constitutions, by which the legislature may by an unusual majority, declare a law to be necessary to the public welfare and thus put it into operation immediately upon its enactment. This application of the emergency clause destroys the procedural possibility of using the referendum.

D. Another method for referring a statute is through the referendum petition. If the legislative body does not voluntarily refer a law, citizens may circulate a petition for the signatures of qualified voters requiring that the law be submitted to a referendum election. The number of bona-fide signatures required for submission varies from 5 per cent to 15 per cent of the total vote in the last general election, depending upon the constitutional provision and the statute governing the referendum's use. The completed petition must be filed in the office of a designated public official (for instance, the secretary of state or the clerk of the municipality) usually within ninety days after the enactment of the law. Thereafter, if the designated public official certifies to the sufficiency of the signatures, the law is suspended pending the referendum decision and the executive provides for submission of the challenged law to the voters, either in a special or a general election.

E. Constitutions include various protections against a referendum decision by an insignificant portion of the eligible electorate. Usually, a majority of the total vote in an election is necessary to defeat a measure, which means that in elections where two or more measures are submitted, or where candidates are elected, the failure of a voter to express his preference on a referred measure constitutes a vote in favour of it. The total of these voting omissions comprise the 'silent vote' by which many referendum petitions are defeated.

F. A plebiscite is also sometimes designated as a referendum, but it is really direct, popular legislative participation or symbolic approval of state policies rather than a device to purify representative government. Thus Hitler held a plebiscite in Germany on 12 November 1933, in order to demonstrate public support for Germany's withdrawal from the Disarmament Conference and from the League of Nations. When in 1945 Winston Churchill was discussing with Attlee the possibility of a prolongation of Britain's wartime coalition regime he wrote: 'If you should decide to stand in with us, all united until the Japanese surrender is compelled, let us discuss means of taking the nation's opinion, for example, a referendum on the issue whether in these conditions, the life of this Parliament should be further prolonged'. To this proposal (the most recent occasion of its kind in British politics) Attlee replied: 'I would not consent to the introduction into our national life of a device so alien to all our traditions as the referendum which has only too often been the instrument of Nazism and Fascism. Hitler's practice in the field of referenda and plebiscites can hardly have endeared these expedients to the British heart' (letters published in *The Times*: London, 22 May 1945). In the light of Mr. Attlee's remarks it is interesting to note that in democratic France, by the end of 1946, no fewer than three referenda had taken place on matters connected with constitutional reform. More recently the French tradition of recourse to referenda has been continued, by General de Gaulle, in the referendum on the future of Algeria in January 1961.

Cortez A. M. Ewing

See also: INITIATIVE
PETITION
PLEBISCITE

Region

A. The term *region* denotes a geographical area which either possesses certain homogeneous characteristics that distinguish it from adjacent areas or other regions, or which serves as a unit of government or administration. Among many various uses of the word, the following may be noted: (a) ethnic or cultural regions possessing a common racial, cultural, or linguistic heritage (Provence, Wales); (b) industrial or urban regions—major centres of industrial production and population concentration (the Ruhr, the West Midland conurbation); (c) topographical or climatic regions, especially where some prominent natural feature (such as a river valley) is significant for the functioning and growth of the whole area (the Tennessee or Volta valleys); (d) economically specialized regions, strongly dependent upon some particular branch of primary production (the cotton or wheat belts of North America, the coalfields of Durham or South Illinois); (e) administrative regions, sub-divisions of a state or other major governmental unit, devised for purposes of administrative convenience (Standard Government regions in Great Britain); (f) supranational political regions, comprising states which share similar political institutions and interests or which represent focal areas of international politics (Western Europe, the Middle East).

B. Some of the areas frequently described as regions exhibit a combination of these characteristics. For example, the 'Deep South' region of U.S.A. exhibits specialized cultural, political, and economic (monocultural) features. The 'Middle East' region combines a common ethnic and cultural background, economic specialization (oil production), and a special position in international politics. The limits of such *extended regions* cannot be traced with any precision. The tendency for a specialized culture to co-exist with a specialized economy (particularly in isolated areas) deserves to be noted.

C. The great variety and vagueness of use of the word derives from a tendency to describe as *regions* any geographical areas of special interest which do not correspond to the areas of states or their main political sub-divisions. As a political concept, the word has traditionally been mainly used to refer to major historic sub-divisions of the larger national states, but recently it has been extended to supranational groupings of states. Both natural and human geography makes extensive use of the term *region*. The term has also, in recent years, acquired increased significance in connection with public schemes of planning and development, both within states and in the international sphere.

P. J. O. Self

See also: REGIONALISM (Political Science)
REGIONALISM (Sociology)

Regional Devolution (See Local Government)

Regionalism (Political Science)

A. *Regionalism* as a movement may be defined as (a) a cultural and political movement, seeking to protect and foster an indigenous culture and to promote autonomous political institutions in particular regions; (b) an administrative and political movement, aiming at the creation of a democratized and integrated governmental structure at an intermediate level between the state and traditional organs of local government. Alternatively, (c) regionalism may be taken to refer to the actual developments in public administration and public planning which have been and are occurring at this intermediate level.

B. 1. In many European states regionalism has ancient roots in traditional ethnic and cultural divisions which predate the formation of modern unitary states. Social and economic developments have progressively weakened these influences, although the very strength of centralization within the modern state—and in particular the concentration of power, wealth, and opportunity in capital cities—has resulted in some efforts to reverse the trend. For example, the French regional movement (which enjoyed the support of Comte and Le Play) advocated a broad measure of political autonomy for regions loosely based on the ancient French provinces. The Fédération Regionaliste Française was formed in 1900, and a similar movement developed rather earlier in Spain, but regionalist movements of this type have had little success with their general aims, although they have helped to draw attention to the special needs of particular areas. In Great Britain, for example, some measure of political and administrative devolution has been granted to Scotland and (more recently) to Wales in recognition of their separate ethnic and cultural traditions.

2. More recently, a new type of administrative regionalism has come into existence. The growth of public services has caused governments to develop an elaborate network of 'field services' and to devolve much work upon regional and local offices. Wartime requirements accelerated this trend—for example in Britain the expedient of regional commissioners, possessing broad co-ordinating powers, was followed by the post-war determination of standard government regions for administrative purposes. In U.S.A., a network of Federal regional offices dealing with a variety of functions (land management, resources conservation, social security) has come into existence. A converse trend has stemmed from the shortcomings of many established units of local government in relation to the widening requirements of efficiency. In large urban areas, special regional agencies (the Port of New York

Regionalism

Authority, the Metropolitan District Commission of Greater Boston, the London Transport Executive) have been set up. In Britain a number of services (including hospitals and gas and electricity distribution) have been transferred from local government to special regional agencies.

3. A further factor has been the development of *regional planning*, brought about by a widening conception of the responsibilities of government for the control of land use and for the conservation and development of natural resources. In Britain after the war a series of regional plans were prepared for the major urban and industrial areas (Greater London, the West Midlands, the Clyde Valley, etc.) which have served as a basis for the more detailed statutory development plans prepared by local authorities in these regions. A different type of regional plan deals with the development and utilization of natural resources in 'under-developed' areas, and several such plans have been prepared. In some states, special regional agencies have been established for developing resources and harnessing their use to broad social goals. The best known is the Tennessee Valley Authority.

These administrative developments have led to various proposals for the creation of elective political institutions at the regional level. Such proposals may be conceived in part as a means for reorganizing and modernizing systems of local government and in part as a device for 'democratizing' the regional activities of central governments or special agencies. An additional aim may be that of relieving the burden of national legislatures. This modern form of regionalism has only a limited connection with the older regionalist movements, and it generally aims at a much more limited devolution of political power. Essentially it is a recipe for securing effective administration and democratic control for a congeries of public services and activities held to require some form of 'regional' treatment.

P. J. O. Self

See also: REGION
REGIONALISM (Sociology)

Regionalism (Sociology)

A. *Regionalism* denotes the study of social phenomena in relation to their location in regions (q.v.) and with reference to the natural environment as well as to the culture of the region. The ideas of relationship between the region and the whole of which it is a part and of the mutual interdependence of the cultural and physical elements of the region are basic to such study.

B. 1. Practically all of the social sciences use the term *region* in somewhat the same sense, though emphases differ. At one extreme may be found the idea of some geographers that society is little more than a reflection of natural environment (e.g. Ratzel) and that therefore the region must be seen as a complex of climate, physiography, topography, soil, minerals, and the like; at the other extreme there is the somewhat mystical idea of Zimmerman (C. C. Zimmerman & R. E. Du Wors, *Graphic Regional Sociology*, Cambridge, Mass.: Phillips, 1952, pp. 10–11) of regional personalities. But, of course, not all geographers are followers of Ratzel, any more than all social scientists would accept Zimmerman's concept. In fact, most geographers, probably would come nearer agreeing with R. B. Hall, who advised geographers that 'probably the greatest single need of the [geographic] regionalist is a series of systematic studies of culture forms and complexes *per se* ... a great deal of value might come from approaching the region through the medium of culture rather than through the orthodox approach of surface configuration' ('The Geographic Region: A Résumé', in *Annals of the Association of American Geographers*, vol. XXV, 1935, p. 129).

2. E. E. Eubank, in his *Concepts of Sociology* (Boston: Heath, 1932), sets up nature of contact as one of the essential characteristics in terms of which the region may be distinguished from other areal units. He says that while the term *area* is of utility with reference to those portions of the world where contact is limited to short range, and restricted space, 'The concept of the *region*, on the other hand, rests upon the fact that barriers between sections have broken down, with the result that some degree of cosmopolitanism has taken the place of localism. ... In the case of the ... [area] ... all members of an area live in the same cultural world as all the rest; whereas in the region while there is a broad cultural background which all have access to, there are many separate cultural worlds within it, and one who lives in one can only know that of another vicariously, if at all' (ibid., pp. 376, 379).

3. This leads in the direction of the insistence of the North Carolina school of regionalists that the region always be seen as a part of a larger whole. R. B. Vance puts it quite explicitly: 'In its simplest form the relation of the regions to the nation is the relation of the parts to the whole—the old problem of securing unity out of diversity expressed in our [national] motto— "E pluribus unum" ' (*All these People*, Chapel Hill: University of North Carolina Press, 1946, p. 477). H. W. Odum and H. E. Moore emphasize the synthesizing character of the region: 'The regionalist sees the region as a unit, a microcosm of society, a set of factors combining to form a regional pattern; and believes that these elements can be understood only when conceived as a part of the whole ... it seems possible to characterize regionalism as a cultural *gestalt* in which are balanced all the constituent factors of culture in the making' (*American Regionalism*, New York: Henry Holt, 1938, pp. 16–17). Further, these writers see the '... region as a *gestalt* in which the various factors find their meaning through their relationship to other factors; a complex of inter-relationships. Within any given region the elements of society will arrange themselves into a pattern, a configuration, which is peculiar to that region and which gives it a character of uniqueness' (ibid., p. 413).

C. The broad scope of regionalism is revealed by attendance of geographers, geologists, biologists, anthropologists, economists, political scientists, historians, psychologists, statisticians, and agricultural scientists, and sociologists, as well as students of regional literature from the humanities, at meetings dealing with regional problems. M. E. Dimock would seem to have had something of this sort in mind when he wrote: 'Regionalism is a clustering of geographic, economic, sociological and governmental factors to such an extent that a distinct consciousness, the recognition of a separate identity within the whole and the desirability of autonomous planning, cultural peculiarities and administrative freedom are theoretically recognized and actually put into effect' (quoted in ibid., p. 276). Similarly, L. Mumford indicates the cross-disciplinary lines of the concept by pointing out that regional movements are likely to start with a revival of language and poetry, proceed through economic invigoration and some degree of political autonomy to efforts at building regional centres of learning and culture (ibid., p. 276).

Harry E. Moore

See also: ECOLOGY
REGION
REGIONALISM (Political Science)

Regression

1. In its widest sense the term denotes retreat to early stages in a process of development. It is an unconscious mental process implying reversion to earlier stages in the development of an individual's personality and of a social group. In an advanced form it implies pathological behaviour and maladjustment.

2. In psychoanalysis regression consists in an unconscious relapse to modes of libido satisfaction established at an earlier period of an individual's normal development. It is an egodefence mechanism in the sense that the individual avoids failure and responsibility by reverting to an earlier less mature mode of adjustment. Most mental disorders involve regressive behaviour in various degrees. In some cases the adult patient behaves as if he has lost the ability to dress, or to feed himself. Some important symptoms in schizophrenia such as egocentrism, animistic beliefs, and the feelings of self-transparence, can be described as regressive infantile behaviour.

3. *Filial regression* refers to Galton's law which states that offspring tend to revert to the average level of the family.

4. The *law of regression* is a rule of memory established by Theodule Ribot (1839–1916) which states that in mental deterioration the process of forgetting starts with recent events and goes towards early memories from childhood.

5. *Social regression* denotes the reversion of certain groups undergoing conditions of stress to modes of adjustment characteristic both of early stages in the life of the individual, and of former periods in the historical development of the group. German society under the Nazi rule is often given as an example in this sense. The main symptoms of regression were, in this case, as follows: strong ethnocentric feelings in the members of the group (narcissism); emergence of a providential leader as the symbol of an almighty father; delusional behaviour of a paranoid type, i.e. group megalomania parallelled by suspicion of an aggression against outgroups; increased inclinations towards mythical animistic thinking. G. M. Gilbert speaks in this context of 'authoritarian regressiveness', i.e. '... the common tendency to avoid mature social responsibility, ... to submit to protective leadership ...' (*The Psychology of Dictatorship*, New York: Ronald Press, 1950, p. 267. See also Z. Barbu, *Democracy and Dictatorship*, London: Routledge & Kegan Paul, 1956, pp. 140–50). According to A. Strachey most

Reinforcement

social groups set up in various degrees regressive processes in the individual in the sense that they 'heighten his instinctual impulses'. 'The sovereign State and in especial the national sovereign State, is well qualified to figure as a regressive group' (*The Unconscious Motives of War*, London: Allen & Unwin, 1957, pp. 182, 201).

Z. Barbu

See also: Defence Mechanism
Projection
Rationalization (Social Psychology)

Reinforcement

A. *Reinforcement* denotes (a) in classical conditioning, the experimental procedure of following the conditioned stimulus by the unconditioned stimulus; (b) in operant or instrumental conditioning, the analogous procedure of following the occurrence of the operant response by the reinforcing stimulus (typically, a reward); (c) the inferred process that increases the strength of conditioning as a result of these arrangements.

B. Within psychology the general meaning of strengthening has become limited now to the strengthening of conditioned responses. Earlier the term *reinforcement* and the term *facilitation* were used synonymously (E. R. Hilgard, 'Reinforcement and Inhibition of Eyelid Reflexes', *Journal of General Psychology*, vol. VIII, 1933, pp. 85–113).

The contemporary meaning derives from Pavlov, and refers to the strengthening of conditioned responses by presenting the conditioned stimulus followed by the unconditioned stimulus, and, conversely to its weakening if the unconditioned stimulus is omitted. 'Repeated application of a conditioned stimulus which is not followed by reinforcement leads to a weakening of the conditioned reflex' (I. P. Pavlov, *Conditioned Reflexes*, London: Oxford University Press, 1927, p. 49). Correspondingly, in instrumental or operant conditioning, the acquired response is also strengthened or weakened by the appearance or absence of the reinforcing stimulus, which in this case is alternatively known as a reward (e.g. food at the end of a maze).

C. There are a number of distinctions to be made among the types of stimuli serving reinforcement, and among the arrangements under which reinforcement takes place.

1. A *primary* reinforcing stimulus (or reinforcer) is one yielding an innate or reflex response (such as food in the mouth producing salivation); a *secondary* reinforcer is one whose properties as a reinforcer have been acquired by association with another reinforcing agent. A special case is the *token reinforcement*, in which the token can itself be exchanged for a primary reinforcer. Thus pay in money is reinforcing because of the reinforcers that money can buy. Secondary reinforcers have reinforcing properties in many situations, and social reinforcements are usually of this kind (B. F. Skinner, *Verbal Behavior*, New York: Appleton-Century-Crofts, 1957).

2. A *positive* reinforcer is the equivalent of a reward, something provoking approach responses; a *negative* reinforcer is usually something noxious or punishing, evoking avoidance responses, although it may be simply removal of a positive reinforcer.

3. The specific arrangements of reinforcement include: (a) the time order and interval between the conditioned stimulus and the reinforcing unconditioned stimulus (forward and backward conditioning, simultaneous, trace and delayed conditioning) (I. P. Pavlov, *Conditioned Reflexes*) and (b) the contingencies that determine the presence or absence of reinforcement on any one trial, or following any one operant response; such contingencies, leading to reinforcement on but a fraction of the times when conditioned responses appear, have been subsumed under *partial reinforcement* (E. R. Hilgard & D. G. Marquis, *Conditioning and Learning*, New York: Appleton-Century, 1940, pp. 148–53), or *intermittent reinforcement* (E. R. Hilgard, *Theories of Learning*, New York: Appleton-Century-Crofts, 1948, p. 112); more recently an elaborate study has appeared exploring a great variety of arrangements (C. B. Ferster & B. F. Skinner, *Schedules of Reinforcement*, New York: Appleton-Century-Crofts, 1957).

D. As is so often the case, the same term is used to describe arrangements and to imply process. Thus a reinforcement trial means, as an arrangement, that it is a trial in which the intended reinforcer (say, a food reward) is present, whether or not it has any demonstrable effect. If it has an effect, it is 'because' the food does something, i.e. it 'reinforces' the running response. In practice, the context reduces both the ambiguity and the circularity of the dual usage, so that little trouble arises because the term is used now in a descriptive sense, now in an explanatory sense.

Ernest R. Hilgard

See also: CONDITIONING
LEARNING
PUNISHMENT
REWARD

Rejection (See **Acceptance** (also **Rejection**))

Relativism (See **Cultural Relativity**)

Reliability

A. *Reliability* is used by social scientists in the sense of degree of stability or reproducibility of empirical results. Science is based on the assumption that its findings are not unique but can be duplicated under identical conditions. Experience, however, has shown that identity is an ideal which can only be approximated in the empirical world. No matter how controlled the conditions, measurements vary. This variation may be due to systematic influences (non-random or constant errors) or to non-systematic influences (random or variable errors). The latter are the ones of importance in a determination of reliability, although both are of concern to the validity (q.v.) of the results. Thus reliability is a necessary though not sufficient factor in determining validity, for without stability of results their relevance to the purpose of the research could not possibly be determined.

Reliability can be estimated only by comparing multiple instances of the 'thing' whose reliability is under study. The comparison may be between the several recorded results of two or more observers or coders, between the several responses to individual items or group of items on the same or different instruments, between the responses of individuals in a sample or between samples, or between the individual and himself at different times. Coefficients can be determined but their interpretation is based on the assumption that the experimental situation was the same for each instance. A high coefficient lends credence to the assumption; a low coefficient denies it, but does not in itself point to the source or sources of the unreliability which may represent the infiltration of systematic errors, an unknown combination of random errors, or both.

B. As stated by H. Peak in the Michigan compendium on research methods, 'Reliability raises the ... important question of how stably ... units or processes [of observation and analysis] can be observed, measured, and inferred. When investigators inquire into the reliability of their observations, they are asking themselves how well they can control the determinants of the key response on repeated attempts to re-establish the same observational situation [for] it is a basic scientific assumption that when conditions are constant, the results must be the same' ('Problems of Objective Observation', in L. Festinger & D. Katz (eds.), *Research Methods in the Behavioral Sciences*, New York: Dryden Press, 1953, p. 292).

1. R. K. Merton points out that: 'The lone scholar is not constrained by the very nature of his work situation to deal systematically with reliability as a technical problem. It is a remote and unlikely possibility that some other scholar ... would independently hit upon precisely the same collection of empirical materials, utilizing the same categories, the same criterion for these categories and conducting the same intellectual operation'. But in contemporary survey research, he continues, 'the problem of reliability becomes so compelling that it cannot be neglected ... different researchers at work on the same empirical materials and performing the same operations must presumably reach the same results' (*Social Theory and Social Structure*, Glencoe, Ill.: The Free Press, 1949, p. 214).

2. Thus it should not be surprising that references to *reliability* in social science literature are found almost exclusively in statistical or measurement contexts. In fact reference to *reliability* has increasingly given way to reference to degree of *error*, a substitution which some believe to be advisable. For example, W. A. Wallis and H. V. Roberts (*Statistics, A New Approach*, Glencoe, Ill.: The Free Press, 1956, p. 134) comment that 'One aspect [of the quality of data] is *precision* or reproducibility—often called, misleadingly, "reliability"'. However, the New York University compendium on methods (M. Jahoda, M. Deutsch, & S. W. Cook, *Research Methods in Social Relations*, New York: Dryden Press, 1951, p. 100), produced under the auspices of the Society for the Psychological Study of Social Issues (SPSSI) finds a use for both terms by defining *reliability* in terms of *error*. 'The evaluation of the reliability of any measurement procedure', it says, 'consists in determining how much of the variation in scores among individuals is due to true differences (and to constant errors) and how much to inconsistencies in measurement. When a measurement is repeated under the same

Religion

conditions, it will yield the same results to the extent that it is free from *random* or *variable* errors'. 'Random error is due to those transient aspects of the person, of the situation of measurement, of the measurement procedure, etc., which are likely to vary by chance from one measurement to the next. ... Estimates of reliability take into account only random errors ...' (ibid.).

3. Concerning the *types* of reliability that have been identified by social scientists, L. Guttman (in S. A. Stouffer, et al., *Measurement and Prediction*, Princeton, N.J.: Princeton University Press, 1950, p. 277) lists 'three kinds of reliability ... three important sources for variation in empirical results ... one is the sampling of people; the second is the sampling of items or questions; and the third is the sampling of trials ... the stability of responses of individuals to the items'. Both the Michigan and N.Y.U. methodological volumes add a fourth type of random variability—that concerned with the reliability of the observer, the coder, the analyst, etc.

4. The determination of reliability is the problem of estimating the effect of the random errors on one's results. This estimate is usually expressed in some form of *reliability coefficient*, perhaps the most authoritative statement on which is to be found in the 'Technical Recommendations for Psychological Tests and Diagnostic Techniques' (prepared by a Joint Committee of the American Psychological Association, American Educational Research Association and National Council on Measurement in Education, *Psychological Bulletin*, Supplement, vol. 51, 1954). The report (ibid., p. 29) lists three types of such coefficients and says that 'The several types of reliability coefficient do not answer the same questions and should be carefully distinguished. We shall refer to a measure based on internal analysis of data obtained on a single trial of a test as a *coefficient of internal consistency*. ... A correlation between scores from two forms given at essentially the same time we shall refer to as a *coefficient of equivalence*. The correlation between test and retest, with an intervening period of time, is a *coefficient of stability*. Such a coefficient is also obtained when two forms of the test are given with an intervening period of time' (ibid.). The interpretation of such coefficients is, however, generally recognized as a complex matter. Ideally, the coefficient is measuring the usefulness of the instrument, all other factors (nonrandom and random) being held constant, but

as H. Peak ('Problems of Objective Observation', p. 293) points out: 'It is misleading to speak of the reliability of a test or a tool with the implication that the reliability or unreliability is a property only of the instrument itself, for the error observed is the result of variation in the whole complex of determinants of the measured event'.

Raymond V. Bowers

See also: VALIDITY

Reliability Coefficient (See **Reliability**)

Religion

A. The term is usually derived from the Latin verb, *religere*: the conscientious fulfilment of duty, awe of higher powers, deep reflection. The related noun *religio* refers to both the object of such inner preoccupation, and the goal of the activity associated with it. Another, later, Latin verb has been cited as a source of the term: *religare*, implying a close and lasting relationship to the supernatural. The scriptures of the various religions hardly contain general terms for religion.

The complex etymology of the term is not fortuitous: the complexity and diversity of human religions, as well as the profound and ambivalent feelings they arouse, have produced a heterogenous set of scientific definitions of the phenomenon. Usually, and perhaps inevitably, these definitions include some evaluative assumptions: many emphasize unduly one aspect of religious systems. It may be useful, therefore, to eschew formal definition and to see inductively what precisely the historical religions entail.

B. Religions are systems of *belief*, *practice*, and *organization* which shape an *ethic* manifest in the behaviour of their adherents.

1. Religious *beliefs* are interpretations of immediate experience by reference to the ultimate structure of the universe, its centres of power and destiny; these are invariably conceived in supernatural terms. Any one set of religious beliefs usually includes a cosmogony and a philosophy of history, a psychology, and a sociology. (It is only in the process of secularization that these become detached from religion.) Belief in the supernatural entities of a religion is, emotionally, highly charged: the believer imputes a special quality, sacredness, to them and this extends to the directives for behaviour imputed to the supernatural or deduced from its existence.

588

2. Such behaviour is in the first instance ritual behaviour: standardized practices by which the believers enact in symbolic form their relationship to the supernatural. Ritual may include adoration, supplication, and attempts to control the supernatural: the distinction between religion and magic is difficult to maintain. Ritual, further, provides a codex of behaviour about which the believers may organize.

3. Religious organization defines membership in the community of believers, attempts to maintain tradition and encapsulate dissent, and through its internal differentiation assigns religious tasks to the believers.

4. Finally, religion entails an *ethic*. Max Weber has stressed ('The Social Psychology of the World Religions', in H. Gerth & C. W. Mills (eds.), *From Max Weber*, London: Routledge & Kegan Paul, 1947) that the ethic of a religion is the result of the interaction of its formal ethical directives with (often recalcitrant) social circumstances. A religious ethic may be psychologically consonant with the rest of the religious system whilst in formal contradiction to it, or it may entail both psychological and formal tensions within a religion. It is these tensions which provide those new religious impulses produced by changes in the social situation.

C. The formal properties of religious systems have been abstracted from historical systems which exhibit an enormous range of variation.

1. Conceptions of the supernatural include the polytheistic pantheon of the ancient Greeks and of Hinduism, the Trinitarian Godhead of Christianity, the jealous Jaweh of the ancient Israelites, the omniscient sovereign of Islam. These are relatively concrete images of the supernatural; there are also the refined metaphysical conceptions of Buddhism and Taoism, the Confucian notions of divine and human order. But concrete notions of the supernatural are often elaborated metaphysically, and metaphysical systems are frequently concretized.

2. Primitive religious systems, defined by the absence of a written tradition, vary as much as the world religions in their conceptions of the supernatural. No distinction between 'higher' or 'lower' religions on this score seems tenable. It has been suggested that in primitive religions, ritual proliferates more than in others; this, too, is doubtful.

3. Religions do differ in the weight they lay upon ritual and in the complexity of their ritual procedures. Rituals have quite distinctive ends;

expiation and purification rituals may co-exist in the same religion with attempts at mystical union with the supernatural. Within Christianity itself, Roman Catholicism and Eastern Orthodoxy have developed ritual orders which contrast sharply with those of Protestantism. Buddhism began as a movement of protest, in part, against Hindu ritual and subsequently developed its own ritual system. Frequently, special performances are reserved for ritual specialists: this is the role of shaman and priest.

4. Religious organization is no less varied than the other aspects of the phenomenon. Tribes, nations, states, social classes, occupational groups may be the bearers of specific religions, or may develop their specific variants of a more widely diffused system. There are *churches* (q.v.) which claim universality and *sects* (q.v.) which define themselves by exclusiveness, organizations self-consciously parochial or militantly proselytising. Religious organizations may be rigidly hierarchical or may be based on the priesthood of all believers, a conception by no means exclusively Protestant.

5. Religious ethics exhibit equally striking differences. Some are world-affirming (Confucianism), others world-denying (Buddhism). Some seek the immediate transformation of the world (chiliasm is not confined to the medieval Christian sects), others disparage the world as but a transitory phenomenon, still others justify it as the best of all possible ones. Christianity has encompassed, at different times and in different places, a number of contradictory ethical attitudes. The relationship of the religious organization to other social structures is, of course, the single most decisive factor in the development of an ethic from the other components of a religious system.

N. Birnbaum

See also: Church
Cult
Protestant Ethic
Sect
Sociology of Religion

Rent

A. *Rent* denotes an item of revenue or payment to any factor of production which has the characteristic of limited supply. It is also used to denote any surplus earned by reason of superior quality or ability.

B. In popular and commercial usage *rent* is the price paid for the use of any durable good: we

Rent

rent farms, we rent city houses, we rent automobiles, we rent tuxedos. After L. Walras (*Elements of Pure Economics*, trans. by W. Jaffe, London: Allen & Unwin, 1954, p. 40) had made clear the importance of including 'the immaterial services of capital goods in the same class of social wealth as material income goods' and of understanding the pricing of these services, it would have been well if the popular usage had been adopted as the economist's usage, for we need a name for the price of such services. (If they are not actually offered for rent, it is necessary to impute the rent they might have commanded if they had been hired rather than owned).

C. 1. Rent appears to have meant in early usage *any item of revenue*, but by the 17th century attention was centred on rent as revenue drawn from land.

In classical political economy rent continued to refer to land. In Adam Smith it referred to the whole income of the landlord and 'is frequently no more than a reasonable profit or interest for the stock laid out by the landlord upon its improvement' (*An Inquiry into the Nature and Causes of the Wealth of Nations* (1776), New York: The Modern Library, 1937, p. 144). Smith was very conscious of the varying proportion of the rent which could be considered return on investment, particularly the variation between different uses of land, e.g. hop gardens or vineyards. D. Ricardo limited the term to that part of the payment to the landlord which is paid 'for the use of the original and indestructible powers of the soil' (*The Principles of Political Economy and Taxation* (1817), New York: Dutton, 1917, p. 33). J. S. Mill, while recognizing the value of distinguishing that part of the payment of a tenant which might be considered return on the investment in buildings, etc., considered that the return made to capital sunk in improvements of a permanent character 'loses altogether the character of profit and is governed by the principles of rent' (*Principles of Political Economy* (1848), London: Longmans, Green, 1929, p. 430). It would indeed be difficult to identify the 'original' powers of the soil and, one might add, few if any of those powers are 'indestructible'.

2. A. Marshall, while preferring to use *rent* in connection with land and other free gifts of nature, recognized that 'there is a continuous gradation from those true gifts which have been appropriated by man, through the income derived from permanent improvements of the soil, to those yielded by farm and factory buildings, steam engines and less durable goods' (*Principles of Economics*, New York: The Macmillan Co., 1948, p. 629). Keeping rent for the free gifts, he coined the word 'quasi-rents' to indicate the return to any piece of industrial equipment the supply of which could not be augmented for a short period of time.

When Marshall wrote of the rent of land as 'the leading species of a large genus' he was thinking of the economic characteristics of the rent of land and recognizing that these characteristics were not peculiar to land. Marshall's parable of the meteoric stones with a series of hypotheses from fixed supply to elastic supply at constant cost, from indestructible to brittle, ends as follows: 'this series of hypotheses stretches continuously from the one extreme in which the income derived from the stones is rent in the strictest sense of the term, to the other extreme in which it is to be classed rather with interest on free or floating capital' (ibid., p. 418). Following this lead, *rent* (sometimes qualified as 'economic' rent) has come to mean any payment to any factor of production which has the characteristic of the payment for land or free gifts: namely, payment determined by limited supply. Putting it another way: Ricardo showed that rent was price determined rather than price determining; rent then comes to be used for any price-determined item. So, except in long run analysis the earnings of man-made durable production goods are rents (and the long run can be defined as the period long enough for them not to be rents, i.e. long enough for the supply of such durable goods to change in response to the price of their services). With this definition wages and salaries become, or contain elements of, rent (rent of ability).

3. One other characteristic should be noted: Ricardo also dealt with the case of differential quality so that rent of the better lands was the surplus earned on the better lands when the price of the product just covered cost on the marginal land, i.e. the poorest land actually cultivated (*The Principles of Political Economy and Taxation*, pp. 34–5). Again, by analogy, any surplus related to differential quality or ability comes to be called *rent*. The scarcity and differential aspects have sometimes been contrasted but they are clearly related: if the better quality factor were not scarce no use would be made of the poorer quality; the existence of the poorer quality limits the rise in the rent of the better quality.

At first this use of rent had reference to the

total supply of particular agents of production: it was conceived, as J. Robinson wrote, (*The Economics of Imperfect Competition*, London: Macmillan, 1933, p. 102) as 'a surplus ... above the minimum earnings necessary to induce it to do its work'. But in the analysis of particular industries, where cost came to be related to alternative opportunity, *rent* came to be used, for example by K. E. Boulding (*Economic Analysis*, London: Hamish Hamilton, 3rd edn. 1955, p. 211) as the 'excess [over] the minimum amount necessary to keep that factor in its present occupation'. Similarly the word is extended, in analysis of the individual firm, to the excess over the minimum amount necessary to keep it in the employ of that firm: and in J. Robinson's analysis to such payments when they are the result of contrived scarcity (monopoly revenue) as well as of natural scarcity.

D. When rent came to be related to 'surplus', by analogy such surpluses as consumer's surplus or saver's surplus came to be referred to, by some writers, as rents.

V. W. Bladen

See also: Interest (Economics)
Profit
Wages

Replication (See Verification)

Representation

A. *Representation* denotes an aspect of the relationship between political personages and those whom they lead within a political system: the leaders are said to 'represent' those who are led in so far as they are nominated, appointed, or elected by them; are responsible to them, and can be recalled or removed by them; and in addition, in so far as they are empowered to make (on behalf of their constituents) arrangements whose force is binding.

B. Like most political relationships, that of *representation* is a matter of degree and range. Representation of the membership of a political system can be full or partial: the devices chosen to effect the relationship are not uniform—nor are they uniformly successful. The binding quality of decisions reached by representatives is also variable and, at times, controversial.

1. The practice of representation is an old one. But its most fruitful political origins were in the constitutional developments in England from the 13th century onwards. From 1264 'the knights of the shire and the burgesses of the boroughs received a summons at the same time' to meet with the King (S. B. Chrimes, *Constitutional History of England*, London: Oxford University Press, 1948, p. 107). From the late 13th century onwards the writ of summons declared that the representatives 'should have full and sufficient power to do and consent to those things which then and there by the common counsel of our realm . . . shall happen to be ordained' (quoted in ibid., p. 109). Thus the English Parliament uniquely developed into a representative assembly in a political sense during the course of the 14th, 15th, and 16th centuries' (ibid., p. 109). The origins of this development in the judicial arrangements and fiscal requirements of medieval England have been much discussed (a classic account is to be found in C. Stephenson, *Medieval Institutions*, Ithaca, N.Y.: Cornell University Press, 1954, p. 126 et seq.). Stephenson insists 'we must keep our eye on actual representation, that is, the practice of electing and commissioning deputies' (ibid., p. 128), and he concludes that the growth of representative institutions was 'a matter of political necessity, occasioned on the one hand by the king's lack of money and on the other by the growing strength of social groups who could supply it' (ibid., p. 138).

Other aspects have been commented upon elsewhere. Thus O. von Gierke (*Political Theories of the Middle Ages*, Cambridge: Cambridge University Press, 1900, ch. VII) insists upon the medieval corporate concept: 'Representatives, who in the first instance are charged with the representation of the several particular communities which compose a people, must, if they are to represent the People as a Whole, act as one single Assembly which resolves and decides in a corporate fashion'. Recent scholarship gives major credit to the church organizations of the late Middle Ages, particularly the Dominican Order, for originating the kinds of political practices (elections, delegations, corporate theory, constituencies, majority rule) that freed the concept for its modern career (M. V. Clarke, *Medieval Representation and Consent*, London: Longmans Green, 1936).

2. The actual word *representation* came into prominence during the long-drawn-out struggles over the distribution of powers in the English Parliament (16th to 20th centuries), and in other nations of the Western world, particularly the United States and France. In 1583, Sir Thomas Smith (*De Republica Anglorum*) wrote that Parliament '. . . representeth and hath the power of the whole realme both the head and the

Representation

bodie'. Here are the notions of some entity imitating, expressing, and making manifest a quality otherwise diffused. Hobbes (*Leviathan* 1651, vol. I, ch. 16) declares: '... to Personate is to Act, or Represent himselfe, or an other; and he that acteth another is said to beare his Person, or act in his name; ... and is called in diverse occasions, diversly; as a Representer, or Representative, a Lieutenant, a Vicar, an Attorney, a Deputy, a Procurator, an Actor, and the like. ... A Multitude of men, are made One Person, when they are by one man, or one Person, Represented.' The absolutist tendency of the definition should be noted.

3. Political theorists have not been unanimous in evaluating representation. T. Paine made the important distinction between 'simple' and 'representative' democracy. 'Simple democracy was society governing itself without the use of secondary means. By ingrafting representation upon democracy, we arrive at a system of government capable of embracing and confederating all the various interests and every extent of territory and population. . . . Athens by representation would have surpassed her own democracy' ('The Rights of Man', in Part Second [1792] *The Complete Writings of Thomas Paine*, ed. by P. S. Foner, New York: Citadel Press, 1945, vol. 1, pp. 371–2). And for J. S. Mill 'the meaning of representative government is that whole peoples or some numerous portion of them exercise through deputies periodically elected by themselves the ultimate controlling power' ('Representative Government', in *Utilitarianism, Liberty, and Representative Government*, London: Dent, 1910, p. 228).

Rather different views were held by Burke and Rousseau. Burke was vigorous in his defence of the independent representative, preferring 'virtual' to 'actual' representation: 'Virtual representation is that in which there is a communion of interests, and a sympathy in feelings and desires, between those who act in the name of any description of people, and the people in whose name they act, though the trustees are not actually chosen by them' ('Letter to Sir Hercules Langriske, Bart., M.P., on the subject of the Roman Catholics of Ireland. ...' [1792], reprinted in R. J. S. Hoffman & P. Levack (eds.), *Burke's Politics*, New York: Knopf, 1949, p. 494). Burke thus divorces elections from representation.

Rousseau (1762) argued that 'Sovereignty, for the same reason as makes it inalienable, cannot be represented: it lies essentially in the General Will, and will does not admit of representation:

it is either the same, or other; there is no intermediate possibility. The deputies of the people therefore are not and cannot be its representatives: they are merely its stewards, and can carry through no definitive act ('Social Contract', in *Social Contract and Discourses*, trans. by G. D. H. Cole, London: Dent, 1913).

A sharp populist or pro-constituency motif is noticed in the definition by W. Paterson, delegate in the Constitutional Convention (*Records*, I, p. 561): 'What is the principle of representation? It is an expedient by which an assembly of certain individuals chosen by the people is substituted in place of the inconvenient meeting of the people themselves'. The same type of definition is congenial to T. Hare, the father of proportional representation, who declares: 'Representation is the vicarious performance of duties which cannot be personally executed' (*A Treatise on the Election of Representatives*, London, 3rd edn., 1865, p. xxxv).

More recently in the United States C. J. Friedrich, following R. von Mohl, defines representation as 'the process through which the influence which the entire citizenry or a part of them have upon governmental action is exercised on their behalf by a smaller number among them, with binding effect upon those represented' (*Constitutional Government and Democracy*, Boston: Little, Brown, 1941, p. 260). E. M. Sait says simply that representation 'occurs whenever one person is authorized to act in place of others' (*Political Institutions*, New York: Appleton-Century, 1938, p. 476). H. D. Lasswell and A. Kaplan define representation, in a system of related definitions, as 'agency formally exercised in the interest of the principal' (or constituency) (*Power and Society*, New Haven: Yale University Press, 1950, p. 165).

Political scientists have tried to abstract the universal quality inherent in historical usage. In this sense, the important ingredient of representation is a *relation*, evidenced by behaviour or extracted by questioning. 'Representation is then a relation (or condition) that exists when the characteristics and acts of one vested with public functions are in accord with the desires of a person(s) to whom the functions have objective or subjective importance' (A. de Grazia, *Public and Republic*, New York: Knopf, 1951, p. 4). A *device* of representation is an attempt to enforce or ensure representation between a representative and a constituent. Such would be an election, a lottery, a reduced term of office, a particular formula of apportionment (often representation is tightly defined as a *device* of representation, especially 'elections', but this presumes an effect that often is not present). Representative government would then be a system of rule in which the legitimacy of the government is grounded upon a numerous and presumably effective set of procedures designed to ensure representation. A typical system of representative government (and of privately organized representative 'governments' such as unions, trade associations, or universities) will number several dozen devices of representation.

Yet the apparatus thus set up is only predictive of representation; that is, representation must be demonstrated. A despotism can provide much representation, a formal democracy little. Numerous problems arise in this connection. Though it is one of the primary situations of political science, the representative condition is most difficult to study and assess. An election itself is one test and definition, though difficult to understand. Another common operational definition occurs in the question addressed to a person (or constituency): 'Do you think the President is doing a good job?' However, as has been shown (H. F. Gosnell, *Democracy: Threshold of Freedom*, New York: Ronald Press, 1948, ch. VIII), the meaningful, imagined dimensions of the representative relation are far too numerous and inaccessible for the present instruments of inquiry; there are meanings extending into the conscious and unconscious levels of representative and constituents; correlates relating to the traits of leaders and followers; variations in so far as one studies long-run and short-run expectations and demands; considerations having to do with electoral information and ignorance; and questions of whether party or personality is the thing being represented to the constituency.

Alfred de Grazia

See also: Constituency
Democracy
Legislative Body
Office

Representative Democracy (See **Democracy**)

Repression

A. The general meaning of the term denotes the restraint, by external force or the power of the mind, of someone or something that threatens to erupt.

B. 1. In psychoanalytic literature it has come to mean an *unconscious defence mechanism* against the recognition of an unconscious instinctual impulse, whereas the term *suppression* refers to a conscious inhibition of a conscious impulse. Freud spoke of repression (*Verdrängung*) in this sense for the first time in 1892 when he described the case of Miss Lucy R., an English governess in Vienna who had developed neurotic symptoms after 'repressing' sexual impulses towards her employer (see J. Breuer & S. Freud, 'Studies on Hysteria' (1895), trans. by A. A. Brill, New York: Nervous and Mental Disease Publishing Co., 1950).

The repressing force derives from cultural standards which have been incorporated by the individual to serve as his 'ego-ideal' or 'super-ego'. According to Freudian theory, repression is primarily directed against the omnipresent Oedipus complex and erases from consciousness the memory of the child's sexual and murderous impulses that had been aroused by either of his parents.

The repressed impulses inevitably succeed in finding devious outlets in more or less disguised ways. Some of these have been culturally accepted in the camouflaged form of folk-lore, myth, fairy tale, ritual, artistic production, etc. Unacceptable outlets give rise to neurotic suffering and to behaviour which is censured as perverted, criminal, or depraved.

2. This view was an application of the theories of Herbart to clinical observations. Herbart, the successor of Kant, wrote a *Textbook in Psychology* [1816] (trans. by M. K. Smith, New York: Appleton, 1901, p. 14), in which he stated that, if two elementary ideas were incompatible one of them 'may be removed entirely out of consciousness. ... In this case, however, the striving of the ... [repressed] ... concept is not to be considered wholly ineffective ...; it works with all its force against the concepts in consciousness'. When the resistance disappears the repressed idea will enter consciousness.

C. At one time Freud held the view that the mechanism of repression served the purpose of keeping from consciousness the ideas and emotions excited by traumatic sexual experiences. Those ideas could never achieve direct conscious expression, though a distorted and disguised expression was possible in dreams, jokes, and at times of inattention. The repressed emotions could find conscious, but disturbing, outlets through either converting psychic energy into physical 'conversion' symptoms or lending excessive emotional force to harmless ideas.

Republic

Clinical experience induced Freud to alter his view. Ideas and emotions could be repressed, not only because they related to a traumatic event, but also because they were the rather direct manifestations of primitive instinctual desires in fantasy, action, or memory. In the first five years of life, primitive instincts are powerful activators of mental processes which therefore suffer extensive repression so that only rudimentary and distorted 'screen' memories of those years are available to adults.

F. Kräupl Taylor

See also: INSTINCT
LIBIDO
PROJECTION
RATIONALIZATION (Social Psychology)
REGRESSION
UNCONSCIOUS

Republic

A. A *republic* is a form of government without a monarch, associated for the most part with representation of the people through some form of elective process and to varying degrees the principles of liberal democracy.

B. Although in Europe before the 17th century the term meant only a well-organized state, the primary and historical antithesis of *republic* is *monarchy* (q.v.). The term, as R. M. MacIver (*The Web of Government*, New York: The Macmillan Co., 1947, p. 155) pointed out, 'has been rather freely applied to almost any kind of state that has no monarchical headship and has, with whatever limitations, some system of election to political offices'. Thus, the Roman republic, the republics of South America, or even the republics of the Soviet Union fall under this rubric. Madison (in A. Hamilton, J. Madison & J. Jay, *The Federalist*, ed. M. Beloff, Oxford: Basil Blackwell, 1948, no. XXXIX, pp. 190–1) wished to distinguish between a *democracy* in which the people meet together and rule directly and a *republic* where the government 'derives all its powers directly or indirectly from the great body of the people, and is administered by persons holding their offices during pleasure, for a limited period, or during good behavior'. But this distinction between a liberal democracy and a republic tended to become obsolete in the 19th century. In all modern societies hardly anyone denies popular will as a theoretical base of government so that the former emotional tones of 'republicanism' versus monarchical principles associated with *republic* have faded and the extreme radicalism

suggested by the Jacobin use of *republicanism* no longer attaches to the term.

C. 1. Though *republic* is often equated with *democracy*, J. A. Corry (*Elements of Democratic Government*, Toronto: Oxford University Press, 1947, p. 4) notes that 'There are republics where the forms clearly point to democracy, but the practices point unequivocally to rule by one or a few, and not to rule by the many'. Moreover, *republic* does not embrace such forms of government as parliamentary monarchy or democratic Caesarism which may meet many tests of popular rule. On a more contemporary theoretical plane, L. Lipson (*The Great Issues of Politics*, New York: Prentice-Hall, 1954, p. 257) speaks of a *republic* as a 'flat rejection of the authoritarian, elitist view that the rulers are the state and that the people are subjects who belong to them'. Again the tendency is to identify a republican form of government with the salient principles of liberal democracy.

2. The word *democracy* was almost feared as much in the 17th and 18th centuries as the word *republic* (C. A. Beard, *The Republic*, New York: Viking Press, 1943, p. 29); and while the latter has lost its radical tinge, the former still retains it for many people, mostly but not always conservatives. For these people republic means limited government, 'rule of law', and constitutionalism, while democracy means mere 'mob' rule or the rule of the fifty-one per cent. Thus men as far apart as Felix Morley and Harry Truman continue to insist that the United States is not a democracy but a republic.

Gerard J. Mangone

See also: DEMOCRACY
MONARCHY
REPUBLICANISM

Republicanism

A. *Republicanism* denotes a variety of political movements and philosophies sharing in common an opposition to monarchy and a preference for representative government and, to varying degrees, the values of equality and liberty.

B. 1. Before the 17th century, the term *republic* (q.v.) or *res publica* was used in Europe to denote a well organized state whether ruled by a hereditary monarch or by elected officials. Thus, the theoretician of the modern French absolute monarchy, Jean Bodin, published his discourses on government under the title *Les Six Livres de la République* (1576). Similarly, Sir Thomas Smith analysed the monarchical government of England under the title *De Republica*

594

Anglorum (1583). After the defeat of the monarchist party in Britain (1645), the term 'a free Commonwealth' was used by the radical Republican Wing of the opponents of the Stuart dynasty as denoting a democratically controlled state as opposed to a state governed by a hereditary monarch. Ludlow thought that the people should decide 'whether the king should govern as a God or whether the people should live under a government derived from their own consent' (G. P. Gooch (ed.), *English Democratic Ideas in the Seventeenth Century*, Cambridge: University Press, 1927, p. 146). Among the Republican pamphletists of the age the most distinguished was John Milton, who in his *Defence of the English People against Salmasius* (1651), declared that hereditary government was contrary to the 'law of nature'. In the army of Cromwell the radical wing, the so-called 'Levellers', who were inspired by Lilburne, demanded the abolition of the House of Lords and of the monarchy, and a biennial House of Commons elected by universal suffrage (see for instance, J. Lilburne's 'England's Birthright justified against arbitrary usurpation, royal or parliamentary' (1645), in T. W. Haller (ed.), *Tracts on Liberty in the Puritan Revolution 1638-1647*, New York: Columbia University Press, 1933, vol. III, pp. 257–307).

Harrington, writing in the same period, uses the term *commonwealth* to describe the system of government in classical Athens, Rome, Venice, and the Netherlands. He shows his preference for those commonwealths in which liberty is assured: '... the liberty of a commonwealth consists in the empire of her laws, the absence whereof would betray her to the lust of tyrants. And these I conceive to be the principles upon which Aristotle and Livy ... have grounded their assertion, "that a commonwealth is an empire of laws and not of men" ' (*The Commonwealth of Oceana* (1656), London: Routledge, 1887, p. 26).

2. In France the term *republic* was used in the 17th century—for instance by La Fontaine and Madame de Sévigné—to describe the 'government' of 'the state'. The term was also being used in contradistinction to monarchy and in the 18th century Montesquieu further extended the use of the term *republic* in the modern sense and claimed that 'a *republican government* is that in which the body, or only a part of the people, is possessed of the supreme power; *monarchy*, that in which a single person governs by fixed and established laws, a *despotic government*, that in which a single person directs everything by his

own will and caprice' (see his *Esprit des Lois* (1748), in the translation of T. Nugent, *The Spirit of the Laws*, 2 vols., London: Bell, 1909, vol. 2, p. 8).

The forerunner of French Republicanism, J.-J. Rousseau, used the term *republic* both in the modern and in the traditional sense. In his *Contrat social* (1762), trans. by G. Hopkins, *Social Contract*, London: Oxford University Press, 1947, pp. 288–340), he writes on the one hand that 'By a Republic, then, I understand any State ruled by law, quite irrespective of the form its government may take', whilst on the other hand, he asserts that 'Monarchy has one fundamental and inevitable blemish which must ever make it inferior to the republican form of government. In the latter it is men of ability and intelligence only who are entrusted by the public vote with the duties of administration, whereas, in a monarchy, the places of power and privilege go always to intriguing and rascally meddlers'. He equates monarchical government with 'despotism' and republics with 'free states' and calls the supporters of 'democracy' as opposed to 'aristocracy' or 'monarchy', 'republicans' (ibid., pp. 328, 339, 349).

During the French Revolution, the republican leaders used frequently the language of Rousseau and Mably. Condorcet insisted that Republican government must be based on equality of rights and of education. Robespierre inserted into the preamble of the republican constitution of 1793 the following sentence, 'The people is the Sovereign: the government is its work and its products: the public functionaries its clerks'.

3. The most widely read spokesman of radical democratic republicanism in the period of the American and French Revolutions was Paine. In his *Rights of Man* (1791–2) he uses the term *republic* in the sense of 'the State' or 'the public good' and calls the non-monarchical state with popular representative institutions a 'democracy'. Nevertheless, he insinuates that the 'common weal' is best served in a 'democracy' and equates *republic* with representative democracy (see T. Paine, *The Rights of Man*, Everyman's Library, London: Dent, 1915, pp. 174–7). In 1801 the President of the U.S.A., Jefferson, spoke in his inaugural address of the 'absolute acquiescence in the decisions of the majority' as 'the vital principle of republics' and opposed it to 'appeal to force, the vital principle of despotism' (see A. B. Hart, *American History Told by Contemporaries*, New York: The Macmillan Co., 1950, vol. III, p. 346).

Residence

4. A new type of republicanism emerged in continental Europe in the early 19th century which is described by Salvemini as 'absolute, mystical and romantic', for instance the republicanism of Mazzini, which he opposes to the 'freethinking and classical republicanism' of the earlier generation. According to Mazzini, 'the Republic is not only the natural expression of our nationhood ... but a *principle* of Education ... a formula of equality for all, of liberty and therefore of responsibility for all ... [it] bestows office only on merit and achievement, not upon birth or wealth' (see G. Salvemini, *Mazzini*, London: Cape, 1956, p. 60).

5. British radical leaders of the Victorian age used the term in a more cautious and sober way, claiming that it is a political philosophy tending towards a democratic organization of government. J. Chamberlain for instance, said in a speech in 1874, 'if to be a Republican is to have a deep unswerving faith in representative institutions ... to hold as a matter of theory at all events, that that is the best government for a free and intelligent people in which merit is preferred to birth, then I hold it an honour to be associated with nearly all the greatest thinkers of the country, and to be called a Republican' (see *J. Chamberlain's Speeches*, London: Constable, 1914, vol. I, pp. 47-8). C. W. Dilke—radical M.P.—declared in 1871 that 'promotion by merit alone and of the non-recognition of any claims founded upon birth—is commonly accepted as republican. I care not whether you call it republican or whether you do not, but I say that it is the only principle upon which, if we are to keep our place among the nations, we can for the future act' (see S. Gwynn & G. M. Tuckwell, *The Life of the Rt. Hon. Sir Charles W. Dilke*, London: Murray, 1917, vol. I, p. 142).

6. During the Third Republic—after 1875—a positivist and anti-clerical variant of republicanism triumphed in France. Its main representative—J. Ferry—defined its aims with the following sentence: 'My aim is to organize humanity without God and without Kings'. Jaurès, the most eloquent spokesman of the idea of a 'social republic' commented: 'He stopped at the threshold of the social question' (J. Jaurès, *Discours Parlementaires*, Paris: E. Cornély, 1904, vol. I, pp. 27-9).

In France since 1875 the term *republicanism* was usually equated with readiness to defend the democratic system of government as well as the laws establishing a secular system of education. Since the end of World War II, however, the term *republican* came to be used more frequently by antidemocratic groups in self-description—but more recently, as used by De Gaulle and other of his circle, the meaning has been close to that of *democratic* in the Anglo-Saxon tradition.

J. S. Erös

See also: DEMOCRACY
            MONARCHY
            REPUBLIC

Residence

A. *Residence* as used in anthropology is applied specifically to the post-nuptial location of the couple with reference to their kinsmen. It is not normally used to refer to the geographic location of a society, to one of its segments, or to an individual apart from the context of marriage and kinship. The word *residence* is thus an abbreviated form of the term *marital residence*. The significance of residence lies partly in the alignments which arise from choosing one or another site, and partly in the re-alignments, readjustments and potential breaks in relationships which may follow change of residence by one or both spouses. G. P. Murdock, for example, regards the change of alignment which follows a change in residence rule as the initial step in the sequence of changes which alter the whole kinship system (*Social Structure*, New York: The Macmillan Co., 1949, ch. 8).

B. Although there is clear consensus on the importance of modes of marital residence and on its initial definition with reference to kinsmen of the couple, consensus collapses with the attempt to define types of residence rules useful in comparative analysis.

1. Historically the first terms introduced were *patrilocal* and *matrilocal*, defined with reference to the 'family', 'people', and 'home' of the bride and groom. *Patrilocal residence* is thus defined by W. H. R. Rivers as '... the wife goes to live with her husband ...' implying the husband's family, and *matrilocal* is defined as '... the husband goes to live with his wife ...' implying her family (*Social Organization*, London: Kegan Paul, Trench, Trubner, 1926, p. 90). Later, *avunculocal residence* was separated out from patrilocal residence to describe the couple living with the groom's mother's brother. Where the couple could choose either patrilocal or matrilocal residence, the rule was termed *bilocal*.

Consideration of etymology prompted the introduction of *virilocal* and *uxorlocal* as substitutes for patrilocal and matrilocal respectively. This usage has become frequent, but by no means universal. *Neolocal* was later distinguished as a separate type in which residence was independent of the families of both bride and groom. More recently *duolocal* has been suggested for those cases in which bride and groom are not co-resident, but each resides with his natal unit. Recognition of the fact that in many societies a marriage may begin with one rule but soon permanently follow a different rule led to the suggestion that such types be designated by the combined terms in the actual order of their sequence. Thus *matri-patrilocal* is applied where the marriage is matrilocal for a period and becomes permanently patrilocal thereafter.

2. Definitions of such specific types have been highly variable. E. B. Tylor's point of reference was the 'family' or 'home' ('On a Method of Investigating the Development of Institutions', *Journal of the Royal Anthropological Institute*, vol. 18, 1889, p. 247). W. H. R. Rivers used the groom and the bride explicitly as the point of reference, but implicitly seemed to include their respective kinsmen (*Social Organization*, p. 90). G. P. Murdock first specifically used the parents as the point of reference, defining *matrilocal* as follows: 'If custom requires the groom to leave his parental home and live with his bride, either in the house of her parents or in a dwelling nearby ...' (*Social Structure*, p. 16). Later his reference point shifted to the kingroup, so that the matrilocal residence is defined as '... normally with or near the wife's female matrilineal kinsmen' ('World Ethnographic Sample', *American Anthropologist*, vol. 59, 1957, p. 670). H. I. Hogbin and C. H. Wedgwood use both kingroup and community as the points of reference in their definitions. *Patri-virilocal* residence is, for instance, defined by them as '... residence of a married couple in the hamlet, ward, or village of the husband's male patrilineal relatives' ('Local Grouping in Melanesia', *Oceania*, vol. XXIII, 1953, p. 243).

3. It is not surprising, therefore, that many anthropologists have abandoned the use of such simple terms as *patrilocal*, *matrilocal* and so forth, and prefer to rely on concrete description buttressed where possible with carefully collected census and interview material in dealing with residence.

W. H. Goodenough ('Residence Rules', *Southwestern Journal of Anthropology*, vol. 12, 1956, pp. 22–37) suggests that the ethnographer investigate those considerations which actually affect the decision about marital residence in a sufficient number of cases to develop a theory of residence for that particular society. He must then test that theory against further data collected in that society and readjust his theory to conform with his findings. He cannot be satisfied with census data alone, but must use this along with whatever data he discovers to be relevant. Only then can typologies be built.

David M. Schneider

See also: KINSHIP AND KINSHIP SYSTEM
MARRIAGE

Residues

A. The word *residue* has a specific and technical sense in V. Pareto's general theory of social action, viz. the manifestation of universal drives and sentiments in universal principles, assumptions, or beliefs underlying non-logical action or reasoning (*The Mind and Society*, trans. from *Trattato di Sociologia generale* by A. Bongiorno & A. Livingston, ed. by A. Livingston, 4 vols., London: Cape, vol. II, par. 868, particularly fn. by A. Livingston). Since residues in every case correspond to certain drives or sentiments, the term can be used also for such drives and sentiments in their capacity of motivating non-logical action. Such non-logical action is distinguished from logical action which follows what Pareto calls the logical experimental method and which is to be found in economic—especially market—behaviour, in scientific research, etc.

B. Pareto believes that residues can be placed in six main classes (*The Mind and Society*, pars. 889–1396): (a) residues of combination (the human tendency to relate things to one another) (pars. 889–990); (b) group persistence or persistence of aggregates (pars. 991–1088); (c) the need to manifest sentiments through external action (pars. 1089–1112); (d) sociability (pars. 1113–1206); (e) integrity of the individual (pars. 1207–1323); (f) sex (pars. 1324–1396).

C. All classes of residues are to be found in all societies, but the proportions in which they are present vary from society to society, and, more important, from group to group within a given society. Social equilibrium (q.v.) in any given society is a consequence of the interaction of residues with one another and with the thin current of logical behaviour of which, Pareto admits, men are capable.

D. G. MacRae

See also: CIRCULATION OF ELITES
DERIVATION

Response

Response

A. *Response* in its most general usage denotes any behaviour or act of an organism which results from a stimulus (q.v.). It is used occasionally to denote the giving and receiving of signs of appreciation and affection.

B. 1. It is difficult historically to think of the term *response* apart from its dyadic position in the famous formula S–R, or stimulus-response. Early psychological approaches sought to reduce experience (or behaviour) into simple constituents or elements. This form of atomism, or elementarism, goes back at least as far as Avenarius (1843–96) who hypothesized that consciousness depends upon a body and nervous system. He broke up experience into its sense-perception elements (D. D. Runes, *The Dictionary of Philosophy*, London: Vision Press, 1951, p. 30). Structuralists, such as Titchener, approached the problem of mind in terms of its structure. All mental states were atomized into their component parts—sensation, images, and feelings. These responses were related to the stimuli which induced them. Gestalt psychology later viewed these structural patterns at the psychological level as *Gestalten*, or configurations.

2. Social psychology came into being as a separate discipline partly as a result of the severe limitations of a psychology that saw individual behaviour in terms of the elements or atoms of consciousness. But the halo effect of elementarism was still strong on this young field. We see it especially reflected in the social psychology of F. H. Allport and his more devoted followers. In looking upon the individual in his social aspects, he said, 'Behavior may be defined as the process of responding to some form of energy in the environment by an activity generally useful to life. The energy, or less exactly, the object from which it is derived, is known as the "stimulus", while the resulting activity is called the "response". ... The bodily structures and functions operating in behavior are of the same general sort whether the stimulus is furnished by a social or non-social object. The first step, therefore, in the approach to social behavior is the understanding of those physiological processes involved in behavior in general' (*Social Psychology*, Boston: Houghton Mifflin, 1924, p. 17).

In both psychology and social psychology, the view just expressed was usually followed up by an analysis of behaviour in terms of the reflex arc as the functional unit of behaviour, along with graphic diagrams of the main structural elements of the central and autonomic nervous system. In addition, Pavlov's law of the conditioned response shed further light upon the learning process. This experimentally derived law had it that if sufficiently repeated, a once biologically inadequate or 'unnatural' stimulus will take the place of a biologically adequate stimulus. For some time, the law of the conditioned response strengthened the elementaristic S–R approach to the learning process.

3. The idea that social scientists can reduce the complexity of consciousness, the role of language in thought and communication, the social process or interaction, the rise and problems of the self, role taking, etc., to such a simple formula as S–R, is open to the charge of oversimplification if not vagueness (G. H. Mead, *Mind, Self and Society*, Chicago: University of Chicago Press, 1934; E. C. Jandy, *Charles Horton Cooley, His Life and His Social Theory*, New York: Dryden Press, 1942; R. E. L. Faris, *Social Psychology*, New York: Ronald Press, 1952; A. R. Lindesmith & A. L. Strauss, *Social Psychology*, New York: Dryden Press, 1956; and S. H. Asch, *Social Psychology*, New York: Prentice-Hall, 1952).

As Mead aptly expressed it, 'The social act is not to be explained by building it up out of stimulus plus response; it must be taken as a dynamic whole—as something going on—no part of which can be considered or understood by itself—a complex organic process implied by each individual stimulus and response involved in it' (*Mind, Self and Society*, p. 7).

It would be rash to propose that such responses as tropisms, reflexes, reflex arcs, and various forms of conditioning be dispensed with. They may well have their uses in the study of animal behaviour, or even that of early human infancy. But increasingly it became evident that the S–R formula was being applied to a wider and wider area of behaviour that strained it to the point of incredibility. Too much emphasis was placed upon the role of simple nervous mechanisms or even the cortex itself. This reached its apogee, for example, in a sweeping generalization by Allport when he said, 'Socialized behavior is thus the supreme achievement of the cortex' (*Social Psychology*, p. 31). This choice bit of biological dogmatism and determinism on the part of the greatest champion of the individualistic approach to social behaviour, was already at the time of its writing (1924), facing the same fate as the doctrine of instincts.

4. The assumptions and presumptions of the psychology of S–R met with the greatest objection and opposition mainly from those social psychologists who looked primarily to sociological concepts for the explanation of human behaviour. They held an organic point of view regarding human nature, personality, and society (C. H. Cooley, J. Dewey, G. H. Mead, E. Faris; less so, W. I. Thomas). Mead perhaps expressed most succinctly what they all thought of the Allportian sort of thinking in social psychology. He said, 'The act, then, and not the tract, is the fundamental datum in both social and individual psychology ...' (*Mind, Self and Society*, p. 8). It was these theorists, more than any others, who insisted upon the qualitative difference between such responses human beings make to objects and the responses they make to other persons. It was they, moreover, who faced squarely the epistemological question of how we come to know other minds and selves. These difficulties the elementarists either evaded or misunderstood.

5. In recent years the over-simple use of stimulus-response theory has been abandoned among social-psychologists trained primarily in psychology rather than sociology. This has been partly due to the development of the concept of the intervening variable (q.v.) in the stimulus-response theory of C. L. Hull and his students which has done much to overcome the 'mechanical' implications of earlier stimulus-response thinking (see for example, T. M. Newcomb, *Social Psychology*, New York: Dryden Press, 1950, pp. 30–3). It has also been due to the increasing interest of these social psychologists in the social conditions of action and their relation to the intervening variables of attitude, motivation, etc. In this context stimulus and response are assumed, but stress is placed on larger organic units of action, so that even the very terms stimulus and response recede into the background (see, for example, D. Krech, R. S. Crutchfield & E. L. Ballachey, *Individual in Society*, New York: McGraw-Hill, 1962).

C. In a somewhat eccentric use, although one that occurs with a degree of frequency in sociology, W. I. Thomas in his theory of the four wishes (*The Unadjusted Girl*, Boston: Little, Brown, 1931, p. 17) defined the wish for response as 'primarily related to the instinct of love and shows itself in the tendency to seek and give signs of appreciation in connection with other individuals'.

Edward C. Jandy

See also: CONDITIONING
MOTIVATION
SOCIAL
SOCIAL ACT
STIMULUS

Responsibility

A. The term, in its core meaning, denotes answerability for the performance of an office, a charge, or a duty.

B. Various authorities emphasize differing parts of this definition, thereby contributing to the ambiguity and inconsistency of its usage.

1. Answerability implies (a) *accountability*, which focuses attention upon the sanctions or procedures by which public officials may be held to account for their actions, e.g. electoral defeat; legislative investigation and publicity with attendant loss of reputation; executive removal, demotion, deprivation of promotion or privileges; judicial process, liability, etc. Other authorities emphasize (b) *discretionary capacity implicit in a public role or office* which the occupant feels required or is expected to fulfil over and beyond his formal, legal authority. A third denotation refers to (c) a professional, group, or legal *standard* (*code*) *of performance* by which the holder of a public trust considers himself bound. A fourth is that of (d) *loyalty to a determinate or indeterminate, personal or institutional, source of authority*, from which emanates a material-ideological interpretation of the ends that the official structure of authority is supposed to serve, and to which official incumbents render obedience.

2. Notwithstanding its ambiguity, the relationship denoted by the term *responsibility*, while applicable to individuals as institutions, approaches as much as any other the essence of government. 'In framing a government which is to be administered by men over men, the great difficulty lies in this: you must first enable the government to control the governed; and in the next place, oblige it to control itself' (*The Federalist*, 1787–8, no. 51). Responsibility is expected capacity of public officials to undertake specified discretionary tasks without detailed direction; such public functions (powers) have to be organized, disciplined, co-ordinated with other official agencies and purposes; public officials and organizations must be freed to act without intolerable restraints yet controlled by the consent, acceptance and resistance of other public officials and human beings participating in the political

Responsibility

control system (J. M. Gaus, *The Frontiers of Public Administration*, Chicago: University of Chicago Press, 1935; G. A. Graham, 'Essentials of Responsibility', in F. M. Marx, *Elements of Public Administration*, New York: Prentice-Hall, 1946, pp. 501–18). The historical process tests the survival value of differing institutional conceptions of political responsibility (G. C. Homans, *The Human Group*, London: Routledge & Kegan Paul, 1950).

3. The problem of political responsibility, whether conceived at the constitutional level of whole governmental systems or as a division of function between politically-responsive officials and administrative technicians or experts, arises partly from conflict of views as to what standard of value constitutes the public interest in specific controversial situations, partly from conflict as to *who* shall control the governmental decision. The conception of 'public office as a public trust' is not a formula or equation which can be solved by applying preferred definitions and logical operations: it provides a partly legal, partly symbolic standard that imposes the welfare of the commonwealth, the common good, as a general principle upon the exercise of official discretion. Responsible government implies effective representation of the public in the selection of rulers and in the formulation of public purpose anticipating the application of official discretion to specific cases. The distinction between political and administrative responsibility does not require an absolute separation of administrators from politics, but a protection of such officials in their obligation to balance and apply with integrity both technical skills and political values to their limited roles in the processes of policy formulation and execution.

C. In its political connotations *responsibility* is variously employed.

1. It establishes *a criterion for differentiating political systems.* Although responsibility implies some basis of legality, its explicit referent usually is that of a standard of conduct, obligation, or performance controlling the exercise of public office. Standards may be spiritual or ethical, social-psychological, or institutional, but these categories overlap and are not mutually exclusive. In the analysis of political systems, perhaps the most critical distinction lies between *democratic* and *authoritarian* regimes. In the former category, responsibility for the conduct of government is institutionalized and vested in constitutional procedures for sharing governmental authority. These norms place effective choice in the whole body of adult citizen-members (the electorate or its representatives) for selecting rulers periodically and thus determining the broad directions of public policy. Authoritarian systems legitimize the monopoly of a ruling class or group in conducting political affairs; the responsibility of the ruler(s) is personalized and exclusive. There is no intermediate human authority between the ruling political group and an external standard imputed to and imposed upon the body politic, e.g. a divine being or will, a dynamic or hereditary principle, a concept of biological or racial fitness, a utopian plan of socio-economic structure and organization—a political formula or ruling myth which it is this group's exclusive function to interpret and apply.

2. The idea of *responsible office* is sometimes used to refer to official positions whose occupants are in various ways accountable to the electorate (or the ultimately ruling group) as compared to those positions which are technical or managerial in character. Analytically, the critical point turns on whether the office is presumed to be responsive directly to the ultimate ruling authority or group, which determines the occupancy and tenure of office, or whether the office is evaluated upon a basis of competence in effectuating policies established by politically-responsible officials, in which case access to and tenure of office are supposedly based upon merit, performance and good behaviour. Empirically, the number of political offices is usually small in comparison to the administrative, but upon changes of government it is potentially capable of either expansion or contraction.

3. A distinction somewhat similar in its effects is made between *political decisions or acts* which are made in controversial situations when the standard of judgement is indeterminate and which are presumed to be responsible to values established by representative processes of political conflict: force, authority, or the electoral and legislative channels of discussion, negotiation and compromise, and *administrative decisions*, which are presumed to be primarily policy-executing and where the standard of judgement is legal, professional, or technical.

4. The term is also used rather widely to denote a variety of professional and technical obligations, e.g. as in such sentences as 'the job carries with it certain responsibilities'—the sense being that the job involves the exercise of some authority and calls for the observance of implicit or explicit standards of competence. In

600

this sense the term is used in 'private' as well as in 'public' government.

D. Important considerations arise in regard to the concept of legal responsibility and its application. In a general discussion 'The Nature of Responsibility' (in *On the Diversity of Morals*, London: Heinemann, 1956, pp. 79 et seq.) M. Ginsberg writes that in all the senses of the term 'there seem to be three elements: causation, obligation, and accountability' and further argues that irrespective of the findings of the psychology of the unconscious mind or of the philosophical debates over determinism 'responsibility ... implies freedom. ... Responsibility and freedom are correlative and since there are degrees of freedom, it follows that there are degrees of responsibility' (ibid., p. 81). This leads straight into a concern with the problems of crime and punishment. This concern has been very vigorously expressed in recent years and some of the ambiguities in the doctrines of legal responsibility and liability have been carefully explored. H. L. A. Hart points out: '... only recently has the word "responsibility" crept into our [British] criminal statutes' (*Punishment and the Elimination of Responsibility*, London: Athlone Press, 1962, p. 20); but the issues raised by 'responsibility' have long been central to discussions of and legislation on punishment. Hart observes that '... though the law approximates in its doctrine of the mental conditions of responsibility to what the moralist requires for moral blame, it is an approximation only and not a complete convergence' (ibid., pp. 20–1). After analysing various legal and sociological discussions of the concept, Hart sets out the case for retaining the principle of responsibility and for its reinterpretation. 'The principle of responsibility, which may be sacrificed when the social cost of maintaining it is too high, has a value and importance quite independent of retributive or denunciatory theories of punishment which we may well discard' (ibid., p. 32).

Avery Leiserson

See also: ADMINISTRATION
AUTONOMY
CONSTITUTIONALISM
CULTURAL DETERMINISM
PARTY RESPONSIBILITY
PUBLIC OFFICE
RULE OF LAW

Revenue

A. *Revenue* denotes a continuous or intermittent flow through time of things having value, accruing to some claimant, usually in payment of a service imputedly rendered by the claimant. In traditional theory there are four factors of production rendering services, their owners claiming the appropriate revenue, i.e. owners of labour claiming wages, of capital claiming interest, of land claiming rent, and of entrepreneurship claiming profits.

Thus a producer of economic goods and services refers to revenue as being the return he receives from his output, or from what he produces for the market. Adam Smith (*An Inquiry into the Nature and Causes of the Wealth of Nations* (1776), New York: Random House, 1937, p. 52) stated that wages, profit, and rent are the three original forms of revenue, and he further stated that land and capital stock are the two original sources of all revenue both private and public (ibid., p. 879). The revenue or income of a corporation arises from one, two, or all of three sources: (a) regular operations, (b) outside operations, and (c) investments.

B. 1. In economic analysis under the theory of pricing, or value theory, the terms *total revenue*, *average revenue*, and *marginal revenue* are used. (a) *Total revenue* refers to total receipts, or all revenue derived from the sale of the entire output or product. (b) *Average revenue* refers to total receipts divided by the number of units of output or product sold, or under conditions of pure or perfect competition as price per unit. (c) *Marginal revenue* is defined as being the additional revenue derived from producing one additional unit of output or product.

2. (a) *Gross revenue* consists of the entire gross receipts with no costs or expenses deducted. (b) *Net revenue* would be the revenue or profit after costs and expenses have been deducted. (c) In accounting of railroads and public utilities, gross receipts from services are termed *operating revenues*.

C. *Government revenue* or *public revenue* includes all public moneys which the state collects and receives from whatever source with the exception of proceeds from loans or borrowing, even though the latter add to current receipts. Government revenue, therefore, includes taxes, fines, licences, fees, special assessments, income from publicly owned and operated projects or services, and miscellaneous receipts such as proceeds from sale of publicly owned properties, interest on government funds, etc. According to Smith (ibid., p. 777) every tax—which is one of the greatest sources of government revenue—

Revitalization Movement

must be paid from wages, profit, and rent, either from some one of them, or from all three, since wages, profit, and rent are the original sources of all income or revenue. J. R. McCulloch (*A Treatise on the Principles and Practical Influence of Taxation*, London: Longman, Brown, Green & Longmans, 1852, p. 40), states that 'it is not from capital, therefore, but from revenue that permanent taxes should be derived'.

Kathleen E. Dunlop

See also: INCOME

Revitalization Movement

A. A *revitalization movement* may be defined as '... a deliberate, organized, conscious effort by members of a society to construct a more satisfying culture' (A. F. C. Wallace, 'Revitalization Movements', *American Anthropologist*, vol. 58, 1956, pp. 281, 265). A. F. C. Wallace, who introduced the term, uses it to designate a wide range of phenomena. While the following are examples of the type of phenomena included as sub-classes of revitalization movements, they should not be thought of as mutually exclusive for '... a given revitalization movement may be nativistic, millenarian, messianic, and revivalistic all at once; and it may [in fact, usually does] display ambivalence with respect to nativistic, revivalistic, and importation themes' (ibid., p. 267): (a) nativism (q.v.) or nativistic movements; (b) revivalistic movements which '... emphasize the institution of customs, values, and even aspects of nature which are thought to have been in the mazeway of previous generations but are not now present ...' (ibid., p. 267); (c) cargo cults (q.v.); (d) vitalistic movements which '... emphasize the importation of alien elements into the mazeway but do not necessarily invoke the ship and cargo as the mechanism' (ibid., p. 267); (e) millenarian movements which '... emphasize transformation of culture in an apocalyptic world transformation engineered by the supernatural' (ibid., p. 267); (f) messianic movements which '...emphasize the participation of a divine saviour in human flesh in the mazeway transformations' (ibid., p. 267).

B. Revitalization movements have been of great historical importance: 'Both Christianity and Mohammedanism, and possibly Buddhism as well, originated in revitalization movements. Most denominational and sectarian groups and orders budded or split off after failure to revitalize a traditional institution. One can ask whether a large proportion of religious phenomena have not originated in personality transformation dreams or visions characteristic of the revitalization process. ... In fact, it can be argued that all organized religions are relics of old revitalization movements, surviving in routinized form in stabilised cultures, and that religious phenomena *per se* originated in the revitalization process—i.e., in visions of a new way of life by individuals under extreme stress' (ibid., pp. 267–8).

Thus it is possible to see the origin of all sacred (q.v.) institutions in a society—as opposed to secular (q.v.) technologically adaptive institutions—in revitalization movements of peoples reacting to various forms of stress.

Weston La Barre

See also: NATIVISM
SOCIAL MOVEMENT

Revolution

A. The term *revolution* is used by most modern authors to denote (a) sudden, radical changes which take place both in political and social conditions, that is when an 'established' government (as well as a social and legal order) is suddenly, sometimes violently, replaced by a new one; (b) changes of a radical, non-political character even if the change in question takes place slowly and without violence (terms like *scientific revolution*, *artistic revolution*, *cultural revolution* and even *sexual revolution* are often used in our century to describe thorough-going changes in various spheres of cultural life).

B. The most widespread modern interpretations of revolution can be summarized in the following:

1. The progressive—evolutionary—optimistic interpretation dominated during the 19th century amongst the parties and the thinkers of the Left and still dominates radical democratic and Marxist theory today. According to this view, great political and social revolutions are the instruments of the 'inevitable' progress of mankind towards a society in which freedom, self-government, social harmony, and equality will dominate. The various 'progressive' schools of thought are, however, divided into those who insist that 'egalitarianism' is the supreme mark of progress and are ready to use dictatorial methods in its service (Leninism) and 'liberal democratic' thinkers who regard only those mass upheavals as genuine progressive revolutions which are directed against tyrannical rulers and aim at establishing freedom and democratic government. There are, of course, many who attempt to achieve both liberty and equality (e.g. democratic socialists).

2. There is also a conservative, pessimistic school of thought which was represented during and after the period of the French Revolution by political thinkers of a feudal, traditionalist, 'theocratic', or royalist turn of mind, and during the latter half of the 19th century by men with a disillusioned political or psychological outlook, such as Nietzsche or Le Bon. These thinkers insist that revolutions are outbreaks of semi-barbaric, uncontrolled, destructive popular emotions. Modern dynamic psychologists sometimes fall back on this interpretation of revolutions, as expressions of 'mass-psychology' and compare them to the 'regressions' to primitive mentality observable in mental breakdowns.

3. The 'scientific', sociological, or positivist view holds that the term *revolution* has a descriptive meaning and no value connotations. On this view all sudden, radical and more or less violent changes in the system of government and society are genuine *revolutions*, as long as it can be established that the political movement which brought about this change was supported by a broad stratum of the population.

4. A balanced modern view opposed both to the optimistic-progressive, and the pessimistic-conservative view is expressed by F. Fejto, who believes that a revolution 'is always a complex contradictory affair, full of an unexpectedness, into which the whole "subconscious" of a people erupts, with all that this implies of the reactionary, the progressive. ... Everything in it is pell-mell ... the splendid and the violent' ('Hungary and Socialism', *Universities and Left Review*, Winter 1958, p. 13).

C. 1. Late 18th-century revolutionary agitation was based on the theory of the 'natural equality' of all men and on the theory of 'popular sovereignty'—a theory which denied the authority of the traditional, absolutist monarchies as well as the legitimacy of the privileges of the nobility. M. Beloff claims that the American 'Declaration of Independence' of 1776 was, and still is, a 'revolutionary document' as it announces the natural equality of all men as well as the right of the governed to change their government by peaceful means, or, if they resist, by the use of force (*Thomas Jefferson and American Democracy*, London: Hodder & Stoughton, 1948, p. 69). The same applies of course also to the French 'Declaration of Human Rights' of 1789.

The most effective propagandist of the liberal democratic theory of revolution was Paine (*Rights of Man*, Dublin: G. Burnet, 1791). He was the prophet of 'a new era' which shall 'blot despotism from the earth' and establish 'the great Republic of man' (see his 'Address to the People of France', in *Selected Writings*, N. Gomgulee (ed.), London: Nicholson & Watson, 1948, pp. 176–8).

2. Saint-Simon, Comte, and Marx ridiculed the 'natural rights' theory of politics as 'unscientific'. Marx vehemently emphasized the *inevitable* character of revolutions which, according to him, were brought about by economic necessities. He claimed that the 'productive forces' of society come at a certain stage of their development in conflict with the 'property relations' and with the existing social and political framework. When the latter become the 'fetters of production' a crisis develops and 'the epoch of social revolutions' begins. The ruling classes cannot, and the oppressed, exploited classes do not want to live any longer under the existing conditions and this conflict of economic classes leads to a violent revolution. Marx regarded revolutions as indispensable factors of progress and claimed that they are 'the locomotives of history' (see K. Marx, *The Class Struggles in France*, 1848–1850, reprinted in K. Marx & F. Engels, *Selected Works in Two Volumes*, London: Lawrence & Wishart, 1951, vol. I, p. 198). For Marx's views on the economic basis of revolutions see his 'Preface to a Contribution to the Critique of Political Economy' (ibid., p. 329).

This deterministic and economistic theory of revolutions was to some extent modified by V. I. Lenin. In 1916 and 1917 Lenin expounded the thesis that 'predatory' war and national oppression can become the starting-point of revolutions and of the break-up of the old order. He believed that the 'imperialist epoch', the epoch of World War I, 'must also necessarily engender and foster the politics of struggle against national oppression and the politics of the proletarian struggle against the bourgeoisie'. He saw 'the inevitability, first, of revolutionary national rebellions and wars; second, of proletarian wars and rebellion *against* the bourgeoisie; and third, of a combination of both kinds of revolutionary war ...' (see: *The Essentials of Lenin in Two Volumes*, London: Lawrence & Wishart, 1947, vol. I, p. 743).

He also emphasized, more than other Marxists, the need for a secret, disciplined, centralized organization of theoretically trained and experienced 'professional revolutionaries' to prepare armed risings and to guide the revolutionary movements of the masses (see his 'What

Reward

is to be done' reprinted in *The Essentials of Lenin*, vol. I, pp. 149–274).

3. In contrast to Marxist writers, proponents of anarchist theory such as Proudhon and P. Kropotkin point out that all revolutions have attempted to realize 'justice' by force but in the process one tyranny took the place of another. Nevertheless, however 'degenerated' they became, all revolutions introduced into society 'a certain degree of justice' at least partially and these 'partial realisations' will lead, so Proudhon and Kropotkin believe, 'to the complete triumph of justice on earth'. They meant, of course, by 'revolutions' the great political and social upheavals which took place in Europe and North America since 1775 (see P. Kropotkin, *Ethics*, London: Harrap, 1924, pp. 273, 279, as well as P. J. Proudhon, *De la Justice dans la Revolution et dans l'Eglise*, 1858, Paris: Librairie des Sciences Politique et Sociales, Marcel Riviere, new edn., 1930–35).

4. Various value-free, sociological definitions of the term *revolution* were given by 20th-century sociologists and political scientists. K. Mannheim claims that during the revolution no genuine state exists because we can only speak of the existence of a state if there is a 'frame group' possessing the monopoly of 'legitimate coercions'. During revolutions 'partial bodies acquire parts of the power of the state to coerce' (see his *Systematic Sociology*, ed. by J. S. Erös & W. A. C. Stewart, London: Routledge & Kegan Paul, 1957, p. 119). P. Sorokin defined revolutionary change as 'a comparatively sudden, rapid and violent change of the obsolete official law of the group or of the institutions and system of values which it represents', and contrasted it to 'orderly change'. It is a result of a 'widening discrepancy between the official law of the group and the unofficial law convictions of some of its members', as well as of an 'irreconcilable antagonism respecting the main values of the group'. It involves the participation of a 'considerable part' of the membership of the group (see his *Society, Culture and Personality*, New York: Harper & Brothers, 1947, pp. 481–2). He distinguishes a 'political revolution' which transforms 'the ruling class and the government' from an 'economic revolution' which attempts 'a violent change in the economic system' and also from a 'religious', 'racial' or a 'nationalistic' revolution. He calls a revolution which attempts to transform 'all the important institutions and values of the group' a 'total revolution' (ibid., p. 482). It must be remarked that

historians and sociologists talking of *revolution* in the wider sense (as applicable to events which took place in France during the 1790s or in Russia after 1917) usually mean what Sorokin terms *total revolution*—a term which did not obtain general acceptance.

C. Brinton uses the term *revolution*—in accordance with general modern usage—as denoting 'the great overturns in previously stable political societies'. He claims that it is a 'drastic, sudden, substitution of one group in charge of the running of a territorial political entity for another group ...' (*The Anatomy of Revolution*, London: Cape, 1953, p. 2).

D. W. Brogan defines *revolution* as 'the overthrow of an established practical order, not merely to replace one Amurath by another, but to replace one social, religious, political system by another'. According to Brogan the problem of revolution was well known to the thinkers of antiquity, yet it is only since the American Revolution that revolution as a 'violent medicine for the ills of the State' acquired the status of an 'institution'. Whilst the American 'Declaration of Independence' became the basis of the 'new revolutionary doctrine', the 'effective' example for revolutionary procedures was furnished by the French Revolution (*The Price of Revolution*, London: Hamish Hamilton, 1951, pp. 1, 2).

J. S. Erös

Reward

A. *Reward* is a term used in psychology to denote any stimulus which increases the probability of occurrence of, or strengthens a response (or class of behaviour) upon which it was contingent.

Such a definition appears applicable to the whole continuum of simple to complex stimuli which various writers have singled out for discussion. Thus a hungry rat may be rewarded by food, an upward-mobile person by a symbol of prestige, and a person with moral principles may reward himself by voluntary adherence to some moral standard in the face of temptation.

B. In learning theory the term reward generally corresponds to the term positive reinforcement. R. S. Woodworth (*Contemporary Schools of Psychology*, London: Methuen, 8th edn., 1951, p. 66) states: 'It has become clear from all this work that Pavlov's "reinforcement" and Thorndike's "reward" are the same. They stand for the same positive factor in establishing an association. Psychologists today are apt to prefer the term reinforcement ...'

E. L. Thorndike's 'law of effect' (*The Elements of Psychology*, New York: Seiler, 1905, p. 203) describes the operation of reward as follows: 'Any act which in a given situation produces satisfaction becomes associated with that situation, so that when the situation recurs the act is more likely than before to recur also'.

C. L. Hull (*Principles of Behavior*, New York: Appleton-Century-Crofts, 1943, p. 131) states: 'The concept of incentive in behavior theory corresponds roughly to the common-sense notion of reward. More technically, the incentive is that substance or commodity in the environment which satisfies a need, i.e., which reduces a drive'.

B. F. Skinner's position is that a reward is that consequence of behaviour which increases the probability of that *class* of behaviour occurring again. 'We first define a positive reinforcer as any stimulus the *presentation* of which strengthens the behavior upon which it is made contingent' (*Science and Human Behavior*, New York: The Macmillan Co., 1953, p. 185).

C. 1. Social psychologists use the term *reward* more broadly. E. L. Hartley and R. E. Hartley (*Fundamentals of Social Psychology*, New York: Knopf, 1952, pp. 274, 275) describe the additional considerations necessary in dealing with the concept of reward in the social psychological framework: 'Reward ... must be very broadly defined when we consider human learning. Because human beings are capable of retaining the effects of their experiences for long periods of time and because they are capable of generalization and transfer, functional rewards ... may be far removed from physical rewards. ... When we speak of reward we mean anything that operates as a source of satisfaction for the individual ... the attitudes other people display and the individual's own feelings may come to serve as rewards'.

2. In personality theory, and especially in psychoanalytic theory, there is a distinction between external and internal sources of reward. O. Fenichel (*The Psychoanalytic Theory of Neurosis*, New York: Norton, 1945, pp. 105, 106) describes the rewarding power of the superego: 'The superego is the heir of the parents not only as a source of threats and punishments but also as a source of protection and as a provider of reassuring love. ... Complying with the superego's demands brings not only relief but also definite feelings of pleasure and security of the same type that children experience from external supplies of love'.

D. There is an important difference between the learning theorists, on the one hand, and the social psychologists and personality theorists, on the other. In general, the first group concerns itself with definitions which are in terms of operations performed by an experimenter or an observer which result in change in behaviour in the organism under study, while the second group considers the subjective experience of the organism as well as the aforementioned factors in arriving at definitions.

Study of the various usages shows that their divergences concern the *explanation* of the effects of reward, rather than the effects per se.

Robert J. Havighurst

See also: PUNISHMENT
REINFORCEMENT
SANCTION

Right (See Left and Right)

Risk (and Uncertainty)
A. 1. In its general meaning *risk* denotes the chances of loss. In economics the term is used to denote (a) a situation characterized (either objectively or subjectively) by incomplete predictability of alternative events; or (b) a situation characterized by knowledge of the parameters of a probability distribution of a set of alternative events, but in which no event carries a probability of 1.

2. *Uncertainty* in its general meaning denotes a situation characterized (either objectively or subjectively) by incomplete predictability of alternative events. In economics the term denotes either (a) a situation characterized by lack of knowledge of the parameters of a probability distribution of a set of alternative events; or (b) a situation such as (a) above and/or pragmatic lack of insurability or seriability of events. In psychology it denotes an effective state of doubt and unsureness and/or of indecisiveness.

B. 1. Except in economics, the term *risk* is usually a non-technical word implying, as in ordinary speech, the chance of incurring damage or a loss of some kind (physical, psychological, military, political, economic, etc.). Risk is in this sense a characteristic of the environment, external to the individual, and thus 'objective'. Risk exists whether or not the individual is aware of it.

2. Uncertainty, on the other hand, is to the psychologist a state of mind, not a character-

605

Risk

istic of the external environment per se. It is thus a subjective term. But the uncertainty may be cognitive, as in the economist's uses of the term *subjective uncertainty*, or it may be affective. Affective uncertainty involves a feeling of doubtfulness and unsureness and/or indecisiveness. Psychologists point out that cognitive uncertainty, meaning the unpredictability of the outcomes of particular lines of action, is not necessarily stressful and does not necessarily give rise to affective uncertainty; in fact situations involving cognitive uncertainty may be welcomed as a challenge. Thus psychologists have attacked an assumption often made by economists—that men seek to avoid situations characterized by cognitive uncertainty or that they demand what economists term *risk premiums* as the price of deliberately undertaking ventures the outcomes of which are not cognitively certain.

C. 1. In its broadest definition the term *uncertainty* is used by economists to refer to any situation in which a set of alternative outcomes is not fully predictable. The uncertainty may be objective in that even an individual possessing all the available information (acquired at no matter how great cost) would still be unable to predict accurately. Or it may be subjective in that with the information the individual in fact has (or considers worth the cost of acquiring) he is unable, or believes he is unable, to predict with accuracy. Increasingly in recent years the term has been defined in the subjective rather than the objective sense. Subjective certainty then implies a firm belief in ability to predict exactly, whether or not this belief is objectively justified.

2. Since F. H. Knight's work in the 1920s (*Risk, Uncertainty and Profit*, New York: Houghton Mifflin, 1921) the terms *risk* and *uncertainty* have come to be used in a mutually exclusive sense. Starting out to analyse the nature of profits, Knight distinguished between insurable and other kinds of unpredictabilities, using the term *risk* to refer to insurable, and *uncertainty* to non-insurable variabilities in outcomes. The clue to this was the possibility of measuring risk by actuarial methods. This led to a modern definition of risk as a situation in which the parameters of the distribution of future events are fully known and mathematical expectations can be computed, while uncertainty refers to situations in which those parameters are not known. Usually the analysis refers to the individual's belief concerning how much he knows, i.e. to subjective risk and subjective uncertainty.

3. To some economists, however, full knowledge of the parameters of a probability distribution constitutes a necessary but not sufficient condition to identify a situation as characterized by risk rather than uncertainty. Basically, they ask the question: what are the conditions necessary for action on the basis of mathematical expectations (whether direct or as utility transformations) derived from a known probability distribution? The conditions of this are that either (a) there must be a large number of independent homogeneous events (or a divisibility into such events) either within the firm or among firms, or (b) within the firm the events must be fully seriable, i.e. repeatable a large number of times with a financial base strong enough to survive an initial chance run of bad outcomes. It is then argued that given a situation in which the parameters of a probability distribution are known (or believed to be known), subjective uncertainty will still prevail if neither of the two above conditions is met.

4. Despite the modern emphasis on the distinction between risk and uncertainty (whether in the pure probability or the more pragmatic approach), there are also tendencies to reintroduce the more general definition of uncertainty as everything that is not certain. In part this is undoubtedly a reflection of refinements in analysis that demonstrate that uncertainty in the broadest sense has varying 'degrees', perhaps along more than one continuum. The dichotomy between risk and uncertainty is seen as both arbitrary and too simple. More emphasis is being placed on variance and on kinds and degrees of knowledge. Thus J. Marschak ('Role of Liquidity Under Complete and Incomplete Information', *American Economic Review*, vol. XXXIX, 1949, pp. 183–4), for example, though he clings to the probability approach, sets up four type situations. Denoting by p the set of probabilities $p_1, p_2 \ldots$ of a set of alternative events $u_1, u_2 \ldots$, he then distinguishes four cases: (a) the firm does not know p; (b) the firm does not know p, but it knows data permitting it to estimate p; (c) the firm (believes it) knows p; (d) the firm (believes it) knows p and that every element of p is either 1 or 0. The first case, which is clearly Knightian uncertainty, Marschak terms *ignorance*. The second case is in a twilight zone between Knightian uncertainty and Knightian risk. The first two cases together Marschak terms *incomplete information*. The last two cases he terms *complete information*, case (d) being *certainty*. All except case (d) are thus variants of uncertainty.

5. Finally, from the beginning the term *risk* has been used in economics in the lay sense to denote merely the danger or chance of loss, without any consideration of possible gain. It is still so used.

Mary Jean Bowman

See also: PROFIT

Rite (See Ceremony and Ritual)

Rites de Passage
A. This term was first used by A. van Gennep (*Les Rites de passage*, Paris: Nourry, 1909) to describe two types of rite: those which accompany the passage of an individual from one social status to another in the course of his life, and those which mark recognized points in the passage of time (new year, new moon, solstice or equinox). The term has come to be restricted to the former type, which are now sometimes called life crisis rites. Typical *rites de passage* in the modern sense are those which accompany birth, the attainment of adult status, marriage, and death.

B. Van Gennep analysed these rites into a sequence of three stages, rites of separation, marginal rites and rites of aggregation (or of entry into, waiting in and leaving the intermediate no-man's-land). The three elements are not equally marked in all *rites de passage*; according to Van Gennep the element of separation is more important in mortuary ritual, that of aggregation in marriage. The marginal rites, marking the period in which an individual is detached from one status but not yet admitted to the next, are most conspicuous in those initiation ceremonies which involve the participants in a long period in the bush cut off from their normal social contacts.

The sacralization of these crucial periods in individual life is itself a matter of sociological interest. Van Gennep drew attention to the characteristic symbolism of *rites de passage*, such as a simulated death and resurrection, or a ritual passing through a door or archway. He interpreted birth rituals as signifying the separation of the infant from the world of the dead (or not-living) and his aggregation to that of the living. Recent ethnography (e.g. M. Wilson, *Rituals of Kinship Among the Nyakyusa*, London: Oxford University Press, 1957) has sup-

plemented his analysis of mortuary ritual by showing how it can explicitly include the aggregation of the dead person to the society of the ancestors.

L. P. Mair

Ritual
A. *Ritual* denotes those aspects of prescribed formal behaviour which have no direct technological consequence. The 'prescription' is ordinarily provided by cultural tradition, but may in some cases be a spontaneous invention of the individual. The majority of 'religious' and 'magical' actions are ritual in this sense but the concept *ritual* is not usefully limited to religious and magical contexts. Ritual actions are 'symbolic' in that they assert something about the state of affairs, but they are not necessarily purposive— i.e. the performer of ritual does not necessarily seek to alter the state of affairs.

B. Following the Latin, *ritus*, the English term *rite* was at first synonomous with custom in general; later it became specifically appropriate only to religious and/or magical custom. As such, it refers to the fixed observances of cult behaviour as distinct from any system of beliefs which may be associated with such observances. Some Christian ecclesiastical writers equate *ritual* with *liturgy*—i.e. the prescribed forms of public worship (E. Underhill, *Worship*, New York, Harper & Bros., 1937); they then use other terms such as *ceremony* to cover individual acts of cult behaviour. Some anthropological writers distinguish *ritual* and *ceremony* on the basis of the sacred-secular dichotomy. Thus in the *Encyclopedia of the Social Sciences*, *ritual* is said to be 'prescribed formal behavior for occasions not given over to technological routine' (R. Benedict, 'Ritual', in E. R. A. Seligman (ed.), *Encyclopedia of the Social Sciences*, New York: The Macmillan Co., 1934, vol. XIII, p. 396) but *ceremony* is 'a formal series of acts indicating . . . the exceptional importance of an occasion' (C. D. Burns, 'Ceremony', in ibid., 1930, vol. III, p. 314). The practical applications of these definitions are barely distinguishable. Some writers assert that ritual is not only formal but purposive. Thus 'Ritual, like etiquette, is a formal mode of behaviour recognized as correct, but unlike the latter it implies belief in the operation of supernatural agencies or forces' (*Notes and Queries on Anthropology*, London: Routledge & Kegan Paul, 6th edn., 1951, p. 175); R. Firth (*Elements of Social Organization*, London: Watts, 1951, p. 222) is even more complicated and specific: ritual is 'a kind of patterned

Ritual Pollution

activity oriented towards control of human affairs, primarily symbolic in character with a non-empirical referent, and as a rule socially sanctioned'.

Definitions of this last sort clearly include not only religious acts but also magical acts of a non-religious kind and the difficulty then arises of how to distinguish such 'magical routines' from 'technological routines'. Thus S. F. Nadel (*Nupe Religion*, London, Routledge & Kegan Paul, 1954) includes as ritual all behaviour exhibiting a degree of rigidity not accounted for by its professed aims and remarks that in medical matters the Nupe 'abandon their own "scientific" principles, diluting them with rules of a different order—with ritual ...' (ibid., p. 134).

On somewhat similar grounds E. R. Leach (*Political Systems of Highland Burma*, London: Bell, 1954, pp. 12–13) has criticized Durkheim's clear-cut distinction between sacred acts (rites) and profane (technological) acts. Almost all actions which are carried out according to traditional routines have their symbolic aspect which can be said to 'say' something about the social condition of the actors. It is this symbolically significant aspect of routine which Leach calls ritual (ibid., p. 13).

C. For anthropologists and ecclesiastics *ritual* always refers to social customs, traditionally sanctioned, but some psychoanalytic writers use the term to include prescribed and elaborated behaviour which has been spontaneously invented by the individual—as by compulsion neurotics (for examples, see M. Klein et al. (eds.), *New Directions in Psycho-analysis*, London: Tavistock Publications, 1955).

E. R. Leach

See also: CEREMONY

Ritual Pollution

A. *Ritual pollution* denotes a state, permanent or temporary, of 'uncleanliness' to which (especially in primitive societies and notably in India) ritual significance is attached.

B. A condition of pollution is considered mystically dangerous either for the defiled person or for those with whom he comes into contact, or both together. If the appropriate cleansing is not undertaken, pollution may result in illness or misfortune in this life, or, where a belief in the after-life exists, may bring penalties in the next world. Ideas about purity and defilement are found in all primitive societies and in many advanced societies. Discussions

have, broadly speaking, concerned firstly the idea-systems of which pollution concepts are a part, and, secondly, the social correlates of these ideas.

C. The following discussion concerns Hindu India, which exhibits pollution beliefs and behaviour in a most developed and most sophisticated form. Beliefs about purity and impurity form an important part of Hindu mystical ideas, and at the same time are connected with the relationships of segregation and hierarchy in the Hindu caste system. But it is to be emphasized that India is an extreme case of a set of phenomena which are manifested, to a greater or lesser degree, in all known societies.

1. Pollution among the Hindus may be either temporary or permanent: that is to say, a man may be defiled by accidental or wilful contact with a polluting object or person, and may later purify himself by the proper ritual means; or his polluting status might be an incident of birth into a particular category of persons.

Accidental or 'situational' pollution is the result of such events as child-birth, menstruation, intercourse, death, or the bodily functions. Persons defiled in this way, or others who are in a defined relationship to the polluted person, may not resume their normal social status until they have performed purifying rites. For example, a menstruating woman is forbidden the kitchen and certain other parts of the house, and at the end of her period she must bathe in a prescribed fashion before she can resume her household duties.

2. Those whose livelihood is gained by handling polluted objects (for example, by washing defiled clothes or by scavenging) or those who carry out an activity in itself polluting (for example, the taking of life) form categories or groups of persons (castes or sub-castes) considered always to be polluting by other persons who do not make their living in such a way.

3. Pollution, however, does not attach only to those who are specialized in dealing with polluting objects. Other castes, including those with traditional occupations which are not defiling, have an ascribed ritual status which makes them an object of ritual danger to castes of higher rank, and subjects them to pollution by contact with castes ranked lower. The relevant forms of contact are limited to defined situations, and these situations vary according to the activity and according to relative positions in the caste hierarchy. For example, in some parts of India the Untouchables at the bottom of the hierarchy pollute others merely by coming within a defined distance of them, even though there be no physical contact. At the other extreme some high castes accept water and certain foodstuffs from castes which are not too far below them in the hierarchy.

4. H. N. C. Stevenson ('Status Evaluation in the Hindu Caste System', *Journal of the Royal Anthropological Institute*, vol. 84, 1954) has argued that objects can be ranked according to a criterion of purity and impurity, and that in an analogous fashion castes fall into ritual rank according to the extent to which their behaviour patterns involve them in or enable them to avoid pollution. Thus changes in diet, or occupation, or in marriage customs, for example, so long as these have reference to pollution ideas, may raise or lower the collective ritual status of a sub-caste. The rank of a caste or sub-caste is said to be fixed by ritual values attached to behaviour customary in that caste.

5. M. Marriott ('Interactional and Attributional Theories of Caste Ranking', *Man in India*, vol. 39, 1959) has pointed out that there are many difficulties in the way of such an 'attributional' theory. Firstly, the presumed values of customary behaviour do not correlate well with actual caste ranking: for example, vegetarian castes are sometimes ranked below meat-eaters. Secondly, many of the customs said to be a source of group pollution and therefore an index of low rank are in fact common to all castes: a woman, for example, of whatever caste, sweeps out her own household or may wash her own or her family's clothes. Thirdly, there is no criterion by which the several forms of impure activity can be ranked: for example, in itself hair-cutting is not deemed necessarily more or less impure than washing clothes or butchering meat. Fourthly, there are many discriminations in rank between castes which ought, on a purely attributional theory, to be ranked equally. M. Marriott notes that the attributional theory works better at the extremes of the caste hierarchy—the Brahmin at the top and the Untouchable at the bottom—than it does in the middle ranges of the caste system.

D. This brief discussion of some theories which relate beliefs about pollution to caste behaviour and the structure of a caste society may be taken as an example of the way in which an understanding of a society is sought through an examination of its religious values. It should be emphasized that theories about pollution and

purity are not to be understood in themselves alone, but are part of, and to be understood in the light of general theories of ritual and religion. (Reference should also be made to M. N. Srinivas, *Religion and Society among the Coorgs of South India*, Oxford: Clarendon Press, 1952, and L. Dumont & D. Pocock (eds.), 'Pure and Impure', *Contributions to Indian Sociology*, vol. 3, 1959, pp. 9–39).

F. G. Bailey

See also: CASTE

Role

A. The term *role* is used in two overlapping but nevertheless different ways in sociology, social psychology, and anthropology.

1. As an aspect of social structure (q.v.) a role may be defined as a named social position characterized by a set of (a) personal qualities and (b) activities, the set being normatively evaluated to some degree both by those in the situation and others. This definition does not preserve the distinction made by R. Linton between *status* (q.v.) and *role* (see B.1 below).

2. As an element in role-playing or social interaction (q.v.) *role* may be defined following T. R. Sarbin (see B.2 below), as a patterned sequence of learnt actions performed by a person in an interaction situation.

B. *Role* has been used in a number of ways, often without clear meaning, in social science (see L. J. Neiman & J. W. Hughes, 'The Problem of the Concept of Role—a Re-survey of the Literature', *Social Forces*, vol. 30, 1951–2, pp. 141–9). The two most common usages are *role* as a unit in society, and *role-playing* as another name for social interaction. The former dates from the definition of role by R. Linton; the latter has developed from the ideas of G. H. Mead.

1. To Linton, status is a 'collection of rights and duties', and a role is the 'dynamic aspect of a status'; to put rights and duties into effect is to perform a role (*The Study of Man*, New York: Appleton-Century, 1936, pp. 113–4). This definition of role and status is also used by T. Parsons (*The Social System*, Glencoe, Ill.: The Free Press, 1951, p. 25), by A. R. Radcliffe-Brown (*Structure and Function in Primitive Society*, Glencoe, Ill.: The Free Press, 1952, pp. 11, 37–8), and by R. K. Merton (*Social Theory and Social Structure*, Glencoe, Ill.: The Free Press, rev. edn., 1957, pp. 368–9). Merton proposes that, where a status entails more than one social relationship, we use

Rule of Law

role-set instead of role. In British and American sociological and anthropological writings, Linton's distinction between status and role is not always preserved; role, status, and social position are used as synonyms.

S. F. Nadel, in a recent important analysis of this concept, objects to Linton's definition of status and role, on the grounds that it is pointless to have different names for a rule of behaviour and its application (*The Theory of Social Structure*, Glencoe, Ill.: The Free Press, 1957, pp. 20–44). He also argues that it is misleading to think of the two concepts as complementary and co-existing, since a rule of behaviour is perceived, either by an observer or by a member of the society, only by abstraction from behaviour on a number of occasions. Nadel's discussion of this concept can be summarized as follows: a *role* is a category of persons distinguished by a normative set of personal and behavioural attributes. He also points out that roles mark the distribution of activities and of socially recognized characteristics (such as age, kinship, or lunacy) among the members of a society.

2. The study of role-playing by social psychologists began with the lectures of G. H. Mead at the University of Chicago in the early 1900s (published as *Mind, Self and Society*, ed. by C. W. Morris, Chicago: The University of Chicago Press, 1934). Mead set forth a theory in which society, the development of personality, and communication are linked. To be able to communicate is, in Mead's famous phrase, to be able to 'take the role of the other' toward one's own vocalizations and behaviour.

Phrases such as 'playing a role' are often used by social psychologists. The reference is to how the self is presented or to what people who interact expect of each other. For a survey of the theory and experimental work which has developed from Mead, see T. R. Sarbin 'Role Theory' (in G. Lindzey (ed.), *Handbook of Social Psychology* (Cambridge, Mass.: Addison-Wesley, 1954, vol. I, pp. 223–58). Sarbin defines *role* as 'a patterned sequence of learned *actions* or deeds performed by a person in an interaction situation' (ibid., p. 225).

3. In both kinds of conceptualizing roles are '... intermediary between "society" and "individual" ... in that strategic area where individual *behavior* becomes social *conduct*, and where the qualities and inclinations distributed over a population are translated into differential attributes required by or exemplifying the obtaining social norms' (S. F. Nadel,

The Theory of Social Structure, p. 20). Nevertheless, the two traditions do not use *role* in quite the same way, and the problems they study are different.

Dorrian Apple Sweetser

See also: STATUS

Role-Playing (See Role)

Role-Set (See Role)

Romantic Love (See Love)

Rule of Law

This concept has been much invoked by publicists and writers about law and government in the English-speaking world since the late 19th century, but its shifting usages make precise definition a matter of some difficulty.

1. (a) In so far as the term is used with reference to the legal ordering of a municipal society, it owes its modern popularity to A. V. Dicey. Although he himself owed something to earlier writers, it is to Dicey that credit is given for elevating a concept of the Rule of Law into a central dogma of British constitutional theory.

According to Dicey the *Rule of Law*, a 'fundamental principle' of the constitution, lay (as he saw it) in three principles (*The Law of the Constitution* (1885), London: Macmillan, 10th edn., 1959): (i) 'The absolute supremacy or predominance of regular law as opposed to the influence of arbitrary power', excluding 'the existence of arbitrariness, or prerogative, or even of wide discretionary authority on the part of the government' (ibid., p. 202); (ii) 'equality before the law, or the equal subjection of all classes to the ordinary law of the land administered by the ordinary Law Courts; ... there can be with us nothing really corresponding to the "administrative law" (*droit administratif*) or the "administrative tribunals" (*tribunaux administratifs*) of France' (ibid., p. 203); (iii) 'the law of the constitution, the rules which in foreign countries naturally form part of a constitutional code, are not the source but the consequence of the rights of individuals, as defined and enforced by the Courts; ... the constitution is the result of the ordinary law of the land' (ibid., p. 203).

Dicey clearly wrote in the context of late 19th-century political thought and in the Whig tradition, but he chose to describe the Rule of Law, not in terms of political philosophy, but in terms of certain specific rules and institutions of the English legal system he knew. The content of the Rule of Law was, to him, itself a matter of law, and he laid his especial emphasis upon the role of the ordinary judiciary in checking the Executive, and the absence of any system of administrative justice beyond the Common Law.

(b) Dicey's formulation exercised an enormous influence upon his own generation and the next, and still receives much attention. In so far as the concept had to do with restraints upon authority, it found its historical roots in the political thought of the ancient world and the Middle Ages, and in feudal Germanic ideas of the reciprocal rights and duties of lord and subject, and had undergone many formulations over the centuries. But Dicey's supporters and his early critics accepted his chosen legal principles as the ultimate expression of that concept; for fifty years, the Diceyan analysis *was* the Rule of Law. The Committee on Ministers' Powers, appointed by a British Labour Government in 1929 to examine the growing practice of delegating legislative and judicial functions to the Executive, and specifically requested 'to report what safeguards ... [were] ... desirable or necessary to secure the constitutional principles of the sovereignty of Parliament and the supremacy of the law', accepted the Diceyan analysis as a basic premise: 'The best exposition of the modern doctrine ... is that contained in Dicey's Law of the Constitution'.

Since the 1930s, there has been a marked reaction against Dicey's formulation, and a restatement of the concept in significantly different terms, although its place in the theory of British government seems secure. Writers such as C. T. Carr, W. Jennings, W. A. Robson, and E. C. S. Wade have demonstrated that Dicey's observation was inaccurate and his conclusions questionable; his principles were not strictly observed in Great Britain in his own day, and they have become increasingly inapplicable to the conditions of modern society, which in every developed country have led to the growth of *administrative law* and its apparatus of discretionary powers and special tribunals.

(c) Most recent writers have found it more useful, therefore, to discuss the concept of the Rule of Law in terms of political rather than legal principles, to emphasize certain community beliefs which operate upon the law (through its makers and executors) to modify its content and application, rather than laws and institutions themselves. This approach is thought to have the further merit of avoiding

any logical inconsistency with the legal doctrine of the legislative supremacy of Parliament. The Rule of Law is seen as a manifestation of a democratic community. 'There is a tradition of life in these islands', said Lord Radcliffe, a Lord of Appeal (*The Problem of Power*, London: Secker & Warburg, 1952, p. 107), 'that both ennobles and restrains authority. Only it lives in the spirit, and has no special form to express it'. 'It is an attitude, an expression of liberal and democratic principles'.

The 1957 British Committee on Administrative Tribunals and Enquiries, heir though it was to the great Committee of 1929, did not repeat its sweeping adoption of Diceyan principles; 'the rule of law', it stated, 'stands for the view that decisions should be made by the application of known principles or laws. ... On the other hand there is what is arbitrary'.

Clearly the central idea remains a liberal repudiation of authoritarian arbitrariness, as it was with Dicey, but the restatement of the concept in terms more of democratic political morality than of law (and particularly British law) frees it from the limitations of time and place with which Dicey encompassed it, and restores to it the eternal relevance of philosophy. It is this conception of the Rule of Law which The International Commission of Jurists seeks to elaborate.

2. The concept of the Rule of Law is occasionally used to mean little more than the existence of public order and an habitual observance of law, as, for example, when it is urged that a Rule of Law be established in international relations. The two usages are linked by a common rejection of arbitrary behaviour, but in this case the arbitrariness condemned is that which may obtain in relations amongst members of a society observing no common code, rather than that which may mark the relationship of government and governed. Even this usage, however, may on occasions reflect liberal-democratic ideas of justice.

R. L. Sharwood

See also: DUE PROCESS

Rural

The term *rural* is used with the antonym *urban* either explicit or implied.

1. As a dichotomy these categories form an important demographic classification and are used in national censuses throughout the world. The dividing point between rural and urban communities varies from country to country:

Rural

in the United States rural communities are those with a population of less than 2,500 people.

2. A society or community may be classified as rural rather than urban by the following criteria which denote areas of a continuum: lower population density; less social differentiation; less social and spatial mobility; slower rates of social change; agriculture (q.v.), as a major occupation; and the centring of the politico-economic system in the holding of land. These and other rural elements have been used in the formulation of various typologies: folk-culture (q.v.), *Gemeinschaft* (q.v.), sacred society (q.v.), etc.

3. The degree of difference between rural and urban populations varies from country to country, the extreme contrast being much reduced in nations like the United States and those of northwest Europe, where urbanization (q.v.) is more advanced. Even in the United States, however, indices of social disorganization and of levels of living, for example, show a decided relationship to size of place: the more rural the population, the lower the rank on both indices.

Harold F. Kaufman

See also: AGRICULTURE (also HORTICULTURE)
FOLK CULTURE
GEMEINSCHAFT
SACRED SOCIETY
URBAN SOCIOLOGY

S

Sacred

This word has both a broader and a narrower reference and usage in the social sciences has given acceptance to both. But although the meanings are not at variance, they cannot satisfactorily be conveyed with one definition.

1. In the broad meaning the *sacred* is that which is protected, whether or not by religion, against violation, intrusion, or defilement. It covers the religious but is not limited to it. Nor is it synonymous with *holy*. H. P. Becker strongly defends the broad use of the term: ' "sacred" is *not* limited to the meanings of "holy", "religious", "spiritual", "godly", "blessed", "hallowed", "pious", "devout", "ecclesiastical", "churchly", "clerical" and so on and so on' (*Through Values to Social Interpretation*, Durham, N.C.: Duke University Press, 1950, p. 274). In this sense *sacred* carries the meaning of respected, venerated, and inviolable. Accordingly a wide variety of religious and non-religious objects, practices, places, customs, and ideas may acquire a sacred character.

2. In the context of religion, the meaning of *sacred* is both narrower and stronger. Here the *sacred* is that which is protected specifically by religion against violation, intrusion, or defilement. It is, therefore, that which is holy, sacrosanct, or consecrated to or by religion. In this usage *sacred* is the opposite of *profane*. Durkheim argued that 'The sacred thing is *par excellence* that which the profane should not touch, and cannot touch with impunity' (*The Elementary Forms of the Religious Life*, trans. by J. W. Swain, London: Allen & Unwin, 1915, p. 40).

Luke Ebersole

See also: PROFANE
            SACRED SOCIETY
            SECULAR
            SECULAR SOCIETY

Sacred Society

Following the broader usage of *sacred* (see *Sacred*), the term came to be used from the 1920s onwards by R. E. Park ('Human Migration and the Marginal Man', *American Journal of Sociology*, vol. XXXIII, 1927–8, pp. 881–93), and by several of his students. As used, for example, by E. C. Hughes, it clearly refers to a society bearing a value-system that, although not necessarily religious in any supernatural way, is held inviolable to the greatest extent possible ('Social Change and Status Protest', in E. C. & H. M. Hughes, *Where Peoples Meet*, Glencoe, Ill.: The Free Press, 1952, pp. 188–99). Shortly afterwards H. Becker began to publish articles and books wherein the term was systematically developed.

A sacred society can be viewed as one that engenders in its members, by means of all the appropriate kinds of socialization, social control, and the like, reluctance to change customary orientation toward, and/or definition of, values regarded as essential in that society, which reluctance exceeds in degree readiness to change in the same respects. More briefly, a sacred society is one bringing its members to be unwilling or unable, in whatever measure, to accept the new *as the new is defined in that society*.

Howard Becker

See also: SACRED
            SECULAR SOCIETY

Sacrifice

A. *Sacrifice* may be defined as the ritual (q.v.) offering of a living human being or animal—in slightly looser usage, crops and perhaps any other objects—or symbolic representation thereof, to a supernatural being for his consumption. Sacrifice is thus a special type of ritual offering, to be distinguished from ritual offerings to human authorities, and from other offerings to supernatural beings not involving consumption by them, e.g. dedication of individual labour to a god's service, simple consecration of animals, or not involving the presentation of living creatures in direct or symbolic form, e.g. church tithes. The term is used principally in anthropological and sociological studies of religion. It is rarely used in social science in its popular meaning of relinquishing anything valued to any superior authority or object of respect or duty.

B. The stated purpose of sacrifice varies widely among different cultures.

Sampling

1. W. R. Smith's view was for a time widely accepted by students of comparative religion, but has more recently been rejected by many anthropologists (*Lectures on the Religion of the Semites*, London: Black, 2nd edn., 1894; E. E. Evans-Pritchard, *The Institutions of Primitive Society*, Glencoe, Ill.: The Free Press, 1954). Smith maintained that in its original and most characteristic form, sacrifice among the Semitic peoples, and probably other groups, was a communal meal in which human participants and the deity shared the same food, bringing them closer to each other, and that the meal, moreover, consisted of an animal identified in some way with the god himself.

2. Regardless of the evolutionary development of sacrifice, which is considered an unresolvable problem by many modern students of comparative religion, the term has been widely applied by Smith and others to ritual offerings which are characterized neither by the communal meal nor by the identification of the object sacrificed with the god. More characteristically sacrifice is regarded primarily as an offering to a god or spirit, and the frequent human consumption of a large part of the offering is treated as an incidental feature. R. Benedict, for example, in discussing sacrifice equates it with a gift and says, '… all possible human attitudes toward a gift are found in various religions' ('Religion', in F. Boas (ed.), *General Anthropology*, Boston: Heath, 1938, pp. 627–65, esp. 644). Thus: (a) the sacrifice may be regarded as a means of ritually compelling a god to perform certain desired acts; (b) it may be regarded as a means of thanking a god for past favours, or acquiring his goodwill for desired but uncertain future acts; (c) it may be regarded as a means of avoiding punishment for past or future sins of individuals or whole communities; (d) it may be a means of expressing the religiously oriented attitude of awe, reverence, and respect.

John L. Fischer

See also: RELIGION

Sampling

A. 1. The term *sampling* is a fairly recent derivative of *sample* and is used variously to refer to one or more aspects of the general process of drawing inferences from a part of something to the whole of it—of generalizing about a 'population' or 'universe' from some examples (or samples) of it. Thus as stated by W. A. Wallis and H. V. Roberts (*Statistics, A New Approach*, Glencoe, Ill.: The Free Press, 1956, p. 101), 'The two most fundamental concepts of statistics are those of a *sample* and a *population*. A sample is often referred to as "the data" or "the observations". … The "population" [or universe] on the other hand is the totality of all possible observations of the same kind. … The problems of sampling [concern] how much evidence should be assembled to answer a given question of whether the evidence actually presented is enough to justify conclusions someone has drawn'. And W. E. Deming (*Some Theory of Sampling*, New York: Rutledge, 1950, p. 2) says that this involves three operations: 'the specification of the precision to be aimed at, the design of the survey or experiment to attain this level of precision, and the appraisal of the precision actually attained'. Moreover, as many have pointed out, the researcher, as the person in ordinary life, is always working with samples —and from necessity in almost all cases.

2. *Sampling*, through all its various uses, consistently denotes some one or more aspects of the process of establishing confidence in general conclusions that are derived from limited (sample) data. At times the term is used, as a noun, for the whole process; at others it is used as an adjective in such combinations as 'sampling statistic' or 'sampling distribution'. So also in some cases the reference is to rigorously formalized procedures; in others to loose judgements. But the trend is to use *sampling* in as precise a manner as the particular context permits at the time.

B. The range of uses of *sampling* extends from the loose to the mathematically precise, and from the general to the specific. Certainly the original, and still probably the most frequent use, stems from the common English usage. A 'sample' of anything is an 'example' or set of examples of it. Thus a person may talk of 'sampling' someone's cooking or someone's hospitality. Certainly so long as the universe from which we are taking examples is uniform little attention needs to be paid to the process of selection. Any kind of sample of one's blood will give almost the same result. It is only, as W. G. Cochran (*Sampling Techniques*, New York: Wiley, 1953, p. 1) points out, 'When the material is far from uniform, as is often the case, the method by which the sample is obtained is critical, and the study of techniques that ensure a trustworthy sample becomes important'.

1. The process of selecting data has always been a concern to careful social scientists. The usual way has been for the researcher to select his data by his own judgement or by a combination of judgement and some more objective procedure. These have been designated 'Judgemental sampling methods' by M. H. Hansen, W. N. Hurwitz, and W. G. Madow (*Sample Survey Methods and Theory*, New York: Wiley, 1953, vol. I, p. 9), and listed as one of two main categories of sampling methods, the other being 'random or probability methods' which will be discussed below. Judgemental methods are most simply defined as those where 'the probability that an individual case is included in the sample is unknown' (ibid., p. 9). Thus the methods of the comparative scholars in the late 19th century in selecting data for their prodigious works were judgemental. So also are all methods concerned with 'typical' or 'representative' cases. So also is the method of a consulting expert who informally 'samples' the opinions of local groups with reference to some topic. On a more sophisticated level, S. A. Stouffer et al. (*Measurement and Prediction*, Princeton, N.J.: Princeton University Press, 1950, p. 286) talk about sampling items from an attitude or opinion study as being judgemental rather than subject to precise sampling procedures.

In cases where probability and judgemental methods are both used in a sampling design, M. H. Hansen et al. (*Sample Survey Methods and Theory*, vol. I, p. 9) list them as judgemental. One such mixed model is *quota sampling* where the investigator is required 'to collect information from an assigned number of individuals [of specified characteristics] but the individuals are left to his personal choice' (M. G. Kendall & W. R. Buckland, *A Dictionary of Statistical Terms*, prepared for the International Statistical Institute with the assistance of Unesco, Edinburgh: Oliver & Boyd, 1957, p. 236).

W. E. Deming (*Some Theory of Sampling*, p. 11) even goes so far as to include under judgemental methods studies carefully based on probability methods but where the 'survey itself through failure of proper design, failure of the questionnaire, or for lack of sufficient response, fails to elicit certain information that is needed in calculating the final estimates'. According to him, 'The usefulness of data from ... [judgemental methods] ... is judged by expert knowledge of the subject matter and comparisons with the results of previous surveys, not from knowledge of probability' (ibid., p. 11). However, he points out that 'judgement-samples will undoubtedly continue to play an important role in research, and they will become more and more useful as their strong points and weak points

are more generally understood' (ibid., p. 12). The trend in judgemental sampling is definitely toward greater explicitness and precision. Quota sampling, for example, is in general an improvement on the expert's personal canvass, and such methods as *scale analysis* are beginning to provide a check on the sampling of items.

2. The major developments in sampling have, however, been in the area of random or probability methods. These are defined by M. H. Hansen et al. (*Sample Survey Methods and Theory*, vol. I, p. 9) as those where 'specific steps are taken to control the probabilities of selection of the sample'. The basic random or probability sampling design is *simple random sampling*, 'a sample ... selected from a population in such a manner that each combination of n elements has the same chance or probability of being selected as every other combination' (ibid., p. 12). This design is not used very frequently in practice but is of the greatest theoretical importance. In fact, all other designs are but refinements to increase efficiency—'ways of making more effective use of available knowledge and resources, so as to get the maximum return for the money expended' (ibid., p. 11).

There are three major types of probability designs that have been developed to meet this requirement of greater efficiency, and which are based on simple random sampling. In actual practice combinations of these three methods are generally used:

(a) *Stratified sampling* is the sampling employed whenever a 'population is divided into groups according to some relevant characteristic and a simple random sample is taken from each group' (W. A. Wallis & H. V. Roberts, *Statistics, A New Approach*, 1956, p. 339).

(b) *Cluster sampling* is the sampling employed whenever 'the basic sampling unit in the population is to be found in groups or clusters (e.g. human beings in households) and sampling is carried out by selecting a sample of clusters and observing all [or a random sample of] the members of each selected cluster' (M. G. Kendall & W. R. Buckland, *A Dictionary of Statistical Terms*, p. 45).

(c) *Systematic sampling* is the sampling employed whenever 'a sample is obtained by some systematic method, as opposed to random choice; for example, sampling from a list by taking individuals at equally spaced intervals—or sampling from an area by determining a pattern of points on a map' (ibid., p. 288).

Raymond V. Bowers

See also: STATISTICS

Sanction

Sanction

A. A *sanction*, in the most general sense of the term, is a punishment or reward whose aim is to procure conformity with the standards of behaviour regarded as desirable by a social group. This usage has long been established in the social sciences. So, for example, Bentham: 'There are four distinguishable sources from which pleasure and pain are in use to flow: considered separately, they may be termed the *physical*, the *political*, the *moral*, and the *religious*; and inasmuch as the pleasures and pains belonging to each of them are capable of giving a binding force to any law or rule of conduct, they may all of them be termed sanctions' (*An Introduction to the Principles of Morals and Legislation*, London: Payne, 1789, ch. III, section II).

B. 1. From a sociological point of view, the most precise analysis of the term is that of A. R. Radcliffe-Brown ('Sanction, Social', in E. R. A. Seligman (ed.), *Encyclopedia of the Social Sciences*, London: Macmillan, 1934, vol. XIII, p. 531). He distinguishes between *positive* and *negative*, and between *diffuse* and *organized* *sanctions* as follows: 'A sanction is a reaction on the part of society or of a considerable number of its members to a mode of behaviour which is thereby approved (positive sanctions) or disapproved (negative sanctions). Sanctions may further be distinguished according to whether they are diffuse or organised: the former are spontaneous expressions of approval or disapproval by members of the community acting as individuals, while the latter are social actions carried out according to some traditional and recognized procedure'.

Of the four possible resultant types, *organized negative sanctions*', backed by the physical force of a constituted political authority (penal law) are most clearly defined, and most consonant with common usage. On the other hand, the least well defined type is that of *diffuse positive sanctions* (esteem), which term forms part of sociological rather than common usage.

2. The use of the term in sociology tends to reflect a concern with the relationship between sanctions and the social solidarity of the community, e.g. the attempt of E. Durkheim, for example, to classify types of social cohesion (*mechanical* and *organic*) by reference to the predominance of types of legal sanctions (*repressive* and *restitutive*) (*The Division of Labour in Society*, trans. by G. Simpson, New York: The Macmillan Co., 1933, p. 69). See also, more recently, the use of the term in the sociology of T. Parsons, *The Social System*, Glencoe, Ill.: The Free Press, 1951). In this context, too, it is worthy of note that the sociological usage differs from the conventional in that it has focused on the latent or unintended consequences of sanctions for the society as well as the consequences intended by the person(s) applying the sanctions (see, for example, the discussion of punishment in E. Durkheim *The Division of Labour in Society*, pp. 85–96, and G. Rusche & O. Kirchheimer, *Punishment and Social Structure*, New York: Columbia University Press, 1940, p. 207).

3. Despite the fact that common usage restricts the term to its negative and organized aspects, it would seem advantageous to retain the wider meaning indicated above. This is especially true where the term is used in a technical sociological sense, for any discussion of institutions as modes of sanctioned conduct must take into account the full range of indulgences and deprivations at the disposal of society for ensuring conformity with its standards.

D. Lockwood

See also: PUNISHMENT
REWARD

Saving

A. The term *saving* denotes (a) the process of accumulating money or material goods for future use; (b) the flow of money or resources that is accumulated during a particular period by such a process; (c) the process of economizing or conserving on resources; (d) those resources which are kept in being by such economizing.

B. In economics saving in sense A(a) is treated as the foregoing of consumption to accumulate assets. The outcome of such a process is saving in sense (b). Here the tendency to interchange *saving* and *savings* has been a frequent source of confusion. *Savings* is best defined as the *stock* of money or resources at a particular *point* in time, i.e. the amount that has been accumulated over all past periods to that particular point. *Saving*, on the other hand, represents the flow of money or resources that is accumulated during a particular period, the interval between two points in time. Mathematically, therefore, saving represents the change in the stock of savings between two points of time.

In analytical terms, 'everyone is agreed that *saving* [in sense A(b)] means the excess of income over expenditure on consumption' (J. M.

Keynes, *The General Theory of Employment, Interest and Money*, London: Macmillan, 1936, p. 61), a definition used by government agencies as a basis for estimating consumer saving. An alternate definition, allegedly more meaningful for studying the impact of income on consumer behaviour, has been advanced by D. H. Robertson ('Saving and Hoarding', *Economic Journal*, vol. XLIII, 1933, pp. 399–413) to the effect that current saving is equivalent to income received in the last period less current consumption expenditures. While both these definitions of *saving* are of value for certain aspects of economic theory, they are of doubtful empirical value. The Keynesian definition tends to produce underestimates of actual saving, as shown by various statistical studies, and the Robertson definition is manageable, or meaningful, only when pay periods are frequent and standardized. The most desirable approach appears to lie in estimating saving directly.

C. Definition A (c) can be partly derived from A (a) for the process of accumulating resources by postponing consumption does 'conserve' them for future use. This applies particularly to productive facilities in so far as postponement of their utilization conserves them for future productive purposes. Largely independent of this facet, however, is the problem of saving or conserving resources while attaining given levels of production or, more broadly, given levels of social welfare. This is an economic problem as well as an engineering problem for saving can be achieved through more efficient allocation of resources as well as through more efficient production processes. This optimization problem has received increasing attention in recent years, involving the application of input–output analysis, linear programming, and various techniques developed in operations research. Much the same considerations enter into problems of social welfare, where a 'saving' can be said to be attained if the welfare of society is increased at no loss in individuals' welfare. It is important to note that given this definition of *saving*, *savings* then simply represents the plural of saving and is not synonomous with *savings* as a measure of stocks.

D. All four usages of the term can occur with reference to either money or material goods. Emphasis in economics has consistently been placed on the former, because the statistical and financial characteristics of modern industrial society render the estimation of saving in non-monetary forms a very difficult task. However, the fact that the saving of money and the saving of material goods can serve as substitutes for one another (as evidenced by an inverse relation between expenditures on consumer durables and monetary saving) has become abundantly clear in the postwar years and more attention can be expected for this problem in the future.

Robert Ferber

See also: CONSUMPTION
CONSUMPTION FUNCTION
EFFICIENCY
PROPENSITY TO CONSUME

Savings (See **Saving**)

Savings Function (See **Consumption Function**)

Scaling

A. In general, *scaling* has been defined as 'the assignment of numerals to objects (including people), according to some rule, in order to represent their properties' (F. M. Lord, 'Scaling', *Review of Educational Research*, vol. 24, 1954, p. 375). The objects are then said to be 'scaled' in respect to these properties. Hence, *a scale* may be either (a) any given 'rule for the assignment of numerals … to aspects of objects or events' (S. S. Stevens, 'Mathematics, Measurement, and Psychophysics', in S. S. Stevens (ed.), *Handbook of Experimental Psychology*, New York: Wiley, 1951, p. 23); or (b) the particular 'set of numerals given to the objects by using a certain rule of assignment' (B. F. Green, 'Attitude Measurement', in G. Lindzey (ed.), *Handbook of Social Psychology*, Cambridge, Mass.: Addison-Wesley, 1954, p. 337).

B. Many specific sets of rules have been developed during the past several decades; and these have been used, initially in psychophysics and mental testing and more recently in other social science fields, both to clarify and to measure a wide range of variables. In psychophysics, G. Fechner, attempting to specify the relationship between sensation and the physical stimulus, developed basic techniques which, together with their various elaborations, form the basis of many modern scaling methods. Educational psychologists, stimulated by the work of J. McK. Cattell and A. Binet, constructed *age scales* and *point scales* of intelligence, which permitted an individual's score to be compared with those of others of the same age. Such men as J. P. Guilford and L. L. Thurstone, combining knowledge of various fields, did much to codify and create interest in scaling techniques;

Scarcity

and Thurstone is himself identified with *rating scales*, *paired comparisons*, and *equal-appearing interval scales*. Much work in attitude measurement, building upon these foundations, has resulted in such procedures as: *Likert-type scales*, L. Guttman's *scalogram analysis*, C. H. Coombs's *unfolding technique*, P. F. Lazarsfeld's *latent structure analysis*, etc. These methods have been widely applied in related fields to such variables as social distance, status, cohesion, consensus, economic utility, and many others.

C. A classification of types of scales has been developed by Stevens in terms of the distinctive points of correspondence 'between the properties of the numeral series and the empirical operations that we can perform with the aspects of objects' (ibid.). He distinguishes among *nominal*, *ordinal*, *interval*, and *ratio scales*, the first two of which are the more widely used in the social sciences. In a nominal scale, objects are classified into mutually exclusive categories, so that all objects in the same category are equivalent to one another. In an ordinal scale, objects are arranged in rank order, so that those in the same category are not only equivalent to one another, but are also 'greater than' those in a category of lower rank. An interval scale, in which the distances between any two numbers on the scale are of known size, has the further formal property that the ratio between any two intervals may be specified. A ratio scale, since it has a true 'zero point', has the still further property that the ratio between any two scale values is known. Stevens's classification has been elaborated by various other writers. Coombs, for example, specifies a *partially ordered scale* which falls between the nominal and ordinal types, and an *ordered metric scale* between ordinal and interval; he suggests that the term *scaling theory* be applied only to the ordered metric and less powerful scales, with the term *measurement theory* applied to the interval and ratio scales ('Theory and Methods of Social Measurement', in L. Festinger & D. Katz (eds.), *Research Methods in the Behavioral Sciences*, New York: Dryden, 1953, pp. 471–535). W. S. Torgerson adds an *ordinal scale with natural origin* to Stevens's classification, noting that zero points have also been located for certain ordinal scales (such as the point of indifference on a scale of attitudes) (*Theory and Methods of Scaling*, New York: Wiley, 1958).

D. Methods of scaling are often divided according to whether or not each 'rests upon a verifiable hypothesis as to the existence of some specific self-consistence in the data' (F. M. Lord, 'Scaling', p. 375). Since many social science variables are conceived as abstractions from a large number of observable acts or responses, a decision must be made, as Lazarsfeld says, as to precisely how 'inferences from concrete observations to "underlying" concepts are to be made' ('A Conceptual Introduction to Latent Structure Analysis', in P. F. Lazarsfeld (ed.), *Mathematical Thinking in the Social Sciences*, 1954, p. 354). According to Green, a mathematical model is needed for this purpose, and each 'scaling method either states or implies such a model' ('Attitude Measurement', p. 336). Some methods contain inherent procedures for testing whether or not the model actually does fit the observable data, while others rely upon the investigator's judgement for the selection of properties to be observed and the numerical values to be assigned. The term *scaling* is sometimes reserved for methods containing a built-in test of the model. An example of this type of method is the Guttman scale, which he describes as follows: 'The purpose of scale analysis is to test the hypothesis that a universe of items comprises but a single factor in the sense that from but a single set of scores ... the responses to each of the items can be reproduced' (L. Guttman, 'Relation of Scalogram Analysis to Other Techniques', in S. A. Stouffer et al., *Measurement and Prediction*, Princeton, N.J.: Princeton University Press, 1950, p. 181).

Matilda White Riley

See also: MEASUREMENT

Scarcity

A. *Scarcity* is the quantitative insufficiency of goods or resources to satisfy demands.

1. *Webster's Collegiate Dictionary* (London: Bell, 1939) defines scarce, in the economic sense, as 'deficient in quantity or number compared with the demand; not abundant'. The scarcity of economic resources to fulfil all human wants or desires is considered the basic condition of economic life, and scarcity is perhaps the most central concept of traditional economic theory. Scarcity gives meaning to 'economizing' behaviour, or the intelligent use of scarce resources to satisfy human ends.

2. The concept has little special usage in other social science fields. Where used, it has either its common-sense meaning or the somewhat more technical meaning given it in economics. Political science and sociology may deal, inter alia, with the scarcity of power and status respectively. Experimental psychology has recently been giving considerable attention to behavioural situations involving economizing, as in certain decision problems or goal-oriented behaviour (see W. Edwards, 'The Theory of Decision Making', *Psychological Bulletin*, vol. LI, 1954, pp. 380–417).

3. Economic scarcity is a relational concept, not an absolute one. It measures the supply of a thing in relation to demand for it; whatever the supply of a thing, if it is abundant in relation to the desire for it, the thing is not scarce. Economic scarcity is normally measured by value or by price in relation to the prices of other things.

B. Many contemporary theorists adopt a 'scarcity definition' of economics, as distinguished from other and older views of its subject-matter —such as 'the nature and causes of the wealth of nations' (Adam Smith); the study of 'mankind in the ordinary business of life' or of 'the attainment and ... use of the material requisites of wellbeing' (A. Marshall, *Principles of Economics*, London: Macmillan, 1890; 8th edn. 1920, p. 1). Objecting to the implications of these views that economics studies some particular 'compartment' of life, that it centres on 'material' things, or that it is necessarily infused by a normative 'welfare' element, a number of economists—including H. J. Davenport (*Economics of Enterprise*, New York: The Macmillan Co., 1913); F. H. Knight (*Risk, Uncertainty and Profit*, New York: Houghton Mifflin, 1921); and L. Robbins (*An Essay on the Nature and Significance of Economic Science*, London: Macmillan, 1932)—have sought a more neutral and, in Robbins's view, *analytical*, definition. Robbins's definition, with which there is nowadays much but far from universal agreement, runs as follows: 'Economics is the science which studies human behaviour as a relationship between ends and scarce means which have alternative uses' (ibid., p. 15).

According to this view, all behavioural and social problems, in so far as there is scarcity of means, possess an economic aspect. Economics is limited, however, to scarcity situations in which (a) the ends are various and competing, and (b) the means are capable of satisfying more than one end (ibid.). The 'economic problem' then is viewed as resource allocation, and economic behaviour (see Economic Man) is the 'rational allocation of scarce means to alternative ends'. Most theorists who accept this conception would nevertheless confine the relevant means to economic resources and the relevant ends to those which are or can be measured by price. Most economists, moreover, refuse to accept the implication in the scarcity definition that their discipline is not intimately concerned with welfare (see A. C. Pigou, *The Economics of Welfare*, London: Macmillan, 1920; 4th edn., 1932; and K. E. Boulding, *Economic Analysis*, New York: Harper & Brothers, 3rd edn., 1955).

1. All meanings in economics imply measurability on some quantitative scale, as in a price system. On the other hand, it does not appear advisable to limit the references of scarcity to *relative* scarcities or to the technical conditions of the allocation problem. Clearly scarcity may exist even though there be only one object (e.g. money-making), or only one means thereto in a particular context. Likewise even though a thing (e.g. highly specialized ability) have only one use, it may be scarce.

2. More important, there may be scarcity of opportunity as well as of resources, as when a lack of job opportunities, however casual, creates 'poverty in the midst of plenty'. If a community is rich, and especially if it has difficulty maintaining aggregate effective demand, there may be good sense in referring to it as an *economy of abundance*, to distinguish it from an *economy of scarcity*. In such a society, certainly, the problem of allocation of scarce resources to alternative ends is not the over-riding one that it has been historically, or is in underdeveloped areas.

3. Another important change in economic analysis that raises some question of the adequacy of the scarcity definition has been the increasing emphasis upon economic growth, where one of the ends to be considered is expansion of the economy. Since economic expansion involves, even more than allocation of given resources, both uncertainty and disturbance, the economic theory of 'economizing scarce resources' loses much of its precision where the growth dimension is introduced (D. McC. Wright, *Capitalism*, New York: McGraw-Hill, 1951).

4. Yet in a fundamental sense it remains true that it is scarcity, in the sense of 'unsatisfied wants at the margin'—whether of real income or of opportunities or both—that gives economics its significance. In this broadest sense all branches of economics deal with scarcity problems, in so far as scarcity can be mitigated by proper management of the economy.

Science

C. With regard to the theory of value scarcity is a unifying principle of the highest importance. This 'modern' view differs from earlier 'classical' ones that 'normal' values were determined by labour, by 'toil and trouble', or by real costs (see Cost, Labour Theory of Value). The co-ordination of the utility (later, 'preference') principle with opportunity costs (see Cost) unified conventional value and distribution theory into a system of general interdependence in which the values of goods and resources are traced to their scarcities at the margin (see Marginal Analysis). This type of theory remains at a very high level of abstraction, however, and interpretation requires scrutiny of the objective and subjective conditions governing supplies and demands and thereby determining scarcities. Not infrequently *scarcity values* (e.g. those of items in short or fixed supply such as rare paintings, necessities in times of great need, or special site values of land) are still distinguished from *normal values*, where competitive forces are able to adjust abnormal scarcities to bring values more in line with relative costs.

James S. Earley

See also: Cost
ECONOMICS
VALUE (Economics)

Scarcity Value (See **Scarcity**)

Science

A. In modern social science usage, the term *science* denotes the systematic, objective study of empirical phenomena and the resultant bodies of knowledge. It is believed by social scientists that their disciplines are themselves sciences in this sense, and that science as a human activity is itself an object of social science investigation.

B. While most contemporary social scientists would tentatively agree with the definition of science given above, difficulties arise in relation to each of the qualifying adjectives: *systematic*, *objective*, and *empirical*.

1. Historically in the social sciences, there has been a gulf between those who believe that the systematic quality of science applies primarily to the body of interrelated propositions of empirical reference that constitute the theory of a science and those who believe that it applies primarily to the realm of methods of investigation. Even today, there is a hiatus between the research done by those stressing theory and by those stressing methods of research. In some disciplines, economics, for example, the stress still seems to be placed primarily on theoretical

models. In others, such as sociology, there is a great body of research carried out according to the rules of careful quantitative research that still does not articulate with the most systematic theory. The tone of debate in this area is not as shrill as it once was and there are efforts on the one side to make theory researchable in a quantitative manner if possible, and on the other side to construct theoretical methods—although, because these are frequently quantitative in a highly technical sense, they still do not articulate with older systematic theory.

In part this controversy has rested on the meaning of the term *measurement*—the act or process of ascertaining the extent, dimensions, quantity, degree, or capacity of a thing, and the argument of those oriented towards method that measurement is the very core of science. This controversy too has diminished with the recognition of systematic theorists that measurement is indeed central and of those interested primarily in method that qualitative phenomena can in a sense be measured as attributes which are present or absent.

There has also been controversy over method itself. Those interested primarily in systematic theory have developed methods of research, but it remains true that these methods have not for the most part been codified, and they are still seriously challenged as to the level of reliability and validity which they can achieve. Theorists, on the other hand, have accused those who have worked out the more systematic methods of sacrificing knowledge of the phenomena being studied to the requirements of respectable method. Here too there seems an increasing possibility of reconciliation as the theoretically oriented attempt to codify their methods and to make them more precise, and as those interested in method recognize increasingly the truth that in scientific research there is something to be said for a 'no holds barred' approach to the problem of grappling with significant data.

Finally, there is an argument in this area as to whether or not systematic necessarily means *generalization*. There are those who have claimed that science is always *nomothetic* in the sense of attempting to build systematic bodies of generalizing propositions. But there is present in social science today, as an historical survival from the German idealist emphasis on the *Geisteswissenschaften*, the view that so long as what is studied is empirical and there is the recognition that general concepts are relevant to the phenomena, the stress can be placed for some purposes on the comprehension of the

620

unique historical event. There is still a difference here between those who believe the social sciences should be primarily historical or biographical and those who believe that the fundamental task is the building of a generalizing discipline, but it is fundamentally a difference in emphasis today, not a difference as to what can be done scientifically (see, for example, C. W. Mills, *The Sociological Imagination*, New York: Oxford University Press, 1959).

2. *Objectivity*—the capacity of a scientific observer to see the empirical world as it 'actually' is, and the resultant quality of the body of knowledge—in the social sciences has been the object of controversy primarily with respect to the ultimate value commitments of the scientist, although radical doubt about objectivity with respect to economic interests, and other social and psychological forces, has been raised by some of the more extreme forms of the sociology of knowledge. The most famous statement on the issue of the relation between values and social science knowledge is that of Weber ('The Meaning of "Ethical Neutrality" in Sociology and Economics' (1917), in *Max Weber on the Methodology of the Social Sciences*, trans. and ed. by E. A. Shils & H. A. Finch, Glencoe, Ill.: The Free Press, 1949, pp. 1–47). Because of the ambiguities of this piece, Weber has been quoted on both sides of the argument. There is no doubt that Weber opposed the claiming of scientific validity for ethical value judgements or the mixing of such judgements with teaching. There is greater doubt in light of his conception of the relevance of values for the selection of problems, of non-empirical normatively valid truths as a basis of empirical science, and finally, of the ultimate decisions by which a man chooses his fate, that there can, in his view, be the complete separation between such ultimate decisions, the non-empirical assumptions, and the value-relevance of problems on the one hand and the theoretical models within which factual data are interpreted on the other hand as is claimed by the strongest advocates of the value-freedom of science today. Thus T. Parsons (*The Structure of Social Action*, New York: McGraw-Hill, 1937, p. 593) points out, while disagreeing, that for Weber the process of analysis which leads to the building up of general concepts 'will not issue in one ultimately uniform system of general concepts but in as many systems as there are value points of view or others significant to knowledge. There can be no one universally valid system of general theory in the social sciences'. Parsons (ibid., pp. 594–7) believes that the

logical disjunction between fact and value, the dependence of the demonstration of causal relations on a formal schema of proof that is independent of any value system except that of scientific truth, and the tendency of theoretical structures of science to close will permit the development of a single objective social science. G. Myrdal, however, believes that despite the presence of the elements of which Parsons speaks —which he believes will permit the growth of an increasing area of scientific consensus—scientific investigation in the social sciences must be related to the value systems of the people concerned (*Value in Social Theory*, New York: Harper & Bros., 1958). While in a somewhat different vein, W. L. Kolb argues that the theoretical models of social science are more closely related to the ultimate commitments of the scientist and of the society of which he is a part than most social scientists think, even though the elements of which Parsons speaks are present and the only legitimate test of a model is its scientific fruitfulness ('Images of Man and the Sociology of Religion', *Journal for the Scientific Study of Religion*, vol. I, 1961–2, pp. 1–29).

3. There is general agreement among social scientists that *empirical* phenomena are phenomena that can be observed by trained scientific observers. There has been, historically, however, a continual disagreement about whether or not it is necessary to deal with phenomena that cannot be directly so observed but can be inferred from a set of observations and then checked against a different set of predicted observations. This has taken different forms. There have been those who have argued that *only* phenomena that can be directly observed should be conceptualized in the social sciences. Thus F. Adler has argued that the concept of value is unnecessary and undesirable in sociology ('The Value Concept in Sociology', *American Journal of Sociology*, vol. LXII, 1956–7, pp. 272–9). There have been others who have argued that conceptualization of intervening variables can occur, but that no reality should be attributed to them. Against this has been placed the tradition that the central variables of the social sciences are frequently 'subjective' variables such as value and motive.

In recent years this controversy has tended to die down as those stressing 'subjective' variables have come to recognize that they must always be inferred from and checked against 'objective' variables, and that indices of such variables are always needed; and as those stressing 'objective' variables have come to realize that they have

Scientism

been forced to deal with the same complexes of problems as those dealing with 'subjective' variables.

Another controversy with respect to the empirical social world has had to do with the question of the social scientist's relationship to it. There have been those who have simply stressed the purpose of science as being the prediction and control of the empirical phenomena concerned. Others have insisted that this position combined with an absolute stress on freedom from values leads in the direction of manipulation and the sale of social science to the highest bidder. They have insisted that social science must at least in part serve as critic of society and as an instrument of human emancipation.

C. As indicated in the section on definition, science is an object of social science investigation as well as a conception of what social science should be. The sociology of science is basically a part of the sociology of knowledge (q.v.). In general there has not been as much stress on the rooting of social science in and distortion of it by the social location of the social scientists, as there has been in the case of modes of knowledge not directed towards the empirical world. It has been felt, however, that the social sciences are more subject to this rootage and distortion than the natural and physical sciences, and, in a few extreme cases, this determination is almost complete. In general the sociology of science has directed itself to the study of science as a social enterprise. Thus R. K. Merton's studies of the relation of Protestantism and science and of priorities in discovery have been more typical of the field than studies like Mills's 'The Professional Ideology of Social Pathologists (R. K. Merton, 'Puritanism, Pietism and Science', in his *Social Theory and Social Structure*, Glencoe, Ill.: The Free Press, 1957, pp. 574–606; R. K. Merton, 'Priorities in Scientific Discovery', *American Sociological Review*, vol. 22, 1957, pp. 635–59; C. W. Mills, 'The Professional Ideology of Social Pathologists', *American Journal of Sociology*, vol. XLIX, 1943–4, pp. 164–80).

William L. Kolb

Scientific Method (See **Science**)

Scientism
A. *Scientism* is a pejorative term denoting for its users the belief and practice of those whom it is used against that (a) science can solve all problems of value and of value-implementation in human life; (b) science can solve all problems of value-implementation in human life; (c)

science can, to some degree, on the basis of empirical observation predict and control human behaviour.

B. There is little doubt that some social scientists and philosophers of social science have claimed that human salvation resides, if it resides anywhere, in the application of the methods of science to problems of value and of human life. Dewey, perhaps, has been the greatest of these men. But the humility and the humaneness of these men have frequently softened criticism against them, so that the term *scientism* has usually been applied against *them* by writers of conservative political bent who see in social science a threat to certain organic types of social order or to a particular order of property (see, for example, A. H. Hobbs, *Social Problems and Scientism*, Harrisburg, Pa.: Stackpole, 1953).

Other critics, however, have been bothered not so much by the *completeness* of the claim on the part of social scientists—although this is always a subject of debate—but by what they take to be the complete determinism and manipulative approach of some who place primary stress on social science. Thus it is doubtful that B. F. Skinner argues that science can determine the validity of values—rather he seems to assume that there is general agreement as to the nature of the humane life—but he does assume the possibility of practically complete control and manipulation of human behaviour through the use of the social sciences (*Science and Human Behavior*, New York: Macmillan, 1953). Unfortunately, attacks on scientism of this sort have a tendency to become attacks on the very idea that the empirical study of human action can in any way *add something* to our powers of prediction of human activity and the control of our own destiny (J. W. Krutch, *The Measure of Man*, New York: Bobbs-Merrill, 1954). In this sort of attack it is not complete determinism that is rejected but any assertion that human action is predictable; not the needless jargon of the social sciences, but any idea that technical language can have any use in the study of human action. Thus *scientism* becomes a term lacking in precision and predominantly a form of verbal abuse.

William L. Kolb

Secession
A. *Secession* denotes the withdrawal of a constituent unit from a political (or other) grouping to which it belongs.

622

B. 1. The term is used in those social sciences which examine the formal consolidation of organized groups as effected through the agency of rules or law. Though it is most frequently found in political science, the term is also found, e.g. in discussions of ecclesiastical polity or of trade union organizations where group withdrawal from a common organization is effected.

2. The word is used as a translation of the Latin *secessio* denoting *withdrawal*. Perhaps its earliest political use is in accounts of the 'withdrawal' of the Roman plebs from the Roman polity (*secessio plebis*) (in 494, 449, and 287 B.C.). The idea developed subsequently in the internal struggles of the Presbyterian Church. The Presbyterian polity lay between congregationalism (confederation) and episcopacy (consolidated unitary organization). When individual churches disagreed with the official national churches they seceded and formed their own independent organizations, viz. in Scotland, the intransigent Cameronians of 1688, the Associate Synod of 1733, and the Free Church of 1843 (*The New Schaff-Herzog Encyclopedia of Religious Knowledge*, Grand Rapids, Mich.: Baker Book House, 1950, vol. 9, pp. 209, 210, 219).

C. In political science *secession* often refers to the right of constituent member-states to withdraw from a federation.

A federal system is one in which the union of individual groups is of such a character as to create a new and distinctive authority but which is not complete enough to destroy the individual integrities of the uniting groups. Federation lies between confederacy and the unitary state. Secession is effected when a unit leaves the federation. In a confederacy this departure would constitute a mere withdrawal, for the legal discretion of the unit is not alienated by the organization of the confederation. Such action in the consolidated unitary state could be effected only through revolution, peaceful or violent.

1. In the United States, from 1789 to 1865, there persisted two distinct constitutional theories upon the right of secession. The Jefferson-Calhoun doctrine was constructed upon three postulates: (a) that the thirteen contracting states were free and independent sovereignties in 1789; (b) that they merely delegated some of their authority to the central government; and (c) that delegated power could be withdrawn at the will of the delegators. In other words, the American Union was the product of a multilateral treaty with thirteen signatories. Member-states admitted after the formation of the Union were tacit signatories to the compact.

The Story-Webster-Lincoln doctrine, in opposition to the states-rights theory, was based upon the contention that the federation of 1789 resulted in the consolidation of the Union and established the citizenry of the United States in a 'collective capacity'. This national political entity thereupon became superior to the interests or whimseys of any fractional portion of the Union. Under this doctrine, secession by a fractional part was nothing more nor less than revolution. Peaceful withdrawal could be effected only through the will or permission of the United States.

The secession of the eleven Southern states in 1861 was countered by the Union's policy of coercion. Four years after the surrender of the Southern armies, the Supreme Court of the United States (U.S. Supreme Court Reports, 7 Wall. 700-43, p. 237, sect. 725-6, State of Texas v. White, 1869) solemnly declared that the Southern states had not seceded, that a state entered into an 'indissoluble relation' when it came into the Union, and that the Constitution 'looks to an indestructible union, composed of indestructible states'.

2. Experience with federalism usually leads to formal discussions on the situs of sovereignty in the federal system. M. von Seydel (1846-1901), Bavarian jurist, became the German Calhoun in supporting the right of member-states to secede from the German federation. In Switzerland, the great debate occurred in the two decades before the Swiss confederation was transformed into the Swiss federation in 1848. K. Welcker (1790-1869) ably advocated the Story-Webster-Lincoln doctrine on the nature of the federal union.

3. The two older federations of the British Commonwealth of Nations—Canada (1867) and Australia (1900)—have not experienced actual secessions though, in 1934, Western Australia unsuccessfully petitioned the British Parliament to let it vacate its membership in the Australian federation (for a discussion of this point see K. C. Wheare, *Federal Government*, Oxford: Oxford University Press, 1953, p. 91 and fn.). In recent years the problem has become crucial in the controversy over the future of the multiracial Federation of Rhodesia and Nyasaland. The *Report of the Advisory Commission on the Review of the Constitution of Rhodesia and Nyasaland* (Cmd. 1148 of 1960)—the Monckton Report—stressed the benefits to be derived through the granting of a 'right of secession' at

Secret Society

an appropriate time or stage, to constituent members of the Federation.

D. The term does not *necessarily* refer to withdrawal from a federal structure. Thus British authorities discuss 'the problem of secession from the Commonwealth' (Sir Ivor Jennings & C. M. Young, *Constitutional Laws of the Commonwealth*, Oxford: Clarendon Press, 1952, p. 141), e.g. 'steps taken by the Southern Irish to secede' in the 1930s (ibid., p. 144). More recently K. C. Wheare has observed that it is now 'accepted that part of membership in the Commonwealth is a unilateral right to secede' (*Constitutional Structure of the Commonwealth*, Oxford: Clarendon Press, 1960, p. 125).

Cortez A. M. Ewing

See also: FEDERALISM
                 REVOLUTION

Secondary Group (See Group)

Secondary Marriage (See Polyandry)

Secret Ballot (See Ballot)

Secret Society

A. This term denotes a form of association for which *secrecy* tends to be an end in itself and in which secret ritual such as passwords, signs, symbols and medicines as well as material paraphernalia form a large part of the society's *raison d'être* and gain in psychological significance through being concealed.

A *secret society* differs from many other associations ranging from bachelor lodges, guilds, initiation groups, bush schools, and age groups in primitive society to modern social clubs, churches or political parties which frequently conceal part of their activities or proceedings from the general public but do not treat secrecy as a matter of primary significance.

B. It is difficult in this respect to discuss the nature of modern institutions, such as Freemasonry, but in primitive cultures secret societies generally constitute an integral part of the social systems concerned. Thus, in the Guinea Coast of West Africa secret associations, including the Poro of Sierra Leone and Liberia, provide tribal education, supervise political and economic affairs, regulate sexual conduct, and operate various social services ranging from 'medical' treatment to forms of entertainment and recreation.

The fact that secret societies play a large part in community affairs means that membership is important for reasons of status as well as economic gain. Quite often, the initiate enjoys privileges unaccorded to non-members, including the right to marry, to use certain titles, to own private property, and to have his case heard in the society's own tribunal. In turn, by sharing in the society's secrets he incurs obligations to his fellow members which transcend whatever allegiance he already owes to kin and other groups in the outside community.

K. Little

Sect

A. A *sect* is a type of religious group formed in protest against, and usually separating from, another religious group; its formation represents support of beliefs, ritual practices, and moral standards, most commonly believed by sect members to be a return to earlier and purer forms of the particular religion; the membership is limited and earned by individual performance; the sect therefore stands apart from, and in contrast to, groups which are carriers of the dominant norms of the societal system; and the sect moves in time either to a position of limited isolation from the surrounding system, or to a state of adaptation to it.

B. The concept has been given a specialized development in an extensive literature of sociology and history, stemming especially from the analysis of M. Weber and E. Troeltsch's effort to provide a typology of religious groups in the context of the study of reforming movements in western society. There thus emerged the distinction between two stages of social change, one representing the final stage of adapted and functional stabilization in the social structure, and the other the innovating stage. The first is the church (q.v.) and the second the sect. The sect, in its pure form, is a protest against and a separation from an existent cult group, a church, or even another sect; the grounds of dissent are avowedly religious and moral but the sect's emergence is likely to be a channel for discontent created in the secular realm. Both as an innovating agency and because of its attack upon the church, the sect tries to change existing society or to withdraw from it; the terms of membership in the sect are always contingent upon performance and thus of continuing individual qualification; leadership is personal and charismatic not sacerdotal or bureaucratic; and finally, all of these are likely to endow the sect with a dynamic and a direction leading either to transition into a church, if the sect survives in the given societal system, or to a religious society if it withdraws to a point of effective isolation from the surrounding society.

C. Some writers have attempted to generalize the sense of the term and to extend its usage beyond its limited reference to religious groups. They view religious *sects* as manifestation of a more general group type, defining a sect as a group based upon a process of change in which an emerging group initiates a set of ideas and practices opposed to a societally adapted group or groups, and then if the former survives becomes itself a societally integrated and adapted group or a tolerated societal sub-culture.

Wellman J. Warner

See also: CHURCH
CULT
RELIGION

Section

1. The term *section* may be applied to any subdivision of an aggregate of persons and is therefore a very general term in sociological analysis. It has thus been used to describe administrative units in a tribal society (e.g. groupings of local administration units of the Kgatla and Ngwato tribes in South Africa have been referred to as sections by I. Schapera in *A Handbook of Tswana Law and Custom*, London: Oxford University Press, 1938, p. 101).

2. A precise meaning has however been attached to the term in the analysis of Australian aboriginal kinship systems, originating in the study by A. R. Radcliffe-Brown, *The Social Organization of Australian Tribes*, London: Macmillan, 1931). He proposed *section* to replace *marriage class*, which he considered a misleading definition of the subdivisions concerned.

3. *Section* now usually refers to one of the four parts into which aboriginal kinship systems are divided over a large area of Western Australia, Queensland and New South Wales, and part of Central Australia.

The working of a four-part section system may be represented as follows (where each letter stands for a section):

$$\uparrow \begin{array}{c} A = B \\ C = D \end{array} \downarrow$$

The sign of equality links sections that may marry and the arrows connect the section of a mother with that of her child. For example, a man of A section may marry a woman of B section, and their children will belong to D section. The effect of a section system of this type is to categorize all relatives into four groups, in one of which a spouse may be found.

The above paradigm of a sector system gives the following grouping of the genealogically closer relatives when the person who is the point of reference (Ego) is taken to be in section A:

Section A: Ego, father's father, mother's mother, brother, sister, son's son, son's daughter

Section B: mother's father, father's mother, mother's brother's son, mother's brother's daughter, daughter's son, daughter's daughter

Section C: mother's brother, mother, sister's son, sister's daughter

Section D: father, father's sister, son, daughter

A section system may be further subdivided: if it contains eight parts it is called a *sub-section* system.

L. F. Baric

See also: KINSHIP AND KINSHIP SYSTEM

Secular

1. In its most universal usage in social science the term refers to the worldly, the civil, or the non-religious, as distinguished from the spiritual and the ecclesiastical. The secular is that which is not dedicated to religious ends and uses. This is the meaning employed in phrases such as 'separate secular schools' and 'orientation to the secular world' (R. M. Williams, *American Society*, New York: Knopf, 1951, pp. 269, 338).

2. *Secular* has also come to be used in a way that does not place it in contrast with the religious only. In supporting this usage H. P. Becker writes: '... the secular is not synonymous with the profane, unholy, infidel, godless, irreligious, heretical, unhallowed, faithless, or any similar terms. It subsumes them, but ... includes a great deal more ...' (*Through Values to Social Interpretation*, Durham, N.C.: Duke University Press, 1950, p. 275). In this sense *secular* is the opposite of the total meaning of *sacred* (q.v.); i.e., it is the opposite of venerated and inviolable. Thus culture is secular when its acceptance is based on rational and utilitarian considerations rather than on reverence and veneration.

3. The term *secular* carries another meaning, unrelated to those given above. It is applied to trends and conditions which continue over a long period of time, as distinguished from short-run fluctuations and temporary changes. Economics provides a number of examples of this usage: a continuing period of inadequate investment and consumption is known as *secular*

Secular Society

stagnation; long-range inflationary conditions are referred to as *secular exhilaration*; long-run trends in prices or in income are called *secular trends*. Similarly, demographers refer to cumulative population trends as secular trends.

Luke Ebersole

See also: SACRED
         SACRED SOCIETY
         SECULAR SOCIETY

Secular Society

This is a term used by H. Becker and others to denote a type of society which is *secular* in the sense set out under *Secular*, Section (2) above.

A secular society can be viewed as one that engenders in or elicits from its members, by any or all appropriate means, readiness to change customary orientation toward, and/or definition of, values regarded as essential in that society. More succinctly, a secular society is one bringing its members to be willing and able, in whatever measure, to accept or pursue the new *as the new is defined in that society*.

Howard Becker

See also: SACRED
         SACRED SOCIETY
         SECULAR

Security (Economics) (See **Money**)

Security (Political Science)

A. The usage of this term in the social sciences reflects the principal ordinary meanings: (a) the condition of being safe; (b) a financial pledge which is at the same time a form of investment.

B. 1. Thus in its most direct sense, security is virtually identical with *safety* and signifies absence of, or protection from, physical danger. This is the basic meaning assigned to the phrase *national security* by political scientists and underlies the variant meaning given to individual security. Law guarantees 'life and limb' as inviolable, and democratic governance has extended individual immunity against coercion to limit the use of force even by such legally-authorized persons as police officers and enemy soldiers. Lawyers, criminologists, and penologists are concerned with individual security as physical safety. So also security is sometimes used in such phrases as *state security*, *security risk*, *security police*, etc., to denote (a) the safety or protection of the state; and/or (b) the agencies to which the safety of the state is entrusted. A more recent and comprehensive usage of security is linked with absence of, or protection from, psychological anxiety. This usage was given public standing by the Atlantic Charter, which referred specifically to freedom 'from want' and 'from fear' as conditions of security.

2. Popular parlance has made *insecurity* synonomous with virtually all types of anxiety. Thus, psychologists, physicians, social workers use security to designate both the absence of specific anxieties and a generalized sense of well-being.

3. In a larger sense, security is virtually identical with *welfare* and signifies absence of, or protection from, material want. This usage of national, and particularly individual, security has underlain much of the controversy over modern conceptions of the *welfare state*. Economists, sociologists, planners frequently use security to mean material welfare. It is in this context that *social security* denotes protection against social hazards or contingencies; freedom from anxiety concerning such hazards; or the steps taken to protect or insure a population against such hazards.

4. Economists use the term as indicated in A. (b) above to denote a financial pledge and investment.

Daniel Lerner

See also: INSECURITY

Sedition

A. There is little difference in the various social science fields in the use of the word *sedition* although the vagueness of the term permits various possible classifications of action that might be listed as seditious. In all fields it means all language, either printed or spoken, and disloyal actions short of treason (q.v.) that arouse distrust and tend to incite to rebellion against the constituted authority of the state. In addition to the possible criminal nature of such an act it is accompanied by a spirit of disloyalty that enhances the heinous nature of the offence.

B. Offences against the peace of the nation in Great Britain are not classified under sedition but consist of seditious libel, seditious words, or seditious conspiracies. It is the adjectival form of the word that has significance in England. Whatever the types of action that are considered seditious all express a sharp dissatisfaction with the government, with those in authority, and a desire for change. English law 'prefers to classify those offences against internal tranquillity which are not accompanied by, or which do not lead to, open violence, and which are loosely described as Sedition, as Seditious Offences'

(E. J. C. Neep, *Seditious Offences*, London: The Fabian Society, 1926, p. 7). It has been stated that English law 'considers as sedition all those practices which have for their object to incite discontent or dissatisfaction, to create public disturbance or to lead to civil war; to bring into hatred or contempt the Sovereign or the Government, the laws or constitution of the realm, and generally all endeavours to promote public disorder' (Reg. v. Sullivan, Reports of Cases in Criminal Law 1867–71, 11 Cox, C. C. Reg. v. Sullivan (1868)). J. Cave (in Regina v. Burns (1886) 16 Cox, C. C. 356) observed that 'an intention to excite ill-will between different classes of Her Majesty's subjects may be a seditious intention; whether or not it is so in any particular case must be decided upon by the jury after taking into consideration all the circumstances of the case'. 'Sedition', he continues, 'embraces everything, whether by word, deed or writing, which is calculated to disturb the tranquillity of the State and lead ignorant persons to subvert the Government and laws of the Empire' (see also Criminal Libel Act 1819, section 1).

C. In the United States sedition is defined by law. Sedition, according to federal law, is to advocate wilfully the destruction or overthrow of the government. A person is guilty of sedition who, with an intent to overthrow the government, 'prints, publishes, edits, issues, circulates, sells, distributes, or publicly displays any written or printed matter advocating, advising or teaching the duty, necessity, desirability or propriety of overthrowing or destroying any government of the United States by force or violence or attempts to do so' (18 U.S.C., Sec. 2385). Sedition is also committed by those persons who organize or attempt to organize or become a member of a group which has for its purposes the destruction of the government by force or violence. In addition to federal law, forty-two states list different offences that are classified as seditious. These laws, like federal law, describe sedition as the use of words and actions having for their purpose the inciting of persons to overthrow or destroy the government. While there is much similarity in these laws, they frequently differ in their listing of seditious practices. These state laws must give way to the federal law should they conflict, for the Supreme Court has recently held that 'Sedition against the United States is not a *local* offence. It is a crime against the *Nation*' (Penn. v. Nelson, 350 U.S. 497, 505 (1956)). Broadly speaking, these laws pro-

hibit the wilful advocacy of the use of force against the government of the United States or of the states.

Acts classified as seditious during wartime have in the past differed from acts classified as seditious during peacetime. During wartime sedition has consisted of disturbance of the public peace by deeds, words, and writing which were short of treason and which were not accompanied by violence. During peacetime most writings and words, in spite of their nature, have not been classified as seditious and the use of the term has been limited to overt acts which had for their purpose the overthrow of the government by acts of violence. Recent legislation by Congress (the Smith Act, Title 18 U.S.C., Sec. 2385; the Internal Security Act of 1950, Title 50 U.S.C., Sec. 781; the Communist Control Act of 1954, Title 50 U.S.C. (1955 Supplement), Sec. 841) tends to remove any differences between peacetime or wartime sedition if the purpose of these seditious acts is the overthrow of the government. This is a result of cold war concepts and is offensive to those who think that no writings should in peacetime be classified as seditious regardless of their content. Ultimately, the responsibility rests on the Supreme Court of the United States to maintain freedom of speech and at the same time to classify as seditious only those acts that advocate the change of established government by violence.

Robert S. Rankin

See also: TREASON

Segment (Also **Segmentation**)

A. The word *segment* means a piece or fragment, and has been used loosely in anthropology to refer to any part or section of a unit. Recently S. F. Nadel's suggestion that *segment* should refer to subdivisions of a totality that are exhaustive and *section* refer to those that are not has generally been accepted (*Foundations of Social Anthropology*, London: Cohen & West, 1951, p. 178). *Segments* may be organized into segmentary series, in which they are in a state of continual segmentation and of complementary opposition. The use of this term in anthropology has been complex only in the forms *segmentation* and *segmentary* (or *segmental*), the former referring both to a process and to a state of relationship between units, the latter to systems in which either the process or the state were observable.

B. 1. Durkheim distinguished two ways in which units merge within a total system,

Segregation

consistent with two forms of social solidarity. In one there is *organic* solidarity, the units being functionally differentiated and interdependent. In the other there is *mechanical* solidarity, found in 'segmental societies with a clan base, [formed by] peoples who are constituted through an association of clans' (E. Durkheim, *The Division of Labour in Society* (1893), Glencoe, Ill.: The Free Press, 1947, pp. 174–5).

2. M. Fortes and E. E. Evans-Pritchard (eds.) (*African Political Systems*, London: Oxford University Press, 1955, p. 6) use the term *segmentary* as an attribute of those politically uncentralized systems in which the political structure was based upon, or associated with, a 'segmentary lineage system' (see *Lineage*). They stressed that the lineages were in a state of continual segmentation and of complementary opposition, segments which were equal and opposed in one situation being merged together and in opposition with another equivalent lineage (in turn segmented) in another; for example, lineages that were at feud with one another in one situation may ally themselves against a common enemy lineage in another, and possibly these foes would temporarily settle their differences and unite to oppose yet a third group in a third situation. This system of alliances and balances may provide the means of settling disputes in a society lacking any centralized form of political authority. The essential features of any such segmentary series (of which the units need not be lineages, but may be age-sets, councils, village groupings, etc.) include the 'nesting' of units within one another to form a series and the characteristic of being in a state of continual segmentation and complementary opposition.

3. Segmentation must be distinguished from fission. By fission a group breaks once and for all into two or more new groups; by segmentation a group merely divides in certain contexts but retains its identity in others.

4. Besides Fortes and Evans-Pritchard, writers who have discussed the nature of segmentary organization include J. A. Barnes ('Seven Types of Segmentation: Human Problems in British Central Africa', *Rhodes-Livingstone Journal*, No. 17, 1955, pp. 1–22); M. G. Smith ('On Segmentary Lineage Systems', *Journal of the Royal Anthropological Institute*, vol. 86, pt. II, 1956, pp. 39–80); J. Goody ('Fields of Social Control Among the Lodogaba', *Journal of the Royal Anthropological Institute*, vol. 87, pt. I, 1957, pp. 75–104); A. W. Southall (*Alur Society*, Cambridge: Heffer, 1956); J. Middleton & D. Tait (eds.) (*Tribes without Rulers*, London: Routledge & Kegan Paul, 1958).

J. Middleton

See also: Lineage

Segregation

1. The major use of the term *segregation* in the social sciences for some years was to denote that ecological process by which people settle or locate in those areas of a community occupied by people of similar social characteristics or activities. The term appears in this usage in R. E. Park and E. W. Burgess, *Introduction to the Science of Sociology* (Chicago: University of Chicago Press, 1924, pp. 252–4). It is still defined in this way in modern works, e.g. G. A. Lundberg et al., *Sociology* (New York: Harper & Bros., 1954, p. 141): '... people of similar social, biological, or other characteristics, or people who engage in similar activities, locate in areas occupied only by their own kind'.

2. In recent years greater stress has come to be placed on that usage of the term in which it denotes that geographic separation *and* separate use of facilities which is *forced* upon subordinate categories and groups of persons by law, custom, or 'gentlemen's agreement'. This usage applies mainly with respect to ethnic, religious, and racial categories and groups. This kind of segregation is exemplified by Jewish ghettos in medieval Europe, current practices in South Africa and to varying degrees in various parts of the United States, and in the treatment of pariah categories and groups in south India and Burma.

3. By extension, in the United States particularly, *segregation* has come to denote the entire range of discriminatory practices including the denial of certain employment or voting rights and the prohibition of miscegenation by means of which ethnic, religious, and racial categories and groups have been denied equal opportunity for social mobility. In this usage it has become almost synonymous with discrimination (q.v.) in one of its usages.

Read Bain

See also: Discrimination
 Prejudice
 Race and Minority Group
  Relations
 Racism

Selection (See **Social Selection**)

Self

A. In its broadest sense *self* is synonymous with the broadest usage of ego (q.v.) denoting the core of the personality system (q.v.) organized around its awareness of itself and its conscious and unconscious orientation toward its most vital interests and values, involving identity, status, commitment, and desire. In this broadest sense the self is what it is to the 'objective' observer drawing upon all possible resources of information. The reflexive character of the self, however, i.e. the fact that it can be an object to itself, has led some social psychologists to narrow the definition so that *self* denotes the individual as viewed (defined) by the individual, a social object among social objects. An intermediate definition of *self* has it denote a process of communication internal to the personality in which symbolic responses of the personality themselves become objects of further response in an internal conversation.

B. The concept of the self has been a key one in sociology and sociologically oriented social psychology for the interpretation of personality. It was brought into these disciplines from the work of W. James and of J. M. Baldwin largely through C. H. Cooley and G. H. Mead (W. James, *Principles of Psychology*, 2 vols., New York: Henry Holt, 1890; J. M. Baldwin, *Social and Ethical Interpretation in Mental Development*, New York: The Macmillan Co., 3rd edn., 1902; C. H. Cooley, *Human Nature and the Social Order*, New York: Charles Scribner's Sons, 1902; G. H. Mead, *Mind, Self and Society*, Chicago: University of Chicago Press, 1934). It dropped out of attention in psychology in the 1910s and for that reason did not receive a great deal of attention in psychologically oriented social psychology until revived, together with *ego*, by G. W. Allport ('The Ego in Contemporary Psychology', *Psychological Review*, vol. 50, 1943, pp. 451–78).

1. Sociology and sociologically oriented social psychology are mostly under the influence of the treatment of the self by G. H. Mead. He regarded the self as dependent on language for its development, and as arising in the context of social experience and activity. '... the word self, which is a reflexive ... indicates that which can be both subject and object. ... The self is ... entirely distinguishable from an organism. ... The self, as that which can be an object to itself, is essentially a social structure, and it arises in social experience ...' (*Mind, Self and Society*, pp. 135–40). The distinguishing feature of the self, according to Mead, is self-consciousness. He saw the self carrying on an internal conversation with the self, a part of the whole process of social communication. In this emergence of the self and its internal conversation with itself, the self comes to direct its own behaviour through the reflected appraisals and expectations of reciprocal others (the 'me') and the more spontaneous responses of the self toward these internalized others (the 'I').

There can be little doubt that Mead's interpretation of the self is overwhelmingly cognitive and social. On the other hand, neither Cooley nor Mead meant by this that the self had no emotional dimension or that the self was simply a reflection of already existing social relations. Mead's view that emotions, like ideas, are essentially social in origin does not mean that they are purely conventional or unspontaneous. Even more important, the social nature of the self and its self-awareness did not mean for Mead that the self was purely object rather than subject or that it was purely reflective of the society rather than itself being to some extent a spontaneous element of the social. The 'I' is a spontaneous agent, not a reflected object.

Perhaps because of problems in Mead's behaviourist frame of reference, sociological social psychologists came to place increasing emphasis on the cognitive and the socially reflective. The self comes to be identified with the process of internal conversation rather than the active agent within which the conversation occurs, and the 'I' becomes increasingly subordinate to the 'me'. By the time of the publication of A. R. Lindesmith and A. L. Strauss's *Social Psychology* (New York: Dryden Press, 1949), '... in a sense, the self is just this process of intraindividual communication ...' and 'the "I"' has come to stand merely for 'impulsive responses' within this conversation (ibid., pp. 156, 198). For others this reduction of the self has proceeded to the point where the self is simply a reflected image (see E. L. Hartley & R. E. Hartley, *Fundamentals of Social Psychology*, New York: Knopf, 1952, p. 316).

2. Psychologically oriented social psychologists have derived their views of the self from a variety of theoretical perspectives and from the empirical study of the child, the adolescent, and social perception. This has meant that there is considerably less unity in viewpoint regarding the self. In general, however, there is nothing incompatible in most of these conceptions with Allport's identification of the self with a broad definition of the ego as a central sector of the personality system which is aware of itself but which is also a dynamic agent knowing, feeling, and striving in the deepest senses. In this

Self-Conception

conception the self as subject knows the self as object, but it is the self as subject and object which is the focus of attention of the scientific observer. Despite Mead's emphasis on the social and on the reflexive character of the self, his stress on the self as object *and* subject, and his stress on the spontaneity of the 'I' would seem to be more compatible with Allport's conception than with the reductions of the self that have occurred in much of so-called Meadian social psychology.

Manford Kuhn

See also: EGO
INTERNALIZATION
SOCIAL INTERACTION

Self-Conception

A. An individual's *self-conception* is his view of himself. It is derived from taking the role of significant others in social interaction (q.v.). Self-conception is equivalent to the self (q.v.) if the latter is defined as the *'individual as perceived by that individual in a socially determined frame of reference'* (T. M. Newcomb, *Social Psychology*, New York: Dryden Press, 1950, p. 328).

Operationally, *self-conception* may be defined therefore in any of the operational ways indicated under self *which are non-projective in nature*. Projective instruments elicit responses which are *not* derived, theoretically at least, from the consciously-held, verbal plans of action (attitudes) which are generally considered to constitute the self-conception. In general, any instrument which is constructed to elicit responses from the individual defining his views of his characteristic ways of acting and feeling toward, and evaluating of, himself as a social object, should yield responses operationally definable as his self-conception. It is possible to use open-ended instruments (M. H. Kuhn, 'Factors in Personality: Socio-Cultural Determinants as seen through the Amish', in F. L. K. Hsu (ed.), *Aspects of Culture and Personality*, New York: Abelard-Schuman, 1954, ch. 3) if one is concerned with saliency of attitudes; or one may use check-list questionnaires of various sorts (e.g. S. F. Miyamoto & S. M. Dornbusch, 'A Test of Interactionist Hypotheses of Self-Conception', *American Journal of Sociology*, vol. LXI, 1955–6, pp. 399–403).

B. *Self-conception* has been used in sociology as the equivalent of the self, that is, one's self is the way one conceives oneself, or one's self-conception. Since the self is by no means universally equated with an individual's consciously held conception of himself in the social science literature, however, it is necessary to delineate the varying relationships between the two concepts.

1. It is useful to know that if the two terms are not used synonymously, then the self is the more general, inclusive term. Certainly self-conception, for example, would not be applicable to the 'somatic self', 'the receptor-effector self', or the 'primitive construed self' used by T. Sarbin ('Role Theory', in G. Lindzey (ed.), *Handbook of Social Psychology*, Cambridge, Mass.: Addison-Wesley, 1954, pp. 241–2), and probably not to the 'introjecting-extrojecting self', for none of these refers to an internalization of language.

2. For those who use the terms *self* and *self-conception* interchangeably, the antecedents of the self lie wholly in the communicative (social) life into which a new individual is being inducted; for those who make self-conception only a part of the self, the antecedents of the latter lie partially or wholly in somatic maturation, and form the basis for the later verbal importations. Some, like Newcomb, see the development of the self to begin with the infant's meeting obstacles to 'motive satisfaction', sometimes in the form of objects which resist his movement. He begins to learn to treat these objects, and himself, as others do, since in so doing he is frustrated less often. 'In learning to make such distinctions, he learns to respond to himself as an object to be perceived, just as he responds to other objects by perceiving them as distinctive' (*Social Psychology*, p. 315). Probably most sociologists would reject these views regarding the emergence of a prelingual self, agreeing with A. R. Lindesmith and A. L. Strauss that 'Conceptions of self arise from social interaction ...' (*Social Psychology*, New York: Dryden Press, rev. edn., 1956, p. 604) which rests on the use of significant symbols (language).

3. Psychologists often use the term *self-concept*, the meaning of which is apparently nearly identical with *self-conception*, although the former seems to be more often found in a context of terminology implicitly or explicitly individualistic rather than social; this context of concepts often omits reference to language and communication and stresses instead perception and cognition.

C. 1. Central to an individual's conception of himself is his *identity*; that is, his generalized

630

position in society deriving from his statuses in the groups of which he is a member, the roles which stem from these statuses, and the social categories which his group memberships lead him to assign himself (sex, age, class, race, etc.) 'The person has an identity of his own and an identity for others. ... Furthermore ... to have an identity involves, in addition to my knowing who I am, that others, too, know me as the same person' (S. E. Asch, *Social Psychology*, Englewood Cliffs, N.J.: Prentice-Hall, 1952, p. 282). His identity may be thought of as deriving from his 'social anchorages' (M. Kuhn & T. McPartland, 'An Empirical Investigation of Self-Attitudes', *American Sociological Review*, vol. 19, 1954, pp. 68–76). Such self-identification may be construed as the basis for motivation (N. Foote, 'Identification as the Basis for a Theory of Motivation', *American Sociological Review*, vol. 16, 1951, pp. 14–21).

2. A self-conception consists, in addition to (a) a view of identity, of (b) notions of one's interests and aversions (i.e. his attitudes toward objects, cognitively, affectively and evaluatively, (c) a conception of one's goals and his successes in achieving them, (d) a picture, sometimes quite sketchy, of the ideological ('world view') frame of reference through which he views himself and other objects, and (e) some kind of self-evaluation (M. Kuhn, 'Self-Attitudes by Age, Sex & Professional Training', *The Sociological Quarterly*, vol. I, 1960, pp. 39–55).

D. The crucial importance of self-conception in the study of human behaviour is attested to by virtually all who use the term or its equivalents.

1. It is said to form the basis for (a) the organized character of personality as well as to be the requisite for (b) the integration of the person into the on-going group process of interaction. '... a structural condition of human interaction. ... To understand more concretely how pivotal our sense of identity is, we would have to observe what happens when a confusion of characters actually occurs' (S. E. Asch, *Social Psychology*, p. 282).

2. Little is known empirically about the constancy or continuity of the self-conception, although there is much speculation and pontification which passes unwarrantedly for scientific generalization. On the one hand there are the many dogmatic statements in sociological and psychological literature regarding the early formation of the personality, which would logically imply the formation in the early family and other primary groups, and consequent im-

mutability, of the self-conception. On the other hand we have such statements as 'Changing groups bring changed self-perceptions ...' (T. M. Newcomb, *Social Psychology*, p. 324) and 'Selves can only exist in definite relationships to other selves' (G. H. Mead, *Mind, Self and Society*, Chicago: University of Chicago Press, 1934, p. 164).

3. Disturbances in self-conceptions of the following varieties have been delineated: (a) accurately reflected views from groups which are themselves normatively deviant from the larger society; (b) inconsistent self-ideas reflected from differing significant others; (c) self-derogating views from derogating others; (d) distorted self views arising from social isolation. These have been theoretically related to mental-emotional disturbances, sociopathy, and delinquent-criminal behaviour.

Manford Kuhn

See also: ROLE
SELF
STATUS

Self-Determination

A. *Self-determination* denotes (a) the process by which national entities establish themselves as independent states and, more importantly, (b) the idea or theory that such entities have the right, recognized and enforced by the international community, so to do. Thus the bare term taken out of the context of its application seems to indicate primarily the process by which nations or national minorities establish themselves as independent states and determine their own governmental form and policies. In most contemporary contexts, however, when collective action of such an agency as the United Nations is used to establish independence or autonomy of minority groups and colonial areas or to protect weak states from strong states, the factual connotation of the term points in the direction of the collective enforcement of the right to independence.

B. The phrase 'self-determination of peoples' is used in the United Nations Charter (Articles 1 and 55) without explanation. 'The concept which lies behind the term ... reaches back to the "consent of the governed" in the American Declaration of Independence; to the "divine right of the people" in the French Revolution; to the democratic nationalism of Mazzini' (C. Eagleton, 'Excesses of Self-Determination', *Foreign Affairs*, vol. 31, 1953, pp. 592–604). Self-determination has no established meaning in

Semantics

international law, but it is used at least four different ways in international affairs.

1. Self-determination refers to the process by which nations or national minorities acquire statehood, or independence (H. W. Briggs, *The Law of Nations*, London: Stevens, 1953, p. 65). H. Kelsen equates self-determination and sovereignty (*The Law of the United Nations*, London: Stevens, 1950, pp. 52–3). A. Cobban, in his study of the history and growth of the idea, links it very closely to the development, in 19th-century Europe, of various forms of nationalism. He observes that 'The right of national independence, which came to be called, during the first World War, the principle of self-determination, is, in general terms, the belief that each nation has a right to constitute an independent state and determine its own government' and that '... it is a theory about the relationship that should prevail between the nation and the state, the latter being understood as any separately governed political community' (*National Self-Determination*, London: Oxford University Press, 1944, p. 4). It is evident that the notion developed along with the growth of self-conscious nationalism and that its meaning in any historical context is linked with the problems, analytical and practical, of distinguishing one 'nation' from another, i.e. the problems of delineating the unit which holds the right of self-determination. The emphasis is on 'self'; Briggs points out that 'the last one hundred and fifty years reveal few cases in which the creation of new states was ordained or greeted by collective community action' (*The Law of Nations*, p. 65). Nevertheless, there is much reference to the term in connection with contemporary efforts to establish independent states under auspices of the United Nations, although *self*-determination is somewhat strained by such usage (see C. Eagleton, 'Excesses of Self-Determination', p. 594).

2. It is used to support claims for independence or autonomy of minority groups or colonial areas within established states. President Wilson spoke in his Fourteen Points (*Address of President Wilson to the Congress of the United States*, 65th Congress, 2nd Session, Document No. 765 in *House Documents*, vol. 113, Washington: Government Printing Office, 1918, p. 5) of adjustment of colonial claims 'based upon a strict observance of the principle that in determining all such questions of sovereignty the interests of the populations concerned must have equal weight with the equitable claims of the government whose title is to be determined'.

'Self-determination of peoples' in the United Nations Charter does not indicate which groups have self-determining powers. 'Large compact national groups' and 'groups widely separated from the parent state by distance' have been listed as having such powers (see C. Eagleton, 'Excesses of Self-Determination', p. 596).

3. The term refers to self-government and freedom of an established state to determine its own form of government and policies. 'As often invoked, it means the right to do as one pleases. It refers to freedom from all external influences and pressures after independence has been attained' (P. C. Jessup, 'Self-Determination Today in Principle and in Practice', *The Virginia Quarterly Review*, vol. 33, 1957, p. 184).

4. Self-determination has been used in support of claims for more than independence and freedom to determine governmental forms and policies. It means that 'weak peoples ought not to be dominated by strong peoples. ... Thus self-determination becomes collective security' (C. Eagleton, 'Excesses of Self-Determination', p. 598). In the view of the United States delegation to the United Nations, it applies 'to politically independent states which needed protection from external pressure, threats, the use of force, and subversive activities' (quoted by C. Eagleton, 'Self-Determination in the United Nations', *American Journal of International Law*, vol. 47, 1953, p. 90).

John M. Howell

See also: NATION
NATIONALISM

Semantics

A. *Semantics* may be defined as consisting of those branches of the study of symbols, particularly linguistic symbols, which deal *primarily* with the *meanings* of such symbols. If all symbols, rather than just linguistic symbols, are included in the following, the definition offered by M. Pei and F. Gaynor serves very well: 'A science dealing with the relations between *referents* and *referends*—linguistic symbols (words, expressions, phrases) and the objects or concepts to which they refer—and the history and changes in the meanings of words' ('Semantics', in *A Dictionary of Linguistics*, New York: Philosophical Library, 1954).

This definition is not simple, however, since it can be used to refer to at least three different sorts of investigation, carried on by quite different groups of scholars; (a) the investigation and analysis of systems of *meanings*, closely related to or part of modern linguistics; (b) the investigation of the nature of meaning; (c) the investigation of the difficulties people experience as a result of confusions and distortions of meaning.

B. While linguists disagree as to whether the study of *semantic* systems is a part of linguistics or a sister discipline, they do agree on the significance of such study and the necessity of relating it to the study of *grammatical* systems (C. F. Hockett, *A Course in Modern Linguistics*, New York: The Macmillan Co., 1958, pp. 138–9).

This linguistically related semantics or semasiology presupposes a theory of the nature of meaning—frequently of a moderately behaviouristic type—but the primary emphasis is on the comparison and analysis of *systems* of *meanings* in actual languages in their interrelations with the grammatical systems of the languages. Such analysis is done for its own sake, and also for the light it may throw on the other branches of linguistics such as the study of grammatical systems or of historical linguistics, as for example the use of semantic criteria for defining the basic vocabulary of a group's language—these criteria referring to the things and situations for which every human community has terms—which is a necessary step for glottochronology (q.v.) (C. F. Hockett, *A Course in Modern Linguistics*, p. 529).

C. The investigation of the nature of meaning and the formulation of a theory of meaning is a much more dispersed enterprise, being found in linguistics, social psychology and the social psychological aspects of the other social sciences, the study of literature, and philosophy. It is frequently indistinguishable from the study of communication (q.v.) or from the general study of symbols (q.v.) and symbolization. Moreover the term *semantics* is not always applied to such investigation and theory formulation.

1. As indicated earlier linguists do have a theory of meaning, usually of a behaviouristic variety. Thus L. Bloomfield has a situational concept of meaning on the basis of which he believes that 'The meaning of speech-forms could be scientifically defined only if all branches of science, including especially psychology and physiology, were close to perfection' (*Language*, New York: Henry Holt, 1933, p. 78). The reason for this is that '... the study of speakers' situations and hearers' responses ... is equivalent to the sum total of human knowledge' (ibid., p. 74). While Bloomfield recognizes that the linguist is interested in *shared* meanings he believes that accuracy is impossible. Hockett, however, also using a behaviourist theory of meaning, believes that the problem of studying meanings can be reduced to manageable proportions. This can be done by stressing (a) the habitual nature of the tie between morphemes and situations or types of situation as contrasted with the unique antecedent and consequent occurrences of particular, unique acts of speech; and (b) the shared, conventional nature of group meanings.

2. The theories of meaning involved in social science studies of the nature of meaning, the learning of meanings, the use of meanings in communication, and the impact of grammar and meaning on culture have at the least a *semantic* dimension and could probably be called *semantics*. This, however, is rarely the case. B. L. Whorf's grappling with the problems of the impact of language on culture and the discussions of similar problems by others have been termed *metalinguistics* (*Language, Thought, and Reality*, ed. by J. B. Carroll, New York: The Technology Press and Wiley, 1956; H. Hoijer (ed.), *Language in Culture*, Chicago: University of Chicago Press, 1954). The term could also be relevantly applied to studies of the emergence, learning, and functions of symbolic meanings by such social psychologists as J. Piaget and G. H. Mead (J. Piaget, *The Language and Thought of the Child*, New York: Harcourt, Brace, 1926; G. H. Mead, *Mind, Self and Society*, Chicago: University of Chicago Press, 1934).

3. Areas of philosophical and literary analysis of meaning—among which Mead's work could be legitimately included—meet the definition of *semantics* on which there is consensus, and yet are not designated by that name. Central here too is the concern with the fundamental nature of meaning—what is implied when it is said that a symbol has meaning (e.g. C. K. Ogden & I. A. Richards, *The Meaning of Meaning*, New York: Harcourt, Brace, 3rd edn. rev., 1930; C. Morris, *Signs, Language, and Behavior*, New York: Prentice-Hall, 1946; S. Langer, *Philosophy in a New Key*, London: Oxford University Press, 1951).

D. The term *semantics*—usually *general semantics*—has been used by a group of scholars who, following A. Korzybski, have been primarily interested in the reform of the uses of languages for the sake of promoting human co-operation

Sentiment

(cf. A. Korzybski, *Science and Sanity*, Lancaster, Pa.: Science Press Printing Co., 1933; S. I. Hayakawa, *Language in Thought and Action*, New York: Harcourt, Brace, 1949; *ETC: A Review of General Semantics*, published since 1943 by International Society for General Semantics). This group drawing on the resources of all studies of language go far beyond the limited conceptions of the problems of meaning found in other scholars. S. I. Hayakawa, for example, defines semantics as '... the study of human interaction through the mechanisms of linguistic communication' (*Language in Thought and Action*, p.v). Yet it must be recognized that they have concentrated primarily on genuine problems of meaning such as the confusion of symbol and object symbolized and the confusion of levels of abstraction in determining the referents of symbols.

Morris Swadesh

See also: Communication
Meaning
Symbol
Symbolism

Sentiment

A. In contemporary social psychology and sociology the term is variously defined as (a) the basic unit of the organization of affect (q.v.); (b) broad, relatively undifferentiated, elements of affect; (c) overt activity on the part of members of a group indicating to those members the existence of affective states.

B. The conception of *sentiment* as the basic unit of the organization of affect derives from the writings of A. F. Shand ('Character and the Emotions', *Mind*, vol. 21, 1896, pp. 203–342) and W. McDougall (*Introduction to Social Psychology*, London: Methuen, 1908). McDougall, elaborating upon the work of Shand, views a sentiment as a unit standing between an emotional propensity and character. Emotional propensities (largely, although not completely, instinctive in nature) are generalized tendencies to act on the basis of feeling in certain ways. Thus, for example, animals, including men, have an instinctive propensity to feel responsibility for the nurturing of offspring. When this propensity on the part of a particular woman becomes linked to her own offspring, the propensity has become organized into a sentiment. The character of the woman, in turn, is constituted by an organization of her sentiments (W. McDougall, *The Energies of Men*, New York: Charles Scribner's Sons, 1933, pp. 205–11).

The attack which the doctrine of human instincts involved in this conception of sentiment provoked has obscured, particularly in the United States, the importance of the concept of sentiment. Certainly this term denotes one of the most important kinds of human motive, and in several respects the concept is more precise than that of attitude (q.v.) with which it has been largely replaced in the United States. Thus, G. W. Allport points out that (a) an attitude is a disposition within the organism considered without regard to its origin, while a sentiment presupposes propensities; (b) an attitude may be diffuse or specific in its object, while a sentiment is centred around a definite object; and (c) sentiments are more lasting and hierarchical than attitudes need be ('The Historical Background of Modern Social Psychology', in G. Lindzey (ed.), *Handbook of Social Psychology*, Cambridge, Mass.: Addison-Wesley, 1954, vol. I, pp. 45–6).

C. The use of *sentiment* to denote broad, relatively undifferentiated, elements of affect (precisely the opposite of the first usage), has been brought into sociology and social psychology from the work of V. Pareto (*The Mind and Society*, A. Livingston (ed.), trans. by A. Bongiorno and A. Livingston, New York: Harcourt, Brace, 1935, 4 vols.). Pareto uses the term in a loosely synonymous fashion with instinct and inclination, to denote the motivational element in the broad residual category of the 'non-logical' which manifests itself in residues (q.v.) and derivations (q.v.). Most commentators on Pareto have considered the 'non-logical' and therefore sentiments as falling solely in the realm of the irrational, but T. Parsons (*The Structure of Social Action*, New York: McGraw-Hill, 1937, pp. 178–300) has argued that there is a non-rational (but not irrational) normative element in Pareto's use of sentiment that may be manifested in residues in cognitive and moral elements as well as affective elements and which is therefore closely linked with such other normative concepts as ultimate ends and moral values which transcend the rational and the logical but cannot be considered irrational. It is in this usage that K. Davis says 'The source of the value in turn lies chiefly in the *sentiments*, broad backgrounds of feeling which make some things seem valuable, others not valuable' (*Human Society*, New York: The Macmillan Co., 1949, p. 124).

D. The third usage is to be found in the work of G. C. Homans (*The Human Group*, New York: Harcourt, Brace, 1950, and *Social Behavior, Its Elementary Forms*, New York: Harcourt, Brace, 1961). Homans says 'The activities that the members of a particular verbal or symbolic community say are signs of the attitudes and feelings a man takes toward another man or other men—these we call *sentiments*' (*Social Behavior, Its Elementary Forms*, p. 33). Homans employs this definition in part because of his reluctance to deal with subjective states from the point of view of the observer: 'The behavior we include under the word "sentiment" must of course be observed or we should not, as scientists, be entitled to make generalizations about it (*The Human Group*, p. 241); and in part because of his wish to take account of the important fact that members of a group engaged in interaction do impute motives. Whether or not this idiosyncratic usage survives will depend largely on whether or not social scientists feel increasingly that 'science' demands that subjective states cannot be spoken about from the point of view of the scientific observer because they are not directly observable. This is an old argument, and not one likely to be resolved through the discussion of a single concept.

T. H. Pear

See also: ATTITUDE
DERIVATIONS
EMOTION
RESIDUES
VALUE

Separation of Powers

A. *Separation of powers* refers to a dispersion of power among the various branches or agencies of government, as a result of which each branch is primarily concerned with the performance of a different function and to this end is more or less independent of the others.

B. Within this general sense of the term there have arisen problems of analysis as well as normative issues. There have been differences of opinion with regard to the precise functions to be separated, the degree of independence necessary, the extent to which checks and balances (q.v.) are a necessary concomitant, and the question of whether the end result requires co-ordinate branches of government. Thus, although everyone agrees that the United States has separation of powers, there is considerable difference of opinion as to whether Britain has, the disagreement hingeing upon the stands taken

with regard to the above points of difference. On the normative issues it has been felt that some such functional dispersion is essential to constitutionalism or liberalism as opposed to authoritarianism; but that, especially when connected with certain types of checks, it makes for conservatism rather than liberalism.

1. The principle or doctrine of separation of powers is one providing for the division of the powers of government along functional as opposed to territorial lines. In theory this pre-supposes that there are different functions of government and that these functions can and should be carried on by different governmental officials, or agencies, or branches. There has, of course, been debate as to the precise functions to be separated and as to their 'separability'. Following Montesquieu, Americans in particular have argued that there are three basic governmental functions which should be separated. C. J. Friedrich, for example, seems to imply that these three functions are inherent in the governmental process and in that sense are 'natural', since there is always the making of rules or general commands (the legislative function), the application of these rules in particular given instances (the executive function), and the adjudication of controversies regarding the applicability of these rules (the judicial function) ('Separation of Powers', in E. R. A. Seligman (ed.), *Encyclopedia of the Social Sciences*, New York: Macmillan, vol. XIII, 1934, pp. 663–6). H. Finer on the other hand sees 'nothing absolutely inherent in the nature of different functions, nothing eternal and unchangeable, which will settle the question of whether there ought to be a separation of powers, and if so, in what it ought to consist. The answer is relative to one's needs and to the organization, procedure, and mentality of the institutions as they actually function' (*The Theory and Practice of Modern Government*, London: Methuen, rev. edn., 1949, p. 107). From this point of view, one which seems to be more nearly the British approach, it is possible to argue that the traditional threefold division does not meet modern needs, and this is what Finer does, along with H. J. Laski and others. Actually Friedrich states elsewhere, 'It may be wise to modify the threefold scheme' by distinguishing between the executive and administrative functions, thus establishing a fourfold scheme (*Constitutional Government and Democracy*, Boston: Little, Brown, 1941, p. 186).

2. There does seem to be considerable agreement that there *ought* to be *some* functional

Sexuality

dispersion of power if there is to be a libertarian rather than an authoritarian government. Montesquieu insists that 'there can be no liberty' if all powers are united in the same person or body of persons. And speaking for the American founding fathers Madison declares, 'The accumulation of all powers, legislative, executive, and judiciary, in the same hands, whether one, a few, or many, whether hereditary, self-appointed, or elective, may justly be pronounced the very definition of tyranny' (*The Federalist* (1788), New York: Heritage Press, 1945, no. XLVII). The founding fathers undoubtedly would have added that separation of powers not only protects individual liberty but also protects private property. Indeed in the opinion of some this was their primary reason for wanting the separation. In view of this dual purpose of securing both liberty and property and the implications of such a duality, it probably should be pointed out that although separation of powers is essential to constitutionalism or liberalism as opposed to authoritarianism, it is not even a characteristic of liberalism as opposed to conservatism. For in so far as the separation is a device that makes change difficult, a device that favours the status quo especially in property relations, it tends to be an instrument of conservatism rather than of liberalism. Indeed many of its chief exponents ever since Montesquieu have tended to assume a rather static order in which there was little need for change.

3. The degree to which separation of powers lends itself to change depends in part upon the degree to which the doctrine is associated with that of checks and balances. If checks and balances are considered to be of the essence of the doctrine, as they are by Montesquieu, the founding fathers, Friedrich, and countless others, especially Americans, then obviously change is much more difficult since all branches of government would have to agree to it. The American supporters of checks and balances argue that these devices are essential if each of the three 'grand departments' is to be able to protect itself against encroachment. But in protecting itself one branch often uses a power which is characteristic of another; thus checks and balances lead to a partial breakdown of separation of powers. As a result each function is only largely or primarily in the hands of a single branch, and each branch is only partly, even though it may be in large part, independent of the others. Of course this could be the case even without checks and balances, but it cer-

tainly seems to be more so with them. Just as the British often differ from the Americans regarding the functions to be separated, so they differ on the necessity for checks and balances as an essential element of separation of powers. There are some, however, who argue for checks as a part of the system and claim that the British have such checks. But even they would tend to agree with those who do not consider checks and balances necessary in pointing out that the British system is different from the American. For in Britain 'the supremacy of Parliament is the chief organic principle of the Constitution' (H. R. G. Greaves, *The British Constitution* (1938), London: Allen & Unwin, 6th impression, 1958, p. 13) whereas in the United States the three branches are presumably co-ordinate with no one subordinate to another. Essentially then the checks lead to a different kind of balance and those insisting upon the American balance of co-ordinates as essential to separation of powers naturally tend to deny the existence of separation of powers in the British system. In terms of the problem of change, it is interesting to note that the American system of three co-ordinate branches checking and balancing each other probably makes change more difficult than the British system of checking and balancing within the framework of parliamentary supremacy and cabinet government.

Warren Roberts

See also: CHECKS AND BALANCES

Sexuality

A. *Sexuality* denotes the complex of drives, attitudes, habits, and actions of an organism organized around coition. Social science disciplines differ in the elements they include in the complex and in the emphases they place on the various elements included.

B. The dominant current view of *sexuality* in psychology may be exemplified in the work of C. L. Hull, who developed a general theory in which *drive* (q.v.) and *need* (q.v.) are central concepts. He says that the primary drives are 'innate or reflex tendencies to action'; among them is the one related to the maintenance of species, which leads to sexual intercourse (*Principles of Behavior*, New York: Appleton-Century-Crofts, 1943, pp. 59–60). Hence the sexual drive is hereditary. Most of the laboratory studies utilize animals, especially the albino rat, on the assumption that there is considerable psychological equivalence between these species

636

and the human. G. Murphy subsumes 'sexual tension, deriving initially from gonad and other endocrine tensions', under 'visceral drives' (*Personality*, New York: Harper & Brothers, 1947, p. 105). Another work asserts that 'society is far from being completely successful in thwarting' the sexual drive, which is listed as a 'primary drive state' and which has proved to be 'clearly related to the action of ... the gonads, or sex glands' (D. D. Wickens & D. R. Meyer, *Psychology*, New York: Dryden Press, 1955, pp. 130, 118, 121).

C. The psychoanalytic conception of sexuality is the most inclusive of all. 'We call the doubtful and indefinable pleasure activities of earliest childhood sexual' (S. Freud, *A General Introduction to Psychoanalysis*, trans. by G. S. Hall, New York: Boni & Liveright, 1935, p. 285). Sexuality includes not only heterosexual intercourse, but also 'friendship, ideals, parent-child affection, love of abstractions, self-love, etc., and all pleasant bodily sensations' (I. Hendricks, *Facts and Theories of Psychoanalysis*, London: Kegan Paul, Trench, Trubner, 1934, p. 29). Sexuality is also held to express itself in concealed, non-sexual behaviour known as 'symbolism'. One's allegedly repressed sexual impulses exert themselves in ways that one cannot control. Thus a detective or a scientist is held to be unconsciously motivated by an unrequited infantile sexual curiosity; a violator of the immigration laws really is either rejecting his mother by his emigration or expressing his incestuous wishes through his illegal entry; and so on. Law and order are held to be sublimations of anal eroticism. Psychoanalysis has had much influence in clinical psychology and psychiatry.

D. The approach of anthropology, social psychology, and sociology is radically different. Most generally, their position can be stated as follows. The patterning of human sexual responses is learnt through symbolically mediated experience in particular groups; every society embodies in its customs, institutions, and language, the biological distinction between the sexes, exemplified in the differentiation of social roles for the respective sexes; the system of sexual social roles tends to change with socio-cultural change.

Human sexuality has six distinct characteristics.

1. It is contained within and controlled by a normatively governed process of selection. The selection is guided in part by the dual tendencies of rules of endogamy and exogamy (q.v.). The incest taboo, in either custom or law, dictates the degree of relationship within which marriage and mating are prohibited. Endogamy guides the degree of relationship outside of which marriage ought not to occur. In the United States there are legal definitions of incest but not of exogamy, except for those states that prohibit interracial intermarriage. The tendency is for marital choice to be made on racial, religious, ethnic, financial, and occupational lines, perhaps in that order.

2. Emotionally intense and more or less permanent unions are formed. In stark contrast are the sexual relations of animals, which are periodic, momentary, and unselective. No animal's sexual behaviour is ever guided by any form or degree of incest taboo, or by moral beliefs.

3. Human sexual behaviour is not necessarily procreative. The differential birth rates and sexual practices, and their trends, show that it can be recreational also. In Western society at least, and in the United States in particular, sex has developed into an interpersonal relationship of love, a significant component of which is the personality of the participants. Sex can be aesthetic and symbolic, as shown in the various arts. It can also be put to commercial use, without involving prostitution, as exemplified by advertising.

4. Human sexual behaviour is partly rational in that there is a decision to have or not to have sexual relations; this sexual decision involves both parties. A sexual thought, a sexual feeling, or sexual relations depend on a process of thinking by which a man concludes that a given female is a member of a certain category—such as girl, woman, sweetheart, wife, sister, mother, friend, stranger—and tends *then* to react toward her both with the behaviour appropriate to one of her class and his interpretation of the current situation. This reasoning precedes whatever overt sexual gesture toward her that he may make. Women are likewise selective and deliberate, since they evidently do not offer themselves indiscriminately to the nearest male. Thus human beings decide to engage in or to abstain from sexual relations; it is not known whether men or women more often take the initiative. The decision is guided by religious, moral, esthetic, or other values, and perhaps by fear of the consequences.

5. Human sexuality is subject to cultural variation among societies and sub-groups of societies. Forms of mating acceptable in one

Shaman

group may be prohibited in other groups. Sexual practices, including homosexuality, forms of sex play prior to intercourse, and means of sexual attraction, among other elements of the sexual complex, vary from society to society and within societies. Such variation is due primarily to social and cultural approval and disapproval.

6. In all human societies sexuality manifests itself to some degree in ways which run counter to the values of the society. In part this may be due to variation in strength of sex drive or to other biological factors. In such cases what is deviant will depend on the content of the cultural value system. But to a considerable degree deviation in sexuality from the normative pattern may itself derive from social and cultural sources, and manifest itself in sub-culture patterns.

Frank E. Hartung

See also: ENDOGAMY
INCEST
LIBIDO
LOVE
MARRIAGE

Shaman (Also Shamanism)

A. The most general usage of *shaman* denotes a specialist in healing, divination and allied social functions, allegedly by techniques of spirit possession and spirit control.

Shamanism denotes that particular form of spirit mediumship in which a specialist (the *shaman*) normally himself a medium, is deemed to exercise developed techniques of control over spirits, sometimes including mastery of spirits believed to be possessing another medium.

B. 1. The word *shaman* is from the Russian—derived from a Siberian term usually transliterated as *saman*, commonly said to be Tungus (see S. M. Shirokogoroff, *Psychomental Complex of the Tungus*, London: Kegan Paul, Trench, Trubner, 1935, pp. 268–9). The precise attribution varies. Thus Czaplicka derives *saman* from the Manchu, meaning one who is moved, exalted, excited. (Derivation from Pali, *samana* (Skr. *sramana*) a Buddhist monk or mendicant, through Chinese *sha men*, is dubious).

2. The term was introduced to Western literature by Russians who first met with the Tungus in the 17th century. 'In all Tungus languages this term refers to persons of both sexes who have mastered spirits, who at their will can introduce these spirits into themselves and use their power over the spirits in their own interests, particularly helping other people, who suffer from the spirits; in such a capacity they may possess a complex of special methods for dealing with the spirits' (ibid., p. 269).

Shamans were at first regarded as 'pagan sorcerers' but later studies attributed divinatory and healing functions to the shaman.

3. Opinions have differed as to the degree to which the phenomena associated with *shamans* may be generalized as *shamanism*. L. Schott, W. Radloff, and others working in the North Asian field saw in the phenomena a systematic set of ritual practices. Schott seems to have been responsible for generalizing the material. 'By shamanism we understand, as is known, the spirit worship connected with exorcism, which already from time immemorial was widespread in the highlands of inner Asia, in the whole of North Asia, and in north-east Europe' ('Uber den Doppelsinn des Wortes Schamene ...', *Abhandlungen der Preussischen Akademie der Wissenschaften*, Berlin, 1842, pp. 461).

Later anthropologists have also used the term *shamanism* and some, e.g. W. Howells, have followed Radloff (*Das Schamentum und Sein Kultus*, 1885) in using the verb *shamanize*. But others, e.g. A. L. Van Gennep, have asserted that there are no shamanistic beliefs or cults; there is only a certain category of persons, playing a specific social and religious role.

4. The terms *shaman* and *shamanism* have been relatively infrequently used by British writers, who have often used *spirit possession* (q.v.) instead, or interchangeably, e.g. S. F. Nadel (*The Nuba*, London: Oxford University Press, 1947, p. 440): 'Like the classical shamanism of North America and Central Asia, the spirit cult of these Nuba tribes centres round individuals capable of producing a state of trance and mental dissociation, which is interpreted as spirit possession'. But *spirit possession* seems too broad a term to specify the social functions and active controlling role characteristic of the shaman.

C. 1. In modern ethnography the terms *shaman* and *shamanism* have been extended to cover a range of analogous phenomena in many parts of the world, especially among Eskimos and American Indian peoples, but there has not been agreement as to their scope. Thus, by some writers the term shaman has been used very broadly for *any specialist who is concerned with the maintenance or restoration of the equilibrium of individuals or a society by ritual means*.

(a) E. D. Chapple and C. S. Coon (*Principles*

of Anthropology, London: Cape, 1947, pp. 397–9, 407) used the term *shaman* as synonymous with priest. They conceived of shamans becoming increasingly specialized, each class of specialist handling a narrow field of ritual techniques, e.g. canoe magic, fishing magic, garden magic (ibid.).

(b) Other American anthropologists equate shaman with medicine man.

(c) R. H. Lowie regarded the shaman as one who has communication with spirits.

(d) Emphasis upon different functions of the shaman in different societies has produced combined terms such as *shaman-priest* (R. Redfield, *Folk Culture of Yucatan*, Chicago: The University of Chicago Press, 1941, p. 128), *shaman-doctor* (A. L. Kroeber, *Anthropology*, New York: Harcourt, Brace, 1948, pp. 298, 565).

(e) W. Howells (*The Heathens: Primitive Man and his Religions*, London: V. Gollancz, 1949) tends to align *shaman* and *witch-doctor*. He points out that when a shaman goes into action, the result is not a rite but a seance.

2. Other writers have made various distinctions between shamans and other kinds of ritual practitioners.

(a) R. Piddington defines one difference thus: 'Shamans are broadly distinguished from priests, in that their activities are related to private or individual magic, such as diagnosing and curing illness, exorcizing evil spirits and providing charms to ensure success or good luck. The term *priest*, on the other hand, is usually restricted to the functionaries who carry out public ceremonies on behalf of the community at large. But in many cultures, for example among the Eskimo, we find the two functions combined in the same individual' (*Introduction to Social Anthropology*, London: Oliver & Boyd, 1950, vol. I, p. 365).

(b) W. Howells distinguishes priests as servitors of gods, properly speaking, from typical magicians who ignore gods or spirits and typical shamans who try to 'bullyrag' them (*The Heathens: Primitive Man and his Religions*, p. 226).

3. The difference of usage depends primarily upon the *criteria regarded as distinctive of a shaman*. M. Eliade (*Le Chamanisme*, Paris: Payot, 1951) has expressed a general view in stating that it is inacceptable to assimilate the typical condition of a shaman to the category of a *mental malady*.

(a) But it has often been pointed out that a typical shaman belongs to a particular *psychological type*. A. Goldenweiser (*Anthropology*,

London: Harrap, 1937, p. 260) contrasts the highly-strung, often neurotic shamans of Siberia and Central America with the 'perfectly normal' magicians of Australia, distinguished by their commonsense and shrewdness rather than by psychic qualities.

(b) W. Howells and others have emphasized the *intellectual qualities* of the shaman as a *leader*.

(c) Other definitions of shamanism focus on the *content* of the performances—drumming, singing, etc. Again the specific *functions* performed have been taken as critical—as by Bouteiller, who equates shamanism with magical healing.

(d) More commonly, the most significant criterion of shamanism is taken to be the *state* attained by the practitioner—that of dissociation, trance behaviour or 'ecstasy'.

R. W. Firth

See also: SPIRIT MEDIUMSHIP
 SPIRIT POSSESSION
 SPIRITUALISM

Short Ballot (See **Ballot**)

Sib

A. A *sib* is a social group in which all of the members recognize a kinship bond based upon the assumption of common descent in the matrilineal or patrilineal line, to the exclusion of the other line; and in which the demonstration of genealogical relationships between and among the various members is not considered necessary or pertinent.

B. 1. F. S. Philbrick used *sib* in the modern sense in 1918 in his translation of R. Huebner's *History of Germanic Private Law* (Boston: Little, Brown, 1918, pp. 114–6). However, it was R. H. Lowie who was responsible for introducing the word to the anthropological profession. In 1920 he called attention to the 'hopeless confusion of nomenclature' in the designation of kinship units which reckon descent unilaterally and observed that the situation 'imperatively calls for a new word and the one chosen is recommended alike by its alluring brevity and phonetic suggestiveness'. Lowie equated *sib* with the *clan* (q.v.) of British anthropologists and defined it simply as a 'unilateral kinship group' (*Primitive Society*, New York: Boni & Liveright, 1920, p. 111).

2. In the years immediately following, the bulk of American anthropologists, and a good many others adopted the clarifying new term

Sibling

which, for the first time, provided a designation for unilateral reckoning with no commitment or implication as to whether the system be matrilineal or patrilineal. Lowie, however, was disturbed by the failure of British anthropologists to employ the term. In 1934 he reverted to the more ambiguous term *clan* (*An Introduction to Cultural Anthropology*, New York: Farrar & Rinehart, 1934, p. 254). In 1948 he explained his abandonment of *sib*: 'Because of the former conflict between British and American usage, I suggested the Anglo-Saxon "sib" for unilateral groups irrespective of descent, but since the proposal was not generally adopted, I have reverted to prevalent British and French terminology' (*Social Organization*, New York: Rinehart, 1948, p. 237). Lowie's evaluation of continental usage as worthy of emphasis superior to that accorded American practice is a view obviously not shared by his many North American colleagues who have continued to use *sib*. G. P. Murdock, for example, comments that 'This exceedingly useful term has not yet achieved the universal acceptance which it deserves' (*Social Structure*, New York: The Macmillan Co., 1949, p. 47).

C. According to Lowie, *sib* organization is characterized by the following:

1. In sib organization the immediate or *nuclear family* (q.v.) is bilateral; but beyond it kinship is traced '... through *either* parent to the total neglect of the other' (*Primitive Society*, p. 111).

2. 'Sib mates of the same generation usually call one another siblings, and from this, given the primitive attitude towards names, it is but a step to feeling that marriage between sib-mates would be incestuous. Hence we find as one of the most common traits of the sib the law of exogamy' (ibid., p. 113).

3. 'In my opinion the transmission of property rights and the mode of residence after marriage have been the most effective means of establishing the principle of unilateral descent...' (ibid., p. 157).

4. The levirate (q.v.) and sororate (q.v.) appear to be older than the sib and 'they can and often have produced the classification of relatives characteristic of the sib' (ibid., p. 163).

5. The sib is extremely variable in its associations. It may be linked with plants and animals but need not be. It may be local or non-local; political or non-political (ibid., pp. 121–2).

D. As a consequence of his recent extensive and exacting exploration of patterns of kinship, in

which he used data from 250 societies, G. P. Murdock refined *sib* without, however, changing the basic criteria. He found it necessary to expand the terminology for associated patterns and practices and to recognize that not all unilateral kinship groups are properly sibs: 'When the members of a consanguineal kin group acknowledge a traditional bond of common descent in the paternal or maternal line, but are unable always to trace the actual genealogical connections between individuals, the group is called a *sib*. ... Some unilinear societies lack true sibs, possessing only lineages. The great majority, however, possess sibs, which are the most characteristic of all unilinear consanguineal kin groups. A sib normally includes several lineages, though these need not be culturally defined. Groups intermediate between sibs and lineages, which are found in some societies, may be called *sub-sibs*' (*Social Structure*, p. 47).

E. As mentioned by Lowie, sibs often are associated by name or tradition with an animal, plant or some other object of nature. In some instances this has significance in terms of the older concept of *totemism* (q.v.). However, it is abundantly proved that totemism is no necessary criterion of sib organization. It is furthermore highly probable that the pattern of unilateral descent sometimes derives from the concept of descent from a common ancestor with the simplification of reckoning which gives the unilateral scheme so great an advantage over the bilateral. But descent from a single named and celebrated common ancestor is not by any means a necessary criterion of sib grouping. It is merely the bond of assumed common descent which must be present.

Verne F. Ray

See also:　Clan
　　　　　　Descent
　　　　　　Gens
　　　　　　Lineal
　　　　　　Residence
　　　　　　Totemism
　　　　　　Unilineal

Sibling

A. A *sibling* is a brother or sister. A male sibling is a brother; a female sibling is a sister. Where one sibling has only one parent in common with another sibling, each is a half-sibling. Sibling is always a relational term but the relationship is not always restricted to blood brother and sisters or even to blood relations at all: the relationship may be a classificatory one extending to blood relatives of the same generation, or it may be purely social as resulting from marriage or adoption.

B. The term *sibling* has been borrowed by social scientists from biology, where it is often used in the shorter form, *sib*, and designates a brother or sister. 'Sibling: full siblings are persons of either sex who have the same father and mother. Two persons who are children of the same mother and different fathers, or of the same father by different mothers, are half-siblings' (*Notes and Queries in Anthropology*, London: Routledge & Kegan Paul, 6th edn., 1951, p. 71). A. R. Radcliffe-Brown makes explicit the nature of the situation where there may be plural marriages: 'A group of siblings is constituted by the sons and daughters of a man and his wife in monogamous societies, or of a man and his wives where there is polygyny, or of a woman and her husbands in polyandrous communities' ('The Study of Kinship Systems', *Journal of the Royal Anthropological Institute*, vol. LXXI, 1941, p. 7).

C. In anthropology the term occurs principally in studies of kinship filling a gap in common English parlance, where there is no generic expression for indicating a brother or sister without designating sex. The word not only makes for simplicity but fits cases where the designation of sex is unnecessary or undesirable. Psychologists have given wide currency to the term through the expression *sibling rivalry*.

D. The study of sibling relationships is an important part of the kinship investigations of anthropologists. R. Linton, for example, suggests that the brother-sister relationship is the core of the consanguine family (*The Study of Man*, New York: Appleton-Century, 1936, p. 159). Whether this is true or not, it can be said that important obligations are assigned in consanguine family systems to brothers and sisters. These obligations or similar ones can be assigned to blood relatives who are not biological siblings by socially classifying them as siblings. Thus in an agnatic consanguine family system, parallel cousins (q.v.) may be classed as siblings. In a still more attenuated fashion, the members of an extended blood grouping may be considered to have sibling obligations, hence the term sib (q.v.) for such groupings.

W. A. Lessa

See also: SIB

Sign

A. *Sign* denotes any stimulus which, because of association with another stimulus, elicits a response appropriate to but in the absence of the original stimulus.

Usage is affected by the distinctions drawn between sign and symbol (q.v.). Much discussion has also turned on the relationship between signs and language. 'Words', writes B. Russell 'are a particular case of *signs*. We may say that a given organism O, a member of a class of stimuli A is a sign of some member of a class of objects B if the occurrence to O of a stimulus of Class A produces a reaction appropriate to an object of Class B' (*Human Knowledge*, London: Allen & Unwin, 1948, p. 199).

For W. James 'Language is a system of *signs*, different from the things signified but able to suggest them' (*Principles of Psychology*, New York: Henry Holt, 1905, vol. II, p. 356).

B. In social science, the use of the term *sign* is generally associated with the attempt to differentiate between man and the other animals. In this context it is usually noted that, although all animals respond to signs, only man responds systematically to symbols (q.v.). Sign is normally used as a generic term under which symbol is subsumed as a particular type. (This relationship between sign and symbol is not universally accepted, however. Cf. H. Bonner, *Social Psychology*, New York: American Book Co., 1953, pp. 45–6). In this most general sense, the definition of *sign* used by A. R. Lindesmith and A. L. Strauss (*Social Psychology*, New York: Dryden Press, 1949, p. 40) is probably as representative as any: 'a stimulus which calls for a response that is the same as or similar to the response previously evoked by some other stimulus'. C. Morris equates sign with cue and states that a sign serves 'to control behavior in the way something else would exercise control if it were present' (*Signs, Language and Behavior*, New York: Prentice-Hall, 1946, p. 95). Morris also uses the term signal for those signs which are not symbols, but this terminology is not widely accepted.

C. This broad definition of *sign* encompasses everything from the simple associated stimuli in basic conditioning experiments to the most complex abstractions of a written language. Thus sign-behaviour is found in all levels of animal life. As S. K. Langer puts it: 'The use of signs is the very first manifestation of mind. It

Slavery

arises as early in biological history as the famous "conditioned reflex", by which a concomitant of a stimulus takes over the stimulus-function. The concomitant becomes a *sign* of the condition to which the reaction is really appropriate' (*Philosophy in a New Key*, Cambridge, Mass.: Harvard University Press, 1942, p. 29).

There is little difference of opinion in this aspect of the use of the term. Differences do occur, however, when attempts are made to differentiate between symbols and other kinds of signs and to define the nature of the relationship between the sign and the thing it signifies. This latter relationship is the central core of the 'problem of meaning' which has plagued philosophers, psychologists, and social scientists for centuries.

Alan C. Kerckhoff

See also: COMMUNICATION
MEANING
SYMBOL

Simple Random Sampling (See **Sampling**)

Slavery

A. *Slavery* is an institution involving a degree of domination-subordination between persons, ranging from the right of life and death of the owner over the slave to carefully detailed legal provisions for mutual rights and privileges; the essential element of the arrangement being the right of a master to force a slave to labour or render other services for the master's benefit. *Commercial slavery* has, in recent times at least, been associated almost wholly with plantation agriculture in regions of labour scarcity; *domestic slavery* has had a more widespread association with the provision of household and personal services. The institution has at its centre not only a set of normative rules, but also a set of rationalizations justifying the practice: usually these rationalizations set forth the supposed religious and economic benefits to the slaves, and the alleged biological inferiority of the slaves.

B. Slavery is a very old institution, although it is not often found in collecting, hunting, or pastoral economies, since some degree of complex agriculture or industrialization is necessary before slavery is profitable (although industrialization also tends to make more efficient use of free labour). It was present in the ancient world, even in Athens, where Aristotle (*Politics*, trans.

by B. Jowett, Oxford: Clarendon Press, 1905, I 4 : 2, p. 31) regarded slavery as a natural consequence of the occurrence of dominance and submission and defined a slave as 'a living possession'. Under Roman law the slave was legally defined as not a person, but a thing serving as a medium for the master's aims (G. Landtman, *The Origin of the Inequality of the Social Classes*, London: Kegan Paul, Trench, Trubner, 1938, p. 228). Landtman makes it clear, however, that Roman slaves were given certain legal rights and protection.

Slavery lasted in parts of Europe throughout the Middle Ages, but was ameliorated by the influence of the Christian religion. In the early days of slavery in European culture, slavery was rationalized as being a means by which the slaves were elevated from barbarism, brought into a superior culture, and offered religious salvation—particularly aiding the slave to fulfil and work out the curse placed on his original ancestor, Noah's son Ham, for the sin of ridiculing his father. In the later days of Western slavery, particularly in the United States, the biblical argument tended to be replaced by the arguments concerning the biological inferiority of the slaves and the goodness of slavery as a 'part of a greater social order which established an ideal division of labor and of responsibility . . . [in which] . . . the principle of rational co-operation was realized; "By making the labor itself capital, the conflict of interest, so evident in other labor systems, lost its foundation" ' (G. Mydral et al., *An American Dilemma*, New York: Harper & Bros., 1944, p. 442).

In modern times, slavery has been confined to the plantation areas of the Western hemisphere settled by Europeans, and the Moslem countries where there is a demand for concubines and other household servants. The 20th century saw the revival of slavery in those industrial societies which underwent totalitarian revolutions, e.g. Nazi Germany. The tenacity of the institution is indicated by the fact that in September 1956, 33 members of the United Nations signed a supplementary convention, seeking to correct conditions of slavery reported by a study commission in 1949 ('Thirty-Three Nations Sign Anti-Slavery Convention', *United Nations Review*, vol. 3, no. 4, 1956, pp. 6–7). The topic of slavery has remained one of interest to scholars (see, for example, M. I. Finley (ed.), *Slavery in Classical Antiquity*, Cambridge: Heffer, 1960, and S. M. Elkins, *Slavery*, Chicago: University of Chicago Press, 1959).

Harry E. Moore

Social

A. In its broadest usage the term, as applied to human beings, refers to any behaviour or attitude that is influenced by past or present experience of the behaviour of other people (direct or indirect), or that is oriented (consciously or unconsciously) toward other people. Normally the term is morally neutral.

B. Various elements of what is *social* in the above broad interpretation may be emphasized or excluded in narrower definitions.

1. A major ambiguity is the uncertainty about whether *social* refers only to situations in which there is interaction. Feeding a newborn baby when it cries is not usually considered interaction and certainly does not involve symbolic interaction, yet the act of the mother does take account of the behaviour of the infant.

2. The relations between the terms *social* and *cultural* (see *Culture*) are confused. *Social* may be defined so broadly that *cultural* is a sub-category of the social. Thus prayer may be regarded as social because it is 'socially' influenced by the 'cultural heritage'; culture is then part of what is social. Or, by contrast, this act and other phenomena may be regarded as cultural but not social, in which case the term *social* is relevant only when direct interaction among humans is involved. Finally these usages may be modified in such a way that *social* is limited to behaviour that is modified by culture *and* involves interaction; *social* then becomes a sub-category of cultural. The common elements in these seemingly contradictory usages are clear, however. *Social* refers to interaction, whatever else it refers to and *cultural* stresses normative and cognitive patterns for action rather than interaction as such.

3. The term *social* is sometimes confined, in what seems an unduly restrictive view, to corporate, purposefully organized group action.

4. *Social* is sometimes given a moral connotation, implying action directed in some sense toward the welfare of others—and usually toward the welfare either of a whole society or its less privileged members.

5. *Social* is often used, without any necessary moral colouring, to imply an awareness of the feelings and attitudes of others, and behaviour influenced by such awareness. Here the stress is on sensitivity, regardless of how it comes into existence or is sustained.

C. Arnold Anderson

Social Accounting (See National Income and Social Accounting)

Social Act

A. *Social act* denotes any attitudinally-organized and goal-directed activity by one or more participants who are objects to themselves (selves). It consists of three parts: (a) *attitudinal anticipations* in the form of plans of action, entering on agenda, scheduling, etc.; (b) *organized, directed activity according to role definition*, established by social norms and invoked through expectations by significant others (reference groups), accompanied by continuing communication, self-indication and self-appraisal; (c) *symbolic goal achievement*, which may have no more relevance to satisfying organic needs than would any ritualistic manipulation of social objects.

B. The term *social act* is widely used by social psychologists, both in sociology and psychology, as the basic unit for observation of human behaviour. The term has a great many divergent referents, however, depending on the overall orientation involved.

1. To those who hold some variety of 'learning theory' orientation, the general scheme for viewing human behaviour is to regard all behaviours as emanating, in the first instance, from *individual* (genetically formed and physiologically definable) drives and motives. Interpersonal and social phenomena are derivative and consequent to these antecedent matters. In such a scheme a social act is most likely to be described as a sequence of behaviours in which some movement of *A* serves as a stimulus to *B*, whose response serves in turn as a stimulus to *A*, and so on, for the duration of such interstimulation and thus of the social act. Some go further and see a given individual's response, say *B*'s, as serving further as a secondary stimulus to *B* himself (see, inter alia, L. W. Doob, *Social Psychology*, New York: Henry Holt, 1952, esp. ch. 19).

2. A similar view of the social act divides it sequentially into *perceptual*, *motoric*, and *consummatory* parts, made social by there being the necessary involvement, in the motoric part, with one or more other persons. K. Young, otherwise much influenced by symbolic-interactionist views, defines the act in much this way: '... the process from drive through cue and response to reinforcement or reward requires the intercession of another individual' (*Social Psychology*, New York: Appleton-Century-Crofts, 3rd edn., 1956, p. 120). 'Reduced to its simplest form a *social act* is an act of a person [which is not completed without the intercession ... of

643

Social Anthropology

another person or persons]' (*Personality and Problems of Adjustment*, New York: Appleton-Century-Crofts, 2nd edn., 1952, p. 154).

3. The critics of the view which conceives the act from perceptual stimulation through motoric action to goal consummation argue that the scheme is derived from animal psychology; human beings, they say, initiate acts, often as *teams*, in terms of *institutional definitions* (rather than being individually triggered into action by external perceptual cues). They argue further that perception is a constant accompaniment to action, but far from being the independent variable (to which human behavioural direction is the dependent variable) perception is generally describable as being in significant respects a *dependent* variable in regard to which intention, goal or plan of action (attitude) is the *independent* variable.

4. The basic issue appears to be whether human behaviour can be successfully studied by taking into account only 'externally' or objectively visible variables (stimuli, serving either as cues or drives, and responses); or whether one must take into account 'meanings for the individual actors'—selves, social objects, attitudes, meaningful others (reference groups), and the meanings of the goals (or outcomes of acts) for the participants *themselves*.

5. G. H. Mead probably did more than anyone else to promote this latter point of view (*Mind, Self and Society*, Chicago: University of Chicago Press, 1934; *The Philosophy of the Act*, Chicago: University of Chicago Press, 1938). 'An act is an impulse that maintains the life-process by the selection of certain sorts of stimuli it needs. Thus, the organism creates its environment'. 'I wish ... to restrict the social act to the class of acts which involve the co-operation of more than one individual, and whose object as defined by the act ... is a social object ... one that answers to all the parts of the complex act, though these parts are found in ... the life-process of the group, not in those of the separate individuals alone' (from footnotes in *Mind, Self and Society*, pp. 6–7). Mead thus substituted for the perceptual, the *attitudinal* as the first or anticipatory part of the act. Given the appropriate attitudes the individual *searches* for the relevant percepts. It is chiefly a derivative of Mead's position which the contemporary symbolic interactionist represents, with his paradigm of the social act furnished with the concepts of attitude, social object, self and significant others (reference groups).

6. Mead stressed other covert features of the act as well as that of anticipatory attitude (e.g. thinking, continuous self-appraisal). It remained for E. Faris to classify acts as *immediate*, *delayed*, *frustrated*, and *retrospective* ('The Retrospective Act', *Journal of Educational Sociology*, vol. 14, 1940, pp. 79–91). In his discussion of the retrospective act (one which 'has for its end the consideration of another act') Faris extended Mead's basic idea that it is in the the social act that self and meaning arise. He also extended Mead's general notions about the relation of *time* to human behaviour. It is time which has proved most troublesome to the proponents of the stimulus-response model of the act, for that model is appropriate only to 'immediate' acts in Faris's terms. Most human acts extend considerably through time; further, they involve, in their covert aspects, attitudes and expectations that may extend quite far, forwards and backwards in time.

7. Even Mead's and Faris's models of the social act appear individualistic when compared with the contemporary dramatistic models of K. Burke, E. Goffman, and N. Foote. Burke's collateral concepts with act include Scene, Agent, Agency, Purpose (*A Grammar of Motives*, New York: Prentice-Hall, 1945, pp. x, xi). He stresses consciousness or intent as the necessary ingredient of the act (ibid., p. 14). Goffman, who does not use the concept, act, as such, uses such suggestive terms from the theatre as performance, scene, setting, audience, team, routine. His accounts of team-performances are good 'representative anecdotes' for describing the social act (see *The Presentation of Self in Everyday Life*, Garden City, N.Y.: Doubleday Anchor Books, 1959).

Manford Kuhn

See also: REFERENCE GROUP
ROLE
SELF
SOCIAL INTERACTION

Social Anthropology

A. The usages of the term *social anthropology* are too varied and too overlapping with *cultural anthropology* and *ethnology* and *ethnography* to permit the formulation of a single definition.

B. The term is more widely used in Great Britain and the British Commonwealth than in the United States, but it is used in both areas (see, for example, P. Radin, *Social Anthropology*, New York: McGraw-Hill, 1932). One of the earliest British discussions in the field was that of J. G. Frazer (*The Scope of Social Anthropology*, London: Macmillan, 1908). Frazer reserved the term for 'one particular department' (ibid., p. 4) of the study of society: '... the sphere of Social Anthropology as I understand it, or at least as I propose to treat it, is limited to the crude beginnings, the rudimentary development of human society' (ibid., p. 6). 'Its province,' he contends, 'may be roughly divided into two departments, one of which embraces the customs and beliefs of savages, while the other includes such relics of these customs and beliefs as have survived in the thought and institutions of more cultured people' (ibid., p. 11). A later discussion which was influenced by the work of Durkheim and his successors in France is that of A. R. Radcliffe-Brown, 'The Methods of Ethnology and Social Anthropology' (*South African Journal of Science*, vol. 20, 1923, pp. 124–47, reprinted in A. R. Radcliffe-Brown, *Method in Social Anthropology*, Chicago: University of Chicago Press, 1958, pp. 3–38). He distinguishes social anthropology from ethnology (q.v.) throughout —both from legitimate ethnology and from the forms of conjectural history with which 19th-century ethnologists had been obsessed. He believed (ibid., p. 8) that the term *social anthropology* should apply to 'the study that seeks to formulate the general laws that underlie the phenomena of culture'. Such a study would yield 'inductive generalizations' which 'can tell us how and why things happen, i.e. according to what laws' (ibid., p. 30); whereas ethnology 'with its strictly historical method can only tell us that certain things have happened or have probably or possibly happened' (ibid., pp. 29–30). Following the tradition of Durkheim and the *Année Sociologique*, he was also at pains to distinguish psychology from social anthropology, holding that '... the former deals with individual behavior in its relation to the individual; the latter deals with the behavior of groups or collective bodies of individuals in its relation to the group' (ibid., p. 17). For later discussion of the scope of the field, following the Radcliffe-Brown tradition, reference should be made to E. E. Evans-Pritchard, *Social Anthropology* (London: Cohen & West, 1951).

C. Some American anthropologists regard social anthropology and cultural anthropology as identical or nearly identical in scope, taking ethnology to be the theoretical and generalizing aspect and ethnography the descriptive aspect of such a discipline. Thus M. Titiev says in his general textbook '... no distinction will be made between an ethnologist and a cultural or social anthropologist. Some shades of difference might be brought out by the use of separate terms, but there is too much overlap to warrant keeping them apart' (*The Science of Man*, New York: Henry Holt, 1954, p. 329, fn.). A. L. Kroeber (*Anthropology*, New York: Harcourt, Brace, 1948), either speaks of 'social and cultural anthropology' jointly or fuses them into a single term, *sociocultural anthropology*. Those writers who consider the distinction unnecessary tend to argue that all human social behaviour is influenced by cultural standards and definitions, and conversely that culture itself is essentially social, in its transmission and distribution among the members of a society.

D. Other American writers distinguish social from cultural anthropology usually on grounds similar to E. A. Hoebel's, who says that social anthropology studies '... social behavior *per se* and only very incidentally ... the technical aspects of material culture' (*Man in the Primitive World*, New York: McGraw-Hill, 1949, p. 5). Such works as G. P. Murdock's *Social Structure* (New York: The Macmillan Co., 1949) and R. H. Lowie's *Social Organization* (New York: Rinehart, 1948) would be examples of this discipline. Frequently, as is true of Hoebel, such writers view social anthropology as a part of cultural anthropology. This is not, however, necessarily the case.

Contemporary British anthropologists tend to conceive of *social anthropology* as denoting a broader field than do many Americans, making it synonymous with the broad usage of *cultural anthropology* in America or with *sociocultural anthropology*. Thus according to R. Firth, social anthropologists '... are usually said to study a society, a community, a culture ...' (*Elements of Social Organization*, London: Watts, 1951, p. 22). And S. F. Nadel, in discussing the scope of social anthropology, says '... neither "social" nor "cultural" anthropology defines our subject matter satisfactorily ... it is essentially two-dimensional, being always both "cultural" and "social" ' (*The Foundations of Social Anthropology*, Glencoe, Ill.: The Free Press, 1951). However, a great deal of the emphasis of British social anthropology is on organization and social structure, particularly kinship structure. Moreover, most British anthropologists do exclude one branch of sociocultural anthropology completely from social anthropology, namely, the pure historical study of the genetic

Social Causation

connections of cultures and the diffusion over time of cultural traits (E. E. Evans-Pritchard, *Social Anthropology*). This is because of strong British emphasis on the importance of understanding the functional relationships of culture traits in full context, which is generally impractical in historical-genetic studies. The British generally classify such studies under ethnology (q.v.) which they thus rigorously separate from social anthropology.

E. A number of writers, British and American, have commented on the essential similarity between sociology (q.v.) and social anthropology (an earlier discussion of this problem may be found in A. R. Radcliffe-Brown, *Method in Social Anthropology*, p. 8, fn.). Most anthropologists who discuss the difference hold that it lies in specific traditions, interests, and methods of work rather than in ultimate theoretical objectives. Specifically, social anthropology is held to be differentiated from sociology by being more concerned with small, non-literate societies, and by relying more on direct and intensive observations of social behaviour. But few anthropologists would exclude the study of large literate societies from their discipline, nor would they proscribe more typically 'sociological' methods of data collection such as the use of standard questionnaires on an extensive sample, or the examination of local documents where available.

John L. Fischer

See also: ETHNOLOGY (Also ETHNOGRAPHY)

Social Causation (Social Causality)

A. In its most general sense the term denotes the process whereby events are linked in terms of cause and effect. To say that one event is the cause of another is usually to intend either (a) that there is an invariable conjunction of the two events and that one is temporally prior to the other, or (b) that the events are related in such a way that, through general propositions and rules concerning their frame of reference and content, a relationship of logical implication holds between the appropriate elements of the descriptive system.

B. 1. In psychology, history, and sociology the word may also be used in a teleological sense. The cause of specific acts of goal attaining behaviour (or what is believed to be such) may be a desired goal of the individual or group.

2. Where attempts have been made to analyse causation involving the consideration of some larger number than two elements, R. M. MacIver (*Social Causation*, Boston: Ginn, 1942, ch. 6) has usefully introduced the notion of a *precipitating cause*: that is, of crucial events *without which* circumstances in a particular social situation remain *unchanged*; *with which*, they *change*. Something of the idea of biological and/or *Aristotelian* potentiality may be found here, but there is no necessary teleological implication.

C. 1. Much of sociological theory on causation or causality has been in terms of uni-causality; that is, the idea that one single species of events alone is efficient in social life. Examples of such theories are to be found in certain technico-economic interpretations of Marxism, in theories that would make culture a function of the earliest experiences of social life and training, etc. Such attempts to simplify social causation are often stimulating and useful but they have never been found ultimately effective. Sociological analysis has therefore tended to proceed in terms of a plurality of causes—which may or may not have been arranged in a hierarchy of importance—and in terms of seeing the answer to causal questions as differing with the differing purposes of investigation.

2. There is an attempt to escape by way of the idea of function from the whole concept of causation in the social sciences. In fact, it is very doubtful whether functionalism can operate in this manner. To explain institutions, etc., in terms of the function that they fulfil or the needs they satisfy for individuals and groups may replace the theory which places the primary emphasis on historical causality by one of necessary simultaneous (and continuing) relationships. This, however, is not to banish the idea of cause; it is merely to stress one kind of causality as against another. Most writers have found both theories of causality are in fact necessary in the causal analysis of concrete social situations.

3. Attempts have frequently been made, with most persistence in American sociology but also elsewhere, to limit the area of purely *social* causation and to try to find the causal basis of social phenomena in the structure of individual motivation and personality. It is probably true to say that there is a strong, if not always conscious bias, towards social nominalism (q.v.) or 'methodological individualism' in most modern American sociology, and in the work of Weber in Germany. This does not, of course, mean that there is any attempt to remove the category of cause, though there is one to identify it as taking place outside the sphere of the purely social. The opposite tendency, to treat societies as having real existence sui generis and apart from the particular individuals who constitute them is to be found in its most extreme form in Durkheim and his School in France, and in the followers of Radcliffe-Brown in British social anthropology. To these writers, social causality is to be explained by structural analysis and the necessities which such an analysis displays. It is probably true to say that the most fruitful methodological procedure—it is not necessarily a methodological principle—for sociology is to push structural analysis as far as is possible and only then turn to what can be learned from the study of motivation and personality.

It seems improbable that in fact any fruitful sociological system—as distinct from the statistical measurement of social phenomena—can proceed without the use of causal concepts and it can be taken as certain that no system of uni-causality is likely to do justice to the phenomena with which sociology and the social sciences are concerned.

D. There has been much discussion about the relationship between ideas of social causation and the problem of the freedom of the individual will, the role of the individual in history, and the possibility that societies are completely deterministic systems. Such discussion is important from the point of view of ethics and metaphysics, but there is little reason to believe that attempts to establish the existence of social causation in particular cases or to classify its varieties need involve themselves in these questions, although it is obvious that the successful solution of such problems would enable more precise delimitation of the role of individual freedom in social affairs.

D. G. MacRae

See also: DETERMINISM
FUNCTION
SOCIAL NOMINALISM

Social Change

A. 1. *Social change* denotes an observed difference from antecedent states of the social structure, institutions, habits, or equipment of a society *in so far as it is* (a) the outcome of legislative or other overt measures to control conduct; or (b) the product of a change either in a specified substructure or dominant sector of social existence, or in the physical or social environment; or (c) the repercussive effect of social actions pursued in conformity with the systematically related modes of fulfilling needs and meeting expectations which prevail in a society.

2. The term also denotes the process through which such differences occur.

B. 1. L. von Wiese ('Sociological Study of Social Change', *Trans. Third World Congress of Sociology*, London: International Sociological Association, 1956, vol. I, pp. 1–9) has recently attempted a review of the uses of the term, which has 'very largely displaced the terms "evolution" or "development" ' (ibid., p. 6). He specifies two main uses: (a) an almost, but not quite, neutralized, non-tendentious rendering of the idea of progress; and (b) statistical usage which makes *change* a purely quantitative conception (ibid., p. 7). He distinguishes social change from cultural change used mainly in regard to technique, and from social 'impact' which refers to influences on one sphere of life from another, and reserves the term for denoting 'alterations in man-man relationships' (ibid., p. 7).

M. Ginsberg ('Factors in Social Change', *Trans. Third World Congress of Sociology*, vol. I, pp. 10–19) understands by *social change* 'a change in social structure, e.g. in the size of a society, the composition or balance of its parts, or the type of organisation' (ibid., p. 10), and also concedes that artistic or linguistic changes may fall within the reference of the term. A. M. Rose proposes a reference exclusively intellectual and moral: 'Finally, we would define *social change* as modifications in the meanings and values held by society or by important sub-groups in the society' ('The Use of Law to Induce Social Change', *Trans. Third World Congress of Sociology*, vol. VI, p. 54).

2. There are other complications. *Social change* as the semantic heir of *progress* (q.v.) (and possible predecessor of *social dynamism*) had to be brought into service to account for the facts previously organized in terms of progress, social development, or even *social change* when this term is identified with progress. This is especially so with regard to attempts to describe or account for 'the laws according to which any state or society produces the state which succeeds it' (J. S. Mill, *A System of Logic*, London: John W. Parker, 1843, vol. II, p. 587); see for instance, N. Birnbaum, 'Conflicting Interpretations of the Rise of Capitalism: Marx and Weber' (*British Journal of Sociology*, vol.

Social Class

IV, 1953, pp. 125–41). There is a further interpretative act needed, and now customarily performed, in relating change as progress to earlier views such as 'The History of the Human Species as a whole may be regarded as the unravelling of a hidden Plan of Nature for accomplishing a perfect State of Civil Constitution for society' (I. Kant, 'Idea of a Universal History on a Cosmo Political Plan' (1784), trans. by T. de Quincey, *Collected Writings*, London: Black, vol. IX, p. 439). Similar mutations occur back to Aristotle, who reports, simpliciter, the 'invention' of social classes by the Egyptians (*Politics;* 1329 b).

3. Beyond the problem of scale, however, is the problem of the units to which it must be presumed social change is reducible. Thus Condorcet: 'Progress is subject to the same general laws that can be observed in the development of the individual, and it is indeed no more than the sum of that development realized in large numbers of individuals joined together in society'. The study of this developmental process 'is a record of change, and is based on the observation of human societies throughout the different stages of their development. It ought to reveal the order of this change and the influence that each moment exerts upon the subsequent moment' (*Sketch for a Historical Picture of the Progress of the Human Mind*, (1795), trans. J. Barraclough, London: Weidenfeld & Nicolson, 1955, p. 4). *Social change* may, accordingly, be regarded as 'everything that happens'. Questions of reductionism (q.v.), therefore, may and do complicate the meaning of the term; while reduction to basic units arranged in series according to rather mechanistic notions of cause is now unfashionable, psychological reductionism has appeared: 'Many of the changes which are recorded in the long time spans of conventional history (such as "the decay of the monarchy", or "the rise of popular government") occur sporadically in the behaviour of individuals, and only gradually become consolidated into identifiable pattern changes. While such changes are going on, innumerable moments of choice occur' (M. Mead, 'Character Formation and Diachronic Theory', in M. Fortes (ed.), *Social Structure*, London: Oxford University Press, 1949, p. 19).

4. The convenient lack of consistency in the referent of the term *social change* revealed in the first three citations (B. 1), all taken from papers delivered on the same occasion, is possibly a consequence of preoccupation with elucidating cause-effect sequences in human circumstances and conduct. Indeed, the one common feature of all contexts studied is the demonstration, or the presumption, that social change, in so far as it is attended to by sociologists, is the product of ascertainable causes.

Tom Burns

See also: CULTURE CHANGE

Social Character (See Basic Personality Structure)

Social Class (Also Class)
A. In its generic sense the term *class* is synonymous with the term *category* (q.v.). While it is frequently used in the social sciences in this sense, it has come to be more closely associated with the term *stratification* (q.v.). In its association with stratification it has sometimes been loosely used to denote all those individuals (or families) who possess within the framework of some society or community relatively the same amounts of power, income, wealth, or prestige or some loosely formulated combination of these elements. More strictly, however, *class* has denoted those holding a common position along some continuum of the economy. While this has sometimes been a continuum of wealth or income, and, at other times, occupations, in the strictest Marxist usage it has denoted basic forms of relationship to the modes of material production—i.e. those who control the instruments of material production and those who do not. Thus in a capitalist economy according to Marx the capitalist class controls the instruments of production, the proletariat does not. In contrast to *class*, *social class* has also been used loosely to denote any of the phenomena described above, but more strictly it has been used to denote all those families and/or individuals in a society or community that possess relatively equal status or prestige. In this usage *social class* has usually been restricted to such groups existing in relatively open systems of stratification, while *caste* (q.v.) has been used to denote them as they exist in closed systems of stratification.

B. 1. It should be possible, following M. Weber (*From Max Weber*, trans. and ed. by H. H. Gerth & C. W. Mills, New York: Oxford University Press, pp. 180–95), to separate analytically *class* as denoting market position, *social class* (or *status group*) as focused on prestige, style of life, and intimate interaction, and *party* as centred on power. But for several reasons, this has not been the case. Marxists, taking economic power based on the social relations related to the means of material production as the central variable, have assimilated market chances, other modes of power, occupational prestige, and style of life to class. Similarly, modern sociological functionalists, stressing the differential distribution of prestige as a basic motivating reward within a society based on value consensus, have tended to assimilate power to authority and market chances to the same occupations that receive prestige, so that class and party have become assimilated to social class (or status group). Thus it is not surprising that *class* and *social class* have become the most variable of major sociological terms. Some investigators may speak of a simple income category as a *class*, a *social class*, or an index of either, while others may use the term *class* to denote a stratum of positions whose members enjoy common life chances, common styles of life, common attitudes and ideologies towards self and society, consciousness of kind, and a sense of fundamental antagonism to other strata. And very frequently the terms are used interchangeably.

2. Be this as it may, increasing recognition is being given to the prevalence of 'multiple class' structures in Western societies, i.e. the presence of various interrelated hierarchies of invidiously ranked positions and of unequal privileges and powers. Since in theoretical discussion, *class* and *social class* are distinguished from other forms of closed and semi-closed systems of stratification, such as caste and estate systems, most modern Western societies are studied in terms of 'class', aside from the 'caste-like' elements which characterize some of them, e.g. the system of treatment of Negroes in the United States now undergoing major challenge. In such modern class systems kinship ties as marks of class position have almost vanished, most particularly in the United States, less so in England, France, and Italy.

C. 1. Empirical studies of class tend predominantly to concentrate on the methods of placing persons and families in their appropriate class position, upon mobility, and upon the consequences of differentiated class positions, rather than on the processes by which classes are formed or formalized. Among the consequences of social class position which have been studied among various kinds of population are: child-rearing practices; mental health and the treatment of mental illness; physical health; infant mortality; general demographic rates; various pathologies such as drug addiction, alcoholism, prostitution; educational facilities and accomplishments; rates of delinquency, crime, arrest, and imprisonment; voting behaviour; consumer preferences; marriage, divorce, and desertion rates; organizational memberships; racial and religious prejudice and discrimination; national and international political attitudes and preferences.

2. A noticeable trend in the past ten years has been an increase in the study of the patterns of social mobility, i.e. the patterns of social class disruption, and the circulation of new memberships into class structures. The emergence of labour unions and of government as powerful countervailing forces to big business, along with the impact of the GI Bill in the United States with its provision for free education, have fostered this new interest. So also, in the United States, the fears that social mobility is slowing down have played a part in motivating such studies. Important studies in this area are N. Rogoff, *Recent Trends in Occupational Mobility* (Glencoe, Ill.: Free Press, 1953), S. M. Lipset & R. Bendix, *Social Mobility in Industrial Societies* (Berkeley: University of California Press, 1959), and D. V. Glass, *Social Mobility in Britain* (London: Routledge & Kegan Paul, 1954).

3. Studies in political behaviour, particularly voting, organizational participation, party activity, etc., have shown considerable sensitivity to class position as a major independent variable. Some investigators have tended to insist that class and social class with their Marxian overtones fail adequately to capture the emerging congeries of interests around which political groups form, particularly in the United States. Lobby groups and interest groups have been suggested alternative concepts (cf. D. B. Truman, *The Governmental Process*, New York: Knopf, 1951). Against this tendency such other writers as C. W. Mills and R. Dahrendorf have formulated powerful arguments in such studies as *The Power Elite* (New York: Oxford University Press, 1957) and *Class and Class Conflict In Industrial Society* (Stanford, Cal.: Stanford University Press, 1959). These studies continue the earlier approaches in which class and social class were considered central to social organization, such as one finds in the Lynds' two books on Middletown (R. S. & H. M. Lynd, *Middletown*, New York: Harcourt, Brace, 1929; and *Middletown in Transition*, New York: Harcourt, Brace, 1937) and W. L. Warner et al., *Yankee*

Social Contact

City Series (New Haven: Yale University Press, 5 vols., 1941–59).

4. Considerable literary-sociological and sociological-journalistic attention has been focused on fringe class phenomena, particularly the formations and styles of urban living, the effects of egregious emphasis on standards of living, the quest for status, and the 'search for identity'. A considerable number of studies of race relations, particularly in the United States, have documented the importance of class differences between Negroes and Whites as an obstacle to desegregation, and of class differences within the Negro group as reflecting the same patterns of social distance as within the White group. Ethnic group differences and those among various religious groups have been shown to lose their clear-cut quality under the impact of equalization of style of life which results from sharing a common standard and level of living.

More recent approaches in social anthropology sometimes include simple class measures, even among non-literate groups. The emerging field of study concerned with culture and personality tends frequently to orient itself toward class variables. Various studies of emerging 'underdeveloped areas' of the world have suggested the problems being encountered and those yet to come when the impact of Westernization, industrialization, and 'status through wealth' are more fully felt.

Melvin M. Tumin

See also: CASTE
           MIDDLE CLASS
           STATUS
           STRATIFICATION
           WORKING CLASS

Social Cohesion (See Cohesion)

Social Contact

A. *Social contact* denotes the reciprocal orientation of persons or groups toward each other that is necessary both for the initiation of social interaction and/or its continuance. As in interaction the major elements involved in social contact are attitudes (q.v.) and values (q.v.), and when these are organized and integrated, roles (q.v.).

B. Among the early leaders of American sociology A. W. Small, R. E. Park, and E. W. Burgess introduced the term *social contact*. In his *General Sociology* (Chicago: University of Chicago Press, 1905, p. 487) Small defined the term as 'the different ways in which individuals are connected with each other', Park and Burgess (*Introduction to the Science of Sociology*, Chicago: University of Chicago Press, 1924, pp. 280, 282) wrote that 'contact may be considered as the initial stage of social interaction and preparatory to the later stages'. It 'conditions and controls the later stages of the process'.

The quotations above indicate that *social contact* is contact between persons and/or groups and that it is a prerequisite for the initiation of social interaction. This is true enough but somewhat superficial—not unlike saying that 'biological contact' is contact between plants and/or animals. The essence of *social contact* is that it is constituted by the meeting of persons who relate to one another in terms of attitudes and values, and that these latter are frequently organized into roles. Further it is apparent that such reciprocal orientation is a prerequisite not only for the initiation of social interaction, but also its continuance.

Rex D. Hopper

See also: ATTITUDE
           ROLE
           SOCIAL INTERACTION
           VALUE

Social Control

A. The term *social control* has two interrelated but significantly distinguishable meanings.

1. It denotes the fact that a person is conditioned and limited in his actions by the groups, community, and society of which he is a member; and that this limitation and conditioning of action performs functions (q.v.), latent or manifest, for the groups, community, and society, and in so far as the person shares the goals and norms of the social units, for the person himself.

2. It denotes the fact that in all social interaction, in so far as the person limits or conditions the actions of others or has his actions limited and conditioned by others, by social groups, communities, or societies of which he may or may not be a member, the mechanisms by which this limiting and conditioning occur are themselves *social* (q.v.) in character. The mechanisms are social in that they themselves in one way or another involve the actions of others: the use of sanctions (q.v.), the process of socialization (q.v.), internalization, the deliberate manipulation of symbols, etc. This usage leaves open the question of whose interests and goals are served by such control. While not incompatible with the usage in (1) above, it includes control which serves the interests of individuals and groups whose interests are at odds with those of the person or persons controlled.

B. In one tradition of sociology, that stressing social unity and shared normative systems, usage A.(1) above has been and is dominant. Although the phenomena denoted by this usage had long been studied, one of the earliest definitions of the term itself in this sense occurred during the building up of the young discipline of sociology in America. This was the usage of E. A. Ross who defined *social control* as 'social domination which is intended and which fulfills a function in the life of society (*Social Control: A Survey of the Foundations of Order*, New York: The Macmillan Co., 1901, p. viii). A similar definition set forth during the early developmental stage of sociology in America is that of R. E. Park and E. W. Burgess: 'all social problems turn out finally to be problems of social control' (*Introduction to the Science of Sociology*, Chicago: University of Chicago Press, 1921, p. 785).

This usage of the term soon was extended to include a social-psychological dimension. Thus for G. H. Mead social control is constitutive of the self, for it depends 'upon the degree to which the individual does assume the attitudes of those in the group who are involved with him in his social activities ... upon the degree to which the individuals in society are able to assume the attitudes of the others who are involved with them in common endeavor' ('The Genesis of the Self and Social Control' (1925), *The Philosophy of the Present*, Chicago: University of Chicago Press, 1932, pp. 192, 193).

In modern structural-functional theory the conception of social control is fundamentally the same. For T. Parsons social control is from the actor's standpoint, his motivation to counteract deviant (norm-violating) behaviour, while from the standpoint of the social system, it is the complex of forces resulting in the system's re-equilibration (*The Social System*, Glencoe, Ill.: The Free Press, 1951, pp. 206–7). In his functional analysis of society, S. F. Nadel distinguishes between 'self-regulation' and social control, the former being traditional behaviour which needs few social controls because it is related to an 'instrumental nexus' and has 'value' attached to it, and the latter operating when self-regulation is weakened ('Social Control and Self-Regulation', *Social Forces*, vol. XXXI, 1952–3, pp. 265–73). In this case, of course, the concept is separated into two parts and only one retains the term *social control*.

In a polemical vein R. Nett argues in favour of a conception of social control as regulating a society so as 'to tap, organize, and adapt its creative strength'; instead of the customary consideration of conformity as a product of social organization, he proposes to focus on deviance as engendering 'continuous social organization' ('Conformity-Deviation and the Social Control Concept', *Ethics*, vol. LXIV, 1953, p. 41).

Another definition of social control in the same tradition makes the study of social control difficult to distinguish from the general sociology of culture if not identical with it. G. Gurvitch defines social control as 'the whole of cultural patterns ... whereby inclusive society, every particular group, and every participating individual member overcome tensions and conflicts ... through temporary equilibria and take steps for new creative efforts' ('Social Control', in G. Gurvitch & W. E. Moore (eds.), *Twentieth Century Sociology*, New York: Philosophical Library, 1945, p. 291). A final example of such usage is that of G. C. Homans, who defines social control as 'the process by which, if a man departs from his existing degree of obedience to a norm, his behavior is brought back toward that degree, or would be brought back if he did depart' (*The Human Group*, New York: Harcourt, Brace, 1950, p. 301).

The study of social control on the part of those just cited has not ignored the mechanisms of control—indeed many of the most subtle analyses of such mechanisms have been made by those in this group. But without exception, in defining the term, they have stressed the functions for the group of which the controlled persons are members.

C. In a second tradition of sociology, that stressing conflict, power, and control as related to the diverse and sometimes opposing interests, individuals, and groups in society, the usage in A.(2) has been stressed. In the extreme version of this tradition, as in orthodox Marxism, the functions for the group, society, or community of which the controlled person is a member may be totally denied (except in so far as the members of the dominating and controlling groups are themselves controlled) as is the very possibility of genuine moral consensus in all historical societies. In more moderate versions, the possibility of social control performing functions for the group of which the person is a member is admitted, but attention is also rightly called to the fact that *control* which is *social* in its

Social Control of Industry

mechanisms may not be *social* or *societal* in its functions, and that much control which appears to be social in its functions may actually be serving better the interests of dominant groups (R. Dahrendorf, *Class and Class Conflict in Industrial Society*, London: Routledge & Kegan Paul, 1959, pp. 156–240). H. Gerth and C. W. Mills write in the same tradition. For them social control is exercised in and through institutional orders; among its types are custom, fashion, convention, law, ethical rules, and institutional controls. Yet there is no guarantee that these orthodox mechanisms serve societal needs or the needs of the persons controlled (*Character and Social Structure*, New York: Harcourt, Brace, 1953, passim). Finally K. Mannheim distinguishes between direct and indirect social controls, and, among the latter, among methods of influencing human behaviour in unorganized masses (crowds), in groups (communities, associations), by means of 'field structures', situations, and social mechanisms. Here again the possibility of exploitation of the person and the society is stressed (*Man and Society in an Age of Reconstruction*, London: Kegan Paul, Trench, Trubner, 1940, pp. 285–311).

Kurt H. Wolff

See also: Conflict
Function
Mechanism
Socialization

Social Control of Industry

A. The phrase *social control of industry*, together with *social control of business*, *public regulation of business*, etc., denotes an area of study and research in which the participants attempt to wed economics and political science in an effort to understand the interaction of the political and economic spheres of social life. Major works devoted to the subject run the gamut from the economics of war to the regulation of trade practices, from constitutional law to compensatory spending, from the conservation of natural resources to collective bargaining. The important characteristics of this study of polity and economy are institutional description, legal interpretation, and economic analysis, with emphasis shifting with changes in time and the related disciplines.

B. In contrast with theories and studies of the economics of socialism (q.v.), those working in the area of academic economics and political science designated by *social control of industry* began with an investigation of the institutional

framework of an individualistic market economy. One of the classic texts in this field (J. M. Clark, *Social Control of Business*, New York: McGraw-Hill, 2nd edn., 1939), in the preface to the first edition reprinted in the second edition, indicates that 'One of the difficult tasks, then, is to exhibit individualism as itself a system of control, and to analyze the institutions of control on which it rests' (ibid., p. xi). Unlike the classical theorist, however, who in building his economic models depicts a rational individual vigorously pursuing his own self-interest in a free market, the student of industry and politics views the economy in the context of highly organized and effective pressure groups. Thus the approach highlights the interaction of government and industry. Again, according to Clark, 'It is at bottom the problem of adjusting conflicting interests and claims of "rights" and harnessing selfish interests to that mutual service which the division of labor has made one of the most fundamental and most commonplace features of industry' (ibid.).

1. Recognizing that the free market itself is dependent upon a system of institutional controls, the earliest emphasis in this field of investigation was upon the creation of institutional patterns that would maintain the freedom of the market, namely anti-trust controls. This is reflected as late as 1942 in a selection of readings compiled by a committee of the American Economic Association (*Readings in the Social Control of Industry*, Philadelphia: The Blakiston Company, 1942) in which over half the material is concerned with anti-trust threats and countermeasures, monopoly franchises, and pricing agreements. While a great deal of stress in such investigations is placed on governmental control, economic analysis is, of course, an important tool for evaluating the effectiveness of government in directing economic activities along accepted channels. Legislation and its administration by public agencies is studied in light of resource allocation and utilization criteria. Recommendations are made which, if carried out, would presumably increase resource mobility, price flexibility, competition, economic stability, employment, and material welfare.

2. The study of government and industry is not confined, however, to examining government as a determinant of economic activity; economic activity is investigated as a determinant of the structure and functioning of government. As population shifted from agricultural to industrial pursuits, and as the economy itself increased in complexity and economic groups in number and diversity, students of the relation of government and the economy have pointed out that governmental intervention had to expand and to become more technical and complex. In turn then the government's role in promoting, protecting, and impairing the position of various interest groups in the economy had to be investigated. Thus the second edition of Clark's *Social Control of Business* contained a new fourth part concerned with the government's dealing with problems of unemployment, depression, and production.

3. As time has passed and the role of governmental intervention has become greater, still new fields of control have been investigated. Increasingly, for example, government has intervened in the area of employee-employer relations, so that this area of activity has come to be included in the sub-field of research (see, for example, H. Evans, *Governmental Regulation of Industrial Relations; A Comparative Study of United States and British Experience*, Ithaca, N.Y.: New York State School of Industrial and Labor Relations at Cornell University, 1961). As the principle of intervention has been increasingly accepted in free-market societies and the scope of intervention has increased, and as at least among some socialists dogmatic collectivism has been abandoned, there has been some fusion of the fields of *social control of industry* and socialist welfare economics. This is reflected for example in the work of A. P. Lerner (see, for example, his *The Economics of Control*, New York: The Macmillan Company, 1944).

Harvey C. Bunke

See also: CAPITALISM
PUBLIC UTILITY
SOCIALISM
WELFARE

Social Cost (See **Cost**)

Social Differentiation (See **Differentiation**)

Social Disorganization

A. *Social disorganization* denotes a breach of social organization (q.v.). It is any kind or degree of weakening or disruption of the pattern of social relations which constitutes a society, an association, or any social system. Complete disorganization destroys the *system*, though not necessarily the components.

The term is also used to designate the process in which such disruption occurs.

B. 1. Most sociologists appear to employ the term in the sense of a relative decline of control. 'We can define [social disorganization] briefly as a decrease of the influence of existing rules of social behavior upon individual members of the group' (W. I. Thomas & F. Znaniecki, *The Polish Peasant in Europe and America*, Boston: Badger, 1920, vol. 4, p. 2). In such a sense, observers can agree on a specific instance of disorganization whether or not they desire or deplore the condition or process.

2. A variation may be found in which the term connotes a 'social problem' or variation from a value standard, for example, 'Disorganization is a departure from some norm of organization and efficiency' (J. O. Hertzler, *Social Institutions*, Lincoln: University of Nebraska Press, 1946, p. 257). Others have laid special emphasis on social change as the essential element in disorganization, and on individual deviation from norms as the essential element.

Robert E. L. Faris

See also: ANOMY
SOCIAL ORGANIZATION
SOCIAL PROBLEM

Social Distance

A. The term *social distance* is used in sociology and social psychology to denote the degree of sympathetic understanding (intimacy) felt by one party to a social relationship towards the other party as measured from a point of complete sympathetic understanding. The further from this point the feelings of the party concerned, the greater is the social distance. On occasion the term used in the meaning above is qualified by the adjective *horizontal*, in which case it is complemented by the term *vertical social distance* which is used loosely to denote degrees of superordination-subordination in a social relationship together with degrees of difference in prestige, power, authority, etc.

B. The term was introduced into sociological terminology by R. E. Park and E. W. Burgess, who in speaking of tendencies towards approach and avoidance said, 'If instead of thinking of these two tendencies as unrelated, they are thought of as conflicting responses to the same situation, where the tendency to approach is modified and complicated by a tendency to withdraw, we get the phenomenon of *social distance*' (*Introduction to the Science of Sociology*, Chicago: University of Chicago Press, 1924, p. 440). While they regarded the distance created

Social Equilibrium

by the tendencies towards approach and avoidance as basic, they spoke of a second *vertical* type of social distance as existing in relationships of inequality (ibid., p. 441).

C. The term was diffused widely in sociology as a result of the creation of a social-distance scale by E. S. Bogardus ('A Social Distance Scale', *Sociology and Social Research*, vol. XVII, 1933, pp. 265–71). 'Social distance was defined in this instance ... as "the degree of sympathetic understanding" that exists between two persons or between a person and a group (personal distance and personal-group distance)' (*Introduction to Social Research*, Los Angeles: Suttonhouse, 1936, p. 100). The scale was made up of items classified by judges as indicating various degrees of 'sympathetic understanding'. It is apparent from the nature of the items, e.g. 'would marry', 'would work in same office with', that 'sympathetic understanding' means 'intimacy', and that vertical distance attitudes are being tapped as well as horizontal distance attitudes. Bogardus recognized that because he was attempting to measure attitudes and feelings, the social distance relationship between two parties would not necessarily be symmetrical, so that he used the term *social distance differential* to denote 'the difference in the distance reactions of each of two parties toward each other' (*Sociology*, New York: The Macmillan Co., 3rd edn., 1949, p. 536).

D. It has been indicated that feelings of closeness and nearness in sympathetic feeling are so intimately bound up with attitudes of superiority and inferiority, that it is difficult to separate *horizontal social distance* from *vertical social distance*. This has led to the increasing and somewhat less precisely defined usage of the term with the adjective 'vertical' attached to it. E. T. Hiller in 1933 spoke of social distance as denoting 'the aloofness and unapproachability of persons, especially those of different social strata' (*Principles of Sociology*, New York: Harper & Bros., 1933, p. 41). And in 1947 he used the term *vertical social distance*: '... differences in rank, prestige, power, and renown may be thought of as "vertical" social distance between two categories' (*Social Relations and Social Structures*, New York: Harper & Bros., 1947, p. 643). This use of the term thus involves superordination and subordination as well as gradations in approachability.

H. Otto Dahlke

See also: ACCOMMODATION
SEGREGATION

654

Social Equilibrium

A. In a broad sense *equilibrium* denotes some kind of balance among a plurality of interrelated social phenomena. This balance may be manifest or merely latent; it may be posited as objectively real or as purely analytical; it may be either static or dynamic.

B. 1. Equilibrium is an ubiquitous expression in sociological literature, and one to which varying degrees of precision attach. P. A. Sorokin (*Social and Cultural Dynamics*, New York: American Book Co., 1941, vol. 4, pp. 677–93) has noted five distinct usages of the term, viz: (a) a state of rest in a social phenomenon, such as the status quo in a political system; (b) a momentary balance in a social phenomenon, e.g. the apex in an organization's curve of growth and decline; (c) a mutual limitation or inhibition among social forces, as in the checks and balances of a constitutional government; (d) an adaptive, adjustive or harmonious property of social phenomena, such as the satisfaction of personal needs within a social order; and (e) '... *a tendency of a social system, when disturbed, to return to its previous status, or to hold its "normal" trend or level*' (italics Sorokin's), such as the short-run stability of workers' methods of production in the face of technical or managerial innovations.

2. Rigorous definitions of the term tend to be variations upon the last of these five usages. Though H. Spencer was first to give equilibrium a central place in his theoretical system, it is from V. Pareto that most present definitions derive. In Pareto's conception (*The Mind and Society*, London: Cape, 1935, vol. 4, p. 1436) a social system is in equilibrium if, when '... it is artificially subjected to some modification different from the modification it undergoes normally, a reaction at once takes place tending to restore it to its real, its normal, state'. A recent refinement upon this definition has been proposed by G. C. Homans (*The Human Group*, New York: Harcourt, Brace, 1950, p. 303): 'A social system is in equilibrium ... when the state of the elements that enter the system and of the mutual relationships between them is such that any small change in one of the elements will be followed by changes in the other elements tending to reduce the amount of that change'.

C. 1. Frequently a distinction is made between static and dynamic equilibrium. Thus G. A. Lundberg (*Foundations of Sociology*, New

York: The Macmillan Co., 1939, p. 210) writes: 'From a static viewpoint, *if the elements under consideration in any closed system are so arranged or so acting relative to some point of reference within the system as to balance each other, in terms of the measures employed, the system is said to be in equilibrium. ... From the dynamic point of view that most probable state toward which any system is constantly moving is, therefore, for that system, the state of equilibrium*' (italics Lundberg's).

2. A further differentiation may be made in terms of the epistemological status which authors give to its referent. Equilibrium may, on the one hand, be considered an objective attribute of a class of social events, or it may, on the other hand, be viewed as an artifact of the investigator's frame of reference. The former point of view is indicated in R. M. MacIver's observation (*Social Causation*, Boston: Ginn, 1942, p. 173) that: 'It is more in keeping with the historical record to think in terms of a constant tendency towards equilibrium, beset always, even in simple or primitive society and still more obviously in the higher civilizations, by forces threatening to unbalance or disrupt it. So the nature of the equilibrium is itself forever changing'. The second point of view is indicated by T. Parsons (*The Social System*, Glencoe, Ill.: The Free Press, 1951, p. 298), who conceives of an equilibrium state as '... a theoretical point of reference. In empirical fact no social system is perfectly equilibrated and integrated'.

Walter Firey

See also: ECONOMIC EQUILIBRIUM

Social Evolution (See Cultural Evolution; Evolution)

Social Fact

A. This term is used to characterize the objects of social enquiry as seen by those who stress the view that (a) institutions are generally quite independent of the particular individuals who occupy roles within them, and (b) the important characteristics of the human personality presuppose, logically and causally, the existence of a social context.

B. 1. Those who reject this standpoint and thus 'deny' the existence of irreducible social facts argue primarily (a) that societies are not something that could exist apart from the individuals composing them, and (b) that therefore statements about societies, institutions and so forth must be interpreted as statements about individual people.

This dispute is not merely philosophical but has methodological and political implications. The rejection of social facts is methodologically suggestive of the use of explanations in terms of individual aims and beliefs, whilst those who argue for social facts will incline to stress institutions. Politically, it has been claimed that belief in social facts leads to collectivism whilst their rejection aids political individualism. It should, however, be noted that such correlations as may exist, logically and historically, between these various views, are complicated rather than simple.

2. The classic discussion of *social facts* is that of Durkheim who uses the term to cover 'a category of facts with very distinctive characteristics; it consists of ways of acting, thinking and feeling, external to the individual and endowed with a power of coercion by reason of which they control him' (*The Rules of Sociological Method*, Chicago: University of Chicago Press, 1938, p. 3).

E. A. Gellner

See also: FACT

Social History

A. *Social history* is the study of the changing network of social relationships, of the development of social institutions, and of shifts in social concepts and values.

B. 1. Both social and economic history (q.v.) are products of a reaction against narrowly defined political history, particularly the history of government and statecraft. Giambattista Vico in his *Scienza Nuova* (1725) (see either: G. Vico, *La Scienza Nuova*, giusta l'edizione del 1744, Bari: Gius. Laterza & Figli, 1928; or *The New Science of G. Vico*, trans. from 3rd edn. 1744 by T. G. Bergin & M. H. Fisch, Ithaca, N.Y.: Cornell University Press, 1948) shifted the balance of interest in historical studies from personal feats and exploits, wars, treaties, and alliances to customs, laws, institutions, forms of economic and social organization, languages, arts, religions, sciences, and 'climates of opinion'. His work, influenced many 19th-century writers during the 'historical revival'. They included Herder, Michelet, and Coleridge. Marx and Engels also acknowledged their debt to Vico, and took over his formula that 'men make their own history' as a starting-point in their historical analysis.

2. To Marx and Engels economic relations

Social Integration

are a 'function of the social productive forces', and in the long run the state of the productive forces determines all social relations—economic, class relations, legal and moral relations, and indirectly, all the creations of the mind and the imagination. Marx never isolated economic from social history or separated economic factors from social factors. Such a separation 'dismembers the activity of social man and converts its various aspects and manifestations into separate forces, which are supposed to determine the historical movement of society ... The progress of social science was bound to lead to the replacement of the theory of factors ... by a synthetic view of social life' (G. V. Plekhanov, *The Materialist Conception of History* (1897), London: Lawrence & Wishart, 1940, p. 21).

3. The growth of industrial society, with the emergence of a new kind of social structure and new views of society, stimulated interest in social history as a 'popular' subject. J. R. Green's *A Short History of the English People* (1864), London: Macmillan, 1875), with its demand for 'knife and fork history' instead of 'drum and trumpet history' was a best seller, while A. Toynbee's *Lectures on the Industrial Revolution in England* (London: Rivingtons, 1884), which popularized that term, were first delivered to 'educated working men'. There was no corresponding parallel development, however, of an academic discipline of social history in Britain, and much popular social history was restricted to the history of 'everyday things'. When G. M. Trevelyan wrote his 20th-century best-seller *English Social History* (London: Longmans, Green, 1944), he defined social history narrowly as 'history of a people with the politics left out' (Introduction). Leaving aside its inadequacies, this definition does not fit the facts of contemporary practice. Some social historians treat social history as economic history with the politics put in, some try to relate it to sociology in the same way that economic historians relate economic history to economic theory; others view it as 'total history', the framework within which all other kinds of history are best considered. The second group divided it into the study of (i) historical social structures and institutions; (ii) social change; (iii) developments in social concepts and terminology; and (iv) shifts in social values.

4. In the course of French and German discussions of methodology and the relationship between sociology and social history there has been a sharper classification of concepts and scope. In France, Marc Bloch, who derived many of his principles from Emile Durkheim, borrowed an older definition of history from Fustel de Coulanges—'History is not the accumulation of all sorts of events which have occurred in the past. It is the science of human societies' (M. Bloch, *Apologie pour l'histoire ou métier d'historien*, Paris: Librairie Armand Colin, 1949, p. 110). His stimulating paper 'Towards a Comparative History of European Societies' (*Revue de synthèse historique*, 1928) sets out his views, which can be further illustrated from the detailed historical articles in the *Annales d'histoire économique et sociale* which he edited with Lucien Febvre.

In Germany, where Comtean precepts were never widely accepted in the 19th century, Max Weber's 'ideal types' transcended historical experience, and Weber drew a sharp distinction between sociology and history. 'The abstract character of the concepts of sociology is responsible for the fact that, compared with actual historical reality, they are relatively lacking in fullness of concrete content' (*Wirtschaft und Gesellschaft* (1913), English trans., *The Theory of Social and Economic Organisation*, London: Hodge, 1947, p. 99). Weber disclaimed the intention, however, of constructing a system of sociological theory, and with his intense interest in social history he stimulated many subsequent investigations of different branches of the subject. In particular, with his study of economic sociology, he built a sturdy bridge between social and economic history.

A. Briggs

See also: CULTURE HISTORY

Social Integration

A. *Integration* may be defined as the process of making whole or entire. *Social integration* refers this process or its resultant state to the social system, and is in turn constituted by the dimensions of *cultural integration* (q.v.) defined in this instance as the consistency of normative patterns with one another; *normative integration* defined as the articulation of normative patterns with motivational processes so that conformity is achieved; *consensual* and *communicative integration* defined as the sharing and transmission of normative patterns among the members of the social system; and *functional integration* defined as the interlocking of claims, expectations, and overt acts.

B. Although the term integration can be and is applied to cultural systems (q.v.) and personality systems (q.v.) in the social sciences, its primary reference in almost all cases is to social systems (q.v.). An analysis of the literature reveals that social integration is conceived to exist in several dimensions, including those of personality and cultural integration, and that the mechanisms (q.v.) functioning in these dimensions contribute to maintenance of the social system as a going concern with respect to the properties of cohesion, boundary maintenance, procedural and functional efficiency, and adaptation to changes in the environing situation.

1. According to P. A. Sorokin (*Society, Culture, and Personality: Their Structure and Dynamics*, New York: Harper & Bros., 1947, p. 314) cultural phenomena conceived as symbolic formulations are integrated when '... two or more interacting, that is, causally connected cultural phenomena stand *in a logical or, for art phenomena, aesthetic consistency with one another*' (italics Sorokin's). This mode of integration, which might be regarded as purely cultural becomes a dimension of social integration in the following passage concerning Durkheim's concept of anomy (q.v.) by T. Parsons (*The Structure of Social Action*, New York: McGraw-Hill, 1937, p. 377): 'Coordinate with and opposite to the state of *anomie* is that of "perfect integration": which implies two things—that the body of normative elements governing conduct in a community forms a consistent system and that its control over the individual is actually effective—that it gets itself obeyed'.

2. Included in the statement by Parsons above is a second dimension of social integration, that of *normative integration*. This dimension involves the articulation of motive with norm so that the actor conforms to the requirements of the normative system. Such conformity in the ideal type of case represents an internalization of the normative system into the personality of the actor.

3. Normative integration, in turn, requires a third dimension of integration, a social dimension of communication, sharing, and consensus. This third dimension is clearly delineated in the following passage from R. M. Williams (*American Society: A Sociological Interpretation*, New York: Knopf, 1951, p. 517): 'Integration is more than a balance-of-power situation or a symbiotic interdependence. Modern sociology seeks to find this something else by investigating the extent and kind of common-value orientations in a social system. A basic postulate is that the integration of a society can be defined in terms of the sharing of common prescriptions

and proscriptions for conduct, belief, valuation'.

4. The sharing of and conforming to a consistent system of cultural norms makes possible a fourth dimension of social integration consisting of reciprocal sets of claims and expectations at the orientation level, and of a reciprocal compatibility of acts at the overt behavioural level. This dimension is delineated by E. T. Hiller (*Social Relations and Structures*, New York: Harper & Bros., 1947, p. 251): 'Integration ... is illustrated by the unified action of every association, even an athletic team. The efforts of a team are based on a division of tasks parceled out to the different players. These tasks must then be purposively synchronized and combined'.

William L. Kolb

See also: CULTURAL INTEGRATION
PERSONALITY INTEGRATION

Social Interaction

A. *Social interaction* denotes the reciprocal influencing of the acts of persons and groups, usually mediated through communication (q.v.). This definition includes the interaction of a person with himself.

B. Usage of the term is of three readily distinguishable kinds.

1. The simplest notion of social interaction when applied to man is that of reciprocal influencing among persons or social forces, as exemplified in the following definitions: 'The reciprocal influence of the social factors that result in human nature and ... culture is ... social interaction' (E. B. Reuter & C. W. Hart, *Introduction to Sociology*, New York: McGraw-Hill, 1937, p. 256); and '[social] interaction is necessarily reciprocal in some degree' (L. von Wiese, *Systematic Sociology*, adapted and amplified by H. Becker, New York: Wiley, 1932, p. 169).

2. The second kind of definition, used by most sociologists and anthropologists, specifies that human interaction is a variety of 'reciprocal influencing', that peculiar to socialized persons. They assert that interaction, as applied to human beings, should be called *symbolic interaction*: e.g. 'Social interaction is based upon communication ... The individual interacts with others through the medium of communication. The result of this activity is the broad and inclusive process of *social interaction*' (F. E. Merrill & H. W. Eldredge, *Culture and Society*, New York: Prentice-Hall, 1952, p. 486). But although some authors equate communication and interaction, others state that interaction involves additional

Social Movement

properties: 'Social interaction may be defined operationally as what happens when two or more persons come into contact (not necessarily physical contact) and a modification of behavior takes place' (L. Wilson & W. L. Kolb, *Sociological Analysis*, New York: Harcourt, Brace, 1949, p. 681).

3. The third kind of definition is offered by some social scientists who wish to view the self (q.v.) as socially interacting with itself, e.g. 'A single individual in a room working at a problem, talking to himself or thinking out loud is ... technically regarded as engaged in interaction, and insofar as the interaction is with the self—a social object—the actor is regarded as engaged in social interaction' (R. F. Bales, 'A Theoretical Framework for Interaction Analysis', in D. Cartwright & A. Zander (eds.), *Group Dynamics*, Evanston, Ill.: Row, Peterson, 1953, p. 31).

Howard Becker

See also: COMMUNICATION
           PROCESS

Social Mobility (See Mobility)

Social Movement
A. The term *social movement* denotes a concerted and continued effort by a social group aimed at reaching a goal (or goals) common to its members. More specifically, the effort is directed at modifying, maintaining, replacing, or destroying an existing social institution. The term is also used to denote the group so engaged. This general formulation leaves open the question, e.g. of degrees of organization and continuity or of clarity of purpose—all of which may vary from one social movement to another or within any one social movement in the course of its history.

B. H. Blumer ('Collective Behavior', in A. M. Lee (ed.), *New Outline of the Principles of Sociology*, New York: Barnes & Noble, 1946, pp. 167–222; 'Collective Behavior', in J. B. Gittler (ed.), *Review of Sociology*, New York: Wiley, 1957, pp. 127–58) has made the outstanding contribution toward attempts to clarify the term *social movement*, within the context of collective behaviour. In the earlier work *social movements* are defined as '... collective enterprises to establish a new order of life. They have their inception in a condition of unrest, and derive their motive power on one hand from dissatisfaction with the current form of life, and on the other hand, from wishes and hopes for a new scheme or system of living. ... As a social movement develops, it takes on the character of

a society. It acquires organization and form, a body of customs and traditions, established leadership and enduring division of labour, social rules and social values—in short, a culture, a social organization, and a new scheme of life' ('Collective Behavior', in A. M. Lee (ed.), *A New Outline of the Principles of Sociology*, p. 199). Blumer classifies social movements as (a) general social movements, such as the labour movement, (b) specific social movements, such as the anti-slavery movement, and (c) expressive social movements such as religious movements and fashion movements (ibid., pp. 199–219). In the later work, Blumer states that 'a social movement signifies either a collective effort to transform some given area of established social relations, or else a large unguided change in social relations involving, however unwittingly, large numbers of participants' ('Collective Behavior', in J. B. Gittler (ed.), *Review of Sociology*, p. 145).

Blumer points out that the usage of the term *social movement* in social sciences has focused on political orientation or upon histories of movements. He points out that R. Heberle's excellent book (*Social Movements: An Introduction to Political Sociology*, New York: Appleton-Century-Crofts, 1951) is confined to movements with political objectives (H. Blumer, 'Collective Behavior', in J. B. Gittler (ed.), *Review of Sociology*, p. 146).

Preston Valien

Social Nominalism
A. *Social nominalism* is any view which denies the reality of collectives and other wholes as independent agents and sees the object of study of the social sciences in individuals, in the items of behaviour of individuals, or in the probabilities which can be inferred from them. It is the view that sociological concepts are 'simply verbal names for collections of individuals or for certain common elements in their behavior' (F. N. House, *The Development of Sociology*, New York: McGraw-Hill, 1936, p. 416).

B. In medieval philosophy nominalism was the view of those who denied 'that general concepts exist in reality ... They declared all concepts to be free creations of the human mind—mere *nomina* or *flatus vocis* arrived at by way of abstractions; ... thus they ascribed to the human mind perfect freedom in forming and defining general concepts in accordance with the objectives which these concepts are intended to serve ... knowledge and understanding of the phenomena were held to be attainable primarily by experience ...' (K. Pribram, *Conflicting Patterns of Thought*, Washington, D.C.: Public Affairs Press, 1949, p. 11). 'Reasoning was ... an operation in which hypothetical concepts are adjusted to various purposes without any faith in the absolute validity of such concepts. [They rejected] the belief in the "identity of thinking and being" ' (ibid., p. 12). According to this view, 'the particulars of immediate experience are the true realities; general ideas or conceptual terms are only names—*nomina*' (F. N. House, *The Development of Sociology*, p. 63).

C. Philosophical, that is epistemological, nominalism is basic to the ways of thinking and, hence, to the methodology of the natural sciences as well as of the social sciences as far as the latter aim at emulating the former. 'In the last analysis, the principles of freedom of thought, of freedom to express, defend and propagate one's views and of general tolerance regarding any conviction, creed, or assumption, owed their acceptance to the rejection of the belief in the "identity of thinking and being" ' (K. Pribram, *Conflicting Patterns of Thought*, p. 12). Social nominalism is definitely implied in philosophical nominalism.

1. P. A. Sorokin specifically identifies 'sociological singularism' as 'a sociological variety of nominalism'. He defines it as the view that 'ontologically, any society is a mere sum of its members and ... does not have any true reality per se' (P. A. Sorokin, *Social and Cultural Dynamics, Fluctuations of Systems of Truth, Ethics, and Law*, New York: The American Book Co., 1937, vol. 2, p. 263). He distinguishes between (a) extreme or consistent sociological singularism, the view 'that the individual is the only social reality ontologically, and also that he is the supreme ethical value'; (b) moderate sociological singularism which 'assumes the ontological reality of the singularistic individuals; but in its ethical aspects it insists that for any given individual not only he himself is the supreme value, but all the other individuals and society as the sum of the individuals, are also the supreme values; and (c) collectivistic sociological singularism according to which 'society is the sum of the individuals ... it claims the priority and superiority of the value of the collectivity compared with that of the individual' (ibid., pp. 263–5).

2. According to R. E. Park and E. W. Burgess nominalism is 'represented by social psychology [which] emphasizes, or seems to emphasize, the independence of the individual'. By contrast, 'realism, represented by collective psychology, emphasizes the control of the group over the individual, of the whole over the part' (*Introduction to the Science of Sociology*, Chicago: University of Chicago Press, 1924, p. 41). They designate as nominalists 'those who thought a concept a mere class-name applied to a group of objects because of some common characteristics ... in this sense Tarde and Giddings and all those writers who think of society as a collection of actually or potentially *like-minded* persons would be nominalists ...' (ibid., p. 36).

Franz Adler

See also: SOCIAL REALISM

Social Object

A. 1. A *social object* may be defined as any thing, idea, event, or state of affairs to which distinctive meaning is attached by the norms of a given group. In this sense of the term all experience is contained within a universe of social objects, inside which human beings (as self-conceiving social objects) interact. Such a universe constitutes a system of objects of which selves are members. The norms of the group constitute the relational plans of action which give meaning to (create) the objects.

2. A *social object* may also be defined as any object which is conceived as an actor, or as having expectations with relation to the actions of ego.

B. 1. The term, in its broadest usage, refers to any distinguishable aspect of social reality. It may be a thing, a quality, an event, or a state of affairs. All that is necessary is that it have been given a unity and a disjunctiveness from other matters by having been given a name which distinguishes it and assigns it a meaning. The sum total of one's social objects constitute his social reality.

This constructed view of social reality was first introduced into social psychology by W. Lippmann: 'For the most part we do not first see, and then define, we define first and then see' (*Public Opinion*, New York: Harcourt, Brace, 1922, p. 81); by W. I. Thomas: 'If men define situations as real, they are real in their consequences' (from the last chapter of *The Child in America*, with D. S. Thomas, reprinted in *Social Behavior and Personality: Contributions of W. I. Thomas to Theory and Social Research*, ed. by E. H. Volkart, New York: Social Science Research Council, 1951, p. 81); and pre-eminently by G. H. Mead, whose influence was largely

Social Order

through his teaching, since his books were for the most part published posthumously: 'Symbolization constitutes objects not constituted before, objects which would not exist except for the context of social relationships ...' (*Mind, Self and Society*, Chicago: University of Chicago Press, 1934, p. 78).

Behind this concept of social object is the general view expressed by E. Cassirer: 'Between the receptor system and the effector system, which are to be found in all species, we find in man a third link which we may describe as the *symbolic system*. ... No longer in a merely physical universe, man lives in a symbolic universe. ... No longer can man confront reality immediately; he cannot see it, as it were, face to face. Physical reality seems to recede as man's symbolic activity advances' (*An Essay on Man*, New Haven: Yale University Press, 1944, pp. 24–5).

2. The more restricted usage is found in Parsons's general theory of action. In this theory a social object 'is an actor or system of action whose reactions and attitudes are significant to the actor ... The social object, the alter, is seen by ego to have expectations which are complementary to ego's own' (T. Parsons & E. A. Shils, 'Values, Motives, and Systems of Action', in T. Parsons & E. A. Shils (eds.), *Toward a General Theory of Action*, Cambridge, Mass.: Harvard University Press, 1951, p. 65). For Parsons and his followers, anything which is seen by ego as an actor is a social object; anything else is experienced as a non-social or physical object. Although there are exceptions both ways, generally speaking another human being (or one's self) is a social object, while a non-human object is a non-social object in Parsons's system.

Manford Kuhn

See also: CULTURE
        DEFINITION OF THE SITUATION
        SOCIAL INTERACTION
        SYMBOL

Social Order

A. *Social order* refers to ascertainable patterns of regular structure, process, or change occurring in and resulting from human interaction. This broader conception embraces regularities of what are often called *pathology* or *disorganization*; the breakup of stable interaction may itself be orderly, i.e. it may take specific forms under given conditions.

A narrower conception of *social order* limits itself to those regularities of interaction that meet with the approval of (a vaguely defined) consensus in a society or are alleged to be *functional*. Dysfunctional processes are then interpreted as signs of 'disorganization'.

B. As with so many concepts in the social sciences, discussions of social order often contain a moral or utopian flavour mixed with the empirical content. By many writers conflict is regarded as disorder and absence of order, a breakdown of stable regularities.

Social order cannot be defined by the absence of 'pathology' or of disorganization, for there are no such situations. Specific pathologies may exhibit a regular *order*, for example, the occurrence of high homicide with low suicide rates in Appalachia and of the opposite combination in Sweden is not *accidental*. Furthermore, while modifications of attitudes or social structures may diminish *disorganization*, it is known that every society has disparate conceptions of the desirable or weak articulation of norms and values in some spheres of life. In short, we are learning to predict the conditions under which various types of *disorder* will occur and their relations to *social order*.

C. Arnold Anderson

See also: SOCIAL INTEGRATION

Social Organization (Anthropology)

The term has a long history in anthropological writing and covers a wide range of not always well-defined ideas. It has often been used synonymously with terms such as *social structure*, *social order*, *social pattern*, and other phrases implying systematic arrangement. Only in the 20th century have efforts been made to give more exact denotation to the term. Variations in usage can conveniently be put into three groups.

1. The earlier and more general usage of the term is exemplified in successive editions of *Notes and Queries on Anthropology*. In the fourth edition, for instance, it is said that 'a full comprehension of the social organization of any people only becomes possible after the complete study of their institutions and of the function of their social groupings' (B. Freire-Marreco & J. L. Myres, *Notes and Queries on Anthropology*, London: The Royal Anthropological Institute, 4th edn., 1912, p. 143). Thirty years later R. H. Lowie still speaks of organization in this same general sense. 'The study of social organization deals primarily with the significant grouping of individuals' (*Social Organisation*, London: Routledge & Kegan Paul, 1950, p. 3). W. H. R.

Rivers (*Kinship and Social Organisation*, London: Constable, 1914, p. 1) and A. R. Radcliffe-Brown (*The Social Organisation of Australian Tribes*, Melbourne: Macmillan, 1931, p. 3) in works of theoretical importance to social anthropology also spoke of organization in this way, and made no effort to distinguish it from *social structure*, though Radcliffe-Brown subsequently attached importance to the distinction.

2. In contrast with earlier writers, Malinowski used the term to indicate the way in which members of society organize themselves and their material environment to satisfy their biological, psychological, and social needs (*A Scientific Theory of Culture*, Chapel Hill: University of North Carolina Press, 1944, pp. 39, 44, 52). In this usage he was probably influenced more by sociological writers than by his anthropological predecessors. M. Weber, for example, used organization to mean 'a system of continuous purposive activity of a specified kind', which was connected with corporate groups and their administration (*The Theory of Social and Economic Organisation*, trans. by A. M. Henderson & T. Parsons, London: Hodge, 1947, p. 138). In economic activities organization was 'a technical category which designated the way in which various types of services are continuously combined with each other and with non-human means of production' (ibid., p. 204).

3. (a) The term is used in yet another way in an article published by G. G. Brown and J. H. Barnett in 1942. The authors remarked that the use of the terms social organization and social structure in current anthropological writings was imprecise, and that both might be used synonymously, even in the same paragraph. They, therefore, suggested the following definition: '... social organisation refers to the systems of obligation-relations which exist among and between the groups constituting a given society, while social structure refers to the placement and position of individuals and of groups within that system of obligation-relations' ('Social Organisation and Social Structure', *American Anthropologist*, vol. 44, 1942, p. 31). In such a system of obligation-relationships 'the degree of elasticity in interpretation of roles permitted by a given social organisation' varies from one society to another, and also allows ideal, expected, and actual behaviour to be taken into account (ibid., p. 34).

(b) The view put forward in this use of the term was not unrepresentative of anthropological opinion at that time. In 1940 Radcliffe-Brown contrasted social structure with social organization. The former he considered to be a system of persons occupying positions related to one another and directly associated with a social organization or system of roles whose interpretation was socially controlled (*Structure and Function in Primitive Society*, London: Cohen & West, 1952, pp. 188–204).

(c) To some anthropologists, however, this formulation was unsatisfactory for handling situations in which a formal social structure was not easily discernible. R. Firth considered the notion of role to 'imply a too mechanical view of social action', in that by 'defining the limits of a person's activities, [it] can imply that a person does only what is assigned for him to do by his social position' ('Social Organization and Social Change', *Journal of the Royal Anthropological Institute*, vol. 84, 1954, p. 9). For Firth social organization is rather 'the working arrangements of society. It is the processes of ordering of action and of relations in reference to given social ends, in terms of adjustments resulting from the exercise of choices by members of the society' (ibid., p. 10). Moreover, organizational devices may alter an existing social structure; and to define organization in this way may therefore be useful in a study of social change.

H. S. Morris

See also: SOCIAL ORGANIZATION (Sociology)
SOCIAL STRUCTURE

Social Organization (Sociology)

A. 1. *Organization* denotes both a structure and a process. As structure, an organization is any stable pattern of interrelations among component parts which forms a whole having characteristics not manifest in the separate parts. Thus a molecule, a jellyfish, a corporation are embraced by this general definition. As process, organization is used to refer to the manner in which these entities are formed.

2. In social science usage, *social organization* denotes a relatively stable set of functioning interrelations among component parts (persons or groups) which results in characteristics not present in the components and produces an entity sui generis. Social organizations evolve as structures of such relations in such a way as to fulfil functions in a manner more efficient and durable than could be achieved by unorganized persons. All society can be understood as a complex system of organizations. Organization, in general, is a magnifier of power, and also the basis of much of the order and predictability in society.

Social Problem

The term is also used to refer to the process by which the pattern of relationship is formed.

B. 1. A social organization may be composed of individual persons—usually acting in a specific capacity (role or office). Groups and organizations themselves may be the components of larger systems, as in the case of such bodies as the Association of American Universities, which is an organization of organizations.

2. An organization is not necessarily composed of identical units, nor does it usually tend to assimilate its components into an identical character. Rather it makes use of complementary differences which fit into an effective pattern relating to the achievement of its functions.

3. It is generally held that the form of social organizations is to a certain extent dominated by their functions, and some theorists have held that without one or more live functions no structure would be able to endure. In actual fact, however, organizations may exist with either precise and unitary functions, or vague, multiple and changing functions. Persons may belong to an organization without a clear conception of its purpose, and members may disagree on what the function is. A university, for example, may be conceived of as a training agency for the young, a storehouse of accumulated knowledge, an instrument for the discovery of knowledge, an agency for building character and arranging marriages of students, and in other ways, and it may in fact achieve all of these to some extent.

4. The stability of the relations among the components of an organization is generally recognized, but this need not be an absolute lack of change. In modern life most organizations are in continuous change—growing, adapting, altering both function and structure, but in a sufficiently orderly manner that the integrity of the organization is maintained.

Robert E. L. Faris

See also: SOCIAL ORGANIZATION
(Anthropology)
SOCIAL STRUCTURE

Social Pathology (See Social Disorganization)

Social Problem

A. A *social problem* may be defined as 'a situation affecting a significant number of people that is believed by them and/or by a significant number of others in the society to be a source of difficulty or unhappiness, and one that is capable of amelioration. Thus a social problem consists of both an objective situation and a subjective social interpretation. The social problems of long standing in most Western societies include juvenile delinquency, crime, chronic alcoholism, suicide, mental disorder, mental deficiency, divorce, desertion, intergroup prejudice and discrimination, industrial conflict, inadequate housing and slum neighbourhoods, unemployment, chronic dependency, corruption in government' (A. M. Rose, *Sociology: The Study of Human Relations*, Toronto: McClelland & Stewart, 1956, p. 452).

B. 1. L. Wirth (*Contemporary Social Problems*, Chicago: University of Chicago Press, 1939, p. 4) drew a distinction (one with which there is general agreement) between a *social problem* and a 'sociological problem' or 'scientific problem'. In Wirth's terms, 'Scientific problems are problems of knowledge; they exist when the relationship between two or more events or series of events is unknown'. He held that a *social problem* 'may be said to arise when an existing situation diverges from a situation which is preferred in accordance with certain values'. A social problem thus 'exists only when certain persons regard an existing situation as a problem. These persons may be either participants or spectators'.

2. There are currently two major theories on the causation of social problems.

(a) One major theory is generally called the 'social disorganization' theory which holds that social problems arise out of situations in which individuals are so divorced from their culture that they are unable to understand each other enough to act meaningfully in relation with each other. This idea seems to have begun with E. Durkheim's concept of *anomie* in his study of the social problem of suicide (*Suicide* (1897), trans. by J. A. Spaulding & G. Simpson, London: Routledge & Kegan Paul, 1952), and received great impetus with W. I. Thomas and F. W. Znaniecki's concept of social disorganization in their study of the social problems of immigrants (*The Polish Peasant in Europe and America*, 2 vols., Chicago: Badger, 1919). In recent years, R. E. L. Faris (*Social Disorganization*, New York: Ronald Press, 1948) may be cited as offering the most consistent analysis of social problems in terms of social disorganization theory.

An important variation of the social disorganization theory is offered by A. P. Herman

662

(*An Approach to Social Problems*, Boston: Ginn, 1949), who built on W. F. Ogburn's concept of the 'cultural lag' (*Social Change with respect to Culture and Original Nature*, New York: Viking Press, 1922). According to Herman, 'Social problems arise, and existing problems are aggravated, when a society creates or accepts instruments of change, yet fails to understand, anticipate, or deal with the consequences of such action' (ibid., p. 51). This approach moves away from considering social problems solely as arising from significant difficulties of communication, but remains within the social disorganization framework by attributing social problems to society's inability to cope with something (specifically with social change).

(b) The second major line of theory attributes social problems to conflicts of interest or value. Problems do not arise out of people's inability to communicate with one another or to engage in collective action but out of fundamental and rational opposition because of different interests and values. K. Marx, L. Gumplowicz, J. Novicow, G. Ratzenhofer, G. Simmel, G. Sorel, and A. Small may be considered to be the formulators of conflict theory. Recent proponents of conflict theory, as applied to social problems, include R. C. Fuller, H. Sheppard, H. Blumer, J. Bernard, G. Myrdal, and G. Vold.

Arnold M. Rose

See also: ANOMY
CONFLICT
SOCIAL DISORGANIZATION

Social Process (See **Process**)

Social Psychology

A. *Social psychology* may be defined as the overlapping portions of psychology and sociology which are particularly concerned with describing and explaining how selves are modified through interaction with others and how their reciprocating behaviour is directed accordingly. It includes or overlaps with such areas of study as culture and personality, collective behaviour, and group dynamics.

B. Although every social science utilizes social-psychological assumptions in formulating its propositions, only psychology and sociology include social psychology as part of their explicit subject-matter. W. McDougall gave an early psychological view of social psychology when he said, '... the fundamental problem of social psychology is the moralization of the individual by the society into which he is born as a creature in which the non-moral and purely egoistic tendencies are so much stronger than any altruistic tendencies' (*Social Psychology* (1908), London: Methuen, 22nd edn., 1931, p. 16). A similar early sociological view is to be found in L. F. Hobhouse's statement (*Social Development*, London: Allen & Unwin, 1924, p. 132) that: 'We may take it that the two most important problems that lie before this science are: (a) What are the distinctive elements in the human mind which determine man's social relations? and (b) How do social relations react upon the mind, developing or modifying its inherent tendencies?' Despite these similarities of definition the characteristic emphases of these two disciplines have provoked informal distinctions between psychologically oriented social psychology and sociologically oriented social psychology. Thus social psychology usually stands not as an independent discipline but as an appendage to psychology or sociology, and its students employ the entire range of methods of investigation found in both parent disciplines from the use of case histories and typological analysis at one extreme to the most 'objective' and sophisticated modes of mathematical description and analysis at the other. Moreover, as in the case of its parent disciplines, it also suffers from the abuse or the misunderstanding of both qualitative and quantitative methods, so that there is both much sloppy theoretical overgeneralization about the human self and also much over-simple reduction of complex human attributes to simple countable elements.

C. The three main current divisions of theory in psychologically oriented social psychology are the *psychoanalytic*, the *behaviourist*, and the *gestaltist*.

1. The psychoanalytic social psychologist tends to approach the description and explanation of human behaviour in terms of the fairly specific motivation of the individual as he copes with the more or less frustrating social world about him. Theory in such social psychology ranges from the orthodoxy of Freud, which while it assigns culture a limiting and frustrating role vis-à-vis human personality also stresses the independent dynamics of the personality system, to the deviants from orthodoxy, such as E. Fromm, who have assigned to social relations and culture a much more determinative and constitutive role in the shaping of personality (S. Freud, *Civilization and Its Discontents*, trans. by J. Riviere, London: Hogarth Press,

Social Psychology

1953; E. Fromm, *Escape from Freedom*, New York: Rinehart, 1941).

2. The behaviourist social psychologist tends similarly to conceive the individual as driven by diffuse needs to confront an environment which may gratify or frustrate them. But learning is stressed in accounting for regularities in behaviour: the individual is seen as learning through reinforcement or extinction by the rewarding or punishing of his initially exploratory responses to stimuli. The most thoroughgoing attempt to establish a theory of human social behaviour on this basis is that of B. F. Skinner in his *Science and Human Behavior* (New York: The Macmillan Co., 1953). Other behaviourists have included more of the standard concepts of social psychology derived from sociology, but have none the less stressed the directly observable aspects of human behaviour, as opposed to imputed subjective elements (G. C. Homans, *Social Behavior: Its Elementary Forms*, New York: Harcourt, Brace & World, 1961; E. L. & R. E. Hartley, *Fundamentals of Social Psychology*, New York: Knopf, 1952).

3. The gestalt social psychologist stresses perception in his approach; the individual is construed as acting toward others in the ways perceived by him as best adapting him as an organism to his environment ('reducing tension'). These perceptions, however, are recognized as heavily influenced if not fully determined by the concepts or concerted behaviour of those other persons who form the social environment of the actor. Probably the most influential gestalt social psychologist has been K. Lewin whose work has had significant consequences for the study of personality and has in large measure brought into existence the field-theory (q.v.) group-dynamics (q.v.) approach to social psychology (*A Dynamic Theory of Personality*, New York: McGraw-Hill, 1935; *Field Theory in Social Science*, ed. by D. Cartwright, New York: Harper & Bros., 1951). In recent years particularly those influenced by the gestalt approach have perhaps gone further than other psychologists in assessing the influence of the self-concept or self-conception (q.v.) as a factor governing behaviour, although ego-psychology has meanwhile become a strong corresponding trend among the psychoanalytically oriented (C. Rogers, *Client-Centered Therapy*, Boston: Houghton Mifflin, 1951; A. Freud, *The Ego and the Mechanisms of Defence*, trans. by C. Baines, New York: International Universities Press, 1946).

4. Theoretically all psychologically oriented social psychologists claim to study the same range of phenomena and the differences in terminology are more marked than their differences in theoretical stance. All three unite in setting off the individual as coping with his environment, more or less heavily influenced by it, but basically viewed as separable from it in thought and investigation. The major theoretical schism thus lies not among the psychologically-oriented social psychologists, but between them and the sociologically oriented.

D. 1. The term *symbolic-interactionists* has been applied to the main representatives of sociologically oriented social psychology, because of the stress which this group places upon social interaction and communication as the matrix from which human selves arise. This stress stems from some of the relatively early theorizing in American sociology concerning the nature of the human self in the writings of C. H. Cooley, G. H. Mead, and J. Dewey (C. H. Cooley, *Human Nature and the Social Order*, New York: Scribners, 1902; G. H. Mead, *Mind, Self and Society*, Chicago: University of Chicago Press, 1934; J. Dewey, *Human Nature and Conduct*, New York: Henry Holt, 1922). The symbolic-interactionist starts his observations with the ongoing social process into which the individual is born, and in which he imediately acquires beginning statuses derived from his sex and parentage. Out of the social experience available to him thenceforth he fashions his self, by progressive redefinitions which more or less comply with the expectations of others (see for example, A. R. Lindesmith & A. L. Strauss, *Social Psychology*, New York: Dryden Press, 1949, pp. 186–204). The kinds of experience available to the individual, being differentially distributed in his society, are sufficiently specific to account for most of the regularities in behaviour which distinguish him as a person from others in his own and other groups. His *self* is conceived as regulating his conduct in much the same manner as it is conceived in the three schools of psychological social psychology which also stress the directive function of the self. Similarly, also, while in any given momentary episode of behaviour involving others, the self of each actor may be taken as given. Over time the self continually changes, acquiring new definitions through the interplay of intentions, group norms, and real outcomes.

2. Action of both individual and group is, in sociological social psychology, basically characterized as the *interaction* of selves. Because so much of the interaction of selves is conducted through the medium of communication, employing language and many other conventional signs, rather than overt physical movements of bodies, the symbolic character of interaction is heavily stressed, and particularly the various attributes of identity, i.e. the naming of qualities of selves. This relativistic conception of personal identity employed by symbolic interactionists, and the confident ascription of unconscious motives to behaviour by the psychoanalytically oriented, are extremes so far apart as to virtually bound the field of social psychology. Yet both the psychoanalytically inclined and the sociologically oriented unite in recognizing identification (q.v.) as the master concept of social psychology, although they may disagree concerning the basic motivational unit, the former tending to stress instinct or drive and the latter attitude. It is the concept of identification that exactly captures the simultaneity of the individual and social aspects of behaviour, and the dependence of self on others for individuality. For all the nominal discrepancies and theoretical and methodological arguments which abound, therefore, few partisans of any faction would deny the title of social psychology to the approach of another.

Nelson N. Foote

See also: ATTITUDE
             BEHAVIOURISM
             COLLECTIVE BEHAVIOUR
             COMMUNICATION
             EGO
             FIELD THEORY
             GROUP DYNAMICS
             HABIT
             INDIVIDUAL
             INSTINCT
             LEARNING
             MOTIVATION
             PERSONALITY SYSTEM
             SELF
             SELF–CONCEPTION
             SOCIAL INTERACTION
             SOCIALIZATION

Social Race (See Race)

Social Realism

A. *Social realism* may be defined as any view that considers wholes like the state, society, culture, groups, institutions, relationships, processes, etc. as something other than or above and beyond the individuals acting them out or the behaviour manifesting them.

B. 1. In medieval philosophy *realism* (also called *universalism*) referred to the view which 'ascribes to the universals objective and real existence, even an existence superior to that of individuals, sometimes even flatly denying the autonomous existence of individuals ...' (L. von Mises, *Theory and History*, New Haven: Yale University Press, 1957, p. 250).

Realistic or universalistic reasoning is based 'on the conviction that the human mind is able to grasp eternally valid rigid ideas, underlying the order of the universe and existing in reality, thus guaranteeing true knowledge without resort to any other source' (K. Pribram, *Conflicting Patterns of Thought*, Washington, D.C.: Public Affairs Press, 1949, p. 163).

2. The relationship between philosophical realism and social realism appears obvious and necessary. Pribram asserts that 'when universalistic methods were applied to social phenomena, reality was attached to such social collectivities as were assumed to owe their existence to the divine order; that is to say, these collectivities were held to be endowed with ends of their own which were independent of the wills of their members' (ibid., p. 8). This medieval philosophy is closely related to what L. Lévy-Bruhl calls 'primitive mentality' (*Primitive Mentality*, trans. by L. A. Clare, New York: The Macmillan Company, 1923; *How Natives Think* [*Les Fonctions mentales dans les sociétés inférieures*] trans. by L. A. Clare, New York: Knopf, 1925), or what H. Kelsen calls 'primitive consciousness' (*Society and Nature*, Chicago: The University of Chicago Press, 1943, pp. 1–23). Kelsen points out that this type of consciousness, by no means limited to non-Caucasoid races or other than Euro-American Cultures, contains 'a peculiarity of thinking, which may be termed a "substantializing tendency"' (ibid., p. 13) by virtue of which 'primitive man substantializes the social group as such' (ibid., p. 16). While Pribram stresses rationalist realism, Lévy-Bruhl and Kelsen stress irrational manifestations.

J. A. Schumpeter, on the other hand, points out that 'the view ... that postulates existence for society per se ... is found also in non-universalist writings' (*History of Economic Analysis*, ed. by E. B. Schumpeter, New York: Oxford University Press, 1954, p. 785n.). He also maintains that according to scholastic philosophy the idea of 'society would claim logical precedence over any individual empirical

Social Selection

society ... but not over individual men' (ibid., p. 85). Actually, there are authors who combine a nominalist epistemology with *social realism* or a realist epistemology with *social nominalism* (q.v.).

C. 1. Within social realism—he refers to it as social universalism—P. A. Sorokin distinguishes three main types: (a) an ontological type: 'Society is the true and primary reality, while the individual is the derivative phenomenon'; (b) an ethical type: 'Society is the primary value and the individual or singularistic interests should be subordinated to it'; and (c) a sociological type: 'Society is much more than a mere number of individuals ... an ontological social entity which embraces all the individuals externally as well as permeates them internally ... is social reality *sui generis* irreducible to individuals'. He also distinguishes between (i) extreme sociological universalism which 'regards the individual as mere part ... much inferior to the value of society as a whole', and (ii) moderate sociological universalism which 'concedes some independent reality to the individual as well as his value ... sometimes ... [even] equal to that of society' (*Social and Cultural Dynamics*, New York: American Book Co., 1937, vol. 2, pp. 262–6).

2. R. E. Park and E. W. Burgess designate as realists all 'those who thought the concept was *real* and not the name of a mere collection of individuals. ... In this sense ... Simmel, Ratzenhofer and Small, who think of society in terms of interaction and social process, may be called realists. They are realist, at any rate, in so far as they think of the members of a society as bound together in a system of mutual influences which has sufficient character to be described as a process' (*Introduction to the Science of Sociology*, Chicago: University of Chicago Press, 1924, p. 36). By contrast F. N. House agrees with O. Spann that an interaction theory of society 'precludes the entertaining of a tenable concept of the social group as a real unity' (*The Development of Sociology*, New York: McGraw-Hill, 1936, p. 406).

Franz Adler

See also: Social Nominalism

Social Relations (See **Social Interaction**)

Social Role (See **Role**)

Social Security (See **Security**)

Social Selection

A. The term denotes the singling out and preservation, either by conscious choice or by the operation of impersonal, more or less automatically working tests, of those forms of life which are particularly adapted to their conditions of existence, notably their physical or social setting, and hence, comparatively speaking, the fittest for survival.

As this definition shows, the word and the idea connoted by it are common to the natural and the social sciences. The concept first developed in a field which lies across the borderline between the two, namely demography, it then found acceptance and elaboration in biology, especially the science of evolution, and from there it penetrated into sociology in the narrower sense of the word, where it was first used in a specific, but later in a more general meaning.

B. 1. In the demographic discussions of the late 18th century, the processes for the designation of which the term selection has since come into use were more or less clearly recognized. In *A Dissertation on the Poor Laws* (by a Wellwisher to Mankind, London: C. Dilly, 1736), Joseph Townsend speaks of an island populated by goats and greyhounds, the latter feeding on the former. 'As many of the goats retired to the scraggy rocks, where the dogs could never follow them, descending only for short intervals to feed with fear and circumspection in the valleys, few of these, besides the careless and the rash, became a prey; and none but the most watchful, strong and active of the dogs could get a sufficiency of food. ... The weakest of both species were among the first to pay the debt of nature; the most active and vigorous preserved their lives' (Sect. VIII). The concept of selection and survival of the fittest is adumbrated in this passage and in several passages of Malthus's *An Essay on the Principle of Population* (T. E. Malthus, *An Essay on the Principle of Population*, London: Johnson, 1798) which inspired Darwin, who gave the term its wide currency and classical connotation.

The following quotation shows in which sense Darwin used the term. 'Can it ... be thought improbable ... that ... variations useful in some way to each being in the great and complex battle of life should sometimes occur in the course of thousands of generations? If such do occur, can we doubt (remembering that many more individuals are born than can possibly survive) that individuals having any advan-

666

tage, however slight, over others, would have the best chance of surviving and of procreating their kind? On the other hand, we may feel sure that any variation in the least degree injurious would be rigidly destroyed. This preservation of favourable variations and rejection of injurious variations I call Natural Selection' (*On the Origin of Species by Means of Natural Selection*, London: Murray, 1859, pp. 69–70, reprint London: Watts & Co., 1950).

2. Social Darwinism took over Darwin's definition of natural selection as it stood and tried to apply it to social reality. It divided, however, into two sub-schools, one of which conceived social selection, in the manner of natural selection, as a process with positive results (survival of the fittest), whereas the other saw it as a process with negative or dysgenic consequences (survival of the unfit).

(a) Writers such as A. O. Ammon (*Die Gesellschaftsordnung und ihre natürlichen Grundlagen*, Jena: Fischer, 1895) maintain that social life shows selecting agencies at work which lie parallel to, and lead to the same weeding out of the worthless as, the tendencies in nature making for preservation of the higher and annihilation of the lower types. The school and economic competition identify the fit, the criminal law the unfit, provided these mechanisms of selection are not impeded by 'unnatural' humanitarian interference.

(b) On the other hand, writers such as G. Vacher de Lapouge (*Les Sélections Sociales*, Paris: Librairie Thorin et Fils, 1896) think of the social processes of selection as running counter to the corresponding processes in nature. In war and politics, in religious, economic, and occupational life, in the application of legal and moral codes, and in the separation of the urban from the rural sector of society, the inferior types are said to be constantly favoured and to gain progressively the upper hand. The prognosis of social evolution which this sub-school put forward was extremely pessimistic: progressive degeneration, physical, mental and moral, and ultimate disappearance of the human race. The whole of social life is here made to appear as 'unnatural'.

(c) Under the influence of Darwin and Social Darwinism, some sociologists, and above all G. Sumner (*Folkways*, Boston: Ginn, 1907) widened the scope of the concept so as to include human conduct and even social institutions because these grow out of human interaction. When men have to act, they will select those 'ways of doing things', which allow them to achieve their aim without incurring pain and in particular without arousing ill-will and possible aggression on the part of their fellow-men. The 'ways' thus selected are 'folkways' (q.v.), firstly because they are normally enacted by all members of a society, and secondly because, as the guarantees of social peace and survival, they are supported by sanctions enforced, if the need arises, by all members of society.

W. Stark

Social Situation

A. The weight of present usage indicates that *social situation* should be defined in terms of the stimulus field or objects to which the actor is oriented. Since sociological theory has long emphasized the importance of the actor as an object to himself (e.g. 'looking-glass self', 'taking the role of the other'), conceptual consistency suggests the desirability of including the actor as a part of the concept of the stimulus field. It also seems desirable not to restrict the term to social objects in the sense of persons and collectivities. A definition which includes all stimuli that 'mean something to the actor' appears to be most serviceable.

These considerations suggest that *social situation* be used to denote the total set of objects, whether persons, collectivities, culture objects, or himself, to which the actor responds.

B. In definitions of this type virtually the only point of disagreement is whether the actor is to be considered as a part of the situation in the sense of being an object to himself or whether the situation is that which is completely external to him.

J. H. S. Bossard and E. S. Boll (*Family Situations*, Philadelphia: University of Pennsylvania Press, 1943, p. 25) are representative of the latter point of view when they define a situation as: 'a number of stimuli, external to the organism but acting upon it, organized as a unit and with special relatedness to each other as stimuli of the specific organism involved'. The classic definition by W. I. Thomas and F. Znaniecki appears to include the actor as an object himself. 'The situation is the set of values and attitudes with which the individual or the group has to deal in a process of activity and with regard to which this activity is planned and its results appreciated. ... The situation involves three kinds of data: (1) The objective conditions under which the individual or society has to act, that is, the totality of values ... which at the given moment affect directly or indirectly the

Social Structure

conscious status of the individual or the group. (2) The pre-existing attitudes of the individual or the group which at a given moment have an actual influence upon his behavior. (3) The definition of the situation, that is, the more or less clear conception of the conditions and consciousness of the attitudes' (*The Polish Peasant in Europe and America*, New York: Knopf, 1927, vol. I, p. 68).

Although the final phrase of the foregoing quotation strongly suggests that the actor or, more precisely, his attitudes, is to be regarded as an element of the situation as object to himself, one of the most explicit statements of this position is that of T. Parsons and E. A. Shils ('Categories of the Orientation and Organization of Action', in T. Parsons & E. A. Shils (eds.), *Toward a General Theory of Action*, Cambridge, Mass.: Harvard University Press, 1951, pp. 53–109). A situation is defined as 'that part of the external world which means something to the actor ... it is that part to which the actor is oriented and in which the actor acts. The situation thus consists of objects of orientation' (ibid., p. 56). Despite their use of the phrase 'the external world' Parsons and Shils add that 'The situation of action may be divided into a class of social objects (individuals and collectivities) and a class of non-social (physical and cultural) objects' (ibid., p. 57). With reference to the former they state explicitly that 'The actor-subject may be oriented to himself as object as well as to other social objects' (ibid., p. 57).

The classification of social and non-social objects opens the possibility of distinguishing between *situation* or *total situation* and social situation, with the latter referring only to social objects. K. Davis (*Human Society*, New York: The Macmillan Co., 1949, p. 83) appears to accept this view when he writes, 'All approaches to social phenomena may be drawn together in terms of the interacting situation in which two or more persons are in contact'. On the other hand, M. & C. W. Sherif (*An Outline of Social Psychology*, New York: Harper & Bros., rev. edn., 1956, p. 4) define social psychology as 'the scientific study of the experience and behavior of individuals in relation to social stimulus situations'. The latter are classified 'under two broad headings: (I) other people and (II) cultural products'. They are emphatic in insisting that social stimulus situations are not limited to the first of these: 'Restricting the definition to the study of experience and behavior in relation to other people, leaving out their cultural products would amount to writing

social psychology as though people were living in a pre-Stone Age' (ibid., p. 21).

H. J. Friedsam

See also: Definition of the Situation
System of Orientation

Social Status (See **Status**)

Social Stratification (See **Stratification**)

Social Structure

A. 1. In the sense in which Spencer and many more recent sociologists have used the concept, *social structure* refers to a more or less distinctive arrangement (of which there may be more than one type) of specialized and mutually dependent *institutions* (q.v.) (and the institutional organizations of positions and/or of actors which they imply) all evolved in the natural course of events as groups of human beings, with given needs and capacities, have interacted with each other (in various types or modes of interaction) and sought to cope with their environment. The units of social structure in this case are themselves structures (either of culturally patterned practices, expectations, norms, or of established relationships among given actors, or both) and the assumption is that 'integration' and/or the survival and well-being of the whole, if not also of all the durable parts severally, and especially the preservation of the general form or arrangement of the whole, depend upon the adequate discharge or performance by each part of functions assigned to or associated with it, under conditions laid down by nature.

2. In contrast with this general conception of social structure is that introduced and maintained by analytic (or 'formal') sociologists (e.g. L. von Wiese, H. Becker, E. T. Hiller) in which *social structure* is seen as consisting of (a) an arrangement of *positions*, or statuses, variously created and maintained and/or (b) a *network* of relationships among persons, or actors. Thus, for example, 'The structure or organization of a society consists of statuses such as occupations, offices, classes, age and sex distributions, and other circumstance-occasioned reciprocities and rules of conduct' (E. T. Hiller, *Social Relations and Social Structures*, New York: Harper & Bros., 1947, p. 330). R. Firth's conception approximates this: 'In the types of society ordinarily studied by anthropologists, the social structure may include

668

critical or basic relationships arising similarly from a class system based on relations with the soil. Other aspects of social structure arise through membership in other kinds of persistent groups, such as clans, castes, age-sets, or secret societies. Other basic relations again are due to position in a kinship system. ...' (*Elements of Social Organization*, London: Watts, 1951, p. 32).

B. The general concept of structure appears to have been borrowed and adapted from physics (especially classical mechanics) on one hand, and, more extensively, from biology (especially the morphology and physiology of animals and of plants) on the other. Although the comparison of social structures to machines or other inorganic structures or to organisms was generally intended to be merely analogous, confusion concerning the precise denotation and the various connotations of the concept has resulted from this practice. This becomes evident when one asks such questions as (a) how, exactly, and by whom or by what the structure is to be regarded as having been brought into existence and 'held together' (viz. fabricated or constructed by some agent with all parts 'mechanically' interconnected; 'genetically' produced in a natural environment with constituent parts or units 'functionally' interrelated in some non-teleologically (or teleologically) viewed process; or intentionally or unintentionally produced in and through the interaction of motivated actors to whom some choices are conceived to be available), (b) in what exactly it consists and whether the constituent units are themselves structures composed of still other units, (c) how, i.e. on what basis or in what way the units are, or must be, 'integrated', (d) how, and in what way, or by what means, it is altered, (e) whether it is essentially motionless or whether it may be conceived of as essentially vibrant, in motion, but along lines that, for analytic purposes, may be regarded as fixed or unchanged as to arrangement. Variations in social science usage could best be pointed out, perhaps, by noting different answers which a sample of social scientists give either implicitly or explicitly, to one or more of these questions. It should be pointed out, however, that few if any social scientists, for one reason or another, appear to have answered all of them explicitly.

C. In current sociological usage the concept of social structure is applied to small groups as well as to larger associations, communities, and societies. There is also implicit recognition of variations in the clarity and degree of prescription and of reliability in the 'definition' and perception of social structure among actors in a situation. In some situations positions (or statuses) are prescribed in detail in culture patterns (and firmly established in the habit patterns of participating or potential actors). There are other situations in which positions (or statuses) and role-expectations are not so sharply defined *in culture* but where there are clear understandings and expectations among the actors concerning their relationships to each other as defined and established in their response patterns. At the extreme there are situations in which neither of these kinds of patternings is firmly established.

Allan W. Eister

See also: SOCIAL ORGANIZATION (Sociology)
SOCIAL SYSTEM

Social Survey
The term *social survey* is used to denote accounts of descriptive or explanatory field research which include first-hand and quantitative information about a particular social problem.

This type of study developed from travellers' tales and personal accounts in various natural contexts. In British practice it has denoted a body of field research literature, from the 18th century onwards, which confines itself to specific social problems, with the particular aim of influencing social policy rather than the more general aim of offering a scientific explanation of social phenomena. 'A fact finding study dealing chiefly with working class poverty and with the nature and problems of the community' (A. F. Wells, *The Local Social Survey in Great Britain*, London: Allen & Unwin, 1935, p. 13). More recently, C. A. Moser, commenting on the variety of enquiries now known as social surveys, argues for a wider use of the term noting that 'the only factor common to surveys is that they are concerned with the demographic characteristics, the social environment, the activities or opinions and attitudes of some group of people' (*Survey Methods in Social Investigation*, London: Heinemann, 1958, p. 1).

In Great Britain, the phrase the 'Social Survey' often denotes the Government Social Survey instituted in 1941 to provide, for the guidance of the administration, social data on public need and demand. This body has also been associated with, or has given advice to,

Social System

many non-governmental groups engaged in socio-economic research.

J. Mogey

See also: CENSUS

Social System

A. A *social system* is the system constituted by the interaction of a plurality of individual actors whose relations to each other are mutually oriented (i.e. are defined and mediated by a system of culturally structured and shared expectations).

B. As a technical term, *social system* has a central place in the work of T. Parsons and E. A. Shils (*Toward a General Theory of Action*, Cambridge, Mass.: Harvard University Press, 1951) and T. Parsons (*The Social System*, Glencoe, Ill.: The Free Press, 1951). It had a wide informal use in prior works by sociologists, social philosophers, and social psychologists. Another term, *social organization* (q.v.) or *organization*, is commonly used by sociologists and some anthropologists to refer to the same or similar phenomena.

Parsons and Shils offer a definition of *social system* at several points in their work. That which follows seems to be the most complete: 'A *social system* is a system of action which has the following characteristics: (1) It involves a process of interaction between two or more actors; the interaction process as such is a focus of the observer's attention. (2) The situation toward which the actors are oriented includes other actors. These other actors (alters) are objects of cathexis. Alter's actions are taken cognitively into account as data. Alter's various orientations may be either *goals* to be pursued or *means* for the accomplishment of goals. Alter's orientations may thus be objects for evaluative judgment. (3) There is [in a social system] interdependent and, in part, concerted action in which the concert is a function of collective goal orientation or common values, and of a consensus of normative and cognitive expectations' *Toward a General Theory of Action*, p. 55).

In other places they are more succinct: 'A social system is a system of the actions of individuals, the principal units of which are roles and constellations of roles. It is a system of differentiated actions, organized into a system of differentiated roles' (ibid., p. 197). Again, 'A social system ... is a system of interaction of a plurality of actors in which the action is oriented by rules which are complexes of complementary expectations concerning roles and sanctions' (ibid., p. 195). In *The Social System*, Parsons states '... a social system consists in a plurality of individual actors interacting with each other in a situation which has at least a physical or environmental aspect, actors who are motivated in terms of a tendency to the "optimization of gratification" and whose relation to their situations, including each other, is defined and mediated in terms of a system of culturally structured and shared symbols' (*The Social System*, pp. 5–6). A bit later he declares, '... a social system is a mode of organization of action elements relative to the persistence or ordered processes of change of the interactive patterns of a plurality of individual actors' (ibid., p. 24).

Certain elements of Parsons's definitions are dispensable. Thus his judgements about the internal dynamics of the actors concerned—as, for example, their tendency to optimize gratification or to cognize and cathect one another—do not seem intrinsic to the definition of social system.

We may notice that the idea of social system does not include cases of interaction in which an individual engages in reciprocal influence with himself. Further, it excludes interaction in which the actors, while influencing one another, are unaware of each other's presence or, if aware, are not interacting in terms of culturally structured and shared expectations. Instances of these types of interaction are especially conspicuous in studies of human ecology (q.v.) and of social change (q.v.).

Guy E. Swanson

See also: FUNCTION
ORGANIZATION
ROLE
SOCIAL ORGANIZATION (Sociology)
SOCIAL STRUCTURE

Social Welfare (See Welfare)

Socialism

A. The *Oxford English Dictionary* defines *socialism* as 'A theory or policy that aims at or advocates the ownership or control of the means of production—capital, land, property, etc.—by the community as a whole and their administration in the interests of all'.

Such a definition is clearly over-formal and ambiguous, and if followed unequivocally would give a misleading picture of the complex nuances of this term.

1. 'Ownership or control' by the community is not of itself very precise. Hitherto the only practical alternative to private enterprise for a modern industrial society has been found in State Capitalism—though the state may delegate its powers to boards which it appoints. *Municipal socialism*—with which many English writers were concerned at the beginning of this century—would in principle avoid some of the problems created by large *national* boards: but this expedient has not been widely followed.

2. A formal definition such as that cited above does not make clear whether the socialization of *all* the means of production is envisaged or only of what Engels called 'the commanding heights'. The former might seem the more logical, seeing that in principle socialists are opposed to private enterprise as exploitation. But again, in practice, many movements now regard themselves as socialist without feeling committed to so broad an objective.

3. No narrow definition can deal adequately with the problem of the differences in actual or conceivable socialist systems which arise (or may arise) from the extent to which such systems coexist with *democracy*. To some *socialism* embodies a form of social or economic democracy which is deemed to possess such merits (as a goal or as a mechanism) that the presence or absence of other patterns of democracy alongside *socialism* is a matter of small importance. To others *socialism* is what is deemed to make the other democratic mechanisms work more smoothly.

4. A good deal of the emotional drive behind socialism has come from the assumptions about 'workers' control of industry' which for many have been central to the issue. Yet few ventures in practical socialism have in fact conceded any wide or significant measure of self-government to the 'workers' in the industries concerned. Nor has there been a consistent clarity in the thinking of socialists upon the potential conflict between the imperatives of 'workers' control' and the norms of administrative efficiency. The problem arising from such conflict cannot be settled or dismissed a priori.

5. A formal definition of the kind cited may be further inadequate if it implies that *socialism* entails a concern with means as distinct from ends. Means and ends are in this, as in so much else, inextricably interwoven—but socialism has always implied, and often articulated, an ideal or vision of the good society in the attainment of which *socialist* economic instrumentalities would be employed. Such a view

has sometimes slipped over into imputing to *socialism* a static quality, often also a negative quality—the nature of the ideal society being described in terms of its distance from currently observable features of non-socialist societies, e.g. exploitation, etc. It may even be that these defects are, to some extent, correlated with a tendency to equate some of the economic instrumentalities with the *goals* of socialism. In recent years a more sociological approach to the goal of the good society has led socialists to contemplate the modern dilemmas of status and equality, and to build into their 'ideals' potentially dynamic and concretely positive features. This is especially true in the debates on *socialism* within advanced societies. In the emergent states *socialism* is more intimately concerned with problems of nationalism and economic development than with the nuances, paradoxes, and symbols of social status. The vision of the 'good society' in such states is of one in which problems of acute poverty have been abolished. *Socialism*, as an economic instrumentality, here has the prime aim of fostering economic growth—an aim to which many other economic, political, and social values may be subordinated.

C. It is not possible to list the many varieties of socialist doctrine and methods that have emerged over the last century and a half. Some of the leading issues which divide the various schools will appear from the following:

1. Marxists have attempted to distinguish 'utopian' from 'scientific' forms of socialism. Marx himself argued that earlier advocates had been 'utopian' in proposing certain changes, because they were desirable—whereas his own brand of socialism purported to show that the changes were 'inevitable' as well as desirable, and to indicate the grounds of this inevitability.

2. Within the camp of self-styled Marxists there has been heated debate as to the path whereby this 'inevitable' goal might be attained. The course of actual social development in advanced societies has produced much scepticism as to this 'inevitability' and led to various forms of revisionism—the concern of which has been to reassess the Marxist view of an 'inevitable' proletarian revolution as the instrument for the attainment of *socialism*.

3. For many Communists today *socialism* implies a stage (which has been claimed variously to have been attained or to be imminent in countries ruled by Communist governments) on the road to Communism proper.

671

Socialization

4. Within the ranks of non-Marxian socialists there has been dispute between the adherents of state socialism (or comprehensively planned socialism) and the defenders of guild socialism. This controversy has been muted in recent years —due to the recognition of the part necessarily played by forms of central planning with regard to economic growth. But the issue of freedom and autonomy raised by the guild socialists remains a central concern for those socialists who regard themselves as being also liberal empiricists and who do not claim that any one form of social or economic organization can instantiate or express *socialist* ideals in a context of constant change.

D. In varying degrees, most clearly in Britain, new motifs have been introduced into *socialism* and, in general, accepted by all socialists as in conformity with the movement's conception of social justice. This has been the outcome of three main demands on the part of the masses: (a) for the establishment of a society in which the workers will be guaranteed not only the political rights they already possess, but also a degree of economic security, including latterly full employment, such as is thought unattainable under the 'free market' system of private enterprise (this has led to a greater measure of State intervention in industry); (b) for a 'Welfare State' to be brought about by a large-scale extension of the social services; (c) for such a redistribution of income as is necessary to iron out class distinctions, and at the same time to enable the living standards of the wage-earners to be maintained and improved.

E. 1. The word *socialism* seems first to have been used in Italy in 1803, but in a sense unconnected with its later meaning. In 1827 *socialist* was employed in the *Co-operative Manager* to denote the followers of Robert Owen's co-operative doctrine; while *socialism* made its appearance in 1832 in the Saint-Simonian organ *Le Globe*, to characterize the Saint-Simonian doctrine. Thereafter both terms were commonly employed in France, England, Germany, and the United States.

2. From the first they implied opposition to *individualism* (q.v.), the early socialists being those who advocated one or another of the various competing 'social systems' which, according to G. D. H. Cole, 'agreed in their hostility to the prevailing individualist order in economics, and to the pre-eminence given to political over social and economic questions'.

Thus, throughout its history, socialism has emphasized the claims of man as a member of society rather than his claims as an individual. This fundamental idea has found expression in many forms—in Anarchism, Syndicalism, Guild Socialism, Christian Socialism, Menshevism and Bolshevism, to name only some of the more important of them. Each is a study in itself, but the ultimate objective of them all has been to create an economy in which society will be responsible for the way in which the means of production are used.

3. There have been differences of view as to the method by which this goal could be realized. Proudhon sought to realize this objective by returning to a simplified economy in which production would be carried out by small decentralized communities. On the other hand, the leaders of the other early socialist schools— Saint-Simon, Fourier, and Owen—all accepted the Industrial Revolution, and their systems so far agreed in envisaging an authoritarian economy, albeit one in which the productive forces would be developed in the interests of society as a whole. Similarly, Marx based his case against the capitalist system on the ground that it had become a 'fetter upon production', and contended that the 'social anarchy' to which it had allegedly led must inevitably yield to production according to a 'common plan', this clearly implying, as his anarchist opponents early discerned, some form of centralized direction, though Engels claimed that it would be one in which 'the administration of persons is replaced by the administration of things'.

R. N. Carew Hunt

See also: CAPITALISM
COMMUNISM

Socialization

A. *Socialization* in social psychology denotes the process by which an individual learns to adjust to the group by acquiring social behaviour of which the group approves.

B. The term *socialization* is used primarily by social psychologists, sociologists, and students of child development: 'All infants whose capacities ... are not severely limited take part in social interaction and, in so doing, acquire social behaviours. The process ... known as socialization ... is essentially one of learning' (T. M. Newcomb, *Social Psychology*, New York: Dryden Press, 1950, p. 51).

This definition from Newcomb rather equates individual socialization with all social learning.

According to others, socialization refers rather to learning which meets with group approval (W. F. Ogburn & M. F. Nimkoff, *Sociology*, Boston: Houghton Mifflin, 3rd edn., 1958, ch. 12).

C. The differences in conception of the term socialization extend also to the mechanisms (q.v.) by which it is achieved. After noting that 'the central focus of the process of socialization lies in the internalization of the culture of the society into which the child is born', T. Parsons and R. F. Bales indicate that the crucial aspects of culture for this purpose are the patterns of value of the society, and that the effective conditions for socialization consist of 'being placed in a social situation where the more powerful and responsible persons are themselves integrated in the cultural value system in question, both in that they constitute with the children an institutionalized social system, and that the patterns have previously been internalized in the relevant ways in their own personalities'. Parsons and Bales also believe that socialization entails alternating differentiation and integration of roles (*Family: Socialization and Interaction Process*, Glencoe, Ill.: The Free Press, 1955, p. 17).

From the Freudian perspective, which Parsons and Bales have adapted to their theory of social action and social systems, socialization is the process whereby the child internalizes parental norms and acquires a superego (q.v.). This is said to occur through cathectic-evaluative and cognitive mechanisms. The former includes reinforcement-extinction, based upon reward and punishment. The latter involves imitation and identification, based on feelings of esteem or love (G. J. Hinkle, 'Sociology and Psychoanalysis', in H. Becker & A. Boskoff (eds.), *Modern Sociological Theory In Continuity and Change*, New York: Dryden Press, 1957, p. 16). The symbolic interactionists (see *Social Psychology*) emphasize the role of speech in the process of socialization: 'The child becomes socialized when he has acquired the ability to communicate with others and to influence and be influenced by them through the use of speech. This implies socially acceptable behavior toward named objects' (A. R. Lindesmith & A. L. Strauss, *Social Psychology*, New York: Dryden Press, rev. edn., 1956, p. 124).

D. Although the term *socialization* is generally used in relation to children the process is a general one and is therefore applicable also to adults. A person may at any age be introduced to new groups and acquire their values.

Meyer F. Nimkoff

See also: INTERNALIZATION
SOCIAL INTERACTION
SOCIAL PSYCHOLOGY

Socialization (Political Science)
(See **Nationalization**)

Societal

The term *societal* was first used by A. G. Keller in his *Queries in Ethnography* (New Haven: Yale University Press, 1903), a manual for laymen who proposed to travel abroad. The term was not explicitly defined, but was used in the phrase 'societal system' to refer to a set of questions dealing with government, law, authority, class structure, and those customs governing relations among men. Keller later explained and justified his introduction of this new term: 'I do not wish to apologize for it in any way, for I think an adjectival form corresponding to the noun "society" and signifying something much more definite than "social" is a present necessity in the development of a science of society. Some of the vagueness chargeable to sociological writing is undoubtedly due to the use of "socius" where "societas" is or should be the real conception in mind' (*Societal Evolution*, New Haven: Yale University Press, rev. edn., 1931, p. 18 n).

The precise meaning assigned to *societal* therefore depends upon the conception of *society* (q.v.) with which it is associated. Since society, for Keller, was 'a group of human beings living in a cooperative effort to win subsistence and to perpetuate the species' (W. G. Sumner & A. G. Keller, *The Science of Society*, New Haven: Yale University Press, 1927, vol. I, pp. 6–7), *societal* referred to the organizational features of group life. Although the term has occasionally been used loosely to refer to anything 'existing throughout a society' (R. Freedman et al., *Principles of Sociology*, New York: Henry Holt, 1952, p. 600), its more frequent application (when the term is used at all, since many sociologists avoid it entirely) has remained more or less consistent with Keller's initial meaning. J. O. Hertzler, for example, recently defined *societal* as referring to 'the social action of individuals and groups as they are involved in the structural-functional, the organizational and operational aspects of a

Society

human community or society' (*Society in Action*, New York: Dryden Press, 1954, p. 6 n).

Ely Chinoy

See also: SOCIAL
SOCIETY

Society

A. There is as yet no single, generally accepted definition of *society*, for each of its three major uses refers to significant aspects of social life.

1. In its broadest meaning *society* refers to the totality of social relationships among men.

2. Each aggregate of human beings of both sexes and all ages bound together into a self-perpetuating group and possessing its own more or less distinctive institutions and culture may be considered *a society*. In practice, it should be noted, the limits of specific societies in this sense frequently have been based on political boundaries, a procedure which raises fundamental questions about the relations between state and society.

3. Society has also been defined as the institutions (q.v.) and culture (q.v.) of an inclusive and more or less distinctive and self-perpetuating group of both sexes and all ages. Obvious connections exist between the second and third definitions, for they refer to the two fundamental and interrelated premises of sociological inquiry, that men live everywhere in groups and that their behaviour is substantially affected by shared norms and values.

B. In medieval social and political theory society as such was not differentiated from the political community. Man belonged to this political community and to the Church; all groups and associations, except the Church, whose political role was subject to controversy, and the family, which was viewed as a 'natural unit', were considered as subordinate to or part of the state. The distinction between state and society emerged gradually during the religious and political upheavals of the 16th and 17th centuries; by the 18th century many influential French and English writers no longer looked upon the two as coterminous. The state was merely one segment, however important, of the larger reality of society.

C. Until Comte and Spencer sought to establish sociology as a separate science in the middle of the 19th century, society was generally considered an aggregate of individuals whose collective character could be deduced from the fundamental nature of man. Both Comte and Spencer insisted, however, that society is not merely 'a collective name for a number of individuals' (H. Spencer, *Principles of Sociology*, London: Williams & Norgate, 3rd ed. rev., 1885, vol. I, p. 435), but is a distinctive 'entity' transcending the individuals who belong to it. Despite continued criticism by those who contended that society is essentially a psychic phenomenon to be explained in terms of individual psychology, the view of society as a reality sui generis gradually gained acceptance as a legitimate premise of sociological inquiry. Even when they accepted this premise, however, sociologists were by no means agreed concerning the nature of the reality that is society.

1. In its most inclusive meaning the term was used to refer to humanity or to mankind at large, or, more frequently, to the basic fact of human association. M. Ginsberg, R. M. MacIver, and T. Parsons all suggested at about the same time that *society* refers to 'the whole tissue' or 'the whole complex scheme' of social relationships (M. Ginsberg, *Sociology*, London: Oxford University Press, 1932, p. 39; R. M. MacIver, *Society: Its Structure and Changes*, New York: Long & Smith, 1932, p. 6; T. Parsons, 'Society', in E. R. A. Seligman (ed.), *Encyclopedia of the Social Sciences*, New York: The Macmillan Co., vol. 14, 1934, p. 225).

2. Society in this general sense was usually distinguished from *a society* (or, in MacIver's case, *a community* (q.v.)), which could then be defined in several different ways. Spencer used *a society* chiefly to denote an organized collectivity, a group of persons held together by co-operative bonds. W. G. Sumner and A. G. Keller followed Spencer's lead by defining a society as 'a group of human beings living in a co-operative effort to win subsistence and to perpetuate the species' (*The Science of Society*, 4 vols., New Haven: Yale University Press, 1927, vol. 1, p. 7). Others who conceived of society as a collectivity did not emphasize co-operation as had Spencer and his followers. R. Linton, for example, identified a society as 'any group of people who have lived and worked together long enough to get themselves organized or to think of themselves as a social unit with well-defined limits' (*The Study of Man*, New York: Appleton-Century, 1936, p. 91). In many instances the difference between society and other groups was virtually ignored in the definitions which were proffered. Thus Ginsberg saw a society as 'a collection of individuals united by certain relations or modes of behaviour which mark them off from others who do not enter into those relations or who differ from them in behaviour' (*Sociology*, p. 40). Even less precise was G. Simmel's influential definition of a society as 'a number of individuals connected by interaction' (K. Wolff (ed.), *The Sociology of Georg Simmel*, Glencoe, Ill.: The Free Press, 1950, p. 10).

3. In order to avoid the ambiguity of these later definitions which seem to equate *society* with any social *group* (q.v.), the term has frequently been confined to 'the largest group to which an individual belongs' (A. W. Green, *Sociology*, New York: McGraw-Hill, 2nd edn., 1956, p. 31), or to that group 'within which the members share the basic elements and conditions of a common life' (L. Wilson & W. L. Kolb, *Sociological Analysis*, New York: Harcourt, Brace, 1949, p. 267). From this perspective society is viewed as a complex network of interconnected and overlapping groups which together form a larger whole sharing a common culture and a distinctive institutional system.

4. The fact that a society was seen to possess a more or less distinctive way of life led, in some cases, to the identification of its institutions and culture as the society itself. This conception stemmed, in part, from Spencer, who had focused his attention chiefly upon institutions rather than upon the relations among the parts which form the collective whole. As R. E. Park and E. W. Burgess pointed out, many sociologists equated *society* with 'the sum total of institutions' (*Introduction to the Science of Sociology*, Chicago: University of Chicago Press, 2nd edn., 1924, p. 161), though they themselves defined it more broadly as 'the social heritage of habit and sentiment, folkways and mores, techniques and culture, all of which are incident or necessary to collective human behaviour' (ibid., p. 161).

Ely Chinoy

See also: SOCIAL
SOCIAL SYSTEM
SOCIETAL

Sociological Theory

A. A *sociological theory* is a statement, using abstract language, which seeks to explain a range—however broad or limited—of phenomena defined as social (q.v.). The field of sociology which has as its task the presentation of sociological theory may, on the one extreme, be constituted by a historical survey of orientations or points of view towards social phenomena, or may, at the other extreme, consist only of those logically integrated, conceptually well defined, sociological propositions for which a good deal of supporting evidence has already been accumulated.

B. While there might be agreement concerning this general definition of theory, sociologists use at least three referents when employing the word theory.

1. First, there is the conception of a theory as a general explanation of, or comprehensive point of view for analysing, most social phenomena. H. Spencer's theory of social evolution would be such a sociological theory (*Principles of Sociology*, London: Williams & Norgate, 1877). In recent years the outstanding works of this nature are P. A. Sorokin, *Social and Cultural Dynamics* (4 vols., New York: American Book Co., 1937–41), T. Parsons, *The Social System* (Glencoe, Ill.: The Free Press, 1951) and T. Parsons, E. A. Shils et al., *Toward a General Theory of Action* (Cambridge, Mass.: Harvard University Press, 1951). Parsons believes that theory must be broad: 'The theoretical system which is basic to sociology must be broader than that of the science of sociology itself. It must be a theory of social systems' (T. Parsons, *Essays in Sociological Theory*, Glencoe, Ill.: The Free Press, 1949, p. 4). Each of the comprehensive theories would exclude all the others, although presumably they would accept extensions and amendments.

2. A second kind of theory might be called limited theory, to contrast it with the comprehensive kind of theory mentioned first. A limited theory 'may be defined as an integrated body of definitions, assumptions, and general propositions covering a given subject matter from which a comprehensive and consistent set of specific and testable hypotheses can be deduced logically' (A. M. Rose, *Theory and Method in the Social Sciences*, Minneapolis: The University of Minnesota Press, 1954, p. 3). R. K. Merton calls theories of this type 'theories of the middle range' (thereby explicitly considering a single isolated hypothesis as a small-scale theory, an equivalence which most sociologists seem to avoid). Merton provides a cogent argument for theories of the middle range as against the comprehensive type of theory: 'Complete sociological systems today, as in their day complete systems of medical theory or of chemical theory, must give way to less imposing but better grounded theories of the middle range. We cannot expect any individual to create an architectonic system of theory providing a manual for the solution of problems, social

Sociology

and sociological. Science, even sociological science, isn't that simple. ... Sociology will advance in the degree that its major concern is with developing theories of the middle range and will be frustrated if attention centers on theory in the large. I believe that our major task *today* is to develop special theories applicable to limited ranges of data' (*Social Theory and Social Structure*, Glencoe, Ill.: The Free Press, rev. edn., 1957, pp. 7, 9). Merton provides well developed examples of theories of the middle range relating to reference group behaviour and to social structure and anomy. A limited theory is subject to extension and amendment, but cannot be used to explain most social phenomena and thus is tolerant of other sociological theories which seek to explain other social phenomena.

3. While both comprehensive and limited theories are generally presented along with empirical data, which are usually used as illustrative for the comprehensive theory and as providing a fairly systematic test for the limited theory, the history of theory is usually presented without empirical data and frequently combined with the history of social thought in general. A history or survey of social thought, describes points of view toward social phenomena in chronological or topical sequence. N. S. Timasheff (*Sociological Theory: Its Nature and Growth*, New York: Doubleday, 1955) notes that: 'Inspection of the sociological theories of the past and present shows that they revolve around a few problems, the most important of which are indicated by the following questions:

What is society and culture?

What are the basic units into which society and culture should be analysed?

What is the relationship between society, culture, and personality?

What are the factors determining the state of a society and a culture, or change in society or culture?

What is sociology and what are its appropriate methods?'

C. Sociological theory might be further described in terms of its purposes or functions. In the joint statement by the authors of *Toward a General Theory of Action* (Cambridge, Mass.: Harvard University Press, 1951, p. 3), the following functions of theory in the social sciences are listed: codification of existing concrete knowledge, guide to research, facilitation of the control of biases of observation and interpretation. H. L. Zetterberg (*Sociology in the*

United States of America, Paris: Unesco 1956, p. 19) holds that it is 'the task of social theory to formulate the minimum number of definitions and hypotheses which are needed for the description and explanation of the topical areas of sociology'.

D. B. Moore ('Sociological Theory and Contemporary Politics', *American Journal of Sociology*, vol. 61, 1955, pp. 107–15), points out that specific sociological theories fall into two categories, in terms of the kinds of propositions they state: theories of causal processes and theories of functional relationships.

Arnold M. Rose

See also: FRAME OF REFERENCE
MODEL

Sociology

A. While there is agreement among modern sociologists that *sociology* denotes the scientific study of the social behaviour or social action of human beings, there continues to be disagreement concerning (a) the nature of scientific method as applied to social phenomena; (b) the conceptualization of social phenomena as including or not including aspects which are not directly observable; and (c) the scope and range of social phenomena to be considered as the proper subject-matter.

B. Disagreement concerning the nature of sociology centred on issues of scientific method usually has to do either with (a) whether or not sociology is primarily a generalizing discipline or an 'historical' discipline or with (b) the legimacy of methods of research which depart from rigorous experimentation or its more usual alternative, careful statistical sampling and data analysis.

1. In the history of sociology there has been considerable controversy as to whether the sociologist should seek to build a systematic body of sociological generalizations or alternatively to develop only those general categories necessary for understanding particular historical configurations of social phenomena. The origin of this controversy lies in the difference between the German concepts of *Naturwissenschaften* and *Geisteswissenschaften*. The latter, which included the study of human activity, were regarded as disciplines which dealt with the unique, and which therefore could not use general concepts or hope for scientific generalization. Since the work of M. Weber, however,

676

there has been little debate about the possibility of using general concepts and of achieving limited scientific generalizations. In his case, however, and in the instances of many others, stress has been placed on the use of general categories and limited generalizations to understand particular historical societies.

In contrast to such 'historically' oriented sociologists have been those who have stressed the 'natural' character of human behaviour and from the beginning have believed that it is possible and desirable to build up a body of sociological principles of universal applicability. In the past such an emphasis was usually associated with a stress on rigorous experimental method, and with the disavowal of non-directly observable phenomena as proper objects of sociological investigation. This is clearly no longer the case, so that a social theorist like T. Parsons (*The Social System*, Glencoe, Ill.: The Free Press, 1951), who takes Weber as one of his points of departure and who is willing to embrace a broad range of research methods and to use 'subjective' categories of motive, value, etc., still desires sociology to move in the direction of the broadest possible range of systematic generalization. At the same time, many sociologists who nominally accept such a conception of sociology as a generalizing science continue to make studies of communities and other social phenomena in which general concepts are used primarily to explain and understand particular cases.

2. The answer to the question of what methods of research are to be used, if sociology is to be legitimately called a science, depends in part, of course, on the definition of science (q.v.) employed, and on the nature and range of the phenomena to be investigated. More importantly, however, it may depend upon the minimum level of verifiability that any descriptive or generalizing statement must have before such a statement can be regarded as a scientific statement. There can be little doubt that natural sciences, such as chemistry and physics, require and are capable of achieving extremely high levels of verifiability made possible by controlled experiment and exact measurement. In general sociologists have followed three paths: (a) the use of any method of research which promises to result in generalization superior to common sense, such method to be determined by the nature of the phenomena and the level of technique of the science at the moment; (b) the insistence on quantification and experimental method (with the use of statistical controls if manipulative control is impossible) and the limitation of research to phenomena which can be so treated; and (c) the effort to find methods of quantification and experimentation adequate to the kind of problems which the sociologists wish to study. It would appear that all three paths have their merits and that a generous definition of science and of sociology might embrace them all, leaving to the future the determination of which of the three will finally endure.

3. The controversy concerning whether or not sociology should contain conceptualizations of social phenomena as including non-observable elements such as motives, attitudes, values, etc. also stems in part from the *Naturwissenschaften-Geisteswissenschaften* dichotomy. German idealists included such elements as the core of social action, but as we have seen, declared them to be non-amenable to scientific observation and generalization. At the other extreme, some sociologists, particularly in the United States, who regarded sociology as a natural science insisted that such phenomena are either non-existent or that if they do exist they cannot and need not be studied by sociologists, since adequate description of and systematic generalization about directly observable human behaviour will be able to account for everything that such non-observable variables attempt to account for.

This controversy is still unresolved, but it has to some extent softened. Thus there are those who still insist that non-observable elements are theoretically necessary (e.g. T. Parsons, *The Social System*, pp. 543-5), but recognize that such elements must be linked with observable elements in a system of causes, effects, and indices and that only the latter can be used for purposes of verification; and there are those that insist that such elements are not necessary but attempt to find observable behaviour that in some sense will play a similar role in a theoretical schema (e.g. G. C. Homans, *Social Behavior: Its Elementary Forms*, New York: Harcourt, Brace and World, 1961, pp. 39-49).

4. The controversy over the scope of the subject matter of sociology is still not settled, and sociologists can be found working within the framework of each available definition.

(a) The original conception of the nature of sociology, stemming from Comte, was that sociology is the most general science dealing with the totality of symbol-mediated social behaviour. In this sense it supplants Aristotle's idea of man as 'the political animal' and all other terms that

Sociology

have been used to denote the study of social-cultural behaviour in the most inclusive sense. It has had older rivals which have claimed this inclusiveness, e.g. *Kulturgeschichte* and *Völkerpsychologie*, but these have largely disappeared. While practically all specialized social sciences have at one time or another through single-factor determinism claimed the role of the basic, generalized social science, the refutation of such determinisms has killed their claims.

At present sociology has two main competitors for the role of basic, general social science: psychology and anthropology. Psychology as such would seem to be a poor claimant. It does not pretend to exhaust the study of social-cultural behaviour, and it includes the study of animal behaviour and—in the case of both animal and human behaviour—the study of the physiologically and neurologically grounded laws of behaviour. Social psychology (q.v.) has roots in both psychology and sociology and if it were to broaden the scope of its subject-matter sufficiently might become the basic social science.

Anthropology must also be regarded as a poor contender. For many years it was more of a biological than a social or cultural speciality, and the biology of man is still one of its major interests. Also it has been and still is mainly concerned with the culture of extinct, pre-historic, and contemporary nonliterate cultures. Recently anthropologists have begun making studies of contemporary literate 'folk' societies and of modern societies which has brought the discipline in this effort into closer relation to sociology.

Despite its shortcomings sociology appears to be the discipline most likely to be the basic, general social science, if there is to be one. From this perspective sociology is the basic, general science of symbolically-mediated social behaviour, and is the discipline which has the task of generalizing, synthesizing, and systematizing the findings and methods of the special social sciences. It can be defined as the science of social relations and processes, the science of society, if society is regarded as the totality of social relations and processes, or the science of culture (q.v.), if the latter term is defined to denote this same totality.

(b) Not all sociologists, however, have been willing to have sociology make the claim of being the basic, general social science. Some have argued that it is a *basic* social science in the sense that it is necessary to the other social sciences, but that it is also a specialized social science centring either on social interaction or on society as an inclusive, organized system of social relations. Thus Simmel insisted on abstracting the 'social' or 'group' aspects of the total behaviour of men and making these aspects the subject-matter of sociology. On the basis of such abstraction he defined two sociologies: general sociology and formal sociology. The first of these is constituted by the study of all of historical life *in so far* as this life is socially determined; the second is constituted by the study of the 'forms' of interaction, e.g. the study of competition regardless of whether the process occurs in the economic, political, or other realm. Such studies are basic to but not inclusive of the work of the other social sciences (G. Simmel, *The Sociology of Georg Simmel*, trans. and ed. by K. H. Wolff, Glencoe, Ill.: The Free Press, 1950, pp. 3–25). So also C. W. Mills in his conception of the sociological imagination would seem to define sociology implicitly as the study of historical life as occurring within and subject to the pressures of the complex whole of society as constituted by its highly structured and organized 'social order' (*The Sociological Imagination*, New York: Oxford University Press, 1959). Both of these conceptions can give rise to special sociologies of knowledge, religion, etc., without, however, implying that such special sociologies include all forms of the study of human behaviour in these areas. M. Ginsberg (*Sociology*, London: Oxford University Press, 1934, p. 17) defines sociology as including (i) a morphology of types and forms of social life; (ii) a study of the interrelations of the parts or factors of social life; and (iii) the study of the conditions of social change. But he still does not regard it as the inclusive social science discipline.

(c) Other sociologists have attempted to narrow the field in other ways. Some have defined it as the study of social groups; others as the study of society as an inclusive organized system. In a recent instance T. Parsons has defined sociology as the study of social institutions and of institutionalization (*The Social System*, pp. 545–55). It is interesting to note, however, that he speaks of the theory of action and the theory of social action, which implies the existence of some discipline concerned primarily with such theory. It is not clear whether such a discipline would be a special, basic science or one capable of including the findings of all the social sciences.

5. If sociology gains acceptance as the generalized science which systematizes all scientific

678

knowledge produced by the special social sciences, the present quibbling about which is the 'most basic' or 'most important' social science will cease and all simplistic, single-factor 'determinisms' will go into oblivion along with phlogiston, vitalism, and souls. Furthermore, if the symbol-mediated social behaviour of human beings, which is the subject-matter of such a sociology, is conceived as structured, then sociology will be clearly seen as the science which investigates the origin, development, and functioning of *all* classes of social structures. We offer the following as a tentative classification of all possible social structures and of the special sciences immediately concerned with them:

(a) Biosocial: All *symbols* immediately sensed, that have culturally defined meanings: verbal, gestural, written, and symbolic artifacts such as flags, uniforms, and monuments. *Special sciences:* Linguistics, philology, logic, mathematics, semantics, semeiology, and possibly grammar and rhetoric.

(b) Personal: All classes and types of *personalities. Special sciences:* Social psychology, psychiatry, psychoanalysis, psychometrics, etc.

(c) Groupal: All general classes of human *groups*—not to be confused with *categories. Special sciences:* Small group research (groupology (?)), morale studies, etc., not well developed even at the descriptive level. Perhaps 'game theory' belongs here.

(d) Institutional: The ten major institutions —art, economics, education, family, government, health, recreation, religion, science, social welfare. *Special sciences:* Aesthetics, economics, education, 'familiology' (nascent), political 'science' (nascent), medical sociology (nascent), none for recreation, theology, sociology of knowledge, social work.

(e) Societal: Residual category for all *social structures* not covered above such as social classes, social movements, *Weltanschauungen* (pl. of 'ethos'?), publics, crowds, social 'contagions' (fads, fashions, hysterias), audiences, regions, etc. *Special sciences:* Not well developed, but opinion-polling, stratification studies, cultural 'lags', social conflict and control or 'social change', etc., represent areas of research which eventually may become special social sciences, as demography and ecology already have done. From these residual categories, new classes of social structures may be isolated and give rise to special sciences as clearly defined as the first four now are (cf. botanical and zoolo-gical classification, with corresponding special sciences).

Read Bain and William L. Kolb

See also: CASE STUDY METHOD
CULTURE
ECONOMICS
METHODOLOGY
POSITIVISM
SCIENCE
SOCIAL
SOCIAL PSYCHOLOGY

Sociology of Education (See **Educational Sociology**)

Sociology of Knowledge

A. The most general significance of the term may be inferred from the following definitions: 'The proper theme of our study is to observe how and in what form intellectual life at a given historical moment is related to the existing social and political forces' (K. Mannheim, *Ideology and Utopia*, London: Kegan Paul, Trench, Trubner, 1952, pp. 237–60). 'Sociology of knowledge is the analysis of the functional interrelations of social processes and structures on the one hand and the patterns of intellectual life, including the modes of knowing, on the other' (H. Becker & H. O. Dahlke, 'Max Scheler's Sociology of Knowledge', *Philosophy and Phenomenological Research*, vol. II, 1941–2, p. 310). 'The sociology of knowledge ... is concerned with the way in which systems of thought ... are conditioned by other social facts' (W. J. H. Sprott, *Science and Social Action*, London: Watts, 1954, p. 141).

As these definitions speak of 'intellectual life' or 'mental acts' or 'systems of thought' in general, and as it is openly or tacitly assumed by them that art, too, is to be included in the field studied, they appear to cover a wider field than that literally suggested by the term *sociology of knowledge*. There is, however, no discrepancy as the underlying assumption is that the mode of knowing, or of meeting with or experiencing reality, lays down a fundamental pattern with which the rest of intellectual life conforms.

B. After W. Jerusalem had in 1909 published an article entitled 'The Sociology of Perception' (*Die Soziologie des Erkennens*) in the weekly paper *Die Zukunft* (reprinted in *Gedanken und Denker. Gesammelte Aufsätze. Neues Folge*, 2nd edn., Vienna & Leipzig: W. Braumuller, 1925),

Sociology of Knowledge

E. Durkheim opened in his *Année Sociologique* a new division entitled *Les Conditions Sociologiques de la Connaissance* (cf. vol. XI, Paris: Felix Alcan, 1910, p. 41). It seems, however, to have been above all M. Scheler, who, in 1924, edited a collective work *Versuche zu einer Soziologie des Wissens* (München: Ungsinstitute für Socialwissenschaften) and, in 1926, published his own *Die Wissensformen und die Gesellschaft* (Leipzig: Der Neue Geist Verlag, 1926) who established the term in the canon of sociological language.

A scientific definition of the term would have to conform to the following requirements: (a) The first is that of strict objectivity, i.e. exclusion of the valuational element. The first aim of the sociology of knowledge conceived as a branch of learning is to *understand* the *origin* of ideas, not to judge of their political bearing and/or their validity (W. Stark, *The Sociology of Knowledge*, London: Routledge & Kegan Paul, 1958, ch. 2). (b) The second is the exclusion of unprovable ontological, i.e. metaphysical assumptions concerning the connection between social sub-structure and mental superstructure. The sociology of knowledge, if it is to be a scholarly discipline, must avoid dogmatic pronouncements about the problem of determinism and freedom in thought and constitute itself as a method for the *interpretation* of the *meaning* of ideas in the light of their (social) parent situation. (c) The third requirement is the provision of a clear definition of what is to be meant by 'social substructure', i.e. the social circumstances within which ideas come into being and in the light of which they can be interpreted.

C. Some of the problems and divergencies of usage become clear in an analysis of (1) Marxist usage; (2) usage in the writings of K. Mannheim; (3) sociology of knowledge as part of epistemology.

1. While the expression as such is not of Marxist origin, it was freely adopted by some of the Marxist writers who felt that the sociology of knowledge is either identical with, or at least a variant of, the so-called 'materialistic conception of history' put forward by K. Marx. In support of this opinion, the following sentences from the Preface to Marx's *A Contribution to the Critique of Political Economy* (1859), trans. N. I. Stone from 2nd German edn., New York: International Library Publishing Co., 1904, pp. 11–12) were habitually quoted: 'In the social production which men carry on they enter into definite relations that are indispensable and independent of their will; these relations of production correspond to a definite stage of development of their material powers of production. The sum total of these relations of production constitutes the economic structure of society—the real foundation, on which rise legal and political superstructures and to which correspond definite forms of social consciousness. The mode of production in material life determines the general character of the social, political and spiritual processes of life. It is not the consciousness of men that determines their existence, but, on the contrary, their social existence determines their consciousness'. The terms structure ('substructure') and 'superstructure', which appear in these sentences, have been freely used even by non-Marxist authors. The decisive difference between them and the Marxists consists, however, in the introduction by the latter of a discrimination between delusionary (or 'ideological') and realistic forms of thought, of which the first is said to be characteristic of declining, the last of ascending social classes.

2. Mannheim's usage of the term was also influenced by these Marxist conceptions, though he tried to fuse them with a basically pragmatic interpretation. As the very title of his main contribution to the subject, *Ideology and Utopia*, indicates, he regarded the sociology of knowledge as essentially the study of three distinct types of thought: firstly, realistic thought, i.e. thought pragmatically adjusted to and functioning as the truth within a given society—thought which contains 'neither less nor more than the reality in whose medium it operates' (ibid., p. 87); secondly, ideological thought, i.e. thought characteristic of conservative and reactionary groupings which is unrealistic because it is determined, not by the will to objective truth, but by the desire to forestall change; thirdly, utopian thought, i.e. thought characteristic of revolutionary groupings whose programme is as yet incapable of realization, and which is therefore also unrealistic because it is again determined, not by the will to objective truth, but by the wish-image of an imagined future. In so far as Mannheim's idea of the sociology of knowledge is characterized by a definite preoccupation with 'ideology' and 'utopia', as against scientific and truthful thought, he tends to conceive it, with the Marxists, as predominantly a technique for the 'unmasking' of delusionary thought-structures.

3. *Sociology of knowledge* can also be re-

680

garded as an investigation of the *validity* of thought-structures with a special view to their explanation, provided by the (non-philosophical, purely empirical or positive) sociology of knowledge on the basis of their (social) circumstances of origination. The sociology of knowledge, if understood in this sense, would become part and parcel of the philosophical discipline called epistemology. It goes without saying that it would have to abstain from political judgements as practised by the Marxists and Mannheim and to submit to the strict principles of all epistemological speculation.

W. Stark

Sociology of Law

A. In its most common usage, the phrase *sociology of law* means the study of law and legal institutions within their social context, as distinguished on the one hand from an analytical study of norms, and on the other hand, from a purely philosophical or teleological approach. It is a description for a multitude of approaches, concerned, in J. Stone's words, 'with the relations between the law and the social, political, economic and psychological facts, which are relevant to an understanding of its ... sociological substratum' ('Problems Confronting Sociological Enquiries Concerning International Law', in *Recueil des Cours*, 89, 1956, vol. I, p. 65).

The emergence of sociology of law as a separate branch of study owes a great deal to the sociological trends and movements discussed in B. below. Still in its infancy, the science of sociology of law suffers from a lack of exact definition and does not yet have clearly defined boundaries (G. Gurvitch, 'Major Problems of the Sociology of Law', *Journal of Social Philosophy*, vol. 6, 1940–1, pp. 197–215). It would seem more appropriate, however, if the term were to be restricted to that still inarticulated science which will be a converging place for the refined, integrated and crystallized efforts of the sociological and juristic movements discussed below as well as of future scholars. Those who claim that sociology of law is an autonomous science, distinguish it from sociological jurisprudence in that it is part of sociology (sociology of the spirit, thereby meaning ideas, beliefs, convictions) rather than jurisprudence (ibid., pp. 198–9) which centres around law and only incidentally draws on the social sciences for animation. Sociology of law as part of the study of sociology proceeds *from the study of law as an observable fact and as one of many social phenomena forming part of a broader cultural pattern*. It is a descriptive science which is not concerned with values as such, except in so far as regards testing the validity of such values in society. Its only relation to jurisprudence is in the raw material it provides to the latter in the form of objective data for a better legislation and application of law.

The autonomy and range of the subject-matter of sociology of law depend on the definition of sociology and law respectively. Hence, to Comte, who did not give a pre-eminent position to the legal phenomenon among other social phenomena, there could be no sociology of law apart from general sociology (cf. G. Gurvitch, *Sociology of Law*, London: Kegan Paul, Trench, Trubner, 1947, p. 12). H. Kelsen, on the other hand, who excludes any sociological definition of law from his 'pure theory of law' also would not recognize the legitimacy of a science of sociology of law apart from general sociology ('Zur Soziologie des Rechtes', *Archiv Für Sozialwissenschaft und Sozialpolitik*, vol. XXXIV, 1912, pp. 601–14). To H. Sinzheimer, sociology of law is a science of legislation: a practical science showing the law-makers the better way to proceed in their task (*De Taak der Rechtessociologie*, Haarlem: Tjeenk Willink & Zoon, 1935), while J. Hall defines sociology of law as a theoretical science consisting of generalizations regarding social phenomena, in so far as they refer to the contents, purposes, applications, and effects of legal rules (*Theft, Law, and Society*, Boston: Little, Brown, 1935). E. Ehrlich's confusion of legal phenomena with social phenomena makes the study of sociology of law far from systematic beyond an empirical sociological study of multifarious legal institutions, although it emphasizes thereby the sociological nature of the science. Again, the more recent exponents of sociology of law, such as B. Horvath (*Rechtssoziologie*, Berlin: Verlag für Staatswissenschaften und Geschichte, 1934), N. S. Timasheff (*An Introduction to the Sociology of Law*, Cambridge, Mass.: Harvard University Press, 1939) and G. Gurvitch (*Sociology of Law*), disagree on the nature and limits of the competence of sociology of law, because of the different definitions of law taken by them as a starting point; and on methodology, because of disagreement on matters of methodology among students of sociology. In Horvath's opinion, law is a substitute for strife and a limitation on powers, while Timasheff sees in law a combination or cross between ethics and power not necessarily conflicting in nature ('What is

681

Sociology of Law

Sociology of Law?' in *The American Journal of Sociology*, vol. XLIII, 1937–8, p. 231). Gurvitch, on the other hand, disagrees with both Horvath and Timasheff (*Sociology of Law*, pp. 150, 153–4). He objects to a definition of law which he thinks belongs to another discipline. 'The task of sociology is not at all to define law or to work out a system of jural categories or jural values', writes Gurvitch (ibid., p. 66), thereby implying the acceptance of the normative definition of law or whatever definition lawyers and legal philosophers choose to adopt, and distinguishing sociology of law from philosophy of law and legal theory. Viewed in this perspective, however, the science of sociology of law becomes dependent for its existence on the limits imposed by sociologists and lawyers on their respective fields.

B. Observations on the interaction of law and other social forces have been made, from time to time, by various writers and jurists, since antiquity. (Obvious examples are to be found in the work of Montesquieu and Weber.) However, the phrase *sociology of law* was only coined in 1892 by D. Anzilotti (*La filosofia del diritto e la sociologia*, Firenze: Tipografia Bouducciana, A. Meozzi, 1892), and the systematic study of sociology of law as a science may be said to have begun at the beginning of the 20th century with the publication of E. Ehrlich's book, *The Fundamental Principles of the Sociology of Law* (*Grundlegung einer Soziologie des Rechts*, München: Duncke & Humblot, 1913, trans. by W. L. Moll, Cambridge, Mass.: Harvard University Press, 1936).

The failure of law to catch up with the modern advances of technology and to control some of the negative effects of industrialization and urbanization have brought about a reaction among jurists and writers against the formalistic study of law and more concentration on its *functional aspect*.

The scepticism characteristic of social scientists and jurists during the latter half of the 19th century and the beginning of the 20th century expressed itself in such extreme movements as the rejection of law altogether as an indispensable factor in the social order of things (Comte, Marx); or in the more moderate views of Durkheim, who looked at law as the expression of collective consciousness or social solidarity rather than as a normative factor in society (*On the Division of Labor in Society* (1893), trans. by G. Simpson, New York: The Macmillan Co., 1933, pp. 64–70). Scepticism among

lawyers and jurists, especially those who were exposed to the sociological teachings of their time, took the form of a rebellion against the hitherto accepted analytical and positivist schools of jurisprudence propounded by Austin and Kelsen.

One such reaction expressed itself in the 'living law' movement of Ehrlich (*The Fundamental Principles of the Sociology of Law*). In Ehrlich's opinion, the source of all law may be found in society itself rather than in legislation, judicial decision, or even state authority. Such law he called 'living law' as distinguished from the 'norm for decision' laid down by the judge, which is not, according to him, the real spirit of law. Ehrlich's work, though criticized, had a great influence in stimulating both sociologists and lawyers to study the functional aspects of law more systematically and to concentrate on the end of law as a means of *social control* (q.v.) rather than on the analytical aspects of jurisprudence (see W. Friedmann, *Legal Theory*, London: Stevens, 4th edn., 1960, pp. 202–4).

The reaction against formalism in America, partly inspired by Ehrlich's teachings and in part original—inspired by O. W. Holmes ('The Path of the Law', in *Collected Legal Papers*, New York: Harcourt, Brace, 1920, pp. 167–202) and B. N. Cardozo (*The Nature of the Judicial Process*, New Haven: Yale University Press, 1921)—has found expression in the American School of Sociological Jurisprudence founded by R. Pound ('The Scope and Purpose of Sociological Jurisprudence', *Harvard Law Review*, vol. XXIV, 1910–11, pp. 591–619; vol. XXV, 1911–12, pp. 140–68, 489–516) and the so-called 'realist movement' represented by such lawyers as K. N. Llewellyn ('A Realistic Jurisprudence', *Columbia Law Review*, vol. XXX, 1930, pp. 431–65) and J. Frank (*Law and the Modern Mind*, New York: Coward-McCann, 1930, and *Courts on Trial*, Princeton, N.J.: Princeton University Press, 1949). The former is essentially concerned with the direction and ends of the law, the latter essentially sceptical and dissecting. Pound's 'Sociological Jurisprudence', while not completely rejecting the positivist approach of the analytical school, shows that *law is a product of social forces* and not merely the formal command of a sovereign. Law is a process of balancing conflicting interests and securing the satisfaction of maximum wants with the minimum of friction. The emphasis on balancing claims, demands and interests rather than the protection of rights makes Pound's definition of law a 'social engineering' device for the improvement of the social and economic order by conscious and intelligent effort (see R. Pound, *Interpretation of Legal History*, Cambridge: Cambridge University Press, 1923, p. 152; and *Introduction to the Philosophy of Law*, New Haven: Yale University Press, 1922, p. 99). The Realistic movement in American jurisprudence means little more than an attitude of 'rule-scepticism' (for a more detailed treatment of the Realist movement see W. Friedmann, *Legal Theory*, pp. 245–58). Unlike Ehrlich, it is overwhelmingly concerned with judicial and administrative decision. It seeks *to discover the social facts behind the judicial norm*, whether such an inquiry is directed to the treatment of injunctions in labour matters by various courts, the study of human prejudices in the interpretation of the Constitution, or the impact of traffic accidents on the development of the tort of negligence.

W. Friedmann

See also: Law

Sociology of Religion

A. Sociologists of religion typically give very broad definitions of their field. Thus, J. Wach, in an extensive mapping of the field (*Sociology of Religion*, Chicago: University of Chicago Press, 1943, pp. 11, 205), writes of studying 'the interrelation of religion and society and the forms of interaction which take place between them', and gives it as an assumption basic to the sociology of religion that 'religious impulses, ideas, and institutions influence, and in turn, are influenced by, social forces, social organization, and stratification'. A similarly broad conception is suggested by E. K. Nottingham (*Religion and Society*, New York: Doubleday, 1954, p. 1), who comments that the sociologist of religion is concerned with religion 'as an aspect of group behavior and with the roles religion has played through the ages'. And Wach's definitional view is virtually repeated in the assertion by J. M. Yinger (*Religion, Society and the Individual*, New York: The Macmillan Co., 1957, pp. 20–1) that 'the sociology of religion is the scientific study of the ways in which society, culture, and personality ... influence religion ... [as well as of] the ways in which religion affects society, culture and personality ...'.

B. 1. If we take the view that 'the sociology of religion is as the sociology of religion does' (and rely on a rough agreement about what may be pointed to as coming under the heading of *sociology of religion*), we find researches and reflections concerned with or centring upon: general group influences on religion; the functions of ritual for societies; typologies of religious organizations and of religious responses to 'the world' or the social order; the direct and indirect influences of religious idea-systems on society and 'components' or elements thereof (such as classes, nationality groups, ethnic groups) and of society on the idea-systems; specific analysis of numbers of religious sects and movements such as Christian Science, Mormonism, and Jehovah's Witnesses; the interaction of significant religious entities at local or 'community' levels; occasional self-conscious appraisals by spokesmen for major religious groups of the social circumstances in which the groups find themselves. This listing is incomplete and its items are necessarily less specifically suggested than they might be. But the general character of concerns in the sociology of religion is thus reasonably well indicated.

2. One problem close to the heart of the field as it is currently developing, and to the whole question of how it is conceived and defined, may be mentioned. In general (though with significant exceptions), sociologists of religion, operating with notions like that of *social interaction*, have not been notably successful in coming to grips with, and saying something sociologically significant about, the *content* of religion, its *cultural* components. Students of comparative religion and a number of theologians, although often working without a distinctive sociological apparatus, present a challenge in this regard. Presumably, much of the future of *sociology of religion* depends upon the mode of response to this challenge.

Louis Schneider

See also: Ancestor Worship
Animism
Church
Consensus
Cult
Institution
Magic
Mana
Monotheism
Moral Order
Non-Empirical
Polytheism
Religion
Revitalization Movement
Ritual
Sacrifice
Sect
Value

Sociometry

Sociometry

A. *Sociometry* is a form or field of social psychology which emphasizes the quantitative aspects of interpersonal phenomena—with special concern for the measurement of preferences.

B. Perhaps the first to use the word *sociometry* (sociométrie) was A. Coste (*Les Principes d'une sociologie objective*, Paris: Alcan, 1899, ch. XV). Coste devised an index of social power (population x the density of the population) and an index of sociality (social power ÷ population); this was a *sociometric* approach to demography (see P. Sorokin, *Contemporary Sociological Theories*, New York: Harper & Bros., 1928; and A. Bjerstedt, *Interpretations of Sociometric Choice Status*, Copenhagen: Munksgaard, 1956, pp. 13–14).

In 1934 J. L. Moreno (*Who Shall Survive?*, New York: Beacon House, 1953, pp. 51, 251) stated that 'Sociometry deals with the mathematical study of psychological properties of populations, the experimental technique of and the results obtained by application of quantitative methods'. He emphasized 'attraction—repulsion—neutrality systems'. Yet Moreno includes in his actual work the dynamics of small group life, especially the creativity and spontaneity of the individual.

C. Apparently, there has come to be a psychological (or individual) and a sociological (or group) approach to sociometry. Psychologists emphasize *the individual* and *his choices* (M. L. Northway, *A Primer of Sociometry*, Toronto: University of Toronto Press, 1952; and H. M. Jennings, *Leadership and Isolation*, New York: Longmans, Green, 1943) while sociologists tend to be more interested in the small groups, which may be organized after sociometric preferences have been made (L. D. Zeleny, 'Selection of Compatible Flying Partners', *American Journal of Sociology*, vol. LII, 1946–7, pp. 424–31).

A British analysis of this difference is of interest. J. E. Richardson ('Classification by Friendship', in C. M. Fleming (ed.), *Studies in the Social Psychology of Adolescence*, London: Routledge & Kegan Paul, 1951, p. 21) declares that Moreno 'explains the group in terms of the individual' while G. H. Mead would 'explain the individual only in terms of the group'. This may not be an entirely accurate analysis; but it recognizes the two approaches; probably the difference is often over-emphasized, however.

D. An early attempt at a synthesis of the various concepts of sociometry was made in 1943 by R. Bain ('Sociometry and Social Measurement', *Sociometry*, vol. VI, 1943, p. 212). Bain suggested that sociometry 'will remain a generic term to describe *all* measurement of societal and interpersonal data'. More recently Bjerstedt (*Interpretations of Sociometric Choice Status*, pp. 15–28) identified thirteen definitions of sociometry ranging from (a) 'every kind of quantitative' social psychology and sociology, through (b) quantitative treatment of 'preferential' interhuman relations, to (c) 'Everything Moreno has been associated with' including 'spontaneity' and 'creativity', etc. These thirteen definitions were sent to 269 'experts' for rating. The first 131 returns were analysed. All possible definitions received some 'votes'. But the most commonly mentioned was that of 'the quantitative treatment of "preferential" interhuman relations'; and the second most commonly mentioned was the 'quantitative treatment of every kind of *interhuman relations*', a sort of 'quantitative social psychology' (ibid., pp. 15, 16).

Bjerstedt was not satisfied, however, with a mere tabulation. He examined all less frequently chosen definitions including the reasons given therefore, and endeavoured to 'draw out' all useful ideas. He finally arrived at a definition on the following lines: *sociometry is the measurement of all kinds of interrelations both human and animal; but the primary emphasis is upon the measurement of human preferences*. Bjerstedt would contend that the first part of the definition should be considered a definition of *sociometry* and the second part a definition of *preferential sociometry*; thus, sociometry may be defined as the 'measurement of every kind of interhuman and interanimal relations' (ibid., p. 28).

Leslie D. Zeleny

See also: GROUP DYNAMICS

Solidarity (See Cohesion)

Sorcery (Also Witchcraft)

A. Beliefs in supernatural attack necessarily imply belief in methods of detecting the attacker. Hence ideas of witchcraft and sorcery are always entangled with those concerning divination (q.v.), but the last is best treated as a separate concept.

Most of the practices specified in accusations of supernatural attack are imaginary but for analytical purposes it may be useful to distinguish (a) *sorcery*: a performance or alleged performance by a magician (sorcerer) which is, in itself, technically possible but which, from a scientific point of view, could not be the cause of consequences attributed to it—especially the consequences of bringing evil upon others; (b) *witchcraft*: a quality or attribute or capacity of witches which has the consequence that they bring evil upon others even though they themselves, in their ordinary human capacity, go through no specific technical performance to achieve this end. Witches, so defined, are not necessarily conscious agents of the evil consequences which flow from the witchcraft which attaches to them or by which they are possessed.

B. Medieval writers did not distinguish sorcery and witchcraft from magic (q.v.). English statutes from the 8th century A.D. mention various offences including *veneficium* (magical poisoning), *incantatio* (creating illusions by spells), *sortilegio* (divinations), *invultuacio* (injuring through the making of wax images) all of which rated as *maleficium* which in Imperial Rome had been the offence of working (magical) evil against the state or against a neighbour. All these concepts remained imprecise. Cifford in *A Discourse of the subtill Practises of Deuilles by Witches and Sorcerers* (1587) defines a witch as 'one that woorketh by the Deuill' but includes under this head 'the conjurer, the enchaunter, the sorcerer, the deuiner, and whatsoever other sort there is'. Modern general dictionaries and encyclopaedias likewise make no clear distinctions. While witches in English folklore are always feminine, males were sometimes convicted of witchcraft in English courts down to the middle of the 17th century (C. L'E. Ewen, *Witch Hunting and Witch Trials*, London: Routledge, 1929).

C. Following E. E. Evans-Pritchard (*Witchcraft, Oracles, and Magic among the Azande*, Oxford: Clarendon Press, 1937) some anthropologists now distinguish witchcraft from sorcery by the following criteria:

1. *Sorcery* is the conscious performance of a technically possible act which has the imaginary consequence of bringing evil upon a victim. Sorcery is thus the craft of evil magic; it can be learnt by anyone.

2. *Witchcraft* is a quality which is innate to the witch, and all manifestations of witchcraft are intrinsically supernatural. Thus the pricking of wax images of an intended victim is *sorcery* but flying through the air on broomsticks is a natural capacity which European *witches* inherit from their mothers.

Though valuable for analytical purposes this distinction is not always reflected in the ethno-graphic sources (C. Kluckhohn, *Navaho Witchcraft*, Cambridge, Mass.: Peabody Museum, 1944) and some authorities have used quite a different terminology. E. Westermarck (*Ritual and Belief in Morocco*, London: Macmillan, 1926, vol. I, chs. VIII, XI) contrasts (a) the Evil Eye and (b) Witchcraft. But in Evans-Pritchard's usage (a) would be witchcraft and (b) sorcery. Again while the 17th-century witches of England and New England were witches, in that they conversed with demons and bore marks of the devil upon their bodies, most of the specific acts of which they were accused were those of sorcery (C. L'E. Ewen, *Witch Hunting and Witch Trials*, p. 267).

D. The terms *witchcraft* and *sorcery* ordinarily denote offences, but, where belief in such powers is unquestioned, their exercise is only an offence if illegally exercised. Medieval Church authorities were entitled at times to pronounce curses (i.e. to practice legitimate sorcery) and ethnography provides many instances of 'legal' sorcerers (B. Malinowski, *Crime and Custom in Savage Society*, New York: Harcourt, Brace, 1926). Similarly, belief in evil witchcraft may be associated with belief in 'good witchcraft'--an innate beneficial power exercised as a protecting influence by those in authority (M. Wilson, *Good Company*, London: Oxford University Press, 1951).

Actual cases of witchcraft and sorcery are ordinarily met with only in the form of accusations. An individual A believes himself to be victim of a supernatural attack and accuses another individual B of sorcery and/or witchcraft. There are societies where the notion of death from 'natural causes' is altogether lacking. Every human illness or death is then attributed to 'witchcraft' of some sort. The anthropologist tends, therefore, to focus his attention on the mode of divination whereby the victim or the victim's kin claim to be able to identify the witch assailant and also upon the nature of the hostile relationship between assailant and victim which is reflected in the accusation.

In any particular cultural situation the pattern of accusations tends to follow a set convention and it is principally a matter of such convention whether the accused is said to be a witch or a sorcerer or simply an employer of sorcerers. Most accusations fall into one of three categories: (a) accuser and accused are in close personal relationship as kinsmen or neighbours and this makes the overt expression of hostility difficult; (b) the accused witch is an individual of low status or an 'outsider' who is made a scapegoat for local misfortunes; (c) the accused is thought to be a member of some unpopular, or illegal, religious or political movement.

According to this definition sorcerers *perform* sorcery but witches are *possessed by* witchcraft, the witchcraft being thought of as either a substance of the witch's body or as some form of familiar spirit.

E. R. Leach

See also: DIVINATION
MAGIC

Sororate

Sororate denotes the custom of contracting marriage with the deceased wife's sister. In some societies her kin have an obligation to provide a girl as substitute for the dead woman. The custom is not nearly so widespread as levirate (q.v.) or widow-inheritance—where it exists the widower can ask for a sororate marriage as a favour, and not claim it as a right. I. Schapera says of the Kgatla that if the parents were not satisfied with the treatment of their dead daughter they would refuse to send a substitute but would refund the bridewealth instead (*Married Life in an African Tribe*, London: Faber & Faber, 1940, p. 324).

In another less frequent usage *sororate* is sometimes confused with *sororal polygyny*.

M. Douglas

See also: LEVIRATE
POLYGAMY

Sovereignty

A. *Sovereignty* denotes (a) the authority to make and amend law conferred by the rules of a legal system; (b) the political or moral authority of the state; (c) the effective source of or influence upon the exercise of political or legal power; (d) the independent legal or moral status of a community.

B. The term has been used from the earliest times to indicate the supreme power exercised by a deity, secular ruler, ruling body or ruling class. Bodin's *Les Six Livres de la Republique* (1576) describes the sovereign power vested in a commonwealth ('which in Latin is termed *majestas*') as 'absolute and perpetual'. In general, Bodin held, the sovereign is not bound by his predecessors' or his own laws since the lawmaker cannot bind himself in any matter which is the subject of his own free exercise of will (though the absolute power of princes and sovereign lords does not extend to the laws of God and of nature (bk. 1, chap. 8). The best known exposition in English of the necessity for the concession by those coming together to form a political society of absolute authority to the ruler or ruling collectivity occurs in Hobbes's *Leviathan* (1651). In its legal aspect the name most closely associated with the concept of sovereignty in Great Britain is that of J. Austin, whose definition of sovereign authority turns upon the political fact of habitual obedience given by the bulk of the population in an independent society to a determinate human superior (or superior body) not itself in a habit of obedience to any superior (*The Province of Jurisprudence Determined*, London: Murray, 1832, Lect. VI).

C. The sovereignty of Parliament in the United Kingdom is the capacity of Crown, Lords, and Commons acting in due form to make or amend any rule of law (see A. V. Dicey, *Law of the Constitution*, London: Macmillan, 10th edn., 1959, ch. 1). Under a federal system of government or one which contains provision for more than one type of legislative procedure (e.g. simple majority procedure for some purpose and special majority procedure for others) legislative sovereignty is sometimes said not to exist. Alternatively it is supposed to be divided or shared between different legislative entities.

D. There are three principal and distinct spheres in which the term sovereignty is to be found.

1. In constitutional law and political science it is commonly used to indicate the Crown or the person of the King but must be distinguished from the wider sense in which the legal sovereign may be defined as (a) the legislative authority defined by a constitution from which all the rules of a legal system derive their validity and by whose action all the rules may be amended or (b) the entity or collectivity in whose name a constitutional system is promulgated. Attributions of the latter kind would be 'The People of the United States' (in the U.S.A.), 'Allah Almighty' (formerly in Pakistan), and 'The working people of town and country as represented by the Soviets of Working People's Deputies' (in the U.S.S.R.).

2. In international law and international politics it is used to denote the independence or autonomy of a state in relation to other states (e.g. 'The nations of the free world must make an even more significant contribution of their national sovereignty to the common cause than hitherto' (Mr. Harold Macmillan, House of Commons, 5 Nov. 1957). *National sovereignty* may be used less stringently to indicate the right or claim of a national group to self-determination or free choice of government.

3. In political philosophy the term usually suggests or indicates the source or moral authority of legitimate government. It may also be used in a factual and sociological sense to indicate the body or class of persons who exercise decisive influence on the wielders of legal authority, e.g. 'That body is "politically sovereign" or supreme in a state, the will of which is ultimately obeyed by the citizens of the state' (A. V. Dicey, *Law of the Constitution*, p. 73). *Sovereignty* in this sense might be attributed to such diverse entities as 'the secret police', 'the Civil Service', 'backstairs influence', or 'the middle classes'.

G. Marshall

See also: LEGITIMACY
STATE

Soviet
A. 1. The term derives from the Russian *Soviet*, i.e. council, and first acquired its specific political meaning during the Russian Revolution of 1905–7, when Soviets of workers' deputies were formed in various industrial towns. These Soviets conducted mass strikes and served as a vehicle of revolutionary agitation for the Socialist parties and anarchist organizations. The Soviets reappeared after the February revolution in 1917, usually as Soviets of Workers' and Soldiers' Deputies. There were also separate Soviets of Peasant Deputies.

2. The Soviets became an extremely influential pressure group, competing for power with the Provisional Government and creating in fact conditions of 'diarchy'. The leaders of the Bolshevik Party regarded the Soviets as organs of uprising and embryonic organs of a new regime. Lenin developed the theory of Soviets as the state form of the dictatorship of the proletariat. Accordingly, the Bolsheviks both seized power in Russia in October 1917 and subsequently exercised it in the name of the Soviets.

3. I. V. Stalin described the Soviets as a 'transmission belt' linking the Party with the masses, 'organizations which rally the labouring masses ... under the leadership of the Party' (*Problems of Leninism*, Moscow: Party Publishing House, 11th Russian edn., 1940, p. 149). The Constitution of 1936 formally re-introduced universal suffrage in Russia, but the designation Soviet was retained for the elected assemblies.

B. The *Large Soviet Encyclopaedia* (Moscow: State Scientific Publishing House, 2nd edn., vol. 39, 1956) defines the Soviets of Working People's Deputies as 'popularly elected organs of state power in the centre and locally ... The Soviets are a higher form of state organization, fitted not for purposes of oppression and suppression of the working people, as befits any bourgeois state form, but for purposes of their full emancipation from oppression and exploitation, for purposes of dictatorship of the proletariat and building communist society'. Because under Article 126 of the 1936 Constitution 'the Communist Party of the Soviet Union ... is the leading core of all organizations of the working people, both public and state', including the Soviets, Stalin's description of Soviets as a 'transmission belt' remains valid.

C. 1. Colloquially and rhetorically the word Soviet (often in Pl.) is also used (particularly outside Russia) to denote the Russian Communist authorities in general.

2. As an adjective, the word Soviet has several meanings: (a) (mostly in Russia) pertaining to Soviets as the governmental and administrative apparatus (e.g. Soviet organs, Soviet work), particularly as opposed to the party, trade union, etc. organs; (b) relating to the present state form in Russia (e.g. Soviet power, Soviet state); (c) relating to Communist Russia in general (e.g. Soviet frontiers, Soviet literature).

S. V. Utechin

See also: BOLSHEVISM
COMMUNISM

Specialization (See Division of Labour)

Speculation
A. *Speculation*, in economics, denotes the action of forecasting fluctuations in the prices of commodities or stocks, and buying and selling them in order to profit by the forecasted price changes.

B. 1. If taken in this sense speculation is to be distinguished from regular trading as done by middlemen whose principal source of gain is the permanent price differences existing between different markets, not price fluctuations in the same market. It also is to be distinguished from investment, in which the principal source of profit is the income earned by the enterprise invested in.

2. The term *speculation* is usually used to describe one of two fundamentally different types of activity. It is sometimes used to mean

Sphere of Influence

any investment of resources or funds involving more than ordinary risk or uncertainty of results. It is more frequently used to describe the buying and selling of commodities, securities or land with the intent of profiting from fluctuations in the prices thereof. Speculation is occasionally used in a third sense, especially in the writings of critics of the organized stock and commodity exchanges. Here it is used as synonymous with gambling.

Of the three meanings the second is the most common and the one usually found in the professional literature of economics and business. It is the only meaning given in B. J. Horton's *Dictionary of Modern Economics* (Washington: Public Affairs Press, 1948). The reason for not using the term *speculation* to describe a risky investment is that there is a fundamental difference between investment and speculation, and such usage only leads to confusion. In investment the assuming of risk is incident to the enterprise undertaken. In speculation the assuming of risk is the essence of the enterprise. Investment is done for purposes of receiving income from the earnings of an enterprise. Speculation is done for purposes of making capital gains from fluctuations in price. Finally, investment is based on long-term expectations as to earnings whereas speculation is based on anticipations of short-term changes in the market. J. M. Keynes (*The General Theory of Employment, Interest and Money*, London: Macmillan, 1936, p. 154) makes a clear distinction between investors and speculators when he describes the latter as 'largely concerned, not with making superior long-term forecasts of the probable yield of an investment over its whole life, but with foreseeing changes in the conventional basis of valuation a short time ahead of the general public'.

Paul G. Craig

See also: INVESTMENT
RISK (AND UNCERTAINTY)

Sphere of Influence

A. *Sphere of influence* has usually been used to denote a geographical region or territory within which a particular power is acknowledged to have preferential or exclusive rights of a political or economic kind. It came into common usage with the expansion of Europe from the 15th century onwards.

B. The determination of a *sphere of influence* is, in a sense, a warning to other powers not to trespass. In the context of the expansion of European power into areas where little or no effective government has existed a *sphere of influence* might well be described as the 'half-way house of imperialism'. Through the exercise of political and economic tutelage the power concerned (and its nationals) may obtain most of the benefits of annexation whilst avoiding the responsibilities and antagonisms to which outright annexation might give rise.

In this century the demarcation of what to all intents and purposes are *spheres of influence* (even though not formally described as such) has also emerged from the carving up of power vacuums consequent upon the defeat of a Great Power (the Ottoman Empire in 1918 and Germany in 1945). Despite the disfavour into which the term now seems to have fallen the more customary designation of a country as a *client state* or a *satellite* of a Great Power might well be regarded as merely another way of saying that that country is within the latter's *sphere of influence*.

C. The use of the term may be illustrated by instances of the different grounds that have historically been found for bases of influence. For example such a sphere has been set up by 'higher edict' as was the result of the Papal Bull 'Aeterni' in 1481 which assigned all discoveries south of the Canaries and west of Africa to Portugal; similarly the Alexandrine Bulls of the last decade of the 15th century constituted the basis of the claims of the Spanish Crown to the lands of the New World. Alternatively *spheres of influence* may be set up by *joint agreement*, e.g. the series of agreements between France, Germany, and England between 1886 and 1906 dividing their respective spheres of influence in North-West Africa; or the agreement between Germany and England of 1890 delineating their respective spheres in East Africa. Amongst the most notable was the Anglo-Russian agreement of 31 August 1907 dividing Persia into a Russian sphere of influence in the north adjacent to the Caucasus, a British sphere in the south-east adjacent to India, and a neutral sphere between.

A third basis might be described as 'unilateral declaration' a category which, according to some writers, would cover the three principles embodied in President Monroe's message to the U.S. Congress on 2 December 1823, known as the Monroe Doctrine, in which the United States put on record her opposition to any attempt by any European Power to extend its political system to any part of the Western hemisphere 'for the purpose of oppressing' the

688

nations or 'controlling in any other manner their destiny'.

G. L. Goodwin

See also: IMPERIALISM

Spirit Mediumship

The term denotes a set of practices and ideas based upon belief that a specific human being possessed by a spirit (or closely controlled by a spirit) can serve as a means of communication between other human beings and the spirit world.

R. W. Firth

See also: SHAMAN
SPIRIT POSSESSION
SPIRITUALISM

Spirit Possession

Spirit possession denotes a set of practices and ideas based upon belief in the entry of a spirit into the body of a human being (or close control by a spirit of the body of a human being) so that the actions of the person affected are thought to be either those of the spirit, or to be immediately dictated by the spirit.

R. W. Firth

See also: SHAMAN
SPIRIT MEDIUMSHIP
SPIRITUALISM

Spiritualism

Spiritualism denotes a set of practices and ideas based upon belief in the existence of disembodied intelligences or personalities (spirits), and in the ability of human beings to communicate with them. The term may also refer more specifically, particularly in Western countries, to an organized movement employing mediums (often professionally) to obtain what is regarded as communication and guidance from spirits.

R. W. Firth

See also: SHAMAN
SPIRIT MEDIUMSHIP
SPIRIT POSSESSION

Spoils (See Patronage)

Standard of Living (Also Level of Living)

A. The phrase *standard of living* denotes (a) the conditions in which people actually live; or (b) the conditions of life to which people aspire but which they may not yet enjoy. In addition there is, as we are reminded by the U.N. *Report on International Definition and Measurement of Standards and Levels of Living* (New York: United Nations, 1954, p. 1) a third concept sometimes described as a standard of living, i.e. 'desirable conditions of living as defined for specific purposes, such as the fixing of minimum wages, of working hours, arrived at by national or international convention or agreement' (ibid., p. 2).

B. 1. Recent discussions and expert analysis by statisticians and others working in this field attempt to separate these various usages and to describe (a) above (the standards attained) as *level of living* (sometimes *plane of living*); (b) above as *standards of living;* and to distinguish the 'third concept' in A. above as *norm of living*.

It is clearly useful to distinguish what appear to be more 'normative' senses of the word *standard* from that sense which is essentially 'descriptive', but recent studies, through emphasizing the use of the term *level of living* and advocating research into its content and measurement, have shown themselves aware that some normative elements adhere to the descriptive term *level*, e.g. the U.N. Report cited above observes that 'The Committee recognized that any decision regarding the aspects or factors to be included in the concept of the level of living in itself involves a value judgement. For example, the recommendation that expectation of life at birth or literacy rate be used to indicate certain aspects of the level of living involves the value judgement that longevity and literacy are desirable. The Committee did not hesitate to make value judgements of this type concerned with content, although it refrained from attempting to establish specific norms ...' (ibid., p. 3).

2. Again in another expert report (*Definition and Measurement of Standards of Living*, Report on Conference of U.S. Experts, Chicago: Public Administration Clearing House, 1953, p. 35), the point is brought out that 'As soon as one begins to measure the actual level of living and to seek to determine whether it is higher or lower than in the past of the society in question, or in another society, it immediately becomes necessary to employ, explicitly or implicitly, some standard or value criterion by which to define the direction in which progress lies. A dimension or scale to measure actual conditions becomes a practical guide only when one can say that a movement towards this or that point of the scale (not necessarily the highest or lowest point) indicates improvement of conditions'.

3. Problems of analysis emerge very promptly when we reflect upon the different possible sources of such normative *standards* or *value criteria*. The *standards* in terms of which efforts may be made to improve existing levels may be

State

drawn from social values, arbitrary legal criteria, or the findings of scientific, e.g. nutritional, research. For an interesting discussion of these problems, see the Report of the U.S. Experts mentioned above (ibid., p. 36 ff.).

The concept of *living* standards, or levels, would include and perhaps emphasize, 'material' quantitative elements such as the consumption of goods and services. But in addition to consumption the idea of *living* includes some reference to conditions, e.g. of work and safety, and also to social amenities which may be qualitative and/or non-quantitative, e.g. education. Here again, the separation of components often demands some degree of subtlety. The provision, for example, of education, not only has long-term 'material' results, but makes 'material' demands upon the economy, e.g. in construction or repair of schools. Furthermore, by provoking *choices*, it at once introduces consideration of *value* which administrators and sociologists alike cannot ignore.

J. Gould

See also: CONSUMPTION
VALUE

State

A. The term *state* denotes a body of people living in a defined territory organized in such a way that a designated few of their own number can expect to control, directly or indirectly, by means of appeal to real or imputed group values or by force if necessary, a more or less restricted range of activities of the body of the people.

B. 1. It will be evident that such a definition of the state—like any other—is in some respects too broad and in others too narrow. Sociological usage—increasingly paralleled by usage in political science takes the state to be an association which provides political leadership—the term is defined, in the sense set out by M. Weber ' . . . only in terms of the specific *means* peculiar to it . . . namely the use of physical force ('Politics as a Vocation', in *From Max Weber*, ed. by H. H. Gerth & C. W. Mills, London: Kegan Paul, Trench, Trubner, 1947, p. 78). Influential also has been the formulation given by R. M. MacIver and C. H. Page: 'The state is distinguished from all other associations by its exclusive investment with the final power of coercion' (*Society: An Introductory Analysis*, New York: Rinehart, 1949, p. 456). The variety of state forms and origins is stressed by M. Ginsberg: 'As a minimum, we may say that the state exists in all communities in which the pro-

tection of the members and the enforcement of common rules are functions of a differentiated system of organs. Communities in which rules are not enforced by collective action, or in which the protection of individuals is left to the kindreds or other groups, or perhaps even to chiefs possessed of no defined authority, are not states' (*Sociology*, London: Oxford University Press, 1934, pp. 147–8). More descriptive and formalistic is the succinct definition given by H. D. Lasswell and A. Kaplan—for them the state is a 'sovereign territorial group' (*Power and Society*, New Haven: Yale University Press, 1950, p. 181). This definition selects four elements—people, territory, government, and independence—as criteria for distinguishing the state from other political entities, and those elements are sufficient to distinguish the state from dependent colonies, the United Nations, the Catholic Church, and a beehive. Borderline cases do exist, nonetheless, such as the Vatican, the Order of Malta, countries like Monaco, and 'satellites' of a powerful state.

2. All these approaches—different though they are—have it in common that they do not raise the philosophical issues inseparable from such questions as 'why does the state exist?' or 'why should we obey the state?' or 'on what grounds is the state justified?' The difficulty there is in keeping clear of such questions may be shown by citing another sociological 'definition'. L. V. Ballard (*Social Institutions*, New York: Appleton-Century, 1936, p. 253) says, 'Sociologically conceived, *the state is the institution which organizes the will of a people, politically constituted, with respect to its collective interests*'. This definition introduces the notion that the coercive power of the state is somehow related to the will of the people and that the people have a common interest or purpose. On the first point, it is difficult to demonstrate that there is a link between the will of the people and the use of power within a state. On the second point, there is variation as to the conception of what the ends, purposes, and functions of the state are. L. Wilson and W. L. Kolb (*Sociological Analysis*, New York: Harcourt, Brace, 1949, pp. 516–17) say that the 'basic function' of the state 'is to maintain social order'. E. T. Hiller (*Social Relations and Structures*, New York: Harper & Bros., 1947, p. 222) describes the aim of the state as 'the promotion of general welfare and maintenance of social order'. P. A. Sorokin (*Society, Culture, and Personality: Their Structure and Dynamics*, New York; Harper & Bros., 1947, p. 206) describes the state as 'a kind of clearing house, for the interrelations and inter-pressures of all the groups in a given population over which the state government extends its power'.

3. The *state* is frequently distinguished from *society*. Wilson and Kolb (*Sociological Analysis*, p. 517) declare that the 'state is a part of society, not the whole of it'. Some writers like Ballard (*Social Institutions*, p. 254) emphasize that the state 'is concerned with many general interests; other associations concentrate on a few special interests'. But E. B. Reuter and C. W. Hart (*Introduction to Sociology*, New York: McGraw-Hill, 1933, pp. 130–1, maintain that 'the state is an organization for a particular purpose and corresponds closely to the church and, except for the extent of its power, with other control and interest groups'.

The *state* is also distinguished from *government*. Ballard (*Social Institutions*, pp. 233–4) thinks of the government as the mechanism through which the state acts. R. M. Williams, Jr. (*American Society: A Sociological Interpretation*, New York: Knopf, 1951, p. 202) argues that 'Government is the legitimate power-holding *group*: the state is the structure by which the group's activity is defined and regulated'.

Finally, some writers view the state primarily as a juristic concept. H. Kelsen (*General Theory of Law and State*, Cambridge, Mass.: Harvard University Press, 1949, pp. 182–3) expresses this view when he says the state is 'a legal order'. An elaboration of this view—one which sets out to solve the perennial philosophical problem—may be found in K. B. Smellie's *Reason in Politics* (London: Duckworth, 1939, pp. 244–9). Ballard (*Social Institutions*, p. 253) insists that the state is 'no mere juristic abstraction'.

William L. Kolb

See also: GOVERNMENT
NATION
SOCIETY

Statics and Dynamics

A. An excellent summary of current usage has been made by J. A. Schumpeter: 'By static analysis we mean a *method* of dealing with economic phenomena that tries to establish relations between elements of the economic system—prices and quantities of commodities—all of which have the same time subscript, that is to say, refer to the same point of time. The ordinary theory of demand and supply in the market of an individual commodity as taught in every textbook will illustrate this case: it relates demand, supply, and price as they are supposed to be at any moment of observation—nothing else is taken into consideration.

'But the elements of the economic system that interact at a given point of time are evidently the result of preceding configurations; and the way itself in which they interact is not less evidently influenced by what people expect future configurations to be. Thus, to keep to our example, we may conceive of the situation in our market as determined, or at least influenced, by previous decisions of producers which cannot be understood from the conditions of the point of time chosen for observation but only from the conditions that prevailed at the time when those decisions were taken. Hence we are led to take into account past and (expected) future values of our variables, lags, sequences, rates of change, cumulative magnitudes, expectations, and so on. The *methods* that aim at doing this constitute economic dynamics' (*History of Economic Analysis*, New York: Oxford University Press, p. 963).

B. The terms *statics* and *dynamics*, historically, have been used in all the social sciences, particularly sociology and economics, but modern usage tends to be restricted to economics. The terms were probably borrowed from Comte by J. S. Mill and were first applied to economic method in the Introduction to Book IV of his *Principles of Political Economy* (1848): 'The three preceding Parts include as detailed a view as our limits permit, of what, by a happy generalization of a mathematical phrase, has been called the Statics of the subject . . .We have thus obtained a collective view of the economical phenomena of society, considered as existing simultaneously . . .We have still to consider the economical condition of mankind as liable to change, and indeed (in the more advanced portions of the race, and in all regions to which their influence reaches) as at all times undergoing progressive changes. We have to consider what these changes are, what are their laws, and what their ultimate tendencies; thereby adding a theory of motion to our theory of equilibrium—the Dynamics of political economy to the Statics.'

More definite ideas concerning statics and dynamics could hardly be formulated prior to the development of a specifically dynamic theory. Consequently, statics remained until recently a loose synonym for traditional or equilibrium theory, and dynamics an expression applied to almost anything else. In 1930, for example, F. H. Knight wrote 'In actual usage economic dynamics, or dynamic economics,

Statistics

has become merely a critical and negative term to refer to the limitations of "static" analysis, or more exactly to any particular author's objections to any other author's use of the equilibrium concepts' ('Statics and Dynamics', trans. from *Zeitschrift für Nationalökonomie*, vol. ii, 1930, in his *The Ethics of Competition*, New York: Harper & Bros., 1935, p. 167).

As late as 1939, J. R. Hicks found it necessary to say, 'The definition of economic dynamics (that much controverted term) which I have in mind here is this. I call Economic Statics those parts of economic theory where we do not trouble about dating; Economic Dynamics those parts where every quantity must be dated' (Oxford: The Clarendon Press, 1939, p. 115). The definitions used by Hicks have proved to be adequate for most purposes, though some writers prefer the more precise distinctions developed by R. Frisch ('On the Notion of Equilibrium and Disequilibrium', *Review of Economic Studies*, vol. III, 1935–6, pp. 100–6) and especially by P. A. Samuelson (*Foundations of Economic Analysis*, Cambridge, Mass.: Harvard University Press, 1947, pp. 311 ff.). In Samuelson's words: 'We may say that *a system is dynamical if its behavior over time is determined by functional equations in which "variables at different points of time" are involved in an "essential" way*' (ibid., p. 314). All other systems are static.

Richard V. Clemence

See also: ECONOMIC EQUILIBRIUM

Statistics

A. The term denotes both (a) the mathematical methods for dealing with data secured through enumeration and measurement; and (b) the data so dealt with (cf. M. J. Hagood, *Statistics for Sociologists*, New York: Holt, 1941). The methods denoted by the term 'are not to be considered as co-ordinate either with research methods or with devices for obtaining and recording responses, but rather as tools for analyzing data collected by whatever means, (Q. McNemar, *Psychological Statistics*, New York: Wiley, 1955, p. 1).

B. 1. The simplest form of the methods of statistics is that of *descriptive statistics* which produce such summary 'statistics' as averages, measures of central tendency, etc.

2. A second set of methods is devoted to determining how representative a sample, or a statistic of the sample, is of the population from which the sample was drawn. Much of these methods is devoted to the significance of observed differences, relationships, or descriptive statistics. A typical question is that of how many chances in a hundred are there that the sample or the statistic of the sample would fall beyond a certain range with respect to the total population or a series of further samples. These methods are designated as *inductive* or *sampling statistics*.

3. A third kind of statistics is the *statistics of relationship*. In a very general sense the word *correlation* can be applied here, although usually the latter term is applied to specific measures of relationship between purely quantitative variables rather than between frequencies of attributes or such frequencies and quantitative variables.

4. The inductive or sampling statistics mentioned above usually make many assumptions about the nature of the populations from which the samples were drawn. These characteristics about which assumptions are made are parameters of the population, so the statistics are *parametric*. More recently there have developed several techniques of inference which do not make such assumptions and therefore are *non-parametric* (cf. S. Siegel, *Nonparametric Statistics for the Behavioral Sciences*, New York: McGraw-Hill, 1956, pp. 1–5).

William L. Kolb

See also: SAMPLING

Status

A. In modern social science *status* denotes (a) position in a social system (q.v.) involving reciprocal expectation of action with respect to occupants of other positions in the same structure; (b) place with respect to the distribution of prestige within a social system, and sometimes, by implication, with respect to the distribution of rights, obligations, power and authority within the same system—as in the phrases *high status*, *low status*; (c) high place with respect to the distribution of prestige within a social system—as in the phrase *status seeker*.

B. This word came into use in social science through a long-standing preoccupation in European social philosophy with authority, law, and social order; particularly in the works of Hobbes, Locke, and Smith. It was assumed by these men that there was a necessary connection between the continued existence of society and the fact that some people have more power and privileges than others, though the philosophers differed as to how various distributions of rights would affect the maintenance of society.

Social theory has inherited from social philosophy the idea that the essential feature of social organization is the allocation of rights and obligations. It also inherited the term *status*. 'Status is essentially a legal term and connotes the sum of the legal capacities of an individual, his powers to enforce legal rights and obligations either for himself or for others' (M. Radin, 'Status', in E. R. A. Seligman (ed.), *Encyclopedia of the Social Sciences*, New York: The Macmillan Co., 1934, vol. 14, p. 373). H. S. Maine used the term in his well-known statement that society evolves from 'status to contract' (*Ancient Law*, London: Murray, 10th edn., 1884, p. 170): 'Starting, as from one terminus of history, from a condition of society in which all the relations of persons are summed up in the relations of Family, we seem to have steadily moved towards a phase of social order in which all these relations arise from the free agreement of individuals' (ibid., p. 169).

C. It is presumably from this intellectual background that R. Linton chose *status* to mean the place of an individual in society and defined it as a 'collection of rights and duties', with *role* (q.v.) defined as the putting into action of these rights and duties (*The Study of Man*, New York: Appleton-Century, 1936, pp. 113–4). Linton's twin definitions of status and role are often quoted but not consistently followed. Status (very occasionally described as *social* status), role, and social position are often used interchangeably.

D. 1. Statuses as positions in a social system are differentiated not only by different sets of rights and duties, but also by different amounts of honour or prestige distributed according to standards shared, at least in part, by the participants in the system. In modern writings on social stratification Weber has written most clearly on this and *status* has been used in the translating of Weber's work as the English term to designate the place that a position holds with respect to the distribution of prestige or honour. Thus R. Bendix translates Weber's definition of *status situation* and *status group* as follows: 'In contrast to the economically determined "class situation" we wish to designate as "status situation" every typical component of the life fate of men that is determined by a specific, positive or negative, social estimation of *honor*. ... In content, status honor is normally expressed by the fact that a specific *style of life* can be expected from all those who wish to belong to the

circle. ... The decisive role of a "style of life" in status "honor" means that status groups are the specific bearers of all "conventions"' (*Max Weber: An Intellectual Portrait*, London: Heinemann, 1960, pp. 105–6).

2. By loose extension of this usage *status* is sometimes used as a synonym for prestige or honour, and by loose implication is sometimes used to denote the power, authority, rights and obligations associated with prestige.

3. The adjective *social* is frequently used with *status* when it is intended in this sense (T. H. Marshall, 'The Nature and Determinants of Social Status', *The Year Book of Education*, 1953, London: Evans Brothers, 1953, p. 34).

E. For Weber and those following him, *status situation* as denoting place with respect to the distribution of prestige is distinguished from *class situation* as denoting the 'typical chance for a supply of goods, external living conditions, and personal life experiences' as determined by the power 'to dispose of goods or skills for the sake of income in a given economic order ...' (ibid., p. 105). Yet in the long run class and status are closely related for Weber, with the former tending to be an important determinant of the latter. In recent usage the concept of status has tended to become divorced from this connection with class and to centre on the struggle for prestige within the middle class, thus avoiding the problems of the relationship between class and status (cf. L. Reissman, *Class in American Society*, Glencoe, Ill.: The Free Press, 1960). In this usage *status* denotes high place on the prestige continuum, as, for example, in V. Packard's popularized work, *The Status Seekers* (New York: McKay, 1959).

Dorrian Apple Sweetser

See also: ROLE
        SOCIAL CLASS
        STRATIFICATION

Statute

A. The term *statute* may be defined as 'a law established by legislative authority as distinguished from unwritten "common law"' (*Foster v. Brown*, 34 S.E. 2d 530, 199 Ga. 444). In more specific usage, it means a law created by a legislative body and is virtually synonymous with the word *act*. In all definitions it refers to 'written' as opposed to 'unwritten' law.

B. In its earliest usage, now largely obsolete, *statute* applied to any act of sovereign authority, including an enactment of the monarch, a

Stereotype

decree of God, or the rules made by a guild for the government of its members. With the growth of the modern state and the development of the concept of law as its enacted will, the term has come to take on more precise meaning primarily to distinguish the 'written' law from the 'unwritten' common law and equity.

The most common line of modern English usage descends from Sir Edward Coke's definition, 'An Act of Parliament made by the King, the Lords and the Commons' (since modified by the Parliament Act of 1911, eliminating in specified cases the necessity of participation by the Lords). A statute in this sense is an act of a duly authorized legislative body. In this form, the term may cover either a public (general) or a private (special) law. It may refer to laws designed to substantiate, to remedy, to replace, or to add to the common law or to earlier statutory law.

More broadly, *statute* is used to refer to 'Any enactment, to which a state gives the force of law, whether it has gone through the usual stages of legislative proceedings, or been adopted in other modes of expressing the will of the state ...' (*Stevens* v. *Griffith*, 4 S. Ct. 283, 111 U.S. 48, 28 L. Ed. 348). Law made by executive or administrative agencies in pursuance of constitutional or legislatively delegated authority, however, is much more commonly called by other names (e.g. treaty, ordinance, decree, rule, regulation); in England, where legislative delegation is the rule, the term *statutory instrument* now is assigned to statutory orders in council. In this sense, the continental European law codes are statute law, however established.

In international law, *statute* refers to the entire body of the internal law of a state, however prescribed; a *personal statute* is that part of the municipal law that has the person as its object and the jurisdiction of which extends beyond national boundaries, while a *real statute* is that part that deals with property and has no extra-territorial validity. As a marked variant, *statute* has likewise lately been employed to denote certain agreements reached by agencies of international legislation, as in the 'Statute of the International Court of Justice'.

John M. Swarthout

See also: LAW
 LEGISLATION

Stereotype

A. *Stereotype* denotes beliefs about classes of individuals, groups, or objects which are 'preconceived', i.e. resulting not from fresh appraisals of each phenomenon but from routinized habits of judgement and expectation. No general statement can be made about the degree or kind of distortion, exaggeration, or simplification manifested in such beliefs.

The term should properly be distinguished clearly from prejudice, for it belongs to the category of beliefs. A *stereotype* cannot, however, be distinguished from other beliefs by asserting its falseness, for there are many examples in the literature which demonstrate at least a kernel of truth in what is called stereotype. Neither can it be identified as an oversimplification of attributes of the external world. Many stereotypes actually present an elaboration of such attributes. Nor does the idea of its organizing function (see B (2) below) do justice to the variety of usages in which it occurs. This function is fulfilled by all perceptual hypotheses. There is, however, one distinguishing element implicit, if not explicit, in all usages of the term: A stereotype is a belief which is not held as an hypothesis buttressed by evidence but is rather mistaken in whole or in part for an established fact.

B. 1. The term was introduced into the social sciences by W. Lippman (*Public Opinion*, New York: Harcourt, Brace, 1922) to refer to preconceived ideas or beliefs about attributes of the external world. Lippman points out that these 'pictures in our heads' serve the purpose of thought economy. Since man has neither the time nor the energy to respond to every event with complete and intelligent discrimination of its unique aspects, he acts in terms of relatively crude expectations about the external world. Inextricably linked to this economic purpose of stereotypes is the danger of premature generalization which distorts attributes of the external world.

2. Much in line with this usage is the idea that stereotypes represent 'the knowledge which men imagine they possess' (L. W. Doob, *Propaganda, Its Psychology and Technique*, New York: Henry Holt, 1935, p. 36). Doob recognizes that neither his own nor Lippman's use of the term distinguishes it clearly from concepts in general which have the function of organizing perception. He concludes that stereotypes are of interest only when they form part of an attitude (q.v.). This is indeed the most frequent usage of the term in social science where stereotypes are as a rule referred to as the cognitive component of one particular attitude—prejudice (q.v.). In the past this has often led to a synonymous use

694

of the terms *prejudice* and *stereotype*. This is implicit in the idea that a stereotype is 'a false classificatory concept to which, as a rule, some strong emotional feeling tone of like or dislike, approval or disapproval, is attached' (K. Young, *Social Psychology*, New York: Appleton-Century-Crofts, 3rd edn., 1956, p. 189) and explicit in the following statement: 'Attitudes which result in gross oversimplifications of experience and in prejudgements ... are commonly called biases, prejudices or stereotypes. The latter term is less normative and therefore on the whole to be preferred' (G. W. Allport, in C. Murchison (ed.), *Handbook of Social Psychology*, Worcester, Mass.: Clark University Press, 1935, p. 809).

3. More recent usages regard stereotypes as beliefs which are in themselves free from evaluation and affect. R. K. Merton (*Social Theory and Social Structure*, Glencoe, Ill.: The Free Press, 1957, pp. 426–7), for example, points to the fact that the stereotype of Abraham Lincoln --thrifty, hard-working, eager for knowledge, ambitious, etc.—which serves to justify his exalted place in American hero worship, is not much different from the stereotype of American Jews, which serves to justify anti-Semitism.

4. In psychiatry, stereotyped behaviour refers to the apparently mechanical repetition of mannerisms in speech and motion which is encountered in some patients suffering from organic or functional disturbances.

Marie Jahoda

See also: ATTITUDE
           PREJUDICE

Stimulus

A. Any change of energy which excites a receptor of an organism can correctly be labelled a *stimulus*.

B. E. D. Adrian (*The Basis of Sensation*, London: Christophers, 1928, p. 18) defines a stimulus as 'any change in the environment of an excitable tissue which, if sufficiently intense, will excite the tissue, i.e. will cause it to display its characteristic activity. The stimulus is thus the external change, and it may be ineffective—the stimulation may not have been intense enough to excite'. Adrian here defines a stimulus such that it need not necessarily mean that excitation is aroused, but the more usual definition is by virtue of its having aroused excitation. Although a precise definition concerns any change of energy, the term is also, more loosely, employed to designate any object or event which excites.

There has arisen in psychology, largely due to behaviourism, a framework of stimulus-response, in which events are interpreted. So it is that a stimulus is connected very closely with the response, in the same sort of way that a reflex arc is considered, although of course at a higher level of integration. It is within this framework that stimulus has a wider connotation than merely a change of energy.

D. R. Price-Williams

See also: CONDITIONING
           RESPONSE

Stimulus-Diffusion (See Diffusion)

Stockholder's Equity (See Net Worth)

Stockholder's Interest (See Net Worth)

Stratification

A. In its generic sense *stratification* denotes the process of placing any set of items along a continuum and the grouping of those items which share a relatively common position on the continuum; in this generic sense it also denotes the resulting arrangement of items. In the social sciences, however, the term has come to mean more narrowly the process by which or the resulting structure in which families become differentiated from one another and arranged in graded strata with varying degrees of prestige, and/or property, and/or power.

B. 1. Historically, the most influential tradition dealing with stratification has been the body of Marxian social theory. In this tradition it was and is theoretically possible to study the stratification of society along continua of power, prestige, or income; or by the delineation of social groups whose members enjoy common life-chances, common styles of life, common attitudes and ideologies of self and society, consciousness of class position, and a sense of fundamental antagonism toward such other groups. Yet in each case the same fundamental reality was being studied—the power relationships of men with respect to the control of the instruments of material production. All the rest was ultimately and in the long run derivative: political power, prestige, and position with respect to the market.

2. In opposition to Marx, Weber wished, analytically, to separate economic power, which for him took the form of position in the market from other modes of power, particularly political

Stratification

power, and from prestige. Thus he argued that classes (determined by market position), parties (groups seeking and holding power), and status groups (groups characterized by the members of each having relatively the same amount of prestige and the same style of life) are correlated with one another, but that it is a matter of empirical determination as to the degree of correlation and as to the causal relations that prevail among them in any particular historical context (*From Max Weber*, trans. and ed. by H. H. Gerth & C. W. Mills, New York: Oxford University Press, pp. 180–95).

3. Among formal definitions in the contemporary literature, that of T. Parsons tends to dominate: 'Social stratification is . . . the differential ranking of the human individuals who compose a given social system and their treatment as superior and inferior relative to one another in certain socially important respects' ('An Analytical Approach to the Theory of Social Stratification', *Essays in Sociological Theory, Pure and Applied*, Glencoe, Ill.: Free Press, 1949, p. 166). Stratification is thus seen as 'ranking', and ranking in turn is understood to be only one form of social differentiation— along the prestige dimension. The fundamental character of stratification and its universal presence are attributed to the requirement for moral distinction in any social system, when viewed as a normative order, and to the requirement (for integration) of some agreement on the quality and quantity of such moral evaluations.

In the elaboration of this theory by B. Barber (*Social Stratification*, New York: Harcourt, Brace & World, 1957) prestige (or status) is the fundamental continuum along which stratification occurs. Power tends to be subsumed under authority as a facility of society and to be associated with certain high prestige occupations because it is functionally necessary for them. Income and wealth are also correlated with prestige both as rewards and facilities for various occupations. The fundamental variables determining the others are the degree of responsibility and the amount of knowledge required for those occupations which are of great functional importance. A consensus model of society rather than a conflict model is assumed. In most instances the family is the social unit stratified.

In this theory stratification is considered to be fundamental to all social systems. The bases or criteria of stratified ranking are variable, although as indicated above knowledge and responsibility in functionally important occupations are crucial. But in no society is ranking based on any one criterion alone. The ideal criteria and distinctions are called the scale of stratification. The actual system in operation is called the system of stratification. Kinship, wealth, and power or property are among the criteria on the basis of which ranking occurs.

It is conceived as theoretically possible to have a case where each member is ranked higher or lower than all others, and also to have a society in which all members are ranked as exact equals. The extremes are seen as the limiting cases or points on the continuum of possible ranking systems. K. Davis and W. E. Moore ('Some Principles of Stratification', *American Sociological Review*, vol. 10, 1945, pp. 242–9; also K. Davis, 'A Conceptual Analysis of Stratification', *American Sociological Review*, vol. 7, 1942, pp. 309–21), however, claim positive functionality for systems of stratification where people are ranked as unequals in which, they say, efficient recruitment of scarce and required high talents occurs by means of rewards with differentiated amounts of property, power, and prestige. M. M. Tumin ('Some Principles of Stratification: A Critical Analysis', *American Sociological Review*, vol. 18, 1953, pp. 387–94; see also Davis's reply in the same issue of the *Review*, pp. 394–7, and Tumin's rejoinder, in the same volume, pp. 672–3), among others, has argued the mixture of 'positive' and 'negative' functions of stratification, indicating alternative modes of recruitment and motivation, with special emphasis on rewards for conscientious performance, regardless of level of talent and pointing to certain substantial losses in manpower, motivation, morale and social cohesion which are traceable to inequality in material rewards and invidiousness in social distinctions.

C. In empirical studies of stratification, methods of research have been labelled 'objective' and 'subjective'. The 'objective' researches have historical roots in Marxism or Weber's conception of class as related to market position. 'Objective indices' such as wealth, property, or occupation have been used to place persons in the system of stratification. The 'subjective' researches have historical roots in Weber's conception of 'status' groups and the later functional theory of stratification. Researchers in this tradition have used the gathering of reputational data concerning persons in the community as a means of placing them in the system of stratification. There is apparent in the 'objectivist' group, however, an increasing concern with the prestige of various occupational categories, so that many recent

696

studies employ some variant of the North-Hatt scale of occupations (cf. C. C. North & P. K. Hatt, 'Jobs and Occupations: A Popular Evaluation', *Opinion News*, vol. IX, 1947, pp. 3–13). At the same time, 'subjectivists' like W. L. Warner have moved in the direction of substituting occupational ratings, house type, source of income, and dwelling area for the various modes of reputational analysis (W. L. Warner, M. Meeker, & K. Eels, *Social Class in America: The Evaluation of Status*, New York: Harper Torchbooks, 1960). There is still a difference in the two groups in that the 'subjectivists' tend to stratify modern Western societies, particularly the U.S., into a six-class system, while the 'objectivists' still tend to cling to some version of the Marxist three-class system.

D. Systems of stratification can be distinguished on the basis of the following characteristics: (a) degree of openness or closedness (e.g. class vs. caste); (b) criteria used for ranking (e.g. wealth, kinship, etc.); (c) mode of allocation to stratum (e.g. by ascription or achievement); (d) diffusion or constriction of consequences of ranking (e.g. how seriously are life-chances affected?); (e) amount and quality of collective consciousness of kind within strata (e.g. class-consciousness present or not?); (f) extent to which ideology that justifies the system and scale of ranking is shared among various strata; (g) consonance or dissonance between ranks as imputed by others and as self-perceived; (h) consonance or dissonance between themes which govern stratification in various societal institutions (e.g. is the criterion of 'level of performance' in economic sphere also applied in family sphere?); (i) amount of hostility and conflict as compared with accommodation and acceptance among the various strata; (j) degree and quality of dissonance between the ideal scale of stratification and the actual system in operation.

Melvin M. Tumin

See also: CASTE
       SOCIAL CLASS
       STATUS

Stratified Sampling (See **Sampling**)

Stratum (See **Stratification**)

Sub-Committee (See **Committee**)

Sub-Culture (See **Culture**)

Subject (See **Citizenship**)

Sublimation

A. *Sublimation* is a psychological process which, according to psychoanalytic theory, has the function of neutralizing the primitive urges of sexual and aggressive instincts and of diverting them into channels which are remote from the original instinctual aims.

B. In alchemy the term *sublimation* denoted the transformation of a substance from the solid into the gaseous state. As this transformation often purified the substance, sublimation came to mean conversion into something purer and nobler. In this sense the term was used for centuries.

In recent years the term has become popular in a specific psychoanalytic sense. Freud's early theories rested on the premise that our manifold sexual instincts are the prime movers of our actions. Sexual instincts were supposed to have a primitive 'aim' which was to discharge libidinal energy through sensual stimulation with the help of special 'objects' or persons. This pan-sexual interpretation of the springs of human behaviour was only possible on the assumption that there existed various psychological processes whose function it was to block or modify this primitive libidinal discharge. Sublimation was one of these psychological processes. It was assumed to refine and de-sexualize primitive instinctual aims. 'Sublimation', Freud said, 'is a process that ... consists in the instinct's directing itself towards an aim other than, and remote from, that of sexual gratification' (*On Narcissism* (1914), in *Collected Papers*, trans. by J. Riviere, London: Woolf, 1925, vol. IV, p. 51). It changes sexual lust into emotions of love, tenderness, and admiration; it transforms crude physical desires into artistic and intellectual aspirations; it substitutes socially acceptable objects and persons for those to which the primitive instincts had been attached. It explains how incestuous desires not only turn into filial affection, but into fond regard for friends and perhaps even a concern for strangers; how sexual curiosity becomes the scientist's search for general knowledge; how anal-erotic interests in faeces changes into aesthetic appreciation and collection of art treasures or a preoccupation with law and order; how maternal desires and fantasies of propagation are converted into gardening or farming interests. It explains so much that E. Jones complained that 'analysts were prone to cite the blessed word "sublimation" as the deus ex machina in all social and idealistic impulses' ('Evolution and Revolution'

Subsistence Economy

(1939), in *Essays in Applied Psychoanalysis*, London: Hogarth Press, 1951, vol. I, p. 267).

In the course of time, psychoanalysts also credited aggressive instincts with the capacity of sublimation. Through it the murderous rage of these instincts is tamed or 'neutralized' and emerges in the guise of competitive sport, business rivalry, or intellectual debate.

Freud assumed that in the healthy person instinctual energy needed a modicum of direct satisfaction. The remaining energy could be sublimated to inspire pursuits which are of cultural value. 'We probably owe the highest achievements of our culture to energy which has been liberated in this way' (S. Freud, *The Origins of Psychoanalysis* (1887–1902), London: Imago, 1954). In recent times, however, psychoanalysts have tended to divorce the concept of sublimation from any value judgement. It is assumed that sublimated instincts can make their appearance in individuals in the most diverse forms as hobbies and preoccupations. It depends on unrelated social conditions whether such sublimated activities are acclaimed as valuable, rejected as detrimental, or tolerated as harmless eccentricities.

F. Kräupl Taylor

See also: INSTINCT
LIBIDO

Subsistence Economy

A. *Subsistence economy* may be defined as an economic organization involving simple technology; the social units in which it is found are small and may be families or folk cultures (q.v.) or peasant societies (q.v.). It (a) provides only the essentials of life, and/or (b) serves to make the social unit relatively independent of other groups by producing most of the goods it consumes.

B. The term *subsistence economy* is rarely explicitly defined in its usages in the social sciences. It is employed principally in connection with rural societies in technologically poorly developed countries and is often synonymous with the terms *subsistence farming* and *subsistence agriculture*. In the field of anthropology, application of the term to a primitive hunting and gathering society would, however, also be meaningful as an economy providing bare subsistence (M. J. Herskovits, *The Economic Life of Primitive Peoples*, New York: Knopf, 1940, p. 11). Two principal and overlapping interpretations emerge from writings in economics, economic geography, rural sociology, social welfare, and cultural anthropology: (a) an economic organization which provides only the necessities of life, and (b) an economic organization which serves to make a social unit self-sufficient through producing a variety of goods or limiting consumption to the goods it produces. When the latter interpretation occurs alone or in connection with a modern national society, *autarky* (self-sufficiency) may be the better term, although both interpretations are found in all of the individual disciplines concerned.

1. By implication or direct statement, the social unit of production, distribution, and consumption is limited to the family or other small social group. Rural sociologists, e.g. identify subsistence farms as family farms which are small and impoverished.

2. The low level of technological development is usually associated with a relatively simple division of labour.

3. Subsistence economies may be imposed by circumstances beyond the control of the human beings concerned—poverty of the physical environment, ignorance of efficient techniques of exploiting natural resources, lack of capital for investment in efficient mechanical equipment, or, in highly stratified societies, inequality along lines of social class (q.v.) in access to the resources of nature. They may, however, also represent witting intent or preference, as among the traditional European peasantry whose attachment to family, the land, tradition, and possibly economic autonomy, has been said to override desire for economic gain; or among agriculturists lacking incentive to produce market goods beyond a subsistence level (cf. J. H. Boeke, *Economics and Economic Policy of Dual Societies*, Haarlem: Willink & Zoon, 1953).

4. *Subsistence economy* often implies a lack of trade or its existence in the form of barter, but the raising of cash crops is not entirely ruled out in all interpretations. Modern agriculturists who raise produce for the market, or hunters and trappers who sell their catch or part of it, but whose efforts either aim only at meeting basic needs or yield little beyond minimal requirements for support, may be described as having subsistence economies, even when the cash crops or catch they produce are important in national commerce (see N. J. G. Pounds, *An Introduction to Economic Geography*, London: Murray, 1951, pp. 40–1).

Edward Norbeck

See also: AGRICULTURE
FOLK CULTURE
PEASANT SOCIETY

Substitution

A. *Substitution* has a specialized sense in economic theory deriving mainly from A. Marshall (*Principles of Economics*, London: Macmillan, 8th edn. 1920, p. 170). 'The "substitution" of more for less appropriate means' is the way in which the businessman seeks that 'distribution of resources between various expenditures which yields a better result than any other', just as the 'primitive housewife seeks to approach to an ideal distribution of wool between the different needs of the family'. Not only did Marshall discuss the process, he also enunciated the *principle of substitution*: the process of substitution of one factor for another continues to 'a margin on which either will be indifferently applied', where the 'net efficiency of either will be proportionate to the cost of applying it' (ibid., p. 405). He saw the process as one of changing inputs with a view to least cost production of output; but also of changing outputs (e.g. more or less hops in the rotation of crops) with a view to maximum profit. He saw that it was 'one form of competition'; and he saw that the consumer's behaviour involved a similar process of substitution. The consumer seeks the most satisfactory combination of goods having in mind the 'principle of diminishing utility'; the producer seeks the most satisfactory combination of factors having in mind the 'principle of diminishing returns'; both seek the 'margin of indifference'.

B. In more recent literature terms have been developed which permit quantitative analysis of the process of substitution.

1. Thus J. Robinson and J. R. Hicks at about the same time began to use the term *elasticity of substitution*. This was defined by Mrs Robinson (*The Economics of Imperfect Competition*, London: Macmillan, 1933, p. 256) as 'the proportionate change in the ratio of the amounts of the factors employed divided by the proportionate change in the ratio of their prices to which it is due'. It may vary from zero, where factor proportions are fixed, to infinity where the two factors may be considered to be one: the elasticity will be different for different periods of time, generally higher the longer the period.

2. There followed the development by R. G. D. Allen and J. R. Hicks of the concept of the *marginal rate of substitution*, applicable to consumers and producers alike, and representing the slope of the appropriate indifference curve. Thus J. R. Hicks in *Value and Capital* (Oxford: The Clarendon Press, 1939, p. 20): 'We may define the marginal rate of substitution of X for Y as the quantity of Y which would just compensate the consumer for the loss of a marginal unit of X'. The concept applied to production refers to the slope of the 'iso-product' curve: the quantity of input A which would have to be substituted for one unit of B if the total product must remain unchanged.

3. Along with the introduction of the *marginal rate of substitution* went the distinction between the *income* and *substitution effects* of changing prices on the amount of the commodity which would be bought. When the price of X falls, the consumer moves to a new equilibrium point on a higher indifference curve (q.v.): the changed (in most cases increased) amount that he would have bought at the old price if he had reached that higher curve by an increase of income may be said to be the 'income' effect of the changed price: the further amount he will buy as he moves along the new indifference curve to the point of tangency is said to be the substitution effect. (Both 'income' and substitution effects would be in the opposite direction following upon a *rise* in the price of X). Similarly in production the *substitution effect* can be separated from the *scale effect*; the effect of a change in the price of factor A on the demand for it resulting from the change in the proportion in which the factors will be employed being separated from the effect of the change in the output of the product as a result of the change in the cost of production.

4. Discussion of the *substitution* effect led to further consideration of the problem of *complementarity*. Marshall had seen that substitution was a form of competition: modern theories of imperfect and monopolistic competition are concerned with the competition between imperfect substitutes, and competition in the pure theorists' models are seen to involve producers of an economically homogeneous commodity, i.e. products for which there are perfect substitutes. R. Triffin in *Monopolistic Competition and General Equilibrium Theory* (Cambridge, Mass.: Harvard University Press, 1940) sets up market categories, and defines an 'industry' by reference to degrees of substitutability as measured by cross elasticities.

V. W. Bladen

See also: COMPETITION
ELASTICITY
INDIFFERENCE CURVE
MONOPOLISTIC COMPETITION

Succession (Anthropology)

Until about 1920 anthropological writers

Succession

seem to have followed the legal usage which refers to the transmission of rights of all kinds but particularly *property rights*. H. Maine (*Ancient Law* (1861), London: Murray, 1905, p. 177) distinguished between inheritance and succession thus: 'Inheritance is a form of universal succession'. He went on to exemplify the variety of rights and duties which may be bundled together in such a universe; they include both property rights and rights to office etc., but the majority of examples quoted concern property.

Since 1924, when W. H. R. Rivers published his *Social Organisation*, anthropologists have employed a rather specialized usage in which the referents for the terms *descent*, *inheritance*, and *succession* are carefully distinguished from one another: e.g. 'Whenever I use this term [descent] it will apply to membership of a group and to this only ... Whenever ... I speak of inheritance, it is understood that I am referring to the transmission of property. The third process to be considered is the transmission of office, and I propose to use the term succession for this process' (*Social Organisation*, London: Kegan Paul, Trench, Trubner, 1924, pp. 86–7). Rivers himself considered this use of succession 'not altogether satisfactory, for it conflicts to some extent with legal usage in which the term applies to property. It would perhaps be more satisfactory if we could find some other word for the transmission of rank and office' (ibid., p. 87). Both British and American anthropologists appear to follow the Rivers usage today.

Barbara E. Ward

See also: Descent

Succession (Political Science)

A. *Succession* may be defined as the process (actual or legal) by which one person (natural or jural) follows another in the possession of property, dignity, office, function, sovereignty or territory, and to the body of rights and duties acquired by the successor.

B. In political science *succession* is primarily a term of law, both municipal and international. In municipal law systems the connotation of the term is usually different in private and public law.

1. In private law the concept succession arose with that of private property and referred to its disposition on the death of the owner by operation of law (intestacy) or of the will of the deceased (testacy). Roman law distinguished *universal succession* in which the *heres* was conceived as continuing the personality of the deceased and was, therefore, liable for all his debts as well as entitled to all his assets, from *partial succession* in which the successor acquired certain assets with the liabilities attached to them. The concept of universal succession did not exist in Germanic and common law, and is not important in most systems of modern law. Titles, dignities and offices are sometimes conceived as private property and transmitted by the private law of succession.

2. In the systems of public law, succession refers to the transmission of public office, especially that of the Chief of State, on the death, incapacity, resignation or termination of office of the incumbent. Different states have used different methods to reconcile the need for competence to perform the functions of the office with the need for certainty and immediacy of succession to avoid the danger of an interregnum. That danger is indicated by numerous instances of civil or international violence such as the wars of the Spanish, Polish, and Austrian succession in the 18th century, and the revolutions in France, Germany, Russia, and China more recently.

3. Laws prescribing precise rules of heredity, as the British Act of Succession in Queen Anne's reign, resemble private law rules for succession to land and assure certainty and immediacy. ('The king is dead, long live the king'). Such laws do not, however, assure personal competence. So modern constitutions tend to reduce the political functions of the hereditary Chief of State to formal choice of a Prime Minister selected by the predominant political party and, therefore, presumably competent to govern.

4. Succession of the Chief of State by the process of popular or legislative election presumably assures personal competence (though capacity to get elected does not necessarily demonstrate capacity to govern) but is not necessarily certain and immediate.

The latter characteristics may be assured by laws providing for election of the successor before ending of a fixed term of his predecessor, as in the United States presidency, and for a fixed order of succession in case of death, disability, or resignation. In the United States succession runs from the President to the Vice-President and then to the Speaker of the House of Representatives, the President Pro Tem of the Senate, the Secretary of State and other members of the Cabinet.

5. Actually succession in rulership may take place by revolution ignoring the existing law.

Ability to rule is sometimes said to be assured by that process, but certainty and immediacy is sacrificed. Usurpers find it difficult to re-establish a rule of succession or legitimacy either hereditary or elective, and the state continues liable to new revolutions, as in the case of ancient Greek tyrannies, Latin-American caudillos and fascist or communist dictators, though such de facto rulers may acquire legitimacy in international law through success, followed by general recognition.

C. Succession in international law is derived by analogy from the private law usage. The term, however, refers to the rights and duties which attach to the acquisition of territory by a state, rather than to the process by which such acquisition is effected.

1. Universal succession occurs when a state is extinguished through transfer of all its territory to one or more other states. In international law the universal successor does not assume the personality of the predecessor, as did the universal successor of Roman law. It does not succeed to unliquidated tort claims or to the obligations of executory treaties. It does, however, succeed not only to the rights and duties attached to the acquired territory, as does a partial successor, but also to the public debt and to the assets abroad of the predecessor state, such as embassy buildings. In case there are several successor states, as in the partition of Poland in the 18th century, those non-territorial assets and obligations are distributed among them according to some criterion, such as the tax-producing value of the territories acquired by each.

2. Partial succession occurs when a state, either pre-existing or established by successful insurrection, acquires territory from a state which survives, as when Spain lost territory to Cuba and the United States in 1898. The partial successor succeeds to rights and duties of its predecessor relating to the acquired territory but not, unless by special agreement, to the ceding state's general debt.

3. The term *succession* has also been applied in international law to the succession of governments within a state, especially when the succession takes place by revolution. However, in principle the state, not the government, is a subject of international law; consequently change in government, whether by constitutional process or revolution, is controlled by the public law of the state not by international law. So long as the state persists without change of territory, there is no breach in the continuity of its rights and duties under international law and the government which actually rules (the general de facto government) is presumed to be prepared to fulfil the state's obligations under international law, as well as to exercise its jurisdiction ('The Tinoco Arbitration, Great Britain—Costa Rica', *American Journal of International Law*, vol. 18, 1924, p. 147 ff; *Annual Digest of Public International Law Cases, 1923–4*, no. 15, London: Longmans, Green, 1933, p. 34 ff.). Complications, however, arise in practice, in case of revolution, because of considerable periods when several governments, each claiming to represent the state, control portions of its territory, or when a de jure government in exile continues preparations to eliminate the de facto government in control of the state's territory.

D. The term *succession* is used to refer, not only to the process of succeeding, to the right or privilege of succeeding, and to the body of rights and obligations succeeded to, but also to a series of successions to a property, throne, territory or function (the Apostolic succession), and to the body of law determining the conditions and modes of succession and the rights and duties of the successor.

Quincy Wright

Succession (Sociology)

The term *succession* was developed by plant and animal ecologists and later borrowed and modified by sociologists seeking to extend ecological theory into the realm of human social phenomena.

1. Among plant and animal ecologists the term denotes a series of replacements of plant associations (communities) in an area, culminating in a climax phase, i.e. an association which is able indefinitely to withstand further threats of invasions (q.v.) (F. E. Clements, *Plant Succession*, Washington, D.C.: Carnegie Institution, 1916). For the most part, succession is regarded as the process by which life forms colonize a bare area. Presumably each combination of climate and soil condition is associated with a characteristic succession of plant associations (C. S. Elton, *The Ecology of Animals*, New York: Wiley, 1933).

2. Sociologists introduced several modifications into their applications of the concept.

(a) They construed succession to mean a single replacement, as when one set of occupants is dislodged and replaced by a different set of

701

Suggestion

occupants (R. D. McKenzie, 'The Ecological Approach to the Study of the Human Community', in R. E. Park, E. W. Burgess, & R. D. McKenzie (eds.), *The City*, Chicago: University of Chicago Press, 1925). Accordingly, their mode of analysis has taken the form of identifying stages in the single cycle of change, such as invasion stage, developmental stage, and climax stage.

(b) The application has usually been made to already occupied areas, notably zones or sections of cities, rather than to vacant areas, though occasionally the concept has been used in the study of colonization (R. D. McKenzie, 'Ecological Succession in the Puget Sound Region', *Publications of the American Sociological Society*, vol. XXIII, 1928, pp. 60–80; and N. S. Hayner, 'Ecological Succession in the San Juan Islands', ibid., pp. 81–92). This second modification is generalized in E. W. Burgess's hypothesis that city growth proceeds as expansion from a centre in the course of which clustered land uses are pressed outward and consequently succeed to one another's areas ('The Growth of the City: An Introduction to a Research Project', in R. E. Park et al., *The City*, pp. 47–62). Burgess's meaning of succession is well illustrated by O. D. Duncan and B. Duncan in the following: 'During year t_0 a given area is exclusively inhabited by members of population group A. In year t_1, some members of group B move into the area, and, by the end of year t_n, all the residents of the area are members of group B. We would then say that over an n-year period the area underwent a succession from an area of A residents to an area of B residents' (*The Negro Population of Chicago: A Study of Residential Succession*, Chicago: University of Chicago Press, 1957, p. 104).

(c) The most drastic adaptation of succession is R. E. Park's effort to enlarge the meaning of the concept to include all forms of complex change. The concept, he stated, should encompass 'every possible form of orderly change so far as it affects the interrelations of individuals in a community or the structure of the society of which these individual units are a part' ('Succession, An Ecological Concept', *American Sociological Review*, vol. 1, 1936, pp. 171–9).

Amos H. Hawley

See also: INVASION

Suggestion

A. *Suggestion* denotes the process (the nature of which still remains in doubt) by which an uncritical response is evoked by a stimulus. In social psychology the term usually refers this process to a relationship in which a person or group uses symbols as the stimuli to provoke uncritical responses from other persons or groups, or, in the case of self-suggestion, from themselves.

B. 1. Although G. Tarde is perhaps primarily known for his employment of the concept *imitation* (q.v.), he was also among the earliest sociologists to utilize the concept of *suggestion*. Indeed he regarded suggestion as the handmaiden of imitation, and defined the latter with a cognitive emphasis so that it was conceived as containing elements of suggestion (*The Laws of Imitation*, New York: Henry Holt, 1903). In G. LeBon's word (*The Crowd*, London: Unwin, 1903) the influence of Tarde, as well as that of Durkheim, is evident. LeBon was interested in such crowd phenomena as the collective mind, mental unity, crowd mind, and the character of crowd behaviour. Many of these phenomena he explained by the mechanism of suggestion and the conditions that make for suggestibility. In the United States J. M. Baldwin and E. A. Ross gave considerable importance to both suggestion and imitation in their works. Ross regarded suggestion and imitation as but two aspects of the same thing in which suggestion functioned as cause and imitation as effect (*Social Psychology*, New York: The Macmillan Co., 1908, p. 13).

2. Sooner or later there was bound to arise strong objection to the wide and loose use of the concepts of suggestion and imitation by social psychologists and sociologists. As early as 1902, C. H. Cooley was already departing from the older tradition (*Human Nature and the Social Order*, New York: Charles Scribner's Sons, 1902, p. 51). Cooley preferred to stress suggestion rather than imitation, because he thought the latter term in many instances covered too much ground and in other respects not enough. He said 'The word suggestion is used here to denote an influence that works in a comparatively mechanical or reflex way, without calling out that higher selective activity of the mind implied in choice and will' (ibid.). A somewhat similar definition, that of W. McDougall, came to be widely adopted both in psychology and social psychology: 'Suggestion is a process of communication resulting in the acceptance with conviction of the communicated proposition in the absence of logically adequate grounds for its acceptance' (*Social Psychology*, London: Methuen, 21st edn., 1928, p. 83).

C. In contemporary social psychology the term has remained in use, despite the fact that it, together with imitation, is no longer regarded as a central explanatory concept for all social behaviour. It has retained its importance in the analysis of crowd and other forms of collective behaviour, advertising, public opinion, and propaganda. As psychological theories have become more sophisticated, the scope of phenomena to which *suggestion* refers has been reduced. Thus if the meaning of the term is still to indicate the lack of rational, critical response it cannot be used to designate the process in which the entire meaning of the situation is cognitively restructured by a change in a single stimulus. For example, the concept of suggestion does not necessarily explain a response in which the term 'rebellion' is approved by American subjects when used by Jefferson, and disapproved when used by Lenin. It may be true that they conceive Jefferson as 'good' and Lenin as 'bad' and therefore respond uncritically, but it is also possible that the subjects know that rebellion meant different things to these two men, and that their approval or disapproval is based on such knowledge (G. W. Allport, 'The Historical Background of Modern Social Psychology', in G. Lindzey (ed.), *Handbook of Social Psychology*, Cambridge, Mass.: Addison-Wesley, 1954, vol. I, pp. 28–9).

So also have the theoretical explanations of suggestion changed over time. Older theories of 'animal magnetism', ideo-motor response, and simple associationism have in part been expanded and in part replaced by theories of reintegration in which complex responses are triggered, after having been previously formed, by a simple cue (sometimes interpreted as a conditioned response); by theories of identification in which stress is placed on the need for close ties of some sort between the initiator of the process of suggestion and the person who reacts uncritically to the suggestion; and by theories of the reduction of effective determinants of suggested behaviour (by reducing the field of effective or relevant stimuli or by taking advantage of the absence of such stimuli from the situation, the initiator of the process is able to elicit the response he desires through the few stimuli he employs) (G. W. Allport, 'The Historical Background of Modern Social Psychology', pp. 25–9). Elements of all these recent theories, for example, will be found in the treatment of the suggestibility of the child and the manner in which he can overcome such suggestibility (A. R. Lindesmith & A. L. Strauss, *Social Psychology*, New York: Dryden Press, 1949, pp. 152–5).

Edward C. Jandy

See also: IMITATION
SYMPATHY

Superego

A. The *superego* is that part of the personality structure, evolving out of the ego (q.v.), which incorporates those moral inhibiting forces which have been experienced by the individual in the course of his early life; it is the result of identification with the society's standard-bearers—especially the parents—and it acts as an internal controlling agency much as these standard-bearers did externally at an earlier period.

B. *Superego* is a term coined by Freud to refer to a 'standard' which is 'created in the Ego which opposes the other faculties by observation, criticism and prohibition' (*Moses and Monotheism*, trans. by K. Jones, London: Hogarth Press, 1939, p. 134). It is thus the third element in the structure of the personality, the other two being the id (q.v.) and the ego (q.v.). Although Freud's conceptualization changed somewhat during his lifetime, the following is an adequate representation of his definition of superego: 'The Super-Ego is the successor and representative of the parents (and educators) who superintended the actions of the individual in his first years of life; it perpetuates their functions almost without a change' (ibid., p. 184). 'It belongs to the [Ego], sharing with it its intricate psychological make-up. On the other hand, it entertains very close relations with the [Id]. The Super-Ego is in reality the record of first impressions as conceived by the [Id]; it is the heir of the dissolved Oedipus Complex. ... The Super-Ego is the agent of that phenomenon we call our conscience' (*The Problem of Lay Analysis*, New York: Brentano's, 1927, pp. 124–5). 'The superego may bring fresh needs to the fore, but its chief function remains the *limitation* of satisfactions' (*An Outline of Psychoanalysis*, New York: Norton, 1949, p. 19).

C. No systematic use is currently made of the term *superego* that does not acknowledge its Freudian origin, and few attempts have been made to alter Freud's concept while at the same time retaining the term. Thus any reference to the superego that does not explicitly state non-Freudian qualifications is likely to be using the term as Freud originally defined it. There have been many criticisms of the Freudian concept of superego, however.

Superorganic

1. K. Horney (*New Ways in Psychoanalysis*, London: Kegan Paul, Trench, Trubner, 1939) objects to the Freudian notion that there is a natural organic striving (localized in the id) that is necessarily in conflict with the moral code of the superego.

2. E. Fromm and A. Kardiner (cf. A. Kardiner, *The Individual and His Society*, New York: Columbia University Press, 1939, pp. 63–75) emphasize the social dynamics of the formation of the superego and variations found in different societies. In this regard, such evidence as that offered by B. Malinowski (*Sex and Repression in Savage Society*, London: Kegan Paul, Trench, Trubner, 1927) concerning the inter-societal differences in the dynamics of the so-called Oedipus complex and the more recent anthropological emphasis on the differentiation between shame and guilt (cf. D. Leighton & C. Kluckhohn, *Children of the People*, Cambridge, Mass.: Harvard University Press, 1947, pp. 170–1) have been indications of dissatisfaction with the Freudian treatment of the role of social and cultural forces in the development of the structure and content of the individual personality.

3. The orthodox Freudian position has also been criticized by G. Murphy for its extreme emphasis on the unconscious elements of the superego to the exclusion of its conscious aspects (*Personality*, New York: Harper & Bros., 1947, pp. 543–4). A further criticism has involved the tendency to conceive of the superego as a compartment of the mind or self rather than as an analytically separable function of the total personality (cf. A. Kardiner, *The Individual and His Society*, pp. 72–3).

D. One of the most systematic attempts to evaluate the original Freudian concept of superego from the point of view of social science was made by T. Parsons (*Working Papers in the Theory of Action*, Glencoe, Ill.: The Free Press, 1953, ch. I). He notes: 'Freud's view was too narrow ... Not only moral standards, but *all the components of the common culture* are internalized as part of the personality structure' (ibid., p. 18) 'Freud introduced an unreal separation between the superego and the ego. ... Freud's view seems to imply [as in the "reality principle"] that the object, as cognitively significant, is given independently of the actor's internalized culture, and that superego standards are then applied to it. This fails to take account of the extent to which the constitution of the object and its moral appraisal are part and parcel

of the *same* fundamental cultural pattern' (ibid., p. 19).

'... It is not only the superego which is internalized—that is, taken over by identification from cathected social objects ... there are involved other important components which presumably must be included in the ego—namely, the system of cognitive categorizations of the object world and the system of expressive symbolism' (ibid., p. 17).

Parsons's concern is with the interrelations between the personality system and the larger social system. In this sense, his work is representative of the social scientist's approach to Freudian theory. The superego refers to that portion of the personality structure which, in Freudian theory, has the most direct relationship with the socio-cultural context in which human behaviour occurs and as such is the locus of the Freudian explanation of social order and cultural continuity. As Parsons's treatment indicates, however, this explanation is not wholly acceptable to many social scientists.

Alan C. Kerckhoff

See also: EGO
GENERALIZED OTHER
ID
REPRESSION
SOCIALIZATION

Superorganic

A. As an adjective the term *superorganic* is sometimes used to modify the term *culture* (q.v.) in such a way as to indicate that (a) while culture is limited by man's organic structure it is not determined by it; (b) culture transcends not only the organic nature of individual men but even to some degree their processes of social interaction. Deriving from its use as an adjective *superorganic* is sometimes used as a noun synonymously with culture.

B. 1. H. Spencer introduced the term *superorganic* in his evolutionary sociology. Evolution took place first in the inorganic realm, then in the organic, and ultimately in the superorganic. 'If there has been Evolution, that form of it here distinguished as super-organic must have come from insensible steps out of the organic. But we may conveniently mark it off as including all those processes and products which imply the co-ordinated actions of many individuals' (*The Principles of Sociology*, 3 vols., London: Williams & Norgate, 3rd edn., 1885, vol. I, p. 4). This identification of the social and the superorganic is not restricted to man, but includes the social life of insects and vertebrates (ibid., pp. 4–7).

2. A. L. Kroeber in his essay, 'The Superorganic' (*American Anthropologist*, vol. 19, 1917, pp. 163–213), found it likely that culture or civilization had some of its roots in the organic, but he thought it better to regard the origin of culture as a kind of 'leap' comparable to the first manifestations of life in matter, even though the matter itself might be made up of inorganic substances. Another important element in this essay is the idea that the superorganic implies the independence of culture not only of the organic life of the individual but also of the group. In this regard Kroeber has said more recently that to say that culture is superorganic does not mean that it is non-organic, non-individual, or non-societal. ' "Superorganic" means simply that when we consider culture we are dealing with something that is organic but which must also be viewed as something more than organic. … The mass or body of culture, the institutions and practices and ideas constituting it, have a persistence and can be conceived as going on their slowly changing way "above" or outside the societies that support them' (*Anthropology*, New York: Harcourt, Brace, 1948, pp. 253–4).

C. In recent years the term *superorganic* has fallen into disuse. It does not appear in such works, all of which recognize the importance of culture, as A. Kardiner, *The Individual and His Society* (New York: Columbia University Press, 1939); R. Linton, *The Cultural Background of Personality* (New York: Appleton-Century-Crofts, 1945); or T. M. Newcomb, *Social Psychology* (New York: The Dryden Press, 1950). Contemporary social scientists are somewhat less interested in whatever dichotomy there may be between the organic and the superorganic, than they are in trying to understand such relationships as are thought to exist between them. Stated another way, there is at present more concern with the working of psychosomatics than with the precise nature of the superorganic. Terms like extra-biologic or extra-somatic, as applied to the distinctive behaviour of human beings when contrasted with other animals, express modern notions of ideas that were originally discussed under the heading of superorganic. Nowadays, social scientists are inclined to take it for granted that culture is superorganic, since it does not seem to arise spontaneously from the organic activities either of individuals or of groups of individuals.

Once they develop, however, superorganic (cultural) requirements have a profound effect on the activities of men and women. The nature of the impact of cultural traditions on the members of every society is presently at least as important to social scientists as were previous efforts to understand how or when the superorganic came into existence.

Mischa Titiev

See also: CULTURAL EVOLUTION
CULTURE
CULTUROLOGY

Supply

A. *Supply* may be defined as the rate of flow of a commodity into a market. More importantly, however, economic analysis centres its attention on the *supply function* or *curve*—concepts which refer to a line connecting a series of points representing the prices required by suppliers to furnish given quantities of a commodity under specified conditions and to the conditions which determine the varying amounts that will be supplied as the price varies. Thus the *supply curve* changes only if there is a change in the amount supplied without a change in price. In partial equilibrium analysis the specified conditions usually imply no change in technology, in prices of closely related commodities, or in supply curves of factors of production used in the production of the commodity. In general equilibrium analysis the variables that are taken as 'given' in partial equilibrium analysis may be introduced explicitly into the analytical model. The development of imperfect and monopolistic competition theory and the growth of general equilibrium economics have reduced interest in the industry supply curve and have focused increasing attention on firm cost (q.v.) curves. In imperfect competition the supply curve of the industry disappears and is replaced by the marginal revenue curve of the firm.

B. At least since Marshall, understanding of marketing behaviour in economics has traditionally been sought through the analysis of the forces of demand and supply. The idea of supply is not, however, as neat or as simple a concept as the idea of demand. Considerable confusion is frequently generated by the lack of symmetry in the technical usage of the two terms. The basis for this lack of symmetry is implicit in Marshall but it is stated explicitly by F. H. Knight (A. Marshall, *Principles of Economics*, London: Macmillan, 8th edn., 1920, bk. IV, ch. 1 and

Supply

bk. V; F. H. Knight, 'Supply', in E. R. A. Seligman (ed.), *Encyclopedia of the Social Sciences*, New York: The Macmillan Co., vol. 14, 1934, pp. 470–4). According to Knight, demand and demand function or curve are synonomous while *supply* designates the rate of flow itself of a commodity into the market. Thus the supply function or curve which is based on the relationship between price and supply under stated conditions must be specified. Thus 'The crucial fact preventing symmetry in the usage of the two terms is that in the natural view of demand price determines quantity taken, but only under restricted conditions [perfect competition and increasing cost] and never in a parallel sense can the quantity supplied be treated as determined by price' (F. H. Knight, 'Supply', p. 470).

C. The response of supply to changes in demand has been discussed mainly with relation to the time period required to bring about changes in the quantity supplied as a result of changes in the relatively 'variable' and 'fixed' cost components (see for example J. M. Cassels, 'The Nature of Statistical Supply Curves', *Journal of Farm Economics*, vol. XV, 1933, pp. 378–87). Knight argues, however, that it is not possible to use the time required by separate cost elements to adjust to demand changes as a basis for construction of supply curves since '... in the event of a change expected to be permanent all the changes considered will begin at once and go on concurrently. A realistic supply curve must be drawn independently in both directions ... from a point representing an initial condition; and the two parts will usually not be continuous'. However, '... the longer the period allowed for adjustment the greater will be the elasticity of supply ... [i.e.] the ratio between the relative price change and the relative change in output of the commodity computed for changes of negligible magnitude' (F. H. Knight, 'Supply', p. 471).

D. The classic discussion of the relationship between firm cost curves and industry supply curves is J. Viner's 'Cost Curves and Supply Curves' (*Zeitschrift für Nationalökonomie*, vol. III, 1931, pp. 23–46). According to Viner, when prices of the several cost components remain unchanged in responses to changes in output at the industry level the aggregate supply curve for the industry can be obtained by summing the marginal cost curves of the individual firms. When the prices of productive factors vary in

response to changes in output at the industry level, either as a result of external technical or pecuniary economies or diseconomies, the marginal cost curves of the individual firms no longer remain unchanged as output expands. In this event the effect of an increase in demand on output at the firm level can be visualized as consisting of two components: (a) a planned increase in output to the level indicated by the intersection of the new demand curve with the original marginal cost curve; (b) a second hypothetical change in output to the level indicated by the intersection of the new marginal cost curve which reflects changed cost conditions in the industry. These *price* and *cost* effects can be thought of as roughly comparable to the *income* and *substitution* effects in demand theory. This analysis is limited to conditions of perfect competition.

E. The literature of imperfect competition has resulted in a reconsideration of supply concepts. According to R. Triffin (*Monopolistic Competition and General Equilibrium Theory*, Cambridge, Mass.: Harvard University Press, 1940, p. 148) 'For the discussion of pure monopoly as well as of heterogeneous [monopolistic] competition, the *industry* is a useless and inapplicable device. Only the *firm's* curve thus remains of interest...' Output under imperfect competition is no longer a function of marginal cost and price but of marginal cost and marginal revenue. And there is no specific relationship between marginal revenue and price such as exists under pure competition.

F. While the growth of imperfect competition theory increased interest in the empirical study of cost functions, it has resulted in only a minor interest in the study of industry supply curves. Only in agriculture has any appreciable effort been devoted to the empirical investigation of supply curves. In the literature dealing with the supply functions for agricultural products, major interest has been focused on the responsiveness of agricultural output to price changes. Early studies emphasized the short-run inelasticity of farm output with respect to price (D. G. Johnson, 'The Nature of the Supply Function for Agricultural Products', *American Economic Review*, vol. XL, 1950, pp. 539–64). More recently M. Nerlove has obtained somewhat higher estimates of supply elasticities ('Estimates of the Elasticities of Supply of Selected Agricultural Commodities', *Journal of Farm Economics*, vol. XXXVIII, 1956, pp. 496–

509). In spite of the improvements in Nerlove's model, investigation of supply relationships are still plagued by the same two limitations faced by students of cost curves: (a) the index number problem posed by a changing product and input mix, and (b) the problem of separating the effects of scale and technology (H. Staehle, 'The Measurement of Statistical Cost Functions', *American Economic Review*, vol. XXXII, 1942, pp. 321–33). In addition there is the problem posed by the inability to determine whether each price observation corresponds to a supply curve with the same time reference.

Vernon W. Ruttan

See also: COST
            DEMAND
            MARGINAL ANALYSIS
            PRICE

Supply Curve (See Supply)

Supply Function (See Supply)

Suppression (See Repression)

Surplus

The term has four main uses in the literature of economics.

1. It is a concept used in analysing profit, rent, value and tangible wealth. In this sense it is more fully described as producer's surplus.

(a) As early as the mercantilists, attention was paid to this surplus or profit considered to arise in exchange, when a commodity is sold above value. Sir James Steuart (*The Works, Political, Metaphysical, and Chronological of the Late Sir James Steuart*, London: Cadell & Davies, 1805, vol. I, pp. 275–6) subscribed to this view but distinguished between two types of surplus: positive profit or surplus which arises from a general increase in labour, industry and skill and adds to the public good; and relative profit or surplus which is the 'vibration of the balance of wealth between parties' and does not add to the public good.

(b) The physiocrats took a different view. They opposed the mercantilist's position that wealth and surplus are due to exchange and maintained that production gives rise to wealth and surplus, which they called *produit net*. Only labour that creates a surplus, i.e. yields an output over and above the wealth which is consumed in order to make production possible, is productive. The *produit net* in the eyes of the physiocrats was not a surplus of social wealth in the abstract sense, but it was the concrete material wealth of useful goods. Only agriculture, in their view, could produce such a surplus. Here it was easiest to point to this difference between the amount of food consumed by the worker plus what is used as seed on the one side and the crop raised on the other side. This surplus was looked upon as a gift of nature and not of labour. With the help of Quesnay's *tableau économique* they attempted to trace the circulation of this surplus among the different classes of society.

(c) The physiocrats laid the foundation for two new surplus theories. Adam Smith (*Wealth of Nations* (1776), New York: The Modern Library, 1937) was dissatisfied with the notion that the surplus was a gift of nature. In his view the surplus was the product of labour. It is in this sense that surplus figures in the labour theory of value. The second theory is associated with Karl Marx (*Das Kapital*, ed. by F. Engels, Hamburg: O. Meissner, 1890) and is known as surplus value theory. Surplus value, for Marx, is based on the premise that the value of a commodity is the amount of human labour necessary to produce it. From this premise it is argued that although the worker is entitled to the entire value thus created, he received only that portion that is necessary to assure the labourer's means of subsistence. The remainder is the surplus value which is taken by the capitalist.

(d) Finally, D. Ricardo's differential rent (*Principles of Political Economy and Taxation*, ed. by P. Sraffa, Cambridge: The University Press, 1951, pp. 67–84) is in a sense a surplus. Differential rent is an unearned increment in value. This producer's surplus is determined by the differences in the productivity of one piece of land over the poorest piece of land which it pays to keep in cultivation. It is measured by the difference in the value of products obtained from its use and the value of the products which could be obtained from the cultivation of marginal land with an equal amount of labour and capital.

2. *Surplus* as *consumer's surplus* is also a concept in welfare economics. According to A. Marshall (*Principles of Economics*, London: Macmillan, 8th edn., 1920, p. 124) consumer's surplus is the 'excess of the price which [the consumer] would be willing to pay rather than go without the thing, over that which he actually does pay'. While he recognized the impossibility of measuring this surplus, he used the concept to demonstrate effects of taxes. J. R. Hicks (*Value and Capital*, Oxford: Clarendon Press, 1939, pp. 40–1) uses an indifference map

Survival

to advance a concept quite similar to Marshall's. According to Hicks, consumer's surplus is '... the *compensating variation* in income, whose loss would just offset the fall in price and leave the consumer no better off than before'.

3. *Economic surplus* is a concept used by K. E. Boulding ('The Concept of Economic Surplus', *American Economic Review*, vol. XXXV, 1945, pp. 851–69). It may be said to be present whenever a seller makes a sale for a sum greater than the least sum for which he would have been willing to make the sale, or whenever a buyer makes a purchase for a sum smaller than the greatest sum for which the buyer would have been willing to make the purchase. Like Marshall's consumer's surplus, this concept too does not lend itself to measurement.

4. *Surplus* is also an accounting concept. For the accountant a surplus represents the difference between a corporation's assets and liabilities as well as capital stock. Earned surplus is the balance of net profits and gains of a corporation after deducting losses and after distributions to stockholders and transfers to capital stock accounts.

Werner Z. Hirsch

See also: Labour Theory of Value
　　　　　Rent

Surplus Value (See **Surplus**)

Survival

A. *Survival* is used in three senses in the social sciences. One corresponds to general popular usage, the second to technical biological usage, and the third to a technical anthropological usage.

1. The first usage is the general 'continuing to live after some event' of the *Oxford English Dictionary*.

2. The second usage carries over into social science the idea of the survival of species brought about by the processes of random mutation and natural selection. Much social science theory is built around this concept, but the concept itself is biological.

3. The third meaning is given by the *Oxford English Dictionary* as follows: '... continuance of a custom, observance, etc., after the circumstances in which it originated or which gave significance to it have passed'. Only this definition requires extended comment.

B. E. B. Tylor brought the concept and method of *survivals* into prominence in anthropology in his *Primitive Culture* first published in 1871. With this term he referred to '... processes, customs, opinions, and so forth, which have been carried on by force of habit into a new state of society different from that in which they had their original home, and they thus remain as proofs and examples of an older condition of culture out of which a newer has been evolved' (*Primitive Culture*, London: Murray, 5th edn., 1913, vol. 1, p. 16). Tylor distinguished between 'mere permanence in culture' and 'survival' by applying for the latter the criteria of loss of utility, function, or meaning. Few carried this to the extent of denying all utility to the survival, and Tylor pointed out that survival frequently becomes revival, though he did not develop this idea. With this 'loss of function' went the further notion, more fully developed by later writers, that the survival was not fully integrated with the rest of the culture. Generally, thinking about the survival itself emphasized, in a static way, its use in reconstructing hysothetical earlier stages in cultural evolution (q.v.). J. F. McLennan, who, among many others, sought the origins of the institution and forms of marriage in folk customs that seemed survivals, thought of them as '... symbolical [or disintegrated] forms [with] corresponding realities ... in the past life of the peoples employing them' (*Primitive Marriage*, Edinburgh: Black, 1865, p. 12).

M. Hodgen points out that the 'anthropological method' ascribed to Tylor 'envisaged the social whole ... as the outcome of a developmental process, subject to demonstration and documentation by the use of the comparative method and the employment of survivals' (*The Doctrine of Survivals*, London: Allenson, 1936, pp. 133–4).

Others treated survivals in a less static manner. R. R. Marett and others raised the question, 'How and why do survivals survive?' Marett saw in them an opportunity to study the 'transformation', 'transvaluation', and 'transposition' of parts of a culture (*Psychology and Folklore*, London: Methuen, 1920, chs. 5, 6). In discussing survival the emphasis shifted from the loss of function and lack of functional integration to the theme of change or variation of function and integration; cultural elements could persist with relatively little change in function, status, or value within the culture, or they could persist, changing in any or all these respects, or they could drop out or change form to an extent that they are seen as replaced.

C. In spite of this broadening of the concept beyond its original limits, B. Malinowski directed an extreme criticism against its use, against the idea that a part of culture could lack function or integration with the rest of culture. He stated that, '... no crucial system of activities can persist without being connected, directly or indirectly, with human needs and their satisfactions' (*A Scientific Theory of Culture*, Chapel Hill: University of North Carolina Press, 1944, p. 142). This sort of criticism led to a decrease in interest in survivals, so that Hodgen could say, '... the doctrine of survivals is gone' (*The Doctrine of Survivals*, p. 187).

D. Important use is still made of *survivals* by folklorists, by students of cultural evolution, and by some interested in the dynamics of cultural continuity and change. 'The fact that a considerable period of time must ordinarily elapse before all adaptive readjustments have been completed in the transition from one form of social organization to another—the phenomenon known as "culture lag"—results in the presence of "survivals" from previous forms of organization in most social systems. Analysis of these can frequently yield reliable indications of historically antecedent types of social structure' (G. P. Murdock, *Social Structure*, New York: The Macmillan Co., 1949, p. 323). They will most often be found in those areas of culture in which they are least subject to pragmatic, functional, or empirical pressure—thus, in children's play, in adult leisure activity, in systems of belief, mythology, folklore, art, adornment, manners, or the less important relationships of a kinship system.

Margaret Mead

See also: CULTURAL LAG

Sweat Shop (See Putting-Out System)

Swing

Swing denotes the amount of the movement of support from one party to another in two-party contests and it is calculated as the average of the percentage gain in the share of the poll by one party and the percentage loss by the other (D. E. Butler, *The British General Election of 1951*, London: Macmillan, 1952, p. 242 and passim; D. E. Butler, *The British General Election of 1959*, London: Macmillan, 1960, pp. 235–40).

The term was first popularized by D. E. Butler in the statistical analysis of the election results in the Nuffield Studies of the British General Elections since 1945.

R. T. McKenzie

See also: VOTING

Symbiosis

A. In human ecology, most definitions agree on these points: that *symbiosis* is a relation that underlies the sustenance structure of a human group; that it may refer to either (or both) the spatial or the division-of-labour aspects of this structure; and that it always involves (although it is not necessarily limited to) reciprocally advantageous relations among *dissimilar* participants. Within this area of agreement, differences occur with respect to such considerations as these: whether symbiosis is limited strictly to relations among dissimilars and does not embrace relations among similars; or whether it is limited to a subsocial type of interaction and, therefore, excludes those human social forms of interaction that necessarily involve exchanges of meaning through language.

B. The term is borrowed from biology where it means the living together in close association, as in a nest or colony, of two or more dissimilar kinds of organisms. In biology it refers to sustenance relations which are either antagonistic or mutually advantageous or both.

In social science, several authors employ the biological definition of symbiosis when referring to plant communities or animal groups for purposes of analogy, or when studying the entire biotic community that embraces men, plants, and beasts. In a more restricted sense, the concept is used to refer to the complex network of sustenance relations that binds together the human population of a community or an economy. This latter usage obviously does not imply biologically different species of organisms but only men of a single species who occupy specialized functional positions within a division-of-labour structure.

C. When *symbiosis* is limited to relations among men, several variations in usage occur, of which three may be cited as illustrative:

1. R. E. Park and E. W. Burgess (*Introduction to the Science of Sociology*, Chicago: University of Chicago Press, 1921, ch. III) conceive symbiosis as a *subsocial type of interaction* among men, similar to that found among members of a plant community or between ants and aphids in an insect colony. It operates indirectly

Symbol

through the reciprocal interaction of human beings with their environment and, in pure form, does not take place by means of communication (q.v.). Among men, this form of interaction is accompanied and modified by cultural norms and by social interaction.

2. A. H. Hawley (*Human Ecology*, New York: Ronald Press, 1950, pp. 209–10) defines *symbiosis* as a reciprocally advantageous kind of sustenance relation that binds together men who perform dissimilar specialized functions within the division-of-labour structure in contrast with *commensalism* (q.v.), which occurs among persons who occupy similar functional positions. This conception does not distinguish between subsocial and human social levels of interaction.

3. L. Wirth (*The Ghetto*, Chicago: University of Chicago Press, 1928, pp. 282–3) uses *symbiosis* to describe the fact that human groups with dissimilar cultures can live in close physical proximity and yet retain their respective social milieux. This conception is based on a distinction between social relations that are impersonal and external as contrasted with those that are personal and intimate. It does not involve either the distinction between subsocial and social relations as made by Park and Burgess or that between symbiosis and commensalism as made by Hawley.

James A. Quinn

See also: COMMENSALISM
             COMMUNITY
             DIVISION OF LABOUR
             ECOLOGY

Symbol

A. While the term *symbol* is sometimes used as synonomous with *sign* (q.v.), it is more frequently recognized as a sub-class of *sign* whose defining characteristics are either the intentional or conventional type of relation holding between the symbol and the symbolized.

B. The advantage of insisting upon the 'intentionality' of symbol-situations is one of 'specificity', highlighting an important difference between human response-types and sub-human (non-human) sign-behaviour. The advantage of insisting upon the 'conventionality' of symbol-situations is one of 'comprehensiveness', highlighting the type-similarity of both deliberately 'intentional' and unconsciously 'intended' symbolic productions and realizations. In view of the still controversial state of inquiry into symbols and symbolizations, it will be safer to

characterize them as 'intentional' and 'conventional' jointly rather than as one to the exclusion of the other.

1. Some writers use *sign* to denote anything that serves as a vehicle of meaning, and *symbol* to denote the sign and the meaning combined (W. L. Warner, *The Living and the Dead*, New Haven: Yale University Press, 1959, pp. 451–5). This usage is unattractive both to those who seek a sharper differentiation of symbols as a sub-class of signs and to the analysts of meaning who emphasize that both signs and symbols occur in triadic and semiotic contexts which involve (a) a respondent (interpreter), (b) a sign-vehicle (physical sign-event), and (c) a referent, designated by the sign-vehicle for the respondent (e.g. C. W. Morris, *Foundation of the Theory of Signs*, Chicago: University of Chicago Press, 1938, p. 4).

2. Other writers, by contrast, tend to overstress the 'conventional' symbolic response, characteristic of human behaviour, by identifying it with arbitrary or deliberate assignment of meaning to symbols which is manifested by language (see, e.g. A. R. Lindesmith & A. L. Strauss, *Social Psychology*, New York: Dryden, 1949, pp. 40–1).

3. According to the *Dictionary of Philosophy* (D. Runes (ed.), New York: The Philosophical Library, 1942, p. 308) symbols are defined as conventional (rather than natural) 'signs which function as such in virtue of a convention, explicit or implicit, between their users'. The value of this definition depends upon a liberal interpretation of 'convention', usually by way of determining the 'symbol-symbolized' relation in terms of (semantic, syntactic, pragmatic, or axiologic) rules. By contrast, all causally-necessary connections (e.g. 'smoke signifies fire') become definitory of natural (rather than conventional) sign-situations.

4. G. H. Mead (*Mind, Self and Society*, Chicago: University of Chicago Press, 1934, p. 156) has had increasing influence on social scientists with his emphasis on the 'symbolic' nature of all intelligent and conscious behaviour. If the self is constituted by reacting to its own acts from the standpoint of those with whom it intereacts, it can do so only by 'taking the role of the generalized other' in a process of using significant symbols. Here a considerably wider conception of 'meaning-conventions' is allowed than by those writers who, after identifying symbols with conventional signs, determine the latter by semantic (language) rules exclusively.

5. Among sociologists, T. Parsons has identified the 'symbolic elements of a cultural tradition' with all 'cultural objects, ... ideas or beliefs so far as they are treated as situational objects by ego ...' (*The Social System*, Glencoe, Ill.: The Free Press, 1951, p. 4). 'A social system consists in a plurality of actors ... who are motivated in terms of a tendency to the "optimization of gratification" and whose relation to their situations, including each other, is defined and mediated in terms of a system of culturally structured and shared symbols' (ibid., pp. 5–6).

6. Among political scientists H. D. Lasswell and A. Kaplan (*Power and Society*, New Haven: Yale University Press, 1950, p. 53) have stressed that the 'political interactions of various powers and groups are constituted by patterns of influence and power, manifested in and affected by symbols'. Political symbols are defined as 'symbols that function to a significant extent in power-practices' (ibid., p. 103). Non-political symbols are defined, more broadly, as characterizing all social conduct which consists of 'practices rather than merely operations, and the subjective factors on which the difference depends may be studied by way of the symbols in which they are expressed' (ibid.).

7. Some writers in philosophy have occasionally moved on to a more radical version of symbols and symbolic-forms, operating with most general definition of *symbol* as covering not only all (culturally extant or possible) representations of reality, but exhausting the very meaning of all physical, social, aesthetic, religious, or moral reality. 'Symbolic functions', instead of permitting alternatives, characterize all human experiences and productions, and man himself (see, e.g. E. Cassirer, *Essay on Man*, New Haven: Yale University Press, 1941, pp. 23–6) is defined as 'the symbolic animal' which, for better or worse, has interposed between stimuli and response a network of symbolic meanings through which he perceives, interprets, and behaviourally conducts himself in a world whose essential features are made out in human history, i.e. as temporal developments of the various symbolic (cultural) forms as which reality is felt, understood, or acted upon.

Carl H. Hamburg

See also: COMMUNICATION
　　　　　CULTURE
　　　　　MEANING
　　　　　SIGN
　　　　　SYMBOLISM

Symbolic Interaction (See Social Interaction)

Symbolism

A. *Symbolic behaviour* is possible because stimuli can be responded to for the significances they have acquired in previous experiences, so that it is possible to speak of the representational nature of stimuli and response patterns. To the extent that stimuli are responded to for the meaning they have acquired in past experiences and to the extent that response patterns or behaviour have meanings beyond that which is directly manifested, they are symbols (q.v.). *Symbolism* then refers to the system of symbols employed or to the fact that behaviour is patterned in symbolic fashion in those cases where it is so patterned.

B. 1. Early writers at times imposed special theoretical limitations on the term. Thus G. H. Mead insisted that a symbol, and therefore symbolism, must involve consciousness: 'The symbol is thus more than a mere substitute stimulus—more than a mere stimulus for a conditioned response or reflex. For the conditioned reflex—the response to a mere substitute stimulus—does not or need not involve consciousness; whereas the response to a symbol does and must involve consciousness' (*Mind, Self and Society*, Chicago: University of Chicago Press, 1934, p. 122). Few writers today would be willing to accept a distinction among processes based upon the presence or absence of accompanying consciousness. Behaviour theorists currently tend to maintain an avoidance of problems of consciousness. Thus, 'Cognitive interpretations of symbolic and abstract behavior contrast sharply with two current theories, of which one reduces symbols to signs and the other tends to reduce concepts to stimulus generalization' (M. Scheerer, 'Cognitive Theory', in G. Lindzey (ed.), *Handbook of Social Psychology*, Cambridge, Mass.: Addison-Wesley, 1954, vol. I, p. 128).

2. In addition to general theoretical evasion of problems of consciousness, psychiatric usage frequently emphasizes *unconscious* symbolism, that is not simply stimulus substitution without consciousness as might occur in a conditioned response, but conscious experiences or behaviour units which have special significance for the unconscious processes of the individual. While detail of usage will vary with the particular variety of analytic theory involved, the trend is well described thus: 'In psychoanalysis, symbolization is the unconscious process in which emotional values are displaced from one object to another, so that repressed wishes may achieve a

Sympathy

measure of disguised satisfaction; but the conscious mind is entirely ignorant of the fact that symbols have been employed' (P. L. Harriman, *The New Dictionary of Psychology*, London: Vision Press, 1947, p. 317).

3. The importance of symbolism in the social process derives from the existence of collective symbols rather than the individually developed symbols. Language, units of economic exchange and credit, flags, religious practices, all represent socially shared symbolism. Collective symbolism in the form of language aids in the solution of problems by permitting vicarious manipulation and by establishing means of communication in interpersonal contacts. Collective symbolism in the form of the use of emblems or of expressive actions aids in the maintenance of the collective by arousing responses which increase solidarity and cohesion.

Eugene L. Hartley

See also: COMMUNICATION
LANGUAGE
SIGN
SYMBOL

Sympathy

A. The term *sympathy* is used to denote a broad range of ways in which one person may participate in the feelings and experiences of others.

B. According to G. H. Allport *sympathy* was historically one of the three major bases for the explanation of social behaviour together with suggestion (q.v.) and imitation (q.v.) in so far as modes of explanation going beyond rational self-interest were used ('The Historical Background of Modern Social Psychology', in G. Lindzey (ed.), *Handbook of Social Psychology*, Cambridge, Mass.: Addison-Wesley, 1954, vol. 1, pp. 18–21). The term covered a range of human responses varying from a reflexive emotional response, similar to the response of the other when one observes the other undergoing some experience, to the highly abstract and intellectualized idea of Love as a way of life. Although the concepts denoted by the term were used by writers such as Smith, Spencer, and McDougall as fundamental explanations of social life, the term itself has not survived and the concepts have been reformulated and renamed by students of group dynamics and practitioners of psychotherapy (ibid., p. 21).

C. One writer in whose work the term *sympathy* played a prominent part, and, if the current interest in phenomenology on the part of some social scientists increases, may yet give new life to the term, is M. Scheler (*The Nature of Sympathy*, trans. by P. Heath from the 5th German edn., New Haven: Yale University Press, 1954). For Scheler the German *Sympathie* denotes a generic concept covering again a wide range of participation on the part of one person in the experience of another. Of particular importance is his distinction between the forms of fellow feeling: immediate community of feeling, fellow feeling about something, emotional infection, and true emotional identification, on the one hand; and the reproduction of the other's feeling 'without its being transmitted to us, or evoking a similar real emotion in us' on the other (ibid., pp. 9–12). Also important is his rejection of empathy (q.v.) as a basis for sympathy and his insistence on a direct and immediate perception of feeling in the gesture of the other.

William L. Kolb

See also: EMPATHY
IMITATION
INTERNALIZATION
UNDERSTANDING

Syndicalism

A. The term, adapted from the French *le syndicalisme* meaning trade unionism, has two main usages: (a) a social doctrine or movement which holds that workers' unions should be the basis of social and industrial administration in a socialist society; (b) militant industrial action by workers' unions.

B. 1. The term became current in English after 1907 to designate the movement among radical sections of industrial workers which has as its central object the transference of the means of production and distribution from their present owners to unions of workers. The method generally favoured to achieve this object is 'direct' (as opposed to parliamentary political) action in the form of sabotage, working to rule, strikes, etc., culminating in a General Strike, which is to be the prelude to a social revolution, e.g. 'The object of syndicalism was to expropriate the capitalists by continued hostilities and to get the factories, workshops and agricultural industries into the hands of the trade unionists' (M. Beer, *A History of British Socialism*, London: G. Bell, 1919, vol. I, p. 321).

The social order envisaged by the syndicalists is summarily described in the following definition of the term made by one of the most prominent leaders of the British movement: 'a condition of society where industry will be controlled by those engaged therein, on the basis of free societies; these to co-operate for the production of all the requirements of life in the most efficient manner, ... a Society in which Parliaments and Governments will have disappeared, having served their purpose with the capitalist system' (T. Mann, *From Single Tax to Syndicalism*, London: Guy Bowman, 1913, p. xiv).

2. In France the movement, whose principles were first clearly formulated by F. Pelloutier (1867–1901), came to be known as *le syndicalisme révolutionnaire*. In England and the U.S.A. likewise the implication is that syndicalism is a *revolutionary* movement.

3. In current usage the term may designate syndicalist tactics whether or not these are directed towards the achievement of control of industry by workers' unions (see L. von Mises, *Socialism* (1936), New Haven: Yale University Press, 1951, p. 270). It is also used loosely as descriptive of situations in industrial organizations in which employees are believed to exercise considerable influence in decision-making.

Since the decline of the movement after World War I, the chief exponents of the doctrine have been anarchists. To emphasize its anti-statist and decentralist character, they have added the prefix 'anarcho-' (see R. Rocker, *Anarcho-Syndicalism*, London: Secker & Warburg, 1938).

G. N. Ostergaard

See also: LABOUR (Political Science)
REVOLUTION

Syntax (See Linguistics)

System of Orientation

A. A *system of orientation* is a web or complex of items of knowledge, attitudes, values, and norms of diverse sorts in terms of which a group (or person) orients itself (or himself) to a situation (comprehends the situation and chooses appropriate courses of action).

B. The core idea of this concept is needed in the social sciences since human action is determined neither by the 'real environment' nor by fixed mechanisms internal to the individual but by selective behaviour expressing ways of looking at or orienting to the situation. American sociologists conventionally have spoken of a person's or a group's definition of the situation (q.v.), embodying cultural prescriptions and personal attitudes. Recently experimentation and analysis in psychology has made *perceptual set* a powerful tool of analysis. Earlier the concept of *attitude* (q.v.) as 'readiness to react in a particular manner' to a given perceived situation served the same purpose.

C. Orientation, therefore, is essentially an alternative to *definition of the situation* or *perceptual set*. Its justification lies mainly in its compatibility with the recently fashionable 'action frame of reference'. The assumption of this approach is that people do 'choose' a course of action; normally there is a quasi-rationality implied, though this is not necessary. Action may be deliberate with either a conscious or a partially non-conscious orientation. It may be non-deliberative (either idiosyncratic or customary) with a non-conscious orientation; it may be merely habitual, and here the idea of orientation is less applicable.

In the most developed version of the 'theory of action' an actor must take account of unmodifiable conditions in the situation, select appropriate means, and take certain postures (cognitive, cathectic, evaluative) toward the situation. He must make an appropriate cognitive assessment of the context within which he is to act. Action presupposes also that certain objects attract or repel. And he must evaluate alternative means or courses in terms of culturally supplied norms of morality, economy, legality, etc.

Thus different aspects of the complex action are influenced, respectively, by distinct *systems of orientation*. It is not merely that different aspects of a situation are affected by separate criteria, such as cognitive or moral. Each culture provides criteria for choice, and these criteria are parts of distinctive *systems* of orientation. Cognitive criteria are selected from a complex: facts or principles of a given science, rules of the number system, 'laws' of psychological behaviour, a marginal principle from economics, etc., not to mention 'superstitions' believed to be veridical. Cathectic judgements reflect culturally specified hierarchies of valuations for assorted objects. The rules for evaluation in a given sphere, such as moral rules, also form an ordered system.

C. Arnold Anderson

See also: ATTITUDE
DEFINITION OF THE SITUATION

Systematic Sampling (See Sampling)

T

Taboo

A. The most general reference of *taboo* is to a ritual restriction or prohibition.

B. 1. The word *taboo* first came into European languages as a result of Captain James Cook's third voyage. Observations in Polynesia—on behaviour in regard to chiefs, human sacrificial victims, persons who had touched a dead body, etc.—established the meaning of *taboo* as '*consecrated*' and as '*not to be touched*' (J. Cook, *Journal of Captain Cook's Last Voyage to the Pacific*, London: E. Newbury, 1781, vol. II, pp. 40, 249). *Taboo* then soon came to be used as a term for a *thing either prohibited, forbidden* (cf. L. de Freycinet, *Voyage autour du monde*, Paris: Chez Pillet Aîné, 1829, vol. II, pt. 1, p. 597), *or sacred* (W. Williams, *A Dictionary of the New Zealand Language*, Paihia: C.M.S. Press, 1844).

1. At the same time, there developed a conception of taboo as *a system or institution*, with implications of a social and religious kind for the order of the society concerned. This led to further sociological consideration of its meaning.

C. In sociology, and more especially anthropology, taboo was soon generalized far beyond its Oceanic ethnographic range.

2. Great attention was paid to the *duality* thought to be inherent in the notion of *taboo*, though this duality was sometimes differently conceived. Thus to the quality of the *sacred or holy* was linked that of the *forbidden, or the unclean, or the dangerous*. It was held that this duality was due to a lack of development of primitive categories. 'In *taboo* proper are combined two notions which with the progress of civilization have become differentiated—(i) sacred and (ii) impure or unclean' (N. W. Thomas, *Encyclopaedia Britannica*, Cambridge: Cambridge University Press, 11th edn., 1911). Another form of duality has been emphasized by S. Freud (*Totem and Taboo*, new trans. by J. Strachey, London: Routledge & Kegan Paul, 1950) who conceived taboo as a series of socialized rules given a mystical sanction to guard individuals from committing acts for which they had strong unconscious inclination.

2. Conceived as a principle or sphere of religious life, taboo was also defined *in opposition to some other principle or sphere*. Thus taboo was defined as negative magic by J. G. Frazer, and as negative *mana* by R. R. Marett, A. R. Radcliffe-Brown, and others. By Durkheim taboo was defined as *religious interdiction* and identified with the respect for the sacred, in opposition to magical interdiction, associated with the sphere of the profane. The religious interdictions are categorical imperatives, the magical interdictions are merely useful maxims (*Elementary Forms of the Religious Life*, London: Allen & Unwin, 1915, pp. 300–1). (Another view, adopted by Freud, by which taboo, the withdrawal from common use, is contrasted with *noa*, the common or profane sphere, is ethnographically inadequate. The term *noa* is found in only a few Polynesian languages, and then only in fairly limited contexts.)

3. The *positive* function of taboo rules in social control was realized at an early period, as by de Freycinet, and by F. E. Maning (pseud. A Pakeha Maori) (*Old New Zealand*, London: Smith, Elder, 1863, pp. 83, 94, 97). J. G. Frazer also saw this: 'Although the restrictions imposed by taboo were often vexatious and absurd, and the whole system has sometimes been denounced by Europeans as a degrading superstition, yet observers who looked a little deeper have rightly perceived that its enactments, enforced mainly by imaginary but still powerful sanctions, were often beneficial' (*Psyche's Task*, London: Macmillan, 1909, p. 20).

The conception of taboo as having general significance for social order was still further expressed by Durkheim: the negative cult—taboo—'is found to exercise a positive action of the highest importance over the religious and moral nature of the individual' (*Elementary Forms of the Religious Life*, p. 309). This view was developed by A. R. Radcliffe-Brown (*Structure and Function in Primitive Society*, London: Cohen & West, 1952, pp. 133–52) who, translating taboo as 'ritual prohibition' emphasized that taboos had a very important function in the establishment and expression of social values.

4. Modern conceptions of taboo have led to variation of emphasis. An essential quality of taboo has been thought to be its *danger aspect*. Since breach of taboo is regarded as being followed automatically by some misfortune to the offender, one view has stressed the significance of automatic, mechanical punishment as being the essence of the definition. 'Tabu may be defined as a negative sanction, a prohibition whose infringement results in an automatic penalty without human or supernatural mediation. ... It must ... be restricted to describe prohibitions against participation in any situation of such inherent danger that the very act of participation will recoil upon the violator of the tabu' (M. Mead, in E. R. A. Seligman (ed.), *Encyclopedia of the Social Sciences*, London: Macmillan, vol. XIV, 1934, p. 502). Another view seeks a broader definition. F. B. Steiner argues '*Taboo is an element of all those situations in which attitudes to values are expressed in terms of danger behaviour*' (*Taboo*, London: Cohen & West, 1956, p. 147). He attributes to it two quite separate social functions: (a) classification and identification of transgressions, (b) institutional localization of danger. 'For until taboos are involved, a danger is not defined and cannot be coped with by institutionalized behaviour' (ibid., p. 146).

R. W. Firth

Take-off (See Industrial Revolution)

Tariff

A. The term *tariff* denotes either (a) a tax or duty imposed on goods passing between nations or regions; or (b) 'the classificatory instrument in which such duties are embodied' (T. E. G. Gregory, *Tariffs*, London: C. Griffin, 1921, p. 2).

B. 1. G. von Haberler distinguishes among tariffs according to the purpose for which they are imposed. 'Revenue duties are usually taken to be those duties whose primary purpose is to provide the State with revenue. ... The main motive for the imposition of protective duties ... is not to create a new source of income for the State but to maintain and encourage those branches of home industry protected by the duties' (*Theory of International Trade*, New York: The Macmillan Co., 1950, p. 238). As time goes on, however, clear distinctions of this kind become blurred and the original objectives of tariff policy become blended into the wider context and problems of international trade policy.

2. There are three major ways in which a tariff may be imposed. It may be an *ad valorem tariff* which is imposed as a percentage of the price of the imported product. It may be a *specific tariff* which is imposed as a levy of so much per physical unit of an imported product. Or finally, if a product is subject to one or the other of those duties, depending upon which is the lower duty, it is a *combined duty*.

3. In earlier periods tariffs were often imposed not only on imports but also on exports. 'Such export duties were a common device of medieval statecraft. ... The last example in Britain was the tax of 1s. a ton on coal, imposed from 1901 to 1906' (W. Beveridge (ed.), *Tariffs: The Case Examined*, London: Longmans, Green, 1932, p. 31).

Norman J. Wood

See also: EXPORTS
IMPORTS
INTERNATIONAL ECONOMICS

Tax (Also Taxation)

A. A *tax* is a compulsory contribution to government with little reference to benefits received. *Taxation* is a government's exacting from those subject to its jurisdiction (individuals, groups, corporations) a compulsory contribution with little reference to benefits bestowed.

B. 1. The term *taxation* is used uniformly in the social sciences to refer to a government's exercise of its power to exact contributions from those subject to its laws. One of the most widely accepted definitions of a tax and the one from which many definitions have been adapted is E. R. A. Seligman's: 'a compulsory contribution from the person to the government to defray the expenses incurred in the common interest of all, without reference to special benefits conferred' (*Essays in Taxation*, New York: The Macmillan Co., 10th edn., 1925, p. 432). H. Dalton defines a tax as 'a compulsory contribution imposed by a public authority, irrespective of the exact amount of service rendered to the taxpayer in return, and not imposed as a penalty for any legal offence' (*Principles of Public Finance*, London: Routledge & Kegan Paul, 4th edn., 1954, p. 23).

2. A government may divert income from individuals to itself by several means: prices, fees, special assessments, or taxes, the last three being manifestations of the taxing power. A price is a charge for a good or service of an economic character, such as water from a public water system; reference is mainly to the special benefit received by the payer, not the public purpose. A fee is a charge for a service of a governmental or administrative character, such as recording a deed; reference is to both the public purpose and the special benefit. A special assessment is a levy against property benefiting from a particular public improvement to help defray the cost of the public improvement; reference is to both the public purpose and the special benefit. A tax is a compulsory levy imposed for general public purposes; reference is mainly to the public purpose, not the special benefit.

3. Taxation is generally thought of as an instrument of revenue, but revenue is not the only purpose of taxation. It is, for example, employed by government to regulate the production and consumption of certain goods and is regarded as a major instrument of national economic policy. Some go so far as to claim that 'The purpose of taxation is never to raise money but to leave less in the hands of the taxpayer' (A. P. Lerner, *Economics of Control*, New York: The Macmillan Co., 1944, p. 307).

4. Taxes are commonly classified according to the tax base, or the object against which the tax is levied. Thus the income tax is a tax on the income of the taxpayer; the property tax a tax on the things in which the taxpayer possesses property rights; and the excise tax a tax levied on commodities before they are sold to consumers. Regardless of the base, however, all taxes are paid by persons, not things.

C. Two terms with wide, but varied, usage are *direct taxes* and *indirect taxes*. The most generally accepted meaning of these terms is that direct taxes refer to the type in which the 'taxpayer' is expected to be the tax bearer while indirect taxes refer to the type in which the taxpayer is expected to shift the tax on to other parties. Examples, respectively, are the personal income tax and an excise tax. Since economic actualities are not always in accord with these expectations, some prefer to disregard incidence and say that 'indirect taxes are those levied on the sale or purchase of any goods or services other than personal services, and that all other taxes are direct' (H. Dalton, *Principles of Public Finance*, p. 25). Others, because of 'confused and contradictory usage', refuse to employ the terms (W. J. Schultz & C. L. Harriss,

American Public Finance, New York: Prentice-Hall, 6th edn., 1954, p. 165, fn. 2).

Charles E. Ratliff, Jr.

See also: PUBLIC DEBT
  PUBLIC FINANCE
  REVENUE

Technology

A. Two general meanings of this term have become fairly well established.

1. In regard to primitive or backward peoples and to periods of prehistory or history prior to industrialization in the modern sense, and in the context of archaeology and social anthropology—the term denotes the body of *knowledge* available for the fashioning of implements and artifacts of all kinds, for the practice of crafts and manual skills (except religious, magical, military, or culinary performances) and for the extraction or collection of materials of all kinds (except those used for food and for religious or magical rituals).

2. In regard to societies already industrialized or becoming so—the term denotes the whole, or an organized sector of, the body of *knowledge* about (a) scientific principles and discoveries and (b) existing and previous industrial processes, resources of power and materials, and methods of transmission and communication, which are thought to be relevant to the production or improvement of goods and services.

B. 1. Early uses of the term, at the very beginning of the 18th century, adhere closely to the sense of the original Greek: the first *Oxford English Dictionary* reference is to a book title (1706) 'Technology, A Description of Arts, especially the Mechanical'.

2. A wider currency of the word was begun by the Encyclopédie, which added the notion of technology as the rational exploitation of arts and crafts through scientific study. Thus technology not only 'describes industrial processes', but traces their development and reveals the improvements of which they are susceptible. The divisions of technology cited by the Encyclopaedists suggest a much wider range of 'study' comprised by technology: i.e. not only of raw materials but also 'dwellings, furniture, clothing, food, drink, hygiene, lighting, heating, instruments and tools'.

3. This amplified meaning was carried over into the 19th century. Thus K. Marx refers to 'natural technology, i.e. in the formation of the organs of plants and animals, as instruments of production for sustaining life', and goes on to say 'Technology discloses man's mode of dealing with Nature, the process of production by which he sustains his life' (*Capital*, trans. by S. Moore & E. Aveling, ed. by F. Engels, London: Sonnenschein, 1904, vol. I, p. 367).

4. The sense of technology as knowledge pertaining to the fashioning and use of tools and instruments, and knowledge of the uses of raw materials (except food) has been followed by anthropologists. Thus R. Firth identifies the 'technological system' as 'the material equipment and body of knowledge at command of the participants in an economy' (*Primitive Polynesian Economy*, London: Routledge, 1939, p. 78). This is also the archaeological usage.

5. Historians and sociologists tend to limit the reference of the word to industrial processes in societies already industrialized or becoming so. Latterly the word has acquired in common usage, followed by sociologists, more limited reference still in (a) serving to distinguish the industrial 'application of the results of science', which is the work of 'technologists' and 'engineers', from 'science' or 'pure science' (D. S. L. Cardwell, *The Organization of Science in England*, London: Heinemann, 1957, p. 11); (b) denoting the practical activity of improving old industrial methods and equipment without reference to scientific principles, i.e. a concern with 'the invention of new things and processes or the improvement of older ones ... perhaps most frequently technical inventions and improvements were made without any help from pure science' (A. Wolf, *A History of Science, Technology and Philosophy in the Eighteenth Century*, London: Allen & Unwin, 1938, pp. 498–9); (c) denoting, especially in American writing, a body of knowledge and skill which is the precursor of, or potentially available for, technical improvements and inventions: 'technology was mediated through the social relations of production, but these were bound sooner or later to catch up with technology' (D. Riesman, *Thorstein Veblen: A Critical Interpretation*, New York: Charles Scribner's Sons, 1953, p. 64).

Tom Burns

Temperament

A. 'Temperament refers to the characteristic phenomena of an individual's emotional nature, including his susceptibility to emotional stimulation, his customary strength and speed of response, the quality of his prevailing mood, and all peculiarities of fluctuation and intensity in mood; these phenomena being regarded as dependent upon constitutional make-up and therefore largely hereditary in origin' (G. W. Allport, *Personality*, New York: Henry Holt, 1937, p. 54).

B. The concept of temperament has had a long and remarkably consistent history from Hippocrates's four (choleric, melancholic, phlegmatic, and sanguine) temperaments described about 400 B.C. up to the present day. Temperament was used with the same essential meaning, although the specific dimensions and types were redefined, by Aristotle, Galen, Kant, Ribot, Gall, Schelling, Muller, Wundt, Fouillée, Kretschmer, Alexander Stewart, Neumann, Ach, Jastrow, and Jaensch, and numerous others whose concepts are reviewed in A. A. Roback's *Psychology of Character* (New York: Harcourt, Brace, 1927).

1. W. McDougall's *Outline of Psychology* (London: Methuen, 5th edn., 1931, p. 358), conceives temperament as largely innate and qualifying the process of mental and character development. 'Temperament is a complex resultant of many factors, each of which is in the main natively determined, though susceptible in various degrees to modification by environmental influences and mental discipline. The mental development of the individual is constantly biassed in this or that direction by the peculiarities of his temperament; the trend of the selective activity of the mind, in all its processes of assimilation, discrimination, apperception, and habit formation, is largely determined by temperament; so that two individuals, similarly endowed as regards disposition and intellectual capacities, would develop very differently if they were of widely different temperament. Temperament largely influences the growth both of intellect and of character'.

'Temperaments being resultants of so many diverse factors, it necessarily follows that the varieties of temperament are innumerable, and that the temperament of any man cannot be adequately characterized by one or a few adjectives. And, in fact, our terminology is here most inadequate. We have only a few appropriate terms, which partially characterize certain types of temperament, adjectives such as buoyant, quick, slow, nervous, active, excitable, sluggish, melancholic, stable, and especially introvert and extrovert' (ibid., p. 358).

2. G. W. Allport distinguishes the American emphasis on basic constitutional temperament from a usage, among certain British writers, which included many additional personality

717

Tension

traits (*Personality*, p. 53): 'The classical doctrine that ascribed peculiarities of temperament to the humors of the body has persisted throughout the ages so that the meaning of the term has varied but little. The term found its way into English in the Middle Ages along with the doctrine of the humors. It meant then and still means a "constitution or habit of mind, especially depending upon or connected with physical constitution". Today in America psychological usage stresses particularly the constitutional basis; for them temperament is the "internal weather" in which personality develops; it is the subjective climate provided by native physiological and kinetic endowment. The usage of the term in Great Britain is somewhat different, tending to equate temperament with personality, as in the phrase "temperament tests" (rather than "tests of personality")'. Titchener, however, seems close to what Allport regards as the British view in defining temperament as the 'general term for innate (or very largely innate) susceptibility of the individual to emotive situations and for the typical character of his emotive responses' (quoted in G. Murphy, *Personality*, New York: Harper & Bros., 1947, p. 998). This would apparently include all innate affective susceptibility, however specific, and the character of learnt as well as innate emotional responses.

Goodwin Watson

See also: EMOTION

Tension

A. In psychology and psychiatry *tension* denotes (a) motive (see *Motivation*) or Drive and (b) a state of strain within personality arising from conflicting motivations. While sociologists and social psychologists also use the term in these senses, they have extended it to denote strains within a group or between groups arising from conflicting attitudes, motives, and values. In all cases one speaks of degrees of intensity or severity of tension measurable in terms of physiological manifestations, subjective feelings, or overt behaviour.

B. Even where *tension* is used as a synonym for *drive* or *motive* there is implied a conception of an opposing force. Thus C. E. Osgood (*Method and Theory in Experimental Psychology*, New York: Oxford University Press, 1953, pp. 606–8), following the Gestaltists, uses the term to denote a drive toward the solution of a problem. This is a case of strain arising from the opposition between the motivation to solve a

problem and the problem's state of not being solved and it manifests itself as a drive towards completion of a task when the work is interrupted before completion. A measure of the degree of tension can be derived from knowledge of the strength of the opposing forces. D. Krech and R. S. Crutchfield (*Elements of Psychology*, New York: Knopf, 1958, p. 311), for instance, state: 'The degree of tension produced by frustration is a function of (1) the strength of aroused motives and (2) the power and persistence of the blockage. The thwarting of weak motive states produces less tension than the thwarting of strong motive states'. The opposing forces involved in the creation of tension may exist within the personality as in the case of demands of incompatible needs; in the relation of the organism to the natural environment; or in the relation of the person to his cultural and social environment.

C. Psychoanalysts emphasize the extent to which tensions are unconsciously created and even unconsciously experienced. According to Freud the ego in its efforts to reconcile the demands of the id, the superego, and reality is 'governed by consideration of the tension produced by stimuli present within it or introduced into it' (*An Outline of Psychoanalysis*, trans. by J. Strachey, New York: W. W. Norton, 1949, p. 16). Such stimuli may have their origins in consciousness but they are much more likely to stem from the unconscious. Though unconsciously evoked, endopsychic tensions will affect behaviour. Projection, sublimation, regression, fantasy, all are seen as tension-reducing mechanisms.

D. The concept of tension and tension systems form an integral part of K. Lewin's field theory (q.v.) (*Field Theory in Social Science*, New York: Harper & Bros., 1951, pp. 4–20). Tension, Lewin suggests, exists within an individual whenever a psychological need or intention (quasi-need) exists. It is released when the need is satisfied. It has several conceptual properties: it will lead to outgoing activity designed to reach the goal or else to withdrawal or substitute activity where the attainment of the goal is perceived as unlikely. Phenomena which Gestalt psychologists have demonstrated, the Zeigarnick effect, rigidity, the consequences of frustration, can all be seen as various reactions to tension. What activity is used to reduce tension will depend on the strength of the tension and also on the individual's perception of the possibilities that the environment offers to reduce tension, i.e. to make possible the achievement of his goal.

E. Through the work of Lewin the concept of tension and tension system has been extended to motivations and/or strains existing within and between groups. Thus tension as drive toward task completion and tension as strain possibly leading to conflict are present in the concepts of those interested in group dynamics (q.v.) (M. Horwitz, 'The Recall of Interrupted Group Tasks: An Experimental Study of Individual Motivation in Relation to Group Goals', in D. Cartwright & A. Zander (eds.), *Group Dynamics*, Evanston, Ill.: Row, Peterson, 1953, pp. 361–84; and K. Lewin, 'The Background of Conflict in Marriage', *Resolving Social Conflicts*, ed. by G. W. Lewin, New York: Harper & Bros., 1948, pp. 89–91). It is interesting to note, however, that the term tends to lose technical preciseness as it is used in relation to the group, and to be replaced by sub-terms that are precisely defined. Thus in the book by R. M. Williams, Jr., *The Reduction of Intergroup Tensions* (New York: Social Science Research Council, 1947), the term is used in the title but it is not defined in the text. Instead the author points out that 'in any research on problems of inter-group relations it is essential to distinguish at least three aspects of negative interaction: prejudice (hostility), discrimination, and conflict' (ibid., p. 36); and then proceeds to define carefully these three terms.

H. Himmelweit

See also: CONFLICT
EGO
FIELD THEORY
GROUP DYNAMICS
ID
MOTIVATION
SUPEREGO

Territorial Jurisdiction (See **Jurisdiction**)

Terror
Terror may be defined as a special kind of tyranny (q.v.). Its characteristics are: (a) that no observance of commands—no matter how punctilious—on the part of prospective victims can insure their safety; (b) that punishments are inflicted indiscriminately with the deliberate aim of creating an atmosphere of fear, and thus paralysing resistance.

These features distinguish terror from policies of extermination. Moreover, terror must be distinguished from robbery and indulgence in sadism, although it is always accompanied by them.

S. Andreski

See also: TYRANNY

Theoretical Model (See **Model**)

Total Cost (See **Cost**)

Total Equity (See **Net Worth**)

Total Revenue (See **Revenue**)

Totalitarianism
A. *Totalitarianism* is the extension of permanent governmental control over the totality of social life. A movement or an ideology may be called totalitarian if it advocates such an extension. Totalitarianism in this sense is, of course, an ideal type to which concrete cases can only approximate, since no government can control every instance of social interaction. The qualification 'permanent' is important because it excludes a large number of cases, such as various sultanates and primitive kingdoms, where sporadic interference with all aspects of life of the subjects was common, but where there was little of systematic regulation.

B. In *Wörterbuch der Soziologie* (ed. by W. Bernsdorf & F. Bülow, Stuttgart: F. Enke Verlag, 1955, p. 551) O. Stammer says: 'we can speak of totalitarianism only where a centralistically oriented mass movement, led by a political minority in an authoritarian manner, relying on the monopoly of power, and with the aid of a dictatorially ruled state, builds an apparatus of power which bears upon all parts of the society'. Z. Brzezinski (*The Permanent Purge: Politics in Soviet Totalitarianism*, Cambridge, Mass.: Harvard University Press, 1956, p. 7) writes: 'Totalitarianism can, therefore, be defined as a system where technologically advanced instruments of political power are wielded without restraint by centralized leadership of an elite movement, for the purpose of effecting a total social revolution, on the basis of certain arbitrary ideological assumptions proclaimed by the leadership, in an atmosphere of coerced unanimity of the entire population'. These definitions, which are fairly typical, raise a general methodological issue.

A scientific term can be useful only if it is sufficiently general to be applied to a number of cases: there is hardly much to be gained by

Totemism

having a term so highly specified that it merely replaces one or two proper names. Stammer's definition fits only Hitler's regime in Germany: the Bolsheviks were never a mass movement, and neither they nor the Chinese communists received help from a 'dictatorially ruled state' in building up their apparatus of power. Brzezinski's definition fits only Soviet Russia before 1935: the efforts of the Soviet rulers of today are aimed rather at preventing than at effecting a revolution, and the party could hardly be called 'a movement' nowadays; the Chinese communists turned from a mass movement into an elite, but were never 'an elite movement'; Hitler never attempted to carry out a total social revolution. Many other definitions of totalitarianism could be likewise accused of unprofitable restrictiveness. Secondly, scientific thought proceeds by decomposing complex individual entities into simpler units (material or conceptual), among whose mutual relations some uniformity might be detected: our concepts should enable us to analyse concrete cases—not merely to name them.

The definition proposed in A. above leaves entirely open the question of antecedents, determinants, consequences and correlates of totalitarianism, though it does imply the absence of any independent centres of power. In fact, a very high degree of totalitarianism can go together with very primitive technology (e.g. the Inca empire or Egypt under the Ptolemies). The late Roman Empire as well as Tokugawa Japan were both highly totalitarian without the aid of any revolutionary ideas. Calvin's Geneva provided an example of theocratic totalitarianism. Whereas effective control over the totality of social life must produce outward unanimity, the reverse is not true: in Spain under the Inquisition there was forced unanimity without totalitarianism. Moreover, there are reasons for thinking that totalitarianism is compatible with considerable variations in the distribution of power within the governmental apparatus, and in the methods of governing.

S. Andreski

See also: ABSOLUTISM
AUTOCRACY
TYRANNY

Totemism

A. This term is derived from an Ojibwa (Algonkin tribe of North America) word, variously written *totem, tatam, dodaim*. (Max Muller argued that the form should be *otem*, leading Andrew Lang to write semi-ironically of 'otemism or totemism'.

Its basic use refers to a system of beliefs and practices embodying concepts of a *mystical or ritual relationship* between members of a social group (usually a descent group) and members of a class of objects (usually a species of animal or plant).

Recognition of the relationship may take many forms. Commonly it is expressed in: (a) respect injunctions—'taboos' (q.v.) such as prohibitions against killing or eating any animal (or interfering with any plant) of the species concerned; (b) kinship beliefs—that the members of the human group are descended from a mythical totem ancestor, or that they and the members of the natural species are 'brothers'. Other expressions of the relationship may be: use of the totem as a group symbol; belief that the totem is a 'protector' of members of the group; recognition of an obligation to perform 'increase rites' to cause the totem species to multiply.

B. There has been much variation of usage in what is taken to be the essential character of totemism, or alternatively, in what phenomena are allowed to be properly classed as totemic.

1. *Amerindian Usage* (a) John Long, who first introduced the terms, emphasized *the tutelary aspect of totemism for the individual*, whose fate was bound up with that of the totem animal. 'One part of the religious superstition of the Savages consists in each of them having his *totam*, or favourite spirit, which he believes watches over him. ... This idea of destiny, or, if I may be allowed the phrase, "*totamism*", however strange, is not confined to the Savages' (*Voyages and Travels of an Indian Interpreter and Trader* ..., London: Robson and others, 1791, pp. 86–7).

(b) From other early Amerindian data the totem (though not always called by this term) was regarded as the emblem, badge or armorial bearings of the social group—though Jonathan Carver (1778) objected to the analogy with blazonry. Related to this usage is the equation of totem with *family name*, as by H. R. Schoolcraft (1834) who also first used the term *totemic system* to describe the schematic use of animal symbols for social groups.

2. *Wider Usage*. (a) Usage of the term began to widen after Grey (1841) drew attention to the similarity between the *kobong* of some western Australian tribes and the *totam* of Long.

(b) Further development of the term as a

general concept stemmed from the work of J. F. McLennan who (i) predicted that totemism would be found to prevail also in Oceania and other regions and (ii) postulated a 'totemic stage' through which, e.g. classical nations had passed, thus associating totemism with a specific state of society involving both exogamy and matriliny.

C. A more sociological conception emerged in the work of W. Robertson-Smith, who associated totemism with sacrifice and communion feasts, and of S. Freud who, while adopting the common definition of totemism, drew attention to ambivalence as a characteristic of the totemic relationship.

D. The conception of totemism as a form of symbolic expression representing the collective life of a social group and serving as a basic integrative force was primarily developed by Durkheim. From Australian evidence he pointed out that totemism could not be defined simply as 'the religion of the clan', but is a complex religious system, operating for the tribe as a whole (*The Elementary Forms of the Religious Life*, trans. by J. W. Swain, London: Allen & Unwin, 1915, pp. 154–5, 295).

E. The unitary nature of totemism as a general phenomenon was a conception rejected by some writers (Toutain, Goldenweiser, Westermarck, Kroeber). From ethnographic evidence it was shown that when a symbolic relationship between a natural species and a social group is recognized, the associated features may vary greatly; in particular, there may be no rule of exogamy for the totem kin members. A. Goldenweiser claimed 'Totemism is one of those cultural complexes which, though distinctive enough when understood, are not distinguishable by content alone' (*Anthropology*, London: Harrap, 1937, p. 323).

F. A. R. Radcliffe-Brown agreed in part. 'Totemism is not one thing but is a general name given to a number of diverse institutions which all have, or seem to have, something in common' (*Structure and Function in Primitive Society*, London: Cohen & West, 1952, pp. 117–18).

Thus granted this diversity, totemism has been regarded as providing a basic organizing principle for the society concerned. Radcliffe-Brown held that:

(1) Totemism is a special development of a more general relation between man and natural species.

(2) Totemism is part of a structural system which organizes not only the relation of human beings to one another, but also the relation of man to his environment.

(3) Natural species are selected as representatives of social groups such as clans, because they express social values, that is, they have important effects upon the material or spiritual well-being of a society.

G. The view of totemism as a ritualization of empirical interests has been contested, in particular by C. Lévi-Strauss. Drawing inter alia on some late statements by A. R. Radcliffe-Brown, he has demonstrated by structural analysis the significance of totemic attributions as expressions of principles of resemblance and contrast, of union and opposition, conceived in logical manner by speculative thought to operate both in nature and in society (*Le Totemisme Aujourd'hui*, Paris: Presses Universitaires de France, 1962, pp. 119–31).

R. W. Firth

Trade

1. *Trade* has a number of possible meanings in economics: (a) a means of earning one's living, an occupation, work, especially skilled work as distinguished from unskilled work, or from a business or a profession or from farming, a craft; (b) buying and selling, barter, commerce; (c) all the persons in a particular line of business; (d) customers, clientele; (e) a purchase or sale, deal, bargain; (f) an exchange, swap; (g) the amount of business done in a particular place.

In addition, as a verb, trade is used in the sense of treating as an asset for example 'trading on the equity', or 'trading on one's good name'. Trade is also combined with other terms such as trade union, trade mark, trade barrier, free trade, or trade association, and in these cases it has one of the meanings ascribed to it above.

2. It is not possible to synthesize these meanings, as they have grown up over time to describe different classes of economic activity. In general we may narrow the meanings down to two specific classes: (i) Trade denotes an occupation or business, a group of people in the same occupation or business, or a group of people who are purchasing the same commodity. This would encompass categories (a) (c), (d), above. (ii) Trade is synonymous with exchange which is carried on between individuals, between countries and within a market place. This would

Trade Union

encompass categories (b), (c), (e), (f), and (g) above.

George H. Borts

Trade Cycle (See **Business Cycles and Business Fluctuations**)

Trade Union (Also **Labour Union**)

A. The exact form which trade unions take varies between countries but there is common agreement about the general meaning of the term. An early definition, frequently cited by non-legal authorities, is that of S. and B. Webb, which states: 'A trade union ... is a continuous association of wage earners for the purpose of maintaining or improving the conditions of their working lives' (*The History of Trade Unionism*, London: Longmans, Green, 1920, p. 1). This is an accurate short description if by wage earners is meant all people who sell their labour irrespective of the precise form their payment takes and if for 'conditions of their working lives' is substituted 'their standard of living'.

The adequacy of such a definition may be tested in the light of four principal criteria:

1. The first criterion is that of a union's *personnel*. The only stipulation is that they must be free to sell their labour for money. A trade union may consist of members of one trade, occupation, profession or industry, a number of these or a combination of them. The members may be wage or salary earners, labourers or higher management. Trade unions are no longer peculiar to manual workers.

2. A second criterion is that of *objectives*. These must be primarily industrial but they can, and often do, have a political content. This occurs when it can be seen that the primary industrial objectives can only be secured by government action and/or when the government plays a dominant role in economic affairs. Political aims then are normally subsidiary to industrial ones and, in the main, supplement them. The objectives are continually widening. At first they were confined to workshop activities. Now they cover a wide range of workers' interests, indeed everything which enters into their standard of living. Trade unions are mainly sectional organizations and their objectives directly concern the interests of their members.

3. A third criterion is that of *structure*. A trade union must have a permanent organization in that its activities run from one industrial incident to another. This is what is meant by 'continuous'. Various bodies, possessing the personnel and objects of trade unions, have existed but they have been formed for specific objects and have disbanded on the fulfilment of those objects. Strike committees are a case in point. Shop stewards' organizations come nearer to the definition of a trade union. They have the personnel and often are permanent, but they normally have restricted objects and are considered as *part* of trade union organizations. But a workshop organization could proclaim itself a trade union, as could any branch of a trade union which felt itself able to deal completely with the range of trade union objects. As with objectives there has been an evolution in structure. Trade unions began as small, localized organizations in which all members could share control. They developed first into loose national alliances then into centralized national organizations which are controlled by representative government. There are also national central organizations of trade unions and international federations of trade unions. A trade union is sometimes described as a voluntary society, i.e. a society which permits eligible persons to join or secede as they wish. But it is not necessary that this should be so. Compulsory membership has an historical basis; it can be enforced by trade unionists in workshops, by a trade union in agreement with an employer, or by law. In practice a high degree of compulsion in one form or another is exercised to obtain and retain members.

4. The fourth criterion is that of *environment*. Trade unions belong only to societies which have a permanent, free, employed class. Unless the employed class is *permanent* the impulse to combine will not exist, and without freedom the facilities to combine will be denied. Variations in industrial and political environments have altered the methods and functions of trade unions. Such variations may affect the range of cases to which definition applies. Thus in the U.S.S.R. trade unions must operate within a planned society, dominated by the Communist Party. Such unions do not possess the function of wage bargaining but have acquired social and welfare functions. Trade unions remain *legally* free organizations in the U.S.S.R. and are not formally a part of the state apparatus, but they are supervised by the Communist Party so their activities in practice differ from those in Western capitalist countries. It is arguable, therefore, that the restrictions on trade unions in the U.S.S.R. which the political and economic conditions impose are such as to disqualify them from use of the description. On the other hand, trade unions in *all* countries are affected by conditions within those countries and have greater or less freedom, wider or narrower functions. They can adapt themselves to local and national needs without altering their main qualifications for recognition as trade unions.

B. 1. The term *trade union* is of relatively recent origin. Until the second half of the 19th century, the terms *combinations of journeymen*, *trade clubs*, *trade societies*, *friendly societies*, and *sick clubs* were commonly used. These were not in all respects trade unions as known today, but they were so in embryo. 'Unions' in the 1830s meant unions of the working class, or workers from various trades, hence the term *trades union*. During the last quarter of the 19th century *trade union* became the acknowledged term. It referred to an association of workers in a single trade. It possessed a more dynamic connotation than did the other terms and more accurately described the intentions of the workers who joined it. But it ceased to be accurate almost as soon as it came into use. Workers at that time started to combine on a class and industrial basis into common organizations. Since then organizations which were formed to cater for workers of a particular *trade* have tended to widen their bases. A trade union, now, strictly speaking, is a *labour union* and it is known as such in North America.

2. There is no internationally valid legal definition of a trade union. In some countries trade unions have not been defined by law; in other countries legal emphasis has been placed in different ways on the personnel, the methods, or the objects of trade unions. Some trade unions in law include employers; others are confined to a narrow category of workers. Where the law has intervened it has been to restrict the trade union as a social phenomenon, for example by regulating its activities or the conduct of its organization. Because of this factor the legal definition often varies from common usage.

V. L. Allen

See also: Labour (Economics)
  Labour (Political Science)
  Labour Market

Tradition

A. 1. *Tradition*, in the strict sense, is a neutral term used to denote the 'transmission', usually oral, whereby modes of activity or taste or belief are handed down ('given across') from one generation to the next, and thus perpetuated Thus as applied to social institutions tradition is the vehicle through which every child learns something of the mores and stock of accumulated knowledge and prejudice of his forefathers. 'The forces of imitation are so much more potent than any adult technique for exploiting them; the child's receptivity to its surroundings is so much more important than any methods of stimulation, that as long as every adult with whom he comes in contact is saturated with the tradition, he cannot escape a similar saturation' (M. Mead, *Growing Up in New Guinea*, London: Routledge, 1931, p. 195).

2. The term *tradition* is also applied to some of the elements of culture so transmitted, but not to all elements. Those elements which are singled out and given the status of *traditions* are usually valued, and it is strongly implied that they are especially worthy of acceptance. Thus a tradition is a mode of behaviour or standard produced by a group as distinct from an individual; and serves to intensify group consciousness and cohesion.

B. 1. The term (a) emphasizes the notions of continuity, stability, and venerability; and (b) stresses the body of collective wisdom embodied in the tradition of the group. In this sense, the weight of tradition, its 'authority', derives from implied criticism of those who would rely upon their own individual stock of reason. Burke in his denunciation of the revolutionaries in France was concerned to indict the 'presumption' of supposing that a violent break with tradition could be justified by appealing to abstract, universal right. In order to point the contrast, he sought to emphasize the strength of the British Constitution in its reliance on tradition. 'You will observe, that, from Magna Charta to the Declaration of Right, it has been the uniform policy of our Constitution to claim and assert our liberties as an *entailed inheritance* derived to us from our forefathers, and to be transmitted to our posterity' (Burke, *Reflections on the Revolution in France*, *Works*, London: Rivington, 1852, vol. IV, p. 177). Here tradition has ceased to be a descriptive term; it is prescriptive.

2. Thus tradition is often advanced as the source of legitimacy; and it has in fact proved the base of many forms of authority (q.v.). 'Patriarchalism is by far the most important type of domination the legitimacy of which rests upon tradition' (M. Weber, *From Max Weber: Essays in Sociology*, trans. by H. H. Gerth & C.

Transhumance

W. Mills, London: Kegan Paul, Trench, Trubner, 1947, p. 296).

3. The term has also been much used in contemporary writings by those who reject the view that existing grievances can be remedied by radical institutional changes. It is here sharply contrasted with *rationalism* or *ideology*. Tradition is on this view an accumulation of pragmatic experience. Thus, 'The rationalist idea substituted social utility for tradition as the main criterion of social institutions and values' (J. L. Talmon, *The Origins of Totalitarian Democracy*, London: Secker & Warburg, 1952, p. 3). Thus also, M. Oakeshott claims that tradition is the source of authentic knowledge of political behaviour in contrast to behaviour inspired by an ideology which is at best an inadequate abridgement of a tradition. He draws the conclusion that a proper political education consists of the assimilation of the nuances and intimations of the parent tradition (see M. Oakeshott, 'Political Education' in *Rationalism in Politics*, London: Methuen, 1962, p. 111 et seq.). It is doubtful whether these more modern formulations succeed in removing from the term its highly emotive content.

R. V. Sampson

See also: IDEOLOGY
LEGITIMACY

Transhumance

A. *Transhumance* refers to a mode of life emphasizing seasonal livestock movements of restricted scope, and a composite subsistence base utilizing farming and herding. Livestock cycles of this type may be found in societies with a complex type of interdependence in the division of labour, where livestock keepers and cultivators form separate but mutually dependent communities. The transhumance pattern ordinarily involves at least one permanent settlement; the entire community may take part in seasonal moves, or the stock may be accompanied only by herders.

B. *Transhumance* is used most extensively in human geography and in anthropology. Variations in usage tend to be associated with different problem emphases in the two disciplines.

1. The meanings assigned to *transhumance* by human geographers usually are broad in scope, as exemplified by A. Fribourg's definition: '... le déplacement alternatif et périodique des troupeaux entre deux régions déterminées de climat différent' ('La Transhumance en Espagne', *Annales de Géographie*, vol. 19, 1910,

p. 231, n. 1). J. Brunhes (*Human Geography*, trans. by E. F. Row, London: Harrap, 1952, pp. 139–46), notes that the human agents involved in these seasonal livestock movements may be limited to a few herders, or may include the entire community of livestock holders. Other geographers, like P. Vidal de la Blache, emphasize alternate pasturing of livestock in plains and mountains (*Principles of Human Geography*, London: Constable, 1952, pp. 130–4).

2. Anthropological usage tends to link transhumance with a subsistence pattern combining farming and herding. Associated with this dual subsistence is a permanent settlement from which both livestock and people move seasonally, as reported for the Nuer by E. E. Evans-Pritchard, or from which herdsmen *only* drive livestock to seasonal pastures (*The Nuer*, Oxford: Clarendon Press, 1940, pp. 51–93; L. Krader, 'Ecology of Central Asian Pastoralism', *Southwestern Journal of Anthropology*, vol. 11, 1955, pp. 301–26). However, anthropologists also use the term with reference to seasonal livestock movements, as when P. H. Gulliver (*The Family Herds*, London: Routledge & Kegan Paul, 1955, pp. 27–31) contrasts the Turkana system of cattle transhumance between mountains and plains with the same people's nomadic cycle for animals dependent upon browsing.

3. Usages of transhumance, notwithstanding the special emphases of particular writers, agree in contrasting the term with *pastoral nomadism*, and with accessory livestock-keeping by sedentary farmers. Thus, the livestock movements of transhumants are depicted as limited in geographical range and in time as compared with nomadic pastoralists. Another dimension of contrast often remarked is the greater importance of farming among transhumants, though the interests of the latter are seldom concentrated upon cultivation in the manner of settled horticultural or agricultural communities. It should be noted, finally, that the term *transhumance* is restricted in general application as compared with *nomadism*—it is seldom used with reference to the cycles of movement of hunting peoples, collectors, or mobile farmers.

Harry W. Basehart

See also: SUBSISTENCE ECONOMY

Transportation

A. *Transportation* is used in its common meaning by social scientists to denote all the means of conveying material goods and persons through space. Most generally interest has been focused on revenue carriers and closely related personal means of conveyance as these have constituted a system for the movement of goods and persons within communities and societies, and between societies. While all the social sciences have given some attention to transportation, only in economics has there been enough work and study to result in the extension of the term to denote a highly developed and technical sub-field of research.

B. While anthropologists and other students of technology have studied transportation as a form of material culture, the other social sciences, with the exception of economics, have stressed the consequences of developing modes of transportation for other phenomena with which they are concerned. Transport development is of interest to political scientists because it provides a guide for estimating the geographical limits of the political unit. Any significant advance in transport technology may be taken as a harbinger of pressures for extending the boundaries of the political unit, be it at the local, national, or international level. To the student of government, a change in transport may herald a shift in international politics or even a change in the balance of power.

Nor are sociologists and geographers oblivious to transport advance. Group and community life is strongly influenced by advances in the methods of overcoming the friction of space. Improved transport technology not only increases physical comfort and reduces fatigue and mental strain, it also redistributes population, transforms neighbourhoods, produces blighted areas, gives rise to urban configurations, and may give rise to quite different behaviour patterns within the same neighbourhood.

C. While economists have not been indifferent to changes in modes of transportation as causes of change in the economy of a society or the world, they have also focused a great deal of attention on the technological-economic complex, that constitutes the system of transportation of a society, itself.

1. Traditionally, this technical economic study of transportation has been carried on within the framework of the study of the *social control of industry* (q.v.). In such studies 'descriptive material on the institutional and legal aspects of the industry's regulated status usually has been the dominant concern' (J. R. Meyer, M. J. Peck, J. Stenason & C. Zwick, *The Economics of Competition in the Transportation Industries*, Cambridge, Mass.: Harvard University Press, 1960, p. 1). Subject to regulation during a period when the doctrine of laissez-faire (q.v.) reached a high-water mark, the control of the transport industry is extraordinarily well documented and has provided data for testing economic models (D. P. Locklin, *Economics of Transportation*, Homewood, Ill.: Irwin, 1960). Of continuing interest are the historical factors which led to the imposition of regulation and the extent to which a negative and restrictive governmental policy can be effective in curbing and redirecting monopolistic powers traditionally associated with railroad organizations. Monopolistic exploitation which appeared in the form of exorbitant rates, rate discrimination, and clever manipulation of financial structures have always been of interest to economists. In addition to evaluating the effectiveness of governmental restraints, economic analysis is employed to determine the efficacy of government to foster an economic and efficient transport system. Legislation is analysed to determine its effect on resource allocation and utilization. Laws related to specific modes of transport are reviewed in terms of the entire transport system. Court decisions are carefully studied to determine whether they promote or impede minimum cost transport. The quasi-judicial bodies responsible for administering and implementing transport legislation are of particular interest to the economist. What are the external pressures emanating from organized groups and institutions including other federal agencies with which the administrative tribunal must cope? Through the application of organization theory and a careful examination of the internal structure and functioning of the quasi-judicial bodies, what can be concluded as to the motives of the regulators and do these motives coincide or conflict with maximizing economic welfare? And if promoting public interest is not consistent with promoting the interest of the quasi-judicial body, which shall prevail? These are questions to which the economist interested in the traditional approach to transportation will address himself.

2. Closely allied with and a logical outgrowth of the traditional approach to the study of transportation is one which places emphasis on meticulously outlining the hierarchy of the cartel-like associations developed by the common carriers for the purpose of improving and integrating carrier service and reducing price competition among carriers of the same type. Under this approach legal documents associated

Treason

with the offering of common carrier service and the levying of rates and fares are interpreted and examined in view of the carriers' tendency to practice price discrimination. Although helpful to a fuller understanding of the implications of regulation, research along these lines does not lend itself to generalization.

3. The recent study of *The Economics of Competition in the Transportation Industries* by J. R. Meyer, M. J. Peck, J. Stenason & C. Zwick cited earlier departs from both these perspectives by stressing the possibilities of competition and the degree to which they believe that overzealous governmental regulation has created the very ills it is trying to correct. They conclude that what is required is 'a substantial reduction in governmental regulation of transportation and heavy reliance on the forces of market competition to insure services and rates in the best interest of the public' (ibid., p. 270). At the other extreme, of course, are those who argue that the ills of the transportation system can be cured only by governmental ownership.

4. A recent literature of great interest to the student of transportation is found in the areas of spatial theory and mathematical programming. Programming techniques are relatively new; location theory is not. Spatial theory as developed by von Thünen and Weber, among others, traditionally has had a place in the study of transportation. The works of A. Lösch (*The Economics of Location*, trans. by W. H. Woglom with the assistance of W. F. Stolfer, New Haven: Yale University Press, 1954) brought a resurgence of interest in location theory. W. Isard (*Location and Space-Economy*, New York: Wiley, 1956) and M. L. Greenhut (*Plant Location in Theory and in Practice, The Economics of Space*, Chapel Hill: University of North Carolina Press, 1956) furthered this interest with their major works, as have myriad articles appearing in the journals. The work in programming has been more concerned with technique than with expanding theory. The studies by M. Beckmann, G. B. McGuire, & C. B. Winston (*Studies in the Economics of Transportation*, New Haven: Yale University Press, 1956) are an excellent example of the application of linear programming and queuing theory to transport problems.

Harvey C. Bunke

See also: ECONOMIC COMPETITION
  MONOPOLISTIC COMPETITION
  PUBLIC UTILITIES
  SOCIAL CONTROL OF INDUSTRY

Treason

A. *Treason*, in its most general meaning, denotes the commission of acts against the safety of the state, by a citizen who owes it allegiance.

B. 1. The act of treason being a classic subject of constitutional law, its definition has varied through the centuries, reflecting the governing conceptions of the state and the individual in every epoch and society. As the high crime of attacking the safety of a sovereign state, treason has been punishable since the beginning of legally constituted government, and early English law was mainly a restatement of Roman law on comparable points.

Current usage in British law follows the Treason Act of 1351 in which the main elements of treason are set out as the offence of levying war against the King or of adhering to his enemies in his realm or giving them aid and comfort in the realm or elsewhere. Generally it is 'an offence against allegiance to the Crown' (Halsbury's *Statutes of England*, London: Butterworth, 2nd edn., 1948, vol. 5, p. 453 n). Recent cases have held that resident aliens may be liable to conviction for such an offence; and so may an alien holding a British passport who commits such an offence while resident in an enemy country (see Joyce v. Public Prosecutions Director, 1946, 62 TLR. 208).

This usage is what is sometimes referred to as High Treason. An earlier usage specified also the offence of *petit treason*—a minor form of treason—denoting 'the murder of a superior by an inferior by whom allegiance was owed in a natural, civil, or spiritual relation' (see Halsbury's *Statutes of England*, vol. 15, p. 790). This formulation dates from the Treason Act of 1351 —but the offence of petit treason was abolished in 1829 (9 Geo. 4c. 31).

2. Because of a desire to prevent such interpretations of treason as found under the concept of petit treason or 'constructive treason' whereby an act not included under Statute could be declared and punished as treasonable, the U.S. Constitution defines *treason* very narrowly as consisting 'only in levying war against them [the United States], or in adhering to their enemies, giving them aid and comfort. No person shall be convicted of treason unless on the testimony of two witnesses to the same overt act, or on confession in open court' (Article 3, Section 3). The same reason played a part in the express prohibition of bills of attainder and ex post facto laws. The narrow Constitutional definition may not be enlarged by Congress, and the overt act (not merely conspiracy) of treason must occur. M. Ploscowe ('Treason', in E. R. A. Seligman, *Encyclopedia of the Social Sciences*, New York: The Macmillan Co., 1935, vol. 15, p. 95) argues that in the treason trial of Burr the phrase 'levying war in the constitution was a technical term employed by the framers in the sense which had been affixed to it by English law. This interpretation impliedly adopts the constructive extension of the phrase . . . in strange contradiction to the wishes of the framers of the constitution. Thus treason . . . in war time includes any act by a citizen which furthers the hostile designs of the enemies of the United States . . . . In times of peace treason may consist not alone in any forceable attempt to overthrow the government but also in organized violent resistance to the execution of any law of the United States'. Similarly, because treason is so hard to prove in the United States, 'lesser' crimes, such as subversion, have been distinguished so as to be more easily punishable.

C. As treason is rare and is enacted by individuals, social psychologists have been more concerned with it than other social scientists, and they have been particularly interested in its 'personality profile'. The new and widespread phenomenon of 'brainwashing' carried out by the Chinese during the Korean conflict, apparently designed to mass-produce treasonable activities among their captives, has led to considerable research by social psychologists on the social determinants of the 'treasonable' personality profile. The yields of knowledge and consequences for law from such researches still lie in the future.

Daniel Lerner

See also: SEDITION

Treaty

A. *Treaty* is used in both a generic and a restricted sense.

1. There is considerable agreement on the meaning of *treaty* in the generic sense. Thus M. Brandon ('Analysis of the Terms "Treaty" and "International Agreement" for Purposes of Registration under Article 102 of the United Nations Charter', *American Journal of International Law*, vol. 47, 1953, p. 56) writes that it is 'the generic term of a great variety of international instruments each recording the fact of an agreement reached by the mutual consent of the parties thereto, and each possessing a different name according to its title or context' (see also A. D. McNair, *The Law of Treaties*, Ox-

ford: The Clarendon Press, 1938). Even under this broad definition, however, it is debatable whether some international instruments are treaties, e.g. the International Law Commission of the United Nations (U.N.Doc. A/CN.4/ SR. 51, p. 11) discussed the appropriateness of including within the scope of the term an agreement effected by an exchange of notes.

2. In its restricted sense the term is more ambiguous. In this sense an instrument that is called a *treaty* is ordinarily more formal and comprehensive and relates to fundamental relations. These characteristics, however, do not sufficiently differentiate *treaties* in the limited sense from other instruments which may qualify to be called *treaties* in the more generic sense but not, in the minds of many, in the narrower sense. Thus there may be formal, comprehensive instruments relating to fundamental relations which should not be called or are not called treaties when the term is used in its limited sense, but it is difficult to determine why this should be so.

B. Within the category denoted by the usage in A. (1) would be included such items as treaty (restricted sense), protocol, agreement, arrangement, accord, act, general act, declaration, modus vivendi, statute, regulations, provisions, pact, covenant, compromise, and charter ('Research in International Law, Under the Auspices of the Faculty of the Harvard Law School, Part III, 'Law of Treaties', *American Journal of International Law*, *Supplement*, vol. 29, 1935, pp. 686, 688, 711–13; D. P. Myers, 'The Names and Scope of Treaties', *American Journal of International Law*, vol. 51, 1957, p. 576). The number of names for instruments included under the generic term *treaty* increases. Writers in the field of international law generally conclude that the names are employed without discrimination (see H. W. Briggs, *The Law of Nations*, London: Stevens, 1953, p. 837). Myers, on the other hand, contends that foreign offices name instruments of the 'genus *treaty*' with 'much consistency' ('The Names and Scope of Treaties', p. 577). The Harvard Research concludes that 'the international juridical effect of a treaty is not dependent upon the name given to the instrument' ('Law of Treaties', p. 710).

There has been discussion on several minor points. Is the treaty the agreement between the parties or the instrument which records the agreement? (see Briggs, *The Law of Nations*, p. 838, for bibliography). The parties may be states, heads of states, governments, or

Trial

international organizations. Oral agreements are not treaties ('Law of Treaties', p. 728).

C. In the restricted sense, a treaty is one of the more *formal* instruments of the genus. The Harvard Research uses *treaty* to describe 'a formal instrument of agreement by which two or more States establish or seek to establish a relation under international law between themselves (ibid., p. 686). Brandon ('Analysis of the Terms "Treaty" and "International Agreement"', pp. 55–6) says 'it denotes a particular but imprecisely defined kind of international instrument which records the fact of an agreement reached by the mutual consent of the parties thereto, and which is thus designated for reasons not based upon any rule of international law . . . .' Myers ('The Names and Scope of Treaties', pp. 579–80) designates *treaty*, in this sense, as 'the most formal instrument of the genus, used to record comprehensive inter-state agreement upon fundamental relations or status', but he adds that although ' "treaty" remains the highest name in the system, fashion has invented substitutes', of which he gives *pact*, *constitution*, and *charter*, as examples.

John M. Howell

See also: INTERNATIONAL RELATIONS

Trial

A. In social science usage a rather broad definition of the term *trial* seems to be desirable. For these purposes, a *trial* is the examination before a competent tribunal, according to the law of the land, of the facts or law, or both, put in issue in an action at law for the purpose of determining such issue. Since the word *hearing* has an established meaning in legal terminology, it should be used instead of *trial* in equity proceedings and in administrative adjudication.

B. The word *trial*, aside from its general meaning of a testing or a putting to proof, is used in the social sciences to describe one of the steps in judicial procedure. Earlier, the term meant the examination of matters of fact in issue in common law cases (Blackstone's *Commentaries*, 1773, bk. 3, p. 350). This limited meaning continued to be used for some time in both England and America. Sweet's *Dictionary of English Law* (ed. by E. Jowitt, 1882) defines 'trial' as 'that step in an action, prosecution, or other judicial proceeding, by which the questions of fact in issue are decided' (see also W. J. Byrne, *A Dictionary of English Law*, London:

Sweet & Maxwell, 1923; and *Bouvier's Law Dictionary*, 1883). A later edition of Bouvier (*Baldwin's Century Edition*, ed. by W. E. Baldwin, Cleveland, O.: Banks-Baldwin Law Publishing Co., 1940, p. 79 in the Supplement) contains this statement: 'But the word [trial] has often a broader significance, as referring to that final examination and decision of matter of law as well as fact, for which every antecedent step is a preparation, which we commonly denominate "the trial"'. Similarly in F. Stroud, *The Judicial Dictionary* (London: Sweet & Maxwell, 3rd edn., 1953), 'A trial is the conclusion, by a competent tribunal, of questions in issue in legal proceedings, whether civil or criminal'. Again, 'A "trial" denotes, in a restricted sense, that step in an action by which issues of fact are decided, and, in a broader sense, is a judicial examination of issues between the parties, whether they be issues of law or of fact' ('Trial', *Words and Phrases*, St Paul, Minn.: West, 1952, vol. 42A, p. 161).

In legal dictionaries and in the literature of jurisprudence a distinction is made between a *trial* and a *hearing*. 'The term "trial" is uniformly, although perhaps not universally, applied to the actual litigation of the merits in an action at law, as contradistinguished from the debate on the merits in a case in equity. The term "hearing" is more precisely applied to equity cases and others savoring of a civil-law form, as contradistinguished from the proceedings which are either grounded on common law or are shaped by analogy to its forms and methods' ('Trial', in *American Jurisprudence*, Rochester, N.Y.: Lawyers Co-operative Publishing Co., 1936, vol. 53, sec. 2, p. 28, fn. 7).

In a more general sense, however, C. N. Callender (*American Courts*, New York: McGraw-Hill, 1927, p. 148) uses the expression 'trials in equity'; and L. Mayers (*The American Legal System*, New York: Harper & Bros., 1955, p. 271) speaks of 'trials' in equity, probate, and admiralty. Apparently the term *hearing* is preferred with reference to administrative adjudication; but here too there are sometimes found such phrases as *trial techniques*, *trial memorandum*, *pre-trial agreements*, and *organization for trial* (E. B. Prettyman, in Bar Association of the District of Columbia, *A Manual on Trial Techniques in Administrative Proceedings and Illustrative Federal Administrative Agencies*, Washington, D.C.: Bar Association of the District of Columbia, 1950).

J. S. G. Carson

See also: LAW

Tribe

A. The *tribe* is a system of social organization which includes several local groups—villages, bands, districts, or lineages—and normally includes a common territory, a common language, and a common culture. The elements constituting the tribe may or may not be co-ordinated by formal or centralized political power. Ideally the term *tribe* implies a large element of solidarity based on strongly shared primary sentiments. Such solidarity becomes contractual in nature as the tribal organization becomes more formally organized. The point at which these latter characteristics become pronounced is, perhaps, a convenient place to distinguish between the *tribe* and the *nation* (q.v.).

B. In general, anthropologists agree on the criteria by which a tribe may be described: common territory, a tradition of common descent, common language, common culture, and a common name—all these forming the basis of the joining of smaller groups such as villages, bands, districts, or lineages.

1. One of the early statements of some of these criteria is that of A. W. Howitt who defines a tribe as '... a larger or smaller aggregate of people who occupy a certain tract of hunting and food ground in common, who speak the same language with dialectical differences, who acknowledge a common relatedness and who deny that relatedness to other tribes' ('Australian Group Relations', *Anthropological Institute*, vol. 37, 1907, pp. 279–89).

2. G. P. Murdock (*Social Structure*, New York: The Macmillan Co., 1949, p. 80) divides local communities into migratory bands, clustered and sedentary villages, and neighbourhoods of dispersed families. Several units of one or more types may coalesce into a larger social system, the tribe. The basis of coalition is afforded, according to Murdock, by common language, contiguous territory, common culture, and a tradition of common descent, and is recognized by the sharing of a common name. The nature of the group thus formed involves a union of kin groups larger than the community to which people ordinarily think that they 'belong' (ibid., p. 81–5).

3. R. Piddington conforms to this general usage when he distinguishes kinship groups from local, i.e. territorial-groupings, and under the latter places the tribe, the 'largest unit of social organization usually recognized in social anthropology, ... a term which is somewhat loosely employed'. He defines a tribe as '... a group of people speaking a common dialect, inhabiting a common territory and displaying a certain homogeneity in their culture' (*An Introduction to Social Anthropology*, Edinburgh: Oliver & Boyd, 1950, pp. 164–5). The group is not exogamous and is a political unit for purposes of internal and external administration.

It should be noted that Piddington's criterion of the tribe as being the 'largest unit of social organization usually recognized in anthropology' overlooks the possibility of federations of tribes, a possibility which has on occasion been realized.

C. While there is general agreement on the characteristics already stated, difficulties arise when the political characteristics of the tribe are discussed. While the notion of territoriality is integral to the notion of tribe, other political criteria are difficult to specify. For example, what political characteristics can be attributed to the pre-contact north-eastern Athabaskans? A number of bands—true local groups that often shifted residence—occupied a fairly circumscribed territory, shared the criteria of *tribe*, and occasionally came together. But no formal leadership appeared in the groups thus formed, nor is there much reason '... to suppose that all or most local groups had a ... leader' (J. H. MacNeish, 'Leadership Among the North-eastern Athabascans', *Anthropologica*, vol. 2, 1956, pp. 131–62). Confronted with this sort of problem anthropologists have distinguished three kinds of tribal units with reference to political organization:

1. *Simple acephalous tribes* are constituted of autonomous bands or villages. In these component units membership is based largely on kinship which is often bilaterally recognized (S. N. Eisenstadt, *From Generation to Generation*, London: Routledge & Kegan Paul, 1956, p. 120). Examples include the Mende, Ibo, Great Whale Eskimo, pre-contact Kaska Indians, and practically all northern forest Athabaskans and Algonkin groups. These tribes are *acephalous* because they lack a clearly designated head or council. Half the communities known to anthropology are of this type.

2. *Acephalous segmentary tribes* also lack a clearly defined head. They are comprised of localized unilinear kin groups—lineages and clans, each of which claims a territory and itself may possess formal political organization (M. Fortes & E. E. Evans-Pritchard, *African*

Trusteeship

Political Systems, London: Oxford University Press, 1940, pp. 1–24). Politically each kinship segment is independent of the other, although a few provisions—mainly ceremonial—exist which allow two or more to act in concert on certain occasions.

3. *Centralized tribes* possess a single power source—king, council, or other form of administration. Such tribes generally are larger than either of the foregoing types. In Africa some centralized tribes emerged when one kinship segment in a segmentary system won political ascendancy over other unilinear groups.

D. It is apparent that the *tribe* is somewhat similar to the *nation*. The line of distinction—while difficult to draw—can be drawn along the lines of the primary nature of tribal ties. The community of language and culture which characterizes the *tribe* is found in many, but not all, nations. More important is the fact that the tradition of common kinship in the tribe—while sometimes spurious—is at its very centre. In the nation if these traditions endure at all they are purely figurative, although a leader may try to convince the people that they are more than that. As the primary ties diminish, they are replaced by secondary or contractual ties, so that these come increasingly to characterize the nation.

John J. Honigmann

See also: COMMUNITY
NATION

Trust (See **Cartel**)

Trusteeship

A. *Trusteeship* has a long-established meaning in municipal law (the office or function of a person, real or juristic, holding property in trust) and a newer application under the international system of the United Nations. Only the latter will be dealt with here. Although the term has been put into use in this new connotation with little explanation, there appears to be general agreement that it denotes an international institution under which states, as trustees, assume an obligation under the supervision of the United Nations to administer trust territories in such a manner that the latter will progress toward self-government or independence. Although independence might not always be a goal (the area might be administered as an autonomous unit), the trustee would never be authorized to absorb the territory.

On the question of the supervisory powers of the United Nations, agreement is not so general. The administering powers claim more freedom as trustees than the 'anti-colonial' members of the United Nations are willing to concede.

B. Trusteeship under the United Nations is not used in the original legal meaning. 'The term itself indicates merely a certain analogy to private trusteeship. The difference is that the trustee of the system established under the authority of the United Nations is not a private person but a state or an international organization and that what it is holding in trust is not property but the power of administering a territory' (H. Kelsen, *The Law of the United Nations*, London: Stevens, 1950, p. 566; see also C. E. Toussaint, *The Trusteeship System of the United Nations*, London: Stevens, 1956).

United Nations trusteeship is patterned after, and is successor to, the mandates system established in Article 22 of the Covenant of the League of Nations. The territories in trust (under mandate) had 'ceased to be under the sovereignty of the States which formerly governed them', but were 'inhabited by peoples not yet able to stand by themselves under the strenuous conditions of the modern world'. Instead of annexing territories of the defeated powers, the victors assigned them to mandatory powers who would administer them according to the 'principle that the well-being and development of such peoples form a sacred trust of civilization' and under the supervision of a Permanent Mandates Commission and the Council of the League.

Chapters 12 and 13 of the United Nations Charter (in *Everyman's United Nations*, New York: United Nations Office of Public Information, 6th edn. 1959, pp. 553–6) establish a trusteeship system that is broader in objective and application than the League system. A basic objective of the system is to advance the inhabitants of the territories toward 'self-government or independence as may be appropriate to the particular circumstances of each territory and its peoples and the freely expressed wishes of the peoples concerned' (ibid.). The system is designed to apply to: (a) territories transferred from the mandates system (with the exception of South West Africa, all such territories have either been so transferred or have become independent); (b) territories which were detached from enemy states as a result of World War II (Somaliland, detached from and administered by Italy); (c) territories placed under the system by states responsible for their administration (no examples). The administering power places territories under the system on a voluntary basis.

Trust territories may be designated as strategic or non-strategic. The distinction is not clear (*Repertory of Practice of United Nations Organs*, New York: United Nations, 1955, vol. 4, p. 238) and only one territory has been designated as strategic (Territory of the Pacific Islands administered by the United States). Supervision of strategic trusts is the responsibility of the Security Council; the General Assembly is responsible for non-strategic areas. The Trusteeship Council assists both by considering reports submitted by the administering authorities, examining petitions from inhabitants of the territories, making periodic visits to the territories, and taking other actions which may be in conformity with the terms of each trusteeship agreement.

John M. Howell

See also: MANDATE

Tyranny

1. In its original sense (in Ancient Greece) it signified the type of authority to whose more recent exemplifications the name *dictatorship* (q.v.) is given. More precisely, a tyrant was a man who held kingly authority in a polity where there is no king by law. As the Greek writers sometimes speak of 'good tyrants', it is evident that the word was not entirely derogatory.

2. In other contexts *tyranny* usually means oppressive and cruel treatment. Often, however, any government of which the speaker disapproves is dubbed a tyranny. As there is no universal agreement on the proper way of governing we could not derive from such a description much information about the behaviour of the government in question without the knowledge of the preferences of the speaker. Further confusion stems from the indiscriminate application of the word *tyranny* to the manner of exercising authority, to the body of persons who practise it, and to the state in which this takes place. In any case the word is strongly evocative of opprobrium.

3. (a) One way of making *tyranny* into a general ethically neutral concept would be to define it as 'regime which is felt by a substantial part of its subjects to be cruel and oppressive'. But it must be remembered that all regimes are deemed to be cruel and oppressive by some of their subjects.

(b) Alternatively, we might define *tyranny* as 'the type of government which secures obedience mainly or entirely through the fear of punishment'.

(c) Most useful heuristically seems to be the following definition: 'tyranny is the manner of exercising authority which involves very frequent recourse to punishments of utmost severity'. A tyranny, as thus defined, can be regular or erratic, according to whether the punishments follow some rules laid down beforehand, or whether they are meted out whimsically.

Tyranny in this sense is compatible with various types of government: autocratic—whether of revolutionary (e.g. Robespierre) or traditional (e.g. Ivan the Terrible) variety; oligarchic (e.g. Sparta) and even democratic, where a minority may be tyrannized by the majority (e.g. the treatment of sinners and dissenters by Savonarola's democratic and levelling regime in Florence). The same is true of smaller social aggregates.

4. In diagnosing tyranny we must bear in mind not only that this is a matter of degree, but also that conditions prevailing in various parts of any social aggregate may differ. To illustrate this point: in Russia, Peter I tyrannized the nobles and the nobles tyrannized the serfs, whereas in Poland of that time a royal tyranny over the nobles was out of the question, but the way in which the latter ruled the peasants was undoubtedly tyrannous. On the whole the governance of the British Isles in the early 19th century could not be described as a tyranny, yet it could be argued that the urban poor as well as the Irish peasantry lived at that time under a tyranny.

Despotism (q.v.) does not absolutely necessitate tyranny, although it undoubtedly tends to be accompanied by it. Despotism without tyranny may occur if the despot is of benevolent disposition and his authority unchallenged. The reign of Marcus Aurelius seems to prove that this unlikely conjunction is not impossible.

S. Andreski

See also: ABSOLUTISM
AUTOCRACY
DESPOTISM
DICTATORSHIP
TOTALITARIANISM

U

Uncertainty (see **Risk (and Uncertainty)**)

Unconscious

A. The term *unconscious* refers broadly to all mental processes of which the subject is not aware. Its use in social psychology is most frequently in the Freudian sense of *preconscious* —distinguishing thoughts which are latent, or 'preconscious' (of which the subject can become aware by a voluntary effort of attention) from those which are 'dynamically' unconscious, repressed from consciousness in a self-protective attempt to ward off their painful associations. The social sciences rarely use the term in the Jungian sense (see C. below).

B. In the United States of America, where the links between clinical and social psychology are closer than elsewhere, the further psycho-analytic distinction between descriptive and dynamic senses is usually followed.

Freud distinguished (unlike Janet, whose concept of the *subconscious* was purely descriptive) between the descriptive and systematic senses of the term *unconscious*. 'The unconscious comprises, on the one hand, acts which are merely latent, temporarily unconscious, but which differ in no other respect from conscious ones and, on the other hand, processes such as repressed ones, which if they were to become conscious would be bound to stand out in the crudest contrast to the rest of the conscious processes' (S. Freud, 'The Unconscious', *Works* (1915), standard edn., London: The Hogarth Press, 1957, vol. XIV, p. 172). The latent but available processes are said to be 'preconscious'.

Unconscious mental processes function according to what Freud termed the 'primary process' as distinct from the 'secondary process' of rational thought and judgement. 'Primary process' thinking takes the form of symbolic phantasy images; it represents a primitive level of discharge of wish-impulses, without their modifications by the impact of reality. The 'primary process' is 'exempt from mutual contradictions' and wishes whose aims would appear incompatible in conscious thought may therefore co-exist unconsciously, producing the incongruities of dreams and neurotic behaviour.

C. In the works of Jung a racial or collective unconscious is postulated as well as a personal one; a postulate derived from the appearance of universal or archetypal symbols in a wide variety of thought forms. This is based upon Jung's distinction between a 'personal' and a 'collective' unconscious. The 'collective' unconscious is the 'all-controlling deposit of ancestral experience from untold millions of years, the echo of prehistoric world events to which each century adds an infinitesimally small amount of variation and differentiation' (*Contributions to Analytical Psychology*, London: Kegan Paul, Trench, Trubner, 1928, p. 162). This racial deposit is expressed in the form of archetypes, or collective symbols. These do not appear frequently in normal waking thought, but according to Jung may be seen in religious symbolism, literature and art, as well as in psychotic breakdown.

D. The word *unconscious* first appeared in English in 1712, but until the formulation of Herbart's dynamic theory of the unconscious, the concept was of the most general kind, indicating no more than a vague background to consciousness. J. F. Herbart (*Psychologie als Wissenschaft*, 1824) introduced the idea of conflict between conscious and unconscious ideas, and described a threshold of the mind beyond which wholly repressed ideas are still in a state of rebellious activity directed against those in consciousness.

C. de Monchaux

See also: REPRESSION
SUBLIMATION

Underdeveloped Areas

A. The term *underdeveloped areas* denotes areas in which, in the light of given criteria, the development of (a) natural, or (b) human resources is below certain levels.

B. 1. The term *underdeveloped* is commonly applied, in economic writings, to 'countries in which per capita real income is low when compared with the per capita real incomes of the United States of America, Canada, Australasia and Western Europe. In this sense, an adequate

732

synonym would be "poor countries" ' (*Measures for the Economic Development of Under-Developed Countries*, Report by a Group of Experts appointed by the Secretary-General of the United Nations, New York: Columbia University Press, 1951, p. 3).

2. By an extension of this definition the term may be applied to an area within a country which, as a whole, is not considered underdeveloped, or to a geographical area embracing more than one country.

C. The practical application of this definition is seen in the classification of countries as developed or underdeveloped according to their level of per capita national income (see, for example, A. E. Staley, *The Future of Underdeveloped Countries*, New York: Harper Bros., 1954, ch. 1; and *Point Four, Co-operative Program for Aid in the Development of Economically Underdeveloped Areas*, U.S. Department of State Publications 3719, Washington, D.C.: Government Printing Office, 1950, Appendix C). There is, however, widespread recognition of certain difficulties and ambiguities which are inherent in this use of the term and of the per capita national income indicators which follow naturally from it.

1. The term carries the implied suggestion that the underdeveloped areas *ought to be developed*. But on what grounds, it may be asked, should the United States, and the other countries mentioned by the United Nations experts, be taken as the standard to which all other countries should conform?

2. Further, it has been argued that it is fallacious to 'compare … national income aggregates for societies with different laws, rules, conventions, hopes and ideals' (S. H. Frankel, *The Economic Impact on Under-Developed Societies*, Oxford: Blackwell, 1953, p. 43; see also, p. 56). Against this point of view, however, it can be said that emulation of the standards of income and consumption characteristic of the countries mentioned is becoming more and more important as the economic aim of peoples all over the world.

3. *Underdeveloped* implies that the countries and areas to which it is applied are *capable of development*, and also that they are 'poor' *because their resources are underdeveloped*. The United Nations experts admitted that a country could still be 'poor' even when the limited resources it possessed were fully developed, but they believed that the possibility was of slight practical importance. Other writers are less

convinced of resource deficiency as a cause of poverty. At the same time, it is clear that countries with extensive undeveloped resources are not necessarily poor.

4. These considerations have given rise to the suggestion that the term underdeveloped should be applied to 'a country which has good potential prospects for using more capital or more labour or more available natural resources, or all of these, to support its present population on a higher level of living, or, if its per capita income level is already fairly high, to support a larger population on a not lower level of living' (J. Viner, *International Trade and Economic Development*, Oxford: Clarendon Press, 1953, p. 98). *Underdeveloped* is not, however, normally used in this sense.

D. The meaning of *underdeveloped* is further complicated when the term is applied to human as well as to natural resources. It has been objected to such an application that it is essential to distinguish between underdevelopment of natural resources and economic backwardness of populations, and that the problems of the so-called 'underdeveloped areas' are, in fact, often associated with the latter rather than with the former condition (see H. Myint, 'An Interpretation of Economic Backwardness', *Oxford Economic Papers*, vol. 6, 1954, pp. 132–63).

The tendency to assume that underdeveloped countries have stagnant economies has also been criticized. It has been pointed out that 'in several under-developed countries some of the current social, political and economic problems and tensions arise not from stagnation but from the rapid and unequal rate of development' (P. T. Bauer & B. S. Yamey, *The Economics of Under-developed Countries*, Cambridge: Cambridge University Press, 1957, p. 7). In some countries there has been rapid development of modern economic activity in a particular sector which has, however, failed to stimulate progress in the rest of the economy. Thus, 'the anachronistic co-existence of the primitive and the modern and of the tribal and the individualistic is a conspicuous feature of many under-developed economies' (ibid.). Where people have been drawn into modern economic activities, they have generally obtained higher incomes in money and material terms, but often at the cost of a disruption of existing social patterns and institutions without the creation of adequate alternatives.

A. Hazlewood

See also: ECONOMIC GROWTH

Understanding

Understanding

A. 1. *Understanding* in the social sciences refers (a) to shared expectations which are the core of culture, (b) to products of learning in human development, and (c) to utilization of role-taking skills in structuring and interpreting social and other relationships.

2. The term also denotes a methodological device for observing social behaviour and giving a 'plausible' explanation of it; which explanation may then be used as the starting point for the development of an account possessing causal adequacy.

B. 1. Definitions of *understanding* as a group phenomenon refer to the knowledge people have about each other's behaviour when they share expectations in a common cultural setting. In this view, culture and 'common understandings' are essentially synonymous. As A. Rose states (*Sociology: The Study of Human Relations*, New York: Knopf, 1956, p. 34), 'there is a core of our culture which practically all people in it do know and understand. This core includes knowledge about behavior toward other people and about behavior toward certain commonly used objects. ... So there is a core of common understandings in our culture, and on the basis of these understandings we have correct expectations most of the time regarding the behavior of others. ... The limits of a culture have to be described in terms of the extent of common understandings regarding how people can be expected to behave toward one another'.

2. As an individual phenomenon, *understanding* is defined in terms of levels of personal development which result from a combination of maturation and learning. For example, E. Hurlock indicates (*Child Development*, New York: McGraw-Hill, 1950, p. 390), '[At birth, the child] has no understanding of his environment or of what he observes around him. Gradually, as a result of maturation and learning, the child begins to understand what he observes and consequently his environment begins to be meaningful to him. But, as no two children have the same intellectual abilities or the same experiences, no two individuals can be expected to have the same understanding of an object or situation'.

3. On both the individual and the group level, understanding is limited and shaped by attitude, sentiment, and other affective factors. Accordingly, some social scientists feel that a definition of understanding should take such factors into account. While distinguishing between two kinds of understanding, knowledge about something and sympathetic understanding of it, G. Stratton remarks (*Social Psychology of International Conduct*, New York: Appleton, 1929, p. 133), 'A larger kind of understanding [than mere "knowledge about"] is necessary, where tolerance and appreciation are fused with the knowledge, as in the understanding between a man and his dog, or between friends, ...' Similarly, C. A. Ellwood notes (*The Psychology of Human Society*, New York: Appleton, 1925, p. 377), 'In general, we find it difficult to understand or sympathize with others unless we think of them as essentially similar to ourselves'.

4. When defined as a type of behaviour, understanding may be viewed as a process of interaction in which significant symbols are shared, or as a product of interaction having various dimensions. One way in which understanding is considered in terms of process is illustrated by G. Higginson, who states (*Psychology*, New York: The Macmillan Co., 1936, pp. 437–8), 'Understanding a situation depends upon the emergence of particular meanings. The individual who understands is able to act in a decidedly different manner from one who does not understand. To understand is to do more than perceive, remember, or imagine. In understanding, man deals with a thing in terms of its relations with other things. ... Generally speaking, understanding is an activity that touches a great variety of life situations. It is a mode which is involved when an individual remarks that he is aware of what is expected of him or that he knows what he can or cannot do. To the extent that he realizes such ordinary relationships, man understands'. Another definition of understanding as process is that which points out how objects are given meaning according to ways in which one is prepared to act toward them in a given situation. E. Freeman (*Principles of General Psychology*, New York: Henry Holt, 1939, p. 514) defines the term in this way: 'Understanding is to be taken here in the broad sense of *meaning something*, anything, to the organism. It implies the absence of indifference. A sharp knife may not be understood by a child as an adult understands it. ... That he will understand it as the adult does, after cutting himself, is another matter involving an old item in a new relationship. In that case he will understand it again, but differently. It will have become related to him as quite a different object, a pain-giving thing and no longer a toy'.

5. When considered in relation to products of interaction, *understanding* is often defined in terms of role-taking skills which result from meaningful interactions, and which are used to explain social phenomena. M. Weber identifies (*The Theory of Social and Economic Organization*, trans. by A. M. Henderson & T. Parsons, New York: Oxford University Press, 1947, pp. 94–5) two levels of such understanding. 'The first is the direct observational understanding of the subjective meaning of a given act as such, including verbal utterances'. Having such actions in our experience, according to Weber, we can immediately find meaning in them. The second is what Weber calls 'explanatory understanding', which is a matter of perceiving observed action as part of larger social acts in which the actors are engaged.

C. Weber also defines *understanding* as a methodological device to study human behaviour. He indicates (ibid., p. 90) that 'subjectively understandable' behaviour, as distinguished from 'merely reactive behaviour' (i.e. psychophysical and other processes which are idiosyncratic), may be investigated by using 'intuition' and other role-taking skills. The investigator thus gains insight into observed behaviour, and can go so far as to suggest plausible explanations of it. But, in order to obtain 'verifiable accuracy of interpretation of the meaning of a phenomenon', the investigator must take into account both the directly understandable and non-understandable components of behaviour. To do this, the investigator utilizes ideal typical analyses to identify and explain interrelations between directly understandable, or rational, and non-understandable, or irrational, aspects of behaviour (see ibid., pp. 88–96). This latter methodological procedure enables what would otherwise be merely plausible explanations to become scientifically adequate, tested accounts of social action.

Ray L. Gold

See also: CULTURE
         EXPECTATION
         IDEAL-TYPE ANALYSIS

Unemployment

A. *Unemployment* denotes the state of not being used. It is especially applied to the state of those persons normally in remunerative occupation. The measure of unemployment is often the number or percentage of people who, not having work, register at employment exchanges or are otherwise recorded as seeking work.

B. There are early references to the unemployed in Elizabethan times. Milton in *Paradise Lost* (iv. 617, wrote in 1667 'Other creatures all day long rove idle, unemployed', also A. Yarranton, in *England's Improvement By Sea and Land* (1677, p. 61): 'there be in England and Wales a 100,000 poor people unemployed'. Elizabethan poor law imposed upon local authorities the obligation to set the unemployed to work. The Poor Relief Act, 1601 was '... for setting to work, all such persons, married or unmarried, having no means to maintain them, use no ordinary and daily trade of life to get their living by'. Throughout the period to 1914 it was generally recognized in Great Britain that local authorities had a moral obligation to provide work in times of exceptional distress (e.g. a circular to the Local Government Board, 1886).

C. Unemployment is primarily a feature of specialization and competitive production— some would say of capitalistic production. In underdeveloped countries with subsistence production, primitive trades, and street marketing, the degree of occupation could not be depicted satisfactorily in terms of employment and unemployment. Indeed, there are good arguments for suggesting that employment involves an employer and that persons normally working on their own account cannot become unemployed though they might become unoccupied. Such a definition avoids difficulties over farmers, shopkeepers, and other self-employed persons who have absolute freedom in determining the time and effort they will put into their work. With increasing age their activities often become progressively slighter, and it is difficult to say when they leave the labour force. Similarly, a woman ordinarily engaged in domestic duties at home is not normally considered to be subject to unemployment.

The International Labour Office consider a standard definition important. They would include as employed all persons who work on their own account or in the employ of others and also unpaid family workers who are engaged in tasks directly related to the operation of a family enterprise for a minimum of fifteen hours a week, not including time spent in unpaid domestic work. The unemployed should be defined as all persons seeking work on a given day who are not employed and are able to take a job if offered one. Workers should not be rejected as 'unemployable' because this depends upon the type of work required, many a useful navvy might be unemployed as a clerk; while in a

Unemployment

boom many a man can find employment who would find it difficult to do so in a depression because of slight physical or mental handicap. Obviously, however, ability to take a job does imply some freedom from sickness, mental or physical (see I.L.O.'s *Employment, Unemployment and Labour Force Statistics*, 1948).

D. The measurement of unemployment implies the acceptance of information which may be far from ideal. There are two major possibilities: (a) The use of a sample survey such as is already regular practice in the United States and Canada and is recommended by O.E.E.C. on the basis of a detailed report by a mixed working party including representatives of I.L.O. (cf. E/C.N. 3/170, para 37). In the United States the monthly report on the Labour Force is part of the census bureau's Current Population survey. It is a measure of the number of persons available for work but for whom the economy provides no job attachment of any kind. The measure is based on a sample of about 25,000 households and has been available monthly since April 1940. Estimated annual data for 1929 to 1939 appear in the 1951 labour statistics handbook (see P. M. Hauser & W. R. Leonard, *Government Statistics for Business Use*, New York: Wiley, 2nd edn., 1956, p. 351 et seq.).

(b) The use of statistics arising from legislation to help the unemployed to get work or to provide them with income while not gainfully occupied. It is usually objected that such statistics are liable to changes because of legislation and of administrative decisions, they rarely cover all occupations and are dependent upon action by the unemployed who, for a variety of reasons, may not choose to seek work through official employment exchanges or may not be entitled to monetary benefits while unemployed. Nevertheless, such statistics are normally the most reliable for indicating trends in many countries, and the trends shown need be seriously suspect only over periods when there were major changes in the operation of the schemes— as when unemployment insurance in the United Kingdom was extended and became National Insurance in 1948. These statistics are not very satisfactory for international comparisons.

Attitudes towards unemployment have changed with time. Originally, it was thought to be due to defects of persons, then that it was a problem of organization, and now that it is a problem of governments, money, and banking. All approaches have some measure of truth. Defects of persons may have some influence upon

who is unemployed but are not primarily the cause of the phenomenon.

In 1909 W. H. Beveridge was saying that the problem of unemployment was the problem of the adjustment of the supply of labour and the demand for labour (*Unemployment: A Problem of Industry*, London: Longmans, 1909, p. 4). Over-production of one particular good thing is possible and not uncommon. Over-production of all good things of life is an impossibility. The solution was a problem of industry, primarily to provide a market for labour to make transfers easier; to reduce seasonal demand in such occupations as agriculture, luxury trades, and the docks; to limit cyclical unemployment, which particularly affects industries producing durable and especially capital goods; and to limit the friction which delays changes rendered necessary by decaying industries, new processes, and machines, demand for new types of labour and for labour in new places. A lack of mobility and adaptability is especially important amongst those of advanced age. The setting up of Labour Exchanges, later called Employment Exchanges, would reduce the size of the minimum reserve of labour needed. Some reserve is needed to cover the fact that because of distance, ignorance, and custom the supply of labour cannot move with perfect freedom and instantaneously.

Experience of a continued high level of unemployment after World War I led to the addition of a 'general' theory of unemployment to the specific explanations already given. It seemed true that there could be a general deficiency of demand for all the good things of life at the same time. 'There is a vital difference between the theory of the economic behaviour of the aggregate and the theory of the behaviour of the individual unit' (J. M. Keynes, *The General Theory of Employment, Interest and Money*, London: Macmillan, 1936, p. 85). When unemployment has become general it is not primarily a problem of unsuitable labour force or even a problem or organization whereby the unemployed are told where the work is available. Reducing wages might be a solution for the decline in the demand for the product of one industry if it enabled that industry to reduce prices relative to other prices, but the employer must hope for the maintenance of wages elsewhere. A general reduction of wages is not an effective remedy if aggregate demand is deficient. It might reduce prices, but it would comparably reduce the effective purchasing power of the wage recipients with no benefit to the economy.

The aggregate deficiency in effective demand

arises when some people (individual or collective) save more than others borrow and spend (normally on capital equipment). Saving itself is a negative act, simply refraining from buying and hence from creating employment. If that saving is not matched, somewhere, by someone spending more than his income, then demand will fall and employment is likely to be reduced. Unemployment is therefore due to a general deficiency of demand and can be reduced either by persuading the savers to save less or the spenders of borrowed money to spend more. Methods used might be mainly financial, such as reducing the rate of interest, and increasing the supply of liquid assets, or by actions of Governmental bodies in increased spending. The reduced saving should not be that which happens automatically when incomes are reduced by unemployment but should be a reduced 'propensity to save' at a given income; the increased expenditure should not be of a type that causes someone else to reduce expenditure in consequence. Thus additional government expenditure on new houses would not be effective if that meant a corresponding reduction in private provision of new houses (Keynes, *ibid.*, p. 130).

This does not mean that unemployment can be abolished. In a progressive economy there will always be people losing jobs and a time-lag before others are found. What is usually considered a reasonable objective is the maintenance of an approximate equality in the number of vacant jobs and the number of unemployed. (W. H. Beveridge, *Full Employment in a Free Society*, London: Allen & Unwin, 1944). It is, however, usually agreed that the objective of full employment has only been achieved successfully if it is associated with reasonable stability in the level of prices. That is where the practical difficulties of full-employment policies arise. Action which encourages spending may be successful in raising expenditure in such a way that it affects prices rather than production and employment. As the proportion of unemployed gets smaller so that it becomes more difficult to obtain additional employees, it becomes more likely that any additional expenditure raises wage rates and hence prices rather than employment. Empirical studies have attempted to relate changes in wages to the level of unemployment. One such study for the United Kingdom suggested that wage rates tended to remain constant with $5\frac{1}{2}$ per cent unemployment, to increase by 1 per cent per annum with 3 per cent unemployment, by 3 per cent per annum with 2 per cent unemployment, and very rapidly indeed with less than 2 per cent unemployed (A. W. Phillips, 'The Relation between Unemployment and the Rate of Changing Money Wage Rates in the U.K., 1861–1957'; *Economica*, 1958, N.S., vol. XXV, p. 283 et seq.).

The new general theory of unemployment means that solution of the main problems is set firmly upon and usually accepted by governments as illustrated by the American recovery programme of 1933 and the British Government's White Paper on Employment Policy (Cmd. 6527, 1944) 'The Government are prepared to accept in future the responsibility for taking action at the earliest possible stage to arrest a threatened slump. This involves a new approach and a new responsibility for the State' (para. 41, p. 16).

H. S. Booker

Unicameral (See **Bicameral**)

Unilateral

Unilateral is sometimes used in kinship studies as a synonym for *unilineal*. That is, the term is applied to groups (clans, lineages) recruited on the basis of descent traced in one line (either male only or female only) from a common ancestor.

Unilateral is also used (as an alternative to *asymmetrical*) in the context of cross-cousin marriage.

Maurice Freedman

See also: Cross-Cousins
  Descent
  Kinship and Kinship System
  Unilineal

Unilineal

A. *Unilineal* is used to describe descent and descent groups in which a single line of descent, through males only (patrilineal or agnatic), or through females only (matrilineal or uterine), is recognized as socially significant as a means of organizing such social activities and institutions as inheritance, ritual congregations, economic groups, marriage rules, and especially residential and political groups, for example clans, sub-clans, lineages, moieties. Where both lines of descent are recognized as a basis for corporate grouping, a system is called *double-unilineal* (q.v.). Where a line of descent may use both male and female links, the term *ambilineal* is used.

B. A. R. Radcliffe-Brown has suggested that the main function of the recognition of unilineal

Urban Sociology

descent as a basis for the organization of kinship groups is the need of defining the 'rights *in rem* over persons' ('Patrilineal and Matrilineal Succession', in his *Structure and Function in Primitive Society*, London: Cohen & West, 1952, p. 46). D. Forde has suggested that the unilineal transmission of both individual and collective rights, giving rise to the formation of unilineal descent groups, is instituted, in those societies that have acquired a certain degree of stability and density of settlement, as a consequence of the operation of the processes of parent-child succession and the sexual division of responsibility for the provision of economic needs ('The Anthropological Approach in Social Science', Pres. Address, British Association for the Advancement of Science, *Advancement of Science*, vol. IV, 1947, pp. 213–24).

J. Middleton

See also: AGNATION
CLAN
COGNATIC
LINEAGE
MATRILINEAL
SEGMENT

Unit Cost (See Cost)

Urban Society (See Urban Sociology)

Urban Sociology

A. In general terms *urban sociology* is the sociological study of cities, city life or urbanism (q.v.), or selected topics in this field.

B. The definition of this term, denoting a subfield of sociology, is made especially difficult by the problem of defining urbanism and of isolating the sub-field's special topics or aspects, many of which are covered or touched upon by other social science specialisms.

C. 1. In the United States much influence has been exerted by L. Wirth's view that the urban community (implicitly contrasted with the folk society or the rural society) is typified by secondary-group associations, segmentation of roles, a high incidence of mobility, and the like ('Urbanism as a Way of Life', *American Journal of Sociology*, vol. XLIV, 1938–9, pp. 1–24). Wirth considered the urban community, as characterized by size, density, heterogeneity, to be the basic factor in terms of which the typical forms that arise in the city might be explained. He stressed the roots of the subject

in the work of Weber, Simmel, and Park, and urged the need of a clear conception of the city as a social entity in order to develop a 'unified body of reliable knowledge, which what passes as "urban sociology" is certainly not at the present time' (ibid., p. 24).

2. There have been other theoretical approaches in which the urban community has not been considered the explanatory or formative factor. W. Firey's *Land Use in Central Boston* (Cambridge, Mass.: Harvard University Press, 1947) is a classic study wherein cultural values are taken as formative factors in explaining urban ecological and social organization. Urban social structure, as well as urban ecology, has also been illuminated by views which place stress on social power (G. Sjoberg, 'Urban Community Theory and Research: A Partial Evaluation', *American Journal of Economics and Sociology*, vol. 14, 1955, pp. 199–206).

3. In Great Britain, R. Glass has criticized many fashionable approaches including the view that urban sociology is or should be mainly concerned with the contrast between urban and rural society and has argued for a more positive approach in which urban sociology would be concerned with 'identifying types of town and city, past and present' ('Trend Report on Urban Sociology', *Current Sociology*, vol. 4, no. 4, Paris: Unesco, 1955).

Gideon Sjoberg

See also: ECOLOGY
RURAL
URBANISM
URBANIZATION

Urbanism

A. *Urbanism* denotes a distinct quality of human community, a special mode of existence or way of life, which is characteristic of the 'city'.

B. 1. The writings of G. Simmel, P. A. Sorokin and C. C. Zimmerman, R. Park, N. J. Spykman, and L. Wirth present a more or less common number of characteristics of urbanism as a special mode of existence or way of life. The work of L. Wirth is particularly representative of this approach in American sociology ('Urbanism as a Way of Life', *American Journal of Sociology*, vol. XLIV, 1938–9, pp. 1–24). These include (a) a complex division of labour with a diversified occupational structure which forms a major basis of the system of social stratification; (b) high territorial and social

738

mobility; (c) marked functional dependence of the population; (d) substantial personal anonymity in interpersonal contacts and segmentalization of social roles and role interactions; (e) reliance on indirect modes of social control; (f) normative deviance. A growing number of sociologists appear to share the point of view that the formal criteria of a scientific definition of what is urban follows from the definition of an urban community in terms of its demographic uniqueness, that is its absolute size and density of settlement.

2. A commonly accepted but controversial approach defines *urbanism* in terms of a rural-urban continuum *where a continuous gradation from rural to urban* is postulated such that all human communities can be theoretically and empirically placed at some point. The definitions of folk and urban *polar* ideal-types of communities (e.g. in the work of R. Redfield) similarly imply a continuum of community where all empirical communities are to be placed somewhere on the continuum. R. Glass, presenting a critique of definitions (and explanations of urbanism) that are set forth 'in terms of non-rural characteristics', argues that 'definitions of the common denominator "urbanism" are not meaningful 'unless they are used as terms of reference ... identifying types of town and city, past and present' (*Current Sociology*, vol. 4, no. 4, 1955, Paris: Unesco, p. 5).

Albert J. Reiss, Jr.

See also: URBAN SOCIOLOGY
URBANIZATION

Urbanization

1. *Urbanization* may denote a diffusion of the influence of urban centres to a rural hinterland. The 'influence' diffused usually refers to the customs and traits of these urban centres. This definition of urbanization is close to the ecological definition of the dominance function of cities. A major disadvantage of this definition is that it confuses the process of concentration in cities (also called urbanization by some) with the 'influence' of these centres.

2. A second major type of definition holds urbanization is synonymous with the appearance of 'urban traits or characteristics' in a population. This definition is commonly found in the literature of rural sociology. The appearance of certain culture practices (usually associated with cities) in a rural area is said to be evidence that the rural population is being 'urbanized', or that it is undergoing urbaniza-

tion. This definition poses the special difficulty that the traits or practices must first be clearly differentiated as urban, which naturally, in turn, presupposes some other process of urbanization.

3. Most demographers see urbanization as a process of population concentration. H. Tisdale for example, defines urbanization as a process of population concentration, with the process proceeding in two main ways: 'the multiplication of points of concentration and the increase in size of individual concentrations' ('The Process of Urbanization', *Social Forces*, vol. 20, 1941–2, pp. 311–6).

The definition of urbanization as a process of population concentration implies a process of moving from a non-urban to a completely urban state of population concentration. There is no implication in this definition, however, that the process is a continuous one, for there can be de-urbanization or equilibrium states short of complete urban concentration.

It should be clear that the definition of urbanization as a process of population concentration implies a definition of the points of concentration as well, viz. cities are defined simply as points of population concentration. The other definitions of urbanization given above also imply definitions of the city in terms of their criteria of urbanization, but they often appear to involve an inherent circularity, e.g. an urban trait is one found in cities, and a city is a place characterized by urban traits.

4. A fourth type of definition holds that urbanization is a process of population concentration in which the ratio of urban people to the total population in a territory increases. This definition implies a definition of cities independent of the urbanization process. From this point of view, an increase in both the size of individual points of concentration and of the number of points of urban concentration may occur without an increase in the urbanization of a territory. Only when a larger proportion of the inhabitants in an area come to live in cities is urbanization said to occur.

Albert J. Reiss, Jr.

See also: URBAN SOCIOLOGY
URBANISM

Utilitarianism

A. *Utilitarianism* in its broadest sense denotes a moral and social theory which asserts or assumes that nothing is desired for its own sake except pleasure, that no kind of pleasure is intrinsically superior to any other kind, and that the function of moral rules is (or ought to be)

Utility

to encourage behaviour that tends to increase pleasure and reduce pain and to discourage behaviour that tends to do the opposite.

B. 1. To be Utilitarian in this wider sense, a theory of morals need not include the notion of pleasure in the definition of a right action; it can hold, for example, that to call an action right is to express approval of it or to commend it or say that it is generally approved. But it cannot be Utilitarian unless it holds that actions come to be called right because their usual tendency is (or was) to increase happiness conceived in terms of pleasure and the absence of pain. No theory that derives moral rules from the 'essential nature' of man or from his 'proper end' as a rational being is Utilitarian; for Utilitarianism explains all moral rules as rules which experience has taught men lead on the whole to the successful pursuit of happiness. It admits that what gives pleasure or pain may differ from person to person, from country to country, from age to age; and also that actual rules, moral and legal, can outlive their utility or can be useful to one section of the community to the detriment of others. But all established rules are or have been useful to all or part of the community.

2. The term *utilitarian* (with a small 'u') is sometimes applied to doctrines and theories even though they are not forms of Utilitarianism as defined above. Every theory which is properly Utilitarian assumes that happiness alone is desired or desirable for its own sake, treating happiness as pleasure and the absence of pain; but not every theory called *utilitarian* makes this assumption. Thus, economics is sometimes called a utilitarian science, not because economists take it for granted that happiness alone is desired or desirable, but because it is not thought their business, as economists, to pass judgements on men's wants. As economists, they are supposed to consider only what men's wants are and how they can be satisfied at the least cost. Utilitarianism is a utilitarian theory, but not all utilitarian theories are varieties of Utilitarianism.

C. The term was first applied to the doctrine of Bentham, James Mill, and their school in the late 1820s.

1. Bentham and the elder Mill held either that men always desire only pleasure and are averse only to pain (sometimes defining desire and aversion so as to make this an analytic proposition), *or* else that, if they also desire and are averse to other things, it is only because they have learnt by experience that these things bring pleasure and avert pain.

2. They defined the utility of an action as its tendency to cause pleasure and to avert pain, and the right action as the one most likely to give the greatest balance of pleasure over pain to the persons liable to be affected by it. The doctrine thus assumes that pleasure and pain can be measured and also that pleasure is commensurable with pain.

3. The greatest happiness principle is the rule: So act that the persons affected by what you do get between them as much happiness as possible. It is the one universal rule of morality, public and private, because it applies everywhere and at all times to governments and to private persons.

Benthamism, or Utilitarianism in the narrower sense, is essentially a radical doctrine. The greatest happiness principle is used to test all rules, moral and legal, and all institutions, and to suggest improvements. Since it is easier for governments to control the behaviour of their subjects by threatening punishments than by offering rewards, their prime duty is to discourage the kinds of behaviour that impede happiness at the cost of inflicting as little pain as possible.

D. The term Utilitarianism has also been used in a wider sense to cover moral and social theories having close affinities with Benthamism, even when they give no rules for measuring happiness and reject the assumption which Bentham and James Mill usually (but not always) make, that every man desires for its own sake only his own pleasure. Thus, Hume's moral theory has been called Utilitarian, though it gives no rules for measuring happiness and denies that one person can desire another's happiness only as a means to his own; whereas John Stuart Mill, a professed Utilitarian, has been accused of departing from the creed by holding that some pleasures are better than others, not because they are more intense or more frequent or more certain, but because they are intrinsically superior.

J. P. Plamenatz

See also: HEDONISM
UTILITY

Utility

A. *Utility* is now generally understood to mean the direct satisfaction that goods and services yield to their possessors.

B. In economics the word *utility* has long since ceased to carry any of the moral or ethical connotations that it has in ordinary usage. As early as 1849, J. S. Mill (*Principles of Political Economy*, London: Parker, 1849, bk. III, ch. II, p. 540) wrote: 'That a thing may have any value in exchange, two conditions are necessary. It must be of some use; that is (as already explained), it must conduce to some purpose, satisfy some desire. No one will pay a price, or part with anything which serves some of his purposes, to obtain a thing which serves none of them. But, secondly, the thing must not only have some utility, there must also be some difficulty in its attainment'.

In A. Marshall's *Principles of Economics* (London: Macmillan, 8th edn., 1920, p. 92) the point is emphasized that 'Utility and Want are used as correlative terms, having no ethical or prudential connotations'.

The following statements from K. E. Boulding's *Economic Analysis* (New York: Harper & Bros., 3rd edn., 1955, pp. 700, 682) are characteristic of contemporary usage: ' "Utility" does not connote mere pleasure or physical satisfaction. It refers to the satisfaction of *any* want, physical or spiritual'. 'The *marginal utility* of any quantity of commodity is the increase in total utility which results from a unit increase in consumption'.

C. The chief use of the term is in connection with the theory of consumers' behaviour. P. A. Samuelson (*Foundations of Economic Analysis*, Cambridge, Mass.: Harvard University Press, 1947, pp. 97–8) writes: '*The utility analysis rests on the fundamental assumption that the individual confronted with given prices and confined to a given total expenditure selects that combination of goods which is highest on his preference scale*'. The utility of any good is different to different people. To any one person, the utility of a 'last' unit (marginal utility) of any good varies inversely with the number of units available to him (Law of Diminishing Utility). In the theory of consumer behaviour, the total utility of any household is said to be maximized when its rates of purchases are such as to make the marginal utilities of all available goods proportional to their prices.

D. Whether utility is properly to be regarded as a cardinal magnitude, or whether it is no more than an ordinal one, is a question concerning which economists continue to differ. Those insisting that it is only an ordinal magnitude claim, for example, 'We can say that 4 units each of Good A and B have more utility for a particular consumer than do three units of each, but we cannot say how *much* more'. This makes any interpersonal comparison of utility very difficult, if not impossible, in the view of those who deny the validity of cardinal utility. One of the major objections made to the indifference curve (q.v.) approach to demand theory has been to its restriction of the concept of utility to an ordinal one (B. F. Haley, 'Value and Distribution', in The American Economic Association, *Survey of Contemporary Economics*, Philadelphia: Blakiston, 1948, p. 5).

Richard V. Clemence

See also: INDIFFERENCE CURVE
MARGINAL ANALYSIS
VALUE (Economics)

Uxorlocal (See Residence)

V

Validity

A. *Validity* and its cognates (valid, validate, validation) are used by social scientists in three related senses: denoting (a) soundness of conceptualizing, (b) applicability of research techniques, and (c) pertinence of data. In all three cases the emphasis is on the value or worth of the idea, the technique, or the datum for some specified objective, as judged in relation to some standard or criterion.

1. The standard referred to may be (a) logical consistency with more established conceptual elements; (b) statistical relationship to some other technique whose applicability to the objective has been demonstrated; or (c) compatibility with other data whose pertinence to the objective is recognized. But whatever the standard, *validity* concerns the degree of confidence we should have in the less known by relating it to something which is better known, of indicating to us the degree of relevance of our tools to the research objective we have in mind. Thus when we speak of the elegance of our formulations, the power of our instruments, or the confirmation of our data, we are speaking in terms of their validity, informal though the references might be. Precision, however, is a matter of reliability (q.v.) rather than validity, as is the stability or reproducibility of the results. It is thus to be recognized that reliability and validity are partners in the research process, for a relevant but unstable instrument is of as little use as a stable but irrelevant one.

2. The most penetrating analysis of validity has been made with reference to measurement techniques. Here two main types of validity are discussed below: the relationship of the instrument to the concept (variable or universe) it is supposed to measure, and its relationship to other concepts (variables or universes). The question is how effectively can the instrument be used to predict either the behaviour contained in the concept (variable or universe) it is supposed to measure, or the behaviour contained in others. In both cases the major problem is the definition of these universes, for without an explicit and 'sound' definition of the underlying concepts, and an explicit and clear delineation of their empirical universes, it is not possible to know what the test measures. To attempt to measure a vague concept or universe cannot possibly yield more than a vague measure.

B. 1. *Validity*, as well as its cognates (valid, validate and validation), is used by social scientists in a variety of senses: (a) soundness or strength of argument or proof; (b) confirmation, corroboration or substantiation of evidence; (c) the quality of being well-founded and applicable to the circumstance. Usage in the first sense is probably the oldest, appearing in such phrases as 'the validity of one's conclusions' R. C. Angell and R. Freedman (in L. Festinger & D. Katz (eds.), *Research Methods in the Behavioural Sciences*, London: Staples Press, 1954, p. 308) provide a typical example in a discussion of the use of documents: 'Lastly there is the problem of validity. How does one know that the interpretation, even if agreed upon by competent social psychologists, is correct?' Usage in the second sense—corroboration of one's data—is likewise an old concern both in connection with documentary evidence and the results of interview, participant observation or questionnaire methods, as exemplified in M. Parten (*Surveys, Polls and Samples*, New York: Harper & Bros, 1950, p. 485) where special attention is devoted to 'the validity of the data yielded by [survey and polling] procedures'. Usage in the third sense is, however, the most recent and certainly the most technical. It is found particularly in connection with research techniques, especially measurement, and concerns 'how well founded and applicable' each is to the research objective involved, as illustrated by such a statement as: 'This social participation scale has shown—validity coefficients of from r = .52 to r = .62' (F. S. Chapin, *Experimental Designs in Sociological Research*, New York: Harper & Bros., 1947, p. 63), and in the recent authoritative statement on technical standards for psychological test construction, which includes 'test validity' as a major topic ('Technical Recommendations for Psychological Tests and Diagnostic Techniques', prepared by a joint committee of the American Psychological Association, American Educational Research Association, and the National

Council on Measurements used in Education, *Psychological Bulletin*, vol. 51, 1954, pp. 13–28).

2. The common element in all three uses of the term is the degree of relevance of the concepts, data or research techniques to the research objectives for which they have been developed, and hence the degree of confidence we should have in them. 'Validity information indicates to the test user' says the 'Technical Recommendations' (ibid., p. 13) 'the degree to which the test is capable of achieving certain aims'. These aims, in the case of all measurement devices, can be divided into two categories: (a) the extent to which an instrument measures what it is supposed to measure; and (b) the extent to which it is useful in measuring or predicting other phenomena. These are referred to as the 'logical' and 'empirical' approaches to validity by M. Jahoda, M. Deutsch, and S. W. Cook (*Research Methods in Social Relations*, New York: Dryden Press, 1951, pp. 109–11), following L. J. Cronbach (*Essentials of Psychological Testing*, New York: Harper & Bros., 1949), and are called 'internal' and 'external' validity by L. Guttman (in S. A. Stouffer et al., 'Measurement and Prediction', vol. IV, *Studies in Social Psychology in World War II*, Princeton, N.J.: Princeton University Press, 1950, pp. 57–9). The two types are complementary rather than mutually exclusive.

(a) In determining logical or internal validity there are three steps to be taken: first, 'define conceptually the characteristic which is being measured ... specify the conditions under which an observable phenomenon will be taken as evidence of the characteristic posited in the concept' (M. Jahoda et al., *Research Methods in Social Relations*, p. 109); second, select instances of these observable phenomena to constitute 'an appropriate operational definition or empirical meaning of the theoretical construct' (ibid.); third, check how well the individual items, and the device as a whole, represent the concept by such means as scale and intensity analysis (S. A. Stouffer et al., 'Measurement and Prediction', p. 59) or such others as item analysis, inter-test correlation, factor analysis and demonstration of dynamics relations (H. Peak, 'Problems of Objective Observation', in L. Festinger & D. Katz, *Research Methods in the Behavioural Sciences*, p. 282).

(b) With reference to empirical or external validity, S. Stouffer et al. ('Measurement and Prediction', p. 57) point out that whereas 'a universe has but one internal validity—it has many possible external validities since it can

be used for many different prediction purposes'. They state that to establish each such external validity, 'The thing to be predicted must first be defined, and then observations must be made to determine the correlation between the predictor and this particular criterion. ... A particular external validity for a universe cannot be determined except by [empirical study]'. M. Jahoda et al. (*Research Methods in Social Relations*, pp. 111–2) add, however, that 'To the extent that the empirical approach limits itself to discovering empirical correlations without any concern for an underlying theoretical explanation of the relationships—it results in knowledge which is insular and barren rather than multiconnected and logically fertile'. Thus is validity closely dependent on the state of scientific theory, a position propounded by R. V. Bowers in 1936 ('An Analysis of the Problem of Validity', *American Sociological Review*, vol. 1, pp. 69–74).

(c) The statement on 'Technical Recommendations for Psychological Tests and Diagnostic Techniques' (pp. 13–14) is consistent with this classification but prefers a break-down into four types of aims for psychological tests: a logical type (content validity), two empirical types (predictive validity and concurrent validity), and one mixed type (construct validity).

Raymond V. Bowers

See also: RELIABILITY

Value

A. In its most general usage in the social sciences *value* denotes any object of any need, attitude, or desire.

1. In most instances in the social sciences the word is used only in those cases where an actual interactive relationship exists between needs, attitudes, and desires on the one hand and objects on the other hand. Thus objects perceived by a scientific observer to have relevance for the needs, attitudes, and desires of the people whom he is observing are not values unless this relevance has somehow been translated into an observable relationship between the thoughts and actions of the people observed and the objects observed.

2. In some instances the word is used not to denote the object in its total concreteness, but rather the elements of the object which are relevant to the relationship between the people observed and the objects.

3. In other instances the term no longer denotes the object or its elements, but rather the relevance of the object or its elements to the

Value

attitudes, needs, and desires of the people observed. In this sense the object or its elements have 'value'.

4. There is an additional usage which is perhaps the one most frequently found in sociology and anthropology. The term has come to denote the shared cultural standards according to which the relevance—moral, aesthetic, or cognitive—of the objects of attitudes, desires, and needs can be compared and judged. There is the belief among those who share a set of such standards that they are valid and should be employed in valuing an object, i.e. relating it to needs, desires, or attitudes, and in evaluating an object, i.e. comparing its relevance with that of another object or other objects.

B. The study of values has been primarily a philosophical task. This is particularly true of efforts to determine the validity of values, i.e. the 'true' relevance of objects for human needs or the 'correctness' of standards for judging such relevance. Social scientists for the most part have not believed that such truth or correctness can be solely the product of empirical observation. Thus by and large they have confined their attention to values, however defined, as empirical variables in social life whose *scientific* importance is not so much dependent upon their validity and correctness as it is upon the fact that they are believed to be true and correct by those who hold them. Hence in their efforts to define value they have attempted to refrain from smuggling in hidden conceptions of true and false values, valid and invalid values. Apart from the efforts of economists whose work is treated in another essay, and whose usage tends to approximate A. (3) above, most attempts at definition have been made by sociologists and anthropologists.

1. W. I. Thomas and F. Znaniecki (with the latter primarily responsible for the passages hereinafter quoted) give in their famous *The Polish Peasant in Europe and America* (New York: Knopf, 1927, pp. 21, 22, 44) a definition of value as reciprocal with attitude which is the most notable example of usage A. (1) and implicitly at least contains usage A. (2): 'By a social value we understand any datum having an empirical content accessible to the members of some social group and a meaning with regard to which it is or may be an object of activity. ... By attitude we understand a process of individual consciousness which determines real or possible activity of the individual in the social world. ... The attitude is thus the individual counterpart

of the social value; activity, in whatever form, is the bond between them. ... The cause of a value or of an attitude is never an attitude or a value alone, but always a combination of an attitude and a value'.

2. W. L. Kolb ('The Changing Prominence of Values in Modern Sociological Theory', in H. Becker & A. Boskoff (eds.), *Modern Sociological Theory in Continuity and Change*, New York: Dryden Press, 1957, pp. 94, 95) calls attention to the shift from usages A. (1) and A. (2) to A. (4) in sociology and anthropology: 'From this [*Polish Peasant*] definition of value as objects meaningful to subjects, combined with the emphasis on rules [or group norms] as the values important for sociologists, the meaning of the value-concept for sociologists has gradually shifted, so that the element of the *normativeness* characteristic of rules has become the determining criterion rather than the element of *objectivity*. In discussing the development of the concept it will be necessary, for the sake of clarity, to use the word "value" to designate this normative element and to abandon the definition of Thomas and Znaniecki'.

In this shift of meaning *value* has come to denote not all social norms, but only the broader standards which when related to the actualities of social life can give rise to complexes of institutionalized norms. Thus C. Kluckhohn ('Values and Value-Orientations in the Theory of Action: An Exploration in Definition and Classification', in T. Parsons & E. Shils (eds.), *Toward a General Theory of Action*, Cambridge, Mass.: Harvard University Press, 1951, p. 395) defines a *value* as 'a conception, explicit or implicit, distinctive of an individual or characteristic of a group, of the desirable which influences the selection from available modes, means, and ends of action'; and T. Parsons (*The Social System*, Glencoe, Ill.: The Free Press, 1951, p. 12) holds that 'An element of a shared symbolic system which serves as a criterion or standard for selection among the alternatives of orientation which are intrinsically open in a situation may be called a value'.

In such conceptions value is identified with broad, fundamental norms, which are generally shared by the members of a society or subgroup and which serve to integrate as well as to guide and channel the organized activities of the members, in part by giving rise to complexes of derivative norms regulating functionally important areas of life. In such definitions the axiological problem of the subjectivity or objectivity of values is not explicitly considered, although the values are conceived by the people sharing them as possessing objective validity.

C. Because the objective *validity* of values has been regarded as constituting a problem which falls outside the realm of science (except by a few positivists their objectivity as phenomena characteristic of the actions of human beings has not been questioned) social scientists have not for the most part devoted themselves to this matter. At the same time, however, this belief that the question of the validity of values is not a scientific problem has created great controversy concerning the place of the scientist's own values in his scientific work. Certainly since the publication of Weber's 'The Meaning of "Ethical Neutrality" in Sociology and Economics' in 1917 (published in English in *Max Weber on the Methodology of the Social Sciences*, trans. and ed. by E. A. Shils & H. A. Finch, Glencoe, Ill.: The Free Press, 1949, pp. 1–47) there have been those who have insisted that the social sciences be value-free in the sense that the value-commitments of the social scientist should play no role in his analysis of social data. No agreement has been reached on this matter. Many of those arguing for the value-free character of social science have overlooked Weber's own belief concerning the limited degree to which such freedom is possible. While he did not want the scientific rostrum turned into a political arena or a religious pulpit, he believed that the ultimate value commitments of each social scientist would determine the problems he was interested in, the presuppositions and assumptions built into his fundamental theoretical conceptions, and the range of data he would investigate; in other words that there would be as many different social sciences as there were modes of ultimate commitment. While aware of the complexities of the relationship of values to science, sociologists like T. Parsons and H. Becker have believed that a high degree of freedom and objectivity in social science is possible (T. Parsons, *The Structure of Social Action*, New York: McGraw-Hill, 1937, pp. 591–601; H. Becker, 'Supreme Values and the Sociologist', *American Sociological Review*, vol. 6, 1941, pp. 155–72). Others like G. Myrdal, while recognizing that respect for empirical data can lead to overlapping areas of verified knowledge on the part of perspectives rooted in varying value commitments, nevertheless believe that the value commitments of the scientist *or* of the people studied must be built into the very framework of investigation (G. Myrdal, *Value*

in Social Theory, New York: Harper & Bros., 1958).

Howard Becker

See also: CONSENSUS
NORM
VALUE (Economics)

Value (Economics)

A. Definitions of *value* in economics, in the order of their frequency in recent literature, appear to be: (a) exchange value, or price—a concept of positive economics which does not have utilitarian or normative connotations; (b) use value or utility (q.v.) defined in various narrower or broader ways which govern the concept's relevance for various types of utilitarian ethics; and (c) 'just price', or the price which should be paid—a sum which may be derived from either a utilitarian or a non-utilitarian ethic.

1. Exchange value, or price, always refers to relative prices or relative value. Thus when we ask what will be the effect of a change in the demand for bread on its 'price', we always assume that the prices of all other goods and services remain constant. This distinction is necessary to distinguish traditional 'price theory', which emphasizes particular prices, from theories directed toward explaining changes in the general price level.

2. Reference to use value occurs most frequently in analysis of consumer demand, where its meaning is an individual's valuation of the usefulness of a good (and varying amounts of it). Thus defined, value becomes a link between economics and that variety of utilitarian ethics which stresses the role of consumer choice. Belief in the use-value theory of demand, however, does not per se imply acceptance of utilitarian ethics. Moreover, persons who believe that utilitarianism is, in some sense, the 'correct' ethic may nevertheless hold that it can never lead to policy conclusions, because policy makers can never measure, and thus add together, different persons' utilities. In recent decades many economists have attempted to construct a meaningful (non-empty) body of 'welfare economics' which has (ordinal) use value as its central concept but which explicitly rejects all interpersonal comparisons.

B. 1. 'The word *value* ...', remarked Adam Smith, 'has two different meanings and sometimes expresses the utility of some particular object, and sometimes the power of purchasing other goods which the possession of that object

Variable

conveys. The one may be called "value in use"; the other, "value in exchange" ' (A. Smith, *Wealth of Nations*, Modern Library, New York: Random House, 1937, p. 28).

2. In textbooks and other writings economists have usually defined the word as *value in exchange*. A. Marshall commented that 'experience has shown that it is not well' to employ the word in the former of Smith's two senses; he preferred the definition which made the term express 'the relation between two things at a particular place and time' (*Principles of Economics*, London: Macmillan, 8th edn., 1920, p. 61). In a money economy this relationship is generally expressed as money price. Both in Marshall's time and since, most books and chapters entitled 'Theory of Value' could accurately be renamed 'Theory of Price'—the title which is more usually given to such writings today, especially in the United States.

3. Neither Marshall nor his successors, however, have restricted their discussion of exchange value to 'the relation between two things at a particular place and [*actual*] time'. Economists have placed much emphasis upon *normal value*, that relationship toward which exchange value would move in a hypothetical, semi-static 'long run'. Moreover, the exact nature of exchange value has been in dispute. To most economists the term has appeared to imply a sum; exchange values can be added to form a total. Thus: Economic theory must ask whether 'free contractual relations under competitive control lead to the maximum production of value as measured in price terms' (F. H. Knight, *The Ethics of Competition*, London: Allen & Unwin, 1935, p. 218). Another view is that 'the valuations which the price system expresses are not quantities at all. ... Value is a relation not a measurement' (L. Robbins, *An Essay on the Nature and Significance of Economic Science*, London: Macmillan, 1932, p. 56).

C. Nor, to many economists, has it seemed that standard economic literature has truly confined —or should confine—*value* within the boundaries of a non-normative theory of exchange. G. Cassel found in value theory elements akin to the old doctrine of 'just price': 'Men urgently want to know more than what prices *are* actually paid ... they want to know what prices *should* be paid ... they want to know the *value* of the different commodities and productive services' (*Nature and Necessity of Interest*, London: Macmillan, 1903, p. 71). Those con-

temporary British and American economists who expound a modernized labour theory of value are especially likely to insist that a meaningful value theory must deal with more than price. Thus: '... production and exchange involve social relations and ... value should, consequently, have some social implication ... the marginal theorists [exemplified by Robbins] ... have made it impossible for seekers after social significance to find any *point d'appui* in the structure of orthodox theory' (H. D. Dickinson, 'Review of R. L. Meek, *Studies in the Labour Theory of Value*', *Economic Journal*, vol. LXVII, 1957, p. 502).

D. Once economic value becomes a normative concept, however, the logical possibilities for redefinition become virtually infinite, and the distinction between economic value and ethical value becomes blurred if not non-existent. In some economic literature the value question which is raised concerns exchange hardly at all; *value* or *social value* here means the contribution which a good or service somehow makes to 'social welfare', and this contribution need not be correlated with any price paid in any actual or ideal situation. Most frequently, it has a utilitarian tinge.

Henry Oliver

See also: Labour Theory of Value
Price
Utility

Variable

A. The term *variable* is being used increasingly in social science to designate any element in an empirical investigation. Deriving from this usage a concept, or conceptual construct, is also a variable when empirical instances of it are being observed and studied. 'Social cohesion' would thus be labelled a concept in a theoretical frame of reference but a variable in an empirical one. The next step, already under way in such usage as T. Parsons's *pattern variable* (q.v.) (*The Social System*, Glencoe, Ill.: The Free Press, 1951, pp. 101–12), is for the term *variable* to be used in the theoretical frame of reference as well.

In this broad empirical reference variable is thus used for qualitative as well as quantifiable observations—for nationality, political party, occupation, or sex as well as for age, intelligence, or wealth—the former being called *qualitative variables* and the latter *quantitative variables*.

Such variables can also be classified in terms of their relations to one another in any particular empirical context. Thus some may properly be called *independent* and some *dependent* in the classical experimental sense. In addition, however, some social scientists have found it useful to identify a third type of relationship—*intervening variables* (q.v.)—which represent relevant factors that have not been neutralized by the experimental design and hence whose effects must be taken into analytical consideration.

B. 1. Until recent years the term was employed primarily in quantitative contexts, and the term *attribute* was used for qualities which were either present or absent in the situation being observed. Today, however, *variable* is used increasingly to represent both. For example, we find R. K. Merton (*Social Theory and Social Structure*, Glencoe, Ill.: The Free Press, 1957, p. 89) describing concepts as *variables*: 'Concepts ... constitute the definitions ... of what is to be observed; they are the variables between which empirical relationships are to be sought', and listing as examples such concepts as status, role, social distance, and anomie. And S. A. Stouffer et al. ('Measurement and Prediction', vol. 4, of *Studies in Social Psychology in World War II*, Princeton, N.J.: Princeton University Press, 1950, p. 63) state that 'We use the term [variable] in its conventional logical or mathematical sense, as denoting a set of values. These values may be numerical (quantitative) or non-numerical [qualitative]. We shall use the term "attribute" interchangeably with "qualitative variable"'. This broader definition is increasingly used by the statisticians themselves. For example, M. G. Kendall and W. R. Buckland, (*A Dictionary of Statistical Terms*, prepared for the International Statistical Institute, Edinburgh: Oliver & Boyd, 1957, p. 310) state that a variable is: 'Generally, any quantity which varies. More precisely, a variable in the mathematical sense, i.e. a quantity which may take any one of the specified set of values. It is convenient to apply the same word to denote non-measurable characteristics, e.g. "sex" is a variable in this sense since any human individual may take one of two "values", male or female'. On the other hand P. F. Lazarsfeld and A. H. Barton ('Qualitative Measurement in the Social Sciences', in D. Lerner & H. D. Lasswell (eds.), *The Policy Sciences*, Stanford, Calif.: Stanford University Press, 1951, p. 170), appear to conceive the term in a somewhat more limited way

as 'permitting any number of gradations and, in addition, implying the possibility of measurement in the most exact sense of the word'.

2. Variables can be classified by their formal content. Two types of quantitative variables are usually distinguished: *continuous variables*, such as distance or age, 'in the sense that between any pair of numbers, however close together, it is possible to have another number' (W. A. Wallis & H. V. Roberts, *Statistics, A New Approach*, London: Methuen, 1957, p. 146); and *discrete variables*, such as cash income or population, where the numbers increase by steps or jumps (there is no number between one cent and two cents or between one person and two persons). Also, under the broader definition of *variable*, two types of qualitative variables are usually distinguished: *attributes*, which are two-valued (dichotomous) variables such as male-female or Democrat-Republican; and *serials* which are multi-valued variables whose values can be arranged in rank order only, such as alphabetic school grades.

3. Variables can also be classified in terms of their relationship to each other. Under conditions of controlled experimentation it is usual to speak of only two types of relationship: the *independent variable* and the *dependent variable*. The independent variable is the one whose changes or differences 'are associated with changes or differences in the dependent variable in any lawful fashion. Observations of the independent variable thus afford a basis for prediction' (A. L. Edwards, *Experimental Design in Psychological Research*, New York: Rinehart, 1950, p. 13). The independent variable is the one that is manipulated in experiments and is often called the *experimental*, *predictor* or *causal variable*. The dependent variable, whose behaviour is presumed to be predictable from the independent variable, is often called the *criterion* or *effect variable* (M. Jahoda et al., *Research Methods in Social Relations*, New York: Dryden Press, 1951, p. 63). This clear-cut direct relationship between two variables has, however, been a most evasive goal for social scientists, and there are some who question its attainability except in trivial or transitory situations, due to the nature of social phenomena. One of the principal reasons is the difficulty of controlling other relevant variables in the experimental situation. However, the importance in many social studies of such other variables, particularly for interpretative purposes, has led to the coining of a special classification for them—*intervening variables* (q.v.)—

Verification

although this term is neither widely nor uniformly used as yet.

Raymond V. Bowers

See also: INTERVENING VARIABLE

Variable Cost (See **Cost**)

Verification

A. *Verification* denotes both the process and the act of establishing the truth of a proposition or a series of propositions whose validity is unestablished. Common synonyms include testing, support, confirmation, and proof. Three basic operations are involved in verification. (a) The unverified proposition is stated as a hypothesis or a prediction of what will be found to be true under specified conditions. (b) Empirical observations of the facts to which the proposition refers are made and analysed. (c) The observations are related to the proposition to see whether and how closely it corresponds to the reality it purports to represent.

The degrees of correspondence form a continuum whose lower end of no correspondence, slight correspondence, etc., constitute rejection, and whose upper end of moderate, great, up to perfect correspondence constitutes verification. Verification thus conceptualized can be calculated statistically, and is the degree of correspondence adequate for the purpose in hand. This step is regarded as the conclusion of a successful scientific research.

B. Verification constitutes a key element in the scientific method. R. Bierstedt (*The Social Order*, New York: McGraw-Hill, 1957, p. 20) writes: 'Science, . . . has no notions so sacred, no propositions so privileged, no truths so absolute that they are not subject to change when new evidence arises to challenge them'. Verification has at least four functions in scientific method.

1. Verification is a source of new theory and a means of integrating new propositions into existing theoretical systems. Theoretical innovation and systematization occur both by empirical verification and by logical deduction.

2. Verification is the method of establishing propositions of such secure validity that they may be called 'scientific laws'. This calls for repeated verifications of the propositions by the original and by different methods of research and under the same and different conditions. The term 'scientific law' simply means that the propositions have been repeatedly verified and

therefore have high predictive value and confidence.

3. Verification is the means of accumulating scientific knowledge—both tested and testable theory and organized relevant facts. The structure of science and the frontiers of research are advanced in this way. For example, S. Stouffer ('Intervening Opportunities, A Theory Relating Mobility and Distance', *American Sociological Review*, vol. 5, 1940, p. 846) constructed a mathematical formula to describe population movements in relation to distance by testing the hypothesis that 'the number of persons going a given distance is directly proportional to the number of opportunities at that distance and inversely proportional to the number of intervening opportunities'.

4. Verification produces the tested propositions and organized facts upon which prediction (q.v.) and control must rest. These processes require specifically applicable knowledge.

C. With reference to aim and method, three basic types of verification can be identified.

1. *Replication verification* refers to the repetition of a research procedure to check the accuracy or truth of the findings reported. The aim here is to establish truth by confirming or supporting findings and to test methods. Thus G. A. Lundberg, C. C. Schrag and O. N. Larsen (*Sociology*, New York: Harper & Bros., 1954, p. 9) observe '. . . , some other investigators must be able to *verify the findings* by repeating the study'. 'Repetition of studies is therefore required for the verification of scientific conclusions and generalizations' (ibid., p. 64).

2. *Consistency verification* refers to the establishment of the truth, or at least the acceptability of theoretical propositions by demonstrating their logical consistency with the elements of established theoretical systems. Validity of the propositions in question may be inferred if the theoretical system with which they are rendered consistent has been previously established empirically. Thus S. C. Dodd (*Dimensions of Society*, New York: The Macmillan Co., 1942, p. 64) states: 'To test truth the philosophy of science offers two general criteria, those of (a) *internal consistency* and (b) *external correspondence*. Is this theory proposed logically consistent within itself and with the current body of theory that constitutes that science at a given date . . . ? Supplementing these two principles of consistency and correspondence are two corollaries. These are the practical subcriteria of *agreement* and *utility*'.

3. *Correspondence verification* refers to the process of relating empirical observations to theoretical propositions to determine whether and to what degree the theory describes external reality. This type of verification begins with theoretical propositions which are treated as hypotheses and which contain a prediction of the fact and the degree of correspondence to external reality. T. Parsons (*The Structure of Social Action*, Glencoe, Ill.: The Free Press, 1949, pp. 8–9) writes: 'The process of verification, fundamental to science, does not consist merely in reconsideration of this applicability to known facts by others than the original formulator of the theory, and then simply waiting for new facts to turn up. It consists in deliberately investigating phenomena with the expectations from the theory in mind and seeing whether or not the facts actually found agree with these expectations. ... In so far as the expectations from the theory agree with the facts found, making allowances for "errors of observation", etc., the theory is "verified".... There is then a reciprocal process: direction, by the expectations derived from a system of theory, toward fields of factual investigation, then reaction of the results of this investigation on the theory'.

Joseph S. Himes

See also: EXPERIMENT
        HYPOTHESIS
        PREDICTION
        RELIABILITY
        SOCIAL CAUSATION
        VALIDITY

Vertical Mobility (See **Mobility**)

Veto

A. To *veto* is to prevent action; the *veto power* is the right or capacity to do so. Thus the common denominator of veto, or veto power, is the legal authority of one public organ, or members of such an organ, to impose an absolute or qualified barrier to action by that organ, or another organ, or by its members.

1. In public municipal law, veto usually means the legally regulated and exercised refusal by an executive organ to approve bills passed by a legislature, thus preventing or delaying their coming into effect. Less frequently it means suspensive action by one legislative body over the legislative action of another.

2. The term has a special sense in the procedures of the United Nations. Here the veto power means the right of one member of the Security Council to prevent the Organization from carrying out action which it could otherwise legally undertake.

3. The term is also used figuratively to denote any action by which one agency or organ of government prevents or delays the carrying out of action by another agency or organ.

4. By still greater extension, the term is used loosely to denote the prevention or delaying of action on the part of one individual or group by another individual or group.

B. 1. In public national law veto refers to the right of an authorized body to prevent or impede action, usually legislative in character. The People's Tribune in ancient Rome was said to exercise a veto power when it countermanded the orders of other officials. The modern use of the veto originated in Great Britain. At first possessed of full legislative authority, in time the Sovereign could only forbid action by Parliament. With the development of cabinet responsibility this power fell into disuse. 'It is true ... that the veto in England remained with the Crown as the mere negative half of the once round and complete power of legislation at first exercised by the Sovereign ...' (W. Wilson, 'Review of E. C. Mason, *The Veto: Its Origin, Development, and Function in the Government of the United States (1789–1889)*', *Annals of The American Academy of Political and Social Science*, vol. I, 1891, p. 696).

The veto has historically referred almost exclusively to negative legislative action by a national executive organ. In exceptional cases a legislative body, such as the British House of Lords, was said to have a 'suspensive veto', or power to delay action. Aside from the unused absolute veto of the British monarch, the power is usually a qualified one, as in the case of the American Presidency where it can be overridden by a two-thirds vote of Congress.

A remarkably wide and disruptive power of veto was enjoyed in the 17th and 18th centuries by each member of the Polish Diet. There free veto—*liberum veto*, which was used extensively until its abolition in 1791, was 'a constitutional arrangement which enabled any member of a diet to nullify the whole of its proceedings' (*The Cambridge History of Poland 1697–1935*, Cambridge: At the University Press, 1951, p. 94).

2. (a) The term has somewhat different meaning in the United Nations. Article 27 of the Charter requires that, on other than procedural matters, and in dealing with a dispute under pacific settlement provisions in which case

Voluntarism

a party to the dispute may not vote, decisions are made by an affirmative vote of seven members of the Security Council, 'including the concurring votes of the permanent members ...' The members of the Soviet bloc refer to the latter requirement as the 'principle of unanimity'; elsewhere it is usually called the veto, or, interchangeably 'the unanimity rule' or principle.

Since decisions of the Security Council are at least quasi-judicial, quasi-legislative, and quasi-executive, and since a veto may not be overridden, the power is absolute over all these types of authority. Although most vetoes have been by a single negative vote (by custom, abstention is not regarded as a veto), the term has been applied also to instances when two permanent members voted in the negative. Thus the veto power in the Security Council is the right of one or more of the permanent members to prevent action by the Council whenever a decision is favoured by at least seven votes. What was usually referred to as the 'rule of unanimity' of the League of Nations is, in United Nations terminology, a veto power.

(b) Many writers on the United Nations also use the term *veto* to apply to another type of decision—that which, to be effective, requires the consent of a permanent member of the Security Council, but when such a member is not acting in that capacity. Thus, commenting on proceedings for amending the U.N. Charter some writers have claimed that 'The great power veto holds, therefore, in both methods [of amending the Charter], and it is impossible to amend the Charter over the opposition of these powers' (M. M. Ball & H. B. Killough, *International Relations*, London: Stevens, 1956, p. 244). Thus it is said that a permanent member of the Council may veto an amendment to the Charter since, to go into effect, it must be approved by all five of them.

Some writers make a distinction between the 'rule of unanimity' and the veto. 'The rule of unanimity declares: Without my consent your decision does not bind me. The veto declares: Without my consent there is no decision at all' (H. J. Morgenthau, *Politics Among Nations*, New York: Knopf, 2nd edn., 1954, p. 291; also see J. L. Brierly, *The Outlook for International Law*, Oxford: At the Clarendon Press, 1944, p. 99).

Since an amendment comes 'into force for all members', the requirement of approval by the 'big five' plays a dual role: It gives each of them a veto power, but it also fulfills the requirement of the rule of unanimity. The veto as applied to

the amending process prevents the application of the amendment to the permanent members without their consent. Since the principle of unanimity does not apply to the other members, by ratifying the Charter they agreed to deprive themselves of an essential element of sovereignty, unless of course they may withdraw, which is disputed. It should be noted that the veto, as it applies to the amending process, does not take place in the Security Council.

3. The term *veto group* has come to be used in contemporary analyses of political power. Such a veto group '... has struggled for and finally attained a power to stop things conceivably inimical to its interests and, within narrower limits to start things' (D. Riesman, *The Lonely Crowd*, New Haven: Yale University Press, 1950, p. 244).

Charles P. Schleicher

Veto Group (See **Veto**)

Veto Power (See **Veto**)

Virilocal (See **Residence**)

Vision (See **Dream**)

Voluntarism

A. *Voluntarism* in social science denotes any theory that stresses the place of choice, decision, purpose, and norms in social action.

B. In its crudest form *voluntarism* means that all social phenomena are directly traceable to the deliberate decisions of human beings. History has often been written in this tradition as though the actions of 'great' men and leaders are the main, if not the sole, cause of all social institutions. This approach ignores the large number of institutions and structures that are culturally significant but are not the result of conscious design.

C. In its sophisticated development voluntarism focuses upon persons as the starting point of social science investigation and upon the acts of such persons. Throughout his *Structure of Social Action* (New York: McGraw-Hill, 1937), T. Parsons refers to his theory of action as voluntaristic in that it includes normative elements, choice, 'subjective' categories, and effort. At the end of the book he drops the term, since he feels that *any* adequate theory of action must be voluntaristic (ibid., p. 762).

D. Voluntarism in social science raises the question of the doctrine of free will. While

750

Parsons and others, e.g. R. M. MacIver, F. Znaniecki, and H. Becker, who stress human choice, goal-seeking, and norms in their sociological theories are careful to dissociate their ideas from those of a positivistic determinism in which such elements are omitted, there is considerable ambiguity as to whether or not they renounce all forms of determinism, particularly of a psychological, social, or cultural character: i.e. whether or not they would agree that at least within limits a person could have done otherwise than he did, given all variables including social, cultural, and psychological variables. Choice does not mean freedom unless within limits the will is free to will what it wills. Determinism is not eliminated, even though social action is not reduced to physical and biological variables (cf. P. Furfey, *The Scope and Method of Sociology*, New York: Harper & Bros., 1953, pp. 61–2; and W. L. Kolb, 'A Social-Psychological Conception of Human Freedom', *Ethics*, vol. 63, 1953, pp. 180–9).

Joseph H. Fichter

Voting

A. *Voting* denotes the means whereby a number of persons are enabled to indicate their agreement or disagreement with some proposition, or their preference as between two or more proposals or between two or more candidates for some office.

B. 1. Usually when a vote is taken the decision of a majority prevails; for some types of decision, it may be provided that there must be an absolute majority of those qualified to vote, or some majority greater than half, either of all those qualified to vote or of all those actually voting, for a particular decision to be valid.

2. The votes ought always to be counted in a way that is manifestly fair. A voice vote, in which the voters shout 'Yes' or 'No', is simple and quick, but acceptable as a final decision only if those declared to be in a minority are satisfied that they really are in a minority. For greater certainty those voting may raise their hands, or stand up, or walk through doors, etc., being counted as they do so; or they may mark papers, which are then counted. It is usual to appoint representatives of both sides to take part in the process of counting. Mechanical methods of counting votes are also sometimes used.

The process of voting is used also to allow people to choose between rival candidates for various offices.

P. A. Bromhead

See also: Ballot
           Election
           Majority
           Plebiscite
           Referendum

W

Wage Rate (See Wages)

Wages

A. 1. 'Wages are the price of labour' (J. R. Hicks, *The Theory of Wages*, London: Macmillan, 1932, p. 1). They are paid for the expenditure of physical and/or mental effort in the production of goods and services. In its broad sense, the term includes implicit 'wages of management' earned by working proprietors, salaries received by supervisory, clerical, and other employees paid by the week, month, or longer periods of time, as well as payments made for shorter intervals of time to manual and mechanical workers.

2. Some writers, however, prefer to confine the term to payments made to hourly rated or other non-supervisory and non-clerical employees (D. Yoder, *Personnel Principles and Policies*, New York: Prentice-Hall, 1952, p. 402). The amount of wages paid may be based upon the number of hours worked or upon the number of pieces or other results produced. Although normally paid in money, wages may be given in kind (goods and services), and may include tips and a wide variety of 'fringe benefits' (G. F. Bloom & H. R. Northrup, *Economics of Labor Relations*, Homewood, Ill.: Irwin, 1954, pp. 293–4). Indeed, the term may denote the entire functional share of national income going to labour.

B. The exact meaning of wages varies with the context and point of view taken. Wages may be conceived of either as a rate or as an amount. To delineate some of these special meanings, related terms have emerged.

1. *Wage rate* or *basic rate* refers to the 'normal' or 'standard' amount paid per hour of work or per unit of product.

2. *Earnings* may be hourly, weekly, monthly, or annual and thus are influenced not only by the wage rate, but also by the number of hours worked. The term *earnings* refers to the 'total remuneration for services rendered or time worked, including overtime premiums, bonuses, commissions and other extra rewards' (F. Peterson, *Survey of Labor Economics*, New York: Harper & Bros., 1941, p. 247). *Average straight-time hourly earnings* is a refinement of this concept which seeks to eliminate the influence of overtime, night-shift differentials, and other premium payments. 'The distinction between the wage rate and his earnings is probably the most important for the wage earner' (D. J. Robertson, *The Economics of Wages*, London: Macmillan, 1961, p. 4).

3. *Take-home pay* is the actual amount received from the employer after deductions made for income tax, social security, insurance, union dues, etc.

4. Of especial importance for comparisons over time designed to take into account changes in 'price levels' is the concept of *real wage rates*. Thus E. H. Phelps Brown and S. V. Hopkins ('The Course of Wage Rates in Five Countries 1860–1939', *Oxford Economic Papers* [New Series], vol. II, no. 2, 1950, p. 226 et seq.) includes tables of (a) money wage rates, (b) the wage earner's cost of living, (c) the price level of final output. They calculate various quotients including a ÷ b which 'we may call the wage rate in consumption-units or, according to common usage, the real wage rate'. They also calculate a ÷ c: 'the wage rate in units of final product or, briefly the product wage rate'.

5. *Labour costs*, though sometimes used interchangeably with *wages*, are affected also by productivity and include all the *fringe payments*, which in addition to *direct wage payments* constitute the total *wage bill* (D. Yoder, *Personnel Principles and Policies*, pp. 406–7).

6. *Fringe payments* or *wage supplements* are payments made without any directly associated employee effort. Such payments are of increasing importance and include: pay for time when the employee does not report for work; monetary awards and prizes for special activities; bonuses, contributions, and profit sharing for which the employee renders no direct service; payments to provide employee security and financial protection against various hazards and contingencies; and other practices and services that benefit employees primarily (A. L. Gitlow, *Labor Economics and Industrial Relations*, Homewood, Ill.: Irwin, 1947, p. 485).

C. The concept of wages as the price of labour has formed a focus for specialized economic

752

theory as well as entering into the body of general economic theory. Broad theories of wage determination, within the theory of price, first centred upon the wage fund concept, came later to be based upon marginal productivity analysis, and more recently have been underpinned by more detailed study of wage structures and the dynamic interplay of causal factors affecting wage-structures in a variety of socioeconomic contexts (see J. T. Dunlop (ed.), *The Theory of Wage Determination*, London: Macmillan, 1957, passim).

H. Ellsworth Steele

See also: INCOME

Wants

A. The term denotes, primarily in economics, both the psychological state of need and the range of goods, services, and other items which both satisfy and stimulate those needs (cf. A. Marshall, *Principles of Economics*, New York: Macmillan, 8th edn., 1920, pp. 86–91).

B. In a very important sense the concept of *wants* together with *scarcity* form the central concern of economics. Thus, for example, G. L. S. Shackle in his book, *Economics for Pleasure* (Cambridge: Cambridge University Press, 1959) opens his analysis with a description of wants, the inevitable scarcity of the means of satisfying them, and the problem this inevitably poses of choosing an arrangement of varying degrees of satisfying the several wants (ibid., pp. 1–5).

Most economists have not then pursued the cultural, sociological, and psychological roots of wants further, but rather have assumed the existence of wants for scarce goods and services as the basis upon which economic activity is elaborated. In this regard, incentive (q.v.) has been a narrower term for economists than wants, since it has usually focused on monetary rewards (and punishments) instrumental for the satisfaction of wants. One of the most ambitious attempts to develop a theory of wants in specific relation to economics was that of C. R. Noyes (*Economic Man in Relation to His Natural Environment*, New York: Columbia University Press, 1948, vol. I, pp. 21–394). It is dubious whether this venture in the psychological roots of economics has been fruitful for economics, and it remains an open question as to whether differences in psychological theories of needs and wants are significant for the assumption of the existence of wants in this broad sense on the part of economists. No psychology or social psychology denies the existence of needs and wants, and if scarcity is granted, then a problem of allocation of effort and rewards remains, regardless of the other aspects of the nature of man.

William L. Kolb

See also: NEED

War

A. Three distinct definitions are important for the social sciences:

1. *War* may denote a socially recognized situation in which armed hostilities of considerable magnitude are conducted more or less continuously between two or more nations, states, or governments.

2. The municipal law of a state may lay it down that war is a condition of armed hostilities carried on between that state and another state or political faction, or between two other states or political factions, which has been declared or recognized as 'war' by the organ invested with that power by the state's constitution and laws.

3. War in contemporary international law is armed conflict between two or more nation-states, each of which claims to be sovereign, and which stand in a relationship of legal equality vis-à-vis other states with respect to the conflict.

B. 1. War primarily denotes armed conflict between nation-states though it is used (a) metaphorically to refer to any conflict as 'a war of words', 'the war of science and religion', 'industrial warfare', 'the war of men and women', 'the war against disease'. Less metaphorically it is applied (b) to hostilities between factions within a state (civil war); (c) to lethal hostilities between any systems of action which closely resemble each other, as primitive tribes, individuals, or even animals; (d) to international hostilities not involving armed force, as 'economic warfare', 'psychological warfare', 'ideological warfare' and 'cold war'.

But, as indicated above, in its most concrete sense the term refers to hostilities of considerable magnitude conducted by armed forces of particular states during a defined period of time, as the Crimean War, the Russo-Japanese War. In this sense a war is a more or less continuous series of battles and campaigns between the belligerents, though in some cases considerable intervals of armistice or suspension of active hostilities, as in the 'Hundred Years War' and the 'Thirty Years War', or changes in the list of active belligerents and division of hostilities among separate theatres as in World Wars I and

War

II, make it difficult to decide whether the conflict should be considered one war or many wars.

2. The difficulty of deciding the magnitude of hostilities which justify the appellation *war* has led some writers to subsume the concept in the more general one of 'a deadly quarrel'. L. F. Richardson has classified such quarrels according to the exponent to base 10 of the number killed, from those of magnitude 10^0, in which only one person is killed (a murder) to those of magnitude 10^7 in which over 10 million were killed—(World Wars I and II)—(*Statistics of Deadly Quarrels*, ed. by Quincy Wright and C. C. Lienau, Pittsburgh: The Boxwood Press, 1960).

3. There has been debate on whether the essential feature is the physical fact of violent contention (in which case the term can be applied to hostilities between animals, primitive tribes, gladiators and insurgents as well as to those between states and nations) or the socially recognized situation in which such contention actually is occurring or probably will occur, in an accepted pattern of behaviour and technology. In the latter sense war is a cultural phenomenon applied only to human groups. This distinction was brought out by Grotius, who criticized Cicero's definition of war as 'a contending by force' (*On Duties* I, XI, 34) because he said that war was not a 'contest but a condition' (*De Jure Belli Ac Pacis*, I, 1, 2, trans. by F. W. Kelsey, Oxford: At the Clarendon Press, 1925, vol. II, p. 33). Hobbes said to the same effect 'the nature of war consisteth not in actual fighting but in a known disposition thereto during all the time there is no assurance to the contrary' (*Leviathan* (1651), ed. by M. Oakeshott, Oxford: Basil Blackwell, 1957, p. 82, I, c. 13).

C. A distinction has been made by U.S. Courts between 'war in the material sense'—with regard to what might be called the 'factual situation' of armed conflict between nation-states (see B. (1)—and 'war in the legal sense' perhaps more appropriately 'war as defined by law, both municipal and international' (The Three Friends 1897, 166 U.S.; and Q. Wright, *A Study of War*, Chicago: University of Chicago Press, 1942, pp. 8 ff.). The 'legal sense' is extremely complex —since different legal systems may employ different criteria in determining the condition of war. Moreover 'legal' and 'material' senses of war can and do overlap.

1. In the muncipal law of a state hostilities involving that state do not have the character of 'legal war' unless the appropriate national authorities have so declared or recognized it. In the United States only Congress can 'declare' war but the President may 'recognize' hostilities initiated by a domestic faction or by another state as legal war (The Prize cases, 1863, 2 Black 635). Since the criteria applied by the political authorities of different governments may be different, hostilities between two governments may be considered legal war by one but rebellion, insurrection, intervention, or defensive action by the other. War, in the sense of the municipal law of non-participating states may similarly vary. National courts usually follow the attitude on this matter of the political authorities of their government, but if that attitude has not been expressed, they may apply the term according to the definition(s) prevailing in international law.

2. International lawyers have however differed on whether the criterion for determining the existence of war in the 'legal sense' is observance of required formalities in the initiation and conduct of hostilities, or the juridical equality of the parties in respect to third states. Modern international law has tended to emphasize the latter. If the United Nations has recognized one belligerent as an aggressor and the other as a defender, members of the United Nations are bound to treat them differently. Consequently the belligerents would not be judicially equal and the hostilities would not be 'war' in the sense in which the term has generally been used by international lawyers during the 18th and 19th centuries. Medieval jurists and the classical writers on international law, however, distinguished the legal character of war, not by the legal equality of the belligerents but by the regularity of initiation and conduct of the hostilities. Gentili, for example, defined war as 'a properly conducted contest of armed public forces' (*De Jure Belli*, trans. by J. C. Rolfe, Oxford: At the Clarendon Press, 1933, vol. II, 1588, pp. 1, 2). Consequently they applied the term *war* to hostilities in which one side was waging a 'just war' and the other an 'unjust war', although in such a case they advocated different treatment of the belligerents by non-participating states.

Since the Kellogg-Briand Pact and the U.N. Charter impose a duty on practically all states not to resort to hostilities except in individual or collective self-defence, on invitation of the state in whose territory the fighting occurs, or with the authority of the United Nations, a situation in which the belligerents are juridically equal can seldom exist if the United Nations functions. The initiator of hostilities is an aggressor and his enemy a defender or a participant in international police action. Consequently war, in the sense of a duel, in which the parties are legally equal, can be said to have been 'outlawed' though war in the material sense may of course occur. War in the legal sense may also occur according to the municipal law of particular states, or even in the sense of international law if the organs of the United Nations fail to function or consider it desirable to tolerate a duel-war in which the parties fight it out as equals.

D. Tribunals called upon to interpret the meaning of war in legal instruments, such as insurance, contracts, charter parties and other instruments which modify the obligations of the parties in case of 'war', are guided by the context of the particular instrument, but they have tended to treat the term in such instruments as meaning war in the material (see above) sense, which is socially but necessarily legally recognized conflict. Thus, for example, the Korean hostilities of 1950-3, though not war in the sense of international law or of the municipal law of many states, has usually been regarded by Courts as 'war' in the sense in which that term was intended in such instruments (Weissman vs. Metropolitan Life Insurance Co., 112 Fed. Suppl. 420, 1953).

Quincy Wright

See also: PEACE

Wealth

A. *Wealth* in ordinary speech means in the first instance *riches*, i.e. an abundance of material possessions. From this it has come to have two further senses: (a) the material possessions themselves, whether or not abundant; (b) an abundance of anything, whether material or not and whether possessed or not—as in such phrases as 'a wealth of illustrations' or 'a wealth of metaphors'.

Economic terminology has in general made exclusive use of the first of these derived meanings, i.e. an aggregate, whether large or small, of material objects.

B. From a study of more specific usages, four important points arise here.

1. *Wealth as a stock of useful and exchangeable goods.* Since neither all material objects constitute wealth, nor all wealth consists of material goods, more precise definitions have been attempted. In this stricter sense, *wealth* refers to the stock of *economically significant items* owned by an individual or a group (such as a class or a nation). For an item to be economically significant, it must satisfy two conditions: it must (a) be useful (capable of satisfying human wants) and it must (b) be actually or potentially exchangeable. Exchangeability requires (i) that ownership can be, legally and physically, transferred and (ii) that the item be scarce in relation to wants. A difficulty arises because 'It would be very paradoxical to have to maintain that, if "economic" goods, by reason of multiplication became "free" goods, wealth would diminish' (L. Robbins, *An Essay on the Nature and Significance of Economic Science*, London: Macmillan, 1932, p. 47 fn.). We may therefore have to define it as including all *potentially* economic goods, irrespective of whether they have or have not a value in any given situation.

2. *The relation between Wealth and Welfare.* Although wealth has an objective counterpart in the physical stock of useful and exchangeable goods, it derives its significance from the ability of this stock to minister to human wants and is thus related to economic welfare (see *Welfare*). The relation to welfare is obvious when we measure wealth by prices, which are intended to reflect individual or social satisfactions. But even other measures of the stock of wealth (such as weight or cubic yards, etc.) have significance only in relation to want satisfaction. The same physical object can be wealth or its opposite, waste. A well in the desert is precious, a flood is a disaster (negative wealth). Today's newspaper is wealth, yesterday's may be rubbish. Or again, what is rubbish in one country may be wealth in another (empty petrol cans), or what is wealth at one moment is waste the next (ammunition when war ends). 'Wealth is not wealth because of its substantial qualities. It is wealth because it is scarce. We cannot define wealth in physical terms as we can define food in terms of vitamin content or calorific value. It is an essentially relative concept' (ibid., p. 47).

3. *Individual and National Wealth.* An individual's wealth consists of the sum of all his assets—whether tangible, like real property and stocks of goods, or intangible, like copyrights, patents, securities and money—minus his debts or obligations. In computing a *nation's* wealth, however, securities and money are not included. Although they constitute the assets of some individuals, exactly equivalent obligations of others lead to cancellations. The only exception

Welfare

are paper claims on foreigners, which form part of the nation's wealth, just as debts to foreigners must be subtracted. Claims on foreigners do not, however, form part of the wealth of the world as a whole, where again they cancel out.

4. *Wealth, Income, Capital.* It should be noted that in its strict usage as discussed above the concept denotes a *stock* or inventory existing at a point of time. It is thus distinguished from *income*, which is a *flow* (of earnings) over a period of time, although in looser usage wealth can stand either for the stock (*capital*) or for the flow (*income*). In the stricter usage it is equivalent to *capital*, though *wealth* suggests the ability to yield satisfactions, whereas *capital* stresses the productive capacity of the stock of economically significant items.

P. Streeten

See also: CAPITAL
          INCOME
          SCARCITY
          WELFARE

Welfare (Also **Welfare Economics**)

1. In the widest sense the term *welfare* denotes well-being. More narrowly it refers to the comfort and improvement of the people, over and above money incomes earned, in so far as they are affected by the policies of the central or local government, private firms or voluntary institutions. It is in this sense that the term is used in such phrases as *welfare work, industrial welfare, welfare state,* etc.

2. *Economic welfare* is the subject matter of one branch of economics, viz. *welfare economics*, and as such has only a very loose connection with (1). The economics of welfare is concerned with the discrepancies between an actual organization of economic affairs and an ideal organization (according to some criterion of economic or non-wasteful organization). In welfare economics, economic welfare is that which is maximized in an ideal organization of the economic system, or that which is increased whenever the organization is improved. Welfare economics attempts to provide a method of evaluating the social gain or loss accruing from economic changes.

A. C. Pigou defines economic welfare as 'that part of general welfare that can be brought directly or indirectly into relation with the measuring-rod of money', where 'the elements of welfare are states of consciousness and, perhaps, their relations' (*The Economics of Welfare* (1920), London: Macmillan, 4th edn., 1932, pp. 11, 10).

3. Special problems arise in defining *social welfare* and in relating it to economic welfare. How is the welfare of individuals related to that of society as a whole?

(a) On the utilitarian view individual welfare is, in principle, measurable, and social welfare is simply the sum of the welfare of all individuals.

(b) L. Robbins and others have denied the measurability and scientific comparability of the welfare of individuals and dismissed the analysis of welfare from economic science.

(c) Others have attempted to endow economic welfare with a precise meaning, without assuming measurability and comparability. If measurability of individual welfare is rejected, it may still be possible to compare differences in welfare and thus to pronounce on social welfare. If an economic change benefits John and harms Bill, we may ask whether John can compensate Bill for his loss and still be better off. On this principle, one school has thought it possible to construct a theory of welfare economics 'which assumes no more than the consistency of preference scales; if one does this the social gains to a group of consumers from a favourable change in prices is measured by the sum of their individual consumer's surpluses, which may be interpreted as the total money income which they (as a group) would have to lose if they were to be reduced, in the new price situation, to the same levels of utility as they were able to reach in the old situation' (J. R. Hicks, 'Demand', in *Chambers' Encyclopaedia*, London: Newnes, 1950).

(d) Others again, while insisting that it is not possible to construct a theory of welfare economics which assumes no more than the consistency of *individual preference scales*, have argued that a scientific study of social welfare is possible if a *social preference scale* is introduced explicitly, which contains, amongst other value judgements, ethical judgements on distribution. All that is required for such a 'social welfare function' is that the various possibilities in which we are interested can be ordered on a line so that any possibility on one side of any point is regarded as 'better' than any possibility on the other side of it. Economics cannot tell us which of these welfare functions is best, but it can analyse the formal properties and general characteristics of welfare functions with economic variables.

4. Welfare economists have attempted to formulate rules of policy of the following kind: taxation should be progressive; direct taxes are better than indirect taxes; prices should equal the extra costs incurred by producing one more unit of the product; countries can gain by imposing certain tariffs, etc.

P. Streeten

Welfare Economics (See Welfare)

White-Collar Class

1. In its most general sense *white-collar class* (derived from U.S. colloquial usage) denotes non-manual employees in contrast to manual wage-earners, or *blue-collar* workers. It is roughly equivalent to the English *black-coated* (which it has to some extent replaced), to the German *Angestellte*, and to the French *employé*.

2. More specifically the term refers *to the lower ranks* of the 'new' (i.e. economically dependent) middle class. Thus, for example, R. Centers excludes managerial and professional personnel and limits the term to 'clerks and kindred workers, salesmen, agents, semi-professional workers, technicians' (*The Psychology of Social Classes*, Princeton, N.J.: Princeton University Press, 1949, p. 49). J. Bonham gives a similar definition: 'On the lower fringe of the middle class, near the boundary where the manual wage earners begin, lies the varied group of employees who are vaguely known as "white collar" workers' (*The Middle Class Vote*, London: Faber & Faber, 1954, p. 65). His criteria for inclusion are threefold: (a) that the worker is an employee; (b) that he is engaged in 'brain' work; and (c) that his qualifications are not recognized as professional.

3. Although the above is the usual meaning of the term, it is sometimes (logically) extended so as to make it synonymous with *the new middle class as a whole*. Thus C. W. Mills, in his study of the American middle class (*White Collar*, New York: Oxford University Press, 1951), includes as *white collar* all occupied persons who are neither entrepreneurial nor manual wage-earning, i.e. managerial and professional as well as sales and clerical workers.

4. It is sometimes equated with *salariat*. This usage is less satisfactory since it technically excludes non-manual wage-earning employees who are normally regarded as white collar.

5. There is a fair measure of agreement that the white-collar group constitutes a 'stratum' rather than a 'class' in the strict (Marxian) sense of that term. 'In terms of property, the white-collar people are *not* "in between Capital and Labour"; they are exactly in the same pro-

perty-class position as the wage-earners' (ibid., p. 71).

D. Lockwood

See also: SOCIAL CLASS

Widow Inheritance (See Levirate)

Will

A. While *will* is sometimes used to denote any impulse to act, the personality in action, or the totality of irrational, emotional, and conative responses which have primacy over intellectual activity, it is more usually used in the sense of deliberate decision in contrast to impulsive action. In this latter sense there is in an act of will a choice of one from several alternatives, and often there is a conscious reference to the subject's self. Thus in this more restricted sense will denotes a sequence of mental acts eventuating in decision or choice. An act of will may then be resolved into (a) envisaging alternative courses of action, (b) deliberating on, examining, and comparing the alternative courses with special reference to the dominant ideals of the self, and (c) deciding.

B. 1. The 'accommodation of feeling and will to the rational side of human nature is characteristic of classic Greek psychology, which seeks always to model itself after the cognitive functions' (M. Dessoir, *Outlines of the History of Psychology* [1911], trans. by D. Fisher, New York: Macmillan, 1912, p. 25). Hence the Greek, or more particularly the Socratic, conception of *will* is a degree of freedom possessed by an individual which is wholly dependent upon intellectual insight, wrong actions being due to lack of right knowledge. The evildoer has no freedom; only the wise man is free.

2. In St Augustine (354–430) the 'primacy of the idea' characteristic of Greek rationalism was displaced by the 'primacy of the will' (*voluntas*). He considered *will* the fundamental moving principle in mental life which is manifested in other mental functions. The later scholastics see *will* and *intellect* as the two rational faculties of the human soul. Man alone has will. Animals must obey the laws of their nature, whereas man is free in so far as he directs himself towards the action he chooses, and his will may act against his intellect. The proper object of rational will is the good in its universal aspect. In this wide sense, medieval usage follows Aristotle in subsuming under *will* all the non-intellectual conative and effective processes. Duns Scotus (c. 1265–1308), like Augustine, also insisted on

the primacy of will. A 'first thought' enters consciousness, serving as stimulus to the *will*, which responds by embracing or rejecting it. If the former, then the 'first thought' becomes a 'second thought' to which the agent's responsibility and freedom of will now attach.

3. At the beginning of the modern epoch we find Hobbes (1588–1679), influenced by the mechanics of Galileo as well as by Aristotle, interpreting *will* as a natural striving towards or away from an exciting cause as it is pleasurable or painful. This activity gradually becomes associated with images and modified by deliberation and appears finally as the 'last appetite'. Both Locke (1632–1704) and Spinoza (d. 1677), however, declare that there is no faculty of *will* apart from particular acts or processes of willing.

4. Intellectualist systems of psychology of the 19th century, like associationism, tended to avoid the problem of *will*. A. Bain (*The Emotions and the Will*, London: Parker & Son, 1859) faced the problem, but he tried to explain away the argument for freedom of will based on the experience of volition. Spontaneous action, he declared, like reflex or instinctive action, is determined by the constitution of the nervous system (E. G. Boring, *A History of Experimental Psychology*, 1929, New York: Century, p. 230). Unlike Bain, James (1842–1910) held that the mechanistic explanation of mind broke down when faced with the problem of *will*. He believed in some integrating and organizing force beyond the separate experiences, volition not being explicable in terms of elements preceding the decision, and he employed the expression *will-to-believe* in an essay by that title (1896). By this, he meant the necessity to believe even when evidence is incomplete, the adventurous spirit of man, the heroic character of all creative thinking, the mind open to possibilities.

5. Among the continental thinkers, Wundt (*Grundriss der Psychologie*, 1896), taking an evolutionary standpoint, made the *will* 'a central and primordial reality', but he nevertheless tried to reduce it to a series of feelings. Höffding (*Outlines of Psychology*, trans. by M. E. Lowndes, London: Macmillan, 1891) however refused to reduce the *will* to more elementary constituents. The *will* for him is a primacy and ultimate way of *acting* and he traced it from the most forms of blind reflex activity and approach or withdrawal in the simplest organisms to conscious human decision in a complex situation.

6. One of the few contemporary psychologists (F. Aveling, *Personality and Will*, London: Nisbet, 1931) who have made a systematic study

of the *will* sums up his views, following Ach and Michotte, as follows: the spontaneous and universal distinction we make between voluntary thought and action, on the one hand, and involuntary action and thought, on the other, lies 'not only at the root of one's own personal conscience, but at that also of all systems of social morality, all codes of positive law, and all forms of institutional religion' (ibid., p. 6). An act of will in order to be understood, must be 'lived, or experienced and known personally' (p. 102). It is not reducible to feelings of strain or effort or striving. 'It is experienced as something other than all those elements which together we usually consider as constituting our bodies so far as these are present in consciousness' (ibid., p. 102). Furthermore, 'Nothing is willed unless it is foreseen. We can only will when we anticipate the consequences of our willing. We must know what we will...' (ibid., p. 240). 'A person', he concludes, 'is an individual, incommunicably existing by himself, who is not merely will, or energy elicited by goals and determined by motives, but an intelligent will contemplating means to ends and making its own motives' (ibid., p. 242).

C. The ancient and unresolved problem of free-will still has its repercussions in current usages of the word *will* and more generally in conceptions of voluntary action. A belief in *free-will* means that the course of thought and volition is or may be directed by the individual himself, regardless of external influences and (according to some) regardless of his physical or mental constitution. This doctrine may be contrasted with determinism of the psychoanalytic or genetic-behavioural variety which leaves no room for *freedom of will* in any sense. However 'far more progress must be made before it will cease to be arrogant of the experimenter to suppose that he has solved the age-old problem of volition' (E. R. Hilgard & D. G. Marquis, *Conditioning and Learning*, New York: Appleton-Century, 1940, p. 276). And there the problem remains.

J. Cohen

See also: MIND

Witchcraft (See Sorcery)

Working Capital (See Capital)

Working Class
A. Conceptual and statistical difficulties combine to make a short definition of this term extremely difficult. A broad measure of assent

would be accorded to the view that the term denotes the lower, subordinate strata—especially those who work as wage-workers and 'with their hands'—within an urban industrial economy, together with the families and dependents of such workers. Yet any such a view may seem superficial or, in part at least, circular. The difficulties that arise are, to some extent, the general difficulties presented to social scientists by the concept of social class (q.v.); these difficulties are compounded by the history of the term, one that has been central to Marxist critiques of society. There are further problems presented by the actual historical development of 'low' strata within industrial society; the movements of individuals into and out of such strata; the changing *relative* positions of the social strata; the shifting boundary lines between the 'middle' and 'lower' strata; the changing inner composition of the 'low' strata; the impact upon all strata of technological and political change.

B. The term 'working classes' antedates that of 'working class'—and was used steadily in the England of the early 19th century. Thus John Wade wrote in 1833 his *History of the Middle and Working Classes*, in which he studied the changing conditions of industrial England in historical, economic, and philosophical terms. It is evident that the notion of class—'middle' or 'working'—emerged from the confrontation in early 19th-century England of the 'manufacturing interest' and those whom they employed. 'Pre-industrial' hierarchies had, of course, included working populations both of skilled artisans and others at the base of the social system. The social divisions in terms of *rank* did not ignore these groups—but although the words 'middle rank' were commonly employed in 17th-century England the phrase 'working rank' had no currency whatever. The notion of a 'working class' as distinct from 'working classes') arose along with hypotheses concerned with the inner solidarity of the 'labouring poor', as they had hitherto been known, and their hostile confrontation (in the new conditions) with the 'middle class' or 'bourgeoisie'. There is evidence, as summarized by A. Briggs, that, by the 1840s, such 'solidarity' as these opposed groups secured *within* their respective ranks was a function of their apprehensions concerning *each other* ('The Language of Class in Early Nineteenth Century England', in A. Briggs & J. Saville (eds.), *Essays on Labour History*, London: Macmillan, 1960, p. 43 et seq.). It was, of

course, upon this working class that Marx reposed his hopes for the revolutionary transformation of 'capitalist' society—an end which he campaigned for and predicted.

C. Contemporary social scientists have been especially concerned with two key problems that relate to the working class. (a) They have been concerned, first, with the empirical study of the shape of the 'working class', its growing heterogeneity and the consequent socio-political orientation. They have thus been led to examine, for example, the extent of *actual* class antagonism. Some have concluded, with D. G. MacRae that 'classes as entities construed by their members as massive, on-going and necessarily opposed realities are ... but quasi-groups, capable certainly rapidly of becoming internally structured and self-conscious, but only intermittently existent as responses to a variety of precipitating causes ... At no previous period have classes in an industrial society ... less closely approximated to the image of their constant, furious existence as embattled sectors within society' (*Ideology and Society*, London: Heinemann, 1961, pp. 74–5). Others, like S. M. Lipset, have explored the controversial topic of 'working-class authoritarianism' (see S. M. Lipset, *Political Man*, London: Heinemann, 1960, p. 97 et seq.). These themes may be contrasted with the more 'romantic' view—still a vocal one in Britain—of the working class as a solidary entity with a history, if not always the current reality, of a viable 'culture'. (b) Social scientists have also been concerned with mapping the boundaries within and between the 'working' and 'middle' classes in the light of development, e.g. in the degree of skill as well as in 'the regularity of employment and ... the wage-differentials between different grades of workers' (G. D. H. Cole, *Studies in Class Structure*, London: Routledge & Kegan Paul, p. 55). Two authorities surveying the pattern of the American working population in 1956 wrote that 'the "working-class" has grown only slightly since 1910 [from 37·4 per cent to 38·9 per cent] but there has been a dramatic change in the occupational composition. The percentage of non-farm laborers dropped sharply from 12 per cent of the labor-force to 6 per cent. The semi-skilled (generally machine operators) have increased from 14 per cent to 20 per cent; and "skilled craftsmen, foremen and kindred" showed overall modest gains from 11·7 per cent to 13·3 per cent' (H. L. Wilensky & C. N. Lebeaux, *Industrial Society and Social*

Working Class

Welfare, New York: Russell Sage Foundation, 1958, p. 93).

While these and similar analyses are, beyond doubt, meaningful and broadly accurate, social analysts do not, even within the same country, adopt identical criteria for assessing the composition of the working class. Thus K. Mayer assesses the working class in the U.S.A. as comprising 'something over 55 per cent of the population' and includes within it 'skilled, semi-skilled and unskilled urban manual workers, farm laborers, and some categories of farm tenants' (*Class and Society*, New York: Doubleday, 1955, p. 40). For some purposes, e.g. mobility studies, this approach presents difficulties. S. M. Miller, observing that 'in many studies urban workers are included with farm workers and cannot be separated out', goes on to term this 'mixed catergory' as ' "manual" to distinguish it from the "working-classes" which exclude farm workers and purport to represent those non-agricultural employees who work with their "hands" ' ('Comparative Social Mobility', UNESCO *Current Sociology*, vol. IX, no. 1, 1960). There are, of course, comparable difficulties in classifying, on a uniform basis, different degrees of skill. These are more significant in Great Britain than the problems of the relatively small 'farm' population. In Britain another common issue arises, as was recently pointed out by A. M. Carr-Saunders, D. C. Caradog Jones, and C. A. Moser, 'in regard to the boundary of the working class; some black-coated workers, a proportion of shop assistants and even of clerks, for example, would seem to be placed properly within this class, whereas others belonging to these categories might be assigned to the lower middle class even though their incomes are below those of skilled manual workers' (*A Survey of Social Conditions in England and Wales*, Oxford: Clarendon Press, 1958, p. 116).

J. Gould

See also: MIDDLE CLASS
        SOCIAL CLASS
        STRATIFICATION

Z

Zonal Hypothesis

A. *Zonal hypothesis* refers to the hypothesis of E. W. Burgess ('The Growth of the City: An Introduction to a Research Project', in R. E. Park et al. (eds.), *The City*, Chicago: University of Chicago Press, 1925, pp. 47–62) that the spatial patterning of types of land use, occupancy, and interaction in the city takes the form of a series of concentric zones with the business district at the centre, surrounded by a zone of transition, and then followed by a series of concentric zones of increasingly expensive residential use out to the suburban fringe.

B. Burgess, in his suggestions for the study of urban growth, *assumed* a concentric zoning of types of occupants in the city. Physical growth then emanates from the centre and involves 'the tendency of each inner zone to extend its area by the invasion of the next outer zone' (ibid., p. 50). Subsequent attention fastened mainly on the assumption rather than the growth hypothesis, and the assumption was raised to the status of an hypothesis. This brought forth vigorous criticism of the zonal hypothesis as an over-simplification both in respect to the symmetry and the homogeneity attributed to the zones. To that criticism J. A. Quinn ('The Burgess Zonal Hypothesis and Its Critics', *American Sociological Review*, vol. 5, 1940, pp. 210–18) replied that the apparent regularities would disappear, if distance were measured in units of time and cost of travel instead of in purely spatial units.

So far as a single set of concentric zones is presumed to describe the total urban pattern, there is involved an assumption of a uni-centred city. A conception of a multi-centred or nucleated city, however, does not necessarily negate the principle of concentric zonation, for it may be possible to view the urban pattern as a congeries of sets of concentric zones.

H. Hoyt ('The Structure of American Cities in the Postwar Era', *American Journal of Sociology*, vol. XLVIII, 1942–3, pp. 475–81) has argued that the patterning takes the form of sectors rather than concentric zones. Thus various types of occupants may settle near the centre in different sectors. From this first settlement, each type of occupancy may then proceed to spread from the centre, and as the means of transportation improve may actually jump over areas to start anew in another place. Thus there will be homogeneous areas, but these will not take the form of concentric zones.

Amos H. Hawley

See also: INVASION
SUCCESSION

9